7, 8, 9 Years

Brown, Marcia. *Once a Mouse.* Scribner, 1961.

Cleary, Beverly. *Ramona Forever,* illustrated by Alan Tiegreen. Morrow, 1984.

Fritz, Jean. *Where Do You Think You're Going, Christopher Columbus?,* illustrated by Margot Tomes. Putnam, 1980.

Grimm, Jacob and Wilhelm Grimm. *Snow White and the Seven Dwarfs,* illustrated by Nancy Ekholm Burkert. Farrar, Straus, 1972.

Hickman, Janet. *The Thunder-Pup.* Macmillan, 1981.

Larrick, Nancy, ed. *Piping Down the Valleys Wild.* Delacorte, 1985.

L'Engle, Madeleine. *A Wrinkle in Time.* Farrar, Straus, 1962.

Lobel, Arnold. *Fables.* Harper, 1980.

MacLachlan, Patricia. *Sarah, Plain and Tall.* Harper, 1985.

Miles, Miska. *Annie and the Old One,* illustrated by Peter Parnall. Little, 1971.

Shulevitz, Uri. *Dawn.* Farrar, Straus, 1974.

Steig, William. *Abel's Island.* Farrar, Straus, 1976.

_____. *Amos & Boris.* Farrar, Straus, 1971.

Steptoe, John. *The Legend of Jumping Mouse.* Lothrop, 1984.

Van Allsburg, Chris. *Jumanji.* Houghton Mifflin, 1981.

Walsh, Jill Paton. *The Green Book,* illustrated by Lloyd Bloom. Farrar, Straus, 1982.

White, E. B. *Charlotte's Web,* illustrated by Garth Williams. Harper, 1952.

9, 10, 11 Years

Alexander, Lloyd. *The Black Cauldron.* Holt, 1965.

Babbitt, Natalie. *Tuck Everlasting.* Farrar, Straus, 1975.

Burnett, Frances Hodgson. *The Secret Garden,* illustrated by Tasha Tudor. Harper, 1962.

Byars, Betsy. *The Pinballs.* Harper, 1977.

Fritz, Jean. *Homesick: My Own Story,* illustrated by Margot Tomes. Putnam, 1982.

George, Jean. *Julie of the Wolves.* Harper, 1972.

Hodges, Margaret. *Saint George and the Dragon,* illustrated by Trina Schart Hyman. Little, Brown, 1984.

Hunter, Mollie. *A Stranger Came Ashore.* Harper, 1975.

Kennedy, X. J., and Dorothy Kennedy. *Knock at a Star: A Child's Introduction to Poetry.* Little, 1982.

Lewis, C. S. *The Lion, the Witch and the Wardrobe.* Macmillan, 1968.

Little, Jean. *Mama's Going to Buy You a Mockingbird.* Viking, 1984.

Low, Alice. *The Macmillan Book of Greek Gods and Heroes,* illustrated by Arvis Stewart. Macmillan, 1985.

O'Brien, Robert C. *Mrs. Frisby and the Rats of NIMH.* Atheneum, 1971.

O'Dell, Scott. *Island of the Blue Dolphins.* Houghton, 1960.

Paterson, Katherine. *Bridge to Terabithia,* illustrated by Donna Diamond. Harper, 1977.

Speare, Elizabeth George. *The Sign of the Beaver.* Houghton, 1983.

Taylor, Mildred. *Roll of Thunder, Hear My Cry.* Dial, 1976.

11, 12, 13 Years

Alexander, Lloyd. *Westmark.* Dutton, 1981.

Amon, Aline. *The Earth Is Sore: Native Americans on Nature.* Atheneum, 1981.

Armstrong, William H. *Sounder.* Harper, 1969.

Cleaver, Vera, and Bill Cleaver. *Where the Lilies Bloom.* Harper, 1969.

Collier, James, and Christopher Collier. *My Brother Sam Is Dead.* Four Winds, 1974.

Cooper, Susan. *The Dark Is Rising.* Atheneum, 1973.

Dunning, Stephen, et al., eds. *Reflections on a Gift of a Watermelon Pickle . . . And Other Modern Verse.* Lothrop, 1966.

Fox, Paula. *One-Eyed Cat.* Bradbury, 1984.

Hautzig, Esther. *The Endless Steppe: A Girl in Exile.* Crowell, 1968.

Hunt, Irene. *Across Five Aprils.* Follett, 1964.

Le Guin, Ursula. *A Wizard of Earthsea.* Houghton, 1968.

Paulsen, Gary. *Dogsong.* Bradbury, 1985.

Rawls, Wilson. *Where the Red Fern Grows.* Bantam, 1974.

Sutcliff, Rosemary. *Sun Horse, Moon Horse.* Dutton, 1978.

Tolkien, J. R. R. *The Hobbit.* Houghton Mifflin, 1973 (1966).

Voigt, Cynthia. *Homecoming.* Atheneum, 1981.

Yep, Laurence. *Child of the Owl.* Harper, 1977.

CHILDREN'S LITERATURE
IN THE ELEMENTARY SCHOOL

CHILDREN'S LITERATURE

IN THE ELEMENTARY SCHOOL

FOURTH EDITION

CHARLOTTE S. HUCK

THE OHIO STATE UNIVERSITY

SUSAN HEPLER

JANET HICKMAN

THE OHIO STATE UNIVERSITY

HOLT, RINEHART AND WINSTON, INC.

Fort Worth   Chicago   San Francisco   Philadelphia   Montreal
Toronto   London   Sydney   Tokyo

Publisher Robert Woodbury
Acquisitions Editor Nedah Abbott
Special Projects Editor Jeanette Ninas Johnson
Design Supervisor Robert Kopelman
Production Manager Pat Sarcuni
Interior Design Susan Brooker, Levavi & Levavi, Inc.
Cover Levavi & Levavi, Inc.

Acknowledgments of copyright ownership and literary and
photographic permissions begin on page 749.

Library of Congress Cataloging-in-Publication Data

Huck, Charlotte S.
    Children's literature in the elementary school.

    Bibliography: p.
    Includes index.
    1. Literature—Study and teaching (Elementary)—
United States.   2. Children's literature—United States.
I. Hepler, Susan Ingrid.   II. Hickman, Janet.   III. Title.
LB1575.5.U5H79   1987   372.6′4   86-29467

ISBN   0-03-041770-8

Printed in the United States of America

0123 040 10987654

Holt, Rinehart and Winston, Inc.
The Dryden Press
Saunders College Publishing

*To all those students whom we have taught
and from whom we have learned . . .*

PREFACE

This Fourth Edition of *Children's Literature in the Elementary School* provides many new features and two new authors. Dr. Janet Hickman, an assistant professor at The Ohio State University, is a children's author in her own right, having published several well-received children's books. She has worked behind the scenes on every edition of this text, doing the index and updating the chapter on biography and informational books in the previous edition. Dr. Susan Hepler also has taught children's literature courses and assisted in making the index for the last edition. All three of the authors have taught in the elementary school as well as at the university level.

Our primary purpose in writing this text has remained the same as in the previous editions—to share our knowledge and enthusiasm for the literature of childhood with students, teachers, and librarians in the hope that they in turn will communicate their excitement about books to the children they teach. As a nation we have become so concerned with teaching the skills of reading that we have often neglected to help children discover the joys of reading. We believe that children become readers only by reading many books of their own choosing and by hearing quality literature read aloud with obvious delight and enthusiasm. It is our hope that the students, teachers, and librarians who read this text will be able to create in children a love of good books and joy in reading them.

The field of children's literature is rapidly changing and becoming increasingly important to the development of a literate nation. Preservice and inservice teachers need to know children's books—yet there are over 40,000 in print! How can students learn to select those which are best from this huge number? How can they assist the emergent reader to find predictable books which he or she can read? How can they help students to become discriminating readers? They can't—unless they know and appreciate the literature of childhood. Another consistent purpose of this book then is to help each person reading it to develop a frame of reference about children's literature; developing criteria for the evaluation of various kinds or genres of literature, discovering favorite books of children at various developmental levels, knowing the quality of writing and illustrating of many writers and artists, building a personal list of favorite books to share with children, and being able to recommend the right book for the right child.

In keeping with these purposes, every chapter has been updated and much has been rewritten. Chapter 1 emphasizes the personal and educational values of children's literature and provides criteria for the selection of materials. Chapter 2 has been given a new focus "Understanding Children's Response to Literature," and includes the latest theory and research on children's response to books. Attention to response to literature shows a teacher where children are in their growth of cognitive development and literary understandings. An updated version of the chart "Books for Ages and Stages" in this chapter provides useful information for selecting books based on children's development, beginning with infants. Chapter 3 on the history of children's literature has been retitled "The Changing World of Children's Books" to reflect not only the past but to incorporate current trends, both in children's literature and the publishing business itself. The problem of censorship is addressed here and as a concern for the selection of materials in the first chapter.

Chapter 4, "Books to Begin On," is another new chapter which reflects the growing interest in early literacy and the role of children's literature as a foundation for reading development. Chapters 5 through 11, the genre chapters, have been completely updated and provide many new titles, while retaining some of the earlier books we consider too good for children to miss. Over one-half of the poems in the poetry chapter are new, while over two-thirds of the 157 illustrations are new to this edition.

Part 3 on "Developing a Literature Program" shows students how to make literature central to the curriculum. Chapter 12 on "Planning the Literature Program" emphasizes creating the learning environment in which literature can grow and provides practical suggestions for moving from a basal reading type program to one that is rich with literature. Chapter 13 provides the rationale for using various literature extensions and emphasizes the increasing importance of children's writing. Various ways to evaluate children's growth in reading and appreciation of literature conclude this text.

Many new charts have been added in order to present information in a compact, usable form. Some of these new charts include "Poetry–Prose Connections," "Recurring Themes in Historical Fiction," a chart of "Types of Questions," and other charts on "ABC Books," "Counting Books," "Specialized Poetry Anthologies," "Single Editions of Poetry," updated charts of the previous edition for folktales, "Books to Read Aloud," "Books for Ages and Stages," and others.

Rather than having a separate section on research, pertinent studies are cited throughout the text to provide the foundation for such topics as children's response to books, the development of a concept of story, the role of literature in producing literacy, children's preference for poetry, the relationship between reading and writing, and other areas of concern. We have also discussed books which would meet the needs of minorities throughout all the different genre chapters. At the same time we have highlighted particular books and criteria in the section in Chapter 9 titled "Living in a Pluralistic Society."

While Part 3 focuses directly on learning experiences in the classroom, we have incorporated throughout the text many teaching ideas and real-life episodes that come from actual classrooms. Rather than to suggest teaching ideas to try, we have reported successful activities and programs that teachers have tried. Similarly, most of the suggested learning experiences at the end of each chapter have been tested in our own classes in children's literature.

The organization of *Children's Literature in the Elementary School* highlights the triple focus of this text, namely the reader, the text, and teaching. Part 1 emphasizes the values and criteria for choosing and using literature with children at their various stages of development and response. Part 2 provides an in-depth look at the various genre of children's literature, while Part 3 focuses attention back to the child and teaching in a literature based program.

Some instructors may want to follow this organization, while others may prefer another approach. Many teachers tell us that they assign Parts 1 and 3 first, and then have their students read Part 2. The genre chapters are complete in themselves and do not have to be read in any particular order, although Chapter 4, "Books to Begin On," and Chapter 5, "Picture Books," probably should be read in sequence. Students should not be expected to read every word in these genre chapters or feel they have to know every title, author, or illustrator! They should be encouraged to study the criteria for evaluating particular kinds of books and then skim the rest of the chapters to find titles that appeal to them and that they might wish to read for a particular assignment or share with the class.

From the cover of this book to the endpapers with their "100 Books to Read Aloud" we have hoped to produce a practical text that will serve as a reference book once students begin their teaching, or for teachers and librarians already in the field. We believe teachers and librarians are professional people who want a book with substance, documented with pertinent research and based on real practice in the classrooms. This is the kind of book we have tried to write.

If the future of our country depends on developing a "nation of readers," then each classroom must become a small community of children and teachers who know the value of books and discover the joy of reading. We hope that all who read this book will join with us in creating these reading communities.

No one writes a text of this magnitude without the help of friends. We are deeply indebted to many persons: the teachers, librarians, and children in the schools where we have always been welcomed; our students at The Ohio State University, both undergraduate and graduate, who have shared insights of children's responses and interpretations of literature with us; who have sent pictures and allowed us to take pictures in their classes. We thank them all and hope they continue to share their classroom experiences and enthusiasm for books with children.

Specifically we wish to express our appreciation to the following teachers and schools who shared their children's work and pictures with us: Marlene Harbert and other faculty members at Barrington Road School, Upper Arlington, Ohio; Kristen Kerstetter and the staff at Highland Park School, Grove City, Ohio; Marilyn Parker at Columbus School for Girls; Peggy Harrison and Peg Reed at Ridgemont School, Mt. Victory, Ohio; Arleen Stuck and Melissa Wilson at Columbus Public Schools, and Roy Wilson from Dhahran Hills Elementary School at Dhahran, Saudi Arabia.

We also wish to thank Sally Oddi and her staff at Cover to Cover Bookstore in Columbus for her gracious help in obtaining and loaning us some hard-to-find books and to Elizabeth Wilkens and the staff at the Windsor Public Library in Connecticut for their service. We are grateful to The Ohio State University Photography Department for their careful work in photographing many of the pictures, to Helen Ball and Frances McClure for allowing us to have photographs taken of some of the rare children's books in The Walter Havighurst Special Collections at Miami University Libraries, Oxford, Ohio, and to James Ballard for the cover photographs, two of the colored pictures, and two black and white section photos.

We are also indebted to Elizabeth Strong for her work on Appendix C and to Dianne Frasier for help in obtaining the many permissions for poems and pictures. Special thanks are due to Dr. Jane Porter, Dan Hade, Mary Lee Hahn, and Christtine Fondse for their help with the index.

We express gratitude to the following reviewers, whose comments and suggestions were most helpful: Joanne Bernstein, Brooklyn College; Patricia Cianciolo, Michigan State University–East Lansing; Thomas Godfrey, Kearney State College; Barbara Harrison, Simmons College; James Jacob, Brigham Young University; Janice Kristo, University of Maine–Orono; Arthea Reed, University of North Carolina–Asheville; Wilma Scrivner, Spring Hill College; Ena Shelley, Butler University; Marilou Sorensen, University of Utah–Salt Lake City; James Walden, Indiana University–Bloomington; Mary Lou White, Wright State University.

To Richard C. Owen, who took time from his own publishing business to work on special assignment for this book, we give particular thanks for his organizational skills, his praise, and his proddings! We also are indebted to Jeanette Ninas Johnson and Nedah Abbott of Holt, Rinehart and Winston for their editing and administrative skills. We are pleased that Dr. Mary Lou White of Wright State agreed to write an instructor's manual for this text.

Finally, we are grateful for four favorite Barbaras in our lives—to Dr. Barbara Chatton, a former librarian now teaching children's literature at the University of Wyoming, for preparing Appendix B, "Book Selection Aids"; to Barbara Peterson, a Ph.D. student at The Ohio State University for her pictures of Tomie de Paola's visit to Highland Park and help in preparing bibliographies; to Barbara Friedberg and the staff at Martin Luther King, Jr., Laboratory School in Evanston, Illinois, for pictures, examples of children's work, and constant support; and to Barbara Fincher, a faithful friend and superb typist. Finally, we want to thank our families for their patience, tolerance, and sheer endurance. There is no adequate way to thank friends and family except to wonder at the glory of having had their company and support in creating this text.

C.S.H.
S.H.
J.H.

Columbus, Ohio

CONTENTS

CHILDREN'S LITERATURE
IN THE ELEMENTARY SCHOOL

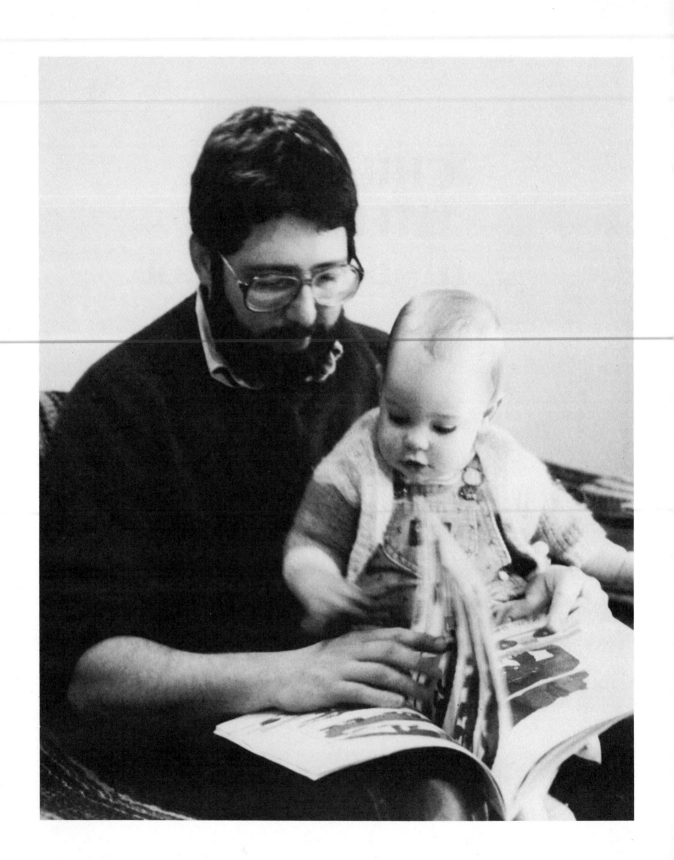

1

LEARNING

ABOUT

BOOKS

AND CHILDREN

VALUING LITERATURE
FOR CHILDREN

*An asterisk in these chapter-opening outlines indi-
cates evaluation criteria presented in chart form.

Was there ever a baby who didn't giggle with delight when her toes were touched to the accompaniment of "This little pig went to market/This little pig stayed at home"? Response to literature begins in the crib with babies listening to Mother Goose rhymes and nursery songs. It continues with the toddler's discovery of Dorothy Kunhardt's *Pat the Bunny* or Eric Carle's *The Very Hungry Caterpillar*. Later, children beg to hear Margaret Wise Brown's *Goodnight Moon* or Beatrix Potter's *Peter Rabbit* one more time.

If he is fortunate in his teachers the primary child will hear stories two and three times a day. He will see his own jealous behavior mirrored by Frances' and Peter's reaction to their siblings in Russell Hoban's *A Baby Sister for Frances* and Ezra Jack Keats' *Peter's Chair*. He will identify with the feelings of Max, who when scolded takes off in his imagination in his very private boat to *Where the Wild Things Are* by Maurice Sendak. And somewhere in those early years he will discover that he can read, and then the magical world of literature will open before him.

The growing child experiences loneliness and fear as she imagines what it would be like to exist as Karana did alone on her *Island of the Blue Dolphins* by Scott O'Dell for some eighteen years. She encounters a toughness and resiliency as she lives the life of Katherine Paterson's *The Great Gilly Hopkins*, a foster child of today. She can experience man's inhumanity to man in the story of *Sounder* by William Armstrong; and she can learn of the horrors of the Holocaust by reading *Anne Frank, The Diary of a Young Girl*.

All that people have ever thought, done, or dreamed lies waiting to be discovered in books. Literature begins with Mother Goose. It includes Sendak as well as Shakespeare, Milne as much as Milton, and Carroll before Camus. Children's literature is a part of the mainstream of all literature, whose source is life itself.

KNOWING CHILDREN'S LITERATURE

Literature Defined

Today, there is an abundance of literature for children that has never existed before in the history of the world. Different kinds of books, vastly increased production of books, and widespread distribution techniques make thousands of books available to children. Revolving racks in drugstores, supermarkets, bus depots, and airports display brightly illustrated books designed to attract young readers. Parents select books as they pile groceries into the cart. Encyclopedias are found next to frozen foods. Children's paperbacks have become as popular as adult ones. Following adult patterns, selections from children's book-of-the-month clubs and children's magazines find their way into thousands of homes. Most schools today recognize the importance of a library media center and trained librarian for every elementary school. Thousands of children also visit attractive rooms in public libraries each week where trained librarians give them assistance.

From the more than 40,000 books now available for boys and girls, how can teachers, librarians, and parents select the ones that are literature? How can we distinguish the trees from the forest? In this plethora of books, there is the great danger of overlooking really fine literature. The number of books published each year increases the difficulty of book selection and, at the same time, emphasizes its importance. Two questions need to be considered: (1) What is literature? and (2) What literature is appropriate for children?

Literature is the imaginative shaping of life and thought into the forms and structures of language. The province of literature is the human condition: life with all its feelings, thoughts, and insights. The experience of literature is always two-dimensional, for it involves both the book and the reader. Some critics consider Lewis Carroll's *Alice in Wonderland* the greatest book ever written for children. However, if the child has no background in fantasy, cannot comprehend the complexity of the plot, nor tolerate the logic of its illogic, she will not be able to interact with the book and so experience literature. We need then to consider the function of the words and pictures. How do the symbols produce an aesthetic experience? How do they help the reader perceive pattern, relationships, feelings that produce an inner experience of art? This aesthetic experience may be a vivid reconstruction of past experience, an extension of experience, or creation of a new experience.

> We all have, in our experience, memories of certain books which changed us in some way—by disturbing us, or by a glorious affirmation of some emotion we knew but could never shape in words, or by some revelation of human nature. Virginia Woolf calls such times "moments of being," and James Joyce titles them "epiphanies."[1]

Literature illuminates the human condition by shaping our insights. W. H. Auden differentiated between first-rate literature and second-rate literature, writing that the reader responds to second-rate literature by saying:

> "That's just the way I always felt." But first-rate literature makes one say: "Until now, I never knew

how I felt. Thanks to this experience, I shall never feel the same way again.[2]

Good writing, or effective use of language, on any subject may produce aesthetic experiences. The imaginative use of language produces both intellectual and emotional responses. It will cause the reader to perceive characters, conflicts, elements in a setting, and universal problems of mankind; it will help the reader to experience the delight of beauty, wonder, and humor or the despair of sorrow, injustice, and ugliness. Vicariously, he will experience other places, other times, and other life styles; he may identify with others or find his own self-identity; he may observe nature more closely or from a different perspective; he will encounter the thrill of taking risks and meeting mystery; he will endure suffering; he will enjoy a sense of achievement and feel he belongs to one segment or all of humanity. He will be challenged to dream dreams, to ponder, and to ask questions of himself.

WHAT IS CHILDREN'S LITERATURE?

It might be said that a child's book is a book a child is reading, and an adult book is a book occupying the attention of an adult. Before the nineteenth century only a few books were written for the specific readership of children. Children read books written for adults, taking from them what they could understand. Today, children continue to read some books intended for adults; for example, Judith Guest's *Ordinary People* and *All Creatures Great and Small* by James Herriot. And yet some books first written for children—such as Margery Williams' *The Velveteen Rabbit*, A. A. Milne's *Winnie the Pooh,* and J. R. R. Tolkien's *The Hobbit*—have been claimed as their own by college students.

Books *about* children may not necessarily be *for* them. Richard Hughes' adult classic *A High Wind in Jamaica* shows the "innocent" depravity of children in contrast to the group of pirates who had captured them. Yet in Harper Lee's novel *To Kill a*

---

[1]Frances Clarke Sayers, *Summoned by Books* (New York: Viking, 1965), p. 16.

[2]W. H. Auden, as quoted by Robert B. Heilman in "Literature and Growing Up," *English Journal*, vol. 45 (September 1956), p. 307.

The best in children's literature earns approval from both critics and children.

Columbus Public Schools, Columbus, Ohio. Photo by Fred Burton.

Mockingbird, also written for adults, 8-year-old Scout Finch reveals a more finely developed conscience than the small Southern town in which she is raised. The presence of a child protagonist, then, does not assure that the book is for children. Obviously, the line between children's literature and adult literature is blurred.

Children today appear more sophisticated and knowledgeable about certain life experiences than those of any previous generation. They spend more time viewing television than they spend in school; average daily viewing is now recorded at 7 hours, 10 minutes per household. The evening news has shown them actual views of war while they ate their dinners. They have witnessed the attempted shooting of a president and a pope. While the modern child is separated from first-hand knowledge of birth, death, and senility, the mass media bring the vicarious and daily experiences of crime, poverty, war, sex, divorce, and murder into the living rooms of virtually all American homes. This generation is exposed to more violence in the name of entertainment than any other generation in the past.

Such exposure has forced adults to reconsider what seems appropriate for children's literature. It seems unbelievable that a few years ago Madeleine L'Engle's *Meet the Austins* was rejected by several publishers because it began with a death; or that some reviewers were shocked by a mild "damn" in *Harriet the Spy* by Louise Fitzhugh. Such publishing taboos have long since disappeared. Children's books are reflecting the problems of today, the ones children read about in the newspapers, see on television and in the movies, and experience at home.

However, the content of children's literature is limited by the experience and understanding of children. Certain emotional and psychological responses seem outside the realm of childhood. For example, the feeling of nostalgia is an adult emotion that is foreign to most boys and girls. Children seldom look back on their childhood, but always forward. Such a sentimental, nostalgic book as *Childhood Is a Time of Innocence* by Joan Walsh Anglund is not for children but is about childhood. One also wonders what frame of reference a child can bring to the recent Newbery award winning book, *A Visit to William Blake's Inn*. Knowing few of the eighteenth-century poems by Blake, how can a child appreciate the references to the "tyger's symmetry" or to the sunflowers in Nancy Willard's superb but abstract poems? Surely this book will need a careful introduction by a knowledgeable teacher or librarian, if middle-graders are going to enjoy it. Children are not elitist; they will seldom read a book because it is the intellectually stylish thing to do. They are not interested in reading the great books of the past unless they think they are really outstanding books today. The young child does not revere the past or his own childhood; he is too busy living in the present.

Cynicism and despair are not childlike emotions. Today's children have a kind of surface cynicism about authority, politics, and the nuclear bomb. But despite their apparent sophistication, they still expect good things to happen in life. The real cynic is bitter, angry, frustrated about the loss of values he once believed in. Some books, such as *Don't Play Dead Before You Have To* by Maia Wojciechowska, are destructive of values before children have had time to develop them. Few children have known despair. They may have endured pain, sorrow, or horror; they may be in what we would consider hopeless situations, but they are not without hope. The truth of the Russian folktale by Becky Reyher, *My Mother Is the Most Beautiful Woman in the World*, shines clear. Children see beauty where there is ugliness; they are hopeful when adults have given up. This is not to suggest that all stories for children must have happy endings; many today do not. It is only to say that when you close the door on hope, you have left the realm of childhood. The only limitations, then, that seem binding on literature for children are those that appropriately reflect the emotions and experiences of children today. Children's books are books that have the child's eye at the center.

WRITING FOR CHILDREN

The skilled author does not write differently or less carefully for children just because he thinks they will not be aware of style or language. E. B. White asserts:

> Anyone who writes *down* to children is simply wasting his time. You have to write up, not down. . . . Some writers for children deliberately avoid using words they think a child doesn't know. This emasculates the prose and . . . bores the reader. . . . Children love words that give them a hard time, provided they are in a context that absorbs their attention.[3]

Authors of children's literature and those who write for adults should receive equal approbation. C. S. Lewis[4] maintained that he wrote a children's story because a children's story was the best art form for what he had to say. Lewis wrote both for adults and children, as have Rumer Godden, Madeleine L'Engle, Paula Fox, E. B. White, Isaac Bashevis Singer, and many other well-known authors.

The uniqueness of children's literature, then, lies in the audience that it addresses. Authors of children's books are circumscribed only by the experiences of childhood, but these are vast and complex. For children think and feel; they wonder and they dream. Their lives may be filled with love or terror. Much is known, but little is explained.

[3]E. B. White, "On Writing for Children," quoted in Virginia Haviland, ed. *Children and Literature: Views and Reviews* (Glenview, Ill.: Scott, Foresman, 1973), p. 140.
[4]C. S. Lewis, "On Three Ways of Writing for Children," *The Horn Book Magazine*, vol. 39 (October 1963), p. 460.

Children are curious about life and adult activities. They live in the midst of tensions, of balances of love and hate within the family and the neighborhood. The author who can fill these experiences with imagination and insight, give them literary shape and structure, and communicate them to children is writing children's literature.

Valuing Literature for Children

PERSONAL VALUES

Literature should be valued in our homes and schools for the enrichment it gives to the personal lives of children, as well as for its proven educational contributions. We shall consider these intrinsic values of literature before we discuss the more obvious extrinsic educational ones.

Provides Enjoyment

First and foremost, literature provides delight and enjoyment as it enlarges the child's horizons by providing new experiences and new insights. Much of what is taught in school is not particularly enjoyable. Our Puritan backgrounds have made literature somewhat suspect. If a child enjoys it, we reason, it can't be very good for her. Yet literature can educate at the same time it entertains.

Children need to discover delight in books before they are asked to master the skills of reading. Then learning to read makes as much sense as learning to ride a bike; they know that eventually it will be fun. Four- and 5-year-olds who have laughed out loud at Judi Barrett's funny book, *Animals Should Definitely Not Wear Clothing,* can hardly wait to read it themselves. After hearing the ugly troll's cry of "Who's that tripping over my bridge?" children are eager to take parts in playing out *The Three Billy Goats Gruff* by Marcia Brown. They respond to the bobbing rhythm of the poem "Mrs. Peck Pigeon" by Eleanor Farjeon as she goes pecking for bread; or the sound of David McCord's "The Pickety Fence." Six- and 7-year-olds giggle at the silly antics of Arnold Lobel's Frog and Toad books, and they laugh uproariously when Beverly Cleary's *Ramona Quimby, Age 8* mistakenly cracks a raw egg on her head thinking it is hard-boiled. Later they empathize with her when she overhears her teacher calling her a nuisance and a showoff.

Judy Blume's book *Are You There, God? It's Me, Margaret* is so popular in the middle grades that there is usually a waiting list for it. This age group also identifies with Lois Lowry's *Anastasia Krupnik*, a fourth-grader who is horrified that her parents are having another baby. A warm, loving family relationship helps her to change her mind in this very funny yet touching novel. Sad books also bring a kind of enjoyment, as the children who have read *Bridge to Terabithia* by Katherine Paterson will tell you. Most children love being frightened by a story. Watch 6's and 7's respond to a scary sharing of Paul Galdone's *The Tailypo* and you will have no doubt of their shivery delight. Many older children revel in the suspense of *Blackbriar* by William Sleator, and they even find a certain kind of thrill in experiencing the grim horror of Nazi Germany in the story of *Friedrich* by Hans Richter.

The list of books that children enjoy can go on and on. There are so many fine ones—and so many that children won't find unless teachers, librarians, and parents share them with children. A love of reading and a taste for literature are the finest gifts we can give to our children, for we will have started them on the path of a lifetime of pleasure with books.

Reinforces Narrative as a Way of Thinking

Storytelling is as old as human history in every culture studied. The most basic human mind is a storytelling one. Ask any of your friends about their weekends or last vacations and they will organize their remarks in narratives about when their car stalled in the middle of a freeway or their child broke his leg or the marvelous place they stayed at the ocean. Barbara Hardy of the University of London suggests that all our constructs of reality are in fact stories that we tell ourselves about how the world works. She maintains that the narrative is the most common and effective form of ordering our world today:

We dream in narrative, day-dream in narrative, remember, anticipate, hope, despair, believe, doubt, plan, revise, criticize, construct, gossip, learn, hate, love by narrative. In order really to live, we make up

stories about ourselves and others, about the personal as well as the social past and future.[5]

Susanne Langer underscores the importance of narrative as a way of thinking with the dramatic statement that "Life is incoherent unless we give it form." She adds, "Usually the process of formulating our own situations and our own biography . . . follows the same pattern—we 'just put it into words,' tell it to ourselves, compose it in terms of 'scenes,' so that our minds can enact all its important moments. The basis for this imaginative work is the poetic art we have known, from the earliest nursery rhymes to the most profound, or sophisticated, or breath-taking drama and fiction."[6]

If thinking in narrative form is characteristic of adult thought, it is even more typical of children's thinking. James Moffett declares that "children must, for a long time, make narrative do for all . . . they utter themselves almost entirely through story."[7] Watch young children and observe all the stories that they are playing out in their lives. They are naughty and sent to their rooms and what do they do? They tell themselves a story about how they will run away—and then won't their parents be sorry? Does this plot sound familiar? Of course, for it is the basis for Maurice Sendak's modern classic *Where the Wild Things Are*. No doubt the universality of this story accounts for its tremendous popularity, for it taps the very well-springs of all stories children have been telling themselves for years.

Literature can bring order to these self-told stories. For example, in the ending of *Where the Wild Things Are*, Max returns to his room after his fantastic dream "where he finds his supper waiting for him—and it was still hot."[8] Ask 5- or 6-year olds who brought Max his supper and they will reply "His mother." Then ask them what this

[5]Barbara Hardy, "Narrative as a Primary Act of the Mind," in *The Cool Web: The Pattern of Children's Reading* by Margaret Meek, Aidan Warlow, Griselda Barton (New York: Atheneum, 1978), p. 13.
[6]Susanne K. Langer, *Feeling and Form* (New York: Scribner's, 1953), p. 400.
[7]James Moffett, *Teaching the Universe of Discourse* (New York: Houghton Mifflin, 1968), p. 49.
[8]Maurice Sendak, *Where the Wild Things Are* (New York: Harper & Row, 1963), unpaged.

ending means, and they will answer "that she's not mad at him any more." Adults recognize the symbolism of love and reconciliation, but children are satisfied that all is well. The outer story has reflected the inner story that they have told themselves and provided a reassuring ending.

Develops the Imagination

Literature develops children's imagination and helps them to consider nature, people, experiences, or ideas in new ways. Tana Hoban's exciting photographic puzzle, *Look Again!*, gives children a rich visual experience and helps them to see a sunflower or a snail or a zebra from a new perspective. Children love to discover secrets hidden in certain illustrations: the little secondary story of the mouse in the informational book *"Charlie Needs a Cloak"* by Tomie de Paola; the fairy-tale characters and those from Sesame Street in *Anno's Journey* by Mitsumasa Anno; or the shipwreck seen through the window of Sendak's *Outside Over There*.

Good writing may pique the child's curiosity just as much as intriguing art. Literature helps children to entertain ideas they never considered before—"to dwell in possibility," as one of Emily Dickinson's poems suggests. Literature frequently provides answers to the child's "what if?" questions. *The Indian in the Cupboard* by Lynne Banks answers the question: what if I could bring my plastic toys to life? Then it asks another of Omri, the protagonist: what responsibility do I have for a live 2-inch Indian? Madeleine L'Engle explores the idea of changing the past in *A Swiftly Tilting Planet*. What if we could enter history? Could we change certain major decisions? Charles Wallace has to find that out and so does the reader. Literature explores possibility. In *The Green Book* by Jill Paton Walsh the family is migrating to a new planet. Each member of the group is allowed to take only one book. Was Patty's choice of the green book a good one? What would you choose if you were limited to one book?

One of the values of fairy tales and myths is the way in which they stretch the child's imagination. What child could imagine creating a coach out of a pumpkin, horses from mice, and coachmen from lizards? Yet they readily accept it all in the well-loved tale of Cinderella. Bettelheim maintains: "Fairy tales have unequaled value, because they offer new dimensions to the child's imagination which would be impossible for him to discover as truly on his own."[9]

Today television has made everything so explicit that children are not developing their interior landscapes. Teachers need to help them see with their inner eye to develop a country of the mind. Mollie Hunter paints the landscape of a Shetland Island fishing village in her exciting story, *A Stranger Came Ashore*. One can see and feel the night of the wild storm and shipwreck with its sudden appearance of the stranger; or the magic night of the ancient celebration of the Up Helly Aa as the skuddler and the guisers dance under the northern lights and Robbie tries to save his sister from the dark powers of the stranger. The reader is witness to the vivid clash by moonlight on the beach between the earth magic and the sea magic. All of Mollie Hunter's books have this power to create the visual image in the mind of the reader and to stretch the imagination. She herself says that the whole reward of reading is:

> . . . To have one's imagination carried soaring on the wings of another's imagination, to be made more aware of the possibilities of one's mind, to be thrilled, amazed, awed, enchanted—in worlds unknown until discovered through the medium of language and to find in those worlds one's own petty horizons growing wider and wider.[10]

Gives Vicarious Experiences

New perspectives are derived as the child has vicarious experiences through literature. Good writing may transport the reader to other places and other periods of time and expand his life space. The reader experiences identification with others as he enters an imaginary situation with his emotions tuned to those of the story. One 10-year-old boy, sharing his love of Jean George's survival story *My Side of the Mountain*, said, "You know, I've always secretly felt I could do it myself." This boy had experienced Sam Gribley's adventure of "living off the land" in his tree home in the Catskill Mountains. Sam's experiment in self-sufficiency

[9]Bruno Bettelheim, *The Uses of Enchantment: The Meaning and Importance of Fairy Tales* (New York: Knopf, 1976), p. 7.

[10]Mollie Hunter, "If You Can Read," Part II, *The Horn Book Magazine*, vol. LIV (August 1978), p. 435.

had strengthened the conviction of a 10-year-old that maybe he could do it, too. James Britton asks, "Why do men improvise on their representations of the world?" He answers, "Because we never cease to long for more lives than the one we have . . . [a reader can] participate in an infinite number."[11]

How better can we feel and experience history than through a well-told story of the lives of its people and times? The reader experiences the loneliness of 10-year-old Ann Hamilton, who is the only girl living in the wilderness of early western Pennsylvania. Ann's father and brothers are so determined to forget their past home in the East that they even build their new home looking west in *The Cabin Faced West* by Jean Fritz. The young reader does not need to be told that slavery is wrong in Paula Fox's *The Slave Dancer;* instead, the author shows him the devastation that it wreaks on slave and master. A history textbook tells; a quality piece of imaginative writing has the power to make the reader feel, to transport him to the deck of a slave ship and force him into the hold until he chokes on the very horror of it.

Literature provides vicarious experiences of adventure, excitement, and struggle against the elements or other obstacles. In fantasy, Will Stanton, seventh son of a seventh son, must do battle against the forces of evil, the power of the dark, and the unbelievably intense cold before he can complete the circle of the old ones. The strength of this fantasy, *The Dark Is Rising* by Susan Cooper, is the degree to which the author involves the reader in Will's struggle. In *Banner in the Sky* by James R. Ullman, Rudi meets many dangers, but must choose between responsibility to others and his consuming desire to scale the mountain peak where his father died. Whether reading takes her to another land, another time period, or an imaginative country of the mind, the young reader will return home enriched by these vicarious experiences. She will then see herself and her immediate world in a new way. Reading gets us out of our own time and place, out of ourselves; but in the end it will return us to ourselves, a little different, a little changed by this experience.

[11]James Britton, *The Dartmouth Seminar Papers: Response to Literature,* edited by James R. Squire (Champaign, Ill.: National Council of Teachers of English, 1968), p. 10.

Develops Insight into Human Behavior

Literature reflects life, yet no book can contain all of living. By its very organizing properties literature has the power to shape and give coherence to human experience. It may focus on one aspect of life, one period of time in an individual's life, and so enable a reader to see and understand relationships that he had never considered. In *Dicey's Song* by Cynthia Voigt a 13-year-old girl learns to release her brothers and sisters to the care of her independent, feisty grandmother. Only as she grows into loving and respecting this eccentric mother of her own mentally ill mother does Dicey begin to understand her grandmother's advice to reach out and let go. Gradually Dicey realizes how hard it is for Gram, whose own three children are lost to her, to reach out to this new family, to let herself love again. As Dicey sands down the rough places on the old derelict boat she has found, she symbolically smooths out her own rough life and readies herself for her independent voyage into maturity.

So much of what we teach in school is concerned with facts. Literature is concerned with feelings, the quality of life. It can educate the heart as well as the mind. Chukovsky, the Russian poet, says:

> The goal of every storyteller consists of fostering in the child, at whatever cost, compassion and humanness, this miraculous ability of man to be disturbed by another being's misfortune, to feel joy about another being's happiness, to experience another's fate as your own.[12]

Good Night, Mr. Tom by Michelle Magorian is a long, yet powerful, novel of an 8-year-old boy who is evacuated from London during World War II to a tiny village in the English countryside. An abused child of a single deranged mother, Willie is placed with a kindly but gruff widower who has almost become a recluse since the death of his wife and infant son. Though sickeningly violent in parts, this is a deeply moving story in which a boy and a lonely old man nurture each other through mutual love. Others in the village are portrayed as real

[12]Kornei Chukovsky, *From Two to Five,* translated by Miriam Morton (Berkeley: University of California Press, 1963), p. 138.

persons who also show compassion and understanding for both Will and Tom. It is a novel that educates the heart as well as the mind.

Literature can show children how others have lived and "become," no matter what the time or place. As children gain increased awareness of the lives of others, as they vicariously try out other roles, they may develop a better understanding of themselves and those around them. Through wide reading as well as living, the child acquires his perceptions of literature and life

Presents the Universality of Experience

Literature continues to ask universal questions about the meaning of life and human relationships with nature and other people. Literature helps children toward a fuller understanding of the common bonds of humanity. By comparing the stories of *Stevie* by John Steptoe and *Thy Friend, Obadiah* by Brinton Turkle, they discover the universal truth that we seldom know how much we like a person (or even a pet gull) until we've lost him. The theme of *Warrior Scarlet* by Rosemary Sutcliff is far more than the attainment of manhood; it is the story of every runt in every litter.

The story of Max leaving home to go to the island of *Where the Wild Things Are* follows the ancient pattern of Homer's *The Iliad* and *The Odyssey*. This pattern is repeated again and again in myth and legend and seen in such widely divergent modern stories as *Sounder* by William Armstrong, *Sign of the Beaver* by Elizabeth Speare, *Call It Courage* by Armstrong Sperry, and *A Wrinkle in Time* by Madeleine L'Engle. These are all stories of a person's journey through terror and hardship and eventual return home. It is the story of everyone's journey through life.

War stories frequently portray people's many acts of humanness in the midst of inhumanity. *Boris* by Jaap ter Haar, *The Upstairs Room* by Johanna Reiss, *Rose Blanche* by Christopher Galloz and Roberto Innocenti—all tell of the uncommon bravery of common people to do what they can to right a wrong. The first story ever recorded by man was the story of *Gilgamesh* (retold by Bryson), the story of a friendship. Children's literature is replete with other stories of such true friendships, as seen in Katherine Paterson's *Bridge to Terabithia*, E. B. White's *Charlotte's Web,* and Ursula LeGuin's *A Wizard of Earthsea*. There is also

the terrible renunciation of friendship in *Friedrich* by Hans Richter. Literature illumines all of life; it casts its light on all that is good in human life; but it may also spotlight that which is dark and debasing in the human experience.

Literature enables us to live many lives and to begin to see the universality of human experience. It provides a record of all that people have ever thought or dreamed of throughout the ages. Nearly 150 years ago, Sir John Herschel, in an address at the opening of a library at Eton, had this to say about the value of literature:

> Give a man a taste for reading and the means of gratifying it, and you cannot fail to make him a happy, as well as a better, man. You place him in contact with the best minds in every period of history, with the wisest and the wittiest, the tenderest and the bravest, those who really adorned humanity. You make him a citizen of all nations and a contemporary of all ages.

EDUCATIONAL VALUES

The intrinsic personal values of literature should be sufficient to give it a major place in the curriculum. Unfortunately, our society assigns a low priority to such aesthetic experiences. Only when literature can be shown to be basic to the development of measurable skills will it receive attention in the elementary schools. Fortunately, research has proven the essential value of literature in helping children learn to read and write.

Language Development

Characteristic of the development of all children is the phenomenal growth of language during the pre-school years. Chukovsky, the Russian poet, refers to the tremendous "speech-giftedness of the pre-school child" and maintains that "beginning with the age of two, every child becomes for a short period of time a linguistic genius."[13]

While there are different points of view concerning how children acquire language, most language theorists would subscribe to the importance of providing a rich language environment for the young child. Cazden maintains that the child's oral language develops "when a richly supplied cafeteria [of language] is available from the begin-

[13]Kornei Chukovsky, *From Two to Five*, pp. 7, 9.

ning. . . ."[14] While it is not the purpose of this text to give a detailed description of language acquisition, it is appropriate to discuss the role literature plays in developing the language power of children.

One study by Irwin[15] indicates that the systematic reading of stories to infants over an eighteen-month period will increase the spontaneous vocalizations of 2½-year-old children. Mothers of the experimental group spent 15 to 20 minutes daily reading and talking about the story and pictures with the child. Few differences were noted during the first four months of the experiment; then the differences became significant in favor of the experimental group. Cazden[16] contrasted two methods of providing young children with adult language input. One treatment was to expand the child's short telegraphic utterance into a complete sentence. For example, when he said "Dog bark," the mother replied "Yes, the dog is barking." The other treatment focused on the idea of the child and extended it through discussion and reading stories. A third group of children in the experiment received no treatment. Contrary to Cazden's expectations that the direct expansion of the child's language would provide the greatest gain, it was the second treatment which focused on meaning and extended that through story that gained the most on all six measures of language development. Cazden points out the value of reading to the young child in a review of her study.

> Reading to an individual child may be a potent form of language stimulation for two reasons. First, the physical contact with the child and second, such reading seems inevitably to stimulate interpolated conversation about the pictures which both adult and child are attending to.[17]

[14]Courtney B. Cazden, *Child Language and Education* (New York: Holt, Rinehart and Winston, 1972), p. 138.

[15]O. C. Irwin, "Infant Speech: Effect of Systematic Reading of Stories," *Journal of Speech and Hearing Research*, vol 3 (June 1960), pp. 187–190.

[16]Courtney B. Cazden, "Environmental Assistance to the Child's Acquisition of Grammar" (unpublished Ph.D. dissertation, Harvard University, 1965).

[17]Courtney B. Cazden, "Some Implications of Research on Language Development for Preschool Education," paper prepared for Social Science Research Council Conference on Preschool Education, Chicago, February 7–9, 1966 (ERIC, Ed. 011 329), p. 9.

Ninio and Bruner[18] found that one of the first language patterns or frames to be developed occurred when a parent shared a picture book with a child from 8 months to 1½ years old. The parent supported the child's dialogue, adjusting her comments as the child gradually could participate more. This the researchers referred to as "scaffolding" or supporting the child's language growth (see Chapter 4, page 148).

These studies show the effect of planned exposure to literature on improving language facility in children. Chomsky[19] measured the language acquisition of thirty-six children between the ages of 5 and 10 and found a high positive correlation between their linguistic stages of development and their previous exposure to literature, as measured by a simple inventory of their literary backgrounds. She concluded that a valid relation between reading exposure and linguistic stages exists.

This study confirms the findings of the others; evidently reading to children increases their language development, while those children who have a high linguistic competence are the ones who have been exposed to much literature.

Literature and Reading

READING ALOUD   Many studies have sought to determine the reasons some children learn to read early and easily, without formal teaching at school. All of them report the significance of having been read to at an early age. In Durkin's studies[20] of children who learned to read before entering school, family respect for reading was found to be a significant factor. This was evidenced by the fact that all her early readers had been read to from the age of 3 or before. Margaret Clark's study[21] of *Young Fluent Readers* in Scotland confirmed the value of being read aloud to at

[18]A. Ninio and J. Bruner, "The Achievement and Antecedents of Labelling," *Journal of Child Language,* 1973, vol. 5, pp. 1–15.

[19]Carol Chomsky, "Stages in Language Development and Reading Exposure," *Harvard Educational Review,* vol. 42 (February 1972), pp 1–33.

[20]Dolores Durkin, *Children Who Read Early* (New York: Columbia Teachers College Press, 1966).

[21]Margaret Clark, *Young Fluent Readers* (London: Heinemann Educational Books, 1976), p. 102.

Reading aloud to all children is essential for their development as readers.

Martin Luther King Laboratory School, Evanston, Illinois, Public Schools. Photo by Fred Wilkins.

an early age. Not all of the children in her study came from wealthy homes, but they all came from homes that valued books. The families made good use of the local library and one father was a superb storyteller, telling his family fairy tales every night. Thorndike's study[22] of reading in fifteen different countries also found that books in the home and reading aloud were potent factors in children's learning to read.

Dorothy Butler[23] has recorded the powerful influence that reading aloud had on a multiple-handicapped child in her moving book, *Cushla and Her Books.* Doctors predicted a future of severe retardation for this little girl, who confounded them

[22]Robert Ladd Thorndike, *Reading Comprehension, Education in 15 Countries: An Empirical Study,* vol. 3, International Studies in Education (New York: Holstead Wiley, 1973).

[23]Dorothy Butler, *Cushla and Her Books* (Boston: The Horn Book, Inc., 1980).

completely by learning to read at a level well beyond her actual age. Cushla was read to from the time she was 4 months of age and literally discovered the world through books.

A long-term effect of reading to children was determined by Sostarich,[24] who compared 12-year-old "active readers" with non-active readers at the sixth-grade level. Both groups of children could read equally well; one group chose to read frequently, while the other group seldom did. In looking into their backgrounds, she found that in every instance the active readers had been read to from the time they were 3 years old, and, in some cases, families were still sharing books aloud.

Libraries and schools can provide rich literature experiences for those children deprived of books in the home, or where parents and children are watching television seven hours a day rather than reading. Dorothy Cohen[25] sought to determine if reading aloud to 7-year-olds who had not previously been exposed to literature would make a difference in their ability to read. Books were read aloud to children in ten experimental classrooms in New York City on a daily basis for a period of one year. Following the 20-minute story time, the children were asked to do something with the book to make it memorable. For example, they might act out the story, draw a picture of their favorite characters, or compare it with a similar story—something to make them think about the story and revisit the book several times. At the end of the year, Cohen found the experimental group was significantly ahead of the control group on reading vocabulary and reading comprehension. Evidently, reading *to* children had helped them learn to read.

A group of researchers from New York University[26] extended the Cohen study to include 500 black children from kindergarten through third grade in four New York City schools. The experi-

mental group participated in a literature-based oral language program which included the daily story followed by creative dramatics, role-playing, storytelling, puppetry, or discussion. The control groups participated in the literature program, but not in the language activities. The conclusions of the study were that the use of literature did expand the language skills of both groups significantly, but the experimental group made the larger gains. Also, the greatest gain was evident among the kindergarten group, suggesting that such a program should start at as early an age as possible.

DEVELOPING A SENSE OF STORY Hearing stories read aloud is a powerful motivation for the child to begin to learn to read. Children learn that reading provides enjoyment and they want to learn themselves. They also see someone important in their lives valuing books. Too frequently we tell children that reading is important, but we show by our actions that we really value only television.

Early exposure to stories also provides a rich input of literary language. Frank Smith maintains:

> Children need to become acquainted with the language of books; it is not the language they hear spoken around them in their daily life, and it is unrealistic to expect them to learn this unfamiliar style at the same time they learn to read.[27]

Listening to stories introduces children to patterns of language and extends vocabulary and meaning. Young children love to repeat such refrains as "Not by the hair on my chinny chin chin" from Paul Galdone's *Three Little Pigs* or the well-loved rhyme from Wanda Gág's *Millions of Cats:*

> Cats here, cats there,
> Cats and kittens everywhere,
>   Hundreds of cats,
>   Thousands of cats,
> Millions and billions and trillions of cats.[28]

They delight in new words such as "humiliated" in Lynd Ward's *The Biggest Bear* or the line from Beatrix Potter's *The Tale of Peter Rabbit* in which

[24]Judith Sostarich, "A Study of the Reading Behavior of Sixth Graders: Comparisons of Active and Other Readers" (unpublished doctoral dissertation, The Ohio State University, 1974).

[25]Dorothy Cohen, "The Effect of Literature on Vocabulary and Reading Achievement," *Elementary English*, vol. 45 (February 1968), pp. 209–213, 217.

[26]Bernice E. Cullinan, Angela Jaggar, and Dorothy Strickland, "Language Expansion for Black Children in the Primary Grades: A Research Report," *Young Children*, vol. 29 (January 1974), pp. 98–112.

[27]Frank Smith, *Reading Without Nonsense* (New York: Teachers College, Columbia University, 1979), p. 136.

[28]Wanda Gág, *Millions of Cats* (New York: Coward McCann, 1928), unpaged.

the friendly sparrows "implored him to exert himself" when Peter was caught in the gooseberry net. A first-grade teacher read to her class Charlotte Zolotow's *Say It!*, in which a mother and her little girl go for a walk on a beautiful autumn day—"a splendiferous day," the mother calls it. Later on, a child asked her to reread the "splendiferous book." Children love the sound of words and enjoy repeating them over and over.

Knowing the structure of a story and being able to anticipate what a particular character will do helps the young child predict the action and determine the meaning of the story he is reading. For example, children quickly learn the rule of three which prevails in most folk tales. They know that if the first Billy Goat Gruff goes trip-trapping over the bridge, the second Billy Goat Gruff will go trip-trapping after him, and so will the third. In reading or listening to the story of the Gingerbread Boy, the child who has had a rich exposure to literature can anticipate the ending on the basis of what he knows about the character of foxes in stories. As one little boy said, "Foxes are clever. He won't be able to get away from him!"

The more experience with literature, the greater the child's ability to grasp the meaning of the story and predict what will happen next. In Gordon Wells' longitudinal study of children in Bristol, England, it was found that the most important indicator of reading comprehension at 7 was the frequency of listening to stories.[29]

DEVELOPING FLUENCY Wide reading of many books is essential to the development of fluency in reading. This was the kind of reading, even re-reading, of favorite stories that Margaret Clark found to be characteristic of her avid readers.[30] Such reading is characteristic of middle-grade students who get "hooked" on a particular author or series of books. Frequently, a sign of a good reader is the child who re-reads favorite books.

In a year-long study of children's reading behavior in a literature-based program in a combination fifth and sixth grade, Hepler found these children read an average of forty-five books per child for the year, with the range being twenty-five to 122 books.[31] Compare this record with the usual two basal texts read in a year by children in the typical basal reading programs. Only such wide reading will develop fluency. Children used to do this at home, but the advent of television and video games has drastically curtailed the amount of children's home reading. If children do not have the opportunity to read widely at school, they will not become fluent readers.

Literature and Writing

Those of us who have taught have always believed that there was a relationship between reading and writing—the good readers seemed to be the good writers, and the good writers were avid readers. While we now have research that validates our observations, little is known about how reading and writing are related.

Walter Loban conducted one of the most extensive studies of the relationship between reading achievement as measured by reading scores and the ratings of writing quality. He discovered a high correlation, particularly in the upper elementary grades, and concluded: "Those who read well also write well; those who read poorly also write poorly."[32]

Studying over 500 children in grade 3, Woodfin[33] examined the multiple relationships between language ability, socioeconomic status, intelligence, reading level, sex, and free writing. The best consistent predictors of writing ability were reading ability and language scores.

Exposure to much good literature appears to make a difference in children's writing abilities, just as it does in their linguistic abilities. Fox and Allen maintain: "The language children use in writing is unlikely to be more sophisticated in ei-

---

[29]Gordon Wells, *The Meaning Makers: Children Learning Language and Using Language to Learn* (London and Portsmouth, N.H.: Heinemann Educational Books, 1986), p. 157.

[30]Clark, p. 103.

[31]Susan Hepler, "Patterns of Response to Literature: A One-Year Study of a Fifth- and Sixth-Grade Classroom" (unpublished doctoral dissertation, The Ohio State University, 1982).

[32]Walter Loban, *The Language of Elementary School Children*, Research Report No. 1 (Urbana, Ill.: National Council of Teachers of English, 1963), p. 75.

[33]M. Woodfin, "Correlations Among Certain Factors and the Written Expression of Third-Grade Children," *Educational and Psychological Measurement*, vol. 2 (1968), pp. 1237–1242.

ther vocabulary or syntax than the language they read or have had someone else read to them."[34]

After a four-year longitudinal study, Mills[35] reported that fourth-grade children who read or listened to and then discussed children's literature as a springboard to writing scored significantly higher in their free writing than a control group that did not use children's literature in this way. Children learned how to write from hearing and discussing quality literature.

Glenda Bissex[36] studied the evolution of her own child's writing and published the results in a book titled after the sign 5-year-old Paul posted over his workbench: "DO NAT DSTRB GNYS AT WRK." This "genius" learned to write and read at the same time. Reading appeared to have a broad influence on the forms of writing Paul did. He first demonstrated his awareness of print by making signs, labels, and advertisements. He then went on to write shopping lists, little stories, notes, newspapers, and a science-fiction book. Books at all times served as models for Paul's increasing sense of form.

If reading provides models for children's writing, then the kinds of reading children are exposed to becomes even more important. Barbara Eckhoff's[37] research clearly shows that the writing of children reflects the feature and style of their reading texts. Comparing children who read from the typical simplified text of most basal readers with those who read from one whose text more nearly matched the style and complexity of literary prose, she found that the children's writing closely resembled the style of writing used in their texts. One group wrote more complex sentences, while the basal group copied the style and format of their reader, writing simple sentences, one sentence per line.

Diane DeFord's[38] study of children's writing in three first grades taught by different methods (i.e., phonics, skills, and a whole-language model using children's literature) shows the influence of both method and texts on children's writing. The first two groups created repetitious drill-type texts, while the children's literature group produced a wider variety of literary forms, including stories, informational prose, songs, poetry, and newspaper reports. This same group was also more competent at retelling stories. Simplified stories produced simplified stories, both written and oral.

The content of children's stories also reflects the literature they have heard. Whether consciously or unconsciously, children pick up words, phrases, parts of plots, even the intonation pattern of dialogue from books they know. The following story was requested as part of a research study on writing. No directions other than "write a story" were given to this second-grader. Notice the number of stories that he "borrows" from in telling his own. The titles of his probable sources are given at right.

THE LONESOME EGG

Once there lived a Lonesome Egg	*The Golden Egg Book* (Brown)
And nobody liked him because he was ugly. And there was an Ugly duck too but they didn't know each other.	*The Ugly Duckling* (Andersen)
One day while the Lonesome Egg was walking, he met the Ugly duck. And the Egg said to the Duck,	
"Will you be my friend?"	*Do You Want To Be My Friend?*
"Well, O.K."	(Carle)
"Oh, thank you."	
"Now let's go to your house, Duck"	
"No, let's go to your house"	Dialogue from the *Frog and Toad* series (Lobel)
"No, we'll go to your house first and my house too."	
"O.K."	

[34]Sharon Fox and Virginia Allen, *The Language Arts: An Integrated Approach* (New York: Holt, Rinehart and Winston, 1983), p. 206.

[35]Editha B. Mills, "Children's Literature and Teaching Written Composition," *Elementary English*, vol. 51 (October, 1974), pp. 971–973.

[36]Glenda Bissex, *GNYS AT WRK: A Child Learns to Write and Read* (Cambridge, Mass.: Harvard University Press, 1980), p. 197.

[37]Barbara Eckhoff, "How Reading Affects Children's Writing," *Language Arts*, vol. 60 (May 1983), pp. 607–616.

[38]Diane DeFord, "Literacy: Reading, Writing, and Other Essentials," *Language Arts*, vol. 58 (September 1981), pp. 652–658.

And while they were walking they met a Panda Bear and they picked it up and took it to Duck's house. And then the baby Panda Bear said: "I'm tired of walking." So they rested.

And soon came a tiger. And the tiger ate them up except for Duck. And right as he saw that he ran as fast as he could until he saw a woodcutter and he told the woodcutter to come very quickly. And when they got there the tiger was asleep. So the woodcutter cut open the tiger and out came Egg and Baby Panda Bear. And they ate the tiger and lived happily ever after.[39]

Little Black Sambo (Bannerman)
or
The Fat Cat (Kent)

Gingerbread Boy (Galdone)
Little Red Riding Hood (Grimm)

Not only can one discern parts of many stories in the content of this writing, but also certain conventions of the text reflect previous exposure to literature. The conventional beginning, "once there lived," and the traditional ending, "lived happily ever after," are obvious examples. Phrases such as "and soon came a tiger" and "out came Egg and Baby Panda Bear" have a literary ring to them. Discussion of whose house they will go to echoes the many conversations in the *Frog and Toad* series by Arnold Lobel. There can be little doubt of the influence of previous exposure to literature on the shape and content of this story told by a 7-year-old child.

The role of reading, then, is significant to the development of writing. For " . . . the development of composition in writing cannot reside in writing alone, but requires reading and being read to. Only from the written language of others can children observe and understand convention and idea together."[40]

[39]Collected for NIE Research Project, "Study of Cohesion Elements on Three Modes of Discourse, "Martha L. King and Victor Rentel, Co-Researchers, The Ohio State University, 1983.
[40]Frank Smith, *Writing and the Writer* (New York: Holt, Rinehart and Winston), 1982.

Literature across the Curriculum

The widely read person is usually the informed person. The content of literature educates while it entertains. A 10-year-old reading *The Cry of the Crow* by Jean George learns much that is authentic and true about crow behavior. Written by a naturalist who has studied animal behavior and owned several pet crows, this story includes such concepts as crow communication, imprinting, and dispersal. More important than the factual information, however, is the story's theme of the significance of choice and growing up.

My Brother Sam Is Dead by the Colliers gives authentic information about one part of the American Revolution while it contrasts different points of view held by the various characters toward the war itself. This story helps the reader to imagine what it was like to live in a family torn apart by divided loyalties. And it raises the larger political question concerning the role of neutrality in a revolution.

Sutcliff's *Sun Horse, Moon Horse* tells a superb story about the possible origin of the White Horse of Uffington. Basing the tale on a theory that the Iceni, an early Iron Age people, are the same as the Epidi of Argyle and Kintyre, who were driven North by invaders, Sutcliff weaves a story in which the great white horse is built as a price for the freedom of the "Horse People." It is a story that could be true, but certainly the reader who is engrossed in the story is also learning much about a culture that existed nearly 2000 years ago in the high chalk downs of England. But since well-written fiction gives more than facts, the reader of *Sun Horse, Moon Horse* also learns about the quality of an artist's dedication and sacrifice for the freedom of his people.

History books tell us little about the evacuation of all West Coast Japanese Americans to prison camps on the barren desert of Utah following the Pearl Harbor attack in 1941. In *Journey to Topaz* by Yoshiko Uchida, readers can see the effect of that relocation order on the life of one family. Facts can be expressed in one line in a history book; feelings can be communicated through story, the true story of one family in particular.

All areas of the curriculum may be enriched through literature. Children may start with a story and research the facts; or they may start with the facts and find the true meanings in the stories surrounding those facts. Literature has the power to educate both the heart and the mind.

Introducing Our Literary Heritage

Children's literary experiences begin when they are introduced to the rhythm and rhymes of Mother Goose, the repetitive structures and universal characters of folk tales, and well-loved classics like Wanda Gág's *Millions of Cats,* Virginia Lee Burton's *The Little House,* and Beatrix Potter's *The Tale of Peter Rabbit.* As children compare the different variants of Cinderella or Rumpelstiltskin they learn about the motifs of transformations, magical objects, and trickery. And they discover something of the universality of folklore from all cultures.

Through in-depth discussions of such books as *The Great Gilly Hopkins* by Katherine Paterson, *Julie of the Wolves* by Jean George, or *Tuck Everlasting* by Natalie Babbitt, children become aware of what constitutes fine writing. While children will usually focus on plot or story, teachers can help them see the gradual character development of Gilly, for example, or ask them why they think Jean George began her book when Julie was lost on the vast tundra rather than starting with the beginning of her story. Children can be led to discover the motifs for the recurring references to the wheel, the toad, and the music box in *Tuck Everlasting* as a way of shedding light on their understanding of this lovely fantasy. Children's appreciation for literature and knowledge of their literary heritage should be developed gradually in the elementary school as a way to add to the enjoyment of literature rather than as an end in itself.

Evaluating Children's Books

A young child's initial response to a book, story, or poem is emotional; the child will tell you how he feels about it and what it means to him. Once a child begins to deal with the "whys" of his feelings he will discover the ways in which the author builds plot, develops characters, and uses language to create meaning and feeling. While teachers and librarians will begin at the affective level of response, they will want to extend children's discriminatory powers to help them discover what constitutes a well-written book. This means that teachers and librarians must know something of the structures and forms of literature; at the same time, they will want to learn much about the structure of children's thought, language acquisition, social and emotional development, and changing interests.[41] For only when teachers and librarians are knowledgeable about both children and books can they ever hope to bring the two together for a meaningful experience of literature.

The traditional criteria by which we evaluate a work of fiction include such elements as plot, setting, theme, characterization, style, point of view, and format. Specialized criteria need to be applied to different types of literature, such as picture books, biographies, and informational books. Additional criteria are also needed to evaluate certain forms of fiction. For example, criteria for a realistic story would not be the same as those used for modern fantasy. Historical fiction requires the added criteria of authenticity of setting and mood. Perhaps the first task of both the teacher and the children is to identify the kind of book they are reading in order to apply the appropriate criteria for evaluation. In evaluating fiction, we usually begin with these criteria:

PLOT

Of prime importance in any work of fiction for children is the plot. Children ask first, "Does the book tell a good story?" The plot is the plan of action; it tells what the characters do and what happens to them. It is the thread that holds the fabric of the story together and makes the reader want to continue reading.

A well-constucted plot is organic and interrelated. It grows logically and naturally from the actions and the decisions of the characters in given situations. The plot should be credible and ring true rather than depend on coincidence and contrivance. It should be original and fresh rather than trite, tired, and predictable.

The appeal of the series books is based completely on action and happenings. Their stories are

[41]See Chapter 2, "Understanding Children's Response to Literature," which relates aspects of child development to children's choice of books.

always predictable; Nancy Drew never fails to solve a mystery and Tom Swift accomplishes one major feat after another. The action is usually beyond the capabilities of the characters and becomes contrived and sensational. These books move rapidly from one improbable happening to another, but they are addictive in the way potato chips are: children read them one after another until they have had their fill.

In books that have substance, obstacles are not quickly overcome, and choices are not always clearcut. In *Cry of the Crow* by Jean George, Mandy must make a cruel decision in order to protect her younger brother. This is not the predictable animal story in which the tamed horse wins the race or the runt of a litter saves his master, but one that is true to nature and has the integrity of life itself.

Books may be exciting, fast-moving, and well-written. Armstrong Sperry's *Call It Courage* gains increasing momentum with each of Mafatu's courageous feats until the climax is reached at the close of the book. Suspense is maintained with the rising action of the story. The climax of a story should be easily identifiable and develop naturally from the actions of the characters to the events of the story. Children prefer a swift conclusion following the climax, but the denouement should knit together the loose ends of the story.

Most of the plots in children's literature are presented in a linear fashion. Usually children do not have the maturity to follow several plots or many flashbacks in time or place. However, several excellent books for middle-graders do make use of these devices. In the Newbery award book *Mrs. Frisby and the Rats of NIMH* by Robert O'Brien, the mouse's story is interrupted by a long flashback in which Nicodemus relates the strange tale of the escape of the intelligent rats from the national laboratory. The flashback reveals the debt the rats owe to Mrs. Frisby's deceased husband and creates suspense as the reader is left worrying about the fate of Mrs. Frisby's very ill son, Timothy.

In *Ash Road*, Ivan Southall skillfully portrays the actions of some five families in a roaring bushfire in Australia. The plot is complex, as it shifts from one group of children to another, but individuals are sharply delineated as they react to the searing horror of the fire. The effectiveness of

the structure, then, depends on the clarity of the author's presentation and the child's ability to comprehend complexity.

Plot is but one element of good writing. If a book does not have a substantial plot, it will not hold children's interest long. But well-loved books contain indefinable qualities and are memorable for more than plot alone.

SETTING

The structure of the story includes both the construction of the plot and its setting. The setting may be in the past, the present, or the future. The story may take place in a specific locale, or the setting may be deliberately vague to convey the universal feeling of all suburbs, all large cities, or all rural communities.

Both the time and place of the story should affect the action, the characters, and the theme. The setting for the haunting tale of *Sounder* by William Armstrong is the rural South sometime near the turn of the century. The story portrays the injustices and cruelties inflicted on a black sharecropper because he had stolen a ham for his hungry family. While the story has a specific setting in time and place, for many it represents the plight of all blacks in the rural South before Selma. The filmed version of *Sounder* changed the locale from Virginia to Louisiana and the time from the early 1900s to the depression year of 1933, with little loss in the impact of the story. Such a change suggests the universality of this story and its setting.

Whenever a specific period of time or locale is presented, it should be authentic and true to what the author knows of that period, place, or people. Part of the challenge of writing accurate historical fiction is believable reconstruction of the time and place of the action. *The Valley of the Shadow* by Hickman chronicles a grim massacre of the Christianized Indians at Gnadenhutten in what is now Ohio. Based on careful research into the diaries of the early missionaries, even an accurate description of the weather and its influence on the action of the story is included. In an award-winning biography by Elizabeth Yates, the setting both reflects, and helps to create, the strength and quiet dignity of *Amos Fortune, Free Man*. The physical and symbolic presence of Monadnock Mountain looms large in the story of this remarkable man. Always,

Amos looks to "his" mountain for fortitude and courage. In return, it is as if the strength of the hills were his also. The setting of a story can do much to create the mood and theme of a book.

The imaginary settings of fantasy must be carefully detailed in order to create a believable story. In *Charlotte's Web*, E. B. White has made us see and smell Wilbur's barnyard home so clearly that it takes little stretch of the imagination to listen in on the animal's conversations. The microcosm that is the world of *Winnie-the-Pooh* by A. A. Milne has been detailed in a map by Ernest Shepard. It pictures the "100 Aker Wood," "Eeyore's Gloomy Place," "Pooh's Trap for Heffalumps," and "Where the Woozle Wasn't"—all familiar places to a *Winnie-the-Pooh* buff. In *A Wizard of Earthsea*, a more serious fantasy by Ursula Le Guin, the tale of wizards, dragons, and shadows is played out in an archipelago of imagined islands. Ruth Robbins has provided a map of Earthsea; for its geography is as exact as the laws and limits of magic used by the wizards of the isles. The Yorkshire setting of *The Secret Garden* by Frances Hodgson Burnett looms large in the memories of generations of children who have loved this mysterious tale. In the mind's eye, the reader can see the many-roomed Misselthwaite Manor with its long corridors and tapestry-covered doors and hear the faint sound of the far off crying of Colin mixed with the mournful wind from the moor. By contrast, the walled garden that Mary discovers is still and quiet, holding the promise of spring and restored health for both the lonely forgotten children.

The setting of a story, then, is important in creating mood, authenticity, and credibility. The accident of place and time in a person's life may be as significant as the accident of birth, for places may have tremendous significance in our life story.

THEME

The third point for the evaluation of any story is its overarching *theme*. The theme of a book reveals the author's purpose in writing the story. Most well-written books may be read for several layers of meaning—plot, theme, or metaphor. On one level the story of *Charlotte's Web* by E. B. White is simply an absurd but amusing tale of how a spider saves the life of a pig; on another level, it reveals

the meaning of loneliness and the obligations of friendship. A third layer of significance can be seen in the acceptance of death as a natural part of the cycle of life. Finally, E. B. White himself wrote that it was ". . . an *appreciative* story. . . . It celebrates life, the seasons, the goodness of the barn, the beauty of the world, the glory of everything."[42] The story of *The Yearling* may appear to be the story of a boy and his pet deer; in reality, Marjorie Kinnan Rawlings has described the painful experience of achieving manhood. The theme of Lynd Ward's picture book, *The Biggest Bear*, is similar to *The Yearling*, although its ending is more appropriate for younger children.

Theme provides a dimension to the story that goes beyond the action of the plot. The theme of a book might be the acceptance of self or others, growing up, the overcoming of fear or prejudice. The theme of a story should be worth imparting to young people and be based on justice and integrity. Sound moral and ethical principles should prevail. Paul Hazard, writing in *Books, Children and Men*, made these comments concerning the kind of children's books that he felt were good:

> . . . and books that awaken in them not maudlin sentimentality, but sensibility; that enable them to share in great human emotions; that give them respect for universal life—that of animals, of plants; that teach them not to despise everything that is mysterious in creation and in man. . . . I like books that set in action truths worthy of lasting forever, and inspiring one's whole inner life. . . .
>
> In short, I like books that have the integrity to perpetuate their own faith in truth and justice. . . .[43]

One danger in writing books for children particularly is that the theme will override the plot. Authors may be so intent on conveying a message that story or characterization may be neglected. Didacticism is still alive and well in the twentieth century. It may hide behind the façade of ecology, drug abuse, or alienation, but it destroys fine writing.

[42]Dorothy L. Guth, ed., *Letters of E. B. White* (New York: Harper & Row, 1976), p. 613.
[43]Paul Hazard, *Books, Children and Men* (Boston: The Horn Book, Inc., 1944), pp. 42–44.

CHARACTERIZATION

True characterization is another hallmark of fine writing. The people portrayed in children's books should be as convincingly real and lifelike as our next-door neighbors. Many of the animal characters in modern fantasy have real personalities, also. The credibility of characters will depend on the author's ability to show their true natures, their strengths, and their weaknesses.

Just as it takes time to know a new friend in all his various dimensions, so, too, does an author try to present many facets of a character. In revealing character an author may tell about the person through narration, record the character's conversation with others, describe the thoughts of the character, show the thoughts of others about the character, or show the character in action. While children prefer action in their stories and dislike too much introspection, a character that is revealed in only one way is apt to lack depth. In many series books the characters are stock characters, not realistic human beings. If only one dimension of a character is presented, or one trait overemphasized, the result is likely to be stereo-typed and wooden. In the Tom Swift stories the reader is always told *how* the hero performs his daring exploits rather than letting the actions and the feelings grow out of the circumstance of the story. Children do not need to be told that Gus overcomes his fear of the dark in *The Stone-Faced Boy* by Paula Fox; he shows his bravery by rescuing a dog for his sister in the middle of the night.

In addition to realism in characterization, there should be consistency in character portrayal. This consistency should not conform to a pattern but to the true nature of the character as the author has presented him. The characters should be depicted so that everything they do, think, and say will seem natural and inevitable. It is as appropriate for Johnetta to use a black dialect when she is speaking in the first person to tell about her kid brother's running away from home in Lucille Clifton's *My Brother Fine with Me* as it is for Obadiah and his family to use the plain talk of the Quakers in Brinton Turkle's *Obadiah the Bold*. While old Nantucket provides the setting for Obadiah, *My Brother Fine with Me* takes place in the city today. Characters should act and speak in

From *Ramona Quimby, Age 8* by Beverly Cleary. Illustration by Alan Tiegren.

From *Winnie-the-Pooh* by A. A. Milne.

accordance with their age, culture, and educational background.

Another aspect of sound characterization is growth and development. Do the characters change in the course of the story, or do they remain the undaunted and self-sufficient personalities that they were in the beginning of the tale? Not all characters will change, of course, but many are memorable for their personality development. No girl will ever forget the struggle of headstrong, self-centered Jo of Louisa May Alcott's *Little Women* in taming her rebellious ways. Marguerite de Angeli has created a vivid character study of Robin in her outstanding book, *The Door in the Wall*. Robin, crippled son of a great lord, must learn to accept his infirmity and find a useful place in life. The gradual development of his character is made clear as he solves these problems. In today's more enlightened world it is easy to empathize with the tomboy *Caddie Woodlawn* in her struggle against the far-reaching demands of the mid-nineteenth century that she become a lady even in the wilds of Wisconsin. When Caddie has finally put away her tomboy ways, she says: "How far I've come! I'm the same girl and yet not the same. I wonder if it's always like this? Folks keep growing from one person into another all of their lives. . . ."[44]

[44]Carol Ryrie Brink, *Caddie Woodlawn* (New York: Macmillan, 1936), p. 27.

In all these books, and many more, the characters seem real and alive. To appear truly human they must grow and change before the reader's eyes. In keeping with life itself, that change is usually gradual and convincing, rather than mercurial and unrealistic.

A character may be three-dimensional, stand out in sharp relief, and still not change. It is as though the character were frozen in a particular time period of his or her life. Such characters may be very interesting, with many facets of their personalities clearly delineated. Homer Price, Ramona Quimby, and Pippi Longstocking show little development of character, yet they remain consistent to their natures in all their adventures. There is a difference, then, between character delineation and character development.

From *Frog and Toad Are Friends* by Arnold Lobel.

From *Little House in the Big Woods* by Laura Ingalls Wilder. Illustration by Garth Williams.

Long after we have forgotten their stories, we can recall some of the personalities of children's literature. We recognize them as they turn the corner of our memories, and we are glad for their friendship. The line is long; it includes animals and people. It is hard to tell where it begins, and we are happy there is no end. In our mind's eye we see the three loyal friends, Mole, Toad, and Rat returning from their adventures on the open road; Mary Poppins flies by holding tightly to her large black umbrella with one hand and carrying her carpet bag in the other; she passes right over those comic friends, Frog and Toad, who are out looking for the corner that spring is just around; while Georgie hops down the road announcing "New folks coming" and nearly interrupts Pooh and Piglet in their search for a Woozle. In the barnyard Wilbur has just discovered a wonderful new friend, Charlotte A. Cavatica, much to the amusement of the wise geese and the sly rat, Templeton. If we look closely, we can see tiny Arrietty and Pod, out for a Borrower's holiday; Stuart Little paddles his souvenir canoe along the drainage ditch; and our favorite Hobbit, Bilbo Baggins, outwits the terrifying Gollum. Gathered in the schoolyard are the Great Gilly Hopkins and her tag-along friend, Agnes Stokes; sitting on the steps, Carlie is instructing Thomas J. about his first day of school and the fact that they are no longer "pinballs"; while Meg Murry is consulting with the principal, Mr. Jenkins, about her little brother, Charles Wallace. Ramona, who is learning to ride her new 2-wheel bicycle wobbles by and Harriet with flashlight and notebook is just beginning her spy route.

The line is long in this procession of real personages in children's literature. It reaches back in our memories to include Beth, Jo, Amy, and Meg; it stands outside a Secret Garden and listens to the laughing voices of Mary, Colin, and Dickon; and, with Laura, it delights in the warm coziness of the fire and the sound of Pa's fiddling in *Little House in the Big Woods*. We know all these characters well because their authors created them and blew the breath of life into each one of them. They have come alive in the pages of books; and they will live forever in our memories.

STYLE

An author's style of writing is simply selection and arrangement of words in presenting the story.

Good writing style is appropriate to the plot, theme, and characters, both creating and reflecting the mood of the story. An author's style is individual and unique. Compare the different ways in which DeJong and O'Dell have described characters who have been left alone:

> The dog had no name. For a dog to have a name, someone must have him and someone must love him, and a dog must have someone. The dog had no one, and no one had the dog. . . . The dog had only himself, so the dog had nothing, and he was afraid.[45]

> The thought of being alone on the island while so many suns rose from the sea and went slowly back into the sea filled my heart with loneliness. . . . Now I was really alone. I could not eat much, nor could I sleep without dreaming terrible dreams.[46]

Meindert DeJong presents layered dimensions of aloneness, drumming sympathy for the little lost dog in a series of staccato, one-syllable words. Scott O'Dell evokes images of vastness and isolation with references to the sun and the sea, yet the tone has directness and simplicity. The lack of emotion in these words that describe how Karana feels after her brother has been killed by wild dogs reflects stoicism in the Indian girl's character.

Certain authors can tap into the feelings and emotions of childhood itself. Janet Hickman has captured the joy of a 9-year-old girl through real childlike comparisons. Linnie is anticipating the glory of her own birthday dog:

> Linnie was so happy that she was afraid to move. It was like having a jigsaw puzzle with the last piece just in, and not wanting anyone to jiggle the table. Or like being in the very best part of a good book and not wanting the end to come.[47]

Children do not enjoy a story that is too descriptive, but they can appreciate figurative language, provided the comparisons are within their background of understanding.

The style of writing should mirror the setting of

[45]Meindert DeJong, *Hurry Home, Candy* (New York: Harper & Row, 1953), p. 1.
[46]Scott O'Dell, *Island of the Blue Dolphins* (Boston: Houghton Mifflin, 1960), p. 60.
[47]Janet Hickman, *The Thunder-Pup* (New York: Macmillan, 1981), p. 37.

the story and the background of the characters. The beautifully spare prose of *Sarah, Plain and Tall* by Patricia MacLachlan reflects its prairie setting and the straightforward manner of Sarah, a mail-order bride from Maine. The tension of the story revolves around the theme of longing and belonging—Sarah's understated longing for the sea and the children's longing for a mother who will stay and belong to this family. The beauty of the sea is contrasted with that of the prairie, particularly after a severe storm when the yellow green light of the prairie reminds Sarah of a sea squall. She paints a picture of her "prairie-sea" and decides to stay. At the end of the story, Anna, the older sister and narrator, reflects on the future:

> Autumn will come, then winter, cold with a wind that blows like the wind off the sea in Maine. . . . There will be Sarah's sea, blue and gray and green, hanging on the wall. And songs old and new. And Seal with yellow eyes. And there will be Sarah, plain and tall.[48]

Katherine Paterson's island setting for *Jacob Have I Loved* is so vividly described that the reader can almost smell the salt-water marsh and the fisherman's catch of the day. In the introduction, Louise is returning to the island after having been away for many years. She strains to see the first sight of it, calling up island images as she imagines how it will look.

> The ferry will be almost there before I can see Rass, lying low as a terrapin on the faded olive water of the Chesapeake. Suddenly, though, the steeple of the Methodist Church will leap from the Bay, dragging up a cluster of white board houses.[49]

Children in the middle grades can also comprehend symbolic meaning and recurring motifs. Literary symbols are the fusion of some concrete object with an abstract concept or meaning. Eight- and 9-year-olds, for example, were able to understand the significance of Jean Fritz' title *The Cabin Faced West* with the brothers' admonition that no

one was to mention their former home on the eastern side of the mountain. Children as young as 7 and 8 realized the symbolic meaning of the cloak Sarah Noble's mother had given her to wear when she went into the wilderness with her father in the story of *The Courage of Sarah Noble* by Alice Dalgliesh. The double meaning of Eiveen Weiman's title *Which Way Courage?* refers to the decision that an Amish girl named Courage must make about the traditions of her family's beliefs.

Motifs contribute to the structure of a story, for they provide the meaningful threads that run through it and help to unify it. Three motifs reappear throughout Natalie Babbitt's story of *Tuck Everlasting*: a toad, a music box, and the concept of a wheel. The wheel is the one that represents the theme of this gentle fantasy, the cycle of life and death that the Tuck family would never experience. The story opens with a reference to a Ferris wheel. Later the author uses the idea of a wheel to hint at things to come:

> The wood was at the Center, the hub of the wheel. All wheels must have a hub. A Ferris wheel has one, as the sun is the hub of a wheeling calendar. Fixed points they are, and best left undisturbed, for without them, nothing holds together.[50]

Again in the story when Tuck takes Winnie out in the rowboat, he uses the example of a wheel to represent life:

> It's a wheel, Winnie. Everything is a wheel, turning and turning, never stopping. The frog is part of it, and the bugs, and the fish and the wood thrush, too. And people. But never the same ones. Always coming in new, always growing and changing, and always moving on. That's the way it's supposed to be. That's the way it *is*.[51]

The tastes of children place some demands on the writer's style. Children tend to want action in their stories and prefer a style that has movement rather than too much description or introspection. Children also demand conversation in their stories. They feel as *Alice in Wonderland* did when she looked into her sister's book and said, "What's the

[48]Patricia MacLachlan, *Sarah, Plain and Tall* (New York: Harper & Row, 1985), p. 58.

[49]Katherine Paterson, *Jacob Have I Loved* (New York: Crowell, 1980), p. 1.

[50]Natalie Babbitt, *Tuck Everlasting* (New York: Farrar, Straus and Giroux, 1975), p. 4.

[51]Babbitt, p. 62.

use of a book without pictures or conversation?" Master craftsmen at writing dialogue that sounds natural and amusing are A. A. Milne in *Winnie the Pooh,* E. B. White in *Charlotte's Web,* and Arnold Lobel in the Frog and Toad stories. Writing contemporary dialogue is difficult indeed, for current expressions and slang quickly become dated. The dialogue in *Freaky Friday* by Mary Rodgers is witty and believable. Both E. L. Konigsburg and Betsy Byars skillfully capture the sound of today's idiom in their popular stories.

The best test of an author's style is oral reading. Does it read smoothly and effortlessly? Is the conversation stilted, or does it really sound like people talking? Does the author introduce variety in the sentence patterns and use of words? Several years ago the expression "Tom Swifties" was coined to characterize the kind of writing in series books in which every verb was modified by a descriptive adverb—for example: "Tom said earnestly," or "Tom fought gallantly." In one recent children's book the author uses the word "said" some eighty times in just one chapter. Read aloud, this book seems repetitious and dull.

Although it is difficult for children to analyze a particular author's style, they do react to it. Children are quick to detect the patronizing air of an author who talks down to them in little asides, for example. They dislike a story that is too sentimental; and they see through the disguise of the too moralistic tales of the past. Adults respond to the clever, the slyly written, and the sarcastic; children do not. Frequently, children are better able to identify what they dislike about an author's style than to identify what they like. Obviously, the matter of style is important when adults evaluate books for children.

POINT OF VIEW

The author's choice of point of view (or points of view) will necessarily influence style, structure, and revelation of character.

Natalie Babbitt utilizes the storytelling voice of the ominiscient narrator in *Tuck Everlasting.* In this way she can include all thoughts and conversations, even stepping back and warning the reader about "the man in the yellow suit" who had heard Tuck's story. This point of view also enables the author as narrator to provide a prologue and epilogue for the playing out of this fantasy. Using the

third person, the omniscient point of view allows the author the complete freedom to crawl inside the skins of each of the characters, thinking their thoughts, speaking their words, and observing the action of the story.

A limited omniscient point of view also uses the third person, but the author chooses to stand behind one character, so to speak, and tell the story from over his or her shoulder. This concealed narrator point of view is limited to what that character can see, hear, believe, or feel. Katherine Paterson has told the story of *The Great Gilly Hopkins* from this perspective. Gilly is "on stage" throughout and we see the world as Gilly sees it. We know what others think about her through their reactions to her and her interpretations of their thoughts. For example, Gilly is having her first dinner at the home of Trotter, her latest foster mother:

> The meal proceeded without incident. Gilly was hungry but thought it better not to seem to enjoy her supper too much. William Ernest ate silently and steadily with only an occasional glance at Gilly. She could tell that the child was scared silly of her. It was about the only thing in the last two hours that had given her any real satisfaction. Power over the boy was sure to be power over Trotter in the long run.[52]

Increasingly, authors today are using the more direct voice of the first person. The Colliers used this perspective in their historical novel, *My Brother Sam Is Dead.* Told from the point of view of Tim, Sam's younger brother, this story reveals the many viewpoints held concerning the American Revolution. Tim, the younger son, is torn between his admiration for his older brother, who is a Rebel, and love for his Loyalist family. Caught in the middle, he tells his story with an immediacy that draws the reader into the past and makes him live through the despair of one family's conflicting decisions. In the hands of such skillful writers as the Colliers, Madeleine L'Engle in *Ring of Endless Light,* or Katherine Paterson in *Jacob Have I Loved,* the first-person narrative creates a kind of "you are there" feeling.

In the hands of less qualified writers, the use of

[52]Katherine Paterson, *The Great Gilly Hopkins* (New York: Harper & Row, 1978), p. 14.

the first person may limit the author to viewing the world from a 10-year-old perspective. In *Blubber* by Judy Blume, a fifth-grader details the many crude ways that her classmates tease a fat girl named Linda. Jill is describing where the various students live in this passage:

> Linda lives in Hidden Valley. . . . It's called hidden valley because there are a million trees and in the summer you can't see any of the houses. Nobody told me this. It's something I figured out by myself.
>
> My stop is next. Me and Tracy are the only ones who get off there. The Wu family lives across the road from us. They have a lot of animals. All of this doesn't mean we live in the country. It's kind of pretend country. That is, it looks like country because of all the woods but just about everyone who lives here works in the city, like my mother and father. I don't know one single farmer unless you count the woman who sells us vegetables in the summer.[53]

Such writing may make for easy reading, but it does not stretch the reader's vocabulary or imagination. The short, choppy sentences simply reflect a 10-year-old's idioms and grammatical errors. Mollie Hunter warns that the first-person point of view can be restricting:

> The result of this device may be a story to which a reader can relate in very direct terms; but simply because of the narrator's limited vocabulary, there is no scope for adventure in language which allows the reader's mind to soar.[54]

Many authors are writing stories in which several points of view are represented. Betsy Byars utilizes two points of view in *The Animal, the Vegetable & John D Jones*. While vacationing with her divorced father on an island, Clara is swept out to sea on her raft as Deanie, her sister, is left on the beach. The action and point of view switch back and forth from Clara's desparate situation to the frantic rescue efforts of Deanie, their father, his friend Delores, and her son John D Jones. Tensions build while petty differences fall away as they all join in the seemingly hopeless

search for Clara. In *A Chance Child*, Jill Paton Walsh extends a search through time, alternating the action and point of view to focus first on Christopher in England today and then on his horribly neglected half-brother, Creep, who has slipped down the canal into the time of the Industrial Revolution.

The last two chapters in Elaine Konigsburg's *The Mixed-Up Files of Mrs. Basil E. Frankweiler* appear to be written in the first person of Mrs. Frankweiler herself as she describes Claudia and Jamie's visit to her house. Her comments include the chauffeur's report of their trip home in her Rolls Royce and written instructions to her lawyer concerning the final disposition of the drawing of the Michelangelo statue which had so intrigued Claudia and Jamie. Daniel Pinkwater utilizes diaries, announcements, even notes on a policeman's blotter to tell his amusing story of *Slaves of Spiegel*. Such unconventional approaches to storytelling reflect a broader trend in contemporary literature toward experimentation with narrative form. In evaluating all these books, we need to ask why the author chose the particular point of view and how the choice influenced the style of writing, moved the action, and revealed character.

FORMAT

The format of a book includes its size, shape, the design of pages, illustrations, typography, quality of paper, and binding. Frequently, some small aspect of the format, such as the book jacket, will be an important factor in a child's decision to read a story.

Today we have beautiful picture storybooks and informational books for all ages of children. This may be one of the reasons, along with cost of production, that books with more text have fewer illustrations than they did in the past. Transition or chapter books, such as the Ramona stories by Beverly Cleary, do have black and white illustrations that help to emphasize the warm humorous situations in which Ramona becomes involved. Alan Tiegreen's pictures enrich the story of *Ramona and Her Father*, but they are not essential to the telling, as they would be if it were a picture book.

The total format at Marguerite de Angeli's *The Door in the Wall* complements the medieval background of this well-written historical fiction. Her many black and white pictures realistically portray

[53]Judy Blume, *Blubber* (New York: Bradbury Press, 1974), p. 10–11.
[54]Mollie Hunter, *Talent Is Not Enough* (New York: Harper & Row, 1976), p. 23.

the castle, churches, and people of that period. Three illustrations are as rich in color and detail as an original illuminated manuscript. The design of the title and dedication pages reminds the reader that fine books can be works of artistic as well as literary merit.

The design and decorations by Maurice Sendak reflect and extend the theme of Randall Jarrell's haunting fantasy, *The Animal Family*. Based upon man's need for a family, no matter how strange, this is the story of a boy growing to manhood on a deserted island and the family that he gradually acquires. Preceding each chapter that describes the members of the family is a picture of their former habitat; the home of the hunter, the sea of the mermaid, the cave of the bear cub, the rocky cliffs of the lynx, and the drifting canoe of the boy. Only the scenes of their origins are portrayed; the family is left to your imagination. The book itself seems to be almost the shape of a little rectangular house

This well-designed title page reflects the theme of the story at the same time it suggests its medieval setting by creating the look of an illuminated manuscript.

From *Door in the Wall* by Marguerite de Angeli.

put together with thick binder's board covered in blue homespun. Wide margins appear to make a home for the print. The impact of the total format of this book is one of complete harmony with its theme of man's need for home and family.

There are factors other than illustrations that need to be considered in the format of a book. Typography is very important. The type should be large enough for easy reading by the age level for which it was intended. At the same time, if type face is too large, children will consider the book "babyish." The space between the lines (leading) should be sufficient to make the text clear.

The quality of the paper must also be considered. A cream-tinted, dull-finished paper that is thick enough to prevent any penetration of ink is most desirable. The binding should be durable and practical, one that can withstand the use of many interested, but frequently grimy, hands. For library and classroom use, books that are bound in cloth, with soil-resistant, washable covers are recommended. However, a book should never be selected on the basis of format alone, without an accompanying evaluation of its content. No book is better than its text.

ADDITIONAL CONSIDERATIONS

A book should not be considered in isolation but as a part of the larger body of literature. Books need to be compared with other books on the same subject or theme. Is this just another horse story, or does it make a distinctive contribution? Every teacher and librarian should know some books so well that each has developed a personal list of books of excellence that can serve as models for comparison. How does this adventure story compare with Sperry's *Call It Courage,* this fantasy with *A Wrinkle in Time* by L'Engle, or this historical fiction with Speare's *The Sign of the Beaver?* These reference points of outstanding books will help to sharpen evaluations.

An author's new book should be compared with his or her previous works. Contributions by the same author may be uneven and inconsistent in quality. What is the best book Jean George has written? Is *My Side of the Mountain* as good as *Julie of the Wolves?* How does *Cry of the Crow* compare with *Gull Number 737?* Too frequently, books are evaluated on the basis of the author's reputation rather than for their inherent worth.

Many informational and biographical series are

written by different authors. The quality of the book will vary with the ability of the writer, despite similarities in approach and format. Rather than condemning or approving an entire series, one should evaluate a book on its own merits.

A book needs to be compared with outstanding prototypes, with other books written by the same author, and with other books in the same series. What have reputable reviewers said about this book? Where have they placed it in relation to others of its type? A comparison of reviews of one book would probably reveal more similarities than differences, but the elusive factor of personal preference of both adults and children should be respected.

In summary, the basic considerations for the evaluation of fiction for children are a well-constructed plot that moves, a significant theme, authentic setting, a credible point of view, convincing characterization, appropriate style, and attractive format. Not all books achieve excellence in each of these areas. Some books are remembered for their fine characterizations, others for their exciting plots, and others for the evocation of the setting. The "Guides for Evaluating Children's Literature" on pages 28–29 may help the reader look at a book more carefully. However, not all questions will be appropriate for each book.

Classics in Children's Literature

Knowledge of children's classics, those books that have stood the test of time, may provide further guidance for evaluating children's books. What makes a book endure from one generation to another? Jordan states: "Until a book has weathered at least one generation and is accepted in the next, it can hardly be given the rank of a classic. . . ."[55]

Many books and poems have achieved an honored position among the best of children's literature through a combination of adult adoration, parent perpetuation, and teacher assignments. Most adults remember with nostalgia the books they read as children. They tend to think that what they read was best and ignore the possibility of the production of any better books. It is easy to forget that every "classic" was once a new book; that

some of today's new books will be the classics of tomorrow. Times have changed, but some adults seem unaware of the change in children's reading interests. Teachers and librarians should begin with the modern child and his interests, not adults' interests when *they* were children.

Certain books became classics when there were very few books from which children could choose. In fact, many classics were not children's books at all, but were written for adults. In their desire to read, children claimed these adult books, struggled through the difficult parts, and disregarded what they did not understand. They had no other choice. Today's child is not so persevering because he sees no reason for it. The introductory sentence of *Robinson Crusoe* runs the length of the entire first page and contains difficult vocabulary and syntax. Defoe wrote the story in 1719 for adult readers, but children quickly discovered this story of shipwreck and adventure and plunged into it. However, they can find the same tingling excitement and more readable prose in Hunter's *A Stranger Came Ashore* or O'Dell's *Island of the Blue Dolphins*.

The classics should not be exempted from re-evaluation by virtue of their past veneration. They should be able to compete favorably with contempary books. Unimpressed by vintage or lineage, children seldom read a book because they think they should. They read more for enjoyment than edification. Some books have been kept alive from one generation to the next by common consent; these are the true classics of children's literature. No teacher or parent has to cajole a child into reading them. These books can hold their own amid the ever-increasing number of new and beautiful books of today.

What is the continuing appeal of these well-loved books for the contemporary child? Primarily, they are magnificent stories. There are adventure and suspense in *Treasure Island, The Adventures of Tom Sawyer,* and *The Adventures of Huckleberry Finn.* Mystery and excitement fill the stories of *Hans Brinker, or The Silver Skates* and *The Secret Garden.* The characterization in most of the classics is outstanding. There is very little plot in the story of *Little Women,* but what reader can forget the March sisters? They could have been your next-door neighbors. This is also true of Tom and Aunt Polly and Huck. The animal personalities of Christopher Robin's stuffed toys are unmis-

[55]Alice M. Jordan, *Children's Classics* (Boston: The Horn Book, Inc., 1947), p. 4.

takable. Even adults have known a Bear of Little Brain and a gloomy Eeyore! And anyone, young or old, who has weathered the disappointments of friendship can admire the enduring loyalty of Ratty and Mole for the rich conceited Toad who drags them away from their beloved riverbank on one wild escapade after another.

The appeal of many of the classics is based upon the type of story they represent. Family chronicles such as *Little Women* and "The Little House" books give the reader a sense of warmth and security. A feeling of place and atmosphere is skillfully developed in the well-loved *Heidi.* Animal stories are represented by *Black Beauty, The Jungle Book,* and *Bambi. Black Beauty* is a sentimental tale filled with short essays on the prevention of cruelty to animals. The theme was timely in 1877 when Anna Sewell wrote this story. However, the genuine emotion in *Black Beauty* appears to be timeless, for it remains popular despite its Victorian airs. Boys and girls still enjoy the beautifully written story of Mowgli who was adopted by the wolf pack when he was a baby and taught the law of the jungle by Bagheera, the panther, and Baloo, the bear. Other favorites in Rudyard Kipling's *The Jungle Book* include "Rikki-Tikki-Tavi," the story of a mongoose, and "Toomai of the Elephants." Most children respond favorably to Felix Salten's sensitively written, if somewhat sentimental, life story of *Bambi,* a deer of the Danube forest.

Many classics are fantasies. Children's reactions to fantasy are similar to those of many adults, who thoroughly enjoy or completely reject the fantastic. For some people, *Alice in Wonderland, Peter Pan, The Wind in the Willows, Winnie the Pooh,* and *The Wizard of Oz* have never been surpassed in the field of children's literature. Others actively dislike these books. Many readers do not "discover" these fantasies until they are adults, and then they applaud them as excellent fare for children! True classics appeal to both children and adults. As one father reported: "I've learned one important thing in three years. It's possible to read to a young child without boring either child or parent. I think parent's boredom is just as important as the child's."[56]

[56]Edward Eager,"A Father's Minority Report," reprinted in *A Horn Book Sampler* (Boston: Horn Book, 1959), p. 166.

GUIDES FOR EVALUATING CHILDREN'S LITERATURE

• Before reading:
What kind of book is this?
What does the reader anticipate from the:
    Title?
    Dust jacket illustration?
    Size of print?
    Illustrations?
    Chapter headings?
    Opening page?
For what age range is this book appropriate?

• Plot:
Does the book tell a good story? Will children enjoy it?
Is there action? Does the story move?
Is the plot original and fresh?
Is it plausible and credible?
    Is there preparation for the events?
    Is there a logical series of happenings?
    Is there a basis of cause and effect in the happenings?
Is there an identifiable climax?
How do events build to a climax?
Is the plot well constructed?

• Setting:
Where does the story take place?
How does the author indicate the time?
How does the setting affect the action, characters, or theme?
Does the story transcend the setting and have universal implications?

• Theme:
Does the story have a theme?
Is the theme worth imparting to children?
Does the theme emerge naturally from the story, or is it stated too obviously?
Does the theme overpower the story?
Does it avoid moralizing?

• Characterization:
How does the author reveal characters?
    Through narration?
    In conversation?
    By thoughts of others?
    By thoughts of the character?
    Through action?
Are the characters convincing and credible?
Do we see their strengths and their weaknesses?
Does the author avoid stereotyping?
Is the behavior of the characters consistent with their ages and background?
Is there any character development or growth?
Has the author shown the causes of character behavior or development?

• Style:
Is the style of writing appropriate to the subject?
Is the style straightforward or figurative?
Is the dialogue natural and suited to the characters?
How did the author create a mood? Is the overall impression one of mystery, gloom,
    evil, joy, security?
What symbols has the author used to intensify meaning?

• Point of view:
Is the point of view from which the story is told appropriate to the purpose of the
    book?
Does the point of view change?
Does the point of view limit the reader's horizon, or enlarge it?
Why did the author choose this particular point of view?

• Format:
Do the illustrations enhance or extend the story?
Are the illustrations consistent with the story?
How is a format of the book related to the text?
What is the quality of the paper?
How sturdy is the binding?

• Additional considerations:
How does the book compare with other books on the same subject?
How does the book compare with other books written by the same author?
How have other reviewers evaluated this book?

The Award Books[57]

Teachers and librarians will find it helpful to be familiar with books that have won awards. These awards, which have been established for various purposes, provide criteria for what experts consider to be the best in children's literature. Such awards have helped to counteract the judgment of the market place by focusing attention on beautiful and worthwhile books. In an age of mass production, they have stimulated artists, authors, and publishers to produce books of distinction and have helped children's literature achieve a worthy status.

Occasionally, one hears the criticism that the award books are not popular with children. This is true of some of them. However, most of the awards are not based on popularity but on well-known recognized excellence. They were never intended to rubber-stamp the tastes of children, but to raise them. Children's reactions to books are significant, and there are many awards, particularly state awards, which are voted on by children. However, popularity of a book, whether for children or for adults, is not necessarily a mark of distinctive writing. How many best-sellers win the Pulitzer Prize for literature? Because there are now more than 100 awards for various categories of children's literature, only the best-known ones will be discussed here.

NEWBERY AND CALDECOTT AWARDS

The two most coveted awards in children's literature are the Newbery and Caldecott awards, determined every year by two fifteen-member committees of the Association for Library Service to Children, a division of the American Library Association. A candidate for either of the awards must be a citizen or resident of the United States.

The John Newbery Medal, established in 1922, is the oldest award for children's books. It is named for John Newbery, a British publisher and bookseller of the eighteenth century. Appropriately called the "father of children's literature," he was the first to conceive the idea of publishing books expressly for children. The Newbery Medal is awarded to the author of the most distinguished contribution to American literature for children published the preceding year.

The Randolph J. Caldecott Medal is named in honor of the great English illustrator of the nineteenth century, Randolph Caldecott. Caldecott was well known for his sprightly picture books depicting the country life of England. The Caldecott Medal, established in 1938, is awarded to the most distinguished American picture book for children chosen from those first published in the United States during the previous year. The text should be worthy of the illustrations, but the award is made primarily for the artwork.

Students of children's literature would do well to acquaint themselves with some of these award-winning books and their authors and illustrators. It is also enlightening to review the Honor Books for these awards. While the highly praised *Charlotte's Web* was an Honor Book, the winner that year was, *Secret of the Andes,* a beautifully written and sensitive story that, unfortunately, is not popular. It is interesting to see the number of times a particular author has been nominated and still has failed to win. Books by Laura Ingalls Wilder were honored for five different years, but never received the award. Final restitution was made, perhaps, by the establishment of the Laura Ingalls Wilder Award, which serves a different purpose. *what purpose?*

Since the selection for the Newbery award must be limited to books published in one year, the quality of the award books varies, for certain years produce a richer harvest than others. The selection in 1964 must have been very difficult, for committee members had to choose from among Emily Neville's *It's Like This, Cat,* Sterling North's *Rascal,* and Esther Weir's *The Loner.* Again in 1971 it must have been frustrating to make a choice from among Betsy Byars' *Summer of the Swans,* Natalie Babbitt's *Kneeknock Rise,* Sylvia Engdahl's *Enchantress from the Stars,* and Scott O'Dell's *Sing Down the Moon.* In the majority of cases, the years have shown the choices to have been wise ones. Many age ranges are represented, but most of the Newbery books are for able, mature readers. Frequently, these books have to be read aloud and discussed with an adult before children develop a taste for their excellence.

[57]See Appendix A for various children's book awards, criteria, and winners. For a complete listing of awards for children's books, consult *Children's Books: Awards and Prizes* published by the Children's Book Council Inc., 67 Irving Place, New York, NY 10003.

In this Caldecott Award winning book, the father loads up his ox-cart with the many things his family have been making and growing all year long to take to market. Barbara Cooney's paintings on wood accurately reflect the New England landscapes and early American primitive art.

From *Ox-Cart Man* by Donald Hall.

There has been less controversy over the choices for the Caldecott award. The list again shows variety as to type of artwork, media used, age appeal, and subject matter. The range of artwork includes the lovely seascapes of Robert McCloskey's *Time of Wonder*, the comic, almost cartoon, style of William Steig's *Sylvester and the Magic Pebble*, the stylized patterns in *Drummer Hoff* by Ed Emberley, or the surrealism of Chris Van Allsburg in *The Polar Express*. Various media are represented among the winners, including collage, woodcut, watercolor, opaque paints, and various combinations of pen and ink and paint. Marcia Brown has won the Caldecott award three times, while Chris Van Allsburg, Robert McCloskey, Nonny Hogrogian, Leo and Diane Dillon, and Barbara Cooney have been honored twice. Joseph Krumgold, Elizabeth Speare, and Katherine Paterson have each received two Newbery awards, while Robert Lawson continues to be the only person who has won both the Newbery and Caldecott awards.

INTERNATIONAL BOOK AWARD

The Hans Christian Andersen Medal was established in 1956 as the first international children's book award. It is given by the International Board of Books for Young People every two years to a living author and an illustrator (since 1966) in recognition of his or her entire body of work. Meindert DeJong, Maurice Sendak, Scott O'Dell, and Paula Fox are the only Americans to have received a medal so far.

LIFETIME CONTRIBUTIONS

To honor an author or illustrator for a substantial and lasting contribution to children's literature, the Laura Ingalls Wilder Award was established in 1954 and is given by the Association for Library Service to Children of the American Library Association. It was presented first to Laura Ingalls Wilder herself, for her "Little House" books. First presented every five years, and now every three years, the award makes no requirement concerning the number of books that must be produced, but a body of work is implied and the books must be published in the United States. Recipients of this major award after the first presentation are: Clara Ingram Judson, Ruth Sawyer, E. B. White, Beverly Cleary, Theodore Geisel (Dr.Seuss), Maurice Sendak, and Jean Fritz.

In 1959 The Catholic Library Association established a somewhat similar award to be presented annually for "continued distinguished contribution to children's literature." The Regina Medal "is not limited to one creed, nor one country, or to one criterion, other than excellence." It may be given to writers, illustrators, editors, and others who have given unstintingly of their creative genius to the field.

There was no major award for children's poetry until 1977, when the National Council of Teachers of English established the Award for Excellence in Poetry for Children, to be given to a living American poet. Like the Wilder Award and the Regina Medal, the poetry award recognizes the writer's entire body of work. Octogenarian David McCord was the first recipient; others have included Aileen Fisher, Karla Kuskin, Myra Cohn Livingston, Eve Merriam, John Ciardi, and Lilian Moore.

No one but the most interested follower of children's literature would want to remember all the awards that are given for children's books. Like the coveted "Oscars" of the motion picture industry and the "Emmys" of television, the awards in children's literature focus attention not only on the winners of the year but also on the entire field of endeavor. They recognize and honor the best and also point the way to improved writing, illustrating, and producing of worthwhile and attractive books for children.

GUIDELINES FOR SELECTION OF MATERIALS

The Need for Selection

Evaluation of a single book involves knowledge of literary criticism. Evaluation of a particular book for a particular child involves an understanding of both literature and the background and development of the child as a reader. Evaluation of many books, films, filmstrips, discs, tapes, and other media for many children who will use them for a variety of purposes requires the establishment of criteria for selection.

While the subject of this text is primarily children's books, the authors do approve the concept of a school library media center for each school. With more than 40,000 children's books in print, it becomes almost impossible for one text to include criteria for both books and media. The adequate evaluation of films, filmstrips, tapes, and computer software demands another text. The explosion of knowledge is part of the reality of the twentieth century. It has been estimated that beginning with the year 1 A. D., knowledge doubled by 1750, again by 1900, the third time by 1950, the fourth time by 1960, and has continued to double every eight to ten years since. Children should have the opportunity to obtain information on any subject within their comprehension, regardless of format or "packaging" of the source. Today we have an abundance of materials in a diversity of formats covering all areas of human knowledge. School and library budgets can be stretched only so far, which increases the complexity of selecting from such a vast array of material.

Since the subject matter of contemporary children's books is changing, the need for written criteria of selection has increased. The new realism in children's books and young adult novels simply reflects the new freedom that can be seen on TV, at the movies, and in current best-sellers. It makes no sense to "protect" children from well-written or well-presented materials on such controversial subjects as abortion, narcotics, or sexual deviations, yet allow them to see sensational stories on the same subjects on TV. Increased sensitivity to sexism, racism, and bias in books and nonbook materials is another area of recent concern that points up the need for a clear statement on selection policies.

The period of childhood is decreasing; our children are growing up faster today than twenty years ago. In the limited time children have to be children, we want to give them the very best books available. The adage of "the right book at the right time" still holds true. Most children's books have to be read at the appropriate age and stage in the development of a child or they will *never be read.* The 8-year-old does not read *The Tale of Peter Rabbit;* the 12-year-old doesn't want to be seen reading *Ramona Quimby, Age 8;* and the junior high student has outgrown *Little House in the Big Woods.* Introduced at the right time, each of these books would have provided a rich, satisfying experience of literature.

The number of books that any one child can read is limited, also. Assuming that a child reads one book every two weeks from the time he is 7 (when independent reading may begin) until he is 13 or 14 (when many young people start reading adult books), he will read about twenty-five books a year, or some 200 books during this period of childhood. With over 40,000 children's books in print, it is possible that a child may read widely, *yet never read a significant book.* Under these circumstances, the need for good book selection becomes even more imperative.

Principles of Selection

With the increase of both numbers of books published and challenges to the selection of certain books, it is essential that schools develop a selection policy. All library groups strongly recommend that each school district develop such a written statement that governs its selection of material. This policy statement should be approved by the school board and subsequently supported by them if challenged. Factors to be considered in such a policy would include: who selects the materials; the quality of material; appropriate content; needs and interests of special children; school curriculum needs; providing for balance in the collection; procedures to follow for censorship and challenged material.

WHO SELECTS THE MATERIALS?

Teachers, students, and parents may recommend particular titles, but the final selection of materials for the school library should be determined by professionally trained personnel. Larger school systems frequently have book selection meetings of all their librarians. At these meetings individual librarians review publishers' advance copies or books that have been ordered on approval. They give their own evaluations but usually say how they agree or disagree with reviews of the book in professional journals. Some librarians from smaller school systems or communities must select the books from reviews without seeing the books themselves. Reliable reviews of children's books play an important part, then, in the selection of books. Four well-known review journals are: *The Booklist, The Bulletin of the Center for Children's Books, The Horn Book Magazine,* and *School Library Journal.* Other sources for reviews are listed in Appendix B.

QUALITY OF MATERIAL

Criteria for evaluation and selection of all types of instructional materials should be established. Such criteria should be available in written form. Books for the collection should meet the criteria of fine writing described earlier in this chapter. More detailed criteria for each genre are given in the chapters in Part II of this text.

Decisions have to be made concerning the conflict between popular demand and quality literature. Librarians have agonized over whether to buy such popular formula books as the Nancy Drew mysteries, the Hardy Boys or the "Choose Your Own Adventure" series. Some have voted in favor of including them in their libraries on the

In Mickey's dream he falls out of his clothes and into the fanciful world of the "night kitchen." More than one librarian censored Mickey's nudity by painting black tempera diapers on him.

From *In the Night Kitchen* by Maurice Sendak.

basis that they "hook children on books." Others have held the line for better-written stories, maintaining that it is possible to find the same kind of excitement and suspense in well-written books. This is a decision that must be made by individual librarians, based on their knowledge of the reading ability and interests of the children they serve and their own basic philosophy of book selection.

Arguments for and against rewritten classics have followed the same line of reasoning. If a child can't read Mark Twain's *Tom Sawyer,* shouldn't we provide an edition that he can read? But immediately we realize that it is the *original* book that has become a classic. When it is rewritten, though it may retain the original plot line, it is likely to lose the qualities that made it a classic in the first place.

Any book that Walt Disney adapts for a film im-

mediately becomes Walt Disney's . . . , as in *Walt Disney's Winnie the Pooh,* for example. The quality and language of these stories are drastically changed, and yet these are the books that children know and ask for. Many children seeing the film about Mrs. Brisby and "The Secret of NIMH" do not even know O'Brien's Newbery award winner, *Mrs. Frisby and the Rats of NIMH,* on which it was based. Do we give them the book based on the film and let them compare it to the original, or do we give them just the award-winner? These are hard and difficult decisions, but they must be made when selecting books. A written policy statement of the criteria to be used when purchasing books will help solve this dilemma.

APPROPRIATE CONTENT

The content of the materials to be selected must be evaluated in terms of the quality of the writing or presentation. Almost any subject can be written about for children depending on the honesty and sensitivity of its treatment by the author. In order to be specific, two examples are given. The first book is recommended; the second is not.

The story of the growing up of 13-year-old Davy Ross is sensitively told by John Donovan in the book, *I'll Get There, It Better Be Worth the Trip.* Following the death of a loved grandmother, Davy is sent to live in a New york City apartment with a mother he hardly knows, a mother who drinks too much. Davy adjusts to his new life and school, but he is desperately lonely until he finds a real friend in Douglass Altschuler. While the boys are on the floor roughhousing with their dog, an incident of open sexuality between them occurs. Davy's mother makes much more of the incident than either of the boys felt, but this adds to Davy's feelings of fear and guilt. The problem is resolved, and Davy develops a better sense of who he is as he moves toward maturity. The incidence of sex in the story is essential to its theme. It grows naturally out of the characters' backgrounds and present situation. The author's point of view is one of sympathy and compassion for an adolescent who feels very alone in his world.

A brief encounter with sex is also part of the story of *Gone and Back* by Nathaniel Benchley. Obadiah, a 13-year-old boy, and his family join the race for new lands in the West. During their trek Obadiah meets Lennie, a girl about his age.

Talking in a barn one day Lennie asks Obadiah if he knows what it is to mate and if he would like to learn. He does; he would; so they do. And that's the end of the scene. It could be removed from the story and never missed in much the same way as the obligatory sex scenes of some adult fiction. Such writing may have shock value, but it does not constitute quality literature.

Controversy about the inappropriateness of violence in books for young children has long been a subject for discussion. After protests by some psychologists, fairy tales were rewritten to temper the grim details that were once included. However, folk tales represent the plight of the human condition and are symbolic of good and evil. The horror may serve as catharsis for fears and anxieties that may be larger than those depicted in the stories. In Grimm's story of *The Seven Ravens* the little girl must cut off her finger in order to enter the crystal palace and save her brothers. Neither pain nor blood is described. In the broad context of the story the action represents the sacrifice of the girl who was partially responsible for the original curse placed upon her brothers. The rewards of the fairy tale are not easily won, and something must be given for each favor received. The monsters in *Where the Wild Things Are* by Sendak have been criticized for being too grotesque and frightening for young children. Yet children do not seem frightened of them at all. And the important theme of that story is that Max does return home where he finds the reality of warmth and love.

In some instances, books may be the very instruments by which children first encounter death or the horrors of war. How many countless children have wept over the death of Beth in *Little Women,* the necessary destruction of the faithful dog in *Old Yeller,* and even the end of a loyal spider in *Charlotte's Web?* We hope that no children will ever again know the horror of a nuclear attack. *Hiroshima No Pika* by Toshi Maruki with its starkly vivid writing and expressionistic pictures, helps children see the tragic events in the lives of one family. Seven-year-old Mii, her mother and father are enjoying their breakfast of sweet potatoes when the United States Air Force bomber, the *Enola Gay,* drops the first atomic bomb on the city. Mii survived but she never grows in mind or body after "the flash." Her mother saves her father, only to have him die later of radiation sickness. The book clearly shows that Americans caused "the flash." The author wrote it for children in the hope that never again would one nation inflict such horror on another. This may not be a book all children are fortified to withstand, yet our very survival may depend upon today's children understanding the facts surrounding Hiroshima. This simple account of one family's survival particularizes their suffering in a way that social studies texts fail to do.

We should not deliberately shock or frighten a child until such time as he or she may have developed the maturity and inner strength to face the tragedies of life. However, literature is one way to experience life, if only vicariously. In the process, a reader can be fortified and educated.

NEEDS AND INTERESTS OF CHILDREN

Materials should always be purchased in terms of the children who will be using them. Chapter 2 emphasizes the needs and interests of all children in terms of their response to literature. As more and more schools mainstream children with special needs, libraries should be certain to include materials for them. Partially sighted children require books with large type; blind children, books in Braille. Children who come from nonliterate homes (and increasingly television has made the climate in many homes today nonliterate) may need more easy-reading books. At the same time our sophisticated culture has pushed the child into growing up faster and faster. As a result middle-graders are clamoring for young adult books. All children, regardless of their background, should have access to a wide diversity of multi-cultural books to choose from. Black children should have many books that reflect the black experience, just as Latinos and Asian-Americans should have an opportunity to see themselves in books. In a pluralistic society, all children should have an opportunity to read about children of different racial, religious, and ethnic backgrounds. Children need books that will give them insight into their own lives, but they should also have books to take them out of those lives to help them see the world in its many dimensions. Suburban children need to read of life in the ghetto—it may be their only contact with it. And slum children must be introduced to the best literature we have. We cannot tolerate the notion that somehow it is all right to give poor children poor books. Regardless of a child's background, a good selection policy should provide a wide range of quality books and diversity of materials for all children.

SCHOOL CURRICULUM NEEDS

Librarians will consider the particular needs of the school curriculum when ordering materials. Particular units in social studies—such as "The Role of Women in History" or a science unit on ecology and pollution or a study of African folklore in literature—may require special books, films, filmstrips, or artifacts. Intensive study of the local region will require additional copies of books about the particular state, industries, and people of the region. Children may want to go out and videotape interviews of persons in the neighborhood, or they could film sites of local interest. Teachers and librarians will want to have the equipment ready for children's first-hand research. Many teachers want changing classroom libraries of paperback books. These are best ordered and kept in the school library media center, where teachers can select from them. Such arrangements must be made jointly with the personnel of the center and the rest of the faculty. The function of the school library media center is to provide a wide range of materials specially chosen to meet the demands of the school curriculum.

BALANCE IN THE COLLECTION

Every school library needs to maintain a balanced collection. Keeping in mind the total needs of the school, the librarian will consider the following balances: book and nonbook material (including videotapes, tapes, records, films, discs, filmstrips, and other materials), hardback and paperback books, reference books, and trade books, fiction and non-fiction, poetry and prose, classics (both old and "new"), realistic and fanciful stories, books for younger and older children, books for poor and superior readers at each grade level, books for teachers to read to students and use for enrichment purposes, and professional books for teachers and parents.

The librarian must always select materials in terms of the present library collection. What are the voids and needs in the collection now? What replacements should be considered? How many duplicate copies of a particularly popular book should be ordered? Every book added to a collection should make some distinct contribution to it. Just because children are interested in magnets does not mean that all new books on magnets should be ordered. What is unique about a particular book? Perhaps it presents new information; perhaps the experiments are more clearly written than in similar books; or it may be for a different age group than the one already in the library. Only the person who knows the total collection can make these book-buying decisions.

SELECTION VS. CENSORSHIP

There is a fine line between careful selection of books for children and censorship. The goal of selection is to include a book on the basis of its quality of writing and total impact; the goal of censorship is to exclude a book in which the content (or even one part) is considered objectionable. Selection policies recommend a balanced collection representative of the various beliefs held by a pluralistic society; censors would impose their privately held beliefs on all.

The National Council of Teachers of English has published a statement contrasting the characteristics of censorship with those of professional guidelines set up to provide criteria for selection of materials (see facing page).

The American Library Association has issued a "Library Bill of Rights," adopted in 1948 and amended in 1967, 1969, and 1980. This statement contains six policies relating to censorship of books and the right of free access to the library for all individuals or groups. This statement has been endorsed by the American Association of School Librarians, also.

Almost every school and each children's librarian in a public library has faced some criticism of the books in the children's collection. Criticism is not necessarily censorship, however. Parents, other faculty members, or citizens have a right to discuss the reasons for the selection of a particular book. It is only when they seek to have the book banned, removed from the shelves, restricted in use, or altered that they are assuming the role of censors.

In the early 1980s, censorship increased dramat-

CENSORSHIP DISTINGUISHED FROM PROFESSIONAL GUIDELINES: EXAMPLES [58]

EXAMPLES OF CENSORSHIP	EXAMPLES OF PROFESSIONAL GUIDELINES
1. EXCLUDE SPECIFIC MATERIALS OR METHODS *Example:* Eliminate books with unhappy endings.	**1. INCLUDE SPECIFIC MATERIALS OR METHODS** *Example:* Include some books with unhappy endings to give a varied view of life.
2. ARE ESSENTIALLY NEGATIVE *Example:* Review your classroom library and eliminate books that include stereotypes.	**2. ARE ESSENTIALLY AFFIRMATIVE** *Example:* Review your classroom library. If necessary, add books that portray groups in nonstereotypical ways.
3. INTEND TO CONTROL *Example:* Do not accept *policeman.* Insist that students say and write *police officer.*	**3. INTEND TO ADVISE** *Example:* Encourage such nonlimiting alternatives for *policeman* as *police officer, officer of the law,* or *law enforcer.*
4. SEEK TO INDOCTRINATE, TO LIMIT ACCESS TO IDEAS AND INFORMATION *Example:* Drug Abuse is a menace to students. Elimate all books that portray drug abuse.	**4. SEEK TO EDUCATE, TO INCREASE ACCESS TO IDEAS AND INFORMATION** *Example:* Include at appropriate grade levels books that will help students understand the personal and social consequences of drug abuse.
5. LOOK AT PARTS OF A WORK IN ISOLATION *Example:* Remove this book. The language includes profanity.	**5. SEE THE RELATIONSHIP OF PARTS TO EACH OTHER AND TO A WORK AS A WHOLE** *Example:* Determine whether the profanity is integral to portrayal of character and development of theme in the book.

[58] *Statement of Censorship and Professional Guidelines,* approved by the Board of Directors of the National Council of Teachers of English, 1982. Reproduced with permission.

ically throughout the country. Individuals and groups from both the right and the left, like the Moral Majority, the religious fundamentalists, members of the feminist movement, and The Council on Interracial Books for Children, all demanded the removal of certain children's books from libraries for various reasons. Targets of the censor generally include profanity of any kind; sex; sexuality; obscenity; the "isms," including sexism, racism, ageism; and the portrayal of witchcraft; religion; nudity; and drugs.

Award books are objects of censorship as readily as other books. The Caldecott award-winning book, *Sylvester and the Magic Pebble* by William Steig, was objected to by law-enforcement groups because it portrays police as pigs. It made no difference that all the characters in the book are animals, that Sylvester and his family are donkeys, and that other characters besides police are also shown as pigs. Steig obviously enjoys telling about and drawing pigs; his first book for children was *Roland, The Minstrel Pig,* and the main character in *The Amazing Bone* is Pearl, an attractive and exceptional pig.

Madeleine L'Engle's Newbery award book, *A Wrinkle in Time,* has been attacked as being non-Christian because of its references to the Happy Medium and Mrs. Who, Mrs. Whatsit, and Mrs. Which, supernatural beings that some have labeled witches. Madeleine L'Engle is well-known for her adult writings on Christianity; nevertheless, ironically, religious literalists have paid no attention to the total message of good overcoming evil in this well-written fantasy, but have seen only "witches."

LIBRARY BILL OF RIGHTS[59]

The American Library Association affirms that all libraries are forums for information and ideas, and that the following basic policies should guide their services.

1. Books and other library resources should be provided for the interest, information, and enlightenment of all people of the community the library serves. Materials should not be excluded because of the origin, background, or views of those contributing to their creation.

2. Libraries should provide materials and information presenting all points of view on current and historical issues. Materials should not be proscribed or removed because of partisan or doctrinal disapproval.

3. Libraries should challenge censorship in the fulfillment of their responsibility to provide information and enlightenment.

4. Libraries should cooperate with all persons and groups concerned with resisting abridgment of free expression and free access to ideas.

5. A person's right to use a library should not be denied or abridged because of origin, age, background, or views.

6. Libraries which make exhibit spaces and meeting rooms available to the public they serve should make such facilities available on an equitable basis, regardless of the beliefs or affiliations of individuals or groups requesting their use.

The Great Gilly Hopkins, a National Book Award winner written by Katherine Paterson, a minister's wife and twice the winner of The Newbery award for excellence in writing, was criticized because Gilly uses an occasional "damn." Yet surely a foster child who has been in three homes in three years is not likely to be a model of refinement. What is noteworthy about this book is the gradual and believable *change* in Gilly's behavior and character. In Jean Fritz's well-received picture-book biography *And Then What Happened, Paul Revere?,* an English Redcoat swears as he apprehends Paul Revere riding to rouse Concord. Fritz was criticized for using "damn," even though it is a matter of historical record.

Contemporary fiction for older children has come under increasing attack as these books began to show the influence of the new freedom allowed in books and films for adults. Such titles as Holland's *The Man Without a Face,* which deals sensitively with a homosexual relationship, Klein's *Mom, the Wolf Man and Me,* which openly accepts alternative family patterns, or Blume's *Deenie,* which includes several references to masturbation, have all been targets of criticism and

censorship attempts. Criteria for these books will be thoroughly discussed in Chapter 9.

A more subtle and frightening kind of censorship is the kind practiced voluntarily by librarians and teachers. If a book has come under negative scrutiny in a nearby town, it is carefully placed under the librarian's desk until the controversy dies down. Or, perhaps the librarians and the teachers just do not order controversial books. "Why stir up trouble when there are so many other good books available?" they falsely reason. Some librarians have even defaced books in their misguided efforts to avoid controversy. More than one librarian censored Sendak's *In the Night Kitchen* by painting black tempera diapers on the naked hero, Mickey! In-house censorship or "closet censorship" is difficult to identify. Selection is a positive process; books are added to a collection for their excellence, to meet a curriculum need, to bring balance to the curriculum. Censorship is negative. Whenever books are rejected for non-literary reasons, for fear of outside criticism,

[59]*Intellectual Freedom Manual,* 2d ed. (Chicago: American Library Association, 1983), p. 14.

for example, librarians and teachers need to ask themselves if they are practicing selection or censorship.

DEALING WITH CENSORSHIP

If there is a demand for censorship, how should it be handled? The first rule is to recognize that anyone has the right to question specific selections. The second rule is to be prepared—have an accepted response process. The written selection policy statement should contain a standardized procedure to follow when materials are challenged. The following guidelines may be useful:

1. Do not discuss the issue until you can be prepared. Give the person a form for "reconsideration of a book" and make an appointment to discuss the book.
2. Make copies of reviews of the questioned book from professional reviewing journals.
3. Notify your principal of the expressed concern. Give him or her copies of the reviews and a memo outlining your reason for selecting the book.
4. At your conference explain the school's selection policy and present copies of the reviews of the book and your memo on your reason for selecting it.
5. Listen to the stated concern as objectively as possible.
6. Inform the person that the material will be reconsidered by the selection committee if he or she wishes it to be.
7. Submit the reconsideration form to the book selection committee of librarians, teachers, and parent representative for their discussion and decision.
8. Inform the person expressing the concern what the committee decided and why.

Several forms for Reconsideration of Materials are available upon request. The National Council of Teachers of English provides one in their booklet *The Students' Right to Know*.[60] The American Library Association has shortened their form to really just two questions: (1) What brought this title to your attention? (2) Please comment on the resource as a whole, as well as being specific about those matters which concern you.[61] The major consideration, then, is to have a form available when you need it and to make it specific to the book itself and simple enough to fill out.

Generally, if parents or other citizens feel their voices have been heard and that they have been dealt with fairly, they will abide by the decision of the book selection committee. If, however, they represent a group which is determined to impose its values on the schools, they will continue their pressure. This is why it is essential that every library have a Library Selection Policy supported by the board and administration. Librarians and teachers also need to be aware of the support they can obtain from such organizations as the Office for Intellectual Freedom of The American Library Association, Freedom to Read Foundation of ALA, The National Council of Teachers of English, The International Reading Association, American Civil Liberties Union, and People for the American Way.

Any challenge to a book is a matter to be taken seriously. Ultimately, what is involved is the freedom to learn and freedom of information, both essential to American rights based on our democratic heritage and principles.

[60]*The Students' Right to Know* (Urbana, Ill.: National Council of Teachers of English, 1982).
[61]"Statement of Concern about Library/Media Center Resources" in *Intellectual Freedom Manual* (Chicago: American Library Association, 1983), p. 167.

SUGGESTED LEARNING EXPERIENCES

1. Write your reading autobiography. What memories do you have of your early reading? Did either of your parents read to you? Do you recall any of the books they read? Did any teachers or librarians read aloud to you? What books did you own as a child? What were some of your favorites? Do you recall any that you did not like? Do you know why?
2. Can you think of any one book that you read and reread as a child? What particular qualities of the story appealed to you? Reread it and evaluate it according to the criteria established in this chapter. Would you still recommend it for children?

3. Read one of the series books: the Bobbsey Twins, the Hardy Boys, or the Nancy Drew series. Look closely at the literary craftsmanship of this book. How many contrived incidents can you find? Do the characters have real strengths *and* weaknesses? If you read this book aloud, how would it sound?
4. Form a mock Newbery award committee and review the winners and Honor Books for one year. Do you agree with the opinions of the actual judges? Be prepared to state your reasons why or why not.
5. Read a recently published children's book; then find reviews from two or more sources. Compare the reviews with your own reaction. Do the reviewers seem to use the same criteria as you do in judging this book?
6. Using at least three of the selection aids described in Appendix B, make a list of appropriate poems, books, and materials that you would want to use to explore a particular topic with a selected age grouping. You might choose "mice," "night," or "friends" for primary grades; "the role of women," "pollution," or "journeys" might be topics for older children.
7. Interview a teacher or librarian to find out what use he or she makes of the award books. How important do they think children's book awards are?
8. Interview a librarian and ask to see the current Policy for Selection. Ask if the library has had censorship problems and what was done about them.

RELATED READINGS

1. Butler, Dorothy. *Cushla and Her Books*. Boston: Horn Book, 1980.
   A moving account of the power of books in the life of a multi-handicapped little girl. Charts at the end of the report show all of Cushla's interactions with books for one typical day, while another one lists the books shared with her for the first four years of her life.
2. "Censorship: Don't Let It Become an Issue in Your School" by NCTE Committee. *Language Arts,* February, 1978. Reprints available from the National Council of Teachers of English, Urbana, Ill.
   Provides excellent guidelines for establishing a selection policy that would help prevent censorship from occurring. Also outlines strategies for dealing with censors.
3. *Children's Books: Awards and Prizes*. New York: The Children's Book Council, 1986.
   A complete listing of all awards and prizes given to children's books. Updated frequently.
4. Chukovsky, Kornei. *From Two to Five,* translated and edited by Miriam Morton. Berkeley: University of California Press, 1963; paperback, 1974.
   A fascinating discussion by a Russian children's poet on the child's growth in language, linguistic creativity, and love of poetry and fantasy.
5. Clark, Margaret M. *Young Fluent Readers*. Exeter, N. H., and London: Heinemann Educational Books, 1976.
   An intensive detailed study of thirty-two Scottish children who were reading fluently and with understanding at approximately 5 years of age, before they started school.
6. Davis, James E., ed. *Dealing with Censorship*. Urbana, Ill.: National Council of Teachers of English, 1979.
   This useful and readable book presents eighteen essays that deal with the current climate regarding censorship, issues and pressures influencing the teaching of language arts, and suggestions for dealing with censorship.
7. Egoff, Sheila, G. T. Stubbs, and L. F. Ashley. *Only Connect: Readings on Children's Literature,* 2nd ed. Toronto: Oxford University Press, 1980.
   An excellent collection of essays on children's literature encompassing literary criticism, standards, changing tastes, child's responses to books, and writing and illustrating books. Many well-known contributors, including Rumer Godden, Nat Hentoff, C. S. Lewis, John Rowe Townsend, and others.
8. Jenkinson, Edward B. *Censors in the Classroom*. New York: Avon Books, 1982.
   A handbook on censorship cases detailing what books are being censored and who the censors are. Well-documented, this should be in every school library.

9. Kimmel, Mary Margaret, and Elizabeth Segel. *For Reading Out Loud! A Guide to Sharing Books With Children*. New York: Delacorte Press, 1983.
   An excellent guide for reading aloud, including what to read, how to read,and ways of fitting it in. Also included is an annotated list of 140 outstanding books for reading aloud to children from about third grade through eighth grade. A unique feature provides the total reading time for many of the titles.
10. Kingman, Lee, ed. *Newbery and Caldecott Medal Books 1966–1975*. Boston: Horn Book, 1975.
    The acceptance speeches of the award winners are included, along with biographical sketches, photographs,and illustrations or quotes from their work. In addition there are critical essays by John Rowe Townsend, Barbara Bader, and Elizabeth Johnson. Speeches of recent award winners are published each year in the August issue of *The Horn Book Magazine*.
11. Meek, Margaret, Aidan Warlow,and Griselda Barton. *The Cool Web: The Pattern of Children's Reading*. New York: Athenaeum, 1978.
    From England, a rich and provocative collection of essays, organized into four areas of concern—the reader, the author, approaches to criticism, and new directions in the study of literature. An excellent annotated bibliography suggests further reading.
12. Taylor, Mary, ed. *School Library and Media Center Acquisition Policies and Procedures*. Phoenix, Ariz.: Oryx Press, 1981.
    Provides sample policies, procedures, and forms from a variety of city, suburban, and county library systems.
13. Trelease, Jim. *The Read-Aloud Handbook*. Rev. ed. New York: Penguin Books, 1985.
    Written for a popular audience by a father who discovered what fun it was to share books with his family, this is a delight to read and a good gift for parents.
14. Vandergrift, Kay E. *Child and Story: The Literary Connection*. New York: Neal-Schuman Publishers, 1980.
    Literary form, critical theory, and elements of story are some of the topics explored in this discussion of the aesthetics of children's literature. One of the book's strengths is that the author sustains her critical perspective without losing sight of contemporary children.

REFERENCES[62]

Alcott, Louisa. *Little Women*, illustrated by Barbara Cooney. Crowell, 1955 (1868).
Andersen, Hans Christian. *The Ugly Duckling*, illustrated by Lorinda B. Cauley. Harcourt, 1979.
Anno, Mitsumasa. *Anno's Journey*. Philomel, 1978.
Armstrong, William H. *Sounder*, illustrated by James Barkley. Harper, 1969.
Babbitt, Natalie. *Kneeknock Rise*. Farrar, Straus, 1970.
_____. *Tuck Everlasting*. Farrar, Straus, 1975.
Banks, Lynne Reid. *The Indian in the Cupboard*, illustrated by Brock Cole. Doubleday, 1980.
Barrett, Judi. *Animals Should Definitely Not Wear Clothing*, illustrated by Ron Barrett. Athenaeum, 1970.
Barrie, James M. *Peter Pan*, illustrated by Nora S. Unwin. Scribner, 1949 (1911).
Baum, L. Frank. *The Wizard of Oz*. World Publishing, 1972 (1900).
Benchley, Nathaniel. *Gone and Back*. Harper, 1971.
Blume, Judy. *Are You There, God? It's Me, Margaret*. Bradbury, 1970.
_____. *Blubber*. Bradbury, 1974.
_____. *Deenie*. Bradbury, 1973.
Brink, Carol Ryrie. *Caddie Woodlawn*. Macmillan, 1936.

[62]Books listed at the end of this chapter are recommended, subject to qualifications noted in the text. See Appendix for publishers' complete addresses. In the case of new editions, the original publication date appears in parentheses.

Brown, Marcia. *The Three Billy Goats Gruff.* Harcourt, 1972.

Brown, Margaret Wise. *The Golden Egg Book,* illustrated by Leonard Weisgard. Western, 1976.

_____.*Goodnight Moon,* illustrated by Clement Hurd. Harper, 1947.

Burnett, Frances Hodgson. *The Secret Garden,* illustrated by Tasha Tudor. Lippincott, 1962 (1910).

Burton, Virginia Lee. *The Little House.* Houghton Mifflin, 1942.

Bryson, Bernada. *Gilgamesh, Man's First Story.* Holt, 1967.

Byars, Betsy. *The Animal, the Vegetable & John D Jones.* Delacorte, 1982.

_____.*Summer of the Swans,* illustrated by Ted CoConis. Viking, 1970.

Carle, Eric. *Do You Want to Be My Friend?* Crowell, 1971.

_____.*The Very Hungry Caterpillar.* Philomel, 1969.

Carroll, Lewis, pseud. (Charles L. Dodgson). *Alice's Adventures in Wonderland and Through the Looking Glass,* illustrated by John Tenniel. Macmillan, 1963 (first published separately, 1866 and 1872).

Clark, Ann Nolan. *Secret of the Andes,* illustrated by Jean Charlot. Viking, 1952.

Cleary, Beverly. *Ramona and Her Father,* illustrated by Alan Tiegreen. Morrow, 1977.

_____.*Ramona Quimby, Age 8,* illustrated by Alan Tiegreen. Morrow, 1981.

Clifton, Lucille. *My Brother Fine with Me,* illustrated by Moneta Barnett. Holt, 1975.

Collier, James Lincoln, and Christopher Collier. *My Brother Sam Is Dead.* Four Winds, 1974.

Cooper, Susan. *The Dark Is Rising,* illustrated by Alan Cober. Atheneum, 1976.

Dalgliesh, Alice. *The Courage of Sarah Noble,* illustrated by Leonard Weisgard. Scribner, 1954.

De Angeli, Marguerite. *The Door in the Wall.* Doubleday, 1949.

Defoe, Daniel. *Robinson Crusoe,* illustrated by N. C. Wyeth. Scribner, 1920 (1719).

DeJong, Meindert. *Hurry Home, Candy,* illustrated by Maurice Sendak. Harper, 1953.

de Paola, Tomie. *"Charlie Needs A Cloak".* Prentice-Hall, 1974.

Donovan, John. *I'll Get There, It Better Be Worth the Trip.* Harper, 1969.

Emberley, Barbara. *Drummer Hoff,* illustrated by Ed Emberley. Prentice-Hall, 1967.

Engdahl, Sylvia Louise. *Enchantress from the Stars,* illustrated by Rodney Shackell. Atheneum, 1970.

Fox, Paula. *The Stone-Faced Boy.* Bradbury, 1968.

Farjeon, Eleanor. "Mrs. Peck Pigeon" in *Roger Was a Razorfish,* compiled by Jill Bennett, illustrated by Maureen Roffey. Lothrop, 1980.

Fitzhugh, Louise. *Harriet the Spy.* Harper, 1964

Frank, Anne. *Anne Frank: The Diary of a Young Girl,* translated by B. M. Mooyart. Doubleday, 1967.

Fritz, Jean. *And Then What Happened, Paul Revere?,* illustrated by Margot Tomes. Coward-McCann, 1973.

_____.*The Cabin Faced West,* illustrated by Feodor Rojankovsky. Coward-McCann, 1958.

Gág, Wanda. *Millions of Cats.* Coward-McCann, 1928.

Galdone, Joanna. *The Tailypo.* Houghton Mifflin, 1977.

Galdone, Paul. *The Gingerbread Boy.* Clarion, 1975.

_____.*Three Little Pigs.* Houghton Mifflin, 1970.

Galloz, Christopher and Roberto Innocenti. *Rose Blanche,* illustrated by Roberto Innocenti. Creative Education, 1985.

George, Jean C. *Cry of the Crow.* Harper, 1980.

_____.*Gull Number 737.* Crowell, 1964.

_____.*Julie of the Wolves,* illustrated by John Schoenherr. Harper, 1972.

_____.*My Side of the Mountain.* Dutton, 1959.

Gipson, Fred. *Old Yeller,* illustrated by Carl Burger. Harper, 1956.

Grimm Brothers. *Little Red Riding Hood,* illustrated by Trina Schart Hyman. Holiday, 1983.

Guest, Judith. *Ordinary People.* Viking, 1976.

Haar, Jap ter. *Boris,* translated by Martha Mearns, illustrated by Rien Poortvliet. Delacorte, 1970.

Herriot, James. *All Creatures Great and Small.* St. Martin, 1972.

Hickman, Janet. *The Thunder-Pup*. Macmillan, 1981.
_____.*The Valley of the Shadow*. Macmillan, 1974.
Hoban, Russell. *A Baby Sister for Frances,* illustrated by Lillian Hoban. Harper, 1964.
Hoban, Tana. *Look Again!* Macmillan, 1971.
Holland, Isabelle. *The Man Without a Face*. Lippincott, 1972.
Hughes, Richard. *A High Wind in Jamaica*. Harper, 1972 (1929).
Hunt, Irene. *Across Five Aprils*. Follett, 1964.
Hunter, Mollie. *A Stranger Came Ashore*. Harper, 1975.
Jarrell, Randall. *The Animal Family,* illustrated by Maurice Sendak. Pantheon, 1965.
Keats, Ezra Jack. *Peter's Chair*. Harper, 1967.
Kent, Jack. *The Fat Cat: A Danish Folktale*. Parents, 1971.
Kipling, Rudyard. *The Jungle Books,* illustrated by Robert Shore. Macmillan, 1964, (1894).
Klein, Norma. *Mom, the Wolf Man and Me*. Pantheon, 1972.
Konigsburg, E. L. *From the Mixed-Up Files of Mrs. Basil E. Frankweiler*. Atheneum, 1967.
Kunhardt, Dorothy, *Pat the Bunny*. Golden Press, 1962 (1940).
Lee, Harper. *To Kill a Mockingbird*. Harper, 1960.
LeGuin, Ursula K. *A Wizard of Earthsea,* illustrated by Ruth Robbins. Parnassus, 1968.
L'Engle, Madeleine. *Meet the Austins*. Vanguard, 1960.
_____.*Ring of Endless Light*. Farrar, Straus, 1980.
_____.*A Wrinkle in Time*. Farrar, Straus, 1962.
Lobel, Arnold. *Frog and Toad Together*. Harper, 1972.
Louie, Ai-Ling. *Yeh-Shen: A Cinderella Story From China,* illustrated by Ed Young. Philomel, 1982.
Lowry, Lois. *Anastasia Krupnik*. Houghton Mifflin, 1979.
Magorian, Michelle. *Good Night, Mr. Tom*. Harper, 1982.
McCloskey, Robert. *Time of Wonder,* Viking, 1957.
McCord, David. "The Pickety Fence," in *Every Time I Climb a Tree,* illustrated by Marc Simont. Little, Brown, 1967.
MacLachlan, Patricia. *Sarah, Plain and Tall*. Harper, 1985.
Maruki, Toshi. *Hiroshima No Pika*. Lothrop, 1980.
Milne, A. A. *Winnie the Pooh,* illustrated by E. H. Shepard. Dutton, 1926.
Neville, Emily. *It's Like This, Cat,* illustrated by Emil Weiss. Harper, 1963.
North, Sterling. *Rascal: A Memoir of a Better Era,* illustrated by John Schoenherr. Dutton, 1963.
O'Brien, Robert C. *Mrs. Frisby and the Rats of NIMH,* illustrated by Zena Bernstein. Atheneum, 1971.
O'Dell, Scott. *Island of the Blue Dolphins*. Houghton Mifflin, 1960.
_____.*Sing Down the Moon*. Houghton Mifflin, 1970.
Paterson, Katherine. *Bridge to Terabithia,* illustrated by Donna Diamond. Crowell, 1977.
_____.*The Great Gilly Hopkins*. Crowell, 1978.
_____.*Jacob Have I Loved*. Crowell, 1980.
Pinkwater, Daniel. *Slaves of Spiegel*. Four Winds, 1982.
Potter, Beatrix. *The Tale of Peter Rabbit*. Warne, n. d.
Rawlings, Marjorie Kinnan. *The Yearling,* illustrated by Edward Shenton. Scribner, 1938.
Reiss, Johanna. *The Upstairs Room*. Crowell, 1972.
Reyher, Becky. *My Mother Is the Most Beautiful Woman in the World,* illustrated by Ruth Gannett. Lothrop, 1945.
Richter, Hans Peter. *Friedrich,* translated by Edite Kroll. Holt, 1970.
Rodgers, Mary. *Freaky Friday*. Harper, 1972.
Salten, Felix. *Bambi,* illustrated by Barbara Cooney. Simon & Schuster, 1970 (1929).
Sendak, Maurice. *In the Night Kitchen*. Harper, 1970.
_____.*Outside Over There*. Harper, 1981.
_____.*Where the Wild Things Are*. Harper, 1963.
Sewell, Anna. *Black Beauty,* illustrated by John Groth. Macmillan, 1962 (1877).
Sleator, William. *Blackbriar*. Dutton, 1972.
Southall, Ivan. *Ash Road,* illustrated by Clem Seale. St. Martin, 1965.
Sperry, Armstrong. *Call It Courage,* Macmillan, 1940.
Spier, Peter. *Noah's Ark*. Doubleday, 1977.

Spyri, Johanna. *Heidi,* illustrated by Greta Elgaard. Macmillan, 1962 (1884).

Steig, William. *The Amazing Bone.* Farrar, Straus, 1976.

_____.*Roland, the Minstrel Pig.* Harper, 1968.

_____.*Sylvester and the Magic Pebble.* Windmill, 1969.

Steptoe, John. *Stevie.* Harper, 1969.

Stevenson, Robert Louis. *Treasure Island,* illustrated by N. C. Wyeth. Scribner, 1911 (1883).

Sutcliff, Rosemary. *Sun Horse, Moon Horse.* Dutton, 1978.

_____.*Warrior Scarlet,* illustrated by Charles Keeping. Walck, 1958.

Tolkien, J. R. R. *The Hobbit.* Houghton Mifflin, 1938.

Turkle, Brinton. *Obadiah the Bold.* Viking, 1965.

_____.*Thy Friend, Obadiah.* Viking, 1969.

Twain, Mark, pseud. (Samuel Clemens). *The Adventures of Huckleberry Finn.* Harper, 1884.

_____.*The Adventures of Tom Sawyer.* Harper, 1876.

Uchida, Yoshiko. *Journey to Topaz,* illustrated by Donald Carrick. Scribner, 1971.

Ullman, James R. *Banner in the Sky.* Lippincott, 1954.

Van Allsburg, Chris. *The Polar Express.* Houghton Mifflin, 1985.

Viorst, Judith. *Alexander and the Terrible, Horrible, No Good, Very Bad Day,* illustrated by Ray Cruz. Atheneum, 1972.

Voigt, Cynthia. *Dicey's Song.* Atheneum, 1982.

Walsh, Jill P. *A Chance Child.* Farrar, Straus, 1978.

_____.*The Green Book,* illustrated by Lloyd Bloom. Farrar, Straus, 1982.

Ward, Lynd. *The Biggest Bear.* Houghton Mifflin, 1952.

Weiman, Eiveen. *Which Way Courage?* Atheneum, 1981.

Weir, Esther. *The Loner.* McKay, 1963.

White, E. B. *Charlotte's Web,* illustrated by Garth Williams. Harper, 1952.

_____.*Stuart Little,* illustrated by Garth Williams. Harper, 1945.

Wilder, Laura Ingalls. The *Little House* Series, illustrated by Garth Williams. Harper, 1953.
   On the Banks of Plum Creek, 1937.
   Little House in the Big Woods, 1932
   Little House on the Prairie, 1935.
   Little Town on the Prairie, 1941.
   The Long Winter, 1940.
   By the Shores of Silver Lake, 1939.
   These Happy Golden Years, 1943.

Willard, Nancy. *A Visit to William Blake's Inn,* illustrated by Alice and Martin Provensen. Harcourt, 1981.

Williams, Margery. *The Velveteen Rabbit,* illustrated by William Nicholson. Doubleday. 1958 (1922).

Wojciechowska, Maia. *Don't Play Dead Before You Have To.* Harper, 1970.

Wuorio, Eva-Lis.*To Fight in Silence.* Holt, 1973.

Wyss, Johann. *Swiss Family Robinson,* illustrated by Lynd Ward. Grosset & Dunlap, 1949 (1814).

Yates, Elizabeth. *Amos Fortune, Free Man,* illustrated by Nora Unwin. Dutton, 1950.

Zolotow, Charlotte. *Say It!,* illustrated by James Stevenson. Greenwillow, 1980.

2

UNDERSTANDING CHILDREN'S RESPONSE TO LITERATURE

Five-year-old Michael hurried to the block corner from the story circle, where his teacher had just read *Little Red Riding Hood*. He whispered parts of the story under his breath as he worked to build a low enclosure around himself. When an aide walked by, Michael stood and made a growling noise. "I'm the big bad wolf!" he announced.

One rainy noon hour Sean and Dan, both 7, found a quiet corner by the bookcase and read to each other from Shel Silverstein's book of verse, *Where the Sidewalk Ends*. "Listen to this one!" (Giggles) "I can read this one!" (More giggles) Two other children discovered the fun and joined them. All four were soon arguing heatedly about which poem was "the best one."

A small group of 9- and 10-year-olds searched the well-stocked library corner of their own classroom for something to read at sustained silent-reading time. Jason picked a book, glanced at the cover, and quickly reshelved it. "Who would want to read a book like *that*?" he muttered. Emily clutched her choice like a prize and whispered to Julie that she had found another Lois Lowry book about Anastasia Krupnik. "I get it next," the friend said, and went on looking for a book about horses.

At regular silent-reading time, 10-year-old Evie curled up in her class' reading-and-rocking chair with Katherine Paterson's book, *The Great Gilly Hopkins*. She read steadily through that period and well into the free work time that followed. When she finished, she went directly to her teacher without stopping to speak to any of her friends. "The way it ended wasn't fair," Evie protested. "Gilly should have gone back to Trotter. This way just isn't right!"

A teacher asked her sixth-graders to explain why they thought Jean George had written *Cry of the Crow*. Katie wrote: "I think what the author was trying to tell you is that once something has lived in the wild, it should stay there even if it's just like your brother or sister. . . . When you catch a bird and try to make it do something, it is like being in prison for the bird."

These glimpses of children responding to literature show some of the many different ways in which they may express their preferences, thoughts, and feelings. Although each of these responses is personal and unique, each one also reflects the child's age and experience. Young children like Michael are often so totally involved in a story that they relive it through dramatic play. Those like Dan and Sean, who are developing independent reading skills, seem particularly eager to demonstrate that ability and to share newly discovered favorites. Middle-graders choosing books, like Jason, Emily, and Julie show definite preferences. In Evie's case, both the expectation of a happy ending and her concern with injustice in a character's life are typical of middle childhood. Katie's success in generalizing a theme about all wild things from the story of one crow and her fluency in discussing the author's purpose are representative of older children's ability to deal with abstract ideas about a story.

In order to have a successful literature program, teachers and librarians must know books well, but that is only half the task. It is also necessary to understand children and the changing patterns of their response to literature.

READING INTERESTS AND PREFERENCES

The term "response to literature" is used in a variety of ways. "Response" may refer to what happens in the mind of the reader or listener as a story or poem unfolds. Or, a "response" may be something said or done that reveals thoughts and feelings about literature. (A 6-year-old's drawing of a favorite character and a book review in the *New York Times* are both responses in this sense.) Teachers or librarians who predict that a book will bring "a good response" use the term in a slightly different way, emphasizing children's level of interest and expressed preferences.

Most of the early research on children and literature was focused on this third area of response to discover what reading material children liked or disliked. Children's interests and preferences are still a major concern for teachers, librarians, parents, publishers, and booksellers. Everyone who selects children's books can make better choices by knowing which books are likely to have immediate appeal for many children and which ones may require introduction or encouragement along the way.

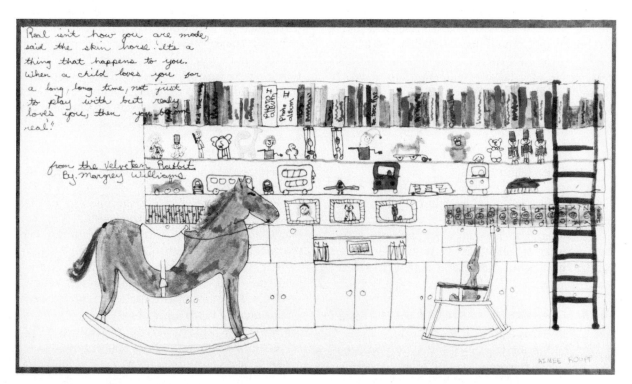

Choosing favorites and interpreting them are both a part of response to literature. Notice how the details of the modern playroom setting in this child's illustration for *The Velveteen Rabbit* provide a glimpse of her unique personal perspective on the book.

Martin Luther King, Jr., Laboratory School, Evanston, Illinois, Public Schools.

Studies of reading interests over the years have consistently identified certain topics and elements of content that have wide appeal.[1] *Animals* and *humor,* for instance, are generally popular across age levels. Among other elements that are frequently mentioned for reader appeal are *action, suspense,* and *surprise.* A study by Greenlaw and Wielan[2] confirms that contemporary children continue to refer to such familiar categories when giving personal assessments of books. The researchers looked at the comments of more than 1000 Georgia school children who were reviewing and "grading" new books in a program called Children's Choices, sponsored by the Children's Book Council and the International Reading Association. They found that most student comments referred to traditionally popular topics and elements of appeal, with humor, riddles and jokes, adventure, how-to, and animals among the most mentioned themes.

Even though we can identify commonly chosen topics and story features that have wide general appeal, it is still impossible to concoct a formula for books that would have unfailing popularity with *all* children. Teachers and librarians need to be sensitive to children's individual tastes, which are often unique and very particular. Nevertheless, the variations in interests among different *groups* of children can be accounted for by certain overall influences.

Age and Sex Differences

The most obvious change in children's interest patterns occurs with age as they take on more complex material and new areas of concern. Good book choices for first- and sixth-graders seldom overlap, even when the general topic is the same.

Robert McCloskey's picture book *Make Way for Ducklings* is a favorite animal story among 4- and 5-year-olds; 12-year-olds prefer their animal characters to be part of something more dramatic, like Wilson Rawls' story about two coon dogs, *Where the Red Fern Grows.* Seven-year-olds laugh at Peggy Parrish's *Amelia Bedelia* and her literal interpretation of instructions like "Draw the drapes" and "Dress the chicken." Eleven-year-olds like "funny" books, too, but prefer a different brand of humor, such as the unusual situations, puns, and wisecracking dialogue of *Fat Men from Space* by Daniel Manus Pinkwater.

Some of the broader shifts in preference that have been reported for elementary school children are summarized in the extensive review of research by Purves and Beach.[3] For instance, most children move away from a preference for fairy tales toward more interest in realistic subject matter. According to these studies, adventure becomes more important through the middle grades, while upper-grade students begin to show marked content preferences according to their sex.

The influence of sex differences on reading interests is not entirely clear. Most studies do report that interests vary with gender as well as age level. In the 1960s Huus reviewed twenty years of interest research and listed seven conclusions that point up age and sex differences in children's preferences for books:

- Interests of children vary according to age and grade level.
- Few differences between the interests of boys and girls are apparent before age 9.
- Notable differences in the interests of boys and girls appear between ages 10 and 13.
- Girls read more than boys, but boys have a wider interest range and read a greater variety.
- Girls show an earlier interest in adult fiction of a romantic type than do boys.
- Boys like chiefly adventure and girls like fiction, but mystery stories appeal to both.
- Boys seldom show preference for a "girl's"

[1]Angela M. Broening, "Factors Influencing Pupils' Reading of Library Books," *Elementary English Review,* vol. 11 (1934), pp. 155–158; Fannie Wyche Dunn, *Interest Factors in Reading Materials* (New York: Teachers College, Columbia University, 1921); Jeanie Goodhope, "Into the Eighties: BAYA's Fourth Reading Interest Survey," *School Library Journal,* vol. 29 (December 1982), p. 33; George W. Norvell, *What Boys and Girls Like to Read* (Morristown, N.J.: Silver, Burdett, 1958).
[2]M. Jean Greenlaw and O. Paul Wielan, "Reading Interests Revisited," *Language Arts,* vol. 56 (April 1979), pp. 432–434.

[3]Alan Purves and Richard Beach, *Literature and the Reader: Research in Response to Literature, Reading Interests, and the Teaching of Literature* (Urbana, Ill.: National Council of Teachers of English, 1972), pp. 69–71.

book, but girls will read "boys'" books to a greater degree.[4]

In the 1970s Robinson and Weintraub[5] reported a trend toward the appearance of sex differences at a younger age. Even early primary children may show sex-related preferences, which assume increasing importance as the children grow older.

However, as consciousness of sex-role stereotyping in our society has increased, some of the conventional wisdom about reading interests has come under new scrutiny. Which of children's choices reflect true interest rather than conformity to cultural expectations? Most observers report that boys give significantly more attention to informational books than girls do, and we might suspect (though we cannot prove) that this is a learned preference. In school and home settings where values do not dictate strict sex-role division, boys and girls share enthusiasm for many common favorites. Elizabeth Segel writes that "the still prevalent tendency of boys to shun books with a female protagonist probably testifies more to the power of peer pressure than to any difficulty of cross-gender identification."[6] Segel stresses that it is important to keep the options for book choice open so that boys and girls can have a chance to explore each other's perspectives.

Other Determinants of Interest

Many factors other than age and sex have been investigated in relation to children's reading interests. At one time the influence of mental age as measured by standardized tests received considerable attenion. Russell came to three major conclusions after comparing the studies of reading interests and intelligence:

- Bright children like books that dull children two to three years older like.
- Bright children read three or four times as many books as do average children and do not taper off in reading at 13 as most children do.
- There is little variation in the reading interests of bright, average, and dull children, except bright children have a wider range of interests.[7]

Recent studies linking intellectual ability and children's response, as we will see in later sections of this chapter, are more likely to focus on precise

Although reading preferences are influenced by age, sex, and many other factors, children often make specific choices based on the book itself—its length, format, cover, or the appeal of a sample paragraph.

Martin Luther King, Jr., Laboratory School, Evanston, Illinois, Public Schools. Photo by James Ballard.

[4]Helen Huus, "Interpreting Research in Children's Literature" in *Children, Books and Reading* (Newark, Del.: The International Reading Association, 1964), p. 125.

[5]Helen M. Robinson and Samuel Weintraub, "Research Related to Children's Interests and to Developmental Values of Reading," *Library Trends*, vol. 22 (October 1973), pp. 81–108.

[6]Elizabeth Segel, "Choices 'For Girls'/'For Boys': Keeping Options Open," *School Library Journal*, vol. 28 (March 1982), p. 106.

[7]David Russell, *Children Learn to Read* (Boston: Ginn, 1961), pp. 394–395.

descriptions of cognitive abilities rather than general measures of "intelligence."

Illustrations, color, format, length, and type of print are all features of the books themselves that may influence children's choices. In one study of 2500 kindergarten children, Cappa[8] found that illustrations were the most important source of appeal, edging out story content. When Brown[9] compared fifth-graders' choices based on actual handling of books with choices made from annotations alone, she found that seeing the cover and illustrations did make a difference. Fenwick's[10] study of school library circulation among junior school pupils revealed high popularity for books with a high percentage of illustrations. The editor[11] of one series of informational books has reported that when market research was undertaken to find what format the intended audience would prefer, middle-grade children resoundingly chose a 70/30 picture-text ratio over a 50/50 one. Conventional findings about children's color and style preferences were underscored in a recent study by Watson,[12] who found younger children drawn to bright, opaque colors, and all ages showing most interest in a realistic style of illustration.

It is tempting to oversimplify the effect of pictures on children's book choices, especially since so much of the research is done outside the context of normal reading and choosing situations. Kiefer[13] studied primary children choosing and using books in their own classroom setting and found their reactions to pictures and picture books were more complex than controlled experiments or surveys could reveal. A child in Kiefer's study commented about one of Lloyd Bloom's illustrations for *We Be Warm Till Springtime Comes* by Lillie Chaffin that it made her feel "like I'm on my Mommy's lap." Realizing that a black and white picture can give such strong feelings of satisfaction helps us see generalizations about children's preference for color in a new perspective. Since books are in increasing competition with media as a source for both entertainment and information, we can expect that studies of their visual impact will become more common and more important.

Social and environmental influences also affect children's book choices and reading interests. While interests do not seem to vary greatly according to geographical location, the impact of the immediate environment—particularly the availability and accessibility of reading materials in the home, classroom, and public and school libraries—can be very strong. Children in classrooms where books are regularly discussed, enjoyed, and given high value tend to show livelier interest in a wider range of literature than children from situations where books are given less attention. It is hard to tell how much of this effect is due to contact with the books and how much is social. Teachers' favorite books are often mentioned by children as their own favorites, perhaps because these are the stories closest to hand, or perhaps because of positive associations with the teacher. Children frequently influence each other in their choice of books. In the pop culture of the classroom, a title or an author or a topic may rise to celebrity status for a time. Shel Silverstein's *A Light in the Attic* may be "the book" to read in one group of third-graders; children may make their own sign-up sheets to read the classroom's only copy of Judy Blume's *Superfudge;* a sixth-grade class may collect as many of Betsy Byars' titles as possible. Younger children may spend time on a theme study of bears and long afterward point out "bear stories" to each other. Media presentations like the oft-repeated animated version of George Selden's *The Cricket in Times Square* or the summer "Reading Rainbow" series from the Public Broadcasting System create demand for specific books.

Peer recommendations are especially important

[8]Dan Cappa, "Sources of Appeal in Kindergarten Books," *Elementary English,* vol. 34 (April 1957), p. 259.

[9]Carol Lynch Brown, "A Study of Procedures for Determining Fifth Grade Children's Book Choices" (unpublished doctoral dissertation, The Ohio State University, Columbus, 1971).

[10]G. Fenwick, "Junior School Pupils' Rejection of School Library Books," *Educational Research,* vol. 17 (February 1975), pp. 143–149.

[11]Pat Robbins, ed., *National Geographic Books for World Explorers,* in a talk before the Children's Literature Assembly, Washington, November 22, 1982.

[12]Jerry Watson, "A Comparison of Picture Book Illustrations Preferred by Teachers and Children," *The Bulletin of the Children's Literature Assembly,* vol. 6 (Autumn 1980), pp. 13–15.

[13]Barbara Kiefer, "The Responses of Children in a Combination First/Second Grade Classroom to Picture Books in a Variety of Artistic Styles," *Journal of Research and Development in Education,* vol. 16 (Spring 1983), pp. 14–20.

to middle-graders in choosing what to read. Some fifth- and sixth-graders are very candid:

> "Everyone else in the class read it, so I figured I ought to, too." . . . "I usually read what Tammy reads." ". . . most of my friends just like the same type of book I like. So, if they find a book, I'll believe them and I'll try it."[14]

The Developmental Perspective

How can children influence each other's book choices so readily? Part of the answer may be simply that age-mates are likely to enjoy the same kinds of stories because they share many developmental characteristics. As children grow and learn, their levels of understanding change, and so do their favorites in literature. Thought-provoking studies within the last several years explain it this way: Children are the most satisfied with those stories that best embody their own conception of the world.

André Favat[15] has argued that children reach the peak of their liking for fairy tales between 6 and 8 years because the reasoning and belief system of the tales is the one most compatible to the child's thinking pattern at that age. Favat analyzed the fairy tales of Perrault, the Grimms, and Hans Christian Andersen. He then compared characteristics of the stories to characteristics of young children's thinking as described by Piaget. Favat found several similarities. For one, young children seem to believe that unrelated objects or actions can have magical influence on each other, just as in the fairy tales the kiss of the prince can magically waken Sleeping Beauty. Animism is another belief common to childhood; toys or even trees are thought to have humanlike lives and thoughts. Likewise in fairy tales the moon and stars speak, objects travel of their own accord, and animals talk as if they were human. The moral judgment of early primary children with its emphasis on punishment and its dependence on adult authority is also echoed in the fairy tales, where those in power pronounce harsh sentences on wrongdoers. Egocentrism and a disregard for causal relationships are two other similarities of child and tale noted by Favat. Most 6- to 8-year-olds are beginning to grow beyond the belief system described here, however. Favat maintained that children who are growing into another stage may find comfort in stepping back, through the story, into their old familiar patterns of thinking. According to Favat, "With its construction of animism, magic, morality of constraint, and its whole egocentric cast, the fairy tale retains in stable form, impervious to change, the very conception of the world the child now finds challenged."[16]

Norma Schlager's[17] study of literature choices in middle childhood reaches a similar conclusion; books with main characters who reflect the emotional and psychological aspects of the reader are the ones that gain a wide readership. Schlager compiled behavioral characteristics of 7- to 12-year-olds based on the developmental theories of Piaget and Erikson. Then she analyzed Newbery award-winning books that showed the highest and lowest circulations in a large library system. She found that the most popular books portray the world of childhood much the same as children see it, according to the child development experts, while the least popular books show a different view.

The analysis of Scott O'Dell's *Island of the Blue Dolphins*, the most widely circulated book in Schlager's study, shows that Karana, the story's main character, displays many of the mental attributes common in 7- to 12-year-olds. Karana lives virtually alone on her island off the California coast for eighteen years and must learn to survive without adult help. Children in the middle grades are similarly concerned with testing their own self-sufficiency, although the circumstances are usually much less dramatic. Karana's success is due to her ability to plan ahead, think logically, and work to make the things she needs. Schlager points out that children in the 7–12 age range are also developing the power of syllogistic reasoning which allows pre-planning and problem solving

---

[14]Susan I. Hepler and Janet Hickman, " 'The Book Was Okay. I Love You'—Social Aspects of Response to Literature," *Theory Into Practice*, vol. 21 (Autumn 1982), p. 279.

[15]André Favat, *Child and Tale: The Origins of Interest* (Urbana, Ill.: National Council of Teachers of English, 1977).

[16]Favat, p. 49.

[17]Norma Marian Schlager, "Developmental Factors Influencing Children's Responses to Literature" (doctoral dissertation, Claremont Graduate School, 1974).

and that they too are task-oriented, with newfound abilities in craftsmanship. In contrast, Schlager's analysis of the least-circulated book in the sample (*Dobry* by Monica Shannon) shows the protagonist looking at the world as a very young child does (he talks to the moon as if it could answer him). The book also portrays him later as an adolescent, with conscious thoughts about his own uniqueness. Schlager suggests that middle-grade readers show little interest because it doesn't include the characteristic behavior and thinking of their age level.

The argument that children's favorite types of stories depend on their current intellectual and psychological development can be extended downward to infants and up into the teen years. Tucker[18] has provided a thorough discussion of the characteristics of children and their favorite literature up to age 14. For example, for children up to age 3, nursery rhymes fit the child's perspective in several ways: they make the adult world seem more childlike; they fit children's sketchy understanding of cause and effect; and they reflect a young child's inconsistent behavior. Three- to 7-year-olds become able to pick out a pattern of events, not just disconnected episodes, and so can really enjoy a book like *Rosie's Walk* by Pat Hutchins. Many popular books for 7- to 11-year-olds reveal a changing relationship with parents, and children's hope of proving themselves to be as capable as adults. In the 11-to-14 range, Tucker points out that books often echo ". . . more complex intellectual and emotional processes, with fictional characters also sometimes standing back from their immediate reactions in order to take a more analytic look at what is really happening."[19]

We must be careful not to oversimplify any explanation of children's book choices, since there are apparently many interrelating personal, social, and environmental factors. Even so, it is important not to underestimate the developmental perspective. Knowing a child's most comfortable level of thought and behavior is a powerful tool for predicting reading interests and for understanding other aspects of response to literature.

[18]Nicholas Tucker, *The Child and the Book: A Psychological and Literary Exploration* (Cambridge: Cambridge University Press, 1981).
[19]Tucker, p. 145.

GROWTH PATTERNS THAT INFLUENCE RESPONSE

The child development point of view begins with recognizing and accepting the uniqueness of childhood. Children are not miniature adults but individuals with their own needs, interests, and capabilities—all of which change over time and at varying rates.

In the early decades of child study, emphasis was placed on discovery of "normal" behavior patterns for each age. Growth studies revealed similarities in patterns of physical, mental, and emotional growth. More recently, longitudinal studies have shown wide variables in individual rates of growth. One child's growth may be uneven, and a spurt in one aspect of development may precede a spurt in another. Age trends continue to be important in understanding the child, but recent research has also been concerned with the interaction of biological, cultural, and life experience forces. We know, for example, that development is not simply the result of the maturation of neural cells but evolves as new experience reshapes existing structures. Experience affects the age at which development may appear.

Studies in children's cognitive and language growth as well as in the other areas of human development have direct application for the choice of appropriate books and the understanding of children's responses. While this text can highlight only a few recent findings, it can serve to alert the student of children's literature to the importance of such information.

As we begin it seems worthwhile to offer a word of caution about graded school organization, which falsely appears to provide homogeneous classroom groups. Not only may there be a two-to-three-year chronological age range within one class but children of the same age will reflect wide and varied levels of individual development. Many of our schools have developed multi-age units or family groupings which further increase diversity of interest and ability. In order to provide appropriate literature experiences for these children, the teacher needs to know each of them as individuals—their level of development, their rate of development, and their varying interests. To meet their needs, the school must provide an ex-

Toddlers have the visual acuity to enjoy searching for familiar details in picture books.

Photo by Susan Fertig.

tensive collection of books and media covering a wide range of topics at various interest and reading levels.

Physical Development

Children's experiences with literature can begin at a very early age. Studies of infant perception show that even tiny babies hear and see better than was thought possible twenty-five years ago. For instance, newborns show more response to patterned, rhythmic sounds than to continuous tones. They also show preferences for the sound frequencies of the human voice.[20] This supports the intui-

tion of parents who chant nursery rhymes or sing lullabies that the sound of songs and rhymes provides satisfaction even for the youngest.

Infants gain visual perception very rapidly within their range of focus. According to Cohen's[21] summary of research, babies in their first 2 months of life see lines, angles, and adjacent areas of high contrast. They progress to seeing simple dimensions such as forms or colors, and before 6 months are perceiving more complex patterns (faces or colored shapes) as whole units. Books designed for babies and toddlers like those by Dick Bruna often acknowledge this developmental pattern by featuring simple, clearly defined illustrations with firm outlines, uncluttered backgrounds, and bright colors.

As visual perception develops, children begin to show fascination with details and often enjoy searching for specific objects in illustrations. One 18-month-old boy spotted a clock in Margaret Wise Brown's *Goodnight Moon* and subsequently pointed out clocks in other books when he discovered them. Older preschoolers make a game of finding "hidden" things in pictures, like the apple in each scene of Clyde and Wendy Watson's *Applebet* or the Mother Goose and fairy tale characters tucked into each illustration of Janet and Allen Ahlberg's *Each Peach Pear Plum*.

Children's attention spans generally increase with age as well as interest. Frequently in their first school experiences young children have trouble sitting quietly for even a 20-minute story. It is better to have several short story times for these children than to demand their attention for longer periods and so lose their interest. Some kindergarten and primary teachers provide many opportunities for children to listen to stories in small groups of two or three by using the listening center or asking parent aides or student-teachers to read to as few as one or two children.

Physical development influences children's interests as well as their attention span. Growth in size, muscularity, and coordination is often reflected in children's choice of a book in which characters share their own newly acquired traits or abilities. *Whistle for Willie* by Ezra Jack Keats, for

[20]Aidan Macfarlane, *The Psychology of Childbirth* (Cambridge, Mass.: Harvard University Press, 1977).

[21]Leslie B. Cohen, "Our Developing Knowledge of Infant Perception and Cognition," *American Psychologist*, vol. 34 (1979), pp. 894–899.

example, seems most rewarding for young children who have just learned to pucker. The demand for sports books increases as boys and girls gain the skills necessary for successful participation.

American children are growing up faster, both physically and psychologically, than they ever have before.[22] Many children, especially girls, reach puberty during the elementary school years. They remain fascinated by Judy Blume's *Are You There, God? It's Me, Margaret* not because it is a religious story but because it accurately reflects the heroine's concerns about menstruation and when she will begin her periods. Margaret has frequent chats with God which include such pleas as: "Are you there God? It's me, Margaret. I just told my mother I want a bra. Please help me grow God. You know where . . ."[23]

Both physical maturity and social forces have led to younger heterosexual interests. Sophisticated 7-year-olds are teased about their "boy friends" or "girl friends," and one report indicates that 6 percent of young females beginning junior high school are already sexually active.[24] It is somehow as if childhood were something to be transcended rather than enjoyed. One result of this shortened childhood is a decrease in the length of time in which boys and girls are interested in reading children's literature. Many of them turn to reading teenage novels or adult fiction before they have read such fine books as *A Solitary Blue* by Cynthia Voigt or *A Gathering of Days* by Joan Blos, both well-written complex stories about young adolescents.

Cognitive Development

The work of the great Swiss psychologist, Jean Piaget[25] has cast much light on our understanding of children's intellectual development. One important idea proposed by Piaget is that intelligence develops as a result of the interaction of environment and the maturation of the child. Piaget's findings suggest distinct stages in the development of logical thinking. All children go through these stages of intellectual development in the same progression, but not necessarily at the same age. Each stage is incorporated into the next stage as new thinking structures are developed.

Some authorities have suggested that these stages may be linked to growth spurts in the physical development of the brain.[26] While the relationship between brain growth and cognitive growth has not been fully explored, it is interesting to see that the reported ages for growth spurts do correspond roughly to the beginning points for the stages of cognitive development as described by Piaget.

According to Piaget, the *sensory-motor period* is the earliest period of cognitive development and is characteristic of the learning of infants to toddlers of about 2 years. The child learns during this period through coordinating sensory perceptions and motor activity. By 1½ to 2 years children enjoy many of the action or game rhymes of Mother Goose. They pay little attention to the words of "Pat a Cake, Pat a Cake," but they delight in the anticipation of the pinching and patting that accompany these rhymes. Tactile books such as *Pat the Bunny* by Dorothy Kunhardt or *Misty's Mischief* by Rod Campbell appeal to their sensory perceptions by encouraging them to touch special materials pasted on the page. Such an introduction to books incorporates what the young child responds to best—sensory-motor play and participation with a loving adult.

The child in the *preoperational period* (ages 2–7 years) learns to represent his world symbolically through language, play, and drawing. His thinking is still egocentric and is based on immediate perception and direct experience. He has not yet learned to *conserve*. (A child who conserves can hold an idea or image constant in his mind regard-

[22]For hypotheses to explain this change, see Marie Winn, *Children Without Childhood* (New York: Pantheon, 1983), chapter 10.

[23]Judy Blume, *Are You There, God? It's Me, Margaret* (Englewood Cliffs, N.J.: Bradbury Press, 1970), p. 37.

[24]Cullen Murphy, "Kids Today," *The Wilson Quarterly*, vol. 6 (Autumn 1982), p. 80.

[25]Barbel Inhelder and Jean Piaget, *The Growth of Logical Thinking* (New York: Basic Books, 1962); John Flavell, *The Developmental Psychology of Jean Piaget* (Princeton, N.J.: Van Nostrand, 1963); Hans G. Furth, *Piaget for Teachers* (Englewood Cliffs, N.J.: Prentice-Hall, 1970).

[26]Herman T. Epstein, "Growth Spurts During Brain Development: Implications for Educational Policy and Practice," in Jeanne S. Chall and Allan F. Mirsky, eds., *Education and the Brain*, Seventy-seventh Yearbook of the National Society for the Study of Education (Chicago: University of Chicago Press, 1978), pp. 343–370.

less of how much it is changed in form. A cup of milk is a cup, despite the shape of the glass that it is in.) This explains why young children so enjoy such cumulative stories as "The Gingerbread Boy" or *Mr. Gumpy's Outing* by John Burningham. The repetition of these tales carries the sequence of the story along for them. Older children, who have learned to conserve, can remember the sequence of events and frequently reject the slowness and repetition of such cumulative stories.

As children's ideas of seriation develop, they are intrigued with stories like "The Three Bears" that emphasize the concept of gradation of size. The structure of many folktales is based on the relating of three events with rising action. Thus, young children can anticipate the climax of the "Three Billy Goats" and the final overthrow of the troll.

Characteristic of the cognitive growth of the child during the preoperational stage is the tremendous increase in language development and concept formation. In *One Morning in Maine*, McCloskey gives us a beautiful example of a child attempting to conceptualize the notion of "toothness." Young Sal shows her first loose tooth to everyone she meets including her parents, a fish hawk, loon, seal, sea gull, clam, and the men at the general store. She wonders for the first time if each of these creatures has teeth that come loose. When Sal finally does lose her tooth on the beach and can't find it, she substitutes a gull's feather to put under the pillow. Sal also compares a tooth to the worn-out spark plug that must be replaced in the motor of the family's boat. Such over-generalized attempts at conceptualization are characteristic of the thinking of this period.

Sal's behavior illustrates what Piaget calls the *assimilation process,* in which the child assimilates what he hears, sees, and feels by accepting new ideas into an already existing set of schema. By watching the loon swallow a herring whole without chewing, Sal decides he doesn't have teeth. She learns from her mother that her sister Jane doesn't even have all of her baby teeth yet. And so Sal constantly assimilates knowledge about teeth and *accommodates* to the notion that there are creatures who do not need to chew. Literature may give rise to this accommodating process as children see themselves or their world in a new light. When new insights are developed, the child is accommodating.

Egocentrism is characteristic of the thinking of children during the preoperational period. Egocentricity, in this sense, does not imply selfishness or putting one's own desires ahead of others. It simply means that the young child is not capable of assuming another person's point of view. Piaget maintained that preschoolers cannot figure out, in the literal sense, what objects will be seen from vantage points different from their own. However, recent work by Donaldson[27] and others suggests that children as young as 3 or 4 can demonstrate this ability when the situation is concrete and has meaning for them. In one study, children from 3½ to 5 years were asked to manipulate toy figures along a model of intersecting walls and to place a boy doll where two policemen dolls in fixed positions would not be able to see him. Ninety percent of the children were able to coordinate the points of view represented by the dolls and successfully complete the task.

Still, in the figurative sense, the young child "sees" everything from a personal perception. A book that clearly demonstrates this kind of egocentrism is *Fish Is Fish* by Leo Lionni. In this picture book a tadpole and a fish are inseparable friends. When the tadpole becomes a frog he crawls out of the pond and discovers the wonders of a new world. He splashes back into the pond and describes these extraordinary things to the fish. As he describes birds with wings and legs, the fish imagines large feathered fish with wings. He sees a cow as a "fish cow," people as "fish people." In fact, he sees everything from his own fishy point of view. Egocentrism also leads young children to respond best to stories in which they can identify with the major character, and in which the plot or theme closely resembles their own actions and feelings. The appeal of *Bedtime for Frances* by Russell Hoban lies in the fact that although Frances is a badger, she always behaves like a rather typical 4- or 5-year-old. The young child has no difficulty in identifying with her.

As children move from the preoperational to the *concrete-operational* level of thought (ages 7–11), their response to literature and poetry changes. Characterized by thought that is flexible and reversible, children in the concrete-operational stage can

[27]Margaret Donaldson, *Children's Minds* (New York: Norton, 1979), chapter 2.

The fish's conception of birds as fish with wings in Leo Lionni's *Fish Is Fish* is like the young child's egocentric, personalized view of the world.

see the structure of such books as Leo Lionni's *The Biggest House in the World*, with its story within a story. Flashbacks and shifts in time periods as seen in *Julie of the Wolves* by Jean George or *Tom's Midnight Garden* by Philippa Pearce are understood as children begin to develop a time sense and can imagine themselves into the future or past. Shifting from an egocentric pattern of thought, children in the concrete-operational period can

more easily identify with different points of view.

One interesting aspect of concrete-operational children's thinking is described by psychologist David Elkind[28] as "cognitive conceit." As children begin to have some success in reasoning and problem solving, they tend to get the idea that they

[28]David Elkind, *Children and Adolescents* (New York: Oxford University Press, 1970).

must be as able as adults, or even smarter. They enjoy besting an older child, parent, or teacher. Although children's visions of superiority may seldom come true in real experience, books for middle-graders often feature young protagonists on their own who manage just as well as, or better than, their elders. In E. L. Konigsburg's *From the Mixed-Up Files of Mrs. Basil E. Frankweiler,* for instance, young Claudia is clever enough to outwit adults by living undetected in New York's Metropolitan Museum of Art and shrewd enough to make an important discovery about one of the statues there.

The last period of cognitive development, described by Piaget as the period of *formal operations,* appears in early adolescence at age 11 or 12 years and on. Students are now capable of abstract theoretical thought, reasoning from hypotheses to logical conclusions. They can hold several plots or sub-plots in mind and see the interrelations among them as developed by Edward Fenton in *The Refugee Summer,* for example. While they have understood the use of such obvious symbols as Sarah Noble's cloak or the broom in *Hurry Home, Candy* by Meindert DeJong, they can now interpret the many symbols and layers of meaning found in some poetry and in such complex books as Alan Garner's *The Stone Book.* They can think about the form and pattern of reasoning, as well as its content, which is why it is referred to as the period of formal thought. This would appear to be the time, then, when literary critcism would be most appropriately introduced. While teachers would have been steadily building some knowledge and appreciation of literature at all levels, detailed analysis of a work would probably not be undertaken before this period of intellectual development. Even then, teachers would want such a discussion to arise from the child's personal response to the book.

It is also important to remember that not all young people entering middle schools or junior high schools have reached the level of formal operations.[29] Some appear to use this type of thinking in one domain and not another, breezing through math but blanking out at critical approaches to literature, or vice versa. At the same time, some younger children demonstrate considerable analytical competence as they talk about books that are familiar and meaningful to them. Cognitive stage theory serves best as a guide for planning literature experiences when it is not interpreted too rigidly.

Language Development

The pattern of early language learning moves from infant babbling and cooing to the use of single words, frequently ones that name familiar people or things, like "Mama" or "kitty." Next, somewhere around 2, children begin to use two words together. They develop the ability to change inflection, intonation, or word order to expand their range of meaning ("Daddy go?" "*Bad* kitty!"). Theorists disagree on just how children are able to acquire a functional command of such a complex system as language so early in life. There is strong evidence, however, that the child is more than just an imitator. Children seem to construct on their own the system for making themselves understood; M. A. K. Halliday calls this "learning how to mean."[30] To do so they must *use* language—talk as well as listen.

Verbal participation with an adult is an important element in sharing literature with young children. ABC or picture identification books like Helen Oxenbury's *Family* provide special opportunities if they are "talked through" rather than simply read as a string of nouns. Toddlers learn more than vocabulary from such encounters. Very early experiences with books encourage many aspects of language development. (See Chapter 4 for more on this point.)

Language development proceeds at a phenomenal pace during the preschool years. By the end of that time children will have learned to express their thoughts in longer sentences that combine ideas or embed one idea within another. In short, they will have gained access to the basic structure of grammar—all this by about age 4, and regard-

[29]David Elkind, "Investigating Intelligence in Early Adolescence," in Mauritz Johnson and Kenneth J. Rehage, eds., *Toward Adolescence: The Middle School Years,* Seventy-ninth Yearbook of the National Society for the Study of Education (Chicago: University of Chicago Press, 1980), pp. 282–294.

[30]M. A. K. Halliday, *Explorations in the Functions of Language* (New York: Elsevier, 1974).

less of native language.[31] The Russian poet and linguist Kornei Chukovsky referred to the tremendous "speech-giftedness of the pre-school child" and maintained that "beginning with the age of two, every child becomes for a short period of time a linguistic genius."[32]

Chukovsky also pointed out what many later researchers have noticed, that children improvise and explore words[33] as they learn, chanting and playing with language as they gain confidence. Rythmic rhymes and nonsense verses are natural choices for preschoolers because they fit this pattern so well. However, children's fun in playing with language as various forms are mastered is not limited to the very young. Middle-grade children, with their wider range of language competence, are fascinated by the variety of jokes, riddles, tongue-twisters, and folklore miscellany offered by Alvin Schwartz in collections like *Tomfoolery: Trickery and Foolery with Words*. They are also intrigued by ingenious uses of language in a story context, as in Norton Juster's *The Phantom Tollbooth* or Ellen Raskin's *The Westing Game*.

We know that children's language growth continues through the elementary grades and beyond, although the rate is never again as dramatic as during the preschool years. The average length and complexity of children's statements, both oral and written, increase as they progress through school.[34] We also know, however, that children's capacity to produce language consistently lags behind their ability to understand it. This suggests that we owe students of all ages the opportunity to read and hear good writing which is beyond the level of their own conversation. Seven-year-olds, for instance, cannot speak with the eloquence and humor that characterize William Steig's picture books, such as *Amos & Boris* or *Doctor De Soto*.

Still, they can understand the language in its story context, and hearing it will add to their knowledge of how language sounds and works. Books by Virginia Hamilton or Natalie Babbitt might serve the same function for older students. Unlike novels that do little more than mirror contemporary speech, the work of these and other fine writers can give children a chance to consider the power of language used with precision and imagination.

Moral Development

Piaget's extensive studies of children included special attention to their developing ideas about fairness and justice. According to Piaget,[35] the difference between younger and older children's concepts is so pronounced that there are really "two moralities" in childhood. Kohlberg's well-known studies of moral development build on Piaget's work, providing a hierarchy of six stages reaching into adulthood.[36] The general direction of development described by both Piaget and Kohlberg indicates how children, as they grow in intellect and experience, may change their interpretation of conflict and moral dilemmas in stories.

Children's moral judgment moves away from the constraints of adult authority toward the influence of group cooperation and independent thinking. Some major areas of change are:

- Young children judge the goodness or badness of an act according to its likelihood of bringing punishment or reward from adults; in other words, they are constrained by the rules that adults have made. Older elementary children usually understand that there are group standards for judging what is good or bad and by then are very conscious of situations where they can make their own rules.
- In a young child's eyes, behavior is totally right or totally wrong, with no allowance for an alternate point of view. More mature children are willing to consider that circumstances and

[31]Dan I. Slobin, "Children and Language: They Learn the Same Way All around the World," in E. Mavis Hetherington and Ross D. Parke, eds., *Contemporary Readings in Child Psychology*, 2nd ed. (New York: McGraw-Hill, 1981), pp. 122–126.
[32]Kornei Chukovsky, *From Two to Five*, translated by Miriam Morton (Berkeley: University of California Press, 1963), pp. 7, 9.
[33]Ruth Weir, *Language in the Crib* (The Hague: Mouton and Co., 1970).
[34]Walter Loban, *Language Development: Kindergarten through Grade Twelve* (Urbana, Ill.: National Council of Teachers of English, 1976).

[35]Jean Piaget, *The Moral Judgment of the Child*, translated by M. Gabain (New York: Free Press, 1965).
[36]Lawrence Kohlberg, "Development of Moral Character and Moral Ideology" in M. L. Hoffman and L. W. Hoffman, eds., *Review of Child Development Research* (New York: Russell Sage Foundation, 1964).

situations make for legitimate differences of opinion.

- Young children tend to judge an act by its consequences, regardless of the actor's intent. By third or fourth grade, most children have switched to considering motivation rather than consequences alone in deciding what degree of guilt is appropriate.

- Young children believe that bad behavior and punishment go together; the more serious the deed, the more severe the punishment they would prescribe. Its form would not necessarily be related to the offense, but it would automatically erase the defender's guilt. Older children are not so quick to suggest all-purpose pain. They are more interested in finding a "fair" punishment, one that somehow fits the crime and will help bring the wrongdoer back within the rules of the group. Several children who had heard Taro Yashima's *Crow Boy* were asked what the teacher in the story would do about shy Chibi, who hid under the school-house on the first day. Most of the first-graders who were questioned said "Spank him!" Nine- and ten-year-olds suggested explaining to him that there was nothing to be afraid of or introducing him to classmates so he wouldn't be shy.

Stories for children present different levels of moral complexity. In Edna Preston's *Squawk to the Moon, Little Goose,* the refrain "Good's good and bad's bad" clearly reflects a young child's unilateral view. After Little Goose has completed her forbidden late-night adventures, her mother first spanks her and then lovingly tucks her into bed,

According to their level of moral development, children of different ages may suggest different ways for the teacher to deal with shy Chibi, who hides on the first day of school.

From *Crow Boy* by Taro Yashima.

neatly encompassing the child's notion that punishment wipes away all fault even as it acknowledges the seriousness of the misdeed.

Some stories are not as simple as they look. Unlike the clear-cut distinctions between good and evil in most European fairy tales, the African story *Why Mosquitoes Buzz in People's Ears* retold by Verna Aardema requires its audience to consider each animal's intentions. A trial is held to determine responsibility for the death of a baby owlet. The tale moves backward through a chain of events to suggest that the culprit is the mosquito whose actions began the original disturbance, although he did not come into contact with the owl. In order to get the full impact of this story, children must see that both intentions and consequences have a bearing on guilt, and that responsibility must sometimes be shared.

Fables are often used with young children because they are brief, have appealing animal characters, and appear to teach a moral lesson. However, in Pillar's[37] research on the response of second-, fourth-, and sixth-graders to fables, few of the second-graders could give explanations that indicated full understanding of important questions raised by the stories, such as why the shepherd boy cried "Wolf!" Significantly more sixth-graders—but not all of them—were successful in explaining the fables, grasped subtle aspects that younger children missed, and were able to generalize that the stories represented broader human qualities. All this suggests that most fables may be lost on children in the early stages of moral development.

The selection of stories and novels for older children also has much to do with the moral complexities they present. For instance, *Mama* by Lee Bennett Hopkins will not find its ideal audience among 9-year-olds because they have strong expectations about the behavior roles of family members. Mothers should follow the rules, but Mama is a shoplifter. The dilemma facing her son is whether to justify his actions by what is best for his family, or what is approved by a wider social group. Our information about moral development indicates that children moving into middle school are better equipped to reason through such questions of conflicting loyalties, even though they may not agree on satisfactory answers. It is the working through of dilemmas, the experts suggest, that allows us to move from one level of moral judgment to another. And literature does present a means by which children can work through situations of conflict without risk, trying out alternative stances to problems as they step into the lives and thoughts of different characters.

Personality Development

Every aspect of a child's growth is intertwined with every other. All learning is a meshing of cognitive dimensions, affective or emotional responses, social relationships, and value orientation. This is the matrix in which personality develops. The process of "becoming" is a highly complex one indeed. To become a "fully functioning" person the child's basic needs must be met. He needs to feel he is loved and understood; he must feel he is a member of a group significant to him; he has to feel he is achieving and growing toward independence. Maslow's research suggests that a person develops through a "hierarchy of needs" from basic animal-survival necessities to the "higher" needs that are more uniquely human and spiritual:

- Physiological needs
- Safety needs
- Love and affection, belongingness needs
- Esteem needs
- Self-actualization needs
- Needs to know and understand
- Aesthetic needs[38]

While some higher-level animals, such as the apes, appear to have needs of belongingness and even esteem, only humans seek to reach their greatest potential in the self-actualizing process in which they are at last free to be themselves. The search for self-actualization may take a lifetime, or it may never be achieved. But the concept that the individual is continually "becoming" is a more positive view than the notion that little change can take place in personality.

[37]Arlene M. Pillar, "Aspects of Moral Judgment in Response to Fables," *Journal of Research and Development in Education*, vol. 16 (Spring 1983), pp. 39–46.

[38]Abraham H. Maslow, *Motivation and Personality*, rev. ed. (New York: Harper & Row, 1970).

Erikson[39] has noted eight stages in this process of becoming, each linked to a critical period of human development. A sense of *trust* must be gained during the first year; a sense of *autonomy* should be realized by age 3; between 3 and 6 years the sense of *initiative* is developed; and a sense of duty and *accomplishment or industry* occupies the period of childhood from 6 to 12 years. In adolescence a sense of *identity* is built; while a sense of *intimacy,* a parental sense of *productivity,* and a sense of *integrity* are among the tasks of adulthood.

The elementary school audience for children's books falls into the categories *initiative, accomplishment,* and *identity.* Preschool and early primary children can be described as preoccupied with first ventures outside the circle of familiar authority. The majority of elementary children are caught up in the period of industry or "task orientation," proud of their ability to use skills and tools, to plan projects, and to work toward finished products. Middle-school students are more concerned with defining values and personal roles. Writers of children's books sometimes suggest a natural audience for their work by bringing one of these orientations into the foreground. In Beatrix Potter's *The Tale of Peter Rabbit,* Peter's adventures demonstrate a developing sense of initiative like that of the preschoolers listening to his story. *A Gift for Mama* by Esther Hautzig focuses on the industriousness of its middle-childhood protagonist, while Helen Cresswell's *Dear Shrink* speaks directly to the adolescent's struggle for identity.

Some researchers interested in response to literature have found special value in the theory of personality developed by Kelly.[40] His *theory of personal constructs* does not describe a particular pattern of development. Instead it provides a framework for understanding how the changing pattern of children's experience leads them to form and change ideas about their world, including the stories they read or hear. According to Kelly, each person's behavior is channeled by continuous prediction about the world based on the set of constructs the person holds at that time. Constructs are unique, personal patterns of perception that define the range of possibilities we see within a particular domain. "Bravery" and "cowardice," for instance, are likely to be construed differently by a fifth-grade gymnast and a test pilot; the limits of bravery will be seen differently, and so will its relative importance. One of the applications of this idea for the classroom helps explain children's varying reactions to the same book. For instance, a child who has read stories of King Arthur and Lloyd Alexander's Prydain series will have a different understanding of what constitutes a hero in literature than someone who has not read beyond the Hardy Boys. Every child brings to literature a different lifetime of experiences and a set of constructs that is not quite the same as any other's. Whenever we consider the broad outlines of similarity that mark developmental levels, we have to remember that each reader is also one of a kind.

The Growing Concept of Story

The way a child's concept or sense of story grows and changes is a developmental pattern of crucial interest to teachers of reading and literature. The educational value of nurturing this development was outlined in Chapter 1. Technically, sense of story is a part of the construct system through which we see the world. It is what we *expect* a story to be, a frame of interwoven ideas about what will happen and how it will be told. This frame guides our interpretation of the story. Our concept of story is a product of all aspects of development interacting with the experience of narrative in our own culture.

One way to understand growth in concept of story is through longitudinal studies that focus on one or a few children, keeping track of a broad range of data. This might include contacts with literature, responses, and developing skills in reading and writing. One such study, *Books before Five,*[41] is Dorothy White's diary account of her daughter Carol's experiences with books. It shows the beginnings of Carol's curiosity about authorship and the origin of stories, her concern about whether things represented in stories are "real" or "true," and other aspects of her changing ideas

[39]Erik H. Erikson, *Childhood and Society,* rev. ed. (New York: Norton, 1964).
[40]George A. Kelly, *A Theory of Personality* (New York: Norton, 1963).
[41]Dorothy White, *Books before Five* (Portsmouth, N.H.: Heinemann Educational Books, 1954, 1984).

He was the strongest king in the world. He could get anything he wanted.

He had the beautifulest castle and the beautifulest queen. He was the kindest king.

Children's expectations about stories are influenced by the stories they know. "Spot the King" was composed by first graders who combined their knowledge of fairy tales with a favorite character from the books of Eric Hill.

Elizabeth Strong, research participant. Dana Avenue Elementary School, Columbus, Ohio, Public Schools.

about literature. Hugh and Maureen Crago[42] have also published accounts of their young daughter's response to books during the preschool years, giving special attention to her understandings and expectations about the illustrations.

Glenda Bissex's study of her son Paul, *GNYS AT WRK*,[43] follows the development of his reading and writing abilities from ages 5 to 11. Although his early development in concept of story is not included, Bissex shows how his later expectations about literary form are influenced by his reading and brought to light through his spontaneous writing. For instance, at 10 years he wrote a sequel for the *Battlestar Galactica* novel he had read and also produced his own newspaper and magazine, demonstrating his knowledge of a variety of forms in writing.

The most comprehensive research on children's sense of story has been done by Applebee. Since young children do not easily examine or explain their own ideas, Applebee drew inferences about their understanding of story structure from the patterns he found in stories told by 2- to 5-year-

[42]Hugh Crago and Maureen Crago, "The Untrained Eye? A Preschool Child Explores Felix Hoffman's 'Rapunzel'," *Children's Literature in Education*, no. 22 (Autumn 1976), pp. 133–151; Maureen Crago, "'Incompletely Shown Objects in Children's Books, One Child's Response," *Children' Literature in Education*, vol. 10 (Autumn 1979), pp. 151–157.

[43]Glenda L. Bissex, *GNYS AT WRK; A Child Learns to Write and Read* (Cambridge, Mass.: Harvard University Press, 1980).

olds. These patterns reflect an increasing ability to chain events together and to develop at the same time a thematic center. The structures he identified, in order of increasing complexity, were:

- heap—collection of unconnected items
- sequence—arbitrary linking of similar events to a common center
- primitive narrative—a concrete center with events related to it by cause and effect or other complementarity
- unfocused chain—linking through a common attribute that shifts from one pair of incidents to the next
- focused chain—chaining of events which are all related to the common center
- narrative—focused chain in which each item develops the theme or character at its center[44]

Most of the 2-year-olds' stories were already beyond the "heap" stage of organization, and some 5-year-olds could manage to tell true narratives. The most commonly told pattern, however, was the focused chain, the "continuing-adventures-of" type of story. This is a pattern which professional writers sometimes use, also; it can be found in many picture books. It is worth noting that the more complex organizational forms really make stories simpler; they become easier to understand and to remember because they are more predictable and make more sense.

Some of the other expectations that children develop about stories concern character roles and the distinction between the real world and the story world. Applebee interviewed 6- and 9-year-olds in London to find out what they thought certain characters were "usually like" in a story. The 9-year-olds were much more confident than the younger group about the stock roles that lions play (brave) and the fact that fairies should be good. Half the 6-year-olds expected witches to be wicked, but with 9-year-olds it was unanimous.[45] It is sometimes much later, however, before students begin to notice and expect multiple dimensions in characterization.

In order to find out what children knew of the relation of stories to real life, Applebee asked the question, "Where does Cinderella live?" Their answers indicated that "stories are astonishingly real even for 6-year-olds who have had a year in a school environment where they hear stories at least daily."[46] By 9, most children had given up thinking that Cinderella is far away over a river or "just a dolly" and could say that it's just a story or that it isn't true.

The difference between real and made-up is an important dimension when children think about stories. *Realism* was one of three "superordinate constructs" that Applebee[47] identified in the responses of children aged 6 to 17. In the beginning children's concern is with the difference between "true" and "made up"; older children shift their attention to how well the "reality" of the story matches the reality of their own lives. *Simplicity* and *evaluation* were other constructs important to children. Nine-year-olds were negative about a "disturbing" story, but 17-year-olds thought "disturbing" was something of a plus. The younger children felt that it was good for a story to "work out as you would expect in the end," but the older adolescents saw that as a slight drawback.

Like other areas of development, continued growth in concept of story depends on the interaction of new capabilities and experiences. All children are exposed to a variety of narrative forms through the media, but this will not guarantee their growth toward fully developed literary expectations. Children must be steadily nurtured with books that help them discover new possibilities and increasing complexity in literature.

Guides for Ages and Stages

Adults who are responsible for children's reading need to be aware of these guides from child development and learning theory and of children's interests. They must keep in mind characteristics and needs of children at different ages and stages of development. At the same time, it is important

[44]Arthur N. Applebee, *The Child's Concept of Story: Ages Two to Seventeen* (Chicago: University of Chicago Press, 1978), chapter 2.
[45]Applebee, chapter 3.
[46]Applebee, p. 42.
[47]Arthur N. Applebee, "Children's Construal of Stories and Related Genres as Measured with Repertory Grid Techniques," *Research in the Teaching of English*, vol. 10 (Winter 1976), pp. 226–238.

to remember that each child has a unique pattern of growth. The following charts summarize some characteristic growth patterns, suggest implications for selection and use of books, and provide examples of suitable books for a particular stage of development.

BOOKS FOR AGES AND STAGES

BEFORE SCHOOL—INFANCY, AGES 1 AND 2

CHARACTERISTICS	IMPLICATIONS	EXAMPLES
Rapid development of senses. Responds to sound of human voice, especially rhythmic patterns. Vision stimulated by areas of color and sharp contrast; increasingly able to see detail.	Enjoys rhymes, songs, and lullabies. Likes simple, bright illustrations. Looks for familiar objects.	*Nursery Rhyme Peek-a-Book*, Hill *Tomie de Paola's Mother Goose*, de Paola *Singing Bee!*, Hart *Hush, Little Baby*, Zemach *B Is for Bear*, Bruna *My Pets*, Hill *Colors*, Reiss
Uses all senses to explore the world immediately at hand; learns through activity and participation.	Gets maximum use from sturdy books with washable pages. Needs to participate by touching, pointing, peeking, moving.	*Peek-a-Boo!*, Ahlberg *Where's Spot?*, Hill *Pat the Bunny*, Kunhardt *Working*, Oxenbury *Tuffa and the Bone*, Schroeder
Very limited attention span; averts eyes or turns away when bored.	Needs books that can be shared a few pages at a time or in a brief sitting; many short story times are better than one long one.	*Playing*, Oxenbury *Max's Ride*, Wells *Dear Zoo*, Campbell *1, 2, 3*, Hoban
Building foundations of language; plays with sounds, learns basic vocabulary along with concepts, begins to learn implicit "rules" that govern speech and conversation.	Needs to hear many rhymes and simple stories. Needs encouragement to use language in labeling pictures and in sharing dialogue with adults as they read aloud.	*Crash! Bang! Boom!*, Spier *Catch Me and Kiss Me and Say It Again*, Watson *Sam Who Never Forgets*, Rice *The First Words Picture Book*, Gillham *What?*, Lionni *Home Sweet Home*, Roffey
Building basic trust in human relationships.	Needs love and affection from care-givers, in stories as well as in life. Thrives on dependable routines and rituals such as bedtime stories.	*Goodnight Moon*, Brown *The Blanket*, Burningham *But Not Billy*, Zolotow *Me and My Kitty*, Rubel
Limited mobility and experience; interests centered in self and the familiar.	Needs books that reflect self and people and activities in the immediate environment.	*The Baby's Catalogue*, Ahlberg *The Cupboard*, Burningham *Sam's Cookie*, Lindgren *I Play in My Room*, Rockwell
Learning autonomy in basic self-help skills.	Enjoys stories of typical toddler accomplishments such as feeding self or getting dressed.	*Alfie's Feet*, Hughes *Mother's Helper*, Oxenbury *How Do I Put It On?*, Watanabe *What a Good Lunch*, Watanabe

BOOKS FOR AGES AND STAGES (continued)

PRESCHOOL AND KINDERGARTEN—AGES 3, 4, AND 5

CHARACTERISTICS	IMPLICATIONS	EXAMPLES
Rapid development of language.	Interest in words, enjoyment of rhymes, nonsense, and repetition and cumulative tales. Enjoys retelling simple folktales and "reading" stories from books without words.	*Pigs Say Oink*, Alexander *Brian Wildsmith's Mother Goose*, Wildsmith *Roll Over*, Gerstein *Mr. Gumpy's Outing*, Burningham *Millions of Cats*, Gág *The Three Bears*, Rockwell *Sunshine*, Ormerod
Very active, short attention span.	Requires books that can be completed in one sitting. Enjoys participation such as naming, pointing, finding, and identifying hidden pictures. Should have a chance to hear stories several times each day.	*John Burningham's ABC*, Burningham *The Very Hungry Caterpillar*, Carle *The Elephant's Wish*, Munari *Each Peach Pear Plum*, Ahlberg *1 Hunter*, Hutchins *Have You Seen My Duckling?*, Tafuri
Child is center of own world. Interest, behavior, and thinking are egocentric.	Likes characters that are easy to identify with. Normally sees only one point of view.	*Where Did My Mother Go?*, Preston *Fix-It*, McPhail *Noisy Nora*, Wells *New Blue Shoes*, Rice
Curious about own world.	Enjoys stories about everyday experiences, pets, playthings, home, people in the immediate environment.	*Will I Have a Friend?*, Cohen *The Snowy Day*, Keats *The Dancing Class*, Oxenbury *Benny Bakes a Cake*, Rice *My Back Yard*, Rockwell
Building concepts through many firsthand experiences.	Books extend and reinforce child's developing concepts.	*Freight Train*, Crews *What's Inside?*, Daughtry *I Read Signs*, Hoban *Trucks*, Gibbons *Is It Red? Is It Yellow? Is It Blue?*, Hoban
Child has little sense of time. Time is "before now," "now," and "not yet."	Books can help children begin to understand the sequence of time.	*When You Were a Baby*, Jonas *Seasons*, Burningham *The Grouchy Ladybug*, Carle *The Little House*, Burton
Child learns through imaginative play; make-believe world of talking animals and magic seems very real.	Enjoys stories that involve imaginative play. Likes personification of toys and animals.	*Martin's Hats*, Blos *May I Bring a Friend?*, DeRegniers *Alexander and the Wind-Up Mouse*, Lionni *Bear Hunt*, Browne *Corduroy*, Freeman

BOOKS FOR AGES AND STAGES (continued)

CHARACTERISTICS	IMPLICATIONS	EXAMPLES
Seeks warmth and security in relationships with family and others.	Likes to hear stories that provide reassurance. Bedtime stories and other read-aloud rituals provide positive literature experiences.	*The Runaway Bunny*, Brown *Betsy's Baby Brother*, Wolde *Little Bear*, Minarik *Even If I Did Something Awful?*, Hazen *Ten, Nine, Eight*, Bang
Beginning to assert independence. Takes delight in own accomplishments.	Books can reflect emotions. Enjoys stories where small characters show initiative.	*I Hate to Go to Bed*, Barrett *No More Baths*, Cole *Alfie Gets in First*, Hughes *Titch*, Hutchins *The Carrot Seed*, Krauss
Makes absolute judgments about right and wrong.	Expects bad behavior to be punished and good behavior rewarded. Requires poetic justice and happy endings.	*The Three Billy Goats Gruff*, Brown *The Little Red Hen*, Galdone *The Tale of Peter Rabbit*, Potter *Binky Gets a Car*, Gackenbach *A Lion for Lewis*, Wells

PRIMARY—AGES 6 AND 7

CHARACTERISTICS	IMPLICATIONS	EXAMPLES
Continued development and expansion of language.	Frequent storytimes during the day provide opportunity to hear the rich and varied language of literature. Wordless books and simple tales encourage story-telling.	*A Pocketful of Cricket*, Caudill *Sylvester and the Magic Pebble*, Steig *Say It!*, Zolotow *A House Is a House for Me*, Hoberman *Strega Nona*, de Paola *The Old Woman Who Lived in a Vinegar Bottle*, Godden *The Snowman*, Briggs *Peter Spier's Rain*, Spier
Attention span increasing.	Prefers short stories; may enjoy a continued story provided each chapter is a complete episode.	*Everett Anderson's Friend*, Clifton *Frederick*, Lionni *Frog and Toad Together*, Lobel *The Courage of Sarah Noble*, Dalgliesh *James and the Giant Peach*, Dahl *Ramona the Brave*, Cleary
Striving to accomplish skills expected by adults.	Proud of accomplishments in reading and writing. Needs reassurance that everyone progresses at own rate. First reading experiences should be enjoyable, using familiar or predictable stories.	*When Will I Read?*, Cohen *Petunia*, Duvoisin *Leo the Late Bloomer*, Kraus *Brown Bear, Brown Bear*, Martin *Farmer in the Dell*, Zuromskis *The Chick and the Duckling*, Ginsburg

BOOKS FOR AGES AND STAGES (continued)

CHARACTERISTICS	IMPLICATIONS	EXAMPLES
Learning still based on immediate perception and direct experiences.	Uses information books to verify as well as extend experience. Much value in watching guinea pigs or tadpoles *before* using a book.	*How My Library Grew by Dinah,* Alexander *Houses from the Sea,* Goudey *Look Again!,* Hoban *How My Garden Grew,* Rockwell *Frogs,* Tarrant
Continued interest in own world, but curious about a wider range of things. Still sees world from an egocentric point of view.	Needs wide variety of books. TV has expanded interests beyond home and neighborhood.	*What Do You See?,* Domanska *Fish Is Fish,* Lionni *How My Parents Learned to Eat,* Friedman *Digging Up Dinosaurs,* Aliki *New Road,* Gibbons *In the Driver's Seat,* Goor
Vague concepts of time.	Needs to learn basics of telling time and the calendar. Simple biographies and historical fiction may give a feeling for the past, but accurate understanding of chronology is beyond this age group.	*Clocks and More Clocks,* Hutchins *Ms Glee Was Waiting,* Hill *All Year Long,* Tafuri *Ox-Cart Man,* Hall *The Glorious Flight,* Provensen *When I Was Young in the Mountains,* Rylant *Little House in the Big Woods,* Wilder
More able to separate fantasy from reality; more aware of own imagination.	Enjoys fantasy. Likes to dramatize simple stories or use feltboard, puppets.	*Where the Wild Things Are,* Sendak *And to Think That I Saw It on Mulberry Street,* Seuss *Sam, Bangs, and Moonshine,* Ness *Abiyoyo,* Seeger *Stone Soup,* Brown *The Fat Cat,* Kent
Beginning to develop empathy and understanding for others.	Adults can ask such questions as "What would you have done?" "How do you think Stevie felt about Robert?"	*Stevie,* Steptoe *We Are Best Friends,* Aliki *Now One Foot, Now the Other,* de Paola *The Balancing Girl,* Rabe *My Mama Needs Me,* Walter *Crow Boy,* Yashima
Has a growing sense of justice. Demands application of rules, regardless of circumstances.	Expects poetic justice in books.	*Let's Be Enemies,* Udry *Dandelion,* Freeman *Python's Party,* Wildsmith *Once a Mouse,* Brown
Humor is developing.	Reading aloud for pure fun has its place in classroom. Enjoys books that have surprise endings, plays on words, incongruous situations, and slapstick comedy. Likes to be in on the joke.	*Where the Sidewalk Ends,* Silverstein *Alexander and the Terrible, Horrible, No Good, Very Bad Day,* Viorst *Do Not Open,* Turkle *Amelia Bedelia,* Parish *Perfect Pigs,* Brown/Krensky *Roger's Umbrella,* Pinkwater

BOOKS FOR AGES AND STAGES (continued)

CHARACTERISTICS	IMPLICATIONS	EXAMPLES
Shows curiosity about sex differences and reproduction.	Teachers need to accept and be ready to answer children's questions about sex.	*A Kitten Is Born*, Fischer-Nagel *The Wonderful Story of How You Were Born*, Gruenberg *"Where Did I Come From?"*, Mayle
Physical contour of the body is changing; permanent teeth appear; learning to whistle and developing other fine motor skills.	Books can help the child accept physical changes in self and differences in others.	*You'll Soon Grow into Them, Titch*, Hutchins *One Morning in Maine*, McCloskey *Whistle for Willie*, Keats
Continues to seek independence from adults and to develop initiative.	Needs opportunities to self-select books and activities. Enjoys stories of responsiblity and successful ventures.	*I Can Do It by Myself*, Little/Greenfield *Ira Sleeps Over*, Waber *The Climb*, Carrick *We Be Warm Till Springtime Comes*, Chaffin *By Myself*, Hopkins
Continues to need warmth and security in family relationships.	Books may emphasize universal human characteristics in a variety of life styles.	*Daddy*, Caines *David and Dog*, Hughes *Mr. Rabbit and the Lovely Present*, Zolotow *A Chair for My Mother*, Williams *The Relatives Came*, Rylant

MIDDLE ELEMENTARY—AGES 8 AND 9

CHARACTERISTICS	IMPLICATIONS	EXAMPLES
Attaining independence in reading skill. May read with complete absorption; others may still be having difficulty learning to read. Wide variation in ability and interest.	Discovers reading as an enjoyable activity. Prefers an uninterrupted block of time for independent reading. During this period, many children become avid readers.	*Follow That Bus*, Hutchins *Something Queer at the Lemonade Stand*, Levy *Mummies Made in Egypt*, Aliki *You're Not for Real, Snoopy*, Schulz *A Lion to Guard Us*, Bulla *Ramona Quimby, Age 8*, Cleary *The Thunder-Pup*, Hickman *Charlotte's Web*, White
Reading level may still be below appreciation level.	Essential to read aloud to children each day in order to extend interests, develop appreciation, and provide balance.	*The Random House Book of Poetry*, Prelutky *Jumanji*, Van Allsburg *Dawn*, Bang *Abel's Island*, Steig *The Green Book*, Walsh *Sarah, Plain and Tall*, MacLachlan
Peer group acceptance becomes increasingly important.	Children need opportunities to recommend and discuss books. Sharing favorites builds sense that reading is fun, has group approval. Popular books may provide status, be much in demand.	*Superfudge*, Blume *A Light in the Attic*, Silverstein *Choose-Your-Own Adventure Series*, Packard *Bunnicula*, Howe

BOOKS FOR AGES AND STAGES (continued)

CHARACTERISTICS	IMPLICATIONS	EXAMPLES
Developing standards of right and wrong. Begins to see viewpoints of others.	Books provide opportunities to relate to several points of view.	*Danny the Champion of the World,* Dahl *The Indian in the Cupboard,* Banks *The Bully of Barkham Street,* Stolz *A Dog on Barkham Street,* Stolz
Less egocentric, developing empathy for others. Questioning death.	Accepts some books with a less than happy ending. Discussion helps children explore their feelings for others.	*Hickory,* Brown *Mustard,* Graeber *A Taste of Blackberries,* Smith *Annie and the Old One,* Miles *How Does It Feel To Be Old?,* Farber
Time concepts and spatial relationships developing. This age level is characterized by thought that is flexible and reversible.	Interested in biographies, life in the past, in other lands, and the future. Prefers fast-moving, exciting stories.	*What's the Big Idea, Ben Franklin?,* Fritz *The Secret Soldier,* McGovern *Trouble for Lucy,* Stevens *The Forgotten Door,* Key *The Land I Lost,* Huynh
Enjoys tall tales, slapstick humor in everyday situations. Appreciates imaginary adventure.	Teachers need to recognize the importance of literature for laughter, releasing tension, and providing enjoyment.	*Paul Bunyan,* Kellogg *The Celery Stalks at Midnight,* Howe *The Magic Moscow,* Pinkwater *McBroom's Almanac,* Fleischman *Whoppers: Tall Tales,* Schwartz
Cognitive growth and language development increase capacity for problem solving and word play.	Likes the challenge of solving puzzles and mysteries. High interest in twists of plot, secret codes, riddles, and other language play.	*Anno's USA,* Anno *The Polar Express,* Van Allsburg *The Case of the Phantom Frog,* Hildick *The Code and Cipher Book,* Sarnoff/Ruffins *A Book of Riddles,* Beisner
Improved coordination makes proficiency in sports and games possible and encourages interest in crafts and hobbies.	Interest in sports books; wants specific knowledge about sports. Enjoys how-to-do-it books.	*Rabbit Ears,* Slote *Football Players Do Amazing Things,* Cebulash *A Very Young Gymnast,* Krementz *The Paper Airplane Book,* Simon *Dollhouse Magic,* Roche *The Little House Cookbook,* Walker
Sees categories and classifications with new clarity; interest in collecting is high.	Likes to collect and trade paperback books. Begins to look for books of one author, series books. Enjoys books that collect facts, informational identification books.	The *Little House* Series, Wilder *Ramona Forever* and others, Cleary *Encyclopedia Brown's Record Book of Weird and Wonderful Facts,* Sobol *A First Look at Insects,* Selsam/Hunt *Trucks: Of Every Sort,* Robbins

BOOKS FOR AGES AND STAGES (continued)

CHARACTERISTICS	IMPLICATIONS	EXAMPLES
Seeks specific information to answer questions; may go to books beyond own reading ability to search out answers.	Requires guidance in locating information within a book and in using the library.	*A Medieval Feast,* Aliki *A Great Bicycle Book,* Sarnoff/Ruffins *Billions of Bats,* Schlein *If You Lived with the Sioux Indians,* McGovern *My Backyard History Book,* Weitzman

LATER ELEMENTARY—AGES 10, 11, 12

CHARACTERISTICS	IMPLICATIONS	EXAMPLES
Rate of physical development varies widely. Rapid growth precedes beginning of puberty, with girls about two years ahead of boys in development. Boys and girls increasingly curious about all aspects of sex.	Guide understanding of growth process and help children meet personal problems. Continued differentiation in reading preferences of boys and girls.	*The Human Body,* Bruun *Are You There, God? It's Me, Margaret,* Blume *Then Again, Maybe I Won't,* Blume *Hold On to Love,* Hunter *Playing Beatie Bow,* Park *The Goof That Won the Pennant,* Kalb *Nightmare Island,* Roy
Understanding and accepting the sex role is a developmental task of this period. Boys and girls develop a sense of each other's identity.	Books may provide identification with gender roles as well as impetus for discussion of stereotypes.	*The Agony of Alice,* Naylor *Philip Hall Likes Me. I Reckon Maybe,* Greene *I'm Deborah Sampson,* Clapp *A Solitary Blue,* Voigt
Increased emphasis on peer group and sense of belonging.	Book choices often influenced by peer group; many requests for books about "kids like us."	*Anything for a Friend,* Conford *The Real Me,* Miles *The 18th Emergency,* Byars *There's a Bat in Bunk Five,* Danziger
Deliberate exclusion of others; some expressions of prejudice.	Books can emphasize unique contribution of all. Discussion can be used to clarify values.	*Alan and Naomi,* Levoy *Blubber,* Blume *Legend Days,* Highwater *A Secret Friend,* Sachs *Roll of Thunder, Hear My Cry,* Taylor
Family patterns changing; may challenge parents' authority. Highly critical of siblings.	Books may provide some insight into these changing relationships.	*Dear Mr. Henshaw,* Cleary *Anastasia Krupnik,* Lowry *The Animal, the Vegetable and John D Jones,* Byars *Journey to an 800 Number,* Konigsburg *Dicey's Song,* Voigt *Justice and Her Brothers,* Hamilton *Jacob Have I Loved,* Paterson

BOOKS FOR AGES AND STAGES (continued)

CHARACTERISTICS	IMPLICATIONS	EXAMPLES
Begins to have models other than parents drawn from TV, movies, sports figures, books. Beginning interest in future vocation.	Biographies may provide models. Career books broaden interests and provide useful information.	*What Can She Be? A Scientist,* Goldreich *How I Came to Be a Writer,* Naylor *Superstars of the Sports World,* Gutman *Sports Star: Fernando Valenzuela,* Burchard
Sustained, intense interest in specific activities; children spend more time in reading at this age than any other.	Enjoys books related to sports, hobbies, special content interests.	*Baseball Access,* Wurman *Drawing from Nature,* Arnosky *Basic Programming for Kids,* Ault *A Horse for X.Y.Z.,* Moeri Prydain Series, Alexander
Seeks to test own skills and abilities; looks ahead to a time of complete independence.	Enjoys stories of survival and "going it alone."	*Julie of the Wolves,* George *My Side of the Mountain,* George *The Sign of the Beaver,* Speare *The Wild Children,* Holman *The Hideaway,* Renner *From the Mixed-Up Files of Mrs. Basil E. Frankweiler,* Konigsburg
Highly developed sense of justice and concern for others.	Likes "sad stories" about death, illness, or people dealing with special problems.	*Goodnight, Mr. Tom,* Magorian *Beat the Turtle Drum,* Greene *How It Feels When a Parent Dies,* Krementz *A Night Without Stars,* Howe *The Alfred Summer,* Slepian
Increased understanding of the chronology of past events; developing sense of own place in time. Begins to see many dimensions of a problem.	Literature provides opportunities to examine issues from different viewpoints. Guidance needed for becoming critical of biased presentations.	*The Night Journey,* Lasky *Friedrich,* Richter *Homesick,* Fritz *Across Five Aprils,* Hunt *To Be a Slave,* Lester *My Brother Sam Is Dead,* Collier
Increased cognitive skill can be used to serve the imagination.	Tackles complex and puzzling plots in mysteries, science fiction, fantasy. Can appreciate more subtlety in humor.	*The Westing Game,* Raskin *Lizard Music,* Pinkwater *Sizzle and Splat,* Kidd *The Haunting,* Mahy *The Dark Is Rising,* Cooper *A Swiftly Tilting Planet,* L'Engle

BOOKS FOR AGES AND STAGES (continued)

CHARACTERISTICS	IMPLICATIONS	EXAMPLES
Searching for values; interested in problems of the world. Can deal with abstract relationships; becoming more analytical.	Valuable discussions may grow out of teacher's reading aloud prose and poetry to this age group. Questions may help students gain insight into both the content and literary structure of a book.	*Hiroshima No Pika*, Maruki *Reflections on a Gift of Watermelon Pickle, and Other Modern Verse*, Dunning *Tuck Everlasting*, Babbitt *Mrs. Frisby and the Rats of NIMH*, O'Brien *Westmark*, Alexander *The Great Gilly Hopkins*, Paterson

RESPONSE IN THE CLASSROOM

Understanding response to literature would be much easier if it were possible to peer inside a child's head. Then we might see firsthand what concept of story guides progress through a book or just what thoughts and feelings are called up as a story unfolds. Instead, teachers must be satisfied with secondary evidence. Children's perceptions and understandings are revealed in many different ways—as they choose and talk about books, as they write, paint, play, or take part in other classroom activities.

Classroom responses may be obvious and direct (primary children have been known to kiss a favorite book) or hidden within a situation that appears to have little to do with literature (block corner play). Many responses are verbal, many come without words. Some are spontaneous, bubbling up out of children too delighted to be still or shyly offered, in confidence. Other responses would not be expressed at all without the direct invitation of teachers who plan extension activities or discussions (see Chapters 12 and 13) to generate thoughtful reaction to literature. To understand any of these observed responses, it is helpful to be acquainted with a few basic theoretical perspectives.

Theories of Response

What really goes on between a reader and a story or poem is a complex question with many answers. Theories about reader response draw from many disciplines, including psychology, linguistics, aesthetics, and, of course, literature and education.

Some theories focus on what is read, while others focus on the reader. Psycholinguists, for instance, examine in careful detail the structure of a story, noting the precise arrangement of words and sequence of ideas. These patterns are called story grammars, and some research indicates that they can affect the way readers understand and recall the story.[48] Psychoanalytic theorists, on the other hand, look at the way readers' own personalities influence their ideas about what they read.[49]

One important point on which scholars agree is that the process of reading and responding is active rather than somehow automatic. Response is dynamic and open to continuous change as readers anticipate, infer, remember, reflect, interpret, and connect. The "meaning" and significance of a story like Patricia MacLachlan's *Sarah, Plain and Tall* will vary from reader to reader, depending on age and personal experience as well as experience with literature. However, the response of a single reader will also change given time for reflection, discussion, or repeated readings.

Some scholars avoid the word "response" be-

[48]Nancy L. Stein and Christine G. Glenn, "An Analysis of Story Comprehension in Elementary School Children," in Roy O. Freedle, ed., *New Dimensions in Discourse Processing* (Norwood, N.J.: Ablex Publishing, 1977); Bertram Bruce, "What Makes a Good Story?" *Language Arts*, vol. 55 (April, 1978), pp. 460–466.
[49]Norman H. Holland, *Five Readers Reading* (New Haven, Conn.: Yale University Press, 1975).

"William Ernest lay a bolster pillow behind Mrs Trotter's back like"

Children's pictures or other classroom work may furnish important evidence about their understanding of literature.
Ellen Esrick, teacher. Martin Luther King, Jr., Laboratory School, Evanston, Illinois, Public Schools,

cause they do not want to suggest the predetermined reaction of a behaviorist point of view (stimulus-response) rather than the lively process they envision. Louise Rosenblatt uses the term "transaction" to describe this process, explaining:

> The literary work exists in the live circuit set up between reader and text: the reader infuses intellectual and emotional meanings into the pattern of verbal symbols, and those symbols channel his thoughts and feelings.[50]

Teachers who focus on rigidly prescribed materials and questions with set answers when talking about

literature are narrowly interpreting what happens when a reader reads. This dynamic theory of response, on the other hand, suggests that children will see many variations of meaning in a poem or story. Sensitive teachers can then begin to encourage a more conscious participation in predicting, reflecting, making inferences, and other parts of the process.

Reader response theory also points out that readers approach works of literature in a special way. James Britton[51] proposes that in all our uses of language we may be either *participants* or *spec-*

[50]Louise M. Rosenblatt, *Literature As Exploration*, 3rd ed. (New York: Noble and Noble, 1976), p. 25.

[51]James Britton, et al., *The Development of Writing Abilities (11–18)*, Schools Council Research Studies (London: Macmillan Education Limited, 1975).

tators. In the participant role we read in order to accomplish something in the real world, as in following a recipe. In the spectator role we focus on what the language says as an end in itself, attending to its forms and patterns, as we do in enjoying poetry.

Rosenblatt[52] also suggests that reading usually involves two roles and that we shift our emphasis from one to the other according to the material and our purposes for reading it. In one role we are most concerned with what information can be learned from the reading. In the other the reader's concern is for the experience of the reading itself, the feelings and images that come and go with the flow of the words. Most readers, or course, find themselves switching back and forth from one stance to the other as they read, but it is important to know where to begin. One thing that teachers can do to help children share the world the author has created is to help them find the appropriate stance from which to respond.

Types of Responses

The most common expressions of response to literature are statements, oral or written. In their most polished form such responses are known as literary criticism. One traditional line of research in literature involves measuring young people's statements against this standard of mature critical ability. Many years ago when I. A. Richards[53] was concerned that college English students were not making "correct" literary judgments, he categorized a sample of their written statements about poems according to what seemed to keep them from speaking like professional critics. For example, the students often failed to get the "plain sense" of the work, they had inappropriate preconceptions, they made stock responses, and they tended to be, at least in Richards' view, overly sentimental.

In a later study of verbal response, Squire[54] in-terviewed ninth- and tenth-graders at various stopping points in the reading of short stories. One of his most interesting observations was a tendency he called *happiness binding,* the students' inclination to expect and interpret a happy ending regardless of contrary evidence in the story. This is the same phenomenon observed by middle-grade teachers when children predict that Hop in Palmer Brown's *Hickory* will survive the cold winter despite eloquent clues about the brevity of a grasshopper's life.

Verbal responses can be categorized in a number of ways, but many researchers begin with a system developed by Alan Purves[55] from the responses of 300 teenagers in four countries. All of the categories in this system have descriptive labels. They help teachers see what *kinds* of statements about literature are made by students without indicating whether the statements are "right" or "wrong."

Most early studies of response involved high school students or young adults rather than elementary or preschool children. Young children also talk about books, and write about them, but their verbal responses have not yet received as much systematic attention. Applebee's study of children's statements about stories, the base for his work on concept of story discussed on pages 62–63, shows how the characteristics of responses change as students gain in age and experience. Only recently have other researchers begun to look carefully at what elementary children have to say about literature, often collecting data from intensive interviews or long periods of observation.[56]

Where children are concerned, it is important to remember that direct comment is only one of many ways of revealing what goes on between the book and its audience. Language used in other ways—to tell or write stories based on other stories, for instance—often provides good clues about a child's

[52]Louise M. Rosenblatt, *The Reader, the Text, the Poem: The Transactional Theory of the Literary Work* (Carbondale, Ill.: Southern Illinois University Press, 1978).

[53]I. A. Richards, *Practical Criticism* (New York: Harcourt Brace, 1929).

[54]James R. Squire, *The Responses of Adolescents While Reading Four Short Stories* (Urbana, Ill.: National Council of Teachers of English, 1964).

[55]Alan C. Purves with Victoria Rippere, *Elements of Writing about a Literary Work: A Study of Response to Literature* (Urbana, Ill.: National Council of Teachers of English, 1968).

[56]Lee Galda, "Assuming the Spectator Stance: An Examination of the Responses of Three Young Readers," *Research in the Teaching of English,* vol. 16 (February 1982), pp. 1–20; Rudine Sims, "Strong Black Girls: A Ten Year Old Responds to Fiction about Afro-Americans," *Journal of Research and Development in Education,* vol. 16 (Spring, 1983), pp. 21–28.

feelings and understandings about the original. Parents and teachers of young children also recognize nonverbal behaviors as signs of response. For instance, young listeners almost always show their involvement, or lack of it, in body postures and facial expressions. Children's artwork, informal drama, and other book extension activities (see Chapter 13) also provide windows on response.

Interpreting Children's Responses

RECOGNIZING GROWTH

Children's responses, like their interests and preferences, change in character over the years. The content of a 10-year-old's response will be different from a 5-year-old's. Their chosen form of responding may also be different. This section outlines some general characteristics of children's responses and the way they change with age.[57] Because there is such wide variation among individual children, it is hard to pinpoint "typical" responses at any level; but it is useful to know the general direction of changes.

YOUNGER CHILDREN (PRESCHOOL–PRIMARY)

- Are *motor-oriented*. As listeners they respond with their whole selves, chiming in on refrains or talking back to the story. They lean closer to the book, point at pictures, clap their hands. They use body movements to try out some of the story's action, "hammering" along with *John Henry* by Ezra Jack Keats or making wild faces to match the illustrations in Ruth Park's *When the Wind Changed*. Actions to demonstrate meaning ("like this") may be given as answer to a teacher's questions. These easily observable responses go under cover as children mature; older children reveal feelings through subtle changes of expression and posture.
- Spontaneously act out stories or bits of stories using actions, roles, and conventions of literature in their *dramatic play*. Witches, kings, "Wild Things," and other well-defined character types appear naturally, showing how well children have assimilated elements of favorite tales. Examples of story language ("We lived happily ever after") are sometimes incorpo-

[57]These outlines are based on the authors' observations but owe a particular debt to Applebee, *The Child's Concept of Story: Ages Two to Seventeen*, pp. 123–125.

rated. Spontaneous dramatic play disappears from the classroom early in the primary years (although it persists out of school with some children) and is replaced by more structured drama of various kinds. Older children are usually much more conscious of their own references to literature.

- Respond to stories piecemeal. Their responses are likely to deal with *parts rather than wholes*. A detail of text or illustration may prompt more comment than the story itself, as children make quick associations with their own experience: "I saw a bird like that once" or "My sister has bunk beds just like those." This part-by-part organization can also be seen in very young children's art where the pictures show individual story items without any indication of relationship ("This is the baby bear's chair, and this is Goldilocks, and this is the house the bears lived in, and here is the bed . . ."). This is the same sort of itemization or catalog of characters, objects, and events that children sometimes use when asked to tell something about a story.
- Resort to *retelling* all or part of a story when asked for a general comment. Without an adult's questions to guide them, children at this stage do not differentiate between the story itself and comments about it.
- Use *embedded language* in answering direct questions about stories. Because young children see the world in literal, concrete terms, their answers will not be generalized but will be couched in terms of the characters and events and objects found in the story. One first grader made a good attempt to generalize the lesson of "The Little Red Hen," but couldn't manage without some reference to the tale: "When someone already baked the cake and you haven't helped, they're probably just gonna say 'no'!" A teacher or other adult who shares the child's context—who knows the story, has heard or read it with the child, and knows what other comments have been made—will understand the intent of such a statement more readily than a casual observer.

CHILDREN IN TRANSITION (PRIMARY–MIDDLE GRADES)

- Change from listeners to readers. They go through a period of focus on the *accomplish-*

ment of independent reading. There are many comments about quantity—number of pages read, the length of a book, or the number of books read. Conventions of print and of book-making may draw attention. One third-grader refused to read any of the poems from Shel Silverstein's *Where the Sidewalk Ends* without locating them in the index first; a classmate was fascinated with the book's variety of word and line arrangements for poetry. Another child studied the front matter of a picture book and pronounced it "a dedicated book." So-called independent reading may be more sociable than it sounds, since many children like to have a listener or reading partner and begin to rely on peers as sounding boards for their response.

• Become more adept at *summarizing* stories in place of straight retelling when asked to talk about them. This is a skill that facilitates discussion and becomes more useful as it is developed. Summarizing is one of the techniques that undergirds critical commentary, but adults use it more deliberately and precisely than children do.

• Classify or *categorize* stories in some of the same ways that adults do. Middle graders who are asked to sort out a random pile of books use categories like "mysteries," "humorous books," "make believe," "fantasy." If you ask kindergarteners to do the same, they are more likely to classify the books by their physical properties ("fat books," "books with pretty covers," "red books") than by content.

• *Attribute personal reactions to the story* itself. A book that bores an 8-year-old will be thought of as "a boring book," as if "boring" were as much a property of the story as its number of pages or the first-person point of view. Children judge a story on the basis of their response to it, regardless of its qualities as literature or its appeal to anyone else. This is a very persistent element in response; it can affect the judgment of students of children's literature and occasionally of professional book reviewers as well as children in elementary school. It takes a great deal of objectivity to manage the separation of a book's literary merits from its personal appeal.

• *Use borrowed characters, events, themes, and patterns from literature in writing,* just as younger children do in dramatic play. In the earliest stages much of this is unconscious as well as spontaneous, as in the case of the 7-year-old who was convinced her story about a fish with paint-splashed insides was "made up out of my own head," even when reminded that the class had just heard Robert McCloskey's *Burt Dow, Deep Water Man.* A 9-year-old spontaneously combined a favorite character with a field-trip experience in his story "Paddington Bear Goes to Franklin Park Conservatory," but he was aware of his idea sources. Other children produce their own examples of patterns, forms, or genres. The direction of growth is toward more conscious realization of the uses of literature in writing (see Chapter 13 on "Extending Literature Through Writing").

OLDER CHILDREN (MIDDLE GRADES–MIDDLE SCHOOL)

• Express *stronger preferences,* especially for personal reading. Younger children seem to enjoy almost everything that is reasonably appropriate, but older ones do not hesitate to reject books they do not like. Some children show particular devotion to certain authors or genres at this time. Some children also become more intense and protective about some of their reactions, and they should not be pressed to share those feelings that demand privacy.

• Are more skillful with language and more able to deal with abstractions. They can *dis-embed* ideas from a story and put them in more generalized terms, as in stating a universal moral for a particular fable.

• Begin to *see* (but not consistently) *that their feelings about a book are related to identifiable aspects of the writing.* Responses like "I love this book because it's great" develop into "I love this book because the characters say such funny things" or *"Are You There, God? It's Me, Margaret* is my favorite because Margaret is just like me."

• Go beyond categorizing stories *toward a more analytical perception* of why characters behave as they do, how the story is put together, or what the author is trying to say. They begin to test fiction against real life and understand it better through the comparison. They use some critical terminology, although their understanding of the term may be incomplete. In talk and writing, children who are encouraged to express ideas freely begin to stand back from their own involvement and take an evaluative look at literature. One sixth-grader had this to say about *A Taste of Blackberries* by Doris Buchanan Smith:

I thought the author could have put more into it. I really didn't know much about the kid who died. I mean, it really happened fast in the book. It started out pretty soon and told about how sad he was and what they used to do. All the fun things they used to do together. I wished at the beginning they would have had all the things that he talked about and then have him thinking about what a good friend he is and then all of a sudden he dies—a little closer to the end. Because when he died, you didn't much care cause you didn't really know him. But I guess the author wanted to talk about how it would be, or how people feel, or maybe what happened to her—how it felt when one of her friends died like that.[58]

In general, children's responses move toward this sort of conscious comment. Young children sometimes make stunningly perceptive observations about stories, but without realizing the worth of what they have said. Older children begin to know what they know, and can then take command of it. This is the circumstance that allows us to layer mature appreciation on top of the beginner's natural delight.

However, older children's increasing capacity for abstraction, generalization, and analysis should *not* be interpreted as a need for programs of formal literary analysis or highly structured study procedures. Opportunities to read, hear, and talk about well-chosen books under the guidance of an interested and informed teacher will allow elementary school children to develop response to their full potential.

One way to demonstrate the differences in response that teachers may notice from one grade level to another is to compare what children at different ages have to say about a particular book.

The following transcript[59] shows the various talk reactions of a 5-year-old, a 7-year-old, a 9-year-old, and an 11-year-old to the story of *Little Blue and Little Yellow* by Leo Lionni, in which the pictures are simply torn pieces of paper. The children's recorded comments follow:

Page 1 introduces Little Blue.
5-YEAR-OLD: "Hello, Blue!" [Shows automatic acceptance and wants to participate in the story.]

Page 2 shows Little Blue at home with his mother and father.
7-YEAR-OLD: "The tall one is papa and the fat one is mama." [Attempts to categorize the abstract shapes.]

Page 3 shows Little Blue's friends.
9-YEAR-OLD: "They're all different colors."
11-YEAR-OLD: "Those are black and yellow children and the red one is an Indian and they are all together." [Deeper analysis, recognizing symbolism.]

Page 4 states that of all the children Little Yellow is Little Blue's best friend.
5-YEAR-OLD: "My best friend is . . ." [At this point all the children had something to say about their best friends!]

Page 5 shows where Little Yellow lives.
7-YEAR-OLD: "The big brown thing is their house, huh?" [The 5-year-old just accepted it as their house; 7-year-old needed reassurance.]

Page 6 shows the children playing hide-and-seek and Ring-a-Ring-o-Roses.
9-YEAR-OLD: "That's supposed to be Ring around the Rosies."

Page 7 pictures them at school seated in neat rows.
11-YEAR-OLD: "Yuch!"

Page 8 shows them playing after school.
7-YEAR-OLD: "See the red one is way up in the air."

Page 9—Mama Blue goes shopping and tells Little Blue to stay home, but he goes out to find Little Yellow.
5-YEAR-OLD: "Oh, oh." [Anticipating punishment.]

[58]Recorded in the classroom of Lois Monaghan, teacher, Barrington School, Upper Arlington, Ohio.

[59]Recorded by Marianne Kubat, student, The Ohio State University.

7-YEAR-OLD: "Awwwww." [Tattling tone.]
11-YEAR-OLD: "He's too little to be left alone."

Page 10—The house is empty.
5-YEAR-OLD: "They moved away in the middle of the night 'cause his mommy couldn't pay for stuff." [Drawing on his own life experience or knowledge of others.]

Page 11 shows Little Blue looking for his friend.
9-YEAR-OLD: Looking at dark background: "That's outside and that's an old dark building." [Wanting to give meaning to abstract picture.]

Page 12—Suddenly he sees Little Yellow.
7-YEAR-OLD: "Yeah!"

Page 13—They hug each other until they become green!
7-YEAR-OLD: "Oh, oh I know what would happen if I went home green." [Anticipates action and consequences.]

Pages 14 and 15—The friends play. [No comments.]

Page 16—They chase Little Orange.
11-YEAR-OLD: "Orange looks scared." [Orange, like all the other colors, is a torn circle of paper.]

Page 17—They climb a mountain. [No comments.]

Page 18—They become tired and go home.
7-YEAR-OLD: "See he's sitting down now." [Green circle is shown near the bottom of the page.]

Page 19—Mama and Papa Blue do not recognize Little Green as their child.
5-YEAR-OLD: "They are too!" [Defiant.]
7-YEAR-OLD: "Poor Little Blue and Little Yellow." [Sympathetic.]
9-YEAR-OLD: "They didn't even know their own kids?" [Incomprehensible.]
11-YEAR-OLD: "Man, they don't know who their kids are!" [Disgust.]

Page 20—Then Little Blue and Little Yellow began to cry blue and yellow tears.
5-YEAR-OLD: "Is cry really that color?"
7-YEAR-OLD: "The blue and yellow is coming out."

Page 21—They pull themselves together and once again they are Little Blue and Little Yellow.
11-YEAR-OLD: "Ya mean, they got it together?"

Page 22—The Blues were very happy.

5-YEAR-OLD: [Giggled.]
7-YEAR-OLD: [Clapped.]

Page 23—They hugged and kissed their son and also Little Yellow—then they became green.
5-YEAR-OLD: "Oh, no, not again!" [Puts his hand to his forehead.]

Page 24—Now at last they understood what had happened, so they went across the street to tell the Yellows.
7-YEAR-OLD: "I think Little Blue and Little Yellow have their arms around each other." [Child is interpreting the picture through her understanding of the theme.]

Last Page—"They all hugged each other with joy and the children played until supper time."
5-YEAR-OLD: "And they lived happily ever after." [Wants the security of the traditional ending.]

Looking at the *endpapers* after reading the story.
7-YEAR-OLD: "The black is at darktime and the white is at daytime."
9-YEAR-OLD: "Black is when they're sad and white is when he's home again."

In the discussion that followed, the 9- and 11-year-olds saw larger meanings in the story than did the 5- and 7-year-olds:

9-YEAR-OLD: "It just means that these two kids liked each other so much that they became just alike."
11-YEAR-OLD: "Everybody knows that blue and yellow make green; their parents should have known that."
9-YEAR-OLD: "I think their parents understood how two people can be real good friends and get a whole lot like each other, but I'd feel awful bad if my parents didn't know who I was."
11-YEAR-OLD: "The kids don't care what anybody looks like or what color you are. It's grownups that hassle you about it. The kids taught the parents that it doesn't matter what color you are, just that you like each other."

From this discussion, it is easy to see the child's growing understanding of complexity and meaning. The 5-year-old put himself into the story true to his egocentric nature. He compared parts of the story to his own experiences. He enjoyed the illustrations and began to talk to them rather than about them. He seemed to be quite concerned when the child was left alone and when the parents didn't recognize the children. He never tried to analyze the abstract shapes, but just accepted them on a literal level. *Little Blue and Little Yellow* left him with no real message or moral, just the good feeling of having heard a story with a happy ending.

The 7-year-old seemed just right for this story. She comprehended the simple abstract pictures and frequently took on the role of narrator by explaining the pictures in her comments. Her comments also showed a developing empathy for the characters.

The 9-year-old was able to see the story in terms of symbolic meanings. He asked if all the different colors signified the races of the world. The others agreed on this theme. He also made the astute observation that persons become very much alike when they are such close friends. His attitude toward the parents not recognizing their own children was one of disgust at their stupidity!

The 11-year-old's responses revealed the greatest maturity in thinking. He readily indentified the theme of friendship and saw the various shapes as different types of people, instead of just representations of races. He imposed different emotions on the pictures—such as "scared," "hurt," "sad," "excited," and so on. He saw the story as a kind of puzzle that he enjoyed "psyching out."

On one level, *Little Blue and Little Yellow* appears to be a simple picture book based on the age-old theme of loss and recovery. On a higher level, however, it moves to the theme of friendship and getting along with those who may be different from you. Each age level responded to the story on their own terms of understanding. It would have done little good (and could have been destructive of enjoyment of literature) if the younger children had been pushed to try to formulate the abstractions achieved by more mature ones. However, Britton maintains that teachers may refine and develop the responses that children are already making, by gradually exposing them to stories with increasingly complex patterns of events.[60]

LEARNING FROM LITERARY MISCUES

In one sense, it is impossible for any child to make a "wrong" response to literature. Each reader's own feelings and personal interpretations are valid because each reader is different. After all, everyone has a different correct answer for the question "What do *you* think?" But some reponses that readers make, although they may reflect true feelings, contradict the objective evidence of the text.

In the teaching of reading, deviations from the text in oral reading are sometimes called *miscues*. According to Goodman and others[61] who have developed this idea, it is not very useful to see miscues simply as mistakes. It is more profitable to see them as clues that reveal what thinking process or cueing systems the child uses during reading. For instance a child who reads "talk" for "talked" and "walked" for "walk" seems to be cueing on the graphic and sound similarities of these word pairs. Another example is the child who reads "Daddy" for "Father," cueing on the meaning but not paying attention to the form of the word. The whole notion of miscues focuses the teacher's attention on the kind of thinking children are doing, not just on the number of errors they make.

This positive point of view is just as important in considering children's attempts to make meaning from whole stories or episodes as it is at the level of words and phrases. We cannot say that a 6-year-old is wrong, for instance, in calling "The Three Little Pigs" a sad story, but the label does not really seem to fit a tale of diligence, cleverness, and success. If we take the attitude that this is a literary miscue and not simply a lack of understanding, we will go on to try to find out what kind of thinking led to that response. The child in this example explained to his teacher that he thought it would be terrible to fall into a pot of boiling water, and it was sad for the wolf. This helped the teacher to see that he was basing his judgment on just a part of the story rather than the whole; other observations showed that this was often the strategy behind his responses.

Sometimes a response will seem so at odds with the original text that an adult may wonder if the child has read or heard an entirely different story.

[60]James Britton, in *Response to Literature,* James R. Squire, ed., (Champaign, Ill.: National Council of Teachers of English, 1968), p. 4.

[61]Yetta M. Goodman and Carolyn L. Burke, *Reading Miscue Inventory* (Chicago: Richard C. Owen, Publisher, 1972).

One 7-year-old girl, after several experiences with Leo Lionni's *Little Blue and Little Yellow*, made a tissue-paper collage picture and wrote a caption which she read aloud as follows:

> I made a pretty picture of Little Yellow and Little Blue. They want to go home but they can't lead back home because the birds has eatened all the crumbs.

In the book, the paper-shape characters play together and then hug each other so tightly that they blend into one green shape. They do not get lost, but when they go home neither set of parents recognizes them until they literally dissolve in tears and regain their own shape and color. When asked about the trail of bread crumbs, the child did not immediately remember any connection to "Hansel and Gretel," and she repeated that Little Blue and Little Yellow were lost and couldn't find their way home. To say that this student confused two familiar stories only describes the surface of things. She cued in on an image that exists in both stories— that of separation from parents—and this seems to have linked them solidly in her perception. This controlling idea was so powerful for her that it crowded out whatever other perceptions she might have expressed. The teacher talked to her about both stories but wisely did not try to "correct" the writing, recognizing that only maturity and continued experience with stories could help her toward a clearer understanding.

Many other examples of response can be profitably interpreted as literary miscues. A group of third graders who were reading and discussing Laura Ingalls Wilder's *By the Shores of Silver Lake* misread the passage that describes the death of Jack, the Ingalls family's beloved dog:

> . . . Pa was going to do the chores. He spoke to Jack, but Jack did not stir.
>
> Only Jack's body, stiff and cold, lay curled there on the blanket.
>
> They buried it on the low slope above the wheat field, by the path he used to run down so gaily when he was going with Laura to bring in the cows. Pa spaded the earth over the box and made the mound smooth . . . .
>
> "Don't cry, Laura," Pa said. "He has gone to the Happy Hunting Grounds."
>
> . . .

Teachers need to listen carefully to children's responses to literature in order to discover their thinking strategies.

The Ohio State University Workshop, Moira McKenzie, visiting teacher.

> Perhaps, in the Happy Hunting Grounds, Jack was running gaily in the wind over some high prairie, as he used to run on the beautiful wild prairies of Indian Territory. Perhaps at last he was catching a jack rabbit.[62]

The children told their teacher that Jack was stiff when he woke up and cold because of the weather, and that later he was out chasing rabbits in the Happy Hunting Grounds. These students seem to have reacted to part of the clues in the text while blocking out others. Their concept of story included such a firm expectation that things in stories will work out all right ("happiness binding") that they didn't see the dog's death as a possible meaning for the text at all. Children who make responses like this one are not so much slow to

[62]Laura Ingalls Wilder, *By the Shores of Silver Lake* (New York: Harper & Row, 1953), pp. 12–13.

pick up meaning as they are quick to operate out of trust in what they already know. Their teacher's questioning acknowledged their competence but refocused their attention on other details that changed their perception of "stiff" and "cold."

This group of students also struggled with another passage in the same book that deals with Pa Ingalls receiving government land from "Uncle Sam." Laura's Aunt Docia is a prominent character in the same chapter, and some children identified Uncle Sam as Aunt Docia's husband. The logic was sound, but based on insufficient world knowledge. This type of literary miscue is common in the reading of historical fiction or other books with unfamiliar background context.

Misinterpretation of key items in literature can occur in a read-aloud audience as well as with independent reading. In one group of fifth-graders where the teacher had just begun Susan Cooper's *The Dark Is Rising,* she stopped to invite predictions about the characters, including the mysterious "Walker." One boy ventured that the Walker was an old man who would cause a lot of trouble in the story, while another, accustomed to a different style of language, argued quite seriously that the Walker must be a woman. He was interpreting the line "The Walker is abroad" as five words rather than four!

Recognizing the origin of children's misinterpretations is important because it suggests how teachers can intervene to help students clarify their thinking or adjust their expectations for certain types of stories. Sometimes, however, the evidence will suggest that a more conventional interpretation is not within reach for a particular child or group at a particular time. Sensitive teachers accept this and do not press for signs of superficial understanding but go on to selections that may be more suitable.

Collecting Children's Responses

Finding out how children understand literature and which books they like is such basic information for elementary teachers and librarians that it should not be left to chance. Luckily there are good techniques for discovering responses that are simple and fit naturally into the ongoing business of classrooms and library media centers.

OBSERVING CHILDREN

Observation provides many clues to the reading interests and habits of children. Watching children as they select books will help adults determine what their interests in books are. Do they go directly to a specific book section? Do they know where to find science books, poetry, biography, or fiction? Do they look at the chapter headings or illustrations before selecting a book? Do they ask for help in locating books? Do they seem to follow the lead of one or two others, selecting in accordance with the leader's choice? Are they really browsing and getting to know books, or are they engaged in aimless wandering? Do they select books that are too difficult to read in order to gain status?

Observing children as they begin to read reveals other helpful information. Do they begin quickly? Can you sense their appreciation of the illustrations? Does body position reflect relaxation and interest in the book? How long is spent in actual reading? If children are truly absorbed in their books, they are not distracted by ordinary movements or sounds in the library or classroom.

Regardless of how much we know about the general characteristics and interest patterns of children at various age levels, it is only after studying individual children that we can say, "David loved Madeleine L'Engle's *A Wrinkle in Time.* I must tell him about the sequel, *A Wind in the Door.* Beth enjoys ballet so much—I wonder if she has seen this new book on it. Peter is somewhat slow in reading, but he enjoyed *A Snake-Lover's Diary* by Barbara Brenner; he might like to try to make a terrarium for his snake. I saw one in that new book on terrariums." And so the teacher plans for the extension of children's reading interests with care. This information can be shared with the school librarian, who is in a unique position to study the child over a period of years.

Understanding of the child and the accumulated effect of past experiences is gained through observation in many situations. The teacher or librarian observes the child studying or reading alone, reacting to others in work and play situations, and meeting problems. The teacher will note what the child does not do or say, as well as active behavioral responses. The teacher seeks to understand the child's perception of self, for this self-concept influences behavior and choices as well as achievement.

It is especially useful to watch and listen to children as they work at book extension activities such as the ones described in Chapter 13. For instance, making a gameboard that traces the adventures of Matt and Attean in Elizabeth George Speare's *The Sign of the Beaver* requires deciding which events are important enough to represent and remembering their sequence—or referring back to the book to check. Watching the work in progress allows the teacher to see false starts and self-corrections as well as to note how the child uses the book for information. It is a bonus if two or three students are working together, for then the teacher may listen as they negotiate next steps. Sometimes the most revealing comments a child makes about literature are offered to another child in just such a setting.

Obviously teachers will not have time for daily, detailed observation of each individual child. In planning for reasonable use of observation techniques, it is first important to be alert for serendipitous moments and random opportunities. One efficient primary teacher in a classroom busy with activities takes a moment as she moves from one group to another to stand back and focus on what just one child is doing. A teacher may single out certain children to watch when they seem to be having difficulties or when they are having special success. Some teachers find that a self-designed checklist is a useful tool. This gives some structure to the observation (Chooses fiction____; chooses nonfiction____; Reads alone____; reads with a friend . . . , etc.) and makes it possible to share the task with classroom aides or parent volunteers.

ELICITING RESPONSES

Children do not always express their ideas about literature spontaneously, and even when they do, the teacher may not be there to see or hear them. There are many ways, however, of deliberately evoking children's responses.

Talking over a story that has just been read aloud or one that a child has just read independently is a natural and satisfying thing to do. Such discussions are a primary teaching tool in helping children build a framework for literature (see Chapter 12). Discussions with a slightly different tone are just as useful in helping teachers get a more complete picture of where the children are to start with. When the focus is on finding out what children are thinking, it is important to begin with general questions that invite talk and do not suggest their own answers: What do you like about the story? What do you notice about it? How does it make you feel? What does this story make you think of? While many comments may not seem relevant from an adult perspective, the careful listener will find out what is in the foreground of the children's perception of the story. This is a time when it is especially important to be accepting, to offer encouraging comments, nods, and other signals of affirmation. Children who fear giving a "wrong" answer will say what they think the teacher wants to hear or perhaps not say much at all. It takes time for readers of any age to frame their thoughts about a book; a little reflection time between reading and discussion may make for a more productive session.

More directive questioning can also be used to explore a particular area of children's understanding. Again, however, the emphasis should be on discovering children's own ideas and not on reaching predetermined answers. To find out more about her children's perception of fantasy, one teacher asked, about Maurice Sendak's *Outside Over There,* "Just where *is* 'outside over there'?" and encouraged them to explain their answers. Another, wanting clues to the sense of moral judgment her children brought to stories, asked them what the teacher in Rebecca Caudill's *A Pocketful of Cricket* should do about Jay, who brought his cricket to school and caused a minor disruption.

Teachers can direct many extension activities to bring out certain aspects of response. One teacher of 6- and 7-year-olds used a picture-making strategy to determine their level of understanding of *Fish Is Fish* by Leo Lionni. This is the story of the fish who imagines that the creatures of the land are all much like himself—"fish people" or "fish birds" or "fish cows." When the teacher finished reading the story to three of the children she said: "Now let's imagine that the frog told the fish all about a furry little black kitten. How do you suppose the fish would see it? Could you draw me a picture of what the fish would see?" One little girl carefully drew a picture of a black furry kitten. Another child started her picture by saying: "Now let's see, I think he'd see the whiskers as gills, so

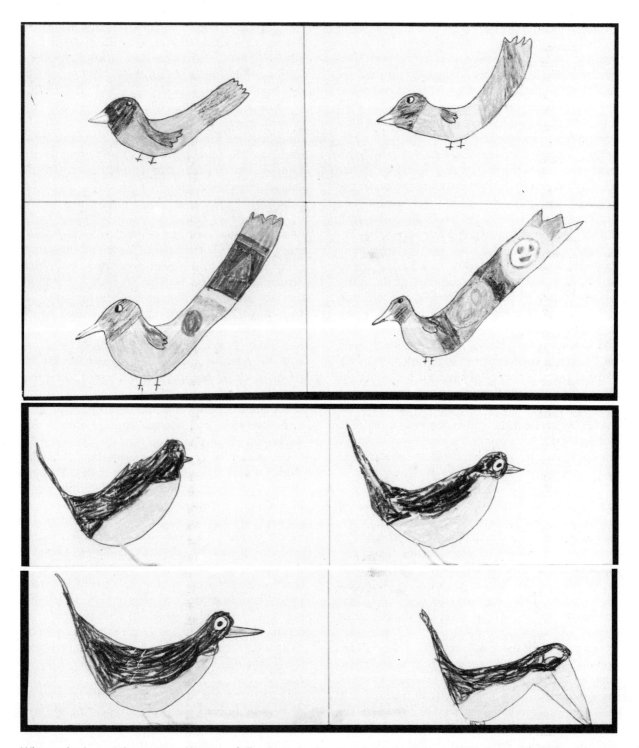

When asked to replicate Lionni's story of *The Biggest House in the World* using a new main character, these two children demonstrated different levels in their understanding of the theme. The 8-year-old (top picture) showed a bird growing more elaborate; the 10-year-old (bottom) portrayed a change leading to the bird's self-destruction.

Tremont Elementary School, Upper Arlington, Ohio, Jill Boyd, teacher.

I'll make them stick out like gills." She then went on to draw a "fish-cat." The third went off on his own creative tangent and told a long story about the cat falling in the water so the fish really did see him as a fish-cat! All of these children had heard the same story at the same time, but their responses as shown in their artwork suggested different levels of understanding.

The pictures on page 83 show two children's responses to the story, *The Biggest House in the World,* also by Lionni. After reading this book, the children were asked to choose any animal and grant it the same wish as the little snail had; namely, that it could change itself in any way. Julia, age 8, chose a bird, and she made his tail large, more elaborate, and more colorful. Rick, age 10, also drew a bird. He used the vocabulary of the story, saying: "The bird twitched his tongue in order to make his beak bigger so he could eat more." Finally, his beak becomes so heavy that he can't see over it or lift it up. The boy's comment was: "He'll have to get a derrick to lift it up now." This 10-year-old got the notion of the bird becoming the cause of his own self-destruction, as in the story of the snail, whereas the 8-year-old girl saw only the change of size and the elaboration of color. Both had translated the story into their own creative drawings, but one child appeared to have a fuller understanding of the meaning of the story.

A middle-school teacher whose students had heard *Tuck Everlasting* by Natalie Babbitt asked them to chart out, with words and pictures, the cycle of their own lives, including what they knew of their past and what they predicted for the future. Many of the children could not transfer the ideas about life and death from the book to their own speculations. They did not get beyond young adulthood in their plans, skipping directly from getting a job and getting married to death at an advanced age. Of those who revealed a deeper connection with the book, some portrayed the possibility that their lives might be troubled or brief; some represented life as a circle with themselves in the older generation giving way to the new. The teacher then used these charts to begin a discussion relating the value system in the book to the students' own lives.

Writing activities can easily be tailored to bring out personal responses. A letter of advice to a friend about what to read helps the teacher judge what kinds of books are important to the writer. Asking a middle-grader to write an updated folktale or a story based on the information about medieval times in Sheila Sancha's *The Luttrell Village* will show something about the child's knowledge of genre as well as a more general concept of story. Children should never have to be subjected to formal testing to determine their response. The number of ways for inviting natural responses in the classroom is limited only by the teacher's ingenuity.

KEEPING TRACK

Observing and inviting children's responses have more value if the teacher can somehow keep track of what has been discovered. Because of the time demands that exist in all classrooms, it is wise to use the simplest methods. Many teachers take advantage of existing reading records (see Chapter 13) to jot down brief notes about children's responses. A teacher's journal or log, even one with brief entries, provides a good overview account of classroom responses. It can also be narrowed in focus to record children's changing attitudes and understandings during a theme of study or to follow the progress of a popular title through the group.

Personal files of children's writing and other work samples are even easier than notes, although they require space. A real advantage of this sort of file is that it provides a history of growth in response that can be accessible to the child as well as the teacher. Children who have this concrete evidence of how far they have come are helped in their progress toward self-awareness and are assured that their work is valued. Some of children's most interesting products may not fit in any file, but they can be photographed. Photos capture the setting of response or the larger context of an activity and serve as a reminder of what prompted this particular work or how it was tied to other concerns in the classroom. Files like this can be collected with minimum effort if children share the responsibility for choosing and updating the contents.

Another valuable tool for keeping track of responses is the audiotape recorder. Taping read-aloud sessions and the talk that follows gives the teacher a chance to sort out patterns of comments that are not easy to catch while in the midst of leading the discussion. Young children or those struggling with the mechanics of writing may be more fluent in their comments on a story if they can speak them directly into a tape recorder rather than writing them. Two or more children may record their private small-group discussion about a book with the idea that the teacher will hear it later. Or the teacher may tape book conferences with one or two children to save for comparison with later responses.

Videotape equipment can be used to record drama experiences or other large-scale activities. While video can capture nonverbal responses beautifully, the apparatus is too intrusive (and expensive) to make this an everyday possibility for most individual classrooms.

Microcomputers, of course, keep track of practically anything. Librarians find them indispensable for many tasks, and teachers familiar with their operation know that they adapt to many record-keeping functions in the classroom. A particular advantage of computerized data is that it may be recalled and compared in so many different combinations. For instance, general information about children and their favorite books might be transformed into a comparison of boys' favorites and girls' favorites or sorted to make a list of readers of non-fiction.

As elementary-school teachers become aware of the way they can tune in to children's responses to literature, they will see the value of examining the nature of children's thinking about it. While we all believe that literature is important for children, we do not truly know what difference it makes in a child's life, if any. An in-depth study of children's responses to books is just as important, if not more important, than the studies of children's interests in books. We should explore the developmental nature of response and conduct longitudinal studies of a child's responses over the years. As teachers and librarians, we need to be still and listen to what the children are telling us about their involvement with books and what it means to them.

SUGGESTED LEARNING EXPERIENCES

1. If there is a young child in your household, keep a log for four to five weeks of his or her interaction with literature. What do the child's choices, reactions, comments, and questions reveal about cognitive skills or moral judgment? Do you see any changes that reflect experiences with books?
2. Observe young children as a parent or teacher reads to them. Note as many behaviors (verbal, nonverbal, or artistic/creative) as you can. What clues do you get about the value of reading aloud and about means of effective presentation?
3. Ask three children of various ages (5, 7, 9) to retell the story of "Goldilocks and the Three Bears" from the point of view of Baby Bear. Who is able to begin the story as Baby Bear? Who can maintain the role change? What problems do 5-year-olds have with the language that 9-year-olds seem to solve easily?
4. Choose one of the many books without words and share it with a 4-year-old. Then ask the child to tell you the story from the pictures. Repeat the procedure with a 6-year-old and with an 8-year-old. What differences do you note in response to the story?
5. Set up a play corner in a primary classroom, including props from stories such as a magic wand, a witch's hat, a cardboard crown. What happens over the course of time? What seem to be the sources for children's imaginative play?
6. Choose one of the book extension activities described in Chapter 13 and try it with two or more children. Pay careful attention to their working procedures and analyze the products. What variations or individual differences do you see? What similarities?
7. In a middle-grade classroom, assemble 20–30 books that are mostly familiar to the children. Ask a small group to categorize and label these for a table-top display. Tape their comments as they work. What do you notice about their categories? About the process? If possible, repeat the activity with younger children and books that they have heard. What differences do you notice? Arrange to see the Weston Woods film, *What's a Good Book?* Discuss the categories suggested by children in contrast to those mentioned by the adult experts interviewed.
8. If you can meet with a class of children, ask them to submit the names of their ten

favorite books. How do their choices reflect their particular ages and stages of development?

9. Visit the children's room of a public or school library to watch children in the process of choosing books. Keep a list, if you can, of the books examined and rejected, as well as those finally chosen. What factors seem to influence the children's choices?

10. With a small group of fellow students or teachers, read and discuss an award-winning children's book. Working together, plan two sets of questions that could be used with children, one to discover children's initial response to the story, the other to direct their thinking toward the characters' motivations and decisions, the author's effective use of language, or other noteworthy features of the writing.

RELATED READINGS

1. Agee, Hugh, and Lee Galda, eds. *Journal of Research and Development in Education,* vol. 16, No. 3 (Spring 1983).

   An entire issue devoted to "Response to Literature: Empirical and Theoretical Studies." Ten diverse articles examine a variety of topics from classroom responses to theoretical notions of the secondary world and the child as implied reader. It is unusual to find a collection of writings based on research that gives so much attention to elementary children.

2. Applebee, Arthur. *The Child's Concept of Story: Ages Two to Seventeen.* Chicago, Ill.: University of Chicago Press, 1978.

   A report of systematic research on children's developing perceptions of stories. Applebee provides fresh insight on the child's sense of story and response to literature. Among the contributions of this important work are a description of organization and complexity in the structure of stories children tell and a model of developmental stages in the formulation of children's response.

3. Cochran–Smith, Marilyn. *The Making of a Reader.* Norwood, N.J.: Ablex Publishing, 1984.

   A monograph based on an ethnographic study conducted in a Philadelphia preschool. The purpose of the study was to look at the many ways that adults "socialize their children into particular patterns of literacy." A great deal of attention is given to the preschool's story-reading sessions. Of particular interest are the frequent charts that juxtapose the teacher's verbal and nonverbal read-aloud behaviors with her listeners' verbal and nonverbal responses.

4. Cooper, Charles R., ed. *Researching Response to Literature and the Teaching of Literature: Points of Departure.* Norwood, N.J.: Ablex Publishing, 1985.

   This collection furnishes a comprehensive scholarly introduction to major theories and research methodologies. Among the contributors are Louise Rosenblatt, Arthur Applebee, Shelley Rubin and Howard Gardner, and James R. Squire. Although few of the chapters refer specifically to elementary school children, the background is valuable for the serious student of children's literature.

5. Elkind, David. *The Hurried Child: Growing Up Too Fast Too Soon.* Reading, Mass.: Addison-Wesley, 1981.

   In a book addressed mainly to parents, a noted psychologist argues that contemporary children are under too much pressure. They are rushed toward adulthood both at home and at school without regard for normal patterns of development or individual differences. Chapters 5 and 6 present a very readable overview of intellectual, emotional, and social development, with particular reference to Piaget. Chapter 4, which deals with the influence of books and media in "hurrying" children, provides good discussion material for adults considering selection policies.

6. Purves, Alan C., and Dianne L. Monson. *Experiencing Children's Literature.* Glenview, Ill.: Scott, Foresman and Company, 1984.

   A research-based overview of literature and its uses in the school, emphasizing the reader's relation with the text.

7. Rosenblatt, Louise M. *The Reader, the Text, the Poem: The Transactional Theory of the Literary Work.* Carbondale, Ill.: Southern Illinois University Press, 1978.

A scholarly discussion of the reader's role in evoking a literary work from an author's text. The distinction between aesthetic and efferent reading stances is clearly explained. Although elementary children are seldom mentioned, the book gives a valuable basis for understanding the responses of readers at any age.

8. Roser, Nancy, and Margaret Frith, eds. *Children's Choices: Teaching with Books Children Like*. Newark, Del.: International Reading Association, 1983.

Nine brief essays deal with children's tastes and with teaching practices that encourage response. Also included is a composite bibliography of children's favorites as determined by a broad sample of student votes in seven years of the Children's Choices program (sponsored by the International Reading Association/Children's Book Council). Although there are no annotations, headings indicate books for Beginning Independent Reading, Younger Readers, Middle Grades, Older Readers, Informational Books, and Poetry/Verse.

9. Schlager, Norma. "Predicting Children's Choices in Literature: A Developmental Approach." *Children's Literature in Education*, vol. 9 (Autumn 1978), pp. 136–142.

Concise report of a study that explored Newbery award winners' relative popularity with children. The comparison of Scott O'Dell's much-read *Island of the Blue Dolphins* with Monica Shannon's largely ignored *Dobry* is clearly presented and thought-provoking.

10. Tucker, Nicholas. *The Child and the Book: A Psychological and Literary Exploration*. Cambridge: Cambridge University Press, 1981.

A British psychologist with wide knowledge of literature outlines the "changing imaginative and intellectual outlook" of children from infancy to age 14. Although his major concern is explaining why certain types of stories are popular at various ages, he also considers why some children show more general interest in reading than others.

REFERENCES[63]

Aardema, Verna. *Why Mosquitoes Buzz in People's Ears: A West African Tale,* illustrated by Leo and Diane Dillon. Dial, 1975.

Ahlberg, Janet, and Allen Ahlberg. *The Baby's Catalogue*. Little, 1983.

_____. *Each Peach Pear Plum*. Viking, 1978.

_____. *Peek-a-Boo!* Viking, 1981.

Alexander, Lloyd. The Prydain Series. Holt.
  The Black Cauldron, 1965.
  The Book of Three, 1964
  The Castle of Llyr. 1966.
  The High King, 1968.
  Taran Wanderer, 1967.

_____. *Westmark*. Dutton, 1981.

Alexander, Martha. *How My Library Grew by Dinah*. Wilson, 1983.

_____. *Pigs Say Oink*. Random, 1981.

Aliki (Brandenberg). *Digging Up Dinosaurs*. Crowell, 1981.

_____. *A Medieval Feast*. Crowell, 1983.

_____. *Mummies Made in Egypt*. Crowell, 1979.

_____. *We Are Best Friends*. Greenwillow, 1982.

Anno, Mitsumasa. *Anno's USA*. Philomel, 1983.

Arnosky, Jim. *Drawing from Nature*. Lothrop, 1983.

Asbjornsen, P. C., and Jorgen E. Moe. *The Three Billy Goats Gruff,* illustrated by Marcia Brown. Harcourt, 1957.

Ault, Roz. *Basic Programming for Kids*. Houghton, 1983.

Babbitt, Natalie. *Tuck Everlasting*. Farrar, 1975.

Bang, Molly, *Dawn*. Morrow, 1983.

[63]All books listed at the end of this chapter are recommended, subject to the qualifications noted in the text. See Appendix for publishers' complete addresses.

_____. *Ten, Nine, Eight*. Greenwillow, 1983.

Banks, Lynne Reid. *The Indian in the Cupboard*. Doubleday, 1981.

Barrett, Judi. *I Hate to Go to Bed*, illustrated by Ray Cruz. Four Winds, 1977.

Beisner, Monica. *A Book of Riddles*. Farrar, 1983.

Blos, Joan. *A Gathering of Days: A New England Girls' Journal, 1830–1832*. Scribner, 1979.

_____. *Martin's Hats*, illustrated by Marc Simont. Morrow, 1984.

Blume, Judy. *Are You There, God? It's Me, Margaret*. Bradbury, 1970.

_____. *Blubber*. Bradbury, 1974.

_____. *Superfudge*. Dutton, 1980.

_____. *Tales of a Fourth Grade Nothing*. Dutton, 1972.

_____. *Then Again, Maybe I Won't*. Bradbury, 1971.

Brenner, Barbara. *A Snake-Lover's Diary*. Young Scott, 1970.

Briggs, Raymond. *The Snowman*. Random, 1978.

Brown, Marc, and Stephen Krensky. *Perfect Pigs: An Introduction to Manners*. Atlantic-Little, Brown, 1983.

Brown, Marcia. *Once a Mouse*. Scribner, 1961.

_____. *Stone Soup*. Scribner, 1947.

Brown, Margaret Wise. *Goodnight Moon*, illustrated by Clement Hurd. Harper, 1947.

_____. *The Runaway Bunny*, illustrated by Clement Hurd. Harper, 1972 (1942).

Brown, Palmer. *Hickory*. Harper, 1978.

Browne, Anthony. *Bear Hunt*. Atheneum, 1980.

Bruna, Dick. *B Is for Bear*. Methuen, 1971.

Bruun, Ruth Dowling, M.D., and Bertel Bruun, M.D. *The Human Body: Your Body and How It Works*, illustrated by Patricia J. Wynne. Random, 1982.

Bulla, Clyde Robert. *A Lion to Guard Us*, illustrated by Michele Chessare. Harper, 1981.

Burchard, S. H. *Sports Star: Fernando Valenzuela*. Harcourt, 1982.

Burningham, John. *The Blanket*. Crowell, 1976.

_____. *The Cupboard*. Crowell, 1975.

_____. *John Burningham's ABC*. Bobbs-Merrill, 1967.

_____. *Mr. Gumpy's Outing*. Holt, 1971.

_____. *Seasons*. Bobbs-Merrill, 1970.

Burton, Virginia Lee. *The Little House*. Houghton, 1942.

Byars, Betsy. *The 18th Emergency*, illustrated by Robert Grossman. Viking, 1973.

_____. *The Animal, the Vegetable, and John D Jones*, illustrated by Ruth Sanderson. Delacorte, 1982.

Caines, Jeanette. *Daddy*, illustrated by Ronald Himler. Harper, 1977.

Campbell, Rod. *Dear Zoo*. Four Winds, 1983.

_____. *Misty's Mischief*. Viking, 1985.

Carle, Eric. *The Grouchy Ladybug*. Crowell, 1977.

_____. *The Very Hungry Caterpillar*. Philomel, 1969.

Carrick, Carol. *The Climb*, illustrated by Donald Carrick. Clarion, 1980.

Caudill, Rebecca. *A Pocketful of Cricket*, illustrated by Evaline Ness. Holt, 1968.

Cebulash, Mel. *Football Players Do Amazing Things*. Random, 1975.

Chaffin, Lillie D. *We Be Warm Till Springtime Comes*, illustrated by Lloyd Bloom. Macmillan, 1980.

Clapp, Patricia. *I'm Deborah Sampson: A Soldier in the War of the Revolution*. Lothrop, 1977.

Cleary, Beverly. *Dear Mr. Henshaw*, illustrated by Paul O. Zelinsky. Morrow, 1983.

_____. *Ramona Forever*. Morrow, 1984.

_____. *Ramona Quimby, Age 8*, illustrated by Alan Tiegreen. Morrow, 1981.

_____. *Ramona the Brave*, illustrated by Alan Tiegreen. Morrow, 1975.

Clifton, Lucille. *Everett Anderson's Friend*, illustrated by Ann Grifalconi. Holt, 1976.

Cohen, Miriam. *When Will I Read?*, illustrated by Lillian Hoban. Greenwillow, 1977.

_____. *Will I Have a Friend?*, illustrated by Lillian Hoban. Macmillan, 1971.

Cole, Brock. *No More Baths*. Doubleday, 1980.

Collier, James Lincoln, and Christopher Collier. *My Brother Sam Is Dead*. Four Winds, 1974.

Conford, Ellen. *Anything for a Friend*. Little, 1979.

Cooper, Susan. *The Dark Is Rising*, illustrated by Alan E. Cober. Atheneum, 1973.

Cresswell, Helen. *Dear Shrink*. Macmillan, 1982.

Crews, Donald. *Freight Train*. Greenwillow, 1978.

Dahl, Roald. *Danny: The Champion of the World*, illustrated by Jill Bennett. Knopf, 1975.

_____. *James and the Giant Peach*, illustrated by Nancy Burkert. Knopf, 1961.

Dalgliesh, Alice. *The Courage of Sarah Noble*, illustrated by Leonard Weisgard. Scribner, 1954.

Danziger, Paula. *There's a Bat in Bunk Five*. Delacorte, 1980.

Daughtry, Duanne. *What's Inside?* Knopf, 1984.

DeJong, Meindert. *Hurry Home, Candy*, illustrated by Maurice Sendak. Harper, 1953.

de Paola, Tomie. *Now One Foot, Now the Other*. Putnam, 1981.

_____. *Strega Nona*. Prentice-Hall, 1975.

_____. *Tomie DePaola's Mother Goose*. Holiday House, 1984.

DeRegniers, Beatrice Shenck. *May I Bring a Friend?*, illustrated by Beni Montresor. Atheneum, 1964.

Domanska, Janina, *What Do You See?* Macmillan, 1974.

Dunning, Stephen, et al. *Reflections on a Gift of Watermelon Pickle and Other Modern Verse*. Lothrop, 1967.

Duvoisin, Roger. *Petunia*. Knopf, 1950.

Farber, Norma. *How Does It Feel to Be Old?*, illustrated by Trina Schart Hyman. Dutton, 1979.

Fenton, Edward. *The Refugee Summer*. Delacorte, 1982.

Fischer-Nagel, Heiderose, and Andreas Fischer-Nagel. *A Kitten Is Born*, translated by Andrea Mernan. Putnam, 1983.

Fleischman, Sid. *McBroom's Almanac*, illustrated by Walter Lorraine. Atlantic-Little, Brown, 1984.

Freeman, Don. *Corduroy*. Viking, 1968.

_____. *Dandelion*. Viking, 1964.

Friedman, Ina. *How My Parents Learned to Eat*, illustrated by Allen Say. Houghton Mifflin, 1984.

Fritz, Jean. *Homesick*, illustrated by Margot Tomes. Putnam, 1982.

_____. *What's the Big Idea, Ben Franklin?*, illustrated by Margot Tomes. Coward, 1976.

Gackenbach, Dick. *Binky Gets a Car*. Clarion, 1983.

Gág, Wanda. *Millions of Cats*. Coward, 1928, 1956.

Galdone, Paul. *The Little Red Hen*. Clarion, 1973.

_____, illustrator. *Little Red Riding Hood*. McGraw-Hill, 1974.

Garner, Alan. *The Stone Book*, illlustrated by Michael Foreman. Philomel, 1978.

George, Jean. *Cry of the Crow*. Harper, 1980.

_____. *Julie of the Wolves*, illustrated by John Schoenherr. Harper, 1972.

_____. *My Side of the Mountain*. Dutton, 1959.

Gerstein, Mordicai. *Roll Over!* Crown, 1984.

Gibbons, Gail. *New Road!* Crowell, 1983.

_____. *Trucks*. Crowell, 1981.

Gillham, Bill. *The First Words Picture Book*, illustrated by Sam Grainger. Coward, 1982.

Ginsburg, Mirra. *The Chick and the Duckling*, illustrated by José Aruego. Macmillan, 1972.

Goble, Paul. *Star Boy*. Bradbury, 1983.

Godden, Rumer. *The Old Woman Who Lived in a Vinegar Bottle*, illustrated by Mairi Hedderwick. Viking, 1972.

Goldreich, Gloria, and Esther Goldreich. *What Can She Be? A Scientist*, illustrated by Sheldon Horowitz. Holt, 1981.

Goor, Ron, and Nancy Goor. *In the Driver's Seat*. Crowell, 1982.

Goudey, Alice. *Houses from the Sea*, illustrated by Adrienne Adams. Scribner, 1959.

Graeber, Charlotte. *Mustard*, illustrated by Donna Diamond. Macmillan, 1982.

Greene, Constance C. *Beat the Turtle Drum*, illustrated by Donna Diamond. Viking, 1976.

Greene, Bette. *Philip Hall Likes Me. I Reckon Maybe*, illustrated by Charles Lilly. Dial, 1974.

Grimm Brothers. *Cinderella*, illustrated by Nonny Hogrogian. Greenwillow, 1981.

Gruenberg, Sidonie M. *The Wonderful Story of How You Were Born*, rev. ed., illustrated by Symeon Shimin. Doubleday, 1970.

Gutman, Bill. *Superstars of the Sports World*. Messner, 1978.

Hall, Donald. *Ox-Cart Man*, illustrated by Barbara Cooney. Viking, 1979.

Hamilton, Virginia. *Justice and Her Brothers*. Greenwillow, 1978.

Hart, Jane. *Singing Bee! A Collection of Favorite Songs*, illustrated by Anita Lobel. Lothrop, 1982.

Hautzig, Esther. *A Gift for Mama*, illustrated by Donna Diamond. Viking, 1984.

Hazen, Barbara. *Even If I Did Something Awful?*, illustrated by Nancy Kincade. Atheneum, 1981.

Hickman, Janet. *The Thunder-Pup*. Macmillan, 1981.

Highwater, Jamake. *Legend Days*. Harper, 1984.

Hildick, E. W. *The Case of the Phantom Frog*, illustrated by Lisl Weil. Macmillan, 1979.

Hill, Donna. *Ms Glee Was Waiting*, illustrated by Diane Dawson. Atheneum, 1978.

Hill, Eric. *My Pets*. Random, 1983.

_____. *Nursery Rhyme Peek-a-Book*. Price, Stern, 1982.

_____. *Where's Spot?* Putnam, 1980.

Hoban, Russell. *Bedtime for Frances*, illustrated by Garth Williams. Harper, 1960.

Hoban, Tana. *I Read Signs*. Greenwillow, 1983.

_____. *Is It Red? Is It Yellow? Is It Blue?* Greenwillow, 1978.

_____. *Look Again!* Macmillan, 1971.

_____. *1, 2, 3*. Greenwillow, 1985.

Hoberman, Mary Ann. *A House Is a House for Me*, illustrated by Betty Fraser. Viking, 1978.

Holman, Felice. *The Wild Children*. Scribner, 1983.

Hopkins, Lee Bennett. *By Myself*, illustrated by Glo Coalson. Crowell, 1980.

_____. *Mama*. Knopf, 1977.

Howe, James. *The Celery Stalks at Midnight*. Atheneum, 1983.

_____. *A Night Without Stars*. Atheneum, 1983.

Howe, James, and Deborah Howe, *Bunnicula*, illustrated by Alan Daniel. Atheneum, 1979.

Hughes, Shirley. *Alfie Gets in First*. Lothrop, 1981.

_____. *Alfie's Feet*. Lothrop, 1983.

_____. *David and Dog*. Prentice-Hall, 1976.

Hunt, Irene. *Across Five Aprils*. Follett, 1964.

Hunter, Mollie. *Hold On to Love*. Harper, 1984.

Hutchins, Pat. *Clocks and More Clocks*. Macmillan, 1970.

_____. *Follow That Bus!*, illustrated by Lawrence Hutchins. Greenwillow, 1977.

_____. *1 Hunter*. Greenwillow, 1982.

_____. *Rosie's Walk*. Macmillan, 1968.

_____. *Titch*. Macmillan, 1971.

_____. *You'll Soon Grow into Them, Titch*. Greenwillow, 1983.

Huynh, Quang Nhuong. *The Land I Lost: Adventures of a Boy in Viet Nam*, illustrated by Vo-Dinh Mai. Harper, 1982.

Jonas, Ann. *When You Were a Baby*. Greenwillow, 1982.

Juster, Norton. *The Phantom Tollbooth*. Random, 1961.

Kalb, Jonah. *The Goof That Won the Pennant*, illustrated by Sandy Kossin. Houghton, 1976.

Keats, Ezra Jack. *John Henry: An American Legend*. Pantheon, 1965.

_____. *The Snowy Day*. Viking, 1962.

_____. *Whistle for Willie*. Viking, 1964.

Kellogg, Steven. *Paul Bunyan*. Morrow, 1984.

Kent, Jack. *The Fat Cat*. Scholastic, 1972.

Key, Alexander. *The Forgotten Door*. Westminster, 1965.

Kidd, Ronald. *Sizzle and Splat*. Lodestar/Dutton, 1983.

Konigsburg, E. L. *From the Mixed-Up Files of Mrs. Basil E. Frankweiler*. Atheneum, 1967.

_____. *Journey to an 800 Number*. Atheneum, 1982.

Kraus, Robert. *Leo the Late Bloomer*, illustrated by José Aruego. Windmill, 1971.

Krauss, Ruth. *The Carrot Seed*, illustrated by Crockett Johnson. Harper, 1945.

Krementz, Jill. *How It Feels When a Parent Dies*. Knopf, 1981.

_____. *A Very Young Gymnast*. Knopf, 1978.

Kunhardt, Dorothy. *Pat the Bunny*. Golden Press, 1962 (1940).

Lasky, Kathryn. *The Night Journey*, illustrated by Trina Schart Hyman. Scribner, 1981.

L'Engle, Madeleine. *A Swiftly Tilting Planet*. Farrar, 1978.

_____. *A Wind in the Door.* Farrar, 1973.

_____. *A Wrinkle in Time.* Farrar, 1962.

Lester, Julius. *To Be a Slave,* illustrated by Tom Feelings. Dial, 1968.

Levoy, Myron. *Alan and Naomi.* Harper, 1978.

Levy, Elizabeth. *Something Queer at the Lemonade Stand,* illustrated by Mordicai Gerstein. Delacorte, 1982.

Lindgren, Barbro. *Sam's Car,* illustrated by Eva Eriksson. Morrow, 1982.

_____. *Sam's Cookies,* illustrated by Eva Eriksson. Morrow, 1982.

Lionni, Leo. *Alexander and the Wind-Up Mouse.* Pantheon, 1974.

_____. *The Biggest House in the World.* Pantheon, 1968.

_____. *Fish Is Fish.* Pantheon, 1970.

_____. *Frederick.* Pantheon, 1966.

_____. *Little Blue and Little Yellow.* Astor-Honor, 1959.

_____. *What?* Pantheon, 1983.

Little, Lessie Jones, and Eloise Greenfield. *I Can Do It Myself,* illustrated by Carole Byard. Crowell, 1978.

Lobel, Arnold. *Frog and Toad Together.* Harper, 1972.

Lowry, Lois. *Anastasia Krupnik.* Houghton, 1979.

McCloskey, Robert. *Burt Dow: Deep Water Man.* Viking, 1963.

_____. *Make Way for Ducklings.* Viking, 1941.

_____. *One Morning in Maine.* Viking, 1952.

McGovern, Ann. *If You Lived with the Sioux Indians,* illustrated by Bob Levering. Four Winds, 1974.

_____. *The Secret Soldier: The Story of Deborah Sampson,* illustrated by Ann Grifalconi. Four Winds, 1975.

MacLachlan, Patricia. *Sarah, Plain and Tall.* Harper, 1985.

McPhail, David. *Fix-It.* Dutton, 1984.

Magorian, Michelle. *Goodnight, Mr. Tom.* Harper, 1981.

Mahy, Margaret. *The Haunting.* Atheneum, 1982.

Martin, Bill, Jr. *Brown Bear, Brown Bear, What Do You See?,* illustrated by Eric Carle. Holt, 1983.

Maruki, Toshi. *Hiroshima No Pika.* Lothrop, 1980.

Mayle, Peter. *"Where Did I Come From?",* illustrated by Arthur Robins. Lyle Stuart, 1973.

Miles, Betty. *The Real Me.* Knopf, 1974.

Miles, Miska. *Annie and the Old One,* illustrated by Peter Parnall. Little, 1971.

Minarik, Else. *Little Bear,* illustrated by Maurice Sendak. Harper, 1957.

Moeri, Louise. *A Horse for X.Y.Z.,* illustrated by Gail Owens. Dutton, 1977.

Munari, Bruno. *The Elephant's Wish.* Philomel, 1980 (1945).

Naylor, Phyllis Reynolds. *The Agony of Alice.* Atheneum, 1985.

_____. *How I Came to Be a Writer.* Atheneum, 1978.

Ness, Evaline. *Sam, Bangs, and Moonshine.* Holt, 1966.

Neville, Emily. *Berries Goodman.* Harper, 1965.

O'Brien, Robert. *Mrs. Frisby and the Rats of NIMH,* illustrated by Zena Bernstein. Atheneum, 1971.

O'Dell, Scott. *Island of the Blue Dolphins.* Houghton, 1960.

Ormerod, Jan. *Sunshine.* Lothrop, 1981.

Oxenbury, Helen. *The Dancing Class.* Dial, 1983.

_____. *Family.* Simon & Schuster, 1981.

_____. *Mother's Helper.* Dial, 1982.

_____. *Playing.* Simon & Schuster, 1981.

_____. *Working.* Simon & Schuster, 1981.

Packard, Edward. Choose Your Own Adventure Series. *The Third Planet from Altair,* illustrated by Barbara Carter. Lippincott, 1979, and others.

Parish, Peggy. *Amelia Bedelia,* illustrated by Fritz Siebel. Harper, 1963.

Park, Ruth. *Playing Beatie Bow.* Atheneum, 1982.

_____. *When the Wind Changed,* illustrated by Deborah Niland. Coward, 1981.

Paterson, Katherine. *Bridge to Terabithia,* illustrated by Donna Diamond. Crowell, 1977.

_____. *The Great Gilly Hopkins.* Crowell. 1978.

_____. *Jacob Have I Loved.* Crowell, 1980.

Pearce, Philippa. *Tom's Midnight Garden,* illustrated by Susan Einzig. Lippincott, 1959.

Pinkwater, Daniel Manus. *Lizard Music*. Dodd, 1976.

_____. *The Magic Moscow*. Four Winds, 1980.

_____. *Roger's Umbrella,* illustrated by James Marshall. Dutton, 1982.

Potter, Beatrix. *The Tale of Peter Rabbit*. Warne, 1902.

Prelutsky, Jack, ed. *The Random House Book of Poetry,* illustrated by Arnold Lobel. Random, 1983.

Preston, Edna Mitchell. *Squawk to the Moon, Little Goose,* illustrated by Barbara Cooney. Viking, 1974.

_____. *Where Did My Mother Go?,* illustrated by Chris Conover. Four Winds, 1978.

Provensen, Alice, and Martin Provensen. *The Glorious Flight: Across the Channel with Louis Blériot July 25, 1909*. Viking, 1983.

Rabe, Berniece. *The Balancing Girl,* illustrated by Lillian Hoban. Dutton, 1981.

Raskin, Ellen. *The Westing Game*. Dutton, 1978.

Rawls, Wilson. *Where the Red Fern Grows*. Doubleday, 1961.

Reiss, John J. *Colors*. Bradbury, 1969.

Renner, Beverly Hollett. *The Hideaway*. Scholastic, 1980.

Rice, Eve. *Benny Bakes a Cake*. Greenwillow, 1981.

_____. *New Blue Shoes*. Macmillan, 1975.

_____. *Sam Who Never Forgets*. Greenwillow, 1977.

Richter, Hans Peter. *Friedrich*. Holt, 1970.

Robbins, Ken. *Trucks: Of Every Sort*. Crown, 1981.

Roche, P. K. *Dollhouse Magic: How to Make and Find Simple Dollhouse Furniture,* illustrated by John Knott and Richard Cuffari. Dial, 1977.

Rockwell, Anne. *The Three Bears and 15 Other Stories*. Crowell, 1975.

_____, and Harlow Rockwell. *How My Garden Grew*. Macmillan, 1982.

_____. *I Play in My Room*. Macmillan, 1981.

_____. *My Back Yard*. Macmillan, 1984.

Roffey, Maureen. *Home Sweet Home*. Coward, 1982.

Roy, Ron. *Nightmare Island*. Dutton, 1981.

Rubel, Nicole. *Me and My Kitty*. Macmillan, 1983.

Rylant, Cynthia. *The Relatives Came,* illustrated by Stephen Gammell. Bradbury, 1985.

_____. *When I Was Young in the Mountains,* illustrated by Diane Goode. Dutton, 1982.

Sachs, Marilyn. *A Secret Friend*. Doubleday, 1978.

Sancha, Sheila. *The Luttrell Village: Country Life in the Middle Ages*. Crowell, 1982.

Sarnoff, Jane, and Reynold Ruffins. *The Code and Cipher Book*. Scribner, 1975.

_____. *A Great Bicycle Book,* new ed. Scribner, 1976.

Schlein, Miriam. *Billions of Bats,* illustrated by Walter Kessell. Lippincott, 1982.

Schroeder, Binette. *Tuffa and the Bone*. Dial, 1983.

Schulz, Charles. *You're Not for Real, Snoopy*. Fawcett, 1978.

Schwartz, Alvin. *Tomfoolery: Trickery and Foolery with Words,* illustrated by Glen Rounds. Harper, 1973.

_____. *Whoppers: Tall Tales and Other Lies,* illustrated by Glen Rounds. Lippincott, 1975.

Seeger, Pete. *Abiyoyo,* illustrated by Michael Hays. Macmillan, 1986.

Selden, George. *The Cricket in Times Square,* illustrated by Garth Williams. Farrar, Straus, 1960.

Selsam, Millicent, and Joyce Hunt. *A First Look at Insects,* illustrated by Harriet Springer. Walker, 1974.

Sendak, Maurice. *Outside Over There*. Harper, 1981.

_____. *Where the Wild Things Are*. Harper, 1963.

Seuss, Dr., pseud. (Theodor S. Geisel). *And to Think That I Saw It on Mulberry Street*. Vanguard, 1937.

Shannon, Monica. *Dobry,* illustrated by Atanas Katchamakoff. Viking, 1934.

Silverstein, Shel. *A Light in the Attic*. Harper, 1981.

_____. *Where the Sidewalk Ends*. Harper, 1974.

Simon, Seymour. *The Paper Airplane Book,* illustrated by Byron Barton. Viking, 1971.

Slepian, Jan. *The Alfred Summer*. Macmillan, 1980.

Slote, Alfred. *Rabbit Ears*. Lippincott, 1982.

Smith, Doris Buchanan. *A Taste of Blackberries,* illustrated by Charles Robinson. Crowell, 1973.

Sobol, Donald J. *Encyclopedia Brown's Record Book of Weird and Wonderful Facts,* illustrated by Sal Murdocca. Delacorte, 1979.

Speare, Elizabeth George. *The Sign of the Beaver.* Houghton, 1983.

Spier, Peter. *Crash! Bang! Boom!* Doubleday, 1972.

_____. *Peter Spier's Rain.* Doubleday, 1982.

Steig, William. *Abel's Island.* Farrar, 1976.

_____. *Amos & Boris.* Farrar, 1971.

_____. *Doctor De Soto.* Farrar, 1982.

_____. *Sylvester and the Magic Pebble.* Windmill, 1969.

Steptoe, John. *Stevie.* Harper, 1969.

Stevens, Carla. *Trouble for Lucy,* illustrated by Ronald Himler. Clarion, 1979.

Stolz, Mary. *The Bully of Barkham Street,* illustrated by Leonard Shortall. Harper, 1963.

_____. *A Dog on Barkham Street,* illustrated by Leonard Shortall. Harper, 1960.

Tafuri, Nancy. *All Year Long.* Greenwillow, 1983.

_____. *Have You Seen My Duckling?* Greenwillow, 1984.

Tarrant, Graham. *Frogs,* illustrated by Tony King. Putnam, 1983.

Taylor, Mildred. *Roll of Thunder, Hear My Cry.* Dial, 1976.

Turkle, Brinton. *Do Not Open.* Dutton, 1981.

Udry, Janice May. *Let's Be Enemies,* illustrated by Maurice Sendak. Harper, 1961.

Van Allsburg, Chris. *Jumanji.* Houghton, 1981.

_____. *The Polar Express.* Houghton, 1985.

Viorst, Judith. *Alexander and the Terrible, Horrible, No Good, Very Bad Day,* illustrated by Ray Cruz. Atheneum, 1972.

Voigt, Cynthia. *Dicey's Song.* Atheneum, 1982.

_____. *A Solitary Blue.* Atheneum, 1983.

Waber, Bernard. *Ira Sleeps Over.* Houghton, 1972.

Walker, Barbara. *The Little House Cookbook: Frontier Foods from Laura Ingalls Wilder's Classic Stories,* illustrated by Garth Williams. Harper, 1979.

Walsh, Jill Paton. *The Green Book,* illustrated by Lloyd Bloom. Farrar, 1982.

Walter, Mildred Pitts. *My Mama Needs Me,* illustrated by Pat Cummings. Lothrop, 1983.

Watanabe, Shigeo. *How Do I Put It On?,* illustrated by Yasuo Ohtomo. Philomel, 1979.

_____. *What A Good Lunch!,* illustrated by Yasuo Ohtomo. Philomel, 1980.

Watson, Clyde. *Applebet: An ABC,* illustrated by Wendy Watson. Farrar, 1982.

_____. *Catch Me and Kiss Me and Say It Again,* illustrated by Wendy Watson. Philomel, 1978.

Weitzman, David. *My Backyard History Book,* illustrated by James Robertson. Little, Brown, 1975.

Wells, Rosemary. *A Lion for Lewis.* Dial, 1982.

_____. *Max's Ride.* Dial, 1979.

_____. *Noisy Nora.* Dial, 1973.

White, E. B. *Charlotte's Web,* illustrated by Garth Williams. Harper, 1953.

Wilder, Laura Ingalls. The Little House Series, illustrated by Garth Williams. Harper, 1953.

  By the Shores of Silver Lake (1939).
  Little House in the Big Woods (1932).
  Little House on the Prairie (1935).
  Little Town on the Prairie (1941).
  The Long Winter (1940).
  On the Banks of Plum Creek (1937).
  These Happy Golden Years (1943).

Wildsmith, Brian. *Brian Wildsmith's Mother Goose.* Watts, 1963.

_____. *Python's Party.* Watts, 1975.

Williams, Vera. *A Chair for My Mother.* Greenwillow, 1982.

Wolde, Gunilla. *Betsy's Baby Brother.* Random, 1975.

Wurman, Richard Saul. *Baseball Access.* Random, 1984.

Yashima, Taro. *Crow Boy.* Viking, 1955.

Zemach, Margot. *Hush, Little Baby.* Dutton, 1976.

Zolotow, Charlotte. *But Not Billy,* illustrated by Kay Chorao. Harper, 1984.

_____. *Mr. Rabbit and the Lovely Present,* illustrated by Maurice Sendak. Harper, 1962.

_____. *Say It!,* illustrated by James Stevenson. Greenwillow, 1980.

Zuromskis, Diane, illustrator. *Farmer in the Dell.* Little, 1978.

3
THE CHANGING WORLD OF CHILDREN'S BOOKS

CRUEL BOYS

"O, what a shame!" a kind child may be ready to say on looking at this picture. You see these boys, little as they are, have hard and cruel hearts. They have been robbing a happy little bird family of one of the young ones; and now they will so hurt it that it will die, or they will let it starve to death. And they have robbed another pair of birds of their nest and eggs. How unhappy must all these birds now be! and how wicked it is to give such needless pain to any of God's creatures! No kind child can think of hurting a dear, innocent little bird. But those who delight in such sport will very likely grow up to be capable of injuring their fellowmen in the various ways of which we so often hear and read. Let us be kind to every thing that lives.

And this isn't the whole story about these wicked boys. Don't you see they are in a *quarrel*, how they shall divide what they have so cruelly stolen from the birds? Ah, that is the way in doing wrong—one wrong step leads on to another; and robbing birds' nests does not usually go alone—a quarrel, or some other wickedness, usually follows it. Beware, then of the *beginnings* of cruelty and wickedness. [1]

EXCERPT FROM *LET'S BE ENEMIES*

James used to be my friend.
But today he is my enemy.
James always wants to be the boss.
James carries the flag.
James takes all the crayons.
He grabs the best digging spoon
and he throws sand. . . .
I'm going right over to James' house and tell him. . . .
"Hullo, James."
"Hullo, John."
"I came to tell you that I'm not your friend
any more."
"Well then, I'm not *your* friend either."
"We're enemies."
"All right!"
"GOOD-BYE!"
"GOOD-BYE!"
" Hey, James!"
"What?"
"Let's roller skate."
"O.K. Have a pretzel, John."
"Thank you, James." [2]

"Cruel Boys."

From *Sunnybank Stories: My Teacher's Gem.* Boston, Mass.: Lee and Shepard, 1863.

[1]Asa Bullard, *Sunnybank Stories: My Teacher's Gem* (Boston: Lee and Shepard, 1863), pp. 22–24.

Let's Be Enemies by Janice May Udry.

Illustration by Maurice Sendak from *Let's Be Enemies* by Janice May Udry. Pictures copyright © 1961 by Maurice Sendak. Reprinted by permission of Harper & Row, Publishers, Inc.

[2]Excerpt from *Let's Be Enemies* by Janice May Udry. Text copyright © 1961 by Janice May Udry. Reprinted by permission of Harper & Row, Publishers, Inc.

C ompare the language, the content, and the illustrations in these two stories—the ways in which society has changed its cultural values and its attitude toward children are strikingly apparent.

"Cruel Boys" is taken from *My Teacher's Gem,* a collection of moralistic stories printed in 1863. Its purpose was to instruct the young by first describing a horrible example of misbehavior and then warning of the dire consequences of, in this instance, stealing. It is told in the third person from the point of view of an adult admonishing all children. The moral of the story is explicitly stated.

The story of "Cruel Boys" contains only one black and white print, the one pictured here. This same illustration was used in many different books at that time. The "pirating" of pictures and stories from other books was a common practice.

Let's Be Enemies (1961), on the other hand, captures the experience, the feelings, and the language of the young child. The story is told in the first person from the point of view of the child protagonist, which makes it easier for the reader to identify with the growing anger of John. But 5-year-olds' quarrels are as fleeting as the brief showers that Sendak includes in his childlike illustrations. The sun soon comes out; and true to the nature of young children, John and James are fast friends by the end of the story.

The contrast between these stories mirrors the changes in literature for children. In *Let's Be Enemies,* children are allowed their childhood; they can be their 5-year-old selves. Their private feelings, thoughts, and language are considered worthy of attention. As much care has gone into conveying the meaning of the story through the pictures as through the text. It has taken nearly 300 years for books to move from the didactic and moralistic to books that delight and entertain.

The literature intended for children always reflects the changing attitude of society toward childhood and the family. As Philippe Ariès[3] contends, the idea of childhood itself was a seventeenth-century invention which has been transformed and reconstituted in every historical period. Consequently, study of the books for children provides a fascinating key to the record of society and the values it has wished to inculcate in its youth.

Children's literature has a brief history when seen in relationship to the history of the world. Nevertheless, it has evolved from a rich and interesting background. Literature reflects not only the values of society but also the books that have preceded it—literature of one generation builds on literature of the past generation. An understanding of family stories of today is enriched by acquaintance with the family stories of the past. How, for example, do the Beverly Cleary stories of the Quimby family (*Ramona and Her Father,* 1977, etc.) or Cynthia Voigt's descriptions of the Tuckermans in *Homecoming* (1981) compare with *The Moffats* (1940) by Eleanor Estes or Edith Nesbit's Bastable children in *The Story of the Treasure-Seekers* (1899) or even that earliest of well-loved family stories, *Little Women* (1868), by Louisa May Alcott?

One danger in evaluating stories of the past is the tendency to use contemporary criteria, rather than recognizing the prevailing values of the period in which a book was published. Some modern-day reviewers criticize *Little Women* as being anti-feminist, but at the time of its publication in 1868, its main character was considered much too independent and tomboyish. Obvious as it may seem, books for children are a product of their times and need to be evaluated in relationship to the other books of the day and against the social and political values of the period. Only then is it

[3]Philippe Ariès, *Centuries of Childhood: A Social History of Family Life,* translated from the French by Robert Baldick (New York: Knopf, 1962).

possible to identify the books that were real break-throughs in creating a changing literature for children.

EARLY BEGINNINGS—THE MIDDLE AGES

The Oral Tradition

Before there were books, there were stories. In the medieval days stories were told around the fires in the cottages or sung in the great halls of the castles. Young and old alike listened, with no distinction being made between stories for children and stories for adults, just as there was little difference in the work they did, the food they ate, or the clothes they wore. All gathered to listen, to be entertained after a hard day's labor. A comparison can be made between this time of the oral tradition and today, when an entire family gathers to view a television show. True, there are children's programs, but many surveys show children watch what adults watch. All are exposed to the same stories.

In the Middle Ages, there were differences in the kinds of stories told in the cottages and the castles and in the way they were told. In the castles and great manor houses wandering minstrels or bards told the heroic tales of Beowulf or King Arthur or the ballad of Fair Isabella, whose stepmother had her cooked and served in a pie. Often these tales were sung, accompanied by harp or lyre. By contrast, the tales told around the peat fires in the cottages or at the medieval fairs were about simple folk: farmers, woodcutters, and millers or beast tales about wolves, foxes, and hens. Frequently, the stories portrayed the poor peasant outwitting the lord of the manor or winning the hand of the princess by a daring deed. These tales were told over and over for generations until they were finally collected by such persons as the Grimm Brothers and thus passed into recorded literature.

It is important to remember that the told tale did not cease with the invention of the printing press. It was many years before the common folk could read or afford to buy books. And the first books did not entertain; their purpose was religious or instructional, frequently both. The told tale continued to delight far into the nineteenth century. Today the storyteller is still a welcome visitor in the classroom, library, or home. A revival of interest in storytelling may be seen in the increased number of storytelling festivals.

The Earliest Manuscripts

Before the invention of movable type, the first books available for children were lesson books handwritten in Latin by monks. Mostly religious or instructional, these were intended only for the wealthy or for use by the teachers in the monastery schools. The value of such handwritten books may be better understood when one realizes that houses and lands were often exchanged for a single volume.[4]

Most of these early lesson books followed one of two forms, which would continue to be used until the early twentieth century: (1) a dialogue between the pupil and teacher, usually in the form of questions and answers, or (2) rhymed couplets, which made for ease in memorization. Aldhelm, Abbot of Malmesbury during the seventh century, is credited with originating the question-and-answer approach. Also during this century, the Venerable Bede translated and wrote some forty-five books for his students at the monastery at Jarrow in England.

Another type of book, the *Elucidarium,* or book of general information for young students, was developed by Anselm, Archbishop of Canterbury during the twelfth century. This type of book, a forerunner of the encyclopedia, treated such topics as manners, children's duties, the properties of animals and plants, and religious precepts.

These early lesson books are only important to the history of children's literature in that they represented some concession to developing specific books for the *instruction* of children. Another six centuries would pass before John Newbery would add the word "amusement" to the word "instruction."

The Gesta Romanorum (Deeds of the Romans), compiled in Latin about 1290, served as a source

---

[4]Louise Frances Story Field (Mrs. E. M. Field), *The Child and His Book* 2nd ed. (London: Wells Gardner, 1892; reprint: Detroit: Singing Tree Press, 1968), p. 13.

book for stories for the clergy for instruction and for enlivening sermons. This compilation of stories included many myths, fables, and tales from as far away as the Orient. Both Chaucer and Shakespeare drew incidents and stories from the Gesta. For example, it contained anecdotes of the three caskets and the pound of flesh found in *The Merchant of Venice* and a synopsis of the medieval romance *Guy of Warwick*. These tales were often dressed up with suitable morals and then told to children.

Only one well-known work remains from this medieval period, Chaucer's *Canterbury Tales*. Although written for adults in 1387, the tales are full of legendary stories and folktales that were known to children as well as adults of the period.

Caxton Begins English Printing

Some historians maintain that printing first began in Holland sometime between 1380 and 1420.[5] However, in the 1450s, Gutenberg in Germany devised a practical method for using movable metal type, producing a quality far superior to printing from the early Dutch type. William Caxton, an English businessman, went to Cologne, Germany, to learn the printing trade. Returning to England, he set up a printing press in Westminster about 1476. Among the first books that he published were *A Book of Curteseye* (1477), *The Historye of Reynart the Foxe* (1481), and *Aesop's Fables* (1484). Malory's *Le Morte d'Arthur* first appeared in printed form in 1485. Caxton is credited with publishing some 106 books, including traditional romance literature, ballads, texts, and religious books. His books were of high quality and expensive, which made them available only to wealthy adults, not children. The impact of the printing press can be seen, however, in the number of books owned by some individuals. Before its invention in the 1450s, even scholars and physicians possessed only a few books. A century later, to give one example, Columbus of Seville (the son of Christopher Columbus) owned a library of more than 15,000 titles.

[5]Elva S. Smith, *Elva S. Smith's History of Children's Literature,* revised by Margaret Hodges and Susan Steinfirst (Chicago: American Library Association, 1980), p. 38.

Hornbooks, ABCs, and Primers

The first children's books to be influenced by the invention of printing were then the only children's books: lesson books or textbooks. Young children learned to read from "hornbooks"; a hornbook was really not a book at all but a little wooden paddle to which was pasted a sheet of parchment printed with the alphabet, the vowels, and the Lord's Prayer. A thin sheet of transparent protective horn bound with strips of brass covered the text. Most of the hornbooks were tiny, measuring 2 3/4 by 5 inches. Sometimes a hole in the handle made it possible for the child to carry the book on a cord around his or her neck or waist. What made these little "books" unique was that now the child could handle them and see the print close up, rather than merely look at a manuscript held by the teacher. Hornbooks were also made of leather, silver, copper, ivory, and sometimes gingerbread! First appearing in the 1440s, they became the first books of instruction for young children for many years. Brought to this country, they were used by the Puritans and in the Colonial Dame Schools.

Children advanced from the hornbooks to ABC books and primers. These had more text than the hornbooks but it was still of a religious nature. The first primers developed from the books of hours intended as private devotionals for lay peo-

ranne in to the forest / And whanne the wyld bestes sawe hym come / they were so ferdfull that they alle beganne to flee/ For they wende/ that it had be the lyon/ And the mayster of the asse sechche and soughte his asse in every place al aboute And as he had soughte longe/he thoughte that he wold go in to the forest for to see yf his asse were there/ And as soone as

Woodcut and type for Caxton's Aesop of 1484.

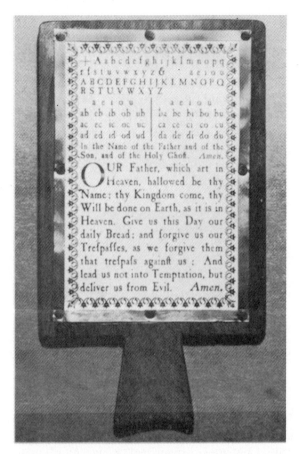

This facsimile of a colonial horn book may be ordered from The Horn Book, Inc., Park Square Building, 31 St. James Ave., Boston, MA. 02116.

ple, with prayers for each hour. In 1514 an alphabet was added to a book of hours for use by children. When Henry VIII came to the throne he authorized printing a set of English primers for children which presented his religious beliefs. These little books, appropriately called King Henry's Primers, appeared about 1548.

John Amos Comenius, a Moravian bishop, planned a book for schools which has been called the first picture book. Titled *Orbis Pictus* (The World Illustrated), the book was translated into English in 1658 and published with many woodcuts illustrating everyday objects.

Lasting Contributions of the Period

Children were no better off after the invention of printing than before. They still derived their enjoy-

ment from the oral tradition of the told story. True, some concession had been made to their youth in devising special books of instruction for them. But only crudely written and printed chapbooks, (sold by peddlers or chapmen) provided a kind of underground literature of enjoyment for both adults and children. The two lasting books of this period are Chaucer's *Canterbury Tales* and Thomas Malory's collection of Arthurian legends, later published in 1485 by Caxton under the title *Le Morte d'Arthur*. Neither of these books was written for children, but they were probably familiar with their content from hearing them told by bards and minstrels.

What strikes a twentieth-century reader as remarkable about this period is how few books there were and how long they stayed in print. Many of the books published by Caxton in the 1440s were still in print in the late 1600s, more than two hundred years later. This seems almost unbelievable when compared with today's publishing world where some books go out of print in less than a year.

CHILDREN'S BOOKS: SEVENTEENTH AND EIGHTEENTH CENTURIES

The "Goodly Godly" Books of the Puritans

Books of the seventeenth century were dominated by the stern spiritual beliefs of Puritanism. As William Sloane has put it, "Nothing in our own diffuse civilization holds quite the pivotal position, the centrality, which religion held in seventeenth-century England and America. To man's relationship with God all the other circumstances of his life were peripheral."[6]

Children were considered to be miniature adults by the Puritans, and they were thus equally subject to sin and eternal damnation. Concern for the salvation of their souls became the central goal of their parents and teachers. Given the high mortality rate of infants and young children (more than half did not live to reach the age of 10), instruction in the fear of God began early.

[6]William Sloane, *Children's Books in England and America in the 17th Century* (New York: King's Press, Columbia University Press, 1955), p. 12.

Children were expected to memorize John Cotton's catechism, *Spiritual Milk for Boston Babes in Either England, Drawn from the Breasts of Both Testaments for Their Souls' Nourishment.* Originally published in England in 1646, it was revised for American children in 1656, the first book written and printed for children in the American colonies. Later books followed its question-and-answer approach. For example, there was the question, "How did God make you?" The child had to memorize the accompanying answer, "I was conceived in sin and born in iniquity." Even alphabet rhymes for the youngest emphasized the sinful nature of humans. *The New England Primer*, first advertised in 1683, includes "In Adam's fall/We sinned all." This primer also provided a catechism, the Ten Commandments, verses about death, and a woodcut of the burning at the stake of the Martyr John Foxe, watched by his wife and nine children. In print for more than a century, about three million copies of this primer were sold.

In England in 1671, James Janeway published his book of gloomy joy titled *A Token for Children, Being an Exact Account of the Conversions, Holy and Exemplary Lives and Joyful Deaths of Several Young Children.* In his preface to Part I, he reminds his readers that they are "by Nature, Children of Wrath." Cotton Mather added the life histories of several New England children and published an American edition of Janeway's book in Boston in 1700 under the title *A Token for Children of New England, or Some Examples of Children in Whom the Fear of God Was Remarkably Budding Before They Died.* Virginia Haviland describes the American edition: "An account of youthful piety, in tune with the doctrine of original sin, this is the first of the few narratives that were available to 18th century children in America and undoubtedly the most widely read children's book in the Puritan age."[7]

The religious leaders also could give approval to the moral and religious instruction in John Bunyan's *Pilgrim's Progress*, first printed in 1678. No doubt children skipped the long theological dialogues as they found adventure by traveling with the clearly defined characters. Another book by John Bunyan, evidently written *for* children, was first published in 1686 under the title *A Book for Boys and Girls or Country Rhymes for Children.* In a later illustrated edition the title was changed to *Divine Emblems or Temporal Things Spiritualized.* In this strange little book, Bunyan would describe a common object in verse and then draw a lesson from the so-called "emblem." His choice of subjects included "Meditations on an Egg" and "A Bee," which provided the following lesson:

> This bee an Emblem truly is of Sin,
> Whose Sweet unto many a Death hath been.
> Now would'st have sweet from Sin, and yet not die,
> Do thou it in the first place mortify.

Darton[8] states that this particular emblem book was popular with both children and ignorant folk throughout the eighteenth century and remained in common use until at least the middle of the nineteenth century.

Chapbooks: Forerunners of Comics

Luckily, there was some relief from the doom and gloom of the religious-oriented books of the Puritans. Chapbooks, small inexpensive folded paper booklets sold by peddlers or chapmen, first appeared in the late 1500s, but it was in the seventeenth and eighteenth centuries that they achieved their popularity. Sold for a few pennies, these crudely printed little books brought excitement and pleasure into the lives of both children and adults with tales about Dick Whittington, Sir Guy of Warwick, Robin Hood, and other heroes. A ballad of a "most strange wedding of the froggee and the mouse" had been licensed as early as 1580. "The Death and Burial of Cock Robin" was another early chapbook that children must have enjoyed. One of the most popular was about Tom Hickathrift, a giant-sized man who accomplished Paul Bunyan-like feats like pulling up trees and felling four highwaymen with a single blow. By contrast, a 1630 story of the tiny Tom Thumb shows him disappearing into a bowl of pudding when he

[7]Virginia Haviland and Margaret N. Coughlan, *Yankee Doodle's Literary Sampler of Prose, Poetry and Pictures* (New York: Crowell, 1974), p. 11.

[8]F. J. Harvey Darton, *Children's Books in England*, 3rd ed., revised by Brian Alderson (Cambridge, England: Cambridge University Press, 1932, 1982), p. 64.

Tom Thumb.

Of *Tom Thumb* running a Tilt, with divers others Knightly exercises by him performed.

A woodcut from a seventeenth-century black-letter chapbook. It contains two episodes; "Tom Thumb running a tilt" and "how Tom Thumb did take his sickness, and of his death and burial." C 1650-1660.

The Walter Havighurst Special Collections, Miami University Libraries, Oxford, Ohio.

was young and later bravely riding into battle astride a mighty warhorse. The earliest known edition of "Jack the Giant Killer" seems to have been in a chapbook of 1711. Other chapbooks gave accounts of crimes and executions, descriptions of the art of making love, and riddles.

While these books were decried by the Puritans, they were read and reread by the common people of England and America. Their popularity with children is said to have influenced John Newbery's decision to publish a book solely for children. The chapbooks' greatly abbreviated texts and crude woodcut illustrations suggest that they were

forerunners of today's comic strips, still read by both adults and children.

Nursery Rhymes or Mother Goose

No one knows for sure the exact origin of the nursery rhymes. Apparently, what we have come to call Mother Goose rhymes, including counting-out rhymes, finger plays, and alphabet verses, originated in the spoken language of both common folk and royalty. Some have been traced as far back as the pre-Christian era. A few writers theorize that "Jack and Jill" refers to the waxing and waning of the moon. It is believed that many of the verses were written as political satires or told of royal tragedy. "Pussycat, Pussycat," for example, was based on an incident in Queen Elizabeth's court. "Three Wise Men of Gotham" reflects stories of the foolish inhabitants of Gotham before the days of King John. Thomas cites the account of a deed in the possession of a Horner family signed by Henry VIII that was a "plum" pulled out of the pie—the King's collection of deeds.[9] However, other scholars have found little evidence of these relationships.[10]

Shakespeare evidently knew these nursery rhymes, for they are referred to in *King Lear* and others of his plays. Yet the oldest *surviving* nursery-rhyme book was published by Mary Cooper in the year 1744 in two or perhaps three little volumes under the title *Tommy Thumb's Pretty Song Book;* a single copy of Volume II is a treasured possession of the British Museum. This second volume includes such favorite verses as "Sing a Song of Sixpence," "There Was an Old Woman," "Hickere, Dickere, Dock," and "London Bridge Is Broken Down." John Newbery is supposed to have published *Mother Goose's Melody or Sonnets for the Cradle* about 1765, although the book was not advertised until 1780, which is the more likely date of its publication. No copy of this edition exists. However, Isaiah Thomas of Worcester, Massachusetts, produced a second edition of *Mother Goose's Melody* in 1794. Since

[9]Katherine Elwes Thomas, *The Real Personages of Mother Goose* (New York: Lothrop, 1930).
[10]Iona and Peter Opie, *The Oxford Nursery Rhyme Book* (London: Oxford University Press, 1952). William S. Baring-Gould and Ceil Baring-Gould, *The Annotated Mother Goose* (New York: Charles N. Potter, 1962).

many of his books were pirated from Newbery, it is assumed that the first edition of about 1786 was a copy of the lost Newbery one.

The legend that Dame Goose is buried in Boston is kept alive for tourists and children who visit the Boston burying grounds, but it has created confusion regarding the origin of the verses. Even the publication of *Songs for the Nursery; or Mother Goose's Melodies* by the son-in-law of Dame Goose has become a legend. According to the story, Thomas Fleet tired of the good woman's frequent renditions of the ditties as she cared for his children, so he decided to collect and publish them in 1719. There has been no actual evidence of this edition.

Other verses and rhymes continued to be added to Mother Goose after their publication as small separate books. *The Comic Adventures of Old Mother Hubbard and her Dog* by Sarah Martin first appeared in 1805. During the same year *Songs from the Nursery Collected by the Most Renowned Poets* was published. For the first time, "Little Miss Muffett" and "One, Two, Buckle My Shoe" were included in a Mother Goose book. *Dame Wiggins of Lee and her Seven Wonderful Cats* was first published in 1823. *The History of Sixteen Wonderful Old Women,* issued by J. Harris and Son in 1820, contains the earliest examples of what we now call the limerick.

Uncertain of her origin as the historians are, they do recognize that the venerable Mother Goose became a welcome part of the nursery on both sides of the Atlantic during the eighteenth century and since then she has never left her post.

Fairy Tales and Adventure

Another source of enjoyment for children came in the form of fairy tales, first printed in France in 1697 by Charles Perrault. Titled *Histoires ou Contes du temps passé; avec des Moralités* (Stories or Tales of Times Past, with Morals), the collection included "The Sleeping Beauty," "Cinderella or the Glass Slipper," "Red Riding Hood," "Puss-in-Boots," and "Blue Beard," among others. These tales were in fashion at the French Court of the Sun King, Louis XIV, where they were told to adults. The frontispiece of Perrault's book, however, showed an old woman spinning and telling stories to children. The caption read *Contes de ma Mère l'Oye* (Tales of Mother Goose), which was the first reference to Mother Goose in children's literature. Translated into English in 1729, these fairy tales have remained France's gift to the children of the world.

Following the success of Perrault, other French authors, including Mme. d'Aulnoy, created original fairy tales. Only one remains well known today and that is "Beauty and the Beast," rewritten from a longer version by Mme. de Beaumont.

The Arabian Nights is another collection of old tales that came from India, Persia, and North Africa. Galland published these tales in French in 1558, but not until about 1706 were they available in English. Intended for adults, such stories as "Aladdin," "Ali Baba," and "Sinbad the Sailor" were appropriated by children. Ridley also published a series of tales modeled after the Arabian Nights under the title *The Tales of the Genii* (1766).

Defoe did not write his account of the eighteenth-century hero Robinson Crusoe for children, but they made his story part of their literature. *The Life and Strange and Surprising Adventures of Robinson Crusoe* (1719) was later printed in an abridged and pocket-sized volume that became a "classic" of children's literature. This book was so popular that it spawned many imitations—so many, in fact, that a word, "Robinsonades," was coined for them.

While children no doubt did not understand the scathing satire of high society in Swift's *Gulliver's Travels,* they did find enjoyment in the hero's adventures with the huge and tiny folk and the talking horses. Thus young and old alike enjoyed this tale of adventure, first published in 1726.

Newbery Publishes for Children

The concept of a literature for children usually dates from 1744, the year the English publisher John Newbery printed *A Little Pretty Pocket-Book*. The title page is shown here. For parents, Newbery included Locke's advice on children, (see page 104). The book itself attempted to teach the alphabet by way of diversion, including games, fables, and little rhymes about the letters of the alphabet. What was significant about the book was

A Little Pretty
POCKET-BOOK,
Intended for the
INSTRUCTION and AMUSEMENT
O F
LITTLE MASTER *TOMMY*,
A N D
PRETTY MISS *POLLY*.
With Two Letters from
J A C K the GIANT-KILLER;
AS ALSO
A BALL and PINCUSHION;
The Use of which will infallibly make *Tommy*
a good Boy, and *Polly* a good Girl.

To which is added,
A LITTLE SONG-BOOK,
BEING
A *New Attempt* to teach Children the Use of
the *English Alphabet*, by Way of Diverſion.

L O N D O N:
Printed for J. NEWBERY, at the *Bible and Sun*
in St. *Paul's Church-Yard*. 1767.
[Price Six-pence bound.]

Little Goody Two Shoes points to her two shoes in a facsimile reprint of John Newbery's best-known publication.

that Newbery deliberately and openly set out to provide amusement for children, something no other publisher had had the courage or insight to do.

No documentary evidence is available to determine whether John Newbery or Oliver Goldsmith wrote *The History of Little Goody Two Shoes*, published by Newbery in 1765. London records do show that Newbery gave Goldsmith lodging above his shop in London called "The Bible and the Sun." It is probable that Goldsmith was the author of some of the 200 books published by Newbery. In the story of *Goody Two Shoes*, Margery Meanwell and her brother are turned out of their home after the death of her parents, for "Her father had succumbed to a fever, in a place where Dr. James' Powder was not to be had." (Newbery also sold Dr. James' Powder and other medicines

in his store.) At first the children are taken in by a kind parson, who properly clothes Tommy and sends him off to sea and provides Margery with two shoes instead of the poor one left to her after their eviction. This kind man hopes to take her into his family, but the evil Graspall threatens to reduce his tithe if he does. Eventually, Margery becomes a tutor who moralizes as she teaches her young pupils to read. She marries a wealthy squire and continues to carry on her good works. *Goody Two Shoes* was read for well over a century. A modern eight-page version of it was sold to be read in air-raid shelters in England in the 1940s.

Newbery was obviously impressed with the advice given by the famous English philosopher John Locke in his *Thoughts Concerning Education* (1693). Locke maintained that as soon as the child knew his alphabet he should be led to read for pleasure. He advocated the use of pictures in books and deplored the lack of easy, pleasant books for children to read, except for *Aesop's Fables* and *Reynard the Fox,* both dating back to Caxton's times.

Newbery's books were all illustrated with pictures based on the text, rather than just any woodcuts available, as was the custom of other printers of the day. Many of his books were bound with Dutch gilt paper covers, which made for a gay appearance. And while the moral lessons were clearly there for young readers, his stories did emphasize love and play rather than the wrath and punishment of God. Except for *Goody Two Shoes,* none of his work has lasted, but we honor the man who was the first to recognize that children deserve a literature of their own.

Didactic Tales

During the last half of the eighteenth century, women writers entered the field of juvenile literature determined to influence the moral development of children. Mrs. Sarah Fielding published *The Governess* in 1749, which included character-building stories about Mrs. Teachum's School for Girls. *Easy Lessons for Children,* published in 1760 by Mrs. Barbauld, contained moral stories supposedly written for children as young as 2 to 3 years. Mrs. Sarah Trimmer thought of herself as the true *Guardian of Education,* the title she later gave to a magazine she published that contained articles on moral subjects and book reviews. Mrs. Trimmer did not approve of fairy tales or Mother Goose. "All Mother Goose tales . . . were only fit to fill the heads of children with confused notions of wonderful and supernatural events brought about by the agency of imaginary beings."[11] She saw no inconsistency, however, in writing a story in which a family of robins could talk about day-to-day problems in their lives. First titled *Fabulous Histories* (1786), it was published for many years afterwards under the title *The Robins.* The conver-

sation between the parent robins and their offspring (called Flapsy, Pecksy, Dicky, and Robin) is stilted and lofty, indeed. Robin, the eldest, is portrayed as a conceited young bird who will take no advice. His parents discuss his behavior in this way:

> "You have been absent a long time, my love," said her mate, "but I perceive that you were indulging your tenderness towards that disobedient nestling, who has rendered himself unworthy of it; however, I do not condemn you for giving him assistance, for had not you undertaken the task, I would myself have flown to him instead of returning home; how is he, likely to live and reward your kindness?"
>
> "Yes," said she, "he will, I flatter myself, soon perfectly recover, for his hurt is not very considerable, and I have the pleasure to tell you he is extremely sensible of his late folly, and I dare say will endeavour to repair his fault with future good behaviour."[12]

Poor Mrs. Trimmer justified the use of this anthropomorphized bird family by calling the stories "fables" and stating that she was following the advice of John Locke, who had advocated the use of *Aesop's Fables* with children. No wonder Beatrix Potter[13] recalled hating this book and refusing to learn to read from it. Some memory of it must have lingered with her, however, for there is a strong resemblance in the sound of names of the young robins to her famous rabbit family, Flopsy, Mopsy, Cottontail, and Peter.

Other didactic writers of this period maintained they followed Rousseau's theory of education by accompanying the child in his natural search for knowledge. These stories frequently contained lengthy "conversations" that tried to conceal moral lessons in the guise of an exciting adventure.

Thomas Day utilized this conversational approach in *The History of Sandford and Merton,* a didactic tale that appeared in three sections (1783, 1786, 1789). Harry Sandford and Tommy Merton were 6-year-old boys who were tutored together, although Harry was the son of a farmer. It was

[11]Darton, p. 97.

[12]Mrs. Trimmer, *The Robins: Or Domestic Life among the Birds,* a revised edition (New York: C. S. Francis & Co., 1851), p. 93.

[13]Jane Crowell Morse, ed. *Beatrix Potter's Americans: Selected Letters* (Boston: The Horn Book, Inc., 1982).

Harry who exemplified the just and righteous for the spoiled Tommy Merton. Day after day, lecture after lecture, the tutor presented long lessons that interrupted the narrative. These priggish children served as models of behavior for nearly one hundred years.

Marie Edgeworth knew Thomas Day, and she also tried to follow the educational priniciples of Rousseau. Her approach was the classical narrative one in which the child learns through bitter experience. Her best-known story is "The Purple Jar," which first appeared in *The Parents' Assistant: or Stories for Children* (1796). In this story, Rosamund, who longed for a purple jar that she saw in an apothecary's window, chose it over the pair of new shoes she needed. Poor Rosamund learns to her great sorrow that the clear glass bottle is only filled with a foul-smelling liquid. Rosamund acknowledges the folly of her choice, saying:

> "Oh Mamma . . . how I wish I had chosen the shoes. They would have been of so much more use to me than that jar; however, I am sure—no, not quite sure—but I hope, I shall be wiser another time."[14]

Poetry

In this period poetry for children also emphasized religion and instruction. Although Isaac Watts spent most of his time writing hymns, he did write some poetry for children. In the preface to *Divine and Moral Songs Attempted in Easy Language for Use of Children* (1715) Watts wrote that his songs were to be memorized, which was how children were to be given "a relish for virtue and religion." Though written by a Puritan, these hymns were kind and loving, and the collection made up a real child's book. Altogether Watts wrote about 700 hymns, some of which are still sung today, notably "Joy to the World," "O God Our Help in Ages Past," and the lovely "Cradle Hymn" which begins "Hush, my dear, lie still and slumber." Charles Wesley was also a prolific hymn writer. His *Hymns for Children* (1763) included "Gentle Jesus, Meek and Mild."

John Newbery printed *Pretty Poems for Children Three Feet High* and added the inscription:

"To all those who are good this book is dedicated by their best friend."

The engraver and artist William Blake wrote poetry that children enjoyed, but the poems comprising *Songs of Innocence* (1789) were not specifically written for children. Blake's poetry was filled with imagination and joy and made the reader aware of beauty without preaching. Children still respond to his happy poem that begins "Piping down the valleys wild, / Piping songs of pleasant glee." His desire to open the "doors of perception" is reflected in his well-known poem "To see a World in a Grain of Sand."

One British artist, Thomas Bewick, emerged during this period as an illustrator of books for boys and girls. He perfected the white-line method of engraving on the end grain of a block of wood to achieve a delicacy of line not found in usual carved woodblock designs. Bewick's *The New Lottery Book of Birds and Beasts* (1771) was one of the first instances of a master illustrator putting his name on a book for children. Among his other

A white line woodcut of "The Fox and the Crow" from *Select Fables* designed and engraved by Thomas and John Bewick C 1784.

The Walter Havighurst Special Collections, Miami University Libraries, Oxford, Ohio.

[14]Quoted by Darton, p. 141.

works were *A Pretty Book of Pictures for Little Masters and Misses; or Tommy Trip's History of Beasts and Birds* (1779), which was a variation of one of Newbery's titles of the early 1760s, and several books of fables, including his own *Fables of Aesop and Others* (1818).

As the century came near its end, most of the stories for children were about how to live the "good life." Information about the natural world was peddled in didactic lectures sugar-coated with conversational style. Little prigs were models for young people to follow. However, there was now a literature for children. Authors and publishers were aware of a new market for books. Parents and teachers were beginning to recognize the importance of literature for children.

CHILDREN'S LITERATURE: THE NINETEENTH CENTURY

Books of Instruction and Information

During the period immediately following the American Revolution, there was a rush to publish textbooks that reflected the changing social purposes and interests of the new nation. A picture of George Washington was substituted for the woodcut of George III in *The New England Primer*. The alphabet no longer intoned "In Adam's fall / We sinned all" but started with a less pious rhyme: "A was an Angler and fished with a hook. / B was a Blockhead and ne'er learned his book."

Noah Webster's *Blue Backed Speller, Simplified and Standardized,* first published in 1783, continued to be widely used in this period. Revised many times, the third part of the series contained stories and became America's first secular reader. It sold more than 80 million copies during the nineteenth century.

Reading for patriotism, good citizenship, and industry was the purpose of the well-loved *Eclectic Readers* by William H. McGuffey. They were used so widely from 1834 to 1900 one could almost say these readers comprised the elementary curriculum in literature. A glance at the *Fifth Reader* reflects the type of material included in these readers: speeches by Daniel Webster, essays by Washington

Irving, selections from Shakespeare (although the play is often not identified), narrative, sentimental, and patriotic poetry, and many didactic essays with such titles as "Advantages of a Well-educated Mind," "Impeachment of Warren Hastings" as reported in the *Edinburgh Review,* and "Eulogy on Candlelight."

Although compulsory education was being extended and the publicly supported common school was being established, parents were also expected to teach children at home. The parent's role was established through stories in which mothers embroidered, sipped tea, and dispensed information to *sweet* children. The following conversation was in *A Key to Knowledge,* published in 1822:

> *Louisa*—By the By, when I come to think of it, what a dirty thing honey is; first swallowed by bees, and then by us.
>
> *Mother*—Your description is certainly not very inviting. Suppose rather that we should call the honey, the syrup of flowers, drawn from the opened buds by the trunk, or proboscis, of the industrious bee.
>
> *Louisa*—Now I like honey again. . . .[15]

In the early nineteenth century Samuel Goodrich was responsible for eliminating the British background in books for American children. Influenced by both the English and American Sunday School movement which produced moral tales for the uneducated masses of children who could attend school only on Sunday, Goodrich wrote more than a hundred books for children. He created the venerable Peter Parley, an elderly gentleman who told stories to children based on his travels and personal experiences. History, geography, and science were included in his *Tales of Peter Parley about America* (1827). Nearly a million copies of *Peter Parley's Method of Telling about Geography to Children* (1829) were published. This series became so popular that Goodrich employed a writing staff to help him which included Nathaniel Hawthorne and his sister, Elizabeth. Sales of Peter Parley's books totaled over 7 million copies, and they were frequently pirated and issued abroad.

The *Little Rollo* series by Jacob Abbott became as popular as the Peter Parley books. Abbott wrote about Little Rollo learning to talk, Rollo learning

15"19th Century Juvenilia," *Times Educational Supplement,* 2262:1412 (September 26, 1958).

to read, and of Rollo's travels to Europe. In the first books of the series, published in 1834, Rollo was a natural little boy, but as he became older and traveled about the world he became another little prig.

The Bodley Family, conceived by Horace Scudder, explored New England, Holland, and other countries in a series of eight books beginning with *Doings of the Bodley Family in Town and Country* (1875). In *Seven Little Sisters Who Live on the Big Round Ball that Floats in the Air* (1861), Jane Andrews told of little girls who lived in the far north, in the desert, in China, and in Switzerland. Without talking down to children or lecturing them, Andrews presented truthful and interesting descriptions of the way foreign children lived. This book was followed in 1885 by *Ten Boys Who Lived on the Road from Long Ago Till Now*.

Only a few writers and publishers seemed to realize that children want to learn about their world. Children had to plod through pages of tiresome conversations with moralistic overtones to gain the information they sought. It was not until much later that informational books on almost every subject were placed on bookshelves for boys and girls.

Folktale Collections

Early in the nineteenth century two German brothers went about asking servants and peasants to recall stories they had heard. In 1812 Jacob and Wilhelm Grimm published the first volume of *Kinder and Hausmarchen* (Household Stories). These serious scholars tried to preserve the form as well as the content of the old tales that were translated and published in England by Edgar Taylor in 1823–1826. "The Elves and the Shoemaker," "Rumplestiltskin," and "Snow White," in addition to many others, became part of the literature of childhood.

In America, Washington Irving included "Rip Van Winkle" and "The Legend of Sleepy Hollow" in his 1819 *Sketch Book*. These tales, written mainly for adults, were also enjoyed by older children.

The origin of the story of "The Three Bears" has been questioned by various authorities. It was first credited to the poet Robert Southey, who pub-lished it in *The Doctor* (1837). Later, Edgar Osborne, the famous English collector of children's books, found the story handwritten in verse by Eleanor Mure in 1831. Both these earlier versions portray a wicked old woman who comes to visit the bears, which are described as wee, middle-sized, and huge. Through various retellings, the story has been changed to the more familiar fair-haired Goldilocks visiting a *family* of bears.

In 1846 Mary Howitt translated Hans Christian Andersen's fairy tales under the title of *Wonderful Stories for Children*. Now both English and American children could enjoy "The Princess and the Pea," "Thumbelina," and "The Emperor's New Clothes." In these stories, inanimate objects and animals like the heroic "Tin Soldier" and "The Ugly Duckling" come to life. The values and foibles of human life are presented in the stories with action and rich language.

Not until the last half of the nineteenth century were folktales and fairy tales completely accepted for children. John Ruskin was influenced by the Grimm tales as he wrote his *King of the Golden River* (1851). Charles Dickens' *The Magic Fishbone* appeared first as a serial in 1868. *The Wonder Book for Boys and Girls* was published by Nathaniel Hawthorne in 1852, followed by *Tanglewood Tales* in 1853. Now children had the Greek myths written especially for them. Sir George Dasent translated *Popular Tales from the North* in 1859, making it possible for children to enjoy more tales from Scandinavia. *The Nürnberg Stove* was another favorite, first published by Louise de la Ramee in a collection of children's stories in 1882. Joel Chandler Harris collected stories from the South for *Uncle Remus, His Songs and Sayings* (1881).

Collections of folktales were made by Andrew Lang in his famous series beginning with *The Blue Fairy Book*. The *Red, Green,* and *Yellow* fairy books followed the 1889 publication of the first volume of folklore. Joseph Jacobs was also interested in retelling folktales especially for children. *English Fairy Tales* was published in two volumes between 1890 and 1894; *Celtic Fairy Tales,* also in two volumes, appeared in 1892 and 1894; while *Indian Fairy Tales* was written in 1892. All these tales were important contributions to the realm of folklore. As the merits of folklore were recognized everywhere, there was increasing interest in such volumes as Howard Pyle's collections of stories titled *Pepper and Salt* (1886) and *The Wonder Clock* (1888).

Family Stories

In the first half of the nineteenth century the didactic school of writing continued to flourish as women writers wielded influential pens. They still condemned fairy stories and relentlessly dispensed information in lengthy dialogues between parent and child. Mrs. Martha Sherwood, a prolific writer, produced over 350 moralizing books and religious tracts. While living in India, she wrote *Little Henry and His Bearer* (1814). This story tells how little Henry converted his Indian servant to Christianity and illustrates her missionary theme. However, she is remembered best for a series of stories about *The Fairchild Family,* the first part published in 1818, the third and last in 1847. Considered one of the first "family" stories, it contained some frighteningly realistic passages. In one scene Lucy, Emily, and Henry (all names in Mrs. Sherwood's own family) quarrel over a doll and say they do not love each other. Mr. Fairchild overhears them and whips their hands with a rod. After dinner he then takes them to Blackwood to see something "very dreadful, . . . a gibbet on which the decomposed body of a man still hangs in irons. The face of the corpse was so shocking the children could not look at it." It seems the man was a murderer who first hated and then killed his brother. Later revisions of this story omitted the grim scene. However, even without this passage Mrs. Sherwood knew how to tell a dramatic vital story, and *The Fairchild Family* was known on both sides of the Atlantic.

In contrast to the religious severity of *The Fairchild Family,* Charlotte Yonge described the milder Victorian experiences of the motherless May family of eleven children in *The Daisy Chain* (1856). Women were always portrayed in the Victorian novel as inferior to men. This attitude is reflected in *The Daisy Chain* when Ethel May is advised not to try to keep up with her brother Norman in his university studies since "a woman cannot hope to equal a man in scholarship." In *The Clever Woman of the Family* (1865) Yonge devotes nearly the whole book to making the heroine "realize how much better and deeper were her husband's ideas than her own."[16] Yonge had an ear for dialogue and frequently recorded her friends' conversations. She was a superb story-teller and wrote over 120 books.

American children wept pools of tears over the pious sentimental story of *Elsie Dinsmore*. Writing under her maiden name, Martha Farquharson, Martha Farquharson Finley initiated the Elsie Dinsmore series in 1867. The best-known scene is the one in which Elsie's father demands that she play the piano and sing for a group of his friends. Because it is the Sabbath, Elsie refuses. Her father will not have his authority questioned and makes her sit on the piano stool for hours until she finally faints and cuts her head in the fall. Filled with remorse, he gently carries her upstairs only to have her insist that she be allowed to pray before going to bed. Elsie at all times is righteous and good. Her favorite book is the Bible, which she knows by heart and quotes regularly. The series contains eighteen books published from 1867 to 1905 which follow Elsie from girlhood through motherhood, widowhood, and into grandmotherhood. Unbelievable as the stories seem to us today, the Elsie Dinsmore books were tremendously popular.

The next year saw the publication of *Little Women* (1868) by Louisa May Alcott. This story must have blown like a fresh breeze through the stifling atmosphere of pious religiosity created by books like *Elsie Dinsmore*. As described by the irrepressible Jo (who was Louisa May Alcott herself), the March family were real people who faced genteel poverty with humor and fortitude. Louisa May Alcott didn't preach moral platitudes, but described the joys, the trials, and the fun of growing up in a loving family. Jo, one of the first tomboys in children's literature, hates the false Victorian standards of the day. When her older sister Meg tells her that she should remember she is a young lady, this follows:

"I'm not! and if turning up my hair makes me one, I'll wear it in two tails till I'm twenty," cried Jo, pull-

[16]Cornelia Meigs, et al., *A Critical History of Children's Literature,* rev. ed. (New York: Macmillan, 1969), p. 158.

The first edition of *Little Women* (published as a single book in 1869) was illustrated by May Alcott, the author's sister.

The Walter Havighurst Special Collections, Miami University Libraries, Oxford, Ohio.

Jessie Wilcox Smith pictured slightly older *Little Women* for the eight full-color illustrations which she painted in oils for the popular 1915 edition.

ing off her net and shaking down a chestnut mane. "I hate to think I've got to grow up and be Miss March, and wear long gowns and look prim as a China-aster. It's bad enough to be a girl, anyway, when I like boys' games and work and manners!"[17]

Little Women was not an immediate success with the critics of the time. One of the first reviewers wrote: "They [*Little Women* was originally two books] are not religious books, should not be read on Sunday, and are not appropriate for the

Sunday School. This is the character of the book before us. It is lively, entertaining, and not harmful."[18]

Children loved it and have read it every day including Sundays since its publication. The first edition of Volume I of *Little Women* (it ended before Beth's death) was sold out within two months of printing. The publisher asked for a second volume, which was ready the next year. Later the two books were combined into one.

Little Men and *Jo's Boys* were sequels to this

[17]Louisa May Alcott, *Little Women* (Boston: Little, Brown and Company, 1868; 1922), p. 3.

[18]Lavinia Russ, "Not to Be Read on Sunday," Centenary of *Little Women*, 1868–1968. *The Horn Book Magazine*, vol. 44 (October, 1968), pp. 521–526.

American family classic. Still loved today, *Little Women* has been translated into many languages throughout the world including Russian, Arabic, Bengali, and Urdu. Fortunately Thomas Niles, Alcott's Boston publisher, persuaded her to take a royalty on her books rather than the usual lump sum for the copyright. Within two years of publication of *Little Women*, Louisa May Alcott had paid off all the family debts, some of which were twenty-five years old. Never again would her family have to endure "genteel poverty."

Another vivacious heroine appeared in the celebrated Katy stories written by Susan Coolidge (pseudonym of Sarah Chauncey Woolsey). This series included such titles as *What Katy Did* (1872), *What Katy Did at School* (1873), and *What Katy Did Next* (1886). Susan Coolidge also wrote many other stories. Harriet Lathrop, under the pseudonym Margaret Sidney, presented a lively family story about a widowed mother and her *Five Little Peppers* in a series starting in 1881 and concluding in 1916 with *Our Davie Pepper*.

Other authors wrote dramatic family stories with foreign settings. In *Hans Brinker: or the Silver Skates*, Mary Mapes Dodge gave accurate glimpses of Dutch life in 1865. The skating race is actually less important than the daring brain surgery performed on Father Brinker, who had been nearly an idiot for several years after an accident. The bravery and courage of Hans and his sister in facing poverty, scorn, and their father's illness provided further examples for child behavior.

Johanna Spyri's well-loved *Heidi* was translated from the German by Louise Brooks and published in this country in 1884. Not only did readers share the joys and sorrows of Heidi's life with her grandfather; they "breathed" the clear mountain air and "lived" in Switzerland.

Frances Hodgson Burnett described family conflict within the English aristocracy in *Little Lord Fauntleroy* (1886). Although born in England, Mrs. Burnett was an American citizen. The well-known English historian of children's literature F. J. Harvey Darton said in 1932, "It [*Little Lord Fauntleroy*] ran through England like a sickly fever. Nine editions were published in as many months, and the odious little prig in the lace collar is not dead yet."[19] Burnett's second book, *Sara Crewe* (1888), told of the pitiful plight of a wealthy pupil who is orphaned and reduced to servitude in a boarding school. Its Cinderella ending delights children and adults, and it was made into a very successful play. Mrs. Burnett then expanded the play into a longer novel under the title *The Little Princess* (1905). As recently as 1981 there was a new edition of *Sara Crewe*, illustrated with appropriate Dickensian pictures by Margot Tomes. Mrs. Burnett's best-written and most popular book is *The Secret Garden* (1910), which presents an exciting plot in a mysterious setting. This story depicts the gradual change wrought in two lonely and selfish children by a hidden garden and the wholesome influence of the boy Dickon. It is still read and loved by children today.

Tales of Adventure

The rise of family stories and series books for girls prompted more attention to tales of adventures and the development of so-called "boys' series." The best known of the Robinsonades, *The Swiss Family Robinson*, was written by Johann David Wyss, a Swiss pastor, and translated into English in 1814. Inaccurate in its description of flora and fauna (almost everything grew on that tropical island), it still delighted children's imaginations. Sir Walter Scott's novels *Rob Roy* (1818) and *Ivanhoe* (1820), while intended for adults, were frequently appropriated by young people. James Fenimore Cooper's Leatherstocking novels of exciting tales of Indians and pioneers in North America were avidly read by young and old alike. The bloody incidents and tragedy of *The Last of the Mohicans* (1826) brought a sense of tingling adventure to all readers. Richard Henry Dana's *Two Years Before the Mast* (1840) describes the author's own adventures as a young seaman sailing around Cape Horn to California. Again written for adults, it provided adventure for children.

An Englishman, Captain Frederick Marryat, had written sea adventures for adults. In an attempt to correct the many errors in principles of navigation and geography which he found in *The Swiss Family Robinson*, he began a series of sea adventures with *The Naval Officer; or Frank Mildmay*, published in 1829. His juvenile adventures included *Masterman Ready* written in three volumes between 1841 and 1842. Unfortunately, he revert-

[19]Darton, pp. 232–233.

ed to the lecture approach used by Thomas Day in *Sandford and Merton* as Masterman Ready instructed *Mr. Midshipman Easy* (1836) on the principles of seamanship. In 1856 another Englishman, Robert Ballantyne, began his series of nearly eighty books with an account of his fur-trading experiences in *The Young Fur Traders*. George A. Henty, an English war correspondent for many years, was determined that English boys should know the military history of the British Empire. *Under Drake's Flag* (1883) ends with the defeat of the Spanish Armada, while *By Pike and Dyke* (1889) details the sieges of Holland and tells of William of Orange. His military history was accurate in the almost ninety books he wrote. However, his characters never changed, as if the same persons were experiencing the wars of all centuries.

These British writers, Marryat, Ballantyne, and Henty, were read with enthusiasm by American children. At the same time the American names Horatio Alger, Oliver Optic, and Harry Castlemon were well known to English readers. The emphasis in American series was more on achievement by the individual, usually against unbelievable odds. The stories by Horatio Alger epitomized this rags-to-riches theme. In fact, since his first successful novel *Ragged Dick* (1868) was based on this formula, he saw no reason to change it in the more than a hundred books that followed. The final paragraph of *Struggling Upwards* presents the theme that was the basis for most of his stories:

> So closes an eventful passage in the life of Luke Larkin. He has struggled upward from a boyhood of privation and self-denial into a youth and manhood of prosperity and honor. There has been some luck about it, I admit, but after all he is indebted for most of his good fortune to his own good qualities. [20]

Oliver Optic was the pen name of William Adams, a New England teacher and principal who wrote such series as *The Yacht-Club Series* (1854), *The Army and Navy Series* (1865), and *The Starry Flag Series* (1867). His stories were lively and well told, and his readers learned some science and geogra-

phy as they traveled with his heroes through more than one hundred of his books.

Harry Castlemon (pseudonym of Charles Austin Fosdick) based his book *Frank on a Gunboat* (1864) on his own experiences in the Civil War. He wrote some fifty-eight more volumes in his Gunboat, Rocky Mountain, Sportsman Club, Boy Trapper, Rod and Gun, and Pony Express series. His stories were exciting, as incident followed incident. He is quoted as saying: "Boys don't like fine writing. What they want is adventure, and the more of it you can get into 250 pages of manuscript, the better fellow you are." [21]

Though most of these series books provided plenty of adventure, the characters and plots tended to be rather superficial and predictable. However, there was one superb adventure story written during the last half of the nineteenth century that included not only a bloody, exciting, and tightly drawn plot but also well-depicted characters. This was Robert Louis Stevenson's *Treasure Island*, serialized in an English magazine called *Young Folks* in 1881 and 1882; it was published in book form in 1883. For the first time adults were drawn to a children's book of adventure rather than children reading adults' books. *Treasure Island* was an immediate success. As Meigs has said, "It is no wonder this book made Stevenson a popular author. It appealed to boys and to the eternal boy in men; to the story-loving spirit which had treasured the chapbooks and perpetuated folk literature by word of mouth for generation after generation." [22]

Other books written for boys changed in their manner. Little prigs became real live boys. Thomas Bailey Aldrich's *The Story of a Bad Boy* (1870) was based on his own life in Portsmouth, New Hampshire. The tale of this Tom's pranks and good times paved the way for another story of a real boy's adventures in Hannibal, Missouri. *The Adventures of Tom Sawyer* was published in 1876 by Mark Twain (pseudonym of Samuel Clemens). This book was soon followed by that American classic *The Adventures of Huckleberry Finn* (1884). Mark Twain combined realism, humor, and adventure in these realistic portrayals of grow-

[20]Horatio Alger, Jr., *Struggling Upwards; or Luke Larkin's Luck* (New York: Superior Printing, n.d.), p. 280.

[21]Jacob Blanck, compiler, *Harry Castlemon: Boys' Own Author* (New York: R. R. Bowker, 1941), pp. 5–6.

[22]Meigs, p. 306.

ing up in a small town near the end of the nineteenth century. While *Huckleberry Finn* has won literary acclaim, children prefer *The Adventures of Tom Sawyer*. This seems only natural, since Tom's adventures involve children their age.

The beginnings of science-fiction adventure stories came to us from France in the translations of Jules Verne's *Journey to the Center of the Earth* (1864), *Twenty Thousand Leagues Under the Sea* (1869), and *Around the World in Eighty Days* (1872). Modern readers may be surprised to note the early dates of these books.

Animal Stories

In *A Dog of Flanders and Other Stories* (1872), Louise de la Ramee presented a collection of stories which included the sad tale of a Belgian work dog and his friend, a boy artist. It has been considered the first modern dog story. *Black Beauty* appeared in 1877 as a protest against cruel treatment of horses. Children skipped the lectures calling for more humane treatment of animals and read the compelling first-person story of the life of Black Beauty. Some children today continue to enjoy Anna Sewell's rather over-drawn and sentimental tale. Rudyard Kipling's *The Jungle Books* (1894–1895) were exciting animal stories. Many children know the story of Mowgli, a child raised by a wolf family, a bear, and a panther.

Ernest Thompson Seton's own drawings and sketches added much to children's enjoyment of *Wild Animals I Have Known* (1898). This book presented true and interesting information in the form of "personal" histories of eight animals and became the forerunner of the modern books written about one animal.

The Rise of Fantasy and Humor

Although many of the early titles of books for children included the word "amusing," their main purpose was to instruct or moralize. Undoubtedly, children enjoyed the broad humor in some of the folktales and the nonsense in Mother Goose, but few books used humor or nonsense before the middle of the nineteenth century.

The first stirrings of modern fantasy may be seen in a tale written by an English clergyman and scientist in 1863. *The Water Babies* by Charles Kingsley is a strange mixture of the fanciful over-laden with heavy doses of morality. It is a story of a chimney sweep who has become a water baby with gills. Hidden within this little tale was Kingsley's social concern for the plight of the chimney sweeps, plus his attempt to reconcile the new science (Darwin's *Origin of the Species* had been published in 1859) with his religious belief that salvation can be obtained through love and compassion as easily as through punishment. Obviously, children were intrigued by the story and not its moral lessons. They probably skipped over the following passage or created their own meanings for the lessons of Mrs. Doasyouwouldbedoneby:

> . . . for you must know and believe that people's souls make their bodies just as a snail makes its shell (I am not joking, my little man; I am in serious solemn earnest). And therefore, when Tom's soul grew all prickly with naughty tempers, his body could not help growing prickly too, so that nobody would cuddle him or play with him, or even like to look at him.[23]

On a summer day in 1862 an Oxford professor of mathematics, Charles Dodgson, told a story to three little girls on a picnic. According to Meigs, this "was the real beginning of modern literature for children."[24] For the tale that was told was about Alice, who followed a White Rabbit down a rabbit hole and found herself a part of a remarkable adventure. At the children's request, Dodgson wrote that story as *Alice's Adventures Underground* and presented it to his young friends as a Christmas gift in 1864. At the insistence of others, he decided to have it published. By 1865 the artist Tenniel had completed the drawings, and *Alice's Adventures in Wonderland*, published under the pseudonym of Lewis Carroll, was ready for the host of readers to come. What made this story absolutely unique for its time was that it contained not a trace of a lesson or a moral. It was really told first, and then written, purely for enjoyment. And it has delighted both children and adults ever since. Allusions to this book and its companion ti-

[23]Charles Kingsley, *The Water Babies* (New York: Platt and Munk, 1863; 1900), p. 149.
[24]Meigs, p. 194.

Although many artists (including Lewis Carroll, himself) have illustrated *Alice in Wonderland*, it is Tenniel who created the most familiar image of the Mad Hatter and The Dormouse.

tle, *Through the Looking-Glass* (1871), have become a part of our everyday speech: "jam tomorrow and jam yesterday—but never jam today"; "curiouser and curiouser"; "much of a muchness"; "begin at the beginning, then go on until you've come to the end: then stop;" "I've believed as many as six impossible things before breakfast"; "O frabjous day," and many more.

Other well-known fantasies were published near the end of the century. George MacDonald was a friend of Lewis Carroll's; in fact he was one of the persons who had urged the publication of Alice. However, his own "invented fairy-tale" *At The Back of the North Wind* (1871) has much more of the sad spiritual quality found in many of Hans Christian Andersen's fairy tales than the mad inconsistencies of the world of Lewis Carroll. MacDonald's other works include *The Princess and the Goblin* (1872) and *The Princess and Curdie* (1883). "The Light Princess" and "The Golden Key" are well-known stories from his other books.

The Adventures of Pinocchio by Carlo Collodi first appeared in a Rome children's newspaper in 1881. Translated into many languages, it was issued in English in 1891 under the title *The Story of a Puppet*, but the title was soon changed back to the original *Pinocchio*. Children still enjoy this story of the mischievous puppet whose nose grew longer with each lie he told the Blue Fairy. Collodi's real name was Carlos Lorenzini.

The prototype for Mary Poppins, Amelia Bedelia, Miss Pickerell, and all the other eccentric women characters in children's literature may be found in the nonsensical antics of Mrs. Peterkin and her family. Published in 1880 by Lucretia Hale, *The Peterkin Papers* provided children with real humor. One of the most amusing stories, "The Lady Who Put Salt in her Coffee," appeared in a juvenile magazine as early as 1868. The antics of the Peterkin family were just as exaggerated and as much fun in 1880 as McCloskey's *Homer Price* was in the 1940s. In this story, Mrs. Peterkin mistakenly substitutes salt for sugar in her coffee. The whole family troops to the chemist and the herb lady to find out what to do. Finally "the lady from Philadelphia" provides the answer—make another cup of coffee!

Also in the category of books for fun may be included the many books with movable parts. Harlequinades, or turn-ups, first appeared in 1766. They consisted of pages of pictures that could be raised or lowered to create other scenes. Later (from the 1840s through the 1890s) pictures were made like Venetian blinds to create another scene. Circular wheels could be turned to provide more action, and whole pop-up scenes created miniature stages. A revival of interest in these books with movable parts may be seen in the number of them that have been reissued in the 1980s. *The Children's Theatre*, for example, shows four scenes of Little Red Riding Hood, Hansel and Gretel, the Nativity scene, and one of a family around a Christmas tree. This book, created by Franz Bonn of Germany in 1878, was reissued by the Viking Press one hundred years later, in 1978. Three books first published in England by Ernest Nister in the 1890s, *Revolving Pictures, Merry Magic Go Round* (first published under the title *Merry Surprises*), and *The Great Panorama Picture Book*, have all been reissued in the 1980s. Children today are as intrigued with the format of these books as children were a hundred years ago.

Poetry

Poetry for children began to flourish in the nineteenth century. In the first part of the century, poetry, like prose, reflected the influence of religion and moral didacticism. The Taylor sisters, Ann and Jane, emphasized polite behavior, morals, and death in the poetry included in their first book, *Original Poems for Infant Minds* (1804). While

Jane Taylor wrote the often parodied "Twinkle Twinkle Little Star" for this collection and Ann provided the lovely "Welcome, welcome little stranger, to this busy world of care," the book also included such a morbid poem as this example:

> You are not so healthy and gay
> So young, so active and bright,
> That death cannot snatch you away,
> Or some dread accident smite.
>
> Here lie both the young and the old,
> Confined in the coffin so small
> The earth covers over them cold,
> The grave-worms devour them all.

William Roscoe's *The Butterfly's Ball and the Grasshopper's Feast* (1807) provided pure nonsense, rhyme, and rhythm that delighted children. There were no moral lessons here, just an invitation: "Come take up your hats and away let us haste / To the Butterfly's Ball and the Grasshopper's Feast. . . ." The arrival of each guest was illustrated by copper engravings of a "snail person" or a "bumble bee child" by William Mulready. Roscoe, an historian and botanist, wrote the book for the pleasure of his own child. It was so fresh and different that it generated many imitations.

Clement Moore, a professor who also wrote to please his own children, gave the world the Christmas classic, *A Visit from St. Nicholas*. One of the first American contributions to a joyous literature for children, it was published with this title in 1823, but is now known as *The Night before Christmas*. Tasha Tudor, Michael Hague, and Tomie de Paola have all created beautifully illustrated editions of this well-loved poem for today's children. Tomie de Paola has also illustrated a new edition of *Mary Had a Little Lamb*, first written by Sarah Josepha Hale in 1830. In 1837 the poem was included in McGuffey's reader and recited by generations of American school children.

Dr. Heinrich Hoffman's *Struwwelpeter* was translated from the German in about 1848. These cautionary tales in verse about "Shock-Headed Peter," who wouldn't comb his hair or cut his nails, Harriet who played with fire, and Augustus, who would not eat his nasty soup until he became as "thin as a thread / and the fifth day was dead,"

There was an Old Man on whose nose, most birds
of the air could repose;
But they all flew away at the closing of day,
Which relieved that Old Man and his nose.

Edward Lear's laughable limericks and humorous illustrations in *A Book of Nonsense* are over one hundred
years old but they are still enjoyed today.

were meant to frighten children into good behavior. Instead, they loved the pictures and gruesome
verse. Surely these poems are the forerunners of
some of the modern verse by Shel Silverstein and
Jack Prelutsky.

The century's greatest contribution to lasting
poetry was the nonsense verse of Edward Lear.
Here was a poet who, like Lewis Carroll, wrote
only to entertain. Lear was by profession a
landscape painter and illustrator. He wrote his first
book, *A Book of Nonsense*, in 1846 for his child
friends, while *More Nonsense* (1872) appeared six
years later. Generations have delighted in "The
Pobble Who Has No Toes," "The Dong with the
Luminous Nose," the elderly "Quangle Wangle,"
and "The Owl and the Pussycat." Lear did not invent the limerick, but he certainly became master
of the form. His black-line illustrations are as clever as his poetry.

Most of Lewis Carroll's nonsense verse is included in *Alice's Adventures in Wonderland* and
Through the Looking-Glass. Many of Carroll's
poems were parodies of the popular poems of his
time. "The Lobster Quadrille" mimics Mary Howitt's "The Spider and the Fly," "Father William"
copies Southey's "The Old Man's Comforts,"
while "How Doth the Little Crocodile" parodies
Watt's "How Doth the Busy Bee." Interest in the

original poems has all but disappeared, but the
parodies continue to delight. "Jabberwocky" is a
"made language" of portmanteau words—namely,
combining the meaning and parts of two words to
create a new one "Slithy," for example, carries the
combined meaning of lithe and slimy, while "mim-
sy" is both flimsy and miserable. The sound and
play of words must have fascinated Carroll, for his
poems and books abound with puns, double meanings, coined words, and wonderful nonsense.

Some of Christina Rossetti's poetry is reminiscent of Mother Goose, such as the well-loved
"Mix a pancake / Stir a pancake / Pop it in the
pan; / Fry the pancake / Toss the pancake / Catch it
if you can." Others such as "Who has seen the
wind?" gave children vivid descriptions of the
world around them. Many poems from her book
Sing Song (1872) are found in anthologies today.
Her long poem *Goblin Market* (1864) has appeared as a separately illustrated book.

William Allingham's name is always associated
with the poem "The Fairies" which begins "Up the
airy mountain, / Down the rushy glen, / We daren't
go a hunting, / For fear of little men." It appeared
in his book *In Fairyland* (1870), which was beautifully illustrated in colored pictures by Richard
Doyle. Allingham's *Ballad Book*, published in
1865, contained "Fourscore of the best of the old
ballads," as stated in his preface. John Greenleaf
Whittier included some of his own poems but also
some by Blake, Shakespeare, Tennyson, Keats,
Shelley, Browning, and Wordsworth in his anthology *Child Life, A Collection of Poems* (1871). He
thought children were capable of understanding
poetry of literary merit.

The century ended with a unique volume of poetry that celebrated the everyday life and thought
of the child. *A Child's Garden of Verses* (1885) by
Robert Louis Stevenson was first published under
the title *Penny Whistles*. Stevenson was a poet who
could enter the child's imagining in such well-
loved poems as "My Shadow," "Bed in Summer,"
"The Swing," "Windy Nights," and "My Bed Is a
Boat." He was the first to discover joy in child's
play.

Two American poets were writing for children
at the close of the nineteenth century. Eugene
Field's *Poems of Childhood* (1896) included "The
Sugar Plum Tree" and "The Duel." James
Whitcomb Riley employed dialect as he described

local incidents and Indiana farm life. This Hoosier dialect has made most of his poems seem obsolete except "Little Orphant Annie" and "The Raggedy Man," which continue to give children pleasure.

Magazines

Magazines formed a significant part of the literature for children in the last half of the nineteenth century. The first magazines for English children, which grew out of the Sunday School movement, were pious indeed. *The Child's Companion* was one of these which continued into the twentieth century. The first true children's magazine for English children appeared in 1853 under the title of *Charm*. It was ahead of its time, however, stating that there would always be room for stories of the little people or fairies on its pages; it lasted only two years. Charlotte Yonge's own stories appeared in her magazine titled *The Monthly Packet*. Mrs. Gatty and her daughter, Julia Horatio Ewing, contributed to this magazine until Mrs. Gatty herself started *Aunt Judy's Magazine* in 1866. The whole Gatty family worked on this, with Dr. Gatty writing articles from time to time, their son setting some of the poems to music, and Mrs. Ewing serving as a regular contributor. This magazine began the policy of reviewing children's books, reporting enthusiastically on *Alice's Adventures in Wonderland* and Hans Christian Andersen's stories.

The first magazine planned for children in America, *The Juvenile Miscellany*, appeared under the editorship of Lydia Maria Child in 1826. Child was a former teacher who wanted to provide enjoyable material for children to read. The magazine was very successful until Child, an ardent abolitionist, spoke out against slavery. Sales dropped immediately, and the magazine stopped publication in 1834. Frank Leslie's *Chatterbox* advertised that its "policy was to improve the mind, diffuse knowledge." It lasted for only seven years, from 1879 to 1886. *Our Young Folks*, edited by Lucy Larcom in Boston, lasted only eight years. Her literary taste was excellent; Dickens' "The Magic Fishbone" appeared in it in 1868 and Thomas Bailey Aldrich's *The Story of a Bad Boy* was first serialized in it in 1869. *Our Young Folks* was sold to Scribner's and became part of the famous *St. Nicholas Magazine* in 1874. Horace

Arthur Rackham has many imitators among today's illustrators, but few have ever been able to equal his ability to create imaginative worlds of gnomes and anthropomorphized trees. From *Mother Goose*.

Scudder edited *The Riverside Magazine* for only three years, from 1867 to 1870. However, he was a moving force for literature for children and wrote true criticism of books and articles on children's reading. *The Youth's Companion* survived the longest of all the children's magazines in America, beginning in 1827 and merging with *The American Boy* in 1929, which in turn ceased publication in 1941. It published such well-known writers as Kipling, Oliver Wendell Holmes, Jack London, Mark Twain, and Theodore Roosevelt, among others. *The Youth's Companion* had a definite editorial policy. It proposed to "exile death from its pages"; tobacco and alcohol were not to be mentioned, and love figured in some of the stories only after 1890. Part of the popularity of this magazine may be attributed to the inviting premiums that were offered each week.

In 1873 Mary Mapes Dodge, author of *Hans Brinker, or the Silver Skates*, became editor of the most famous magazine for children, *St. Nicholas*. The publisher announced that in this magazine "there must be entertainment, no less than information; the spirit of laughter would be evoked; there would be 'no sermonizing, no wearisome spinning out of facts, no rattling of dry bones of history,' while all priggishness was condemned."[25] A promising young writer, Frank Stockton, became Dodge's assistant, and together they published a magazine that would become known throughout the English-speaking world. They attracted such well-known artists and writers as Arthur Rackham, Reginald Birch, Howard Pyle, Frances Hodgson Burnett, Rudyard Kipling, Robert Louis Stevenson, and Louisa May Alcott, among others. Many of the novels which were first serialized in *St. Nicholas Magazine* were published as books and became classics of their day. These included Louisa May Alcott's *An Old Fashioned Girl* (1870), *Jo's Boys* (1873), Frances Hodgson Burnett's *Little Lord Fauntleroy* (1886) and *Sara Crewe* (1888), Rudyard Kipling's *The Jungle Book*, and many others. This magazine guided children's reading for over three quarters of a century and set standards of excellence for the whole publishing field.

Illustrators of the Nineteenth Century

During the nineteenth century illustrators of children's books began to achieve as much recognition as the authors. In the early part of the century, crude woodcuts were still being used, illustrators were not identified, and pictures were frequently interchanged among books. Gradually, however, several outstanding artists emerged as illustrators of children's books. George Cruikshank was an engraver who illustrated the English edition of *Grimm's Fairy Tales* in 1823 with tiny detailed pictures which portrayed much action and humor, real characters, and spritely elves and fairies. His interpretations were so appropriate

and seemed so much a part of these tales that they were republished in Germany with the original text. In 1853–1854 he published four volumes of his *Fairy Library*, which contain some of his best artwork. Unfortunately, he altered some of the stories to conform to what he called certain "temperance truths." For example, after the marriage contract is signed, Cinderella's godmother begs the king not to serve wine at the celebration, saying ". . . your Majesty is aware that this same drink leads also to quarrels, brutal fights, and violent death."[26] Cruikshank was a friend of Dickens and his most famous illustrator, although they had a falling-out over Cruikshank's rewriting of these tales. Fortunately, he is remembered for his enchanting illustrations, not his rewritten texts.

The three best-known illustrators of the nineteenth century are Walter Crane, Randolph Caldecott, and Kate Greenaway. All three were fortunate indeed to have Edmund Evans, the best color printer in England, as their engraver. Walter Crane, the son of a portrait painter, knew that Evans wanted to print some quality illustrated books for children, something that interested Crane also. Crane created beautifully designed pictures for four nursery-rhyme books, *Sing a Song of Sixpence*, *The House That Jack Built*, *Dame Trot and Her Comical Cat*, and *The History of Cock Robin and Jenny Wren*. Evans and Crane convinced Warne to publish these high-quality "Toy Books" during the years 1865–1866. They were very successful, and Crane went on to design some thirty-five other picture books, including two well-known nursery-rhyme collections with music and illustrations. These were titled *The Baby's Opera* (1877) and *The Baby's Bouquet* (1878). Crane had a strong sense of design and paid particular attention to the total format of the book, including the placement of the text, the quality of the paper, even the design at the beginning and end of chapters. He characteristically used flat colors with a firm black outline for his pictures. His pages were usually decorated with elaborate borders. He made a point of studying the Victorian child's attitude toward art, saying: "Like the An-

[25]Alice M. Jordan, *From Rollo to Tom Sawyer* (Boston: Horn Book, 1948), p. 134.

[26]George Cruikshank, *George Cruikshank's Fairy Library; Cinderella and The Glass Slipper* (London: D. Bogue, 1853).

Without alerting Joan, the French had attacked the English bastion of Saint-Loup. The attack failed; the French were retreating in disorder. Joan rushed up, rallied them, and led them once more to the very foot of the bastion. The English, under their commander Talbot, fought back desperately for three hours, but despite their resistance the French overcame them and captured the bastion.

The extraordinary illustrations of Maurice Boutet de Monvel for the picture book of *Joan of Arc* created in 1896 had a pervasive influence on the children's books that followed.

cient Egyptians, children appear to see most things in profile and like definite statements in design. They prefer well-defined forms and frank colour. They don't want to bother about three dimensions."[27]

The picture books by Randolph Caldecott established new standards of illustration for children's books, His drawings were filled with action, joy of living, and good fun. His love of animals and the English countryside is reflected in the illustrations that seem to convey much meaning through a few lines. Although Caldecott, like Crane, illustrated many books, he is best remembered for his series of picture books that included such titles as *The House That Jack Built* (1878), *The Diverting History of John Gilpin* (1878), *Sing a Song of Sixpence* (1880), and *Hey Diddle Diddle Picture Book* (1883). On the Caldecott medal for distinguished illustrations there is a reproduction of one of his pictures taken from John Gilpin's ride,

[27]As quoted by Bryan Holme in his Preface to *An Alphabet of Old Friends and the Absurd ABC* by Walter Crane (New York: The Metropolitan Museum of Art, 1981), unpaged.

a reminder of this famous illustrator of the nineteenth century.

Kate Greenaway's name brings visions of English gardens; delicate, prim figures; and the special style of costume on her rather fragile children. Her art defined the fanciful world of Victorian sentimentality. After the publication of her first book *Under the Window* (1878), it became the fashion to dress children in Greenaway costumes with large floppy hats. Greeting cards, wallpaper, and even china were made with designs copied after Greenaway. Her best-known works include *Marigold Garden* (1885), *A Apple Pie* (1886), and *The Pied Piper of Hamelin* (1888). The Kate Greenaway Medal, similar to our Caldecott Medal, is given each year to the most distinguished British picture book.

From France came the remarkable work of Maurice Boutet de Monvel. An academic painter, he had done some illustrating for magazines and two children's books written by Anatole France. He had also illustrated some selections from La Fontaine's fables. But the work for which he is remembered are the superb pictures for *Jeanne d'Arc*, which he wrote and illustrated in 1896. The power of these paintings—the massed groupings of men and horses and the mob scenes in which every person is an individual, yet the focus is always on the Maid of Orleans—made this a distinctive book for young and old alike. It was translated into English in 1897. This book was reissued in 1980 by Viking Press in cooperation with the Pierpont Morgan Library.

In America, Howard Pyle was writing and illustrating his version of *The Merry Adventures of Robin Hood of Great Renown* (1883), *Pepper and Salt* (1886), and *The Wonder Clock* (1888). He created *real* people in his illustrations for these collections of folktales and legends. His characters from the Middle Ages were strong; the life of the times was portrayed with interesting clear detail. In 1903, he published the first of four volumes of *The Story of King Arthur and His Knights*, reissued by Scribner in 1984. Pyle also illustrated and wrote for *Scribner's Monthly Magazine* and *St. Nicholas*. Another of his important contributions was establishing classes for illustrators of children's books. Some of his students included N. C. Wyeth, Maxfield Parrish, and Jessie Wilcox Smith, all of whom became well-known illustrators in the twentieth century.

By the close of the nineteenth century, children's literature was alive and flourishing. Pious, moralistic, didactic books were no longer being written. Gone were the make-believe accounts of impossible children. In their place were real live persons living in fun-loving families. Pure nonsense and the fanciful were welcomed in both poetry and fantasy. The old folktales and the fairies were accepted once again. Children's books were more beautiful, with illustrations by recognized artists. A few magazines had given consideration to the place of literary criticism. Much would need to be done to bring books to all children in the next century, but a literature for children, designed to bring them joy and happiness, was now firmly in place.

CHILDREN'S LITERATURE: THE TWENTIETH CENTURY

If the nineteenth century saw the firm establishment of a literature for children, the twentieth may be characterized by the recognition of literary and artistic quality in children's books, the growth of children's book departments in publishing houses, and the expansion of both public and school library service to all children. Technological improvements made it possible to create beautifully illustrated well-bound books for children and just as easy to mass-produce shoddy cheap editions. The picture book as we know it today was created early in this century, as well as fine informational books for all ages.

Recognition of Children's Literature

Disturbed by the influence of the fifty-cent juvenile, Franklin K. Mathiews, Chief Scout Librarian, sought to raise the level of reading for children. His suggestion for establishing a Children's Book Week was promoted in 1919 by Frederick Melcher as a project of the American Booksellers Association. Schools, libraries, newspapers, and bookstores supported the event, which became a significant stimulant to the development of children's literature. In 1945 the Children's Book Council was established to promote Book Week and to distribute information on children's books throughout the year.

Melcher also promoted another event that has encouraged the development of children's literature. He proposed the presentation of an annual award for the most distinguished book for children. Initiated in 1922, the Newbery Medal was the first award in the world to be given for "distinguished contribution to literature for children." The Caldecott Medal for the most distinguished picture book of the year was first given in 1938. Both these awards have had great influence in raising the standards of writing and illustrating in children's books. They also gave prestige to the idea of creating books for children. An international award, The Hans Christian Andersen Award, was established in 1956 and is given every two years to a living author for his or her complete body of work. Starting in 1966, an artist was also recognized.

The addition of children's departments to publishing firms indicated the growing importance of literature for the young. In 1919 Macmillan made Louise Seaman children's editor, and other companies were soon to follow this innovation. May Massee became editor of children's books at Doubleday in 1922. The first critical reviews of children's books appeared in *The Bookman* in 1918. Anne Carroll Moore continued this influential work in her *New York Herald Tribune* column, "The Three Owls." *The Horn Book Magazine*, a publication solely devoted to children's literature, was first published in 1924 under the editorship of Bertha Mahony.

Public libraries instituted children's rooms and many elementary schools had libraries. By 1915 the American Library Association had established a School Library division. However, it was not until the enactment of The Elementary and Secondary Education Act of 1965 that the concept of school library media centers for *every* elementary school seemed a viable possibility.

The Junior Literary Guild was established in 1929 and was the first to send children selected books each month. In the late 1950s paperback book clubs made it possible for more children to own books and increased their enthusiasm for reading. Currently, many book clubs offer selections of children's literature.

The Rise of the Picture Book

One of the best-loved stories of all time is *The Tale of Peter Rabbit*, who appeared in Mr. MacGregor's garden at the turn of the century. After writing it in a letter to the ill son of a former governess, Beatrix Potter enlarged the story and submitted it to Warne Publishers. When they rejected it, she had it published privately in 1901. Warne finally accepted and published *The Tale of Peter Rabbit* in 1902. Potter later introduced stories of many other animals, such as Jemima Puddleduck, Benjamin Bunny, and Mrs. Tittlemouse, but the cottontail family is the best known and loved. Unfortunately, the books were not copyrighted in this country and so Peter Rabbit was pirated extensively and appeared with unattractive copied illustrations. A new edition of Potter's stories with illustrations by the English artist Allen Atkinson was published in 1983, but Beatrix Potter's own pictures are so right, so all of a piece with the stories, so timeless, that it seems almost a travesty to try to reinterpret them today.

At the same time that Potter was writing and illustrating, Leslie Brooke was creating wonderfully humorous pictures for his nursery-rhyme picture books. No one could draw such expressive faces on pigs as Brooke did in *This Little Pig Went to Market*, which first appeared in *The Golden Goose Book* (1905). Brooke added whimsical details to his illustrations like a picture of "Home Sweet Home" hanging inside the pigs' house showing a mother pig and her little ones. Leslie Brooke's animals in the popular *Johnny Crow's Garden* (1903) were costumed and personified. They included the lion with "green and yellow tie on" and the bear in his striped pants and tailcoat. Children still love the three Johnny Crow stories with their nonsensical verse.

The other well-known English illustrator of this period was Arthur Rackham. He is recognized for the imaginative detail of his pictures, which frequently portrayed grotesque people and humanlike trees evoking an eerie atmosphere. His illustrations for *Mother Goose* (1913) show imaginative elves and gnomes hiding under mushrooms and in

"If we only had a cat!" sighed the very old woman.
"A cat?" asked the very old man.
"Yes, a sweet little fluffy cat," said the very old woman.
"I will get you a cat, my dear," said the very old man.

And he set out over the hills to look for one. He climbed over the sunny hills. He trudged through the cool valleys. He walked a long, long time and at last he came to a hill which was quite covered with cats.

Wanda Gág's delightful tale *Millions of Cats,* published in 1928, has been called the first American picture storybook.

the roots of trees. He illustrated many other books, including Hans Christian Andersen's *Fairy Tales, Cinderella, Peter Pan in Kensington Gardens, Aesop's Fables,* and many more.

For many years these English books, along with those of Caldecott, Crane, and Greenaway, supplied the American picture-book market. There was much rejoicing, then, when in 1923 C. B. Falls' *ABC Book* with its boldly colored woodcuts was published in this country. Only a few persons knew that it was a rather poor copy of William Nicholson's *Alphabet* (1898) and his *Square Book of Animals,*[28] both published in England.

William Nicholson is credited with creating the first true picture book, *Clever Bill,* published in England in 1926 and in New York in 1927. Farrar, Straus reissued this book in 1972, including the following statement by Maurice Sendak on the jacket flap: "*Clever Bill,* I have long felt, is among the few perfect picture books ever created for children." At the most the text of this book is only two long run-on sentences, while the illustrations carry the story of the little girl who goes to visit her aunt and leaves her favorite toy soldier at home. The toy runs after her and is "just in time to

meet her train at Dover. 'Clever Bill.' " Wanda Gág's delightful tale *Millions of Cats,* published in 1928, has been called the first American picture storybook. This is an outstanding example of how text and pictures work together to provide the unfolding drama of the journey of a very old man in search of the most beautiful cat in the world. The long horizontal format enabled Gág to spread the journey over both pages. The traditional type tale with its repetition and refrain of "hundreds of cats, thousands of cats, millions and billions and trillions of cats" is still popular with children today. It opened the door to what was to become a treasure house of beauty and enjoyment for children, the modern picture book.

Progressive education and the growth of the nursery school movement made an impact on the development of books for the pre-school child. Lucy Sprague Mitchell of the Bank Street School (first called the Bureau for Educational Experiment) published her *Here and Now Story Book* in 1921. She pointed out the young child's preoccupation with self and interest in daily experiences. Her collection of stories provided simple little tales of the small child's everyday activities; none of them have lasted. However, she did conduct classes on writing for children, and Margaret Wise Brown attended these classes. When William Scott and his partner decided to start a new firm to pub-

[28]See discussion and illustrations in Barbara Bader's *American Picture Books From Noah's Ark to the Beast Within* (New York: Macmillan Publishing Company, 1976), p. 24.

lish books just for the very young child, Mrs. Mitchell recommended that they contact Margaret Wise Brown. Their first success and breakthrough book for young children was *The Noisy Book* (1939). In this story a little dog Muffin has bandaged eyes and must guess at the noises he hears, and so must the child listening to the story. These books (there were some seven in the series) invited participation by the child reader-listener.

Writing under her own name and some three pseudonyms, Margaret Wise Brown created nearly one hundred books. Her most frequent illustrator was Leonard Weisgard, who won the Caldecott award for their book *The Little Island* (1946). Many of her books are still popular today, including the most favorite bedtime story of all, *Goodnight Moon* (1947), and *The Runaway Bunny* (1942). Harper reissued *The Little Fur Family* (1946) complete in its "fur coat edition" in 1984. After her untimely death at 42, William Scott wrote "all her books have an elusive quality that was Margaret Wise Brown. . . . [They have] simplicity, directness, humor, unexpectedness, respect for the reader and a sense of the importance of living."[29]

Other author-illustrators of this period include Marjorie Flack, who, like Margaret Wise Brown, knew how to tell a good story for preschoolers. Her *Angus and the Ducks* (1930) and *Ask Mr. Bear* (1952) are still shared with youngsters. Kurt Wiese illustrated her popular *The Story About Ping* (1933), the little runaway duck on the Yangtze River. Lois Lenski began creating her picture storybooks of *The Little Family* (1932) and *The Little Auto* (1934) at about this time. These pictured 5-year-olds as little adults doing what young children wished they could do, such as drive a car, sail a boat, or be a fireman.

Inanimate machines became popular characters in such books as Watty Piper's *The Little Engine That Could* (1929), Hardie Gramatky's *Little Toot* (1930), and Virginia Lee Burton's *Mike Mulligan and His Steam Shovel* (1939). Burton personified *The Little House* (1942), which was first built in the country, then engulfed by the city, and finally rescued and returned to the country again. This story, which won the Caldecott award, has been called a child's first sociology book.

Dr. Seuss wrote and illustrated the first of many hilarious rhymed stories for children, *To Think That I Saw It on Mulberry Street,* in 1937. That delightful dare-devil, *Madeline,* appeared on the Paris streets in 1939. Though not Ludwig Bemelmans' first book, it is certainly his best known. Robert McCloskey's ducklings made their difficult journey across Boston streets in 1941. *Make Way for Ducklings* richly deserved the Caldecott award it received. In the same year H. A. Rey introduced the antics of everyone's favorite monkey, *Curious George.*

During the late 1930s and early 1940s the United States benefited from the influx of many fine European artists seeking refuge in this country. These artists found a legitimate outlet for their creative talents in the field of children's literature. Picture books were greatly enriched through their unique contributions. A glance at a roster of some of the names of well-known illustrators will indicate the international flavor of their backgrounds: d'Aulaire, Duvoisin, Eichenberg, Mordvinoff, Petersham, Rojankovsky, Simont, Shulevitz, Slobodkin, and many more. (Most of their work is discussed in Chapter 5, "Picture Books.") Certainly the variety of their national backgrounds has added a cosmopolitan flavor to our picture books that is unprecedented both in time and place. American children have become the beneficiaries of an inheritance from the whole artistic world.

Growth of Informational Books

Increased understanding of child development brought the recognition that the child was naturally curious and actively sought information. No longer did a discussion of nature have to be disguised as "an exciting walk with Uncle Fred," who lectured on the flowers and trees. Children enjoy facts, and they eagerly accept information given to them in a straightforward manner.

E. Boyd Smith created some of the earliest information picture books in *The Farm Book* (1910), *Chicken World* (1910), *The Seashore Book* (1912), and *The Railroad Book* (1913). The illustrations for these stories were large, double-page spreads filled with fascinating detail. His *Chicken World* tells the life story of a chick, ending with a roast

[29]Louise Seaman Bechtel, "Margaret Wise Brown, 'Laureate of the Nursery,' " *The Horn Book Magazine*, vol. 24 (June, 1958), p. 184.

E. Boyd Smith was one of the first Americans to produce artistic and accurate information picture books. *The Railroad Book* was first published in 1913.

bird on a platter! Each illustration has a border showing the larger context of the farm where the chicken world exists. Smith lived in France for a long period and some of his illustrations remind one of Boutet de Monvel's work for *Joan of Arc*. Smith illustrated many other books; one of the most memorable is his interpretation of *The Story of Noah's Ark* (1909). Certainly his wonderful picture of the seasick animals stretched out on a rolling ark could compete with Peter Spier's more recent Caldecott award-winning *Noah's Ark*.

From Sweden came a translation of *Pelle's New Suit* (1929) by Elsa Beskow. Large colored pictures illustrate the process of making clothes, beginning with the shearing of Pelle's lamb, carding the wool, spinning it, dyeing it, weaving the cloth, making the suit, and ending with a bright Sunday morning when Pelle wears his new suit. It is interesting for children to compare this book, which can still be found in libraries today, with Tomie de Paola's "*Charlie Needs a Cloak*." Maud and Miska Petersham used rich vivid colors on every page of their informational books, which frequently described processes. They published five storybooks, each composed of four parts which were also published as separate books. Thus *The Story Book of Things We Use* (1933), *The Story Books of Wheels, Trains, Aircraft* (1935), *The Story Book of Foods from the Field* (1936), and *The Story*

Book of Things We Wear (1939) spawned some fifteen smaller books. These books were the predecessors of Holling C. Holling's beautifully illustrated story of the travels of a little carved canoe, *Paddle to the Sea* (1941), which gave rich geographical information on the Great Lakes Region, and *Tree in the Trail* (1942), which provided much that was of historical interest about the Southwest.

W. Maxwell Reed, a former professor at Harvard, started to answer his nephew's questions in a series of letters which resulted in two books, *The Earth for Sam* (1932) and the popular *Stars for Sam* (1931). These books exemplify the beginnings of accurate informational books written by recognized authorities in the field.

As a result of the pre-school movement with its emphasis on the "here and now," young children also had their informational books. Mary Steichen Martin produced *The First Picture Book: Everyday Things for Babies* (1930) while her photographer father, Edward Steichen, took the pictures of such common objects as a cup of milk with a slice of bread and butter, a faucet with a bar of soap, a glass holding a toothbrush, a brush and comb set, etc. No text accompanied these pictures, which were clear enough to provoke recognition and discussion for the child. *The Second Picture Book* (1931) showed pictures of children using common objects. Neither one of these books was particularly popular, but they paved the way for other photographic information books. Lewis W. Hine published his *Men at Work* (1932), picturing train engineers, workers on a skyscraper, and cowboys. Lucy Sprague Mitchell created verses for the photos of Clara Lambert in their publication *Skyscraper* (1933). Harriet Huntington's book *Let's Go Outdoors* (1939) portrayed close-up pictures of bugs and flowers just as a child might discover them on a nature walk. Blurring the background, Huntington focused on sharp images in a way similar to the work of Tana Hoban today. This book was followed by *Let's Go to the Seashore* (1941). Both books stayed in print well over twenty-five years. Henry Kane's fine close-ups of a mouse and frog in his *The Tale of the Whitefoot Mouse* (1940) and *The Tale of a Bullfrog* (1941) started the trend to create photographic stories of individual animals.

Since the 1940s, quantities of informational books have rolled from the presses to give children facts on almost every conceivable subject. Series books in the areas of science and social studies were important developments in this period. The *First Books*, *All About Books*, and the *True Books* series are examples of the trend. Many books of experiments by such authors as the Schneiders and Freemans stimulated children's science activities. Developments in the fields of atomic energy and exploration of space have been reflected in books for children. In the 1950s factual books about rockets, satellites, and space almost seemed to be fantasy, but by the 1960s such books were an accepted fact of daily life.

Biographies appeared to satisfy children's interest in national heroes. Ingri and Edgar Parin d'Aulaire, who had lived in Norway and in many other parts of Europe, were fascinated with the heroes of the new world. They presented somewhat idealized images in their large picture-book biographies, *George Washington* (1930), *Abraham Lincoln* (1939), *Leif the Lucky* (1941), *Pocahontas* (1949), and many more. Since these stories were new to them, they were perhaps freer to interpret the lives afresh seeing them as a child discovers them for the first time. James Daugherty portrayed *Daniel Boone* (1939) and many other American pioneers with strong vibrant pictures and ringing epic prose which was awarded the Newbery Medal.

The *Childhood of Famous Americans* series initiated the trend of publishing biographies for boys and girls in series form. By the 1960s biographies gave less emphasis to the early years of great men and women. More biographies for young children became available, including such lively and authentic books as Fritz's *And Then What Happened, Paul Revere?* (1973) and *Poor Richard in France* (1973) by F. N. Monjo. Biographies of Civil Rights leaders honored such well-known persons as Martin Luther King, Jr., and lesser-known participants like Rosa Parks, the woman who refused to give up her seat on a bus in Montgomery, Alabama, in 1955. More concern was evidenced for publishing biographies about women, and Crowell began their series on Women in America, which includes titles on Gertrude Stein, Fanny Kemble, and others.

Early in the twentieth century, historical fiction was written for children. Laura Richards quoted from diaries and letters as she wrote *Abigail Adams and Her Times* (1909). *The Horsemen of the Plains* (1910) by Joseph Altsheler related exciting frontier stories of the Cheyenne War. The legendary approach to history was utilized by MacGregor in *Story of Greece* (1914). *When Knights Were Bold* brought another period of history to life when Tappan published this book in 1911. The sweep of history was shown in Hendrik Van Loon's *The Story of Mankind* (1921), the first Newbery award-winner.

Laura Ingalls Wilder's remarkable series of Little House books started with *The Little House in the Big Woods* in 1932, while Coatsworth began her *Away Goes Sally* series in 1934. Brink wrote of that vivacious tomboy *Caddie Woodlawn* the following year. The "eyewitness" books included *America: Adventures in Eyewitness History* (1962) and *Africa: Adventures in Eyewitness History* (1963), both by Rhoda Hoff. These books, based on original sources, recognized children's ability to read complex materials and draw their own conclusions about history.

Bealer's *Only the Names Remain: The Cherokees and the Trail of Tears* (1972) was representative of a new emphasis on readable, carefully documented history. It also attempted to balance the record of history by presenting the American Indian point of view. The Newbery award-winner for 1974, *The Slave Dancer* by Paula Fox, realistically faced up to the wrongs of the past. Celebration of the Bicentennial spurred publication of many attractive and authentic books on eighteenth-century America.

There is no accurate accounting of the number of nonfiction children's titles that are published in contrast to fiction, but a survey of the new titles would suggest that nearly two-thirds of the children's books published today could be classified as informational. Informational books are discussed in detail in Chapter 11 of this book, while biography is presented in Chapter 10.

Proliferation of Series Books

The dime novel had been initiated in the nineteenth century, and the series books of George Henty, Oliver Optic, and Horatio Alger had introduced the repetitive incident plot and stereotyped characters. In the twentieth century "fiction factories" were developed by Edward Stratemeyer, who manufactured the plots for literally hundreds of books, including *The Rover Boys* (1899–1926), *The Bobbsey Twins* (1904–), the *Tom Swift* series (1910–1941), and *The Hardy Boys* (1927–), to name just a few. Using a variety of pseudonyms, Stratemeyer would give hack writers a three-page outline of characters and plot to complete. When he died in 1930, a millionaire, he had himself written or conceived for others to write more than 1300 fifty-cent juveniles. His daughter, Harriet Stratemeyer Adams, continued his work, writing nearly 200 children's books, including the well-known *Nancy Drew* series (1930–), until her death at 89 in 1982. In all her books, Mrs. Adams portrayed an innocent, affluent, and secure world. Nancy Drew may be kidnapped, knocked unconscious, and locked in a room with no way to escape, but she always solves the crime and survives to spend another day chasing villains in her blue roadster. Although modern versions of the series books deal with nuclear war, space flights, and submarines, the plots and characters have remained the same. The hero or heroine is always a child or adolescent acting with adult wisdom and triumphing over all obstacles—unaided, undaunted, undefeated. Despite bitter criticism from literary critics, these books have been translated into many languages and continue to be sold in our country and throughout the world.

There were books that met with literary approval that were also sold in series. The Lucy Fitch Perkins *Twins* series, beginning in 1911 with *The Dutch Twins*, provided authentic information on children of other lands in the form of an interesting realistic story. The series included books at various levels of difficulty; the story of *The Scotch Twins* (1919) was more complex, for example, than *The Dutch Twins*. The author also wrote stories of twins living in different historical periods, such as *The Puritan Twins* (1921), *The Pioneer Twins* (1927), and many more.

Folktales of the World

The publication of Grimm's *Household Tales* in the early part of the nineteenth century represented only the beginning of interest in recording the told tale. Not until the twentieth century would children have access to the folktales of almost the entire world. A famous story-teller, Gudrun Thorne-Thomsen, recorded stories from Norway in *East o' the Sun and West o' the Moon* in 1912. Kate Douglas Wiggin edited tales from the *Arabian Nights* in 1909, and Ellen Babbitt brought forth a collection of *Jataka Tales* from India in 1912. Constance Smedley provided children with stories from Africa and Asia in her *Tales from Timbuktu* (1923). The next year, Charles Finger published stories that he had collected from Indians in South America in his Newbery award-winning book *Tales from the Silver Lands* (1924). Ruth Sawyer went to Spain in search of folktales like the Irish stories she already knew. *Picture Tales from Spain* (1936) came out of that trip, and other Spanish stories were eventually published in her *Way of the Storyteller* (1942) and *The Long Christmas* (1941). Mary Gould Davis collaborated with Ralph Steele Boggs in creating another collection of Spanish stories, *Three Golden Oranges* (1936).

Pura Belpré grew up in Puerto Rico in a family of story-tellers. She later told these stories to American children in library story hours. Finally they were published in a collection called *The Tiger and The Rabbit* (1946). Philip Sherlock, vice-principal of the University College of the West Indies in Jamaica, told stories of his homeland at a meeting of the American Library Association. A children's book editor heard him and persuaded him to publish *Anansi, The Spider Man* (1954). Harold Courlander, a folklorist and musicologist, made many fine collections of stories in West Africa, Ethiopia, Indonesia, Asia, and the islands of the Pacific. His first collection of tales for children was *Uncle Bouqui of Haiti* (1942). Courlander worked like the Grimm brothers, collecting his stories from the native story-tellers of the country. Some of his best stories are contained in *The Cow-Tail Switch and Other West African Stories* (1947) and *The Hat-Shaking Dance and Other Tales from the Gold Coast* (1957). The tales in *The Terrapin's Pot of Sense* (1957) were collected from black story-tellers in Alabama, New Jersey, and Michigan. Courlander related these stories to their origins in Africa in his interesting notes in the back of the book.

Lim Sian-Tek, a Chinese writer, spent ten years gathering many different Chinese myths, legends, and folktales from her country. These were introduced to American children in *Folk Tales from China* (1944). Frances Carpenter made "Grandmother" collections, such as her *Tales of a Chinese Grandmother* (1949). *The Dancing Kettle and Other Japanese Folk Tales* (1949) contains the favorite stories from Yoshiko Uchida's childhood. She also adapted old Japanese tales for American children in her popular *The Magic Listening Cap* (1955) and *The Sea of Gold* (1965, 1985).

Alice Geer Kelsey introduced American children to the humorous tales of the Hodja of Turkey and the Mullah of Persia in *Once the Hodja* (1943) and *Once the Mullah* (1954).

Many other collections continue to be published each year. What these collections have done is to present American children with the folklore of the world. They have also served as source material for the many individual folktale picture books that became so popular in the 1950s and 1960s and continue to roll off the presses today.

Marcia Brown developed this trend of illustrating single folktales in a picture-book format with her publication of the French tale of trickery *Stone Soup* (1947). Her *Cinderella* (1954) and *Once a Mouse* (1961) won Caldecott Medals, while her other fairy tales, *Puss in Boots*, *Dick Whittington and His Cat*, and *The Steadfast Tin Soldier* were Honor Books for the award. Other illustrators who have brought children richly illustrated picture-book fairy tales include Felix Hoffman, Adrienne Adams, Paul Galdone, Errol LeCain, Nonny Hogrogian, Margot Zemach, and many others.

Greater emphasis was also placed on individual African folktales, Jewish folktales, and legends of native Americans during the decades of the 1960s and 1970s. Gail Haley won the Caldecott award (1971) for *A Story A Story*, an African tale of Anansi, while *Anansi the Spider* by Gerald McDermott won the award in 1973. Leo and Diane Dillon received this award for their illustrations for *Why Mosquitoes Buzz in People's Ears* (1975), an African tale retold by Verna Aardema. Two Jewish tales, *The Golem* (1976) by Beverly Brodsky McDermott and *It Could Always Be Worse* (1977) by Margo Zemach were Honor Books. Folktales from around the world were not only an established part of children's literature but a frequently honored genre.

Fantasy

Fantasy for children in the first half of the twentieth century seemed to come mainly from the pens of English writers. Kipling stimulated the child's imagination in his *Just So Stories* (1902) with his humorous accounts of the origins of animal characteristics—how the elephant got his trunk or the camel his hump. Much of the delight of these stories is in Kipling's use of rich language like "grey green greasy Limpopo River all set about with fever trees" and "the bi-colored python rock snake" who could tie himself in "a double clothes-hitch" around a tree.

Also in 1902, Warne Brothers published Beatrix Potter's diminutive little book *The Tale of Peter Rabbit*, as already noted. Another English storyteller, Kenneth Grahame, brought to life for his son the adventures of a water rat, a mole, a toad, and a badger. *The Wind in the Willows* was published in 1908 with pictures by Ernest Shepard. This story of four loyal friends became a child's classic; it has been reissued in a variety of editions. Arthur Rackham created illustrations for it just before his death in 1940. Michael Hague created new illustrations for the complete book in 1980, while the modern English illustrator John Burningham made new illustrations for it in 1983. Individual chapters have been published as picture books: *The River Bank*, illustrated by Adrienne Adams in 1973: *The Open Road* (1979) and *Wayfarers All* (1981), both illustrated by Beverly Gooding. Obviously *The Wind in the Willows* continues to delight second and third generations of children!

The boy who refused to grow up and lose the beauties of Never Never Land, Peter Pan, first appeared in a London play by J. M. Barrie in 1904. Later the play was made into a book titled *Peter Pan in Kensington Gardens* (1906), with elaborate illustrations by Arthur Rackham. Darton maintains that *Peter Pan*, though in the form of a play, "has influenced the spirit of children's books, and the grown-up view of them, more powerfully than any other work except the *Alices* and Andersen's *Fairy Tales*."[30]

The Wizard of Oz by L. Frank Baum has been called the first American fantasy. Published in 1900, this highly inventive story of the Cowardly Lion, the Tin Woodman, the Scarecrow, and Dorothy in the Land of Oz has been enjoyed by thousands of children! Several publishers felt *The Wizard of Oz* was too radical a departure from the literature of the day and refused to publish it.

[30]Darton, p. 309.

Baum and the illustrator W. W. Denslow finally agreed to pay all the expenses if one small Chicago firm would print it. Within two months of publication, the book had been reprinted twice. The first book of the series is the best and might well have sufficed, but Baum created some thirteen more titles; and after his death at least twenty-six others were added to the series by Ruth Plumly Thompson, John R. Neill, and others. The 1939 film version of *The Wizard of Oz*, starring Judy Garland, has helped to keep interest in this book alive.

Talking animals have always appealed to children. Hugh Lofting created the eccentric Dr. Dolittle, who could talk to animals as well as understand their languages. In *The Story of Dr. Dolittle* (1920), Lofting describes the way Dolittle learns the animals' languages with the help of the parrot Polynesia and begins his animal therapy. There were ten books in this series; the second one, *The Voyages of Doctor Dolittle* (1922), won the Newbery Medal. Later readings would reveal racial stereotypes in these books, but readers in the 1920s were not alert to such flaws in writing.

Remembering her love of toys, Margery Williams wrote *The Velveteen Rabbit* (1922) while living in England. This story, with its moving description of what it means to be real, has delighted children and adults. It was first illustrated by William Nicholson; no fewer than three newly illustrated editions, by Michael Hague, Ilse Plume, and Allen Atkinson, appeared in 1982 and 1983, some sixty years after its first publication.

One of the most delightful stories of well-loved toys was A. A. Milne's story of *Winnie the Pooh*, written for his son in 1926. Eeyore, Piglet, and Pooh may be stuffed animals, but they have real, believable personalities. Their many adventures in the "100 Aker Wood" with Christopher Robin have provided hours of amusement for both children and the parents and teachers fortunate enough to have shared these stories with boys and girls. Ernest Shepard created unsurpassed illustrations of these lovable toys.

Many American children found the books by Walter Brooks about Freddy the Pig highly entertaining. Starting with *To and Again* (1927), Brooks created some twenty-five novels about the high jinks that occurred on Mr. Bean's farm. These books were reissued in 1986. Robert Lawson's *Rabbit Hill* (1944) and *The Tough Winter* (1954) captured the feelings and thoughts of the little wild animals that lived in the Connecticut meadows, farms, and woods near his house. Though the animals speak, each one remains an individual representative of his or her particular species.

All these stories paved the way for the most well-loved animal fantasy to be written by an American, E. B. White's *Charlotte's Web* (1952). This book, with its multiple themes of friendship, loyalty, and the celebration of life, is now delighting second and third generations of children. (See Chapter 7 for further discussion.)

Other significant fantasy appearing in this twentieth century certainly must include J. R. R. Tolkien's *The Hobbit* (1937), first discovered by college students and only recently shared with children, and *The Little Prince* by Antoine de Saint-Exupéry, which also appealed primarily to adults. Translated in 1943 from the French, this tale of a pilot's encounter with a Little Prince who lived alone on a tiny planet no larger than a house is really a story of the importance of uniqueness and love.

Poetry

The turn of the century saw the publication of the first work by a rare children's poet, Walter de la Mare's *Songs for Childhood* (1902). This was a poet who understood the importance and meaning of early childhood experiences. Leonard Clark says of him: "Walter de la Mare wrote as if he were a child himself, as if he were *revealing* his own childhood, though with the mature gifts of the authentic poet. His children are true to childhood."[31] His poems can be mysterious: the "someone" who knocks on the "wee small door"; they can be humorous: whatever Miss T. eats turns into Miss T.; they can capture the delight of a young child's visit to his grandmother's, where there is a cupboard of lollipops and Banbury cakes. In "Silver" de la Mare paints a picture of the beauty of a moonlit night. Eleven years after the publication of his first book, his *Peacock Pie* brought readers new melodies, nursery rhymes, and poems of enchantment.

Eleanor Farjeon, also English, was writing merry imaginative verse for children at the same time Walter de la Mare was creating his poetry. Her

[31]Leonard Clark, *Walter de la Mare* (New York: Henry Z. Walck, 1961), p. 44.

first published work was *Nursery Rhymes of London Town* (1916). *Joan's Door* was published ten years later and *Over the Garden Wall* in 1933. Many of these poems later appeared in a collection titled *Eleanor Farjeon's Poems for Children* (1931, 1951, 1984). We remember her for such poems as "Mrs. Peck Pigeon," "Tippetty Witchet," and "The Night Will Never Stay."

Still another Englishman brought joy and fun into the nursery with *When We Were Very Young* (1924) and *Now We Are Six* (1927). A. A. Milne could tell a rollicking story, as in "Bold Sir Brian" or "The King's Breakfast" or "Sneezles" or he could capture a child's imaginative play, as in "Lines or Squares" or "Binker."

In this country Rachel Field, Dorothy Aldis, and Aileen Fisher were interpreting the delight of the child's everyday world. The transition in children's poetry from the didactic to the descriptive, from moralizing to poems of fun and nonsense, had at last been achieved. No longer were poems *about* children; they were *for* children.

Frances Frost and Elizabeth Coatsworth were writing lovely poems about nature. Many of Coatsworth's were contained within her historical series of books beginning with *Away Goes Sally*. The 1930s and 1940s saw many collections of poetry selected especially for children from the works of well-known contemporary poets. These included Edna St. Vincent Millay's *Poems Selected for Young People* (1917), Vachel Lindsay's *Johnny Appleseed and Other Poems* (1928), Carl Sandburg's *Early Moon* (1930), Sara Teasdale's *Stars Tonight* (1930), Emily Dickenson's *Poems for Youth* (1934), Robert Frost's *Come In and Other Poems* (1943) and later his *You Come Too* (1959), Countee Cullen's *The Lost Zoo* (1940), and many others.

Hildegarde Hoyt Swift gave a poetic interpretation of the American Negro in her book *North Star Shining* (1947), illustrated with powerful pictures by Lynd Ward. The Pulitzer Prize-winning black poet, Gwendolyn Brooks presented the poignant poems of *Bronzeville Boys and Girls* in 1956. Each of these poems carries a child's name as the title and is written as the voice of that child.

Two fine poets for children emerged during the early 1950s, Harry Behn and David McCord. Harry Behn's first book, *The Little Hill* (1949), consisted of thirty-three poems written for his three children. His other books of poetry ranged from pure nonsense to childhood memories to lyrical poems of nature. His vision was a child's, his voice a mature poet's. Much of his poetry draws on his memories of growing up as a child when Arizona was still a territory. David McCord's poetry is more playful and humorous than Behn's. McCord's verse includes poems of nature and everyday experiences and an interest in language and the various forms of poetry. His first book of poetry was *Far and Few: Rhymes of Never Was and Always Is* (1952).

New interests in poetry were seen in the 1960s with many books of poetry written by children. Richard Lewis published his first volume of children's writing from around the world, *Miracles* (1966). The same year the poignant poetry and drawings of the children kept at the Theresienstadt Concentration Camp between 1942 and 1944 were published under the title . . . *I Never Saw Another Butterfly*. The strident voices of the protest of the 1960s were heard in *Young Voices* (1971), an anthology of poems written by fourth-, fifth-, and sixth-grade children in response to a 1969 poetry search by Schaeffer and Mellor. Nancy Larrick published a collection of poems written by American youth titled *I Heard a Scream in the Street* (1970).

Specialized collections of poetry celebrating the uniqueness of blacks, American Indians, Eskimos, and others were published in the 1960s and 1970s. Arnold Adoff published two such collections in 1970, *I Am the Darker Brother: An Anthology of Modern Poems by Black Americans* and *Black Out Loud: An Anthology of Modern Poems by Black Americans*. Hettie Jones edited *The Trees Stand Shining* (1971), a collection of Papago Indian poems, and John Bierhorst presented a scholarly collection of poems, chants, and prayers from Indian cultures of both North and South America, *In the Trail of the Wind: American Indian Poems and Ritual Orations* (1971). Knud Rasmussen was the first to record the virile poetry of the Eskimo in his *Beyond the High Hills: A book of Eskimo Poems* in 1961, while James Houston edited and illustrated *Songs of the Dream People: Chants and Images from the Indians and Eskimos of North America* (1972). The uniqueness of girls was portrayed in two books, *Girls Can Too* (1972), edited by Lee Bennett Hopkins, and *Amelia Mixed the*

Mustard and Other Poems, selected and illustrated by Evaline Ness in 1975.

With such increased interest in poetry for children, it seems particularly fitting that the National Council of Teachers of English established the first award for Excellence in Poetry for Children in 1977.

LANDMARKS IN THE DEVELOPMENT OF BOOKS FOR CHILDREN

• Before 1700
Oral stories told by minstrels—Beowulf, King Arthur, ballads, etc.

c. 700	Question-and-answer form of instruction—Aldhelm
c. 1200	*Elucidarium*, Anslem
c. 1290	*Gesta Romanorum*,
1387	*Canterbury Tales*, Geoffrey Chaucer
c. 1440	Hornbooks developed
1477	*A Book of Curteseye* published by Caxton
1481	*Historye of Reynart the Foxe* published by Caxton
1484	*The Fables of Aesop* published by Caxton
1485	*Le Morte d'Arthur*, Malory
1548	*King Henry's Primer*
c. 1580s	Beginnings of chapbooks

• Seventeenth century

1646	*Spiritual Milk for Boston Babes . . .*, John Cotton
1659	*Orbis Pictus*, Johann Amos Comenius
1678	*The Pilgrim's Progress*, John Bunyan
c. 1686	*The New England Primer*
1697	*Histoires ou Contes du Temps Passé*, Charles Perrault

• Eighteenth century

c. 1706	*The Arabian Nights* translated into English
1715	*Divine and Moral Songs*, Isaac Watts
1719	*Robinson Crusoe*, Daniel Defoe
1726	*Gulliver's Travels*, Jonathan Swift
1729	Perrault's *Fairy Tales* translated into English
1744	*A Little Pretty Pocket-Book*, John Newbery
1765	*The History of Little Goody Two Shoes*, John Newbery, publisher
1771	*The New Lottery Book of Birds and Beasts*, Thomas Bewick
c. 1780	*Mother Goose's Melody* (may have been Newbery)
c. 1786	*Mother Goose's Melodies*, Isaiah Thomas, American publisher
1789	*Songs of Innocence*, William Blake

• Nineteenth century

1804	*Original Poems for Infant Minds*, Ann and Jane Taylor
1807	*The Butterfly's Ball*, William Roscoe
1823	*A Visit From St. Nicholas*, Clement C. Moore
1823	*Grimm's Popular Stories*, translated by Edgar Taylor, illustrated by George Cruikshank
1846	*Book of Nonsense*, Edward Lear
1846	*Fairy Tales of Hans Christian Andersen*, translated by Mary Howitt
1848	*Struwwelpeter*, Heinrich Hoffman (English translation)
1861	*Seven Little Sisters Who Live on the Big Round Ball that Floats in the Air*, Jane Andrews
1865	*The House That Jack Built, Sing a Song of Sixpence*, illustrated by Walter Crane
1865	*Alice's Adventures in Wonderland*, Lewis Carroll, illustrated by John Tenniel
1865	*Hans Brinker, or the Silver Skates*, Mary Mapes Dodge
1868	*Little Women*, Louisa May Alcott
1869	*Twenty Thousand Leagues Under the Sea*, Jules Verne

LANDMARKS IN THE DEVELOPMENT OF BOOKS FOR CHILDREN (continued)

1871	*At the Back of the North Wind*, George Macdonald
1872	*Sing-Song*, Christina Rossetti
1873	*St. Nicholas Magazine* begun, Mary Mapes Dodge, editor
1876	*The Adventures of Tom Sawyer*, Mark Twain
1878	*Under the Window*, Kate Greenaway
1878	*The Diverting History of John Gilpin*, illustrated by Randolph Caldecott
1880	*The Peterkin Papers*, Lucretia Hale
1881	*Adventures of Pinocchio*, Carlo Collodi
1883	*Merry Adventures of Robin Hood*, adapted and illustrated by Howard Pyle
1883	*Treasure Island*, Robert Louis Stevenson
1883	*Uncle Remus Stories*, Joel Chandler Harris
1884	*Heidi*, Johanna Spyri, translated by Louise Brooks
1884	*Adventures of Huckleberry Finn*, Mark Twain
1885	*A Child's Garden of Verse*, Robert Louis Stevenson
1889	*The Blue Fairy Book*, Andrew Lang
1894	*The Jungle Book*, Rudyard Kipling
1897	*Joan of Arc*, Maurice Boutet de Monvel (English translation)
1898	*Wild Animals I Have Known*, Ernest Thompson Seton

• First half of the twentieth century

1900	*Wizard of Oz*, L. Frank Baum
1901	*The Tale of Peter Rabbit*, Beatrix Potter
1902	*Songs of Childhood*, Walter de la Mare
1902	*Just So Stories*, Rudyard Kipling
1903	*Johnny Crow's Garden*, L. Leslie Brooke
1903	*Call of the Wild*, Jack London
1903	*Rebecca of Sunnybrook Farm*, Kate Douglas Wiggin
1906	*Peter Pan in Kensington Gardens*, J. M. Barrie, illustrated by Arthur Rackham
1908	*Wind in the Willows*, Kenneth Grahame, illustrated by Ernest Shepard
1910	*The Secret Garden*, Frances Hodgson Burnett
1910	*The Farm Book* and *Chicken World*, E. Boyd Smith
1921	*Here and Now Story Book*, Lucy Sprague Mitchell
1922	*Rootabega Stories*, Carl Sandburg
1922	Newbery Medal for "most distinguished book for children" established
1924	*When We Were Very Young*, A. A. Milne, illustrated by Ernest H. Shepard
1926	*Smoky, the Cow-Horse*, Will James
1926	*Winnie the Pooh*, A. A. Milne, illustrated by Ernest H. Shepard
1926	*Clever Bill*, William Nicholson
1928	*Millions of Cats*, Wanda Gág
1929	*Pelle's New Suit*, Elsa Beskow (English translation)
1930	*The Earth for Sam*, W. Maxwell Reed
1932	*What Whiskers Did*, Ruth Carroll
1932	*Little House in the Big Woods*, Laura Ingalls Wilder
1934	*The Little Auto*, Lois Lenski
1934	*Mary Poppins*, Pamela Travers
1935	*Caddie Woodlawn*, Carol Ryrie Brink
1936	*Story of Ferdinand*, Munro Leaf, illustrated by Robert Lawson
1936	*Roller Skates*, Ruth Sawyer
1937	*And To Think That I Saw it on Mulberry Street*, Dr. Seuss

LANDMARKS IN THE DEVELOPMENT OF BOOKS FOR CHILDREN (continued)

1937	*The Hobbit,* J. R. R. Tolkien
1938	Caldecott Medal for "most distinguished picture book for children" established
1939	*Madeline,* Ludwig Bemelmans
1939	*The Noisy Book,* Margaret Wise Brown, illustrated by Roger Duvoisin
1939	*Mike Mulligan and His Steam Shovel,* Virginia Lee Burton
1940	*The Moffats,* Eleanor Estes
1940	*Blue Willow,* Doris Gates
1941	*Make Way for Ducklings,* Robert McCloskey
1941	*Paddle to the Sea,* Holling C. Holling
1941	*George Washington's World,* Genevieve Foster
1941	*In My Mother's House,* Ann Nolan Clark
1941	*Curious George,* A. A. Rey
1942	*Little House,* Virginia Lee Burton
1943	*Johnny Tremain,* Esther Forbes
1943	*Homer Price,* Robert McCloskey
1944	*Rabbit Hill,* Robert Lawson
1944	*The Hundred Dresses,* Eleanor Estes, illustrated by Louis Slobodkin
1945	*Two Is a Team,* Lorraine and Jerrold Beim, illustrated by Ernest Crichlow
1945	*Call Me Charley,* Jesse Jackson
1946	*Bright April,* Marguerite de Angeli
1947	*Stone Soup,* Marcia Brown
1947	*White Snow, Bright Snow,* Alvin Tresselt, illustrated by Roger Duvoisin
1947	*Judy's Journey,* Lois Lenski
1948	*The Twenty-one Balloons,* William Pène du Bois

• **Second half of the twentieth century**

1952	*A Hole Is To Dig,* Ruth Krauss, illustrated by Maurice Sendak
1952	*Charlotte's Web,* E. B. White, illustrated by Garth Williams
1952	*Diary of a Young Girl,* Anne Frank
1956	*Bronzeville Boys and Girls,* Gwendolyn Brooks
1957	*The Cat in the Hat,* Dr. Seuss
1959	*Tom's Midnight Garden,* Philippa Pearce
1962	*A Wrinkle in Time,* Madeleine L'Engle
1962	*The Snowy Day,* Ezra Jack Keats
1963	*Where the Wild Things Are,* Maurice Sendak
1964	*Harriet the Spy,* Louise Fitzhugh
1965	*Dorp Dead,* Julia Cunningham
1966	Mildred L. Batchhelder Award for most outstanding translated book established
1969	*Stevie,* John Steptoe
1969	*Where the Lilies Bloom,* Vera and Bill Cleaver
1970	*Are You There God? It's Me, Margaret,* Judy Blume
1970	*In the Night Kitchen,* Maurice Sendak
1973	*Where the Sidewalk Ends,* Shel Silverstein
1974	*My Brother Sam Is Dead,* James and Christopher Collier
1974	"The Little Books": *The Baby, The Blanket, The Cupboard,* John Burningham
1975	*M. C. Higgins the Great,* Virginia Hamilton
1976	*Why Mosquitoes Buzz in People's Ears,* retold by Verna Aardema, illustrated by Leo and Diane Dillon
1977	National Council of Teachers of English Excellence in Poetry for Children Award established

Realistic fiction

One characteristic of books in the past was how long they stayed in print and were read by generations of children. In the beginning of the twentieth century children continued to derive pleasure from *Little Women* (1868) and the other Alcott books, Dodge's *Hans Brinker, or the Silver Skates* (1865), Spyri's *Heidi* (1884), all the Frances Hodgson Burnett books, including *Little Lord Fauntleroy* (1886), *The Little Princess* (1905), and *The Secret Garden* (1910). Many of these titles continue to bring pleasure to children today.

Perhaps the success of the orphaned Little Princess accounted for the number of stories about orphans. L. M. Montgomery wrote the very popular story *Anne of Green Gables* (1908) about a young orphan girl living on Prince Edward Island in Canada. Seven sequels covered Anne's growing up, her adulthood, and her children. Montgomery also wrote *Emily of New Moon* (1923), the story of an orphan who had to draw straws to see which of the family relations would take her. Books were never written in the first person at this time, but Emily's letters to her dead father and her journal allowed the reader to enter into her thoughts and feelings in a way that anticipated the many first-person stories of contemporary children's books. Jean Webster's story of *Daddy-Long-Legs* (1912) is also a story of an orphan and her benefactor. *Pollyanna* (1913) by Eleanor H. Porter was another popular story of an orphan who must learn to live with two disagreeable spinster aunts. Her unfailingly optimistic way of coping made her name last longer than her story. While Dorothy Canfield's *Understood Betsy* (1917) was not an orphan, she was a sickly city child sent to live with relatives on a Vermont farm in order to regain her health. Lucinda of *Roller Skates* (1936) was not an orphan either but was left with her teacher and sister while her father and mother went abroad for a year in the late 1890s. Lucinda had a gloriously free year to explore New York on her roller skates. She made friends with everyone she met—the fruit vendor, the policeman, the hansom cab driver, and Uncle Earle. Lucinda was an unforgettable character who loved life and people. Ruth Sawyer won the Newbery award for this book in 1937.

Kate Douglas Wiggins' *Rebecca of Sunnybrook Farm* (1903) epitomizes the happy family stories that were characteristic of the first half of the century. For younger children, Carolyn Haywood began her many Betsy and Eddie stories in 1939 with *B is for Betsy*; these stories tell of simple everyday doings of children at school and home. In *Thimble Summer* (1938) Elizabeth Enright told an entertaining family story set on a Wisconsin farm. Enright's *The Saturdays* (1941) was the first of several stories capturing the joyous living of the four children of the Melendy family. In three books, *The Moffats* (1941), *The Middle Moffat* (1942), and *Rufus M* (1943), Eleanor Estes detailed the delights of growing up in West Haven, Connecticut. The four children, Jane, Rufus, Sylvie, and Joey, are clearly realized as individuals and grow up in ways consistent with their characters. Sydney Taylor's *All-of-a-Kind Family* (1955) presented the adventures of five Jewish girls growing up on New York's Lower East Side.

Two humorous stories appeared at this time: McCloskey's classic tale of *Homer Price* (1943) and his amusing adventures in Centerburg and Cleary's *Henry Huggins* (1950). Both centered around all-American boys growing up in small towns, they have given two generations of children much laughter.

Not all realistic fiction told happy or humorous tales of growing up in mainstream America. Realistic fiction often reflected war, depression, and social problems in the contemporary scene. As adults became more aware of various ethnic and regional groups in our nation, children's books reflected this interest also. Lois Lenski pioneered in presenting authentic, detailed descriptions of life in specific regions of the United States. By living in the community, observing the customs of the people, and listening to their stories, she was able to produce a significant record of American life from the 1940s into the 1960s. Her first book, *Bayou Suzette* (1943), was set in the Louisiana bayou country, while *Strawberry Girl* (1945), which won the Newbery Medal, told of life among the Florida Crackers. *Judy's Journey* (1947), her most forceful book, concerned the plight of the migratory workers. Doris Gates also dramatized the problems of the migratory worker in her classic story *Blue Willow* (1940), named after the family's one prized possession, a blue willow plate. Eleanor Estes was one of the first to write about poverty and children's interrelationships in their closed society.

Her book *The Hundred Dresses* (1944) enabled teachers to undertake and guide frank discussions of the problem of being "different."

Until the 1950s and 1960s very few books portrayed blacks or other racial minorities. Books that did portray blacks showed stereotypes—the bandana-covered fat mammy and the kinky-haired, thick-lipped "funny" boy. This stereotype was epitomized in the Nicodemus series written by Inez Hogan in the late 1930s with such titles as *Nicodemus and the Gang* (1939). The jacket of this book quotes part of a *New York Herald Tribune* review that said: "A story that will get itself remembered when some longer and louder ones are forgotten." Fortunately, Nicodemus with his gang—who have such stereotyped names as Rastus, Obadiah, and Petunia—have been forgotten. "I'se a comin'," "Yas'm Mammy," and "nex' time, I spec you better stan' on de groun' fo' speech makin'" exemplified the "black-face" dialect used in this series. The segregation of blacks was clearly shown in *Araminta* (1935) by Eva Knox Evans and the photographic essay *Tobe* (1939) by Stella Sharpe. It was nearly ten years later that blacks and whites were shown participating in activities together. The theme of *Two Is a Team* (1945) by the Beims is revealed in both the title and the action as a black and a white boy play together. Prejudice was openly discussed for the first time in Jesse Jackson's *Call Me Charley* (1945) and Marguerite de Angeli's *Bright April* (1946).

Mary Jane (1959) by Dorothy Sterling, *The Empty Schoolhouse* (1965) by Natalie Carlson, and *Patricia Crosses Town* (1965) by Betty Baum discussed the new social problems caused by school integration. By the mid-1960s, a few books showed black characters in the illustrations, but this was not mentioned in the text. Examples included *The Snowy Day* (1962) by Ezra Jack Keats, *Mississippi Possum* (1965) by Miska Miles, and Louisa Shotwell's *Roosevelt Grady* (1963). In the 1970s such books were criticized for "whitewashing" the blacks and attempting to make everyone the same. Books such as *Zeely* (1967) by Virginia Hamilton and *Stevie* (1969) by John Steptoe, both written by black authors, captured something of the special pride of the black experience in children's literature.

M. C. Higgins the Great by Virginia Hamilton, a black author, won the Newbery award for distinguished writing in 1975. Two years later, *Roll of Thunder, Hear My Cry* by Mildred D. Taylor, another fine black author, won the award. Books about blacks and written by blacks had at long last received recognition. However, even today the number of black authors is small indeed when compared to the black population of this country.

The "new freedoms" of the 1960s were reflected in both adult and children's books. The so-called "new realism" in children's literature can probably be dated from the publication of *Harriet the Spy* (1964) by Louise Fitzhugh. Harriet is an 11-year-old anti-heroine who keeps a notebook in which she records with brutal honesty her impressions of her family, friends, and New York neighborhood characters. Unlike Lucinda, who made friends with the people she met in *Roller Skates*, Harriet spies on them. Harriet's parents are psychologically absent, being too engrossed in their own affairs to be overly concerned about their daughter's activities. Children readily identified with Harriet, for she had the courage to think *and* say the things they didn't dare to say, including swearing. Following *Harriet*'s breakthrough, the long-standing taboos in children's literature came tumbling down. The Cleavers wrote about death and suicide in *Where the Lilies Bloom* (1969) and *Grover* (1970); alcoholism and homosexuality are described in *I'll Get There, It Better Be Worth the Trip* (1969) by Donovan; and *George* (1970) by Konigsburg includes divorced parents, a psychologically disturbed child, and LSD. In Judy Blume's popular novel *Are You There God? It's Me, Margaret* (1970), Margaret's vague interest in religion is overshadowed by the more immediate concern of when she will start menstruating. *Mom, the Wolf Man and Me* (1972) by Norma Klein is the candid story of a young girl's fear that her single mother will get married. *Deenie* (1973) by Judy Blume is primarily the story of a beautiful girl who discovers she must wear a back brace for four years. The story contains several references to masturbation. Even picture books reflected the impact of this new freedom. Mickey falls out of bed and out of his clothes in Maurice Sendak's *In the Night Kitchen* (1970). In *My Special Best Words* (1974) by John Steptoe, bodily functions are discussed naturally, as a slightly older sister tries to toilet-train her younger brother.

The literature published for the child's expanding world reflected the changes and challenges of life in the mid-twentieth century. Just as adult literature mirrored the disillusionment of depression, wars, and materialism by becoming more sordid, sensational, and psychological, children's literature became more frank and honest, portraying such problems as war, drugs, divorce, abortion, sex, and homosexuality. No longer were children protected by stories of happy families. Rather it was felt that children would develop coping behaviors as they read about others who had survived similar problems.

All these problems are legitimate concerns of childhood. They have always existed, but only in the last twenty years have they been openly and honestly written about in books for children. Further discussion of realism in children's literature is in Chapter 9.

An International Literature for Children

An exciting development in children's literature was the rise of international interest in children's books during the years after World War II. This was indicated by an increased flow of children's books between countries. In 1950 *Pippi Longstocking* by the Swedish author Astrid Lindgren arrived in our country and was an immediate success. This was the beginning of many such exchanges.

The Mildred L. Batchelder Award for the most outstanding translated children's book originally published abroad and then published in the United States was established in 1966 by the Association for Library Service to Children of the American Library Association to honor their retiring executive secretary who had worked tirelessly for the exchange of books. This award has served as an impetus in promoting the translation of fine children's books from abroad. Such excellent books as *Don't Take Teddy* (1967) by the Norwegian writer Friis-Baastad; *Friedrich* (1970) by Hans Richter of Germany; and two books from Greece, *Wildcat under Glass* (1968) and *Petro's War* (1972) by Alki Zei, have been the recipients of this award.

Another indicator of the growing internationalism of children's literature during the 1950s was the number of congresses, book fairs, and exhibitions of children's books that were held around the world. The first general assembly of the International Board on Books for Young People (IBBY) was held in 1953. Jella Lepman, founder of IBBY, maintained that the organization should serve as a world conscience for international children's books and call attention to the best in the field by awarding international prizes. Consequently, IBBY awarded its first Hans Christian Andersen Medal to Eleanor Farjeon in 1956. In 1966 IBBY decided to extend the award to include a medal for the most outstanding artist as well as author of children's books. Alois Carigiet was the first artist to receive this award. Then, in 1967, Jella Lepman created the annual International Children's Book Day, which was appropriately established on April 2nd, the birthday of Hans Christian Andersen. The IBBY congresses meet every other year.

In 1967 the Biennale of Illustrations in Bratislava, Czechoslovakia (BIB), held its first exhibition. It is now scheduled to meet in the odd-numbered years, alternating with the IBBY congress. Other international displays include the annual Frankfurt Book Fair in September of each year and the Bologna Children's Book Fair in April.

The 1950s and the 1960s, then, saw the formation of international organizations for the exchange and appreciation of children's books throughout the world. These developments paved the way for UNESCO to designate 1972 as International Book Year. Almost 250 years from the time Newbery first conceived of the idea of a literature especially for children's enjoyment, it had achieved worldwide recognition. Literature for children has indeed come of age.

MODERN TRENDS IN CHILDREN'S BOOKS

Children's Books: Big Business

At the present time the publication and distribution of juvenile books comprises a big business—producing a children's book market of nearly half a billion dollars. The number of juveniles published in 1980 was more than ten times the number published in 1880. These statistics show the increased rate of growth for each decade of publication of juveniles over a century.

JUVENILES PUBLISHED[32]	
1880	270
1890	408
1900	527
1910	1,010
1920	477
1930	933
1940	984
1950	1,059
1960	1,725
1970	2,640
1980	2,895

In later years the increase in the number of children's books published can be attributed to the increase in paperback editions, included along with hardbound in these figures. Recent years have seen a dramatic increase in both quality and inferior paperbacks for children. Individual publishing houses are selecting some of the best of their previously published titles for reissue in paperback form. Increasingly, publishers are bringing out new titles in hardcover and paperback simultaneously. However, in order to compensate for some of the books they are no longer able to purchase, paperback houses have started commissioning their own original books to be published directly in paperback. While some of these qualify as imaginative writing, the majority of them are written to formula and go by the name of the series, such as "Romance Series" or "Sweet Dreams Series," rather than the title of the book. These books are reminiscent of the many series churned out by the Stratemeyer syndicate beginning in 1885.

Another factor hidden in the statistics is the large number of titles that go out of print each year. The life of a book is seldom even five years any more, in contrast to ten, twenty, or in the case of the very early books, two hundred years of reprinting. While it appears then that we have many more books being published, title turnover is far greater. However, certain books do stay in print and continue to sell and sell. Judy Blume's publishers maintain that all her books have sold over 25 million copies. And Shel Silverstein's poetry books have also sold over 25 million copies. The *Bowker*

Annual[33] lists nearly fifty hardcover children's books that have sold over 750,000 copies. Heading the list is Beatrix Potter's *Tale of Peter Rabbit*, with 8 million copies, while E. B. White's *Charlotte's Web* has sold over 1½ million copies and *Where the Wild Things Are* by Maurice Sendak has sold 1 million hardback copies. Books by Dr. Seuss, Marguerite Henry, and Laura Ingalls Wilder are among other titles in this rarefied company.

The health of children's literature can also be seen by the increasing number of children's book stores and childrens book fairs. Ten years ago the number of independent children's book stores in the United States was less than a dozen or so; today the number is well over three hundred, not including the children's departments of larger book stores and chains. Unfortunately, many large chain stores buy the cheaper books produced for mass marketing. This also applies to the jobbers whose entire business is supplying book fairs. Generally, book fairs sponsored by independent stores can be more responsive to the schools' needs and provide better-quality books.

Another trend in the publishing business has been the number of mergers of publishing houses with big business conglomerates. There are few independently owned publishing companies left today. A publishing company owned by a large conglomerate must show a profit; it is measured against the success of other companies in the corporation, most of which have nothing to do with publishing. Many of these changes occurred in the late 1970s when the cutback in federal assistance to education was felt in schools throughout the land. The school market had always been the safety net of the publishing companies; they knew they could count on school sales. Suddenly there were budget cuts and more demand for computer hardware and software which left less for books. In order to counteract this loss of school sales, publishers appear to be putting more emphasis on the trade book market than ever before.

Development of New Kinds of Books

As publishers sought continued profits, they searched for new markets. As a result of the many research studies showing the value of reading

[32]The Bowker Annual of Library and Book Trade Information (New York: Bowker, 1983).

[33]*The Bowker Annual of Library and Book Trade Information* (New York: Bowker, 1985).

aloud to children and interest in the so-called "Super Baby Syndrome," publishers discovered the infant market. Many companies are producing their own line of books for babies and toddlers. Helen Oxenbury's series of board books titled *Friends*, *Working*, *Playing*, *Dressing*, and *Family*, all published in 1981, were the first to portray the infant with his or her concerns and accomplishments. Her husband, John Burningham, had done the same thing for toddlers in his little books *The Blanket*, *The Cupboard*, etc., first published in England in 1974. The creation of these new books for the very young, plus the publication of such popular titles as Jim Trelease's *The Read-Aloud Handbook*, appears to have created a new awareness among conscientious parents of the value of reading aloud to youngsters.

Wordless books (more correctly called textless, since many of them do contain words in the introduction or afterword) first made their appearance in 1932 with *What Whiskers Did* by Ruth Carroll. This story of the adventures of a little Scottie dog was reprinted in 1965, when there was a greater

This antique pop-up book, *The Great Menagerie*, was created by the well-known German artist Meggendorfer in 1884. Today new pop-up books are created along with reissues of the old ones. This book was translated into English and adapted for a new publication by the Metropolitan Museum of Art in 1979.

The Walter Havighurst Special Collections, Miami University Libraries, Oxford, Ohio.

emphasis on the importance of "reading pictures" in preparation for learning to read. The wordless books caught on, and the 1960s and 1970s saw a flood of them. Some of them, such as Mercer Meyer's *A Boy a Dog and a Frog* (1967) series, were amusing cartoon sequences, while others reached a fine artistic level, such as *The Snowman* (1978) by Raymond Briggs. Wordless books are no longer only for beginning readers—watch adults and older children pore over the journey books of Mitsumasa Anno. The first of these, *Anno's Journey* (1978), recorded Anno's impressions of his visit to Europe. Clues to the many scenarios portrayed on each page are provided in the afterword.

Toy books, including pop-up books and books with revolving pictures, were quite the vogue in the late Victorian era of the 1890s. First printed in Germany, they became too costly to be continued. A revival of interest in these books is seen in the many reissues of them nearly a hundred years after their original publication. Now produced by cheap labor in Colombia, South America, and Singapore, reissues of books by Ernest Nister, such as *The Great Panorama Picture Book* (1895, 1982), and newly designed ones by such well-known artists as Tomie de Paola, Nicola Bayley, and John S. Goodall are once again delighting children. Unlike the Victorian ones, the modern pop-ups tell a continuous story like Goodall's nostalgic *Lavinia's Cottage* (1982) and Brown's *Goodnight Moon Room* (1984). Unless very well designed and sturdy, these manipulative books are more appropriate for the entertainment of one child than for library use.

Another trend reflected in the publishing industry is the increasing popularity of the "choose-your-own-ending" stories, which ask the child to help in creating plots by selecting various alternatives that then lead to different conclusions. Almost non-books, these stories have plots that are developed along a branching scheme similar to computer programs. Again many publishers have been quick to produce this type of book that meets the demands of today's children for quick action and participation. Written on many reading levels, there are choose-your-own mysteries, westerns, and romances, with dozens of books in each series.

Walt Disney was the first to establish movie-related books, rewriting old classics to suit himself and titling them *Walt Disney's Cinderella*, for example. Unfortunately, this practice has continued, resulting in emasculated distortions of such award-winning books as *Mrs. Frisby and the Rats of NIMH*, appearing as *The Secret of NIMH*. The story of the rats' success in changing their basic nature and establishing a new agricultural society is down-played in favor of telling of "Mrs. Brisby's" attempt to save her son Timothy's life, but even this is done by magic and not through her own bravery, as in O'Brien's original book. A real concern is that children who read these spin-off books are under the impression that they have read the story as it was originally conceived—which is not true.

Another trend is the publication of the print book as a secondary form, a book based on a popular television show, film, or even video game. The ultimate result of this market-oriented approach to publishing is the packaging of cheaply produced books with other items such as stuffed animals, tee shirts, or greeting cards. Quality writing is seldom part of such a package.

Shifts in Publishing Emphases

Recent years have seen far greater emphasis placed on contemporary realistic fiction, for example, than on historical fiction or biography. It is hard to account for this shift—as insolvable as the chicken-and-egg question. Did children stop reading historical fiction and biography, so publishers stopped publishing these types, or vice versa? The cause is not as important as the phenomenon. The popularity of the *Childhood of Famous Americans* series can be documented, also that of the many historical fiction novels by such authors as Meader, Meadowcraft, and Steele, writing in the 1940s and 1950s. Children today appear to be much more interested in stories that reflect their own present concerns than in stories that tell of the past.

Along with the decrease in historical fiction and biography has been a tremendous increase in the number of informational or nonfiction books published. Many of these are superior books indeed, like the David Macaulay books that detail the building of a *Pyramid* or the functioning of a *Mill*. But most non-fiction does not stretch the imagination in the same way that a story might. Neither does it demand the continued attention to plot and

character development required by fiction. Many of these informational books appear to have taken the place of historical fiction, particularly in the pattern of boys' reading.

In an attempt to save costs and produce "safe books" in these conservative times, publishers are reissuing titles on their backlists and producing new editions of classics. It is a joy to have such books as *Treasure Island* and *Robinson Crusoe* back in print with their handsome N. C. Wyeth illustrations and to see new editions of *The Velveteen Rabbit* and *The Lion, the Witch and the Wardrobe*, both illustrated by Michael Hague. At the same time, most of these books are available in libraries, and costly new editions may mean that new authors and artists are not being published. We can legitimately ask the question: how many different editions of *Wind in the Willows* do we need?

With the decrease in federal funds has come a decrease in the number of books published about minorities. This decrease was underlined when a group of authors, publishers, and librarians discussed the lack of black books at a meeting in 1984 of the Countee Cullen Regional Branch of the New York Public Library.[34] The occasion marked the library's publication of the 1984 edition of *The Black Experience in Children's Books* list, which is only about one-half the size of the 1979 edition. The current list includes about 400 titles, with only about 100 titles added since the previous edition.

The progress that was made, then, in the 1960s and 1970s in the publication of books for minorities is endangered by a retrogressive trend. Three factors may account for this slippage: (1) The Council on Interracial Books for Children strongly supports the principle that only a person of a particular minority may write about that experience. (2) The greatest sales of books about minorities are through schools, not book stores. Since school budgets have been cut, this has had an effect on the sales of these books. (3) The move toward conservatism in the nation and in publishing may have had an impact on the production of multi-ethnic books. Such a trend should not be tolerated in a democratic multi-racial society.

[34]Gordon Flagg, in his column "Young People," *American Libraries*, vol. 15 (September, 1984), p. 601.

Experimentation in Writing Styles

For years it was assumed that all books for children were told in the third person; children were not supposed to like introspective first-person accounts. The recognition and popularity of such books as *Meet the Austins* (1960) by Madeleine L'Engle, *It's Like This, Cat* (1963) by Emily Neville, *Dorp Dead* (1965) by Julia Cunningham, and Judy Blume's *Are You There God? It's Me, Margaret* (1970) certainly put an end to this myth. The "me generation" wanted and enjoyed the immediacy of a first-person telling. Such a style allows the author to reveal the thoughts and feelings of the main character, to give the reader a kind of "you are there" feeling. Even historical fiction and biography have assumed this point of view in such books as *My Brother Sam Is Dead* (1974) by the Colliers, *Sarah Bishop* (1980) by Scott O'Dell, and the biography *I'm Deborah Sampson* (1977) by Patricia Clapp.

Another trend in writing may be seen in the books told from various points of view. Mary Stolz wrote two books with the same plot but told from the different protagonists' points of view: *A Dog on Barkham Street* (1960) and *The Bully on Barkham Street* (1963). Hila Colman told the story of a runaway from the girl's point of view interlaced with chapters from her mother's point of view in *Claudia, Where Are You?* (1969). Betsy Byars used two different points of view to dramatize Clara's rescue at sea in *The Animal, the Vegetable & John D Jones* (1982). The use of such shifting points of view, which can heighten the suspense of a story, reflects the use of flashback, cut-ins, and other devices on TV and in films.

Other experimentation in writing includes the use of letters and journals. Such an approach is not necessarily new. In *Little Women* (1868) Alcott included a copy of the "Pickwick Portfolio," a newspaper the four sisters created, a round-robin story they all composed, many letters, and a copy of Amy's "Will." A revival of interest in telling stories through letters or journals is characteristic of some recent books. The Newbery award-winner *A Gathering of Days* (1979) by Joan Blos consists of imaginary entries from a New England girl's diary for the years 1830–1832. Beverly Cleary won the Newbery award in 1984 for her story *Dear Mr. Henshaw*. This story consists mostly of letters Leigh writes to an author, who answers with his own list of questions and demands. When Leigh tires of answering Mr. Henshaw's questions he switches to his own diary. All are included in Cleary's story of the son of a divorcée who is living with his mother but longing for his truck-driver father.

Some authors are combining genres in intriguing new ways. In *A Chance Child* (1978) Jill Paton Walsh tells the story of Creep, an abused child of the twentieth century who drifts down a canal in an old rusty boat and passes from his time to that of England during the Industrial Revolution. His half-brother frantically searches for him only to find through research in the library that he stayed on in the nineteenth century. By mixing historical fiction with contemporary times, Walsh could contrast the grim treatment of children during the Industrial Revolution with some of the cruelties endured by children today. *The Root Cellar* by Janet Lunn also provides a mixture of modern-day living and the Civil War era. *A Girl Called Boy* (1982) by Belinda Humence is based on the oral histories and plantation records of actual slaves. It begins in the present, when a conjure bird of her great, great, great-grandfather sends Blanche Overtha Yancey (called Boy for short) back to the 1850s when her relatives had been slaves of the Yanceys. All these books use an element of fantasy to unite the past with the present. Yet their primary purpose is to present historical fiction. Starting in the present is simply a device to capture children's interest and lead them into the past.

Increased Censorship

It is impossible to speak of trends in the 1960s, 1970s, and 1980s without speaking of the increase in censorship of books in schools and libraries. The number of book challenges has increased every decade since the 1950s. Judith Krug, director of the American Library Association Office for Intellectual Freedom and executive director of the Freedom to Read Foundation, says that in 1980 and 1981 the number of censorship attempts reported to her office was three times greater than for the same period in the previous year—a jump from 300 to between 900 and 1000.[35] According

[35]Joseph Deitch, "Portrait [of Judith Krug]," *Wilson Library Bulletin*, vol. 58 (May, 1984), p. 656.

to research reported by ALA, about half of the censorship attempts in the United States succeed. It should be emphasized that censorship does not mean simply a complaint or challenge; it means an attempt to have a book removed from a library.

The history of censorship can be traced to colonial days, when books were suppressed in this country. One of the early heritages acquired from across the sea was the practice of censorship. Indeed this is the reason for the adoption of the First Amendment. Of course censorship has been particularly widespread in dictatorships. What is important to remember is that in America we have a responsibility to champion the right of free access to ideas for all, children and adults.

Most book challenges are directed at young adult books, However, as the new freedoms of the 1960s were reflected in children's books, censorship and book bannings became more common. Books can be objected to for almost any reason. In his book *Censors in the Classroom: The Mind Benders*,[36] Edward B. Jenkinson lists some 116 targets of the censors, including profanity, conflicts with parents, drug use and abuse, homosexuality, violence, depressing stories of the ghetto, realistic dialogue, secular humanism, values clarification— and the list goes on. Dictionaries, textbooks, trade books, nursery rhymes have all come under attack.

A group of parents in Eagle Point, Oregon, asked the school board to remove *The Three Billy Goats Gruff* from the elementary school library because of its "violent content."[37] After a committee looked closely at the book and its use in the curriculum, the board unanimously decided to reject the challenge. Of all the children's authors who have come under attack, Judy Blume is cited most frequently. Her books have been challenged in Hanover, Pennsylvania, Peoria, Illinois, and Casper, Wyoming, to name just a few. In some instances the books have been removed from the library; in other cases children have had to obtain parental consent to read them.[38] A survey in Ohio showed that even such Newbery award-winning

books as Jean George's *Julie of the Wolves* and Madeleine L'Engle's *A Wrinkle in Time* have been objects of censorship.[39]

There is no doubt that censorship has been on the rise in the elementary schools of our country during the last thirty years. The censors represent both conservatives and liberals. Many of them are administrators, teachers, and librarians themselves! For a further discussion of censorship and what you can do about it, see Chapter 1, "Selection vs. Censorship" and "Dealing with Censorship."

Development of a Multi-literate Society

Dire statements have been made about the death of the book as we know it today, statements that call this the post-literate society. For example, in an article in *The Principal*, Sally Zakariya made this prediction: "For the first time, reading may lose its place as the primary criterion of academic success, with computer literacy overtaking it as education's number one priority."[40] As a matter of fact, computer software companies are presently working with such well-known science-fiction authors as Ray Bradbury and Arthur C. Clarke to adapt their adult novels to "interactive fiction," an electronic form of literature that transforms the reader into an active participant in the plot. While the characters and situations in most of the games are based on the books, the players respond to and actually create variations in the plot lines by typing commands on the computer screen. Given children's interest in the "choose-your-own-ending" books, it seems most likely that "interactive children's stories" may be a trend of the future.

Charles Suhor, deputy executive director of the National Council of Teachers of English, takes a middle position in projecting four possible scenarios for the role of print in the future, ranging from a technological takeover to books remaining the core of educational materials. His most reasoned conclusion is: "Ultimately, the new technologies will not be revolutionary, transforming, or pervasive in the schools. They will have a place,

[36]Edward B. Jenkinson, *Censors in the Classroom: The Mind Benders* (New York: Avon, 1982).
[37]Judith F. Krug, ed., *Newsletter on Intellectual Freedom*, vol. 13 (September, 1984), p. 155.
[38]Judith F. Krug, ed., *Newsletter on Intellectual Freedom*, vol. 14 (March, 1985), pp. 1, 58.

[39]Amy McClure, "Censorship in Ohio: It *Is* Happening Here," *The Ohio Reading Teacher*, vol. 16 (April, 1982), pp. 1–6.
[40]Sally Zakariya, "The Computer Goes to School," *The Principal* (May, 1982), pp. 18-19.

but that place will resemble at best a modified media center in which books, machinery, teachers, and students find more varied ways of relating to each other."[41]

It seems likely, then, that the youth of today will become multi-literate, using the new technologies for the rapid retrieval of information of all kinds, for writing and editing their thoughts, and for creating original programs of their own. But they will still need reading for a wide range of skills and

books for pleasure reading. Just as many youth today are multi-lingual, so the youth of the future will become multi-literate, reading a wide variety of formats.

As we move toward the close of the century, the future of the book is uncertain. Computers, videotapes, cassettes, films, cable TV, all have the potential to give us instant information in almost any form we wish. Will the book be as important as it is today in the year 2000? Those of us who love literature and have witnessed its positive influence on children's lives can only hope that it will be— that it will continue to live and flourish.

[41]Charles Suhor, draft of unpublished paper, "The Role of Print as a Medium in our Society," 41 pp., 1984.

SUGGESTED LEARNING EXPERIENCES

1. Interview five adults of different ages and ask about their favorite childhood books and reading interests. How similar are their responses? How much overlapping of titles is there?
2. Conduct a survey of your literature class to find out how many students have read *Little Women*, *Alice in Wonderland*, *Wind in the Willows*, *Charlotte's Web*, or one of Judy Blume's books. Make a chart of your findings.
3. Prepare a display of early children's books; note the printing and binding, the illustrations, the subject matter. Display a varied selection of recent books as well. What contrasts do you see, and what similarities?
4. Identify adult purposes in several recent books for children. Can you find any examples of didactic stories written in the last ten years? Be sure to look at several books dealing with current social problems.
5. Read and compare two books of realistic fiction with blacks as major characters—one published within the last five years, the other published before 1960. How does each book specifically reflect the time in which it was written?
6. If possible, read two books aloud to a group of children. Choose one old book and one new, but on a similar theme, such as the books about quarreling in the introduction to this chapter. Elicit the children's responses. What do they see as differences? Which book do they prefer?
7. Read one of the books listed as having been censored. Act out a meeting with the concerned person, letting him or her tell you of their reactions to the book. How will you treat this person? What will you say and do?
8. Read one of the new original paperbacks produced for a series. Compare it with a Nancy Drew book or a Sue Barton book. What similarities, differences do you see? Another person could compare it with a modern realistic story for children like those by Cynthia Voigt or Katherine Paterson. Again, how do they compare?
9. Plan a panel discussion on the role of the book in the future. What would you lose if you didn't have books?

RELATED READINGS

1. Ariès, Philippe. *Centuries of Childhood: A Social History of Family Life*. Translated from the French by Robert Baldick. New York: Knopf, 1962.
   A definitive study of the development of the concept of childhood. Ariès maintained that childhood was not discovered until the seventeenth century. While some have disputed this statement, Ariès' book has formed the basis of most historical studies of childhood.

2. Avery, Gillian. *Childhood's Pattern: A Study of the Heroes and Heroines of Children's Fiction, 1770–1950.* London: Hodder and Stoughton, 1975.

   Gillian Avery has made an intensive study of English children's books and the way they reflect the constantly shifting moral and social patterns of their times. A well-written, interesting presentation.

3. Bader, Barbara. *American Picturebooks from Noah's Ark to the Beast Within.* New York: Macmillan, 1976.

   A comprehensive historical study of American picture books, including the influence of foreign artists, the impact of motion pictures and comic books, and the social scene. Over 700 illustrations, some in color, enable the author to discuss and show various styles of art. Emphasis is placed on books produced from the 1920s to the 1970s.

4. Bingham, Jane, and Grayce Scholt. *Fifteen Centuries of Children's Literature.* Westport, Conn.: Greenwood Press, 1980.

   An indispensable reference book for the historical scholar of children's literature. Provides an annotated chronology of both British and American books from 523 A.D. through 1945. The chronology is divided into six time segments, one for each chapter. Historical background, development of books, and the general attitude toward children are presented for each time period. Includes information on series books as well as those that became classics.

5. Carpenter, Humphrey, and Mari Prichard. *The Oxford Companion to Children's Literature.* Oxford and New York: Oxford University Press, 1984.

   An excellent reference source on many aspects of children's literature including authors, illustrators, titles, and characters. The historical span stretches from early chapbooks through books published in the 1980s. Nearly 2,000 entries are included in this one-volume reference source to children's literature.

6. Darton, F. J. Harvey. *Children's Books in England: Five Centuries of Social Life.* Third Edition, revised by Brian Alderson. Cambridge and New York: Cambridge University Press, 1982. (First published in 1932.)

   This updated version of a well-recognized text on the history of children's literature in England makes fascinating reading. Darton had great respect for children's books, seeing their relationship to the history of children, the socioeconomic situation of the times, the cultural-religious beliefs of the period, and the history of publishing. While Alderson added detailed notes to each chapter, he did not revise the text. Therefore the reader does need to remember that the "now" and "today" referred to in the text refers to Darton's time, 1932.

7. Haviland, Virginia, and Margaret N. Coughlan. *Yankee Doodle's Literary Sampler of Prose, Poetry and Pictures.* New York: Crowell, 1974.

   Examples of American children's books selected from the some 17,000 titles of American juvenile literature gathered in the Rare Book Division of the Library of Congress. This volume is available in paperback and is profusely illustrated.

8. Johnson, Diedre. *Stratemeyer Pseudonyms and Series Books.* Westport, Conn.: Greenwood Press, 1982.

   This book provides an annotated checklist of the Stratemeyer syndicated publications, plus historical information on the growth of the company. The bibliography is arranged alphabetically by authors and pseudonyms. Thus it is possible to see how many Laura Lee Hope books were published and note the various authors and publishers.

9. Lystad, Mary. *From Dr. Mather to Dr. Seuss: 200 Years of American Books for Children.* Cambridge, Mass.: Schenkiman Publishing Co., 1980.

   Basing her conclusions on a content analysis of 1,000 books chosen from a random sample of the juveniles in the Rare Book Collection of the Library of Congress, Lystad determined the social values and social behavior reflected in American children's books over the last 200 years. The author traces the changes in literature for children from the religious admonitions of Dr. Mather to the nonsense of the Dr. Seuss.

10. Meigs, Cornelia, et, al. *A Critical History of Children's Literature.* Rev. ed. New York: Macmillan, 1969.

    First published in 1953, this comprehensive history of children's literature was written and revised by four recognized authorities in the field: Cornelia Meigs, Anne Thaxter Eaton, Elizabeth Nesbitt, and Ruth Hill Viguers. The organization by four chronological periods emphasizes the social trends influencing children's literature in England and America from earliest times to 1967.

11. Pellowski, Anne. *The World of Children's Literature*. New York: Bowker, 1968.
   An ambitious volume that presents the development of literature in every country, including the way political and social influences show the world view of children's literature. Annotated bibliographies of books and articles follow each commentary.
12. Smith, Elva S. *Elva S. Smith's The History of Children's Literature*. Revised by Margaret Hodges and Susan Steinfirst. Chicago: American Library Association, 1980.
   This very useful reference book on American and English children's books has been revised and enlarged by Hodges and Steinfirst. An introduction and outline for each period is given from Anglo-Saxon times to the close of the nineteenth century. Annotated references are provided for general works and individual writers of each period.
13. Townsend, John Rowe. *Written for Children: An Outline of English Children's Literature*. Second Revised Edition. New York: J. B. Lippincott, 1983.
   Townsend supplies a readable overview of the development of children's books in England and America, with a brief nod at Canada and Australia. His critical comments add interest to the text and help to put the books in perspective. The survey begins with books before 1840 and carries them through 1973 and beyond.

Note: The contemporary books mentioned in this chapter can be checked in the index for discussions in other chapters.

2

KNOWING
CHILDREN'S
LITERATURE

4

BOOKS
TO BEGIN ON

W hen one of our friends was visiting in England, she was surprised when her door was opened by a pink-cheeked blond toddler clutching her blanket and a copy of John Burningham's book *The Blanket*. She smiled at her visitor and asked her if she wanted her to read to her. With no hesitation the child climbed up on the bed and sat most contentedly while our friend read this story about the child who had lost his blanket and had his whole household scurrying around trying to find it until, at last, he found it under his pillow and went fast asleep. When she finished reading, the little girl took the edge of the book and nudged her for more. So she reread it and this time the toddler joined in with a quiet "M-mum" for Mummy and a "Da" for Daddy. Once again when she finished, she was nudged for more. Our friend said, "All right, I'll read it one more time, only this time you show me where to begin." Whereupon she took the book and turned it upside-down right-side-over and gave it to her. The child promptly turned it around and turned it over, opened the book, and turned past the acknowledgements and title page to the first page of picture and text. Later our friend found out that Kathy was only 18 months old!

DEVELOPING INITIAL LITERACY

What a lot Kathy already knows about books and reading at 18 months! First she knows books are enjoyable and even has a particular favorite. She also knows that adults hold the key to reading and can give meaning to the text. She herself knows how to hold a book and that it has to be right-side-up to read the print. She knows that you begin the story not on the title page but the page with more print. She recognizes the page on which Mummy first looks for the blanket, and she anticipates the next page in which Daddy looks for the blanket. If at 18 months she knows this much about how to read a book, think what she will know when she enters school.

At a year and a half, Kathy already has entered the world of literature. In talking with her mother our friend discovered that Kathy was read to frequently. Her mother, her school-age sister, and her father all shared books with her. She had a special shelf for her own books. The family went to the library at least once a week. Books were valued in their household.

Kathy is learning to love books, as she has many opportunities to snuggle up close to her mother and father for story time. She is also increasing her vocabulary as she points to pictures and names them or hears new words used in the context of the story. The language development of children this age is phenomenal; preoccupation with words and sounds of language is characteristic of the very young child. Books help to fulfill this insatiable desire to hear and learn new words. Hearing literature of good quality helps the child to develop his or her full language potential.

Children cannot be introduced to books too soon. The human baby is first attuned to various sound patterns almost from the moment of birth. She will be startled by a cross voice or a loud noise, soothed by a gentle loving voice or a softly sung lullaby. Gradually the baby begins to develop comprehension skills as she attaches meaning to the sounds around her. Talk is essential at this time. In *A Language for Life*,[1] an educational

[1] *A Language for Life*, The Bullock Report (London: H.M.S.O., 1975).

report from England, parents are advised to "bathe the child with language." One parent read a best-selling novel to her infant son just so he could hear the sound of her voice. Primarily, however, the very young child listens for the "quack quack" of a duck in a picture book or the "rrroar" of a lion. Singing simple nursery rhymes or playing such finger rhymes as "this little pig went to market" will make the baby giggle with delight. Increasingly, publishers are producing books for babies' enjoyment. These will be discussed later.

The young child who has the opportunity to hear and enjoy many stories is also beginning to learn to read. No one taught Kathy how to hold a book or where to begin to read the text. Through constant exposure to stories, Kathy is learning about book handling and developing some begin-

ning concepts about print.[2] She is spontaneously learning some of the attitudes, concepts, and skills that Don Holdaway describes as a "literacy set," including a positive attitude toward books, an understanding about the sense-making aspect of stories, the stability of print to tell the same story each time, and the form and structure of written language itself. All of this learning occurs at the pre-reading stage—what Holdaway refers to as the "emergent level of reading"—and seems to be essential for later success in reading.[3]

This certainly proved to be true in the longitudi-

[2]See Marie Clay, *The Early Detection of Reading Difficulties*, 3rd ed. (Portsmouth, N.H.: Heinemann Educational Books, 1985), for a description of her *Concepts about Print* test.
[3]Don Holdaway, *The Foundations of Literacy* (Sydney: Ashton Scholastic, 1979).

Research suggests that one of the most important gifts a family can give to children is an early love of books.
Photo by Nickalee Jung

nal study that was conducted by Gordon Wells. Following thirty-two children for a full nine-year period, he studied the way differences in the pre-school years affected children's later educational achievement. Of the many measures which he recorded, he found early exposure to books to be the most significant:

> Of all the activities that had been considered as possibly helpful preparation for the acquisition of literacy, only one was significantly associated with the later test scores, and it was clearly associated with both of them. *That activity was listening to stories.*[4]

Researchers have also studied the way in which parents share books with young children. Ninio and Bruner[5] discovered that one of the first language patterns or frames that a parent and child develop is in relation to sharing a picture book. Parents appear to use a consistent language pattern when labeling objects in a picture book. For example, the mother (or father) will first get the child's attention by saying "Look" and point to the picture. Next, she will query the child, asking "What's that?" Third, she usually gives the picture a label and, finally, in response to the child's repeating the name she will smile and say "That's right." If, however, the child can provide the label first, she will fine-tune her response and give him immediate approval. The child and mother (or father) take turns in this dialogue and collaboratively make meaning out of the text. This book-reading context is unique because the attention of the participants is jointly focused on pictures and words that stay the same for each rereading. Thus the child can predict the story and build up vocabulary over numerous readings.

While the way parents share these books follows a distinctive pattern, the quality of the read-aloud time varies tremendously according to the parents' patience and ingenuity in holding the youngster's interest. Linda Lamme[6] videotaped parents sharing

Carle's *The Very Hungry Caterpillar* and obtained a time variation of 1 minute 35 seconds to 16 minutes in reading the book. Evidently, some parents raced through this book, while others progressed in a more leisurely fashion, taking time to talk about the story and let their children poke their fingers in the holes that the caterpillar makes as he "eats" his way through the pages.

Besides length of time given to reading aloud, the quality of that time is important. Two researchers studied the parent as a reader and developed a scale to measure read-aloud sessions. They discovered that a large percentage of the parents of very young children did not know how to use a book to maximize the child's learning and enjoyment. When looking at an identification book many of them gave the name of the object without waiting long enough to see if the child could name it by herself. Some parents, on the other hand, elaborated on the child's response so that when a little girl, on seeing a picture of popcorn, squealed "See the popcorn!" the mother responded by saying, "Yes, look at the popcorn. I wonder if it has butter on it." Only 22 percent of their sample of readers gave such feedback with expansion or repetition.[7] The quality of the read-aloud time for the young child is as important as the selection of the book and the length of time spent.

Early exposure to books with plenty of time for talk and enjoyment of the story appear, then, to be key factors in the child's acquisition of literacy. One father whose child has been exposed to books from infancy said, "You know, I haven't the slightest doubt that David will learn to read, any more than I was concerned that he would talk."

BABIES' FIRST BOOKS

First books for young children are frequently identification books or "naming books" that allow a child to point to one picture after another, demanding to know "wha dat?" It is probably this give and take of language between the adult and the child that makes sharing books at this age so important.

[4]Gordon Wells, *The Meaning Makers: Children Learning Language and Using Language to Learn.* (Portsmouth, N.H.: Heinemann Educational Books, 1986), p. 151 (emphasis added).

[5]A. Ninio and J. Bruner, "The Achievement and Antecedents of Labelling," *Journal of Child Language*, vol. 5 (1973), pp. 1–15.

[6]Linda Lamme and Pat Olmsted, "Family Reading Habits and Children's Progress in Reading." Paper presented at the Annual Meeting of IRA, Miami Beach, May 2–6, l977. ERIC Document ED 138 963.

[7]Barry J. Guinagh and R. Emile Jester, "How Parents Read to Children," *Theory into Practice*, vol. XI, no. 3 (1972), pp. 171–177.

Recognizing the need for the young child to identify and name objects, publishers have produced many of these simple, sturdy "first books." These are usually constructed with heavy laminated cardboard or plastic pages that will withstand sticky fingers. They usually portray familiar objects like favorite toys, clothing, and animals. These identification books may have an accompanying text, but there is little or no plot or sequence to the stories. The fun in sharing them is in naming and talking about the pictures and following the reader's oral instructions: "Show me the doggie—the shoes—the jeans—the train." Illustrations for these books need to be simple, uncluttered, and easily identifiable, with little or no background to distract from the main object. *Baby's First Book*, illustrated by Garth Williams, has long been a favorite. Tana Hoban's board book *What Is It?* presents clear colored photographs of such familiar objects as a sock, a shoe, a bib, a cup, a spoon, and so on. Only one object is pictured on a page, shown against a plain white background, in this sturdy first book. *The First Words Picture Book* by Bill Gillham, based on research carried out at the University of Nottingham and at Harvard, represents the fifteen topics that occur most often in children's words. Each topic is illustrated first by itself and then in some kind of action. Thus "dog" is shown alone and then on the next page the text reads "Jenny is giving the *dog* his dinner" and an appropriate illustration shows the action. Contemporary parents are portrayed. For example, Mother is dressed in blue jeans and seen filling the *car* with gas in one picture, while Dad plays "This little pig went to market" with Jenny's *toes* in another one.

Helen Oxenbury has a series of "Baby Board Books" titled *Playing, Dressing, Working, Friends,* and *Family*. These books feature a delightfully droll round-headed infant doing what toddlers do, such as banging on pots, messily eating food, or sitting on the potty. A single noun such as "bowl,"

Helen Oxenbury's "Baby Board Books" feature a droll roundheaded infant doing what babies enjoy most such as drumming on pots. The object (pot) is clearly shown with its name on the left side of the page, while the baby's use of it is portrayed on the right. From *Playing*.

"potty," or "dog" represents the action on the page in much the same way that the young child uses a single word to carry the force of a sentence. The simplicity of the illustrations is just right for the audience—plain white backgrounds, clearly outlined figures, single focused composition, attractive but not distracting color. Slightly more background is represented in another set of first books by Oxenbury with such titles as *Mother's Helper*, *Beach Day*, and *Shopping Trip*. These portray a toddler in a variety of amusing situations like "helping" mother by licking the cookie bowl and spilling water all over the kitchen while washing up. Though these are wordless books, the pictures portray little stories that nurture the narrative thinking of the child and at the same time entertain parents.

Jan Ormerod's "Baby Books" are unique in that they portray the special relationships between babies and fathers. The series includes *Dad's Back*, *Messy Baby*, *Reading*, and *Sleeping*. In *Reading*, for example, a bearded, handsome father attempts to read his book while a beguiling toddler crawls in and out of his legs, peeps over his book, and finally ends up resting in his arms, reading too. While the texts are minimal in these books, clear pictures capture the love and humor between a father and his child.

Rachel Isadora details the many things a toddler can see, hear, and touch in her companion books titled *I See*, *I Hear*, and *I Touch*. In these books a baby responds to all the familiar things she hears, such as the ticking of a clock, the vroom of a vacuum, the quacks of ducks; or those she sees, such as her teddy bear, her belly button, her stroller, her bath, and so on. Lovely watercolors make these fine books to share. Some interpretation might be necessary, however, for the picture that shows the baby in her crib hearing the footsteps of her parents since no parents are pictured. Toddlers need pictures that match the text.

The many Dick Bruna books, such as *Miffy*, *The Apple*, *The Fish*, and *I Can Dress Myself* appeal to the small child with their stylized, clearly outlined figures against a plain background. Objects are easily recognized and identified in these books. One of Cushla's favorite books at 8 to 9 months (see page 12) was Bruna's alphabet book, *B Is for Bear*.

The bear in the "I Can Do It All By Myself"

series, by the Japanese author Watanabe and illustrator Ohtomo, is a real character. Two-year-olds will giggle at his antics in *How Do I Put It On?* Pictures show the bear putting his pants on over his head, while the text asks "Do I put them on like this?" The child can join in on the resounding "no!" on the next page as the clever bear then puts them on correctly. After demonstrating the right and wrong way to get dressed, the bear finally does it "all by himself." An even messier bear shows children how not to eat in *What a Good Lunch!* Children love the warmth and humor portrayed in these books and they relish the feeling of knowing more than the bear, a feeling psychologists have called "cognitive conceit." Other books in this series about a confident bear include *I Can Ride It*, *I Can Build a House*, *I'm the King of the Castle*, *Get Set! Go!*, and *Where's My Daddy?*

Rosemary Wells' little board books about Max, a lovable rabbity creature, are described as "Very First Books." However, the humor is more for adults than young children. In *Max's First Word* his sister tries to get Max to talk. She names everything she shows him and Max always responds with "Bang." Giving him an apple, Ruby suggests he say "Yum, yum," but Max surprises her with "Delicious." *Max's Ride* emphasizes such directional terms as "down," "over," "out," "under" as Max careens down a hill in his baby buggy. *Max's Toys* becomes a counting story, but objects are grouped together too quickly in the book as a child is asked to find five balloons, six cars, seven trucks, and a beanbag octopus with eight legs all on one page. Four other stories continue big sister Rhoda's struggle to get Max to eat an egg for breakfast, take a bath, and go to bed. Max manages to outsmart her every move.

Lionni's series of four wordless board books about two mice are titled *Who?*, *What?*, *Where?*, and *When?* The subtitle of this series, "Pictures to Talk About," effectively describes its purpose. In *Who?* a typical Lionni mouse made from torn paper visits a squirrel, a turtle, rabbit, hen, owl, and a wonderfully designed porcupine. All animals are done in collage, clearly shown against a pure white background. *What?* answers the question "What is it?" as the little mouse and his mother look at common objects found in the house. *Where?* plays with location, showing the little mouse *inside* a box, *up* in a tree, *inside* a bottle, etc. *When?* relates to weather and seasonal happenings, such as "When will it snow?" or "When can I go swimming?" Only the pictures are shown, so much would depend on the "reader" asking different interesting questions. The subtitle is right; there is much to discuss in these well-designed wordless books for the littlest ones.

The Blanket, described in the anecdote that opens this chapter, is one of a series by the British artist-author John Burningham. Other titles include *The Rabbit*, *The Cupboard*, *The Baby*, *The Snow*, and *The School*. These squarish-shaped books have more text than those of Oxenbury or Watanabe, but they still portray the activities and interests of a 2- or 3-year-old. For example, in *The Cupboard* the little boy gets out all the pots and pans and then puts them back again. In *The Baby*, this same child details what the baby does at his house, such as eating, sleeping, going for a walk. It concludes with the candid statement that "Sometimes I like the baby, and sometimes I don't." In these simple stories the young child is always at the center of the action, reflecting the ego-centered way of thinking that is characteristic of this age group. The plot line is not sequential; episodes could be interchanged at will. This is characteristic of the kind of stories the young children tell themselves.

Janet and Allan Ahlberg, also British, created *The Baby's Catalogue* when they noticed their own daughter's fascination with the mail-order catalogs that came to their house. Full of baby paraphernalia that toddlers will recognize, this book provides much to look at. It follows six babies (including a pair of twins) through their day. Instead of one Dad, it portrays five fathers and five mothers of different economic and ethnic backgrounds. While objects are clearly shown, the many little pictures on a page make it more appropriate for slightly older children. Certainly parents will identify with the page of "accidents" and the last page showing a very tired father walking a baby at night. The Ahlbergs have also published *Peek-a-Boo!*, which pictures a toddler's day. Every other page has a cut-out round circle which centers in on one part of the next picture and provides the recurring phrase "Peek-a-Boo." Turning the page, you then see the complete picture, which has many details to discuss.

"PARTICIPATION" BOOKS

Young children actively respond to a book by pointing or labeling, but some books have a kind of "built-in participation" as part of their design. These books have flaps to lift up and peek under, soft flannel to touch, or holes to poke fingers through. Such books may serve as the transition between toys and real books. *Pat the Bunny* by Kunhardt has been a best-seller for the very young child for more than forty years. In this little book the child is invited to use senses other than sight and sound. A "pattable" bunny made of flannel is on one page, flowers that really smell on another, and Daddy's unshaven face, represented by rough sandpaper, is on still another. Young children literally wear out this "tactile" book.

An increasing number of sophisticated cut-out books and "lift the flap" stories are appearing on the market. *Home Sweet Home* by Maureen Roffey is a good example of this trend in publishing. Questions and answers about the homes of various animals provide the structure; for example, the reader is asked, "Does a cat live in a kennel?" Looking through the open door of a kennel you can see a rounded shape and tail that could be a cat; turning the page of course reveals a dog.

Eric Hill's "lift the flap" stories about the dog Spot never fail to intrigue young children. In *Where's Spot?*, Spot's mother Sally searches for her puppy behind a door, inside a clock, under the stairs, in the piano, and under the rug. As the child opens doors and lifts up flaps to join in the search, highly unlikely creatures such as monkeys, snakes, and lions say "no" to the question "Is he in here?" Since "no" is one of 2-year-olds' favorite words, they love to chime in on the refrain. In *Spot's First Walk* the puppy meets all kinds of adventures behind fences, by chicken coops, and in the pond. These books are sturdily made, the pictures are bright and clear, and the stories are imaginative. Other titles in the series include *Spot's Birthday Party* and *Spot's First Christmas*. The titles are also available in Spanish editions.

Eric Carle's story of *The Very Hungry Caterpillar* is a favorite with children from 3 through 6. This imaginative tale describes the life cycle of a ravenous caterpillar who leaves behind a trail of holes in all the food that he eats. Children love to stick their fingers through the holes and count them. They particularly enjoy the caterpillar's menu for Saturday, which includes "one piece of chocolate cake, one ice cream cone, one pickle, one slice of Swiss cheese, one slice of salami, one lollipop, one piece of cherry pie, one sausage, one cupcake and one slice of watermelon." In Carle's multi-sensory story of *The Very Busy Spider*, children are invited to feel the pictures as well as see them. Brilliant collages depict familiar animals whose questions are never answered by the spider, who is too busy spinning her tactile web. No one can resist feeling these pictures in this story that emphasizes all the senses. The use of animal sounds and the repetition of the spider's actions make this as predictable a story as the well-loved *The Very Hungry Caterpillar*. Carle's story of *The Grouchy Ladybug* describes a nasty-tempered bug who quarrels with everyone she meets until she encounters a whale. Clever die-cut pages reinforce concepts of relative size and time of day. This book is more appropriate for children from ages 5 through 7.

Books that describe different kinds of sounds invite their own special kind of noisy participation. *Noisy* by Shirley Hughes pictures the noises a baby and a toddler can make, as well as the noises they hear. Realistic pictures show a frustrated mother holding a bawling baby while the telephone rings and the stew boils over. Peter Spier's book of animal sounds is titled *Gobble Growl Grunt*, while in *Crash! Bang! Boom!* the reader may compare the quiet crunch of new boots in the snow with the police siren's commanding cry of "you, you, you." *Pigs Say Oink* by Martha Alexander includes sounds of many animals, trains, children at a nursery school, and the quietest sound of all, when everyone is asleep. *Early Morning in the Barn* by Nancy Tafuri begins with a large double-page spread picturing a rooster waking the barnyard with his "cock-a-doodle-doo." A little chick responds with a "cheep," which awakens his brother and sister. All three run out of the henhouse into the barnyard, where they are greeted by an array of animals each making their familiar noise. Finally the story comes full circle as the chicks meet their mother hen. Lovely sunny pictures add to the fun of this noisy book.

If a book does not provide for participation, the

EVALUATING BOOKS FOR THE VERY YOUNG CHILD

The best books for babies and toddlers should meet these criteria:

- Relate to familiar life experiences.
- Provide clear uncluttered illustrations with little or no distracting background.
- Be constructed well, with sturdy durable pages.
- Use clear, natural language.
- Have predictable stories.
- Provide some humor, especially so the child will feel superior.
- Offer opportunities for participation and interaction.
- Hold the attention of the child.

---

adult reader can stimulate it by the kinds of questions he or she asks. For example, when sharing the old favorite *Caps for Sale* by Slobodkina, the parent might say to the child, "Find the monkey—not the one in the red hat, not the one in the blue hat, but the one in the green hat!" Such participation will help children develop visual discrimination, but, more importantly, it will add to the fun of the story hour. However, it is not necessary to elicit the child's participation in reading every book. Parents will know when it is best to ask a child to join in and when it might be best just to let the child listen to the story.

FINGER RHYMES AND NURSERY SONGS

Finger rhymes are one traditional way to provide for young children's participation as they play "Five Little Pigs" or sing "Where Is Thumbkin?" and the ever popular "Eensy, Weensy Spider." Finger plays date back to the time of Friedrich Froebel, the so-called father of the kindergarten movement, who went out in the German countryside and collected the finger plays and games that the peasant mothers were using with their children.

Marc Brown has collected and illustrated fourteen favorite finger plays, including the appropriate action, in his book *Finger Rhymes*. *Hand Rhymes*, a companion book to *Finger Rhymes*, includes fourteen more popular hand games, such as "This is the church / This is the steeple." Illustrated with amusing full-color pictures, these two books are very useful, with clear directions. Tom Glazer's *Eye Winker Tom Tinker Chin Chopper* provides the music and verbal directions for some fifty finger plays. His collection includes some for the youngest, such as "Eye Winker," "Pat-a-Cake," "Here Is the Church," and some longer cumulative songs for older children, such as "I Know an Old Lady Who Swallowed a Fly" and "There's a Hole in the Bottom of the Sea." Piano arrangements and guitar chords accompany each of these rhymes.

Babies and young toddlers often first respond to the sounds of music and singing. After Margot Zemach had sung the lullaby "Hush, Little Baby" to her daughter Rebecca every night for over a year, she decided to illustrate the song. Music is provided for the parents who might want to sing *Hush, Little Baby* and be delightfully entertained at the same time by the humorous visual images of each verse. Zemach's earthy pictures seem just right for this song and also for the cumulative Ozark song that her husband adapted for her pictures in *Mommy, Buy Me a China Doll*. Unfortunately, they did not include the music in their book, but Eliza Lou's ingenious suggestions of ways they can obtain money in order to buy her a doll make for an amusing tale without the music.

Another bit of delightful Americana is Aliki's spirited song *Go Tell Aunt Rhody*. Starting with brilliant endpapers of quilt blocks, this illustrated song book tells the familiar tale of the death of the old gray goose. While the gander and the goslings mourn her death, Aunt Rhody is pleased indeed with her new feather bed.

Children made up additonal verses to the rollicking old folk song *Oh, A-Hunting We Will Go*, adapted by John Langstaff. Nancy Winslow Parker's childlike illustrations are carefully arranged so as not to give away the last lines of each verse. Once children have determined the pattern of the song, they can guess what will be seen in the next picture. They easily predict the goat will end up "in a boat," but they laugh at the bear who gets put "in underwear." Children may want to create their own additions to this song after they hear these verses.

Diane Zuromskis illustrated the well-loved nursery-rhyme song *The Farmer in the Dell* with round pictures that help to recall the circle game that is played to this rhyme. Pictures portray the farmer and his wife, their child, nurse, dog, cat, rat, and cheese. The story ends when they all run after the rat who had eaten part of the cheese, which then stands alone. Children who know the song enjoy "reading" the words from memory. In *Fiddle-I-Fee*, Diane Zuromskis Stanley creates a little girl's lavish dinner party held for all her animal friends in her tree house. Highly imaginative pictures illustrate this traditional American chant. Children love to join in on all the various animal sounds in this long cumulative tale. They will enjoy noticing what the little girl feeds each of her animal guests at this very special dinner party in "yonders tree."

Counting rhymes have also been made into individual song books. *Roll Over*, illustrated by Merle Peek, shows a little boy in bed with nine animals. Each time they roll over, one animal falls out of bed. As the number of animals in the bed dwindles, children can look to see where they have found resting places in the room. Finally, when only the boy is asleep in his bed, a lion in a picture in his room appears to be winking and all the other animals are seen on a wall frieze that rings the ceiling. The music accompanies this tale of a young child's imaginary game. Mordicai Gerstein's *Roll Over!* is a small-sized book featuring a foldout flap on each page. As a little boy calls out "Roll over," the reader lifts the flap to discover which of his animal friends has fallen out of the huge bed. After the little boy is asleep alone in his bed, all the animals come creeping back and crawl in the other side. There is much to observe in this book—the sun design on the end of the bed descends as the moon comes up. The last page shows a darkened room as the moon says "Good night" to the ten humps in the bed.

Ezra Jack Keats illustrated his version of the old counting rhyme *Over in the Meadow* with collage pictures in jewel-like colors. The fine recording by Marvin Hayes for Scholastic increases children's enjoyment of the lilt and rhythm of this favorite nursery song. Primary-grade children can compare Keats' illustrations with those done by Rojankovsky for Langstaff's version of this story of all the animals who lived in the sunny meadow by the cool pond. Rojankovsky received the Caldecott award for his amusing interpretation of an old Scottish ballad telling of the wedding festivities of Frog and Miss Mousie. John Langstaff used the

Southern Appalachian music for this tale of *Frog Went A-Courtin'*.

Peter Spier illustrated several nursery-rhyme songs with meticulous attention to detail. The setting for *The Fox Went Out on a Chilly Night,* a Caldecott Honor Book, portrays the lovely autumn countryside near a New England village. The complete text of the song is provided at the end of the book. Children can sing along with a second showing of the book or join in while viewing the filmstrip from Weston Woods. In *London Bridge Is Falling Down,* Spier depicts the many changes that were made in that well-known structure. Notes on the history of London Bridge and the music for the song appear on the back pages for the adult reader.

MOTHER GOOSE

For many children, Mother Goose is their first introduction to the world of literature. Even a 1-year-old child will respond with delight to the language games of "Pat-a-Cake! Pat-a-Cake!" or "This Little Pig Went to Market." Many of the Mother Goose rhymes and jingles continue to be favorites among the 4s and 5s. What is the attraction of Mother Goose that makes her so appealing to these young children? What accounts for her survival through these many years? Much of the language in these rhymes is obscure; for example, modern-day children have no idea what curds and whey are, yet they delight in Little Miss Muffet. Nothing in current literature has replaced the venerable Mother Goose for the nursery-school age.

Appeal of Mother Goose

Much of the appeal of Mother Goose lies in the musical quality of the varied language patterns, the rhythm and rhyme of the verses, the alliteration of such lines as: "Wee Willie Winkie runs through the town" or "Deedle, deedle, dumpling, my son John." Children love the sound of the words, for they are experimenting with language in this period of their lives. The child learns new words every day; he likes to try them out, to chant them in his play. Mother Goose rhymes help the young

child satisfy this preoccupation with language patterns and stimulate further language development.

Mother Goose rhymes also offer young children many opportunities for active participation and response. The young child loves to get bounced on Daddy's knee to the rhythm of "Ride a Cock Horse" or clap hands to the sound of "Pat-a-cake, pat-a-cake, baker's man." Most of the verses are short and easily memorized; they can be chanted in unison or children may join in the refrains. Some of the rhymes—such as "Pease Porridge Hot," "London Bridge," or "Ring a Ring o' Roses"—are games or involve direct action from the child. Other verses include counting rhymes—as in "1, 2, buckle my shoe / 3, 4, shut the door." Slightly older children enjoy answering the riddles in some of the Mother Goose verses or attempting to say their favorite tongue twisters. Every child likes to fool someone with the well-known riddle: "As I was going to St. Ives, I met a man with seven wives." And they never fail to delight in successful recitation of the entire verse of "Peter Piper picked a peck of pickled peppers."

Another attraction of many of the Mother Goose rhymes is their narrative quality; they tell a good story. In just six lines "Little Miss Muffet" proves to be an exciting tale with action, a climax, and a satisfying conclusion. This is also true of "Simple Simon," "Sing a Song of Sixpence," "The Old Woman in the Shoe," and "Three Blind Mice." These stories in Mother Goose are characterized by their quick action. They are not moralistic, but justice does prevail, as in the ending of "The Queen of Hearts." Pre-school and kindergarten children enjoy pantomiming or dramatizing these well-known verse stories.

Many of the characters in Mother Goose have interesting likable personalities: Old King Cole *is* a merry old soul; Old Mother Hubbard not only tries to find her poor dog a bone but she runs all over town at his special bidding; and although Tommy Lynn puts the pussy in the well, Johnny Stout pulls her out! "The Crooked Man" is a grotesque character, but he has a crooked smile; and one can't help liking poor old "Simple Simon." Unpleasant but intriguing character traits are suggested by "Crosspatch," "Tom, the Piper's Son," and "Lazy Elsie Marley."

The content of the verses reflects the interests of young children. Many favorites are rhymes about animals—"The Three Little Kittens," "The Cat and the Fiddle," and the story of the mouse that ran up the clock in "Hickory Dickory Dock." While many of the animals are personified, others are not. For example, the kitten in "I Love Little Pussy" is very real. Some of the verses are about simple everyday experiences and include such incidents as "Lucy Locket" losing her purse, "The Three Little Kittens" losing their mittens, and "Little Bo Peep" losing her sheep. Children's pranks are enacted in "Ding, Dong, Bell!" and "Georgie Porgie." Everyday misfortunes are included in "Jack and Jill" and "Humpty Dumpty." "Peter, Peter, Pumpkin-Eater" has a housing problem, as does the "Old Woman in the Shoe." There are many verses about seasons and the weather, a concern of both young and old. The pleading request of one child, "Rain, Rain, Go Away," reflects the universal feelings of all children.

A major appeal of Mother Goose is the varied humor. There is the jolly good fun of a ridiculous situation in:

One misty, moisty morning
When cloudy was the weather,
I chanced to meet an old man
Clothed all in leather;
He began to compliment
And I began to grin—
"How do you do" and "How do you do"
And "How do you do" again!

Two 6-year-olds interpreted this verse in action by pretending to pass each other; as one moved to the left, the other moved in the same direction. Their movements were perfect for this amusing and familiar situation.

The young child's rather primitive sense of humor, which delights in other persons' misfortune, is satisfied by the verses about "Jack and Jill" and "Dr. Foster":

Doctor Foster went to Gloucester
In a shower of rain;
He stepped in a puddle up to his middle
And never went there again.

When this kind of humor is exaggerated, it is apt to become sadistic. Children's humor can be cruel, however, and they are quite insensitive to the dire punishment of the "old man / Who would not say his prayers / I took him by the left leg / And threw him down the stairs." For children, such action is fun and thoroughly relished.

Finally, the pure nonsense in Mother Goose tickles children's funny bones. Chukovsky,[8] a Russian poet, reminds us that there is sense in nonsense; a child has to know reality to appreciate the juxtaposition of the strawberries and the herrings in this verse:

The man in the wilderness asked me
How many strawberries grow in the sea.
I answered him as I thought good,
As many as red herrings grow in the wood.

Different Editions of Mother Goose

Today's children are fortunate in being able to choose among many beautifully illustrated Mother Goose editions. There is no *one* best Mother Goose book, for this is a matter for individual preference. The children in every family deserve at least one of the better editions, however. Preschool and primary teachers will also want to have one that can be shared with small groups of children who may not have been fortunate enough ever to have seen a really beautiful Mother Goose.

BRITISH EDITIONS

Three British editions of Mother Goose have been treasured classics for many generations. While they are, perhaps, not the most appropriate selections for the modern American child, they still appeal to children. They are important for the student of children's literature, for they are the forerunners of many of our present editions. *Mother Goose, or The Old Nursery Rhymes,* illustrated by Kate Greenaway, is tiny in format, with quaint, precise, old fashioned pictures. Greenaway's children have a quiet decorum that is in keeping with their nineteenth-century finery. However, there is action in these tiny pictures and a feeling for the English rural countryside and villages.

Quite different in effect is the edition by Arthur Rackham entitled *Mother Goose, Old Nursery*

[8]Kornei Chukovsky, *From Two to Five,* translated by Miriam Morton (Berkeley: University of California Press, 1963), p. 95.

Rhymes. Rackham uses three different types of illustrations for his verses—pen-and-ink sketches, silhouettes, and colored pictures. The latter are painted in the typical Rackham fashion, with eerie trees and weird little men peering from under their mushroom hats.

Leslie Brooke's *Ring o' Roses* presents a very different impression from that of the Rackham edition. Brooke's pictures are delightfully humorous and gay. The pigs in "This Little Pig Went to Market" are happy and complacent, except for the poor dejected fellow who had no roast beef.

Modern British editions of Mother Goose are equally outstanding. *Lavender's Blue,* compiled by Kathleen Lines and illustrated by Harold Jones, has colored pictures in muted tones of blue, green, and brown that are unmistakably British in setting, costume, and mood. Raymond Briggs has produced a comprehensive *The Mother Goose Treasury* which includes over 400 rhymes and more than twice as many illustrations. The book appears crammed with many vivid little scenes, objects, and comic people. Each rhyme has its own illustrations, and in some instances, each verse or line has an accompanying picture. This gives a feeling of clutter, but it provides much for the child to look at and enjoy. Almost all the verses are drawn from the definitive *Oxford Nursery Rhyme Book* with its 800 rhymes collected by Iona and Peter Opie.

A very British and earthy collection of Mother Goose rhymes is titled *Cakes and Custard.* The English critic Brian Alderson deliberately selected some unusual variants of well-known rhymes, as well as favorite ones. For example, Roley Poley kisses the girls rather than Georgie Porgie. In his foreword, Alderson explains that such unfamiliar variants make the reader "hear afresh" what the rhymes are saying. Helen Oxenbury's droll illustrations of common folk caught in the midst of their everyday lives also help us to view these rhymes from a new perspective.

One of the most striking and unusual Mother Goose editions is *Brian Wildsmith's Mother Goose.* Painted in brilliant watercolors, these pictures capture the gaiety of Mother Goose for twentieth-century children. The typical Wildsmith trademark is seen in the harlequin designs on the clothing of his characters. Another unusual characteristic of Wildsmith's style is the frequency with which he shows just the backs of people. By illustrating the back of "Tom, Tom, the Piper's Son" and that of the "Ten O'clock Scholar," Wildsmith invites the reader into the scene. The careful planning of this book is reflected in the combination of rhymes that are presented on facing pages. For example, "Little Boy Blue" is shown opposite "Diddle, Diddle, Dumpling"; both boys are sleeping, one in the haystack and the other in his bed.

AMERICAN EDITIONS

Counterparts of the British editions may be seen in some of the American ones. The good humor that is so characteristic of Brooke is equally characteristic of Rojankovsky's illustrations in *The Tall Book of Mother Goose.* His pictures are bright and happy; his children are natural looking, sometimes homely and disheveled. Rojankovsky is particularly skilled in capturing children's expressions; his "Little Miss Muffet" is terrified; "Lucy Locket" is thoughtful and pensive; "Jack Horner" is a picture of greedy innocence. Rojankovsky has portrayed his Humpty Dumpty as Hitler. Since according to one theory the first nursery rhymes were really political satire, this portrayal seems quite appropriate, particularly in 1942 when this edition was first published.

Michael Hague has created somewhat old-fashioned illustrations for his *Mother Goose,* which is appropriately subtitled *A Collection of Classic Nursery Rhymes.* His dark-toned watercolors with their medieval houses and street scenes are very reminiscent of the art of Arthur Rackham. Some of the illustrations are even silhouettes, a characteristic of Rackham's work.

Tomie de Paola's Mother Goose contains more than 200 rhymes, each illustrated with brilliant jewel tones against a clear white background. Pictures are large enough to hold the attention of a young child. Several include a full-page spread, while many show a sequence of action. Careful placement of the rhymes provides such interesting artistic contrasts as the jagged lines of the crooked man's house next to the rounded haystack of Little Boy Blue. The total format of this comprehensive Mother Goose is pleasing to the eye. The humor and action in the pictures will delight children.

James Marshall's Mother Goose has provided young children with a fresh and funny look at the venerable Old Goose. Most of the rhymes included in this collection are humorous, with hilarious illustrations to match. Children clever enough to spy the knife slipping through the pumpkin shell will realize that Peter Peter is not going to be able to keep his wife forever, despite the last line of the rhyme. Sharing Marshall's funny parody on "Hey Diddle Diddle" might inspire older children to create their own original Mother Goose rhymes.

Arnold Lobel portrays an unusual cast of Mother Goose characters in his book *Gregory Griggs and Other Nursery Rhyme People*. Use of space, well-placed pictures, and splendid watercolors make this a handsome book indeed. Seven- and 8-year-olds would love to meet these humorous and little known characters from Mother Goose. Lobel has created very funny new nursery rhymes in his book *Whiskers and Rhymes*. Older children will delight in both the rhymes and pictures of this book.

Adult readers will enjoy searching for such famous persons as Robert Frost, Princess Anne, Toscanini, Napoleon, and Hitler in Wallace

Tomie de Paola's traditional-appearing Mother Goose is painted in jewel-tones against a clear white background. Good humor abounds in these illustrations for verses selected from the authentic Iona and Peter Opie collection. From *Tomie de Paola's Mother Goose*.

Tripp's hilarious Mother Goose titled *Granfa' Grig Had a Pig*. Young children delight in the brightly colored pictures and the antics of the many funny animal characters, while older children laugh at the frequent puns and comments included in the comic book blurbs of some of the verses. The crooked old man is really a "crook," portrayed with his accomplices, the crooked cat and mouse. This is a vibrant and modern Mother Goose book which will entertain all ages.

The Real Mother Goose by Blanche Fisher Wright has long been an established favorite in American nurseries. The rather flat traditional pictures remind one of Brooke's work but lack his delightful humor. First published in 1916, the book has now been divided into four narrow-sized board books with checkered covers. The original old-fashioned-appearing pictures have not been changed, however.

The Provensens in *The Mother Goose Book* returned to the traditional style of illustrations by using Victorian dress and flat, subdued colors. Through grouping rhymes by subject matter, the illustrators make one picture serve several verses. Variations in shape and design combine the best of the old and the new in illustrating this collection of some 150 rhymes.

The *Mother Goose* by Tasha Tudor is reminiscent of the work of Kate Greenaway. Her soft pastel pictures are quaint and charming; her characters, lovable. The costumes of the characters represent many periods: American colonial, pioneer, Kate Greenaway, and Elizabethan. Miniatures in flowered frames on the endpapers and title page add to the old-fashioned feeling of this book.

One of the most beautiful editions of Mother Goose is *The Book of Nursery and Mother Goose Rhymes* by Marguerite de Angeli. This large book contains nearly 250 pictures, some of which are full-page illustrations painted in soft watercolors. The rich detail of the English countryside is similar to Lines' *Lavender's Blue* and suggests that the illustrator was very aware of the origin of Mother Goose. De Angeli's children and babies are beautifully portrayed, showing her love and knowledge of her own children and grandchildren.

Carefully designed wood engravings in six colors illustrate Philip Reed's *Mother Goose and Nursery Rhymes*. His rustic human characters and spirited animals provide humor and charm. The total format of this book represents superb bookmaking. The fine paper and well-designed use of space give a feeling of quality and richness.

The Rooster Crows by the Petershams has sometimes been called an American Mother Goose for it includes many well-known American rhymes and jingles such as "A bear went over the mountain" and "How much wood would a woodchuck chuck . . ." Another bit of Americana is found in the highly original *Father Fox's Pennyrhymes,* written by Clyde Watson and illustrated by her sister, Wendy Watson. These nonsense rhymes and jingles have the lilt and rhythm of traditional rhymes of folklore. Some are as gay as "Knickerbocker Knockabout / Sausages & Sauerkraut"; while others are as sad as Mrs. Fox's lament, "The rain falls down / The wind blows up: / I've spent all the pennies / In my old tin cup." The little watercolor-and-ink illustrations detail the antics of Father Fox and his friends and relatives in old-fashioned pictures. The Watsons create more original rhymes in *Catch Me and Kiss Me and Say It Again.* Characterized by the sound of traditional folklore, these little rhymes contain the loving humor captured in the title verse. Large watercolor pictures celebrate the daily games and activities of chubby, robust children. These include finger plays, piggy-back rides, and rhymes for dressing, eating, cutting fingernails, watching thunderstorms, and sleeping. A lovely goodnight rhyme goes:

Hushabye my darling
Don't you make a peep
Little creatures everywhere
Are settling down to sleep

Fishes in the millpond
Goslings in the barn
Kitten by the fireside
Baby in my arms

Listen to the raindrops
Singing you to sleep
Hushabye my darling
Don't you make a peep[9]

A delightful nursery-rhyme book is N. M. Bodecker's *It's Raining Said John Twaining.* Re-

calling his childhood in Denmark, Bodecker, a poet and artist, translated and adapted the rhymes into English so he could share them with his three sons. His pictures are as droll and humorous as some of the rhymes, particularly the title verse.

SINGLE-VERSE OR LIMITED-VERSE EDITIONS

A recent publishing trend has been the production of picture books portraying only one Mother Goose rhyme or a limited number of rhymes around a single theme. *The Three Little Kittens,* illustrated by Lorinda Cauley, would delight very young children with its pawprint cover and appealing kittens. Beginning readers would also enjoy "reading" the text of this verse, which they almost know by heart. It would give them the satisfaction of having "read" a whole book.

This would be an appropriate use for Paul Galdone's single-verse editions, including *The Old Woman and Her Pig; The House That Jack Built; Old Mother Hubbard and Her Dog; Tom, Tom, the Piper's Son;* and *The History of Simple Simon.* These narrative verses have action and humor and lend themselves well to individual presentations. Galdone's colorful pictures are large and clear and are equally good for sharing with a group of young children. It is fun to compare Galdone's *Old Mother Hubbard* with the sophisticated humor of the *Old Mother Hubbard* done by Evaline Ness. In this very modern version a harassed Mother Hubbard runs all over town buying delicacies for a huge English sheep dog while the dog romps about the house, reads the funny papers, and smokes a pipe. Another contrast is provided by the lift-the-flap version of *Old Mother Hubbard* created by Colin and Jacqui Hawkins. In this humorous updated tale Mother Hubbard is a rounded, almost comic book, character. The first part of each rhyme appears on the left side of the page with a door on the right. Open the door and the reader discovers a very funny dog doing all kinds of antics, including brushing his teeth and writing a letter. The traditional verses of the supposed death of the dog and Mother Hubbard's trip to the undertaker have been eliminated.

Tomie de Paola stages his version of *The Comic Adventures of Old Mother Hubbard and Her Dog.* Four box seats on the page facing the title page contain Bo-Peep and sheep, Humpty Dumpty, Mother Goose and friend, and a servant awaiting the arrival of the guests in the fourth box. On the

[9]Clyde Watson, *Catch Me and Kiss Me and Say It Again,* illustrated by Wendy Watson (New York: Philomel, 1978), p. 60.

next page, when the King and Queen of Hearts are in their places, the curtain rises on the story of Old Mother Hubbard and the antics of her dog. Children love to look for surprises in their books and Tomie de Paola seldom fails them. In this tale he incorporates some fifteen other nursery rhymes in four oval vignettes on the proscenium of the stage. A comparison of these Old Mother Hubbard books exposes young children to various art styles and helps them see how many different ways one nursery rhyme can be interpreted.

Susan Jeffers features only rhymes with horses in her Mother Goose compilation, *If Wishes Were Horses.* Her horses are beautifully drawn and represent much variety, from Shetland ponies to large hunters. Their riders include children of different multi-ethnic backgrounds and adults riding to hounds and to Banbury Cross. Good humor abounds in these lively pictures. Another one of her books based on a Mother Goose rhyme is *Three Jovial Huntsmen.* This is the tale of the unsuccessful hunting trip of three stupid hunters who

search and search for quarry and never see the many hidden animals watching them. The softly muted colors of the forest provide perfect hiding places for the concealed animals.

Children in the primary grades enjoy the specialized series of Mother Goose rhymes and other poems about dogs, cats, pigs, and houses titled *Hark! Hark! The Dogs Do Bark, Mittens for Kittens, This Little Pig-a-Wig,* and *The Parrot in the Garret.* These poems and verses collected by Lenore Blegvad are beautifully illustrated by her husband Erik Blegvad with tiny detailed full-color and black and white illustrations. These little books provide teachers with a fresh new look at some familiar and less well-known verses and suggest possible themes to study.

In a succession of carefully selected nursery rhymes, Peter Spier tells the story of a farmer's day in New Castle, Delaware, during the early nineteeth century. Spier's detailed, colorful pictures begin before dawn as Mr. Marley (Lazy Elsie is asleep in the log farmhouse) prepares to go to

Eric Hill combines the fun of a "lift the flap" book with riddles about favorite verses. Only when you open King Cole's cloak do you find the answer to the riddle given in the Mother Goose rhyme. From *The Nursery Rhyme Peek-A-Book.*

market. In *To Market, to Market* a cohesive story is told with many nursery rhymes until the Marleys return to the farm on "silver Saturday," for "the morn's the resting day." The scenes of the Market Place show the Town Hall and colonial brick homes facing the Delaware River. Authentic interiors of the church, the smithy, and the sheep barn help children visualize earlier times in U.S. history. The author's notes provide historical background for his setting and make this book one to share with a variety of age groups.

A handsome edition of *The House That Jack Built* has been presented in both French and English, illustrated with woodcuts by Antonio Frasconi. While this verse does not regularly appear in Mother Goose books, it is a well-known traditional nursery rhyme. Frasconi's four-color woodcuts have a strength and rusticity appropriate for this old rhyme.

Two recent books make a kind of game based on children's knowledge of Mother Goose. The easiest one, Eric Hill's *Nursery Rhyme Peek-a-Book,* asks rhyming questions such as "Hickory, dickory, dock, what ran up the clock?" Lifting the flap covering the face of the clock, the child discovers not only a little mouse, but the text of the whole rhyme printed on the inside of the flap. Ten well-known rhymes such as "Old Mother Hubbard," "Sing a Song of Sixpence," "Humpty Dumpty," and "Little Miss Muffet" are included. If children don't know these verses, they will after hearing this book. Sturdily made with lively, clear pictures, it provides for much participation and learning.

Each Peach Pear Plum by the Ahlbergs pulls together characters from Mother Goose and traditional folktales in a kind of "I Spy" game. Starting with Little Tom Thumb, each successive picture hides a new character somewhere in its design. Thus the picture of Baby Bunting carries the text "Baby Bunting fast asleep, I spy Bo-Peep," while the next picture of Bo-Peep challenges the viewer to find Jack and Jill. Children delight in playing this game and they particulary love the ending,

EVALUATING MOTHER GOOSE BOOKS

With so many editions of Mother Goose, what factors should be considered when evaluating them? The following points may be useful in studying various editions:

- *Coverage:* How many verses are included? Are they well-known rhymes, or are there some fresh and unusual ones?
- *Illustrations:* What medium has been used? What colors? Are the illustrations realistic, stylized, or varied? Are the illustrations consistent with the text? Do they elaborate the text? What is the mood of the illustrations (humorous, sedate, high-spirited)? Has the illustrator created a fresh original approach, avoiding cliché-ridden images?
- *Text:* Does the text read smoothly or have verses been altered? Is the text all on the same page, or fragmented by turning page?
- *Setting:* What background is presented—rural or urban? Does the book take place in any particular country? Is the setting modern or in the past? What does the setting add to the collection?
- *Characters:* Do the characters come from a variety of ethnic backgrounds? Do the characters have distinct personalities? Are adults and children featured or only children? How are animals presented—as humans or realistically?
- *Arrangement:* Is there a thematic arrangement of the verses? Is there a feeling of unity to the whole book, rather than just separate verses? Are pictures and verses well spaced or crowded? Is it clear which picture illustrates which verse?
- *Format:* What is the quality of the paper and the binding? Is the title page well designed? Is there an index or table of contents? Is there harmony among endpapers, cover, and jacket?

No matter what edition is selected, children should be exposed to the rhythm and rhyme of Mother Goose. It is part of their literary heritage and may serve as their first introduction to the realm of literature.

which pictures all of the characters together, eating plum pie, of course.

ABC BOOKS

ABC books can also be used for identification or naming, as they provide the young child with large, lovely pictures of animals or single objects to look at and talk about. This is perhaps a better use of these books than to instruct children in "saying their ABCs," for the memorized recital of the alphabet does little to help children to learn to read, while an extended vocabulary will be useful. ABC books do, however, give children practice in the identification of individual letters—necessary when children begin to read and write.

Certain factors need to be considered in selecting alphabet books. Objects should be clearly presented on a page, and these should be easily identifiable and meaningful for the intended age level. Only one or two objects should be shown for the very young child and it is best to avoid portraying anything that might have several correct names. For example, if a rabbit is presented for "R," the very young child might refer to it as a "bunny." Since text is necessarily limited, the pictures usually "carry" the story. For this reason they should be both clear and consistent with the text, reflecting and creating the mood of the book.

Alphabet books vary in both their texts and pictorial presentation from very simple to intricate levels of abstraction. Author/illustrators use a variety of organizing structures to create ABC texts. Four types of ABC books are discussed here (some books incorporate several types): (1) Word-picture formats; (2) Simple narrative; (3) Riddles or puzzles; (4) Topical themes. Today there are so many alphabet books that only the outstanding examples of each type are described. The table on pages 160–162 lists other titles with similar structure.

Dick Bruna's *B Is for Bear* is a clear example of a simple identification alphabet book for the very young child. Clearly designed, with only one object to a page and a single facing letter, this book allows even 1- and 2-year-olds to identify the objects. Plain white backgrounds alternate with clear yellow, blue, green, and red. The last page provides the text in case there is any confusion in interpreting picture and letter.

Striking pictures of realistic animals climb, poke through, or push large black block letters in *Animal Alphabet* by Burt Kitchen. A giraffe chins himself on the huge "G," while a small snail climbs up the "S." Each page contains only the letter and picture of the animal. Names of animals are given on a page at the end of this handsome book.

Some ABC books present a variety of objects that provide a small vignette for each letter. In Helen Oxenbury's *ABC of Things*, for example, the letter "H" is represented by a very funny picture of a *hare* and *hippopotamus* lying in bed in the *hospital*. All three names are given for identification purposes, however.

At first glance Kate Duke's *The Guinea Pig ABC* looks like a one word–one picture identification book. A closer look reveals that the child must interpret the action and meaning of each small vignette on a page. Thus "M" stands for "mean" and shows one guinea pig about to pull a chair out from another. While the vignettes are clear and

A giraffe appears to chin himself on a huge black block letter "G" in *Animal Alphabet* by Bert Kitchen.

ABC BOOKS

TYPE	AUTHOR/ ILLUSTRATOR	TITLE	AGE LEVEL	UNIQUE FEATURES
Word/picture identification				
	Dick Bruna	*B Is for Bear*	1, 2	See text.
	Burt Kitchen	*Animal Alphabet*	2–5	See text.
	John Burningham	*John Burningham's ABC*	2–4	One clear picture for each letter. Unusual choices: "T" is for *t*ractor, while "V" shows a *v*olcano.
	Brian Wildsmith	*Brian Wildsmith's ABC*	2–4	Brilliant colors portray animals, birds, a *q*ueen, a *v*iolin, a *x*ylophone. One picture on a page.
	Helen Oxenbury	*Helen Oxenbury's ABC of Things*	3–6	See text.
	Marcia Brown	*All Butterflies*	4–7	Superb double-page woodcuts illustrate paired letters and words such as *C*ats *D*ance, *E*lephants *F*ly. A butterfly can be found on each page.
	Tana Hoban	*A, B, See!*	5–7	Black and white photograms illustrate familiar objects. The page for "L" depicts a piece of *l*ace, a *l*ollipop, a *l*ock, and two *l*eaves.
	Leonard Baskin	*Hosie's Alphabet*	5–8	A well-known American artist creates a sophisticated book for his son. Brilliant pictures illustrate such wonderful sounding words as a "quintessential quail."
Simple narrative	Wanda Gág	*The ABC Bunny*	2–4	A little rabbit provides the story line for each letter. Beautifully designed woodcuts in black and white illustrate this classic ABC. Each letter is brilliant red, reminiscent of a child's block.
	Bruno Munari	*Bruno Munari's ABC*	2–4	An Italian artist presents a book notable for its simple but beautiful design. A buzzing fly adds a slight story line.
	Eve Merriam, John Wallner	*Goodnight to Annie*	3–5	Wallner creates dreamlike illustrations for Merriam's poetic descriptions of drowsy birds and animals going to sleep. The last page pictures Annie asleep with her alphabet book still open.
	Kate Duke	*The Guinea Pig ABC*	4–6	See text.
	Clyde Watson,	*Applebet*		

TYPE	AUTHOR/ ILLUSTRATOR	TITLE	AGE LEVEL	UNIQUE FEATURES
	Clyde Watson Wendy Watson	*Applebet*	5–7	See text.
	Jane Yolen, Jane Breskin Zalben	*All in the Woodland Early*	5–7	Yolen wrote the verse and music for this ABC which features a bird, animal, insect from the woodlands for each letter. The surprise ending brings all the animals together. Zalben accurately illustrates each forest creature in natural colors.
	Anita Lobel, Arnold Lobel	*On Market Street*	5–7	See text.
Riddles or puzzles	Mitsumasa Anno Jan Garten	*Anno's Alphabet* *The Alphabet Tale*	5–10 5–7	See text. Each letter is introduced on the preceding page by showing just the tail of an animal; turn the page and you see the whole animal. Children can predict the next animal by the rhyming verse, the picture of the tail, and the beginning letter.
	Anne Rockwell	*Albert B. Cub and Zebra*	5–8	This wordless alphabet book is both a puzzle and a story. Albert B. Cub's beloved zebra is abducted. Albert's search for his friend takes him around the world and through the alphabet.
	Miska Miles, Peter Parnall	*Apricot ABC*	6–9	Parnall hides the letters in the grass in this ecological story of the adventures of an apricot seed. Detailed illustrations of a meadow complement the quiet verse of the text.
Topical themes	Francine Grossbart	*A Big City*	4–7	Brightly colored silhouettes show such familiar city objects as a fire escape, garbage can, and hydrant. Simplicity and clarity of graphic design.
	Mary Azarian Rachel Isadora Tasha Tudor	*A Farmer's Alphabet* *City Seen from A to Z* *A Is for Annabelle*	5–12 6–9 5–7	See text. See text. Delicate watercolors portray an old-fashioned doll with her different belongings representing different letters.

TYPE	AUTHOR/ ILLUSTRATOR	TITLE	AGE LEVEL	UNIQUE FEATURES
Topical themes	Alice Provensen, Martin Provensen	*A Peaceable Kingdom: The Shaker ABCEDARIUS*	6–12	The Provensens illustrated this old 1882 alphabet verse of the Shakers in a way that depicts the rhyme of the animals but also provides much information about the way the Shakers lived. Richard Barsain concludes the book with a note on Shaker history and education.
	Muriel Feelings, Tom Feelings	*Jambo Means Hello*	6–12	Muriel Feelings gives children a simple lesson in Swahili while introducing some important aspects of the geography and culture of East Africa. Tom Feelings has produced soft, luminous gray, black, and white illustrations of the people and their villages.
	Margaret Musgrove, Leo Dillon, Diane Dillon	*Ashanti to Zulu: African Traditions*	7–12	This is the only alphabet book to have won the Caldecott Medal. Musgrove describes many of the customs of some 26 African tribes, while the Dillons create stunning illustrations picturing the people, their homes, an artifact and animal for each tribe. Pictures are framed and tied together at the corners with a design based on the Kano Knot which symbolizes endless searching.
	Ted Harrison	*A Northern Alphabet*	7–12	A striking book about northern Canada and Alaska describes people, places, animals, and objects for each letter. Place names beginning with the appropriate letter form a frame around each picture. The flowing lines of the pictures recall the Inuit art.

cleverly done, it is a more difficult task to interpret a story than to simply identify an object or animal.

Applebet by the Watson sisters is a delightful alphabet story told in rhymed verse of a farmer and her daughter Bet who take a cart full of apples to the country fair. The book portrays lovely rural scenes in the autumn and robust action at the fair. In keeping with the title, the binding is apple-green and the opening picture portrays a beautiful crisp red apple while the accompanying verse asks the child to find the apple hidden in each picture. Illustrations and verse celebrate a bit of rural Americana which will delight young children. The last page portrays an apple with several bites taken out as if reading *Applebet* has helped the reader digest a delicious apple experience.

Arnold and Anita Lobel combine their many talents to create a handsome and unique alphabet book. Starting with the picture of a small Victori-

an boy determinedly lacing up his high shoes, sailor hat ready to go and purse fat with change, we follow him on his journey to the title page, *On Market Street*. Then he proceeds on his way through all the shops from A to Z. He returns home in the evening exhausted, with an empty purse, but a gorgeous array of gifts each purchased from a different shop. Rather than portray all the stores, Anita Lobel creates tradespeople and shopkeepers out of their own wares, making intriguing characters from *b*ooks, *c*locks, *e*ggs, *q*uilts, *t*oys, or *z*ippers. Five-, 6-, and 7-year-olds will love looking at this alphabet storybook. They can check out the variety of gifts and see if they can name them from A to Z. They can turn back the pages to look at

Inspired by 17th-century French trade engravings, Anita Lobel creates shopkeepers out of their own wares for the unique alphabet book *On Market Street*. Text by Arnold Lobel.

Crisp black and white woodcuts celebrate rural life in Vermont in this handsome alphabet book. From *A Farmer's Alphabet* by Mary Azarian.

the original storekeeper and try to find the gift the little boy bought. Older children might enjoy creating their own alphabet people.

Some alphabet books incorporate riddles or hidden puzzles in their formats. *Anno's Alphabet* by one of Japan's leading illustrators and designers, Mitsumasa Anno, is filled with visual illusions and puzzles. Each large letter looks three-dimensional, as if it had been carefully carved from wood. Suddenly, however, its perspective will appear to change and surprise you. The "M" is only half there as it disappears into its mirror image. Each letter is matched with a clear yet amusing picture and hidden in all of the borders are even more surprises. A glossary at the end provides clues to the hidden pictures in this visually exciting ABC book.

Topical themes are frequently used to tie the alphabet together. For example, Rachel Isadora brings the city to life with vibrant black and white street scenes for *City Seen from A to Z*. Her city is bustling with people—all ages, all races, all enjoying their city, including the men playing *J*azz, a wonderfully graceful little girl dancing in her too big *T*utu and wearing new socks and sneakers, and a plump grandmother and her granddaughter licking *I*ce cream cones. Isadora captures action through body postures and story-telling vignettes in this city ABC.

A handsome alphabet book that celebrates rural life in Vermont is Mary Azarian's *A Farmer's Alphabet*. Crisp black and white woodcuts portray such scenes as a snow-covered *B*arn on a hillside, *I*cicles hanging from the eaves of a small house, a big old-fashioned wood *S*tove, a hand-made *Q*uilt, and cardboard-stiff *Z*innias. Red capital and lower case letters on creamy white paper provide striking contrast to the black and white pictures. The Vermont Department of Education was so impressed by Azarian's designs that they commissioned her to create this book and then purchased one for each elementary school in Vermont. Young and old will enjoy looking at this beautiful alphabet book.

Obviously there is no lack of ABC books, both general and specialized, for the pre-schooler and for the older child. Each ABC book should be evaluated on its own merits in concept and design, considering the purpose for which it will be used and the projected age level of its audience. The concept of an ABC book is one that can be utilized in every area of study. Children would thoroughly enjoy making their own, such as an "ABC of Pioneer Life" or an "ABC of Favorite Books," and then sharing them with their peers or younger children.

COUNTING BOOKS

Ideally, boys and girls should learn to count by playing with real objects like blocks, boxes, bottle caps, or model cars. They can manipulate and group these as they wish, actually seeing what happens when you add one more block to nine or divide six blocks into two groups. Since time immemorial, however, we have been providing children with counting books, substituting pictures for real objects. The young child can make this transition from the concrete to its visual representation if he or she first experiences the real and the visual illustrations are clearly presented.

In evaluating counting books, then, we look to see if the objects to be counted stand out clearly on the page. Various groupings of objects should avoid a cluttered, confusing look. Illustrations and page design are most important in evaluating counting books. Accuracy is essential.

Counting books, too, vary from the very simple to the more complex. For the purposes of this text they are discussed under three categories: (1) One-to-one correspondence; (2) Other simple mathematical concepts; (3) Number stories and puzzles. Examples of each category are given, while the table on pages 169–171 lists other titles with similar structure.

Tana Hoban's *1, 2, 3* is a sturdy, well-designed first counting book which presents simple one-to-one correspondence. Colored photographs picture such well-known objects as two shoes, five small fingers, six eggs, seven animal crackers, and ten toes. Numbers and names of the numerals are given in this first board book for very young children. Hoban has also used clear black and white photographs to illustrate a counting book for slightly older children, *Count and See*. Again she has photographed objects that are familiar and meaningful to the young child, such as three school

TYPE	AUTHOR/ ILLUSTRATOR	TITLE	AGE LEVEL	UNIQUE FEATURES
One-to-one correspondence	Tana Hoban	*1, 2, 3*	1—3	See text.
	John J. Reiss	*Numbers*	3—5	Clear drawings of such common objects as shoes, kites, baseball players, etc., make this well within the young child's experience. The book ends with a picture representing 1000 rain drops.
	John Burningham	*Count-Up*	4—6	This is the first of six ingenious books that introduce mathematical concepts. By lifting flaps, the child can count various animals.
	Eric Carle	*1, 2, 3 to the Zoo*	4—6	A circus train serves as the vehicle for this counting book as each passing car has an increasing number of animals in it, such as two hippos and nine snakes.
	Molly Bang	*Ten, Nine, Eight*	4—6	Starting with her ten toes, a father begins a countdown until his daughter is in bed. One of the few number books to portray a black father and daughter.
	Helen Oxenbury	*Numbers of Things*	4—6	Delightfully amusing illustrations add to the fun of this number book. Fifty is represented by the appropriate number of lady bugs, while the final page pictures an astronaut on the moon and asks "How many stars?"
	Brian Wildsmith	*Brian Wildsmith's 1, 2, 3's*	4—6	This is a handsome but confusing alphabet book. Using a kind of harlequin design of colors proves to be distracting for accurate counting.
	Tana Hoban	*Count and See*	4—6	See text.
	Muriel Feelings, Tom Feelings	*Moja Means One*	7—12	This is a better informational book on East Africa and the Swahili language than a counting book. For example, the number six is represented by six persons in different kinds of dress, but only five kinds of clothing are identified. Older children will benefit from the information given on Africa and the superb soft brown paintings by Tom Feelings.

COUNTING BOOKS

TYPE	AUTHOR/ ILLUSTRATOR	TITLE	AGE LEVEL	UNIQUE FEATURES
Other simple mathematical concepts	John Burningham	*Pigs Plus*	4–7	A young pig sets off in a red car and meets a succession of difficulties. In each instance another pig helps him out and joins the fun. Young children will never realize they are learning simple addition in this amusing tale.
	John Burningham	*Ride Off*	4–7	The concept of subtraction is presented as one by one five children slip off a big horse which gallops away.
	Mitsumasa Anno	*Anno's Counting Book*	4–7	See text.
	Mitsumasa Anno	*Anno's Counting House*	5–8	Ten little people living in a furnished house move to an empty house next door, taking their belongings with them. Concepts of addition and subtraction can be developed. Die-cut windows pique the child's curiosity to see inside.
Number stories and puzzles	Shirley Hughes	*A Walk in the Park*	3–5	A little girl and her grandfather count all the things they see during their walk in the park. Detailed watercolors show "six runners running" and "ten birds swooping in the sky."
	Eric Carle	*The Very Hungry Caterpillar*	5–7	A very hungry caterpillar eats through one apple, two pears, etc., until he becomes fat, spins a cocoon, and emerges as a beautiful butterfly. Clever die-cut holes invite children to poke fingers through the various foods the caterpillar eats.
	Maurice Sendak	*One Was Johnny*	5–7	Part of the small "Nutshell Library," this is the story of a small boy visited by many obnoxious animals. He threatens to eat them all if they are not gone by the time he counts down from ten.

COUNTING BOOKS (continued)

TYPE	AUTHOR/ILLUSTRATOR	TITLE	AGE LEVEL	UNIQUE FEATURES
Number stories and puzzles	Pat Hutchins	*1 Hunter*	5–7	See text.
	Jane Yolen, Jane Breskin Zalben	*An Invitation to the Butterfly Ball*	5–7	An elf invites various sets of animals to the coming ball. A little mouse ties the story together in her rhymed refrain lamenting her inability to find a "proper floor length dress."
	Fulvio Testa	*If You Take a Pencil*	6–8	This circular tale tells of two children who take a pencil and draw *three* cats which admire *four* birds and so on until the children arrive on a treasure island and discover twelve treasure chests—all empty except for the last one, which contains a single pencil. Older children could create their own number story using this one as a model.

buses, six candles on a birthday cake, nine firemen's hats, a dozen eggs in their carton, fifteen cookies, and amazingly, 100 peas in ten pea shells! A pair of young boys—one black, the other

In the eleventh month, Anno shows eleven evergreen trees, eleven migrating birds, and eleven bare trees. How many other sets of eleven can you discover in this remarkable counting book? From *Anno's Counting Book* by Mitsumasa Anno.

EVALUATING ABC AND COUNTING BOOKS

ABC Books
- Objects or animals should be clearly presented on a page.
- For very young children, only one or two objects should be pictured.
- Common objects or animals which are easily identifiable are best for young child.
- ABC books should avoid the use of objects that may be known by several names.
- The author/illustrator purpose for the book should be clear.
- Illustrations should be consistent with text and reflect the mood of the book.
- The organizing principle of presentations should be clear.
- The intended age level should be considered in both pictures and text.

Counting Books
- Objects to be counted should stand out clearly.
- Accuracy is essential.
- Common objects that children know, such as fingers, toes, eggs, are usually best for young child.
- Groupings or sets should be clearly differentiated.
- Number concepts should not be lost in story.

white— represent the numeral 2. The cover pictures an integrated group of seven boys and girls with balloons. The photographs are reinforced on opposite pages with the number as word, as numeral, and as model set represented by white dots.

Many mathematical concepts are developed in one of the most inventive and perfect counting books of recent years, *Anno's Counting Book,* by Mitsumasa Anno. Delicate watercolors portray a landscape changing with the various times of day, seasons, and year. The clock in the church steeple tells the time of day, while adults, children, and animals go about their daily activities. As the buildings in the village increase, so do the groups and sets of children, adults, trees, trains, boats, and so on. This is one of the few counting books to begin with zero—a cold winter landscape showing only the river and the sky, no village. It ends with a picture of the twelfth month, a snowy Christmas scene and twelve reindeer in the sky. Nothing seems contrived in this book, for all the number relationships are shown in natural situa-

tions of daily living, just the way children would find them in their own communities.

Pat Hutchins provides both a number story and a puzzle in her creative book *1 Hunter*. This is an account of a hunter's humorous walk through a jungle filled with hidden animals. The hunter determinedly stalks past two trees; turn the page and "the trees" are the legs of two elephants. The hunter continues on his way through a grove of trees; the next page shows they were the legs of three giraffes. The hunter is oblivious to all he is missing until the very last page when the animals come out of hiding and the one hunter runs away! Wonderful endpapers add to the story as many eyes peek from their various hiding places. Children love finding hidden animals, and Hutchins reveals just enough of them so that the child reader can predict the next page.

Since many of the criteria for evaluating counting books are similar to those for alphabet books, the list on this page includes both.

CONCEPT BOOKS

A concept book is one that describes various dimensions of an object, a class of objects, or an abstract idea. Concepts need to grow from first-hand experience as children gradually perceive common characteristics and relationships such as color, size, weight, or location. Some concepts like shape or color can be more easily presented in a book than such abstract concepts as growth, time, or distance. Certain concepts like love or death develop gradually over years and may be best understood in the themes of storybooks or informational books for older children.

The books discussed in this chapter are those written for young children with the specific purpose of developing concepts. A concept book is really a young child's first informational book. It should stimulate much talk and help children develop their vocabularies while at the same time it sharpens their perceptions and enlarges their growing understanding of the world. Well-defined concepts are necessary for children's language and cognitive development.

Notice how the young child struggles to define his or her understanding of the concept "dog." At first "doggies" include all dogs and maybe even a few cats and squirrels. Later, after they have abstracted the essential qualities of "dogginess," young children can tell the difference. Still later, they can make finer differentiations—discriminate between the St. Bernard and the German shepherd, for example. Concept books help children to identify these essential elements of an object or a class of objects.

ABC books and counting books are really concept books. So, too, are the books that help children to identify and discriminate colors. John Reiss illustrates his book of *Colors* for very young children with clear, bright graphics showing several pages of familiar objects for each color; for example, the various shades of green are shown by green leaves, grass, a green snake, a frog, turtle, pickles, cucumbers, gooseberries, and peas. It is appropriate that a first book on colors should be as aesthetically pleasing to the eye as this one.

Tana Hoban's *Is It Red? Is It Yellow? Is It Blue?* is subtitled "An Adventure in Color." With clear close-up photographs, Hoban helps the child see the vivid colors in such common sights as fire hydrants, cars, a lollipop, oranges, apples, and bal-

Tana Hoban's clear black and white photographs capture children's interest at the same time they build concepts of "big" and "little" in *Big Ones, Little Ones.*

loons. Small circles of color below the pictures help the child to know what colors to look for on that page. With adult help, the child can explore other concepts like shape and size in these carefully planned pictures.

Hoban has written three books on shapes. The first, *Shapes and Things,* uses black and white photograms of real objects like scissors and a hammer to help children identify unique shapes. Each page shows sets of generic objects; thus shapes of tools are arranged on one page, while objects used in sewing are on the opposite page. *Circles, Triangles and Squares* uses photographs of familiar objects to present these particular concepts. Full-color photographs illustrate her third book, *Shapes, Shapes, Shapes.*

John Reiss helps children find circles, triangles, ovals, rectangles, and squares in vivid colored pictures of common objects in his stunning book *Shapes.* Beginning with the most familiar shapes, squares and circles, Reiss moves to the less familiar ones like cubes, showing how the solid form is really framed by squares. Jan Pienkowski's series of concepts books includes one on *Shapes.* The format of this book helps the youngest child to distinguish shapes by placing a clear drawing of a spiral on the left-hand page and a picture of two snails on a curled frond of a fern on the right. The spirals are clearly indicated within the shapes of the snails.

Fulvio Testa emphasizes the shapes and beauty in the world in his dazzling book *If You Look Around You.* Beginning with a single pinprick of light which is a distant star, Testa ends with a look at the tranquil sphere which is the earth seen from a spaceship window. This is a book to challenge all readers to open their eyes and observe.

Hoban shows relative size with fascinating pictures of mother and baby animals in *Big Ones, Little Ones.* These creatures include zoo animals and domesticized ones. Not daunted by such complex concepts for the young child as opposites and position, Hoban has created *Push Pull, Empty Full* and *Over, Under and Through.* Striking black and white photographs contrast fifteen pairs of opposites. A turtle is pictured with his head tucked in for "in" and poked out for "out," while two eggs are seen whole and then smashed on the floor for "broken." The second book pictures children in a variety of situations going *Over, Under and*

Through. Much actual experience of going over, under, and through is needed to understand these spatial concepts, but this excellent book can reinforce and extend the child's understanding. A more complex book but one that children really enjoy is *Dig, Drill, Dump, Fill.* In this one Hoban turns her fine photographic lens on heavy machinery, including road rollers, trash trucks, street flushers, cranes with electric magnets, and dump trucks. Clear black and white pictures show these big machines in action, while a glossary provides their names and functions.

Peter Spier's *Fast-Slow High-Low: A Book of Opposites* uses many little watercolor pictures to illustrate various aspects of opposites. "Smooth-Rough" includes a porcupine and a ground hog, a poodle and a dachshund, a slimy worm and a hairy caterpillar, a smooth highway and a bumpy road. Parents or teachers might have to help children find the two things being compared, but this book will help the child learn that a single concept can apply to many situations. As usual with Peter Spier's delightful watercolors and pen-and-ink pictures, the child will have much to look at and talk about.

Bathwater's Hot is part of Shirley Hughes' Nursery Collection. Here a little girl discovers that many things have opposites, such as "Bathwater's hot, seawater's cold." Based on the everyday activities of youngsters, these opposites are shown in the context of the child's experiences. As usual, Hughes creates believable children in action-filled pictures.

A little car's journey from the city to the country is used to teach the concept of opposites in *Traffic: A Book of Opposites* by Betsy and Giulio Maestro. The text is in large print and very brief—"There goes a long train. Here comes a short one." Illustrations are brilliant in color and make use of large flat areas. Some of the concepts presented in this book are confusing and developmentally beyond the reach of the young child. Children frequently use such words as big and tall and short and small as synonyms. Kindergarten children have much difficulty in seeing "the long small train" as opposite of the "big short train." While these concepts would be more appropriate for primary children, the look of the book appears to be for younger children.

Young children are intrigued with Donald

Crews' books, *Freight Train* and *Truck*. In the first one, Crews pictures an empty track, then each of the different cars; the red caboose, orange tank car, yellow hopper car, green cattle car, blue gondola, purple box car, and finally the black steam engine. The train goes faster and faster through the tunnels and over bridges until it becomes a rainbow of speeding colors and then fades out of sight. Both colors and specific names for the cars provide real information for young children. Using bold graphics, Crews swings a big red tractor *Truck* across the country from east to west through cities, small towns, night and day, rain and shine. No text appears in this concept book except all the environmental print one naturally encounters on a trip, such as names of other trucks, traffic signs, highway exit signs, tunnels, and truck stops. In *School Bus* children again have an opportunity to see common signs and symbols: the green "walk" sign, the red "don't walk" sign, the school bus stop, and others. The yellow buses are large and small, but all pick up students and bring them home when school is over. In another book titled *Flying*, Crews details the flight of a plane from take-off to landing. Other equally well-designed concept books by Crews include a wonderful ride on a *Carousel* and *Light*, which contrasts the lights in the city with those in the country.

My Kitchen by Harlow Rockwell contains a slight thread of a story as a little boy points out the everyday objects in his kitchen and their uses. The story ends with the preparation of a very satisfying peanut butter sandwich and cup of soup for his lunch. Clear simple pictures with no clutter and plenty of white space allow children to identify these comfortable well-known objects. The double-page picture of the boxes and cans on the shelf provides much opportunity for reading the environmental print that appears on the labels of grocery items.

Rockwell previews and reassures children about potentially threatening situations in his concept books *My Nursery School*, *My Doctor*, and *My Dentist*. Again a first-person narrative describes happy nursery-school activities and the security of being picked up by Mother at the end of the morning. It is good to see a male teacher reading to the children. *My Dentist* and *My Doctor* show the various instruments used by both and explain what the doctor (a woman) and the dentist (a man) will

do. These books can be used to allay fears before new experiences and to recall the event by revisiting it through a book.

More detail is provided in the concept books by Anne and Harlow Rockwell, *Thruway, Machines, The Supermarket,* and *The Toolbox.* The title page of *The Supermarket* shows a large empty brown bag. It begins with the natural remark of the little boy: "I like the way the door opens all by itself at the supermarket." Each object that the little boy or his mother puts in the cart is clearly drawn and named. Interest is added by buying ingredients for the boy's coming birthday party. *The Toolbox* features simple watercolor pictures of tools and a phrase or two to describe their functions; a plane, for example, "smooths wood and makes it curly." *Tools* by Ken Robbins introduces children to many different tools with lovely full-color, hand-tinted photographs. However, just their names are given, not how they are used. And the child's point of view so typical of the Rockwell books is missing in this one.

With a simple straightforward text and bold illustrations using broad flat spaces, Byron Barton takes us on a tour of an *Airport*. We arrive with the buses and cars, and then the tour includes a view of a plane with all the parts pointed out, including the pilot's cockpit. The story ends with the wonder of the take-off. Barton eliminates all unnecessary detail. His pictures remind us of the way children can draw and convey just the essentials of a scene. *Building a House,* also by Barton, describes a process rather than a place or single concept. Beginning with the bulldozer digging the hole, the cement mixer pouring cement, and the carpenters putting up walls, the action continues as the bricklayers, electricians, and painters finish the house, until at last the family moves in. Barton's simple no-nonsense text clearly identifies the workers and their functions. In all of Barton's books people of various racial backgrounds are included in a natural way.

Concept books help children see relationships between objects, develop awareness of similarities or differences, or grasp the various dimensions of an abstract idea. Often these books begin with the familiar and move to the unfamiliar or more complex. Concepts should be presented in a clear, unconfusing manner, with one or more examples given. Where appropriate, functions of objects should be made clear. Concepts should be within the developmental scope of the child. Concept books can be used to enrich or reinforce an experience, not substitute for it.

WORDLESS BOOKS

Wordless books are picture books in which the story line is told entirely through pictures. They are increasingly popular with today's TV-oriented child. Many of them are laid out in the same sequential format as comic books and have wide appeal to different age levels.

Textless books are surprisingly helpful in developing some of the skills necessary for reading. Handling the book, turning the pages, beginning at the left-hand side and moving to the right are all skills that give the young child a sense of directionality and the experience of acting like a reader. These books are particularly useful in stimulating language development through encouraging children to take an active part in story-telling. As the child relates the story, she will become aware of beginnings, endings, the sequence of the story, the climax, the actions of the characters—all necessary for learning how a story works, for developing a sense of story. "Reading" a wordless book also requires specific comprehension of the illustrations. Teachers may want to record children's stories into language experience booklets. Older children may want to write their own creative stories to accompany the illustrations. In order to help the child tell the story, pictures must show action and sequence clearly so children will not be confused in their tellings. Also, children should be given an opportunity to examine the book and look through it completely before they try to tell the story orally. Otherwise, they will describe the action on each page but not understand the sequential relationship of the story.

The Good Bird by Peter Wezel was one of the first wordless picture books, and it is still one of the easiest to share with very young children. In this story a friendly pink bird shares his worm with an unhappy goldfish. The crayoned pictures are simple and childlike, but clearly show the sequence of action. In *Do You Want to Be My Friend?*, Eric Carle has given the child more latitude to create his own story about a little mouse who in seeking a friend follows the lead of one tail after another, only to be very surprised at what is at the other end! The brilliant collage pictures will delight children as much as the opportunity to tell their own versions of this story.

A highly original wordless book is *Changes, Changes* by Pat Hutchins. Here, two wooden dolls arrange and rearrange wooden building blocks to tell a fast-paced circular story. When their block house catches fire, the resourceful couple dismantle it and build a fire engine, whose hose quickly douses the fire, thereby creating a flood! Undaunted, the wooden dolls then build a boat, which becomes a truck, which is changed to a train, until eventually they reconstruct their original block house. Hutchins has written and illustrated an even funnier story with the use of only one sentence. In this book Rosie—a very determined, flat-footed hen—goes for a walk, unmindful of the fact that she is being stalked by a hungry fox. At every turn of *Rosie's Walk*, the hen unwittingly foils the fox in his plans to catch her. The brightly colored comic illustrations help youngsters to tell Rosie's story. Primary children enjoy telling this story from the point of view of the fox.

The first waking thought of a plump little lady is that this is the morning to have *Pancakes for Breakfast*. Tomie de Paola pictures her persistent efforts to make the pancakes despite the fact that she has to go to the hen house to gather the eggs, milk the cow, and churn the butter. Finally thinking she has all the ingredients, she discovers she must go and buy some maple syrup. She returns with a self-satisfied expression on her face only to discover that her dog and cat have tipped over the milk and flour and eaten the eggs. All is not lost, however, for from her neighbor's house comes the delicious aroma of pancakes. Once again she puts on her bonnet and cape and invites herself in to eat an enormous breakfast of pancakes. Sequence is clearly shown in full-page illustrations nicely balanced with two frames to an occasional picture (four frames across). The expressions on the little lady's face and those of her cat and dog help tell this amusing and satisfying story. The recipe for the pancakes is given and asks to be tried out.

In a clear sequence of narrow pictures, Jan Ormerod portrays a young girl getting dressed independently while her parents oversleep. She triumphantly saves the day by wakening them and showing them the time. From *Sunshine.*

Two lovely wordless books, *Sunshine* and *Moonlight* by Jan Ormerod, celebrate a small girl's joy with the simple pleasures of morning and night-time rituals. In a series of watercolor vignettes, often several to a page, a lovable little girl "helps" her mother and father get up in the morning. The little girl wakens first, reads her book, and then tiptoes down the hall to waken her father with a kiss. He slips out of bed and the two of them make breakfast for her mother (first burning the toast). After breakfast her bearded father reads the newspaper and her mother goes back to sleep for some extra shut-eye. The little girl gets dressed in a wonderful sequence of twelve narrow pictures across two pages. She then looks at her clock and goes in to alert her parents that they have overslept. They both dash back and forth in various stages of getting dressed. Finally, her father kisses her goodbye, and the little girl goes off with her school bag and her mother. The sunshine of this story streams through the windows and the radiant love of this family. *Moonlight* concludes the day with dinner, bath, bedtime story, and stalling ploys familiar to all children and parents. Once again the illustrator captures the shining glow of moonlight with beautifully soft watercolors.

Through the ingenious use of half pages, John Goodall manages to add excitement and movement to his many wordless adventure stories. Lovely detailed watercolors portray *The Midnight Adventures of Kelly, Dot, and Esmeralda;* a koala bear, a doll, and a tiny mouse, who climb through a picture on the wall and into a charming landscape of a river and boat. Their river outing meets with disaster, as does their trip to a village fair. The three just manage to make it back to the boat, the river, through the picture, and onto the safety of their own toy shelf. *Shrewbettina's Birthday* and *Surprise Picnic* are also in full color and use the same imaginative format. *Naughty Nancy* is the tale of an irrepressible mouse who is the flower girl in her sister's wedding. *Creepy Castle* appeals to slightly older children as they "read" the mouse melodrama of the brave knight mouse who rescues his fair damsel mouse in distress. Five other books by Goodall detail the amusing adventures of accident-prone Paddy Pork, including a night at the opera, a holiday out camping, and ballooning. Children find these stories very funny and again delight in the added drama the half page provides. Goodall's wordless books are long, with several incidents in each plot, yet the pictures show the action clearly and make them easy and exciting to narrate.

It is interesting to see when children recognize that *Deep in the Forest* by Brinton Turkle is really a variant of "Goldilocks and the Three Bears," with the unique twist that a baby bear wreaks havoc in a pioneer cabin. Usually when the children see baby bear eating porridge from three different-sized bowls, they recall having "heard" something like this before.

Mercer Mayer was one of the first illustrators to create wordless books. His "A Boy, a Dog, and a Frog" series is very popular with children aged 5 and up. Simple line drawings in green and black portray the friendship between a boy, his dog, his frog, and a turtle. The stories are amusing and full of slapstick fun, particularly in *Frog Goes to Dinner,* when frog hides in the boy's pocket and goes to the restaurant with the family. Chaos results when he jumps into the salad and knocks over the champagne. An embarrassed family is evicted from the restaurant and the boy is banished to his room. Jealousy is the theme of *One Frog Too Many* when the boy is given a new baby frog. These stories are humorous and easily told from their pictures.

Emily McCully tells two delightful stories of a large mouse family and their seasonal fun in *Picnic* and *First Snow.* In *Picnic* a little mouse falls out of the truck when they go down a bumpy road. Her loss is not discovered until all eight of her brothers and sisters are ready to eat. Then the whole family piles into the truck to go find her. In the meantime the little mouse and her toy baby mouse have been eating luscious raspberries. She accidentally puts down her toy in her search for the tasty berries. When she is finally reunited with her family, there is a small crisis while she goes back to find her missing "child." In *First Snow,* the same little mouse hesitates to try sledding down the steep hill. After her first slide down, however, she loves it, and the whole family has to wait for her to take one last slide before the sun disappears over the snow-covered hill. These books provide real narratives, with identifiable characters, exciting plots, and lush watercolors.

Peter Spier's Rain captures the delight of a brother and sister thoroughly enjoying playing in a rain-puddled day. It begins with just a few drops on the title page. The children's mother calls them into the house to get their macintoshes, rubber boots, and umbrella and then sensibly sends them outside to play. And play they do! A watery-blue double-page spread pictures the splashing raindrops and the children sloshing through the puddles. They see the shimmering beauty of drops of rain caught in a spider's web, with the spider safe and dry under the limb of the tree. They check on where other animals and birds hide in the rain and feed the ducks and geese and swans who are in their element as much as the children. Finally a strong wind comes up and they run for home where they enjoy all the cozy inside treats of a rainy day: cocoa and cookies, a hot bath, reading, and building a huge block construction. After dinner, a game of marbles, and watching TV, the children go to bed. The moon comes up and the clouds part. Birds greet a rain-washed dawn and the children waken to a glistening sunny day.

The story of *Noah's Ark* has been translated from the Dutch by Peter Spier and appears in verse form on the first page. What follows, however, is virtually the wordless story of all that transpires both inside and outside the ark for forty days and forty nights. Various sized pictures portray Noah's many activities on the ark and capture his every mood, from deep concern to jubilant rejoicing over the dove's return with the olive branch. Mrs. Noah's washline of clothes contrasts sharply with the dirty, messy interior of the ark at the end of its long voyage. Humorous touches run throughout this book, including the number of rabbits which leave the ark and the slow final departure of the snails and tortoise. Each viewing of the book reveals more of Spier's wit and artistic talent. This book richly deserved the Caldecott Medal which it received.

Another beautiful wordless book is Raymond Briggs' *The Snowman.* Using soft watercolors in a comic-strip format, Briggs tells the story of a small boy and his snowman who comes to life one night. The boy invites the snowman inside to see the house but warns him away from the fireplace, the stove, and the hot water tap. The snowman has a childlike fascination for such simple things as an electric light switch, a skateboard, the father's false teeth in a glass, and the family car. The boy and the snowman share a meal and a fantastic pre-dawn flight before returning to bed and the front lawn. In the morning the sun awakens the boy, and his first thought is for his snowman. He looks out the window—alas, his friend has melted. Children who look at this lovely picture book want to look at it over and over again. It is the kind of story that invites revisiting and discussing all the details which Briggs has included.

BOOKS ABOUT THE COMMON EXPERIENCES OF THE YOUNG CHILD

Increasingly, publishers are producing books that mirror the everyday common experiences and feelings of the pre-schooler. These books for 3- through 5-year-olds are usually small in size and suggest individual rather than school sharing. Illustrations are simple and clear, but usually not of the same quality as the more expensive picture books discussed in the next chapter. The young child's activities and concerns are at the center of these books, but frequently the humor is directed at the parent reader.

Anne and Harlow Rockwell collaborated on producing the "My World" series including such titles as *I Love My Pets, Sick in Bed, I Play in My Room, Happy Birthday to Me,* and *Can I Help?* The text in these squarish books presents a straightforward first-person account of a child's response to these experiences. Small, brightly colored illustrations add to the stories. The Rockwells effectively cut across stereotyping; in *Sick in Bed,* the doctor is a woman, and when the child returns to nursery school her teacher is a man. A little girl helps her father polish the car in *Can I Help?,* but it is her mother who helps her fly a kite.

The "Betsy" series by Gunilla Wolde were first published in Sweden. In *Betsy and the Doctor,* Betsy falls off the climbing tree in nursery school and cuts her head. Robert, one of the nursery-school teachers, takes her to the doctor for stitches. Back at school, Betsy becomes the center of attention. In *Betsy's Baby Brother,* Betsy's ambivalent feelings are described when her mother nurses her brother—that's the time she'd like to give him away to another lady! Betsy helps her mother take care of him, changes his dirty diapers, and talks to him until he goes to sleep—then he is "cuddly and sweet." Other titles in the series include *This Is Betsy* and *Betsy's First Day at Nursery School.*

The "Out and About" series by Helen Oxenbury describe first-time experiences with hilarious results. *Eating Out,* for example, is a disaster. The whole adventure is told in a very matter-of-fact manner by the "innocent" 3- or 4-year-old who was the cause of the waiter tripping and spilling all the food. *The Car Trip* reflects the feelings of many families who venture forth too soon on a long day's trip with a preschooler. Oxenbury captures the wonderfully awkward gallop of a little girl in her first *Dancing Class.* Details, expressions, and humor characterize all the pictures and stories in this series. Other titles include *First Day of School, The Birthday Party, The Checkup, Our Dog,* and *Grandma and Grandpa.*

One of the developmental tasks of this age group is learning such physical skills as buttoning or zipping up your clothes or putting the right shoe on the right foot. In *Oh, Lewis!* by Eve Rice, Lewis, his mother, and sister go shopping on a cold winter day. First, Lewis' boots become unbuckled and his patient mother stops to fasten them up again. An unzipped jacket signals another stop, while lost mittens and a slipped hood require more attention. Finally when they return home Lewis is so firmly into his clothes that he doesn't know how to begin to take them off. Gentle pictures detail this universal task of the very young.

In *Alfie's Feet* Shirley Hughes captures a young boy's delight in his new yellow boots but his puzzlement at the way they feel. Finally, he realizes he has them on the wrong feet and switches them himself. In *Alfie Gets in First,* Alfie is so excited to be the first one home from a shopping trip that he races in the door as soon as his mother opens it and locks himself in. Hughes ingeniously uses the center gutter of the book as the door dividing the outside of the house from the inside. In this way the reader can see all the people who come to try to help open the door at the same time it is possible to see what Alfie is doing. Just at the moment when the window cleaner is about to climb up his ladder and go through a bathroom window, Alfie gets a chair, reaches the lock himself, and grandly opens the door. Busy, detailed pictures of a London urban area provide much for children to look at, but primarily they will be delighted by Alfie's accomplishment. A similar situation is described in *Sara and the Door* by Virginia Allen Jensen. However, in this story Sara is all alone when she shuts her coat in the door and she must figure out what to do. The knob is too high for her to reach, but finally she unbuttons her coat and walks away free. Expressive little black and brown pictures

"Open the door, Alfie," said Mom.
But Alfie didn't know how to open the door from the inside. The catch was too high up. Mom looked into the mail slot. .
"Try to reach the catch and turn it," she said. Alfie tried but he couldn't quite reach it.
"Can you put the key through the mail slot?" asked Mom. But Alfie couldn't reach the mail slot either.

Shirley Hughes ingeniously uses the gutter of the book to represent the door separating Alfie from his mom. Increasing frustration is shown on both sides of the door, until Alfie solves the problem. From *Alfie Gets In First.*

show Sara's struggles with her coat and her happy solution.

Many stories for children this age provide reassurance for their fears. In *Michael Is Brave*, Helen E. Buckley tells of a small boy who is too frightened to go down the slide until his teacher asks him to go up and stand behind a little girl who is more afraid than he is. After she goes down the slide, Michael does, too, and discovers that he likes it. Emily McCully's illustrations change perspective and let you see how very high the slide seems to Michael when he is at the top. *The Biggest Meanest Ugliest Dog in the Whole Wide World* describes the way Jonathan feels about Pirate, the neighbor's dog. Jonathan is always very careful to check where Pirate is before he goes outside because he is so frightened of him. One day, however, he is playing in his sandbox and Pirate gets out and joins him. He is too close for Jonathan to run away, so he throws a ball at him. But the biggest meanest ugliest dog in the whole wide world retrieves it and wags his tail, asking Jonathan to throw it again. Rebecca Jones has written a warm satisfying story for any toddler frightened of dogs. Illustrations by Wendy Watson provide just the right touch of gentle humor for

this triumphant tale of overcoming a common fear.

Eve Rice has a way of tapping into the young child's feeling. In *Benny Bakes a Cake*, Benny has a wonderful time helping his mother make his birthday cake. But when they go for a walk, Ralph, their dog, eats the cake. Benny is disconsolate until his father comes home with presents, birthday hats, *and* a beautiful birthday cake. A young child can easily follow the action of this story by looking at the large flat primary-colored pictures shown against a clear white background. Just as father didn't forget Benny's birthday, neither does Sam the zookeeper forget to feed the elephant. In *Sam Who Never Forgets*, Rice shows the keeper feeding all the animals except the elephant, who is really worried. But then Sam comes back with a wagon full of food just for him. This is a fine book to share just before or after a trip to the zoo.

Amifika is certain he is one of the things his Daddy will have forgotten while he was away in the army. Lucille Clifton tells the heart-warming story of a small black child who is worried his Daddy won't remember him because he can't remember his Daddy. Tired of hiding in the back-

and Benny stirs

In this wonderfully predictable story, Benny helps make his birthday cake, while it is clear what role Ralph, his dog, will play. From *Benny Bakes a Cake* by Eve Rice.

yard, he goes to sleep, only to wake up in the arms of his Daddy:

> And all of a sudden the dark warm place came together in Amifika's mind and he jumped in the man's arms and squeezed his arms around the man's neck just like his arms remembered something.[10]

Sam, another small child, feels rejected by all the members of his family—all are so engrossed in

[10]Lucille Clifton, *Amifika,* illustrated by Thomas DiGrazia (New York: Dutton, 1977), unpaged.

their own activities that they tell him to go somewhere else to play. Finally, completely frustrated, Sam begins to cry. Then all members of the family come together and realize the cumulative effect they have had on Sam. Consoled at last, Sam helps his mother make raspberry tarts. Symeon Shimin's illustrations capture all nuances of feelings in this fine book by Ann Herbert Scott.

The youngest child frequently feels left out, the tag-end of the family. Pat Hutchins captures these feelings in her well-loved *Titch.* Titch is too small to ride a two-wheel bicycle or fly a kite or use a hammer. But he is not too small to plant a seed,

Everything is growing in this picture by Pat Hutchins, except Titch. He never seems to reach the promise of the title *You'll Soon Grow Into Them, Titch* until the end when he can at long last say it to someone else.

and Titch's plant grows and grows. The ending of the story of Titch is a classic example of poetic justice for the youngest and smallest of a family. In *You'll Soon Grow into Them, Titch*, it is obvious that once again Titch as the youngest must wear the hand-me-downs. But his mother sees they don't fit and his father takes him out and buys him a whole new outfit. With the arrival of a new baby in the family it is at last Titch's turn to say "You'll soon grow into them." Complementary stories of birth and growth are told only through the pictures of the ingenious tale. Mother's growing pregnancy coincides with a nesting robin seen outside the window. Buds on the tree and bulbs in the garden and in a pot in the house all bloom at the same time the baby robins hatch and the children greet the newest member of the family.

Young children need much love and reassurance that they will always be needed and belong to their family. This is the theme of the favorite story *The Runaway Bunny* by Margaret Wise Brown. A little bunny announces that he is going to run away and his mother tells him that she will run after him.

The little bunny thinks of all the things he will become—a fish in a stream, a crocus, a sailboat. His mother in turn says she will become a fisherman, a gardener, the wind, and come after him. The little rabbit decides just to stay and be her little bunny, after all. This story might seem suffocating for older children, but it is just what the preschool child wants to hear.

Bedtime stories provide the comfort and reassurance that children need to face the dark alone. No book for the very young child ever replaced Margaret Wise Brown's *Goodnight Moon*. First published in 1947, it was reissued in 1975 in paperback and made into a pop-up book, *The Goodnight Moon Room* in 1984. This gentle poetic story shows a little bunny going to bed while a grandmother bunny helps him whisper goodnight to everything in his room. Gradually the room darkens and only the light from the moon is seen when the little bunny is at last asleep. Children love to join in on the rhyme and look for the little mouse which is in each picture of the bedroom. Clement Hurd's gradually darkening pictures show each item mentioned in the room. Two- and 3-year-olds ask to hear this soothing book over and over again. Brown also wrote *A Child's Good Night Book* in which a rhythmical text tells of animals and people preparing for bed. It has never been as popular as *Goodnight Moon*, however.

Charlotte Zolotow has written several bedtime stories. Her *Wake Up and Good Night* contrasts the brilliant sunny day and singing birds with the stillness of the night when "only the trees whisper." Leonard Weisgard's brilliant full-color illustrations contrast the joyous shining day with the dark shadows of the night. In *The Summer Night*, Zolotow tells of a little girl who can't sleep and of the way her father helps her to enjoy the night sights and sounds until she becomes sleepy again.

In *Goodnight, Goodnight* by Eve Rice, goodnights are said outside homes and inside homes as the darkness comes creeping slowly over the city. Up on the roof of a tall building a little kitten purrs for someone to play with him. The end of the story finds his mother cat carrying him away with a final goodnight. Done in crisp black and white with a yellow moon, this is a gentle, beautifully illustrated city bedtime story.

In *Bedtime Story* Jim Erskine provides a story

within a story as a mother tells her child all the things that are happening in the house and outside as he snuggles down to sleep and dreams of all she has told him. In *Close Your Eyes* by Jean Marzollo, Susan Jeffers' pictures show two stories going on simultaneously. Rhyming text suggests things a little girl can do in her dreams, such as play with "wooly lambs on a lazy day." Large close-up pictures show the wooly lambs, while smaller ones show a harassed father getting his little one ready for bed. Despite the soothing visions of animals going to sleep, the little girl fights bedtime throughout the book. At last she does go to bed, with visions of all her father has told her as her dreams. Susan Jeffers' large beautifully composed pictures will intrigue both children and their parents.

Stories that have no relationship to bedtime of course make fine reading at this time, too. So young children should see many of the appropriate picture books described in Chapter 5 and hear the well-loved traditional tales of "The Three Bears," "The Three Billy Goats Gruff," and "The Gingerbread Man" discussed in Chapter 6. For while young children need books that mirror their own feelings and experiences, they also need books to take them beyond those experiences and to help their imaginations soar.

BOOKS FOR THE BEGINNING READER

Learning to read begins at home with children hearing stories on their parents' laps and seeing loved persons in their lives valuing books. The child lucky enough to have had such a wide exposure to books will usually learn to read easily and fluently. The importance of reading aloud to young children for their success in learning to read has been consistently proven by researchers in this country and abroad (see Chapter 1: Clark 1976, Cohen 1968, Durkin 1966, Thorndike 1973, Wells 1986).

The books for the very young child which have been discussed in this chapter may be read again when children of 5 or 6 start to become readers. Increasingly, theories of reading emphasize the importance of reading for meaning and enjoyment from the very start of learning to read. Many pre-

primers and primers have stilted, unnatural language and pointless plots that cut across the child's spontaneous attempts to read; on the other hand, stories that children love and have heard over and over again have natural language and satisfying plots that encourage reading. Many of these books utilize repeated language and story patterns which help the child learn to read naturally as she or he joins in on the refrains or predicts the action of the story.

Jerome Bruner was the first to use the term "scaffold" to characterize adult assistance to children's language development.[11] It is also possible for a book to be an instructional scaffold or kind of temporary help in the child's first attempts to read. Such books include familiar texts like Mother Goose rhymes or songs that children know by heart and can easily "read" or they may be books with repetitive language or story patterns which help children remember or predict the story easily. Bridge and others[12] report a study with slower first-graders that showed sight words were better learned in the context of predictable books and language experience stories than from pre-primers. Primary teachers and school librarians will want to know how to identify such predictable books.

Predictable Books

Books that can help a child learn to read may be identified by such characteristics as repetitive language patterns or story patterns or the use of such familiar sequences as numbers, the days of the week, or hierarchical patterns. Frequently, texts combine several of these characteristics in a single story.

Many stories include repetitive phrases or questions that invite children to share in the reading. Eric Hill's *Where's Spot?* provides for active participation as the child helps search for the dog. Each time a flap is lifted to answer such a question as

[11]Identified by C. B. Cazden, "Adult Assistance to Language Development: Scaffolds, Models, and Direct Instruction" in R. P. Parker and F. A. Davis, *Developing Literacy: Young Children's Use of Language* (Newark, Del.: International Reading Association, 1983), pp. 3–18.
[12]Connie A. Bridge, et al., "Using Predictable Materials vs. Preprimers to Teach Beginning Sight Words," *The Reading Teacher*, vol. 36 (May, 1983), pp. 884–891.

"Is he behind the door?" a hidden animal answers with an emphatic "No." Children quickly learn the language pattern of this very easy text.

Another well-liked patterned question-and-answer book is *Brown Bear, Brown Bear, What Do You See?* by Bill Martin, Jr. The question in the title is put to a large brown bear, who replies that he sees a redbird looking at him. The question is then directed at the redbird: "Redbird, redbird, what do you see?" He sees a yellow duck, who in turn sees a blue horse, and so on. Identification of animal and color in the picture allows the child to chime in on the question for each page. The large, bold collage pictures by Eric Carle are a perfect match for the text and support the child's reading of the story.

Mirra Ginsburg's *The Chick and the Duckling* play a delightful game of follow-the-leader. Each thing the duckling does is copied by the chick, who echoes "Me too." When the duck decides to take a second swim, the chick has learned his lesson and says "Not me." Both the refrain and repeated action in the story make this a very predictable book. Other patterned language books may repeat certain words many times, as in *The Teeny Tiny Woman* by Paul Galdone.

Repetitive story patterns also help the child predict the action in the plot. The easy folktales with their patterns of three, such as *The Three Billy Goats Gruff* by Brown, *The Three Little Pigs* and *The Three Bears*, both illustrated by Galdone, support the child's reading. For once children recognize the story structure, they know that if the great big bear says "Someone has been tasting my porridge," then the middle-sized bear and the baby bear will both say the same thing.

Cumulative tales have repeated patterns and phrases which become longer and longer with each incident. Children love to read the story of *The Great Big Enormous Turnip* by Tolstoy which tells

When young children are provided a rich literary environment in which they are read stories, are surrounded by books, and are given time to read and write, they very quickly begin to "act like readers."
International Stock Photo © 1982 Barbara Loudis, Hunter School, New York City.

of an attempt to pull up a turnip by a whole family including the Old Man, the Old Woman, the granddaughter, the black dog, the house cat, and the little mouse, whose added strength is just what is needed.

Some modern stories contain predictable plots, also. Certainly one of the easiest is Brian Wildsmith's *The Cat Sat on the Mat*. In this simple yet beautifully illustrated book, one animal after another comes and sits on the mat until the cat thinks there are too many. With one hiss he frightens them all away and once again he is left with complete ownership of the mat. *Rosie's Walk* by Hutchins is better for telling than reading since the entire text is only one sentence long. However, children can learn how to predict what is going to happen to the fox by careful observation of where the unsuspecting hen takes her walk. The journey story, *Three Ducks Went Wandering* by Ron Roy, is filled with danger and narrow escapes from an angry bull, a hungry hawk, a family of foxes, and a snake. Children enjoy guessing how the ducks will survive each crisis. Another tale of a narrow escape, by Mirra Ginsburg, is the story of a hen and chicks who get *Across the Stream* and foil the hungry fox. These and other stories help children begin to develop an understanding of how the character of a fox will act in an animal tale. This developing sense of a story also begins to help them predict action.

Building on children's knowledge of numbers and the days of the week provides a kind of scaffold for reading *The Very Hungry Caterpillar* by Eric Carle. They particularly enjoy reciting the part where the caterpillar eats through *one* apple on *Monday, two* pears on *Tuesday, three* plums on *Wednesday,* until he has a huge feast on *Sunday.* In Maurice Sendak's rhyming *Chicken Soup with Rice,* each verse begins with the month and ends with doing something to the soup, such as blowing it or sipping it. Some groups have made up their own verses for the months, using Sendak's pattern and repeated phrases. Hierarchies based on size, such as those in the tales about the three bears and the three Billy Goats Gruff, help children to read these stories. With one reading, children easily discern the pattern of being the littlest in Pat Hutchins' story of *Titch.* They know that if his brother has a *great big* bike and his sister a *big bike,* then Titch will have a *tricycle.* Other stories build on children's knowledge and delight in imitating the various sounds of animals. Eric Carle's *A Very Busy Spider* uses this device as animal after animal tries to dissuade the spider from her task of making her web. *Going for a Walk* by Beatrice Schenk deRegniers also revolves around the sounds made by the many animals the little girl meets on her walk.

Familiar Mother Goose rhymes and songs that children know by heart, such as *Over in the Meadow* by Ezra Jack Keats, *The Farmer in the Dell* by Diane Zuromskis, or *Roll Over!* by Merle Peek all enable a child to act like a reader. Children can hold the books or point to a large chart and "read the words" because they know the verse or song. As they match sentences and phrase cards or point to individual words, they begin to read the text. In the meantime, they are learning that those symbols stand for the words they already know. This enables them to behave like readers.

Some concept books like *Truck* by Donald Crews or *My Kitchen* by Anne Rockwell give children an opportunity to read environmental print. Ron and Nancy Goor have produced a book based only on photographs of common *Signs*. Tana Hoban's books *I Read Signs* and *I Read Symbols* provide excellent photographs of environmental print which is first learned where children see it. These books help teachers see how aware of print their children are becoming. However, children may recognize a stop sign at the corner and not recognize it in a book. The proper context for reading is important.

The following list of titles, then, is a guide to books that help a child learn to read rather than cut across his or her knowledge of how stories work as do the many contrived non-stories that appear in some pre-primers and primers.

OTHER PREDICTABLE BOOKS

Language Patterns: Repetitive Words, Phrases, Questions
Brown, Ruth. *A Dark Dark Tale.* Dial, 1981.
Carle, Eric. *Do You Want to Be My Friend?* Harper, 1971.
_____. *The Very Busy Spider.* Philomel, 1984.
Ginsburg, Mirra. *Good Morning, Chick,* illustrated by Byron Barton. Greenwillow, 1980.

OTHER PREDICTABLE BOOKS (continued)

Kraus, Robert. *Whose Mouse Are You?*, illustrated by José Aruego and Ariane Dewey. Collier, 1970.

_____. *Where Are You Going, Little Mouse?*, illustrated by José Aruego and Ariane Dewey. Greenwillow, 1986.

Tafuri, Nancy. *Have You Seen My Duckling?* Greenwillow, 1984.

Watanabe, Shigeo. *What a Good Lunch!*, illustrated by Yasuo Ohtomo. Philomel, 1980.

_____. *Where's My Daddy?* Philomel, 1982.

Zemach, Margot. *The Teeny Tiny Woman*. Scholastic, 1965.

Story Patterns

Brown, Marcia. *The Three Billy Goats Gruff*. Harcourt, 1957.

Brown, Margaret Wise. *Four Fur Feet*. William R. Scott, 1961.

Galdone, Paul. *The Three Bears*. Scholastic, 1973.

_____. *The Little Red Hen*. Scholastic, 1973.

_____. *The Three Little Pigs*. Clarion, 1970.

Kraus, Ruth. *The Carrot Seed*, illustrated by Crockett Johnson. Harper, 1945.

Preston, Edna Mitchell. *The Sad Story of the Little Bluebird and the Hungry Cat*, illustrated by Barbara Cooney. Four Winds, 1975.

Cumulative Tales

Duff, Maggie. *Rum, Pum, Pum*. Macmillan, 1978.

Emberley, Barbara. *Drummer Hoff*, illustrated by Ed Emberley. Prentice-Hall, 1967.

Galdone, Paul. *The Gingerbread Boy*. Seabury, 1975.

Hayes, Sarah. *This Is the Bear*, illustrated by Helen Craig. Lipincott, 1986.

Kent, Jack. *The Fat Cat*. Parents, 1971.

Peppe, Rodney. *The House That Jack Built*. Delacorte, 1970.

Sutton, Eve. *My Cat Likes to Hide in Boxes*. Scholastic, 1973.

Wood, Audrey. *The Napping House*, illustrated by Don Wood. Harcourt, 1984.

Predictable Plots

Barton, Byron. *Buzz, Buzz, Buzz*. Macmillan, 1973.

Brown, Margaret Wise. *Goodnight Moon*. Harper, 1947.

Burningham, John. *Mr. Gumpy's Outing*. Holt, 1971.

Hutchins, Pat. *Good-Night, Owl!* Macmillan (Penguin), 1982.

_____. *Happy Birthday, Sam*. Puffin/Penguin, 1981.

_____. *You'll Soon Grow Into Them, Titch*. Greenwillow, 1983.

Rice, Eve. *Benny Bakes a Cake*. Greenwillow, 1981.

_____. *Sam Who Never Forgets*. Greenwillow, 1977.

Familiar Sequences: Numbers, Days of Week, Months, Hierarchies

Bang, Molly. *Ten, Nine, Eight*. Greenwillow, 1983.

Becker, John. *Seven Little Rabbits*, illustrated by Barbara Cooney. Walker, 1973.

Galdone, Paul. *The Three Billy Goats Gruff*. Seabury, 1973.

Hutchins, Pat. *1 Hunter*. Greenwillow, 1982.

Keats, Ezra Jack. *Over in the Meadow*. Scholastic, 1971.

Mack, Stan. *10 Bears in My Bed*. Pantheon, 1974.

Skaar, Grace. *What Do the Animals Say?* Scholastic, 1972.

Shulevitz, Uri. *One Monday Morning*. Scribner, 1967.

Familiar Songs and Rhymes

Aliki. *Go Tell Aunt Rhody*. Macmillan, 1974.

Bonne, Rose, and Alan Mills. *I Know an Old Lady*. Rand McNally, 1961.

de Paola, Tomie. *Tomie de Paola's Mother Goose*. Putnam, 1985.

Gerstein, Mordicai. *Roll Over!* Crown, 1984.

Hawkins, Colin, and Jacqui. *Old Mother Hubbard*. Putnam, 1985.

Hill, Eric. *Nursery Rhyme Peek-a-Book*. Price, Stern, 1982.

Langstaff, John. *Oh, A-Hunting We Will Go*, illustrated by Nancy Winslow Parker. Atheneum, 1974. (paper)

Martin, Bill, Jr. *Fire! Fire! Said Mrs. McGuire*. Holt, 1970.

Peek, Merle, adapted and illustrated. *Mary Wore Her Red Dress and Henry Wore His Green Sneakers*. Clarion Books, 1985.

Quackenbush, Robert. *She'll Be Comin' Round the Mountain*. Lippincott, 1973.

_____. *Skip to My Lou*. Lippincott, 1975.

Stanley, Diane Zuromskis. *Fiddle-I-Fee*. Little, Brown, 1979.

Wells, Rosemary. *Noisy Nora*. Dial, 1973.

Use of Environmental Print

Crews, Donald. *Truck.* Greenwillow, 1980.

_____. *School Bus.* Greenwillow, 1984.

Goor, Ron, and Nancy Goor. *Signs.* Crowell, 1983.

Hoban, Tana. *I Read Signs.* Greenwillow, 1983.

_____. *I Read Symbols.* Greenwillow, 1983.

Preston, Edna Mitchell. *Where Did My Mother Go?,* illustrated by Chris Conover. Four Winds, 1978.

Controlled-Vocabulary Books

Most basal reading series control the number of words, the sounds of the words, and the length of the stories for beginning readers. Until the advent of books for babies and pre-schoolers, most picture storybooks were written to be read *to* children and thus were at a reading level of at least third grade. They were written for the young child's interest and appreciation level, not reading ability level. That left very little for the beginning reader to read, except for pre-primers and primers. This is no longer true with the number of easy predictable books available today.

A new genre of book was created when Dr. Seuss wrote *The Cat in the Hat* in 1957. This book was written with a controlled vocabulary (derived from the Dolch vocabulary list of 220 words) for the young child to read independently. In format, such books tend to look more like basal readers than picture storybooks, although they do have illustrations on every page. Some of these books,

such as *Little Bear* by Minarik and the superb "Frog and Toad" series by Arnold Lobel, can take their rightful place in children's literature. In fact, while *Frog and Toad Are Friends* was a Caldecott Honor Book, *Frog and Toad Together* was a Newbery Honor Book two years later, suggesting that quality writing can be achieved with a limited vocabulary. *Mouse Tales,* also by Lobel, consists of seven short bedtime stories which Papa Mouse tells, one for each of his seven mouse boys. The warmth, humor, and literary quality of these tales are complemented by Lobel's amusing illustrations of a tiny world of mouse people. Equally successful stories by Lobel include *Owl at Home* and *Uncle Elephant.*

Today there are literally hundreds of these easy-reading books. Unfortunately, many of them do not achieve such literary excellence as the ones mentioned. They appear to be contrived and restricted by the controlled vocabulary. Research has shown that the meaning of the story is more important for ease of reading than limiting vocabulary. It would seem more useful, then, to produce predictable books with fine literary qualities and matching pictures than the huge number of very uneven controlled-vocabulary books which are not too different from children's basal readers. Few children remember the stories in readers, but they do read Carle's *The Very Hungry Caterpillar,* Brown's *A Dark Dark Tale,* and Ginsburg's *The Chick and the Duckling* over and over again! It is these stories that put children onto the road to reading and increase delight in literature.

SUGGESTED LEARNING EXPERIENCES

1. Share several stories with a child under 1 year of age. What appears to capture his or her attention? How many different ways can you provide for the child's active participation in the story?

2. Learn several finger plays to try with young children. Can they do them? What is difficult for them? Teach these finger plays to your classmates in children's literature.

3. Working in pairs and using the evaluative criteria established in this chapter, compare three different editions of Mother Goose or ABC or counting books.

4. Select a wordless picture book to use with children of various ages. Record the retelling of the story by each child, noting differences in language development, sense of story, descriptive phrases, and complexity of plot. Be sure to let the child look through the book once before beginning to tell the story.

5. Assume you are going to compile a small Mother Goose book of twenty to twenty-five rhymes. Which ones would you choose? How would you arrange them in your book?

6. Find a concept book about one particular subject. *Before* you read it, list all the possible dimensions of that concept. Then compare your list with what the author/artist chose to include.

7. Read three or four bedtime stories to one child or several children. Which ones do they ask to hear repeated? Can you find any patterns among their favorites?

8. Select what you consider to be a predictable book. Share it with 5- and 6-year-olds, waiting for them to join in at various places. What did you learn about your selection?

9. Interview a nursery-school teacher. How often does he or she read aloud to the group? How do the teachers select the books? Do they have any favorites? What are they? What recommendations for change could you make?

10. Compare several pre-primers and primers with the books for the beginning reader described in this text. What do you notice as being different or significant for an emerging reader?

RELATED READINGS

1. Boegehold, Betty Doyle. *Getting Ready to Read*. Bank Street College of Education. New York: Ballantine Books, 1984.

   A practical guide for parents, with appropriate games, activities, books, and book extensions to help further a preschool child's language development and enjoyment of literature.

2. Bridge, Connie A., Peter N. Winograd, and Darliene Haley. "Using Predictable Materials vs. Preprimers to Teach Beginning Sight Vocabulary," *The Reading Teacher*, vol. 36 (May 1983) pp. 884–891.

   This well-written account of the use of trade books with beginning readers would provide a research base for teaching children to learn to read with real books.

3. Butler, Dorothy. *Babies Need Books*. New York: Atheneum, 1980.

   A firm believer in the importance of books for the young child, this New Zealander writes from her experience as a mother, grandmother, and a specialist children's bookseller. She not only recommends books for the 1s through 5s, but she gives practical suggestions of when and how to read to wiggly children.

4. Butler, Dorothy, and Marie Clay. *Reading Begins at Home*. Portsmouth, N.H.: Heinemann Educational Books, 1979.

   A very useful small book of some forty pages which helps parents of pre-schoolers know how to give their children the very best educational start. Needless to say, emphasis is placed on reading to children frequently, plus excellent suggestions on what to read and how to share books with your child.

5. Cochran-Smith, Marilyn. *The Making of a Reader*. Norwood, N.J.: Ablex Publishing, 1984.

   This book focuses on how adults and children observed over an 18-month period in a preschool collaborate on building meaning in books. It emphasizes what the children know about books and ways they seem to be coming to know it. The observational charts will prove useful to other researchers.

6. Goelmann, Hillel, Antoinette Oberg, and Frank Smith, eds. *Awakening to Literacy*. Portsmouth, N.H.: Heinemann Educational Books, 1984.

   Based on a literacy symposium held at the University of Victoria, these fourteen papers provide a thorough review of the research on literacy before schooling. Articles by Yetta Goodman, Frank Smith, and Jerome Bruner are particularly significant. William H. Teale's paper on the importance of reading aloud to young children supports the point of view presented in this chapter.

7. Opie, Iona, and Peter Opie. *The Oxford Nursery Rhyme Book*. London: The Oxford University Press, 1955.

   These well-known authorities of the oral rhymes and games of children collected over 800 traditional rhymes for this book. In their *Oxford Dictionary of Nursery Rhymes* (1951), they provide the histories for many of the verses.

8. Rhodes, Lynn K. "I Can Read! Predictable Books as Resources for Reading and Writing Instruction," *The Reading Teacher*, vol. 34 (February 1981), pp. 511–518.

This article discusses some characteristics of predictable books and gives valuable suggestions on how to use them in the classroom. A bibliography of predictable books is attached.

9. Taylor, Denny, and Dorothy S. Strickland. *Family Storybook Reading*. Portsmouth, N.H.: Heinemann Educational Books, 1986.

These authors provide real-life experiences and photographs of the various ways parents share books in the home. Astute observers, the authors focus on the natural ways parents lead children to developing literacy.

10. Wells, Gordon. *The Meaning Makers: Children Learning Language and Using Language to Learn*. Portsmouth, N.H.: Heinemann Educational Books, 1986.

Wells reports on the importance of story and reading aloud to pre-schoolers for the later educational attainment of children. Based on fifteen years of longitudinal research, this is a significant book.

11. White, Dorothy. *Books before Five*. Portsmouth, N.H.: Heinemann Educational Books, 1954, 1984.

This is a re-issue of the first longitudinal study of a young child's response to books. Written by a young mother who was a former librarian, this book records how she and her daughter Carol explored books from the time Carol was 2 until she went to school. Long out of print, this new edition has a foreword by Marie Clay.

REFERENCES

Ahlberg, Janet, and Allan Ahlberg. *The Baby's Catalogue*. Little, Brown, 1982.
_____. *Each Peach Pear Plum*. Viking, 1979.
_____. *Peek-a-Boo!* Viking, 1981.
Alderson, Brian. *Cakes and Custard,* illustrated by Helen Oxenbury. Morrow, 1975.
Alexander, Martha. *Pigs Say Oink*. Random, 1978.
Aliki (Brandenberg). *Go Tell Aunt Rhody*. Macmillan, 1974.
Anno, Mitsumasa. *Anno's Alphabet*. Crowell, 1975.
_____. *Anno's Counting Book*. Crowell, 1977.
_____. *Anno's Counting House*. Crowell, 1982.
Azarian, Mary. *A Farmer's Alphabet*. Godine, 1981.
Bang, Molly. *Ten, Nine, Eight*. Greenwillow, 1983.
Barton, Byron. *Airport*. Crowell, 1982.
_____. *Building a House*. Greenwillow, 1981.
Baskin, Leonard, illustrator. *Hosie's Alphabet,* words by Hosea, Tobias, and Lisa Baskin. Viking, 1972.
Blegvad, Lenore. *Hark! Hark! The Dogs Do Bark and Other Rhymes About Dogs,* illustrated by Erik Blegvad. Atheneum, 1976.
_____. *Mittens for Kittens and Other Rhymes about Cats,* illustrated by Erik Blegvad. Atheneum, 1974.
_____. *The Parrot in the Garret and Other Rhymes about Dwellings,* illustrated by Erik Blegvad. Atheneum, 1982.
_____. *This Little Pig-a-Wig and Other Rhymes about Pigs,* illustrated by Erik Blegvad. Atheneum, 1978.
Bodecker, N. M. *It's Raining, Said John Twaining*. Atheneum, 1973.
Briggs, Raymond. *The Mother Goose Treasury*. Coward-McCann, 1966.
_____. *The Snowman*. Random, 1978.
Brooke, Leslie. *Ring o' Roses*. Warne, 1923.
Brown, Marc. *Finger Rhymes*. Dutton, 1980.
_____. *Hand Rhymes*. Dutton, 1985.
Brown, Marcia. *All Butterflies*. Scribner, 1974.
_____. *The Three Billy Goats Gruff*. Harcourt, 1957.
Brown, Margaret Wise. *A Child's Good Night Book,* illustrated by Jean Charlot. Addison, 1950.
_____. *Goodnight Moon,* illustrated by Clement Hurd. Harper, 1947.
_____. *The Goodnight Moon Room,* illustrated by Clement Hurd. Harper, 1984.

————. *The Runaway Bunny*, illustrated by Clement Hurd. Harper, 1972 (1942).

Bruna, Dick. *The Apple*. Methuen, 1965.

————. *B Is for Bear*. Methuen, 1967.

————. *The Fish*. Methuen, 1975.

————. *I Can Dress Myself*. Methuen, 1978.

————. *Miffy*. Methuen, 1975.

Buckley, Helen E. *Michael Is Brave*, illustrated by Emily McCully. Lothrop, 1971.

Burningham, John. *The Baby*. Crowell, 1975.

————. *The Blanket*. Crowell, 1976.

————. *The Cupboard*. Crowell, 1976.

————. *The Dog*. Crowell, 1976.

————. *The Friend*. Crowell, l976.

————. *The Rabbit*. Crowell, 1975.

————. *The School*. Crowell, 1975.

————. *The Snow*. Crowell, 1975.

————. *John Burningham's ABC*. Bobbs-Merrill, 1967.

Carle, Eric. *Do You Want to Be My Friend?* Harper, 1971.

————. *The Grouchy Ladybug*. Harper, 1977.

————. *1, 2, 3 to the Zoo*. Philomel, 1968.

————. *The Very Busy Spider*. Philomel, 1984.

————. *The Very Hungry Caterpillar*. Philomel, 1969.

Cauley, Lorinda Bryan. *The Three Little Kittens*. Putnam, 1982.

Clifton, Lucille. *Amifika*, illustrated by Thomas DiGrazia. Dutton, 1977.

Crews, Donald. *Carrousel*. Greenwillow, 1982.

————. *Flying*. Greenwillow, 1986.

————. *Freight Train*. Greenwillow, 1978.

————. *Light*. Greenwillow, 1981.

————. *School Bus*. Greenwillow, 1984.

————. *Truck*. Greenwillow, 1980.

DeAngeli, Marguerite. *The Book of Nursery and Mother Goose Rhymes*. Doubleday, 1954.

de Paola, Tomie. *The Comic Adventures of Old Mother Hubbard and Her Dog*. Harcourt, 1981.

————. *Pancakes for Breakfast*. Harcourt, 1978.

————. *Tomie de Paola's Mother Goose*. Putnam, 1985.

DeRegniers, Beatrice Schenk. *Going for a Walk*. Harper, 1982.

Duke, Kate. *The Guinea Pig ABC*. Dutton, 1983.

Erskine, Jim. *Bedtime Story*, illustrated by Ann Schweninger. Crown, 1982.

Feelings, Muriel. *Jambo Means Hello: Swahili Alphabet Book*, illustrated by Tom Feelings. Dial, 1974.

————. *Moja Means One: Swahili Counting Book*, illustrated by Tom Feelings. Dial, 1971.

Frasconi, Antonio. *The House That Jack Built*. Harcourt, 1958.

Gág, Wanda. *The ABC Bunny*. Coward-McCann, 1933.

Galdone, Paul. *The Gingerbread Boy*. Clarion, 1975.

————. *The History of Simple Simon*. McGraw-Hill, 1966.

————. *The House That Jack Built*. McGraw-Hill, 1961.

————. *Old Mother Hubbard and Her Dog*. McGraw-Hill, 1960.

————. *The Teeny Tiny Woman*. Clarion, 1984.

————. *The Three Bears*. Scholastic, 1973.

————. *The Three Little Pigs*. Clarion, 1970.

————. *Tom, Tom, the Piper's Son*. McGraw-Hill, 1964.

Garten, Jan. *The Alphabet Tale*, illustrated by Muriel Batherman. Random, 1964.

Gerstein, Mordicai. *Roll Over!* Crown, 1984.

Gillham, Bill. *The First Words Picture Book*, illustrated by Sam Grainger. Coward, 1982.

Ginsburg, Mirra. *Across the Stream*, illustrated by Nancy Tafuri. Greenwillow, 1982.

————. *The Chick and the Duckling*, illustrated by José and Ariane Aruego. Macmillan, 1972.

————. *Good Morning, Chick*, illustrated by Byron Barton. Greenwillow, 1980.

Glazer, Tom. *Eye Winker Tom Tinker Chin Chopper*. Doubleday, 1973.

Goodall, John S. *The Adventures of Paddy Pork*. Harcourt, 1968.

_____. *The Ballooning Adventures of Paddy Pork*. Harcourt, 1969.

_____. *Creepy Castle*. Atheneum, 1975.

_____. *Jacko*. Harcourt, 1972.

_____. *The Midnight Adventures of Kelly, Dot, and Esmeralda*. Atheneum, 1972.

_____. *Naughty Nancy*. Atheneum, 1975.

_____. *Paddy's Evening Out*. Atheneum, 1973.

_____. *Paddy's New Hat*. Atheneum, 1980.

_____. *Paddy Pork's Holiday*. Atheneum, 1976.

_____. *Shrewbettina's Birthday*. Harcourt, 1971.

_____. *The Surprise Picnic*. Atheneum, 1977.

Goor, Ron, and Nancy Goor. *Signs*. Crowell, 1983.

Greenaway, Kate. *Mother Goose, or The Old Nursery Rhymes*. Warne, n.d.

Grossbart, Francine. *A Big City*. Harper, 1966.

Hague, Michael. *Mother Goose: A Collection of Classic Nursery Rhymes*. Holt, 1984.

Harrison, Ted. *A Northern Alphabet*. Tundra, 1982.

Hawkins, Colin, and Jacqui Hawkins. *Old Mother Hubbard*. Putnam, 1985.

Hill, Eric. *Nursery Rhyme Peek-a-Book*. Price, Stern, 1982.

_____. *Spot's Birthday Party*. Putnam, 1982.

_____. *Spot's First Christmas*. Putnam, 1983.

_____. *Spot's First Walk*. Putnam, l981.

_____. *Where's Spot?* Putnam, 1980.

Hoban, Tana. *A, B, See!* Greenwillow, 1982.

_____. *Big Ones, Little Ones*. Greenwillow, 1976.

_____. *Circles, Triangles and Squares*. Macmillan, 1974.

_____. *Count and See*. Macmillan, 1972.

_____. *Dig, Drill, Dump, Fill*. Greenwillow, 1975.

_____. *I Read Signs*. Greenwillow, 1983.

_____. *I Read Symbols*. Greenwillow, 1983.

_____. *Is It Red? Is It Yellow? Is It Blue?* Greenwillow, 1978.

_____. *1, 2, 3*. Greenwillow, 1985.

_____. *Over, Under and Through and Other Spatial Concepts*. Macmillan, 1973.

_____. *Shapes, Shapes, Shapes*. Greenwillow, 1986.

_____. *Push Pull, Empty Full: A Book of Opposites*. Macmillan, 1972.

_____. *Shapes and Things*. Macmillan, 1970.

_____. *What's That?* Greenwillow, 1985.

Hughes, Shirley. *Alfie's Feet*. Lothrop, 1983.

_____. *Alfie Gets in First*. Lothrop, 1982.

_____. "Nursery Collection." *Bathwater's Hot. Noisy. When We Went to the Park*. All Lothrop, 1985.

Hutchins, Pat. *Changes, Changes*. Macmillan, 1971.

_____. *Good-Night, Owl!* Macmillan, 1972.

_____. *1 Hunter*. Greenwillow, 1982.

_____. *Rosie's Walk*. Macmillan, 1968.

_____. *Titch*. Macmillan, 1971.

_____. *You'll Soon Grow Into Them, Titch*. Greenwillow, 1983.

Isadora, Rachel. *City Seen from A to Z*. Greenwillow, 1983.

_____. *I Hear*. Greenwillow, 1985.

_____. *I See*. Greenwillow, 1985.

_____. *I Touch*. Greenwillow, 1985.

Jeffers, Susan. *If Wishes Were Horses and Other Rhymes*. Dutton, 1979.

Jensen, Virginia Allen. *Sara and the Door*, illustrated by Ann Sturgnell. Addison, 1977.

Jones, Rebecca C. *The Biggest, Meanest, Ugliest Dog in the Whole Wide World*, illustrated by Wendy Watson. Macmillan, 1982.

Keats, Ezra Jack. *Over in the Meadow*. Scholastic, 1971.

Kent, Jack. *The Fat Cat*. Parents', 1971.

Kitchen, Burt. *Animal Alphabet*. Dial, 1984.

Kunhardt, Dorothy. *Pat the Bunny*. Golden, 1962 (1940).

Langstaff, John. *Frog Went A-Courtin'*, illustrated by Feodor Rojankovsky. Harcourt, 1955.

_____. *Oh, A-Hunting We Will Go,* illustrated by Nancy Winslow Parker. Atheneum, 1974.

_____. *Over in the Meadow,* illustrated by Feodor Rojankovsky. Harcourt, 1967.

Lines, Kathleen. *Lavender's Blue,* illustrated by Harold Jones. Watts, 1964.

Lionni, Leo. "Pictures to Talk About" Series. *Who? What? Where? When?* All Pantheon, 1983.

Lobel, Arnold. "Frog and Toad Series." *Days with Frog and Toad,* 1979. *Frog and Toad All Year,* 1976. *Frog and Toad Are Friends,* 1970. *Frog and Toad Together,* 1972. All Harper.

_____. *Gregory Griggs and Other Nursery Rhyme People.* Greenwillow, 1978.

_____. *Mouse Tales.* Harper, 1972.

_____. *On Market Street,* illustrated by Anita Lobel. Greenwillow, 1981.

_____. *Owl at Home.* Harper, 1975.

_____. *Uncle Elephant.* Harper, 1981.

_____. *Whiskers and Rhymes.* Greenwillow, 1985.

McCully, Emily Arnold. *First Snow.* Harper, 1985.

_____. *Picnic.* Harper, 1984.

Maestro, Betty, and Giulio Maestro. *Traffic: A Book of Opposites.* Crown, 1981.

Marshall, James. *James Marshall's Mother Goose.* Farrar, 1979.

Martin, Bill, Jr. *Brown Bear, Brown Bear, What Do You See?,* illustrated by Eric Carle. Holt, 1983.

Marzollo, Jean. *Close Your Eyes,* illustrated by Susan Jeffers. Dial, 1978.

Mayer, Mercer. *A Boy, a Dog, and a Frog.* Dial, 1967.

_____. *Frog Goes to Dinner.* Dial, 1974.

_____. *One Frog Too Many.* Dial, 1975.

Merriam, Eve. *Good Night to Annie,* illustrated by John Wallner. Four Winds, 1980.

Miles, Miska. *Apricot ABC,* illustrated by Peter Parnall. Little, Brown, 1969.

Minarik, Else Holmelund. *Father Bear Comes Home,* illustrated by Maurice Sendak. Harper, 1959.

_____. *A Kiss for Little Bear,* illustrated by Maurice Sendak. Harper, 1968.

_____. *Little Bear,* illustrated by Maurice Sendak. Harper, 1957.

_____. *Little Bear's Friend,* illustrated by Maurice Sendak. Harper, 1960.

_____. *Little Bear's Visit,* illustrated by Maurice Sendak. Harper, 1961.

Munari, Bruno. *The Birthday Present.* Philomel, 1980 (1959).

_____. *Bruno Munari's ABC.* World Publishing, 1960.

_____. *The Elephant's Wish.* Philomel, 1980 (1945).

Musgrove, Margaret. *Ashanti to Zulu: African Traditions,* illustrated by Leo and Diane Dillon. Dial, 1976.

Ness, Evaline. *Old Mother Hubbard and Her Dog.* Holt, l972.

Ormerod, Jan. "Baby Books." *Dad's Back. Messy Baby. Reading. Sleeping.* All Lothrop, 1985.

_____. *Moonlight.* Lothrop, 1982.

_____. *Sunshine.* Lothrop, 1981.

Oxenbury, Helen. "The Baby Board Books." *Dressing. Family. Friends. Playing. Working.* All Simon & Schuster, 1981.

_____. *Helen Oxenbury's ABC of Things.* Watts, 1972.

_____. *Numbers of Things.* Watts, 1968.

_____. "Out and About Books." *The Birthday Party. The Car Trip. The Checkup. The Dancing Class. Eating Out. First Day of School. Grandma and Grandpa. Our Dog.* All Dutton (Dial), 1983.

_____. "Very First Books." *Beach Day. Good Night, Good Morning. Monkey See, Monkey Do. Mother's Helper. Shopping Trip.* All Dial, 1982.

Peek, Merle. *Roll Over.* Clarion, 1981.

Petersham, Maud, and Miska Petersham. *The Rooster Crows.* Macmillan, 1945.

Pienkowski, Jan. *Shapes.* Harvey House, 1975.

Provensen, Alice, and Martin Provensen. *The Mother Goose Book.* Random, 1976.

_____. *A Peaceable Kingdom: The Shaker ABCEDARIUS.* Viking, 1978.

Rackham, Arthur. *Mother Goose, Old Nursery Rhymes.* Appleton, 1913.

Reed, Philip. *Mother Goose and Nursery Rhymes.* Atheneum, 1963.

Reiss, John J. *Colors.* Bradbury, 1969.

_____. *Numbers*. Bradbury, 1971.

_____. *Shapes*. Bradbury, 1974.

Rice, Eve. *Benny Bakes a Cake*. Greenwillow, 1981.

_____. *Goodnight, Goodnight*. Greenwillow, 1980.

_____. *Oh, Lewis!* Macmillan, 1974.

_____. *Sam Who Never Forgets*. Greenwillow, 1977.

Robbins, Ken. *Tools*. Four Winds, 1983.

Rockwell, Anne. *Albert B. Cub and Zebra: An Alphabet Storybook*. Crowell, 1977.

Rockwell, Anne, and Harlow Rockwell. *Machines*. Macmillan, 1972.

_____. *The Supermarket*. Macmillan, 1979.

_____. *Thruway*. Macmillan, 1972.

_____. *The Toolbox*. Macmillan, 1971.

_____. "My World Series." *Can I Help?*, 1982. *Happy Birthday to Me*, 1981. *How My Garden Grew*, 1982. *I Play in My Room*, 1981. *I Love My Pets*, 1982. *Sick in Bed*, 1982. All Macmillan.

Rockwell, Harlow. *My Dentist*. Greenwillow, 1975.

_____. *My Doctor*. Macmillan, 1973.

_____. *My Kitchen*. Greenwillow, 1980.

_____. *My Nursery School*. Greenwillow, 1976.

Roffey, Maureen. *Home Sweet Home*. Coward-McCann, 1983.

Rojankovsky, Feodor. *The Tall Book of Mother Goose*. Harper, 1942.

Roy, Ron. *Three Ducks Went Wandering*, illustrated by Paul Galdone. Clarion, 1979.

Scott, Ann Herbert. *Sam*, illustrated by Symeon Shimin. McGraw-Hill, 1967.

Sendak, Maurice. *Chicken Soup With Rice*. Harper, 1962.

_____. *One Was Johnny* (Nutshell Library, Vol. 3). Harper, 1962.

Seuss, Dr. (Theodor S. Geisel). *The Cat in the Hat*. Beginner Books, 1957.

Slobodkina, Esphyr. *Caps for Sale*. Addison, 1947.

Spier, Peter. *Crash! Bang! Boom!* Doubleday, 1972.

_____. *Gobble Growl Grunt*. Doubleday, 1971.

_____. *Fast-Slow High-Low*. Doubleday, 1972.

_____. *The Fox Went Out on A Chilly Night*. Doubleday, 1961.

_____. *London Bridge Is Falling Down*. Doubleday, 1967.

_____. *Noah's Ark*. Doubleday, 1977.

_____. *Peter Spier's Rain*. Doubleday, 1982.

_____. *To Market, To Market*. Doubleday, 1967.

Stanley, Diane Zuromskis. *Fiddle-I-Fee*. Little, Brown, 1979.

Tafuri, Nancy. *Early Morning in the Barn*. Greenwillow, 1983.

_____. *Have You Seen My Duckling?* Greenwillow, 1984.

Testa, Fulvio. *If You Look Around You*. Dutton, 1983.

_____. *If You Take a Pencil*. Dial, 1982.

Tolstoy, Alexei. *The Great Big Enormous Turnip*, illustrated by Helen Oxenbury. Watts, 1968.

Tripp, Wallace. *Granfa' Grig Had a Pig and Other Rhymes Without Reason*. Little, Brown, 1976.

Tudor, Tasha. *A Is for Annabelle*. Walck, 1954.

_____. *Mother Goose*. Walck, 1944.

Turkle, Brinton. *Deep in the Forest*. Dutton, 1976.

Watanabe, Shigeo. "I Can Do It All By Myself" Series, illustrated by Yasuo Ohtomo. *Get Set! Go!*, 1981. *How Do I Put It On?*, 1979. *I Can Ride It!*, 1982. *I'm King of the Castle*, 1982. *What a Good Lunch!*, 1980. *Where's My Daddy?*, 1982. All Philomel.

Watson, Clyde. *Applebet*, illustrated by Wendy Watson. Farrar, Straus, 1982.

_____. *Father Fox's Pennyrhymes*, illustrated by Wendy Watson. Crowell, 1971.

Wells, Rosemary. "Very First Books." *Max's Bath*, 1985. *Max's Bedtime*, 1985. *Max's Birthday*, 1985. *Max's Breakfast*, 1985. *Max's First Word*, 1979. *Max's Ride*. 1979. *Max's Toys*, 1979. All Dial.

Wezel, Peter. *The Good Bird*. Harper, 1964.

Wildsmith, Brian. *Brian Wildsmith's ABC*. Watts, 1963.

_____. *Brian Wildsmith's Mother Goose*. Watts, 1963.

_____. *Brian Wildsmith's 1, 2, 3's*. Watts, 1965.

_____. *The Cat Sat on the Mat*. Oxford, 1983.

Williams, Garth. *Baby's First Book*. Golden Press, 1955.

Wolde, Gunilla. "Betsy Books." *This Is Betsy,* 1975. *Betsy's Baby Brother,* 1975. *Betsy's First Day at Nursery School,* 1976. *Betsy and the Doctor,* 1978. All Random

Wright, Blanche Fisher. *The Real Mother Goose*. Rand McNally, 1965 (1916).

_____. *The Real Mother Goose: Green Husky Book*. Rand McNally, 1984.

_____. *The Real Mother Goose: Husky Book Four*. Rand McNally, 1983.

_____. *The Real Mother Goose: Yellow Husky Book*. Rand McNally, 1984.

Yolen, Jane. *All in the Woodland Early,* illustrated by Jane Breskin Zalben. Collins, 1979.

_____. *An Invitation to the Butterfly Ball,* illustrated by Jane Breskin Zalben. Parents', 1976.

Zemach, Harve. *Mommy, Buy Me a China Doll,* illustrated by Margot Zemach. Follett, 1966.

Zemach, Margot. *Hush, Little Baby*. Dutton, 1976.

Zolotow, Charlotte. *The Summer Night,* illustrated by Ben Shecter. Harper, 1974.

_____. *Wake Up and Good Night,* illustrated by Leonard Weisgard. Harper, 1971.

Zuromskis, Diane, illustrator. *The Farmer in the Dell*. Little, Brown, 1978.

5 PICTURE BOOKS

One primary teacher was enchanted with *Say It!* by Charlotte Zolotow, illustrated by James Stevenson. She read it to her first- and second-graders, who were attentive and seemed to enjoy the story. After reading it they reviewed what the mother and the little girl had seen on their walk. Then the teacher asked them where it had taken place and they gave her reasons for their answer of "in the country." She also asked them if there were any words or phrases they particularly liked and several children mentioned "splendiferous." They also discussed what they thought would be a "splendiferous day." *Say It!* was then placed on the display table with other books about the fall and trees.

The following week, the teacher read the book again before taking the group outside for a walk. The children took clipboards, pencils, and papers and sat among the leaves under a group of maple trees where they were to record what they saw, heard, felt, thought, smelled, or wished. Everyone worked on their "thought ramblings" for about 15 minutes. Then they made a giant pile of leaves and jumped and played in them.

The teacher decided to share *Say It!* one more time with this group and she asked them why they thought she was reading it again. Their responses were:

1. It is about trees and we are studying trees.
2. It is about fall and it is fall.
3. You must really like the book.
4. The pictures are pretty.
5. It has "splendiferous" in it.

After sharing the story, the children selected their favorite words and phrases to be listed on the board. These included "swirled," "wondrous," "dazzling," "zigzagging streaks of color," "scrunching," and so forth. This time the children began reading *Say It!* during their silent reading time and displayed it among their favorite books on the window sill.

The following day they looked at each illustration carefully and talked about how James Stevenson had made the pictures. Children were then given watercolors and an opportunity to paint their favorite part of the book or something that it reminded them of. They worked for several days on their painting, frequently referring back to the book. Children were also asked to write about their paintings. Their comments included:

This is a pond of floating colors. The mother said it is a wonderful pond. (Ritchie)
It was a golden splendiferous day in this town and the mommie and the girl walked down the road and saw lots of leaves. (Barbie)
The little girl and her mother went on a walk. And on the walk they found a little floating cloud of seeds. (Valerie)

Children also recorded their thoughts and feelings about *Say It!* Many of them shared it with their "Book Buddies" in second and third grades.

Because a fine book was shared in depth with these children, they developed a far greater appreciation for it than if they had only heard it once. They learned to value the language and unique expressions in *Say It!* Their appreciation for and experience with watercolors were heightened. And their speaking and writing vocabularies were enhanced and enlarged. In the process of looking at one book in depth, children learned much about the way text and illustrations work together to create a story, and their appreciation for quality book-making was developed. [1]

A picture book had provided for the development of these students' visual and verbal imaginations. Repeated readings opened up new meanings and added to their experience of enjoying the beauty of a fall day. For literature extends experiences and helps us see the world afresh.

Picture books may also provide children with the only "real art" which they will encounter in years. Today's child is bombarded with visual images from TV, commercial ads, neon signs, yet seldom has an opportunity to have a quality art experience. Picture books enable children to see through the eyes of an artist.

[1]This description is based on a much longer article by Joetta M. Beaver, *"Say It!* Over and Over," *Language Arts,* vol. 59, (February, 1982), pp. 143–148.

THE PICTURE BOOK DEFINED

Authorities do not always agree on the definition of a picture book. Some maintain that a picture book is one that simply has a picture-book format. Such a broad definition would include picture storybooks, informational books, concept books, even so called "coffee table books."

This chapter is concerned with picture storybooks only. The picture storybook is one that conveys its messages through two media, the art of illustrating and the art of writing. In a well-designed book in which the total format reflects the meaning of the story, both the illustrations and text must bear the burden of narration. Barbara Bader maintains that:

As an art form it [the picture book] hinges on the interdependence of pictures and words, on the simultaneous display of two facing pages, and on the drama of the turning of the page.[2]

Some persons differentiate between the picture book and the picture storybook. The difference is contingent on the development of plot and characters. A picture book may be an alphabet book, a counting book, a first book, or a concept book. In

[2]Barbara Bader, *American Picturebooks from Noah's Ark to The Beast Within* (New York: Macmillan, 1976), Introduction.

these the pictures must be accurate and synchronized with the text; however, it is not essential that they provide the continuity required by a story line. The illustrations for a concept book or an alphabet book may depict a different object or animal on each page, providing for much variety in the pictures. Examples would be Bert Kitchen's *Animal Alphabet,* which shows large individual pictures for each letter, or Tana Hoban's *Big Ones Little Ones,* which includes photographs of various animals and their babies. In a picture storybook, however, the same characters and settings are frequently drawn, while variety is achieved through the action of the characters. The artist must consider plot and character development in the picture storybook, rather than just the unifying idea or concept of the picture book itself.

Diane Goode has drawn warm, sensitive illustrations for Cynthia Rylant's picture storybook *When I Was Young in the Mountains.* The story is episodic—based on the fond memories of a little girl's visits to her grandparents' house in the mountains. Through story and pictures, which work together to create a unified whole, this picture book celebrates the love of an extended family and the beauty of a remote mountain region. For example, each night when the grandfather comes home from work in the mines, he kisses the top of the little girl's head so as not to get her dirty. A compassionate grandmother takes her to the out-

Diane Goode's warm sensitive illustrations reflect the love within an extended family and the beauty of the region in Cynthia Rylant's story of *When I Was Young in the Mountains*.

house at night after she has eaten too much okra. Artistic impressions must change, depending on the story line, but the characters and setting have to be consistent throughout.

While is is important to recognize the characteristics that distinguish a picture book from a picture storybook, in many instances, the two terms are used interchangeably to refer to that large group of books in which pictures and text are considered to be of equal importance. While the fusion of pictures and text is essential for the unity of presentation in a picture book, the fusion does not exist in the illustrated book. In the latter the pictures are mere extensions of the text. They may enrich the interpretation of the story, but they are not necessary for its understanding. For example, Trina Schart Hyman's many pictures capture the beauty of Wales in Dylan Thomas' *A Child's Christmas in Wales*, yet it is best described as a profusely illustrated book, not a picture storybook.

Though the pictures greatly enhance this nostalgic recollection of Christmas, they do not attempt to tell the whole story, which is really evoked by the rich use of words by this well-known poet. This is a book for adults and those children who have achieved the reading skills and maturity required to reflect on Christmas memories of the past.

THE ART AND ARTISTS OF PICTURE BOOKS

A picture storybook, then, must be a seamless whole conveying meaning in both the art and the text. Most frequently a child "reads" the pictures while an adult shares the story. An illustration does not merely reflect the action on that page but shares in moving the story forward. At every level of narration the pictures should convey and enhance the meaning behind the story. Artists do this in a variety of subtle and interesting ways.

Creating Meaning in Picture Storybooks

An outstanding example of a picture storybook which helps to move the plot is the well-loved *Blueberries for Sal* by Robert McCloskey. This is a story that children can tell by themselves just by looking at the clear blue-and-white pictures. The illustrations help the "reader" anticipate both the action and climax as Sal and her mother are seen going berry-picking up one side of Blueberry Hill, and Little Bear and his mother are seen coming up the other side. McCloskey uses a false climax, a good storytelling technique. Sal hears a noise and starts to peer behind an ominously dark rock; the reader expects her to meet the bears, but instead she sees a mother crow and her children. On the next page she calmly meets Mother Bear and tramps along behind her. A parallel plot gives Little Bear a similar experience, but Sal's mother is not so calm about meeting him! The human expressions of surprise, fear, and consternation on the faces of both mothers express emotion as well as action.

Lynd Ward has used another technique to show the climax in his well-loved story, *The Biggest Bear*. In order to dramatize the growth of Johnny's bear, he shows him first as a lovable but mischievous cub. The next four pictures illustrate the chaos the bear created in the kitchen during the summer, Mr. McCarroll's trampled cornfield in the fall, the half-eaten and ruined bacon and hams in the smokehouse during the winter, and the overturned sap buckets in the spring. The bear is not shown in any of these pictures; only the results of his destructive actions are. The text suggests the passage of time, but in no way prepares the reader for the shock of the next picture of a gigantic bear, standing on his hind legs gorging himself on the McLeans' maple syrup! This adventure story has moments of real pathos, compassion, and humor. The illustrations help to create these feelings as well as the text does.

Size of picture may increase with the mounting tension of the story. One of the best-known examples of this is seen in Maurice Sendak's fine story, *Where the Wild Things Are*. The pictures in this book become larger and larger as Max's dream becomes more and more fantastic. Following the climactic wild rumpus, which is portrayed on three full-sized spreads with no text whatsoever, Max returns home. The pictures decrease in size, although never down to their original size; just as symbolically, Max will never be quite the same again after his dream experience.

Picture-book artists also provide clues to the future action of a story. A close look at the first and second pages of *Where the Wild Things Are* shows the mischievous Max dressed in his wild things suit and stringing up a home-made tent. A stuffed toy looking vaguely like a wild thing hangs near by. Later the tent and wild things appear in Max's dream trip to the far off land of the wild things. His drawing of a wild thing on page two shows his preoccupation with creating these creatures which later inhabit his dreams.

In *Ms Glee Was Waiting* by Donna Hill, illustrated by Diane Dawson, the title page and dedication page provide clues for the fanciful story that Laura tells to her piano teacher as to why she was late. The author tells us nothing about how far the piano teacher's house is from where Laura lived. Yet a map held by her brother reveals that it is really the next house once you cross a small bridge

In Marcia Brown's woodcut, the beak-like shape of the hill reinforces the drama of the little mouse about to be snatched up in the beak of the crow. From *Once A Mouse*.

and railroad track. Looking closely at each picture, you can see where Laura has all her imaginary adventures on her "long walk" to Ms Glee's house. The various clocks in the pictures also show the passing of the time for the hour's music lesson. None of this is in the text, but it all adds to the fun of Laura's fanciful story.

Some picture-book illustrations use visual metaphors in the same way poets add to the image-making qualities of their poems. In *Once a Mouse* Marcia Brown reinforces the drama of the little mouse who is about to be snatched up in the beak of a crow by making the shape of a hill in the background look like an open beak. Again, as she creates shadows of the animals, the reader can see the shadow of the tiger is that of a dog, his former self before the hermit transformed him.

Sendak's book *Outside Over There* is filled with visual metaphors and symbols. A comparison of the half-title page and the last picture in the book reveals that the entire action of Ida's dream story happened in one moment of time, the time when her baby sister took one small step. The storm at sea and the shipwreck which the viewer can see outside the window accompany and intensify with Ida's fury over the goblin's stealing of her baby sister. Spenser used the same metaphor of a safe sea journey to accompany his telling of *Saint George and the Dragon*. Trina Schart Hyman faithfully reproduced it in the borders of her superb illustrations for that story as told by Margaret Hodges.

The creative introduction of color provides just the right climax for Arnold Lobel's black and white illustrations in *Hildilid's Night*. This delightful story by Cheli Ryan has a modern folktale quality to it. It tells the story of a little old woman who hates the night above all things, so she tries to chase it away by sweeping it outside with a broom, by spanking it, stuffing it in a sack; she even digs a grave for it, but still it will not go away. After all her vain endeavors she is exhausted and returns home to sleep just as the sun comes up and drives away the detested night. The only use of color is on the last three pages, when Hildilid is too tired to see the faint yellow gold of dawn. On the final page her little hut is ablaze with sunlight and Hildilid is sound asleep.

Pictures should not only reflect the action and climax of the plot, they should help to create the basic mood of the story. In a perfection of words and watercolors, Robert McCloskey captures the changing mood of the Maine coast in his *Time of Wonder*. Using soft grays and yellow, he conveys the warmth and mystery of the early morning fog in the woods. His ocean storm scene, on the other hand, is slashed with streaks of dark blues and emerald greens, highlighted by churning whites. The text is no longer quiet and poetic, but races along with "the sharp choppy waves and slamming rain." The storm subsides; the summer ends; and it is time to leave the island. The beauty of this book will not reach all children, but it will speak forever to young and old alike who have ever intensely loved a particular place on this earth. Words and pictures so complement each other that the reader is filled with quiet wonder when he sees the family's boat slip into the sunset and reads the poetic prose:

> Take a farewell look
> At the waves and sky.
> Take a farewell sniff
> Of the salty sea.
> A little bit sad
> About the place you are leaving,
> A little bit glad
> About the place you are going.
> It is a time of quiet wonder—
> for wondering, for instance:
> Where do hummingbirds go in a hurricane?[3]

Besides creating the basic mood of a story, illustrations also help portray convincing character delineation and development. The characterization in the pictures must correspond to that of the story. There is no mistaking the devilish quality of the incorrigible *Madeline* as she balances herself on the ledge of the Pont des Arts in Paris or says "pooh-pooh to the tiger in the zoo." Madeline is always her roguish self in the four other books that Ludwig Bemelmans wrote about her. She shows little or no character development, but the delineation of her character is unmistakable. Madeline is a real personality.

One of the few picture storybooks that portrays character development is *Crow Boy* by Taro Yashima. In the very first picture of this wonderfully sensitive story, Chibi is shown hidden away in the dark space underneath the schoolhouse,

[3]Robert McCloskey, *Time of Wonder* (New York: Viking, 1957), p. 62.

afraid of the schoolmaster, afraid of the children. Once inside the school, the artist has pictured Chibi and his desk far removed from all the other children. His use of space helps to emphasize Chibi's isolation and intensifies his feelings of loneliness. In subsequent pictures he is always alone, while the other children come to school in two's and three's. With the arrival of the friendly schoolmaster and his discovery of Chibi's talent to imitate crows, Chibi grows in stature and courage. On graduation day he is pictured standing tall and erect, having been the only one honored for perfect attendance at school for six years. Chibi does not completely change with his new name of Crow Boy, for this story has the integrity of life itself. He remains aloof and independent as he assumes his increased adult responsibilities. He has lost the gnawing loneliness of Chibi, however, as the final pages of text and pictures combine to tell us of his character development:

> Crow Boy would nod and smile as if he liked the name. And when his work was done he would buy a few things for his family. Then he would set off for his home on the far side of the mountain, stretching his growing shoulders proudly like a grown-up man. And from around the turn of the mountain road would come a crow call—the happy one.[4]

Another requirement of an excellent picture book is one of accuracy and consistency with the text. If the story states, as Bemelmans does in *Madeline,* that "In an old house in Paris that was covered with vines lived twelve little girls in two straight lines,"[5] children are going to look for the vines; they are going to count the little girls; and they are going to check to see that the lines are straight. Bemelmans was painstakingly careful to include just eleven little girls in his pictures after Madeline goes to the hospital. He failed in one small picture that shows twelve girls breaking their bread, even though Madeline was still hospitalized. A 7-year-old child noticed the error and called attention to it one day during a story hour.

Some picture-book artists do painstaking research to be certain their pictures are authentic to the time and setting of their stories. When Trina

[4]Taro Yashima, *Crow Boy* (New York: Viking, 1955), p. 37.
[5]Ludwig Bemelmans, *Madeline* (New York: Viking, 1939, 1962), unpaged.

Schart Hyman decided to place Hodges' story of *Saint George and the Dragon* in fourth-century England she had to learn about herb-lore and ancient roses and wildflowers in order to decorate the borders authentically. These border flowers symbolically reflect the action of the story. For example, when Saint George engages the dragon in battle for the first time the flowers are agrimony or fairy wand, used as a charm against serpents; as he lies wounded by the river the flowers are mandrake, the root of which is a powerful anesthetic. During the second encounter with the dragon, hawthorne berries decorate the border and symbolize the rebirth of life. And on the next to last page, where the king offers the hand of his daughter, Una, in marriage to George, the borders blossom with the white roses which bloomed so profusely that the Romans gave England the name Albion, from Rosa Alba, or white rose. Red was the richest color of the time, and so Hyman's angels have red wings. She had to learn about pre-Norman sailing vessels and pre-Arthurian armor and wagons to be authentic in reproducing these. All this research went into the art of *Saint George and the Dragon,* which richly deserved the Caldecott award it received.

Not only are settings in the past carefully documented, but settings of today are faithfully presented in children's picture storybooks. Every young American may visit the public gardens of Boston shown in Robert McCloskey's almost classic story, *Make Way for Ducklings.* Foreign settings are authentically represented in Ludwig Bemelmans' books, *Madeline* and *Madeline's Rescue.* In these stories Bemelmans uses well-known landmarks of Paris—such as Notre Dame, the opera building, Sacré Coeur, the Tuileries, and the Pont Neuf—as background for his striking colored pictures of Madeline and her eleven friends.

The authenticity of the setting is not as important to boys and girls as is the plot of the book. However, where a specific setting is suggested, it should be accurate and authentic. It is hoped that young children's horizons will be widened by these occasional glimpses of other worlds that serve as background for their favorite stories.

The Artist's Choice of Media

Children accept and enjoy a variety of media in the illustrations of their picture books. Many artists today are using the picture book as a vehicle for experimentation with new and interesting media. However, the question of what medium the artist used is not nearly as important as the appropriateness of the choice for the particular book and how effectively the artist used it. Nevertheless, teachers and children are fascinated with the how of illustrating and always ask what medium is used. This becomes increasingly difficult to answer as artists these days use a combination of media and printing techniques to achieve a particular effect. Some publishing houses provide information on the art techniques of some of their outstanding books. This may be found in a foreword, on the copyright page, or on a jacket flap. It is a service that teachers and librarians hope more companies will provide.

The following section gives a brief overview of some of the possibilities for the choice of media open to the artist.

WOODCUTS AND SIMILAR TECHNIQUES

In the beginning of printing the woodcut was the only means of reproducing art. It is still used effectively today. In making a woodcut, the nonprinting areas are cut away, leaving a raised surface which, when inked and pressed on paper, duplicates the original design. If color is to be used, the artist must prepare as many woodcuts as colors. Woodcut illustrations produce a bold simplicity and have a power that is not found in any other medium.

Mary Azarian is known for her print-making ability. Her handsome alphabet book, *A Farmer's Alphabet,* was discussed in Chapter 4. She has also illustrated *The Tale of John Barleycorn* and *The Man Who Lived Alone* with woodcuts. The latter story, written in simple lyrical prose by the well-known poet Donald Hall, tells the tale of a man who lives alone in a small cabin because he chooses to do so.

Marcia Brown has used woodcuts superbly in her fable of India, *Once a Mouse,* and her ABC book *All Butterflies.* Taking full advantage of her medium, she has allowed the texture or grain of the wood to show through, adding depth and interesting patterns to these dramatic illustrations. Although Ed Emberley used only three colors for woodcuts for *Drummer Hoff,* the book appears to explode with as much color as the powder of Drummer Hoff's cannon. This effect was created by careful overprinting of Emberley's very stylized designs.

Ashley Wolff uses glowing linoleum block prints to portray *A Year of Birds.* Birds and months are named, but the pictures extend these labels to show seasonal activities of humans—shoveling snow, swimming, going to school. The continuity of life is presented by a pregnant mother, a newborn baby, and the flight of the Canada geese. This same illustrator creates a story of friendship

Marcia Sewall's powerful black and white scratchboard illustrations capture the swift movement of horse and rider in *Song of the Horse* by Richard Kennedy.

between a girl and boy in Elizabethan London to accompany the traditional verses for *The Bells of London.* The pictures also portray the story of the girl's determination to free her pet dove, which the boy has bought in the market. All this goes on while the bells peal their well-known sounds. Wolff's use of linoleum blocks seems particularly appropriate for capturing the bustle of activity of medieval London.

Scratchboard illustrations may be confused with wood engravings, since their appearance is similar. However, the process of making them is very different. In making scratchboard illustrations a very black ink is usually painted on the smooth white surface of a drawing board or scratchboard. When it is thoroughly dry, the picture is made by scratching through the black-inked surface with a sharp instrument. Color may be added with a trans-

parent overlay, or it may be painted on the white scratchboard prior to applying the black ink. Scratchboard technique produces crisp black and white illustrations. Marcia Sewall has created dramatic scratchboard pictures for Richard Kennedy's *Song of the Horse.* Nearly every 10-, 11-, or 12-year-old girl has a dream of owning her own horse—this story makes the dream come true. Barbara Cooney has achieved an equally dramatic effect with this technique combined with brilliant color overlays for her award-winning book *Chanticleer and the Fox.*

COLLAGE

The use of collage for illustrating children's books has become very popular. The effect of this medium is simple and childlike, not unlike pictures children might make themselves. The word "collage,"

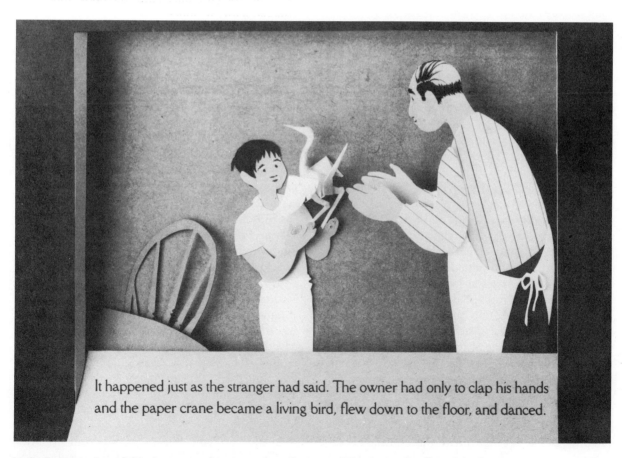

It happened just as the stranger had said. The owner had only to clap his hands and the paper crane became a living bird, flew down to the floor, and danced.

Molly Bang's unique folded paper sculpture, cut-out figures and furniture placed in a shadow box seem most appropriate for illustrating *The Paper Crane.*

derived from the French verb *coller*, meaning "to paste," refers to the kind of picture that is made by cutting out a variety of different kinds of materials—newspaper clippings, patterned wallpaper, fabric, and the like, and assembling them into a unified, harmonious illustration. Ezra Jack Keats proved himself a master of this technique with his award-winning *The Snowy Day*. Using patterned and textured papers and pen and ink, Keats captured young Peter's delight in a snowy day.

Leo Lionni used collage with patterned crayon shapes to create the grass, leaves, and birds in his highly original *Inch by Inch*. Circles of torn paper were used to convey the abstract families of *Little Blue and Little Yellow*. In his own version of the ant and grasshopper fable, Lionni has created a favorite character, *Frederick,* a mouse-poet torn from two shades of gray paper. In the story of *Alexander and the Wind-up Mouse,* Lionni arranges scraps of newspapers, tissue paper, marbleized paper, and wallpaper to tell the story of the friendship of a house mouse with a wind-up toy mouse.

Eric Carle first paints many sheets of paper with various colors to achieve texture. Then he cuts them out and pastes them together to create such interesting characters as *The Very Hungry Caterpillar* or the animals in *The Very Busy Spider*. Mounted on clear white paper, the images are clearly seen or felt, as is the case with the tactile pictures in *The Very Busy Spider*. Jennie Baker creates collage pictures using real natural materials such as grass, leaves, feathers, and hair. In her story of *Millicent*, the old lady who comes to feed the pigeons every day in Hyde Park in Sydney, Australia, Baker actually knitted a sweater for Millicent, cut out the material for her skirt and wove her straw hat with raffia. Baker spent two years in New York City creating scenes of Central Park and the city with real materials. Her book *Home in the Sky* is the result of this research; it tells the story of a white homing pigeon who strays from the flock and has all kinds of adventures in the city, including a subway ride, but eventually returns to his roof-top in the sky. Spectacular endpapers show pigeons with a three-dimensional effect. Children will be fascinated with this unusual book.

Molly Bang's folded paper sculpture, cut-out figures, and furniture seem just right for her modern folktale of *The Paper Crane* which comes to life and restores the restaurant by-passed by a freeway. True to so many Chinese fairy tales, the owner of the restaurant receives his good reward as payment for his kindness to a gentle stranger. Children would love to learn to make their own paper cranes and create collage pictures after hearing this story.

Marcia Brown has made sophisticated use of collage in her stunning interpretation of the French poet Blaise Cendrars' *Shadow*. Rich backgrounds of textured painted shapes have been cut out to form purple and orange mountains, while the people and their shadows are done in black and tissue paper silhouettes. Some woodcuts printed in white represent the eerie spirits in this tale of Africa where shadows are both respected and feared.

PAINTS AND PEN AND INK

The vast majority of illustrations for children's books are done in paint, pen and ink, or combinations of these media. The creation of new materials, such as plastic paints or acrylics, and new techniques frequently make it very difficult to determine the medium used.

Generally, paint may be divided into two kinds, paint that is translucent and has a somewhat transparent quality, such as watercolor, and paint that is opaque and impenetrable to light, such as tempera, gouache, and oils.

We usually think of old-fashioned delicate pictures when we think of watercolor, but this is not necessarily the case. Edward Ardizzone, England's master of watercolor and pen-and-ink sketches, has produced full-color seascapes for his *Little Tim and the Brave Sea Captain* that have tremendous vitality and movement. The storm scenes in McCloskey's *Time of Wonder* have this same power, contrasted with the soft diffused light of the fog scene.

James Stevenson's watercolor illustrations for *Say It!* by Zolotow create a golden windy autumn day. The leaves swirl around the little girl and her mother, they make zigzagging streaks of color in the pond, and the milkweed seeds blow about. Stevenson's impressionistic watercolors convey the mood and beauty of this very special day. Using blurry watercolors of dark blues and grays with suddenly brilliant clear greens and yellows, Shulevitz's book *Dawn* captures the beauty of the change from pre-dawn light to the shimmering brilliance of sunrise.

Watercolors can be warm and cozy too, as seen

in Vera Williams' *A Chair for My Mother.* In this story of a family's struggle to recover from a household fire, we celebrate the day they have saved enough money to buy a big fat comfortable chair for the little girl's mother. Watercolors create the symbolic borders of these pictures and the velvet texture of the chairs in the furniture store. Helme Heine's joyful, comic watercolors help to create his amusing tale of *The Most Wonderful Egg in the World.* Three hens quarrel about who is the most beautiful, so they decide to ask the king. He advises them that beauty is as beauty does and promises them that whichever one of them lays the most wonderful egg he will make a princess. Since they each lay an extraordinary egg, he ends up by crowning each one a princess. The last picture portrays three very satisfied chickens on a chicken-shaped gondola with the king acting as the gondolier. Such elegance in line and use of watercolor heightens the incongruity and humor of this very funny story. Heine's *Friends* and *Pigs' Wedding* make equally good examples of the effective use of watercolor to create slyly comic illustrations.

Acrylics or plastic paints produce vibrant almost shocking colors. José Aruego and Ariane Aruego have used this medium to achieve brilliant pictures for the follow-the-leader story of *The Chick and the Duckling* by Ginsburg (see Chapter 4). Barbara Cooney uses acrylic paints to create the well-loved pictures for *Miss Rumphius.* After her many travels throughout the world, Miss Rumphius settles down in her little gray house in Maine beside a shimmering ocean. Crisp clear colors beautifully capture the Maine landscape, with its purple and blue blooming lupine. Barbara Berger creates luminous pictures which seem to glow with light for her symbolic story of *Grandfather Twilight.* In this tranquil story which personifies twilight, Grandfather Twilight walks through the forest each evening carrying a glowing pearl. The pearl grows larger and larger until he gives it to the silence above the sea where it becomes a luminous moon.

Some of Keats' picture books are a combination of collage and acrylic paintings. The brilliant sky scenes in *Dreams* are made from marbleized paper, first created by floating acrylic paints on water and then lightly placing a piece of paper over it. Contrasted against the dark tenement building, where Amy and Roberto live, these brilliant backdrops give the feeling of a hot city night.

Opaque paint may give a brilliant sparkling

look, such as that Weisgard achieved in *The Little Island,* or it may produce the rather somber colors of Politi's *Song of the Swallows.* Sidjakov has created a stained-glass effect for Robbins' story of *Baboushka and the Three Kings* by using bright blue, red, and yellow tempera paints and a black felt pen to outline his wooden, doll-like figures. Sendak contrasted dark green and blue tempera with shades of purple to create Max's weird fantasy world in *Where the Wild Things Are.* Texture and shading are achieved with pen-and-ink cross-hatching strokes. The characters in Sendak's *In The Night Kitchen* are painted in bold flat colors that resemble a comic-book world, while details are reserved for the intricate labels and pictures that are on the cartons, bottles, and jars that make up the city of the night kitchen.

Gouache paint is the same as powder color or

Lloyd Bloom's superb rendering of black and white oils creates an illusion of warmth from the fire in contrast to the bitter cold light reflected from the frosted windows. From *We Be Warm Till Springtime Comes* by Lillie D. Chaffin.

tempera, with the addition of white. Roger Du-voisin used this medium most effectively to create the fog-shrouded world of *Hide and Seek Fog* by Alvin Tresselt. The use of gouache is also characteristic of the many books illustrated by the Provensens, including their Maple Hill Farm books for younger children and the well-known *A Visit to William Blake's Inn* by Willard (see Chapter 8) and the Caldecott award-winner *The Glorious Flight Across the Channel with Louis Blériot.*

Lloyd Bloom used black and white oil paint to evoke the piercing cold of winter in the Appalachian mountains for Chaffin's haunting story of the impoverished family in *We Be Warm Till Springtime Comes.* The artist's effective use of light and shadow enabled him to create the feeling of the penetrating cold which seeps through the frosted windows. And yet when the young boy successfully gets some coal for the family, the light of the fire generates warmth at last. The choice of oil paints and black and white color seems to balance the cold and the heat in the same way that the family's love for one another offsets the seriousness of their plight.

Full-color oil paints were used by Nonny Hogrogian for her cumulative story of the fox who lost his tail and spent *One Fine Day* in trying to retrieve it. The humor of a humbled fox and demanding woman are captured in line and movement of this circular story.

CRAYON AND CHALK AND PENCIL

Crayon and soft pencil illustrations are frequently employed for children's books. The subtle texture of crayon is easily discernible. Rojankovsky used crayon, brush, and ink to make his delightful illustrations for *Frog Went A-Courtin'.* In *Fish Is Fish,* Lionni creates an underwater world with crayons, but he portrays the fish's conception of the frog's world with the brilliant colors of acrylics. The difference in color and media helps to separate the imagined world from the real one.

The soft grease pencil drawings of Stephen Gammell create a mystical mood for the legend of *Where the Buffaloes Begin* by Olaf Baker. The large full-page and double-page pictures capture the wide sweep of the prairie and the immensity of the buffalo. Yet the impressionistic indefinite shapes suggest the legendary nature of a story in which the buffalo arise from a misty lake and

Soft grease pencil drawings and impressionistic shapes of the buffaloes create a mystical feeling for this legendary tale illustrated by Stephen Gammell. From *Where the Buffaloes Begin* by Olaf Baker.

stampede an enemy tribe, thereby saving Little Wolf's people.

Using only a soft pencil, Chris Van Allsburg creates a surrealistic world for the playing of the game *Jumanji.* His figures have a sculptured three-dimensional effect which makes them appear very real against the bizarre background of a house suddenly inhabited by lions, pythons, and monkeys. His first book, *The Garden of Abdul Gasazi,* was also done in black and white, while *The Wreck of the Zephyr* uses glorious full-color pastels to create an equally astonishing story.

Increasingly artists are using combinations of many media. John Burningham creates the visual jokes in his book *Come Away from the Water, Shirley* by using crayons to depict Shirley's father and mother as they sit in their beach chairs giving frequent admonitions to Shirley. On the other side of the page he employs rich paints, collage and crayon to develop the wonderful pirate adventure story that Shirley creates in her imagination. The use of different media and color tones helps to create the humor of this juxtaposition of parents' and child's thinking. In *Time to Get Out of the*

Bath, Shirley, Burningham uses the same technique for Shirley's exciting adventures down the bath drain.

PHOTOGRAPHY

More and more children's books are being illustrated with photographs. A photograph, like a painting, can simply record an incident or, in the hands of a photo-artist, it can interpret, extend, contrast, and develop real insight. The most exciting photographic work for children's books is being done by Tana Hoban. Her book *Look Again!* does not present a narrative but helps the child develop her perception and sharpen her awareness of the world. A 2-inch-square peep hole allows the viewer to see only a portion of the black and white photograph, while guessing what it is. As the pages are turned, a detailed close-up of a snail, a fish, the face of a zebra appear. As the square frame falls back on the previous photograph, another pattern is seen, causing the reader to *Look Again!* The book provides an exercise in seeing, a way of expanding the child's consciousness. Its total graphic conception is simple, yet superbly complex. In *Take Another Look,* this artist-photographer uses the same format of a cut-out frame for a photograph. Hoban's many concept books and counting books have been described in Chapter 4.

Elements of Design

Artists must also make choices about certain elements of design, particularly the use of line, space, and color.

LINE

Line is so inherently a part of every illustration that we forget that it too can convey meaning. A horizontal line may suggest repose and peace, while a vertical line gives stability, and a diagonal line suggests action and movement. Uri Shulevitz has used diagonal rain lines superbly in his pictures and even endpapers of his book *Rain Rain Rivers.* Parnall's many horizontal lines and rounded womb-like shapes in *Your Own Best Secret Place* and *The Way to Start a Day* suggest peace and a tapping of inner strength.

Even the size of a line may convey meaning. John Steptoe uses a heavy black outline to his figures in his city story of *Stevie,* the little boy Robert resented because his mother baby-sat him in their home. The clear fine lines of M. B. Goffstein for *Brookie and Her Lamb* and *My Noah's Ark* suggest the simplicity and universality of these quiet stories. Marcia Brown used a broken feathery line to create the fairy-tale quality and the elegance of the French origin for her rendition of *Cinderella.*

SPACE

The creative use of space, as we have seen in Yashima's *Crow Boy,* can produce a feeling of isolation or the blurred line between reality and legend, as used by Gammell in *Where the Buffaloes Begin* (Baker). Zwerger uses a soft wash to reduce her backgrounds to almost nothing, thereby making the realistic wistful characters in Grimms' fairy tales stand out. Lizabeth Zwerger pictures the little girl who goes to search for her brothers in *The Seven Ravens* as sitting on her little chair almost looking as if she were alone on the edge of the world. The use of borders as in Williams' *A Chair for My Mother* or as in Hyman's interpretation of *Little Red Riding Hood* can provide a kind of coziness to the story.

In inexpensive mass-marketed books which frequently must conform to one size for all, artists cannot afford the creative use of space. In a well-designed picture storybook, however, the illustrators may use space to enhance the meaning of the story.

USE OF COLOR

Very young children under 4 usually prefer brightly colored pictures. Older boys and girls readily accept black and white illustrations provided the pictures and text tell a good story. Many perennial favorites do not use color in their illustrations—the sepia pictures of McCloskey's *Make Way for Ducklings* and Ward's *The Biggest Bear,* the black and white humorous illustrations by Robert Lawson for *The Story of Ferdinand,* and the well-loved black and white illustrations of *Millions of Cats* by Wanda Gág.

Illustrators today are successfully using black and white graphics to create exciting picture books. The unique story by Ann Jonas titled *Round Trip* describes a trip to the city past farms and silos, steel highway wires, and riding the subway; turn the book around and the reader returns in the dark. The farms and silos become factories, the highway poles support the freeway and the subway becomes a parking garage. Black and white are the appropriate colors for this triumph of design.

Ben's Trumpet by Rachel Isadora vibrates with the rhythms of jazz. Interspersing her black and white with white on black illustrations, the artist creates realistic pictures of the pianist, the saxophonist, and the trombonist, whose trombone almost appears to come out of the double-page spread in its ecstasy of rhythm. Movement is cap-

tured on every page; in the walk and sway of musicians, Ben's pretense at playing the trumpet, and the zig-zaggy lines representing the sounds of jazz. Isadora creates real people in her black and white drawings, contrasting them with the art deco of the Zig Zag Jazz Club which echoes the period of the origin of jazz. The total format of this book suggests the sounds of jazz itself and represents the longings of Ben to be a part of it. Color would not have added to this story. The use of color, then, is no guarantee of success for a book. To be fair to the artists, however, it is important to recognize that they frequently do not have a choice of wheth-

The black and white Art Deco pictures for *Ben's Trumpet* by Rachel Isadora vibrate with the rhythms of jazz and reflect the period in which jazz was born.

er to use color or not for economic reasons. It is far more expensive to produce a book in full color than in black and white.

The choice of color or colors depends on the theme of the book. Certainly, the choice of blue for both pictures and text in *Blueberries for Sal* by McCloskey was appropriate. Tawny yellow and black were the natural choices for Don Freeman's wonderfully funny story of the lion who suddenly decided to live up to the double meaning of his name, *Dandelion*. Quiet stories—such as *Play with Me* and *Gilberto and the Wind* by Marie Hall Ets—are illustrated with pastels of white, browns, and pale yellow against a soft gray background. Taking his designs from the Plains Indians, Paul Goble used brilliant colors to illustrate the award-winning story of *The Girl Who Loved Wild Horses*. Tepees with authentic Indian designs in reds, blues, and tan stand out sharply against the dark mountains, and horses seem to stampede across the pages. You can almost feel the heat of the blazing sun as you look at the orange reds of Marcia Brown's African plains in *Shadow* or feel a cool breeze in the comfort of the dark blue nights. The contrast of the vibrant colors in this book provides for the drama of the turning page.

Certain artists have made effective use of color to show a change in mood for the story. In order to convey the loneliness of *Swimmy* after the tuna fish has gulped down all of his friends, Lionni places the tiny black fish on a large double-page spread of watery gray. The introduction of soft yellow to the pervasive blues in Don Wood's pictures all for *The Napping House* foretells the end of the rain and sleep in this very funny cumulative tale. In Verna Aardema's cumulative tale of *Bringing the Rain to Kapiti Plain,* Beatriz Vidal has pictured starving cattle on a parched and barren African plain which suddenly grows green when Ki-pat shoots down the rain from a cloud with his eagle feather. In Brock Cole's *The Winter Wren* it is Winter who keeps Spring asleep at his farm. When Simon and Meg go to wake her up, Winter hurls sleet and ice at them. Meg is transformed into a Winter Wren and tells Simon what to do. When the two children (Meg is returned to her original state) walk home, "spring rolled before them like a great green wave" and the pictures present a gleaming green panorama.

In order to signify danger Marcia Brown has ad-

ded red to her pictures for *Once a Mouse.* Starting with cool forest green, mustard yellow, and a trace of red, the red builds up in increasing amounts until the climax is reached and the tiger is changed back to a mouse. Only cool green and yellow are seen in the last picture as the hermit is once again "thinking about big—and little. . . ."

It is this rich use of many layers of color to create meaning which helps to distinguish the really fine picture storybooks. The splashy use of color for color's sake, so frequently seen in the "grocery-store" or mass-produced books, does little to develop the artistic eye of children. It is the appropriate use of color which is significant.

POINT OF VIEW OR PERSPECTIVE

Just as an author decides what would be the best point of view from which to tell a story, so too does an artist think about perspective. One way to obtain action in what might otherwise be a static series of pictures is to change one's focus just as a movie camera changes perspective or shows close-ups and then moves back to pan the whole scene. In *The Napping House,* for example, the scene is always the bed where the granny, the dog, the cat, the mouse, and the flea are seen in various postures as they sleep during the quiet rain. Don Wood shows us a fish-eye view of the scene with the bed growing increasingly concave until its final collapse. His perspective is always looking down, but he moves it slowly until he is directly above the sleeping figures for the climax when the flea bites the cat and wakes them all up and the bed falls down.

Leo Lionni uses a change in perspective to help the reader see the amazing snail's shell in *The Biggest House in the World* from the point of view of first the butterflies and then the frogs. The butterflies claim the snail's shell with its colorful turrets looks just like a cathedral or a circus, while the frogs look up at it and maintain it resembles a birthday cake. When the snail is left behind because his large house cannot be moved, the reader sees a smaller crumbled shell pictured from the eye level of the viewer.

The perspective in the surrealistic pictures for *Jumanji* changes from a worm's-eye point of view to a bird's-eye, adding to the constant shifts between reality to fantasy in that story. Seen from the floor level of an ordinary living room, two

Seen from the floor level of a living room, two charging rhinoceroses look much more frightening than at the zoo. The sculptured three-dimensional effect of these animals against the background of an ordinary living room helps to create the surrealistic world of *Jumanji* by Chris Van Allsburg.

charging rhinoceroses look much more frightening than in the zoo! Again in *The Polar Express*, Chris Van Allsburg shows dramatic shifts in perspective from the aerial views from Santa's sleigh to the floor-level view of the children opening their presents.

Not all artists work with changing perspectives, but when they do, it is interesting to ask why and look to see how this adds to the meaning of the story.

The Matter of Style

Style is an elusive quality of an artist's work based on the arrangement of line, color, and mass into a visual image. The style of an illustrator will be influenced by his or her own skill as an artist and the vision of the story that is being interpreted. The primary decision for the artist to make is how to create a style that will harmonize and enhance the meaning of the text. The illustrator also needs to consider how the art might extend or add a new dimension to the message of the story.

Style can also refer to the particular artistic pro-perties associated with eras or culture like Renaissance art or Impressionism. Pictorial styles can be distinguished by certain constant elements or "umbrella conventions" which are widely accepted ways of depicting.[6] Teachers may want to know these terms, just as they develop an understanding of literary terms for more careful evaluation of books for children. However, they are cautioned that it is more important to teach a child to look and really see how an illustrator creates meaning than it is to be glib with terms they may not understand. Also these terms were developed to describe the art of a single picture, not the cumulative effect of many images seen by turning the pages of a picture book.

REALISM OR REPRESENTATIONAL ART

While no designation of an art style can be precise because of the infinite variation within styles, realism is perhaps the easiest to recognize because it presents a picture of the world as we see it in real life. Of course the pictures still incorporate the artist's interpretation of the story, the choice of scenes to visualize, point of view, expressions, and so forth. For example, Thomas DiGrazia has pictured with sensitive black and white realistic drawings the friendship of an 8-year-old boy for the slightly retarded older boy who lives next door. The two boys help each other; Jacob, the older boy, knows all the names of cars, while Sam helps him remember what to buy at the market and to learn what traffic lights mean. *My Friend Jacob* is a realistic story that requires realism in the pictures. DiGrazia also did the expressive pictures for *Amifika*, the story of the little boy who worries that when his Daddy comes home from the army he won't remember him (see Chapter 4). Both of these books are by Lucille Clifton.

One of the superb illustrators who utilizes a representational style is Symeon Shimin. Fine draftsmanship is evident in Shimin's natural sketches of people and animals. His rabbits in Aileen Fisher's long extended poem *Listen Rabbit* make you want to reach out and touch them—they

[6]The authors are indebted to Barbara Kiefer for her description of art styles in the appendix of her dissertation, "The Response of Primary Children to Picture Books" (unpublished dissertation, The Ohio State University, Columbus, 1982).

Randolph Caldecott was one of the first illustrators for children to show action in his pictures. The design for the Caldecott Medal is taken from this picture of *The Diverting History of John Gilpin.*

EARLY ILLUSTRATORS

Walter Crane's decorative borders and fine sense of design are seen in this frontispiece for *The Baby's Own Aesop.*

A trusting *Jemima Puddle-Duck* listens to the "foxy-whiskered gentleman." Beatrix Potter created real personalities in both the text and pictures of her many books.

Full-color linoleum block prints tell a story of friendship and freedom at the same time they illustrate the traditional verses for *The Bells of London*, by Ashley Wolff.

Marcia Brown creates powerful images with her collage of black silhouettes, blue-purple shadows, and white spirit masks printed from woodcuts on tissue paper in *Shadow*.

One winter morning Peter woke up and looked out the window. Snow had fallen during the night. It covered everything as far as he could see.

A colláge of red-patterned paper conveys the warmth of Peter's room in contrast to the snowy city roofs.
From *The Snowy Day* by Ezra Jack Keats.

Warwick Hutton's superb watercolors provide both strength and delicacy for the retelling of the timeless tale of *The Sleeping Beauty.*

Acrylic or plastic paints create luminous twilight pictures which seem to glow with light in Barbara Berger's *Grandfather Twilight.*

A VARIETY OF MEDIA

Van Allsburg's rich use of full-color pastels helps the reader believe in this haunting tale of a boat that could fly, *The Wreck of the Zephyr.*

Vera Williams uses brilliant watercolors to paint slightly distorted body positions. These expressionistic paintings seem childlike and appropriate for the first-person telling of the search for *A Chair for My Mother*.

Style of art can also reflect the culture of a particular country. In *The M Horse*, by Sally Scott, intricate detailed paintings copy the jewel-like sty Persian miniatures.

APPROPRIATE STYLE

The life-size figure of a fish in bed creates the surrealistic world of a butcher who finally turns into a salmon.

Illustration by Richard Egielski from *Louis the Fish* by Arthur Yorinks.

Mattie Lou O'Kelley's primitive paintings capture the joy and beauty of *The Winter Place* by Ruth Yaffe Radin.

James Stevenson's impressionistic watercolors create the illusion of a windy autumn day—"a splendiferous day" in *Say It!* by Charlotte Zolotow.

The frame used by Trina Schart Hyman distances her viewers from the days when dragons disturbed the countryside.

From *Saint George and the Dragon* by Margaret Hodges.

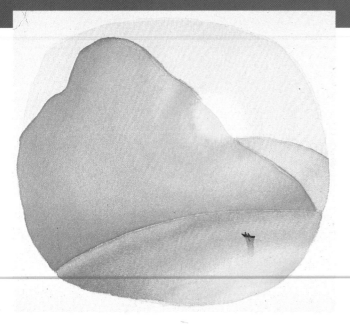

EFFECTIVE USE OF COLOR

The daily miracle of *Dawn* is dramatized by Uri Shulevitz's use of changing shapes and increasing light and color.

The graphic art of Donald Crews captures the end of twilight. The plane descends just as night begins to cover the sky.

From *Flying.*

A wakeful flea
who bites the mouse,

Don Wood's perspective inches slightly higher with each picture until the viewer appears to be directly above the bed for the climax of this funny cumulative story of *The Napping House* by Audrey Wood.

INTERESTING PERSPECTIVES

By placing the viewer above Santa and his reindeer, Van Allsburg creates a feeling of enormous depth and distance.

From *The Polar Express*.

TWO INTERPRETATIONS OF HANSEL AND GRETEL

Why do you think the artist Anthony Browne decided to create a modern setting for *Hansel and Gretel*? Does it change the story in any way?

Paul O. Zelinsky's *Hansel and Gretel* suggests a more traditional setting with his lush use of oil paints and period dress. Why do you think the artist chose this setting? What does it do for the story?

My Friend Jacob by Lucille Clifton is the story of the friendship of an 8-year-old boy with a retarded older boy who lives next door. Realism is the appropriate art style for this very realistic story. Illustration by Thomas DiGrazia.

appear so soft and real. Donald Carrick illustrates his wife's real-life stories about children sleeping out in the woods for the first time, climbing mountains, and having a beloved dog run over. His brown and green natural watercolors realistically portray these experiences in *Sleep Out, The Climb, The Accident,* and others. The illustrations are an integral part of these stories, helping to convey their mood and sensitivity to nature and childhood experiences. Realistic illustrations help the reader to enter more fully into an experience which she or he could actually have.

IMPRESSIONISM

Impressionism is associated with the French artists who worked in and around Paris in the latter part of the nineteenth century, including such well-known names as Monet, Sisley, Pissarro, and oth-

ers. These artists were primarily concerned with the properties of light and color. By placing dots and slashes of unmixed color next to each other, they simulated actual reflected light. This approach creates an illusion of a landscape or building which viewers must then recompose with their eyes.

Probably the best examples of impressionism in picture books are the Monet-like pictures painted by Sendak for *Mr. Rabbit and the Lovely Present,* written by Charlotte Zolotow. In luscious shades of blues and greens, Sendak has created a dream-like world where a very sophisticated rabbit and a little girl wander about the countryside looking for presents of red, yellow, green, and blue (her mother's favorite colors) for the little girl's mother. The dappled endpapers for this book are examples of impressionistic techniques in themselves.

Stevenson's art for *Say It!* by Zolotow is also reminiscent of the impressionists. His speckled pond and blowing leaves create the illusion of a windy autumn day.

The many fine broken lines which Mitsumasa Anno uses to recreate the impression of his trip to Europe in *Anno's Journey* are also impressionistic watercolor illustrations. He even includes scenes from some of the impressionists' and post-impressionists' paintings by Renoir, Van Gogh, and Seurat tucked away in his landscapes as a way of recording his personal views of the culture of Northern Europe.

Impressionism, then, helps to create illusions. It was effectively used, as we saw, to create the mystical world where history and legend blend in Stephen Gammell's paintings for *Where the Buffaloes Begin* and in recapturing the memoirs of time past in his superb illustrations for Cynthia Rylant's poems in *Waiting to Waltz: A Childhood.* (See picture in Chapter 8.) Impressionistic paintings have a way of distancing the viewer, placing you outside the action while at the same time their luminous beauty draws you in.

EXPRESSIONISM

Aspects of expressionistic art include shocking colors, figures slightly out of proportion, and rough rapid brushwork. The emphasis is on the artist's own self-expression rather than the reproduction of what he or she sees.

In illustrations for children's books, expression may take the form of brilliant blue horses or blue cats, as seen in some of Eric Carle's pictures for very young children. His endpapers for the unique picture book *The Very Busy Spider* are splashed with arresting bright colors, for example. The jewel-like but unusual colors for the four animals in Domanska's interpretation of Grimms' *The Bremen Town Musicians* are another fine example of expressionistic paintings. Here the striking colors and unusual angles shown in both animals and robbers help to create the excitement and action of this robust fairy tale. The brilliant colors and distorted body positions of the mother and grandmother as seen in *A Chair for My Mother* by Vera Williams reflect aspects of expressionism. At the same time, the decorative borders with their symbolic motifs give a feeling for naive style.

SURREALISM

Surrealism is characterized more by subject matter than by technique, for the surrealist combines incongruous images in unnatural juxtapositions. In order to make the viewer believe in this unreal scene, the artwork will be meticulously detailed realism.

The illustrations for Molly Bang's wordless book *The Grey Lady and the Strawberry Snatcher* are a lively example of the juxtaposition of the real with the unreal. The style is realistic, but the setting is pure fantasy. A plump little Grey Lady carrying her box of delicious strawberries is pursued down surrealistic streets to a surrealistic swamp by a character in a lime-green cape with electric blue face, hands, and feet. Wherever he walks, mushrooms spring up beneath his feet. The story ends satisfactorily with the Grey Lady eluding her pursuer and finally enjoying her strawberries with her family.

Richard Egielski's surrealist paintings complement the utter nonsense of the story of *Louis the Fish* by Arthur Yorinks. In this tongue-in-cheek tale, Louis, a man brought up to be a butcher because his father and his grandfather were butchers, can't stand it any longer and turns into a silvery scaled salmon. Hints of the action are seen in the cloud-fish on the front cover. As his delusion increases, he sees his customers as fish, and finally he wakes up one morning as a fish. Surreal pictures seem most appropriate for such a funny weird story.

Beginning with the ink blots and snakelike pens on the endpapers of *Simon's Book*, Henrik Drescher has created a scary world where Simon's drawings come to life. The little boy in the picture is chased by a monster and protected by an ink-bottle creature plus pens turned into snakes. After a wild romp through the pages of the book, the monster catches the boy only to give him a kiss. Brilliant colors blend an expressionistic style with a surreal world in this unusual tale with its surprising ending.

PRIMITIVE OR FOLK ART

Primitive or folk art usually refers to the art of peoples or cultures that have no writing systems and so record their history through art. Primitive art is characterized by a simplification of line and use of abstracted forms for symbols of plant or animal life. Gail Haley's African tale *A Story a Story* is an example of the adaptation of primitive art for illustrations. Paul Goble's use of Plains Indian designs in dress and on tepees for the well-known legend of *Star Boy* recall the hide paintings of these native Americans. Gerald McDermott's use of geometric shapes in *Arrow to the Sun* reflects the symbolic artwork of the Southwest Indians.

Another form of primitive art is referred to as naive or folk art. This style is often found in such self-taught artists as Grandma Moses, Henri Rousseau, or the early American limners and can be characterized by a lack of knowledge of such conventions as perspective or so-called real appearances. Mattie Lou O'Kelley created thirteen vibrant paintings for Radin's nostalgic story *A Winter Place*. In lyrical prose she describes a special place in the hills where the children always went to skate. They walked past "the farm with the blue steel silos," through the town, and then took the path through the hills, skated, and returned home. In colors that sparkle as much as the new snow, O'Keefe creates primitive paintings filled with stylized homes, trees, and mountains.

Barbara Cooney adapted her style to imitate that of the Early American limners for *Ox-Cart Man* by Hall. Tomie de Paola uses gouache paints reminiscent of the paintings on wood done by the early itinerant painters for *The Quilt Story* by Johnson and the lively tale of *Tattie's River Jour-*

ney by Murphy. His illustrations for *Mary Had a Little Lamb* by Hale and the brightly colored illustrations for *Tomie de Paola's Mother Goose* all echo the early folk art style.

CARTOON STYLE

Many children's books are illustrated in a cartoon style which depends on a lively line to create movement and humor. Certainly the gross exaggerations of the zany animals of Dr. Seuss are representative of this style. From the weird birds in *Scrambled Eggs Super* to the mess created by *The Cat in the Hat*, Seuss utilizes cartoon·art to tell his far-fetched stories. Sendak used cartoon style very effectively in some of his early art for *A Hole Is to Dig* and *A Very Special House*, both by Ruth Krauss. The little boy who swings on doors and jumps on beds in *A Very Special House* is the only one painted in color, so the reader knows that all the other goings on in this very special house are "root in the noodle" of his "head head head." Flat painted figures representative of cartoon art can be seen in the pictures for *In the Night Kitchen*.

Most of the work of Steven Kellogg reflects the influence of cartoon art. His wonderful large drawings of *The Mysterious Tadpole* who turns into the missing Loch Ness Monster are fine examples of the expression and humor that can be achieved with this style of art.

A close look at the art of José Aruego for such books as *Leo the Late Bloomer* and *Owliver*, by Robert Kraus, reveals the artist's skill at creating animal cartoon characters. Most of his color work has been added by Ariane Dewey, for Aruego prefers to create only the inventive line drawings.

William Steig creates his sophisticated dressed animals in line and wash drawings for *The Amazing Bone, Gorky Rises*, and *Dr. DeSoto*. Although Steig uses background in many of his pictures, the flat looking characters and clever lines remind one of cartoon art. This style of art does require skilled drawing and vivid imagination. It creates and extends much of the humor in children's books.

PERSONAL STYLES

Few picture-book artists use only one style of art; they adapt their work to meet the requirements of a particular story. At the same time, many of them do develop a recognizable personal style which may be identified by their preference for a particular pictorial style of art, use of medium, even choice of content. Thus we have come to associate the use of collage with Leo Lionni, Ezra Jack Keats, and Eric Carle, even though they each use it very differently. The delicate old-fashioned style of Tasha Tudor's watercolors is as easily recognizable as the flowing massive look of the watercolors of Warwick Hutton. Tomie de Paola's use of the symbols of folk art such as hearts, doves, and rabbits is another way of recognizing his work. The amusing animals in the stories by Pat Hutchins are frequently stylized with patterned fur and feathers. Her birds in *Good-Night, Owl!* and that self-assured hen in *Rosie's Walk* are obviously vintage Hutchins.

Several artists are experimenting with both style and media and seem to gather strength with each new book. Sendak's droll little whimsical characters are as recognizable as Jennie, the white sealyham terrier that appears in many of his books. However, his pictures for *The Moon Jumpers, Mr. Rabbit and the Lovely Present, Where the Wild Things Are, In the Night Kitchen*, and *Outside Over There* vary, despite the fact that each has a moonlight setting. The luminous illustrations for *The Moon Jumpers* by Udry give a dreamy effect for the children's dance in the night. The children have a look of almost arrested motion. The "Wild Rumpus" scenes in *Where the Wild Things Are* have an effect almost of caricature and are an extension of the dance in *The Moon Jumpers*. The impressionistic Monet-like pictures for *Mr. Rabbit and the Lovely Present* written by Zolotow are easily identifiable. The trees and endpapers of *Where the Wild Things Are* have been compared to Henri Rousseau's French primitive paintings. However, Max, with his roguish smile, and the big ludicrous beasts with their "terrible eyes and terrible teeth" are very much Sendak. While the illustrations for *In the Night Kitchen* reflect the influence that Disney and the comics had on Sendak in his youth, they are very definitely Sendak's own creation. Max has now become Mickey, who sheds the last of his inhibitions in a dream in which he falls out of his clothes and into the night kitchen. Comic-book characters have been refined to a work of art that captures the feelings and dream-wishes of childhood. The lush watercolors in *Outside Over There* represent a new direction in Sendak's work. Here he is reaching the child at a deeper psychological level through symbolic art. His artistic metaphors call forth the same inner feelings that Ida is struggling with as she imagines in a momentary day-dream what it would be like to be rid of the responsibility of her baby sister. Even though the art is very different in *Where the Wild Things Are, In the Night Kitchen,* and *Outside Over There,* Sendak refers to them as a trilogy, all united by the fact that they represent childhood dreams. Each new book of Sendak's represents a deeper involvement with the child that he was and a greater mastery of interpretation.

Marcia Brown's sensitivity to the varying requirements of different stories has led her to use different media and styles of illustrating. Look at the movement of her wonderful *The Three Billy Goats Gruff* as they come prancing over that bridge in the Norwegian fiord country. Her troll is a muddy, ugly one that you are glad to see crushed to bits! Compare these vigorous crayon and gouache drawings to the fluff and frills of *Cinderella* or to the bold, vigorous concentration of lines and design in the woodcuts for *Once a Mouse.* The striking collage and black silhouettes for *Shadow* by Cendrars richly capture the intense contrasts of the African scenes. It is difficult to recognize a book by Marcia Brown except to say it will be one that will be beautifully composed to reflect the background and meaning of the story.

Style, then, is an elusive quality of the artist, changing and varying over the years and with the particular demands of the work. There is, perhaps, more freedom to experiment in illustrating children's books than ever before. Many of our contemporary artists are taking advantage of this new freedom and producing fresh and original art.

Children who have been exposed to a variety of art styles through fine picture books may develop more visual maturity and appreciation. Certainly there is no *one* style that is appropriate for children or preferred by children. The major consideration in evaluating styles is how well it conveys and enhances *meaning.*

The Format of the Book

A picture book is not made up of single illustrated pictures but conveys its message through a *series* of sequential images. The impact of the total format of the book is what creates the art object known as the picture book.

Book size and shape are often decisions made jointly by the illustrator and the art director of the publishing house. They may search for a size that will enhance the theme of the story. *Owliver* by Robert Kraus is a large book, perhaps because illustrators Aruego and Dewey saw the choice of a career and the problem of pleasing or displeasing parents as "big" issues. The fact that José Aruego was a lawyer before he became a book illustrator might have influenced his feelings. *Noisy Nora* by Rosemary Wells is a very small book and certainly in keeping with the way middle-sister Nora, a small mouse, felt about her left-out state. The size of Raskin's amusing story, *Nothing Ever Happens on My Block,* reflects the small narrow viewpoint of dull Chester, who misses the many exciting events that *are* occurring all around him.

The shape of some books suggests their content. The horizontal shape of Donald Hall's *Ox-Cart Man,* illustrated by Cooney, is very appropriate for portraying the long trek to the Portsmouth market to sell the family's produce in the early fall and the long walk home through leafless trees in late autumn after the father has sold everything, including the ox and his cart. *A Tree Is Nice* by Udry, illustrated by Marc Simont, is tall and vertical in shape, much like the tree described in the text.

Both the cloth cover and dust jacket of a book should receive careful attention. The primary purpose of the jacket is to call attention to the book. It should not be just a duplicate of an illustration from the book but should be carefully designed to express the general character or mood. Too often the binding design or cloth cover of a book is just a repeat of the jacket; yet, the cloth material will not take the color of an illustration in the same way as the paper of the jacket. Good cloth designs are usually small and symbolic of the content. For example, Williams uses an imprint of a chair, heart-shaped to show the family's intense desire for a beautiful, comfortable *Chair for My Mother.* De Paola's touching story of the relationship between a grandfather who has had a stroke and his grandson who helps him learn to walk again is described in *Now One Foot, Now the Other.* Bobby and his grandfather used to see how high they could build a tower of blocks, and it was always the elephant block that made them topple over. After his stroke, Grandfather didn't recognize any of them, but Bobby had faith that he would. The day he played the block game, Grandfather made an attempt to laugh when Bobby said "Now, time for the elephant block." That was the turning point in Grandfather's recovery, so it is appropriate that de Paola placed the elephant block on the front cover of his story. A discussion with children of why de Paola made this choice would help them recognize the meaning of symbols.

The endpapers of a picture book may also add to its attractiveness. These are the first and last pages of the book, one of which is glued to the reverse of the cover, while the other is not pasted down. Endpapers are usually of stronger paper than printed pages. In picture books endpapers are usually of a color that harmonizes with the cover or other pictures in the book, and frequently these are illustrated. Again, their patterns usually give a hint of the general theme of the book. The endpapers for Fulvio Testa's sophisticated counting book, *If You Take a Pencil*, emphasize the theme of the book by showing row after row of brightly colored pencils laid out end to end. Lore Segal's funny tale of *The Story of Old Mrs. Brubeck and How She Looked for Trouble and Where She Found Him* has gray silhouettes of Old Mrs. Brubeck dashing madly about searching for trouble. This timeless tale is illustrated by Marcia Sewall with pictures which are as full of energy as Old Mrs. Brubeck. Tomie de Paola creates an Italian setting for *Strega Nona* by showing the arched piazza and tile roofs of Strega Nona's Calabrian town. The endpapers of *Crow Boy* by Yashima show a flower and butterfly alone against a dark background. They seem to symbolize the metamorphosis of Crow Boy's life from one of dark despair to brilliant hope.

Even the title page of a picture book can be beautiful and symbolic. Marcia Brown has created a striking title page for Cendrars' *Shadow*. She portrays a young boy in silhouette anxiously looking back at his long shadow which falls across a double-page spread, while the spirits of his ancestors shown as white masks look on. This primitive fear and respect for *Shadow* permeates the book. By way of contrast the title page of the well-loved story of *The Happy Lion* by Louise Fatio intro-

duces the reader to the tame nature of this beast. On a double-page spread Duvoisin draws a golden benign lion peacefully sleeping while a small bird eats a meal not more than a paw's length away from his mouth. William Steig emphasizes the friendship of a mouse and a whale at the same time he contrasts their size with his title page for *Amos & Boris*. The clue to what is wrong with the TV set in David McPhail's funny story of *Fix-It* is given on the half-title page and title page. Young children who like to be "in the know" delight in finding this secret.

Attention should be given to the spacing of pictures and text so that they do not appear monotonously in the same position on each page. Full-sized pictures may be interspersed with smaller ones, or a page may show a sequence of four pictures. Beatriz Vidal's placement of pictures and use of shapes complement the rhythm of Verna Aardema's *Bringing the Rain to Kapiti Plain*. This Nandi tale is cumulative, reminiscent of the nursery rhyme "The House That Jack Built." First, Vidal shows a green verdant plain mostly on the right-hand page; then she switches to the left, while the third page rests the eye with a double-page spread showing a heavy cloud mass spreading over the entire plain. Then once again she places her masses on the right and then left page—the reader anticipates this shift just as he or she anticipates the cumulative rhyme. It is not done throughout the book, however; it would be too monotonous. This is a beautiful example of how one image on a page blends into the next to create the total impact of the book.

The spacing of the text on the page, the choice of margins, the white space within a book contribute to the making of a quality picture book. In Virginia Lee Burton's *The Little House* the text is arranged on the page in a way which suggests the curve of the road in the opposite picture.

It is important also that the text can easily be read and not placed on dark paper. In Paul Goble's *The Girl Who Loved Wild Horses*, the text was changed to white when it was placed on the dark pages that represented night.

The appropriate choice of type design is also a matter for consideration. Type is the name given to all printed letters, and typeface refers to the more than 6,000 different styles available today.

These typefaces vary in legibility and the feeling they create. Some seem bold; others delicate and graceful; some crisp and businesslike. Sidjakov describes the difficulty he and his editor had in finding a suitable typeface for *Baboushka and the Three Kings*. When they did find one they liked, it was obsolete and not easily available. They finally located enough fonts to handset *Baboushka* a page at a time.[7]

Other factors in a picture book must be considered from a utilitarian standpoint. The paper should be dull so that it does not easily reflect light, opaque to prevent print showing through, and strong to withstand heavy usage. Its color, texture, and receptivity to ink must be considered. Side-sewing in the binding of many picture books makes them more durable, but may distort double-page spreads, unless the artwork is prepared with the gutter separation in mind. Tall narrow books with side-sewing will not lie flat when the book is open. Many librarians complain that the binding that is being done today is of poor quality and will not last for the life of the book. These, then, are some of the practical considerations which may affect the beauty and the durability of a book. Librarians, teachers, and publishers must be aware of all these factors.

In sum, no one single element creates an outstanding picture book; what does create one is the effective blending of all elements working together to create a cohesive whole which pleases the eye and delights the imagination.

THE LANGUAGE OF PICTURE BOOKS

The words of picture books are as important as the illustrations; they may help children develop an early sensitivity to the imaginative use of language. Since most of these books will be read to children rather than by them, there is no reason to oversimplify or write down to today's knowledgeable and sophisticated child. Television does not talk down to children; neither should parents, teachers, or books. Beatrix Potter knew that given the context

of the story and the picture of Peter caught in the gooseberry net, most children would comprehend the sentence ". . . his sobs were overheard by some friendly sparrows, who flew to him in great excitement, and implored him to exert himself."[8]

Certainly one way to extend children's vocabulary and understanding of complex literary language is by reading aloud well-written books. *Amos & Boris* is a comical story by Steig of the friendship between two such unlikely mammals as a mouse and a whale. Amos, the mouse, delighted by all things nautical, builds himself a jaunty little boat named "Rodent." Admiring the starry skies one night, he rolls overboard and is saved by a huge whale who is amazed to find that the mouse is also a mammal. He gives him a ride to safety and true to the lion and rat fable on which the story is based, Amos is able to reciprocate at a later time. Steig's luxuriant use of language and superb pictures make this an unusual picture book. The description of their trip home details their growing friendship:

> Swimming along, sometimes at great speed, sometimes slowly and leisurely, sometimes resting and exchanging ideas, sometimes stopping to sleep, it took them a week to reach Amos' home shore. During that time, they developed a deep admiration for one another. Boris admired the delicacy, the quivering daintiness, the light touch, the small voice, the gemlike radiance of the mouse. Amos admired the bulk, the grandeur, the power, the purpose, the rich voice, and the abounding friendliness of the whale.[9]

While these may seem difficult words to understand, children do make sense of the story, using the context of both the pictures and text. They sweep back and forth from one to the other, obtaining the general feeling for this unusual friendship even if they do not know the exact meaning of every single word. This is the way that children increase their vocabularies—by hearing or reading words they do not know but in a context which provides the general sense of the meaning.

In contrast to the exuberant use of words in

[7]Nicolas Sidjakov, "Caldecott Award Acceptance" in *Newbery and Caldecott Medal Books: 1956–1965*, edited by Lee Kingman (Boston: The Horn Book, Inc., 1965), pp. 223–225.

[8]Beatrix Potter, *The Tale of Peter Rabbit* (London: Frederick Warne, 1902), p. 45.
[9]William Steig, *Amos & Boris* (New York: Farrar, Straus, 1971), unpaged.

WILLIAM STEIG
AMOS & BORIS

Farrar, Straus and Giroux   New York

The title page of *Amos & Boris* suggests the incongruous friendship of a monstrous whale and a tiny mouse.

Amos & Boris, the well-known New England poet Donald Hall portrays the journey of *Ox-Cart Man* in cadenced language which is as slow and deliberate as the pace of the ox on the ten-day journey to Portsmouth. When the father packs the family's products which had taken them a whole year to make, the author describes them in a kind of litany of words:

> He packed a bag of wool
> he sheared from the sheep in April.

> He packed a shawl his wife wove on a loom
> from yarn spun at the spinning wheel
> from sheep sheared in April.

> He packed five pairs of mittens
> his daughter knit
> from yarn spun at the spinning wheel
> from sheep sheared in April.[10]

Children love the sound of unusual words, as we have seen with the 6- and 7-year-olds' delight in "splendiferous" in *Say It!* in the opening anecdote. Following story time in first grade, one child was heard chanting the word "humiliated, humiliated" after he had heard it used in Ward's *The Biggest Bear.* Children are equally intrigued with the non-

[10]Donald Hall, *Ox-Cart Man,* illustrated by Barbara Cooney (Viking Press, 1979), unpaged.

sense story of what three children do on a "bimulous" night *When the Sky Is Like Lace* by Elinor Horwitz. Cooney's interpretations of this moonlight-drenched night are breathtaking.

Children delight in the repetition of words and will join in the refrains of such books as *Millions of Cats* by Wanda Gág or *Caps for Sale* by Slobodkina. Read Maurice Sendak's *Chicken Soup with Rice* to 6-year-olds and after the third time of reading the refrain: "Sipping once / sipping twice / sipping chicken soup / with rice," all the children will be saying it right along with you.

All children can appreciate figurative language, provided the comparisons are within the realm of their experiences. The vivid word pictures in Tresselt's *White Snow, Bright Snow* are thoroughly enjoyed by 5- and 6-year-olds and reflect a child's point of view:

> In the morning a clear blue sky was overhead and blue shadows hid in all the corners. Automobiles looked like big fat raisins buried in snow drifts.
>
> Houses crouched together, their windows peeking out from under great white eyebrows. Even the church steeple wore a pointed cap on its top.[11]

In his beautiful book *Swimmy*, Lionni has described strange sights in the unknown depths of the ocean in terms children will understand and visualize: "a lobster who walked about like a water-moving machine," "a forest of seaweeds growing from sugar-candy rocks," and "an eel whose tail was too far away to remember."[12] The introduction to *The Sign in Mendel's Window* by Mildred Phillips metaphorically captures the setting and theme of this traditional-sounding story:

> They called Kosnov a town. It was like calling a puddle a pond, a leaf a bush, a branch a tree. The whole town of Kosnov was no more than a dozen old wooden buildings huddled close, each leaning on its neighbor for support, just as the people who lived and worked in them did.[13]

[11]Alvin Tresselt, *White Snow, Bright Snow,* illustrated by Roger Duvoisin (New York: Lothrop, 1947), p. 20.
[12]Leo Lionni, *Swimmy* (New York: Pantheon, 1963), unpaged.
[13]Mildred Phillips, *The Sign in Mendel's Window,* illustrated by Margot Zemach (New York: Macmillan, 1985), unpaged.

Pictures by Margot Zemach help create "Fiddler on the Roof" feeling for tiny Kosnov. The people do stick together and help Mendel when a "simple thinker" rents his room in order to rob him.

The dialogue of a story can be rich and believable, even in a controlled-vocabulary book like *Frog and Toad Are Friends,* or it can be dull and stilted, as in a Dick and Jane basal reader. Arnold Lobel is a master at creating understated humorous dialogue in his Frog and Toad Series. The two friends decide to go for a swim, and Toad admonishes Frog:

> "After I put on my bathing suit, you must not look at me until I get into the water."
>
> "Why not?" asked Frog.
>
> "Because I look funny in my bathing suit. That is why," said Toad.
>
> . . . When Toad came out from behind the rocks, . . . he was wearing his bathing suit. "Don't peek," he said.

All the animals come to watch Toad in swimming, and he is too embarrassed to get out. Finally he is freezing and has to, and they all laugh at his 1920 striped suit. Frog says:

> "You *do* look funny in your bathing suit."
>
> "Of course I do," said Toad.[14]

Similarly, part of the charm of the "Frances stories" by Russell Hoban is the natural-sounding dialogue of everyone's favorite badger, Frances. The expressive pictures are as humorous as the dialogue in both these well-written series.

In evaluating picture storybooks it is well to remember that the attention span of the young child is limited, and so the story must be told rather quickly. Picture storybooks are short—usually thirty-two to sixty-four pages. Even within this limitation the criteria developed in Chapter 1 for all fiction apply equally well to picture storybooks. Both text and illustrations should be evaluated in a picture storybook. The artistry of the words should be equal to the beauty of the illustrations.

[14]Arnold Lobel, *Frog and Toad Are Friends* (New York: Harper & Row, 1970), pp. 42, 52.

THE CONTENT OF PICTURE BOOKS

While story and illustrations must be considered when evaluating picture books, the appropriateness of the content for the age level of its intended audience also needs to be considered. A particular danger in writing for young children is that the author will write *about* a child rather than *for a* child. Look carefully at a book which fits the adjectives "cute" or "sweet" or "dear." There is a way of talking down to children in both pictures and text. Children resent being chucked under the chin, whether by an author or a great aunt! Joan Walsh Anglund's books, *Spring Is a New Beginning* or *Morning Is a Little Child*, are examples of books that are about childhood, not for children. These little books are filled with nostalgia, an emotion seldom felt by the young child.

Sex stereotyping begins early. Examples can be found in pictures as well as text. In the imaginative story *Can I Keep Him?* by Steven Kellogg, Albert asks his mother if he can keep one pet after another, ranging from real to imaginary to human. His distraught mother is always pictured attending to such household chores as scrubbing, ironing, and cleaning the toilet bowl. She explains in very practical terms why Albert cannot keep his pets; for example, a snake's scales could clog the vacuum. While the contrast between Albert's highly original ideas and his mother's mundane preoccupation with household duties is funny, it is also a devastating image of the traditional housewife.

An increasing number of books have been published which counteract sex stereotyping. *William's Doll* by Charlotte Zolotow is one of the best known of them. In this story, William is a little boy who desperately wants a doll. He has a basketball and a tiny train set that his father has given him, but he still wants a doll. His brother thinks he is a creep, and the boy next door calls him a sissy. Only his grandmother understands how he feels and so she brings him a baby doll "to hug . . . so that when he's a father . . . he'll know how to care for his baby. . . ."[15]

[15]Charlotte Zolotow, *William's Doll*, illustrated by William Pène du Bois (New York: Harper & Row, 1972), unpaged.

In the story of *Max* by Isadora, a young baseball player walks his sister to her dancing class on his way to the park for his weekly game. One morning when Max is early he finds that he likes ballet dancing and decides that it is a super way to warm up for baseball. Soft gray pencil drawings show Max in his baseball uniform stretching at the barre and trying to do the split. His enjoyment increases until a jubilant Max does a high leap out the door and runs down to the park to hit a homerun. The humor in the pictures and text save the story from appearing to be too contrived.

In *Everett Anderson's Friend*, Lucille Clifton challenges both ethnic and sex stereotyping. Everett Anderson, a favorite black character in several books by Clifton, is not too pleased when a girl moves into the next-door apartment, particularly a girl named Maria, who can run and win at playing ball. However, when Everett loses his apartment key, he is pleased indeed to visit Maria and her mama, who refers to boys as "muchachos" and gives Everett a delicious taco. Line drawings by Ann Grifalconi match the lively poetic text of this delightful story.

We have few picture books that portray modern Hispanic Americans and Native Americans. These groups have been maligned in print, television, and on commercial games as blood-thirsty warriors and sleeping peons in sombreros. A few stories, such as *Annie and the Old One* by Miska Miles, which portrays the loving relationship between a Navaho girl and her grandmother, are hardly enough to counteract the false pictures given in the marketplace. Marie Hall Ets and Aurora Labastida's *Nine Days to Christmas, a Story of Mexico* tells of a 5-year-old's excitement over having her own Christmas party and piñata game. Leo Politi's picture storybook *Pedro, the Angel of Olvera Street* also centers on the Posada celebration among the Mexican-Americans in Los Angeles. His other Christmas story, *The Nicest Gift*, tells of a little boy's joy when his lost dog Blanco finds him. We need more such picture books to celebrate the experiences of all cultural groups in our country.

While there are more books about the elderly than ever before, one can find stereotypes among these, too. One young-appearing grandfather came to a bookstore recently and said he wanted " a book about a grandfather in which the main char-

GUIDES FOR EVALUATING PICTURE BOOKS*

Content:
- How appropriate is the content of the book for its intended age level?
- Is this a book that will appeal to children, or is it really written for adults?
- When and where does it take place? How has the artist portrayed this?
- Are the characters well delineated and developed?
- Are sex, race, and other stereotypes avoided?
- What is the quality of the language of the text?
- How is the theme developed through text and illustrations?

Illustrations:
- In what ways do the illustrations help to create the meaning of the text?
- How are pictures made an integral part of the text?
- Do the illustrations extend the text in any way? Do they provide clues to the action of the story?
- Are the pictures accurate and consistent with the text?
- Where the setting calls for it, are the illustrations authentic in detail?

Medium and Style of Illustrations:
- What medium has the illustrator chosen to use? Is it appropriate for the mood of the story?
- How has the illustrator used line, shape, and color to extend the story?
- How would you describe the style of the illustrations? Is the style appropriate for the story?
- How has the illustrator varied the style and technique? What techniques seem to create rhythm and movement?
- How has the illustrator created balance in composition?

Format:
- Does the size of the book seem appropriate to the content?
- Does the jacket design express the theme of the book?
- Do the cover design and endpapers convey the spirit of the story?
- In what way does the title page anticipate the story to come?
- Is the type design well chosen for the theme and purpose of the book?
- What is the quality of the paper?
- How durable is the binding?

Comparison with Others:
- How is this work similar to or different from other works by this author and/or illustrator?
- How is this story similar to or different from other books with the same subject or theme?
- What comments have reviewers made about this book? Do you agree or disagree with them?
- What has the artist said about his or her work?
- Will this book make a contribution to the growing body of children's literature? How lasting do you think it will be?

*Note: These questions are listed to help the reader determine the strengths of the book. Not every question is appropriate for every book.

acter doesn't die." Many grandparents today in their 60s and 70s are vigorous and healthy; we might well ask if they are being portrayed this way.

Picture books frequently give children their first impressions of various ethnic and racial groups.

Only when our books portray characters of both sexes, all ages, all ethnic and cultural groups in a wide range of occupations and from a great variety of socioeconomic backgrounds and settings will we have moved away from stereotyping to a more honest portrayal of the world for children.

THEMES AND SUBJECTS IN PICTURE BOOKS

As teachers and librarians it is important that we know all the criteria by which to judge a quality picture book. Children, however, are most interested in one criterion—does it tell a good story? Story is all. Only gradually can they be interested in the art or the background of the authors and illustrators. For this reason, books will be discussed by their themes for the benefit of those selecting particular books or preparing units for study.

Family Stories

Family stories today include single-parent families, divorced and remarried families, and the extended family. John Steptoe's *Daddy Is a Monster Sometimes* depicts some of the difficulties of a single father raising his children. His prismatic pictures capture the feelings and tension in a household where fathers become monsters "when they have monster children."

Daddy by Jeannette Caines is a story of the warm loving relationship between a little girl and her father. Child of divorced parents, she waits for him to come every Saturday. "Before Daddy comes to get me, I get wrinkles in my stomach. . . . Then on Saturday morning he rings one short and one long, and my wrinkles go away."[16] The two of them go shopping, make chocolate pudding, and play hide-and-seek under the kitchen table and in the supermarket aisles. Paula, Daddy's wife, lets the little girl dress up in long, fancy clothes. Ronald Himler's illustrations capture the joy and delight that both father and daughter feel for this magic day together.

Mama One and Mama Two by Patricia Mac-Lachlan is a warm loving story of a child being reassured by her foster mother that she will be loved and cared for until her real mother recovers from her mental depression and the two of them can be together again. Pictures by Ruth Lercher Bornstein capture not only the warmth of the glad times the little girl remembers but also the dark, sad times. The story ends with the hopeful promise of spring, the bluebird's return, and perhaps the return of the little girl's mother.

Like Jake and Me by Mavis Jukes, longer than most picture storybooks, describes a sensitive boy's adjustment to his tough-appearing stepfather, who always wears Stetson hats and has real doubts about Alex's ability to help on the farm. Yet Alex and the reader are allowed to see Jake's softer side in his concern for his pregnant wife and his fear of spiders. When Alex "calmly" saves him from the wolf spider crawling down his neck, a bond of affection is forged between the two. Lloyd Bloom's bold illustrations capture the strong personalities in this well-written story.

Sibling rivalry over the arrival of a new baby is the theme of Martha Alexander's *Nobody Asked Me If I Wanted a Baby Sister*. Oliver is indignant about all the attention that his new baby sister, Bonnie, is receiving, so he puts her in his little red wagon and sets out to give her away. However, Bonnie herself lets him know that he is very special to her when no one else can quell her howls. His self-esteem restored, Oliver changes his mind about giving her away. The humorous little pictures are just right for this childlike story about real feelings. Peter in *Peter's Chair* by Ezra Jack Keats doesn't give his sister away, but he decides to run away himself before all of his possessions are painted pink for his new baby sister. However, when he discovers that he no longer fits in his chair, he decides that maybe it would be fun to paint it pink himself. The collage pictures add greatly to this universally-loved story. Sibling rivalry is also portrayed in *She Come Bringing Me That Little Baby Girl* by Eloise Greenfield. Kevin dislikes all the attention given to his new sister. Then his uncle tells him how he used to take care of his baby sister, and Kevin is surprised to learn that his mother was once a baby girl. Kevin gets over his resentment and goes to get his friends to show them his new sister. Illustrations by John Steptoe capture Kevin's changing emotions in this warm, loving story.

In Mildred Pitts Walter's story *My Mama Needs Me*, Jason is torn between wanting to play with his friends and his sense of responsibility to stay close to home to help his mother with his new baby sister. This story of an older child's desire to be of

16Jeannette Caines, *Daddy*, illustrated by Ronald Himler (New York: Harper & Row, 1977), pp. 30–31.

help and yet his resentment at the changes in their life is a very real one. *Jeremy Isn't Hungry* is a humorous story by Barbara Williams of a 5- or 6-year-old trying to feed his baby brother while his mother is rushing to get ready to go to his sister's school program. Alexander's pictures show a harassed mother in the shower and then on the phone, calling out instructions to Davey. Jeremy is not cooperating. Finally Davey gives up and announces that *Jeremy Isn't Hungry*.

The title of Joan Lexau's book, *Emily and the Klunky Baby and the Next-door Dog* describes how Emily feels about her task of taking care of her baby brother while their mother works on income taxes. Emily decides to run away and go live with her Daddy—only she doesn't know the way. She becomes disoriented while going around the block, but she finally reaches home after a frustrating experience. Martha Alexander's pictures have captured the genuine emotions of a modern divorced mother who has had all the noise she can stand, and those of Emily who is equally vexed with her "klunky baby brother."

Sibling conflict is portrayed more frequently in picture storybooks than are love and compassion. In Shirley Hughes' story of *David and Dog*, a big sister, Bella, lovingly gives up the huge teddy bear which she had won at the fair in order to obtain her little brother's lost, much-loved stuffed dog. Hughes always portrays real, believable characters in messy confusing households in both her pictures and text. In this story Bella shows her love for Dave in her actions, while many family mood stories only talk about love.

A warm jubilant picture storybook by Cynthia Rylant, illustrated by Stephen Gammell, describes the summer when all *The Relatives Came*. Driving up from Virginia in an old station wagon, some six or seven relatives arrive:

> Then it was hugging time. Talk about hugging! Those relatives just passed us all around their car, pulling us against their wrinkled Virginia clothes, crying sometimes. They hugged us for hours.[17]

The relatives stay for weeks and weeks, helping tend the garden and mend any broken things. They

[17]Cynthia Rylant, *The Relatives Came*, illustrated by Stephen Gammell (New York: Bradbury Press, 1985), unpaged.

eat the strawberries and the melons and then they all pile in the station wagon and head back to Virginia. Stephen Gammell uses brightly colored pencil sketches for this award-winning book about a joyous family reunion.

There are an increasing number of stories about grandparents. Two persistent themes can be seen in most of them, namely, enjoyment of the relationship and/or adjustment to the death of a grandparent. A little girl comes to spend the summer in the country *At Grandmother's House* by Elaine Moore. The summer is defined by "beginning with strawberries and ending with plums" as we see the little girl and her grandmother picking fruit and shooing away the birds and squirrels. Two "half-birthday" parties at Chessie's Ice Cream Parlor substitute for their regular birthdays during the year. The soft evocative pictures by Elise Primavera capture the love and warmth of this relationship.

In *Timothy and Gramps* by Ron Brooks, a grandfather helps his shy grandson to overcome his loneliness by going to school with him and telling stories. When the children want to hear more, Timothy dramatically tells them his Grandpa's favorite story. "From then on school didn't seem half as bad." Ron Brooks' large pen-and-ink and wash pictures beautifully portray the Australian school and countryside, while Grandpa is shown as an entertaining story-teller.

Tomie de Paola has written two grandmother stories. In the first one Joey warns his friend as they go to visit his Italian grandmother to *Watch Out for Chicken Feet in Your Soup*. The well-meaning grandmother feeds the two boys the entire time they are there. Eugene gets to help her make bread dolls (a recipe is provided in the text) and thoroughly enjoys his visit. The second story, *Nana Upstairs and Nana Downstairs*, is more serious, describing a boy's visits with his bed-ridden great-grandmother. After she dies, "Nana Downstairs" moves upstairs. *First One Step and Then the Other*, mentioned before, is de Paola's story of the little boy helping his grandfather recover from a stroke and learn to walk again.

Aliki's book *The Two of Them* depicts the loving relations between a grandfather and his granddaughter. The grandfather had made her a ring even before she was born. He made her a bed, a cradle for her dolls, and a bamboo flute. "And every year she loved him even more than the things he made for her." When he dies she is not ready, but knows she will always remember him. Lovely glowing pastel pictures capture the essence of their love for each other.

John Burningham's *Grandpa* is a moving story showing the many experiences which a little girl and her grandfather share, such as planting seeds, playing, building sand castles, and sledding. Alternating pages have simple line sketches that portray the grandfather's memories of his childhood. The parallel conversations are characteristic of the very young and very old, adding to the realism of this story. The grandfather becomes ill but can still sit in his favorite chair with his granddaughter. The next scene pictures the girl alone and her grandfather's chair empty. The contrast brings a gasp from children when the book is read aloud.

Through Grandpa's Eyes by Patricia Mac-Lachlan is a longer story of a little boy who learns to "see" as his blind grandfather does. The two of them make music together, read, listen for the birds, do the dishes. In fact, there is little that this grandfather cannot do despite his handicap. This is a tender story in which the grandson realizes that his grandfather has many ways of seeing.

Every family makes its own history, creates its own mythology by retelling family stories many times over. The delightful story of *How My Parents Learned to Eat* by Ina Friedman tells of an American sailor who learned to eat with chopsticks in order to invite his future wife, a Japanese girl, out to dinner. She in turn learns how to use a fork and knife so he won't be embarrassed by her. Told by their daughter, this is a family story that explains why they sometimes eat with chopsticks and sometimes with knives and forks.

Riki Levinson has told a story within a story in her recounting of the immigrant experience in *Watch the Stars Come Out*. The story, one the small red-haired narrator inherited from her Grandma's mama, describes the journey two young children made alone on a ship from Europe to America—a trip that took some twenty-three days in the late nineteenth century. They were met by their parents, taken to their new and strange home in America, and given a bath. Then they went to bed early and watched the stars come out just as the small red-haired narrator loved to do. Diane Goode's muted colored pictures help to dis-

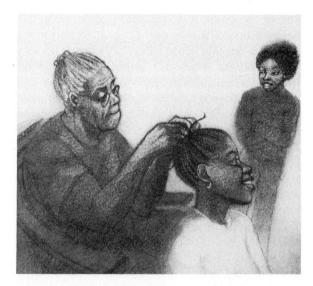

As a black great-grandmother braids Sister's hair, she relates the history of her people to various symbols, including hair styles. From *Cornrows* by Camille Yarborough, illustrated by Carole Byard.

tance the story, creating the feeling of looking through an old family album.

In Camille Yarborough's *Cornrows*, a great-grandmother and mother relate the history of their people to various kinds of hair styles. As the great-grandmother braids Sister's and her brother Me Too's hair, they sing in rhythmic praise of all that cornrowed hair has symbolized in the past. While the children decide what to name their hairstyles, Mama recites a litany of famous blacks, and Sister names her hairstyle after Langston Hughes because she knows one of his poems. In typical little-boy fashion, Me Too names his after Batman. Carole Byard's wonderful charcoal illustrations warmly portray this family time.

Familiar Everyday Experiences

Everything is new to the young child the first time it happens—going to school, making friends, losing his or her teeth, taking a trip, moving away, experiencing the death of a pet. Soon, however, children become accustomed to familiar experiences. Nevertheless, books may help children keep alive the wonder and the anticipation of such experiences. They may also alleviate some of their concerns and worries about the new and unknown. When Ira was invited to sleep overnight at Reggie's house he was very excited; he had never slept at a friend's house before. But then his sister asks him if he is going to take his teddy bear. First Ira decides he will, then he decides he won't. Luckily, Reggie lives right next door, so when he pulls his teddy bear out of a drawer, Ira can go home for his. While adults find this story, *Ira Sleeps Over* by Bernard Waber, very funny, 5- and 6-year-olds are serious about Ira's dilemma.

Miriam Cohen writes believable reassuring stories about young children's concerns. On his first day of school Jim worriedly asks his father, *Will I Have a Friend?* He is equally apprehensive about *The New Teacher* and the skill of reading in *When Will I Read? Best Friends* details the way Jim and Paul cement their friendship by working together to solve the problem about the light in the classroom incubator. In another first-grade experience, Jim and some of his classmates become separated from their teacher in *Lost in the Museum*. These little books describe real children's fears and concerns. Lillian Hoban's illustrations of a first-grade classroom in an old city school are as warm and reassuring as Jim's teachers and friendly classmates.

Willaby by Rachel Isadora is a delightful first-grader who ". . . likes math, lunch, her teacher, Miss Finney, and science." But best of all Willaby likes to draw. When Miss Finney is absent, all the children copy a poem which the substitute teacher puts on the board to send to her—all the children except Willaby, who draws a picture of a fire engine. She neglects to sign her name to her picture and so worries all weekend that Miss Finney will think she forgot her. But on Monday a perceptive teacher shows her appreciation.

Jay, a young farm boy, loves the countryside and decides to take his pet cricket to school in Rebecca Caudill's sensitive story, *A Pocketful of Cricket*. An understanding teacher finds a way for him to keep his noisy cricket in the classroom and share it with others. Descriptive language and expressive pictures by Evaline Ness evoke the beauty of Jay's country walk. Another favorite picture book which seems particularly appropriate for 6- and 7-year-olds in the process of losing their teeth is *One Morning in Maine* by Robert McCloskey. Young Sal awakens one morning to find she has a loose tooth. She announces it to anyone who will listen, including her parents, a fish hawk, loon, seal, sea gull, clam, and men at the general store. When she finally does lose it on the beach, she substitutes a gull's feather to put under her pillow.

For young children, a day on the beach or a special birthday gift may be memorable. A mother tells her daughter about all the things they will discover on the seashore *When the Tide Is Low* by Cole. Virginia Wright-Frierson has painted watery seascapes and accurate pictures of sea animals and shells for this quiet story of a mother and daughter's delightful day. A father and son hike to the California beach and build an elaborate castle in the wet sand in *Johnny Castleseed* by Edward Ormondroyd. Although their castle begins to crumble when it dries, they see that the idea was contagious as people all along the beach are starting castles of their own. It might be interesting to discuss the meaning of the title, before Evan's father makes the comparison to Johnny Appleseed, suggesting they scattered the idea of castle seeds rather than real seeds.

In *Something Special for Me*, Vera Williams makes very real the decision that Rosa, the little girl in *A Chair for My Mother*, must make. Soon it will be her birthday, and this time she can have the money in the large money jar that contains her mother's tips from being a waitress to buy anything she wants. After much soul-searching, Rosa decides to spend the money on a used accordion.

Many picture books portray the joys and vicissitudes of friendship. *Anna Banana and Me* by Lenore Blegvad describes just the right kind of friend for the shy somewhat fearful boy who delights in her sudden appearances and disappearances. She is not afraid of long dark hallways or crawling under park benches or swinging above the treetops. And when she leaves him sitting high up on the lap of a park statue, he draws courage from Anna's "magic" and jumps down. Erik Blegvad's full-color pictures capture the lively exuberance of this daring girl with the wonderful name of Anna Banana.

Samantha (everyone called her Sam) is the highly imaginative heroine in the Caldecott award-winner *Sam, Bangs, and Moonshine* by Evaline Ness. Sam's fantasies are responsible for the near loss of her devoted friend Thomas when she sends him out to Blue Rock at high tide to see a mermaid. When Thomas is safely rescued, Sam decides to give him her pet gerbil named "Moonshine." Symbolically, Sam gives away her "Moonshine" tendencies at the same time.

Ezra Jack Keats' stories about Peter begin with *The Snowy Day, Peter's Chair, Whistle for Willie,* and *A Letter to Amy.* As Peter grows up he is joined by his friend Archie in *Goggles, Hi Cat!,* and *Pet Show!* All these stories take place in the inner city and have exciting story lines and convincing characterization. In *Goggles,* Peter, Archie, and Willie, Peter's dachshund, fool some big boys who want to take away the motorcycle goggles that the two friends have found. In *Hi Cat!* Peter is adopted by a crazy cat. In *Pet Show!* the crazy cat disappears just when Archie needs him for his entry. Being highly creative, Archie substitutes an empty bottle which contains his pet, a germ! He receives an award for the quietest pet. Keats has used bright acrylic paints for these well-loved stories of Peter and his friends.

Keats introduced a new child to the city neighborhood with his story about *Louie.* Louie is entranced by the puppet show that Susie and Roberto give and he particularly loves the puppet Gussie. In a surprise ending the children give him the puppet. When Louie moves away in *The Trip,* he creatively entertains himself by making a shoe-box diorama of his old neighborhood. Suddenly his dream comes true as his old friends come to see him. Both these stories suggest art projects that children could do themselves.

John Steptoe has written a story of city children and their friendship in *Stevie.* At first Robert doesn't like *Stevie,* the little boy who comes and stays at their house every day while his mother goes to work. Robert tells how Stevie plays with his toys and breaks them, climbs all over his bed with his dirty shoes, and gets him into trouble. But then Stevie's mother and father come to take him away for good and Robert realizes that he misses him. The theme of this story is universal; for many of us seldom learn to appreciate what we have until it is gone. A 9-year-old girl described Stevie as "a nice nuisance"—we have all experienced one!

In *I'll Fix Anthony* by Judith Viorst a younger brother dreams of revenge, planning all the different ways that he can think of to "fix Anthony," his older brother. The contrast between his plans and the ending provides much of the humor of this book. Everyone has a bad day occasionally, but

few of us have experienced the kind of day that Viorst has written about in *Alexander and the Terrible, Horrible, No Good, Very Bad Day.* Alexander knew it was going to be a miserable day from the moment he woke up with gum in his hair. And he was right. It was a bad, bad day at school; he had lima beans for supper; and there was kissing on TV. When Alexander went to bed his bath was too hot and he got soap in his eyes; but the worst affront was the fact that he had to wear the railroad-train pajamas that he hated. He thought of moving to Australia, but "Mom says some days are like that. Even in Australia." Alexander has money problems in *Alexander, Who Used to Be Rich Last Sunday.* His brother Anthony has money, his brother Nicholas has money, but all Alexander has is bus tokens. Finally, Alexander decides that maybe bus tokens are all some people are meant to have. This is not quite as funny as the first Alexander story but the pictures by Ray Cruz are hilarious.

Viorst has written a quieter, more serious story about the death of a young boy's cat, *The Tenth Good Thing About Barney.* After Barney died, the little boy's mother told him to think about ten good things to say about Barney, and that they would have a funeral for him the next day. The little boy could only think of nine things, but later, while he was helping his father plant seeds, he thought of the tenth: Barney was in the ground helping the flowers to grow. The little black and white ink sketches by Erik Blegvad help create the sincerity of this story of a boy's first experience with death. The reader feels that somehow the boy will always remember Barney, the cat that purred in his ear and "sometimes . . . slept on my belly and kept it warm."

Hans Wilhelm's tender story *I'll Always Love You* tells of a boy and his dog Elfie who grew up together, Elfie growing rounder while the boy grows taller. The story recalls their good times together; their play, Elfie's escapades, yet doesn't ignore the grief when Elfie dies. The whole family ". . . buried Elfie together." Soft delicate watercolors provide humor in detailing Elfie's plump lines and tenderness as a back view shows the boy and dog sharing his coat against an autumn wind. This story would encourage children to share stories of pets they will always love.

The Accident by Carol and Donald Carrick

describes Christopher's dismay when his dog Bodger is run over by a truck and killed. In *The Foundling,* Christopher's Dad takes him to the local animal shelter hoping that a dog there will attract his attention. However, Christopher feels it would be unfaithful to Bodger's memory and can't respond to any dog. Later, an abandoned pup that he thinks belongs next door starts waiting for him after school. When Christopher finds he doesn't belong to anyone, he decides to keep him.

These stories are part of a series of books about Christopher and his family, including *Sleep Out* when Christopher and his dog do what many children long to do. *Lost in the Storm* details Christopher's concern for his lost dog. *Accident* and *The Foundling* follow this one. In *The Washout* Christopher and his new dog rescue his mother, while *Ben and the Porcupine* describes the inevitable when dog and porcupine meet. These are all exciting, realistic stories illustrated with Donald Carrick's watercolors which create a real feeling for New England villages and sea coast.

Picture Books about Older People

For many years we believed that children only identified with stories about children their own age. More recently we have given them literature which includes persons of all ages. For example, young children delight in the adventures of Mr. Gumpy, the children's literature equivalent of Mr. Rogers on TV. In *Mr. Gumpy's Outing* by John Burningham, he takes two children and an assortment of animals in his boat, first giving such admonitions as not to squabble or hop about or flap or muck about. Of course, they do all these things and tip the boat over. But then kind, patient Mr. Gumpy invites them home for tea. In *Mr. Gumpy's Motor Car,* the long-suffering Mr. Gumpy takes the whole gang for a ride in his old-fashioned car. When the rains come, the car gets stuck in the mud. In onomatopoetic language, Burningham describes them all pushing out the old car:

> They pushed and shoved and heaved and strained and gasped and slipped and slithered and squelched. . . . Slowly the car began to move.[18]

[18]John Burningham, *Mr. Gumpy's Motor Car* (New York: Harper & Row, 1976), unpaged.

Covered with mud, they pile back in the car and Mr. Gumpy invites them home for a swim. When they leave, the patient, enduring man suggests they come back for another drive someday.

In some stories children help older people. For example, in Vera Williams' *Music, Music for Everyone,* the last of the trilogy about Rosa and the family's money jar, Grandma is sick and the big red chair is empty. So too is the money jar, as all extra money must go for her care. After school Rosa plays her birthday accordion for her grandmother and sometimes her three friends come over and they have a real band. This is what gives Rosa her "wonderful idea" of how to make money. The girls form their own Oak Street Band and play for a party for Leora's great-grandmother and great-grandfather. Rosa's grandmother is well enough to attend, and the girls receive money for their entertaining.

Miss Maggie lives all alone in her rotting log house. Nat Crawford brings her milk and some beans from his mother. He always tries to look inside to see if there really is a black snake hanging from the rafters as reported, but he is too frightened to enter. One winter day he doesn't see smoke from her chimney, so he goes over to find a very old Miss Maggie troubled because her pet starling has died. Ned takes her by the hand back to his father. This is the beginning of their friendship. Cynthia Rylant says the story is based on an Appalachian woman whom she knew. Thomas DiGrazia's pictures of the grief-stricken *Miss Maggie* make her look like a little dried apple doll of the region.

Rose lives all alone except for her big hulk of an English sheepdog named John Brown. One night Rose sees something move in the garden, a midnight cat. Each night when John Brown isn't looking she puts milk out for it, and each night when Rose isn't looking John Brown tips it over. One day Rose is sick and announces she is staying in bed indefinitely. John Brown thinks about this all day and then asks Rose if the midnight cat will make her feel better. He lets her in and for the first time, Rose gets up and sits by the fire. The midnight cat sits on the arm of her chair and purrs. Jenny Wagner titled this amusing story of "sibling rivalry" *John Brown, Rose and the Midnight Cat.* Ron Brooks drew the expressive illustrations of a huge spoiled John Brown and a worried round lit-

Barbara Cooney's *Miss Rumphius* is a superb model of an independent older person. Following the advice of her grandfather to make the world more beautiful, she scatters lupine seed all over her little sea coast village.

tle lady. Children love this story, first published in Australia.

Barbara Cooney has illustrated two popular stories about older people, *Emma* and *Miss Rumphius*. *Emma*, written by Wendy Kesselman, is about a woman the author knew who didn't start painting until she was in her late 80s. In this story Barbara Cooney depicts her as a kind of Grandma Moses character who creates many primitive paintings based on her memories of her town. Her family are astonished and people come from all over the world to view her work. *Miss Rumphius* is a superb model of an independent older person.

As a youngster she told her grandfather that she too wished to travel to far-away places as he had and live by the sea. He told her there was a third thing she must do—make the world more beautiful. And so years later she planted lupine all over her little sea coast village. Repetition of the story line is reflected as a very elderly Miss Rumphius passes along her grandfather's advice to her grand-niece. The continuity of life is nicely portrayed by the many objects which we first saw in the grandfather's house, or on her travels, and which now comfortably reside in Miss Rumphius' home.

All these books feature older persons as independent contributing persons in society. A few picture books focus specifically on aging. *How Does It Feel to Be Old?* by Norma Farber presents, in poetic dialogue between a young girl and her grandmother, the pleasures, longings, and some of the anger and fear the grandmother feels and remembers as she grows older. Trina Schart Hyman has used sepia overlays and black line drawings to contrast contemporary scenes with the grandmother's memories.

In *Annie and the Old One* by Miska Miles, a Navajo grandmother openly discusses her approaching death with her loving granddaughter. In fact, the old woman sets a date for it, saying that when the new rug is taken from the loom she will go to "Mother Earth." Annie does everything she can think of to forestall the completion of the rug until her grandmother guesses what she is doing and talks with her:

> You have tried to hold back time. This cannot be done. . . . The sun comes up from the edge of the earth in the morning. It returns to the edge of the earth in the evening. Earth, from which good things come for the living creatures on it. Earth, to which all creatures finally go.[19]

Understanding at last, Annie picks up the Old One's weaving stick and begins to help with the weaving. Parnall's sensitive black and white pictures depict Annie's love for her grandmother.

The Child's World of Nature

Sometimes young children seem more attuned to the world about them than adults do. Watch children on the first day of snow, for example, and see the excitement in their eyes and their eagerness to go outside.

Ronald Himler has captured a young child's joy in seeing the sunrise in *Wake Up, Jeremiah*. Waking early, Jeremiah gets dressed in the dark, runs downstairs and through the dimly lit trees of dawn to the top of the hill to stand in a blaze of sunlight. He then makes the reverse journey back to his house to waken his parents.

Dawn by Uri Shulevitz, based on a Japanese haiku, provides a more sophisticated approach to the beauty of a sunrise. A boy and his grandfather are camping by a lake and awaken in the pre-dawn light. Gradually, almost in a slowed down cinematic fashion, the pictures move from deep blues to subdued grays and finally to the blazing yellow green of the sun. Different perspectives show the boy and the old man moving farther and farther out into the lake until they almost appear to be swallowed up by the brilliance of the sun on the final page. These are both quiet stories which focus on the beauty of an everyday event of nature, and yet they speak to children. One child, when asked why the artist chose to shape some of the pictures the way he did, noted that many were ovals, "like egg-shapes because eggs are beginnings and this story is about a day's beginning."

Rachel Carson tells us in the sensitive essay that she wrote about her grand-nephew, Roger, just a few years before her death: "If a child is to keep alive his inborn sense of wonder . . . he needs the companionship of at least one adult who can share it, rediscovering with him the joy, excitement and mystery of the world we live in."[20] Books are not a substitute for real experiences, but through the sharing of beautiful picture books, teachers can enhance a real experience and keep the wonder of it alive with their own enthusiasm and appreciation.

John Burningham has created a large handsome book on *Seasons*. Full-color scenes follow the cycle of the seasons from Spring, with "birds nesting" and "ducks dabbling," to Summer, with "holidays" and "heat waves," to Autumn, with "leaves flying" and "geese soaring," to Winter, with "ice and snow" and "endless rain," until it is Spring again, with a nest of baby birds. Some of the scenes and captions have an English flavor, as one would expect from one of England's finest illustrators. The text is as terse as the pictures are breathtaking.

Lucille Clifton writes an amusing story of two young city boys who go out to find Spring. Brinton Turkle illustrated *The Boy Who Didn't Believe in Spring* in vivid watercolors. After looking everywhere the boys find spring in a bird's nest in an

[19]Miska Miles, *Annie and the Old One,* illustrated by Peter Parnall (New York: Little, Brown, 1971), unpaged.

[20]Rachel Carson, *The Sense of Wonder,* photographs by Charles Pratt and others (New York: Harper & Row, 1956, 1965), p. 45.

old abandoned car and a patch of yellow flowers, both in a junkyard.

A Winter Place by Ruth Radin is a secret hidden place in the hills where the children go to skate. Mattie Lou O'Kelly's rich, vibrant primitive paintings of winter make this an unusually important book to share with children.

Alvin Tresselt and Roger Duvoisin have presented a contrast between adults' and children's reactions to weather in *White Snow, Bright Snow* and *Hide and Seek Fog.* In the first book adults' displeasure over the inconvenience of a snowstorm is contrasted with the children's joy over its arrival. Repeating this same pattern, Tresselt has described the children's ready response to a fog that came and stayed for three days in a little seaside village on Cape Cod, while their parents grumbled about spending their vacations in the middle of a cloud. Duvoisin's hazy pearl-gray illustrations effectively convey the mystery of a fog-shrouded day.

In *The Storm Book* by Charlotte Zolotow, children may follow the progress of a storm from the oppressive dry stillness broken by the first faint rumble of thunder to the last graceful arch of the rainbow in Margaret Bloy Graham's pictures.

In *Rain Rain Rivers* Uri Shulevitz has produced a strikingly well-designed book that expresses the mood of a rainy day in the city and the country. Indoors, a little girl watches, listens, and feels safe and cozy in her own small room. Outdoors it rains on the windowpanes, the roof tops; it rains on the fields, the hills, and the ponds. The streams, the brooks, the rivers, the seas, surge and swell, rage and roar. Tomorrow will bring puddles and mud. "I'll jump over pieces of sky in the gutter" thinks the little girl. Watercolors in greens and blues are the appropriate media and colors used for these lovely illustrations.

Peter Spier's Rain by Peter Spier is a wordless book that has been described in Chapter 4. However, there is so much to be discerned by looking at this book that it deserves a second mention. All the dimensions of a rainstorm are included here—children's reactions, animals', indoor and outdoor fun in the rain. No unit on weather would be complete without using this book.

Thomas Locker, a well-known landscape artist, has illustrated his first picture book *Where the River Begins* with majestic full-color oil paintings.

In this story two boys and their grandfather journey to the source of the river that flows past their house. The paintings reflect the many moods of nature from that special quality of early morning light to the flash of lightning that bursts through the night sky over their small tent. Locker's rendering of light reminds one of the early landscape painters of the Hudson River school. In *The Mare on the Hill,* Locker has captured the beauty of a wild horse and the two boys who love her. Beautiful as these books are, they seem more a collection of paintings than integrated picture storybooks.

Animals as People

Ever since the day Peter Rabbit disobeyed his mother and squeezed through Mr. MacGregor's garden fence, children have enjoyed stories in which animals act like people, frequently like small children. In fact, many of these stories would be listed as family stories if you read just the text since only in the pictures are the characters revealed as animals. Usually the animals are dressed and live in cozy furnished homes, hollow trees, or burrows and face the same problems as their child readers whose lives are mirrored in these stories. Perhaps it is the child's natural inclination to anthropomorphize their toys and pets that makes animal characters seem so appealing.

Boys and girls can easily see their own behavior mirrored in *Bedtime for Frances* by Russell Hoban, the story of an engaging badger who finds as many excuses to avoid going to sleep as any 5-year-old child. In *A Baby Sister for Frances,* also by the Hobans, Frances decides that Gloria is receiving entirely too much attention, so she packs her knapsack, says goodbye to her parents, and runs away—under the dining room table. Frances continues to want to be the center of attention, even on Gloria's birthday. *A Birthday for Frances* is uproariously funny as the egocentric badger eats most of her present for her little sister! Frances outmaneuvers Albert and the rest of the boys in *Best Friends for Frances;* but Thelma nearly gets the best of her in an easy-reading book titled *A Bargain for Frances.* Frances is a funny, opinionated badger character that all primary-grade children should have the chance to meet.

The Little Bear series by Minarik also serves as a

surrogate animal family. Maurice Sendak's illustrations are in perfect harmony with the tone of this book. He portrays a large Mother Bear whose Victorian dress and apron provide a very ample lap for Little Bear. When Little Bear decides to go to the moon, his mother joins in the fun of pretending that she is on the moon too, until Little Bear tells her to stop fooling:

"You are my Mother Bear and I am your Little Bear, and we are on Earth, and you know it. Now may I eat my lunch?"

"Yes," said Mother Bear, "and then you will have your nap. For you are my little bear, and I know it."[21]

Other stories about Little Bear include *Father Bear Comes Home, Little Bear's Friend, Little Bear's Visit,* and *A Kiss for Little Bear.*

As the middle sister in a mouse family, *Noisy Nora* has to find some unusual way to gain the attention of her parents—and this she does with a flourish. In simple verse and beguiling illustrations, Rosemary Wells has created a very lovable animal character who will gain the attention of every child lucky enough to hear this amusing story. Another attention-getter by Wells is *Hazel's Amazing Mother,* a determined badger who appears at just the right moment to save Hazel from three nasty bullies. The bond between Hazel and her mother is very real even if her propitious air-lift using the picnic tablecloth as a balloon stretches one's credulity. Children will be delighted with the happy ending and enjoy the way Hazel's formidable mother thwarts the three bullies. Wells is also the creator of *Stanley and Rhoda,* an older brother-and-sister combination of little animals that could be hamsters or guinea pigs. Mostly they are children, and big brother Stanley knows all the ways to handle his toddler sister. Facial expressions and very funny dialogue make this book a favorite. Other animal personalities by Wells include child raccoons in *Benjamin and Tulip* and *Timothy Goes to School.*

Another demanding mouse-child is Celestine, who lives with her warm understanding avun-

Soft warm watercolors capture the loving companionship of a large avuncular bear and a small but demanding mouse-child. From *Ernest and Celestine* by Gabrielle Vincent.

cular figure of a bear named Ernest. In *Ernest and Celestine's Picnic,* a pouty Celestine refuses to be consoled when rain interferes with their planned picnic. The resourceful bear pretends the sun is shining and they have their picnic anyway. In *Smile, Ernest and Celestine,* another emotional crisis is precipitated when Celestine discovers that Ernest has no pictures of her in his photograph album. The understanding bear explains the pictures were taken before he knew her, when he was a counselor at a camp. He then tells her to put on her best dress and takes her to a photographer. *Merry Christmas, Ernest and Celestine* continues the adventures of these appealing animal characters. Translated from the French, the stories derive much of their humor from the delicate expressive watercolors of the author-illustrator, Gabrielle Vincent.

The series of stories about a young pig by David McPhail delights young children. In *Pig Pig Grows Up* a very over-protected pig refuses to grow up and act his age. His indulgent mother pushes him in a stroller and falls exhausted to the ground. When the stroller rolls downhill, Pig Pig acts swiftly and averts a crash into a baby buggy. Suddenly Pig Pig has grown up. In *Pig Pig Rides* he tells his mother of all the daring things he is going to do as he goes out to ride his bicycle. She cautions him to be careful because she loves him. In *Pig Pig Goes*

[21]Else Holmelund Minarik, *Little Bear,* illustrated by Maurice Sendak (New York: Harper & Row, 1957), p. 48.

to Camp only the pictures reveal what camp is really like for Pig Pig. McPhail has also written a series of imaginative small books about a bear titled *The Bear's Toothache, Henry Bear's Park,* and *Stanley, Henry Bear's Friend.* These books have far more text than the Pig Pig series and appeal more to primary children. Stanley and Henry Bear are well worth knowing.

Almost all first-graders love the stories of a silly goose, *Petunia,* who thinks she has acquired wisdom when she finds a book. She does not know that it is important to learn to read what is in the book, and as a result gives all kinds of poor advice to her unfortunate friends in the barnyard. Duvoisin has also illustrated his wife's many stories about that sophisticated French lion, *The Happy Lion.* One day, this king of the beasts finds his cage door open and observes that anyone could walk in! It then occurs to him that he could take a stroll himself. He is completely mystified by the strange antics of his friends, the townspeople, when he walks into their village. Only the zookeeper's son, François, calls out "Bonjour, Happy Lion," and seems glad to see him as he calmly walks him back to the zoo. Another sophisticated French "animality" is Tomi Ungerer's *Crictor,* a most affectionate boa constrictor pet of Madame Bodot, who teaches school in a peaceful French village—peaceful until a burglar breaks into her apartment only to meet Crictor!

Other favorite books about animal personalities include Jean de Brunhoff's *The Story of Babar,* a little elephant who runs away from the jungle and goes to live with an understanding lady in Paris. His cousins, Arthur and Celestine, come to visit and persuade him to return to Africa where his poise and elegant wardrobe are so impressive that he is made King of the Jungle. The Babar stories are now being continued by Jean de Brunhoff's son, Laurent. The *Curious George* stories by H. A. Rey are also children's favorites. This comical monkey has one escapade after another, but the man in the yellow hat always manages to save him from real danger. When the Primm family move into their apartment in *The House on East 88th Street,* they find Lyle, a performing crocodile, in the bathtub. They become fast friends and live happily together. Several other stories by Bernard Waber continue the adventures of Lyle. The preposterous animals of Dr. Seuss need little intro-

duction to children. They love the story of *Horton Hatches the Egg* that tells of the good-natured elephant who helps the ungrateful lazy bird, Mazie, to hatch her egg. The incongruity of a great big elephant sitting on a nest in a tree tickles the funny bone in all of us. Another lovable Seuss animal is *Thidwick, the Big-hearted Moose,* whose generosity nearly costs him his life. These earlier books by Dr. Seuss have more spontaneity and originality than many of his recent ones, which are written with a controlled vocabulary and appear to be following a formula of exaggeration.

First-graders faced with the formidable (for some of them) task of learning to read can sympathize with *Leo the Late Bloomer* by Robert Kraus. Leo, a baby tiger, can't do anything right; he can't read, write, or draw; he is a sloppy eater and never talks. His mother assures his father that Leo is a late bloomer. And she is right. Eventually, and in his own good time, Leo blooms! Beautiful, brilliant pictures by Jose Aruego add much to the humor of this story. The same team has written and illustrated *Owliver,* and *Milton the Early Riser.*

Good Night, Owl! by Pat Hutchins is a brilliant, beautifully designed book. In this story poor owl tries to sleep during the day, but the bees buzz; the crows croak; the starlings chitter; the woodpecker taps his hollow nest—and sleep is impossible. Then, when night falls and there isn't a sound, owl screeches and screeches until everyone is wide awake! Young children will be intrigued by the onomatopoetic text that imitates the sounds of the birds and by the surprise ending.

Friends abound in many of the stories of fanciful animals. Three good *Friends,* a mouse, a pig, and a rooster, do everything together; they play hide-and-seek, play pirates, go fishing, pick cherries, and have stomach aches. They vow that as good friends they will always stay together. But then it comes time to go to bed. Their first attempts to stay in Johnny Mouse's house fail when Charlie Rooster gets stuck in the door. Fat Percy invites them for the night, but the mouse refuses to stay in a pigsty. When they try to roost in the henhouse the perch gives way. Finally they decide that "sometimes good friends can't be together" and each goes to his own house. The humorous watercolors by author-illustrator Helme Heine capture the bliss and distress of this friendship. The theme that friendships need some space in their togetherness is one for all ages.

Everyone needs a real friend like Lucy, the country cat in Diane Stanley's delightful Victorian story of the friendship of two cats, *A Country Tale*. When Mrs. Snickers, an elegantly dressed pure white cat, moves into the Butternut manse for the summer, Cleo is enthralled. She makes herself a beautiful frock for Mrs. Snickers' teas and spends less and less time with Lucy. When Mrs. Snickers returns to town she extends to Cleo a vague "you must come and see me sometime" invitation. Cleo dreams about it and finally decides to go. She walks into town and is miserable at Mrs. Snickers' elegant party. On her return home, she is robbed of her beautiful dress and purse and hardly knows who she is. Faithful Lucy meets her and takes her to her own home where she persuades her to bathe and put on her own dress—now she knows who she is, and she confesses to Lucy that she had an awful time. Lucy sympathetically replies, "I knew you would." The beautiful detailed pictures of the cats in their Victorian dresses and the amusing tale will please children in the primary grades. *A Country Tale* also fits a universal theme of many fanciful animal tales, that of being true to one's own nature.

The same theme occurs in *Dandelion* by Don Freeman, the story of a lion who becomes such a "dandy" in order to go to a party that his hostess does not recognize him and shuts the door in his face! The children do not recognize their own dog in the story of *Harry, the Dirty Dog* by Gene Zion. Harry, once a white dog with black spots, hides his scrub brush and so becomes a black dog with white spots! He digs up his scrub brush and when the children give him a bath, they finally recognize him. Waber's book, *"You Look Ridiculous," Said the Rhinoceros to the Hippopotamus*, is as funny as its title. Each animal that the sensitive hippopotamus meets tells her that she looks ridiculous without the distinctive characteristic of his particular species. Even the hippopotamus thinks she looks ridiculous. When she looks at herself in the stream, she laughs so hard that she wakes herself up from her frightening dream and is delighted that she is still herself. Eric Carle's story for younger children, *The Mixed-Up Chameleon*, tells of a chameleon's many wishes when he sees all the animals in the zoo. He becomes so many different things that when a fly goes by, he can't catch it. Then he wants to be a chameleon again. Brilliant colored pictures and cut-out pages help the reader predict what the chameleon's next wish will be.

Modern Folktale Style

Many picture storybooks are written in the traditional folktale style. These stories are original and modern, yet they have the rhythm, repetition, and refrains of the old tales. Many of them also include talking animals reminiscent of the old beast tales. *Squawk to the Moon, Little Goose* by Edna Preston tells the engaging story of Little Goose's disobedient moonlight swim, her escape from the fox, and her return to the inevitable spanking. Folktale elements include trickery, the use of the number three, and the Little Goose's refrain. Beautifully executed watercolors by Barbara Cooney make the most of this book's nighttime setting.

Brian Wildsmith is a far better illustrator than he is an author. Some of his most successful stories, however, are those which have plots that sound like old folktales. *Python's Party* is a beautiful example of double trickery. All the animals are invited to perform tricks at a party. After the pelican shows how many of them he can take into his large bill, the python suggests he can swallow more than that. When he refuses to let the animals out, the elephant steps on his tail and out they all come, far wiser than when they accepted his invitation in the first place. Brilliant expressionistic pictures illustrate the story of *The Owl and the Woodpecker* by Wildsmith. In this tale of a grudge turned into a friendship, the troublesome woodpecker keeps the owl awake all day with his loud drumming, but saves him when owl's tree blows down in a storm.

Leo Lionni frequently writes modern folktales. His story of *Alexander and the Wind-Up Mouse* includes a purple pebble, a magic lizard, and a transformation. Alexander envies a wind-up mouse, Willie, and wants to become one himself. However, fortunes change and in order to save his friend, Alexander asks the magic lizard to make Willie a real mouse, just like Alexander. In *Frederick* Lionni creates his own version of the fable of the "ant and the grasshopper," only this tale celebrates the contribution of Frederick, a mouse poet.

The other mice bring in the harvest for the long winter, but Frederick does not work. He is gathering a harvest of sights and feelings. When the wind is cold and there is no food, Frederick shares his contribution of words and colors with his friends. He makes up poetry about the sun and the flowers and warms their souls. Lionni's statement about the role of an artist in society is direct and to the point. As if to underscore the value of words, the endpapers are nothing but Frederick's name repeated over and over again.

Wit and humor abound in Arnold Lobel's collection of modern *Fables*, as in the pictures of a pirouetting camel in a tutu, an elephant reading "The Daily Trumpet," and a crocodile in bed admiring the perfect order of the flowers on the wallpaper in preference to the riotous growth of real flowers in the garden. The little mouse who sets out to see the world in the picture by the table of contents actually makes it to the ocean in the last illustration of this delightful book. Children love the stories and find the morals funny, too.

Many of William Steig's books use magic or transformations. He won the Caldecott award for his book *Sylvester and the Magic Pebble*. Sylvester is a young donkey who finds a magic red pebble that will grant his every wish. Hurrying home to show it to his family, he meets a lion and foolishly wishes himself a stone. The seasons pass but Sylvester remains a boulder. One day in May his mother and father have a picnic, and by chance use Sylvester's stone as their table! In trying to forget Sylvester, they remember him. Having just found the red pebble, they place it on the stone and Sylvester wishes he were his real self again—and he is!

The Amazing Bone by Steig is truly remarkable, for the bone can talk in any language. Pearl, a young pig, finds it on a beautiful spring day after its former owner, a witch, had dropped it. The bone protects Pearl when robbers attempt to snatch her purse. However, the bone can't prevent a fox from kidnapping her for his main dinner. Just as he is about to pop Pearl in the oven, the bone repeats a magic chant that it had learned from the witch, and the fox becomes as small as a mouse and runs away. A witch also figures in Steig's story of *Caleb and Kate*, for she was the one who put a charm on Caleb, thereby transforming the poor man into a dog. Gorky, a frog in

They could guess what he was dreaming about. Mrs. De Soto handed her husband a pole to keep the fox's mouth open.

In *Doctor De Soto* by William Steig, a mouse dentist and his wife outfox the fox with their very special treatment.

Gorky Rises, makes his own magic potion that enables him to fly. The potion also changes elephant rock into a real live elephant, something his father insisted upon seeing in order to believe it. In *Doctor De Soto,* the dentist and his wife use their ingenuity to outwit the fox who had decided to eat them following his dental treatment. Outfoxing a fox did require a special formula, however. In all these tales the language and illustrations portray the tongue-in-cheek humor that we have come to expect from William Steig.

Certain contemporary stories provide a modern twist on a well-loved tale and require a previous knowledge of the folk tales. *Jim and the Beanstalk* by Raymond Briggs is a marvelous modern retelling of this favorite tale. Children who know the story of the "Three Little Pigs" are rightly suspicious of the babysitter, Mrs. Wolf, in *Mr. and Mrs. Pig's Evening Out* by Mary Rayner. Boys and girls anticipate the climax of this story way before Garth squeals for help and alerts all of his nine brothers and sisters. In *Garth Pig and the Ice-Cream Lady*, Garth is abducted by the sinister Mrs. Wolf in her "Volfswagon" van. The van has engine trouble and Garth escapes just as his siblings cycle into view hot on his trail. In *Mrs. Pig's Bulk Buy* Mary Rayner writes a very funny modern pourquoi story of why little pigs are pink instead of white. She also cures her large family of wanting to eat ketchup on everything. In Harry Allard's tale *It's So Nice to Have a Wolf Around the House* a reformed wolf applies for the job of a companion to an old man and his three pets. James Marshall's comical illustrations complement the zany humor of this tale.

Increasingly authors today are writing modern folk or fairy tales that derive their humor from switching traditionally assigned male and female roles. *Helga's Dowry* by Tomie de Paola is the funny tale of an orphan troll, who having no dowry goes out and earns one for herself. The Troll King secretly observes her and so admires her ingenuity that he marries her. De Paola's pictures of lumpy trolls add much to the humor of this tale.

Steven Kellogg's retelling and illustrations for *Chicken Little* are very funny indeed. The story starts out with Chicken Little's famous warning that "The sky is falling" after she has been hit on the head by an acorn. Foxy Loxy hears the animals cry for the police and quickly changes his "poultry" truck sign to read "poulice." Thinking his Thanksgiving dinner is safely locked in the truck, he shows the foolish fowls the harmless acorn and tosses it up in the air. It gets caught in Sergeant Hippo Hefty's helicopter, which crashes to the earth, landing on the truck and freeing all the birds while Sergeant Hefty "flattens the fleeing fox." Foxy Loxy is sent to prison and Chicken Little plants the acorn. It grows into a fine tall tree by the side of her house, where her grandchildren come to hear her retell her famous story. Action-packed illustrations accompany this hilarious retelling of the Chicken Little story.

Tomi Ungerer creates a different kind of spoof on the usual fairy story in his tale of *Zeralda's Ogre*. This particular ogre only eats little children until he meets 6-year-old Zeralda, who cooks such delicacies as watercress soup, snails, and suckling pigs for him. Under Zeralda's influence the ogre and his friends completely lose their taste for children! Another farce is *The Beast of Monsieur Racine* by the same author-artist.

Humorous Picture Books

Young children's humor is simple and obvious. They laugh uproariously at the large comic pictures in *Animals Should Definitely Not Wear Clothing* by the Barretts. The broad humor of a moose tangled up in his trousers, a chicken trying to lay an egg in stretch pants, and opossums wearing their clothes upside down delights both adults and children. The more subtle joke of the large lady and larger elephant wearing the same dress is not caught by everyone, however. The sequel to this book *Animals Should Definitely Not Act Like People*, while funny, doesn't seem quite as humorous as the first story.

Slapstick and nonsense are the order of the day at the royal party in *May I Bring a Friend?* by Beatrice Schenk de Regniers. A little boy is invited to tea by the King and Queen and each time he goes he takes a friend: a giraffe, monkeys, lions, and hippos—not all of whom are very polite. The monkeys swing on the chandeliers; the hippopotamus puts his foot in the cake; the lions roar; and the seal plays "Long Live Apple Pie" on his bugle. Through it all their royal majesties retain their equanimity. The brilliant purple, pink, and yellow illustrations by Beni Montresor resemble stage settings for the passing parade of incongruities.

Steven Kellogg is a master at drawing utter confusion and slapstick. A bored young girl gives her mother a deadpan account of the class trip to the farm in the hilarious story of *The Day Jimmy's Boa Ate the Wash* by Trinka Noble. The contrast between the girl's reporting of the events and the exuberant illustrations is hilarious. The same approach is used in *Jimmy's Boa Bounces Back*, written and illustrated by the same team. In this instance, Meggie reports what happens when her mother decides to wear Jimmy's boa constrictor in her hat to the garden club meeting. One exaggerated scene after another unfolds in this ridiculous story. The low-key narration is nicely balanced by the action-packed pictures. Kellogg has also produced many books of his own which are equally funny. The tales of his own Great Dane in *Pinkerton, Behave* and *A Rose for Pinkerton* provide the frame for his mad-cap pictures. The first story tells of Pinkerton's failure at obedience school and his accidental capture of a burglar. The surprise ending adds to this funny tale. In *A Rose for Pinkerton*, he and the family cat Rose create bedlam at the International Pet Show. But once again, when it is least expected, Pinkerton saves the day.

Children also enjoy books about funny weird characters who appear in a series of stories. Seven- and 8-year-olds find the deadpan humor of Allard's *The Stupids Die* very funny. When the lights go out, the Stupids decide that they have died. When the lights come back on, they think they are in heaven until Grandpa sets them right—"This isn't Heaven—This is Cleveland." Children love to look for the visual jokes in the Stupids' house; for example, the framed picture of beach balls is labeled "The Pyramids" and one of a dog is titled "Fish." *The Stupids Have a Ball* and *The Stupids Step Out* are other titles in this series. James Marshall's lumpy figures seem just right for the Stupid family. Marshall has created his own funny friends in his many stories about *George and Martha*, large hippopotamuses. Each book usually contains about five episodes, which gives the feeling of a chapter book for 6- and 7-year-olds. For example, in *George and Martha Tons of Fun* the stories include "Misunderstanding," "The Sweet Tooth," "The Photograph," "The Hypnotist," and "The Special Gift."

Marc Brown's Arthur stories are equally popular and include a variety of animal characters. Arthur bears the brunt of a good deal of teasing in *Arthur's Nose* and *Arthur's Eyes* (when he must wear glasses). Never very brave, Arthur is seen as very courageous when he goes into a large spooky house on Halloween to find his baby sister in *Arthur's Halloween*. A surprise ending to *Arthur's Valentine* delights children who have to guess who his secret admirer is. In *Arthur's April Fool* Arthur gets back at Binky Barnes, the class bully. All these Arthur books satisfy 6- and 7-year-olds' sense of humor and demand for poetic justice.

Another favorite character of children this age is Harry Allard's Miss Nelson, the lovely sweet teacher who cannot make the class behave. In *Miss Nelson Is Missing*, she is replaced by Miss Viola Swamp, who wears a dark black dress and is a witch, the children decide. After one week with Miss Swamp's rules and homework, the children are delighted to welcome Miss Nelson back. At home Miss Nelson takes off her coat and hangs it right next to an ugly black dress. Viola Swamp returns to coach the worst team in the state in *Miss Nelson Has a Field Day*. Readers will be delighted with the coach's ugly black sweat shirt which reads "Coach and Don't You Forget It." Children will have to solve the puzzle of how Miss Nelson and her alter ego can be in the same place at the same time.

Silly ridiculous situations tickle children's funny bones. Five- and 6-year-olds love the tale of *Cully Cully and the Bear* by Wilson Gage. In this story Cully Cully, a pioneer hunter, decides the ground is cold and he needs a bearskin rug. He finds the bear, but his arrow misses him and angers the bear, who gives chase. Around and around a tree they go. Sometimes the bear is ahead, sometimes Cully Cully. In fact it is hard to know who is chasing whom. Children will find this tale rollicking good fun. James Stevenson's pictures add to the humor, including one wonderful bird's-eye view that looks down on the chase.

Children also enjoy the fun of Franz Brandenberg's story of an octopus in *Otto Is Different*. Otto would prefer to be like his other friends, but his parents convince him that having eight arms can be a real advantage at times. For example, Otto can do many things at once: "He brushed his teeth, tied his shoes, washed his face and blew his nose" all at the same time. He also appreciated receiving eight-armed hugs rather than two-armed ones! James Stevenson's illustrations are done with much comic energy, showing the swirling activity of all of Otto's arms. The theme of accepting differences is a worthwhile one, but mostly children will enjoy the humor of this book.

John Burningham's book *Would You Rather . . .* gives children a choice of ridiculous situations, such as "Would you rather eat spider stew, slug dumplings, mashed worms or drink snail squash?" While 5- and 6-year-olds respond to the large funny pictures, the choices seem more appropriate for older children. For example, only a 7- or 8-year-old would be embarrassed by the thought of his father dancing at school or his mother having a row in a cafe while a 5-year-old would be more accepting of such parental faults.

Older children will enjoy Arthur Yorinks' bizarre story *It Happened in Pinsk*, illustrated by

Egielski. Based on an adult story by Gogol, "The Nose," this tale describes a man going through an identity crisis. No matter what success he has, he feels he is not as important as someone else. One morning at breakfast he realizes that his head is missing. His wife is exasperated, saying, "Oh, Irv! . . . every day you lose something. Your keys. Your glasses. Now this." She quickly makes him a head of a pillowcase stuffed with socks and sends him off to work. Poor Irv is desperate until he sees his head being used as a dummy's head in a hat shop. He runs in and grabs it and is delighted that at last he has found himself. The inside joke of this story is that the head is a likeness of Maurice Sendak, the artist's mentor. The humor in *Louis the Fish* by this same team will appeal to older children, also.

Young children are past masters at exaggeration, so they appreciate the humor of the tall tale. *Could Be Worse!*, Grandpa's laconic comment on anything that ever happened to anyone, is the title of a tale by James Stevenson. One day grandpa hears Mary Ann asking Louis why Grandpa always says the same thing, and Louis says it is probably because nothing very interesting ever happened to him. The next morning Grandpa tells the children a tall tale that is unsurpassed, and their comment is most predictable: "Could Be Worse." Stevenson continues his Grandpa's epic adventures, recounting what happened to him on *That Terrible Halloween Night* and his memories of all the scary things that could frighten children in *What's Under the Bed?* and the dreadful things that his baby brother did in *Worse Than Willy*. It is hard ever to get the best of Grandpa! Even when Mary Ann and Louis complain about their first day of school, it doesn't compare with his, *That Dreadful Day*. Stevenson's illustrations are as exaggerated as Grandpa's stories.

Burt Dow, Deep-Water Man by Robert McCloskey is a tall tale of an old fisherman who catches a whale by the tail and then binds the wound with a candy-striped bandaid. The grateful whale swallows him whole, boat and all, in order to protect him from a storm. With the help of some bilge water and the giggling gull, Burt Dow is burped back into the ocean and home to his sister Leela, but not before he has put candy-striped bandaids on a whole school of whales. This story has been made into an award-winning film by Weston Woods.

Fantasy in Picture Books

The line is blurred between humorous picture stories for children and fanciful ones. Talking beasts and modern take-offs on folktales are certainly fanciful stories, yet they can be very humorous. However, children appear to make a difference between the make-believe story and the funny one.

Many picture storybooks portray children's fantasies or dreams. In *The Quilt* by Ann Jonas a little girl looks at each square in the patchwork quilt that her mother and father have made for her. When she goes to sleep the quilt becomes three-dimensional and she enters each scene searching for her stuffed dog. She dreams she falls over a cliff and wakes up to find she and her quilt are on the floor, also her stuffed dog. The way the patches gradually assume dimension reminds one of the forest growing up in Max's room in *Where the Wild Things Are*.

In the story *George Shrinks* by William Joyce, George dreams he is small and wakes to find it is true. He discovers a note from his parents listing his chores. The words of the note become the text of the story while the illustrations show how George deals with each task. He uses a sponge to surf across the dishes as he cleans them. He takes the garbage out by hitching a little red wagon to his crawling baby brother, who is now much larger than George. He has a wonderful time flying in a model airplane until it is knocked down by the cat. Suddenly George is his own size again, with his parents at his side, but as in so many other fantasies, he has the damaged plane to remind him of the adventure and to make readers wonder if maybe it really did happen.

John Burningham contrasts daydreams with reality in his two books *Come Away From the Water, Shirley* and *Time to Get Out of the Bath, Shirley*. The first book has been described in this chapter. In the second one, Shirley is taking a bath while her mother weighs herself, cleans the wash bowl, and generally picks up the bathroom, admonishing Shirley most of the time for being so messy. Meanwhile, Shirley in her imagination, shown in richly colored dream pictures, has ridden her duck down the drain and out onto a wider river. She is rescued from going over the rapids by a knight in armor, meets the King and Queen, and defeats them in a tilting match on the river while all are riding ducks. The contrast between Shirley's vivid imagination and her mother's preoccupation with mundane matters is very funny indeed. The endpapers of this book also deserve mention as they combine pipes and sewers with all of Shirley's adventures. Both these books are picture books which will appeal to 8-, 9-, and 10-year-olds.

Another form of fantasy of young children involves anthropomorphism or the personification of inanimate objects, such as toys and machines. Most all children know and love Watty Piper's story of *The Little Engine That Could*, . . . and did get the toys over the mountain. Most of the books written by Virginia Lee Burton contain personification: *Katie and the Big Snow, The Little House,* and *Mike Mulligan and His Steam Shovel.* The modern problem of obsolescence is solved easily in the story of Mike and his beloved steam shovel, Mary Ann. After proving that Mary Ann could dig a basement for the new town hall in a day, Mike is forced to convert her into a furnace, since he has neglected to plan a way for Mary Ann to get out of the excavation. Katie is a snowplow who saves the day by plowing out a whole village. The encroachment of the city on the country is portrayed in Burton's classic story of *The Little House* that stood on the hill and watched day and night and the seasons pass. Gradually, a road is built, cars come, and soon the city grows up around the little house. Elevated cars speed by her; subway trains speed under her; and people rush to and fro in front of her. One day the great-great-granddaughter of the original owner sees the little house, buys her, and has her moved back to the country where she can once again see the stars.

Hardie Gramatky has personified a boat in his well-loved story of *Little Toot*, the headstrong tugboat in New York Harbor who refuses to accept adult responsibilities until a crisis makes him a hero. Gramatky's illustrations of the little boat appear animated, reflecting his years of work at the Walt Disney Studio.

Several picture books personify toys and dolls. All primary children love the story of the little wistful teddy bear named *Corduroy* for his green corduroy overalls. Corduroy waits patiently in the department store for someone to buy him. A little girl, Lisa, sees him and wants him but her mother discourages her by pointing out that he doesn't

look new and that one of the buttons on his shoulder straps is missing. Corduroy has many exciting adventures in the store as he goes in search of a new button. He doesn't find one, but the next morning he does find what he has wanted most—a home and a friend, for Lisa returns with the contents of her piggy bank and buys him. This book by Don Freeman is a completely satisfying story containing pathos, love, and excitement. The sequel to this story is *A Pocket for Corduroy.*

One of the earliest stories to personify toys was *The Velveteen Rabbit* by Margery Williams. Any child who has loved a stuffed animal of his own will understand the conversation between the old skin horse and the velveteen rabbit on the subject of becoming real. The skin horse tells the rabbit, "real isn't how you are inside . . . It's a thing that happens to you when a child loves you for a long long while." When the rabbit asks how it happens, he replies. "It doesn't happen all at once . . . you become. It takes a long while."[22] Four or five newly illustrated editions of this story have been published; the ones by Michael Hague, Ilse Plume, and Alan Atkinson are the most attractive.

Today there are more stories about monsters than there are about toys and dolls. Baby monsters can be very lovable if *Clyde Monster* by Robert Crowe is an example. In a reversal of roles, Clyde is afraid to go to bed because people might be hiding in his cave to get him. His parents assure him that people and monsters came to an agreement years ago not to scare each other. Clyde is not completely convinced, for as he goes to bed he asks that they leave "the rock open just a little." In Mercer Mayer's well-loved story, *There's a Nightmare in My Closet*, a small boy ends up by comforting a monster who has a nightmare. In fact, the ugly yet lovable creature climbs into bed with him.

Sibling rivalry is the theme of *The Very Worst Monster* by Pat Hutchins. When Billy monster was born, his father said he would grow up to be "the very worst monster in the world." But Billy's sister Hazel intended to do that. Every time Billy did something awful, Hazel did something even more monstrous—but no one noticed. Then Hazel did something that did catch their attention—she gave her baby brother away, thereby achieving her goal.

[22]Margery Williams, *The Velveteen Rabbit*, illustrated by William Nicholson (New York: Doubleday, 1922), p. 17.

Hutchins' pictures for this story are much fun—the monsters are all monstrous and live in very cozy well-furnished caves.

A scary ghost story that primary children love is *The Tailypo* by Joanna Galdone. A creature gets in an old man's cabin one night and he cuts its tail off. Every night he hears a scratching alongside his cabin and he calls out "Who's that?" and an eerie voice answers: "Tailypo, tailypo—I'm coming to get my tailypo."[23]

In *Do Not Open*, Brinton Turkle bottled up one of the biggest, nastiest monsters in the world. Miss Moody read the label but she heard a small child's voice inside begging to be let out. The monster tried to scare her by getting bigger and bigger. She then informed him she was only frightened of mice and so of course he became a mouse, which her cat ate. This is an old folktale trick, but Turkle has made it seem new again in this surprising picture book.

Kellogg's funny story of *The Mysterious Tadpole* can almost be predicted when the reader learns that Louis has received a pet tadpole from his Scottish uncle who lives near Loch Ness. However, the ending of this fanciful tale holds a surprise, also.

Tog the Ribber; or Granny's Tale by Paul Coltman is deliciously spooky. The text is a long narrative poem by a British poet who uses nonsense words similar to those in Carroll's "Jabberwocky." His daughter has transformed it into a picture book with eerie yet beautiful full-color pictures. In the story Granny explains "Why her hair is white / And . . . why she don't speak right" by recounting an episode from her childhood. One night as she was coming home alone she was pursued by the ghostly bones of Tog the Ribber:

> . . . Tog hobbed clitter clotter after.
> And still he come. I heard his snork.
> He snorked green breath upon my nick.[24]

The illustrations are filled with menacing shapes of insects, worms, spiders, snakes, owls, bones, disembodied faces all spilling out of the misty pages. It is with great relief that Granny ends her nightmarish tale safe in her "cosly bed." This is a story that begs to be read aloud or told.

Picture Books for Older Children

Increasingly, in our visual world picture books are being produced for children of all ages. Unless teachers and librarians are aware of this, children may miss them, which would be most unfortunate.

Some of these books have universal appeal, such as Karla Kuskin's delightful *The Philharmonic Gets Dressed* with its wonderful illustrations of ninety-two men and thirteen women getting dressed to go to work. The pictures by Marc Simont of the men shaving, getting into their underwear and black trousers, and the women wiggling into their slips and long black skirts are very funny. And yet something of the scope of human involvement in a major symphony orchestra production comes through in this story.

Sue Alexander's story of *Nadia the Willful* has a different kind of universal appeal. When her brother is lost on the desert, his father, Sheik Tarik, declares death to anyone who ever again mentions his name. However the wise Nadia knows that only by remembering and talking about those whom we have loved is their memory preserved forever. The story is distanced by taking place on the desert, but Nadia shows the way to make an oasis of the heart.

The long prose poems by Byrd Baylor are most appropriate for children 8 and above. In *The Best Town in the World* a child narrator repeats all his/her father's claims for the wonderful town where he grew up. But the full-color pictures by Ronald Himler portray a perfectly ordinary small western town at the turn of the century. Older children could recall the tales about family places they have heard their parents discuss all their lives. Many other books by Byrd Baylor have a western setting that has been suggested by the clear firm lines of Peter Parnall's pen and ink and paints. *Hawk, I'm Your Brother* describes the taming and freeing of a boy's hawk. *Your Own Best Secret Place, Everybody Needs a Rock,* and *The Other Way to Listen* are all books that will increase children's sensitivity to nature; they should be shared with children from ages 7 through 12.

Anno's travel stories delight older children. They

[23]Joanna Galdone, *The Tailypo*, illustrated by Paul Galdone (New York: Clarion Books, 1977), unpaged.
[24]Paul Coltman, *Tog the Ribber*, illustrated by Gillian McClure (New York: Farrar, Straus and Giroux, 1985), unpaged.

Eight women dress in long black skirts. They wear black tops, sweaters, or blouses. Four women put on long black dresses. And one wears a black jumper over a black shirt. A few of the women put jewelry on, a necklace, earrings, but no bracelets. Bracelets would get in the way when they're working.

This inside view of ninety-two men and thirteen women getting dressed for their Philharmonic performance appeals to all ages. Illustration by Marc Simont from *The Philharmonic Gets Dressed* by Karla Kuskin.

can pore over *Anno's Journey* finding all the hidden pictures depicting European folktales or, using an art book, match scenes from famous paintings or discover the places where the Japanese artist has employed trompe l'oeil techniques, creating the illusion of children playing ring toss on the spire of a cathedral or of a statue holding the reins of a horse. *Anno's U.S.A.* requires a child to reconstruct the history of the United States going from the West to the East, a complex and intriguing task. Other travel stories include *Anno's Britain* and *Anno's Italy*.

The fantasy of Chris Van Allsburg is certainly for older children. *Jumanji* has been discussed previously. *The Garden of Abdul Gasazi* was Allsburg's first book. Children are intrigued with the stark black and white pictures portraying the strange garden and huge house of the magician. The puzzling ending of the story gives them much to discuss. The ending for *The Wreck of the Zephyr* is another of Allsburg's puzzles. Superb full-color pictures illustrate this fantasy of the one time a boat could fly. *The Mysteries of Harris Burdick* provides puzzles that must be solved with every picture. This book would be superb to use in writing classes with middle-grade children.

The Polar Express by Van Allsburg is a haunting Christmas story for all children and for those who remain children at heart. It is the tale of a boy who on Christmas Eve boards a mysterious train filled with children, bound for the North Pole. When he arrives a large statuesque Santa Claus offers him any gift he wants. The boy modestly chooses to ask for one of the silver bells from the reindeer's harness. On the way home he loses the bell; yet on Christmas morning there it is in a small box under the tree. The boy and his sister can each hear its sound but his parents cannot. Years later the boy, now a grown man, can still hear its silver tone. Changing perspectives from inside the train to outside the train, from floor level to an aerial view from Santa's sleigh create movement and add to the breathtaking quality of these pictures. The interplay of light and dark in these full-color pictures helps to create the memory of a child's dream of a snow-shrouded world. Yet the sound of the bell remains for those who truly believe in Christmas. This picture storybook richly deserved the Caldecott award which it received.

Some picture books should be used only with older children. The moving story of Mii and her family is told by Toshi Maruki in *Hiroshima No Pika*, which means the flash of Hiroshima. Seven-year-old Mii and her family are calmly eating their breakfast of sweet potatoes on August 6, 1945, at 8:15 A.M. when the flash occurs. Mii's mother carries her wounded father to the river. There they all sleep for four days. Mii's father recovers, only to die later from radiation exposure. Mii herself never grows in mind or body beyond her seven years. The expressionistic pictures of the fires, the thunder and lightning and the wounded and dying all create the horror of an atomic attack. Yet the book was written in the hope it would never happen again. In the afterword of this picture book the author-illustrator writes:

> I am now past seventy years old. I have neither children nor grandchildren. But I have written this book for grandchildren everywhere. It took me a very long time to complete it. It is very difficult to tell young

people about something very bad that happened, in the hope that their knowing will help keep it from happening again.[25]

This, of course, is the reason teachers should share this book. For somehow when pain is particularized for a specific family it becomes more real and immediate than when it is depersonalized into mass numbers who were killed that day.

The kindness of one child who cared and provided food for children in a concentration camp is told in the moving story of *Rose Blanche* by Christopher Galloz and Roberto Innocenti. Illustrated with paintings of almost photographic clarity, this picture book is certainly for older children. The courage of Rose Blanche and all persons who in their small ways try to maintain humanity in the midst of inhumanity is something that needs to be discussed with older children.

Picture books, then, are for all children. They can enlarge children's lives, stretch their imaginations, and enhance their living. The phenomenal growth of beautiful picture books for children of all ages is an outstanding accomplishment of the past fifty years of publishing. Children do not always recognize the beauty of these books, but early impressions do exert an influence on the development of permanent tastes for children growing up.

Picture books are also for adults, who find them potentially satisfying art and literature. Frequently they buy them for gifts, or to display as art objects on coffee tables, or for their own personal enjoyment.

[25]Toshi Maruki, *Hiroshima No Pika* (New York: Lothrop, Lee and Shepard, 1980), unpaged.

SUGGESTED LEARNING EXPERIENCES

1. Look closely at three or more picture storybooks to discover how the illustrations carry the story's meaning beyond the words. Note the effect of the artist's choice of medium, style, and color, look for content details present in the pictures but not in the text.
2. Study the work of one Caldecott award-winning illustrator. What media does this artist use? What terms would you use to describe his or her style? How do earlier books compare to the most recent ones? Read his or her acceptance speech for the Caldecott. How has the illustrator's style been influenced by his or her concepts of childhood?
3. Form a mock Caldecott Award committee and review the Honor Books and award-winning book for one specific year. Would you have made the same decision as the ALA committee? Why or why not?

4. Find three or four books which are examples of the use of one medium—such as scratchboard or collage. Experiment with the materials used in this medium to make a picture of your own.

5. Find examples of picture books which you think might increase children's sensitivity to well-used language. Look for vivid descriptions, repetition of unusual words or phrases, figures of speech within the child's experience.

6. Select a group of stories based on a single subject or theme, such as stories about grandparents, first-time experiences, or "Be yourself" theme. Discuss which ones you would use to introduce a unit, which you would read aloud as a teacher, which would be appropriate for children's reading.

7. Collect stories written by one author such as Zolotow, Clifton, or Tresselt, but illustrated by different artists. How does the artist's vision change the mood of the story?

8. Select picture books for older children. Tell how these might fit into a unit of work for this age group.

9. Interview primary-grade teachers to see how often they read to the children, how long a time they read, and what their favorite books are.

RELATED READINGS

1. Anno, Mitsumasa. *The Unique World of Mitsumasa Anno*, translated and adapted by Samuel Crowell Morse. Foreword by Martin Gardner. New York: Philomel Books, 1980.
   An overview of the art of this amazing man, including some of his own pithy comments. Helps the student see the range of Anno's work beyond his picture books. Even the format of this book is unique in that it looks like a package from Japan.

2. Bader, Barbara. *American Picturebooks from Noah's Ark to The Beast Within*. New York: Macmillan, 1976.
   A comprehensive historical study of American picture books including the influence of foreign artists, the impact of motion pictures and comic books, and the social scene. Over 700 illustrations (130 in color) enable the author to discuss various styles of many illustrators. Useful sections on informational books and the mass market are also included. While out of print this book is still available in many libraries.

3. Brown, Marcia. *Lotus Seeds: Children's Pictures and Books*. New York: Scribners, 1986.
   A noted illustrator writes eloquently on picture books, the hero within, publishing, and her own work. Her three Caldecott acceptance speeches are included among these thought-provoking essays.

4. Cianciolo, Patricia, ed., *Picture Books for Children*. Chicago, Ill.: The American Library Association, 1981.
   A thorough discussion and annotated listing of all kinds of picture books for children, including biographies and informational books, picture book editions of single poems, and folktales. Appropriate age levels for each book are suggested; these range from 3 to 18.

5. Kiefer, Barbara. "The Responses of Children in a Combination First/Second Grade Classroom to Picture Books in a Variety of Artistic Styles," *Journal of Research and Development in Education*, Vol. 16, No. 3, 1983, pp. 14–20.
   A report on a ten-week study in the classroom of 7- and 8-year-olds' responses to picture books. Emphasis was placed on how the children's responses to books changed over time and the importance of the setting in fostering response.

6. *The Lion and the Unicorn, A Critical Journal of Children's Literature*, "Picture Books," Vol. 7/8, Department of English, Brooklyn College, 1985.
   A special double issue of this literary magazine focuses only on picture books. It contains some thirteen articles. Stephen Roxburgh takes an in-depth look at *Outside Over There* by Sendak, Leonard Marcus examines the books of Anno, and Nancy Willard interviews the Provensens about their artwork over the years.

7. Kingman, Lee, Joanna Foster, and Ruth Lontroft. *Illustrators of Children's Books: 1957–1966*. Boston: The Horn Book, Inc., 1968.

The third book in a series on children's book illustrators. Contains an interesting article, "Color Separation," by Adrienne Adams. A source for many brief biographical sketches of illustrators.

8. Kingman, Lee, ed. *The Illustrator's Notebook*. Boston: The Horn Book, Inc., 1978.

Some thirty-five illustrators of children's books share their experience and knowledge in articles drawn from *The Horn Book Magazine*. This collection includes the very helpful series, "The Artist at Work," which details various techniques of illustrating with different media.

9. _____. *Newbery and Caldecott Medal Books: 1956–1965*. Boston: The Horn Book, Inc., 1965.

10. _____. *Newbery and Caldecott Medal Books: 1966–1975*. Boston: The Horn Book, Inc., 1975.

These volumes contain the acceptance papers and biographies of the Newbery and Caldecott winners for the decades of 1956–1966 and 1966–1975. In the most recent volume, John Rowe Townsend, the well-known English critic, evaluates the Newbery winners from his rather critical perspective; while Barbara Bader analyzes the art and illustrations of the Caldecott winners.

11. Marantz, Kenneth. "The Picture Book as Art Object: A Call for Balanced Reviewing," *Wilson Library Bulletin*, 52, No. 2 (Oct. 1977), pp. 148–151.

A foundational article on the need to evaluate the illustrations of a picture book as knowledgeably as the story. The emphasis is placed on the picture book as an integral art object.

12. Preiss, Byron, ed. *The Art of Leo and Diane Dillon*. New York: Ballantine Books, 1981.

This interesting book with its beautiful reproductions of pictures by the Dillons again shows the range of art of these talented persons. Art from posters, record covers, wood carvings, and their many folktales is included.

13. Shulevitz, Uri. *Writing With Pictures: How to Write and Illustrate Children's Books*. New York: Watson-Guptill, 1985.

A noted author and illustrator gives a detailed description of how to write, illustrate, and publish a picture book. Using pictures from his own and other well-known artists as examples, he shows how all details in a picture—framing, size, sequencing, blurred edge, shapes—work together to create the story line, characters, settings, and mood demanded by the story. This is an instructional, fascinating overview of picture-book making.

REFERENCES

Aardema, Verna. *Bringing the Rain to Kapiti Plain*, illustrated by Beatriz Vidal. Dial, 1981.

Alexander, Martha. *Nobody Asked Me If I Wanted a Baby Sister*. Dial, 1971.

Alexander, Sue. *Nadia the Willful*, illustrated by Lloyd Bloom. Pantheon, 1983.

Aliki, pseud. (Aliki Brandenberg). *The Two of Them*. Greenwillow, 1979.

Allard, Harry. *It's So Nice to Have a Wolf around The House*, illustrated by James Marshall. Doubleday, 1977.

Allard, Harry and James Marshall. *Miss Nelson Has a Field Day*, illustrated by James Marshall. Houghton Mifflin, 1985.

_____. *Miss Nelson Is Missing*, illustrated by James Marshall. Houghton Mifflin, 1977.

_____. *The Stupids Die*, illustrated by James Marshall. Houghton Mifflin, 1981.

_____. *The Stupids Have a Ball*, illustrated by James Marshall. Houghton Mifflin, 1977.

_____. *The Stupids Step Out*, illustrated by James Marshall. Houghton Mifflin, 1978.

Anno, Mitsumasa. *Anno's Britain*. Philomel, 1982.

_____. *Anno's Italy*. Philomel, 1980.

_____. *Anno's Journey*. Collins, 1978

_____. *Anno's U.S.A.* Philomel, 1983.

Ardizzone, Edward. *Little Tim and the Brave Sea Captain*. Penguin, 1983.

Asbjornsen, Peter Christian, and Jorgen E. Moe. *The Three Billy Goats Gruff*, illustrated by Marcia Brown. Harcourt, 1957.

Azarian, Mary. *A Farmer's Alphabet*. Godine, 1981.
_____. *The Tale of John Barleycorn*. Godine, 1982.
Baker, Jeannie. *Home in the Sky*. Greenwillow, 1984.
_____. *Millicent*. André Deutsch, 1980.
Baker, Olaf. *Where the Buffaloes Begin*, illustrated by Stephen Gammell. Warne, 1981.
Bang, Molly. *The Grey Lady and the Strawberry Snatcher*. Four Winds Press, 1980.
_____. *The Paper Crane*. Greenwillow, 1985.
Barrett, Judi. *Animals Should Definitely Not Act Like People*, illustrated by Ron Barrett. Atheneum, 1980.
_____. *Animals Should Definitely Not Wear Clothing*, illustrated by Ron Barrett. Atheneum, 1970.
Baylor, Byrd. *The Best Town in the World*, illustrated by Ronald Himler. Scribner, 1983.
_____. *Everybody Needs a Rock*, illustrated by Peter Parnall. Scribner, 1974.
_____. *Hawk, I'm Your Brother*, illustrated by Peter Parnall. Scribner, 1976.
_____. *The Other Way to Listen*, illustrated by Peter Parnall. Scribner, 1978.
_____. *The Way to Start a Day*, illustrated by Peter Parnall. Scribner, 1978.
_____. *Your Own Best Secret Place*, illustrated by Peter Parnall. Scribner, 1979.
Bemelmans, Ludwig. *Madeline*. Viking, 1962 (1939).
_____. *Madeline's Rescue*. Viking, 1953.
Berger, Barbara. *Grandfather Twilight*. Philomel, 1984.
Blegvad, Lenore. *Anna Banana and Me*, illustrated by Erik Blegvad. Atheneum, 1985.
Brandenberg, Franz. *Otto Is Different*, illustrated by James Stevenson. Greenwillow, 1985.
Briggs, Raymond. *Jim and the Beanstalk*. Coward-McCann, 1970.
Brooks, Ron. *Timothy and Gramps*. Bradbury, 1978.
Brown, Marc. *Arthur's April Fool*. Little, Brown, 1983.
_____. *Arthur's Eyes*. Little, Brown, 1979.
_____. *Arthur's Halloween*. Little, Brown, 1983.
_____. *Arthur's Nose*. Little, Brown, 1976.
_____. *Arthur's Valentine*. Little, Brown, 1980.
Brown, Marcia. *All Butterflies*. Scribner, 1974.
_____. *Once a Mouse*. Scribner, 1961.
Burningham, John. *Come Away From the Water, Shirley*. Harper, 1977.
_____. *Grandpa*. Crown, 1985.
_____. *Mr. Gumpy's Motor Car*. Harper, 1976.
_____. *Mr. Gumpy's Outing*. Holt, 1971.
_____. *Seasons*. Bobbs-Merrill, 1970.
_____. *Time to Get Out of the Bath, Shirley*. Harper, 1978.
_____. *Would You Rather. . . .* Harper, 1978.
Burton, Virginia Lee. *Katie and The Big Snow*. Houghton Mifflin, 1943.
_____. *The Little House*. Houghton Mifflin, 1942.
_____. *Mike Mulligan and His Steam Shovel*. Houghton Mifflin, 1939.
Caines, Jeanette. *Daddy*, illustrated by Ronald Himler. Harper, 1977.
Carle, Eric. *The Mixed-Up Chameleon*. 2nd ed. Harper, 1984.
_____. *The Very Busy Spider*. Philomel, 1984.
_____. *The Very Hungry Caterpillar*. World, 1968.
Carrick, Carol. *The Accident*, illustrated by Donald Carrick. Clarion, 1976.
_____. *Ben and the Porcupine*, illustrated by Donald Carrick. Clarion, 1981.
_____. *The Foundling*, illustrated by Donald Carrick. Clarion, 1977.
_____. *Lost in the Storm*, illustrated by Donald Carrick. Clarion, 1974.
_____. *Patrick's Dinosaurs*, illustrated by Donald Carrick. Clarion, 1983.
_____. *Sleep Out*, illustrated by Donald Carrick. Clarion, 1973.
_____. *The Washout*, illustrated by Donald Carrick. Clarion, 1978.
Caudill, Rebecca. *A Pocketful of Cricket*, illustrated by Evaline Ness. Holt, 1964.
Cendrars, Blaise. *Shadow*, illustrated by Marcia Brown. Scribner, 1982.
Chaffin, Lillie. *We Be Warm Till Springtime Comes*, illustrated by Lloyd Bloom. Macmillan, 1980.
Clifton, Lucille. *Amifika*, illustrated by Thomas DiGrazia. Dutton, 1977.
_____. *The Boy Who Didn't Believe in Spring*, illustrated by Brinton Turkle. Dutton, 1973.
_____. *Everett Anderson's Friend*, illustrated by Ann Grifalconi. Holt, 1976.

_____. *My Friend Jacob,* illustrated by Thomas DiGrazia. Dutton, 1980.

Cohen, Miriam. *Lost in the Museum,* illustrated by Lillian Hoban. Greenwillow, 1979.

_____. *The New Teacher,* illustrated by Lillian Hoban. Macmillan, 1972.

_____. *When Will I Read?,* illustrated by Lillian Hoban. Greenwillow, 1977.

_____. *Will I Have a Friend?,* illustrated by Lillian Hoban. Macmillan, 1967.

Cole, Brock. *The Winter Wren.* Farrar, Straus, 1984.

Cole, Sheila. *When the Tide Is Low,* illustrated by Virginia Wright-Frierson. Lothrop, 1985.

Coltman, Paul. *Tog the Ribber; or Granny's Tale,* illustrated by Gillian McClure. Farrar, Straus, 1985.

Cooney, Barbara. *Chanticleer and the Fox.* Crowell, 1958.

_____. *Miss Rumphius.* Viking, 1982.

Crowe, Robert. *Clyde Monster,* illustrated by Kay Chorao. Dutton, 1976.

DeBrunhoff, Jean. *The Story of Babar.* Random House, 1960.

de Paola, Tomie. *Helga's Dowry: A Troll Love Story.* Harcourt, 1977.

_____. *Nana Upstairs, Nana Downstairs.* Penguin, 1978.

_____. *Now One Foot, Now the Other.* Putnam, 1981.

_____. *Strega Nona.* Prentice-Hall, 1975.

_____. *Tomie de Paola's Mother Goose.* Putnam, 1985.

_____. *Watch Out for the Chicken-Feet in Your Soup.* Prentice-Hall, 1974.

de Regniers, Beatrice Schenk. *May I Bring a Friend?,* illustrated by Beni Montresor. Atheneum, 1964.

Drescher, Henrik. *Simon's Book.* Lothrop, 1983.

Emberley, Barbara. *Drummer Hoff,* illustrated by Ed Emberley. Prentice-Hall, 1967.

Ets, Marie Hall. *Gilberto and the Wind.* Viking, 1963.

_____. *Play with Me.* Viking, 1955.

_____, and Aurora Labastida. *Nine Days to Christmas,* illustrated by Marie Hall Ets. Viking, 1959.

Farber, Norma. *How Does It Feel to Be Old?,* illustrated by Trina Schart Hyman. Dutton, 1979.

Fatio, Louise. *The Happy Lion,* illustrated by Roger Duvoisin. McGraw-Hill, 1954.

Fisher, Aileen. *Listen Rabbit,* illustrated by Symeon Shimin. Crowell, 1964.

Freeman, Don. *Corduroy.* Viking, 1968.

_____. *Dandelion.* Viking, 1964.

_____. *A Pocket for Corduroy.* Viking, 1978.

Friedman, Ina. *How My Parents Learned to Eat,* illustrated by Allen Say. Houghton Mifflin, 1984.

Gág, Wanda. *Millions of Cats.* Coward-McCann, 1928.

Gage, Wilson. *Cully Cully and the Bear,* illustrated by James Stevenson. Greenwillow, 1983.

Galdone, Joanna. *The Tailypo,* illustrated by Paul Galdone. Houghton Mifflin, 1977.

Galloz, Christopher and Roberto Innocenti. *Rose Blanche,* illustrated by Roberto Innocenti. Creative Education, 1985.

Ginsburg, Mirra. *The Chick and the Duckling,* illustrated by José Aruego and Ariane Aruego. Macmillan, 1972.

Goble, Paul. *The Girl Who Loved Wild Horses.* Bradbury, 1978.

_____. *Star Boy.* Bradbury, 1983.

Goffstein, M. B., *Brookie and Her Lamb,* rev. ed. Farrar, Straus, 1981.

_____. *My Noah's Ark.* Harper, 1978.

Gramatky, Hardie. *Little Toot.* Putnam, 1939.

Greenfield, Eloise. *She Come Bringing Me That Little Baby Girl,* illustrated by John Steptoe. Lippincott, 1974.

Grimm Brothers. *The Bremen Town Musicians,* translated by Elizabeth Shub, illustrated by Janina Domanska. Greenwillow, 1980.

_____. *The Seven Ravens,* translated by Elizabeth D. Crawford, illustrated by Lisbeth Zwerger. Morrow, 1981.

Hale, Sara Josepha. *Mary Had a Little Lamb,* illustrated by Tomie de Paola. Holiday, 1984.

Haley, Gail E. *A Story, A Story.* Atheneum, 1970.

Hall, Donald. *The Man Who Lived Alone*, illustrated by Mary Azarian. Godine, 1984.
_____. *Ox-Cart Man*, illustrated by Barbara Cooney. Viking, 1979.
Heine, Helme. *Friends*. Atheneum, 1982.
_____. *The Most Wonderful Egg in the World*. Atheneum, 1983.
_____. *Pigs' Wedding*. Atheneum, 1979.
Hill, Donna. *Ms Glee Was Waiting*, illustrated by Diane Dawson. Atheneum, 1978.
Himler, Ronald. *Wake Up, Jeremiah*. Harper, 1979.
Hoban, Russell. *A Baby Sister for Frances*, illustrated by Lillian Hoban. Harper, 1964.
_____. *A Bargain for Frances*, illustrated by Lillian Hoban. Harper, 1970.
_____. *Best Friends for Frances*, illustrated by Lillian Hoban. Harper, 1969.
_____. *A Birthday for Frances*, illustrated by Lillian Hoban. Harper, 1968.
Hoban, Tana. *Big Ones, Little Ones*. Greenwillow, 1976.
_____. *Look Again!* Macmillan, 1971.
_____. *Take Another Look*. Greenwillow, 1981.
Hodges, Margaret. *Saint George and the Dragon*, illustrated by Trina Schart Hyman. Little, Brown, 1984.
Hogrogian, Nonny. *One Fine Day*. Macmillan, 1971.
Horwitz, Elinor Lander. *When the Sky Is Like Lace*, illustrated by Barbara Cooney. Lippincott, 1975.
Hughes, Shirley. *David and Dog*. Lothrop, 1981.
Hutchins, Pat. *Good-Night, Owl!* Macmillan, 1972.
_____. *Rosie's Walk*. Macmillan, 1968.
_____. *The Very Worst Monster*. Greenwillow, 1985.
Hyman, Trina Schart. *Little Red Riding Hood*. Holiday House, 1983.
Isadora, Rachel. *Ben's Trumpet*. Greenwillow, 1979.
_____. *Max*. Macmillan, 1976.
_____. *Willaby*. Macmillan, 1977.
Johnson, Tony. *The Quilt Story*, illustrated by Tomie de Paola. Putnam, 1985.
Jonas, Ann. *The Quilt*. Greenwillow, 1984.
_____. *Round Trip*. Greenwillow, 1983.
Joyce, William. *George Shrinks*. Harper, 1985.
Jukes, Mavis. *Like Jake and Me*, illustrated by Lloyd Bloom. Knopf, 1984.
Kantrowitz, Mildred. *Maxie*, illustrated by Emily A. McCully. Parents, 1970.
Keats, Ezra Jack. *Dreams*. Macmillan, 1974.
_____. *Goggles*. Macmillan, 1969.
_____. *Hi Cat!* Macmillan, 1970.
_____. *A Letter to Amy*. Harper, 1968.
_____. *Louie*. Greenwillow, 1983 (1975).
_____. *Pet Show!* Macmillan, 1972.
_____. *Peter's Chair*. Harper, 1967.
_____. *The Snowy Day*. Viking, 1962.
_____. *The Trip*. Greenwillow, 1978.
_____. *Whistle for Willie*. Viking, 1964.
Keeping, Charles. *Joseph's Yard*. Oxford, 1969.
Kellogg, Steven. *Can I Keep Him?* Dial, 1971.
_____. *Chicken Little*. Morrow, 1985.
_____. *The Mysterious Tadpole*. Dial, 1977.
_____. *Pinkerton, Behave!* Dial, 1979.
_____. *A Rose for Pinkerton*. Dial, 1981.
Kennedy, Richard. *Song of the Horse*, illustrated by Marcia Sewall. Dutton, 1981.
Kesselman, Wendy. *Emma*, illustrated by Barbara Cooney. Doubleday, 1980.
Kitchen, Bert. *Animal Alphabet*. Dial, 1984.
Kuskin, Karla. *The Philharmonic Gets Dressed*, illustrated by Marc Simont. Harper, 1982.
Kraus, Robert. *Leo the Late Bloomer*, illustrated by Jose Aruego. Crowell, 1971.
_____. *Milton the Early Riser*, illustrated by Jose Aruego and Ariane Aruego. Windmill, 1972.
_____. *Owliver*, illustrated by Jose Aruego and Ariane Dewey. Windmill, 1974.
Krauss, Ruth. *A Hole Is to Dig*, illustrated by Maurice Sendak. Harper, 1952.
_____. *A Very Special House*, illustrated by Maurice Sendak. Harper, 1953.

Langstaff, John, and Feodor Rojankovsky. *Frog Went A-Courtin'*, illustrated by Feodor Rojankovsky. Harcourt, 1955.

Leaf, Munro. *The Story of Ferdinand*, illustrated by Robert Lawson. Viking, 1936.

Levinson, Riki. *Watch the Stars Come Out*, illustrated by Diane Goode. Dutton, 1985.

Lexau, Joan. *Benjie*, illustrated by Don Bolognese. Dial, 1964.

_____. *Benjie on His Own*, illustrated by Don Bolognese. Dial, 1970.

_____. *Emily and the Klunky Baby and the Next-door Dog*, illustrated by Martha Alexander. Dial, 1972.

Lionni, Leo. *Alexander and the Wind-up Mouse*. Pantheon, 1969.

_____. *The Biggest House in the World*. Pantheon, 1968.

_____. *Fish Is Fish*, Pantheon, 1970.

_____. *Frederick*. Pantheon, 1967.

_____. *Inch by Inch*. Astor-Honor, 1960.

_____. *Little Blue and Little Yellow*. Astor-Honor, 1959.

_____. *Swimmy*. Pantheon, 1963.

Locker, Thomas. *The Mare on the Hill*. Dial, 1985.

_____. *Where the River Begins*. Dial, 1984.

Lobel, Arnold. *Days with Frog and Toad*. Harper, 1979.

_____. *Fables*. Harper, 1980.

_____. *Frog and Toad All Year*. Harper, 1976.

_____. *Frog and Toad Are Friends*. Harper, 1970.

_____. *Frog and Toad Together*. Harper, 1972.

McCloskey, Robert. *Blueberries for Sal*. Viking, 1963.

_____. *Burt Dow, Deep-Water Man*. Viking, 1963.

_____. *Make Way for Ducklings*. Viking, 1941.

_____. *Time of Wonder*. Viking, 1957.

McDermott, Gerald. *Arrow to the Sun: A Pueblo Indian Tale*. Viking, 1974.

MacDonald, Golden, pseud. (Margaret Wise Brown). *The Little Island*, illustrated by Leonard Weisgard. Doubleday, 1946.

MacLachlan, Patricia. *Mama One, Mama Two*, illustrated by Ruth Lercher Bornstein. Harper, 1982.

_____. *Through Grandpa's Eyes*, illustrated by Deborah Ray. Harper, 1979.

McPhail, David. *The Bear's Toothache*. Little, Brown, 1972.

_____. *Fix-It*. Dutton, 1984.

_____. *Henry Bear's Park*. Little, Brown, 1976.

_____. *Pig Pig Goes to Camp*. Dutton, 1983.

_____. *Pig Pig Grows Up*. Dutton, 1980.

_____. *Pig Pig Rides*. Dutton, 1982.

_____. *Stanley: Henry Bear's Friend*. Little, Brown, 1979.

Marshall, James. *George and Martha*. Houghton Mifflin, 1972.

_____. *George and Martha Tons of Fun*. Houghton Mifflin, 1972.

Maruki, Toshi. *Hiroshima No Pika*. Lothrop, 1980.

Mayer, Mercer. *There's a Nightmare in My Closet*. Dial, 1968.

Miles, Miska. *Annie and the Old One*, illustrated by Peter Parnall. Little, Brown, 1971.

Minarik, Else Holmelund. *A Kiss for Little Bear*, illustrated by Maurice Sendak. Harper, 1968.

_____. *Little Bear*, illustrated by Maurice Sendak. Harper, 1957.

_____. *Little Bear's Friend*, illustrated by Maurice Sendak. Harper, 1960.

_____. *Little Bear's Visit*, illustrated by Maurice Sendak. Harper, 1961.

Moore, Elaine. *Grandma's House*, illustrated by Elise Primavera. Lothrop, 1985.

Murphy, Shirley Rousseau. *Tattie's River Journey*, illustrated by Tomie de Paola. Dial, 1983.

Ness, Evaline. *Sam, Bangs and Moonshine*. Holt, 1966.

Noble, Trinka H. *The Day Jimmy's Boa Ate the Wash*, illustrated by Steven Kellogg. Dial, 1980.

_____. *The Day Jimmy's Boa Bounced Back*, illustrated by Steven Kellogg. Dial, 1984.

Perrault, Charles. *Cinderella*, illustrated by Marcia Brown. Scribner, 1954.

Phillips, Mildred. *The Sign in Mendel's Window*, illustrated by Margot Zemach. Macmillan, 1985.

Piper, Watty. *The Little Engine That Could,* illustrated by George Hauman and Doris Hauman. Platt and Munk, 1954 (1930).

Politi, Leo. *The Nicest Gift.* Scribner, 1973.

_____. *Pedro, the Angel of Olvera Street.* Scribner, 1946.

_____. *Song of the Swallows.* Scribner, 1949.

Potter, Beatrix. *The Tale of Peter Rabbit.* Warne, 1902.

Preston, Edna Mitchell. *Squawk to the Moon, Little Goose,* illustrated by Barbara Cooney. Viking, 1974.

Provensen, Alice, and Martin Provensen. *The Glorious Flight Across the Channel with Louis Blériot.* Viking, 1983.

_____. *Our Animal Friends at Maple Hill Farm,* rev. ed. Random, 1984.

Ormondroyd, Edward. *Johnny Castleseed,* illustrated by Diana Thewlis. Parnassus, 1985.

Radin, Ruth Yaffe. *A Winter Place,* illustrated by Mattie Lou O'Kelley. Little, Brown, 1982.

Rayner, Mary. *Garth Pig and the Ice Cream Lady.* Atheneum, 1977.

_____. *Mr. and Mrs. Pig's Evening Out.* Atheneum, 1976.

_____. *Mrs. Pig's Bulk Buy.* Atheneum, 1981.

Rey, H. A. *Curious George.* Houghton Mifflin, 1941.

Robbins, Ruth. *Baboushka and the Three Kings,* illustrated by Nicolas Sidjakov. Parnassus, 1960.

Ryan, Cheli Duran. *Hildilid's Night,* illustrated by Arnold Lobel. Macmillan, 1971.

Rylant, Cynthia. *Miss Maggie,* illustrated by Thomas DiGrazia. Dutton, 1983.

_____. *The Relatives Came,* illustrated by Stephen Gammell. Bradbury, 1985.

_____. *Waiting to Waltz: A Childhood,* illustrated by Stephen Gammell. Bradbury, 1984.

_____. *When I Was Young in the Mountains,* illustrated by Diane Goode. Dutton, 1982.

Segal, Lore. *The Story of Old Mrs. Brubeck and How She Looked for Trouble and Where She Found Him,* illustrated by Marcia Sewall. Pantheon, 1981.

Sendak, Maurice. *In the Night Kitchen.* Harper, 1970.

_____. *The Nutshell Library: Alligators All Around. Pierre. One Was Johnny. Chicken Soup With Rice.* Harper, 1962.

_____. *Outside Over There.* Harper, 1981.

_____. *Where the Wild Things Are.* Harper, 1963.

Seuss, Dr., pseud. (Theodor S. Geisel). *And To Think That I Saw It On Mulberry Street.* Vanguard, 1937.

_____. *The Cat in the Hat.* Random, 1957.

_____. *Horton Hatches the Egg.* Random, 1940.

_____. *McElligot's Pool.* Random, 1947.

_____. *Scrambled Eggs Super.* Random, 1953.

_____. *Thidwick the Big-hearted Moose.* Random, 1948.

Shulevitz, Uri. *Dawn.* Farrar, Straus, 1974.

_____. *One Monday Morning.* Scribner, 1976.

_____. *Rain Rain Rivers.* Farrar, Straus, 1969.

Slobodkina, Esphyr. *Caps for Sale.* W. R. Scott, 1947.

Spier, Peter. *Peter Spier's Rain.* Doubleday, 1982.

Stanley, Diane. *A Country Tale.* Four Winds, 1985.

Stanovich, Betty Jo. *Big Boy, Little Boy,* illustrated by Virginia Wright-Frierson. Lothrop, 1984.

Steig, William. *The Amazing Bone.* Farrar, Straus, 1976.

_____. *Amos & Boris.* Farrar, Straus, 1971.

_____. *Caleb and Kate.* Farrar, Straus, 1977.

_____. *Doctor DeSoto.* Farrar, Straus, 1982.

_____. *Gorky Rises.* Farrar, Straus, 1980.

_____. *Sylvester and the Magic Pebble.* Windmill, 1979.

Steptoe, John. *Daddy Is a Monster . . . Sometimes.* Lippincott, 1980.

_____. *Stevie.* Harper, 1969.

Stevenson, James. *Could Be Worse!* Greenwillow, 1977.

_____. *That Dreadful Day.* Greenwillow, 1985.

_____. *That Terrible Halloween Night.* Greenwillow, 1980.

_____. *What's Under My Bed?* Greenwillow, 1983.

_____. *Worse Than Willy!* Greenwillow, 1984.

Testa, Fulvio. *If You Take a Pencil* . . . . Dial, 1982.

Thomas, Dylan. *A Child's Christmas in Wales*, illustrated by Trina Schart Hyman. Holiday, 1985.

Turkle, Brinton. *Do Not Open*. Dutton, 1981.

Tresselt, Alvin. *Hide and Seek Fog*, illustrated by Roger Duvoisin. Lothrop, 1965.

_____. *White Snow, Bright Snow*, illustrated by Roger Duvoisin. Lothrop, 1947.

Udry, Janice May. *The Moon Jumpers*, illustrated by Maurice Sendak. Harper, 1959.

_____. *A Tree Is Nice*, illustrated by Marc Simont. Harper, 1956.

Ungerer, Tomi. *The Beast of Monsieur Racine*. Farrar, Straus, 1971.

_____. *Zeralda's Ogre*. Harper, 1967.

Van Allsburg, Chris. *The Garden of Abdul Gasazi*. Houghton Mifflin, 1979.

_____. *Jumanji*. Houghton Mifflin, 1981.

_____. *The Mysteries of Harris Burdick*. Houghton Mifflin, 1984.

_____. *The Wreck of the Zephyr*. Houghton Mifflin, 1983.

Vincent, Gabrielle. *Ernest and Celestine's Picnic*. Greenwillow, 1982.

_____. *Merry Christmas, Ernest and Celestine*. Greenwillow, 1984.

_____. *Smile, Ernest and Celestine*. Greenwillow, 1982.

Viorst, Judith. *Alexander and the Terrible, Horrible, No Good, Very Bad Day*, illustrated by Ray Cruz. Atheneum, 1972.

_____. *Alexander Who Used to Be Rich Last Sunday*, illustrated by Ray Cruz. Atheneum, 1978.

_____. *I'll Fix Anthony*, illustrated by Arnold Lobel. Harper, 1969.

_____. *The Tenth Good Thing About Barney*, illustrated by Erik Blegvad. Atheneum, 1971.

Waber, Bernard. *The House on East 88th Street*. Houghton Mifflin, 1962.

_____. *Ira Sleeps Over*. Houghton Mifflin, 1972.

_____. *"You Look Ridiculous," Said the Rhinoceros to the Hippopotamus*. Houghton Mifflin, 1966.

Wagner, Jenny. *John Brown, Rose, and the Midnight Cat*, illustrated by Ron Brooks. Bradbury, 1978.

Walter, Mildred Pitts. *My Mama Needs Me*, illustrated by Pat Cummings. Lothrop, 1983.

Ward, Lynd. *The Biggest Bear*. Houghton Mifflin, 1952.

Wells, Rosemary. *Benjamin and Tulip*. Doubleday, 1973.

_____. *Stanley and Rhoda*. Dial, 1978.

_____. *Timothy Goes to School*. Dial, 1983.

_____. *Noisy Nora*. Dial, 1973.

Wildsmith, Brian. *The Owl and the Woodpecker*. Watts, 1972.

_____. *Python's Party*. Oxford, 1974.

Wilhelm, Hans. *I'll Always Love You*. Crown, 1985.

Willard, Nancy. *A Visit to William Blake's Inn*, illustrated by Alice and Martin Provensen. Harcourt, 1981.

Williams, Barbara. *Albert's Toothache*, illustrated by Kay Chorao. Dutton, 1974.

_____. *Jeremy Isn't Hungry*, illustrated by Martha Alexander. Dutton, 1978.

Williams, Margery. *The Velveteen Rabbit*, illustrated by William Nicholson. Doubleday, 1958 (1922). Illustrated by Alan Atkinson, Knopf, 1983. Illustrated by Michael Hague. Holt, 1983. Illustrated by Ilse Plume. Godine, 1983.

Williams, Vera B. *A Chair for My Mother*. Greenwillow, 1982.

_____. *Music, Music for Everyone*. Greenwillow, 1984.

_____. *Something Special for Me*. Greenwillow, 1983.

Wolff, Ashley. *The Bells of London*. Dodd, Mead, 1985.

_____. *Only the Cat Saw*. Dodd, Mead, 1985.

_____. *A Year of Birds*. Dodd, Mead, 1984.

Wood, Audrey. *The Napping House*, illustrated by Don Wood. Harcourt, 1984.

Yarborough, Camille. *Cornrows*, illustrated by Carole Byard. Putnam, 1979.

Yashima, Taro, pseud. (Jun Iwamatsu). *Crow Boy*. Viking, 1955.

Yorinks, Arthur. *It Happened in Pinsk*, illustrated by Richard Egielski. Farrar, Straus, 1983.

_____. *Louis the Fish*, illustrated by Richard Egielski. Farrar, Straus, 1980.

Zion, Gene, *Harry, the Dirty Dog*, illustrated by Margaret Bloy Graham. Harper, 1956.

Zolotow, Charlotte. *Do You Know What I'll Do?*, illustrated by Garth Williams. Harper, 1958.

————. *If It Weren't for You,* illustrated by Ben Shecter. Harper, 1966.

————. *A Father Like That,* illustrated by Ben Shecter. Harper, 1971.

————. *Mr. Rabbit and the Lovely Present,* illustrated by Maurice Sendak. Harper, 1962.

————. *My Grandson Lew,* illustrated by William Pène du Bois. Harper, 1972.

————. *Say It!,* illustrated by James Stevenson. Greenwillow, 1980.

————. *The Storm Book,* illustrated by Margaret Bloy Graham. Harper, 1952.

————. *William's Doll,* illustrated by William Pène du Bois. Harper, 1972.

6

TRADITIONAL LITERATURE

E ver since human beings realized they were unique among animals in that they could think and talk, they have tried to explain themselves and their world. Who were the first humans? How did they come to be? What made the sun and the moon and the stars? Why were the animals made the way they were? What caused night and day, the seasons, the cycle of life itself? Why were some people greedy and some unselfish, some ugly and some handsome, some dull and some clever? As people pondered these questions and many more, they created stories that helped explain the world to their primitive minds. The storytellers told these tales again and again around the fires of the early tribes, by the hearths of humble cottages, before the great fire in the king's hall; they told them as they sat in the grass huts of the jungle, the hogans of the Navajo, and the igloos of the Eskimo. Their children told them, and their children's children, until the stories were as smooth and polished as the roundest stones in the stream. And so people created their myths and their folktales, their legends and epics; the literature of the fireside, the poetry of the people, and the memory of humankind.

A PERSPECTIVE ON TRADITIONAL LITERATURE

Origin of Folk Literature

We have no one word that encompasses all of the stories that are born of the oral tradition. They are most often grouped under the heading of folklore, folk literature, or mythology. Generally, we say that myths are about gods and the creation of things; legends are about heroes and their mighty deeds before the time of recorded history; and folktales, fairy tales, and fables are simple stories about talking beasts, woodcutters, and princesses who reveal human behavior and beliefs while playing out their roles in a world of wonder and magic.

Children sometimes identify these stories as "make-believe," as contrasted with "true" or "stories that could really happen." Unfortunately, the word *myth* has sometimes been defined as an "imagined event" or a "pagan falsehood," as opposed to "historical fact" or "Christian truth." In literary study, however, *myth* does not mean "un-

true"; rather, the term refers to a generalized meaning or a universal idea, a significant truth about man and his life. A single *myth* is a narrative that tells of origins,[1] explains natural or social phenomena, or suggests the destiny of humans through the interaction of people and supernatural beings. A *mythology* is a group of myths of a particular culture. Myth-making[2] is continuous and in process today. Usually myth is a product of a society rather than of a single author.

The origin of the myths has fascinated and puzzled mythologists, anthropologists, and psychologists. How, they wonder, can one account for the similarities among these stories that grew out of ancient cultures widely separated from each other? The Greek myth "Cupid and Psyche" (15)[3] is very

[1]Sylvan Barnet, Morton Berman, and William Burto, *The Study of Literature* (Boston, Mass.: Little, Brown, 1960), pp. 315-316.
[2]Jerome Bruner, "Myth and Identity," in *The Making of Myth*, Richard M. Ohrmann, ed. (New York: Putnam, 1962), pp. 159–170.
[3]The number in parentheses following the title of a folktale or myth indicates the number of a reference in the bibliography at the end of this chapter. This reference lists the book in which the tale may be found.

much like the Norwegian tale "East of the Sun and West of the Moon" (8). Again, the Norwegian story "The Princess on the Glass Hill" (155) is similar to the French "Cinderella" (212), except that the main character is a boy instead of a girl. And the story of Cinderella is found throughout the world, with nearly 500 versions in Europe alone.

In trying to explain this phenomenon, one group of early mythologists proposed the notion of *monogenesis*, or inheritance from a single culture. The Grimm brothers, who were among the first of the nineteenth-century scholars of folklore, theorized that all folktales originated from one prehistoric group called Aryans, later identified as Indo-Europeans by modern linguists. As this group migrated to other countries the scholars reasoned that they took their folklore with them, which led to the theory of *diffusion*.

Another approach to folklore involves the theory of *polygenesis*, or multiple origins. It is argued that each story could have been an independent invention growing out of universal desires and needs of humankind. Early anthropologists viewed myth as the religion of the people derived from rituals that were recounted in drama and narratives. They identified recurrent themes in myths of different cultures. Kluckhohn's study[4] of the myths of fifty cultures revealed such recurring themes as the flood, slaying of monsters, incest, sibling rivalry, and castration. He also found several patterns repeated in the myth of the hero. Sir James Frazer's twelve-volume analysis of ritual, taboos, and myths, *The Golden Bough*[5] was of major importance. This anthropological study gave sexual symbolic meaning to primitive myths and greatly influenced modern literature.

Freud's analysis[6] of myth as dream, or disguised wish fulfillment, was the beginning of psychological literary criticism. Freud held the view that all myths expressed the Oedipus theme with its incest motive, guilt, and punishment. Another psychological viewpoint was that of Carl Jung, a contemporary of Freud, who thought that a "collective unconscious" is "inherited in the structure of the brain."[7] These unconscious, recurring images created the primitive mythic heroes and still exist as individual fantasies for the civilized person as a kind of "race memory," according to Jung. The folklorist, however, may disagree with such psychological interpretations. Dorson notes that "folk literature cannot all be prettily channeled into the universal mono-myth," and "the folklorist looks with jaundiced eye at the excessive straining of mythologists to extort symbols from folk tales."[8]

Folktales are also of special interest to scholars of narrative theory. Because of the way the tales are honed by many generations of telling, only the most important elements of the story survive. Close study of the patterns of action and character relationships show how language shapes a form we recognize as a story. Vladimir Propp, for instance, analyzed Russian tales and identified a set sequence of 31 "functions" that might occur in a tale, such as: the hero leaves home (departure); one member of a family lacks or desires something (lack); or, a villain attempts to deceive his victim (trickery).[9] Other researchers have used simplified folktale structures to develop models of children's story comprehension. Although looking at tales in such a technical way is definitely an adult perspective, children who have heard and enjoyed many traditional stories begin to discover for themselves that folktales seem to follow certain structural rules. One 10-year-old girl who wrote instructions for "Making a Fairy Story" summed up by saying ". . . fairy tales have to have a sort of pattern or they would just be regular stories."

However scholars choose to look at them, folktales and myths are literature derived from human imagination to explain the human condition. Literature today continues to express our concern about human strengths, weaknesses, and the individual's relationships to the world and to other people. Traditional literature forms the foundation of understandings of life as expressed in modern literature.

[4]Clyde Kluckhohn, "Recurrent Themes in Myth and Mythmaking," in Ohrmann, pp. 52–65.
[5]Sir James Frazer, *The Golden Bough*, 3rd ed. (London: Macmillan, 1911–1915).
[6]Stanley E. Hyman, *The Armed Vision*, rev. ed. (New York: Vintage, 1955).
[7]Carl C. Jung, "On the Relation of Analytic Psychology to Poetic Art," in O. B. Hardison, Jr., ed., *Modern Continental Literary Criticism* (New York: Appleton, 1962), pp. 267–288.
[8]Richard Dorson, "Theories of Myth and the Folklorist," in Ohrmann, p. 45.
[9]Vladimir Propp, *The Morphology of the Folktale* (Austin, Tex.: University of Texas Press, 1968).

The Value of Folk Literature—For Children

When Jacob and Wilhelm Grimm published the first volume of their "Household Stories" in 1812, they did not intend it for children. These early philologists were studying the language and grammar of such traditional tales. In recent years, as we have seen, anthropologists study folklore in order to understand the inherent values and beliefs of a culture. Psychologists look at folktales and myths and discover something of the motivations and inner feelings of humans; while folklorists themselves collect and categorize various stories, types, and motifs from around the world. These are all adult scholars of folk literature, which itself was first created by adults and usually told to an adult community. How, then, did folk literature become associated with children's literature; and what value does this kind of literature have for children?

Originally, folklore was the literature of the people; stories were told to young and old alike. Families or tribes or the king's court would gather to hear a famous storyteller in much the same way that an entire family today will watch their favorite television program. With the age of scientific enlightenment, these stories were relegated to the nursery, kept alive, in many instances, by resourceful nursemaids or grandmothers, much to the delight of children.

Children today still enjoy such tales because they are first and foremost good stories. Born of the oral tradition, these stories are usually short and have fast-moving plots. They are frequently humorous and almost always end happily. Poetic justice prevails; the good and the just are eventually rewarded, while the evil are punished. This appeals to the child's sense of justice and his moral judgment. Wishes come true, but usually not without the fulfillment of a task or trial. The littlest child, the youngest son, or the smallest animal succeeds, while the oldest or the largest is frequently defeated. Youngsters who are the little people of their world thrive on such a turn of events.

Beyond the function of pure entertainment, folktales can kindle the child's imagination. Behind every great author, poet, architect, mathematician, or diplomat is a dream of what the person hopes to achieve. This dream or ideal has been created by the power of imagination. If we always give children stories of "what is," stories that only mirror the living of today, then we have not helped them to imagine what "might have been" or "what might be."

Bruno Bettelheim, in his remarkable book *The Uses of Enchantment*, maintains that fairy tales help children to cope with their dreams and inner turmoil. "Each fairy tale," he says, "is a magic mirror which reflects some aspects of our inner world and of the steps required by our evolution from immaturity to maturity."[10]

Chukovsky, the Russian poet, tells of a time when it was proposed that all folktales and fairy tales be eliminated from the education of the Soviet child in favor of simple realistic stories. Then one of the major Russian educators began keeping a diary of her child's development. She found that her child, as if to compensate for the fairy tales which he had been denied, began to make up his own. He had never heard a folktale, but his world was peopled with talking tigers, birds, and bugs. Chukovsky concludes this story with the statement: "Fantasy is the most valuable attribute of the human mind and should be diligently nurtured from earliest childhood."[11]

Traditional literature is a rightful part of a child's literary heritage and lays the groundwork for understanding all literature. Poetry and modern stories allude to traditional literature, particularly the Greek myths, Aesop's fables, and Bible stories. Northrop Frye maintains that "all theme and characters and stories that you encounter in literature belong to one big interlocking family."[12] As you meet recurring patterns or symbols in mythlike floods, savior heroes, cruel stepmothers, the seasonal cycle of the year, the cycle of a human life, you begin to build a framework for literature. Poetry, prose, and drama become more emotionally significant as you respond to these recurring archetypes.

Our speech and vocabulary reflect many contributions from traditional literature. Think of the figures of speech that come from Aesop's fables: "sour grapes," "dog in the manger," "boy who

[10]Bruno Bettelheim, *The Uses of Enchantment* (New York: Knopf, 1976), p. 309.
[11]Kornei Chukovsky, *From Two to Five*, translated and edited by Miriam Morton (Berkeley: University of California Press, 1963), p.119.
[12]Northrop Frye, *The Educated Imagination* (Bloomington: Indiana University Press, 1964), p. 48.

cried wolf." Our language is replete with words and phrases from the myths—"narcissistic," "cereal," "labyrinth," "siren," and many more. Isaac Asimov has written a fascinating book, *Words from the Myths* (311), which tells the stories of how such words originated. The child who has the opportunity to hear or read traditional literature cannot help but extend the meaning of language.

Every culture has produced a folklore. A study of the folktales of Africa, Russia, or the Native American will provide insights into the beliefs of these peoples, their values, their jokes, their life styles, their histories. A cross-cultural study of folk literature will help children discover the universal qualities of humankind.

FOLKTALES

Definition of Folktales

Folktales have been defined as "all forms of narrative, written or oral, which have come to be handed down through the years."[13] This definition would include epics, ballads, legends, and folk songs, as well as myths and fables. In using folk literature in the elementary school we have tended to confine the rather simple folktales—such as the popular "The Three Billy Goats Gruff," "Little Red Riding Hood," and "Rumpelstiltskin"—to the primary grades; while we recommend the so-called "fairy tales"—such as "Snow White" and "Cinderella"—for slightly older children, since these tales are longer and contain romantic elements. Such a division appears arbitrary; it is based more on use than any real difference in the stories. To complicate matters even further, modern fanciful stories created by a known author are often also referred to as fairy tales. Hans Christian Andersen's fairy tales are becoming part of the heritage that might be described as folktales, but *they originated in written rather than oral form.* Thus they are distinguished from the stories told by the common folk that were finally collected and recorded.

Questions often arise about which of the available print versions of a tale is the "correct" or authentic text. From a folklorist's point of view, a tale is re-created every time it is told and therefore *every* telling is correct in its own way. A great deal of variation is also acceptable in print versions, where literary style carries the same uniqueness as the teller's voice. Authors and illustrators may also add original twists, customize their stories for a chosen audience, or adapt a familiar tale to an unfamiliar setting, as oral storytellers do. There may be a problem, however, when a print version suggests by its title, or lack of an author's note, that it represents a tale derived directly from a previously printed source. Readers of a story identified as recorded and published by the Brothers Grimm, for instance, have a right to find this tale then subsequently published without major additions, omissions, or distortions.

This chapter discusses the folktales and so-called fairy tales in children's literature that come from the oral tradition. It also includes a description of the epics, myths, and stories from the Bible, which are all a part of traditional literature. Modern fanciful stories written by known authors are discussed in Chapter 7.

Types of Folktales

CUMULATIVE TALES

Very young children are fascinated by such cumulative stories as "The Old Woman and Her Pig" (91) with its "Rat! rat! gnaw rope; rope won't hang butcher; butcher won't kill ox; ox won't drink water; water won't quench fire; fire won't burn stick; stick won't beat dog; dog won't bite pig; piggy won't get over the stile; and I shan't get home tonight." The story itself is not as important as the increasing repetition of the details building up to a quick climax. The story of the naughty Gingerbread Boy who ran away from the old woman defiantly crying "Catch me if you can" has been told in many different versions, including the Norwegian "The Pancake" (6), the Russian "The Bun" (31), and the Scottish "The Wee Bannock" (249). Ruth Sawyer's *Journey Cake, Ho!* (230) is an adaptation of this well-loved story.

In another familiar cumulative tale, one day an acorn falls on *Henny Penny* (223). Thinking the sky is falling down, she persuades Cocky-Locky, Ducky-Daddles, Goosey-Poosey, and Turkey-

[13]Frye, p. 48.

Lurkey to go along with her to tell the king. Young children delight in the sound of the rhyming double names which are repeated over and over.

The Fat Cat (180) is a wonderful Danish cumulative folktale that Jack Kent has illustrated in a picture-book format. The fat cat eats the gruel he was watching for the little old lady; then he eats the pot and the little old lady herself! He continues his eating binge, growing larger and larger with each victim. Finally, the fat cat is stopped when he makes the mistake of trying to eat the woodcutter. All his victims are released, and the last picture shows the woodcutter carefully applying a bandaid to the fat cat's tummy. Certainly the best known of all cumulative tales is the popular *The House That Jack Built* (78, 252). You will find repetitive stories in practically all folklore.

POURQUOI STORIES

Some of the folktales are "why" or *pourquoi* stories that explain certain animal traits or characteristics or customs of people. The Norwegians have a story about a fox tricking a bear into thinking that he could catch fish by holding his tail in a hole in the ice. His tail froze and came off when he tried to pull it out, which is "Why the Bear Is Stumpy-Tailed" (155). In "How the Animals Got Their Tails" (36), Ashley Bryan tells an African tale of a time when all animals were vegetarians. Then, Raluvhimba created a mistake, the flies who were flesh-eaters and blood-suckers. "I can't take back what I've done. After all, that's life," the god said. But he did give the rest of the animals tails with which to swish away the flies.

Many American Indian stories are "why" stories that explain animal features, the origin of certain natural features, or how humans and their customs came to be. William Toye has retold the Micmac Indian legend of how Glooskap saved the people from the giant Winter by persuading the lovely Summer to return north with him for half of the year. Elizabeth Cleaver has illustrated this book, *How Summer Came to Canada* (260), with brilliant collage pictures that make intriguing use of torn paper, pine needles, and hemlock. Paul Goble's story of *Star Boy* (101) explains why the Sun Dance was given to the Blackfeet.

A very funny Burmese tale, "The Tiger's Minister of State" (57), explains why the rabbit twitches

Parents and teachers of preschoolers will appreciate Helen Oxenbury's fine collection of simply told, colorfully illustrated folktales.

his nose constantly. Tiger tests the applicants for the position of minister by asking each if his breath is sweet. The boar denies the truth and is rejected as a flatterer. The monkey agrees the tiger's breath is very offensive; he is rejected for being too frank. The rabbit diplomatically twitches his nose and says he has such a cold he can't smell anything. So he is chosen to be minister of state; and to this day he twitches his nose to show he cannot smell.[14]

BEAST TALES

Probably the favorite folktales of young children are the beast tales in which animals act and talk like human beings. The best known of these fre-

[14]For literary pourquoi tales, see the section on Rudyard Kipling's *Just-So Stories* in Chapter 7.

quently appear in newly illustrated versions. In *The Three Little Pigs*, Paul Galdone (94) portrays the wolf as a ferocious doggy creature; Erik Blegvad's version (26) shows a barrel-chested wolf capable of huffing down perhaps even brick houses; Lorinda Bryan Cauley's wolf (172) is presented as a country gentleman among bumpkins; and Tony Ross shows a modern-day wolf (227) in a gray flannel topcoat pursuing the pigs, who have moved to the country to escape an overcrowded city high-rise apartment! Other beast tales found in several versions include *The Three Billy Goats Gruff* (10, 93), *The Little Red Hen* (88, 223, 286), and *Puss in Boots* (92, 215, 226). In *The Three Bears and 15 Other Stories* (223), Anne Rockwell has included many of these favorite beast stories in a delightful collection for the very young child. Clear, glowing watercolors are used throughout to help the child follow the action of the stories.

Primary-age children enjoy comparing versions of these well-known tales, observing contrasting portrayals, illustration technique and medium, or the story-teller's use of language. They notice that authors, illustrators, and translators make different choices. *The Bremen Town Musicians* in Elizabeth Shub's version (105) ends, "And this tale's still warm from the telling, for I've just heard it."[15] Ilse Plume's colorful version (104) leaves the musicians happily at home "making wonderful music under the stars." Children who are used to comparing versions become eager to detect these nuances, and seldom chorus in bored voices, "Oh, we've already heard that one."

Many West African stories are wise beast-foolish beast tales of how one animal, such as the rabbit or the spider, outwits hyena, leopard, or other foes. "Bo Rabbit Smart for True" (175), a West African tale, has been retold by Priscilla Jaquith in the Gullah dialect in which it was originally collected. In this delightful tale Bo Rabbit bets both Elephant and Whale that he can win a tug-of-war. Bo Rabbit obtains a long rope, fastens one end to Whale and the other to Elephant, and stays halfway between the two, laughing heartily. The two large animals never do realize they've been tricked and both vow that Bo Rabbit is one strong animal. Ed Young's expressive pencil drawings, four to a page, illustrate each exchange of the animals in this tale. *The Extraordinary Tug-of-War* (231), a Nigerian version of this tale, pits Hippopotamus and Elephant against each other, much to the enjoyment of Hare. Talking animals appear in folktales of all cultures. Fish are often found in English, Scandinavian, German, and South Sea stories. Tales of bears, wolves, and the firebird are found in Russian folklore. Spiders, rabbits, tortoises, crocodiles, monkeys, lions, and tigers are very much a part of African tales; while rabbits, badgers, monkeys, and even bees are represented in Japanese stories. A study of just the animals in folklore would be a fascinating search.

NOODLEHEAD STORIES

So called "noodlehead" or numbskull stories are a part of every folk culture. These tales frequently follow a set pattern. In the Hodja stories from Turkey (70), the Hodja—a local scholar, teacher, preacher, and judge all rolled into one—could be very clever or very stupid. In one tale the Hodja is sawing the very branch of a tree that he is sitting on. A passer-by tells him that he will fall if he continues to do that. He does fall, so he considers the man a prophet. If this man knew when the Hodja was going to fall, perhaps he can also tell when the Hodja will die. The stranger says the Hodja will probably die when his donkey brays twice. So when his donkey brays twice, the Hodja lies down on the road, shuts his eyes, and announces he is dead. His friends get a coffin and start to carry him home. But when they come to a fork in the road they begin to argue which way to go. Finally, the Hodja can endure it no longer. "'When I was alive,' he snaps, 'I took the left fork!'"[16]

A Russian noodlehead story, "How the Peasant Helped His Horse" (98), tells how, when the horse is having difficulty pulling a heavy load, the peasant gets out, puts one of the bags of wheat on his shoulder, then climbs back into the wagon, saying; "Giddy-up, giddy-up! It's easier for you now! I'm carrying a whole bag on my shoulder!"[17]

[15]Grimm Brothers, *The Bremen Town Musicians*, translated by Elizabeth Shub, illustrated by Janina Domanska (New York: Greenwillow, 1980), unpaged.

[16]Charles Downing, *Tales of the Hodja*, illustrated by William Papas (New York: Walck, 1965), p.42.

[17]Mirra Ginsburg, *Three Rolls and One Doughnut*, illustrated by Anita Lobel (New York: Dial Press, 1970), p. 6.

The Brothers Grimm included the well-known *Hans in Luck* (111) in their collection. After working for seven years, Hans asks for his wages to go home to see his mother. On his way home he trades his gold for a horse, the horse for a cow, the cow for a pig, the pig for a goose, and so forth. By the time he reaches home he has nothing left, but the happy Hans is delighted not to be encumbered by any burdens. Felix Hoffman, the well-known Swiss illustrator, has created a handsome picture-book version of this noodlehead tale.

Several collections of these stories have been compiled. *Noodles, Nitwits and Numbskulls* by Maria Leach (185) and *Noodlehead Stories from Around the World* by Jagendorf (173) are two sources. *The Twelve Clever Brothers and Other Fools* by Mirra Ginsburg (97) is a sparkling collection of noodlehead stories from the Russian people. Most of these stories are short and are good for story-telling. The humor of these tales is their complete nonsense and absurdity. Children delight in knowing that they couldn't possibly happen.

WONDER TALES

Children call wonder tales of magic and supernatural "fairy tales." Very few of them have even a fairy godmother in them, but still the name persists. These are the stories that include giants, such as *Jack and the Beanstalk* (44), or elves and goblins in *The Elves and the Shoemaker* (107). Wicked witches, called Baba Yagas in Russian folklore, demons such as the *oni* of Japanese tales, or monsters and dragons abound in these stories. Traditionally, we have thought of the fairy tale as involving romance and adventure. "Cinderella," "Snow White and the Seven Dwarfs," or "Beauty and the Beast" all have elements of both. *The Provensen Book of Fairy Tales* (217) is a fine collection of twelve classic and literary fairy tales, including "Beauty and the Beast," "The Three Wishes," "The Seven Simons," and "The Prince and the Goose Girl." This collection is beautifully illustrated with the Provensens' rich and colorful paintings. The long quest tales—such as the Russian "Ivan Tsarevich, the Grey Wolf, and the Firebird" (45) or the Norwegian "East of the Sun and West of the Moon" (183)—are complex wonder tales in which the hero, or heroine, triumphs against all odds to win the beautiful princess, or handsome prince, and makes a fortune. Children

know that these tales will end with ". . . and they lived happily ever after." In fact, one of the appeals of the fairy tale is the secure knowledge that no matter what happens the virtues of love, kindness, and truth will prevail; while hate, wickedness, and evil will be punished. Fairy tales have always represented the glorious fulfillment of human desires.

REALISTIC STORIES

Surprisingly, there are a few realistic tales included in folklore. The story of *Dick Whittington* (32) could have happened; in fact, there is historical reason to suggest that a Richard Whittington did indeed live and was mayor of London. The Norse tale of the loving wife who thought her husband could do no wrong is realistically told in "Gudbrand on the Hillside" (11). A funny tale of marital conflict is presented in the Russian story of "Who Will Wash the Pot?" (96). It is based on the familiar folktale pattern of the married couple declaring that the first to speak will have to do some unwanted task—in this instance, wash the pot. The well-loved Japanese tale *The Burning Rice Fields* (40), as told by Sara Cone Bryant, is a realistic story based on the self-sacrifice of the old man who set his fields ablaze in order to warn the villagers of a coming tidal wave.

Zlateh, the Goat (246), the title story in a collection of Jewish tales by Singer, is a realistic survival story. The son of a poor peasant family is sent off to the butcher to sell Zlateh, the family goat. On the way to town he and the goat are caught in a fierce snowstorm. They take refuge in a haystack where they stay for three days. Zlateh eats the hay while the boy exists on Zlateh's milk and warmth. When the storm is over, they return home to a grateful family. No one ever again mentions selling Zlateh, the goat.

Generally, however, while a tale may have had its origin in a real person or experience, it has become so embroidered through various tellings that it takes its place among the folklore of its culture.

The table that follows, "A Cross-Cultural Study of Folktale Types," is the first of three tables that group folktales from various countries in specific ways. These groups provide easy access to similar-tale titles so that teachers may more easily plan curricula. The other charts group tales by motif and by variants.

A CROSS-CULTURAL STUDY OF FOLKTALE TYPES

TYPE OF FOLKTALE	TALE	CULTURE
Cumulative tales	The Old Woman and Her Pig (91)	England
	"The Pancake" (6)	Norway
	"Plop" (274)	Tibet
	The Fat Cat (180)	Denmark
	Henny Penny (86)	England
	One Fine Day (164)	Armenia
Pourquoi tales	"Jack and the Devil" (144)	Black American
	"Why the Bear Is Stumpy-Tailed" (155)	Norway
	Why the Sun and the Moon Live in the Sky (60)	Africa
	How Summer Came to Canada (260)	Native American
	"Tia Miseria's Pear Tree (276)	Puerto Rico
	"How Animals Got Their Tails" (36)	Africa
	Star Boy (101)	Native American
	The Cat's Purr (37)	West Indian
Beast tales	The Three Billy Goats Gruff (93)	Norway
	The Three Little Pigs (24)	England
	"Kantjil and Monkey Business" (30)	Indonesia
	Bo Rabbit Smart for True (175)	Black American
	The Bremen Town Musicians (105)	Germany
	"The Tar Baby" (156)	Black American
	Beat the Story Drum, Pum-Pum (36)	African
Noodlehead tales	"Clever Elsie" (134)	Germany
	"The First Schlemiel" (246)	Jewish
	The Twelve Clever Brothers and Other Fools (97)	Russia
	The Disobedient Eels (48)	Italy
	Three Rolls and One Doughnut (98)	Russia
Wonder tales	"Jack and the Beanstalk" (249)	England
	Beauty and the Beast (62)	France
	The Ring in the Prairie (233)	Native American
	Snow White (131)	Germany
	"Vasilisa the Beautiful" (45)	Russia
	The Elves and the Shoemaker (107)	Germany
	"Green Dragon Pond" (157)	China
Realistic tales	"The Case of the Uncooked Eggs" (276)	Haiti
	"Gudbrand on the Hillside" (11)	Norway
	Dick Whittington and His Cat (32)	England
	"Who Will Wash the Pot?" (96)	Russia
	The Wave (163)	Japan
	Zlateh, the Goat (246)	Jewish
	Two Pairs of Shoes (262)	Persia
	Brothers (79)	Hebrew

Characteristics of Folktales

Since folktales have been told and retold from generation to generation within a particular culture, we may ask how they reflect the country of their origin and their oral tradition. An authentic tale from Africa will include references to the flora and fauna of Africa, to the food that was eaten by the tribesmen, their huts, their customs, their foibles, and their beliefs; and it will sound as if it is being

"Now, I'm coming to gobble you up!" roared the troll.
    "Well, come along! I've got two spears,
    And I'll poke your eyeballs out at your ears.
    I've got besides two great big stones,
    And I'll crush you to bits, body and bones."

As *The Three Billy Goats Gruff* face the troll under the bridge, the repetition of the "trip, trap, trap," the troll's demands, and the goats' responses are essential elements in this traditional Norse tale, illustrated by Marcia Brown.

told. While folktales have many elements in common, it should not be possible to confuse a folktale from Japan with a folktale from the fiords of Norway. What then are the characteristics common to all folktales?

PLOT STRUCTURES OF FOLKTALES

Among the folktales best known in children's literature, the longer stories are usually simple and direct. A series of episodes maintains a quick flow of action. If it is a wise beast–foolish beast story, the characters are quickly delineated; the action shows the inevitable conflict and resolution; and the ending is usually brief. If the tale is a romance, the hero sets forth on his journey, often helps the poor on his way, frequently receives magical power, overcomes obstacles, and returns to safety. The plot that involves a weak or innocent child going forth to meet the monsters of the world is another form of the "journey-novel." *Hansel and Gretel* (116) go out into a dark world and meet the witch, but goodness and purity triumph. Almost all folktale plots are success stories of one kind or another.

Repetition is a basic element in many folktale plots. Frequently, three is the magic number for building suspense. There are three little pigs whose three houses face the puffing of the wolf. Then the wolf gives three challenges to the pig in the brick house—to get turnips and apples and to go to the fair. In the longer tales each of the three tasks becomes increasingly more difficult, and the intensity of the wonders becomes progressively more marvelous. For example, in the Norwegian tale of "The Maid on the Glass Mountain" (11), Espen Cinderlad first rides his horse one-third of the way up the hill; the next day he goes two-thirds of the way up, and the last day he reaches the top. There is a satisfying sense of order that comes from this heightened expectation of recurring tasks.

Repetition of responses, chants, or poems is frequently a part of the structure of a tale. "Mirror, mirror on the wall, who is fairest of them all" and "Fee, fi, fo, fum" are repetitive verses that are familiar to all. Many versions of *Hansel and Gretel* (112, 113, 114) end with a storyteller's coda:

> "My story is done,
> See the mouse run.
> If it's caught in a trap,
> You can make a fur cap."[18]

The somber and beautiful Scottish tale, "The Black Bull of Norroway" (249), is filled with lovely verses. A young girl at last finds her lover after searching for him for many years. She bargains with the witch-woman, who is going to marry him, for just three nights alone with him. However, the witch-bride drugs him and so all night long the lovely girl sighs and sings:

> "Far have I sought for thee,
> Long have I wrought for thee,
> Near am I brought to thee,
> Dear Duke o' Norroway
> Wilt thou say naught to me?"[19]

Time and place are established quickly in the folktale. Time is always past, and frequently described by such conventional terms as "Once upon a time" or "In the first old time" or "In olden times when wishing still helped one." Time passes quickly in the folktale. The woods and brambles encircle Sleeping Beauty's palace (183) in a quarter of an hour, and "when a hundred years were gone and passed," the prince appears at the moment the enchantment ends. The setting of the folktale is not specific, but in some faraway land, in a cottage in the woods, in a beautiful palace.

The introduction to the folktale usually presents the conflict, characters, and setting in a few sentences. In "Anansi and Nothing Go Hunting for Wives" (58) the problem is established in the first two sentences:

> It came to Anansi one time, as he sat in his little hut, that he needed a wife. For most men this would have been a simple affair, but Anansi's bad name had spread throughout the country and he knew that he wouldn't be likely to have much luck finding a wife in near-by villages.[20]

With little description, the storyteller goes to the heart of his story, capturing the interest of his audience.

The conclusion of the story follows the climax very quickly and includes few details. After the small sister finds her brothers who have been bewitched as *The Seven Ravens* (127), she leaves her tiny ring in one of the ravens' cups. He sees it and wishes:

> "Would God that our own little sister were here, for then we should be free!"
>
> When the maiden, who was standing behind the door listening, heard the wish, she came out, and then all the ravens regained human forms again. And they embraced and kissed one another and went joyfully home."[21]

Even this is a long ending compared with, "and so they were married and lived happily ever after."

The structure of the folktale, with its quick introduction, economy of incident, and logical and brief conclusion maintains interest through suspense and repetition. Because the storyteller has to keep the attention of the audience, each episode must contribute to the theme of the story. Written versions, then, should follow the oral tradition, adding little description and avoiding lengthy asides or admonitions.

CHARACTERIZATION IN FOLKTALES

Characters in folktales are shown in flat dimensions, symbolic of the completely good or entirely evil. Character development is seldom depicted. The beautiful girl is usually virtuous, humble, patient, and loving. Stepmothers are ugly, cross, and mean. The hero, usually fair-haired or curly-haired, is strong, virile, brave, kind, and sympathetic. The poor are often kind, generous, and

[18]Grimm Brothers, *Hansel and Gretel*, translated by Charles Scribner, Jr., illustrated by Adrienne Adams (New York: Charles Scribner's Sons, 1975), unpaged.
[19]Flora Annie Steel, *English Fairy Tales*, illustrated by Arthur Rackham (New York: Macmillan, 1962), p. 116.
[20]Harold Courlander and George Herzog, *The Cow Tail Switch and Other West African Stories* (New York: Holt, Rinehart and Winston, 1947), p. 95.
[21]Grimm Brothers, *The Seven Ravens*, translated by Elizabeth D. Crawford, illustrated by Lisbeth Zwerger (New York: William Morrow & Company, 1981), unpaged.

long suffering; while the rich are imperious, hard-hearted, and often conniving, if not actually dishonest. Physical characteristics may be described briefly, but readers form their own pictures as they read: "Pretty children they all were, but the prettiest was the youngest daughter, who was so lovely there was no end to her loveliness."[22] In describing "The Daughter of the Dragon King" the Chinese grandmother says: "Now this young woman was poorly dressed, but her face was as fair as a plum blossom in spring, and her body was as slender as a willow branch."[23]

Qualities of character or special strengths or weaknesses of the characters are revealed quickly, because this factor will be the cause of conflict or lead to resolution of the plot. The lazy daughter and virtuous stepdaughter are contrasted in the Russian tale *The Month-Brothers* (199). "The daughter used to loll about the whole day long on a featherbed devouring sweetmeats, while the stepdaughter never got a chance to rest from morn to night."[24] A rich merchant in Addis Ababa was characterized in one sentence: "Haptom Hasei was so rich that he owned everything that money could buy, and often he was very bored because he had tired of everything he knew, and there was nothing new for him to do."[25]

Seeing folktale characters as symbols of good, evil, power, wisdom, and other traits, children begin to understand the basis of literature that distills human experience.

STYLE OF FOLKTALES

Folktales offer children many opportunities to hear rich qualitative language and a wide variety of language patterns. Story introductions may range from the familiar "once upon a time" to the Persian "there was a time and there wasn't a time" or the African tale that starts: "We do not mean, we do not really mean that what we are going to say is true."

The introductions and language of the folktale should maintain the "flavor" of the country but still be understood by its present audience. Folktales should not be "written down" to children, but they may need to be simplified. Wanda Gág describes her method of simplification in adapting folktales for children:

By simplification I mean:

(a) freeing hybrid stories of confusing passages
(b) using repetition for clarity where a mature style does not include it
(c) employing actual dialogue to sustain or revive interest in places where the narrative is too condensed for children

However, I do not mean writing in words of one or two syllables. True, the careless use of large words is confusing to children; but long, even unfamiliar words are relished and easily absorbed by them, provided they have enough color and sound value.[26]

American children have probably never heard the words "pawkiest piece" or "cosseted," yet they could easily grasp the meaning of them in the context of the Scottish folktale, "The Laird's Lass and the Gobha's Son" (211):

An old laird had a young daughter once and she was the pawkiest piece in all the world. Her father petted her and her mother cosseted her till the wonder of it was that she wasn't so spoiled that she couldn't be borne.[27]

However, in introducing the story, the teacher would need to tell the children that the "gobha" in the title meant a blacksmith.

Unusual phrases appear in many folktales. In *Russian Wonder Tales* (270) the narrative includes "whether the way was long or short," "across three times nine kingdoms," and "the morning is wiser than the evening." Some folktales include proverbs of the country. For example, a king

22P. C. Asbjørnsen and Jorgen E. Moe, *East of the Sun and West of the Moon, and Other Tales,* illustrated by Tom Vroman (New York: Macmillan, 1963), p.1.
23Frances Carpenter, *Tales of a Chinese Grandmother,* illustrated by Malthe Hasselriis (New York: Doubleday, 1949), p. 75.
24Samuel Marshak, *The Month-Brothers: A Slavic Tale,* translated by Thomas P. Whitney, illustrated by Diane Stanley (New York: Morrow, 1983), unpaged.
25Harold Courlander and Wolf Leslau, *The Fire on the Mountain and Other Ethiopian Stories,* illustrated by Robert W. Kane (New York: Holt, Rinehart and Winston, 1950), p. 7.
26Wanda Gág, *Tales from Grimm* (New York: Coward-McCann, 1936), p. ix.
27Sorche Nic Leodhas, *Thistle and Thyme, Tales and Legends from Scotland,* illustrated by Evaline Ness (New York: Holt, Rinehart and Winston, 1962), p. 17.

speaks to his followers after hearing a story of a man whose second wife murdered his son: "Choose whom you want to marry, but if you choose a tree that has fruit, you must care for the fruit as much as for the tree."[28]

Although there is a minimum of description in the folktale, figurative language and imagery are employed by effective narrators. Isaac Singer (244) uses delightful prose to introduce the Jewish tale about the wager between the spirits of good luck and bad luck:

> In a faraway land, on a sunny spring day, the sky was as blue as the sea, and the sea was as blue as the sky, and the earth was green and in love with them both.[29]

In an African tale (254), when Zomo's trick frightens the cock, he has "a feeling in his belly as if the hairy caterpillar that he had swallowed earlier that morning has come to life and is going on a tour of inspection."[30]

Frequently, storytellers imitate the sounds of the story. In Katherine Paterson's poetic translation from the Japanese of the traditional tale *The Crane Wife* (278), Yohei goes out into the winter snow on an errand. "Suddenly, *basabasa*, he heard a rustling sound. It was a crane dragging its wing, as it swooped down and landed on the path."[31] Later in the story, the sound of a weaver at a loom is heard—*tonkara, tonkara*. In Maggie Duff's retelling of a folktale from India, Blackbird beats out *Rum Pum Pum* (71) on his walnut-shell drum, as he marches out to challenge an unjust king. In the Gullah beast tale "Alligator's Sunday Suit" (175), baby alligators curtsy politely to Bo Rabbit, *sazip, sazip;* later, they slither into a nearby field, *kapuk, kapuk, kapuk*. These onomatopoeic words help listeners see the story and are wonderful additions for those who tell and read stories to children.

When the tales are written as though the storyteller is speaking directly to the reader, the oral tradition is more clearly communicated. Arkhurst uses this style effectively in *The Adventures of Spider* (7):

> I have already told you, and you have already seen for yourselves, that Spider was very full of mischief. He was often naughty and always greedy. But sometimes, in his little heart, he wanted very much to be good. . . . He tried hard, but his appetite almost always got in the way. In fact, that is why Spider has a bald head to this day. Would you like to hear how it got that way?[32]

Surely children in the primary grades would be cheated linguistically if the only version they heard was McDermott's *Anansi the Spider* (194):

> One time Anansi went a long way from home. Far from home. He got lost. He fell into trouble. Back home was See Trouble. "Father is in danger!" he cried. He knew it quickly and he told those other sons.[33]

This kind of simplification of text deprives children not only of meaning but also of language of the folktale, a key feature of literature based on an oral tradition. Without the pictures, it would be difficult to comprehend this story.

Most writers of folktales use little description in expressing the feelings of the characters but let the dialogue and events convey emotion. In the well-loved tale of "The Goose Girl" (108), only Falada, the magical horse, knew that the goose girl was the real princess. But the wicked servant who had taken the princess' place had the horse's head cut off. Each day the goose girl stopped and spoke to the horse's head that hung on the gateway, and each day the horse revealed the sadness of her situation:

> "Alas, my queen, I'm sad for thee.
> Thy mother's heart would broken be,
> If this cruel treatment she could see."[34]

[28]Diane Wolkstein, *The Magic Orange Tree and Other Haitian Folktales,* illustrated by Elsa Henriquez (New York: Knopf, 1978), p. 97.

[29]Isaac Bashevis Singer, *Mazel and Shlimazel, or The Milk of a Lioness,* illustrated by Margot Zemach (New York: Farrar, Straus, Giroux, 1967), p. 1.

[30]Hugh Sturton, *Zomo the Rabbit,* illustrated by Peter Warner (New York: Atheneum, 1966), p. 22.

[31]Sumiko Yagawa, *The Crane Wife,* translated by Katherine Paterson, illustrated by Suekichi Akaba (New York: William Morrow, 1981), unpaged.

[32]Joyce Cooper Arkhurst, *The Adventures of Spider, West African Folk Tales,* illustrated by Jerry Pinkney (Boston: Little, Brown, 1964), p. 21.

[33]Gerald McDermott, *Anansi the Spider* (New York: Holt, Rinehart and Winston, 1972), unpaged.

[34]Grimm Brothers, *Favorite Tales from Grimm,* retold by Nancy Garden, illustrated by Mercer Mayer (New York: Four Winds, 1982), p. 70.

Dialect enhances a story, but it is difficult for children to read. The teacher will need to practice reading or telling a story with dialect, but it is worth the effort if it is done well. Richard Chase recorded stories from the Appalachian mountain folk in *The Jack Tales* (47). He notes: "The dialect has been changed enough to avoid confusion to the reading eye; the idiom has been kept throughout." In this dialogue from "The Heifer Hide" the mountaineer vocabulary and dialect are clear:

"Well, now," she says, "hit's just a little I was a-savin' for my kinfolks comin' tomorrow."

"Me and Jack's your kinfolks. Bring it on out here for us."

So Jack and him eat a lot of them good rations. Jack was awful hungry, and he knowed she hadn't brought out her best stuff yet, so he rammed his heifer hide again, says, "You blabber-mouthed thing! I done told you to hush. You keep on tellin' lies now and I'll put you out the door."[35]

In Virginia Hamilton's collection of black American folktales, *The People Could Fly* (144), speech rhythms and patterns have been preserved, though the dialect has been modified. On the other hand, the dialect of the Brer Rabbit stories in *The Complete Tales of Uncle Remus* by Harris (150) is so heavy as to be most difficult to tell and equally hard to understand.

The major criteria for style in the written folktale, then, are that it maintain the atmosphere of the country and culture from which it originated and that it truly seems to be a tale *told* by a storyteller.

THEMES IN FOLKTALES

The basic purpose of the folktale was to tell an entertaining story, yet these stories do present important themes. Some tales may be merely humorous accounts of foolish people who are so ridiculous that the listeners see their own foolish ways exaggerated. Many of the stories provided an outlet for feelings against the kings and nobles who oppressed the poor. Values of the culture were expressed in folklore. The virtues of humility, kindness, patience, sympathy, hard work, and courage were invariably rewarded. These rewards

[35]Richard Chase, *The Jack Tales,* illustrated by Berkeley Williams (Boston, Mass.: Houghton Mifflin, 1943), p. xi.

reflected the goals of people—long life, a good husband or loving wife, beautiful homes and fine clothing, plenty of food, freedom from fear of the ogre or giant. The power of love, mercy, and kindness is one of the major themes of folktales. "The Pumpkin Child" (203), a Persian tale, was a little girl born to a woman who expressed a deep wish for a daughter even if she looked like a pumpkin. When a prince agreed to marry the girl, love released her from the enchantment and she became "as beautiful as the moon on its fourteenth night." The thematic wisdom of *Beauty and the Beast* (62) is that one should not trust too much to appearances. The lesson that inner qualities of love and kindness are more important than the outer semblance is clearly presented.

Many folktales feature the small and powerless achieving good ends by perseverance and patience. In "The Six Swans" (108), a girl saves her six brothers who have been turned into swans, by remaining silent for six years while sewing shirts from flowers. Often it is quick wits and clear thinking that save the day or win the reward. In *A Story, A Story* (141), Anansi the spider man wins stories for his people by outsmarting a leopard, the hornets, and a fairy and presenting them all to the Sky God. The four poor, weak animals in *The Bremen Town Musicians* (105) cooperate by using their wits not only to save their lives but also to win a home and security for themselves. *The Valiant Little Tailor* (138) may be able to kill seven flies with one blow, but what about ogres? He manages to outsmart one by convincing him that he, too, can squeeze water from a stone. But the ogre cannot see that he is really squeezing a round cheese. Colorful illustrations by Victor Ambrus make fun of the ogres, who are dressed in great yellow or red bloomers decorated with cow skulls. The ogres sport tattoos and safety-pin earrings in contrast to the small but natty tailor.

Feminists have expressed concern that folktale themes most often favor courageous, independent boy adventurers, while girls languish at home. Though it is true that it is easier to find tales that feature plucky boys, there are folktales that portray resourceful, courageous, clever, and independent girls. *Mollie Whuppie* (61), the youngest daughter of a woodcutter, rescues her two older sisters and herself from the murderous giant. She then bravely returns to the giant's castle to steal a sword, a purse, and a gold ring. Thus she wins for each sister and herself a king's son for a husband. In Susan Jeffers' Scottish tale *Wild Robin* (176), Janet saves her brother Robin from the fairy band by holding tightly to him even though the fairies cause him to change his true form into many fearsome shapes. *Duffy and the Devil* (282) make a pact, but she finally outwits him—and manages to get out of spinning and knitting for the rest of her days. Clever Oonagh helps her giant husband, *Fin M'Coul* (63), outsmart the giant Cucullin. Tales that feature spirited and courageous heroines have been gathered in several collections. *The Maid of the North* (216), *The Skull in the Snow* (193), and *Womenfolk and Fairy Tales* (205) are three examples of the way collections from the world over preserve and honor stories of strong, clever, and often brave women.

Parents, teachers, and some psychologists have expressed concern about themes of cruelty and horror in folktales. "Little Red Riding Hood," for example, has been rewritten so that the wolf eats neither the grandmother nor the heroine. Cruel deeds occur very quickly with no sense of pain and no details of the action. In *The Seven Ravens* (127), no blood drips from the sister's hand when she cuts off a finger; not an "ouch" escapes her lips. The wolf is cut open so the six kids can escape, and the mother goat sews the stones into his stomach without any suggestion that the wolf is being hurt (124). Children accept these stories as they are—symbolic interpretations of life in an imaginary land of another time.

MOTIFS IN FOLKTALES

Folklorists analyze folktales according to motifs or patterns, numbering each tale and labeling its episodes.[36] *Motifs* have been defined as the smallest part of a tale that can exist independently. These motifs can be seen in the recurring parade of characters in folktales—the younger brother, the wicked stepmother, the abused child, the clever trickster—or in such supernatural beings as the fairy godmother, the evil witch, or the terrifying giant. The use of magical objects—a slipper, a doll,

a ring, or tablecloth—is another pattern found in many folktales. Stories of enchantment, long sleeps, or marvelous transformations are typical motifs. Some of the motifs have been repeated so frequently that they have been identified as a type of folk story. Thus we have noodlehead stories about fools and simpletons, beast tales about talking animals, and the wonder tales of supernatural beings that children generally call fairy tales.

Even the plots of the stories have recurring patterns—three tasks to be performed, three wishes that are granted, or three trials to be endured. A simple tale will have several motifs, a complex one will have many. Recognizing some of the most common motifs in folklore will help a teacher to suggest points of comparison and contrast in a cross-cultural approach to folk literature.

The Long Sleep or Enchantment

The long sleep is a motif that appears time and again in folklore and may symbolically represent the coming of winter or death. Perhaps the best-known tales that include this motif are Grimm's *Snow-White and the Seven Dwarfs* (131, 132) and "The Sleeping Beauty in the Wood" (183), first recorded by Perrault. A Japanese story, "Urashima Taro and the Princess of the Sea" (264), tells of a boy who remains under the sea in a beautiful palace for three years, only to discover he was gone three hundred years. In the modern picture book *Seashore Story*, Yashima has told this tale as a story within a story (279). In the Vietnamese tale "The Fairy Grotto" (267), Tu Thuc also discovers that he has been in the fairy kingdom for three hundred years.

Magical Powers

Magical powers are frequently given to persons or animals in folktales. A common pattern in folklore is the "helpful companions" who all have wonderful powers. In *The Fool of the World and the Flying Ship* (219), the fool's eight companions can do such things as eat huge quantities, hear long distances, or drink whole lakes. Later, these talents help the fool overcome the tasks the czar sets for whoever wishes to win his daughter's hand. This

[36]Stith Thompson, *Motif Index of Folk-literature* (Bloomington: Indiana University Press, 1955–1958), 6 vols.

same motif is found in *Rum Pum Pum: A Folk Tale From India* (71). Here, Blackbird is helped to overcome the cruel king by his friends Cat, Stick, River, and the ants. José Aruego and Ariane Dewey have portrayed Blackbird's quest in lavishly colored illustrations. *The Month-Brothers* (199) have magical powers over the seasons, and each brother oversees his month. In the Chinese version of Cinderella, *Yeh-Shen* (191), a fish can work magic even after its death. The *Little Humpbacked Horse* (162) can fly. All of these magical powers aid each hero in obtaining his or her goal in the story.

Magical Transformations

The transformation of an animal to a person, or vice versa, is a part of many folktales. "Beauty and the Beast" (183) is one of the most familiar of the tales using this motif. "The Frog Prince" (134) is

Strega Nona warns Big Anthony not to touch her pasta pot in Tomie de Paola's popular tale.

one such popular story collected by the Grimm brothers. A frog retrieves the princess' ball in exchange for her promise that he can eat from her plate and sleep with her. He becomes a prince when allowed on her pillow. In a Shawnee Indian story *The Ring in the Prairie* (233), Waupee, the Indian brave, transforms himself into a small mouse so that he can creep up and capture one of the twelve sisters who come down from the sky to dance. A crane can turn into a human being and back into a crane in the Japanese tale *The Crane Wife* (278). Errol Le Cain's decorative illustrations for *Cinderella* (213) skillfully capture the exact moments of two transformations. The mouse is changed into a horse in eight overlapping figures, while in another illustration Cinderella goes in five sequences from riches to rags as floating images of the striking clock pursue her. Illustrations like these might tempt children to represent transformations in their illustrating of other tales in a similar manner.

Magic Objects

Magic objects are essential aspects of many tales that also reflect other themes. In the story of *The Magic Pot* (53), the pot helps a poor old man and woman by going "hucka-pucka" down the road on its three legs to the rich man's house and returning loaded with food or silver. The kindly old witch *Strega Nona* (64) just said "Bubble bubble pasta pot" to make all the pasta she needed. The problem was that Big Anthony didn't know the secret of how to get it to stop. A Goddess takes pity on a poor but good man and gives him *The Magic Cooking Pot* (259). When an innkeeper tricks him out of it, the Goddess gives him another pot full of demons that beat the innkeeper and force him to return the first pot. Faith Towle has used the unique medium of batik to create the illustrations for this "pot tale" from India.

A magic table cloth is a frequently used device for providing food in folktales. In the Norwegian tale "The Lad Who Went to the North Wind" (9) and also the Armenian variant "The Enormous Genie" (256), a table provides food on the command of "Table, spread thyself." Both these stories include an animal that spits out gold coins and a club that beats a person on command. Both a ring and a lamp play an essential part in the story of *Aladdin* (181). The Zemachs have combined their talents to produce a hilarious Italian folktale called *Too Much Nose* (285). In this story each of three poor sons is given a magical object. In a real switch on folktale patterns, the second son outwits the scheming, cheating queen by discovering the magic secret of how to change the sizes of people's noses. In the end he recovers all of the magical objects and leaves the queen with too much nose! Warwick Hutton has retold and illustrated a version of this tale in *The Nose Tree* (168). Here, however, three soldiers eventually outwit the king's daughter, who is really a witch. Hutton's luminous watercolors humorously portray the noses of both the first soldier and the witch princess as the noses appear to slither down the castle walls and through the forests.

Other magic objects that figure in folktales are dolls, purses, harps, the hen that lays the golden egg, and many more. In *A Book of Charms and Changelings* (197), Manning-Sanders has collected a group of tales from all over the world that involve the use of magic objects.

Wishes

Many stories are told of wishes that are granted and then used foolishly or in anger or greed. *The Three Wishes* is the tale of the woodsman who was so hungry that he wished for a sausage; his wife was so angry at this wish that she wished the sausage would stick to his nose; then of course they have to use the third wish to get it off. Paul Galdone's amusing picture-book version of this tale delights primary-grade children (95). A Japanese tale of the foolish use of wishes has been told in picture-book form by Eve Titus under the title *The Two Stonecutters* (257). In return for their kindness the Goddess of the Forest grants two brothers seven wishes between them. The younger brother, who is quite content with his life, gives all his wishes except one to his elder brother, who longs to be rich and powerful. The elder brother promptly uses his six wishes to satisfy his desire for riches and to become a prince. Wanting more and more power, he wishes to become the wind, the sun, a storm cloud, and finally a stone. Luckily, the younger brother, who has remained a contented stonecutter, finds the elder brother and is able to save him with the one remaining wish.

Trickery

Both animals and people trick their friends and neighbors in folk literature. The wolf tricks Little Red Riding Hood into believing he is her grandmother; and Hansel and Gretel trick the mean old witch into crawling into the oven.

Almost every culture has an animal trickster in its folklore. In European folktales it is usually a wolf or a fox; in Japan it is a badger or a hare; Indonesia has Kantjil, a tiny mouse deer; and Africa has three well-known tricksters, Anansi the spider, Zomo the rabbit, and Ijapa the tortoise; while Coyote and the raven play this role in Native American tales.

Harold Berson has illustrated a very funny picture book about how a rich man foiled a robber in *The Thief Who Hugged a Moonbeam* (21). When the man hears a thief on the roof, he tells his wife in a very loud voice that the way he obtained his wealth was to speak a magic word and then ride a moonbeam into the open windows of houses. When the thief tries to do it, disaster follows. *Balarin's Goat* (20), another story by Berson, is the amusing French tale of how a wife decides to trick her husband into giving her as much attention as he showers on his favorite goat, Fleurette. Surely this tale was first told by a woman!

In the black American tale *Wiley and the Hairy Man* (14), Wiley twice tricks the Hairy Man, who lives in the Tombigbee Swamp land. But it is Wiley's mother who plays the third trick. When the Hairy Man comes to take Wiley away, his mother promises, from inside her cabin, to give him "the young 'un." However she does not say *which* young one she means and she has substituted a piglet in Wiley's bed. The Hairy Man, realizing that he has been foiled, angrily snatches the piglet and disappears in a rage. According to tradition, since he has been tricked three times, he can never bother Wiley and his mother again.

Enchantments and long sleeps, magical powers, transformations, use of magic objects, wishes, and trickery are just a few of the motifs that run through the folklore of all countries, as we have seen. Others may include the power of naming, as in "Rumpelstiltskin" (118); the ability to make yourself invisible, as the gardener did in *The Twelve Dancing Princesses* (137); becoming stuck to a person or object, as in the black-American tale "The Tar Baby" (156), or the "Lazy Jack" pattern of the simpleton who follows his mother's directions at the wrong time (204). You can make your own lists of motifs or have the children in your classroom do so. It is one way to understand the common elements of all folklore.

The following table, "A Cross-Cultural Study of Folktale Motifs," mentions both well-known and lesser-known tales as a beginning for those wishing to pursue a study of motifs. There are many other titles that could be added to these five motifs and, of course, there are many more motifs around which to group folklore.

A CROSS-CULTURAL STUDY OF FOLKTALE MOTIFS

SAMPLE MOTIF	TALE	CULTURE
Magical powers	*The Fool of the World and the Flying Ship* (219)	Russia
	The Woodcutter's Duck (263)	Poland
	Rum Pum Pum (71)	India
	The Month-Brothers (199)	Russia
	The Little Humpbacked Horse (162)	Russia
	The Riddle of the Drum (1)	Mexico
	The Fisherman and His Wife (110)	Germany
Transformations	*Beauty and the Beast* (62)	France
	"The Frog Prince" (134)	Germany
	"The Prince Who Was Taken Away by the Salmon" (148)	Native American

A CROSS-CULTURAL STUDY OF FOLKTALE MOTIFS (continued)

SAMPLE MOTIF	TALE	CULTURE
Transformations (cont.)	*Cinderella* (85)	France
	Wild Robin (176)	Scotland
	The Crane Wife (278)	Japan
	"Master Frog" (267)	Vietnam
	The Winter Wife (59)	Native American
	The Sorcerer's Apprentice (84)	Germany
Magical objects	"Bruh Lizard and Bruh Rabbit" (144)	Black American
	Vasilisa the Beautiful (272)	Russia
	Too Much Nose (285)	Italy
	"The Shepherd's Nosegay" (151)	Czechoslovakia
	"Aladdin" (181)	Arabia
	The Magic Cooking Pot (259)	India
	The Nose Tree (168)	Germany
	The Twelve Dancing Princesses (137)	Germany
Trickery	*Balarin's Goat* (20)	France
	"Anansi and the Old Hag" (238)	Jamaica
	"Shrewd Todie and Lyzer, the Miser" (245)	Jewish
	Wiley and the Hairy Man (13)	Black American
	Puss in Boots (92)	France
	Fin M'Coul (63)	Ireland
	"Bo Rabbit Smart for True" (175)	Black American
	Stone Soup (33)	France
	"Never Heard of This Before" (157)	China
Wishes	*The Three Wishes* (95)	England
	The Two Stonecutters (257)	Japan
	The Fisherman and His Wife (110)	Germany
	The Seven Ravens (127)	Germany
Long sleep	*Snow White and the Seven Dwarfs* (132)	Germany
	"Urashima Taro and the Princess of the Sea" (264)	Japan
	"The Fairy Grotto" (267)	Vietnam
	The Sleeping Beauty (129)	Germany
	Seashore Story (279)	Japan

VARIANTS OF FOLKTALES

The number of variants of a single folktale fascinates beginning students of folklore. A variant has basically the same story or plot as the original, but it may have different characters and a different setting and use some some different motifs. For example, a Japanese Rumpelstiltskin story (265) is about an ogre who built a bridge for a carpenter. If the carpenter couldn't discover the ogre's name, he had to forfeit one of his eyeballs. In an Armenian tale, "The Talking Fish" (255), a demon lends a poor peasant a cow for three years, at the end of which the demon will return to ask a question. If the peasant cannot answer it, he and his wife must become the demon's slaves. In a twist to the usual ending a traveler visiting their house answers all the demon's questions correctly. The traveler turns out to have been a fish that the kind peasant had returned to the sea. Other better-known variants of Rumpelstiltskin are the English *Tom Tit Tot* (210); the Scottish "Whippety Stourie" (273); and a tale from Cornwall, *Duffy and the Devil* (282). These are all discussed under "British Folktales."

A comparison of the variants of Cinderella illustrates differences in theme and motif. Scholars have found versions of this story in ancient Egypt, in China in the ninth century, and in Iceland in the tenth century. Cinderella receives her magic gifts in many different ways; in the French and most familiar version, a fairy godmother gives them to her (212); in Grimm's version (106) a dove appears on the tree that grew from the tears she had shed on her mother's grave; in the English *Tattercoats* (250) she receives her beautiful gowns from a herdboy; in the Chinese *Yeh-Shen* (191) magic fish bones bestow gifts on her. She attends three balls in some variants; for example, in the Italian version (153), Cenerentola throws coins as she leaves the ball the first night and pearls on the second escape and loses her slipper on the third night. Her treatment of the stepsisters varies from blinding them to inviting them to live at the palace. The Vietnamese version, "The Brocaded Slipper" (267), is made longer by the narrative of the stepsister finally meeting her own death after "killing" her Cinderella sister, Tam, three times. In "The Indian Cinderella" (156), the lovely young daughter of a chief is cruelly treated by her jealous elder sisters who frequently beat her and burn her face with hot coals. For this reason she is often called "Little Burnt Face" (67) in other versions of this tale. But she is the only maiden who is able to see the invisible Strong Wind and describe him to his sister. He becomes visible when he takes her for his wife. Her own sisters are turned into aspen trees forever destined to tremble and quake whenever Strong Wind passes by.

Other variants occur across cultures. In the *Tops and Bottoms* (52) motif, an industrious farmer and a lazy one agree to share the crops. One receives the top crop; one gets the root crop. But the clever farmer is always sure he plants a crop that can be harvested to his advantage. Another form of trickery provides a second common variant, *Stone Soup* (33). The soup usually begins with a nail, stone, ax, or hatchet and ends with a delicious concoction of all that the villagers have contributed. It is frequently enacted in lower elementary grades, where children make and eat their own group soup after reading or hearing the story. The "helpful companions" usually help someone small or powerless to achieve a goal by each contributing their unique talents. Uri Shulevitz won a Caldecott Medal for his portrayal of this theme in *The Fool of the World and the Flying Ship* (219). "Jack and the Beanstalk" comes in many versions, but Appalachian variants change not only the language in which the story is told; they also present typical rural objects which Jack covets and steals, such as a coverlet with small bells on it or a rifle (47). Humorous variations on this tale have been retold and illustrated by Briggs (*Jim and the Beanstalk*) (29) and by Ross (*Jack and the Beanstalk*) (225).

We have provided tables that organize folktales by tale type and by common motif. The following table, "A Cross-Cultural Study of Folktale Variants," provides yet a third way of organizing tales for classroom presentation. These variants make excellent comparison material and elementary children enjoy discovering the similarities and differences. Classroom-made charts, with the tale titles going down the left margin and topics listed across the top, allow children to compare such aspects as:

- opening and ending conventions
- origin of the tale
- clues to the country or region of origin
- talents of the characters
- tasks to be done
- verses, refrains, chants, and their outcomes
- illustrations
- special or unique vocabulary

Each group of variants will have other categories to compare as well. For example, categories might be "Instructions for Stopping a Pot from Cooking," "How Rumpelstiltskin's Name Is Discovered," or "What the Witch Looks Like." Children should be encouraged to develop their own category titles whenever possible.

Knowledge of the different variants of a tale, common motifs, and common types of folktales will enable a teacher to help children see similar elements in folktales across cultures. Knowledge of the folklore of a particular country or cultural group will aid in identifying the uniqueness and individuality of that group. Both approaches to a study of folklore seem essential.

VARIANTS OF A THEME	CULTURE
Cinderella (200)	France
"Tattercoats" (213)	England
"Aschenputtel" (118)	Germany
"The Princess on the Glass Hill" (155)	Norway
Nomi and the Magic Fish (202)	Africa
Yeh-Shen (191)	China
"The Indian Cinderella" (156)	Native American
Vasilisa the Beautiful (272)	Russia
"The Brocaded Slipper" (267)	Vietnam
"Six Men Go Far Together in the Wide World" (124)	Germany
The Blue Bird (80)	Literary Chinese
The Riddle of the Drum (1)	Mexico
Rum Pum Pum (71)	India
The Fool of the World and the Flying Ship (219)	Russia
Five Chinese Brothers (23)	Chinese
Anansi the Spider (194)	Africa
Jack and the Beanstalk (44)	England
Jim and the Beanstalk (29)	Modern Literary
Jack and the Wonder Beans (251)	Appalachian American
The History of Mother Twaddle and the Marvelous Achievements of Her Son Jack (87)	England
"Jack and the Bean Tree" (47)	Appalachian American
Jack and the Beanstalk (225)	Modern Literary
Jack and the Bean Tree (142)	Appalachian American
Tops and Bottoms (52)	England
The Best of the Bargain (69)	Poland
Why the Jackal Won't Speak to the Hedgehog (22)	Tunisia
"The Peasant and the Bear" (42)	Russia
"The Lad Who Went to the North Wind" (8)	Norway
"Jack and the North West Wind" (47)	Appalachian American
"Bottle Hill" (198)	Ireland
"Clever Peter and the Two Bottles" (218)	Germany
"The Enormoous Genie" (256)	Armenia
The Table, the Donkey and the Stick (133)	Germany
Stone Soup (33)	France
"Boiled Ax" (42)	Russia
"Hatchet Gruel" (98)	Russia
Nail Soup (283)	Sweden
Rumpelstiltskin (126)	Germany
Tom Tit Tot (210)	England
"The Talking Fish" (255)	Armenia
"The Ogre Who Built a Bridge" (265)	Japan
Duffy and the Devil (282)	England
"Whippety Stourie" (273)	Scotland
The Magic Porridge Pot (90)	Germany
The Magic Pot (53)	Modern Literary
Strega Nona (64)	Modern Literary
The Magic Cooking Pot (259)	India
The Funny Little Woman (207)	Japan

Folktales of the World

BRITISH FOLKTALES

The first folktales that most children in the United States hear are the English ones. This is because Joseph Jacobs, the folklorist who collected many of the English tales, deliberately adapted them for young children, writing them, he said, "as a good old nurse will speak when she tells Fairy Tales." His collection includes cumulative tales such as "The Old Woman and Her Pig" and "Henny Penny" and the much-loved talking-beast stories, "The Little Red Hen," "The Three Bears," and "The Three Little Pigs." Paul Galdone has illustrated single editions of all of these nursery tales with large, colorful, and humorous pictures that appeal to the young child. Gavin Bishop's colorful endpapers of swirling oak leaves and an ever-darkening sequence of pictures depict *Chicken Licken* (25) and the folly of following Foxy Woxy's advice. All of the hapless animals eaten by the fox are represented in one illustration of flying feathers, bones, teeth, and tongue, but the lucky chicken escapes. Steven Kellogg has "updated" this tale in his humorous version, *Chicken Little* (178). Today, when children see such beautiful modern picture books, it is good to have these well-loved classic tales in handsome single picture-book editions.

English folktales are known for their humor, particularly those stories that are about fools and simpletons. "Mr. and Mrs. Vinegar" (249) is a cheerful story of a couple who live in a glass pickle jar until Mrs. Vinegar smashes it with her vigorous sweeping. They then set out to find their fortune and do when they frighten away some robbers and retrieve their stolen gold. Mrs. Vinegar sends her husband off to buy a cow, but Mr. Vinegar trades the cow for various articles until he is left with nothing. Another simpleton is "Lazy Jack" (249), who follows the right directions at the wrong time, a motif found in many folktales.

The tale of *The Three Sillies* (287) has comic illustrations by Margot Zemach. It is a droll story about people who borrow trouble before it comes. A young girl goes down in the cellar to draw beer for her suitor and parents. She sees an axe stuck in the cellar beam, and she imagines what might happen if, after her marriage, she has a son and he goes down in the cellar and is struck by the axe. Her parents soon join her in weeping over this imagined tragedy.

There is an element of realism that runs through some of the English folktales. The story of Dick Whittington and his cat has its basis in history. There was once a real Richard Whittington who was three times mayor of London, in 1396, 1406, and 1419. And what an exceptional mayor he must have been—enacting prison reforms, providing the first public lavatory and drinking fountain, and building a library and a wing on the hospital for unmarried mothers. It is no wonder that the common people made him the popular hero of one of their most cherished tales. The story of "Dick and His Cat" was found in some of the very earliest chapbooks of the day. Marcia Brown's picture-story book, *Dick Whittington and His Cat* (32), portrays this realistic tale with handsome linoleum block prints appropriately printed in gold and black.

The British version of Cinderella, called *Tattercoats* (250), is a more poignant romance than the better-known French story. For in this tale the prince falls in love with Tattercoats even when she is dirty and wearing an old torn petticoat. To prove his love he invites her to come as she is with her gooseherd friend and his geese to the king's ball that evening. Only after the prince greets them and presents her to the king as the girl he has chosen for his bride does the gooseherd begin to play his magical pipe and Tattercoats' rags are changed to shining robes while the geese become dainty pages. The goosehead is never seen again. Diane Goode's luminous illustrations seem most appropriate for this romantic tale.

Rumer Godden retells a modern version of her favorite English tale in *The Old Woman Who Lived in a Vinegar Bottle* (102). Mairi Hedderwick's lovely watercolor illustrations show the changes in both the character and condition of the old woman, who first lived in an old house the shape of a stone vinegar bottle. She is very happy and contented until she saves the life of a fish who then grants her every wish. These include a new cottage, new clothes, furniture, and a maid! Finally, when she demands a chauffeur and a big shining car like the queen's, the fish has had enough and returns her to her original house and condition. In the Grimm brothers' story, *The Fisherman and His Wife* (110), the wife never finds contentment even after she has been made emperor and pope.

Giant killers are also characteristic of some English stories. Everyone knows the story of *Jack and the Beanstalk* (44). Less well known in the United States is the story of *Mollie Whuppie* (61). Mollie is a girl who would delight the heart of any feminist, for she is clever enough to trick the giant four times. Each time she narrowly escapes over the Bridge of One Hair. The original version (249) is a somewhat bloody story in that Mollie tricks the giant into choking his own children rather than her sisters and beating his own wife to death after she has traded places with Mollie. However, de la Mare's retelling softens the story so that we don't know what finally happens to the giant's family.

A strong giant in Irish folklore is *Fin M'Coul: The Giant of Knockmany Hill* (63), but the giant Cucullin is stronger. However, clever Oonagh, his wife, makes a plan with the help of the fairies who are everywhere in evidence in Tomie de Paola's humorous illustrations. When Cucullin arrives at the door, the trembling Fin is disguised as his own son in a cradle. Oonagh sets Cucullin to eating what is supposedly Fin's usual bread, except that she has baked iron skillets into each round loaf. When Cucullin complains of lost teeth, Oonagh proves that the "baby" is stronger when he eats his loaf of bread which, of course, has no pan in it. When the giant asks to feel the baby Fin's amazing teeth, Fin bites off the giant's brass finger, the source of all his strength. The details in the borders of this well-known story are taken from early Irish metalwork jewelry patterns. A similar version of the tale that points up Oonagh's resourcefulness is found in "Oonagh and the Giants" (216). Further adventures of Fin, written in a more serious vein and for older readers, are found in *The Green Hero: Early Adventures of Finn McCool* (74), which portrays Finn as a runt of a giant with very human problems.

Three British variants of the "Rumpelstiltskin" or naming theme provide interesting contrasts in language, illustration, and content. Using crude woodcuts in *Tom Tit Tot* (210), Evaline Ness portrays a "gatless" girl who merely cries when she cannot guess the name of the "black impet" who has done her spinning. Its name is revealed to the king, who sees the creature twirling its tail, singing:

> Nimmy Nimmy not
> My name's Tom Tit Tot.[37]

Margot Zemach's "squinny-eyed creature" (282) sings:

> Tomorrow! Tomorrow! Tomorrow's the day!
> I'll take her! I'll take her! I'll take her away!
> Let her weep, let her cry, let her beg, let her pray—
> She'll never guess my name is Tarraway![38]

However, Duffy's outwitting of the Devil makes all of her husband's hand-spun clothes disappear! Both the language and the pen-and-wash illustrations retain the Cornish flavor of this folklore comedy. In the Scottish "Whippety Stourie" (273) six wee ladies help a young wife outmaneuver her husband.

A hauntingly beautiful picture book loosely based on the Scottish folktale "Tamlane" is Susan Jeffers' *Wild Robin* (176). Robin is such a disobedient, wayward boy that even his kind sister Janet loses patience. When Robin runs away he falls under the spell of a fairy queen. Taken to the dazzling fairy palace, Robin is allowed to do anything he wants, but he soon finds he is lonely and grows tired of doing nothing. An elf takes pity on the grieving Janet and tells her how she can rescue her brother: she must hold onto him regardless of how many different repulsive shapes the fairies give him. Finally, through love and courage, Janet overcomes the power of the fairy queen and Robin is restored to his own true self. Susan Jeffers' evocative pictures contrast the cool, heartless fairies of Scottish folklore with the warmth and love of an older sister. Mollie Hunter makes use of the same motif of many changing shapes in her modern fantasy of Scotland, *The Haunted Mountain* (see Chapter 7).

Susan Cooper retells a Welsh story about an equivalent of the Scottish fairies, the Tylwyth Teg, and their revenge on the greedy father in *The*

[37]Evaline Ness, *Tom Tit Tot* (New York: Scribner, 1965), unpaged.
[38]Harve Zemach, *Duffy and the Devil,* illustrated by Margot Zemach (New York: Farrar, Straus, 1973), unpaged.

Silver Cow (54). When a father sends his son out to mind the cows, the boy's harp-playing attracts a strange white cow from out of the lake. It joins the herd and the family's fortunes improve, but the father hoards his gain and eventually plans to slaughter his herd to make even more money. When the son cries desperately to the Tylwyth Teg to save the beautiful cows, a voice calls "Come home, silver cows" and one by one, the cows plunge into the dark water never to be seen again. Warwick Hutton's softly greened watercolor illustrations capture the look of the Welsh countryside and portray with special beauty the white water-lilies which the fairies leave behind upon the water's surface.

British folklore includes giants and wee folk but has developed relatively few of the complicated wonder tales that abound in French and Russian folklore. It is often more robust and humorous than some other European tale traditions. Its greatest contribution has been made to the youngest children in providing such nursery classics as "The Three Little Pigs," "Henny Penny," and "The Little Red Hen."

GERMAN FOLKTALES

Next in popularity to the English folktales are those of German origin. Jacob and Wilhelm Grimm spent over twelve years collecting the tales which they published in 1812 as the first volume of *Kinder und Hausmärchen* (Household Stories). They did not adapt their stories for children as Joseph Jacobs did for British folktales, but were very careful to preserve the form and content of the tales as they were told (without benefit of a tape recorder). These were then translated into English by Edgar Taylor from 1823 to 1826.

New and beautiful collections and single tales of Grimms' stories continue to be published today. Maurice Sendak visited Kassel, Germany, before illustrating his two volumes *The Juniper Tree and Other Tales from Grimm* (119). In the museum there he was fortunate enough to find a version illustrated by none other than the Grimms' younger brother, Ludwig. The size of this little-known version with only six engravings served as the inspiration for Sendak's small volumes. Mindful of the fact that these tales were told to country folk, Sendak used adults as his subjects. His view of Rapun-

Maurice Sendak has given the Grimm stories back to adults with his symbolic, distinguished illustrations. Here, for example, he portrays a pregnant Rapunzel. From *The Juniper Tree and Other Tales* from Grimm.

zel is from within her room looking out, rather than the cliché of Rapunzel hanging her hair out of the castle window. Sendak has pictured a pregnant Rapunzel, for the story states that she had her twin babies with her when she was at last united with her prince. This is an authentic and distinguished edition of Grimm that reflects the origin of the stories, yet makes us look at them with new wonder and delight.

Mercer Mayer in *Favorite Tales from Grimm* (108) has illustrated well-known tales like "Cinderella," "The Valiant Little Tailor," and "Rapunzel" along with several less familiar stories like "The Two Brothers" and "Fitcher's Bird." Wanda Gág's classic *Tales from Grimm* (134) provides a collection to share with younger children. Brian Alderson's distinguished translation of thirty-one tales in *The Brothers Grimm: Popular Folk Tales* (124) is accompanied by Michael Foreman's often humorous and sometimes mysterious paintings and drawings. Fortunately, the number of well illustrated single tales of Grimm is increasing, as well.

German folktales are not as funny as the English ones. They have a few drolls and simpletons, such as "Clever Elsie"(134) whose story is similar to that of *The Three Sillies* (287) in which the girl cries because the baby she might have could someday be cut by the axe in the cellar. When Clever Elsie goes to the fields to reap the rye, she cuts her clothes instead of the rye and does not know herself. She decides to go home to see who she is. Upon arriving at the house, she asks her husband if Elsie is at home. Thinking that his wife is upstairs, her husband answers, "Yes."

"Ach!" cried Clever Elsie."Then I'm already at home, and this is not I, and I'm not Elsie but somebody else, and I don't live here."[39]

Elizabeth Shub has adapted a tale which is similar to the Norwegian *Gone Is Gone* (81) for beginning readers, *Clever Kate* (239). In it, Kate, a bride of only one week, makes unbelievable mistakes, including giving her husband's gold away. All is recovered in the end and the well-meaning, lovable Kate truly earns the title of *Clever Kate*. Anita Lobel's decorative peasant art adds to the fun of this tale. "Goose Hans" (134) is about the foolish boy who receives gifts from a prospective bride. He puts the needle in a haystack, the knife in his sleeve, a goat in his pocket—literally following his mother's directions. Left alone, he causes havoc in the house, but ends the day by rolling in honey and goose feathers to sit on the eggs, replacing the goose he kills.

Monica Laimgruber's version of *The Fisherman and His Wife* (110) presents a foolish woman who wishes her way from being a fishwife in "a night pot near the sea" to being pope in a great church—and back again. When her husband spares the life of an enchanted flounder, the wife insists that the fish owes him a wish. Back goes the husband and, in the style of folktales, asks for the wish in verse:

Flounder, flounder in the sea,
Hear my words and come to me.

Grant the wish of Ilsebill
Though her wish is not my will.[40]

By using increasingly darker colors and showing the water becoming more roiled, Laimgruber convinces us that the fish is progressively more disturbed by the wife's greedy demands. In a raging storm, the fish tells the poor man to return to his wife, whose demands have returned them to the night pot. "And there they are to this very day." Margot Zemach's version (109) portrays a more poverty-stricken couple living in a pigsty, and the housing goes through several transformations before the couple's clothes begin to catch up to their circumstances. In comparison to Laimgruber's well-designed and orderly pages, Zemach crowds her scenes with jumbles of people and portrays the increasingly stormy weather with angry swirls of black watercolor wash. A clever modern variation to compare with these versions is Rumer Godden's *The Old Woman Who Lived in a Vinegar Bottle* (102).

The well-known tale of "The Bremen Town Musicians" is a story of the cooperative efforts of the donkey, the hound, the cat, and the rooster in routing robbers out of their house. Ilse Plume's colorful drawings of the four animals, the forest, and the countryside setttings are warm and appealing (104). Donna Diamond's framed black and white illustrations, created entirely from black dots, simulate turn-of-the-century photographs (103). Janina Domanska's bright but crowded paintings built of geometric shapes accompany a more colloquial version of this tale, translated by Elizabeth Shub (105). All three versions would be interesting to compare in a classroom discussion.

The wolf is usually the villain in the few beast tales in German folklore. Perhaps the best-known wolf appears in the Grimm story "Little Red Cap." In the familiar story, the heroine ignores her mother's warnings and, as a result, she and her grandmother are eaten. Both escape through the intervention of a passing hunter who thinks that the wolf's loud snores couldn't be coming from a healthy grandmother. After her adventure, the little girl vows always to obey her mother's advice. Both Lisbeth Zwerger, in *Little Red Cap* (121),

[39]Wanda Gág, *Tales from Grimm* (New York: Coward-McCann, 1936), p. 132.

[40]Grimm Brothers, *The Fisherman and His Wife*, translated by Elizabeth Shub, illustrated by Monika Laimgruber (New York: Greenwillow, 1978), unpaged.

Trina Schart Hyman places a guardian cat in the background of Little Red Riding Hood's first encounter with the wolf. Children enjoy searching for it in subsequent pictures. From *Little Red Riding Hood.*

and Trina Schart Hyman, in *Little Red Riding Hood* (122), have portrayed this story with striking but differing illustrations. Hyman presents a younger, more innocent child distracted by the wolf. Small vignettes depicting houshold details, wildflowers, and insects are enclosed in changing border frames, giving the whole book a delightfully old-fashioned look. Children will look to find the cat in nearly every illustration which features Little Red Riding Hood. In *Self-Portrait: Trina Schart Hyman* (170), the author-illustrator recounts the importance of this story to her childhood. Beautiful, spare watercolors by Zwerger portray a contrastingly older Red Cap and the essential props against a soft and muted backdrop. Her use of gray and brown washes highlights the essentials while Hyman elaborately details forest and cottage backgrounds. Other versions of this tale have been illustrated by Paul Galdone (89) and Edward Gorey (65).

Tom Thumb (136), the little lad not much bigger than his mother's thumb, also ends up in the wolf's belly. However, quick-witted Tom tricks the wolf into taking him home, where Tom's parents kill the wolf and cut him open to find Tom safe and alive. Felix Hoffmann has illustrated a handsome single edition of this favorite tale.

Some of the Grimm tales can be just that—grim, dark, and forbidding. Small children can be frightened by the story of *Hansel and Gretel* (115), the somber tale of a brother and sister abandoned in the woods by their parents and nearly eaten by a horrible witch. However, justice does prevail in this wonder tale: the witch dies in the same way as she had intended to kill the children; the stepmother also dies, and the children, laden with wealth, are reunited with their joyful father. Several very different illustrated versions present this tale to children. Paul Zelinsky's oil paintings somberly re-create the forest settings and interior of the poor woodcutter's house. One can almost smell the witch's tasty house (117). Lisbeth Zwerger (114) portrays characters against a brown wash that gives the action a dreamlike, long-ago appearance. Susan Jeffers' exquisitely rendered forest scenes detail each leaf and bird, but her renditions of the children's experiences with the witch suffer from a sameness both of color and of size (116). Jeffers' witch is wrapped in a shawl identical to the stepmother's, hinting that the two may be the same person. Anthony Browne, in his startling contemporary version (113), makes the same connection by the placement of a mole on each woman's cheek. Browne's illustrations are full of reflected images, symbols of cages and flight, and the triangular shape that resembles a witch's hat. One writer has suggested that "Hansel and Gretel" is a story about the child's psychological and symbolic journey to independence. The cages and bars represent regression to an earlier infantile dependency, while the many birds represent a child's growth and development into an independent being.[41] The story concludes with hope as blue sky is reflected in the doorway framing the reunion of father and children. On a shelf a green shoot emerges from a potted plant. While adults may feel that Browne's interpretation brings the story too close to children today, this violation of the folktale convention of distancing in "a long time ago"

[41]Jane Doonan, "Talking Pictures: A New Look at 'Hansel and Gretel,' " *Signal,* no. 42 (September 1983), pp. 123–131.

may be treated by older children simply as one more interesting variation.

Other Grimm stories featuring witches have been illustrated and retold. In the less well-known *Jorinda and Joringel* (82), a wicked witch tansforms a lovely girl into a nightingale. Joringel, a shepherd, finds a magic flower. With it and his love to protect him, he goes to the castle in the dense forest and frees Jorinda and the 7,000 other girls who had all been transformed into birds. Another witch, though never unkind to *Rapunzel* (125), nevertheless keeps her locked in a tower until a prince climbs her braids. When the witch discovers the deception, she throws him from the tower and he blinds himself on the thorns below. However, a year later, he and Rapunzel are reunited and her tears restore his sight. Trina Schart Hyman's dark and mysterious illustrations for this story have a Slavic appearance and owe a debt to Russian illustrator Ivan Biliban's use of small rectangular vignettes and borders.

German folklore is enlivened by little elves and dwarfs. Children everywhere love the story of *The Elves and the Shoemaker* (188), the tale of the little men who helped the old shoemaker and his wife. Every night they made shoes for the old couple until one night the shoemaker and his wife made them a beautiful set of clothes. Then off the elves scampered, never to be seen again. Paul Galdone (107) humorously but warmly portrays this favorite tale. *Rumpelstiltskin* is another well-known German tale of a rather demanding dwarf. Donna Diamond has illustrated this tale in stark near-photographic pictures (126).

Some of the German tales are laced together with a heavy thread of morality—kindness is always rewarded, while dire punishment faces the evil doer. In the so-called "grandmother tale" of *Mother Holly* (123), the kind child's diligence earns a reward of gold from old Mother Holly at the bottom of the well, while the lazy sister merits only a shower of pitch. This story has a theme similar to the favorite French tale of "Toads and Diamonds" (183).

Another morality tale is the story of the humbling of a haughty princess by her husband, *King Thrushbeard* (120). Felix Hoffmann has illustrated this classic tale with his usual handsome pictures. The importance of keeping a promise, even to a frog, is emphasized in the story of "The Frog Prince" (134). The princess did not relish sharing her little gold plate with the frog, or her bed, but her father made her honor her promise to do so when the frog retrieved her golden ball from the fountain. When the petulant princess threw the frog against the wall, she broke his enchantment and a handsome prince emerged. Of course they were married and lived happily ever after.

Wicked enchantments and magical transformations are typical of German folktales. Seven boys are changed into *The Seven Ravens* (127, 128) by the curse of their father when they break a jug of water which was to be used to christen their new baby sister. When the sister is old enough to realize what has happened, she sets off for the glass mountain to find them. Coming at last to a locked door, she must cut off her finger in order to pass through. There she is able to release her brothers. "The Six Swans" (108) is a story of treachery and true faithfulness. A king's sons are turned into swans by a wicked stepmother. The price for their transformation is difficult, indeed, for their sister must make them six shirts from star flowers and she may neither laugh nor speak for six years. A king falls in love with her and marries her with the hope that she will speak. She is cruelly tricked by his mother and sentenced to burn at the stake. Just as the fire is about to be lit, the swan brothers appear. She throws the little shirts over them and they are transformed into men, except for one brother whose shirt was not quite finished; he has a swan wing for the rest of his life. Margot Tomes has illustrated this (83), and other Grimm tales told by Wanda Gág in small-size books with old-fashioned-looking sepia-toned and black line drawings. It was from this tale that Hans Christian Andersen took the inspiration for this complex literary tale, *The Wild Swans*, which has been stunningly portrayed by Susan Jeffers (4).

While Walt Disney may be credited with making "Snow White" the best known of fairy tales today, he is also responsible for having bowdlerized it to such an extent that the Grimm brothers would not recognize it. The Disney dwarfs are cute little men with names that came out of the Disney Studio rather than the Black Forest. Snow White is a sweet teenager who dances with the dwarfs and makes them wash before supper! For over thirty years no one challenged this Disney interpretation, until Nancy Burkert (132) created a beautifully illustrated edition translated by Randall Jarrell. Burkert used her own daughter as the model for Snow White, a beautiful 14-year-old girl, not a child, but not yet a woman. Weeks of medical library research revealed the characteristic proportions of dwarfs, and so Burkert drew not funny grotesque elves but real people, who look at Snow White with love and pride in their eyes. The medieval cottage of the dwarfs is authentic: every architectural detail, the rich fabrics on the walls, the braided floor mat, the very plates and mugs on the table were copied from museum pieces. Snow White herself wears a headdress borrowed from an Albrecht Dürer portrait. The white dog, basket of cherries, and the lilies on the table all signify virginity, while the meadow rue that is embroidered on Snow White's apron was believed to have been a protection against witches. No detail has been overlooked in creating this authentic beautiful scene. Disney used the storyteller's prerogative in adding a "Sleeping Beauty" ending to his story, with Snow White being awakened by the kiss of the prince. Randall Jarrell was true to Grimm's story, in which the apple that had become lodged in the heroine's throat was shaken free when the prince carried her off to Italy. For the climax Burkert has painted a triumphal judgment scene. The white dog stands with his tail between his legs as he looks down the long flight of stairs where the jealous queen was taken after she had danced to her doom in red-hot slippers. Snow White and her prince ascend the stairs to their future paradise. Perhaps such a book restores the dignity, the beauty, and symbolic meaning to the story of *Snow White and the Seven Dwarfs*. Another edition of *Snow White* (131) has been faithfully translated by Paul Heins and illustrated by Trina Hyman with more robust, romantic pictures than the symbolic ones of Burkert. In this version the artist skillfully portrays the ravaging effects of the queen's jealous madness through the expressions on her face.

The German *Cinderella* (106) is a somber, gruesome tale. There is no fairy godmother in this version; rather, the little ash girl goes to her mother's grave beneath the hazel tree and a white dove grants her every wish. The stepsisters and stepmother tease the poor girl unmercifully as they throw peas into the ashes and then promise her she can go to the dance if she will pick them out. The eldest stepsister cuts her toe off, trying to fit her foot to the golden slipper, while the second stepsister mutilates her heel. At the wedding of Cinderella to the king's son, the two false sisters are blinded by birds who peck out their eyes.

While there is little mercy for the wicked in these German tales, there is much joy for the righteous. The plots are exciting, fast-moving, and a little frightening. Evil stepmothers, wicked witches, and an occasional mean dwarf hold princes and princesses in magical enchantments that can be broken only by kindness and love. Such were the dreams and wishes of the common folk of Germany when the Grimm brothers recorded their tales.

SCANDINAVIAN FOLKTALES

Most of the Scandinavian folktales are from the single Norwegian collection titled *East of the Sun and West of the Moon*. These stories were gathered in the early 1840s by Peter Christian Asbjørnsen and Jorgen Moe. They rank in popularity with Grimm's fairy tales and for the same reason; they were written down in the vigorous language of the storyteller. Ten years after the publication of these tales in Norway, they were ably translated by an Englishman, George Dasent, and made available to the English-speaking world (8).

Perhaps the best known of all of these stories is *The Three Billy Goats Gruff* (10) who "trip-trapped" across the troll's bridge to eat the green grass on the other side. It is the perfect example of folktale structure: the use of three billy goats, the increasing size of each one, and the anticipated downfall of the mean old troll. Fast action and an economy of words lead directly to the storyteller's conventional ending:

> Snip, snap, snout
> This tale's told out.

Marcia Brown's matchless picture-book version is faithful to the Norwegian origin of this tale in both the setting for her lively illustrations and in the text. Paul Galdone's picture book (93), showing large close-up illustrations of the goats and the troll, will appeal particularly to the younger child.

Two very funny Norwegian folktales deserve to be told together, for they complement each other. One, "Gudbrand on the Hillside" (11), tells of the contented wife who thinks everything her husband does is fine. One miserable day things go wrong for him—he sets out to buy a cow and trades it for one thing after another until he has nothing left, but still certain of his wife's infinite faith in his judgment, he bets his neighbor that she will not say a word against him. The good woman does not disappoint him and he wins his bet. Wanda Gág's *Gone Is Gone* (81) presents a bragging husband who tells his wife how hard he works while she just "putters and potters about the house." His wife suggests that they trade places; he can take care of the house and she'll do his work in the field. The next day is an utter disaster for the husband and he never again says that his work is harder than his wife's!

The Norwegians tell of a Cinderlad, rather than a Cinderella, in "The Maid on the Glass Mountain" (11). In it, a brave youngest son guards a hayfield and captures three horses on three successive nights. With these, he is able to ride up a glass hill, obtain three golden apples, and win the hand of a beautiful princess.

Just as determined as Cinderlad is "The Lad Who Went to the North Wind" (9) and complains about the Wind blowing the grain out of his hand. The gruff North Wind then gives the boy a magic table cloth that will spread and serve a full meal. Unfortunately, he shows it to an innkeeper, who steals it; the brave lad goes back to the North Wind and receives a ram that will make gold coins. Again he is robbed but the North Wind gives him a stick that will beat persons on command. When the innkeeper steals that, he is so beaten that he agrees to return all, and the boy proceeds homeward with his gifts.

The title story of *East O' the Sun and West O' the Moon* (8) is a complex tale that is similar to the French "Beauty and the Beast" (183) and the Scottish "Black Bull of Norroway" (249). In this tale a poor man gives his youngest daughter to a white bear, who promises to make the family rich. The white bear comes to her every night and throws off his beast shape, but he leaves before dawn so she never sees him. When her mother tells her to light a candle and look into his face, she sees a handsome prince, but three hot drops of tallow awaken him. Then he tells her of his wicked enchantment in which for one year he must be a bear by day. Now that she has seen him, he must return to the castle which lies east of the sun and west of the moon and marry the princess with a

long nose. So the girl seeks the castle, finally arriving there on the back of the North Wind. Before the prince will marry, he sets one condition: he will only marry the one who can wash out the tallow spots on his shirt. Neither his long-nose bride-to-be nor an old hag can do it, but the girl who has posed as a beggar can wash it white as the snow. The wicked trolls burst and the prince and princess marry and leave the castle that lies east of the sun and west of the moon.

Kathleen and Michael Hague's retelling of *East of the Sun and West of the Moon* (140) follows the original structure of the story faithfully. However, Mercer Mayer's version (201) is really a fabricated variation in which an enchanted frog-prince is carried away. Instead of the girl going to each of the winds, she travels to a giant salamander, a forest unicorn, and so forth. While the Mayer illustrations are more compelling than the scenes portrayed by Michael Hague, teachers may well wish to read aloud the original version (8) and let children's imaginations make their own images.

In many of the Norwegian tales the hero is aided in the accomplishment of seemingly impossible tasks by animals that he has been kind to. For example, in "The Giant Who Had No Heart in His Body" (9), a raven, a salmon, and a wolf all help to find the giant's heart. Then Boots squeezes it and forces the giant to restore to life his six brothers and their wives who had been turned to stone. In "Lord Per" (11), the Norwegian "Puss in Boots," the cat presents the king with the gifts of a reindeer, a stag, an elk, and a troll's castle. Then she asks him to cut off her head. When he reluctantly does, she becomes a lovely princess and he makes her his queen.

Scandinavian tales, then, seem to reflect the harsh elements of the northern climate. Wild animal helpmates (and horses) assist heroes in overcoming giants or wicked trolls. Frequently, they are human beings who are held by an evil spell. The Scandinavian tales, characterized by many trolls, magic objects, and enchantments, often are also humorous, exciting, and fast-moving. The youngest son performs impossible tasks with ease and a kind of practical resourcefulness.

FRENCH FOLKTALES

French folktales were the earliest to be recorded, and they are also the most sophisticated and adult. This is probably because these tales were the rage among the court society of Louis XIV. In 1697 Charles Perrault, a distinguished member of the French Academy, published a little volume of fairy tales. The title page bore no name and there has been some debate as to whether they were the product of Charles Perrault or his son, Pierre. While the stories were probably very close to the ones told Pierre by his governess, they have the consciously elegant style of the "literary tale" rather than the "told tale" of the Grimms. Eight of these stories, first translated into English in 1729, have been retold by John Bierhorst in *The Glass Slipper* (214). Mitchell Miller's illustrations present often grotesque characterizations with much attention to period detail. From Perrault's collection, certainly "Cinderella," "Red Riding Hood," "Puss in Boots," and "Sleeping Beauty" are very much entrenched in English folklore.

The godmother in Cinderella is Perrault's invention, as are the pumpkin coach, the six horses of dappled mouse gray, and the glass slipper. In this French version Cinderella is kind and forgiving of her two stepsisters, inviting them to live at the palace with her. Marcia Brown was faithful to both the French setting and original text in her Caldecott award-winning book *Cinderella* (212). Ethereal illustrations in delicate blues and pinks portray the splendid palace scenes. Cinderella's stepsisters are haughty and homely, but hardly cruel. Another beautiful picture-book rendition of *Cinderella* has been created by Errol Le Cain (213). The rich, lavish illustrations are interesting to compare with Brown's delicate ones. Paul Galdone has also illustrated a colorful and humorous version for younger children (85).

The sister story to "Cinderella" is the well-known "Sleeping Beauty." The opening suggests that this is not a story told for peasants but one to be enjoyed by a wealthy and traveled society:

> Once upon a time there were a king and a queen who were very unhappy that they did not have any children, so unhappy that it can hardly be expressed. They went to all the watering places in the world, tried vows, pilgrimages, and acts of devotion but nothing would do. Finally, however, the queen did become pregnant and gave birth to a daughter.[42]

[42]Charles Perrault, "Sleeping Beauty" in *The Twelve Dancing Princesses and Other Fairy Tales,* edited by Alfred David and Mary Elizabeth David (New York: New American Library, 1964), p. 125.

It is interesting to compare the wishes that the fairies gave to the newborn baby. In the German tale they endow Briar Rose with virtue, beauty, riches, and "everything in the world she could wish for"; in the French version they bestow her with beauty, an angelic disposition, the abilities to dance, sing, and play music. In both versions the jealous uninvited fairy predicts the child will prick her finger on a spindle and die. This wish is softened by the last fairy who changes it to the long sleep of a hundred years to be broken by the kiss of a prince.

Several beautiful picture-book editions of "Sleeping Beauty" have been published. An English illustrator, Warwick Hutton, has presented the Grimm version in delicate watercolors (129). Another English artist, Errol Le Cain went to the Brothers Grimm for his retelling of the German *Thorn Rose or The Sleeping Beauty* (135). His rich, opulent pictures give the impression of early German paintings and royal tapestries. One wishes that his retelling of the tale might have been as rich as his illustrations. Trina Hyman has painted robust romantic scenes for her interpretation of *The Sleeping Beauty* (130). Her many close-up pictures of the characters place the reader in the midst of the scenes rather than providing the distancing and mystical mood of the others. All are beautiful books, and children's appreciation for them would be enriched by contrasting them.

Marcia Brown's *Puss in Boots* (215) is French from the tip of the feathered plume in his hat to the toes of his grand boots. While he was the only inheritance of the youngest son of a poor miller, he proved to be a very rich inheritance indeed. Each day "Puss" sent fresh vegetables, a hare, or pheasant to the king, telling him that they were from an imaginary Marquis of Carabas, his master. Dashing ahead of the royal carriage, the cat tells the peasants to say the land belongs to the Marquis of Carabas or he will make mincemeat of them. Reaching a castle, he tricks the ogre into changing into a mouse, which he promptly eats. The castle then becomes his master's, and Puss remains the dashing hero in boots and plumed hat. Children would enjoy comparing Marcia Brown's lavishly dressed French Puss with Paul Galdone's swashbuckler (92) or the fierce adventurer of Tony Ross (226).

Adrienne Adams has created a beautiful single-tale edition of the French story, *The Twelve Danc-*

In these contrasting interpretations, Tony Ross portrays *Puss in Boots* as a jaunty adventurer while Marcia Brown's dapper *Puss in Boots* could step into a French court.

ing Princesses (184). The mystery of how the twelve lovely princesses who are locked in their rooms each night wear out their dancing slippers is discovered by a gardener's helper. Although he is entitled to marry one of the princesses, he will not do so until the youngest proclaims her love for him. Then the mysterious enchantment is broken and the princes who had been the dancing partners of the lovely ladies are freed to become their husbands. Both Errol Le Cain (137) and Laszlo Gál (192) have created striking versions of this tale also told by Grimm. Le Cain's ornately bordered pictures portray a very French court observed by a poor soldier. Gál uses soft colors to portray a faraway kingdom populated by almost contemporary-looking royalty.

The best-known French wonder tale, other than those by Perrault, is *Beauty and the Beast* (149), adapted from a long story written by a Madame de Beaumont in 1757. Diane Goode (62) has retold this tale for today's children in spare prose and has provided romantic illustrations of the girl who preferred "virtue to beauty and wit." Goode's lion-maned beast contrasts with the cat like beast of Mercer Mayer's version (200). Mayer attracts the reader's eye by his use of gnarled and tortured forest backdrops and his ornately decorated interiors. A third version, illustrated by Errol Le Cain (149), reflects the tale's French origins with its tapestry borders and the elegant French court costumes of the characters. A version by Warwick Hutton (169) features watercolor illustrations that make stunning use of light and deep shadow to tell this story of a girl who "loved character instead of looks." An overwritten and dialogue-ridden edition has been retold by Deborah Apy and illustrated by Michael Hague (5). While the Hague illustrations may draw children's attention, the other four editions capture the story's essence in far better prose.

The folktales of France were not the tales of the poor but those of the rich. They have all the trappings of the traditional fairy tale, including fairy godmothers, stepsisters, and handsome princes. Tales of romance and sophisticated intrigue, they must surely have been the "soap operas" of their day.

RUSSIAN FOLKTALES

Russian folktales reflect universal folklore patterns with many stories of tasks and trials, transformations, and tricksters. However, the Russian tales are longer and more complicated than those of other countries and frequently involve several sets of tasks, as in "Ivan Tsarevitch, the Grey Wolf, and the Firebird" (45). This story begins with three sons being charged to find the thief who steals the golden apple from a certain tree. The youngest, Ivan, gets the feathers of the firebird and sets out to find it. He is kind to a wolf which later reciprocates this help. However, each time the boy has a task, he disregards the wolf's advice and has an even more difficult task assigned. Finally, on the completion of all the tasks, including obtaining the firebird, the beautiful princess Elena, and the horse with the golden mane, Ivan is murdered by his two brothers who wish to obtain Ivan's reward from their father. Thirty days later his friend the gray wolf finds Ivan and with the help of a crow restores him to life. Ivan arrives at the palace just in time to prevent the marriage of Princess Elena to his evil brother.

In *The Little Humpbacked Horse* (162), a horse rather than a wolf advises his young and foolish master. Ivan must capture a firebird, win a princess, and pass through boiling water. The hot water makes Ivan even more handsome. So the young tsarevna tricks the old tsar into jumping in, the tsar dies, and Ivan and his princess marry and rule happily ever after. A picture-book version of *The Fire Bird* (27) has glowing illustrations by Toma Bogdanovic. Rich in color and design, these pictures beautifully complement this well-loved Russian tale. The firebird theme runs throughout Russian folklore and was the inspiration for Stravinsky's "Firebird" music. Middle-grade children would enjoy both the story and the exciting music.

There is a grim, frightening aspect to many of the Russian tales. For example, *Vasilisa the Beautiful* (272) is the Russian counterpart to Cinderella. But in this tale Vasilisa is sent to the wicked witch Baba Yaga to obtain a light for her stepsister who hopes that the witch will eat Vasilisa up. Ever protected by the little doll Vasilisa's mother had given her before she died, Vasilisa carries the light home in a human skull. Upon her return, the intensity of the light's rays consumes her stepmother and stepsister. A light and humorous variation on this tale, written for beginning readers by Joanna Cole, is *Bony-Legs* (50), another name for Baba Yaga. In the story, little Sasha meets the witch, who lives in a house that stands on chicken legs. Due to Sasha's kindness to a cat, a dog, and a squeaky gate, she is able to escape being eaten by Bony-Legs and returns home safely. Maida Silverman's *Anna and the Seven Swans* (242) is yet another story of a child's escape from being eaten by Baba Yaga. While Anna runs to find her wandering little brother, she pauses to pull cherry dumplings from a pleading oven and to bail milk from a river that is about to overflow its jelly banks. Later, those she has helped aid her in hiding from Baba Yaga's eye. David Small's opaque watercolors are overset with brown line which gives a northern but not wintry look to this adapted Russian tale.

Koshchei, the Deathless One, is another evil character in Russian folklore. In the complex tale of "Marya Moryevna" (271) Prince Ivan disobeys his wife Marya and opens a closet only to find Koshchei, the Deathless, shackled by twelve chains. He takes pity on him and gives him water to drink, which restores Koshchei's strength and enables him to escape. After a long chase and a series of trials, Ivan and Koshchei have a grim fight and the Deathless One is finally killed:

> [Koshchei] jumped to the ground and tried to slash him with a saber. But Prince Ivan's steed kicked Koshchei the Deathless, smashing his head, and the prince finished him off with a club. Then Prince Ivan placed a pile of firewood on top of him, lighted it and Koshchei the Deathless was burned up. Prince Ivan scattered his ashes in the wind.[43]

This and three other tales have been included in a beautiful edition of Russian fairy tales edited by Jacqueline Onassis (209).

[43]Thomas P. Whitney, translator, *In a Certain Kingdom*, illustrated by Dieter Lange (New York: Macmillan, 1972), p. 120.

Cumulative tales have delighted children all over the world. Tolstoy retold the old Russian folktale that emphasizes the theme of cooperation in pulling out *The Great Big Enormous Turnip* (258). The old man did not know that when he planted his turnip and told it to grow sweet and strong that it would do both! The story tells how it required the old man, the old woman, her granddaughter, the dog, the cat, and the mouse to pull the turnip out. Helen Oxenbury's illustrations show a very English family pulling up the turnip. She portrays the struggle from several vantage points—the side, the rear, even a bird's-eye view looking down on the family. The tale is superb for story-telling and dramátization.

A variant on the cumulative tale of the gingerbread boy is *The Bun: A Tale from Russia* (31), illustrated by Marcia Brown. A more frightening cumulative story is about *The Clay Pot Boy* (174), who gobbles up the childless couple that created him and everything else in his way. Lobel portrays the "boy" as a rather rounded monster that grows larger and larger as he goes on his voracious path. Finally he is stopped by a little goat that butts him to pieces. This story, which suggests humanity may be destroyed by that which it creates, has many implications for the twentieth century.

A well-loved Slavic tale personifying the seasons is *The Month-Brothers* (199), illustrated in stunning watercolors by Diane Stanley. A girl is told by her stingy stepmother to go out into the winter snow and not to return until she has gathered snowdrops for her stepsister's birthday. Faced with an impossible task, she comes upon the twelve months of the year all gathered about a fire in the forest. January and February agree to give the youngest month-brother, March, one hour to create a forest floor dappled with snowdrops, and the girl is able to complete her task. However, the greedy stepmother now sends her own spoiled daughter out into the snow to demand special summer food to sell in the wintertime market. The rude girl accosts the month-brothers and is finally frozen in snow by old January. Her greedy mother also perishes while out looking for her daughter. The first girl grows up to raise a family and a wonderful garden, and it is said that she has all the months of the year as guests. While January and February are represented as old men, March is a

Diane Stanley captures a moment of hope for the unfortunate little sister sent into a January storm to gather snowdrops in the Bohemian tale, *The Month-Brothers* by Samuel Marshak.

young boy, reflecting rural people's belief that the year of growing really begins in March.

Another well-loved Russian folktale, *My Mother Is the Most Beautiful Woman in the World* by Reyher (221), contains the universal truth that beauty is in the eye of the beholder. When Varya falls asleep in the wheat fields, she is separated from her mother. Exhausted and crying, she will only say that her mother is the most beautiful woman in the world. After the townsfolk have called all the local beauties together for Varya's inspection, a large toothless woman pushes her way through the crowd to embrace her daughter. Varya had proved the old Russian proverb: We do not love people because they are beautiful, but they seem beautiful to us because we love them.

Russian peasants enjoyed telling their children stories in which the common people succeeded or got the best of their generals and tsars. Uri Shulevitz has illustrated two handsome picture books that glorify the underdog. In *Soldier and Tsar in the Forest* (241), a simple soldier saves a helpless tsar who has become lost in the woods on a hunting trip. *The Fool of the World and the Flying Ship* (219) follows the typical pattern of the youngest son who, with the help of his eight companions, each of whom has a magical power, outwits a treacherous tsar and wins the princess for himself. Magnificent pictures capture the sweep of the Russian countryside and the richness of the tsar's palace, in contrast to the humble huts and dress of the peasants. This book received the Caldecott award.

Russian folklore is replete with stories of fools and noodleheads. Ivan is a clever fool in the Russian tale *Salt* (284) by Harve Zemach. In this well-illustrated single tale, a wealthy merchant gives each of his three sons a ship and cargo to trade in foreign lands. Only Ivan, "the fool," makes his fortune and wins the princess, much to his father's amazement.

The title story of *Three Rolls and One Doughnut* (98) is a lovely noodlehead tale. A peasant walks a long way from his village to the city and is very hungry. He buys one roll, but he is still hungry. He buys another, and another; finally he buys a doughnut and he is no longer hungry.

> "Ah," he clapped himself on the forehead. "What a fool I was to have wasted all that good money on rolls. I should have bought a doughnut to begin with!"[44]

The same collection contains the story "Hatchet Gruel," which is similar to the Swedish *Nail Soup* (283) and the French *Stone Soup* (33). In the Russian version a soldier asks an old woman for a bite of food. "The old woman was rich and stingy. She was so stingy that she would not give you a piece of ice in winter."[45] The enterprising soldier teaches her to make a delicious gruel by boiling an old hatchet; though at his suggestion she adds salt, a handful of oats, and a spoonful of butter! And so the Russian tales celebrate the cleverness of the

peasant and his gullibility. Their wry humor balances the dark grim tales of evil enchantments and horrendous punishments.

JEWISH FOLKTALES

Only recently have Jewish folktales been made available for children in written form. In *Zlateh the Goat* (246) and *When Shlemiel Went to Warsaw* (245), Isaac Bashevis Singer has told warm, humorous stories based on the Yiddish tradition and his own childhood memories. Here are tales of the amiable fools of Chelm (that fabled village where only fools live), lazy Shlemiels, and shrewd poor peasants who outwit rich misers. In Chelm the wise elders are the most foolish of all, and their "solutions" to people's problems make for some hilarious stories. One night they plan to gather the pearls and diamonds of the sparkling snow so the jewels could be sold for money. Worrying about how they might prevent the villagers from trampling the snow, they decide to send a messenger to each house to tell the people to stay inside. But then the "wise elders" realize the messenger's feet will spoil the snow, so their solution is to have him carried on a table supported by four men so that he will not make any footprints as he goes from house to house!

The story of "Shrewd Todie and Lyzer the Miser" (245) is a delightful tale of chicanery in another book by Singer. Todie repeatedly borrows a silver tablespoon from Lyzer and returns it along with the gift of a silver teaspoon, saying that the tablespoon had given birth to the teaspoon. When Todie then asks to borrow some silver candlesticks, Lyzer, eager to increase his wealth, presses eight of them on Todie, who immediately sells them. When Todie does not return them, saying that the "candlesticks died," Lyzer swears that candlesticks cannot die and calls the rabbi for advice. The rabbi hears both sides and then tells Lyzer the miser that if he believes spoons can give birth, then he must accept the "fact" that candlesticks can die! This same tale is told in a slightly different version in the story called "The Borrower" (236) in *Let's Steal the Moon*, a collection of Jewish tales by Serwer. The title story of this book relates to the time the foolish people of Chelm decided to capture the moon in a barrel of water in order to save it for a dark night.

[44]Mirra Ginsburg, *Three Rolls and One Doughnut: Fables from Russia*, illustrated by Anita Lobel (New York: Dial, 1970), p. 7.
[45]Ginsburg, *Three Rolls and One Doughnut*, pp. 25, 26.

Zemach's lively pictures almost shout the utter confusion of the farmer's overcrowded hut in *It Could Always Be Worse.*

In *It Could Always Be Worse* (288), Margot Zemach has told the familiar tale of the poor farmer whose house is so crowded that he seeks the rabbi's advice. Following the rabbi's wise counsel, the farmer brings first one animal after another into the house until the noise and confusion become unbearable; then the rabbi advises their removal, and the house appears to be very large and peaceful. Zemach has created a humorous version of this tale with large robust pictures that seem to swarm with squalling children, rambunctious animals, and horrified adults. Marilyn Hirsch has also told this story in her picture book *Could Anything Be Worse?* (160).

A matchless picture book, also illustrated by

Margot Zemach, is *Mazel and Shlimazel, or the Milk of a Lioness* (244) by Isaac Singer. This is a long, complicated story of a wager between Mazel, the spirit of Good Luck, and Shlimazel, the spirit of Bad Luck, and Tam, a poor peasant lad who is the subject of their bet. The two spirits work their influences, and Tam is nearly hanged before Good Luck gets Bad Luck drunk on the wine of forgetfulness and comes to Tam's rescue. But Tam learns that "good luck follows those who are diligent, honest, sincere, and helpful to others."[46] Using thick black lines and muted royal colors in a

[46]Isaac Bashevis Singer, *Mazel and Schlimazel, or the Milk of a Lioness,* illustrated by Margot Zemach (New York: Farrar, Straus, 1967), p. 42.

variety of patterns, Zemach has contrasted rich scenes of Byzantine Russian palaces with poor peasant huts crowded together in miserable little villages. In almost every picture one can find the joyful figure of Good Luck watching over his special charge. On the last page we see just his jaunty back as he goes on his merry way.

In pictures and text adapted from a Yiddish story by I. L. Peretz, *The Magician* (240), Uri Shulevitz illustrates the legend telling how Elijah in the guise of a magician appears in a village on the eve of Passover and conjures a feast for a desperately poor couple who have nothing to eat. Another Hebrew legend, *Elijah the Slave* (243), has been retold by Isaac Singer and magnificently illustrated by Antonio Frasconi. In this story Elijah, a messenger from God, sells himself as a slave in order to help a poor faithful scribe. The pictures appear to have been made from woodcuts and then cut out and pasted on radiant backgrounds. The effect is breathtaking and reminiscent of medieval art.

These Jewish tales have a poignancy, wit, and ironic humor that is not matched by any other folklore. Many of them have been preserved by the masterful writing of Isaac Bashevis Singer, who has retained the flavor of both the oral tradition and the Yiddish origin.

FOLKTALES OF THE EAST

To describe the folktales of the Near Eastern countries, India and Indonesia, and the Orient would take several books, for this area was the cradle of civilization and the birthplace of many of our stories. Unfortunately, these tales are not as well known in the United States as they deserve to be. Rather than confuse the reader with a description of many unfamiliar stories, only those tales or books that might serve as an introduction to the folklore of these countries will be discussed.

Armenian folktales usually have the formal beginning *Once There Was and Was Not* and end with the traditional phrase *Three Apples Fell from Heaven:* one for the teller, one for the listener, and one for the peoples of the world. Two fine collections of Armenian tales by Virginia Tashjian derive their titles from these traditional beginnings and endings (255, 256). Nonny Hogrogian has created superb humorous illustrations that reflect the folk wisdom of the stories. The tale of "The Enormous Genie" (256) reminds one of the Norwegian story, "The Lad Who Went to the North Wind" (9), while the story of "The Miller-King" (255) is a variant of "Puss in Boots" (92). In this Armenian version, however, the helpful animal who boasts of his master's wealth and then proceeds to get it for him is a fox that a miller let out of a trap. In Hogrogian's Caldecott award-winner *One Fine Day* (164) an old woman catches a fox licking up her pail of milk and she cuts off his tail. She agrees to sew it back on only when he replaces the milk, which proves a difficult task. The matchless simplicity of Hogrogian's drawings is perfect for the rustic humor found in most of these folktales.

The Hodja stories are known throughout the Middle East, the Balkans, and Greece. Nasreddin Hodja was thought to have lived several hundred years ago in Turkey, where he served as a religious leader, teacher, or judge as the occasion demanded. He could be wise or he could be foolish, but he was always able to laugh at himself. The wisdom of Hodja is seen in the way he settles disputes between villagers. One day he watches a woodcutter chopping trees while his companion rests nearby (269). Every time the axe falls, however, the companion groans helpfully. When the woodcutter finishes and sells his load of wood at the bazaar, his companion demands half of the pay. The Hodja carefully listens to both sides of the case and then, taking each of the coins, he drops them on the stone:

> As they rang out with a pleasant jingle he said to the companion, "Do you hear this?"
>
> "Yes," the companion answered.
>
> "Fine," said the Hoca [Hodja]. "The *sound* is yours, and the *coin* is the woodcutter's."[47]

The foolishness of the Hodja is seen in this typical Hodja story (70):

> One day a friend came up to the Hodja with an egg hidden in his hand.
>
> "Hodja," he said, "if you guess what I've got in my hand, I'll treat you to an omelette. An *omelette*."
>
> "Give me a clue," said the Hodja.

[47]Barbara K. Walker, *Watermelons, Walnuts and the Wisdom of Allah and Other Tales of the Hoca*, illustrated by Harold Berson (New York: Parents', 1967), p. 36.

"It's white on the outside, and yellow in the middle."

"I know, I know!" cried the Hodja. "It's a turnip with a carrot inside!"[48]

Just Say Hic! (268) (pronounced "heech") is an amusing Turkish folktale in picture-book form that follows the "Lazy Jack" (249) pattern. However, instead of carrying something in the right way at the wrong time, this boy always says the right thing at the wrong time. Sent by his master to buy some salt, the servant boy, Hasan, repeats the word for salt, "Hic, hic, hic." In Turkey, "hic" also means "nothing." He repeats the word as he watches a fisherman, who tells him to say, "May there be five or ten of them" instead of "nothing." He then repeats *this* phrase as he sees a funeral procession! And so it goes, as Hasan creates comic scenes with his right phrases in the wrong places.

In *Two Pairs of Shoes* (262), P. L. Travers has retold two stories in which old, tattered shoes play an important part. "Abu Kassem's Slippers" belong to a penny-pinching merchant who refuses to part with them even though they are wholly inappropriate for a man of his stature. Each attempt to get rid of the shoes brings Abu Kassem more misfortune and even stiff fines from the local officials. Finally, Abu Kassem begs the Cadi to take them; the Cadi consents but counsels that nothing lasts forever and when a thing is no longer useful, it should be relinquished. "The Sandals of Ayez" are kept by a trusted servant of the king to remind him of his former days in poverty. However, jealous courtiers are convinced that behind the locked door lies treasure which Ayez is stealing from his king. When they force open the door, they see only worthless old sandals and a worn sheepskin jacket. But the king understands and rewards his friend who wished to remember and be faithful to his original self. Leo and Diane Dillon frame their richly colored illustrations in hand-decorated and marbleized paper which adds to the elegant look of this book.

Errol Le Cain has illustrated *Aladdin* (181), a well-known tale from the *Arabian Nights* which was first published in 1712. Le Cain portrays Aladdin's adventures in the cave and later with his magic lamp in pictures that resemble Persian miniature paintings. Details, ornate borders, and interestingly patterned surfaces lend an authenticity to the illustrations for this story. Unfortunately, there are few single-tale editions of stories from this famous collection. Children usually find these tales very long and complicated, even in adapted versions by Padriac Colum (51) or Andrew Lang (182). More single stories retold and in picture-book format might introduce these tales to children once again.

Many of the tales from India are moralistic or religious in nature. The *Jataka* (Birth) tales are stories of the previous reincarnations of the Buddha. The Buddha appears as a lamb, a crane, a tiny deer, and many other animals in stories in which he always serves as a noble example. These beast tales were actually fables and always taught a moral lesson. They were known to have existed as early as the fifth century A.D. Later a guide for princes was composed as a series of moralistic animal stories known as the *Panchatantra*, literally meaning five books. These stories usually had a framing narrative leading into many other narratives that were loosely strung together. The *Panchatantra* was printed in Persia under the title *The Fables of Bidpai*. When these stories are translated into English, the morals and teaching verses are usually eliminated. Without their morals or references to the Buddha, these Indian fables become more like folktales.

One of the thirty *Jataka Tales* retold by Nancy De Roin (66) is "The Monkey and the Crocodile." The crocodile wants to eat a monkey's heart and tricks him into riding across the river where all the wonderful fruits to eat are growing. On the way across, the greedy monkey realizes that he is about to be eaten and in turn tricks the crocodile. He points to the ripe figs hanging on a tree and asks the stupid crocodile to return to shore so he can get his heart, which he has left in that tree. The crocodile obliges and the lucky monkey scampers back to his tree, chanting a verse that states what he has learned.

Marcia Brown has told the story of *The Blue Jackal* (34) that falls into an indigo vat and becomes the color of the sky. When all the animals see him they fall down in terror and awe. The jackal quickly takes advantage of the situation and announces that he has been sent from on high to

[48]Charles Downing, *Tales of the Hodja*, illustrated by William Papas (New York: Walck, 1965), p. 11.

be their king. His rule is short-lived, however, for one day when he hears the jackal's howls, he lifts up his muzzle and reveals his true self as he joins his brothers in a fierce howl. Marcia Brown's strong woodcuts and linocuts flow with the action of the story.

The animal trickster in Indian tales is the jackal, who can also be helpful, as he is in "The Tiger, the Brahman, and the Jackal" (152). In this tale, the Brahman, or wise man, lets a tiger out of his cage. The tiger promptly decides to eat his benefactor, but gives him the opportunity to ask others if the tiger is being unjust. The Brahman meets the jackal and tells him of all that has occurred. The jackal pretends to be very confused and insists on going back to the scene of the incident, where he then attempts to reconstruct it in his mind:

> "Yes! I was in the cage—no I wasn't—dear! dear! Where are my wits? Let me see— the tiger was in the Brahman, and the cage came walking by—no, that's not it either! Well, don't mind me, but begin your dinner, for I shall never understand."
>
> "Yes, you shall!" returned the tiger, in a rage at the jackal's stupidity. "I'll *make* you understand."[49]

The tiger then proceeds to demonstrate what happened, including getting back into the cage, which is precisely what the jackal intended, as he quickly shuts the door on him. This pattern of the ungrateful animal returned to captivity is also found in the black American tale "Rattlesnake's Word" (175).

"The Valiant Chattee-Maker" (152) is the funny story of a poor man who makes pots. He rides a tiger by mistake and then is credited with more courage than he feels. The story has many of the same motifs as *The Valiant Little Tailor* (138). Courlander includes an Indian "Lazy Jack" story in his collection *The Tiger's Whisker* (57). "The Boy and the Cloth" would amuse children no end. The poor boy refuses to take seven rupees offered to him for his mother's cloth because she had told him to sell it for four! Not only does this unfortunate do all the wrong things at the right times, but he says all the right things at the wrong times!

Since Indian tales were originally told to instruct the young, many of them contain a lesson, as has

been noted. "The Prince of the Six Weapons" (57) tells the story of a prince's struggle with a demon covered with long blue hair. The prince tries to kill the demon with his five weapons—bow, spear, shield, war-axe, and sword. He fails for nothing penetrates that thick blue hide. However, the prince is not frightened, for he tells the demon that he has a sixth weapon within him and that if the demon eats him, the demon will be destroyed. The weapon is knowledge. "Whenever they come together knowledge destroys evil."[50]

In *The Magic Plum Tree* (189) Freya Littledale has retold a tale similar in theme to "The Blind Men and the Elephant." A king takes each of his three sons at different seasons to see a plum tree. However, since each son views the tree at a different time, they begin to argue about whether its branches are bare, blossoming, or leafed out. Finally, the king takes all three boys to see the fruited tree. Each is incredulous; the king then reminds them that each has seen this tree with different eyes. Then, they all sit down to enjoy the ripe fruit.

Long a favorite with boys and girls in the United States, the story *Tikki Tikki Tembo* (208) is a Chinese *pourquoi* tale. When the "first and honored" son with the grand long name of Tikki-Tikki-Tembo-no-sa-rembo-chari-bari-ruchi-pipperi-pembo falls in the well, it takes so long for his brother Chang to tell someone that the elder son is nearly drowned! And that is why to this day all Chinese have short names. Young children love to repeat the rhythmical long name of the elder brother. Both the text and Blair Lent's stiff, stylized illustrations capture the tongue-in-cheek humor of the danger of too much respect!

Ed Young, a Chinese artist, has illustrated *The Emperor and the Kite* (280), a delightful story of the faithfulness of the youngest daughter of the emperor. Djeow Seow is so tiny that she is often ignored. But of all his eight children, only she attempts to help her father when he is captured and imprisoned in a high tower. Each day she sends him food in a basket attached to her kite. Finally, one day she sends up a long, strong rope which she has been patiently weaving of vines, grasses, and her own long black hair. The emperor ties it to the

---

[49]Virginia Haviland, *Favorite Fairy Tales Told in India*, illustrated by Blair Lent (Boston, Mass.: Little, Brown, 1973), p. 88.

[50]Harold Courlander, *The Tiger's Whisker and Other Tales and Legends from Asia and the Pacific*, illustrated by Enrico Arno (New York: Harcourt Brace Jovanovich, 1959), p. 57.

iron bar of his window and climbs down to kneel before his tiny daughter. The intricate illustrations, in the authentic Chinese art form of cut-paper design, are as delicate as the sensitive story. While this is not a retelling of an old tale, it does derive from a bit of Chinese history.

Ed Young has also illustrated the oldest written variant of "Cinderella," *Yeh-Shen* (191), which predates European versions by a thousand years. Yeh-Shen, left in the care of a stepmother and stepsister, is made to do the heaviest chores. Her only friend is a fish, which she feeds and talks with each day. When the stepmother kills and eats the fish,

Yeh-Shen discovers that its magic spirit still lives in the bones. Through their magic powers, she is able to go to a festival dressed in a gown, a cloak made of kingfisher feathers, and spun-gold slippers. There the suspicious stepsister causes the girl to run and she loses a slipper. Immediately, her fine clothes turn to rags. The king, however, struck with the mysterious girl's beauty, places the slipper in a roadside pavilion and hides in wait for the girl who will reclaim it. He discovers Yeh-Shen's true identity when she creeps to the pavilion and puts on the slipper. So they are married, but the unkind stepmother and her daughter are said to have been

In this oldest known version of "Cinderella," Young's use of a fish shape on every page reminds the reader of the origin of Yeh-Shen's good fortune. Illustration by Ed Young from *Yeh-Shen* by Ai-Ling Louie.

"crushed to death in a shower of flying stones." Young's authentic costumes reflect the area of China from which this story comes. Paneled pictures resemble those of folding painted screens. In addition, each shimmering pastel and watercolor illustration reminds us in shape or shadow of the contours of the magic fish. A much longer but similar version of the tale comes west by way of Vietnam in *The Brocaded Slipper* (267).

A collection of tales gathered from Chinese minority peoples indicates the diversity of sources for stories in that country. In *The Spring of Butterflies* (157), stories show how talent, common sense, and steadfast loyalty triumph over foolishness, greed, and evil. A practical princess takes to her new home as a dowry not gold and jewels but grains and seeds. A boy sacrifices his life so that his village might once again have water. In "The Wonderful Brocade" a poor old woman's embroidered farmhouse and surrounding fields come to life due to her youngest son's efforts and her own talented fingers. Her two older sons, shamed by the success of the youngest and by their own greed, are afraid to approach and walk "away and away," dragging their walking sticks. Meticulously rendered and richly detailed paintings by two Chinese artists add an exotic beauty to this collection translated by He Liyi, schoolmaster in a village school and a survivor of the Cultural Revolution.

Oriental folktales have a delicacy and quiet sedateness not found in other folklore. Even the humor is dignified and dry—and can be devastating, as seen in the story of "The Ambassador from Chi" (57). According to tradition there is bad feeling between the Prince of Chu and the Prince of Chi. However, the Prince of Chi wants to have better relations with Chu, so he sends an ambassador who is a master of diplomacy and "saving face." The Prince of Chu is determined to ridicule him at a formal banquet given for all the foreign dignitaries. The prince asks him therefore why he was chosen as the ambassador and if a more worthy citizen couldn't have been found. The ambassador from Chi gives this withering explanation:

"Oh, Prince of Chu, you see it is this way. In my country we have a guiding principle about sending ambassadors abroad. We send a good man to a state with a good ruler. To a state with a bad and vulgar ruler we send a bad and vulgar ambassador. So, as I am the most useless and worthless man in all of Chi, I was sent to the court of the Prince of Chu."[51]

Japanese folklore contains several examples of miniature people. In *Little One Inch*, Issun Boshi grows no bigger than a finger (28). When he is older, he floats to the city of Kyoto to seek his fortune. In his rice bowl boat and armed only with a sewing needle for a sword, he tricks two sorts of Japanese demons, a river *kappa* and a birdlike *tengu*. Later when he becomes the bodyguard of a human-sized daughter of a merchant, he defeats two giant *Onis* who drop their magic hammers as they run. Striking a hammer, Issun Boshi is granted one wish, and he chooses that he and the merchant's daughter might become the same size. So she joins him as another one-inch. In *Issun Boshi, the Inchling* (171), he grows to human size. In "Momotaro" (154), the small person comes floating down the river inside a peach. He grows to be a fine young man and at 15 is determined to go off to an island and destroy the demons who live there. Following the typical folktale pattern, he shares his food with three animals who join him in his quest and aid him in conquering the demons and the treasure that they had stolen. He returns home and shares his good fortune with the old couple who had been so kind to him.

One of the best-known Japanese tales is *The Crane Wife* (278), a story of the results of succumbing to poor advice and greed. Yohei, a poor peasant, removes an arrow from a wounded crane and dresses the wound. Later that night, a beautiful young woman appears at his door and asks to be his wife. Yohei accepts gladly, but as there are now two mouths to feed, the woman offers to weave cloth. Each time she weaves, she warns Yohei never to look in on her; each time she weaves, she appears exhausted and more frail. Nevertheless, the cloth she weaves is beautiful, and Yohei sells it for a high price. However, his neighbor persuades the innocent Yohei that he should sell more cloth, and at a higher price, in the city. He also inspires Yohei's curiosity— just what is

[51]Harold Courlander, *The Tiger's Whisker and Other Tales and Legends from Asia and the Pacific,* illustrated by Enrico Arno (New York: Harcourt Brace Jovanovich, 1959), p. 45.

the young woman using for thread? So he looks in on her, only to discover a crane plucking feathers from her own breast in order to weave the beautiful fabric. She can now tarry in human form no longer and away she flies. Suekichi Akaba applied water-thinned ink to textured paper to create haunting and beautiful illustrations. Her representation of a woman weaving behind opaque paper doors reveals hints of the woman's true identity—floating feathers. It would be interesting to compare this traditional tale with Molly Bang's literary use of a similar motif in *Dawn* (13), which is set in a New England seaport. The alert reader spots clues to Dawn's true identity, such as pieces of eggshell that appear under her bed where she has given birth to a daughter.

Arlene Mosel has retold the story of *The Funny Little Woman* (207) who laughs at the wicked *Oni*—demons who capture her and take her underground to cook for them. They give her a magic rice paddle which makes a potful of rice from one grain. She steals the paddle and starts to escape, but the *Oni* suck all the water into their mouths, causing the woman's boat to become mired. Her infectious giggling, however, makes them laugh, and all the water flows back into the river. She floats back to her house and becomes the richest woman in Japan by making rice cakes with her magic paddle. Blair Lent won the Caldecott award for his imaginative pictures showing the wicked green demons underground and the detailed insets of the little woman's house during the passing seasons.

Lent also illustrated *The Wave* (163) as retold by Margaret Hodges. He used intricate cardboard cuts in shades of brown and black to portray this story of the old man who sacrificed his own rice fields in order to warn the villagers of a coming tidal wave. Another version, told by Sara Cone Bryant, is illustrated with simple childlike pictures in bright colors. *The Wave* has a richness of language and a quiet dignity in both the text and illustrations that the more simplified version, *The Burning Rice Fields* (40), does not have. Children enjoy comparing these two interpretations, however.

Many Japanese tales are similar to European folktales. "The Ogre Who Built a Bridge" (265) is a Rumpelstiltskin variant with a different task and reward. A river ogre agrees to build a bridge for a well-known carpenter. If he fails to guess the ogre's name, the carpenter must give him one of his eyeballs! Luckily the carpenter comes upon a group of ogre children who are singing about "Mr. Ogre Roku" so he successfully thwarts the river ogre. When he is named, the ogre disappears into the depths of the river.

The folklore of Japan is more easily characterized than that from other parts of the Orient, perhaps because it has been more readily accessible to Westerners. Here we have stories of poor farmers, many childless couples who have their dreams fulfilled. Gentleness and kindness to others and to animals is rewarded. Respect for older persons and aged parents is a constant pattern in this folklore. Wicked *Oni* are pictured as blue, green, or red ogres. Beautiful picture-book versions of these magical tales are making them more widely available to a world audience.

FOLKTALES FROM AFRICA

Today our children are the fortunate recipients of a rich bounty of folktales collected in Africa by such well-known present-day folklorists as Harold Courlander. His collections often group tales according to content; *The King's Drum and Other African Tales* (55) presents stories that concern important members of the tribe like heroes, hunters, and sorcerers. Another part of this bounty is the many single tales that have been illustrated by noted artists. *A Story, A Story* (141) by Gail Haley won the Caldecott award in 1971; while both Gerald McDermott's brilliant graphics for *Anansi, the Spider* (194) and Blair Lent's distinguished illustrations for *Why the Sun and the Moon Live in the Sky* (60) by Dayrell made them Honor Books for their respective years.

Story-telling in Africa is a highly developed art, particularly in West Africa. These tales have a rhythm and cadence found in no other stories of the world. They ring of the oral tradition and sound as if they really are being told. They are frequently written from the point of view of the storyteller, as in this tale of "How Spider Got a Thin Waist" (7):

Many dry seasons ago, before the oldest man in our village can remember, before the rain and the dry and the rain and the dry that any of us can talk about to his children, Spider was a very big person. He did not look as he looks today, with his fat head and his fat body and his thin waist in between. Of course, he had two eyes and eight legs and he lived in a web. But none of him was thin. He was big and round, and his waistline was very fat indeed. Today, he is very different, as all of you know, and this is how it came to pass.[52]

Short sentences, frequent use of parallel constructions, repetition, and much dialogue characterize the style of many of the African tales. All these elements are apparent in the story of "Ticky-Picky Boom-Boom" (238), an Anansi story that came to us by way of Jamaica. One can almost hear the storyteller increasing his tempo as he tells of the foolish tiger who is chased by the yams that he had tried to dig out of Anansi's garden:

> Tiger began to run. The yams ran, too. Tiger began to gallop. The yams galloped, too. Tiger jumped. The yams jumped. Tiger made for Brother Dog's house as fast as he could, and he called out at the top of his voice,
> "Oh, Brother Dog, Brother Dog, hide me from the yams."
> Dog said, "All right, Tiger, hide behind me and don't say a word."
> So Tiger hid behind Dog.
> Down the road came the yams stamping on their two legs, three legs, four legs:
> "Ticky-Picky Boom-Boom
> "Ticky-Picky Boom-Boom, Boof!"[53]

In a rhythmical tale from the Antilles, *The Dancing Granny* (38) can't resist the song of Spider Ananse, pictured as a vigorous man in the illustrations. Granny Anika dances far out of sight while the clever Ananse raids her vegetable plot. Three more times Brother Ananse tricks the old lady until she gets hold of him and makes him dance with her. The story sings itself with rhythmic prose and repeated refrains. Dark grey drawings capture the movements of the dancing Granny and Brother Ananse. Eight-, 9- and 10-year-olds would love to

dramatize or move to the rhythms of this story, which has been retold and illustrated by Ashley Bryan.

Many of the African tales are about personified animals, including those tricksters Anansi the spider, Zomo the rabbit, and Ijapa the tortoise. Both Anansi and Zomo the rabbit are lazy characters who are continually tricking other animals into doing their work for them. In the story "Zomo Pays His Debts" (254), the rabbit is introduced to the reader in this way:

> Zomo the Rabbit is never a great one for work. He will tell you that he likes using his head, not his hands, but the truth is that unless he has to, he will not use either.[54]

Zomo became Brer Rabbit in the black folklore of the United States when the Hausa peoples of Africa were captured as slaves. Ijapa the tortoise has survived in the black literature of the United States as Brother Terrapin. "Like Anansi, Ijapa is shrewd (sometimes even wise), conniving, greedy, indolent, unreliable, ambitious, exhibitionist, unpredictable, aggressive, generally preposterous, and sometimes stupid."[55]

While all three of these tricksters—the spider, the hare, and the tortoise—have bad characters, one has to admire their ingenuity and wit. They are not always successful, occasionally the tricksters are tricked by someone else. In "Anansi the Spider in Search of a Fool" (39) Anansi looks for someone to do all of his work for him. Anene the Crow agrees to go fishing with him and even volunteers his help in such a way that Anansi ends up doing the work:

> "Now let me make the fish traps," said Crow. "Yes, let me. I'll show you how. You can take the fatigue of my labors."
> Spider replied, "Anene, never! Everyone knows that I'm a great weaver. Leave the trap making to me. You take the fatigue."[56]

[52]Joyce Cooper Arkhurst, *The Adventures of Spider, West African Folk Tales* (Boston, Mass.: Little Brown, 1964), p. 5.

[53]Philip M. Sherlock, *Anansi the Spider Man, Jamaican Folk Tales,* illustrated by Marcia Brown (New York: Crowell, 1954), p. 79.

[54]Hugh Sturton, *Zomo the Rabbit,* illustrated by Peter Warner (New York: Atheneum, 1966), p. 14.

[55]In "Notes on the Stories" by Harold Courlander and Ezekiel A. Eshugbayi, *Olode the Hunter and Other Tales from Nigeria* (New York: Harcourt Brace Jovanovich, 1968), p. 127.

[56]Ashley Bryan, *The Ox of the Wonderful Horns and Other African Folktales* (New York: Atheneum, 1971), pp. 6, 7.

The repetition of forms and patterns in the Dillons' pictures echo the repetition in the cumulative tale, *Why Mosquitoes Buzz in People's Ears* by Verna Aardema.

Leo and Diane Dillon won the Caldecott award for their beautifully illustrated book, *Why Mosquitoes Buzz in People's Ears* (2). In this tale the mosquito tells the iguana a tall tale that sets off a chain reaction which ends in disaster for a baby owl. Until the animals can find the culprit who is responsible for the owlet's death, Mother Owl refuses to hoot and wake the sun. King Lion holds a council and listens to everyone's excuse. Lively action words are used to tell this cumulative tale:

So it was the mosquito
who annoyed the iguana,
who frightened the python,
who scared the rabbit,
who startled the cow,
who alarmed the monkey,
who killed the owlet—
and now Mother Owl won't wake the sun
so that day can come.[57]

The cut-out effect of the stylized watercolors captures the feeling for the story and African design. These are beautiful pictures for a distinguished book. The Dillons have also illustrated Verna Aardema's humorous Masai tale, *Who's in Rabbit's House?* (3) as a play with masked actors.

African folktales are marked by a sophisticated and wry humor that delights in exposing the foibles of human nature. In a Nigerian story Seidu always boasts that he is "The Brave Man of Golo" (55). Seeing some enemy warriors, Seidu and his companions race for the nearest trees. The warriors ridicule him, and when he returns to his own village everyone there laughs at the courage of the great boaster. At last Seidu can stand it no longer and sends his wife to tell them this:

"Seidu who was formerly the bravest of men was reduced to being the bravest in his village. But from now on he is not the bravest in the village. He agrees to be only as brave as other people."[58]

A play on words is another favored form of humor in some African tales. Courlander tells the story of the very wealthy man named Time (58). Change of fortune reduces him to a beggar and persons remark that "Behold, Time isn't what it used to be!"[59] The same collection has a story about the young hunters who try to capture "The One You Don't See Coming," which is their name for sleep. In another Anansi story, there is a character named Nothing. Anansi kills him and all the villagers "cry for nothing!" (58).

Frequently, an African tale will present a dilemma and then the story-teller will invite the audience to participate in suggesting the conclusion. In the story of "Three Sons of a Chief" (55), a chief decides to test the strength of each of his sons in a contest. One son throws his spear at a baobab tree and rides his horse through the hole; the second son jumps his horse over the tree; while the third son pulls the tree up and moves it over his head. The audience is asked to decide which is the

[57]Verna Aardema, *Why Mosquitoes Buzz in People's Ears*, illustrated by Leo and Diane Dillon (New York: Dial, 1975), unpaged.

[58]Harold Courlander, *The King's Drum and Other African Tales* (New York: Harcourt Brace Jovanovich, 1962), p. 55.

[59]Harold Courlander and George Herzog, *The Cow-Tail Switch and Other West African Stories* (New York: Holt, Rinehart and Winston, 1947), p. 77.

greatest among them. The problem of which son should receive the famous Cow-Tail Switch as a reward for finding his lost father is asked in the title story of the book by Courlander (58). The boys undertake the search only after the youngest child learns to speak and asks for his father. Each of the sons has a special talent which he uses to help restore his father to life. It is then that the storyteller asks who should receive the father's cow-tail switch.

Many African stories may also be described as "why" or "how" stories. Ashley Bryan's wonderful retelling of "How the Animals Got Their Tails" is a joy to read aloud (36). Gail Haley's *A Story, A Story* (141) recounts how Anansi brought stories to humankind, while Jan Carew's *The Third Gift* (41) tells how we came to value imagination and faith.

Several African tales compare interestingly with their counterparts from other cultures, suggesting how good tales may be borrowed and adapted by storytellers of different cultures. *Nomi and the Magic Fish* (202) is a Zulu retelling of the "Cinderella" variant from China. *Akimba and the Magic Cow* (224), retold by Anne Rose, sounds very much like the Grimm story "The Table, the Ass, and the Stick." Akimba is tricked when he lends his neighbor Bumba each of his magic possessions. The cow will no longer spit gold coins when he says "Kukuku," nor will the sheep spit silver when he says "Bururu." The chicken will not lay real eggs. When the old man who has given the magical beasts to Akimba gives him a stick, all is set to rights once more. Children enjoy trying to re-create the feel of Hope Meryman's woodcut illustrations by using a printing technique with Styrofoam trays for the print plates (see Chapter 13).

Obviously, there is no dearth of folk literature from Africa. This is where oral tradition has been maintained. Children in the United States who hear these tales will be able to enter another culture, another country, and listen to the rhythmical chord of the ancient storytellers. They will learn of a land where baobab trees grow and people fear crocodiles, leopards, droughts, and famines. More importantly, they will learn something about the wishes, dreams, hopes, humor, and despair of other peoples. They may begin to see literature as the universal story of humankind.

FOLKTALES IN THE UNITED STATES

When the early settlers, immigrants, and slaves came to North America they brought their folktales with them from England, Scotland, and Ireland; from Germany, Russia, and Scandinavia; from West Africa; and China. Children in the United States are the fortunate inheritors of the folklore of the world. As these stories were told over and over again, some of them took on an unmistakable, North American flavor.

A wonderfully funny black American tale that was first recorded by the WPA in Alabama has now been retold and illustrated by Molly Bang as *Wiley and the Hairy Man* (14). Wiley and his mother have to figure out three ways to trick the little hairy monster and then by the laws of the swamp he can never bother them again. Little monsters or the huge characters of the tall tales are more representative of American folklore than the elves and fairies of Northern European origin.

Most folktales that are indigenous to the United States are those that were already here—the folklore of the American Indian and those marvelous tall tales that developed from the pioneer spirit of a young country. In discussing folktales of the United States it is impossible to describe any one body of folklore such as the Grimms discovered in Germany. However, the folklore of the United States can be placed in three large categories:

1. That which was here originally: American Indian, Eskimo, and Hawaiian.
2. That which came from other countries and was changed in the process: Black folklore and European variants.
3. That which developed: Tall tales and other Americana.

In *North American Legends* (156), Virginia Haviland has presented an anthology of tales that illustrate each of these three categories. Her excellent selection enables teachers to become acquainted quickly with common tales, motifs, and characters from each tradition.

Folktales of the Native American

To try to characterize all the folklore of the various American Indian tribes as one cohesive whole is as unreasonable as to lump all of the folklore of

Europe together. For there is as great a diversity between the folktales of the Indians of the Northwest Coast, as compared to the Eastern Woodland Indians, as there is between fierce totem poles of the one group and the delicate beadwork of the other. There are, however, some common characteristics among the various tribes and between the folklore of the Indians and some of the Northern European tales.

Many of the Indian tales are a combination of tribal lore and religious beliefs. Quite properly, some of them should be categorized as mythology, for they include creation myths and sacred legends. As with the Greek and Roman mythology, some of these tales were told as separate stories out of context of the original creation tale. Because history does not give us complete information about the religious beliefs of the individual tribes, we have put all the tales together to form an amorphous body of Indian folklore.

The very act of storytelling was considered of ceremonial importance among various tribal groups. Storytelling was done at night and among certain tribes, such as the Iroquois, it was only permitted in the winter. Men, women, and children listened reverently to stories, which in some instances were "owned" by certain tellers and could not be told by any other person. The sacred number of four is found in all Indian tales, rather than the pattern of three that is common to other folktales. Four hairs may be pulled and offered to the four winds; or the ceremonial pipe will be smoked four times; or four quests must be made before a mission will be accomplished.

The stories, when originally told, were loosely plotted rather than highly structured as were European fairy tales. Thomas Leekley, who retold some of the stories of the Chippewa and Ottawa tribes in his book *The World of Manabozho* (186), says:

> Indian folklore is a great collection of anecdotes, jokes, and fables, and storytellers constantly combined and recombined these elements in different ways. We seldom find a plotted story of the kind we know. Instead, the interest is usually in a single episode; if this is linked to another, the relationship is that of two beads on one string, seldom that of two bricks in one building.[60]

[60]Thomas B. Leekley, *The World of Manabozho: Tales of the Chippewa Indians*, illustrated by Yeffe Kimball (New York: Vanguard, 1965), pp. 7–8.

Elizabeth Cleaver has provided stunning linocut and collage pictures to illustrate the origin of *The Loon's Necklace.*

Many of the Indian tales are nature myths— "how and why" animals have certain characteristics or explanations for natural phenomena. Belting's collection, *The Long-tailed Bear* (319), is a good source for such stories as "How the Birds Came to Have Many Colors" and "How Frogs Lost Their Tails." The title story is similar to the Norse story of how the bear was tricked into using his tail for fishing in ice, where it became frozen tight. In *The Loon's Necklace* (261), the bird receives his markings as a reward for his kindness in restoring the sight of a blind old man. Elizabeth Cleaver has created stunning collage illustrations for this picture-book story of the origin of the "necklace." Several tales in the collection *The Talking Stone* (67), explain how the Winnebago people came to know "Thunderbird," who was formerly the giant Nasan; "Why Blackbird Has White Eyes," a Navajo tale; and the California Indian story of the origin of the Pleiades, "What Happened to Six Wives Who Ate Onions."

Perhaps one of the best-known stories of explanation, which combines religious beliefs, how-and-why explanations, and references to Indian custom, is "Star Boy," which has many versions.

Anna Vojtech's mysterious illustrations for *The Star Husband* (206) work well with Jane Mobley's retelling. A young woman wishes for a star husband and is granted her wish. She goes to live with him in the sky and has a boy child. She has been warned never to dig in the floor of the sky, but one day when she is bored she ignores the warning:

> Suddenly, up through the hole came a wind different from the cold, clean air of heaven. It was a wind from earth, and on it were the fresh scent of green things growing and the pungent smell of animals. On the wind was the smoke of the cooking fires of her people and the sharp odor of the holy herbs used in ceremonies.[61]

So she must leave her husband and son and return to earth, where she finishes out her life watching her star husband and her son, the moon. When she dies, she joins them in the sky world as the evening star shining close by the moon. Paul Goble has retold this tale of *Star Boy* (101) in less poetic prose but with beautiful illustrations drawn from careful references to Blackfoot artistic traditions. In this story, Star Boy, expelled from the sky world with his mother and marked with a mysterious scar because of her disobedience, becomes known as Scarface. In order to marry, he must make a journey to the Sun, who removes the scar. When this happens, Star Boy is able to marry. To commemorate and honor the Sun's gesture, the Blackfeet have a sacred Sun Dance each summer. In Goble's version, Star Boy becomes another star and joins his father, Morning Star, and his mother, Evening Star. The original George B. Grinnell retelling on which Goble built his tale may be found in Haviland's *North American Legends* (156).

Without reference to scholarship, Robert San Souci has also retold this story in *The Legend of Scarface* (229). While the illustrations by Daniel San Souci are often striking, this edition has been criticized for its eclectic and embroidered retelling of this Blackfoot tale. Still another version of this story forms the skeleton of Jamake Highwater's novel, *Anpao* (158). In the tradition of "beads on a string" rather than "bricks in a building," Highwater lets Anpao meet many traditional Indian characters like Coyote, Grandmother Spider,

Raven, and the Mouse People as he journeys to ask the sun for the removal of his scar. Parts of this novel are very humorous and would be fun to read aloud to middle-schoolers familiar with the outline of the tale.

Among the many books Paul Goble has written and illustrated, *The Girl Who Loved Wild Horses* (100) is certainly a favorite with children. Although this story does not retell a traditional Native American narrative, it synthesizes themes and motifs found among the Plains Indians. The girl of the title, from an unidentified tribe, stays near the village horses and becomes lost when the herd is stampeded by a thunderstorm. The girl's people find her at last, still with the horses, under the protection of a wild stallion who has taken them into his band. Returned to her family, she so longs for her wild companions that she is permitted to go back and live with them. Each year she visits her parents, but when these visits cease and a beautiful mare is seen beside the stallion, her people say that "the girl had surely become one of the wild horses at last." Goble has used delicate pen line and full color to give sharp focus and a sense of arrested motion to leaping horses, flying manes, and swirling clouds. Flowers, insects, and animals live in the foreground of each illustration. Goble's use of pattern and form is obviously influenced by Native American art. He has used similar techniques to tell the transformation tale of *Buffalo Woman* (99). The story emphasizes the Plains people's dependency on the buffalo and explains the relationships between the Straight-Up People and the Buffalo Nation.

Another human who becomes involved in the sky world is presented in the romantic story *The Ring in the Prairie* (233), edited by Bierhorst. Waupee transforms himself into a mouse in order to catch the youngest of the twelve princesses who come down from the sky to dance on the prairie. The youngest daughter of the stars marries Waupee and has a child, but she still yearns for her sisters in the sky. So she fashions a basket large enough for her son and herself to return to the sky. Years later, following the instructions of her father, she returns for Waupee, who is to bring back a feather, a paw, or a tail of every kind of bird and animal he kills while hunting. When Waupee presents his gifts, each of the stars is allowed to select one. They then become that animal or bird. Waupee and his wife and son select the feathers

---

[61]Jane Mobley, *The Star Husband*, illustrated by Anna Vojtech (New York: Doubleday, 1979), p. 16.

from a white hawk and together they descend to the earth. This story, originally recorded by Schoolcraft in the early 1800s, is illustrated in glowing colors by Leo and Diane Dillon. "The Red Swan" (232) is a complex, mysterious tale of transformation also recorded by Schoolcraft. This story was mentioned by Longfellow in *The Song of Hiawatha*.

Other collections by Bierhorst provide authentic tales with notes on the story sources. *The Girl Who Married a Ghost* (24) contains nine stories and is illustrated with photographs that link Indian myth to actual images. *The Whistling Skeleton* (139) presents nine other tales, all collected by George B. Grinnell. Robert Andrew Parker's shadowy black and white illustrations add an eeriness to these Native American tales of the supernatural.

Almost all tribal folklore contains various adventures of trickster figures who served as go-betweens for the sky world and earth. The kindly Glooscap of the Woodland Indians was also known as Badger. Badger's loyalty and concern for his little brother caused him to steal summer to cheer up the ill younger one. "The Year Summer Was Stolen" (159) tells of this escapade. Manabozho was a kind of half god, half superpower among the eastern tribes. But some of the stories of Manabozho picture him as less than a superhero; in fact, the story of "Sleepy Feet" (186) is a real noodlehead tale. Waiting for some rabbits to roast, Manabozho puts his feet in charge of watching them, while he goes to sleep! A canoeload of Indians comes by and quickly steals his dinner. Manabozho promptly punishes his feet by burning them because they have failed in their duty to guard his dinner! Both a rascal and a fool, cruel and admirable, Manabozho's favorite disguise is that of a hare. (His name, in fact, means "Great Hare.") He uses this shape to steal fire from the people in "The Theft of Fire" (67). The Great Plains trickster Coyote also snatches fire from the burning mountain in Hodges' *The Fire Bringer* (161), illustrated by Peter Parnall with clean line and an economy of color. To this day, says the legend, Coyote's fur is singed and yellow along his sides where the flames blew backward as he ran down the mountain carrying the burning brand.

A trickster of the Pacific Northwest is Raven. While he is a wily, crafty being who loves to get the better of others, he is also a friend to humankind, bringing fire or salmon to the people (222). Raven is typical of all trickster figures in that he is a strange blend of characteristics:

> Raven can be noble, majestic, wise and godlike. He can be powerful, brave, knowledgeable and heroic. But at the same time—often during the same story—he can be foolish and stupid, selfish and vain, deceitful and even cruel. And that is the most basic and important truth that lies within all the different Trickster tales.[62]

Christie Harris chronicles many of the Pacific Northwest Indian stories which must have been told during gatherings and potlatches—great feasts and gift exchanges among the tribes in that area—in *Once More upon a Totem* (148). One favorite tale was the story of "The Prince Who Was Taken Away by the Salmon." This story explores the mystery of the Pacific salmon, their disappearance and their return to the rivers of the West. Harris has also made fine collections of Mouse Woman stories in *Mouse Woman and the Vanished Princesses* (147), *Mouse Woman and the Mischief-Makers* (145), and *Mouse Woman and the Muddleheads* (146). Mouse Woman was a supernatural being who could appear as either a mouse or the tiniest of grandmothers. Whether it was a Narnank or a human who began the troubles, Mouse Woman missed nothing with her big, busy, mouse eyes and was determined to make everything right. The Mouse Woman stories have been illustrated by Douglas Tait in bold drawings which incorporate the beautiful decorative art so typical of the coastal tribes, with many interesting details of their clothing and textiles.

There are quest stories other than the Scarface variants. One complex Tlingit Indian story, *The Angry Moon* (247), has been retold by William Sleator and illustrated in full-color designs by Blair Lent. An Indian girl, Lapowinsa, who dared to laugh at the moon is spirited away and made his prisoner. Her friend Lupan shoots his arrows into the sky all that night. The arrows link into a ladder, which Lupan climbs into the sky country. An old grandmother gives him four gifts which enable him to impede the moon's chase as it races

---

[62]Gail Robinson, *Raven the Trickster* (New York: Atheneum, 1982), p. 11.

after Lupan and Lapowinsa. Gerald McDermott has created stunning yellow, orange, and brown graphic designs for the Pueblo quest tale *Arrow to the Sun* (195). He received the Caldecott award for his vibrant illustrations of this tale.

In order to encourage the telling of the old legends, Byrd Baylor collected Arizona Indian children's favorite stories and recorded them just as they told them. Baylor used a favorite ending for many Indian legends for the title of this interesting book, *And It Is Still That Way* (16). These recent books, all well-written, carefully researched, and attractive, also should increase children's interest in the folklore of Native Americans.

Though survival themes are constant in Indian tales, they are particularly strong in stories of the Eskimo. A powerful yet simple Eskimo tale (49) tells of Ana, a widow who goes to beg food from her brother-in-law. Instead of food her cruel sister-in-law fills her bag with three stones. Two strangers hear her tale and give her a tiny sealskin poke which, when she awakens, is filled with seal meat and blubber. And the amazing poke is always full! Glo Coalson has illustrated this fine single tale, *Three Stone Woman,* with bold black sumi brush drawings that reflect its Eskimo origin.

Tikta Liktak (166), a legendary Eskimo hunter, is isolated when an ice pan breaks away. In desperate hunger, he becomes obsessed with the idea that the island he reaches is his grave. He builds a coffin and climbs into it to die. The dreams of the past bring refreshment of spirit, and he wakens saying, "I will not die." Still living in the dream, he kills a seal and gains the strength to survive and finally to find his way home. This is a dramatic tale of courage and triumph over nature. James Houston has recorded two other superb Eskimo legends, *The White Archer* (167), and *Akavak* (165). The White Archer seeks only vengeance, but he finally succumbs to the kindness and wisdom of Ittock and his wife. Akavak helps his grandfather survive on their long and difficult journey only to see him die at the end of the trip. These tales reveal the hardships and the difficulties which are the daily pattern of the Eskimo's life. Houston, who spent many years among the Inuit people, is especially sensitive to authentic depictions of Eskimo art and culture. His sketches and drawings for many of his books are suggestive of Eskimo and Indian sculpture or carvings. His use of language reflects the rugged terrain of his settings with such comparisons as "One fell within a dog team's length of the igloo."[63]

The following table, "A Cross-Cultural Study of Folktales," provides a means of comparing characteristics, characters, collectors, and typical tales representative of specific areas.

Black Folklore in the United States

When the slaves were brought to this country from Africa, they continued to tell many African tales, particularly the talking-beast tales. Some of these stories took on new layers of meaning about the relations between the slave and his or her owner. Richard Dorson has collected over a thousand black folktales in the United States and classified them under such headings as "Animal and Bird" stories in his book *American Negro Folktales.* Julius Lester has retold several of these tales for children in his book *The Knee-high Man and Other Tales* (187), amusingly illustrated by Ralph Pinto. Some of these stories are about those favorite characters, Mr. Rabbit and Mr. Bear. Mr. Rabbit always gets the best of Mr. Bear, as in the story in which Mr. Rabbit volunteers to provide Mr. Bear with the answer to "What Is Trouble?" The story of "The Farmer and the Snake" is a realistic one of a farmer who helps a poor frozen snake and is bitten in return. The moral is a sad commentary on the nature of beast or man.

Joel Chandler Harris became interested in collecting the tales he heard black people tell in Georgia. He published these tales in 1880 under the title *Uncle Remus Stories.* The stories are transcribed in Harris' written interpretation of the dialect of the Southern Negro. Unless the dialect is simplified, these tales are almost impossible to tell and even more difficult to understand. Margaret Wise Brown prepared the simplest version in her edition titled *Brer Rabbit* (35). Rees selected three of his favorite Brer Rabbit stories and recreated them in rhyming verse in *Brer Rabbit and His Tricks* (220), including "Brer Rabbit and Tar Baby."

Courlander also includes some of "Buh

[63]See "Profile: James Houston" by Wendy K. Sutton in *Language Arts,* vol. 60 (October 1983), pp. 907–913, for excellent background on this well-known Canadian author.

A CROSS-CULTURAL STUDY OF FOLKTALES

CULTURES AND COLLECTORS	TYPICAL TALES	CHARACTERS	CHARACTERISTICS
British folktales Joseph Jacobs (1854–1916)	*The Old Woman and Her Pig* (91) *The Three Little Pigs* (94) *The Little Red Hen* (88) *Tom Tit Tot* (210) *Jack and the Beanstalk* (225) "Whippety Stourie" (273)	Mr. Vinegar Lazy Jack Giants "Wee folk" Dick Whittington	Cumulative tales for the youngest Well-loved beast tales Droll humorous stories Giant killers Simpletons
German folktales The Grimm Brothers Jacob (1785–1863) Wilhelm (1786–1859)	*Little Red Cap* (121) *The Elves and the Shoemaker* (188) *Rumpelstiltskin* (126) *Hansel and Gretel* (114) "Frog Prince" (134) *The Seven Ravens* (128) *Rapunzel* (125) *Snow-White and the Seven Dwarfs* (132)	"Clever" Elsie Tom Thumb Rumpelstiltskin Hansel and Gretel Snow White Evil witches Dwarfs and elves Bears Wolves	More somber frightening tales Some children as characters Harsh punishment (Snow White) Romances—Rapunzel, Snow White, King Thrushbeard Transformations
Scandinavian folktales Peter Christian Asbjørnsen (1812–1885) Jorgen E. Moe (1813–1882) Translated into English by George Webbe Dasent (1817–1896)	*The Three Billy Goats Gruff* (10) "Why the Sea Is Salt" (155) "Why the Bear Is Stumpy-Tailed" (155) "Gudbrand on the Hillside" (11) "The Lad Who Went to the North Wind" (9) "Princess on the Glass Hill" (155) *East O' the Sun and West O' the Moon* (8) "Lord Per" (11)	Trolls, Tomte Many-headed giants Youngest sons or "Boots" North wind White bears Salmon Cats Reindeer, elk	Tongue-in-cheek humor Some pourquoi stories Helpful animals Magic objects Magic enchantments Many trials and tasks Poor boy succeeds
French folktales Charles Perrault (1628–1703)	*Puss in Boots* (92) *Cinderella* (213) *The Sleeping Beauty* (214) *The Twelve Dancing Princesses* (137) *Beauty and the Beast* (149)	Fairy godmothers Jealous stepsisters Kings and queens Princes and princesses Courtiers	Traditional fairy tale Romance Wicked enchantments Long sleep Unselfish youngest daughter succeeds

CULTURES AND COLLECTORS	TYPICAL TALES	CHARACTERS	CHARACTERISTICS
Russian folktales Alexander Afanasyev (1855–1864)	*The Great Big Enormous Turnip* (258) *Vasilisa the Beautiful* (272) *Salt* (284) *The Fool of the World and the Flying Ship* (219) "Marya Moryevna" (271) "Ivan Tsarevitch, the Grey Wolf, and the Firebird" (42)	Fox is the trickster Vasilisa, the beautiful or the wise Ivan, the youngest brother Baba Yagas, witches Koshchei, the Deathless, an evil wizard The Firebird Wolves Bears	Ivan, the fool, triumphs Peasants and youngest brothers outwit generals and tsars Many sets of tasks and trials Quest of the firebird Helpful animals Dire punishments Frightening, bloody tales Wry humor
Japanese folktales *Little One-Inch* (28) *The Funny Little Woman* (207) *The Crane Wife* (278) *Seashore Story* (279) *The Burning Rice Fields* (40)	Inchling Momotaro, Little Peach Boy Ogres, *Oni* Goblins, *Tengu* Magic badgers, *Tanuki* Urashima	Poor farmers or fishermen Childless couples who have "different" children Cranes Magic fish Ogres	Transformation into bird Respect for the aged Kindness to animals rewarded Self-sacrifice
African folktales Harold Courlander and other present-day collectors	"How Spider Got a Thin Waist" (7) *Why the Sun and the Moon Live in the Sky* (60) "Zomo Pays His Debts" (254) "How the Animals Got Their Tails" (36) *A Story, A Story* (141) *The Cow-Tail Switch* (58)	Anansi, the Spider Zomo, the Rabbit Ijapa, the Tortoise Mama Semamingi Crocodiles Leopards	"How and why" stories Many talking beast tales Animal tricksters Small defenseless animal or man outwits others Wry humor Play on words Dilemma tales
Native American folktales Henry Rowe Schoolcraft (1820s–1850s)	*The Fire Bringer* (161) "Prince Who Was Taken Away by the Salmon" (159) *The Ring in the Prairie* (233) "Red Swan" (232) *Star Boy* (101)	Glooscap Manabozho, "The Hare" Coyote Raven Badger	Many legends and nature myths Tricksters Transformation tales Struggle for survival Use of pattern of four "How and why" stories

Rabbit's" stories in his collection of black folklore in the book *Terrapin's Pot of Sense* (56). He has preacher stories of outsmarting the devil and some variants of European and African tales. "Sharing the Crops" is the old tops and bottoms motif found in many tales. In this one, the sharecropper gets the best of the plantation owner three years in a row by first choosing the bottoms of the crops and planting potatoes; then the tops and planting oats; and finally he agrees to take just the middle of the crops and plants corn! "Old Boss, John, and the Mule" is similar to "Talk" in Courlander's *Cow-Tail Switch* (58), but much funnier somehow. John is frightened by his mule, who starts talking and saying he's going to tell the Boss how lazy John is and how badly he treats the mule. John runs home and says he is going to quit; he won't work with a talking mule. The boss goes out to get the mule and can't make him say a thing. He comes back and scolds John:

> "I'm pretty put out with you," Boss say and start on up to the house. Halfway there he shake his head, sayin', "Don't know what I'm goin' to do with that boy. Sure don't know."
>
> Right then his yellow dog speak up, sayin' "Fire him, Boss. You got no choice."[64]

In four tales of *Bo Rabbit Smart For True* (175), Priscilla Jaquith retells Gullah versions of more rabbit tales. These tales, collected from descendants of former slaves living on the Sea Islands of Georgia, reflect aspects of both African and Native American folklore tradition with their trickster rabbits. Rabbit tricks Elephant and Whale into a tug-of-war and another time tricks Rattlesnake back under his log. He, in turn, is bested by Partridge in a hiding contest. Once again, the wonderful cadences and word usage in these tales from the oral tradition make them a joy to read aloud to children. Ed Young's framed drawings, four to a page margin, give the pictures the look of still frames from an action-packed cartoon.

Virginia Hamilton has assembled a superior collection of stories representing the main body of American black folktales in *The People Could Fly* (144). Twenty-four tales are divided into four sec-

[64]Harold Courlander, *Terrapin's Pot of Sense*, illustrated by Elton Fax (New York: Holt, Rinehart and Winston, 1957), p. 89.

tions. The animal tales contain such familiar stories as "Doc Rabbit, Bruh Fox, and the Tar Baby" and a lesson to the rich folks from their poor neighbors, "Bruh Alligator Meets Trouble." Motifs of transformation, trickery, and tall tales are found in the second section, which includes a version of "Wiley, His Mama, and the Hairy Man" that would compare well with Bang's version (14). A third contains tales of Jacks and one of John de Conquer whose adventures as a mythical hero are more fully developed in Hamilton's extended folktale-like novel, *The Magical Adventures of Pretty Pearl* (143). Here, too, are tales of slaves who outwit slaveowners to win their freedom. "The Peculiar Such Thing" readers may recognize as a variation of the British "Tailypo." Another pourquoi tale, "Jack and the Devil," explains the origins of foxfire or marsh light. The final section contains slave tales of freedom, including one handed down in the author's own family. The poignant title story, a moving one of fieldhands escaping from a cruel overseer, is typical of the stories often told on "Juneteenth," the day on which black people in the South remember Emancipation. Hamilton has preserved the individual voices of the storytellers from whom the stories were collected. Some are in Gullah or plantation dialect and others include African words whose meanings are lost to us today. An excellent classroom resource, the collection contains author notes and an extensive bibliography. Bold black

Virginia Hamilton's "The People Could Fly" is a powerful testament to the many slaves who never had an opportunity to "fly away to freedom" except in their imaginations. Illustration by Leo and Diane Dillon.

and white illustrations by Leo and Diane Dillon evoke the humor, beauty, and liveliness of these traditional stories.

European Variants in the United States

Richard Chase collected and published *The Jack Tales* (47) and *Grandfather Tales* (46), which are American variations of old stories brought to this country by English, Irish, and Scottish settlers in the seventeenth and eighteenth centuries. They are as much a part of Americana as the Brer Rabbit stories. In some respects Jack is an equivalent figure to Brer Rabbit. He is a trickster hero who overcomes his opponent through quick wit and cunning, rather than the strength that triumphs in the tall tales of the United States. All of these stories come from the mountain folk of the southern Appalachians. Cut off from the main stream of immigration and changing customs, these people preserved their stories and songs in the same way that they continue to weave the Tudor rose into their fabrics.

The Jack Tales represent a cycle of stories in which Jack is always the central figure. You'd expect to find him playing this role in "Jack in the Giant's Newground" and "Jack and the Bean Tree." However, he shows up again in "Jack and the Robbers," which is a variant of *The Bremen Town Musicians* (103). The delightful aspect of these tales is Jack's nonchalance about his exploits and the incongruous mixing of the mountaineer dialect with unicorns, kings, and swords. James Still has retold the amusing Appalachian variant of "Jack and the Beanstalk" using the title *Jack and the Wonder Beans* (251). The language is rich in mountaineer dialect and colloquialisms. For example, Jack and his mother are described as being as poor as "Job's turkey," while the winter was as "cold as doorknobs." Jack describes the giant's wife as the "high tall woman" and the giant himself was: ". . . seventeen feet tall, with feet like cornsleds, hands like hams, fingernails to match bucket lids, and the meanest eye ever beheld in this earthly world."[65] Margot Tomes' illustrations of grays, blues, and browns capture the rustic simplicity of the people and their homes. Her huge giant of a man and his "high tall woman" are an appropriate contrast to the size of Jack. Gail Haley's

Jack and the Bean Tree (142) is told in dialect by the storyteller, Poppyseed, who is based on the author's grandmother. Students would enjoy comparing these Appalachian versions with the original tale to see how stories change to reflect the areas in which they are told.

Tall Tales and Other Americana

Ask any visitor to the United States what he has seen and he is apt to laugh and reply that whatever it was, it was the "biggest in the world"—the longest hot dog, the highest building, the largest store, the hottest spot. This is the land of superlatives, "the best." While many countries have tall tales in their folklore, only the United States has developed such a number of huge legendary heroes. Perhaps the vast frontier made settlers seem so puny that they felt compelled to invent stories about superheroes. Whatever the reasons, North American tall tales contain a glorious mixture of the humor, the bravado, the pioneer spirit that was needed to tame a wilderness.

Of all the heroes, only Johnny Appleseed was of a gentle, tame nature who lived to serve others. Johnny Appleseed did exist—his real name was John Chapman. Davy Crockett and Daniel Boone actually lived also, but stories about them have been embroidered or invented. They swagger, exaggerate, and play tricks, yet solve problems with good humor.

Paul Bunyan was a huge lumberjack who bossed a big gang of lumbermen in the North Woods of Michigan, Minnesota, and Wisconsin. Children will enjoy stories about his school problems, for: "Just to write his name Paul had to put five copy books one on top of the other, and even then the teacher would only see part of each letter and he would mark him wrong."[66] Paul's light lunch one day was "three sides of barbecued beef, half a wagon load of potatoes, carrots and a few other odds and ends,"[67] Glen Rounds reports in *Ol' Paul, the Mighty Logger* (228). Rounds asserts, as do most chroniclers of Paul's doings, that he worked for Paul and was the biggest liar ever in camp. By switching from past to present tense,

[65]James Still, *Jack and the Wonder Beans*, illustrated by Margot Tomes (New York: Putnam, 1977), unpaged.

[66]Roberta Strauss Feuerlecht, *The Legends of Paul Bunyan*, illustrated by Kurt Werth (New York: Macmillan, 1966), p. 17.
[67]Glen Rounds, *Ol' Paul, the Mighty Logger* (New York: Holiday, 1949), p. 28.

In *Paul Bunyan,* Steven Kellogg's fanciful endpaper map helps readers locate the sites of the lengendary logger's many exploits.

Rounds gives these eleven tales special immediacy. Esther Shephard's telling of *Paul Bunyan* (237) is somewhat windy and colloquial, but Rockwell Kent's powerful illustrations and unique capital letters intrigue children. Steven Kellogg synopsizes the life of *Paul Bunyan* (179) in his humorously illustrated picture-book version. Tidy endpapers depict Paul's New England seacoast beginnings and a United States map highlights Paul's feats. This action-packed version serves as an introduction to exploits like Paul's digging of the Great Lakes and the Grand Canyon and his famous popcorn blizzard. However, the extended text of the other versions fleshes out individual tall tales and makes them better choices for reading aloud.

What Paul Bunyan meant to the North, Pecos Bill (253) meant to the West. Bill was one of eighteen children, so his parents didn't miss him when he bounced off the wagon when crossing the Pecos River. Raised by a coyote, Bill finally went back to the ranch and became an amazing cowboy. He invented the lasso and taught the cowhands how to rope cattle. Later, he is credited with the idea of branding cattle and developing the round-up, the cowboy song, and many other uniquely Western customs. A famous keelboatman who lived on the Mississippi was Mike Fink. In his words:

> I'm thunder and lightnin' and hurrycane all rolled into one! With a mite o' earthquake throwed in for good measure. I'm a Mississippi whirlpool! I'm a river snag! I'm half hoss and half alligator! I'm all that and a long chalk more! I can outrun, outjump, knock down and mud waller any man as wants to try me! Whoopee! Make way for the king of the keelboatmen![68]

[68]Zachary Ball, *Young Mike Fink,* illustrated by Paul Lantz (New York: Holiday, 1958), p. 196.

Industry has its heroes, too. "Joe Magarac" (253) is a man of steel who came to Hunkietown. Magarac means Jackass, and Joe works like a mule and eats like a mule. He can stir molten iron with his arm, but when there is no more work to be done, he melts himself and becomes part of a new steel mill. "John Henry" (253) is a powerful black who swings his hammer mightily to build the transcontinental railroad. His contest with a steam drill is a dramatic story. Ezra Jack Keats used a picture-book format (177) to create huge, bold figures to tell of this legendary hero. We need more such attractive single editions of these North American tall tales.

Some excellent collections of tall tales have been made by Malcolmson in *Yankee Doodle's Cousins* (196) and Stoutenburg in *American Tall Tales* (253).

The table, "Some American Tall-Tale Heroes," details some of the characteristics of eight of these legendary heroes, including their occupations and their unique childhoods. Other legendary heroes that could be researched and added to the chart might include Casey Jones, *Febold Feboldson* (68), Stormalong (75), Tony Beaver, and more.

Other North American folklore has been collected in *The Hodgepodge Book* (72) by Duncan Emrich. This includes riddles and jokes, proverbs, cumulative stories and songs—such as the favorite "The Little Old Lady Who Swallowed A Fly"—and many more wise and witty bits of American folklore. Emrich has also compiled *The Nonsense Book of Riddles, Rhymes, Tongue Twisters, Puzzles and Jokes from American Folklore* (73). Alvin Schwartz has collected *Witcracks: Jokes & Jests from American Folklore* (235) and examples of *Flapdoodle: Pure Nonsense from American Folklore* (234), which are sure to delight children.

FABLES

Origin of Fables

Fables are usually associated with the name Aesop, a Greek slave who is supposed to have been born in Asia Minor about 600 B.C. Some scholars doubt his actual existence and believe that his works were the product of several storytellers. We know that some of the fables appeared in Greek literature two centuries before Aesop's birth, and in India and Egypt before that. The first written fables were in Greek, translated into Latin and again into English by William Caxton, and printed in 1484.

Another source for fables, as we have seen, was the *Jatakas*, animal stories that told of the previous births of the Buddha, and the *Panchatantra*, which was written for the purpose of instructing the young princes of India. These stories, longer than Aesop's fables, have moralistic verses interspersed throughout. When these are removed, the tales are closer to folktales, where they were discussed. One exception, however, is Marcia Brown's *Once a Mouse* (299), which is obviously a fable, with its implied moral on the pride of self. Beautifully illustrated with striking woodcuts, this fable from India received the Caldecott award.

A third common source for fables is the work of La Fontaine, a French poet, who wrote his fables in verse form. However, he drew largely on the collections of Aesop's fables that were available in the seventeenth century.

Characteristics of Fables

Fables are brief, didactic tales in which animals, or occasionally the elements, speak as human beings. Examples of these might be the well-known race between "The Hare and the Tortoise" or the contest between "The Sun and the North Wind." Humans do appear in a few fables, such as "The Country Maid and the Milk Pail" or "The Boy Who Cried Wolf." The characters are impersonal, with no name other than "fox," "rabbit," or "cow." They do not have the lively personalities of Anansi the spider or Kantjil the mouse deer of folktale fame. The animals are merely representative of different aspects of human nature—the lion stands for kingliness, the fox for cunning, the sheep for innocence and simplicity, and so on. Fables seldom have more than three characters, and the plots are usually based on a single incident. Primarily, fables were meant to instruct. Therefore, all of them contain either an implicit or an explicit moral.

Because of their brevity fables appear to be simple. However, they convey an abstract idea in relatively few words, and for that very reason are highly complex stories. In selecting fables, then, it

SOME AMERICAN TALL-TALE HEROES

NAME	OCCUPATION, LOCALE	CHARACTERISTICS	CHILDHOOD
Johnny Appleseed (John Chapman) (1774–1845)	Wanderer, planter of apple trees Pennsylvania, Ohio, Indiana	Selfless, gentle, a healer Tame wolf as companion Dressed in ragged clothes, with cooking pot for hat Always carried apple seeds	Loved apple trees and animals; could make things grow

NAME	OCCUPATION, LOCALE	CHARACTERISTICS	CHILDHOOD
Pecos Bill	Cowboy Texas, the Southwest	Normal size, great strength and daring (could hug a bear to death or ride a cyclone like a bronco) Clever—invented lasso, six-shooter, spurs, branding iron Owned beautiful white mustang named Widow-Maker	One of 18 children As a baby drank mountain lion's milk; lost by his parents and raised by a pack of coyotes

NAME	OCCUPATION, LOCALE	CHARACTERISTICS	CHILDHOOD
Paul Bunyan	Lumberman North Woods	Of huge proportions, enormously strong, a good problem solver Pet—"Babe," a giant blue ox	Dangerously strong, even as a baby—cradled in a boat at sea

NAME	OCCUPATION, LOCALE	CHARACTERISTICS	CHILDHOOD
Davy Crockett (1786–1836)	Frontiersman Tennessee	Tall, known for wide grin Good hunter and soldier Animal lover Battled comets and cold weather Tamed and rode a bear named "Death-Hug" Rifle named "Betsy"	Very tall Good woodsman and hunter

SOME AMERICAN TALL-TALE HEROES (continued)

NAME	OCCUPATION, LOCALE	CHARACTERISTICS	CHILDHOOD
Mike Fink	Keelboatman Ohio, Mississippi, and Missouri Rivers	Loud and quick-tempered Given to bragging Expert marksman, good fighter Rifle named "Bang-All"	Lived in the woods Not big, but tough

NAME	OCCUPATION, LOCALE	CHARACTERISTICS	CHILDHOOD
John Henry	Railroad man (hammerman) The South	Huge black hero known for strength, great endurance, natural ability for steel-driving Companion—Li'l Willie	First thing he reached for as a baby was a hammer

NAME	OCCUPATION, LOCALE	CHARACTERISTICS	CHILDHOOD
Joe Magarac (Jackass)	Steel worker Pittsburgh ("Hunkietown")	Bigger than usual, made of steel Works and eats like a mule Could stir molten iron with his arm	Born from an ore pit or a rolling mill

NAME	OCCUPATION, LOCALE	CHARACTERISTICS	CHILDHOOD
Alfred Bulltop Stormalong	Sailor, whaler, ship's captain Massachusetts, Northeast Coast	Huge in size and strength: 5 fathoms tall Prodigious appetite Skillful and daring Always needed a bigger ship Made the White Cliffs of Dover with soap	Born with oceanwater in his veins

is wise to look at the quality of both language and illustrations. Compare the following two interpretations of the beginning of "The Town Mouse and the Country Mouse":

A country mouse one day received a visit from his cousin who lived in the town. He did his best to provide the town mouse with good food, but it was clear that his cousin did not care for barley and corn."[69]

Contrast this spare prose of Harold Jones with Heidi Holder's more embroidered version:

A honest, plain, sensible Country Mouse invited her city friend for a visit. When the City Mouse arrived, the Country Mouse opened her heart and hearth in honor of her old friend. There was not a morsel that she did not bring forth out of her larder—peas and barley, cheese and parings and nuts—hoping by quantity to make up for what she feared was wanting in quality, eating nothing herself, lest her guest should not have enough.[70]

While both illustrators frame their pictures, Holder's borders suggest medieval manuscript embellishments and Jones uses vegetation. His blocky full-color animals contrast with Holder's sepia-toned and delicately rendered ones. Both versions reflect the unique and various treatments given to Aesop's stories for children today.

Various Editions of Fables

Eve Rice in *Once in a Wood* (296) has retold for beginning readers ten of the most popular of Aesop's fables. Soft black and white illustrations reminiscent of stone lithography illustrate such choices as "The Crow and the Water Jug," "Belling the Cat," and "The Hare Who Had Many Friends." Unlike the story text, the moral, which is often spoken by one of the animal characters, rhymes. Thus the wise old mouse tells the younger impetuous mice:

Things are easier said than done—
The old and wise will tell you that.

So now, will someone tell me this:
Who is going to bell the cat?[71]

In *The Exploding Frog and Other Fables from Aesop* (293), John McFarland retells more than thirty fables with a contemporary flair. The cheerfully humorous illustrations of James Marshall add much to this version. The moral or point of some of these fables is less obvious, and children might be challenged to try stating one. Eric Carle has selected *Twelve Tales from Aesop* (298) to illustrate in his familiar brightly colored style.

Older editions include the oversized book *Aesop's Fables* edited by Untermeyer (291) and illustrated with large animal cartoon-figures who make comments about the stories. Thus a talking dog usurps the manger and barks words of warning to a hungry cow, donkey, and ram. The animal bystanders who watch the tortoise win the race with the hare murmur such comments as "strange," or "I wouldn't have thought it possible." This is a witty, sophisticated edition of the fables which should delight 9- and 10-year-olds. Boris Artzybasheff's collection (289) is illustrated with superb woodcuts and contains morals or pedantic "applications" reminiscent of earlier editions of Aesop. James Reeves uses modern conversational style and added details in his *Fables from Aesop* (294). Recently, *The Caldecott Aesop* (292) was reissued in a fascimile edition. In it, twenty fables are doubly illustrated—once with a literal animal scene and, second, with a human interpretation. "The Ass in the Lion's Skin" impresses the other animals until the wind blows off his disguise. In Caldecott's satiric second interpretation, the ass is seen as a pompous art critic.

Other illustrators have chosen fables for treatment in picture-book format. Ed Young's pencil drawings for *The Lion and the Mouse* (295) emphasize the contrast between big and little by portraying the lion from the mouse's point of view. Paul Galdone's *Three Aesop Fox Fables* (303) include two stories in which the fox is outsmarted and one in which he triumphs. Galdone's bright-eyed fox provides the continuity for these three lively stories. Other single fables which Galdone has illustrated include *The Town Mouse and the*

[69]Aesop, *Tales from Aesop*, retold and illustrated by Harold Jones (New York: Watts/Julia MacRae, 1982), unpaged.
[70]Aesop, *Aesop's Fables*, illustrated by Heidi Holder (New York: Viking, 1981), p. 5.

[71]Aesop, *Once in a Wood. Ten Tales from Aesop*, adapted and illustrated by Eve Rice (New York: Greenwillow, 1979), p. 27.

Cartoon figures and imaginative conversation extend the meanings of *Aesop's Fables*. A dog in the manger prevents others from enjoying what he cannot eat. Illustration by Alice and Martin Provensen.

Country Mouse (304), *Androcles and the Lion* (301), and a Jataka tale, *The Monkey and the Crocodile* (302).

La Fontaine based many of his fables on Aesop, and two collections introduce his fables to younger readers. Anne Rockwell's cheerful illustrations for *The Turtle and the Two Ducks* (307) depict eleven familiar fables, including "The Grasshopper and the Ant," and "The Fox and the Grapes." Children would enjoy adding their own morals or lessons to some of these stories. Richard Scarry's adapted versions, *The Fables of La Fontaine* (305), depict the characters as large dressed-up animals in bright primary colors.

Various artists have interpreted the story of *The Miller, the Boy and the Donkey,* including a brilliant edition by Wildsmith (306). By way of contrast, *Hee Haw* (309) by Ann McGovern also capitalizes on the comedy act of the miller and his son carring their donkey in their attempt to please everyone.

Children in the middle grades might enjoy comparing different collections, as well as interpretations of single stories. In this way they could become more sensitive to the style and possible meanings of the stories, while appreciating various artistic interpretations. After reading such modern fables as Steig's *Amos & Boris* (310), Lionni's *Frederick* (308), Lobel's collection of *Fables* (190), and Ciardi's *John J. Plenty and Fiddler Dan* (300), they might want to try writing their own. By comparing Frederick and Fiddler Dan with the original fable of "The Ant and the Grasshopper," they could see that both Ciardi and Lionni were saying something significant about the place of the artist in our society. Such a discussion would help children understand the deeper layers of meaning that are inherent in the form of the fable.

MYTHS

The Nature of Myth

Mythology evolved as primitive man searched his imagination and related events to forces, as he sought explanation of the earth, sky, and human behavior. These explanations moved slowly through the stages of a concept of one power of force in human form, who controlled the phenomena of nature; to a complex system in which the god or goddess represented such virtues as wisdom, purity, or love; to a worshipping of the gods in organized fashion. Gods took the forms of men and women, but they were immortal and possessed supernatural powers.

Myths deal with human relationships with the gods, with the relationships of the gods among themselves, with the way people accept or fulfill their destiny, and with the struggle of people within and without themselves between good and evil forces. The myths are good stories, too, for they contain action, suspense, and basic conflicts. Usually, each story is short and can be enjoyed by itself, without deep knowledge of the general mythology.

Types of Myths

CREATION MYTHS

Every culture has a story about how the world began, how people were made, how the sun and the moon got in the sky. These are called creation myths, or origin myths; they give an explanation for the beginnings of things. John Bierhorst's *The Hungry Woman: Myths and Legends of the Aztecs* (321) includes creation myths and legends of pre-Aztec times. Illustrations for this book are reproductions of paintings by early Aztec artists who by tradition drew the stories of the myths as a way of preserving them. Penelope Farmer has collected eighty myths from around the world in her book *Beginnings* (335). They are grouped under categories like man, flood, fire, or food plants. Stories range from a Finnish one that tells how the earth was created from parts of a teal's broken egg and shaped by the Mother of Water, to a Nigerian one telling why we have death in the world. Men and tortoises wanted to see their children. "Only the stones did not want to have children, and so they never die." In *The Beginning* (362), Maria

Leach brings together some sixty myths such as the Haida Indian story that says Raven created man from a clam shell. Leach makes the point that it does not matter if the early explanations were not true, since a wrong answer "does not belittle the seeking for an answer." Another book by Leach, which is more appropriate for children, is *How the People Sang the Mountains Up* (363). The title story of this book tells of the Apaches' belief in the power of song to make the mountains rise. Another good source for creation myths is the book by Fahs and Spoerl, *Beginnings: Earth Sky Life Death* (334). They include the stories of Adam and Eve; the Greek story of the creation of man by Prometheus; and the Norwegian tale of the giant cow who licked an ice block into the shape of a man called Buri, grandfather of Odin.

Betty Baker has retold the hauntingly beautiful creation myths of the Pima and Papago Indian tribes in a continuing narrative, *At the Center of the World* (314). Earth Magician was supposed to have created the world and man three different times while the Buzzard watched him. The first time no one died and soon there was nothing to eat. The second time the people were born old. The third time the people smoked, even the babies! Finally, Buzzard said: "You're still making mistakes. . . . The lizards' legs are too short and the snakes have none at all." But Earth Magician said he was tired and he stopped. This is an exciting well-written story that children in the middle grades would enjoy.

NATURE MYTHS

The nature myths include stories that explain seasonal changes, animal characteristics, earth formation, constellations, and the movements of the sun and earth. Many Indian nature myths are appropriate for children in the primary grades. Belting's collections, *The Long-Tailed Bear* (319) and *The Earth Is on a Fish's Back* (318), contain both nature and creation myths. The familiar story of Narcissus and Echo, as well as the less familiar one "The Two Bears," appears in the book by Green, *Tales the Muses Told* (350). The story of "The Two Bears" tells how the constellations of the Great Bear and the Little Bear were put in the sky. Dayrell's African story *Why the Sun and the Moon Live in the Sky* (60) is a fine example of a nature myth.

The Greek story of "Demeter and Persephone"

explains the change of seasons. Hades, god of the underworld, carried Persephone off to his land to be his bride, and Demeter, her mother, who made plants grow, mourned for her daughter. When she learned of Persephone's fate, she asked Zeus to intercede, and it was granted that the girl might return if she had eaten nothing in Hades. Since she had eaten the seeds of a pomegranate, she was compelled to return for four months each year. Several beautiful picture-book interpretations of this story have been published. Gerald McDermott in *Daughter of Earth* (365) contrasts the cool greens of earth above with the smoke reds of the underworld. By stroking the prepared canvas with a hard-bristle brush, he has given the paintings a surface that resembles the ancient frescoes of Roman art. Ati Forberg has used mixed-media including finger-painting to create the artwork for *Persephone, Bringer of Spring* by Tomaino (395). Her dramatic pictures have the quality of an exquisite Greek vase—particularly the one that shows Persephone within the outline of a pomegranate tasting the four seeds that would bind her to Hades for four months of the year. Margaret Hodges has retold this story under the title *Persephone and the Springtime* (357). The illustrations by Stewart seem overly romantic and old-fashioned in appearance. The text does not read as smoothly as the Tomaino one. *Demeter and Persephone,* in simple clear prose by Proddow (374) is distinguished by the fine illustrations of Barbara Cooney. Children in the middle grades should have an opportunity to compare and contrast all four versions of this well-known nature myth.

HERO MYTHS

Another kind of myth does not attempt to explain anything at all. These are the hero myths that are found in many cultures. These myths have some of the same qualities as wonder stories in that the hero is given certain tasks or, in the case of Heracles, labors, to accomplish. Frequently the gods help (or hinder) a particular favorite (or disliked) mortal. Monsters such as gorgons, hydras, and chimaeras in the Greek stories are plentiful, but these provide the hero with his challenge. Characteristic of the hero role is that he accepts all dangerous assignments and accomplishes his quest or dies in one last glorious adventure.

One of the great Greek hero tales is the story of Perseus. The birth and life of Perseus follow the pattern of many heroes. When it is prophesied to him that a grandson will kill him, Acrisius imprisons his daughter so she will have no children. However, Zeus, the king of the gods comes to her in a shower of golden rain and a child is born from their union. Acrisius puts mother and child to sea in a wooden chest where they are found by a fisherman who adopts the child. When Perseus is but 15 he rashly promises the king of the island the head of the terrible gorgon Medusa. Her hair was made of snakes, and anyone who looked at her turned to stone. The goddess Athena gives Perseus her sword and shield, while Hermes lends him his winged sandals. With directions from the three hideous gray sisters, Perseus goes to the gorgon's isle, where he succeeds in slaying her. He returns to the land of his birth, stopping on the way home to save the beautiful maiden Andromeda from a sea monster. He then becomes king, making Andromeda his queen. Margaret Hodges has retold this story in clear prose, while Charles Mikolaycak has provided dramatic pictures for the book, *The Gorgon's Head* (354). Ian Serrailler has given us a slightly longer but somehow more vivid retelling of this hero tale in his book of the same title (385).

Greek Mythology

The myths with which we are the most familiar are those of the Ancient Greeks which were collected by the poet Hesiod sometime during the eighth century B.C. The Roman versions of these myths were adapted by the poet Ovid during the first century B.C. in his well-known work, *Metamorphoses*. This has caused some confusion in that the Roman names for the gods are better known than the Greek, and yet the stories originated with the Greeks. However, the more recent versions of these myths are using Greek names. In working with children it is best to be consistent in your choice of names, or they will become confused. You might wish to reproduce the following table for their reference.

Greek mythology is composed of many stories of gods and goddesses, heroes, and monsters. The Greeks were the first to see their gods in their own image. As their culture became more sophisticated and complex, so, too, did their stories of the gods. These personified gods could do anything that humans could do, but on a much mightier scale. The gods, while immortal, freely entered into the lives

SOME GODS AND GODDESSES OF GREEK AND ROMAN MYTHOLOGY

GREEK	ROMAN	TITLE	RELATIONSHIP
Zeus	Jupiter or Jove	Supreme Ruler, Lord of the Sky	
Poseidon	Neptune	God of the Sea	Brother of Zeus
Hades or Pluto	Dis	God of the Underworld	Brother of Zeus
Hestia	Vesta	Goddess of the Home and Hearth	Sister of Zeus
Hera	Juno	Goddess of Women and Marriage	Wife and sister of Zeus
Ares	Mars	God of War	Son of Zeus and Hera
Athena	Minerva	Goddess of Wisdom	Daughter of Zeus
Apollo	Apollo	God of Light and Truth, the Sun God	Son of Zeus and Leto
Aphrodite	Venus	Goddess of Love and Beauty	Daughter of Zeus, wife of Hephaestus
Hermes	Mercury	Messenger of the Gods	Son of Zeus and Maia
Artemis	Diana	Goddess of the Moon and Hunt	Twin sister of Apollo
Hephaestus	Vulcan	God of Fire	Son of Hera
Eros	Cupid	God of Love	Son of Aphrodite (in some accounts)
Demeter	Ceres	Goddess of Corn	Daughter of Cronus and Rhea
Dionysus or Bacchus	Bacchus	God of Wine	Son of Zeus and Semele
Persephone	Proserpine	Maiden of Spring	Daughter of Demeter

of mortals, helping or hindering them, depending on their particular moods. Their strength was mighty and so was their wrath. Many of the myths are concerned with conflicts and the loves of the gods. Jealousy and the struggle for power among them often caused trouble for humans. Some of the stories of the loves and quarrels of the immortals, however, are inappropriate for children.

Greek mythology includes the creation story that Earth and Sky were the first gods. Their children were giant Cyclops and the Titans, one of whom was Cronus who drove his father away with a scythe (thus, the picture of Father Time). Cronus swallowed each of his children so they would not usurp his place, but his wife gave him a stone instead of her last child, Zeus. Of course Zeus overthrew his father and made him disgorge his brothers and sisters, who were still alive. Zeus married Hera, a very jealous vindictive woman, who caused all kinds of trouble. Prometheus was a Titan who defied the other gods in order to give man fire. Zeus then chained him to Mount Caucasus, where an eagle devoured his liver each day, but it was renewed each night. Zeus also sent Pandora, with her box of trouble, as a punishment for Prometheus and man. Told not to open the box, Pandora was so curious that she could not help herself. All the evils of the world came forth, and only hope remained in the box.

Children who have a good background in folk-tales will find many of the same elements present in the myths. They will enjoy the story of King Midas, who foolishly wished that everything he touched would turn to gold. While Hawthorne's sentimental version (353) of this story emphasized the evilness of greed, earlier translations suggested that the sin of Midas was his continued defiance of the gods.

The gods could not tolerate human pride any more than they could defiance or arrogance, which the Greeks called *hubris*, a word we still use today. *Hubris* was always swiftly followed by Nemesis, the goddess of retribution. Arachne was transformed into a spider because of her *hubris*. She foolishly claimed to be a better weaver than the goddess Athena, who challenged her to a contest and won. Bellerophon tamed the mighty winged horse, Pegasus, and together they slew the monster Chimaera, defeated the Amazons in battle, and overcame many other dangers. As Bellerophon's fame spread, he grew proud and arrogant. One fatal day he decided to challenge the gods themselves. Springing on the back of Pegasus he shouted aloud that he would fly to Olympus, the home of the gods. This was too much for Zeus, who caused a gadfly to sting Pegasus and Bellerophon was thrown to his death far below. Krystyna Turska has given children a dramatic interpretation of this favorite story in picture-book format simply titled *Pegasus* (396); her glorious pictures of the winged horse capture the excitement of this tale.

Eight- and nine-year-olds delight in the story of *Daedalus and Icarus,* as told by Farmer and illustrated in a picture book by Connor (336). They are intrigued with the idea of the labyrinth designed by Daedalus to house the monstrous Minotaur. The ingenious escape from this maze, climaxed with the first flight of man, makes a fascinating tale. But as in the story of Bellerophon, Icarus became so enchanted with his own power that he flew too close to the sun and the wax of his wings melted and caused his downfall. Serraillier has written a slightly longer version of this story in *A Fall from the Sky* (384).

Another reckless boy was Phaëthon, son of the Sun-God, Hebris, Phaëthon's one consuming wish was permission to drive the sun chariot across the sky for a day. Reluctantly his father granted him this wish, and the results were disastrous. Pollack's poetic retelling of this story (373) describes the flight:

> The horses reared and pawed at the sky, fighting to get more slack. They snorted and neighed and whinnied and kicked, strong and wild and wanting their heads. . . . They climbed more sharply, resisting the driver. . . . Wider and wider the chariot swung, finally out of control.[72]

The love story of *Cupid and Psyche* (317) has been competently retold by Barth and illustrated with dramatic wash drawings by Ati Forberg. Middle-grade students reading this myth for the first time will be struck by its similarity to the motifs of folktales, particularly the tale of *Beauty and the Beast* (149).

After children have been introduced to these exciting single myths, they will be ready for the longer hero tales of Perseus, the gorgon-slayer; Theseus, who killed the Minotaur; the many labors of Heracles; and the tale of Jason and the Argonauts' search for the golden fleece. Serraillier has provided us with fine well-written books about each of these heroes. *The Way of Danger* (387) chronicles the story of Theseus. *Heracles the Strong* (386) is the amazing story of the persistence and accomplishments of this hero (who is better known by his Roman name of Hercules). The story

[72]Merrill Pollack, *Phaëthon,* illustrated by William Hofmann (Philadelphia: Lippincott, 1966), pp. 46–47.

of Jason's quest for the golden fleece is told in the book *The Clashing Rocks* (383). All these retellings by Serraillier provide a continuous narrative of the hero. Written in short chapters, they would be excellent to read aloud to a group of middle-graders.

Bernard Evslin's *Hercules* (332) is told in modern language and allusion, which makes for an exciting and fast-paced narrative. By heightening the action and emphasizing characterization of the villainous Hera or the faithful and brave Iole, Evslin makes Hercules into a hero very much in keeping with those children already know from television and fantasy movies.

Doris Gates has written a series of books featuring all of the stories related to one god or goddess. These provide a continuing theme and avoid the fragmentation of books that attempt to give a complete coverage of the myths. *Lord of the Sky, Zeus* (341) includes the lovely story of the poor couple, "Baucis and Philemon," who were willing to share all that they had with the stranger who stopped at their humble hut, never dreaming that he was Zeus. The longer stories of Theseus and Daedalus are well written, as are the other books in the series: *The Warrior Goddess: Athena* (343), *The Golden God: Apollo* (340), and *Two Queens of Heaven, The Story of Demeter and Aphrodite* (342). These would be fine stories to read aloud to 10- to 12-year-olds.

Several collections introduce children to these Greek myths without overpowering them with names and episodes. The d'Aulaires' *Book of Greek Myths* (312) conveys the sense of the power of the gods in beautiful colored full-page lithographs. The stories are brief but complete. The Provensens' illustrations are outstanding features of two Golden Books, *The Golden Treasury of Myths and Legends* (398) by White and *The Iliad and the Odyssey* (397) by Watson. The design is excellent, and colors create the mood. A masklike quality of the faces painted in charcoal, gray, or brown is in keeping with the myths. There is no pronunciation guide, but the style is readable.

Benson's *Stories of the Gods and Heroes* (320) were derived from *The Age of Fable* (323), written by Thomas Bulfinch in 1855. Benson has kept the flavor of the older storytellers but has presented the tales in very readable style. Conversation is used wisely to create interest. The indicated pronunciation of a word or name follows immediately in the text. Alice Low has efficiently retold many of these tales in *The Macmillan Book of Greek Gods and Heroes* (364). Sections introduce the gods and the creation of mankind; the heroic adventures of Perseus, Heracles, Jason, Theseus, and Zeus; and the origins of several constellations. Watercolor illustrations interspersed with black and white drawings give this collection an inviting look for middle-grade readers. *Tales of the Greek Heroes* (349) by Roger Lancelyn Green is a somewhat more difficult but well-written retelling of these same myths.

Evslin also employs modern vernacular in *Heroes and Monsters of Greek Myth* (333). The pace of the text and the language make this book appealing to today's child. For example, Procrustes is showing Perseus his remarkable six-foot bed into which he fits everyone by the expedient of either cutting off their feet or stretching them. He explains:

> "And I am a very neat, orderly person. I like things to fit. Now, if the guest is too short for the bed, we attach those chains to his ankles and stretch him. Simple."
>
> "And if he's too long?" said Theseus.
>
> "Oh, well then we just lop off his legs to the proper length."
>
> "I see."
>
> "But don't worry about that part of it. You look like a stretch job to me. Go ahead, lie down."[73]

Robert Graves has utilized this same rather flippant approach to the myths in his book *Greek Gods and Heroes* (344). This style makes the stories seem very contemporary, but at the same time they lose part of their mystery and grandeur.

Finally, the most exciting books based on the Greek myths are *The God Beneath the Sea* (338) and *The Golden Shadow* (339) by Leon Garfield and Edward Blishen. The first is a long continuous narrative that evokes an emotional response from the reader. We are captured on the first page with Hephaestus the "fiery shrieking baby" who falls from the sky into the sea and is cared for by sea-goddesses (338). When they finally tell him about his origin, they in effect tell the reader too about

[73]Bernard Evslin, Dorothy Evslin, and Ned Hoopes, *Heroes and Monsters of Greek Myth* (New York: Scholastic, 1970), p. 53.

the making of the gods. The characterizations are remarkably clear—Zeus the lusty patriarch of a huge, quarrelsome family; Hera his cruel and jealous wife; Hermes the lovable rogue. All of them assume a dimension not usually given in simple retellings. These are the gods the Greeks must have known, while we have had only the shells of their stories. Many of the episodes are beyond the maturity and experience of elementary-school children. Blum's strange black and white illustrations are somewhat grotesque. *The Golden Shadow* (339) is also illustrated with startling black and white sketches by Charles Keeping. It is a collection of the Greek legends of Hercules, including the Calydonian boar hunt and his twelve labors, such as the killing of the many-headed Hydra and the cleaning of the Augean stables. Again, these are vital, sensuous dramatic tellings that completely absorb the reader. These books would be appropriate at the junior high school level and are strongly recommended for teachers to provide a new perspective on the Greek myths and legends.

Norse Mythology

A mythology derives its characteristics from the land and peoples of its origin. The land of the Norsemen was a cold, cruel land of frost, snow, and ice. Life was a continual struggle for survival against these elements. It seems only natural that Norse mythology was filled with gods who had to battle against huge frost giants also. These were heroic gods who, unlike the immortal Greek gods safe in their home on sunny Mount Olympus, knew that they and their home on Asgard would eventually be destroyed. And in a way their prophecy was fulfilled, for Christianity all but extinguished the talk of the old gods, except in Iceland. There, in the thirteenth century, Snorri Sturluson—a poet, scholar, and historian—collected many of the Norse myths and legends into a book called the *Prose Edda*. Much of his writing was based on an earlier verse collection called the *Poetic Edda*. These two books are the primary sources for our knowledge of Norse mythology.

It is too bad that children do not know these myths as well as they know those of the Greeks. In some ways the Norse tales seem more suited to children than the highly sophisticated, gentle Greek tales. These stories appeal to the child's imagination, with their tales of giants and dwarfs, eight-legged horses and vicious wolves, magic hammers and rings. Primarily they are bold, powerful stories of the relationships among the gods and their battles against the evil frost giants. Odin is the serious protector of the men he created, willingly sacrificing one of his eyes to obtain wisdom that would allow him to see deep into the hearts of men. The largest and the strongest of the gods is Thor, owner of a magic hammer that will hit its mark and then return to his hands. And Balder, the tragic god of light, is the most loved by all the other gods.

Some of the stories are amusing. Seven- and eight-year-olds would enjoy the picture-book version of *The Hammer of Thunder* (375), retold by Ann Pyk. In this tale the enormous Thor is dressed as a bride and goes with Loki, who is his "bridesmaid," in order to trick the giant Thrym into returning Thor's magic hammer. Loki is a puzzling character who seems a likable mischief-maker in the beginning of the tales but becomes increasingly evil. Finally, he is responsible for the death of Balder. He guides the hand of Hoder, Balder's blind brother, who shoots a fatal arrow made of mistletoe, the only object that could harm Balder. The gods impose a cruel punishment on Loki that reminds one of the punishment of Prometheus. This story has been retold by Edna Barth in *Balder and the Mistletoe* (316).

While the best collection of these myths remains the classic Colum one, *The Children of Odin* (327), there are other notable collections. The d'Aulaires have provided a continuous narrative of these stories along with handsome lithographs, in their book *Norse Gods and Giants* (313). Their retelling of these tales maintains the flavor of the original *Edda*. For example, the description of the making of a special bond to chain the fierce Fenris wolf reminds one of the Witches' Chant in Macbeth:

> [The gnomes] spell-caught the sound of cat paws, the breath of fish, the spittle of birds, the hairs of a woman's beard, the root of a mountain, and spun them around the sinews of a bear. That made a bond that looked as fine as a ribbon of silk, but since it was made of things not in this world, it was so strong nothing in the world could break it.[74]

[74]Ingri d'Aulaire and Edgar d'Aulaire, *Norse Gods and Giants* (Garden City, N.Y.: Doubleday, 1967), p. 52.

With his single eye flashing under his golden helmet, Odin, the all-father of Norse mythology, rides his great eight-legged horse into battle. From *Norse Gods and Giants* by Ingri and Edgar Parin d'Amlaire.

Green has provided a more thorough treatment of these tales in his book *The Myths of the Norsemen* (347). For her long book *In the Morning of Time* (360), Cynthia King has interwoven many of the myths with the central story of the Norse god Balder. The theme of this well-written long narrative runs throughout all the Norse myths, namely the tension between good and evil. Hoder identifies it as he considers the unknowing part he played in his brother's death:

> The blind god said, "Two brothers, two sides of a coin, good and evil, darkness and light, insight and innocence, that is all that any of us have been."[75]

[75]Cynthia King, *In the Morning of Time*, illustrated by Charles Mikolaycak (New York: Four Winds, 1970), p. 136.

If children have time to become acquainted with only one mythology, they should know the Greek stories (or their Roman adaptations). No other tales have so influenced the literature and art of the Western world. Norse mythology, too, has left its mark on Western culture, as in the names for Wednesday (Odin's day) and Thursday (Thor's day). Also, these tales have a special appeal for children. However, there are many other important mythologies that may be sampled as a part of the study of a culture or be simply enjoyed as literature.

EPIC AND LEGENDARY HEROES

The epic is a long narrative or cycle of stories clustering around the actions of a single hero. It grew out of the myths or along with them, since the gods were still intervening in earlier epics like the *Iliad* and the *Odyssey*. Gradually, the center of action shifted from the gods to a human hero, so that in such tales as Robin Hood the focus is completely on the daring adventures of the man himself.

The epic hero is a cultural or national hero embodying all the ideal characteristics of greatness in his time. Thus, Odysseus and Penelope, his wife, represented the Greek ideals of intelligence, persistence, and resourcefulness. He survived by his wit rather than his great strength. Both King Arthur and Robin Hood appealed to the English love of justice and freedom; King Arthur and his knights represented the code of chivalry, while Robin Hood was the champion of the common man—the prototype of the "good outlaw." The epics, then, express the highest moral values of a society. A knowledge of the epics gives children an understanding of a particular culture; but, more importantly, it provides them with models of greatness through the ages.

Many of the epics were originally written in poetic form, although a few, such as Malory's *Morte d'Arthur,* were in prose. Some, such as the story of Robin Hood, came from ballads. The translations used should keep the poetic rhythm, for the epics were sung in measured dignity with rich images and a suggestion of deep emotion. Such tales should not be rewritten in a "thin" style, nor should they omit the dangers, grim horrors, or weakness of humans. For even though the epic hero is a "larger than life" character, he is human and his humanity should show. Rewritten versions should communicate the excitement and the nobility that are characteristic of these great tales.

The *Iliad* and the *Odyssey*

According to tradition, a blind minstrel named Homer composed the epic poems the *Iliad* and the *Odyssey* about 850 B.C.; but scholars generally believe that parts of the stories were sung by many persons and that they were woven into one long narrative before they were written. The *Iliad* is an account of the Trojan War fought by the Greeks over Helen, the most beautiful woman in the world. Paris, son of King Priam of Troy, has taken her away from the Greek king Menelaus. After a siege of ten years, Agamemnon and Achilles, Greek leaders, quarrel bitterly over the spoils of the war. The gods and goddesses have their favorites, and they, too, quarrel among themselves as they witness the battles, almost as one would watch a football game! The complex story is long and difficult to understand, although specific incidents such as the final defeat of the Trojans by the cunning device of the Trojan Horse do intrigue some children. Fortunately, James Reeves has told this classic tale through the eyes of 10-year-old Illias (379). The first-person account gives vitality and excitement to the story, as do the dramatic pictures by Krystyna Turska. This is a great story in a handsome format, which children should have the opportunity to enjoy. *The Siege and Fall of Troy* (345) by Robert Graves gives the complete story of Troy, including one chapter on the return home of Odysseus. This account is written in modern contemporary language.

The *Odyssey* is the story of the hazardous ten-year journey of Odysseus (called Ulysses by the Romans) from Troy to his home in Ithaca, following the end of the war. Odysseus has one terrifying experience after another, which he manages to survive by his cunning. For example, he defeats the horrible one-eyed Cyclops by blinding him and then strapping his men to the undersides of sheep, which were allowed to leave the cave. No one has heard the song of the Sirens and lived, until Odysseus puts wax in his men's ears and has himself bound to the mast of his ship with strict orders to his men to ignore his pleas for release. His ship safely passes between the whirlpool of Charybdis and the monster Scylla, but later is shipwrecked and delayed for seven years. A loyal servant and his son aid the returned hero in assuming his rightful throne and saving his wife; Penelope has had a difficult time discouraging the many suitors who wish to become king. While children or teachers may be acquainted with episodes from the story, it is the total force of all his trials that presents the full dimensions of this hero.

The Iliad and the Odyssey (397) by Watson is enriched by the powerful illustrations of the Provensens. The modern text maintains the flow of action, but it does not recall the stately language of more traditional translations. A pronunciation guide is very helpful. Both of Barbara Picard's retellings, *The Odyssey of Homer Retold* (371) and *The Iliad of Homer* (370), are distinguished and give emphasis to development of characters. The two books written by Church in 1906 and 1907 have been combined and printed as *The Iliad and the Odyssey of Homer* (325). The style seems somewhat formal and includes such phrases as "You speak truly, fair lady." Padraic Colum's version, *The Children's Homer* (328), keeps the essence of the traditional poem and Pogany's illustrations distinguish this book.

The *Ramayana*

The *Ramayana* is the great epic tale of India which tells how the noble Rama, his devoted brothers, and his beautiful virtuous wife Sita manage to defeat the evil demon Ravana. Heir to the throne, Rama is banished from his home through the trickery of his stepmother. Prince Rama, his brothers, and the devoted Sita spend fourteen years in wandering and adventure. One day Sita vanishes, kidnapped by Ravana. Rama searches for her unsuccessfully and then turns to a tribe of monkeys for their help. Finally Sita is found, and with the help of an entire army of monkeys, Rama rescues her. In order to be cleansed from her association with the demon, Sita must stand a trial by fire. Her faithfulness proved, she is united with her beloved Rama. Peace and plenty prevail during the reign of Rama.

Composed in India by the sage Valmiki during the fourth century B.C., the *Ramayana* represented some 24,000 couplets which were memorized and repeated. It constitutes part of the gospel of Hindu scripture, for Rama and his wife are held as the ideal man and woman. Rama is believed to be an incarnation of the god Vishnu come to earth in human form.

Elizabeth Seeger has created a prose version of *The Ramayana* (382) that reads smoothly as one long and exciting narrative. Joseph Gaer has told the story for children in *The Adventures of Rama* (337). Mukerji's version, *Rama, the Hero of India* (368), tells how the Hindus memorize these stories. Surely Western children should know something of this epic hero who is so important to a large part of the world.

Heroes of the Middle Ages

Some historians believe there was a King Arthur who became famous around the sixth century. Defeated by the invading Saxons, his people fled to Wales and Brittany and told stories of his bravery and goodness. Other stories became attached to these, and the exploits of Tristram, Gawaine, and Lancelot were added to the Arthurian cycle. The religious element of the quest for the Holy Grail, the cup used by Christ at the Last Supper, was also added. Whether or not the chalice actually existed, it remains as a symbol of purity and love. In the fifteenth century Sir Thomas Malory's *Morte d'Arthur* was one of the first books printed in England and became a major source of later versions. Margaret Hodges has recounted how Malory came to tell these stories in her nonfiction *Knight Prisoner: The Tale of Sir Thomas Malory and His King Arthur* (355).

While many of the brave deeds of the knights were performed for the love of a fair lady, others, such as the intriguing tale of *Sir Gawain and the Green Knight* (351), contain elements of mystery and wonder. These are noble tales and children delight in them. They are fascinated by the story of "The Sword in the Stone," "How Arthur Gained Excalibur," and the puzzling "Passing of Arthur." T. H. White's *The Sword in the Stone* (399) adds the author's customary arch humor to an imaginative retelling of Arthur's boyhood and growth under Merlin's tutelage. Picard, in her notes for *Hero Tales from the British Isles* (369), relates the old tradition that Arthur and his knights are not dead but sleeping in a cave and that they will awaken and fight again when England has need of them. William Mayne utilized this legend in his eerie modern fantasy titled *Earthfasts* (see Chapter 7).

There are several fine collections of tales of King Arthur. Two earlier editions are still popular: Sidney Lanier's *The Boy's King Arthur* (361), which first appeared in 1880, and Howard Pyle's *The Story of King Arthur and His Knights* (378). Picard's *Stories of King Arthur and His Knights* (372) includes the deceit of Guinivere. The style is stately and follows the old form. Told in simple, direct language, Jay Williams' *Sword of King Arthur* (400) is based on Malory, but is the easiest version to read of the legends of Arthur.

Rosemary Sutcliff brings thirteen stories from the Arthurian cycle to life in *The Sword and the Circle* (393). Beginning with the events surrounding Arthur's accession to the throne, she weaves other stories into the text in separate chapters. "Tristan and Iseult," "Beaumains, the Kitchen Knight," "Sir Gawain and the Green Knight," and "Gawain and the Loathly Lady" are but a few of the tales included. Two other volumes, though concerning important parts of Arthurian legend, deal with less adventurous or romantic aspects of the story and may be of less interest to middle-grade readers. *The Light Beyond the Forest: The Quest for the Holy Grail* (391) details the wanderings of Lancelot, Galahad, Percival, and others in search of the grail but also in search of their own salvation. *The Road to Camlann* (392) tells of the sad end of Arthur and the Round Table fellowship. Sutcliff has also retold the romantic *Tristan and Iseult* in a full-length novel (394). The language has a lyrical quality reminiscent of the old storytellers:

> It was young summer when they came to the hidden valley; and three times the hawthorn trees were rusted with berries and the hazelnuts fell into the stream. And three times winter came and they huddled about the fire in the smoky bothie and threw on logs from the wood-store outside . . . [76]

In *Sir Gawain and the Loathly Lady* by Selina Hastings (352), King Arthur is caught without his sword Excalibur and must answer a riddle to save his life: What is it that women most desire? On the way home, a despairing Arthur meets a Loathly Lady, rendered in truly horrible detail by Juan Wijngaard, who offers him the riddle's answer if he will marry her to one of his knights. Arthur agrees but is heartbroken when valiant Sir Gawain offers himself. They are married, much to the chagrin of the court. However, once alone in the bedchambers, the Lady turns into a beautiful young woman who gives her new husband a choice. Will she be beautiful by day and ugly by night, or the opposite? When Gawain cannot bear to make the decision, he answers "You must decide whichever you prefer." This breaks the spell and is also the key to the riddle. What every woman desires is to have her own way. This exquisitely illuminated story features bordered and decorated illustrations full of medieval detail and suffused with light. The story is a companion to *Sir Gawain and the Green Knight* (351). Winifred Rosen has retold *Three Romances* (381) from the love stories of Camelot. The first story, "Sir Gawain and the Loathly Lady," would make an interesting comparison with the previous version. In the story of "Enid and Geraint," Enid's steadfast devotion to her jealous husband triumphs in the end. The third story tells of Merlin's fatal infatuation with the fairy Ninian and portends the end of the fellowship of the Round Table. Rosen's forthright retellings preserve medieval language use without sacrificing clarity.

Taliesin and King Arthur (380) by Ruth Robbins is extracted from Welsh legendry in the *Mabinogion* and tells of the experiences of a young Welsh poet, Taliesin, when he entered the contest of the bards on Christmas Eve day at King Arthur's court. Youngest of the poets, he wins the high honor of the day by singing the riddle of his birth. Fantasy readers meet Taliesin through a found harp key in Nancy Bond's *A String in the Harp* and discover many Arthurian motifs in Susan Cooper's "The Dark Is Rising" quintet (see Chapter 7). Older readers may want to investigate some of these connections in Joy Chant's *The High Kings* (324). Designed for an adult audience, this strikingly illustrated book looks at Arthur's Celtic ancestors through the device of stories told at Arthur's court.

All of these books contribute to a child's knowledge of the mystique that surrounds the story of King Arthur. Students seldom discover these tales on their own, but once introduced to them, children delight in taking their place at that round table of adventure.

---

[76] Rosemary Sutcliff, *Tristan and Iseult* (New York: Dutton, 1971), p. 90.

Before Arthur could rebuke his steward, Gawain jumped down from his horse and knelt before the Lady. 'Madam,' he said, 'will you honour me with your hand in marriage?'

Highly ornate border patterns, insets of story details, and the opulence of King Arthur's medieval court are an integral part of the illustrations for this traditional tale. Illustration by Juan Wijngaard from *Sir Gawain and the Loathly Lady*, retold by Selina Hastings.

Another legendary hero who captures the imagination of children is Robin Hood. Scholars have been unable to agree over whether there was indeed a medieval outlaw by the name of Robin Hood or whether he was really a mythical character derived from festival plays given in France at Whitsuntide. But by the fifteenth century May Day celebrations in England were called "Robin Hood's Festivals," and the story of Robin Hood had become a legend for all time.

Children love this brave hero who lived in Sherwood Forest, outwitted the Sheriff of Nottingham, and shared his stolen goods with the poor. Others in the band were the huge Little John, Friar Tuck, the minstrel Alan-a-Dale, and Robin's sweetheart Maid Marian. According to one story, the king came in the disguise of a monk and shared their dinner and games. Convinced of their loyalty to him, he granted them pardon. Some stories include Robin's death through the treachery of the false Prioress.

Howard Pyle's *Some Merry Adventures of Robin Hood* (377) is a shorter version of his classic, *The Merry Adventures of Robin Hood* (376). Ann McGovern has retold this familiar legend in clear, direct language. A few words, such as "perchance" and "thou," retain the spirit of the medieval language without making *Robin Hood of Sherwood Forest* (366) too difficult to read. N. C. Wyeth's illustrations make Creswick's *Robin Hood* (330) another appealing choice.

Virginia Lee Burton spent three years making the scratchboard illustrations for *The Song of Robin Hood* (367), edited by Malcolmson and Castagnetta. Every verse of every song has its own small black and white etching similar to the illuminated manuscripts of medieval days. Large full-page illustrations with rhythmical design sweep the eye around a road to a castle or around the cowled figures of men seated by an open fire, and then up with the swirls of the smoke. This is one of the most beautiful examples of bookmaking that we have. Surely it should be shared, for it somehow captures the spirit of that delightful adventurer, Robin Hood.

Another distinctly medieval hero is Saint George, who battled with the dragon as related in Spenser's "The Faerie Queene." It has been vividly retold by Margaret Hodges in *Saint George and the Dragon* (358). Illustrations by Trina Schart Hyman add to the drama and excitement of this tale of triumph (see Chapter 5, the section "Creating Meaning in Picture Storybooks," for an extended discussion of this Caldecott award-winner).

THE BIBLE AS LITERATURE

The Place of the Bible in Literary Study

The Bible has an important and rightful place in any comprehensive discussion of traditional literature. For the Bible is a written record of people's continuing search to understand themselves and their relationships with others and their creator. It makes little sense to tell children the story of Jack the Giant Killer but to deny them the stories about David and Goliath or Samson. They read of the wanderings of Odysseus, but not those of Moses. They learn that Gilgamesh built an ark and survived a flood, but do not know the story of Noah. Our fear should not be that children will know the Bible; rather it should be that they will *not* know it. Whatever our religious persuasion or nonpersuasion, children should not be denied their right to knowledge of the traditional literature of the Bible. For other literature cannot be fully understood unless children are familiar with the outstanding characters, incidents, poems, proverbs, and parables of this literature of the Western world of thought. It is time that we clarified the difference between the practice of religious customs and indoctrination of one viewpoint and the study of the Bible as a great work of literature. In 1963 the Supreme Court asserted that "religious exercises" violated the First Amendment, but the Court also encouraged study of the Bible as literature:

> In addition, it might well be said that one's education is not complete without a study of comparative religion or the history of religion and its relationship to the advancement of Civilization. It certainly may be said that the Bible is worthy of study for its literary and historic qualities.[77]

The literary scholar Northrop Frye believes it essential to teach the Bible, for it presents humans in all their history. "It's the *myth* of the Bible that should be the basis of literary training, its imaginative survey of the human situation which is so broad and comprehensive that everything else finds its place inside it."[78] Some critics will be disturbed by the use of the term *myth* unless they understand its larger literary context as the human search for and expression of truth and meaning.

Books for the Study of the Bible

COLLECTIONS OF BIBLE STORIES

When a school staff agrees that children should have an opportunity to hear or read some of the great stories from the Bible, it faces the task of selecting material. Walter de la Mare's introduc-

[77]Quoted by Betty D. Mayo, "The Bible in the Classroom," *The Christian Science Monitor* (September 30, 1966), p. 9.

[78]Northrop Frye, *The Educated Imagination* (Bloomington: Indiana University Press, 1964), p.111.

tion to *Stories from the Bible* (413) provides an excellent background for understanding the problems of translation. He compares versions of the story of Ruth in the Geneva Bible (1560), the Douai Bible (1609), and the Authorized Version (1611). The old form of spelling is used in his quotations from Wycliffe of 1382, John Purvey of 1386, and Miles Coverdale of 1536. He clearly explains the differences between literal, allegorical, moral, and analogical meanings given words and phrases. This book presents the Creation; the flood; and stories of Moses, Joseph, Samson, Samuel, Saul, and David. The text combines modern style with imagery in description and a biblical form in conversation. For example: "As Joseph grew older, and in all that he was and did showed himself more and more unlike themselves, jealousy gnawed in their hearts like the fretting of a cankerworm."[79]

The text for *Brian Wildsmith's Illustrated Bible Stories* (432) was written by Philip Turner, a winner of the British Carnegie Medal for distinguished writing for children. The Bible story has been presented in chronological order as a consecutive narrative, including stories of both the Old and New Testaments. The writing has dignity and simplicity and Wildsmith's pictures illuminate every page. Alvin Tresselt (431) has retold twelve of the traditional stories from the Old Testament which Lynd Ward illustrated with handsome lithographs. The prose has retained the poetic quality of the Old Testament and at the same time has been artfully simplified. Marguerite de Angeli closely followed the text of the King James version in her edition of *The Old Testament* (412). Her soft watercolor illustrations are superb, and the pencil character studies are especially fine.

SINGLE BIBLE STORIES

Many individual picture-book stories from the Bible are especially useful for sharing with children. Leonard Everett Fisher adapted *The Seven Days of Creation* (417) and created bold colorful paintings to excite the imagination of readers. Helga Aichinger's full-color paintings for *Noah and the Rainbow* (407) have an exquisite simplicity of line that matches the fine retelling of this ancient story translated from the German by Clyde Bulla. Peter Spier contrasts many types of page design to tell in almost wordless picture-book format the story of

[79]Walter de la Mare, *Stories from the Bible*, illustrated by Edward Ardizzone (New York: Knopf, 1961), p. 62.

Noah's Ark (430). Double-page spreads portray the drama of preparing the ark and of the rising waters. Smaller groups of smaller pictures detail the mounting mess inside the ark, Noah's humorous encounters with the huge family of animals, and poignant moments before he sends a dove to find dry land. In *Noah and the Great Flood* (424), Warwick Hutton uses the King James version of the story as his text. His watercolor pictures have the quiet power of a tableau in contrast to the constant activity of Peter Spier's ark.

Hutton has also retold the story of *Jonah and the Great Fish* (423). His powerful watercolors depict the reluctant rose-clad Jonah against an increasingly angry and darkening backdrop of sky and sea. In the belly of the great fish, Jonah rests on a bed of fish, his legs crossed in fin fashion. Hutton has created a vivid interpretation of this Old Testament story. Bulla's retelling (408) features distinguished pictures of great simplicity, again by Aichinger. The all-blue great fish fills a double-page spread, while the sea seems to splash and swirl over the pages. Peter Spier's text for *The Book of Jonah* (429) is taken from his translation of the Dutch equivalent of the King James Bible. Spier's version follows Jonah from the busy Joppa shipyard to his ill-fated journey into the Mediterranean Sea and, finally, to his angry vigil and reconciliation on the hillside near Nineveh. A fascinating four-page historical note provides valuable background information for this well-known tale of the Old Testament. A comparison of text and illustration of different versions of Noah's or Jonah's story would help children appreciate variety in interpretation of the same tale.

In *A Basket in the Reeds* (427) by Saporta, the illustrations are patterned after Egyptian wall paintings. The text includes a poetic description of the river as the basket carrying the baby Moses floats in the reeds. Children should be made aware of the way this author used his imagination to extend the brief account in the Bible. Using her imagination in much the same way, Miriam Chaikin tells of *Joshua in the Promised Land* (409). David Frampton's bordered and stylized woodcuts illustrate the Israelites' fight for the Promised Land, led by Joshua, successor to Moses. *Esther* by Lisl Weil (434) reveals the way Esther saves her Hebrew people by tricking the evil Haman. Her deeds are remembered in the feast of Purim. This picture book would help clarify for children the Purim

play so essential for the family's escape from persecution in Kathryn Lasky's *The Night Journey* (see Chapter 9).

Lorenz Graham has retold five Bible stories in the idiomatic language of African-English, which he heard in Liberia. *David He No Fear* (418) is the well-loved story of David and Goliath. Ann Grifalconi's strong and powerful woodcuts are most appropriate for this story. The other books in the series are *God Wash the World and Start Again* (420), *A Road Down in the Sea* (422); and, from the New Testament, *Every Man Heart Lay Down* (birth of Jesus) (419) and *Hongry Catch the Foolish Boy* (Prodigal Son) (421). These retellings provide an immediacy and simplicity to Bible stories for all children.

The story of *The Tower of Babel* (435) has been retold by William Wiesner in picture-book form. The richly designed illustrations are busy and full of details. The figures are flat and stiff, as in Mesopotamian art, but they become very animated as their language is confused and they can no longer communicate with one another. This is very much a pourquoi story, explaining the division of one people into many nations and languages. It is essentially a good story, but it would also be very useful in a unit on communication.

Isaac Bashevis Singer has vividly retold the Old Testament story of the destruction of Sodom in *The Wicked City* (428). The text is substantial, with a strong sense of story and the underlying layer of meaning for today's world. For example, when Abraham comes to visit Lot, neighbors talk:

> "Why did Lot allow his crazy uncle to come here?" one of the bystanders asked. Others pelted Abraham and his two companions with the dung of asses.
>
> "This is what happens when one admits strangers," said another. "Sooner or later they bring foreigners with them."[80]

The scratchboard pictures by Fisher provide fine details of texture and facial expression.

Older children will be better able to appreciate the many subtleties and symbols in the boldly colorful and sensual illustrations of Charles Miko-

laycak. He has illustrated two Old Testament stories retold by Barbara Cohen as first-person narratives. Isaac, an old grandfather in *The Binding of Isaac* (410), tells how he was nearly sacrificed by his father, Abraham. While there are many proper names introduced as the assembled children question Isaac, the story line remains dramatically clear. In a longer text, *I Am Joseph* (411), Joseph tells how his pride in his "coat of many colors" led to years of unhappiness and estrangement before he was finally reunited with his brothers and father. From the New Testament, Mikolaycak has depicted two stories both adapted by Elizabeth Winthrop. Illustrations for *A Child Is Born* (436) give a more active and protective role to Joseph. *He Is Risen* (437) portrays in strong diagonals and a muted pallette of rusts, browns, and reds the central events of the Easter story. As in all of his stories from the Bible, Mikolaycak's authen-

Yucca and poinsettia bloom in Barbara Cooney's illustrations for this Aztec version of the Nativity story. From *Spirit Child: A Story of the Nativity* by John Bierhorst.

[80]Isaac Bashevis Singer, *The Wicked City*, translated by the author and Elizabeth Shub, illustrated by Leonard Everett Fisher (New York: Farrar, Straus, 1972), unpaged.

tic depictions of textile patterns, everyday detail, armor, and headgear are based on research he conducts in such places as the Metropolitan Museum. Using patterned black, gray, and white, Mikolaycak has also illustrated Bernard Evslin's *Signs and Wonders: Tales from the Old Testament* (416). As in his other work, Evslin creates dialogue, description, and elaboration to clarify what he feels are points that may confuse the reader.

The Christmas story has been retold in words and pictures many times. Everyone has a favorite, but certainly Piatti's *The Holy Night* (433) and Aichinger's *The Shepherd* (401) must be among the most beautiful. *The Christ Child* (404), illustrated by the Petershams, has long been a favorite to share with children. As do many illustrators of this story, Jan Pieńkowski uses gilt borders in his exquisite *Christmas—The King James Version* (405). Detailed black silhouettes against softly colored backgrounds give this telling the look of a pageant. John Bierhorst discovered and translated an Aztec version of the Nativity in *Spirit Child: A Story of the Nativity* (406). Barbara Cooney's beautiful paintings portray the story against a background of rural Aztec villages, mountain landscapes, and traditional ornamentation.

Another legend associated with Christmas is *The Legend of Old Befana* (414). Tomie de Paola's Italian version tells the story of the old woman who was too busy cleaning her house and sidewalks to accompany the wise men and her subsequent destiny—to wander the earth forever. His *The Story of the Three Wise Kings* (415) begins with a historical note of how this story has developed over the centuries and would make a good companion to Befana's story. *Baboushka and the Three Kings*, a Caldecott Medal-winner written by Robbins and illustrated by Sidjakov (426), is a Russian version. Mikolaycak's *Babushka* (425) depicts the Russian Befana journeying and searching through the ages and into contemporary times. These stories would be ripe for reading on January 6, or Twelfth Night, the traditional "Feast of the Three Kings."

In two related books about the Bible, *Words in Genesis* (403) and *Words from the Exodus* (402), Asimov shows how our modern language has been enriched by words derived from the Old Testament. As in his book *Words from the Myths* (311), Asimov presents the story behind the words and our present-day use of them.

The Bible, the myths, the fables, and folktales represent the literature of the people down through the ages. Folk literature has deep roots in basic human feelings. Through this literature, children may form a link with the common bonds of humanity from the beginnings of time.

SUGGESTED LEARNING EXPERIENCES

1. Read as many folktales and myths of one country as you can. Assuming that these stories provided your only basis for understanding the country, chart the characteristics of the country which can be derived from the tales. Include land formations, climate, food, animals, typical occupations, customs, beliefs, values, expressions, and so forth.
2. Choose one motif, such as transformations, wishes, or magical objects, and see how many different tales you can find in that classification.
3. Find as many different editions as you can of such well-known stories as "Cinderella," "Hansel and Gretel," "Sleeping Beauty," "Noah's Ark," or "Puss In Boots." Chart or compare both the language of the retellings and the illustrations.
4. Find as many variations as you can on a particular theme, such as "Helpful Companions," "Jack and the Beanstalk," or "Cinderella." Bring them to class and share them in small groups.
5. Select one folktale that you think you would like to learn to tell. Prepare it and tell it to four or five members of your class or to a group of children. What suggestions do they or you have for improving your presentation?
6. Write a modern fable for such well-known morals as "Pride goeth before a fall" or "Don't count your chicks before they hatch." Use present-day objects, animals, or people.
7. Collect advertisements that show our use of words from the myths; for example, Atlas tires, Mercury cars, Ajax cleanser. Using the book *Words from the Myths* by Asimov determine the story behind the advertisement.

8. Make a list of literary titles or allusions derived from myth or scriptural writings.
9. On the basis of your knowledge of the characteristics of an epic, what do you think the hero of a North American epic might be like? Consider personal qualities, obstacles, achievements.
10. Develop a simple inventory of names from folktales, fables, myths, and Biblical characters. Give it to your class or ask to give it to a group of children. How well known is traditional literature today?

RELATED READINGS

1. Bettelheim, Bruno. *The Uses of Enchantment*. New York: Knopf, 1976.
   A noted child psychologist maintains that fairy tales have a unique place in the development of children, satisfying many of their deepest emotional needs. He offers detailed analysis of several individual tales to show how they enable children to cope with their emotions and their world.
2. Brean, Herbert, and the editors of *Life*. *The Life Treasury of American Folklore*, illustrated by James Lewicki. New York: Time, 1961.
   Picture maps would be of interest to children. Includes lesser-known American heroes and such unsavory characters as Jesse James.
3. Bulfinch, Thomas. *The Age of Fable or Beauties of Mythology*. New York: New American Library, 1962.
   This classical survey of mythology is presented in paperback. Notes and references are very helpful.
4. Cook, Elizabeth. *The Ordinary and the Fabulous*. Cambridge, England: Cambridge University Press, 1969.
   A senior lecturer in English discusses myths, legends, and fairy tales for teachers and storytellers. A particularly helpful section is the author's critical analysis of the presentation of some scenes from myths and legends in various editions.
5. Dundes, Alan, ed. *Cinderella: A Casebook*. New York: Wildman Press, 1983.
   A collection of scholarly essays spanning the history of folklore research on the Cinderella theme. Of special interest to teachers and librarians are discussions of "Cinderella in Africa," a Jungian approach to "The Beautiful Wassilissa," and Jane Yolen's look at Cinderella in the mass market in "America's Cinderella."
6. Favat, André. *Child and Tale: The Origins of Interest*. NCTE Research Report #19. Urbana, Ill.: The National Council of Teachers of English, 1977.
   Favat traces parallels between the components of traditional fairy tales and the concepts of reality as held by children 6 to 8 years of age, the period of peak interest in fairy tales.
7. Frye, Northrop. *The Educated Imagination*. Bloomington: Indiana University Press, 1964.
   A literary critic develops a theory of literature and presents a plan for literary study in the school that includes intensive study of the Bible and other traditional literature.
8. Hamilton, Edith. *Mythology,* illustrated by Steele Savage. Boston: Little, Brown, 1944.
   The introduction summarizes the emergence of Greek ideas. Genealogical tables are helpful. A very readable source presenting Creation, Stories of Love and Adventure, and Heroes of the Trojan War.
9. Opie, Iona, and Peter Opie. *The Classic Fairy Tales*. New York: Oxford University Press, 1974.
   Twenty-four of the best known fairy tales are presented as they first appeared in print in English. Pictures are gleaned from two centuries of illustrators. An invaluable source of information on primary sources is the Opies' introductory essay for each tale.
10. Thompson, Stith. *The Folktale*. New York: Holt, Rinehart and Winston, 1951.
    Various theories of the origins of folktales and folktale themes are presented in a thorough manner in this book.
11. Yolen, Jane. *Touch Magic: Fantasy, Faerie and Folklore in the Literature of Childhood*. New York: Philomel, 1981.
    In short lively essays the author, herself a writer of fantasy and the literary tale, discusses the history of folklore and its role in the social, emotional, and intellectual growth of the child.

REFERENCES[81]

FOLKTALES

1. Aardema, Verna. *The Riddle of the Drum*, illustrated by Tony Chen. Four Winds, 1979. (S—Mexico)
2. _____. *Why Mosquitoes Buzz in People's Ears*, illustrated by Leo and Diane Dillon. Dial, 1975. (S—Africa)
3. _____. *Who's in Rabbit's House?*, illustrated by Leo and Diane Dillon. Dial, 1977. (S—Africa)
4. Andersen, Hans Christian. *The Wild Swans*, retold by Amy Erlich, illustrated by Susan Jeffers. Dial, 1981. (S—Literary)
5. Apy, Deborah. *Beauty and the Beast*, illustrated by Michael Hague. Holt, 1983. (S—France)
6. Arbuthnot, May Hill, compiler. *The Arbuthnot Anthology of Children's Literature*, rev. ed. Scott, Foresman, 1961.
7. Arkhurst, Joyce Cooper. *The Adventures of Spider, West African Folk Tales*, illustrated by Jerry Pinkney. Little, Brown, 1964.
8. Asbjørnsen, Peter Christian, and Jorgen E. Moe. *East O' the Sun and West O' the Moon*, translated by George Webbe Dasent. Dover, 1970 (1888). (Norway)
9. _____. *East of the Sun and West of the Moon, and Other Tales*, illustrated by Tom Vroman. Macmillan, 1963. (Norway)
10. _____. *The Three Billy Goats Gruff*, illustrated by Marcia Brown. Harcourt, 1957. (S—Norway)
11. d'Aulaire, Ingri, and Edgar d'Aulaire, editors and illustrators. *East of the Sun and West of the Moon*. Viking, 1969 (1938). (Norway)
12. Ball, Zachary. *Young Mike Fink*, illustrated by Paul Lantz. Holiday, 1958. (United States)
13. Bang, Molly. *Dawn*. Morrow, 1983. (S—Literary)
14. _____. *Wiley and the Hairy Man*. Macmillan, 1976. (S—United States)
15. Barth, Edna. *Cupid and Psyche: A Love Story*, illustrated by Ati Forberg. Houghton Mifflin, 1976. (S—Greece)
16. Baylor, Byrd, editor. *And It Is Still That Way*. Scribner, 1976. (Native American)
17. Belpré, Pura. *The Dance of the Animals: A Puerto Rican Folk Tale*, illustrated by Paul Galdone. Warne, 1972. (S)
18. _____. *Oté: A Puerto Rican Folk Tale*, illustrated by Paul Galdone. Pantheon, 1969. (S)
19. _____. *Perez and Martina*, rev. ed., illustrated by Carlos Sanchez. Warne, 1961. (S—Puerto Rico)
20. Berson, Harold. *Balarin's Goat*. Crown, 1972. (S—France)
21. _____. *The Thief Who Hugged a Moonbeam*. Seabury, 1972. (S—France)
22. _____. *Why the Jackal Won't Speak to the Hedgehog*. Seabury, 1969. (S—Tunisia)
23. Bishop, Claire Huchet. *The Five Chinese Brothers*, illustrated by Kurt Wiese. Coward-McCann, 1938. (S)
24. Bierhorst, John, editor. *The Girl Who Married a Ghost and Other Tales from the North American Indians*, photographs by Edward S. Curtis. Four Winds, 1978.
25. Bishop, Gavin. *Chicken Licken*. Oxford, 1984. (S—England)
26. Blegvad, Erik. *The Three Little Pigs*. Atheneum, 1980. (S—England)
27. Bogdanovic, Toma, illustrator. *The Fire Bird*. Scroll Press, 1972. (S—Russia)
28. Brenner, Barbara. *Little One Inch*, illustrated by Fred Brenner. Coward, 1977. (S—Japan)
29. Briggs, Raymond. *Jim and the Beanstalk*. Coward, 1970. (S—Modern Literary)
30. Bro, Marguerite Harmon. *How the Mouse Deer Became King*, illustrated by Joseph Low. Doubleday, 1966. (Indonesia)
31. Brown, Marcia. *The Bun: A Tale from Russia*. Harcourt, 1972. (S)
32. _____. *Dick Whittington and His Cat*. Scribner, 1950. (S—England)

[81]Single tales are identified with the code letter S. Where country of origin is not obviously indicated within the reference, it is supplied in parentheses at the end. All books listed at the end of this chapter are recommended, subject to the qualifications noted in the text. See Appendix for publishers' complete addresses.

33. _____. *Stone Soup.* Scribner, 1947. (S—France)
34. _____. *The Blue Jackal.* Scribner, 1977. (S—India)
35. Brown, Margaret Wise. *Brer Rabbit: Stories from Uncle Remus,* illustrated by A. B. Frost. Harper, 1941. (Black American)
36. Bryan, Ashley. *Beat the Story-Drum, Pum-Pum.* Atheneum, 1980. (Africa)
37. _____. *The Cat's Purr.* Atheneum, 1985. (S—Antilles)
38. _____. *The Dancing Granny.* Atheneum, 1977. (S—Antilles)
39. _____. *The Ox of the Wonderful Horns and Other African Folktales.* Atheneum, 1971.
40. Bryant, Sara Cone. *The Burning Rice Fields,* illustrated by Mamoru Funai. Holt, 1963. (S—Japan)
41. Carew, Jan. *The Third Gift,* illustrated by Leo and Diane Dillon. Little, Brown, 1974. (S—Africa)
42. Carey, Bonnie. *Baba Yaga's Geese and Other Russian Stories.* Indiana University Press, 1973.
43. Carpenter, Frances. *Tales of a Chinese Grandmother,* illustrated by Malthe Hasselriis. Doubleday, 1949.
44. Cauley, Lorinda Bryan. *Jack and the Beanstalk.* Putnam, 1983. (S—England)
45. Chandler, Robert, translator. *Russian Folktales,* illustrated by Ivan I. Bilibin. Shambala/Random, 1980.
46. Chase, Richard. *Grandfather Tales.* Houghton Mifflin, 1948. (United States)
47. _____. *The Jack Tales,* illustrated by Berkeley Williams, Jr. Houghton Mifflin, 1943. (United States)
48. Cimino, Maria. *The Disobedient Eels and Other Italian Tales,* illustrated by Claire Nivola. Pantheon, 1970.
49. Coalson, Glo. *Three Stone Woman.* Atheneum, 1971. (S—Eskimo)
50. Cole, Joanna. *Bony-Legs,* illustrated by Dirk Zimmer. Four Winds, 1983. (S—Russian)
51. Colum, Padraic. *The Arabian Nights,* illustrated by Lynd Ward. Macmillan, 1953 (1923).
52. Conger, Lesley. *Tops and Bottoms,* illustrated by Imero Gobbato. Four Winds, 1970. (S—England)
53. Coombs, Patricia. *The Magic Pot.* Lothrop, 1977. (S—Modern Literary)
54. Cooper, Susan. *The Silver Cow,* illustrated by Warwick Hutton. Atheneum, 1983. (S—Wales)
55. Courlander, Harold. *The King's Drum and Other African Tales.* Harcourt, 1962.
56. _____. *Terrapin's Pot of Sense,* illustrated by Elton Fax. Holt, 1957. (Black American)
57. _____. *The Tiger's Whisker and Other Tales and Legends from Asia and the Pacific,* illustrated by Enrico Arno. Harcourt, 1959.
58. Courlander, Harold, and George Herzog. *The Cow-Tail Switch and Other West African Stories,* illustrated by Madye Lee Chastain. Holt, 1947.
59. Crompton, Anne Eliot. *The Winter Wife,* illustrated by Robert Andrew Parker. Little, Brown, 1975. (S—Native American)
60. Dayrell, Elphinstone. *Why the Sun and the Moon Live in the Sky,* illustrated by Blair Lent. Houghton Mifflin, 1968. (S—Africa)
61. de la Mare, Walter. *Mollie Whuppie,* illustrated by Errol Le Cain. Farrar, Straus, 1983. (S—England)
62. De Beaumont, Madame. *Beauty and the Beast,* translated and illustrated by Diane Goode. Bradbury, 1978. (S—France)
63. de Paola, Tomie. *Fin M'Coul: The Giant of Knockmany Hill.* Holiday, 1981. (S—Ireland)
64. _____. *Strega Nona.* Prentice-Hall, 1975. (S—Literary, Italy)
65. de Regniers, Beatrice Schenk. *Red Riding Hood,* illustrated by Edward Gorey. Atheneum, 1972. (S—Germany)
66. De Roin, Nancy. *Jataka Tales: Fables from the Buddha,* illustrated by Ellen Lanyon. Houghton Mifflin, 1975. (India)
67. de Wit, Dorothy, editor. *The Talking Stone: An Anthology of Native American Tales and Legends,* illustrated by Donald Crews. Greenwillow, 1979.
68. Dewey, Ariane. *Febold Feboldson.* Greenwillow, 1984. (S—United States)
69. Domanska, Janina. *The Best of the Bargain.* Greenwillow, 1977. (S—Poland)

70. Downing, Charles. *Tales of the Hodja,* illustrated by William Papas. Walck, 1965. (Turkey)

71. Duff, Maggie. *Rum Pum Pum: A Folk Tale from India,* illustrated by José Aruego and Ariane Dewey. Macmillan, 1978.

72. Emrich, Duncan. *The Hodgepodge Book: An Almanac of American Folklore,* illustrated by Ib Ohlsson. Four Winds, 1972.

73. _____. *The Nonsense Book of Riddles, Rhymes, Tongue Twisters, Puzzles and Jokes from American Folklore,* illustrated by Ib Ohlsson. Four Winds, 1972.

74. Evslin, Bernard. *The Green Hero: Early Adventures of Finn McCool,* illustrated by Barbara Bascove. Four Winds, 1975. (Ireland)

75. Felton, Harold W. *True Tall Tales of Stormalong: Sailor of the Seven Seas,* illustrated by Joan Sandin. Prentice-Hall, 1968. (United States)

76. Feuerlecht, Roberta Strauss. *The Legends of Paul Bunyan,* illustrated by Kurt Werth. Macmillan, 1966. (United States)

77. Finger, Charles, *Tales from Silver Lands,* illustrated by Paul Honoré. Doubleday, 1924. (Latin America)

78. Frasconi, Antonio. *The House That Jack Built.* Harcourt, 1958. (S—England)

79. Freedman, Florence B. *Brothers: A Hebrew Legend,* illustrated by Robert Andrew Parker. Harper, 1985. (S)

80. French, Fiona. *The Blue Bird.* Walck, 1972. (S—Literary China)

81. Gág, Wanda. *Gone Is Gone.* Coward-McCann, 1935. (S—Norway)

82. _____. *Jorinda and Joringel,* illustrated by Margot Tomes. Coward-McCann, 1978. (S—Germany)

83. _____. *The Six Swans,* illustrated by Margot Tomes. Coward-McCann, 1982. (S—Germany)

84. _____. *The Sorcerer's Apprentice.* Coward McCann, 1979. (S—Germany)

85. Galdone, Paul. *Cinderella.* McGraw-Hill, 1978. (S—France)

86. _____. *Henny Penny.* Seabury, 1968. (S—England)

87. _____. *The History of Mother Twaddle and the Marvelous Achievements of Her Son Jack.* Seabury, 1974. (S—England)

88. _____. *The Little Red Hen.* Seabury, 1974. (S—England)

89. _____. *Little Red Riding Hood.* McGraw-Hill, 1974. (S—Germany)

90. _____. *The Magic Porridge Pot.* Seabury, 1976. (S—Germany)

91. _____. *The Old Woman and Her Pig.* McGraw-Hill, 1960. (S—England)

92. _____. *Puss in Boots.* Seabury, 1976. (S—France)

93. _____. *The Three Billy Goats Gruff.* Seabury, 1973. (S—Norway)

94. _____. *The Three Little Pigs.* Seabury, 1970. (S—England)

95. _____. *The Three Wishes.* McGraw-Hill, 1961. (S—England)

96. Ginsburg, Mirra. *The Lazies: Tales of the Peoples of Russia.* Macmillan, 1973.

97. _____. *The Twelve Clever Brothers and Other Fools,* illustrated by Charles Mikolaycak. Lippincott, 1979. (Russia)

98. _____. *Three Rolls and One Doughnut: Fables from Russia,* illustrated by Anita Lobel. Dial, 1970.

99. Goble, Paul. *Buffalo Woman.* Bradbury, 1984. (S—Native American)

100. _____. *The Girl Who Loved Wild Horses.* Bradbury, 1978. (S—Literary, Native American)

101. _____. *Star Boy.* Bradbury, 1983. (S—Native American)

102. Godden, Rumer. *The Old Woman Who Lived in a Vinegar Bottle,* illustrated by Mairi Hedderwick. Viking, 1972. (S—England)

103. Grimm Brothers. *The Bremen Town Musicians,* retold and illustrated by Donna Diamond. Delacorte, 1981. (S)

104. _____. *The Bremen-Town Musicians,* retold and illustrated by Ilse Plume. Doubleday, 1980. (S)

105. _____. *The Bremen Town Musicians,* translated by Elizabeth Shub, illustrated by Janina Domanska. Greenwillow, 1980. (S)

106. _____. *Cinderella,* illustrated by Nonny Hogrogian. Greenwillow, 1981. (S)

107. _____. *The Elves and the Shoemaker,* retold and illustrated by Paul Galdone. Clarion, 1984. (S)

108. _____. *Favorite Tales from Grimm,* retold by Nancy Garden, illustrated by Mercer Mayer. Four Winds, 1982.

109. _____. *The Fisherman and His Wife,* translated by Randall Jarrell, illustrated by Margot Zemach. Farrar, Straus, 1980. (S)
110. _____. *The Fisherman and His Wife,* translated by Elizabeth Shub, illustrated by Monica Laimgruber. Greenwillow, 1978. (S)
111. _____. *Hans in Luck,* illustrated by Felix Hoffman. Atheneum, 1975. (S)
112. _____. *Hansel and Gretel,* translated by Charles Scribner, Jr., illustrated by Adrienne Adams. Scribner, 1975. (S)
113. _____. *Hansel and Gretel,* illustrated by Anthony Browne. F. Watts, 1981. (S)
114. _____. *Hansel and Gretel,* translated by Elizabeth D. Crawford, illustrated by Lisbeth Zwerger. Morrow, 1979. (S)
115. _____. *Hansel and Gretel,* illustrated by Paul Galdone. McGraw-Hill, 1982. (S)
116. _____. *Hansel and Gretel,* illustrated by Susan Jeffers. Dial, 1980. (S)
117. _____. *Hansel and Gretel,* retold by Rika Lesser, illustrated by Paul O. Zelinsky. Dodd Mead, 1984. (S)
118. _____. *Household Stories,* translated by Lucy Crane, illustrated by Walter Crane. Dover. (1886)
119. _____. *The Juniper Tree and Other Tales from Grimm,* translated by Lore Segal and Maurice Sendak, illustrated by Maurice Sendak. Farrar, Straus, 1973.
120. _____. *King Thrushbeard,* illustrated by Felix Hoffmann. Harcourt, 1961. (S)
121. _____. *Little Red Cap,* translated by Elizabeth D. Crawford, illustrated by Lisbeth Zwerger. Morrow, 1983. (S)
122. _____. *Little Red Riding Hood,* illustrated by Trina Schart Hyman. Holiday, 1983. (S)
123. _____. *Mother Holly,* retold and illustrated by Bernadette Watts. Crowell, 1972. (S)
124. _____. *Popular Folk Tales: The Brothers Grimm,* translated by Brian Alderson, illustrated by Michael Foreman. Doubleday, 1978.
125. _____. *Rapunzel,* retold by Barbara Rogasky, illustrated by Trina Schart Hyman. Holiday, 1982. (S)
126. _____. *Rumpelstiltskin,* illustrated by Donna Diamond. Holiday, 1983. (S)
127. _____. *The Seven Ravens,* translated by Elizabeth D. Crawford, illustrated by Lisbeth Zwerger. Morrow, 1981. (S)
128. _____. *The Seven Ravens,* illustrated by Felix Hoffmann. Harcourt, 1963. (S)
129. _____. *The Sleeping Beauty,* retold and illustrated by Warwick Hutton. Atheneum, 1979. (S)
130. _____. *The Sleeping Beauty,* retold and illustrated by Trina Schart Hyman. Little, Brown, 1974. (S)
131. _____. *Snow White,* translated by Paul Heins, illustrated by Trina Schart Hyman. Little, Brown, 1974. (S)
132. _____. *Snow-White and the Seven Dwarfs,* translated by Randall Jarrell, illustrated by Nancy Ekholm Burkert. Farrar, Straus, 1972. (S)
133. _____. *The Table, the Donkey, and the Stick,* illustrated by Paul Galdone. McGraw-Hill, 1976. (S)
134. _____. *Tales from Grimm,* translated and illustrated by Wanda Gág. Coward McCann, 1936.
135. _____. *Thorn Rose or The Sleeping Beauty,* illlustrated by Errol Le Cain. Bradbury, 1975. (S)
136. _____. *Tom Thumb,* illustrated by Felix Hoffmann. Atheneum, 1973. (S)
137. _____. *The Twelve Dancing Princesses,* illustrated by Errol Le Cain. Viking, 1978. (S)
138. _____. *The Valiant Little Tailor,* illustated by Victor G. Ambrus. Oxford, 1980. (S)
139. Grinnell, George Bird. *The Whistling Skeleton: American Indian Tales of the Supernatural,* edited by John Bierhorst, illustrated by Robert Andrew Parker. Four Winds, 1982.
140. Hague, Kathleen, and Michael Hague. *East of the Sun and West of the Moon,* illustrated by Michael Hague. Harcourt, 1980. (S—Norway)
141. Haley, Gail E. *A Story, A Story.* Atheneum, 1970. (S—Africa)
142. _____. *Jack and the Bean Tree.* Crown, 1986. (S—United States)
143. Hamilton, Virginia. *The Magical Adventures of Pretty Pearl.* Harper, 1983. (Black American)
144. _____. *The People Could Fly,* illustrated by Leo and Diane Dillon. Knopf, 1985. (Black American)

145. Harris, Christie. *Mouse Woman and the Mischief-Makers*, illustrated by Douglas Tait. Atheneum, 1977. (Native American)

146. _____. *Mouse Woman and the Muddleheads*, illustrated by Douglas Tait. Atheneum, 1979. (Native American)

147. _____. *Mouse Woman and the Vanished Princess*, illustrated by Douglas Tait. Atheneum, 1976. (Native American)

148. _____. *Once More upon a Totem*, illustrated by Douglas Tait. Atheneum, 1973. (Native American)

149. Harris, Rosemary, reteller. *Beauty and the Beast*, illustrated by Errol Le Cain. Doubleday, 1979. (S—France)

150. Harris, Joel Chandler. *The Complete Tales of Uncle Remus*, compiled by Richard Chase, illustrated by Arthur Frost and others. Houghton Mifflin, 1955. (Black American)

151. Haviland, Virginia. *Favorite Fairy Tales Told in Czechoslovakia*, illustrated by Trina Schart Hyman. Little, Brown, 1966.

152. _____. *Favorite Fairy Tales Told in India*, illustrated by Blair Lent. Little, Brown, 1973.

153. _____. *Favorite Fairy Tales Told in Italy*, illustrated by Evaline Ness. Little, Brown, 1965.

154. _____. *Favorite Fairy Tales Told in Japan*, illustrated by George Suyeoka. Little, Brown, 1967.

155. _____. *Favorite Fairy Tales Told in Norway*, illustrated by Leonard Weisgard. Little, Brown, 1961.

156. _____, editor. *North American Legends*, illustrated by Ann Strugnell. Collins, 1979.

157. He Liyi. *The Spring of Butterflies and Other Chinese Folk Tales*. Lothrop, 1986.

158. Highwater, Jamake. *Anpao*, illustrated by Fritz Scholder. Lippincott, 1977. (Native American)

159. Hill, Kay. *More Glooscap Stories: Legends of the Wabanaki Indians*, illustrated by John Hamberger. Dodd Mead, 1970.

160. Hirsch, Marilyn. *Could Anything Be Worse?* Holiday, 1974. (S—Jewish)

161. Hodges, Margaret. *The Fire Bringer: A Paiute Indian Legend*, illustrated by Peter Parnall. Little, Brown, 1972. (S)

162. _____. *The Little Humpbacked Horse*, illustrated by Chris Conover. Farrar, 1980. (S—Russia)

163. _____. *The Wave*, illustrated by Blair Lent. Houghton Mifflin, 1964. (S—Japan)

164. Hogrogian, Nonny. *One Fine Day*. Macmillan, 1971. (S—Armenian)

165. Houston, James. *Akavak: An Eskimo Journey*. Harcourt, 1968. (S)

166. _____. *Tikta Liktak: An Eskimo Legend*. Harcourt, 1965. (S)

167. _____. *The White Archer: An Eskimo Legend*. Harcourt, 1967. (S)

168. Hutton, Warwick. *The Nose Tree*. Atheneum, 1981. (S—England)

169. _____. *Beauty and the Beast*. Atheneum, 1985. (S—France)

170. Hyman, Trina Schart. *Self-Portrait: Trina Schart Hyman*. Addison-Wesley, 1981.

171. Ishii, Momoko. *Issun Boshi, the Inchling: An Old Tale of Japan*, translated by Yone Mizuta, illustrated by Fuku Akino. Walker, 1967. (S)

172. Jacobs, Joseph. *The Story of the Three Little Pigs*, illustrated by Lorinda Bryan Cauley. Putnam, 1980. (S—England)

173. Jagendorf, Moritz A. *Noodlehead Stories from Around the World*, illustrated by Shane Miller. Vanguard, 1957.

174. Jameson, Cynthia. *The Clay Pot Boy*, illustrated by Arnold Lobel. Coward-McCann, 1973. (S—Russia)

175. Jaquith, Priscilla. *Bo Rabbit Smart for True: Folktales from the Gullah*, illustrated by Ed Young. Philomel, 1981. (Black American)

176. Jeffers, Susan. *Wild Robin*. Dutton, 1976. (S—Scotland)

177. Keats, Ezra Jack. *John Henry, An American Legend*. Pantheon, 1965. (S)

178. Kellogg, Steven. *Chicken Little*. Morrow, 1985. (S—Modern Literary)

179. _____. *Paul Bunyan*. Morrow, 1984. (S—United States)

180. Kent, Jack. *The Fat Cat: A Danish Folktale*. Parents', 1971. (S)

181. Lang, Andrew, reteller. *Aladdin*, illustrated by Errol Le Cain. Viking, 1981. (S—Arabia)

182. _____. *The Arabian Nights*, illustrated by Vera Bock. McKay, 1951.

183. _____. *The Blue Fairy Book*, illustrated by Reisie Lonette. Random House, 1959.

184. _____. *The Twelve Dancing Princesses*, illustrated by Adrienne Adams. Holt, 1966. (S—France)

185. Leach, Maria, *Noodles, Nitwits and Numbskulls*, illustrated by Kurt Werth. World, 1961.

186. Leekley, Thomas B. *The World of Manabozho: Tales of the Chippewa Indians*, illustrated by Yeffe Kimball. Vanguard, 1965.

187. Lester, Julius. *The Knee-high Man and Other Tales*, illustrated by Ralph Pinto. Dial, 1972. (Black American)

188. Littledale, Freya. *The Elves and the Shoemaker*, illustrated by Brinton Turkle. Four Winds, 1975. (S—Germany)

189. _____. *The Magic Plum Tree*, illustrated by Enrico Arno. Crown, 1981. (S—India)

190. Lobel, Arnold. *Fables*. Harper, 1980. (Literary)

191. Louie, Ai-Ling. *Yeh-Shen: A Cinderella Story from China*, illustrated by Ed Young. Philomel, 1982. (S)

192. Lunn, Janet. *The Twelve Dancing Princesses*, illustrated by Lászlo Gál. Metheun, 1979. (S)

193. McCarty, Toni. *The Skull in the Snow and Other Folktales*, illustrated by Katherine Coville. Delacorte, 1981.

194. McDermott, Gerald. *Anansi the Spider*. Holt, 1972. (S—African)

195. _____. *Arrow to the Sun*. Viking, 1974. (S—Native American)

196. Malcolmson, Anne. *Yankee Doodle's Cousins*, illustrated by Robert McCloskey. Houghton Mifflin, 1941. (United States)

197. Manning-Sanders, Ruth. *A Book of Charms and Changelings*, illustrated by Robin Jacques. Dutton, 1972.

198. _____. *A Choice of Magic*, illustrated by Robin Jacques. Dutton, 1971.

199. Marshak, Samuel. *The Month-Brothers: A Slavic Tale*, translated by Thomas P. Whitney, illustrated by Diane Stanley. Morrow, 1983. (S—Russian)

200. Mayer, Marianna, reteller. *Beauty and the Beast*, illustrated by Mercer Mayer. Four Winds, 1978. (S—France)

201. Mayer, Mercer. *East of the Sun and West of the Moon*. Four Winds, 1980. (S—Norway)

202. Mbane, Phumla. *Nomi and the Magic Fish*, illustrated by Carole Byard. Doubleday, 1972. (S—Africa)

203. Mehdevi, Anne Sinclair. *Persian Folk and Fairy Tales*, illustrated by Paul E. Kennedy. Knopf, 1965.

204. Merriam, Eve. *Epaminondas*, illustrated by Trina Schart Hyman. Follett, 1968. (S—United States)

205. Minard, Rosemary, editor. *Womenfolk and Fairy Tales*, illustrated by Suzanne Klein. Houghton Mifflin, 1975.

206. Mobley, Jane. *The Star Husband*, illustrated by Anna Vojtech. Doubleday, 1979. (S—Native American)

207. Mosel, Arlene. *The Funny Little Woman*, illustrated by Blair Lent. Dutton, 1972. (S—Japan)

208. _____. *Tikki Tikki Tembo*, illustrated by Blair Lent. Holt, 1968. (S—China)

209. Onassis, Jacqueline, editor. *The Firebird and Other Russian Tales*, illustrated by Boris Svorykin. Viking, 1978.

210. Ness, Evaline. *Tom Tit Tot*. Scribner, 1965. (S—England)

211. Nic Leodhas, Sorche. *Thistle and Thyme, Tales and Legends from Scotland*, illustrated by Evaline Ness. Holt, 1962.

212. Perrault, Charles. *Cinderella*, illustrated by Marcia Brown. Scribner, 1954. (S—France)

213. _____. *Cinderella, or The Little Glass Slipper*, illustrated by Errol Le Cain. Bradbury, 1973. (S—France)

214. _____. *The Glass Slipper: Charles Perrault's Tales of Times Past*, translated by John Bierhorst, illustrated by Mitchell Miller. Four Winds, 1981.

215. _____. *Puss in Boots*, illustrated by Marcia Brown. Scribner, 1952. (S—France)

216. Phelps, Ethel Johnston. *The Maid of the North: Feminist Folk Tales from Around the World*, illustrated by Lloyd Bloom. Holt, 1981.

217. Provensen, Alice, and Martin Provensen. *The Provensen Book of Fairy Tales*. Random, 1971.

218. Pyle, Howard. *Pepper and Salt, or Seasoning for Young Folks.* Harper, 1913.
219. Ransome, Arthur. *The Fool of the World and the Flying Ship,* illustrated by Uri Shulevitz. Farrar, Straus, 1968. (S—Russia)
220. Rees, Ennis. *Brer Rabbit and His Tricks,* illustrated by Edward Gorey. Young Scott Books, 1967. (Black American)
221. Reyher, Becky. *My Mother Is the Most Beautiful Woman in the World,* illustrated by Ruth Gannett. Lothrop, 1945. (S—Russia)
222. Robinson, Gail. *Raven the Trickster,* illustrated by Joanna Troughton. Atheneum, 1982. (Native American)
223. Rockwell, Anne. *The Three Bears and 15 Other Stories.* Crowell, 1975.
224. Rose, Anne. *Akimba and the Magic Cow,* illustrated by Hope Meryman. Four Winds, 1976. (S—Africa)
225. Ross, Tony. *Jack and the Beanstalk.* Delacorte, 1981. (S—England)
226. _____. *Puss in Boots: The Story of a Sneaky Cat.* Delacorte, 1981. (S—France)
227. _____. *The Three Pigs.* Pantheon, 1983. (S—England)
228. Rounds, Glen. *Ol' Paul, the Mighty Logger.* Holiday, 1949. (S—United States)
229. San Souci, Robert. *The Legend of Scarface: A Blackfeet Indian Tale,* illustrated by Daniel San Souci. Doubleday, 1978. (S)
230. Sawyer, Ruth, *Journey Cake, Ho!,* illustrated by Robert McCloskey. Viking, 1953. (S)
231. Schatz, Letta. *The Extraordinary Tug-of-War,* illustrated by John Burningham. Follett, 1968. (S—Africa)
232. Schoolcraft, Henry Rowe. *The Fire Plume: Legends of the American Indians,* edited by John Bierhorst, illustrated by Alan E. Cober. Dial, 1969.
233. _____. *The Ring in the Prairie: A Shawnee Legend,* edited by John Bierhorst, illustrated by Leo and Diane Dillon. Dial, 1970. (S)
234. Schwartz, Alvin. *Flapdoodle: Pure Nonsense from American Folklore,* illustrated by John O'Brien. Lippincott, 1980.
235. _____. *Witcracks: Jokes & Jests from American Folklore,* illustrated by Glen Rounds. Lippincott, 1973.
236. Serwer, Blanche Luria. *Let's Steal the Moon,* illustrated by Trina Schart Hyman. Little, Brown, 1970. (Jewish)
237. Shepard, Esther. *Paul Bunyan,* illustrated by Rockwell Kent. Harcourt, 1924. (United States)
238. Sherlock, Philip M. *Anansi the Spider Man, Jamaican Folk Tales,* illustrated by Marcia Brown. Crowell, 1954.
239. Shub, Elizabeth, adapter. *Clever Kate: Adapted from a Story by the Brothers Grimm,* illustrated by Anita Lobel. Macmillan, 1973. (S—Germany)
240. Shulevitz, Uri. *The Magician,* adapted from the Yiddish of I. L. Peretz. Macmillan, 1973. (S—Jewish)
241. _____, illustrator. *Soldier and Tsar in the Forest: A Russian Tale,* translated by Richard Lourie. Farrar, Straus, 1972. (S)
242. Silverman, Maida. *Anna and the Seven Swans,* illustrated by David Small. Morrow, 1984. (S—Russian)
243. Singer, Isaac Bashevis. *Elijah the Slave,* translated by the author and Elizabeth Shub, illustrated by Antonio Frasconi. Farrar, Straus, 1970. (S—Jewish)
244. _____. *Mazel and Shlimazel, or the Milk of a Lioness,* illustrated by Margot Zemach. Farrar, Straus, 1967. (S—Jewish)
245. _____. *When Shlemiel Went to Warsaw and Other Stories,* translated by the author and Elizabeth Shub, illustrated by Margot Zemach. Farrar, Straus, 1968. (Jewish)
246. _____. *Zlateh, the Goat, and Other Stories,* translated by the author and Elizabeth Shub, illustrated by Maurice Sendak. Harper, 1966. (Jewish)
247. Sleator, William. *The Angry Moon,* illustrated by Blair Lent. Little, Brown, 1970. (S—Native American)
248. Stamm, Claus. *Three Strong Women, A Tall Tale from Japan,* illustrated by Kazue Mizumura. Viking, 1962. (S)
249. Steel, Flora Annie. *English Fairy Tales,* illustrated by Arthur Rackham. Macmillan, 1962 (1918).
250. _____. *Tattercoats,* illustrated by Diane Goode. Bradbury, 1976. (S—English)
251. Still, James. *Jack and the Wonder Beans,* illustrated by Margot Tomes. Putnam, 1977. (S—United States)
252. Stobbs, William. *The House That Jack Built.* Oxford, 1983. (S—England)

253. Stoutenberg, Adrien. *American Tall Tales,* illustrated by Richard M. Powers. Viking, 1966.
254. Sturton, Hugh. *Zomo the Rabbit,* illustrated by Peter Warner. Atheneum, 1966. (Africa)
255. Tashjian, Virginia. *Once There Was and Was Not, Armenian Tales Retold,* illustrated by Nonny Hogrogian. Little, Brown. 1966.
256. _____. *Three Apples Fell from Heaven, Armenian Tales Retold,* illustrated by Nonny Hogrogian. Little, Brown, 1971.
257. Titus, Eve. *The Two Stonecutters,* illustrated by Yoko Mitsuhasi. Doubleday, 1967. (S—Japan)
258. Tolstoy, Alexei. *The Great Big Enormous Turnip,* illustrated by Helen Oxenbury. F. Watts, 1969. (S—Russia)
259. Towle, Faith M. *The Magic Cooking Pot.* Houghton Mifflin, 1975. (S—India)
260. Toye, William. *How Summer Came to Canada,* illustrated by Elizabeth Cleaver. Walck, 1969. (S—Native American)
261. _____. *The Loon's Necklace,* illustrated by Elizabeth Cleaver. Oxford, 1977. (S—Native American)
262. Travers, P. L. *Two Pairs of Shoes,* illustrated by Leo and Diane Dillon. Viking, 1980. (Near East)
263. Turska, Krystyna. *The Woodcutter's Duck.* Macmillan, 1973. (S—Poland)
264. Uchida, Yoshiko. *The Dancing Kettle and Other Japanese Folk Tales,* illustrated by Richard C. Jones. Harcourt, 1949.
265. _____. *The Sea of Gold and Other Tales from Japan,* illustrated by Marianne Yamaguchi. Scribner, 1965.
266. Upadhyay, Asha. *Tales from India,* illustrated by Nickzad Nodjoumi. Random, 1971.
267. Vuong, Lynette Dyer. *The Brocaded Slipper and Other Vietnamese Tales,* illustrated by Vo-Dinh Mai. Addison-Wesley, 1982.
268. Walker, Barbara K. *Just Say Hic!,* illustrated by Don Bolognese. Follett, 1965. (S—Turkey)
269. _____. *Watermelons, Walnuts and the Wisdom of Allah and Other Tales of the Hoca,* illustrated by Harold Berson. Parents', 1967. (Turkey)
270. Wheeler, Post. *Russian Wonder Tales,* illustrated by Bilibin. A. S. Barnes, 1957.
271. Whitney, Thomas P., translator. *In a Certain Kingdom,* illustrated by Dieter Lange. Macmillan, 1972. (Russia)
272. _____. *Vasilisa the Beautiful,* illustrated by Nonny Hogrogian. Macmillan, 1970. (S—Russia)
273. Wilson, Barbara Ker. *Scottish Folk-tales and Legends,* illustrated by Joan Kiddell-Monroe. Walck, 1954.
274. Withers, Carl. *I Saw a Rocket Walk a Mile,* illustrated by John E. Johnson. Holt, 1965.
275. _____. *A World of Nonsense: Strange and Humorous Tales from Many Lands,* illustrated by John E. Johnson. Holt, 1968.
276. Wolkstein, Diane. *The Magic Orange Tree and Other Haitian Folktales,* illustrated by Elsa Henriquez. Knopf, 1978.
277. Wyndham, Lee. *Tales the People Tell in Russia,* illustrated by Andrew Antal. Messner, 1970.
278. Yagawa, Sumiko. *The Crane Wife,* translated by Katherine Paterson, illustrated by Suekichi Akaba. Morrow, 1981. (S—Japan)
279. Yashima, Taro, pseud. (Jun Iwamatsu). *Seashore Story.* Viking, 1967. (S—Japan)
280. Yolen, Jane. *The Emperor and the Kite,* illustrated by Ed Young. World, 1967. (S—Literary, China)
281. _____. *Greyling,* illustrated by William Stobbs. Philomel, 1968. (S—Literary, Shetland Islands)
282. Zemach, Harve. *Duffy and the Devil,* illustrated by Margot Zemach. Farrar, Straus, 1973. (S—England)
283. _____. *Nail Soup,* adapted from the text by Nils Djurklo, illustrated by Margot Zemach. Follett, 1964. (S—Sweden)
284. _____. *Salt: A Russian Tale,* illustrated by Margot Zemach. Follett, 1965. (S—Russia)
285. _____. *Too Much Nose, An Italian Tale,* illustrated by Margot Zemach. Holt, 1967. (S)

286. Zemach, Margot. *The Little Red Hen*. Farrar, 1983. (S—England)
287. _____. *The Three Sillies*. Holt, 1963. (S—England)
288. _____. *It Could Always Be Worse*. Farrar, Straus, 1977. (S—Jewish)

FABLES

289. Aesop. *Aesop's Fables*, illustrated by Boris Artzybasheff. Viking, 1933.
290. _____. *Aesop's Fables*, illustrated by Heidi Holder. Viking, 1981.
291. _____. *Aesop's Fables*, selected and adapted by Louis Untermeyer, illustrated by Alice and Martin Provensen. Golden Press, 1966.
292. _____. *The Caldecott Aesop*, illustrated by Randolph Caldecott. Doubleday, 1978 (1883).
293. _____. *The Exploding Frog and Other Fables from Aesop*, retold by John McFarland, illustrated by James Marshall. Little, Brown, 1981.
294. _____. *Fables from Aesop*, retold by James Reeves, illustrated by Maurice Wilson. Walck, 1962.
295. _____. *The Lion and the Mouse*, illustrated by Ed Young. Doubleday, 1980.
296. _____. *Once in a Wood. Ten Tales from Aesop*, illustrated and adapted by Eve Rice. Greenwillow, 1979.
297. _____. *Tales from Aesop*, retold and illustrated by Harold Jones. Watts/Julia MacRae, 1982.
298. _____. *Twelve Tales from Aesop*, retold and illustrated by Eric Carle. Putnam, 1980.
299. Brown, Marcia. *Once a Mouse*. Scribner, 1961.
300. Ciardi, John. *John J. Plenty and Fiddler Dan*, illustrated by Madeleine Gekiere. Lippincott, 1963.
301. Galdone, Paul. *Androcles and the Lion*. McGraw-Hill, 1970.
302. _____. *The Monkey and the Crocodile*. Seabury, 1969.
303. _____. *Three Aesop Fox Fables*. Seabury, 1971.
304. _____. *The Town Mouse and the Country Mouse*. McGraw-Hill, 1971.
305. La Fontaine. *The Fables of La Fontaine*, adapted and illustrated by Richard Scarry. Doubleday, 1963.
306. _____. *The Miller, the Boy and the Donkey*, illustrated by Brian Wildsmith. F. Watts, 1969.
307. _____. *The Turtle and the Two Ducks: Animal Fables Retold from La Fontaine*, by Patricia Plante and David Bergman, illustrated by Anne Rockwell. Crowell, 1981.
308. Lionni, Leo. *Frederick*. Pantheon, 1967.
309. McGovern, Ann. *Hee Haw*, illustrated by Eric von Schmidt. Houghton Mifflin, 1969.
310. Steig, William. *Amos & Boris*. Farrar, Straus, 1971.

MYTHS AND EPICS

311. Asimov, Isaac. *Words from the Myths*, illustrated by William Barss. Houghton Mifflin, 1961.
312. d'Aulaire, Ingri, and Edgar Parin d'Aulaire. *Book of Greek Myths*. Doubleday, 1962.
313. _____. *Norse Gods and Giants*. Doubleday, 1967.
314. Baker, Betty. *At the Center of the World*, illustrated by Murray Tinkelman. Macmillan, 1973.
315. Baldwin, James. *The Story of Roland*, illustrated by Peter Hurd. Scribner, 1930.
316. Barth, Edna. *Balder and the Mistletoe*, illustrated by Richard Cuffari. Houghton Mifflin, 1979.
317. _____. *Cupid and Psyche*, illustrated by Ati Forberg. Seabury, 1976.
318. Belting, Natalia. *The Earth Is on a Fish's Back: Tales of Beginnings*, illustrated by Esta Nesbitt. Holt, 1965.
319. _____. *The Long-tailed Bear and Other Indian Legends*, illustrated by Louis Cary. Bobbs-Merrill, 1961.
320. Benson, Sally. *Stories of the Gods and Heroes*, illustrated by Steele Savage. Dial, 1940.
321. Bierhorst, John, editor. *The Hungry Woman: Myths and Legends of the Aztecs*. Morrow, 1984.
322. Bryson, Bernarda. *Gilgamesh: A Man's First Story*. Holt, 1967.
323. Bulfinch, Thomas. *The Age of Fable*. New American Library, 1962 (1855).
324. Chant, Joy. *The High Kings*, illustrated by George Sharp. Bantam, 1983.

325. Church, Alfred J., editor. *The Iliad and the Odyssey of Homer,* illustrated by Eugene Karlin. Macmillan, 1967 (1906; 1907).

326. Clark, Eleanor. *The Song of Roland,* illustrated by Leonard Everett Fisher. Random, 1960.

327. Colum, Padraic. *The Children of Odin,* illustrated by Willy Pogany. Macmillan, 1920.

328. _____. *The Children's Homer: The Adventures of Odysseus and the Tale of Troy,* illustrated by Willy Pogany. Macmillan, 1962.

329. Coolidge, Olivia. *Legends of the North,* illustrated by Edouard Sandoz. Houghton Mifflin, 1951.

330. Creswick, Paul. *Robin Hood,* illustrated by N. C. Wyeth. Scribner, 1984 (reissue).

331. Crossley-Holland, Kevin. *Havelok the Dane,* illustrated by Brian Wildsmith. Dutton, 1965.

332. Evslin, Bernard. *Hercules,* illustrated by Joseph A. Smith. Morrow, 1984.

333. Evslin, Bernard, Dorothy Evslin, and Ned Hoopes. *Heroes and Monsters of Greek Myth,* illustrated by William Hunter. Scholastic, 1970.

334. Fahs, Sophia, and Dorothy Spoerl. *Beginnings: Earth Sky Life Death.* Starr King Press, 1958.

335. Farmer, Penelope. *Beginnings: Creation Myths of the World,* illustrated by Antonio Frasconi. Atheneum/Margaret McElderry, 1979.

336. _____. *Daedalus and Icarus,* illustrated by Chris Connor. Harcourt, 1971.

337. Gaer, Joseph. *The Adventures of Rama,* illustrated by Randy Monk. Little, Brown, 1954.

338. Garfield, Leon, and Edward Blishen. *The God Beneath the Sea,* illustrated by Zevi Blum. Pantheon, 1971.

339. _____. *The Golden Shadow,* illustrated by Charles Keeping. Pantheon, 1973.

340. Gates, Doris. *The Golden God: Apollo,* illustrated by Constantinos CoConis. Viking, 1973.

341. _____. *Lord of the Sky: Zeus,* illustrated by Robert Handville. Viking, 1972.

342. _____. *Two Queens of Heaven, The Story of Demeter and Aphrodite,* illustrated by Trina Schart Hyman. Viking, 1974.

343. _____. *The Warrior Goddess: Athena,* illustrated by Don Bolognese. Viking, 1972.

344. Graves, Robert. *Greek Gods and Heroes.* Doubleday, 1960.

345. _____. *The Siege and Fall of Troy,* illustrated by C. Walter Hodges. Doubleday, 1962.

346. Green, Roger Lancelyn. *A Book of Myths,* illustrated by Joan Kiddell-Monroe. Dutton, 1965.

347. _____. *The Myths of the Norsemen,* illustrated by Brian Wildsmith. Dufour, 1964.

348. _____. *Tales of Ancient Egypt,* illustrated by Elaine Raphael. Walck, 1968.

349. _____. *Tales of the Greek Heroes.* Penguin Books, 1958.

350. _____. *Tales the Muses Told,* illustrated by Don Bolognese. Walck, 1965.

351. Hastings, Selina. *Sir Gawain and the Green Knight.* Lothrop, 1981.

352. _____. *Sir Gawain and the Loathly Lady,* illustrated by Juan Wijngaard. Lothrop, 1985.

353. Hawthorne, Nathaniel. *The Golden Touch,* illustrated by Paul Galdone. McGraw-Hill, 1959.

354. Hodges, Margaret. *The Gorgon's Head,* illustrated by Charles Mikolaycak. Little, Brown, 1972.

355. _____. *Knight Prisoner: The Tale of Sir Thomas Malory and His King Arthur.* Farrar, Straus, 1976.

356. _____. *The Other World, Myths of the Celts,* illustrated by Eros Keith. Farrar, Straus, 1973.

357. _____. *Persephone and the Springtime, A Greek Myth,* illustrated by Arvis Stewart. Little, Brown, 1973.

358. _____. *Saint George and the Dragon,* illustrated by Trina Schart Hyman. Little, Brown, 1984.

359. Hosford, Dorothy G. *Sons of the Volsungs,* illustrated by Frank Dobias. Holt, 1949.

360. King, Cynthia. *In the Morning of Time: The Story of the Norse God Balder,* illustrated by Charles Mikolaycak. Four Winds, 1970.

361. Lanier, Sidney. *The Boy's King Arthur,* illustrated by N. C. Wyeth. Scribner, 1880.

362. Leach, Maria. *The Beginning: Creation Myths around the World,* illustrated by Jan Bell Fairservis. Funk & Wagnalls, 1956.

363. _____. *How the People Sang the Mountains Up: How and Why Stories,* illustrated by Glen Rounds. Viking, 1967.
364. Low, Alice. *The Macmillan Book of Greek Gods and Heroes,* illustrated by Arvis Stewart. Macmillan, 1985.
365. McDermott, Gerald. *Daughter of Earth: A Roman Myth.* Delacorte, 1984.
366. McGovern, Ann. *Robin Hood of Sherwood Forest,* illustrated by Tracy Sugarman. Scholastic, 1970.
367. Malcolmson, Anne, editor. *The Song of Robin Hood,* music arranged by Grace Castagnetta, illustrated by Virginia Lee Burton. Houghton Mifflin, 1947.
368. Mukerji, Dhan Gopal. *Rama, the Hero of India,* illustrated by Edgar Parin d'Aulaire. Dutton, 1930.
369. Picard, Barbara Leonie. *Hero Tales from the British Isles,* illustrated by Gay Galsworthy. Penguin, 1969.
370. _____. *The Iliad of Homer,* illustrated by Joan Kiddell-Monroe. Walck, 1960.
371. _____. *The Odyssey of Homer Retold.* Walck, 1952.
372. _____. *Stories of King Arthur and His Knights,* illustrated by Roy Morgan. Walck, 1955.
373. Pollack, Merrill. *Phaëthon,* illustrated by William Hofmann. Lippincott, 1966.
374. Proddow, Penelope, translator. *Demeter and Persephone,* illustrated by Barbara Cooney. Doubleday, 1972.
375. Pyk, Ann. *The Hammer of Thunder,* illustrated by Jan Pyk. Putnam, 1972.
376. Pyle, Howard. *The Merry Adventures of Robin Hood.* Scribner, 1946 (1883).
377. _____. *Some Merry Adventures of Robin Hood.* Scribner, 1954.
378. _____. *The Story of King Arthur and His Knights.* Scribner, 1984 (1883).
379. Reeves, James. *The Trojan Horse,* illustrated by Krystyna Turska. F. Watts, 1969.
380. Robbins, Ruth. *Taliesin and King Arthur.* Parnassus, 1970.
381. Rosen, Winifred. *Three Romances: Love Stories from Camelot Retold.* Knopf, 1981.
382. Seeger, Elizabeth. *The Ramayana,* illustrated by Gordon Laite. Young Scott, 1969.
383. Serraillier, Ian. *The Clashing Rocks: The Story of Jason,* illustrated by William Stobbs. Walck, 1964.
384. _____. *A Fall from the Sky: The Story of Daedalus,* illustrated by William Stobbs. Walck, 1966.
385. _____. *The Gorgon's Head: The Story of Perseus,* illustrated by William Stobbs. Walck, 1962.
386. _____. *Heracles the Strong,* illustrated by Rocco Negri. Walck, 1970.
387. _____. *The Way of Danger: The Story of Theseus,* illustrated by William Stobbs. Walck, 1963.
388. Sherwood, Merriam, translator. *The Song of Roland,* illustrated by Edith Emerson. McKay, 1938.
389. Sutcliff, Rosemary. *The High Deeds of Finn MacCool,* illustrated by Michael Charlton. Dutton, 1967.
390. _____. *The Hound of Ulster,* illustrated by Victor Ambrus. Dutton, 1963.
391. _____. *The Light Beyond the Forest: The Quest for the Holy Grail.* Dutton, 1980.
392. _____. *The Road to Camlann.* Dutton, 1982.
393. _____. *The Sword and the Circle.* Dutton, 1981.
394. _____. *Tristan and Iseult.* Dutton, 1971.
395. Tomaino, Sarah F. *Persephone, Bringer of Spring,* illustrated by Ati Forberg. Crowell, 1971.
396. Turska, Krystyna. *Pegasus.* F. Watts, 1970.
397. Watson, Jane Werner. *The Iliad and the Odyssey,* illustrated by Alice and Martin Provensen. Golden Press, 1956.
398. White, Anne Terry. *The Golden Treasury of Myths and Legends,* illustrated by Alice and Martin Provensen. Golden Press, 1959.
399. White T. H. *The Sword in the Stone.* Putnam, 1939.
400. Williams, Jay. *Sword of King Arthur,* illustrated by Louis Glanzman. Crowell, 1968.

BIBLE

401. Aichinger, Helga. *The Shepherd.* Crowell, 1967.
402. Asimov, Isaac. *Words from the Exodus,* illustrated by William Barss. Houghton Mifflin, 1963.

403. _____. *Words in Genesis,* illustrated by William Barss. Houghton Mifflin, 1962.
404. Bible, New Testament. *The Christ Child,* illustrated by Maud Miska Petersham. Doubleday, 1931.
405. _____. *Christmas: The King James Version,* illustrated by Jan Pieńkowski. Knopf, 1984.
406. Bierhorst, John, translator. *Spirit Child: A Story of the Nativity,* illustrated by Barbara Cooney. Morrow, 1984.
407. Bolliger, Max, reteller. *Noah and the Rainbow,* translated by Clyde Robert Bulla, illustrated by Helga Aichinger. Crowell, 1972.
408. Bulla, Clyde Robert. *Jonah and the Great Fish,* illustrated by Helga Aichinger. Crowell, 1970.
409. Chaikin, Miriam. *Joshua in the Promised Land,* illustrated by David Frampton. Clarion, 1982.
410. Cohen, Barbara. *The Binding of Isaac,* illustrated by Charles Mikolaycak. Lothrop, 1978.
411. _____. *I Am Joseph,* illustrated by Charles Mikolaycak. Lothrop, 1980.
412. de Angeli, Marguerite. *The Old Testament.* Doubleday, 1959.
413. de la Mare, Walter. *Stories from the Bible,* illustrated by Edward Ardizzone. Knopf, 1961.
414. de Paola, Tomie. *The Legend of Old Befana.* Harcourt, 1980.
415. _____. *The Story of the Three Wise Kings.* Putnam, 1983.
416. Evslin, Bernard. *Signs and Wonders: Tales from the Old Testament,* illustrated by Charles Mikolaycak. Four Winds, 1981.
417. Fisher, Leonard Everett. *The Seven Days of Creation.* Holiday, 1981.
418. Graham, Lorenz. *David He No Fear,* illustrated by Ann Grifalconi. Crowell, 1971.
419. _____. *Every Man Heart Lay Down,* illustrated by Colleen Browning. Crowell, 1970.
420. _____. *God Wash the World and Start Again,* illustrated by Clare R. Ross. Crowell, 1971.
421. _____. *Hongry Catch the Foolish Boy,* illustrated by James Brown, Jr. Crowell, 1973.
422. _____. *A Road Down in the Sea,* illustrated by Gregorio Prestopino. Crowell, 1970.
423. Hutton, Warwick. *Jonah and the Great Fish.* Atheneum/Margaret K. McElderry, 1983.
424. _____. *Noah and the Great Flood.* Atheneum, 1977.
425. Mikolaycak, Charles. *Babushka: An Old Russian Folktale.* Holiday, 1984.
426. Robbins, Ruth. *Baboushka and the Three Kings,* illustrated by Nicolas Sidjakov. Parnassus, 1960.
427. Saporta, Raphael. *A Basket in the Reeds,* illustrated by H. Hechtkopf. Lerner, 1965.
428. Singer, Isaac Bashevis. *The Wicked City,* translated by the author and Elizabeth Shub, illustrated by Leonard Everett Fisher. Farrar, Straus, 1972.
429. Spier, Peter. *The Book of Jonah.* Doubleday, 1985.
430. _____. *Noah's Ark.* Doubleday, 1977.
431. Tresselt, Alvin. *Stories from the Bible,* illustrated by Lynd Ward. Coward-McCann, 1971.
432. Turner, Philip. *Brian Wildsmith's Illustrated Bible Stories,* illustrated by Brian Wildsmith. Watts, 1969.
433. von Jüchen, Aurel. *The Holy Night,* translated by Cornelia Schaeffer, illustrated by Celestino Piatti. Atheneum, 1968.
434. Weil, Lisl. *Esther.* Atheneum, 1980.
435. Wiesner, William. *The Tower of Babel.* Viking, 1968.
436. Winthrop, Elizabeth. *A Child Is Born,* illustrated by Charles Milolaycak. Holiday, 1983.
437. _____. *He Is Risen,* illustrated by Charles Mikolaycak. Holiday, 1985.

7

MODERN
FANTASY

A wonderfully perceptive teacher maintained a diary in which she recorded significant events in her teaching day. These excerpts reveal her students' responses to a reading aloud of the well-known fantasy *Charlotte's Web* by E. B. White:

January 18

A wisp of a girl with dark dreaming eyes, Judy F. sits transfixed, listening to *Charlotte's Web*. When I read aloud, I'm aware of an irreplaceable group feeling. But beyond that, if children aren't read to, how will they see the purpose of such a difficult skill? . . .

February 6

Judy came in glowing.

"We've bought a baby pig. Mother took me to a nearby farm."

"How marvelous. What's his name?"

"Wilbur," she said, in a matter-of-fact voice—as if the name of the pig in *Charlotte's Web* was the only one possible. "He's quite cuddly for a pig. We bathe him every day."

February 20

When I'm alone with Judy, I ask about Wilbur.

"Oh, he's getting along just fine. We bought him a large pink ribbon and only take it off when he goes to bed."

"Where does he sleep?"

"In my bed," said Judy, as if I ought to know.

March 2

Everyone was silent at the end of *Charlotte's Web*. David wept when Charlotte died. Later he asked to borrow the book. It'll be interesting to see how he maneouvers such difficult reading. But there's the motivation they talk about.

April 3

Judy's mother hurried over to me at the P.T.A. meeting.

"What's all this about your pig?" she queried.

"My pig?" I answered incredulously. "You mean your pig; the one you and Judy bought at the farm."

"Come now," said Mrs. F. "This is ridiculous. Judy's been telling me for weeks about the class pig. The one you named for Wilbur in *Charlotte's Web*."

We looked at each other, puzzled, and suddenly the truth dawned upon us.

Wilbur, that immaculately clean pig in his dazzling pink ribbon, belonged to neither Mrs. F. nor me. He was born in dreams—a creature of Judy's wonderful imagination.[1]

A book of fantasy had seemed so real to these children that David had cried at its end, and Judy had continued the story in her imagination, convincing both her teacher and her mother that Wilbur did indeed exist.

[1] Jean Katzenberg, "More Leaves from a Teacher's Diary: On Reading" in *Outlook*, Issue II (Spring 1974), pp. 28–29. Published by the Mountain View Center for Environmental Education, University of Colorado.

FANTASY FOR TODAY'S CHILD

Some educators and parents have questioned the value of fantasy for today's child. They argue that children want contemporary stories that are relevant and speak to the problems of daily living—"now" books about the real world, not fantasies about unreal worlds. They point to books by Judy Blume, Lois Lowry, Betsy Byars, and others (see Chapter 9) as examples of books that speak directly to today's child.

The tremendous increase in the publication of

informational books also indicates that children are seeking "useful" books that provide real facts, such as the most recent NFL statistics on football players or a report on underwater archeology. Of what use, the realists ask, is a 400-page story about talking rabbits (*Watership Down* by Richard Adams) or one about a bizarre family that includes a hunter, a mermaid, a bear, and a lynx (*The Animal Family* by Randall Jarrell)?

Children themselves have denied the truth of some of these statements by choosing many books of fantasy as their favorites. Certainly *Charlotte's Web* is one of the most popular children's books to be published within the past thirty-five years. Lewis' Narnia series, Dahl's *Charlie and the Chocolate Factory*, and L'Engle's *A Wrinkle in Time* are all fantasies that rank high among children's favorite books. And many of the classics, books that have endured through several generations—such as *Winnie-the-Pooh*, *The Wind in the Willows*, and *Alice's Adventures in Wonderland*—are also fantasies.

The great fantasies frequently reveal new insights into the world of reality. Both *Charlotte's Web* and *Wind in the Willows* detail the responsibilities and loyalties required of true friendship. The fundamental truth underlying Le Guin's story *A Wizard of Earthsea* is that people are responsible for the evil they create and are only free of it when they face it directly. Such a theme might appear to be a thinly disguised Sunday School lesson in a book of realism; in fantasy it becomes an exciting quest for identity and self-knowledge. Fantasy consistently asks the universal questions concerning the struggle of good versus evil, the humanity of man, the meaning of life and death.

A modern contemporary novel may be out of date in five years, but well-written fantasy endures. Andersen's tale *The Nightingale* speaks directly to the twentieth century's adoration of mechanical gadgetry to the neglect of what is real. Arkin has portrayed the ultimate hazard of "following the crowd" in *The Lemming Condition;* while in *A Wrinkle in Time*, L'Engle details the loss of freedom on the planet Camazotz, where even the children must skip rope and bounce balls in time to the terrible rhythm of the heartbeat of "It." Fantasy frequently proclaims ancient truths in a way that makes children see their own reality from a new perspective.

Most importantly, however, fantasy helps the child to develop imagination. The ability to imagine, to conceive of alternative ways of life, to entertain new ideas, to create strange new worlds, to dream dreams are all skills vital to the survival of humankind. Paul Fenimore Cooper wrote of the importance of imagination:

> He who lacks imagination lives but half a life. He has his experiences, he has his facts, he has his learning. But do any of these really live unless touched by the magic of the imagination? So long as the road is straight he can see down it and follow it. But imagination looks around the turns and gazes far off into the distance on either side. And it is imagination that walks hand in hand with vision.[2]

The Roots of Fantasy

The modern literature of fantasy is diverse. We have contemporary fairy tales; stories of magic, talking toys, and other wonders; quests for truth in lands that never were; and narratives that speculate on the future. While these types of stories may seem very different, they do have something in common: they are rooted in earlier sources—in folktales, legends, myths, and the oldest dreams of humankind.

All literature borrows from itself, but the fantastic genre is particularly dependent. Motifs, patterns of events, characters, settings, or themes of new fantasy books often seem familiar. And well they should, for we have met them before, in other, older stories.

Jane Yolen, in an essay on the importance of traditional literature, says:

> Stories lean on stories, art on art. This familiarity with the treasure-house of ancient story is necessary for any true appreciation of today's literature. A child who has never met Merlin—how can he or she really recognize the wizards in Earthsea? The child who has never heard of Arthur—how can he or she totally appreciate Susan Cooper's *The Grey King?*[3]

Many authors borrow directly from the charac-

[2]Paul Fenimore Cooper, "On Catching a Child's Fancy," in *Three Owls*, Third Book, Annie Carroll Moore, ed. (New York: Coward-McCann, 1931), pp. 56–57.
[3]Jane Yolen, "How Basic Is Shazam?" in *Touch Magic: Fantasy, Faerie and Folklore in the Literature of Childhood* (New York: Philomel Books, 1981), p. 15.

ters and motifs of folklore. The black-American folk heroes John de Conquer and John Henry Roustabout enliven the unusual fantasy by Virginia Hamilton, *The Magical Adventures of Pretty Pearl*. Mollie Hunter's fantasy books are filled with the magic folk of her native Scotland. There are, among others, worrisome trows; the Selkies, who are seals capable of taking human form on the land; and water sprites called kelpies, often seen as horses.

Such shape-shifting often occurs in folk and fairy tales, and similar transformations are frequently arranged by authors of modern fantasy. In *The Cat Who Wished to Be a Man*, Lloyd Alexander's wizard transforms his cat Lionel into a young man whose catlike ways wear off only gradually. The wizard himself, of course, is a character drawn from the magician-figures of old tales. In the same book, a good-hearted rogue named Tudbelly invites inhospitable townspeople to a feast, promising them a special stew, and then tricks them into furnishing the ingredients themselves. Readers who have had prior experience with folktales may recognize that Alexander's "delicious Pro Bono Publico" stew is made from the same basic recipe as *Stone Soup*, in the retelling by Marcia Brown.

In the case of Robin McKinley's *Beauty*, the debt to an earlier source is immediately clear. McKinley sets out, as a novelist, to recast the tale of "Beauty and the Beast," with the explorations of character and motive and the everyday detail which do not fit within the frame of a conventional fairy tale. The result is a rich and satisfying book that manages to sustain a sense of anticipation even in those readers who know the outcome. Shirley Rousseau Murphy incorporates several variants of the Cinderella story in *Silver Woven in My Hair*, another fully developed fantasy for young readers built on the simpler structure of a familiar tale.

Some bodies of traditional lore have proved to be more popular than others as sources of new stories. Echoes of King Arthur—both the Arthur of the Medieval romances (as in Malory's *Le Morte d'Arthur*) and his historic precursor, Arthur the tribal chieftain of early Britain—are found in a great many modern fantasies. In *The Acorn Quest* by Yolen, a brief book with a light touch, the animal knights searching for the Golden Acorn that will save Woodland from hunger are sly parodies of Arthur's Knights of the Round Table in their profound pursuit of the Holy Grail. Among fantasies that treat the legends more seriously, William Mayne's *Earthfasts* and Jane Louise Curry's *The Sleepers* are just two of those that are much in Arthur's debt. Susan Cooper's five books that make up *The Dark Is Rising* sequence weave together elements of the Arthurian legends and broader themes from Celtic mythology, with its emphasis on ancient powers.

The stories of the Celts also figure heavily in Lloyd Alexander's Chronicles of Prydain; *The Black Cauldron* was known for its grisly work of making invincible warriors from the dead long before the fourteenth century, when the collected tales of Welsh tradition known as the *Mabinogion* were first committed to writing.

Most of the authors who draw on the Celtic stories use those versions most familiar in England and Wales. But many of the same tales have variants or analogues in the Celtic traditions of Ireland, where Finn McCool is the hero of record. Mary Tannen has tapped this source in *The Wizard Children of Finn* and *The Lost Legend of Finn*, in which a modern sister and brother are time travelers to ancient Ireland, caught up in Finn's destiny, Druid magic, and finally Viking bloodshed.

Many fantasies are based on multiple sources. Perhaps it is this striking of several familiar notes at once to sound a chord of satisfaction that brings them such enduring popularity. *The Hobbit* by Tolkien plays out the archetypal hero story of mythology against a smaller-scale setting more common to folklore. C. S. Lewis' Narnia series puts centaurs and fauns from the classical myths in company with modern children fighting Medieval battles in situations parallel to those recounted in Christian theology. Madeleine L'Engle draws on a similar array of referents. The volumes of her Time Trilogy (*A Wrinkle in Time*, *A Wind in the Door*, *A Swiftly Tilting Planet*) explore intriguing possibilities of astrophysics and cellular biology, as befits science fiction; but the books also reflect her knowledge of theology, classical literature, myths, legends, and history.

The ultimate source of all fantasy—the taproot—is the human psyche. Like the ancient tale-tellers and the Medieval bards, modern fantasy writers call up the images of our deepest needs, our darkest fears, and our highest hopes. Maurice Sendak, for instance, speaks to his young audience through such images in his picture books and in the singular small volume entitled *Higglety, Pigglety, Pop!* In this book a dog named Jennie sets out on an unspecified quest because "There must be more to life than having everything."[4] Her experiences are childlike and highly symbolic: the comforts of eating and the fear of being eaten, in turn, by a lion; the importance of one's own real name; the significance of dreams. Jennie's quest, as it turns out, may be read as the search for maturity and personal identity.

This is the same psychic adventure that Ursula Le Guin conducts, for an older audience, in *A Wizard of Earthsea*, where a young magician must learn the power of naming and recognize the Shadow that pursues him as part of himself. Adults may find, in these and similar stories, many of the collective images or shared symbols called archetypes by the great psychologist Carl Jung. Children will simply recognize that such a fantasy is "true." All our best fantasies, from the briefest modern fairy tale to the most complex novel of high adventure, share this quality of truth.

MODERN FAIRY TALES

The traditional folktale or fairy tale had no identifiable author but was passed by word of mouth from one generation to the next. While the names of Grimm and Jacobs have become associated with some of these tales, they did not *write* the stories; they compiled the folktales of Germany and England. The modern literary fairy tale utilizes the form of the old but has an identifiable author.

The Beginnings of the Modern Fairy Tale

Hans Christian Andersen is generally credited with being the first *author* of modern fairy tales, although even some of his stories, such as *The Wild Swans,* are definite adaptations of the old folktales. (Compare Andersen's *The Wild Swans*

[4]Maurice Sendak, *Higglety, Pigglety, Pop!* (New York: Harper & Row, 1967), p. 5.

with Grimms' "The Six Swans," for example.) Every Andersen story bears his unmistakable stamp of gentleness, melancholy, and faith in God. Even his adaptations of old tales were embellished with deeper hidden meanings, making them very much his creations.

Two of Andersen's tales, *The Ugly Duckling* and *The Steadfast Tin Soldier,* are said to be autobiographical. Just as the jest of the poultry yard became a beautiful swan, the gawky Andersen suffered indignities in his youth but was later honored by his king and countrymen. The sad tale of the shy, loyal tin soldier rejected by the toy ballerina is said by some to represent Andersen's rejection by the woman he loved.

Many of Andersen's fairy tales are really commentaries on what he saw as the false standards of society. In *The Princess and the Pea*, sometimes called "The Real Princess," Andersen laughs at the snobbish pride of the princess who claimed she could feel a pea through twenty mattresses and twenty eiderdown beds. The farce of *The Emperor's New Clothes* is disclosed by a young child who had no reason to assume the hollow pretense of his elders and so told the truth—that the Emperor was stark naked!

Andersen was not afraid to show children cruelty, morbidity, sorrow, and even death. In the long tale *The Snow Queen*, the glass splinter enters Kay's eye and stabs his heart, which becomes cold as ice. He then becomes spiteful and angry with Gerda, who is hurt by the changed behavior of her companion but, still loving him, searches for him in the Snow Queen's palace. At last she finds him, and her tears melt the splinter and his icy coldness. "The Little Mermaid" suffers terribly for her selfless love of a mortal prince. *The Little Match Girl* ends in the gentle death of a young girl who is freezing to death and who has seen a vision of her grandmother in the last flicker of her matches. A few stories, such as the tender *Thumbelina,* end happily, but most of Andersen's tales contain a thread of tragedy.

Many of Andersen's stories have been beautifully illustrated in single editions. Adrienne Adams paid a special visit to Denmark to become familiar with Andersen's native land before creating her watercolor illustrations for *The Ugly Duckling.* Lorinda Bryan Cauley's version portrays this story with soft colors and finely detailed pen-and-ink lines. Marcia Brown uses no color in the many fine-line drawings for *The Snow Queen* which emphasize the coldness of the queen's icy halls. Errol Le Cain's version of this tale provides a contrast, with brilliantly colored and ornately patterned surfaces emphasizing the strangeness of Gerda's journey to find her lost companion. Le Cain borrows from a Brueghel painting, "Hunters in the Snow," for an opening scene of children sledding. Nancy Ekholm Burkert has illustrated two Andersen stories, *The Fir Tree* and *The Nightingale*. The latter is richly portrayed in a manner resembling paintings on old Chinese silk screens. Blair Lent's version of *The Little Match Girl* uses towering buildings and a blinding snowstorm to set off the helplessness of the freezing little girl. With simplicity and a sure sepia line, Lisbeth Zwerger depicts detail and personality in both *The Nightingale's* Chinese court and in the small world of *Thumbeline*. Demi uses Chinese techniques of placing outlined landscapes on golden green silk backgrounds in her decorative version of *The Nightingale*. Illustrators such as these have done much to popularize Andersen's work.

Since Andersen's work must be translated for non-Danish readers, some variation in texts occurs. However, when Andersen's words are edited or retold, critics often object. Though translations of *Thumbelina*, such as those by W. R. James or the Winstons, may vary in what words they choose, they have not omitted incidents or parts such as the ending, a coda which alludes to "the man who can tell stories." Amy Ehrlich's retelling which accompanies Susan Jeffers' beautiful illustrations removes much of the leisurely pace of Andersen's writing and omits the coda entirely. While some suggest this makes Andersen more accessible to children, others claim that children are not meeting the true Andersen in adapted texts like this.

The Complete Fairy Tales and Stories of Andersen have been faithfully translated by Erik Haugaard. Eighteen of these stories, selected for a single volume and illustrated by Michael Foreman, provide children with several of the most popular and well known of Andersen's stories. Many other illustrators, such as Michael Hague and Edward Ardizzone, have selected and illustrated their own favorite tales from the body of Andersen's work.

Two other early authors of the literary fairy tale are Oscar Wilde and George MacDonald. Wilde's *The Happy Prince*, strikingly illustrated by Jean Claverie, is the somewhat sentimental story of a bejeweled statue who little by little gives his valuable decorations to the poor. His emissary and friend is a swallow who faithfully postpones his winter migration to Egypt to do the prince's bidding, only to succumb to the cold at the statue's feet. When the town councilors melt down the now shabby statue for its lead, all burns except the heart, which is cast on the same ash heap as the body of the dead bird. Together, the two are received in Heaven as the most precious things in the city. Wilde's *The Selfish Giant* has even more religious symbolism and is less appropriate for children.

Comparing Errol Le Cain's illustration for *The Snow Queen* with Brueghel's "Hunters in the Snow" on the next page shows how one artist may pay homage to another.

Many of MacDonald's fairy tales were religious in nature, including *The Golden Key,* which has been sensitively illustrated by Maurice Sendak. Sendak also illustrated MacDonald's *The Light Princess,* the story of a princess who has been deprived of her gravity by an aunt who was angry at not being invited to her christening. It is interesting to compare Sendak's tender yet humorous illustrations for this story with the detailed, amusing, and colorful pictures by William Pène du Bois. MacDonald is also remembered for *At the Back of The North Wind,* published in 1871, one of the foundations of modern fantasy.

Fairy Tales Today

In many instances modern writers have written farcical versions of the old fairy-tale form. The story may be set in the days of kings and queens and beautiful princesses; the language will reflect the manners of the period; and the usual "Once upon a time" beginning and "They lived happily ever after" ending will be present; but the conflict may have a modern twist. True to all fairy tales, virtue will be rewarded and evil overcome. *A Birthday for the Princess* by Anita Lobel has a unique and unusual ending. It is a story of an over-directed, over-protected, unloved princess. No one ever asks the princess how *she* feels or what *she* wants— even on her birthday. In the midst of her very planned birthday party, the princess slips away and invites an organ-grinder and monkey to be her guests. The horrified king and queen have the poor organ-grinder thrown in the dungeon, but the lonely little princess lets him out and rides away with him forever. Anita Lobel's illustrations are humorous, yet elegantly rich in detail.

Jay Williams is the author of several modern fairy tales. *The Practical Princess* and *Petronella* liberate women from the state of helplessness in which the traditional tale often portrays them. Traditional roles are also altered in *The Good-for-Nothing Prince,* in which the princess has to demand that the lazy prince rescue her. Only after she throws his food out the window does Prince Palagon respond to her request. The story *Everyone Knows What a Dragon Looks Like* has been illustrated in an Oriental style by Mercer Mayer. In this handsome modern tale, Williams suggests that appearances can be deceiving. For no one except Han, the poor little gate sweeper, will believe it when a small fat man with a long white beard announces that he is a dragon come to defend the city against the wild horsemen of the north. Even though the Mandarin and his councilors have been praying for a dragon to save their city, they will not bother with the old man or condescend to grant him his request for food, drink, and polite treatment. When he receives all of this from Han, he quickly turns into a dragon and rescues the city. Now at long last the people know what a dragon looks like—a small, fat, bald old man. The robust humorous illustrations capture the spirit of this tongue-in-cheek modern fairy tale.

John Gardner, known for his critically acclaimed adult fiction, also wrote for children in the fairy-tale form. The collections *Dragon, Dragon and Other Tales* and *Gudgekin the Thistle Girl and Other Tales* are populated with giants, handsome princes, ogres, wise old philosophers, wizards, and other familiar creatures. But the author's choice of detail is often strictly modern. The title character in "Dragon, Dragon," for instance, ". . . tore the last chapters out of novels and . . . stole spark plugs out of people's cars . . ."[5] These stories are products of our own time in an even more basic way, however, since Gardner's surprise twists of plot and character reversals are sometimes bizarre. They force the reader to think again in the same way that contemporary art often forces a second look.

Jane Yolen is a writer of lyrical tales that make use of modern psychological insights while following traditional patterns found in folk literature. Ed Young's illustrations in the style of Oriental cut paper grace *The Emperor and the Kite,* in which the youngest daughter rescues her emperor father from imprisonment by means of a kite. In *The Girl Who Loved the Wind,* Yolen tells of the princess Danina who is protected by her father from all the unlovely things of the world by a high wall he has constructed around the palace. But when Danina hears the wind sing a true song of the world, she spreads her cape and off she flies with the wind. Ed Young studied Persian miniatures before designing the richly textured pictures for this beautiful book. A blind Chinese princess learns to "see" from the remarkable vision of a wise blind man in *The Seeing Stick.* Color is used selectively by Remy Char-

[5]John Gardner, "Dragon, Dragon" in *Dragon, Dragon and Other Tales* (New York: Alfred Knopf, 1975), p. 4.

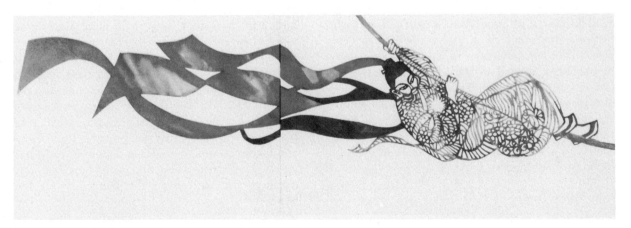

A kite tail streams in the wake of the emperor's escape down a rope made of his daughter's hair. Illustration by Ed Young from *The Emperor and the Kite* by Jane Yolen.

lip and Demetra Maraslis to help the reader see and feel the excitement of the princess. Collections of Yolen stories have been illustrated by David Palladini. *The Hundredth Dove and Other Tales,* for instance, presents seven short tales of love and separation, featuring seal maids or mermen and their human relationships, a loyal fowler and a princess, or childhood sweethearts betrayed by a sorcerer.

Other popular modern fairy tales are James Thurber's *Many Moons* and Louis Slobodkin's *The Amiable Giant. Many Moons* is the story of a petulant princess who desires the moon. The characterizations of the enraged king, the perplexed wise men, and the understanding jester are well drawn. Princess Lenore solves the problem of obtaining the moon in a completely satisfying and childlike manner. Louis Slobodkin received the Caldecott Medal for his illustrations for *Many Moons.* Slobodkin also wrote and illustrated *The Amiable Giant,* which is a disarming tale of a friendly, but misunderstood giant. As in *Many Moons,* a child solves the problem.

The Thirteen Clocks by James Thurber is a more sophisticated and mature fairy tale. A cold duke who was afraid of "now" had frozen time in Coffin Castle, where he kept the beautiful Princess Saralinda. A prince in the disguise of a ragged minstrel accomplishes the impossible tasks set by the duke and wins her hand. However, it is only with the bungling and amusing help of the Golux that the Prince is able to obtain the one thousand jewels and start the thirteen clocks, so that the time is Now and he may marry his princess. This is an imaginative spoof on fairy tales and one that middle-graders thoroughly enjoy.

The 500 Hats of Bartholomew Cubbins by Dr. Seuss is the hilarious tale of a small boy who is commanded to take off his hat for the king. Bartholomew complies, only to find that another hat appears in its place. The king is enraged and sends him to the executioner, who is a very proper kind of person and refuses to execute anyone wearing a hat. The king's horrid nephew, the Grand Duke Wilfred, suggests that he be allowed to push poor Bartholomew off the highest parapet of the castle. As they climb the stairs, Bartholomew desperately tears off his hats, which become more and more elaborate. The 500th hat is so "befeathered and bejeweled" that the king offers to spare Bartholomew's life in exchange for his gorgeous hat. Bartholomew gladly removes it. Much to his relief, his head remains bare. *Bartholomew and the Oobleck* is a sequel to the magical medieval tale of Bartholomew Cubbins.

Children may first be introduced to the characters in Lloyd Alexander's Prydain series by reading the exciting picture-book tale of *Coll and His White Pig.* When King Arawn, the Lord of the Land of Death, spirits away Hen Wen, the magical pig, Coll has no choice but to go after her. By following the traditional folktale motif of providing aid to three animals in distress, Coll is helped to save his pig. Alexander's style of writing captures the sound of the traditional tale. Notice, for example, his ending:

> Such is the tale of Coll and the rescuing of Hen Wen, with the help of the owl, Ash-Wing, the stag, Oak-Horn, and the digging and delving of the moles.
>
> And such is the end of it.[6]

Alexander's *The Truthful Harp* has magical powers. Every time its owner, Fflewddur Flam, exaggerates the truth, the harp breaks a string. Pictures by Evaline Ness contrast the reality of Fflewddur's world with his vivid imaginings: his "wild and mettlesome charger" appears as a plump, sway-backed pony; his "loyal subjects" who come down to wish him farewell are one small child! Despite Flam's truth-stretching, he has a kind and noble heart, as his deeds later show. These and six other stories collected in *The Foundling and Other Tales of Prydain* deal with happenings before the birth of Taran, Assistant Pig-Keeper. As Alexander notes they "take up certain threads left unraveled in the longer weaving."

Kenneth Grahame's *The Reluctant Dragon* is the droll tale of a peace-loving dragon who is forced to fight Saint George. The dragon's friend, called simply the Boy, arranges a meeting between Saint George and the dragon, and a mock fight is planned. Saint George is the hero of the day, the dragon is highly entertained at a banquet, and the Boy is pleased to have saved both the dragon and Saint George. The pictures by Ernest Shepard add to the subtle humor of this book.

A popular fairy tale of our time for adults and

[6]Lloyd Alexander, *Coll and His White Pig,* illustrated by Evaline Ness (New York: Holt, 1965); unpaged.

children is the haunting story of *The Little Prince* by Antoine de Saint-Exupéry. Written in the first person, the story tells of the author's encounter with the Little Prince on the Sahara Desert, where he has made a forced landing with his disabled plane. Bit by bit, the author learns the strange history of the Little Prince, who lives all alone on a tiny planet no larger than a house. He possesses three volcanoes, two active and one extinct, and one flower unlike any other flower in all the galaxy. However, when he sees a garden of roses, he doubts the uniqueness of his flower until a fox shows him that what we love is always unique to us. This gentle story means many things to different people, but its wisdom and beauty are for all.

Something of the same tone pervades *The Violin-Maker's Gift* by Donn Kushner, an award-winning book from Canada. Gaspard the violin-maker rescues a fledgling bird and gives it to the care of his friend the toll-keeper, where it grows into a marvelous creature reputed to have oracular powers. The bird is caged and exhibited, to be rescued once more by Gaspard and at last freed. Before it flies away, it reveals to him the secret of making great violins, which sound "as if a human soul were imprisoned in the wood, not crying for release, but perfectly content to be there."[7] Like Gaspard's instruments, his story can be treasured for its tranquil spirit and elegant construction.

MODERN FANTASY

Fantasy, like poetry, means more than it says. Underlying most of the great books of fantasy is a metaphorical comment on society today. Some children will find the hidden meanings in a tale such as *The Little Prince;* others will simply read it as a good story; and still others will be put off reading it altogether because it isn't "real." Children vary in their capacity for imaginative thinking. The literal-minded child finds the suspension of reality a barrier to the enjoyment of fantasy; other children relish the opportunity to enter the world of enchantment. Children's reactions to

[7]Donn Kushner, *The Violin-Maker's Gift* (New York: Farrar, Straus & Giroux, 1982), p. 71.

books of modern fantasy are seldom predictable or mild; they appear to be either vehemently for or against them. Frequently, taste for fantasy may be developed by having the teacher or librarian read aloud favorite books, such as Cleary's *Ralph S. Mouse,* Merrill's *The Pushcart War,* or Hurmence's *A Girl Called Boy.*

Evaluating Modern Fantasy

Well-written fantasy, like other fiction, has a well-constructed plot, convincing characterization, a worthwhile theme, and an appropriate style. However, additional considerations are needed to guide the evaluation of fantasy. The primary concern is the way the author makes the fantasy believable. A variety of techniques may be used to create belief in the unbelievable. Many authors firmly ground a story in reality before gradually moving into fantasy. Not until Chapter 3 in *Charlotte's Web* does author E. B. White suggest that Fern can understand the farm animals as they talk. And even then, Fern never talks to the animals; she only listens to them. By the end of the story Fern is growing up and really is more interested in listening to Henry Fussy than to the animals.

Another method for creating belief is careful attention to the detail of the setting. Mary Norton's graphic description of the Borrowers' home beneath the clock enables the reader to visualize this domestic background and to feel what it would be like to be as small as *The Borrowers.* This well-written fantasy includes details of sensory imagery helping the reader to experience the sounds, smells, and tastes of this new world.

Having one of the characters mirror the disbelief of the reader is another device for creating convincing fantasy. In *Jeremy Visick,* David Wiseman has portrayed his protagonist, Matthew, as a boy who thinks history is rubbish. Therefore, when even he is persuaded that the past lives again, the reader shares his terror as he descends to sure disaster within the depths of the Wheal Maid mine. In another well-written fantasy, *The Indian in the Cupboard* by Lynne Reid Banks, the boy Omri so respects the integrity of his toy cowboy and Indian come-to-life that the reader also begins to think of them as real. If they did not indeed exist, why should this thoroughly believable child take such pains with them?

The use of appropriate language adds a kind of documentation to fantasy. Underground for nearly two hundred years, the drummer uses such obsolete words as "arfish" for "afraid" in *Earthfasts,* by William Mayne, and his lack of understanding of such modern words as "breakfast" seems very authentic indeed. Richard Adams created his own lapine language for the rabbits in *Watership Down.* "Tharn," for example, describes a state somewhere between panic and exhaustion, a sort of paralysis of fear. By the time you finish reading this remarkable book, you find yourself thinking with some of these words.

The proof of real objects gives an added dimension of truth in books. How can one explain the origin of Greta's kitten or her father's penknife if not from Blue Cove in Julia Sauer's story *Fog Magic?* In *Tom's Midnight Garden* by Philippa Pearce, it is the discovery of a pair of ice skates that confirms the reader's belief in Tom's adventures.

Another point to be considered when evaluating fantasy is the consistency of the story. Each fantasy should have a logical framework and an internal consistency within the rules that the author has developed. Characters cannot become invisible whenever they face difficulty unless invisibility is a well-established part of their natures. The laws of fantasy may be strange indeed, but they must be obeyed.

Lloyd Alexander, master of the craft of writing fantasy, explains the importance of internal consistency within the well-written fantasy:

> Once committed to his imaginary kingdom, the writer is not a monarch but a subject. Characters must appear plausible in their own setting, and the writer must go along with the inner logic. Happenings should have logical implications. Details should be tested for consistency. Shall animals speak? If so, do *all* animals speak? If not, then which—and how? Above all, why? Is it essential to the story, or lamely cute? Are there enchantments? How powerful? If an enchanter can perform such-and-such, can he not also do so-and-so?[8]

Finally, while all plots should be original, the

[8]Lloyd Alexander, "The Flat-Heeled Muse," in *Children and Literature* by Virginia Haviland (Glenview, Ill.: Scott Foresman and Co., 1973), p. 243.

plots of fantasy must be ingenious and creative. A contrived or trite plot seems more obvious in a fanciful tale than in a realistic story.

GUIDES FOR EVALUATING MODERN FANTASY

The following specific questions might guide the evaluation of modern fantasy:
- What are the fantastic elements of the story?
- How has the author made the story believable?
- Is the story logical and consistent within the framework established by the author?
- Is the plot original and ingenious?
- Is there a universal truth underlying the metaphor of the fantasy?
- How does it compare to other books of the same kind or by the same author?

Moving into Modern Fantasy

Books of modern fantasy are usually longer than fairy tales and may take a variety of forms. All contain some imaginary elements that are contrary to reality as we know it today; for example, they may personify animals or toys, create new worlds, change the size of human beings, give humans unusual powers, or manipulate time patterns. Some fantasies utilize several of these approaches. Characteristic of most fantasy, like the fairy tales of old, is the presentation of a universal truth or a hidden meaning—love overcomes hate, the fools may be wiser than the wise men, the granting of wishes may not bring happiness. These ideas are presented by authors in stories that represent a wide range of complexity and reading difficulty. The most complex of these are discussed in the section "High Fantasy" on page 370. But between fairy tales and high fantasy lies that rich treasure of modern fantasy most accessible to novice readers. These stories are read and taken to heart for their own sake. They also serve to make the genre and its conventions familiar and comfortable, so that children may one day move with ease into high fantasy.

ANIMAL FANTASY

Storytellers have long told tales of the origins of certain animal characteristics. The humor of Rudyard Kipling's pourquoi tales, *Just-So Stories,* is based on his wonderful use of words and his tongue-in-cheek asides to the reader. A favorite with children is the story of *The Elephant's Child*, whose nose originally was no bigger than a bulgy boot. His "'satiable curtiosity" causes him all kinds of trouble and spankings. To find out what the crocodile has for dinner he departs for the "banks of the great grey-green, greasy Limpopo River, all set about with fever-trees. . . ." Here he meets the crocodile, who whispers in his ear that today he will start his meal with the Elephant's Child! The Elephant's Child is finally freed from the crocodile, but only after his nose has been badly pulled out of shape. As he waits for it to shrink, the Bi-Colored-Python-Rock-Snake points out all of the advantages of having an elongated nose. It is convenient for eating, for making a "cool-schloopy-sloshy mud-cap all trickly behind his ears," but most of all it would be wonderful for spanking! Some of these stories—such as *The Elephant's Child, How the Leopard Got His Spots,* and *How the Rhinoceros Got His Skin*—have been attractively illustrated in single picture-book editions by Leonard Weisgard. Charles Keeping presents *The Beginning of the Armadillos* in boldly designed and highly patterned shapes seen against strong blues and greens. Lorinda Bryan Cauley's contrasting version features nearly twice the number of illustrations in alternating soft pastels and black and white drawings. Her anthropomorphized animals reflect well Kipling's gentle mocking of the bouncy Jaguar and provide a warmth which the Keeping version lacks.

A humorous introduction to animal fantasy is *Bunnicula* by Deborah and James Howe. When the Monroe family return from seeing "Dracula" with a small rabbit they found on a theater seat, the family cat Chester is immediately suspicious. Evidence mounts up: a note written in an obscure Transylvanian dialect is tied around the rabbit's neck; in the kitchen a white tomato and other vegetables appear drained of their juices; and the rabbit can go in and out of his locked cage. Is Bunnicula a vampire? Chester is convinced of it, and his efforts to protect the Monroes are laconically observed and recounted by Harold, the family dog. Older children can appreciate Harold's clever observations and his very doglike concern for food. Two pun-filled sequels are *The Celery Stalks at Midnight* and *Howliday Inn.*

Other and less demanding introductions to an-imal fantasy are Beverly Cleary's *The Mouse and the Motorcycle, Runaway Ralph,* and *Ralph S. Mouse.* These stories require little suspension of disbelief and are just pure fun. In the first story, Ralph makes friends with a boy staying at the Mountain View Inn who gives him a small toy motorcycle. *Runaway Ralph* continues Ralph's adventures with the motorcycle. In the third story, to escape his jealous mouse relatives, Ralph goes to school in the pocket of his friend Ryan, becomes a class project, and loses his precious motorcycle but gains a sports car. Cleary's excursions into the world of fantasy are as well accepted by children as are her realistic humorous stories of Henry Huggins and Ramona Quimby.

Michael Bond's Paddington series continues to please children who are just discovering the pleasures of being able to read longer books. Bond's first book, *A Bear Called Paddington,* introduces readers to the bear found in a London railway station and taken by the Brown family to their home. Paddington earnestly tries to help the Browns, but

Meadow flowers gently frame a shared moment between the two unlikely friends, a grasshopper and a mouse in *Hickory* by Palmer Brown.

invariably ends up in difficulty. His well-meaning efforts produce a series of absurdities that make amusing reading. One of the funniest incidents in *More about Paddington* describes the day Paddington decides to wallpaper his room. He covers the doors and windows and then can't find his way out! Other adventures of this lovable bear are included in *Paddington at Large, Paddington Helps Out, Paddington Takes the Air,* and many more—all amusingly illustrated by Peggy Fortnum.

Macaroon by Julia Cunningham is the gentle story of a raccoon who thinks he knows how to obtain all the comforts of life without any of the disadvantages. In the fall, when the leaves turn to scarlet and the air becomes crisp, the raccoon knows it is time for him to adopt a human child. Since it has become increasingly difficult each spring to abandon his adopted children, Macaroon decides to find the most impossible of all children, so that the spring departure will be a relief. His choice is the spoiled and unruly Erika. Slowly and quite believably Macaroon reforms Erika and loses his heart to her in the process. Evaline Ness has portrayed the temperament and tenderness of this story with her fine illustrations.

Palmer Brown's *Hickory* had always lived with his family in the bottom of a grandfather clock. A daring mouse, Hickory decides to move on his own to the meadow. There he sets up housekeeping in a rabbit's former burrow and makes friends with a grasshopper named Hope ("Hop" for short). When Hickory hears the ending phrase of Hop's song "Now, when the nights grow cold and long,/The song I sing will soon be done," he realizes that unless they leave the meadow, his friend will surely die in the coming winter. So, ever-conscious of passing time, Hickory and Hop start south to find a sunny meadow. However, the story ends, "That night on these owl-haunted upper ridges there would be a hard frost." While young children hopefully predict that the two friends will live to find the new meadow, Brown has reminded readers throughout that "Time is going/Never staying,/Always flowing,/Ever saying: Gone!" The ending is foreshadowed when Hickory's brother protests at a story-telling session that "It is not fair to begin a story without knowing the end." Their father reminds them that "All stories have their endings in their beginnings, if you know where to look." This well-crafted tale is further enhanced by Brown's many pastel-tinted pen-and-ink drawings which portray intimate details of house and meadow.

Unquestionably the most beloved animal fantasy of our time is E. B. White's delightful tale, *Charlotte's Web.* While must of our fantasy is of English origin, *Charlotte's Web* is as Amercian as the Fourth of July and just as much a part of our children's heritage. Eight-year-old Fern can understand all of the animals in the barnyard—the geese who always speak in triplicate ("certainly-ertainly-ertainly"); the wise old sheep; and Templeton, the crafty rat—yet she cannot communicate with them. The true heroine of the story is Charlotte A. Cavatica—a beautiful, large gray spider who befriends Wilbur, a humble little pig. The kindly old sheep inadvertently drops the news that

A loyal Charlotte spins out her opinion of her friend Wilbur in this best-loved fantasy of our time, *Charlotte's Web* by E. B. White. Illustration by Garth Williams.

as soon as Wilbur is nice and fat he will be butchered. When Wilbur becomes hysterical Charlotte promises to save him. By miraculously spinning words into her web that describe the pig as "radiant," "terrific," and "humble," she makes Wilbur famous. The pig is saved, but Charlotte dies alone on the fairgrounds. Wilbur manages to bring Charlotte's egg sac back to the farm so that the continuity of life in the barnyard is maintained. Wilbur never forgets his friend Charlotte, though he loves her children and grandchildren dearly. Because of her, Wilbur may look forward to a secure and pleasant old age:

> Life in the barn was very good—night and day, winter and summer, spring and fall, dull days and bright days. It was the best place to be, thought Wilbur, this warm delicious cellar, with the garrulous geese, the changing seasons, the heat of the sun, the passage of swallows, the nearness of rats, the sameness of sheep, the love of spiders, the smell of manure, and the glory of everything.[9]

This story has humor, pathos, wisdom, and beauty. Its major themes speak of the web of true friendship and the cycle of life and death. All ages find meaning in this most popular fantasy.

Two other animal fantasies by White are also enjoyed by children. *Stuart Little,* the mouse son of human parents, sets out in the world to find Margalo, a bird who once saved his life. Another animal who walks and talks with humans is presented in *The Trumpet of the Swan.* Louie, a mute swan, must learn to play an instrument in order to woo his would-be mate. While neither book has all the strengths of *Charlotte's Web,* both appeal to children for their curious blend of fantasy and reality.

The English counterpart of Wilbur the pig is Daggie Dogfoot, the runt hero of King-Smith's story *Pigs Might Fly.* Saved by luck and his own determination from the Pigman's club, Daggie watches birds and aspires to fly. He discovers instead a talent for swimming that allows him to help rescue all the pigs from a flood. Like E. B. White's barn, the pigyard and pastures here are

described in sharp, sensory detail, and the animals' conversation reflects the author's shrewd perceptions about human as well as animal nature.

The Mousewife by Rumer Godden is a tender story of the friendship between a small industrious mousewife and a caged turtledove. The dove tells her about dew, about night, and the glory of flying. It is with wonder and awe that the little mousewife learns of the outside world. At last she can no longer stand to think of her friend imprisoned in a cage and she jumps on the catch, releasing the dove. As she sees him fly away she cries, but she knows now what it means to fly, for she has seen the stars and some of the world beyond. There is a gentle sadness in this story that reminds the reader of some of Andersen's tales. The detail of Heidi Holder's realistic pencil drawings emphasizes the limited sphere of the mousewife's world.

These same qualities of wonder and tenderness are found in the story of a small brown bat who becomes a poet. *The Bat-Poet,* written by the well-known poet Randall Jarrell, is both a delightful animal fantasy and a commentary on the writing of poetry itself. A bat who cannot sleep during the days opens his eyes and sees squirrels and chipmunks, the sun, and the mockingbird. He tries to get the other little bats to open their eyes and see the world, but they refuse. Admiring the mockingbird's many songs, the little bat makes up some of his own. He first tries his poems out on the bats, but they aren't interested. The mockingbird deigns to listen, but comments only on the form not the content of his poem. At last, the bat finds the perfect listener, the chipmunk, who is delighted with his poems and believes them. The fine pen-and-ink drawings by Maurice Sendak give the impression of steel engravings. They are as faithful to the world of nature as are the little animals in this story. Although they talk and write poetry, their behavior is otherwise true to life.

Robert Lawson has written a satisfying and tender story about all the little animals who live on *Rabbit Hill.* New folks are moving into the big house on the hill. Will they be planting folks, who like small animals, or shiftless, mean people? Each animal character responds in his own unique way to this sudden bit of news. Mother Rabbit is a worrier and tends to be pessimistic; Father Rabbit,

---

[9]E. B. White, *Charlotte's Web,* illustrated by Garth Williams (New York: Harper & Row, 1952), p.183.

stately and always eloquent, feels that there are many auspicious signs (he is a Southern gentleman and always speaks in this fashion), and young Georgie delightedly leaps down the hill chanting, "New folks coming, new folks coming!" Although on probation for several days after their arrival, the new folks win approval by putting up a large sign that says: "Please Drive Carefully on Account of Small Animals." *The Tough Winter* is a sequel to *Rabbit Hill,* describing the plight of all the animals when the "Folks" go away for the winter and leave a neglectful caretaker and a mean dog in charge.

The urban counterpart of *Charlotte's Web* and *Rabbit Hill* is *The Cricket in Times Square* by George Selden. A fast-talking Broadway mouse named Tucker and his pal, Harry the Cat, initiate a small country cricket called Chester into the vagaries of city living. Chester spends only one summer in New York City, having been transported in someone's picnic lunch basket. The climax of Chester's summer adventures comes when the cricket begins giving nightly concerts from the Bellinis' newsstand, saving his benefactors from bankruptcy. On his last night before his return to Connecticut, Chester brings traffic in New York City to a standstill as he chirps the sextet from *Lucia di Lammermoor.* The three friends plan a reunion visit in the country, which becomes the focus of a second book, *Tucker's Countryside. Harry Cat's Pet Puppy* appeals to the same audience, but the more recent *Chester Cricket's Pigeon Ride* has a shorter text and more emphasis on illustrations. In all these warm and witty books, Garth Williams has created human expressions for each animal to complement their very real personalities.

Garth Williams also illustrated the series of tongue-in-cheek melodramas by Margery Sharp about the pure and beautiful white mouse *Miss Bianca.* The first story, *The Rescuers,* tells of the breathtaking adventure of three mice—Miss Bianca, Bernard, and Nils—as they rescue a Norwegian poet from the grim, windowless Black Castle. *Miss Bianca* is the exciting story of the rescue of a little girl, Patience, from the clutches of a hideous wicked duchess, who lives in the Diamond Palace. She has twelve mechanical ladies-in-waiting who regularly bow to her every hour and say, "as your Grace pleases." The fiendish duchess wants at least

one human being who will react to her cruelty, however, so Patience is kidnapped for this purpose. The beautiful and gracious Miss Bianca and the humble and resolute Bernard rescue Patience with the aid of the mouse members of the Ladies Guild. Williams' illustrations portray the hideousness of the duchess, as well as the gentle beauty of Miss Bianca. *The Turret, Miss Bianca in the Salt Mines,* and *Bernard the Brave* continue the adventures of these intrepid mice.

Dominic, the expansive hound dog created by William Steig, leaves home one day to see the world. Dominic is an adventuring hero in the mold of the classic picaresque character—he meets good fortune and bad (mostly in the form of the wicked Doomsday Gang), a little magic, and, in the end, following the best tradition of fairy tales, he finds a beautiful dog sleeping in an enchanted garden. The book is more than a delightful spoof, however, for it makes its own comment on the personal and social values of our world.

It is in chronicling the year-long survival of a mouse on an island that Steig firmly establishes himself as a superb author as well as illustrator of children's books. *Abel's Island* details the survival of Abel, a very Victorian mouse, who is trapped on an island after having been caught in a torrential rainstorm while attempting to retrieve his wife's scarf. Abel tries one ingenious escape plan after another, all without success. Left on his own, this rodent Crusoe finds a hollow log and learns to feed off the land. He not only battles physical elements such as finding food, existing during the winter, and escaping from his enemy the owl, but he overcomes the psychological fears of loneliness and overwhelming despair. Finally, after almost a year of foraging for himself, Abel is able; and he easily swims the distance to shore. Creating more than a mouse melodrama, Steig has shown us what is of value in surviving life today. Stripped of his possessions, Abel relies on his resourcefulness, but he is kept alive by his love for his wife Amanda, his art, his friendship with the forgetful frog, his hatred of the owl, and his joy of life. He is also sustained by two lucky finds, a pocket watch and a book:

. . . the steady, mechanical tempo of the watch gave him something he had been wanting in this wild place. It and the book helped him feel connected to the civilized world he'd come from. He had no use for the time the watch could tell, but he needed the ticking.[10]

What E. B. White has done to popularize and humanize spiders, Robert O'Brien has accomplished for rats in his Newbery award-winning book, *Mrs. Frisby and the Rats of NIMH*. Really two stories within one, the first is a warm and brave animal tale of Mrs. Frisby, a widowed mouse mother, and her concern for her family. The plot turns on Mrs. Frisby's determination to save the family's winter home in the garden from spring plowing so that her son Timothy will have sufficient time to recuperate from pneumonia. Mrs. Frisby is sent to the rats for help in saving her house and gradually begins to piece together their story, a process speeded up by the device of a long first-person account by Nicodemus, their leader. The rats, as well as Mrs. Frisby's late husband, have escaped from a laboratory called NIMH (National Institute for Mental Health—although it is never so identified in the story), where they had been given DNA and steroid injections to develop their intelligence so they could read and write and also extend their life spans. When Mrs. Frisby meets them, the rats are just completing a plan to move into a wilderness preserve where they hope to establish a self-sufficient farming community and at last live without stealing. In the process of helping the rats prepare to move her house, Mrs. Frisby is able to discover and warn them about the government exterminators who are coming with cyanide gas. All of the rats but two escape to their hidden valley; but the reader never knows if the unlucky ones include Justin, Mrs. Frisby's friend. The epilogue suggests many possibilities for discussion questions or further adventures.

An exodus of a different sort is the focus of Alan Arkin's *The Lemming Condition*. When his friend Crow asks some bothersome questions, young Bubber begins to doubt the wisdom of the other lemmings' intention to march over the cliffs to the sea. Can lemmings swim? How does Bubber feel about water? Still the youngster finds himself unable to resist the run toward mass suicide, finally

feeling "one with his people." Only at the last moment does Bubber recover his senses and manage to cling to safety in a crevice between two rocks. He sets his course away from the handful of survivors, declaring that he is "not a lemming anymore." This book is much shorter than *Mrs. Frisby and the Rats of NIMH*, but it may prove more difficult for inexperienced readers, since the humor is heavily ironic and the crucial meanings lie at the level of allegory.

Penelope Lively also explores some of the conflicts between independent thinkers and those who follow the crowd in *The Voyage of QV 66*. After a disastrous flood that forces the evacuation of the People to Mars, several animals commandeer a flat-bottomed boat and make their way through the English countryside. The group includes a dog (the narrator), a horse, a cow, a pigeon, a cat, and a parrot. Their inspiration, however, is Stanley, a memorable creature full of clever, often bothersome, ideas and ceaseless curiosity. After a series of adventures including a narrow escape from sacrifice by crows at Stonehenge, they all come safely to London. There Stanley discovers his own kind (monkeys) but is horrified by the repressive society they have created for themselves at the Zoo. He persuades his friends to travel on: "Out there, of course. . . . I mean, you can't just sit about, can you? You've got to find out about things."[11] The animals' voyage can be understood on several levels, and there is much to discuss about the actual journey and the questing spirit.

Richard Adams' *Watership Down* was originally published in England as a children's book but as adult fiction in the United States. This remarkable story of a rabbit band who cherish their freedom enough to fight for it is presented in a lengthy and complex book inaccessible to many children. Adams has created a complete rabbit civilization including a history, a religion, a mythology, and even a lapine language with a partial set of linguistic rules to accompany it. The central character of *Watership Down* is Hazel, a young buck who leads a little band of bucks away from their old warren which has been doomed by a new housing tract. He does so reluctantly but at the urging of

[10]William Steig, *Abel's Island* (New York: Farrar, Straus & Giroux 1976), p. 58.

[11]Penelope Lively, *The Voyage of QV 66*, illustrated by Harold Jones (New York: Dutton, 1979), p. 172.

his younger and weaker brother, Fiver, who has a form of extrasensory perception. One of the feats of the author's characterization is the slow, steady growth of Hazel as a leader. He is firm but gentle, wise enough to recognize the talents of others, and always considerate. His actions in saving a terrified mouse from a kestrel and nursing a crippled gull back to health pay handsome dividends, true to the folklore tradition.

This is a surprisingly unsentimental, even tough story. It is more realistic than most "realism" because the story is firmly rooted in a world we know. The details of rabbit life are accurately presented and nothing is passed over or "prettied up." They mate, make droppings, and talk and joke about both, very much as humans do. The rabbits get hurt and bleed and suffer; they grow ugly with age and they die. During their story-telling sessions the reader learns of El-ahrairah, the great chief rabbit and trickster; he hears a remarkable creation legend and a deeply moving story of a rabbit redeemer who braves the palace of death to offer his own life for his people. And at the end of the book, when one of the does tells her little one a new story of El-ahrairah, we know that she is telling a garbled version of the story of the establishment of Watership Down and adding Hazel's accomplishments to those of the legendary rabbit—a comment on the entire process of myth-making.

Watership Down has been compared with *The Wind in the Willows* by Kenneth Grahame. In fact, one English reviewer maintained that the "story is what one might expect had *The Wind in the Willows* been written after two world wars, various marks of nuclear bomb, the Korean and Vietnam obscenities and half a dozen other hells created by the inexhaustibly evil powers of man."[12] Certainly, *The Wind in the Willows* seems slower, much more idyllic, and sentimental by comparison with the Adams book. Yet it is not a story of harsh survival, as is *Watership Down,* but a peaceful, tender, sometimes humorous story of the friendship among four animals; Water Rat, Mole, Toad, and Badger. Kindly Badger is the oldest and wisest of the quartet, the one they all seek when they are in trouble. Rat is a practical soul, good-natured and intelligent. Mole is the appreciative, sometimes gullible, one. The comic relief of the story is provided by Toad, who follows one fad after another. He is always showing off and becoming involved in situations from which Rat, Mole, and Badger are forced to rescue him. Despite his wild fantasies and changing crazes, Toad is a good-hearted, generous friend. As Rat says: "It's never the wrong time to call on Toad. Early or late he's always the same fellow. Always good-tempered, always glad to see you. Always sorry when you go!"[13] It is Toad's expansive, open-hearted personality that enables his loyal friends to put up with him at all. Besides friendship, the sense of home and love of nature are the other two themes that pervade this fantasy. Each of the character's homes is described in detail, from the costly Toad Hall to Ratty's snug little dwelling place in the riverbank. Long, loving descriptions of the riverbank, the wild wood, and more abound in this animal pastoral. All children will not have the background of experience to appreciate its beauty, but there are some who love this book above all others. It is best read aloud a chapter at a time, just as Grahame wrote it for his son. One other way to introduce the book would be to share Adrienne Adams' beautifully illustrated picture book of just the first chapter titled *The River Bank* or one of two excerpts illustrated by Beverly Gooding, *The Open Road* and *Wayfarers All: From The Wind in the Willows.*

THE WORLD OF TOYS AND DOLLS

As authors have endowed animals with human characteristics, so, too, have they personified toys and dolls. Young children enjoy stories that personify the inanimate such as a tugboat or a steamshovel. Seven-, 8-, and 9-year-olds still like to imagine that their favorite playthings have a life of their own. Hans Christian Andersen utilized this approach in his stories of "The Steadfast Tin Soldier," "The Fir Tree," and many others.

One of the most popular of all children's stories, *The Adventures of Pinocchio* by Carlo Collodi, is a personification story. The mischievous puppet that old Geppetto carves out of wood becomes alive and has all kinds of adventures. He plays

---

[12]Aidan Chambers, "Letter from England: Great Leaping Lapins!" in *The Horn Book Magazine,* vol. 49, no. 3 (June 1973), p. 255.

[13]Kenneth Grahame, *The Wind in the Willows,* illustrated by E. H. Shepard (New York: Scribner, 1908, 1940), p. 34.

hookey from school, wastes his money, and tangles with many unsavory characters. Each time he lies to the Blue Fairy his nose grows longer, until it is so long that he has difficulty turning around in a room. When Pinocchio at last is truly kind to someone else, he becomes a real boy. First published in Italy in 1881, this universal favorite has been translated into many languages. It has frequently been adapted to soften the worst of Pinocchio's behavior and the most frightening of his adventures.[14] Observance of the hundredth anniversary of publication rekindled interest in the original version and prompted a new U.S. translation by Marianna Mayer. In this edition, vivid full-page illustrations by Gerald McDermott suggest the terrors as well as the comedy of Pinocchio's story.

Probably no one has made toys seem quite so much like people as has A. A. Milne in his well-loved Pooh stories. Each chapter contains a separate adventure about the favorite stuffed toys of Milne's son, Christopher Robin. The good companions include *Winnie-the-Pooh*, a bear of little brain; doleful Eeyore, the donkey; Piglet, the happy follower and devoted friend of Pooh; and Rabbit; Owl; Kanga; and little Roo. A bouncy new friend, Tigger, joins the group in Milne's second book, *The House at Pooh Corner*. They all live in the "100 Aker Wood" and spend most of their time getting into—and out of—exciting and amusing situations. One time, Pooh becomes wedged in a very tight place and has to abstain from eating his "hunny" for a whole week until he grows thin again. Eight- and 9-year-olds thoroughly enjoy the humor of the Heffalump story and appreciate the self-pity of gloomy Eeyore on his birthday. They like kindly but forgetful Pooh, who knocks at his own door and then wonders why no one answers. They are delighted when Piglet and Roo exchange places in Kanga's pocket, and even more pleased when Piglet gets a dose of Roo's medicine! The humor in these stories is not hilarious but quiet and subtle, with a gentle touch of whimsy. Such humor is usually lost on primary-grade children, but is greatly appreciated by children in the middle elementary grades. However, younger children

may enjoy the Pooh stories when they are read within a family circle. Parents' chuckles are contagious, and soon the whole family has become Pooh admirers.

Rumer Godden makes the world of dolls seem very much alive in several of her books—*The Dolls' House, Impunity Jane,* and *The Fairy Doll.* The idea expressed in all Godden's doll books is stated best by Toddie in *The Dolls' House.* She says: "It is an anxious, sometimes a dangerous thing to be a doll. Dolls cannot choose; they can only be chosen; they cannot 'do'; they can only be done by."[15] Another characteristic of Godden's stories is that many of them are stories about boy dolls, or even boys who enjoy playing with dolls.

Miss Hickory by Carolyn Bailey is the story of a unique country doll whose body is an applewood twig and whose head is a hickory nut. Miss Hickory has all the common sense and forthright qualities that her name implies. She survives a severe New Hampshire winter in the company of her friends—Crow, Bull Frog, Ground Hog, and Squirrel. It was Squirrel who ended it all when he ate Miss Hickory's head; but then some might say that was just the beginning—and so it was.

In *The Indian in the Cupboard* by Lynne Reid Banks, a toy plastic Indian becomes alive when Omri puts it inside a cupboard, locks it, and then unlocks it with a special key. Nine-year-old Omri feels pride and responsibility in caring for "his" Indian, Little Bear, and is quickly involved in providing for his needs. But trouble begins when Omri's friend Patrick places a cowboy in the cupboard. The British author gives stereotypical language to Little Bear ("Little Bear fight like mountain lion. Take many scalps!") and the cowboy Boone ("I ain't sharin' m'vittles with no lousy scalp-snafflin' Injun and that's m'last word!"), but the characters transcend this in their growing concern for each other's welfare. Banks suggests once again to readers that we are responsible for what we have tamed or brought to life.

As in the previous title, Elizabeth Winthrop's *The Castle in the Attic* also examines responsibility for one's own actions. Ten-year-old William, although an accomplished gymnast, lacks confidence in himself. When he hears that Mrs.

[14]See Richard Wunderlich and Thomas J. Morrissey, "The Desecration of *Pinocchio* in the United States," *The Horn Book Magazine*, vol. 58, no. 2 (April 1982), pp. 205–212.

[15]Rumer Godden, *The Dolls' House*, illustrated by Tasha Tudor (New York: Viking, 1962; first published in England in 1947), p. 13.

Phillips, his lifelong friend and live-in babysitter, is returning to her native England, he is crushed but determined to find a way to make her stay. After she brings him her parting gift, a huge model of a castle which has been in her family for generations, William discovers that one tiny lead knight has come to life at William's touch. He reveals the presence of a wizard's amulet from another time and place, a charm that can be used to miniaturize objects or people. Almost at once William regrets his decision to reduce his babysitter to toy size and keep her in the castle. To undo this wrong, he must submit himself to the charm, travel back in time with the knight, and recover the amulet that will reverse the spell. Away from Mrs. Phillips for the first time, he discovers unexpected strengths and returns victorious. He is also prepared to wish his friend farewell and has become a more confident gymnast, as well. The strong grounding in reality and the elaborately described castle give this fantasy special appeal for upper elementary students.

An inventive plot and memorable characters created by Richard Kennedy in *Amy's Eyes* help sustain reader interest in this lengthy but compelling story. Left at an orphanage by her sailor father, Amy is delighted when her sailor doll comes to life and becomes a ship's captain. In spite of wicked doings at the orphanage, and Amy's pining away until she becomes a doll, the captain is able to return for Amy and take her off on a voyage to hunt for treasure. The ship is "manned" by an odd lot: Skivvy who is made from long underwear, a crew of stuffed animals brought to life by a dose of Mother Goose and a needle-prick in the head, an evil cook who is not what she seems, and a lovesick frog. Together, they eventually outwit the pirate Goldnose and discover Amy's father, but not without a terrible price. The language is unusual, often poetic, and frequent humorous passages move the story to its serious conclusion. While fourth-graders have enjoyed hearing the story read aloud, its length and complexity, plus the many diversions both nautical and philosophical, make it most likely to appeal to proficient, appreciative, and slightly older readers of fantasy.

A strangely cruel yet tender tale by Russell Hoban, *The Mouse and His Child*, tells of two wind-up toys and their efforts to become "self-winding." New and shiny in the toy shop the day before Christmas, the naive little toys end up on the rubbish heap in the cruel clutches of Manny Rat. Their long and tedious journey fulfills the prophecy predicted by the frog:

> Low in the dark of summer, high in the winter light; a painful spring, a shattering fall, a scattering regathered. The evening you flee at the beginning awaits you in the end.[16]

The wind-up toys' adventures in the outside world begin when a lonely tramp finds them in the trash can, winds them up, and tells them to "Be Tramps." Searching for a home, a family, and "their territory," the wind-ups seem completely dependent on blind fate. A combination of many coincidences returns them to the dump, where they find "their doll house," establish their family, and defeat Manny Rat. In fact, Manny becomes "Uncle Manny" in his total conversion. In the end the same tramp sees them and advises them to "Be Happy." The story is not a gentle one. It is filled with images of death and decay, violence and vengeance, tears and laughter. The ideas are complex and are conveyed in symbolism and satire. Like *Alice's Adventures in Wonderland*, the story may appeal more to adults than to children. Yet it is a fantasy that is not easily forgotten.

LILLIPUTIAN WORLDS

Children who enjoy Andersen's tale of the lovely *Thumbelina* or who try to read every one of John Peterson's easy chapter books about *The Littles* are following a long-standing fantasy tradition that dates back to Jonathan Swift's exploration of the land of the Lilliputians in *Gulliver's Travels*.

T. H. White has updated the lure of Lilliput by placing descendants of the original little people on an English estate, with their community-in-exile at the foot of a garden cupola known as *Mistress Masham's Repose*. The whimsy, the elaborate descriptions, and the allusions of this story are slanted toward a highly literate, even adult, audience. Yet this is an entertaining story, dazzling in its use of language, and highly rewarding to a motivated student. Written in the 1940s and long out of print, it has been reissued for a new generation of readers.

[16]Russell Hoban, *The Mouse and His Child* (New York Harper & Row, 1967), p. 28.

Arrietty meets a "human bean." The artists, Beth and Joe Krush, have skillfully shown the comparative sizes of the tiny borrower and the boy. From *The Borrowers* by Mary Norton.

Mary Norton has told a fascinating story about tiny people, *The Borrowers,* and their miniature world under the grandfather clock. There are not many borrowers left, for the rush of modern life does not suit them. They derive their names from their occupation, which is "borrowing" from human "beans," those "great slaves put there for them to use." "Borrowing" is a dangerous trade, for if one is seen by human beings, disastrous things may happen. Therefore, it is with real alarm that Pod and Homily Clock learn of their daughter Arrietty's desire to explore the world upstairs. Finally, Pod allows Arrietty to go on an expedition with him. While Pod is borrowing fibers from the hall doormat to make a new brush for Homily, Arrietty wanders outside, where she meets the boy. Arrietty's disbelief about the number of people in the world who are the boy's size, compared to those of her size, is most convincing:

"Honestly—" began Arrietty helplessly and laughed again. "Do you really think—I mean, whatever sort of world would it be? Those great chairs . . . I've seen them. Fancy if you had to make chairs that size for everyone? And the stuff for their clothes . . . miles and miles of it . . . tents of it . . . and the sewing! And their great houses, reaching up so you can hardly see the ceilings . . . their great beds . . . the food they eat . . . great smoking mountains of it, huge bags of stew and soup and stuff."[17]

In the end, the Borrowers are "discovered" and have to flee for their lives. This surprise ending leads directly to the sequel called *The Borrowers Afield.* The characterizations in these stories are particularly well drawn. Homily is a worrier and Pod is her solid, kindly husband. Prim and properly brought up, Arrietty still cannot control her natural curiosity. These are real people that Mary Norton has created. Her apt descriptions of setting and the detailed illustrations by Beth and Joe Krush make the small-scale world of the Borrowers come alive. Other titles in the series include *The Borrowers Afloat, The Borrowers Aloft,* and *The Borrowers Avenged.*

A very readable fantasy from the United States is *The Gammage Cup* by Carol Kendall. This is the

[17]Mary Norton, *The Borrowers,* illustrated by Beth and Joe Krush (New York: Harcourt Brace Jovanovich, 1953), p. 78.

story of the Minnipins, mostly sober, sedate, and tradition-bound little folk in The Land Between the Mountains. When a "best village" contest is announced, a town meeting at Slipper-on-the-Water decides that in order to win the coveted Gammage cup, all homes must be painted green and all Minnipins must wear green. Muggles speaks for the nonconforming few who insist on bright doors and orange sashes:

> ". . . it's no matter what color we paint our doors or what kind of clothes we wear, we're . . . well, we're those colors inside us. Instead of being green inside, you see, like other folk. So I don't think it would do any good if we just changed our outside color." [18]

The rebellious ones are exiled to the mountains, where by chance they discover a threat to the village from the Minnipins' ancient enemies, the Mushrooms. Muggles and her companions sound the alarm, save the village, and are welcomed back as heroes. This well-written fantasy offers tart commentary on false values in society and the theme of the individual versus the group. Ironically, the gentle Minnipins prove to be surprisingly fierce in their encounter with the Mushrooms.

ECCENTRIC CHARACTERS AND PREPOSTEROUS SITUATIONS

Many humorous fantasies for children are based on eccentric characters who are bigger than life or on situations that could not possibly happen. Cars or people may fly, eggs may hatch into dinosaurs or dragons, and boys may shrink. Often these characters and situations occur in otherwise very normal settings—which allows readers to believe more readily.

Pippi Longstocking, a notoriously funny character created by Astrid Lindgren, has delighted children for more than thirty years. Pippi is an orphan who lives alone with her monkey and her horse in a child's utopian world where she tells herself when to go to bed and when to get up! Pippi takes care of herself most efficiently and has a wonderful time doing it. Although she is only 9 years old, Pippi can hold her own with anyone, for she is so strong that she can pick up a horse or a man and throw him into the air. Children love this amazing character who always has the integrity to say what she thinks, even if she shocks adults; actually, children admire Pippi's carefree existence. Seven-, 8-, and 9-year-olds enjoy her madcap adventures in the sequels to the original Pippi book, *Pippi Goes on Board*, *Pippi in the South Seas*, and *Pippi on the Run*.

Third- and fourth-graders thoroughly enjoy the fun of *Miss Osborne-the-Mop* by Wilson Gage. One very dull summer Jody discovers that she has the power to change people and objects into something else and back again. Complications arise when Jody turns a dust mop into a person who strongly resembles her fourth-grade teacher and then finds that she cannot turn the tireless, spindly-legged Miss Osborne back into an ordinary dust mop.

When the east wind blew *Mary Poppins* by P. L. Travers into the Bankses' house in London to care for Michael and Jane, it blew her into the hearts of many thousands of readers. Wearing her shapeless hat and white gloves, carrying her parrot-handled umbrella and a large carpet bag, Mary Poppins is as British as tea, yet many children in the United States love this nursemaid with strange magical powers. Probably their favorite story is that of the laughing-gas party. Jane, Michael, and Mary Poppins visit Mary Poppins' uncle for tea, only to be overcome by fits of uncontrollable laughter. As a result, they all blow right up to the ceiling. Mary Poppins raises the table in some way, and they have birthday tea suspended in midair! Nothing seems impossible for this prim autocrat of the nursery to perform in her matter-of-fact, believable fashion. Not all children enjoy the British flavor of this book, but many adore Mary Poppins as much as Michael and Jane did. Mary Poppins goes serenely on her way through other funny adventures in *Mary Poppins Comes Back*, *Mary Poppins Opens the Door*, and *Mary Poppins in the Park*.

The story of *Mr. Popper's Penguins* by Richard and Florence Atwater has long been the favorite funny story of many primary-grade children. This is the tale of Mr. Popper, a mild little house painter whose major interest in life is the study of the Antarctic. An explorer presents Mr. Popper with a penguin which he promptly names Captain Cook. In order to keep Captain Cook from becom-

[18]Carol Kendall, *The Gammage Cup*, illustrated by Erik Blegvad (New York: Harcourt Brace Jovanovich, 1959), pp. 91–92.

ing lonely, Mr. Popper obtains Greta from the zoo. After the arrival of ten baby penguins, Mr. Popper has a freezing plant put in the basement of his house and his furnace moved upstairs to the living room. The Atwaters' serious recounting of a highly implausible situation adds to the humor of this truly funny story.

In the world of *James and the Giant Peach* by Roald Dahl, James meets many strange characters. James, one of the saddest and loneliest boys in the world, lives with his wicked Aunt Sponge and Aunt Spiker in an old, ramshackle house on a high hill in the south of England. James meets a queer old man who thrusts a bag of green crystals into his hands and tells him to mix them with water and drink them and he'll never be miserable again. After cautioning him not to let the crystals escape, the old man disappears. James is so excited and so intent upon getting to the kitchen without being seen by his aunts that he slips and falls, and all of the magic crystals disappear into the ground right under the old peach tree. In no time at all an enormous peach grows on the tree, bigger than a house. One night James discovers a door in the side of the peach. Upon entering he finds six amazing creatures who say they have been waiting for him—a grasshopper the size of a large dog, a giant ladybug, an enormous spider, a centipede, an earthworm, and a silkworm. Early the next morning the centipede gnaws off the stem and the huge peach starts to roll down the hill, incidentally smashing Aunt Spiker and crushing Aunt Sponge on its mad dash to the sea. The marvelous adventure has begun! Threatened by sharks, James saves the peach by throwing strands of silk and spider webbing over 502 seagulls who gently lift the peach from the ocean and sail away across the sea. This is a wonderful spoof on Victorian morality tales. The characters are well drawn, their grumbling conversations are very believable, the plot is original and ingenious. The illustrations by Nancy Burkert are beautifully detailed and reflect the pathos and joy of James' "fabulous flight." For these reasons as well as because of the many short chapters, this book is popular with children of all ages; it has been read aloud successfully to first- and second-graders, as well as to older children.

Still another fabulous flight is recorded in the story of *The Twenty-one Balloons* by William Pène du Bois. Professor Sherman leaves San Francisco on August 15, 1883, in a giant balloon, telling reporters that he hopes to be the first man to fly across the Pacific Ocean. He is picked up three weeks later in the Atlantic Ocean clinging to the wreckage of a platform which has been flown through the air by twenty-one balloons. The story is told as the professor's speech at the Explorers' Club. On the seventh day of his voyage a seagull plummets through the professor's balloon, and he is forced to land on the island of Krakatoa. There, Professor Sherman discovers that he is to be a permanent visitor, since the twenty families who live over the most fabulous diamond mine in the world wish to remain unknown. They are extremely gracious to the professor and escort him on a tour of their amazing island, which heaves like the ocean from its volcanic activity. However, each of the houses is built on a diamond foundation and so does not move. The houses are amazing; they include a replica of Mount Vernon, a British cottage with a thatched roof, the Petit Trianon, a Moroccan house, and so on. The professor describes in graphic detail the houses, the inventions, and the customs of the Krakatoans and their escape when the volcano erupts. As usual, the minute description of du Bois' text is matched only by the meticulous perfection of his pen-and-ink drawings.

It seems preposterous to try to raise a dinosaur in a small New Hampshire town. However, that is precisely what Nate Twitchell does when *The Enormous Egg* which he is taking care of hatches into a baby Triceratops. When government figures in Washington, D. C., are consulted about the problem, members of Congress attempt to have "Uncle Beazley" (the dinosaur) destroyed, since he is extinct and probably un-American! Oliver Butterworth's satire on politics in the United States is a delightful mixture of humor and truth. Another egg poses problems for *Weird Henry Berg* by Sarah Sargent. This curiously patterned egg, which has been in the Berg family for over a century, hatches into a dragon. As the lizard grows and begins to assume the characteristics of its ancient race, Henry must choose between keeping it as a pet and allowing it to return to its homeland, the dragon lairs high in the Welsh mountains.

It is not dragons but lizards that complicate an 11-year-old's life in Daniel Pinkwater's *Lizard Music*. With his older sister on an unauthorized camping trip and his parents away for two weeks,

Victor has taken to watching late-night television. The only trouble is that he has begun to see large lizards peering over newscasters' shoulders, making music after the late late movie, or answering questions on a lizard quiz show. On a bus, Victor meets the cheerful but strange Chicken Man, so named for the chicken Claudia who roosts under his hat. The Chicken Man seems to know all about lizards. Back home, Victor muses:

> I like things neat. This situation wasn't neat at all, I decided that I was going to do something about it. Up till now, things had just been happening—not even happening *to* me—just happening in front of me. I wanted to know what was going on. I wanted to make some things happen.[19]

Victor's determination eventually gains him a tour of a floating island run by lizards. Pinkwater's story is fast-paced, full of zany names, hilarious observations on contemporary society, and bad puns. After one middle-school teacher jokingly awarded an enthusiastic seventh-grader a "lizard lover's" card, he and other students formed a school club. Potential members in the club had to pass a student-made test on the book, and many students went on to read other Pinkwater books.

Other books by Pinkwater rely on the same crazy blend of humor, eccentric characters, and preposterous situations. *The Magic Moscow* introduces readers to Norman Bleistift, young assistant to Steve Nicholson who owns the diner where such vegetable-and-ice cream specialties as the Nuclear Meltdown and the Day of Wrath are served. In *Slaves of Spiegel*, Norman and Steve are kidnapped by fat men from outer space to participate in their intergalactic junk-food cooking contest. While this series of slim books is more accessible to younger readers than *Lizard Music* is, they are read with enthusiasm by older readers as well.

A satire that is both funny and pathetic is *The Shrinking of Treehorn* by Florence Parry Heide. One day a very strange thing happens to Treehorn, a boy of 7 or 8; he starts shrinking. His mother and father ignore his predicament except to tell him to sit up at the table. His friend Moshie tells him that it is a stupid thing to do, and his teacher

[19]Daniel M. Pinkwater, *Lizard Music* (New York: Dodd, Mead, 1976), p. 47.

says: "'We don't shrink in this class.'" Poor Treehorn spends an unhappy day and night until he finds a magical game that restores his growth. The next night, however, as he is watching one of his fifty-six favorite TV programs, he notices that his hand has turned green. He decides not to tell his parents and see if they notice anything different. They don't. While this book appears in a picture-book format with Edward Gorey's wonderful tongue-in-cheek pen-and-ink drawings, it is not a story for young children. Satire requires maturity. The situation is impossible, but the uncaring self-centered attitude of the parents is possible. Fortunately, most children see it as a very funny story and are very quick to say: "Well, my parents would certainly notice if I started shrinking!" Treehorn's adventures are continued in a sequel, *Treehorn's Treasure*.

If Treehorn's parents ignore him, Pulcifer has the opposite concern in *The Problem with Pulcifer* by Heide. His parents are worried because their son refuses to watch television, can't follow even simple situation comedies, and prefers instead to read. His parents send him to a "special corrective remedial class for non-watchers" where Pulcifer practices reading parts of books interspersed with advertisements in hopes that he will transfer the skills to television watching. When that doesn't

Ironically, no adults, including the school principal, notice that Treehorn is shrinking. Illustration by Edward Gorey from *The Shrinking of Treehorn* by Florence Parry Heide.

help, Pulcifer is sent to a psychiatrist who decides that he doesn't understand the reason for watching television—everyone watches. Pulcifer is not convinced and we leave him, with his supportive but uncomprehending parents, settling down with a stack of books. Judy Glasser's illustrations poke sly fun at our television-ridden interiors and portray with humor this determined reader in the midst of a nonreading adult population.

Freaky Friday by Mary Rodgers hinges on one impossible situation: When Annabel wakes up one morning, she finds she has turned into her mother! She looks like her mother, must meet her mother's obligations and appointments, but thinks and acts as Annabel. In Rodgers' *Summer Switch,* Ape Face suddenly finds himself in the body of his father. Instead of going to summer camp, he is about to leave for Beverly Hills and a new job. While *Freaky Friday* is told by Annabel, *Summer Switch* is hilariously related, in alternating typefaces, first by Ape Face in California and then by his father at Camp Soonawissakit. While both sets of switchers gain new understandings of each other, it is the humor that carries the stories along and makes either a good candidate for reading aloud in fifth- or sixth-grade classrooms.

A preposterous situation is presented in one of the few satires really enjoyed by children, Jean Merrill's *The Pushcart War.* Written from the point of view of 1996, the story is presented as a "documented report" of the famous Pushcart War of 1986. Believing that we cannot have peace in the world unless people understand how wars start, the "author-historian" proceeds to describe the beginning of the war between the giant trucks of New York City and the pushcarts which began when Mack, driver of the Mighty Mammoth, rode down the cart of Morris the Florist. Like the Minutemen of the American Revolution, the 509 pushcart peddlers unite in their fight against the three largest trucking firms in the city. At first their fragile carts are crushed like matchboxes, but then the loyal band of defenders develops the old-fashioned peashooter into a highly effective weapon. The straight-faced account that provides details of the progress of the war and the eventual triumph of the pushcart peddlers is both a funny and pathetic commentary on life today. Children thoroughly enjoy this satire; in fact, one fifth-grade class returned for report cards on the last day of school and stayed an extra hour while their teacher finished reading the book. Few books can claim such devotion!

EXTRAORDINARY WORLDS

When Alice followed the White Rabbit down his rabbit hole and entered into a world that grew "curiouser and curiouser," she established a pattern for many modern books of fantasy. Starting in the world of reality they move quickly into the world of fantasy, where the everyday becomes extraordinary in a believable fashion. The plausible impossibilities of *Alice's Adventures in Wonderland* include potions to drink and edibles to eat that make poor Alice grow up and down like an elevator. At the famous "Mad Hatter's Tea Party" there is no room for tea. The Mad Hatter, the Dormouse, and the Rabbit are just a few of the individuals whom Alice meets in her wanderings. Other characters include the Red Queen, who has to keep running in order to stay "in the same place"; the hurrying White Rabbit, who keeps murmuring that he'll be late—yet no one knows where he is going; Humpty Dumpty, whose words mean exactly what he chooses them to mean; and the terrifying Queen of Hearts, who indiscriminately shouts, "Off with her head." Always the proper Victorian young lady, Alice maintains her own personality despite her bizarre surroundings, and her acceptance of this nonsense makes it all seem believable. She becomes the one link with reality in this amazingly fantastic world.

Children are often surprised to find *Alice* and *Through the Looking Glass* the source of many words and expressions used in the popular culture. While many children do not have the maturity or sense of word play required to appreciate this fantasy, teachers or librarians might read aloud popular selections, such as the Jabberwocky or the Mad Hatter's Tea Party, and encourage those who enjoy them to read the entire book.

The cyclone that blew Dorothy into the Land of Oz continues to blow swirling controversies around this series of books by L. Frank Baum and others. Some maintain that *The Wizard of Oz* is a skillfully written fantasy, a classic in its own right. Others condemn the first book because of some of the poorly written volumes of over forty that followed. *The Wizard of Oz* was the first book and is the most popular. In this story Dorothy, her dog

Toto, the Scarecrow, the Tin Woodman, and the Cowardly Lion make the long, hazardous trip to the Emerald City to seek special gifts from the Wonderful Wizard. Eventually each of the characters achieves his or her particular wish, but the wizardry is in the way they come to think of themselves, rather than in anything that the Wizard does for them. For the most part this fantasy depends on the strange situations and creatures that Dorothy and her companions meet, rather than anything they do or say. One never doubts that the four will overcome all odds and achieve their wishes. Even the Wizard holds no terror for practical, matter-of-fact Dorothy. This lack of wonder and awe—the basic ingredients of most fantasy—make *The Wizard of Oz* seem somewhat pedestrian when compared with other books of its kind.

For many years the Moomintroll family has delighted the children of Sweden. Now children in the United States are taking to these strange but endearing creatures that look slightly like hippopotamuses. The Moomin live in a lonely valley with various peculiar friends. Each member of the Moomin family is an individual and remains faithful to his or her characterization throughout the series of books. *Tales from Moominvalley* is the first and, perhaps, best of this fantastic series. Tove Jansson won the international Hans Christian Andersen Award for this contribution to the literature of children.

One of the most popular fantasies for children is Roald Dahl's tongue-in-cheek morality tale, *Charlie and the Chocolate Factory*. Mr. Willie Wonka, owner of the mysterious locked chocolate factory, suddenly announces that the five children who find the gold seal on their chocolate bars will be allowed to visit his fabulous factory. And what an assortment of children win—Augustus Gloop, a greedy fat pig of a boy; Veruca Salt, a spoiled little rich girl whose parents always buy her what she wants; Violet Beauregarde, the world's champion gum chewer; Mike Teevee, a fresh child who spends every waking moment in front of the television set; and Charlie Bucket, a hero, who is honest, brave, trustworthy, obedient, poor, and starving. One by one the children are disobedient and meet with horrible accidents in the chocolate factory. Nothing, of course, happens to the virtuous Charlie, who by the story's conclusion has

brought his poor family to live in the chocolate factory and is learning the business from his benefactor. The 1964 edition of this book was criticized because the factory was worked by the Oompa-Loompas, black pygmies supposedly imported from Africa by Mr. Wonka, exploited as workers, and presented as a group rather than as individuals.[20] In the 1973 edition, Dahl revised the text so that the Oompa-Loompas were long-haired little people imported from Loompaland. The sequel to this book, *Charlie and the Great Glass Elevator*, lacks the humor and the imaginative sparkle of the first book.

Going through *The Phantom Tollbooth*, Milo discovers a strange and curious world indeed. Norton Juster, the author, creates "The Lands Beyond," which includes the Foothills of Confusion, the Mountains of Ignorance, the Lands of Null, the Doldrums, and the Sea of Knowledge. Here Milo meets King Azoz the Unabridged, the unhappy ruler of Dictionopolis, the Mathemagician who serves them subtraction stew and increases their hunger, and the watchdog Tock, who keeps on ticking throughout all their adventures. The substance of this fantasy is in its play on words rather than its characters or situations. Its appreciation is dependent on the reader's knowledge of the various meanings of words. For this reason children with mature vocabularies particularly enjoy its humor.

Rather than create their own imaginary worlds, many authors have successfully blended fantasy with reality to produce strange elements in the known world. *The Sea Egg* by L. M. Boston is the haunting story of two young boys and their magical summer on the Cornish coast of England. The boys buy an unusual egg-shaped rock which hatches into a baby triton (a merman), with whom they swim and play most of the day. On the last night of the boys' holiday, their companion shares the most remarkable experience of all—a magical night swimming with the seals through the underwater tunnels of Seal Island. Boston evokes an eerie beauty in this strange, suspenseful sea adventure.

[20]Lois Kalb Bouchard, "A New Look at Old Favorites: 'Charlie and the Chocolate Factory' " in *Interracial Books for Children*, vol. 3 (Winter, Spring 1971), pp. 3, 8.

A mermaid is a part of the curious *The Animal Family* created by Randall Jarrell. A man and woman and their son are shipwrecked on an uninhabited coast, where they live an isolated life. The boy's mother and father grow old and die; and the boy, now a man and a hunter, is left completely alone. The hunter's loneliness is assuaged as a mermaid, bear, lynx, and, finally, a shipwrecked baby become his family. This is a strange and haunting story of man's need to create a home and share love and companionship in the context of a family, even if the family consists of a mermaid and animals. Maurice Sendak has wisely illustrated the original home of every member of this family, thereby emphasizing the theme of the story.

Two of Natalie Babbitt's fantasies, *The Search for Delicious* and *Kneeknock Rise,* comment on the truth of myth within the framework of a quest story. Young Gaylen is sent out as the king's messenger to poll the kingdom as to which food should stand for the word "delicious" in the dictionary that the prime minister is compiling. Before he finishes, Gaylen uncovers Hemlock's plot to overthrow the king. With the help of all the creatures that the people no longer believe in, but that are the subject of the minstrel's songs and tales—such as woldwellers, the dwarfs, and Ardis the mermaid—Gaylen is able to foil Hemlock and save his king. In the epilogue the minstrel returns and the prime minister tells him Gaylen's strange story, thinking that it would make a very pretty song indeed! And so mythmaking continues. In *Kneeknock Rise,* Egan climbs the mountain and finds a perfectly rational explanation for the groaning noises of the mythical Megrimum. When he eagerly relates his findings to the villagers, they refuse to listen to him, and Egan discovers that man does not relinquish his myths easily; harmless monsters may be preferable to facts.

MAGICAL POWERS

Folktales are replete with characters or objects that possess particular magical powers of enchantment. Modern authors like Roald Dahl have been quick to utilize this motif in many of their fanciful tales. Zak, an 8-year-old girl, has a terrible power and a highly developed sense of righteous indignation. When she becomes irate at her neighbors for hunting, she puts *The Magic Finger* on them. The next morning when Mr. and Mrs. Gregg awaken, they find that they are duck-sized and have grown wings where their arms were. Imagine their consternation when they are out in the backyard trying out their wings, and see a family of enormous ducks moving into their house! Sizing up the situation, Mr. Gregg builds a nest for the night. They awaken after a damp, rainy night to find themselves peering down the ends of three double-barreled shotguns. After promising the ducks that they will never go hunting again, the Greggs are returned to their own house in their original forms. The theme of this fast-paced fantasy is very much in keeping with today's concern for the preservation of wildlife. There is no mistaking the message in William Pène du Bois' pictures, one of which shows Zak pointing her finger at the reader in the same manner as the well-known poster of Uncle Sam by James Montgomery Flagg.

Commander Caractacus Pott was a famous inventor, but he couldn't account for all the magical abilities of his mysterious green car, *Chitty-Chitty-Bang-Bang.* Chitty-Chitty could be an airplane or a boat as well, so the Potts took a sea voyage across the Channel between England and France only to discover a gangster cave containing the gang's ammunition. With the help of the great green car, Commander Pott and his family blow up the cave, but not before the gangsters have seen them. The children are kidnapped and held as hostages. However, by this time the reader is certain that Chitty-Chitty will use the marvelous radar scanner on her hood and find the twins. And she does! The gangsters are turned over to the police. At the very end of the book Chitty-Chitty soars up to the sky, and the Potts are off on an unknown adventure. This sophisticated parody on a detective story is the only children's book written by Ian Fleming, the creator of the well-known James Bond mysteries.

The children in books of fantasy often possess a magic object, know a magic saying, or have magical powers themselves. In *Half Magic* by Edward Eager, Jane finds what she believes to be a nickel, but it is a magic charm or at least half of a magic charm, for it provides half of all the children's wishes. Soon the children learn to double their wishes, so that half of them will come true. Eager's *Seven-day Magic* tells of a magic book that the children borrow from the library. When they open the book, they find it is about themselves; everything they did that morning is in the book and the rest of the book is shut tight waiting for them to create it. Logic and humor are characteristic of the many books of fantasy which were Eager's legacy of modern magic to today's children.

Frequently, less demanding fantasy relies on magical powers, slight characterization, and fast-moving plots to interest less able readers. For instance, Ruth Chew's *Mostly Magic* features two children whose discovery of a magical ladder and pencil transports them to other places and allows them to transform objects. In *Wish Come True* by Mary Q. Steele, a brother and sister have a magic ring that allows them to change their shapes, appearances, and abilities. Scott Corbett's "trick" books, such as *The Lemonade Trick,* rely on Kirby Maxwell's use of a magic chemistry set belonging to Mrs. Greymalkin, a neighborhood witch. Greedy John Midas suffers the consequences of his newly acquired magical power, *The Chocolate Touch,* in Patrick Skene Catling's new twist on an old story. While none of these stories tax an accomplished reader, many children come to discover the pleasures of wide reading through books such as these.

Jane Langton has created several stories of mystery and magical powers surrounding the Halls, who live in a strange old turreted house in Concord, Massachusetts. In *The Diamond in the Window,* Uncle Freddy had been a world-renowned authority on Emerson and Thoreau until the mysterious disappearance of his younger brother and sister left him slightly deranged. In the tower room two beds are made up in a vain hope for the return of the two children. Edward and Eleanor move to the tower room and search in their dreams for the two missing members of the family. Sequels include *The Swing in the Summerhouse,* which swings the children into several separate adventures, and *The Astonishing Stereoscope,* which allows them to enter the world they view through the glasses.

The fourth story of the Hall family, *The Fledgling,* centers upon 8-year-old Georgie's desire and eventual ability to fly. She is befriended by the Goose Prince, who takes her on his back and teaches her to glide in the air for herself. Although Georgie outgrows her gift, and the Goose Prince falls prey to a gun, the goose leaves her with a magical present, a ball which projects an image of the whole world, and the admonition, *"Take good care of it."* While the villains Preak and Prawn are presented as satirizations of the world's attitudes rather than as whole people, Georgie and her family are lovingly portrayed. Langton's sensory descriptions of common things give the story a warm and comfortable tone (the closet "smelled of warm rubbers and moth flakes and woolen cloth"), while her evocation of flying may make earthbound readers' spirits soar. Another story, *The Summer Birds* by Penelope Farmer, presents child flyers taught by a strange boy who hopes to draw them to his island to restore his birdlike race. However, Farmer's story is darker toned and its conclusion less hopeful than in *The Fledgling,* which was a Newbery Medal Honor Book.

SUSPENSE AND THE SUPERNATURAL

Interest in the occult and the supernatural, a recent adult preoccupation, has captured the imagination of children, also. They enjoy spooky, scary stories, just as they like being frightened by terror in TV or theater horror films. Increasingly, publishers are issuing finely crafted suspense fantasies which are very often superior to the usual ghost story or mystery tale. These well-written tales of suspense and the supernatural deserve attention.

Mollie Hunter mingles long-ago legend with present-day mystery in *The Haunted Mountain.* In the lonely mountain passes of the Scottish Highlands the country folk still heed the ancient lore, which bids them give a parcel of their land to the "Good People," so called to disguise their evil nature. But MacAllister, a strong and stubborn crofter, ignores a warning not to defy these shadowy creatures. He needs money to marry his Peigi-Ann, and so he dares to plow the Goodman's Croft. Later, the Good People capture him and chain him to the haunted mountain for seven years. His young son Fergus, cast in the same rugged mold as his father, breaks the evil spell by enduring a time of terrible testing. *The Walking Stones* is a more gentle, loving story of an old Scotsman called Bodach and his friendship with young Donald. Together the two of them call up their co-walkers from the other world to hold back the flooding of their Highland Glen until after the time of the secret walking of the magic ring of stones. Rings of standing stones are still found in secluded glens in Scotland. If you have ever listened to the silence that permeates the center of one, it would not be difficult to believe this superb story of *The Walking Stones.*

Mollie Hunter has based her eerie tale, *A Stranger Came Ashore,* on the old legends of the Shetland Islands that tell of the Selkie Folk, seals who can take on human form. Only young Robbie Henderson and his grandfather are suspicious of the handsome stranger who appears in their midst on the stormy night of a shipwreck. After Old Da dies, Robbie must put together the clues which reveal the real identity of Finn Learson and the sinister nature of his interest in the golden-haired Elspeth, Robbie's sister. Events build to a fearful climax on a night of ancient magic, when the dark powers of the sea are pitted against the common folk dressed as earth spirits and celebrating the last of the yule festival. Teachers who read aloud *A Stranger Came Ashore* find Jane Yolen's picture book *Greyling* a good introduction to Selkie lore. Children familiar with this story are much more sensitive to Hunter's use of foreshadowing, folk beliefs, mood, and setting in this finely crafted novel.

Paul Fleischman's brief book *The Half-A-Moon Inn* has the tone of a folktale and a setting to match. Born mute, 12-year-old Aaron feels a new independence when his mother lets him stay home while she takes the cart to market. When it later becomes apparent that his mother is lost in a great snowstorm, Aaron sets off to find her. He accidentally stumbles into the Half-A-Moon Inn, where he is imprisoned by the evil Miss Grackle, who needs a boy to tend the bewitched fires none but honest folk may kindle. Aaron soon discovers that Miss Grackle reads her patrons' dreams and robs them, but he is unable to run away because she has stolen his boots and his warm clothes. Aaron's escape, his reunion with his mother, and the folktalelike demise of the witch (she freezes to death beside her unlit fireplace) provide a satisfying conclusion. The telling of the story is lighter than its content, and the well-wrought dialogue makes this a challenging and entertaining choice for reading aloud to 9- and 10-year-olds.

John Bellairs' popular trilogy beginning with *The House with a Clock in Its Walls* owes less to the literary folktale than does *The Half-A-Moon Inn.* Following the death of his parents, Lewis Barnavelt comes to live with his Uncle Jonathan in an old Victorian mansion. Before Lewis' eyes, stained-glass windows change their pictures, worthless poker hands become winners, and telescopes reveal past rather than present events. It comes as no surprise to Lewis that his uncle and his uncle's best friend Mrs. Zimmerman are wizards. Lewis quickly becomes involved in their efforts to locate a ticking clock hidden somewhere in the house by a former owner, Isaac Izard, which has been set to bring about Doomsday. Children enjoy this fast-moving story, which blends details of magic and an intriguing old house with snappy exchanges among likable characters. Lewis makes a friend of Rose Rita Pottinger in *Figure in the Shadows. The Letter, the Witch, and the Ring,* in which Mrs. Zimmerman and Rose Rita try to recover a magic ring before it can be used for evil ends, concludes the series. Readers who have come to know Lewis from the first two books may miss his presence in this third volume.

William Sleator's *Blackbriar* creates a haunting sense of place. From the moment Danny and his guardian, Phillipa, move into the ancient house, Danny can feel its strange powers. He discovers a list of names carved on the cellar door followed by the dates *1665* or *1666,* except for the last name of Mary Peachy. It stands alone. Strange, weird events occur in rapid succession. One night a shadowy figure knocks at the door and asks for Mary Peachy. Another time, upon returning from the village, Danny and Phillipa see a fire burning in their fireplace and a robed figure seated in front of it. When they enter the house the man is gone, but the fire continues to burn. Islington, the Siamese cat, finds a strange little wooden doll that terrifies Phillipa, but somehow fascinates Danny. In fact, Danny consistently draws strength from meeting each of these challenges, while Phillipa becomes more pettish and quarrelsome. With the aid of the girl Lark, Danny finds a tunnel leading from the cellar of Blackbriar and a room full of skeletons. In a dramatic climax the two children uncover the mystery of Blackbriar and Mary Peachy. The woods gradually reclaim Blackbriar for the ghost of Mary Peachy while Danny claims his self-hood and growing independence. This remarkable book, which sustains interest and suspense throughout, is a great one to read aloud to 10- and 11-year-olds.

For sheer nightmare quality no one can compete

with the books of Leon Garfield. He establishes an eerie ominous mood from the very first of *Mister Corbett's Ghost:*

A windy night and the Old Year dying of an ague. Good riddance! A bad Old Year, with a mean spring, a poor summer, a bitter autumn—and now this cold, shivering ague. No one was sorry to see it go. Even the clouds, all in black, seemed hurrying to its burying—somewhere past Hampstead.[21]

Benjamin wishes his harsh taskmaster, Mr. Corbett, dead when he is ordered to go off on a long delivery errand and is likely to miss the New Year's party. The recipient of the delivery, either the devil himself or a close relative, offers to arrange this for a simple fee and Benjamin discovers Mr. Corbett's body in the road on the way home. When eventually the sad ghost begins to plague the guilty boy, Ben must bargain once more with the strange old man for the restoration of Mr. Corbett. Ever afterward, Ben thinks differently about his master. The story is similar to *A Christmas Carol* and children may discover the comparisons: in Dickens' story, the man develops compassion for the boy; here, the boy develops compassion for the man.

Another restless spirit is found in *The Ghost of Thomas Kempe* by Penelope Lively. Released from a bottle dislodged by workmen refinishing James Harrison's room, the ghost is determined to harass James into being his apprentice in matters of "Sorcerie, Astrologie, Geomancie, Alchemie, and Recoveries of Goodes Loste." This seventeenth-century poltergeist blows through rooms, causes some small accidents and a near tragedy, and leaves accusing notes in an effort to control James and make his own presence felt in this century. When at last the ghost is returned to his final resting place, James has experienced a sense of the layers of time coexisting in his English village and has shared his adventure only with old Bert Ellison, a handyman and amateur exorcist. Penelope Lively tells a good story with humor, and readers are left with the feeling of being, like James, in the middle of time which reaches away behind and before us.

The ghosts of Colby Rodowsky's *The Gathering Room* seem somehow more alive than the story's "real" characters, troubled Mudge and his parents, who have moved into the gatehouse of an historic cemetery. Isolated from other children, Mudge makes friends with a young girl killed by a milk wagon, a judge, two victims of the War of 1812, and assorted other cemetery residents. He is so contented with their companionship that he resents the intrusion of a visiting aunt who urges the family back to a more conventional life style. Finding a friend from outside the cemetery walls finally eases the boy's painful transition into the contemporary world. Since the story's beginning is slow-paced and rather complex, readers may need encouragement to keep going until the oddly fascinating atmosphere begins to exert its hold.

The opening paragraph of *Sweet Whispers, Brother Rush* by Virginia Hamilton quickly draws the reader into a remarkable story:

The first time Teresa saw Brother was the way she would think of him ever after. Tree fell head over heels for him. It was love at first sight in a wild beating of her heart that took her breath. But it was a dark Friday three weeks later when it rained, hard and wicked, before she knew Brother Rush was a ghost.[22]

Fourteen-year-old Tree has been taking care of her older brother Dab while her mother, Viola, works in another city as a practical nurse. She comes home sporadically to stock the pantry and to leave money for Tree and Dab. Loving "M'Vy," Tree painfully accepts these absences and devotes her time to schoolwork and caring for her brother. As Dab's occasional bouts of sickness suddenly become more frequent, Brother Rush appears to Tree. He has come to "take her out" through a small space he holds in his hand. Looking into this space, Tree becomes an observer of her family's recent past which, until now, she has not questioned. It is through several times with Brother Rush that Tree begins to understand why her mother has always avoided Dab, the hereditary nature of Dab's sickness, and something about her father. When Dab is moved to a hospital where he succumbs to

[21]Leon Garfield, *Mister Corbett's Ghost,* illustrated by Alan E. Cober (New York: Pantheon, 1968), p. 1.

[22]Virginia Hamilton, *Sweet Whispers, Brother Rush.* (New York: Philomel, 1982), p. 9.

Sweet Whispers, Brother Rush
Virginia Hamilton

Teresa reaches for images in the mirror held by her uncle's ghost to try to grasp what she has seen but has yet to understand. Jacket painting by Leo and Diane Dillon.

the disease, it is the times with Brother Rush that enable Tree to explain to herself what has happened. But it is M'Vy's love and the gentle strength of her companion Silversmith that pull Tree through her anger and despair toward an acceptance of her brother's death and the promise of new extended family relationships. Making use of cadences and inflections of black speakers, Hamilton moves surely from narration to dialogue and into Tree's thoughts. She has created complex characters whose steady or fumbling reachings for each other may linger with middle-school readers long past the reading of this story. A strong sense of family also exists in Hamilton's trilogy, the Justice Cycle, which begins with *Justice and Her Brothers* and explores ESP and its effects on family relationships.

TRICKS WITH TIME

Probably every human being at one time or another has wondered what it would be like to visit the past. We have looked at old houses and wished they could tell us of the previous lives they contained; we have held antique jewelry in our hands and wondered about the former owners. Our curiosity has usually been more than just an historical interest; we have wished to communicate, to enter into the lives of the past without somehow losing our own particular place in time.

Recognizing this fascination with being transported to another age, authors of books for children have written many fantasies that are based on tricks with time. Characters appear to step easily from their particular moment in the present to a long-lost point in someone else's. Usually these time leaps are linked to a certain tangible object or place that is common to both periods. In *Tom's Midnight Garden* by Philippa Pearce, the old grandfather clock that strikes thirteen hours serves as the fixed point of entry for the fantasy. And in *Playing Beatie Bow* by Ruth Park, Abby slips into the 1870s by virtue of the antique crochet work she wears on her dress; she cannot return to her own time without it. The rules of time fantasy are as binding as the relentless ticking of our own time period.

Julia Sauer's *Fog Magic* is the tender, moving story of Greta Addington, a young girl of Nova Scotia. One day, while walking in the fog, Greta discovers a secret world, the village of Blue Cove. This fishing village is only present in the fog; on sunny days there are just empty cellar holes of houses from the past. Midst the fog magic, Greta meets a girl her own age whose mother senses that Greta is from "over the mountain" and quietly reminds her each time the fog is lifting that it is time to go home. Some occasional knowing looks and comments from Greta's father make her realize that he, too, has visited Blue Cove. Greta is particularly anxious that her twelfth birthday be a foggy day. That evening, when she is on the way home from a church picnic with her father, the fog comes in. She runs back to enter Blue Cove, where her friend's mother gives her a soft gray kitten and quietly wishes her a "Safe passage for all the years ahead." Greta senses that this will be the last time that she will be able to visit Blue Cove. She walks slowly down the hill to find her father waiting. As she shows him her kitten, he reaches into his pocket and pulls out an odd little knife that he had received on his twelfth birthday at Blue Cove. This is a hauntingly beautiful story, memorable for its mood and setting. Part of its appeal may come from the underlying view, common in mystical fantasy, that childhood confers special sensibilities which adults can no longer share.

No one is more skillful in fusing the past with the present than L. M. Boston in her stories of Green Knowe, that mysterious old English house in which the author still lives. In *The Children of Green Knowe*, the first in this series, Boston tells the story of Tolly, who is sent to live with his great-grandmother. Over the large fireplace in the drawing room hangs a picture of three children who grew up at Green Knowe in the seventeenth century. Tolly's great-grandmother tells him stories about them: of Toby and his pony Festi, of Linnet and her birds, of Alexander and his flute. The children seem so real that Tolly is convinced they often play hide and seek with him. His great-grandmother believes him, and soon the reader does too. In *The Treasure of Green Knowe*, Boston has included a mysterious search for lost jewels, but the real interest of the book is the story-within-a-story of blind Susan Oldknow's life at Green Knowe some two centuries ago. Children may better appreciate the problems and joys of the blind after hearing Susan's story of misunderstanding and mistreatment. A sinister mood prevails in *An Enemy at Green Knowe*, in which Granny Oldknow tells Tolly and his Chinese friend Ping about a mad alchemist who practiced witchcraft at Green Knowe in the year 1630. Drawn into a search for the alchemist's books by a mysterious neighbor, the boys find themselves fighting evil as dark as that conjured by the madman three centuries before. The old house at Green Knowe is also the setting for *The River at Green Knowe*. New characters are introduced, but the reader misses Tolly and his great-grandmother, who just naturally seem to belong to Green Knowe.

One of the best time fantasies to be written is the mysterious and exciting *Tom's Midnight Garden* by Philippa Pearce. Forced to spend part of a summer with a rather boring aunt and uncle, Tom finds his visit quite dull until he hears the grandfather clock in the hall strike thirteen. That is the time for him to slip into the garden and play with Hatty, a child of the past. Hatty and the gardener, Abel, are the only ones who can see Tom in his pajamas; he is invisible to everyone else. Tom becomes so absorbed in his midnight visits when "there is time no longer," that he does not wish to return home. One fateful night Tom opens the back door and sees only the paving and the fences that stand there in daylight—Hatty and her garden have vanished. When Tom meets the real Hatty, a little old lady who has been dreaming about her past, he understands why the weather in the garden has always been perfect, why some nights it has been one season and the next night a different one, why Hatty was sometimes young and sometimes older; it all depended on what old Mrs. Bartholomew had chosen to remember. Lonely and bored, Tom had joined her in her dreams. This is a fascinating story that should please both boys and girls in the middle grades. The book won the Carnegie Medal as the outstanding English children's book for the year of its publication.

While the characters in most time fantasies slip in and out of the past, the problem in *Tuck Everlasting* is that the Tuck family is trapped forever in the present. Natalie Babbitt's elegant prose leads the reader to expect a quiet Victorian fantasy, but the book holds many surprises—including a kidnapping, a murder, and a jailbreak. The story opens with Winnie Foster, an over-protected 10-year-old, sitting in front of her family's prim touch-me-not cottage on a hot August day talking to a large plump toad. She informs the toad that she wants to do something interesting, something that will make a difference to the world. The very next morning Winnie "runs away" to the nearby woods owned by her parents and sees a young lad of 17 (although he first says he is 104 years old) drinking from a spring. When Winnie asks for a drink, Jesse Tuck warns her not to take one. Just at that moment his mother, Mae Tuck, and brother Miles arrive. With all due apologies to Winnie, they bundle her onto their horse to go back to their home to have a talk with Mae's husband, Angus Tuck. On the way, Mae tells Winnie the strange story that drinking the spring water has given them everlasting life. Back at the shabby three-room cottage of the Tucks, Winnie receives kindly affection from them all as they try to persuade her to guard their secret. In the morning Angus Tuck takes Winnie rowing on the lake and explains to her what it is like to live forever. He longs for a natural conclusion to his life. "I want to grow again, . . . and change. And if that means I got to move on at the end of it, then I want that, too."[23] Although the Tucks intend to let Winnie Foster make her own decision, they do not know that a man in a yellow suit has been searching for them for years, and that he just happened to hear Mae Tuck reveal their secret to Winnie. Caught in the melodrama of the Tucks' lives, Winnie decides to protect and help them, a decision that does indeed change Winnie's life. The simplicity of the Tucks and their story belies the depth of the theme of *Tuck Everlasting*. With its prologue and epilogue, the story reminds one of a play, a kind of *Our Town* for children.

Many fantasies written in the United States seem more light-hearted than those of the British. For example, Edward Ormondroyd's *Time at the Top* is a refreshingly different time fantasy. It starts out with a windy, wretched day when everything goes wrong, until Susan meets and helps a funny little old "Mary Poppins-ish" woman who says she will "give her three." When Susan pushes the elevator button for the top floor where she and her father live, the elevator keeps right on going to the eighth floor—except there is no eighth floor. Susan gets off and finds herself in a different time and at a different place. How she makes friends with Victoria and her brother Robert and solves their financial difficulties and their widowed mother's marital problems makes for a fast-paced, amusing story. *All in Good Time* is a sequel to this time fantasy.

Mystery is also an important part of the complex fantasy by Eleanor Cameron titled *The Court of the Stone Children*. The story of modern-day Nina, who has a "Museum Feeling" and thinks she would like to be a curator, becomes intertwined with the story of Dominique, a young noblewoman of nineteenth-century France whose father was executed by Napoleon's regime and whose family possessions are now housed in a French museum in San Francisco. Domi appears to Nina in the museum and becomes her friend. She enlists Nina's help in the task of clearing her father's name of the charge of murder. What then develops is a suspenseful mystery, with telling clues foreshadowed in one of Nina's "real-life" dreams, in which one of the statues in the museum's Court of Stone Children points the way to a painting which serves as evidence of the count's innocence. The Chagall painting "Time Is a River without Banks," which hangs in the museum, is used throughout the story as a symbolic reference point for Nina's unusual interest in the abstract nature of time. She understands:

> . . . the connection between her Museum Feeling and the painting. "Time is a river without banks"—yes, immeasurable and indefinable. And she understood, with no need for words, that it was the paradox and, somehow, the sadness of Time that drew her to the possessions of those long gone: objects, unthinking, unfeeling objects that yet have their own voices, and that outlast the loving flesh that created them.[24]

This is a profound theme explored by a truly accomplished writer. However, young readers will be more likely to value the book for its exciting events and for the haunting presence of Domi in her museum domain than for its eloquent abstractions.

Another story involving political intrigue is *A Traveler in Time,* which is based on the dream experiences of its author, Alison Uttley. Penelope, who is visiting her aunt and uncle at an old manor house in England, steps through a door and finds herself talking to a woman who is kneading dough in an Elizabethan kitchen. At first, Penelope's visits are brief, but then she finds herself caught up with the old tragedy of Anthony Babington and his plot to save Mary Queen of Scots. Knowing Mary's fate, Penelope tries to communicate the dangers involved, but no one will listen to her pathetic pleas. Penelope slips back and forth in time, but she sadly realizes that she will outgrow her visions.

Some time fantasies draw credibility from leg-

[23]Natalie Babbitt, *Tuck Everlasting* (New York: Farrar, Straus & Giroux, 1975), p. 63.

[24]Eleanor Cameron, *The Court of the Stone Children* (New York: Dutton, 1973), p. 91

endary characters and events. One of these is William Mayne's chilling story, *Earthfasts*. David and Keith meet at dusk at the place where Keith had seen a swelling in the earth the day before. Tonight it is larger, and the ground is vibrating with the sound of drumming. As the noise increases, the boys are frozen in terror as a person emerges from the ground beating a drum and clutching a steady, cold white flame. David identifies this stranger as Nellie Jack John, who according to legend went underground more than two hundred years ago to seek the treasure of King Arthur. The boys protect and feed him, but Nellie Jack John only stays above the earth for two days, leaving his strangely cold candle behind him. Fascinated by the glow of the taper, David realizes that the many bizarre events occurring throughout the countryside are related to Nellie Jack John's disturbance of time. Ancient stones, called earthfasts, work up in a farmer's ploughed field; a family's poltergeist or boggart returns after an absence of many years; and one terror-filled night David vanishes in what looks like a flash of lightning. Trying to find a clue to David's disappearance, Keith stares at the brilliant cold flame of the candle. Suddenly he understands:

> On the skyline, where lightness filled the air, stood a row of huge stones, or giants. Keith was not sure which they were, but it did not matter, because standing stones were giants, and giants became standing stones whilst the King's time was standing still. And the King's time stood still when the candle Keith held was in its proper place under the ground, because King Arthur's time was not yet come.[25]

This is an unforgettable book that owes much of its impact to its language and its finely realized setting.

A String in the Harp also gains strength from its setting, in this case Wales, and from its connection to legend. Nancy Bond tells of an American family's adjustment to living abroad when their newly widowed father accepts a university post. It is a particularly difficult time for 12-year-old Peter, who is stubborn, lonely, and hateful until he finds a strange ancient object later identified as the harp

key of Taliesin, the great sixth-century bard who lived in this part of Wales. While the key draws Peter back in time, his present-day life is adversely affected. Eventually, he is able to return the key to its proper place and assume a responsible place in the family. This strongly characterized but lengthy story mingles past and present time in a believable and involving way.

Like Peter, other time travelers learn to deal with a troubled present through experiences in an equally troubled past. In the Australian prizewinner *Playing Beatie Bow*, Ruth Park presents Abigail, a contemporary 14-year-old who has been deeply hurt first by her father's defection from the family and then by her mother's quick agreement when he wants to come back. In this resentful mood, Abigail follows a strangely dressed child who has been watching a neighborhood street game called "Beatie Bow." The little girl, the original Beatie Bow, leads Abigail through increasingly unfamiliar streets to her home in The Rocks area of Sydney—in the year 1873. Injured in a fall and divested of the dress with antique crochet work which has made her time passage possible, Abigail is trapped with Beatie's family. She comes to care for them all, especially charming cousin Judah, engaged to Beatie's older sister but attracted to Abby as well. Through her courage during a fire in the Bow family's candy shop, Abigail earns her return to the twentieth century, where she finds that she is now more tolerant of her father's lapse of affection. The epilogue-style ending provides an added twist of romance as an older Abigail discovers that her visit to the past is a surprising link to an attractive young man in the present. Few students in the United States are well acquainted with Australian geography, much less its history, but the setting is so vividly portrayed that this lack of familiarity need not stand in the way of a reader's enjoyment. The historical characters rise above their quaintness to become memorable, and the contemporary ones have both sharpness and humor. This is a well-told, highly entertaining story that provides glimpses of everyday life in the past.

Malcolm Bosse's *Cave Beyond Time* puts Ben, a modern teenager, at the site of his uncle's archaeological dig in the American Southwest. Having just suffered the tragic loss of his family in an auto accident, Ben feels grief, resentment, and a terrible sense of displacement. On a solitary excursion

[25] William Mayne, *Earthfasts* (New York: Dutton, 1967), p. 140.

away from camp he is bitten by rattlesnakes and wakes from delirium to find himself displaced in time—not once, but three times. In turn, he shares the dangerous life of Stone Age nomads, the challenge of mastering weapons of a later tribe of bison hunters, and the plight of pueblo farmers suffering a drought. In each of his encounters with the past, the boy must learn to bear a shattering loss and accept the possibility of a new future. Ben's experiences beyond time are given credibility by the author's use of graphic detail in describing the violence of hunting and the harshness of the hunters' rituals. Further credibility is gained through a familiar convention of fantasy in which the protagonist furnishes proof of his adventures by bringing special knowledge of the past back into the present with him. When Ben is found and treated for his wounds, he is able to explain the cave paintings which have puzzled his uncle's colleagues, and he predicts that they will find a large painted figure of the god of hunting, called Who Is Always There. But the author confirms that the significance of fantasy is a matter of personal not practical knowledge, in Ben's final realization:

> . . . it was no longer important what people believed or what was found or not found in the cave. Who Is Always There was always there. What had happened to Ben in the forest and plains would always be with him, real, forever in his heart.[26]

In some books where characters are shifted from modern times into specific periods of history, the concern with social and political issues of the past is very strong. These stories serve the purposes of historical fiction as well as fantasy. One notable example is *A Chance Child* by Jill Paton Walsh. Creep, a present-day English boy who is abused and kept locked in a closet, gets out by chance and follows a canal that takes him back to the period of the Industrial Revolution. As a child laborer, he travels from one exhausting and dangerous job to another, eventually losing his grip on the present altogether. His half-brother, the only person with any clue to his disappearance, searches historical documents from the early 1800s and is at last satisfied that Creep has escaped into the past and

lived out his life there. The amount of technological information about work in the coal mines, the nailer's forge, the pottery, and the textile mill attests to the research necessary for re-creating these settings. Walsh's juxtaposition of the abusive treatment of children in the nineteenth century and Creep's contemporary plight adds a dimension of social conscience infrequently found in fantasy. This is an extraordinary novel that demands much of the reader, partly because it blurs the distinctions between time fantasy and historical fiction.

Another book that explores the condition of a child laborer in nineteenth-century England is *Jeremy Visick* by David Wiseman. Twelve-year-old

Curiosity about a gravestone inscription sends *Jeremy Visick* on a journey into the history of his own small mining town in Britain. From the book by David Wiseman. Jacket illustration by Abigail Rorer.

[26]Malcolm J. Bosse, *Cave Beyond Time* (New York: Thomas Y. Crowell, 1980), p. 187.

Matthew has a school assignment designed to focus attention on the abandoned copper mines in his part of Cornwall. Research in a village churchyard tells him that three men from one family had died in a mine disaster and that a fourth, 12-year-old Jeremy Visick, had also perished, although his body had never been found. Matthew is strangely drawn to the forlorn gravestone which tells this tale and also to a shed in his own yard. Here the Visicks had once lived in poverty, and here they appear to Matthew as they were in their own time. Filled with the idea of somehow saving Jeremy, he accompanies the Visick men down into the mine and experiences the terror of the explosion in which they were killed. The reader's foreknowledge of disaster and death adds to the suspense, as does the growing sense of real-life danger to Matthew, who has discovered the abandoned mines with their grown-over entrances and treacherous vent shafts. Matthew's encounters with the past seem to be as much dream or illusion as time travel. In any case, the boy's careful investigation and documentation of the history that haunts him make all the events seem plausible. In his own way Matthew does rescue Jeremy, an aspect of the story that would be worth discussing with students.

Authors in the United States also use time travel as a way to involve readers in essentially historical themes. Jean Marzollo's *Halfway Down Paddy Lane,* which speaks to an adolescent audience, thrusts modern-day Kate into the labor troubles and dangerous prejudices of a New England mill town in 1850. Younger readers can go through a similar time slip in *A Girl Called Boy* by Belinda Hurmence. Blanche Overtha Yancey (Boy) is bored by her father's obvious pride in their black heritage and no longer impressed by the tiny African soapstone "freedom bird" passed down by his great-great-grandfather. But in response to her sarcastic command, the stone takes her "over the water" (a North Carolina stream near the picnic grounds where she has come for a family outing) and into the past when her father's ancestors were slaves. Boy's panic as she gradually realizes that she has lost touch with the present and, with her jeans and short-cropped hair, is being mistaken for a male runaway slave is entirely believable. The reader who discovers the injustices of slavery as Boy does, surprised and frightened by each new

cruelty and bit of hardship, is likely to develop strong feelings about the issues. Boy's flight toward freedom is exciting, and she becomes a memorable character. Her growing admiration and affection for the slaves who befriend and protect her are a counterpoint to her earlier attitudes and a testimony to the determination and sense of community among her people. The author's use of actual slave narratives and plantation records provides the same authenticity of background that would be expected in historical fiction. Using the device of time travel strengthens this story, however, for it allows the interjection of a contemporary perspective to balance the impact of that era's distorted values.

Janet Lunn, American born but now living in Canada, weaves together a haunting tale of a contemporary child, an old Canadian farmhouse, and the American Civil War in her book, *The Root Cellar.* When her grandmother dies, Rose is sent to live with her Aunt Nan's family in their country home on the northern shore of Lake Ontario. A shy child who has lived only with adults in New York City, 12-year-old Rose feels desperately lonely in the midst of Aunt Nan's and Uncle Bob's lively family. When she discovers an old root cellar door covered with vines and grass, she opens it and finds herself in a world of over one hundred years ago. She is more comfortable in this world and easily makes friends with Susan and Will. When Will runs off to fight in the Civil War and does not return, Rose and Susan set out on a hazardous journey which eventually takes them across the United States to an army hospital in Washington, D. C. Rose, who has traveled to Paris with her grandmother, is not prepared for the difficulties of this trip. She discovers, however, a strength and determination she did not know she had which helps her when she returns to her own time. Some of the reverberations from this well-written fantasy echo the feelings created in other notable books. For instance, Rose's delight in the orchard and finding the root cellar door is reminiscent of Mary's experiences in Burnett's *The Secret Garden.* In another instance, Rose finally realizes that the old Mrs. Morrissay who helped her cook Christmas dinner for the family was really Susan, her friend in the past. A similar moment of understanding occurs in *Tom's Midnight Garden* by Pearce.

Occasionally authors play tricks with time by manipulating history to suit themselves and borrowing a literary style to match. It is difficult to describe Joan Aiken's work as anything but fantastic Victorian melodrama. *The Wolves of Willoughby Chase* has all of the ingredients of a nineteenth-century chiller, including wicked wolves without and an outrageously wicked governess within. It takes place in a period of history that never existed—the Stuarts in the person of good King James III are on the throne in the nineteenth century! *Black Hearts in Battersea* is the mad and exciting sequel, with shipwrecks, stowaways, more wolves, and a desperate climax to save the king by means of a balloon. *Nightbirds on Nantucket* is the tale of the quest for a pink whale. Feminists will applaud the return of the resourceful 11-year-old Dido as much as they will dislike the quaking 9-year-old Dutiful Penitence and her sinister Aunt Tribulation. Dido is also at the center of a still more inventive book, *The Stolen Lake.* Here some of the history of Roman Britain has been superimposed on the geography of South America, with a 1,300-year-old Queen Guinevere awaiting Arthur just for good measure! While these books are not typical fantasies, their perpetual-motion plots represent suspenseful melodrama at its best.

High Fantasy

Many readers who learn to enjoy popular stories of magic, ghosts, time travel, and the like go on to become fans of a more serious and demanding type of story called high fantasy. These are complex narratives characterized by certain recurring themes and motifs. For instance, the stories frequently take place in created worlds or imaginary kingdoms. Characters may call upon ancient and fundamental powers, for good or ill. The conflict between these opposing forces becomes the focus of many stories. Frequently, the protagonists of high fantasy have a quest to fulfill. They pursue their destinies in a series of adventures which may require more than one volume for the telling. Finally, although there may be touches of humor, the overall tone of high fantasy is serious, because its purpose is serious. High fantasy concerns itself with cosmic questions and ultimate values: goodness, truth, courage, wisdom.

In accepting the National Book Award for *The Farthest Shore*, Ursula Le Guin spoke about the intent of fantasy at this level:

> The fantasist, whether he uses the ancient archetypes of myth and legend or the younger ones of science and technology, may be talking as seriously as any sociologist—and a good deal more directly—about human life as it is lived, and as it might be lived, and as it ought to be lived. For after all, as great scientists have said and as all children know, it is above all by the imagination that we achieve perception, and compassion, and hope.[27]

High fantasy's best audience stretches over a wide age range, from pre-adolescents to adults. Some of its most enthusiastic readers are the same young people who are devoted to games of imagined adventures like "Dungeons and Dragons." Many older readers simply call themselves science-fiction fans and make little distinction between the two types of books. In fact, much science fiction is also high fantasy; Madeleine L'Engle's *A Wrinkle in Time* is one familiar example. Some stories, like Anne McCaffrey's *Dragonsong*, appear to be science fiction by their extra-terrestrial settings and the use of precepts of science (in this case, the bonding of a newborn animal and a mother-figure). But *Dragonsong* seems more fantasy than science, since the newborns are traditional dragons and "fire lizards."

Not all critics will agree about the proper categorization of books like these. But it is the book itself, not its label, that matters to the reader. However it may be identified, well-written high fantasy rewards its audience.

ANCIENT POWERS

Stories of the power of creation and the elemental forces of nature must have fascinated audiences since the first tale-tellers. Modern science has not dispelled the ancient mystery of first things, nor diminished the fear of final ones. Some of today's fantasy writers call up these deep-rooted twin senses of wonder and dread in new stories built on myth and legend.

Sulamith Ish-Kishor's *The Master of Miracle* is

[27]Ursula K. Le Guin, "National Book Award Acceptance Speech," in *The Language of the Night: Essays on Fantasy and Science Fiction*, edited by Susan Wood (New York: Putnam, 1979), p. 58.

based on the Jewish legend of the creation of the Golem. The man-of-clay motif is found in the literature of many cultures, including one of the Greek myths about Prometheus. The Golem variant had its origin in sixteenth-century Prague, when the Jews were being severely persecuted. In order to save them from destruction, says the legend, a great rabbi who could invoke the power of God created a huge living being from clay. In Ish-Kishor's story the High Rabbi asks Gideon, an orphan boy, to dig and carry the clay from which the giant man, the Golem, is made. With the Golem's help a plot is foiled, for a greedy count had pretended that ghetto Jews had stolen his daughter to use her blood for the Passover. The Golem and Gideon find Maria Agnes where the count himself has hidden her, and the ghetto is saved. Then Gideon makes one fateful mistake. He does not follow the rabbi's instructions to destroy the Golem once it has fulfilled its purpose. The Golem goes on a rampage. Severely injured by the giant's collapse, Gideon is doomed to live and guard its remains until the return of the Jews to Palestine. This is a familiar cautionary theme—grief comes to those who tamper with forces which are not theirs to direct. In a reflection at the end of the story Gideon says: "I must learn that to put away death is to misunderstand the purpose of life."[28]

Alan Garner's book *The Owl Service* is based on the Welsh legend in the *Mabinogion* about Leu Llaw Gyffes and his wife Blodeuwedd, who was made for him out of flowers and who then destroyed him when she turned into an owl. For retelling the tragic tale in today's world, Garner uses as a symbolic device a set of china dishes with a distinctive flower pattern which can be pieced together to resemble an owl (the "owl service"). The complex cast of characters centers on a group of contemporary teenagers—Alison and Roger, a stepbrother and sister from an English upper-class family, and Gwyn, a Welsh boy whose mother rents part of her large house to summer visitors. Gwyn hopes to leave his Welsh village and become better educated. The next group of characters involves the older generation, particularly Huw, the gardener and handyman who, we later discover, is Gwyn's father. A third layer of characters includes those who make up the ancient legend of Blodeuwedd. The story begins when Alison hears scratchings in the ceiling over her bedroom and Gwyn's investigation turns up nothing but a stack of china in the unused attic. When Alison traces the pattern from a plate and folds the paper to fit the lines together, she sees the picture of an owl. The pattern then disappears from the plates, but the house becomes filled with a strange menace emanating from them. Poltergeist events occur and increase the many tensions among the characters: the English superiority against the Welsh clannishness, upper social class against the servant class, education against superstition, the younger generation against the older. A kind of nastiness in human relations pervades the house, along with owl feathers and droppings. The mounting tension is climaxed by an owl attack on Alison, which is relieved only by Roger's apology to Gwyn and his insistence that Alison see flowers, not owls, on the plate. The conclusion is intense and dramatic and requires close reading.

Garner knows the setting for his work so well that he can write with an uncanny sense of place. A dramatized version of *The Owl Service* was filmed for British television in the author's own house, itself a site of poltergeist activity, where his visitors developed a new respect for his fascination with unseen presences. One of Garner's earlier books, *Elidor*, has the same mounting terror as *The Owl Service* but is less complex. It is the adventure of four children who, while exploring a church that is being dismantled for slum clearance, enter the other world of Elidor which is threatened by the powers of darkness. Students might read this book as a step toward the complexity and overlaid stories of *The Owl Service*.

Patricia Wrightson is an Australian author with a special interest in Aboriginal folklore. She has shaped several fantasy stories around elements of nature—rock, fire, wind—which are strongly felt on that continent and has peopled them with legendary creatures such as Narguns, Ninya, Mimi, and water spirits. In *The Nargun and the Stars*, men disturb the ancient ones at Wongadilla, a sheep ranch in northern Australia. Simon Brent, shocked at the accidental death of both of his parents, arrives to live with middle-aged Charlie

[28]Sulamith Ish-Kishor, *The Master of Miracle: A New Novel of the Golem*, illustrated by Arnold Lobel (New York: Harper & Row, 1971), p. 104.

and Edie, second cousins whom he has never met. Slowly he comes to terms with the simple, direct ways of the lonely countryside itself. A city boy, he is awed by the size and beauty of the ranch and the swamp, where he discovers the Potkoorok, a frog-like creature who likes apples and speaks! Simon learns too of the shadowy, elusive spirits who live in the trees, the Turongs. But on the night of the storm Simon is terrified by another, older presence, the ancient Nargun, the huge stonelike creature that "oozed from rose-red fire into darkness." Disturbed by the vibrations of the bulldozer and the road scraper, the Nargun is moving, searching for his primeval silence, crushing everything in his path. Calmly, courageously Charlie tries to discover all he can about the ancient creature, and then he develops an ingenious plan to trap the Nargun in a cavern. This is a haunting and powerful fantasy which suggests man's unending struggle with primordial forces.

Wrightson has also written a trilogy: *The Ice Is Coming, The Dark Bright Water,* and *Journey Behind the Wind.* The central character is Wirrun, a young man of the People (Aborigines) who is called to save the land from ancient spirits which would disturb it. In the first book, men of ice called Ninya plot to trap the Eldest Nargun, who holds the power of fire, and take the land. Wirrun has to call on the People and the friendly spirits of the land to help him find the Eldest Nargun and save it from the gathering cold. The story of his success is an exciting one, with surprising ironies and touches of humor. In *The Dark Bright Water* Wirrun solves the mystery of why the spirits of the land have become restless, and in *Journey Behind the Wind* he travels to a confrontation with the monstrous Wulgaru, keeper of death.

The little-known traditions underlying these books and their emphasis on magical rather than human characters make unusual demands on the reader. The drama of the narrative and the force of Wrightson's language even the balance, however. These are books that evoke images of awesome, ancient powers and hint that the wise should live, like the Aborigines, in harmony with nature.

THE STRUGGLE BETWEEN GOOD AND EVIL

The age-old conflict between good and evil, light and darkness, life and death is a recurring theme in modern fantasy as well as in traditional literature. The setting for the struggle may be in the world as we know it, or in an invented land like Narnia, which some children know as well as their own backyards or city blocks. C. S. Lewis, a well-known English scholar and theologian, created seven fantasies about the country of Narnia. The best of the series is the first one published, *The Lion, the Witch, and the Wardrobe,* although it was the second in the sequence according to the history of Narnia. Beginning quite realistically in our time and world, four children find their way into the land of Narnia through the back of a huge wardrobe (or closet) in one of the large rooms of an old English house. The land is wrapped in a blanket of snow and ice, under the wicked Snow Queen's spell that controls the weather so it is "always winter and never Christmas." The children and the Narnians pit themselves against the evil witch and her motley assortment of ghouls, boggles, minotaurs, and hags. With the coming of the great Aslan the Lion, signs of spring are seen in the land. The children successfully aid the lion king in destroying the evil forces, and he crowns them Kings and Queens of Narnia. Narnia has its own history and time, and in *The Magician's Nephew* the reader is told of the beginnings of Narnia. Narnian time is brief, as measured against our time, so with each visit of the children several hundred Narnian years have passed. In the seventh and last of the books of Narnia, King Tirian remembers the stories of his ancestors about the Earth Children and calls on them to come to his aid in this, *The Last Battle.* Narnia is destroyed; yet the real Narnia, the inner Narnia, is not. The children learn that no good thing is ever lost, and the real identity of the Great Lion, Aslan, is finally revealed to them. These stories are mysterious, intriguing, and beautifully written. If children do not always understand their religious allegory, they may appreciate them as wondrous adventures that somehow reveal more than they say.

Susan Cooper has written a series of five books about the cosmic struggle between light and dark. *Over Sea, Under Stone* introduces the three Drew children who, on holiday in Cornwall, find an ancient treasure map linked to King Arthur. The third book in the series, *Greenwitch,* continues this quest story. Both stories are less complex than the remarkable second book, *The Dark Is Rising.* On Midwinter Day that is his eleventh birthday, Will

Alan Cober's montage foreshadows the malice and evil intended for Will Stanton by the powers of the Dark in *The Grey King* by Susan Cooper.

Stanton discovers that he is the last of the Old Ones, immortals dedicated throughout the ages to keeping the world from the forces of evil, the Dark. Will must find the six Signs of Life in order to complete his power and defeat, even temporarily, the rising of the Dark. Strange powers enable him to move in and out of Time where he meets Merriman Lyon, the first of the Old Ones, who becomes his teacher and mentor. While rich in symbolism and allegory, the story is grounded in reality so that Will's "real" life and quest in suspended time are distinct, yet interwoven. In the fourth book of the series, *The Grey King,* Will once again must prepare for the coming battle between the Dark and the Light. Special help comes from Bran, a strange albino boy, and his dog Cafall. Set in Wales, the story works on many levels with the feud over a sheep-killing dog taking on more significance when Bran's mysterious background is revealed. *Silver on the Tree* draws characters from the previous four novels together for a final assault on the Dark. Much that was hidden in the other tales is made explicit here and the knowledge of the major threads of the four books is necessary before one reads this exciting and fulfilling climax to the saga.

Authors portray good and evil in many different symbolic forms. In *The Book of the Dun Cow* by Walter Wangerin, Jr., the clash of opposing forces takes place in an unusual barnyard allegory with characters drawn from Medieval beast tales. The evil of the monster Wyrm, who is imprisoned within the earth, is loosed in the form of Cocka-trice, a cruel rooster with a snakelike tail, and the deadly small serpents, Basilisks, who kill with a single bite. Standing against these ominous forces are the animals who are fated to be the Keepers of Wyrm:

> The watchers, the guards . . . the last protection against an almighty evil which, should it pass them, would burst bloody into the universe and smash into chaos and sorrow everything that had been made orderly and good.[29]

This unlikely army is led by the rooster Chaunte-cleer, whose character is revealed in great "hu-man" detail. Among his unique companions are the self-effacing Mundo Cani Dog, blustering John Wesley Weasel, and a mysterious heavenly messenger known as the Dun Cow. Chauntecleer drives away the Basilisks and destroys Cockatrice in a spectacular cockfight; but the evil of Wyrm is not so easily defeated, and the rooster hero's spirit is broken. Only a final act of courage and sacrifice from an unexpected source keeps the great serpent itself from breaking free. The excitement and suspense of the plot, the intriguing characters, and the author's blend of the comic and the profound make this a book worth knowing. However, the animals' sense of despair in the face of evil is more typical of an adult's world view than a child's. Mature readers can find many-layered personal and spiritual themes in this story, written by a Christian minister who is also a scholar of Medieval literature.

A more exotic setting for the encounter between good and evil is created by Meredith Ann Pierce for *The Darkangel*. In some far-off future time on the moon, a young woman is carried away by a "vampyre," a fair young man with "wings of pure shadow." The abductor is pursued by the victim's servant girl, Aeriel, who is in turn captured. Her fate is to wait upon the spirit-forms of the darkangel's thirteen brides, whose souls are held in tiny vials on his neckchain. In her efforts to free them, Aeriel discovers that the darkangel himself is enslaved, and that she is the only one who can save him from becoming completely and utterly evil. The act of faith required is reminiscent of tales such as "Beauty and the Beast," but far more dramatic. For experienced readers, one of the pleasures of this book might be in recognizing its links with other fantasies; for instance, the great lion Pendarlon, who carries Aeriel across the desert, is an echo of Aslan in Lewis' Narnia series. *The Darkangel* stands on its own imaginative mer-its, however, as a fantasy romance that celebrates the power of love over hate.

QUESTS AND ADVENTURES

Many of the books previously mentioned which focus on ancient powers or the struggle between good and evil are also adventure stories which make use of the quest motif. In fact, high fantasy is almost always the story of a search—for treasure, justice, identity, understanding—and of a hero-figure who learns important lessons in the adven-turing.

One of the most famous seekers in all fantasy is J. R. R. Tolkien's Bilbo Baggins, *The Hobbit*. Gen-erally hobbits are very respectable creatures who never have any adventures or do anything unex-pected.

> They are (or were) small people, smaller than dwarves (and they have no beards) but very much larger than lilliputians. There is little or no magic about them, except the ordinary everyday sort which helps them to disappear quickly when large stupid folk like you and me come blundering along making a noise like elephants which they can hear a mile off. They are inclined to be fat in the stomach; they dress in bright colors (chiefly green and yellow); wear no shoes, because their feet grow natural leather soles and thick warm brown hair like the stuff on their heads (which is curly); have long clever brown fingers, good-natured faces, and laugh deep fruity laughs (especially after dinner, which they have twice a day when they can get it).[30]

Bilbo Baggins, however, has an adventure and finds himself doing and saying altogether unex-pected things. He is tricked by the dwarfs and the

---

[29]Walter Wangerin, Jr., *The Book of the Dun Cow* (New York: Harper & Row, 1978), p. 23.

[30]J. R. R. Tolkien, *The Hobbit* (Boston, Mass.: Hough-ton Mifflin, 1938), p. 12.

elves into going on a quest for treasure when he would much rather stay at home where he could be sure of six solid meals a day rather than be off fighting dragons. On the way, he is lost in a tunnel and nearly consumed by a ghoulish creature called Gollum, who is "dark as darkness except for his two big round pale eyes." Gradually the hobbit's inner courage emerges, as he struggles on through terrifying woods, encounters with huge hairy spiders, and battles with goblins to a somewhat enigmatic victory over the dragon (a more heroic figure is allowed to slay it). *The Hobbit* gives children an introduction to Middle-earth and its creatures. Later they may pursue this interest in Tolkien's vastly expanded view of Middle-earth in *The Lord of the Rings,* a 1,300-page trilogy which again draws on the author's scholarly knowledge of the myth and folklore of northwestern Europe.

Welsh legends and mythology are the inspiration for the intriguing chronicles of the imaginary land of Prydain as told by Lloyd Alexander. In *The Book of Three* the reader is introduced to Taran, an assistant pigkeeper who dreams of becoming a hero. With a strange assortment of companions he pursues Hen Wen, the oracular pig, and struggles to save Prydain from the forces of evil. The chronicles are continued in the most exciting of all of the books, *The Black Cauldron.* Once again the faithful companions fight evil as they seek to find and destroy the great cauldron in which the dread Cauldron-Born are created, "mute and deathless warriors" made from the stolen bodies of those slain in battle. Taran is proud to be chosen to fight for Lord Gwydion, for now he will have more opportunity to win honor than when washing pigs or weeding a garden. His wise and sensitive companion, Adaon, tells him:

> "I have marched in many a battle host . . . but I have also planted seeds and reaped the harvest with my own hands. And I have learned there is greater honor in a field well plowed than in a field steeped in blood.[31]

Gradually, Taran learns what it means to become a man among men—the sacrifice of his gentle Adaon, the final courage of the proud Ellidyr, and

the faithfulness of his companions. He experiences treachery, tragedy, and triumph; yet a thread of humor runs throughout to lighten the tension. Good does prevail, and Taran has matured and is ready for his next adventure. In the third book of the series, *The Castle of Llyr,* Taran escorts Princess Eilonwy to the Isle of Mona, where Queen Teleria is expected to teach the temperamental Eilonwy to behave in the manner of a proper princess—not an easy task. In the fourth book, *Taran Wanderer,* Taran goes questing in search of his parentage. More important than the identity of his parents, however, is Taran's self-discovery of who he is and what he dares to become. *The High King,* the masterful conclusion to this cycle of stories about the kingdom of Prydain, received the Newbery award. However, the recognition carried praise for all five of these chronicles. Each may be read independently, but together they represent an exciting adventure in some of the best-written fantasy of our time.

Lloyd Alexander has a gift for portraying comic adventures, and he has written several books in which serious themes lie under a surface of fast action and polished wit. *The Cat Who Wished to Be a Man* and *The Wizard in the Tree* are books of this sort. *The Marvelous Misadventures of Sebastian* is equally light-hearted, with all the trappings of madcap adventure. Sebastian finds an enchanted violin in which he hears the sound of what he might have become and in the end sets off to rediscover that lost self. In *The First Two Lives of Lukas-Kasha,* a young village idler is transported through a conjurer's trick to a kingdom where he finds, to his chagrin, that *he* is king. There he learns leadership and responsibility as he helps restore a spirited slave girl to her birthright as queen of a neighboring land. One 11-year-old referred to this as a "Lloyd-Alexanderish" book that might be read twice "to make sure you didn't miss anything." It does exemplify certain elements typical of the author's work: rich use of language, comic tone, a strong-willed female foil to the likeable, all-too-human hero, and the imaginary kingdom with occasional touches of magic.

The inhabitants of Alexander's mythical kingdom of *Westmark,* however, have no recourse to magic. The Westmark books, by the author's own reckoning, are not fantasy. But they do have a questing hero and serious social and political

[31]Lloyd Alexander, *The Black Cauldron* (New York: Holt, Rinehart and Winston, 1965), p. 43.

themes that make them larger than life. *Westmark* is the story of Theo, a printer's apprentice, who pursues questions of honor, justice, and freedom of the press as he tries to avoid the villainy of the kingdom's chief minister. Theo helps restore his street-urchin friend Mickle to her rightful place as princess, but he also struggles with the concept of monarchy: does anyone have a "rightful" place upon a throne? *The Kestrel* and *The Beggar Queen* are sequels in which Theo and Mickle, now the "Beggar Queen," prove their worth in battle but learn the personal cost of victory.

Unlike *Westmark,* conventional high fantasy does not question birthright. The unsuspecting or reluctant hero born to be leader, princess, or king accepts true identity in a way that symbolizes each young person's own discovery of the powers and burdens of maturity. Just as Lloyd Alexander's pigkeeper Taran discovers that he has been chosen from the beginning for high purpose in the Prydain Chronicles, so does Patricia McKillip's Morgon of Hed find an undreamed-of destiny in the trilogy which begins with *The Riddle-Master of Hed.* Morgon knows that he is a prince and a land-ruler; he does not know the significance of the three stars that he bears on his forehead. As a student at the College of Riddle-Masters, he comes upon riddles which concern those stars, but he is reluctant to accept the powers which are his to claim. In the second book, *Heir of Sea and Fire,* Morgon disappears into Erlenstar Mountain on a search for the High One, and Raederle, the beautiful girl who is pledged to him, comes into full possession of her own magic. In *Harpist in the Wind,* the two are together once more, and the solution to the riddle of the Star-Bearer is known at last. These are difficult books, dense with allusions to the history and geography of their imaginary setting. Fantasy fans who are proficient readers are easily caught up in the compelling narrative, however. To avoid dissatisfaction with the abrupt endings of the first two books, it may be a good idea to begin this series with all three volumes at hand.

In Robin McKinley's *The Blue Sword,* a book with closer ties to the world as we know it, a young woman called Harry discovers that her heritage has destined her to be a "Lady Hero." A ward of her brother, Harry feels vaguely out of place in the military outpost where he has brought her to live. She feels strangely drawn by the mountains where Free Hillfolk still live in an uneasy truce with the conquering Homelanders, Harry's people. When Corlath the Hill-king comes to ask the Homelanders' cooperation in turning back the Northerners, who have demonic powers in battle, he is rebuffed. But his visionary gift of *kelar* drives him back to take Harry off across the desert to the hills, where she is treated as an honored captive, privileged to sit among his select troop of Riders. When she first tastes the Water of Sight, it is apparent that Harry has her own *kelar* and that she is destined to play a part in the Hillfolk's efforts against the hordes of the North. More and more at ease with her abductors, Harry trains for battle and earns the right to be a king's Rider and to bear the treasured Blue Sword, whose special power in her hand must finally stand between the Hillfolk and their enemies. The girl's poignant relationship with Corlath and his people is put in new perspective by her defiant courage and by her discovery of an ancestral link that proves she is in truth one of them. The story is rich with details of horsemanship, combat, and the romance of a nomadic life. It also speaks directly about women's roles and responsibilities, a message all the more intriguing for being set in a frame of military and desert life, where traditional roles for women are often rigid. *The Hero and the Crown* happens in time before *The Blue Sword* and features many of the same themes. It chronicles the coming of the king's only child Aerin into her powers while leaving the reader with the desire to know more of what Aerin's future will bring.

In *Dragonsong,* Anne McCaffrey has written about another young woman, Menolly, whose special power is tied to her remarkable talent for music. Her family denies her dream of becoming a Harper because tradition dictates that the making of music is a man's task. Menolly runs away, taking shelter from her planet's fiery scourge of "Threadfall" in a hollow cliff by the sea. Here she stumbles on the hatching of a clutch of coveted fire lizards, kin to the great dragons that patrol the skies. Being the first to feed and touch the new creatures, she "bonds" with nine of them, commanding their loyalty for life. Menolly's beautiful lizards help give her the confidence she needs to take up a new life when she is rescued by a dragonrider and brought to the attention of the Master Harper. *Dragonsinger* tells of Menolly's trials and successes as an apprentice at the Harper Hall, and *Dragondrums* takes up the story of her fellow student Piemur, who has his own role to play in protecting the kingdom of Pern. Except for the unusual proper names, these books are less complex and easier to read than many of the high fantasies previously discussed. *Dragonsong* in particular has great reader appeal; but it may be worth noting that in comparison to other fantasy protagonists, Menolly pays a low price for getting her heart's desire.

Dragon's Blood by Jane Yolen has some similarity to the McCaffrey books although it embodies a sterner view of the world. Again the action takes place on a mythical planet, and dragons (who fight for sport) must be trained from hatchlings by one who has the gift for mind-bonding with them. Yolen tells the story of Jakkin, a bond-servant who steals a newly hatched dragon and trains it in the hope of earning his bond-price and his freedom. His surprising success is due in part to the help of a girl named Akki, who has distinct ideas about running her own life. Her brusque manner, her skills of healing, and her uncertain identity combine to make her an unusually interesting secondary character. In *Heart's Blood*, Jakkin's plans to enter his own dragon in the gaming pits are disrupted when he agrees to infiltrate a treacherous rebel group.

A superb tale of high fantasy which has become a standard against which others may be judged is *A Wizard of Earthsea* by Ursula Le Guin. This is

Ruth Robbins' detailed map gives substance to the geography of Earthsea, the imaginary land created by Ursula Le Guin. From *A Wizard of Earthsea*.

the story of a young boy studying at the School for Wizards who is taunted by a jealous classmate to use his powers before he is ready. Pride and arrogance drive him to call up a dreadful malignant shadow that threatens his life and all of Earthsea. Thus begins the chase and the hunt between the young wizard and the shadow-beast across stone-peaked islands and the farthest reaches of the waters of Earthsea. Le Guin has created a believable world with its own geography, peoples, beasts, culture, and beliefs. The characterization of young Sparrowhawk, or Ged, his true name known only to his most trusted friends, is well developed; he grows from an intelligent, impatient adolescent to a wise and grateful mage. The loyalty and constancy of his friend Vetch are beautifully portrayed. One of the major themes running throughout the story is the responsibility that each choice carries with it. While attending the School of Wizardry Ged asks the Master Hand how transformation of objects can be made permanent. He is answered:

> . . . you will learn it, when you are ready to learn it. But you must not change one thing, one pebble, one grain of sand, until you know what good and evil will follow the act. The world is in Equilibrium. A wizard's power of Changing and of Summoning can change the balance of the world. It is dangerous, that power. It is most perilous. It must follow knowledge, and serve need. To light a candle is to cast a shadow.[32]

The word "shadow" is one of the recurring motifs of this story. Ged sails in a boat named "The Shadow," and the evil that he has released into the world is called a shadow, since it has no name. In the end he recognizes it as a shadow of himself and the evil he did. True to traditional literature the power of naming or knowing a person's true name is of central importance in this book. Ged's first test on the wizard's island of Roke is to find the password to enter, and five years later his last test is to name the same Master Doorkeeper. In both instances he has to be humble enough to admit his own ignorance. And finally Ged's naming of the shadow with his own name suggests once again

that he has accepted responsibility for the evil he has released.

> Ged's ultimate quest . . . had made him whole: a man: who knowing his whole true self, cannot be used or possessed by any other power other than by himself, and whose life therefore is lived for life's sake and never in the service of ruin, or pain, or hatred, or the dark.[33]

The next story in this trilogy of Earthsea is the sinister tale of a child priestess given at the age of 5 to a cult of darkness and evil. At 15 Arha discovers Ged trapped in *The Tombs of Atuan*, a place no man is allowed, and she must decide between death and life for them both. This is a slower, more somber story than the first, but it provides important insights into human trust and the price of freedom. The last of the trilogy focuses once again on the Wizard of Earthsea. Titled *The Farthest Shore*, it completes the mighty deeds of Ged. In this moving tale Ged uses all his wisdom and wizardry to defeat the evil forces of destruction which threaten to overcome the islands of Earthsea. Its metaphor for today's world is profound and clear. The National Book Award in the Children's Category was given to Ursula Le Guin in 1973 for *The Farthest Shore*.

SCIENCE FICTION

The line between fantasy and science fiction has always been difficult to draw, particularly in children's literature. Children are likely to use the label "science fiction" for any book that includes the paraphernalia of science, although critics make finer distinctions. It has been suggested that fantasy (even "science fantasy") presents a world that never was and never could be, while science fiction speculates on a world that, given what we now know of science, might just one day be possible. Sylvia Engdahl says that "science fiction differs from fantasy not in subject matter but in aim, and its unique aim is to suggest real hypotheses about mankind's future or about the nature of the

---

[32]Ursula Le Guin, *A Wizard of Earthsea*, illustrated by Ruth Robbins (Berkeley, Calif.: Parnassus, 1968), p. 57.

[33]Le Guin, p. 203.

universe."[34] Of course the difficulty comes in deciding what constitutes a "real hypothesis." Are talking cats possible? Plants with a crystalline structure? Space ships that think and are self-repairing? All these ideas have been put forth by science-fiction writers asking themselves "What if . . .?"

The World of Speculation

Science fiction is relevant for today's rapidly changing world. It speculates about future technological advances, and more. Writers must imagine how these new discoveries will affect the daily lives and thoughts of people. In order to do this, the writer must construct a future world in which certain unknowns are accepted as proven fact. As in modern fantasy, detailed descriptions of these "scientific facts" and the characters' acceptance of them make the story believable. H. M. Hoover speaks about the author's responsibility to be consistent with "facts":

> If the story takes place on an alien world, the reader must be able to believe humans can walk there. Everything, from gravity and atmosphere, geology and life forms, must fit and be a part of that world if it is to ring true. . . . If not, somewhere a bright child will say "baloney" or a less polite equivalent, and toss the book aside. Children may be gullible from lack of time to learn, but they're not stupid, and they remember details.[35]

In addition, the author who speaks to today's youth about the future must say what he believes about the interaction of science on every aspect of society, from politics to warfare, from religion to sports, from education to entertainment.

One of the values of science fiction for children is its ability to develop imagination, improvisation, intuition, speculation, and flexibility in the minds of its readers. Most literature offers a static picture of society, whereas science fiction assumes a future that is vastly different from the one we know today. Madeleine L'Engle suggests that children enter this world of speculation more easily than adults do: "Children have always been interested in these cosmic questions and riddles which adults often attempt to tame by placing into categories fit only for scientists or adults or theologians."[36]

Much of the science fiction which considers cosmic questions falls within the realm of young adult literature, but there are exceptions. Occasionally, too, upper-elementary-age children who develop a love of science fiction read well above what adults might consider their usual reading levels. Whether children enter science fiction through space adventure books, science fantasy, or through the full-blown novels of Hoover, Christopher, or Engdahl, they enter a genre that challenges readers' basic assumptions. In his introduction of *Worlds to Come*, Damon Knight makes this statement:

> What science fiction has been doing for the last forty years is to shake up people's thinking, make them skeptical of dogma, get them used to the idea of change, let them dare to want new things. Nobody will ever know for sure how much effect these stories have had, but it is almost impossible to believe they have had none.[37]

THROUGH THE DOOR

Many children come easily to science fiction by way of books which may not fit a purist's definition of the genre but which incorporate some of its trappings, such as robots, spaceships, futuristic settings, or scientific terminology. Some of the easiest science fiction of this kind is found in several series for young readers. Slobodkin's *The Space Ship under the Apple Tree* introduces Eddie Blow to Marty from the planet Martinea who is nearly marooned on Earth when he loses the power source for his spacecraft. *Danny Dunn and the Anti-Gravity Paint* by Williams and Abraskin and *Matthew Looney and the Space Pirates* by Beatty are typical titles in two popular series which

[34]Sylvia Louise Engdahl, "The Changing Role of Science Fiction in Children's Literature," *The Horn Book Magazine,* vol. 47 (October 1971), p. 450.
[35]H. M. Hoover, "Where Do You Get Your Ideas?," *Top of the News,* vol. 39 (Fall 1982), p. 61.
[36]Madeleine L'Engle, "Childlike Wonder and the Truths of Science Fiction," *Children's Literature,* vol. 10 (Yale University Press, 1982), p. 102.
[37]Damon Knight, ed., in the introduction to *Worlds to Come* (New York: Harper & Row, 1967), p. xi.

present enterprising boys in a variety of adventures. MacGregor's *Miss Pickerell Goes to Mars* introduces readers to an intrepid traveler in space as well as on earth. *The Wonderful Flight to the Mushroom Planet* by Cameron offers readers the chance to meet Mr. Bass who lives on the planet Basidium. While few weighty themes are dealt with in series such as these, they provide repeated satisfactions to young readers who can follow the same cast of characters in similar format through adventures or mysteries with ultimately happy conclusions.

Alfred Slote provides much the same satisfaction to readers with *My Robot Buddy*. Ten-year-old Jack Jameson longs for a brother and so, for his birthday, his parents present him with a robot, Danny One. Danny is programmed to play baseball and football, climb trees, do light chores, and learn. The two become inseparable and Jack even learns to mimic the stiff-kneed jerky walk of a robot. It is this skill that causes him to be robotnapped, but Danny One saves him and brings about the capture of the crooks. Slote continues the adventures of the two brothers on the planet nation of *C.O.L.A.R.*, an organization of renegade child robots fleeing the repressive ownership of their earthling employers.

Another kind of manufactured "human" is presented in Christine Nostlinger's *Konrad*. When unconventional Mrs. Bartolotti receives a large can in the mail, she opens it only to discover it contains a crumpled-looking dwarf who says "Hi, Mom!" Following the printed instructions that come with the can, she dissolves a special nutrient solution in six quarts of water, pours it over the dwarf, and it swells into a 7-year-old boy! By the time the factory realizes they have sent Konrad to the wrong address, he and his new mother have developed an affectionate need for each other and so decide to foil the factory investigators. Nostlinger's descriptions of Konrad's disguise, a change from model boy to mischief-maker, and interactions with other characters are humorous and warm.

An exceptional book that presents a hopeful view of the future is Jill Paton Walsh's *The Green Book*. A family escapes Earth with others in a pre-programmed spacecraft before the "Disaster." Father tells Joe, Sarah, and Pattie that they can take very little with them but that this includes

From their departing spaceship, two sisters watch through the porthole as the world shrinks, diminishes, and finally disappears. Illustration by Lloyd Bloom from *The Green Book* by Jill Paton Walsh.

"one book per voyager." Pattie is ridiculed for wasting her choice on a blank green-covered book. When they arrive at their destination planet, Pattie, as the youngest, has the privilege of naming their new home, a place of red foliage and shimmering silver plains. "We are at Shine, on the first day," says Pattie. Ironically, this shine is produced by the crystalline structure of the plant life on the planet. When the wheat seeds brought from Earth produce a crop of grains like "hexagonal yellow beads, shining like golden glass," it appears that the colony will face starvation. The children secretly grind the glasslike beads, mix and bake the dough, and eat the bread without harm. It is then that Pattie's blank book is needed to keep records, and the story-starved people discover that the green book is now full of the most satisfying story of all—their own. An excellent choice for reading aloud and discussing with third- and fourth-graders, this simple book of high quality raises thought-provoking speculations about life and survival on another planet. The writing is vivid and tight, evocative without being obscure, and an interesting twist in the narrative voice neatly brings together the opening and closing sentences. Illustrations by Lloyd Bloom match a solemn tone in the text and are memorable for their rounded shapes softened by light on Shine.

VISITORS TO EARTH

Television and motion pictures have eased our acceptance of the possibility of visitors from other parts of the universe. Whether the visitor arrives purposefully or inadvertently, young readers today are willing to suspend disbelief and are usually prepared to consider the dilemmas which visitor and human interactions present.

The Fallen Spaceman by Lee Harding considers what happens when a giant spaceman falls to earth after being unwittingly abandoned by its starship. Witnessing the crash, Erik is frightened enough to fetch his father but then is curious enough to creep into a small opening in the spaceman's back. A hatch closes and Erik is trapped. While his father and brother search frantically for another opening, Erik makes his way to the hollow spaceman's head only to discover that the craft is lurching through the woods. It is also "piloted" by a boy-sized, terrified alien. While neither can live for long in the other's atmosphere, both unite to stop the spaceman's destruction. Although Erik feels a kinship with the small pilot Tyro, it is Tyro who considers his responsibility to Earth as its first alien visitor:

> But he had done his best—he had saved the earth boy. They would not think badly of him, these people of earth. Perhaps they would remember him if his people ever passed this way again.[38]

The gentle Tyro is rescued by his starship, and Erik and others on earth are left to ponder what has happened.

In *Star Ka'at*, André Norton and Dorothy Madlee introduce readers to a superior breed of cats that visit earth in hopes of saving other cats before the world destroys itself. When orphans Jim and Elly Mae discover the Ka'at spaceship and go aboard, two Ka'ats they have befriended are able to communicate with them and so become their sponsor for the journey from Earth. In other books

[38]Lee Harding, *The Fallen Spaceman*, illustrated by John and Ian Schoenherr (New York: Harper & Row, 1980), p. 90.

in the series, the children continue to aid Ka'ats Tiro and Mer in their efforts to protect Ka'at populations on other planets. Spunky Elly Mae learns quickly and develops her powers of telepathy, but it is regrettable that the authors' representation of this black child's speech relies more on errors in grammar than on use of an authentic dialect.

A purposeful but less benevolent visitor to earth is Nicholas Fisk's *Grinny*. Great-Aunt Emma appears suddenly in the family of 11-year-old Tim and his younger but precocious sister Beth. At first no one can recall having this ever-smiling aunt, but when she murmurs "You remember me," doubts seem to vanish. Tim's diary chronicles the children's gradual realization that "Grinny" has been sent from another planet to determine if earth is "Suitable" for subjugation and colonization. By determining this created being's weaknesses, Tim and Beth force Grinny to signal the waiting invaders that earth is indeed "Not Suitable." The horrible demise of Grinny seems an appropriate end for the evil robot.

Alexander Key presents an unwilling visitor to earth in *The Forgotten Door*, which explores the rights of individuals and challenges readers' assumptions about the nature of human society. Little Jon wakens cold and bruised in a mossy cave and cannot remember who he is or where he came from. He is found by the kindly Bean family, who gradually discover some amazing facts about the quiet, sensitive boy. He cannot speak English, but he understands thought and gradually translates it into words. He can communicate with animals, even their cross dog. He eats only vegetables and knows nothing of money, guns, robbery, murder, war, or other evils. It soon becomes apparent to the Beans that he is not from this world. Rumors spread, however, and soon the federal government demands custody of Little Jon. Other political groups would like to use Jon's powers and the Beans are desperate for help. Finally, Jon is able to hear his parents calling him, and he communicates his concern for his friends, the Beans. As various forces close in on the tiny cabin, Jon and the Beans disappear through the Forgotten Door to the world Jon has described to them—a world so simple as to need no laws, leaders, or money, and one where intelligent people work together. The fast pace of the story and its substantial characters and challenging themes have made this a good discussion choice for small groups of fourth- and fifth-graders. *Star Lord* by Louise Lawrence, for slightly older readers, considers a similar situation, further complicated by the supernatural powers present within a Welsh mountainside where the visitor's spacecraft lands.

VIEWS OF THE FUTURE

Science fiction of the highest level presents the reader with complex hypotheses about the future of humankind. Many of H. M. Hoover's novels raise questions about the organization of society and the nature of the world following a massive ecological disaster. Writers such as John Christopher and Madeleine L'Engle imagine other life forms and their interactions with our world. William Sleator in *The Green Futures of Tycho* asks how present time may be altered to affect the future; in L'Engle's *A Swiftly Tilting Planet*, the past is altered to change the present and future. Throughout these novels of speculation runs the question of which human qualities and responsibilities will become—or remain—essential in time to come.

A Wrinkle in Time suggests that love and individuality will continue to be important for the future. If there is a classic in the field of science fiction for children, it may be this Newbery award-winner by Madeleine L'Engle. The exciting story concerns Charles Wallace, a 5-year-old brilliant beyond his age and time, and Meg, his 12-year-old sister, whose stubbornness later becomes an asset. With the help of Calvin O'Keefe, a 14-year-old on whose stability the two often rely, the children begin a frenzied search for their missing father, a scientist working for the government. They are aided in their search by three women who have supernatural powers—Mrs. Whatsit, Mrs. Who, and Mrs. Which. To rescue Mr. Murry, the children travel by means of a wrinkle in time, or a tesseract, to the evil planet of Camazotz. These people, having given up their identities to It, do everything in synchronization. When Charles Wallace attempts to resist It by reason, he, too, is captured. Though Meg is able to save her father, they must leave Charles Wallace behind. Exhausted and still under the evil influence of It, Meg is slowly nursed back to love and peace by another strange but loving creature, Aunt Beast. When Meg realizes that only she can save Charles Wallace, she returns to confront It with what she knows It does not have or understand—the power of love. This many-layered story may be read for its exciting plot alone. But it may also be read for its themes and the values it espouses.

A Wind in the Door, also by L'Engle, is a companion story involving many of the previous characters with new situations and other creatures. The story concerns the fight to save Charles Wallace from a baffling illness. Meg, Calvin, and Mr. Jenkins, the cold, remote principal of the school, are led to a planet in galactic space where size does not exist. Here they are made small enough to enter Charles Wallace's body and help fight the attacking forces of evil, the Echthroi. Only when Meg names them with her own name does she overcome them and save Charles. The story emphasizes the importance of every minuscule part of the universe in carrying out its purpose in living, to be all that it was meant to be. *A Wind in the Door* is more complex than *A Wrinkle in Time,* but L'Engle is capable of "kything" her message to perceptive children of 9 or 10 and up.

A Swiftly Tilting Planet completes L'Engle's Time trilogy. Charles Wallace has been saved, first from the dehumanization of It, and second from a rare blood disease. Now, in this story, the reader discovers why Charles Wallace has been twice rescued, for his ultimate mission involves saving the world from total destruction. He must journey back in historical time to change some seemingly small part of past relationships so that a potential world war in the present may be averted. The cast of characters has grown older, with Meg now married to Calvin and expecting a baby and Charles Wallace a teenager. This is by far the most demanding of the three volumes, as there are many characters in several time frames to attend to. The Time trilogy is a unique and wonderful combination of science fiction, modern fantasy, traditional lore, and religious symbolism by which L'Engle stretches the minds and the spirits of her readers.

The White Mountains trilogy by John Christopher describes a future world that has been reduced to a primitive society. However, people in this twenty-first-century world are controlled by machine creatures called Tripods. At 14 each human being must be "capped," a ceremony in which a steel plate is inserted into the skull to make the wearer a servant of the state. No one is allowed to discuss the capping ceremony, but Will finds out that his friend Jack has some real reservations about it. After Jack's capping he appears to be a different person—docile, too busy working to be a friend. Will talks to a seemingly crazy Vagrant and finds out that there is a colony of free people living in *The White Mountains* to the south. Will describes the terrifying journey that he and two other boys make to reach this refuge. In the second book, *The City of Gold and Lead,* Will wins an athletic contest in order to have "the privilege" of serving the master Tripods. Actually, he goes as a spy to learn the secrets of this alien culture. In the last book of the series, *The Pool of Fire,* the Tripods are defeated and mankind is free to set up its own government. The reader hopes that Will's plan for world unity will succeed; but Christopher is a realistic writer, so Will is forced by quarreling, dissident groups to give up his plans for world peace.

Christopher's second science-fiction trilogy *(The Prince in Waiting, Beyond the Burning Lands,* and *The Sword of the Spirits)* deals with England in the twenty-first century. People measure time since "The Disaster," a period of volcanic activity, earthquakes, and strong radiation from the sun, which has destroyed all of man's technical accomplishments. Amid the ruins a kind of medieval society has sprung up, with independent city-states not far advanced from barbarian tribes. Religion takes the form of Spiritism in this society, and the use of machines or the pursuit of science is strictly forbidden. These books have much more violence in them than the White Mountain trilogy, which is in keeping with their imagined setting. It may be justified because it raises the ethical questions of whether violence impersonalized by distance and machine is any different from hand-to-hand violence and whether it is possible to keep "rules" in war. All of John Christopher's books help children consider the problems of the future of humankind, but the themes never overburden the suspense or action of the stories.

H. M. Hoover is a prolific writer of science fiction for children and young adults. Many of her novels include complex political and social systems, challenging ideas, multiple species of thinking beings, and large casts of characters. *This Time of Darkness* presents a future in which most people live underground inside domed, many-layered cities, crowded and dirty but safe from the uncertainties of the outside atmosphere. Eleven-year-old Amy has been taught by her learning center that all layers of the city are alike, that there is nothing left or living outside the walls. However, unlike other citizens, Amy can read, and when she befriends Axel, who says he once lived outside, the two plan an escape. Their flight takes them on a terrifying but fascinating tour to the highest levels of the city where they are finally ejected as undesirables. Once outside, they must survive sunburn, starvation, an attack by mutants, and a brush fire before they, and the ever-present watcher following them, are reunited with Axel's people. Hoover imagines a very different view of future civilization after "the Great Destruction" in *Children of Morrow* and its sequel, *Treasures of Morrow.* Twelve-year-old Tia and her friend Rabbit are shunned as different from the repressive tribe in which they live. Although the two think they are merely dreaming, they are both able to communicate with strange others by means of telepathy. When the two participate accidentally in a murder and are themselves threatened, they are told by the telepathic beings to flee toward the sea. These beings are highly civilized technocrats living in a city which was engineered years ago to withstand the Great Destruction. Although the children are saved and begin their life at Morrow, they wish to return in the sequel in hopes of making a change for the better in their former home. They realize for themselves that they must leave their past behind them.

André Norton is another prolific writer of science fiction. Her many titles include *The Crystal Gryphon, The Night of Masks,* and *Zero Stone.* In *Breed to Come,* she uses one of her favorite motifs, that of the intelligent animal mutant. Her stories are absorbing and the questions are worth discussion. There is a minimum of space jargon, lots of action, and good character development, although, in *Breed to Come,* the animal people seem to have greater dimension than the humans. Most of Norton's stories are for teenagers, but some middle-grade science-fiction fans are capable of reading them.

Teenager Ann Burden in *Z for Zachariah* by Robert C. O'Brien thinks she is the last living person on earth. As the radio stations go off the air one by one, it becomes apparent that her family is never going to return to the valley. Ann begins to carve out a solitary life, accompanied only by the family dog, when she sees what appears to be smoke from a campfire on the horizon. Drawing closer, she sees it is indeed another person, who is wearing a radiation-proof safe-suit. After initially hiding from him, Ann becomes his caretaker when he falls ill from radiation sickness. But John Loomis does not provide Ann with hoped-for companionship; instead, he becomes more and more possessive of Ann's work time and property while protecting his safe-suit. Eventually, Ann must hide in the hills to avoid Loomis and the possibility of being killed. At last, she decides on a plan to steal the safe-suit and leave the valley in hopes that she will find other survivors whom she has dreamed about. Her last encounter with Loomis leaves him in the valley and finds Ann headed toward the west where once she saw circling birds. Written in the form of a diary kept by Ann, this story is rich in the details of her survival and growing resolve. Ann traces her doubt and anger about the many choices she must make, but the reader does not doubt that Ann will find the others for whom she searches.

Enchantress from the Stars by Sylvia Louise Engdahl is an unusual story that almost goes beyond science fiction in its scope. The mission of Elana and her party is to save the Andrecians from the Imperialists. Elana belongs to an anthropological service of the future which represents the most advanced humanity in the universe. By contrast, the Andrecians are at a medieval stage of development; people still believe in magic and will reward anyone who can kill the "terrible dragon." It, however, is really an earth-mover with which the Imperialists intend to destroy forests and colonize. Eventually the fourth son of an Andrecian woodcutter and Elana defeat the invaders with the values of love, faith, and sacrifice which transcend all levels of development. The story helps readers see their own world in a different perspective, a function of all good literature. In a somewhat didactic sequel, *The Far Side of Evil,* Engdahl deals with the consequences of misuse of nuclear power. *This Star Shall Abide* and *Beyond the Tomorrow Mountains* are other contributions by this major writer of science fiction for young adults.

Fantasy for children needs no defense. Whether it is a modern fairy tale like *Many Moons* or *The Little Prince,* modern fantasy like *Charlotte's Web* or *The Dark Is Rising,* or the science fiction of *A Wrinkle in Time* or *Enchantress from the Stars,* these lasting books can speak for our time and the times to come. They may stretch children's imagination and help them to view the world with a new perspective.

SUGGESTED LEARNING EXPERIENCES

1. Ask a group of middle-graders, or your friends, to list their ten favorite children's books. How many of these could be categorized as modern fantasy?

2. Write a modern fairy tale, fable, or tall tale using the old forms, but with twentieth-century content and reflecting today's changing values. For example, you might want to consider reversing the stereotyped sex roles of the prince and princess.

3. Working with children, or your peers, make an illustrated map to show an extraordinary world or imaginary kingdom that you have discovered in a book. Make a key to locate events of the story.

4. Compare the Chronicles of Narnia by C. S. Lewis with Lloyd Alexander's Prydain series; or compare two animal fantasies, such as *Charlotte's Web* with *Pigs Might Fly.* In what ways are they alike; how are they different?

5. Choose a book of high fantasy or time fantasy and identify motifs which seem to derive from folklore, myth, or legend. Which of these motifs are common in other modern fantasies?

6. Make a display or a chart of the many symbols and their meaning found in *The Dark Is Rising* by Susan Cooper.

7. The importance of naming or having a secret name is a motif that is central to such books as L'Engle's *A Wind in the Door,* Le Guin's *A Wizard of Earthsea,* and Hunter's *A Stranger Came Ashore.* Find other such examples in traditional literature or in anthropological reports of primitive societies. Prepare a chart of your findings.

8. Ask yourself what might happen to the world of tomorrow if hunger were eliminated or if robots became practical or if hydrogen fusion were made a workable source of energy. Think through the impact of one such scientific advancement.

RELATED READINGS

1. Cameron, Eleanor. *The Green and Burning Tree*. Boston, Mass.: Little, Brown, 1969.
   The title essay in this fine book of literary criticism is a study of time fantasy. As the author of many fantasies herself, Cameron is in a unique position to evaluate the fantasies in this category.

2. Campbell, Joseph. *The Hero with a Thousand Faces*, 2nd ed. Princeton, N. J.: Princeton University Press, 1968.
   This standard scholarly work on the "monomyth," or the archetypal story of the hero, helps the serious student of high fantasy to see the protagonist of the quest in a universal perspective.

3. Egoff, Sheila, G. T. Stubbs, and L. F. Ashley. *Only Connect: Readings on Children's Literature*, 2nd ed. New York: Oxford University Press, 1980.
   All the selections under "Fairy Tales, Fantasy, Animals" would be appropriate reading for this chapter. However, don't miss reading the article by C. S. Lewis, "On Three Ways of Writing for Children," or P. L. Travers' (creator of Mary Poppins) fine article, "Only Connect."

4. Haviland, Virginia. *Children and Literature: Views and Reviews*. Glenview, Ill.: Scott Foresman, 1973.
   The former children's librarian of the Library of Congress has made an excellent selection of readings for this book. All of the entries for Chapter Six would be appropriate, but two seem to have great significance for this chapter: Lloyd Alexander's "The Flat-Heeled Muse" and Sylvia Engdahl's "The Changing Role of Science Fiction in Children's Literature."

5. Hunter, Mollie. *Talent Is Not Enough*. New York: Harper & Row, 1975.
   A talented author discusses writing for children. In the essay titled "One World," Hunter maintains that true fantasy so integrates the real and the imagined world that it becomes believable. She also acknowledges fantasy's debt to ancient folklore, describing the basis for her own writing of *A Stranger Came Ashore*.

6. Le Guin, Ursula. *The Language of the Night: Essays on Fantasy and Science Fiction*. New York: Putnam, 1979.
   Excellent essays by an outstanding writer of fantasy and science fiction discuss "Myth and Archetype in Science Fiction" and ask "Why are Americans Afraid of Dragons?," among others.

7. Lynn, Ruth Nadelman. *Fantasy for Children: An Annotated Checklist*. New York: Bowker, 1979.
   A comprehensive bibliographic guide which groups fantasy titles according to content. Categories include Ghosts, Magical Toys, and twenty-three varieties of mythical beings or creatures. Helpful tool for librarians and teachers developing curriculum resource guides.

8. Meek, Margaret, Aidan Warlow, and Griselda Barton. *The Cool Web: The Pattern of Children's Readings*. New York: Atheneum, 1978.
   This fine collection of some fifty essays on children's literature was first published in England. James Britton's article on "The Role of Fantasy" and Arthur Applebee's "Where Does Cinderella Live?" have particular importance for this chapter.

9. Tolkien, J. R. *Tree and Leaf*. Boston, Mass.: Houghton Mifflin, 1965.
   The author of *The Hobbit* has written a critical essay on the technique and purposes of writing "On Fairy Stories." This discussion is followed by a short story, "Leaf by Niggle," which is an illustration of the points Tolkien makes in his essay.

REFERENCES[39]

Adams, Richard. *Watership Down*. Macmillan, 1974.
Aiken, Joan. *Black Hearts in Battersea*, illustrated by Robin Jacques. Doubleday, 1964.
———. *Nightbirds on Nantucket*, illustrated by Robin Jacques. Doubleday, 1966.
———. *The Stolen Lake*. Delacorte, 1981.
———. *The Wolves of Willoughby Chase*, illustrated by Pat Marriott. Doubleday, 1963.

[39]All books listed at the end of this chapter are recommended, subject to the qualifications noted in the text. See Appendix for publishers' complete addresses.

Alexander, Lloyd. *The Black Cauldron*. Holt, 1965.

———. *The Book of Three*. Holt, 1964.

———. *The Castle of Llyr*. Holt, 1966.

———. *The Cat Who Wished to Be a Man*. Dutton, 1973.

———. *Coll and His White Pig*, illustrated by Evaline Ness. Holt, 1965.

———. *The First Two Lives of Lukas-Kasha*. Dutton, 1978.

———. *The Foundling and Other Tales of Prydain*. Dell, 1982.

———. *The High King*. Holt, 1968.

———. *The Kestrel*. Dutton, 1982.

———. *The Beggar Queen*. Dutton, 1984.

———. *The Marvelous Misadventures of Sebastian*. Dutton, 1970.

———. *Taran Wanderer*. Holt, 1967.

———. *The Truthful Harp*, illustrated by Evaline Ness. Holt, 1971.

———. *Westmark*. Dutton, 1981.

———. *The Wizard in the Tree*, illustrated by Laszlo Kubinyi. Dutton, 1975.

Andersen, Hans Christian. *The Emperor's New Clothes*, illustrated by Virginia Lee Burton. Houghton Mifflin, 1949.

———. *The Fir Tree*, illustrated by Nancy Ekholm Burkert. Harper, 1970.

———. *Hans Christian Andersen: The Complete Fairy Tales and Stories*, translated by Erik Haugaard. Doubleday, 1974.

———. *The Little Match Girl*, illustrated by Blair Lent. Houghton Mifflin, 1968.

———. "The Little Mermaid" in *Hans Christian Andersen: The Complete Fairy Tales and Stories*, translated by Erik Christian Haugaard. Doubleday, 1974.

———. *The Nightingale*, translated by Anthea Bell, illustrated by Lisbeth Zwerger. Picture Book Studio, 1985.

———. *The Nightingale*, adapted by Anna Bier, illustrated by Demi. Harcourt, 1985.

———. *The Nightingale*, translated by M. R. James, illustrated by Kaj Beckman. Van Nostrand, 1969.

———. *The Nightingale*, translated by Eva Le Gallienne, illustrated by Nancy Ekholm Burkert. Harper, 1965.

———. "The Princess and the Pea" in *Seven Tales*, translated by Eva Le Gallienne, illustrated by Maurice Sendak. Harper, 1959.

———. *The Princess and the Pea*, illustrated by Paul Galdone. Seabury, 1978.

———. *The Snow Queen*, illustrated by Marcia Brown. Scribner, 1972.

———. *The Snow Queen*, adapted by Naomi Lewis, illustrated by Errol Le Cain. Viking, 1979.

———. *The Steadfast Tin Soldier*, translated by M. R. James, illustrated by Marcia Brown. Scribner, 1953.

———. *The Steadfast Tin Soldier*, illustrated by Monika Laimgruber. Atheneum, 1971.

———. *Thumbelina*, retold by Amy Ehrlich, illustrated by Susan Jeffers. Dial, 1979.

———. *Thumbelina*, translated by M. R. James, illustrated by Kaj Beckman. Van Nostrand, 1973.

———. *Thumbeline*, translated by Anthea Bell, illustrated by Lisbeth Zwerger. Picture Book Studio, 1985.

———. *Thumbeline*, translated by Richard and Clara Winston, illustrated by Lisbeth Zwerger. Morrow, 1980.

———. *The Ugly Duckling*, illustrated by Adrienne Adams. Scribner, 1965.

———. *The Ugly Duckling*, retold and illustrated by Lorinda Bryan Cauley. Harcourt, 1979.

———. *The Ugly Duckling*, translated by R. Keigwin, illustrated by Johannes Larsen. Macmillan, n. d.

———. *The Wild Swans*, illustrated by Marcia Brown. Scribner, 1963.

———. *The Wild Swans*, retold by Amy Ehrlich, illustrated by Susan Jeffers. Dial, 1981.

Arkin, Alan. *The Lemming Condition*. Harper, 1976.

Atwater, Richard, and Florence Atwater. *Mr. Popper's Penguins*, illustrated by Robert Lawson. Little, Brown, 1938.

Babbitt, Natalie. *Eyes of the Amaryllis*. Farrar, Straus, 1977.

———. *Kneeknock Rise*. Farrar, Straus, 1970.

———. *The Search for Delicious*. Farrar, Straus, 1969.

_____. *Tuck Everlasting.* Farrar, Straus, 1975.
Bailey, Carolyn Sherwin. *Miss Hickory,* illustrated by Ruth Gannett. Viking, 1962 (1946).
Banks, Lynne Reid. *The Indian in the Cupboard,* illustrated by Brock Cole. Doubleday, 1981.
Baum, L. Frank. *The Wizard of Oz.* World, 1972 (1900).
Beatty, Jerome, Jr. *Matthew Looney and the Space Pirates,* illustrated by Gahan Wilson. Young Scott, 1972.
Bellairs, John. *Figure in the Shadows.* Dial, 1975.
_____. *The House with a Clock in Its Walls.* Dial, 1973.
_____. *The Letter, the Watch, and the Ring.* Dial, 1976.
Bond, Michael. *A Bear Called Paddington,* illustrated by Peggy Fortnum. Houghton Mifflin, 1960.
_____. *More about Paddington,* illustrated by Peggy Fortnum. Houghton Mifflin, 1962.
_____. *Paddington at Large,* illustrated by Peggy Fortnum. Houghton Mifflin, 1963.
_____. *Paddington Helps Out,* illustrated by Peggy Fortnum. Houghton Mifflin, 1961.
_____. *Paddinton Marches On,* illustrated by Peggy Fortnum. Houghton Mifflin, 1965.
_____. *Paddington Takes the Air,* illustrated by Peggy Fortnum. Houghton Mifflin, 1971.
Bond, Nancy. *A String in the Harp.* Atheneum, 1976.
Bosse, Malcolm. *Cave Beyond Time.* Crowell, 1980.
Boston, L. M. *The Children of Green Knowe,* illustrated by Peter Boston. Harcourt, 1955.
_____. *An Enemy at Green Knowe,* illustrated by Peter Boston. Harcourt, 1964.
_____. *The River at Green Knowe,* illustrated by Peter Boston. Harcourt, 1959.
_____. *The Sea Egg,* illustrated by Peter Boston. Harcourt, 1967.
_____. *The Treasure of Green Knowe,* illustrated by Peter Boston. Harcourt, 1958.
Brown, Palmer. *Hickory.* Harper, 1978.
Burnett, Frances H. *The Secret Garden,* illustrated by Tasha Tudor. Lippincott, 1962 (1910).
Butterworth, Oliver. *The Enormous Egg,* illustrated by Louis Darling. Little, Brown, 1956.
Cameron, Eleanor. *The Court of the Stone Children.* Dutton, 1973.
_____. *The Wonderful Flight to the Mushroom Planet,* illustrated by Robert Henneberger. Little, Brown, 1954.
Carroll, Lewis, pseud. (Charles L. Dodgson). *Alice's Adventures in Wonderland and Through the Looking Glass,* illustrated by John Tenniel. Macmillan, 1963 (1865, 1872).
Catling, Patrick Skene. *The Chocolate Touch,* illustrated by Margot Apple. Morrow, 1979 (1952).
Chew, Ruth. *Mostly Magic.* Holiday, 1982.
Christopher, John. *Beyond the Burning Lands.* Macmillan, 1971.
_____. *The City of Gold and Lead.* Macmillan, 1967.
_____. *The Guardians.* Macmillan, 1970.
_____. *The Pool of Fire.* Macmillan, 1968.
_____. *The Prince in Waiting.* Macmillan, 1970.
_____. *The Sword of the Spirits.* Macmillan, 1972.
_____. *The White Mountains.* Macmillan, 1967.
Cleary, Beverly. *The Mouse and the Motorcycle,* illustrated by Louis Darling. Morrow, 1965.
_____. *Ralph S. Mouse,* illustrated by Paul O. Zelinsky. Morrow, 1982.
_____. *Runaway Ralph,* illustrated by Louis Darling. Morrow, 1970.
Collodi, Carlo. *The Adventures of Pinocchio,* illustrated by Naiad Einsel. Macmillan, 1963 (1892).
_____. *The Adventures of Pinocchio,* translated by Marianna Mayer, illustrated by Gerald McDermott. Four Winds, 1981.
Cooper, Susan. *The Dark Is Rising,* illustrated by Alan E. Cober. Atheneum, 1973.
_____. *Greenwitch.* Atheneum, 1974.
_____. *The Grey King.* Atheneum, 1975.
_____. *Over Sea, Under Stone,* illustrated by Marjorie Gill. Harcourt, 1966.
_____. *Silver on the Tree.* Atheneum, 1977.
Corbett, Scott. *The Lemonade Trick,* illustrated by Paul Galdone. Atlantic-Little, Brown, 1960.
Cunningham, Julia. *Macaroon,* illustrated by Evaline Ness. Pantheon, 1962.

Curry, Jane Louise. *The Sleepers*, illustrated by Gareth Floyd. Harcourt, 1968.

Dahl, Roald. *Charlie and the Chocolate Factory*, illustrated by Joseph Schindelman. Knopf, 1973 (1964).

_____. *Charlie and the Great Glass Elevator*, illustrated by Joseph Schindelman. Knopf, 1972.

_____. *James and the Giant Peach*, illustrated by Nancy Ekholm Burkert. Knopf, 1961.

_____. *The Magic Finger*, illustrated by William Pène du Bois. Harper, 1966.

du Bois, William Pène. *The Twenty-one Balloons*. Viking, 1947.

Eager, Edward. *Half Magic*, illustrated by N. M. Bodecker. Harcourt, 1954.

_____. *Seven-Day Magic*, illustrated by N. M. Bodecker. Harcourt, 1962.

Engdahl, Sylvia Louise. *Beyond the Tomorrow Mountains*, illustrated by Richard Cuffari. Atheneum, 1973.

_____. *Enchantress from the Stars*, illustrated by Rodney Shackell. Atheneum, 1970.

_____. *The Far Side of Evil*, illustrated by Richard Cuffari. Atheneum, 1971.

_____. *This Star Shall Abide*, illustrated by Richard Cuffari. Atheneum, 1972.

Farmer, Penelope. *The Summer Birds*, illustrated by James Spanfeller. Harcourt, 1962.

Fisk, Nicholas. *Grinny*. Elsevier-Nelson, 1974.

Fleischman, Paul. *The Half-A-Moon Inn*, illustrated by Kathy Jacobi. Harper, 1980.

Fleming, Ian. *Chitty-Chitty-Bang-Bang*, illustrated by John Burningham. Random, 1964.

Gage, Wilson. *Miss Osborne-the-Mop*, illustrated by Paul Galdone. World, 1963.

Gardner, John. *Dragon, Dragon, and Other Tales*. Knopf, 1975.

_____. *Gudgekin the Thistle Girl and Other Tales*. Knopf, 1976.

Garfield, Leon. *Mister Corbett's Ghost*, illustrated by Alan E. Cober. Pantheon, 1968.

Garner, Alan. *Elidor*. Walck, 1967.

_____. *The Owl Service*. Walck, 1968.

_____. *Red Shift*. Macmillan, 1973.

Godden, Rumer. *The Dolls' House*, illustrated by Tasha Tudor. Viking, 1962 (1947).

_____. *The Fairy Doll*, illustrated by Adrienne Adams. Viking, 1956.

_____. *Impunity Jane*, illustrated by Adrienne Adams. Viking, 1954.

_____. *The Mousewife*, illustrated by Heidi Holder. Viking, 1982 (1951).

Grahame, Kenneth. *The Open Road*, illustrated by Beverly Gooding. Scribner, 1980.

_____. *The Reluctant Dragon*, illustrated by Ernest H. Shepard. Holiday, 1938.

_____. *The River Bank* from *The Wind in the Willows*, illustrated by Adrienne Adams. Scribner, 1977.

_____. *Wayfarers All: From The Wind in the Willows*, illustrated by Beverly Gooding. Scribner, 1981.

_____. *The Wind in the Willows*, illustrated by E. H. Shepard. Scribner, 1940 (1908).

Hamilton, Virginia. *Justice and Her Brothers*. Greenwillow, 1978.

_____. *The Magical Adventures of Pretty Pearl*. Harper, 1983.

_____. *Sweet Whispers, Brother Rush*. Philomel, 1982.

Harding, Lee. *The Fallen Spaceman*, illustrated by John and Ian Schoenherr. Harper, 1980.

Heide, Florence Parry. *The Problem with Pulcifer*, illustrated by Judy Glasser. Lippincott, 1982.

_____. *The Shrinking of Treehorn*, illustrated by Edward Gorey. Holiday, 1981.

_____. *Treehorn's Treasure*, illustrated by Edward Gorey. Holiday, 1981.

Hoban, Russell. *The Mouse and His Child*, illustrated by Lillian Hoban. Harper, 1967.

Hoover, H. M. *Children of Morrow*. Four Winds, 1973.

_____. *This Time of Darkness*. Viking, 1980.

_____. *Treasures of Morrow*. Four Winds, 1976.

Howe, Deborah, and James Howe. *Bunnicula*. Atheneum, 1979.

Howe, James. *The Celery Stalks at Midnight*, illustrated by Leslie Morrill. Atheneum, 1983.

_____. *Howliday Inn*, illustrated by Lynn Munsinger. Atheneum, 1982.

Hunter, Mollie, pseud. (Maureen McIlwraith). *The Haunted Mountain: A Story of Suspense*, illustrated by Laszo Kubinyi. Harper, 1972.

_____. *A Stranger Came Ashore*. Harper, 1975.

_____. *The Walking Stones: A Story of Suspense*, illustrated by Trina Schart Hyman. Harper, 1970.

Hurmence, Belinda. *A Girl Called Boy*. Clarion, 1982.

Ish-Kishor, Sulamith. *The Master of Miracle: A New Novel of the Golem*, illustrated by Arnold Lobel. Harper, 1971.

Jansson, Tove. *Tales from Moominvalley*, translated by Thomas Warburton. Walck, 1964.

Jarrell, Randall. *The Animal Family*, illustrated by Maurice Sendak. Pantheon, 1965.

_____. *The Bat-Poet*, illustrated by Maurice Sendak. Macmillan, 1964.

Juster, Norton. *The Phantom Tollbooth*. Random, 1961.

Kendall, Carol. *The Gammage Cup*, illustrated by Erik Blegvad. Harcourt, 1959.

Kennedy, Richard. *Amy's Eyes*, illustrated by Richard Egielski. Harper, 1985.

Key, Alexander. *The Forgotten Door*. Westminster, 1965.

King-Smith, Dick. *Pigs Might Fly*, illustrated by Mary Rayner. Viking, 1982.

Kipling, Rudyard. *The Beginning of the Armadillos*, illustrated by Lorinda Bryan Cauley. Harcourt, 1985.

_____. *The Beginning of the Armadillos*, illustrated by Charles Keeping. Bedrick, 1983.

_____. *The Elephant's Child*, illustrated by Leonard Weisgard. Walker, 1970.

_____. *How the Leopard Got His Spots*, illustrated by Leonard Weisgard. Walker, 1972.

_____. *How the Rhinoceros Got His Skin*, illustrated by Leonard Weisgard. Walker, 1974.

_____. *Just So Stories*, illustrated by Etienne Delessert. Doubleday, 1972.

Kushner, Donn. *The Violin-Maker's Gift*. Farrar, Straus, 1982.

Langton, Jane. *The Astonishing Stereoscope*, illustrated by Erik Blegvad. Harper, 1971.

_____. *The Diamond in the Window*, illustrated by Erik Blegvad. Harper, 1962.

_____. *The Fledgling*. Harper, 1980.

_____. *The Swing in the Summerhouse*, illustrated by Erik Blegvad. Harper, 1967.

Lawrence, Louise. *Star Lord*. Harper, 1978.

Lawson, Robert. *Rabbit Hill*. Viking, 1944

_____. *The Tough Winter*. Viking, 1954.

Le Guin, Ursula K. *The Farthest Shore*, illustrated by Gail Garraty. Atheneum, 1972.

_____. *The Tombs of Atuan*, illustrated by Gail Garraty. Atheneum, 1971.

_____. *A Wizard of Earthsea*, illustrated by Ruth Robbins. Parnassus, 1968.

L'Engle, Madeleine. *A Swiftly Tilting Planet*. Farrar, Straus, 1978.

_____. *A Wind in the Door*. Farrar, Straus, 1973.

_____. *A Wrinkle in Time*. Farrar, Straus, 1962.

Lewis, C. S. *The Horse and His Boy*, illustrated by Pauline Baynes. Macmillan, 1962.

_____. *The Last Battle*, illustrated by Pauline Baynes. Macmillan, 1964.

_____. *The Lion, the Witch, and the Wardrobe*, illustrated by Pauline Baynes. Macmillan, 1961.

_____. *The Magician's Nephew*, illustrated by Pauline Baynes. Macmillan, 1964.

_____. *Prince Caspian, the Return to Narnia*, illustrated by Pauline Baynes. Macmillan, 1964.

_____. *The Silver Chair*, illustrated by Pauline Baynes. Macmillan, 1962.

_____. *The Voyage of the "Dawn Treader,"* illustrated by Pauline Baynes. Macmillan, 1962.

Lindgren, Astrid. *Pippi Goes on Board*, translated by Florence Lamborn, illustrated by Louis S. Glanzman. Viking, 1957.

_____. *Pippi in the South Seas*, translated by Florence Lamborn, illustrated by Louis S. Glanzman. Viking, 1959.

_____. *Pippi Longstocking*, illustrated by Louis S. Glanzman. Viking, 1950.

_____. *Pippi on the Run*. Viking, 1976.

Lively, Penelope. *The Ghost of Thomas Kempe*, illustrated by Anthony Maitland. Dutton, 1973.

_____. *The Voyage of QV 66*, illustrated by Harold Jones. Dutton, 1979.

Lobel, Anita. *A Birthday for the Princess*. Harper, 1973.

Lunn, Janet. *The Root Cellar*. Scribner, 1983.

McCaffrey, Anne. *Dragondrums*, illustrated by Fred Marcellino. Atheneum, 1979.

_____. *Dragonsinger*. Atheneum, 1977.

_____. *Dragonsong*, illustrated by Laura Lydecker. Atheneum, 1976.

MacDonald, George. *At the Back of the North Wind*. Garland, 1976 (1871).

_____. *The Golden Key*, illustrated by Maurice Sendak. Farrar, Straus, 1967.

_____. *The Light Princess*, illustrated by William Pène du Bois. Crowell, 1962.

_____. *The Light Princess*, illustrated by Maurice Sendak. Farrar, Straus, 1969.

MacGregor, Ellen. *Miss Pickerell Goes to Mars*, illustrated by Paul Galdone. McGraw-Hill, 1951.

McKillip, Patricia. *Harpist in the Wind*. Atheneum, 1979.

_____. *Heir of Sea and Fire*. Atheneum, 1977.

_____. *The Riddle-Master of Hed*. Atheneum, 1976.

McKinley, Robin. *Beauty: A Retelling of the Story of Beauty and the Beast*. Harper, 1978.

_____. *The Blue Sword*. Greenwillow, 1982.

_____. *The Hero and the Crown*. Greenwillow, 1985

Marzollo, Jean. *Halfway Down Paddy Lane*. Dial, 1981.

Mayne, William. *Earthfasts*. Dutton, 1967.

Merrill, Jean. *The Pushcart War*, illustrated by Ronni Solbert. W. R. Scott, 1964.

Milne, A. A. *The House at Pooh Corner*, illustrated by Ernest H. Shepard. Dutton, 1928.

_____. *Winnie-the-Pooh*, illustrated by Ernest H. Shepard. Dutton, 1926.

Murphy, Shirley Rousseau. *Silver Woven in My Hair*, illustrated by Alan Tiegreen. Atheneum, 1977.

Norton, André. *Breed to Come*. Viking, 1972.

_____. *The Crystal Gryphon*. Atheneum, 1972.

_____. *The Night of Masks*. Harcourt, 1964.

_____. *Zero Stone*. Viking, 1968.

_____, and Dorothy Madlee. *Star Ka'at*. Walker, 1976.

Norton, Mary. *The Borrowers*, illustrated by Beth and Joe Krush. Harcourt, 1953.

_____. *The Borrowers Afield*, illustrated by Beth and Joe Krush. Harcourt, 1955.

_____. *The Borrowers Afloat*, illustrated by Beth and Joe Krush. Harcourt, 1959.

_____. *The Borrowers Aloft*, illustrated by Beth and Joe Krush. Harcourt, 1961.

_____. *The Borrowers Avenged*, illustrated by Beth and Joe Krush. Harcourt, 1982.

Nostlinger, Christine. *Konrad*. Watts, 1977.

O'Brien, Robert C. *Mrs. Frisby and the Rats of NIMH*, illustrated by Zena Bernstein. Atheneum, 1971.

_____. *Z for Zachariah*. Atheneum, 1975.

Ormondroyd, Edward. *All in Good Time*, illustrated by Ruth Robbins. Parnassus, 1975.

_____. *Time at the Top*, illustrated by Peggy Bach. Parnassus, 1963.

Park, Ruth. *Playing Beatie Bow*. Atheneum, 1982.

Pearce, Philippa. *Tom's Midnight Garden*, illustrated by Susan Einzig. Lippincott, 1959.

Peterson, John. *The Littles*, illustrated by Roberta C. Clark. Scholastic, 1970.

Pierce, Meredith Ann. *The Darkangel*. Atlantic-Little, Brown, 1982.

Pinkwater, Daniel M. *Lizard Music*. Dodd, Mead, 1976.

_____. *Attila the Pun*. Four Winds, 1981.

_____. *The Magic Moscow*. Four Winds, 1980.

_____. *Slaves of Spiegel*. Four Winds, 1982.

Rodgers, Mary. *Freaky Friday*. Harper, 1972.

_____. *Summer Switch*. Harper, 1982.

Rodowsky, Colby. *The Gathering Room*. Farrar, Straus, 1981.

Saint-Exupéry, Antoine de. *The Little Prince*, translated by Katherine Woods. Harcourt, 1943.

Sargent, Sarah. *Weird Henry Berg*. Crown, 1980.

Sauer, Julia. *Fog Magic*, illustrated by Lynd Ward. Viking, 1943.

Selden, George. *Chester Cricket's Pigeon Ride*, illustrated by Garth Williams. Farrar, Straus, 1981.

_____. *The Cricket in Times Square*, illustrated by Garth Williams. Farrar, Straus, 1960.

_____. *Harry Cat's Pet Puppy*, illustrated by Garth Williams. Farrar, Straus, 1974.

_____. *Tucker's Countryside*, illustrated by Garth Williams. Farrar, Straus, 1969.

Sendak, Maurice. *Higglety, Pigglety, Pop!* Harper, 1967.

Seuss, Dr., pseud. (Theodor Seuss Geisel). *The 500 Hats of Bartholomew Cubbins*. Vanguard, 1938.

Sharp, Margery. *Bernard the Brave*. Little, Brown, 1977.

_____. *Miss Bianca*, illustrated by Garth Williams. Little, Brown, 1962.

_____. *Miss Bianca and the Bridesmaid*, illustrated by Erik Blegvad. Little, Brown, 1972.

_____. *Miss Bianca in the Salt Mines*, illustrated by Garth Williams. Little, Brown, 1967.

_____. *The Rescuers*, illustrated by Garth Williams. Little, Brown, 1959.

_____. *The Turret*, illustrated by Garth Williams. Little, Brown, 1963.

Sleator, William. *Blackbriar*. Dutton, 1972.

_____. *The Green Futures of Tycho*. Dutton, 1981.

Slobodkin, Louis. *The Amiable Giant*. Macmillan, 1955.
_____. *The Space Ship under the Apple Tree*. Macmillan, 1952.
Slote, Alfred. *C.O.L.A.R.*, illustrated by Anthony Kramer. Harper, 1981.
_____. *My Robot Buddy*. Lippincott, 1975.
Steele, Mary Q. *Wish Come True*, illustrated by Muriel Batherman. Greenwillow, 1979.
Steig, William. *Abel's Island*. Farrar, Straus, 1976.
_____. *Dominic*. Farrar, Straus, 1972.
Tannen, Mary. *The Lost Legend of Finn*. Knopf, 1982.
_____. *The Wizard Children of Finn*. Knopf, 1981.
Thurber, James. *Many Moons*, illustrated by Louis Slobodkin. Harcourt, 1943.
_____. *The 13 Clocks*, illustrated by Marc Simont. Simon & Schuster, 1950.
Tolkien, J. R. R. *The Hobbit*. Houghton Mifflin, 1938.
Travers, P. L. *Mary Poppins*, illustrated by Mary Shepard. Harcourt, 1934.
_____. *Mary Poppins Comes Back*, illustrated by Mary Shepard. Harcourt, 1935.
_____. *Mary Poppins in the Park*, illustrated by Mary Shepard. Harcourt, 1952.
_____. *Mary Poppins Opens the Door*, illustrated by Mary Shepard and Agnes Sims. Harcourt, 1943.
Uttley, Alison. *A Traveler in Time*, illustrated by Christine Price. Viking, 1964 (1939).
Walsh, Jill Paton. *A Chance Child*. Farrar, Straus, 1978.
_____. *The Green Book*, illustrated by Lloyd Bloom. Farrar, Straus, 1982.
Wangerin, Walter, Jr. *The Book of the Dun Cow*. Harper, 1978.
White, E. B. *Charlotte's Web*, illustrated by Garth Williams. Harper, 1952.
_____. *Stuart Little*, illustrated by Garth Williams. Harper, 1945.
_____. *The Trumpet of the Swan*, illustrated by Edward Frascino. Harper, 1970.
White, T. H. *Mistress Masham's Repose*, illustrated by Fritz Eichenberg. Gregg, 1980 (1946).
Wilde, Oscar. *The Happy Prince*, illustrated by Jean Claverie. Oxford, 1981.
_____. *The Selfish Giant*, illustrated by Herbert Danska. Harlan Quist, 1967.
Williams, Jay. *Everyone Knows What a Dragon Looks Like*, illustrated by Mercer Mayer. Four Winds, 1976.
_____. *The Good-for-Nothing Prince*, illustrated by Imero Gobbato. Norton, 1969.
_____. *Petronella*, illustrated by Friso Henstra. Parents', 1973.
_____. *The Practical Princess*, illustrated by Friso Henstra. Parents', 1969.
Williams, Jay, and Raymond Abrashkin. *Danny Dunn and the Anti-Gravity Paint*, illustrated by Ezra Jack Keats. McGraw-Hill, 1964.
Winthrop, Elizabeth. *The Castle in the Attic*. Holiday House, 1985.
Wiseman, David. *Jeremy Visick*. Houghton Mifflin, 1981.
Wrightson, Patricia. *The Dark Bright Water*. Atheneum, 1979.
_____. *The Ice Is Coming*. Atheneum, 1977.
_____. *Journey Behind the Wind*. Atheneum, 1981.
_____. *The Nargun and the Stars*. Atheneum, 1974.
Yolen, Jane. *The Acorn Quest*, illustrated by Susanna Natti. Crowell, 1981.
_____. *Dragon's Blood*. Delacorte, 1982.
_____. *The Emperor and the Kite*, illustrated by Ed Young. World, 1967.
_____. *The Girl Who Loved the Wind*, illustrated by Ed Young. Corwell, 1972.
_____. *Greyling*, illustrated by William Stobbs. Philomel, 1968.
_____. *Heart's Blood*. Delacorte, 1984.
_____. *The Hundredth Dove and Other Tales*, illustrated by David Palladini. Harper, 1977.
_____. *The Seeing Stick*, illustrated by Remy Charlip and Demetra Maraslis. Crowell, 1977.

8

POETRY

A fifth-grade teacher finished reading aloud Paterson's *Bridge to Terabithia* to her class. This is the well-loved story of friendship between a highly imaginative girl, Leslie, and Jess—middle child in a rural family of five. It was Leslie's idea to create Terabithia, their secret kingdom in the woods that could be approached only by swinging across a stream on a rope. And it was this frayed rope that brought about the tragedy in the story. Following the completion of the story, the group was silent for a moment thinking about Leslie's death and the legacy she had left Jess. Wisely, the teacher respected their silence, recognizing that this book had moved them deeply. They did not discuss it immediately but quietly began to do other work. That evening one of the girls in the class wrote this poem:

As the stubborn stream
    swirls and pulls out a song
The hillside stands in the cold dark sky.
Over the hillside stands
    a lovely palace.
Before
    it shook with joy,
But now
    its queen is dead.

So the sour sweet wind
Blows the tassels of the weak rope.
And the tree mourns
    scolding the rope, saying
Couldn't you have held out a little longer?

Cheri Taylor
Highland Park School
Grove City, Ohio
Linda Charles, teacher

Poetry was as much a part of this classroom as prose was. The teacher shared some poetry every day, as well as reading stories. Frequently she read a poem that reflected the same content or feeling as the novel she was reading. So it was natural for Cheri to write a poem in response to her feelings about *Bridge to Terabithia*.

Poetry is the language of emotions. It can encapsulate a deep response in a few words. For Cheri, poetry was the only way to capture her feelings about a book that had moved her as no other one had ever done before.

THE MEANING OF POETRY

What Is Poetry?

There is an elusiveness about poetry that defies precise definition. It is not so much what it is that is important as how it makes us feel. Eleanor Farjeon tells us that "Poetry" (63) is "not a rose, but the scent of the rose . . . Not the sea, but the sound of the sea." Fine poetry is this distillation of experience that captures the essence of an object, feeling, or thought. Such intensification requires a more highly structured patterning of words than prose does. Each word must be chosen with care, for both its sound and meaning, for poetry is language in its most connotative and concentrated form. Laurence Perrine defines poetry as "a kind of language that says more and says it more intensely than ordinary language."[1]

Poetry may both broaden and intensify experience, or it may present a range of experiences

[1]Laurence Perrine, *Sound and Sense: An Introduction to Poetry,* 3rd ed. (New York: Harcourt Brace Jovanovich, 1969), p. 3.

beyond the realm of personal possibility for the individual listener. It may also illuminate, clarify, and deepen an everyday occurrence in a way the reader never considered, making the reader see more and feel more than ever before. For poetry does more than mirror life; it reveals life in new dimensions. Robert Frost stated that a poem goes from delight to wisdom. Poetry does delight children, but it also helps them develop new insights, new ways of sensing their world.

Poetry communicates experience by appealing to both the thoughts and feelings of its reader. It has the power to evoke in its hearers rich sensory images and deep emotional responses. Poetry demands total response from the individual—all the intellect, senses, emotion, and imagination. It does not tell *about* an experience as much as it invites its hearers to *participate in* the experience. Poetry can only happen when the poem and the reader connect. Eve Merriam writes about the process in this way:

"I," says the poem matter-of-factly,
"I am a cloud,
I am a tree.

I am a city,
I am the sea,

I am a golden
Mystery."

But, adds the poem silently,
I cannot speak until you come.
Reader, come, come with me.

Eve Merriam (176)[2]

Much of what poetry says is conveyed by suggestion, by indirection, by what is not said. As Carl Sandburg put it, "What can be explained is not poetry. . . . The poems that are obvious are like the puzzles that are already solved. They deny us the joy of seeking and creating."[3] A certain amount of ambiguity is characteristic of poetry,

[2]If the source of a poem is not obvious, the number following a poem in this chapter refers to the number in the References of the book where the poem may be found. Many of the poems appear in several anthologies, however.
[3]Carl Sandburg, "Short Talk on Poetry," in *Early Moon* (New York: Harcourt Brace Jovanovich, 1930), p. 27.

for more is hidden in it than in prose. The poet does not tell readers "all," but invites them to go beyond the literal level of the poem and discover its deeper meanings for themselves.

Robert Frost playfully suggested that poetry is what gets lost in translation—and translation of poetry into prose is as difficult as translation of poetry into another language. To paraphrase a poem is to destroy it. Would it be possible to reduce Frost's "Mending Wall" to prose? The scene, the situation, the contrast of the two men's thoughts about the wall they are repairing may be described, but the experience of the poem cannot be conveyed except by its own words.

Poetry for Children

Poetry for children differs little from poetry for adults, except that it comments on life in dimensions that are meaningful for children. Its language should be poetic and its content should appeal directly to children. Myra Cohn Livingston has described "Winter and Summer" in a way that reflects how children might view these contrasting seasons:

WINTER AND SUMMER
The winter
    is an ice-cream treat,
    all frosty white and cold to eat.
But summer
    is a lemonade
    of yellow sun and straw-cool shade.

Myra Cohn Livingston (163)

Such poetry appeals to children's sensory experiences and helps them think about the differences between winter and summer in a creative, imaginative way. It speaks to the child, but in the language of poetry. Poetry for children appeals to their emotions as well as to their senses. Young persons may experience emotions that are similar to adults, but the circumstances that provoked them will generally differ. They get angry, but it may be because they have to go to bed too early. The are easily hurt, but it may be because Daddy spanked them and they are hiding "Up in the Pine" (99), or they are worried because their dog is "Gone" (101).

The scope of poetry for children, then, encompasses all the feelings, all the experiences of childhood.

The limitations of poetry for children are surprisingly few. Poems of passion and nostalgia seem to have little place in childhood, as these are not children's emotions (see Chapter 1). Literary allusions are necessarily limited, and metaphors should be related to children's experiences. Figurative language tends to obscure meaning, unless it is based on familiar experiences or well-known objects. Young children readily respond to the figures of speech in this poem, however:

SIDEWALK MEASLES

I saw the sidewalk catch the measles
When the rain came down today.
It started with a little blotching—
Quickly spread to heavy splotching,
Then as I continued watching
The rain-rash slowly dried away.

Barbara M. Hales (111)

The comparison of the rain marks on the sidewalk with the way someone with the measles looks will appeal to children. The poet has helped children look at a common sight with new vision. By putting two disparate objects together, the characteristic of one becomes the characteristic of the other, enlarging the way a child thinks about the patterns of rain on the sidewalk. Capitalizing on children's interests, this poem helps the child to view the world in a new way, through the language of poetry. Its metaphor is childlike, but not "childish."

Space-age children need fresh comparisons that are relevant to their background of experiences. The child's hero of today works in space and not under the spreading chestnut tree. Many children who would have little understanding of "The Village Blacksmith" (248) would comprehend the comparison that Eve Merriam makes in her poem:

SATELLITE, SATELLITE

Satellite, satellite
The earth goes around the sun.

Satellite, satellite,
The moon goes around the earth.

Satellite, satellite,
I have a little satellite:

My little brother orbits me
And pesters day and night.

Eve Merriam (184)

Children might be encouraged through discussion to think of other satellite situations in their lives—a little dog that faithfully follows its master, a bee buzzing around a clover blossom, even Mary's little lamb.

The emotional appeal of children's poetry should reflect the real emotions of childhood. Poetry that is cute, coy, nostalgic, or sarcastic may be *about* children, but it is not *for* them. Whittier's "The Barefoot Boy" (64) looks back on childhood in a nostalgic fashion characteristic of adults, not children. "The Children's Hour" (64) by Longfellow is an old man's reminiscences of his delight in his children. Some poems patronize childhood as a period in life when children are "cute" or "naughty." Joan W. Anglund's poetry is as cute and sentimental as her pictures of "sweet little boys and girls." Even the best of children's poets occasionally have been guilty of this kind of portrayal of childhood. For example, "Vespers" (188) by A. A. Milne appeals more to adults who are amused and pleased by the sweet description of a child's desultory thoughts during prayer, while children find little humor in this poem which makes them the object of laughter.

Many poems are didactic and preachy. Unfortunately, some teachers will accept moralizing in poetry that they would never accept in prose. Sentimentality is another adult emotion, seldom felt by children. The poem "Which Loved Best," frequently quoted before Mother's Day, drips with sentiment and morality. Poems that are *about* childhood or aim to instruct are usually disliked by children.

Yet children do feel deep emotions; they can be hurt, fearful, bewildered, sad, happy, expectant, satisfied. Some poets have been successful in capturing the real feelings of childhood. For example, Stephen Spender describes the agony of the overprotected child who wants desperately to make friends with the bullies who frighten him:

MY PARENTS KEPT ME FROM CHILDREN WHO WERE ROUGH

My parents kept me from children who were
    rough
Who threw words like stones and who wore
    torn clothes.
Their thighs showed through rags. They ran in
    the street
And climbed cliffs and stripped by the country
    streams.

I feared more than tigers their muscles like iron
Their jerking hands and their knees tight on my
    arms.
I feared the salt-coarse pointing of those boys
Who copied my lisp behind me on the road.

They were lithe, they sprang out behind hedges
Like dogs to bark at my world. They threw mud
While I looked the other way, pretending to
    smile.
I longed to forgive them, but they never smiled.

Stephen Spender (177)

There are two schools of thought concerning what is appropriate poetry for children. Some would disallow any poetry written by the so-called children's poets and present only poems of recognized poets who write for adults. They would search for the few poems of Tennyson, Shakespeare, and Dickinson, for example, that might be appropriate for children. Others have limited poetry in the classroom to such childhood poets as Stevenson, Farjeon, and Aldis. This seems an unnecessary dichotomy.

A third school of thought concerning what is appropriate poetry for children is the school embraced by this text, which would take the best from both worlds. In evaluating a poem for children it makes little difference who the author is, provided the poem speaks *to children* in the *language* of poetry. Children deserve excellence in poetry regardless of its source, but it must speak to them at their point in time.

The Elements of Poetry

A child responds to the total impact of a poem and should not be required to analyze it. However, teachers need to understand the language of poetry if they are to select the best to share with children. How, for example, can you differentiate between real poetry and mere verse? *Mother Goose*, jump-rope rhymes, tongue twisters, and the lyrics of some songs are not poetry; but they *can* serve as a springboard for diving into real poetry. Elizabeth Coatsworth, who has written much fine poetry and verse for children, refers to rhyme as "poetry in petticoats."[4] Such rhymes may have the sound of poetry, but they do not contain the quality of imagination or the depth of emotion that characterizes real poetry.

It is a difficult task to identify elements of poetry for today's children, for modern poets are breaking traditional molds in both content and form. These poems speak directly to the reader about all subjects. Frequently the words are spattered across pages in a random fashion or they become poem-pictures, as in concrete poetry. As children become more sophisticated by their exposure to films and television, the dividing line between what is poetry for adults and what is poetry for children becomes fainter and fainter. It is, however, possible to identify those poems that contain the elements of fine poetry, yet still speak to children.

RHYTHM

The young child is naturally rhythmical. She beats on the tray of her highchair, kicks her foot against the table, and chants her vocabulary of one or two words in a singsong fashion. She delights in the sound of "Pat-a-cake, pat-a-cake, baker's man," or "Ride a cock-horse to Banbury Cross" before she understands the meaning of the words. This response to a measured beat is as old as humans themselves. Primitive people had chants, hunting and working songs, dances, and crude musical instruments. Rhythm is a part of the daily beat of our lives—the steady pulse rate, regular breathing, and pattern of growth. The inevitability of night and day, the revolving seasons, birth and death provide a pattern for everyone's life. The very ebb and flow of the ocean, the sound of the rain on the window, and the pattern of rows of corn in a field reflect the rhythm of the world around us.

Poetry satisfies the child's natural response to

[4]Elizabeth Coatsworth, *The Sparrow Bush*, illustrated by Stefan Martin (New York: Norton, 1966), p. 8.

rhythm. Eve Merriam has described the importance of rhythm in the first verse of the title poem of her book, *It Doesn't Always Have to Rhyme:*

INSIDE A POEM

It doesn't always have to rhyme,
but there's the repeat of a beat, somewhere
an inner chime that makes you want to
tap your feet or swerve in a curve;
a lilt, a leap, a lightning-split:—

Eve Merriam (183)

It is this built-in rhythm or meter that helps to differentiate poetry from prose. A poem has a kind of music of its own, and the child responds to it.

The very young child enjoys the monotonous rocking-horse rhythm of Mother Goose and expects it in all other poems. Mary Ann Hoberman has explored other rhythms in the child's life as she links weather and seasonal patterns to the rhythm of a child's swinging:

Hello and good-by
Hello and good-by

When I'm in a swing
Swinging low and then high,
Good-by to the ground
Hello to the sky.

Hello to the rain
Good-by to the sun,
Then hello again sun
When the rain is all done.

In blows the winter,
Away the birds fly.
Good-by and hello
Hello and good-by.

Mary Ann Hoberman (97)

Stevenson's well-known poem "The Swing" (239) suggests a different meter for the physical sensation of swinging. Read both of these poems to children and let them pantomime swinging as they chant the lines. Then they can discuss which poem was the easier one to respond to.

The galloping rhythm of Stevenson's "Windy Nights" compares the sound of the wild wind to a mysterious horseman riding by. The refrain of the last four lines may be read loudly and then softly to give the effect of the wailing wind:

By, on the highway, low and loud,
By at the gallop goes he:
By at the gallop he goes, and then
By he comes back at the gallop again.

Robert Louis Stevenson (239)

Stevenson has also captured the fast pace of a train with the clipped rhythm of his poem "From a Railway Carriage" (239). The sliding, gliding movement of "Skating" is well portrayed by the rhythm of Herbert Asquith's poem (10), while the slow steady beat of "Lullaby" by Hillyer (60) imitates the strong strokes of the paddle moving a canoe slowly toward the shore. The rhythm of a poem, then, should be appropriate to its subject matter, reinforcing and creating its meaning.

In some poems both the rhythm and pattern of the lines are suggestive of the movement or mood of the poem. The arrangement of these poems forces the reader to emphasize a particular rhythm. The words of Farjeon's "Mrs. Peck-Pigeon" and the repetition of the hard sounds of "b" and "p" help to create the bobbing rhythm of the pigeon herself:

MRS. PECK-PIGEON

Mrs. Peck-Pigeon
Is picking for bread,
Bob—bob—bob
Goes her little round head.
Tame as a pussy-cat
In the street,
Step—step—step
Go her little red feet.
With her little red feet
And her little round head,
Mrs. Peck-Pigeon
Goes picking for bread.

Eleanor Farjeon (63)

In Dorothy Baruch's "Merry-go-Round" (10) the pattern of the line and the rhythm can be read to suggest the increasing and decreasing speed of a merry-go-round. The somewhat pensive mood of A. A. Milne's "Halfway Down" (188) is heightened by the arrangement of the words and lines. The reader has to interpret the slow descent of a little boy going down the stairs until he stops at his favorite step, halfway down.

A change of rhythm is indicative of a new element in the poem: a contrast in mood, a warning, or a different speaker, for example. Mary Austin has contrasted the ominous movement of "The Sandhill Crane" as he goes "slowly solemnly stalking," with the fast scuttling movements of the frogs and minnows who fear for their lives.

THE SANDHILL CRANE

Whenever the days are cool and clear
The sandhill crane goes walking
Across the field by the flashing weir
Slowly, solemnly stalking.
The little frogs in the tules hear
And jump for their lives when he comes near,
The minnows scuttle away in fear,
When the sandhill crane goes walking.

Mary Austin (1)

RHYME AND SOUND

In addition to the rhythm of a poem children respond to its rhyme. For rhyme helps to create the musical qualities of a poem, and children enjoy the "singingness of words." The Russian poet Chukovsky[5] maintains that in the beginning of childhood we are all "versifiers," and that it is only later in life that we begin to speak in prose. He is referring to the young child's tendency to double all syllables so that "mother" is first "mama" and water "wa-wa." This, plus the regular patterning of such words as daddy, mommy, granny, and so on, makes for a natural production of rhyme. Karla Kuskin capitalized on this phenomenon among children with her amusing story of *Alexander Soames* (126) who could only "speak in poems"! The young child's enjoyment of Mother Goose is due almost entirely to the rhyme and rhythm of these verses. "Rope Rhyme" by Eloise Greenfield captures the rhythm of the turning rope and the slapping sound of the rope itself.

[5]Kornei Chukovsky, *From Two to Five,* translated and edited by Miriam Morton (Berkeley: University of California Press, 1963), p. 64.

The Dillons' illustrations for the poems in *Honey I Love* by Eloise Greenfield are as joyous and thoughtful as the poems themselves.

ROPE RHYME

Get set, ready now, jump right in
Bounce and kick and giggle and spin
Listen to the rope when it hits the ground
Listen to that clappedy-slappedy sound
Jump right up when it tells you to
Come back down, whatever you do
Count to a hundred, count by ten
Start to count all over again
That's what jumping is all about
Get set, ready now,
    jump
       right
          out!

Eloise Greenfield (92)

Other rope rhymes, street chants, handclap games, and taunts were collected by Barbara Michels and Bettye White in Texas, in both small towns and Houston. In sharing *Apples on a Stick: The Folklore of Black Children* (187) with your own children, it would be fascinating to see how many of these playground verses are known to all children. Street rhymes are where the sound of poetry begins for many children.

But children need to be freed from the notion that all poetry must rhyme in order to be poetry. They should be introduced to some poetry that doesn't rhyme, such as free verse or haiku, so that they begin to listen to the meaning of a poem as well as the sound of it.

Rhyme is one aspect of sound; alliteration, or the repetition of initial consonant sounds, is another; while assonance, or the repetition of particular vowel sounds, is still another. The repetition of the hard "g" sounds in "Godfrey Gordon Gustavus Gore" (64) adds to the humor of this poem about the boy who would never shut the door. Younger children delight in the "splishes and sploshes and slooshes and sloshes" which Susie's galoshes make in Rhoda W. Bacmeister's poem "Galoshes" (46). The quiet "s" sound and the repetition of the double "o" in "moon" and "shoon" suggest the mysterious beauty of the moon in "Silver" (10). Onomatopoeia is a term that refers to the use of words that make a sound like the action represented by the word, such as "crack," "hiss," and "sputter." Occasionally, a poet will create an entire poem that resembles a particular sound. David McCord has successfully imitated the sound of hitting a picket fence with a stick in his popular chant:

The pickety fence
The pickety fence
Give it a lick it's
The pickety fence
Give it a lick it's
A clickety fence
Give it a lick it's
A lickety fence
Give it a lick
Give it a lick
Give it a lick
With a rickety stick
Pickety
Pickety
Pickety
Pick

David McCord (170)

"Railroad Reverie" (176) by E. R. Young captures the sound of a train far away in the distance and then coming closer and closer. Children love the first loud and then soft refrain of:

Catch-a-teacher, catch-a-teacher, patch-his-
  britches,
Patch-his-britches, catch-a-teacher, patch-his-
  britches
Catch-a-teacher. Whoosh! . . .

Repetition is another way that the poet creates particular sound effects in a poem. Certain words or a phrase may be repeated for special emphasis or to develop a recurring motif or theme, as in a symphony. In "Night Train" Robert Francis creates a different mood from "Railroad Reverie." His is the lonely sound of a far-off train whistle blowing, blowing.

NIGHT TRAIN

Across the dim frozen fields of night
Where is it going, where is it going?
No throb of wheels, no rush of light.
Only a whistle blowing, blowing.
Only a whistle blowing.

Something echoing through my brain,
Something timed between sleep and waking,
Murmurs, murmurs this may be the train
I must be sometime, somewhere taking,
I must be sometime taking.

Robert Francis (94)

Robert Frost frequently used repetition of particular lines or phrases to emphasize meaning in his poems. The repetition of the last line "miles to go before I sleep" in his famous "Stopping by Woods on a Snowy Evening" (89) adds to the mysterious element in that poem.

Children are intrigued with the sound of language and enjoy unusual and ridiculous combinations of words. The gay nonsense of Laura Richards' "Eletelephony" (214) is as much in the sound of the ridiculous words as in the plight of the poor elephant who tried to use the "telephant." Children love to trip off the name of "James James Morrison Morrison Weatherby George Dupree," who complained about his mother's "Disobedience" (188), while "Mean

Song" by Eve Merriam conveys real anger with many made-up words such as

. . .
A nox in the groot,
A root in the stoot
And a gock in the forbeshaw, too.
. . .

Eve Merriam (184)

Poets use rhyme, rhythm, and the various devices of alliteration, assonance, repetition, and coined words to create the melody and sound of poetry loved by children.

IMAGERY

Poetry draws on many kinds of language magic. To speak of the imagery of a poem refers to direct sensory images of sight, sound, touch, smell, or taste. This aspect of poetry has particular appeal for children, as it reflects one of the major ways they explore their world. The very young child grasps an object and immediately puts it in her mouth. Children love to squeeze warm, soft puppies or they squeal with delight as a baby pet mouse scampers up their arms. Taste and smell are also highly developed in the young child.

The sadness of our modern society is that children are increasingly deprived of natural sensory experiences. One of the first admonitions they hear is "Don't touch." In the endless pavement of our cities, how many children have an opportunity to roll in crunchy piles of leaves? Air-pollution laws assure that they will never enjoy the acrid autumn smell of burning bonfires (rightly so, but still a loss). Many also miss the warm yeasty odor of homemade bread or the sweet joy of licking the bowl of brownie batter. Some of our newest schools are windowless, so children are even deprived of seeing the brilliant blue sky on a crisp cold day or the growing darkness of a storm or the changing silhouette of an oak tree on the horizon.

Poetry can never be a substitute for actual sensory experience. A child can't develop a concept of texture by hearing a poem or seeing pictures of the rough bark of a tree; he must first touch the bark and compare the feel of a deeply furrowed oak with the smooth surfaced trunk of a beech tree. Then the poet can call up these experiences, extend them or make the child see them in a new way.

John Moffitt describes how to really "see" with the eyes of the poet:

TO LOOK AT ANY THING
To look at any thing,
If you would know that thing,
You must look at it long:
To look at this green and say
'I have seen spring in these
Woods,' will not do—you must
Be the thing you see:
You must be the dark snakes of
Stems and ferny plumes of leaves,
You must enter in
To the small silences between
The leaves,
You must take your time
And touch the very peace
They issue from.

John Moffitt (60)

Since most children are visual-minded they respond readily to the picture-making quality of poetry. Louise Allen has looked with the eyes of a young child at a familiar world made strange by snow. Her poem "First Snow" may well be the first snow of the season or the child's first experience with snow:

FIRST SNOW
Snow makes whiteness where it falls,
The bushes look like popcorn balls.
And places where I always play,
Look like somewhere else today.

Marie Louise Allen (113)

Robert Frost has made us see a "Patch of Old Snow" (60) in the city as if it were an old blown-away newspaper bespeckled with grimy print. How many different ways can snow be described?

Tennyson's description of "The Eagle" is rich in the use of visual imagery. In the first verse the reader can see the eagle perched on the crest of a steep mountain, poised ready for his swift descent whenever he sights his quarry. But in the second verse the poet "enters into" the eagle's world and describes it from the bird's point of view. Looking down from his lofty height, the might of the waves is reduced to wrinkles and the sea seems to crawl:

THE EAGLE

He clasps the crag with crooked hands;
Close to the sun in lonely lands,
Ringed with the azure world, he stands.

The wrinkled sea beneath him crawls;
He watches from his mountain walls,
And like a thunderbolt he falls.

Alfred, Lord Tennyson (136)

The lonely, peaceful scene is shattered by the natural metaphor of the final line, "And like a thunderbolt he falls." In your mind's eye you can see, almost feel the wind on your wings, as you plunge down the face of the cliff.

Most poetry depends on visual and auditory imagery to evoke a mood or response, but imagery of touch, taste, and smell is also used. Children have always enjoyed the poem that begins, "Mud is very nice to feel / all squishy—squash between the toes! . . ." (46). Zilpha Snyder's "Poem to Mud" (237) also wallows in this delightful feeling. Contrast the crinkled feel of "Gravel Paths" (116) by Patricia Hubbell with the soft squishy delight of playing in the mud. Or you could compare what feet know through their sensory experiences with what hands discover. Dorothy Aldis does this for very young children in her poem "Feet" (9). Mary O'Neill's book *Fingers Are Always Bringing Me News* contains poems about many different kinds of fingers, from those of newborn babies to old fingers reaching out to feel the texture of their world. Listen to the beginning of:

COUNTRY FINGERS

My fingers know hay
And the grummy pull of resin
On pine trees in the Spring,
The oily-wooley, fuzzy feel of sheep,
The satin sides of cows,
And the feather dust of chickens.
My fingers know barn splinters,
The rough of whetstones,
The nick of burrs,
The taut, death-spring of a trap.
My fingers have felt pebbles
In the bottom of a brook,
The dart of fishes
And a turtle's snap. . . .

Mary O'Neill (201)

Psychologists tell us that some of children's earliest memories are sensory, recalling particularly the way things smell and taste. Most children have a delicate sense of taste that responds to the texture and smell of a particular food. In "Hard and Soft" (3) Arnold Adoff contrasts the crunch of eating a carrot with the quiet sound of swallowing raisins. In "A Matter of Taste" (184) Eve Merriam relates the way food tastes to the way it feels and sounds when being chewed. Myra Cohn Livingston expresses most children's distaste for the look and taste of liver in her amusing poem "O' Sliver of Liver" (157), while Aileen Fisher creates a vivid sensory impression by contrasting the various textures of the skins of fruits in her poem "Skins." Before introducing this poem, put a variety of fruit in a paper bag and have children describe the first one they touch. Encourage them to use descriptive words and then see if their classmates can guess the name of the fruit from their description of how it feels. Compare their responses with Fisher's:

SKINS

Skins of lemons are waterproof slickers.
Pineapple skins are stuck full of stickers.
Skins of apples are skinny and shiny
and strawberry skins (if any) are tiny.

Grapes have skins that are juicy and squishy.
Gooseberry skins are vinegar-ishy.
Skins of peaches are fuzzy and hairy.
Oranges' skins are more peely than pare-y.

Skins of plums are squirty and squeezy.
Bananas have skins you can pull-off-easy.

I like skins that are thin as sheeting
so what-is-under is bigger for eating.

Aileen Fisher (78)

Certain smells can recapture a whole experience that may have happened years before. In "That Was the Summer" (46) Marci Ridlon recalls summer smells of grass and hot wet pavement. Joanna Cole contrasts the smells of the road with the smells of the beach.

DRIVING TO THE BEACH

On the road
smell fumes and tar

through the windows
of the car.

But at the beach
smell suntan lotion
and wind
  and sun
    and ocean!

Joanna Cole (99)

In "Swell Smells" (57) Beatrice Schenk de Regniers lists her favorite smells. Such a list could provide a model for children to select their favorites. Zhenya Gay's poem which begins "The world is full of wonderful smells" (91) tells of the luscious smell of hot bread and cake, of a haymow, and a warm dog lying in the sun. Much of children's poetry evokes this rich sensory response from its hearers and serves to sharpen children's perceptions.

FIGURATIVE LANGUAGE: COMPARISON AND CONTRAST

Since the language of poetry is so compressed, every word must be made to convey the message of the poem. Poets do this by comparing two objects or ideas with each other in such a way that the connotation of one word gives added meaning to another. Rowena Bennett in describing the look of "Motor Cars" from a high city window compares them to little black beetles:

MOTOR CARS

From a city window, 'way up high,
I like to watch the cars go by.
They look like burnished beetles, black,
That leave a little muddy track
Behind them as they slowly crawl.
Sometimes they do not move at all
But huddle close with hum and drone
As though they feared to be alone.
They grope their way through fog and night
With the golden feelers of their light.

Rowena Bennett (10)

Having established the "look-alikeness" of cars and burnished beetles in the first simile, the poet then extends the comparison in the metaphor of the last two lines, in which the cars have *become*

beetles, their lights now assuming such beetle properties as "feelers." When writers compare one thing with another, using such connecting words as *like* or *as,* they are using a simile. In a metaphor the poet speaks of an object or idea as if it *were* another object. In recent years we have paid little attention to the difference between these two techniques, referring to both as examples of metaphorical or figurative language.

It is not important that children know the difference between a simile and a metaphor. It is important that they know what is being compared and that the comparison is fresh and new and helps them view the idea or object in a different and unusual way. Two well-known poems that contain metaphors that help children see their world afresh are "The Moon's the North Wind's Cooky" (226) and the first line of "On a Snowy Day" (9), which describes fenceposts as wearing marshmallow hats. Perhaps the reason these poems have endured is that they also reveal a true understanding of a child's point of view.

Some figurative language is so commonplace that it has lost its ability to evoke new images. Language and verse are filled with such clichés as "it rained cats and dogs," "a blanket of snow," "quiet as a mouse," or "thin as a rail." Eve Merriam describes a "Cliché" (183) as what lazy people use in their writing. Her poem "Metaphor Man" (185) also pokes fun at such expressions as "drives a hard bargain," "stands four square," or "flies in a rage."

In her books titled *Small Poems* (257), *More Small Poems* (256), and *Still More Small Poems* (258), Valerie Worth has written simple yet vivid metaphorical poems which describe such ordinary objects as a safety pin, sidewalks, and earthworms. Her free verse is unpretentious, yet crisp and clear. Children who have carefully observed the grasshopper will appreciate her comparison of its shape with that of a tractor.

TRACTOR

The tractor rests
In the shed
Dead or asleep,

But with high
Hind wheels
Held so still

We know
It is only waiting
Ready to leap—

Like a heavy
Brown
Grasshopper

                                        Valerie Worth (257)

Most children are intrigued with the subject of dinosaurs and readily respond to Charles Malam's poem that compares a steam shovel with those enormous beasts. The image, which the poem projects, reinforces the idea of the poem throughout:

STEAM SHOVEL

The dinosaurs are not all dead.
I saw one raise its iron head
To watch me walking down the road
Beyond our house today.
Its jaws were dripping with a load
Of earth and grass that it had cropped.
It must have heard me where I stopped,
Snorted white steam my way,
And stretched its long neck out to see,
And chewed, and grinned quite amiably.

                                        Charles Malam (60)

Judith Thurman compares the beam of a flashlight to a dog straining on a leash. Without showing children a picture, it is interesting to ask them to fold a paper and draw the two things that are being compared. Teachers then have some understanding of children's ability to "see" metaphorically.

FLASHLIGHT

My flashlight tugs me
through the dark
like a hound
with a yellow eye,

sniffs
at the edges
of steep places,

paws
at moles'

and rabbits'
holes,

points its nose
where sharp things
lie asleep—

and then it bounds
ahead of me
on home ground.

                                        Judith Thurman (243)

Carl Sandburg's well-known poem "Fog" (109) likens the fog hovering over the city to a cat that sits "on silent haunches." Langston Hughes sees the city as a bird in the first stanza of this poem, "City," and personifies it in the last:

CITY

In the morning the city
Spreads its wings
Making a song
In stone that sings.

In the evening the city
Goes to bed
Hanging lights
About its head.

                                        Langston Hughes (176)

Personification is a way of speaking about inanimate objects as though they were persons. Aileen Fisher uses personification to describe "The Voice of the Sky" (74) as the oldest voice that has ever been heard. The wind becomes a person in Adrien Stoutenberg's free verse titled:

THE STORM

In a storm
the wind talks
with its mouth wide open.
It yells around corners
with its eyes shut.
It bumps itself
and falls over a roof
and whispers
Oh. . . . Oh. . . . oh. . . .

                                        Adrien Stoutenberg (193)

Ted Hughes presents a forceful picture of autumn as the day that comes and wrings the neck of summer. No child will think nature poems are sissy when they hear this one. The last verse gives a striking image of autumn.

THERE CAME A DAY

. . .

There came this day and he was autumn
His mouth was wide
And red as a sunset
His tail was an icicle.

                    Ted Hughes (118)

Human beings have always personified inanimate objects. Young children personify their toys and pets, while adolescents and adults name their computers, their cars and boats. Poetry simply extends this process to a wider range of objects.

Another way of strengthening an image is through contrast. Elizabeth Coatsworth employs this device in much of her poetry. Her best-known "Poem of Praise" (43) contrasts the beauty of swift things with those that are slow and steady (page 422). Similarly, she compares the speeds at which "Morning and Afternoon" (43) pass, in the poem by that title. Marci Ridlon presents two points of view concerning life in the city in her poem "City City" (214). By contrasting a view of a bridge by day and night, Lilian Moore gives us two images, one of strength and one of lacy lightness.

THE BRIDGE

A bridge
by day
is steel and strong.
It carries
giant trucks that roll along
above the waters
of the bay.
A bridge is steel and might—
till night.

A bridge
at night
is spun of light
that someone tossed
across the bay

and someone caught
and pinned down tight—
till day.

                    Lilian Moore (194)

In the poem "Fueled," the poet compares the launching of a man-made rocket with the miraculous growth of a seedling pushing its way through the earth. The first feat receives much acclaim, while the second goes virtually unnoticed. There seems to be no doubt in the poet's mind which is the greater event, for she has even shaped her poem to resemble half of a tree:

FUELED

Fueled
by a million
man-made
wings of fire—
the rocket tore a tunnel
through the sky—
and everybody cheered.
Fueled
only by a thought from God—
the seedling
urged its way
through the thickness of black—
and as it pierced
the heavy ceiling of the soil—
and launched itself
up into outer space—
no
one
even clapped.

                    Marcie Hans (60)

Even though all children know about rockets and seeds, they may not be able to see the connection between the two images that the poet has created. Among one group of educationally and economically advantaged 8-year-olds, not one child saw both of these ideas; yet 11-year-olds in the same school easily recognized them. This suggests the importance of knowing the developmental level of a group before selecting poetry for them.

THE SHAPE OF A POEM

The first thing children notice about reading a poem is that it looks different from prose. And usually it does. Most poems begin with capital letters for each line and have one or more stanzas.

Increasingly, however, poets are using the shape of their poems to reinforce the image of the idea. David McCord describes the plight of "The Grasshopper" (172) that fell down a deep well. As luck would have it, he discovers a rope and up he climbs one word at a time! The reader must read up the page to follow the grasshopper's ascent. Eve Merriam's "Windshield Wiper" (185) not only sounds like the even rhythm of a car's wiper but has the look of two wipers. Lillian Morrison's poem about a sidewalk racer describes the thrill of the rider at the same time it takes the shape of a skateboard and strengthens her image.

THE SIDEWALK RACER

or

On the Skateboard

Skimming
an asphalt sea
I swerve, I curve, I
sway; I speed to whirring
sound an inch above the
ground; I'm the sailor
and the sail, I'm the
driver and the wheel
I'm the one and only
single engine
human auto
mobile

Lillian Morrison (195)

Children enjoy mounting their own poems on a piece of paper shaped in the image of their poem, such as a verse about a jack-o'-lantern on a pumpkin shape or a poem about a plane mounted on the silhouette of a plane. Later their words themselves may form the shape of the content, as in concrete poetry.

THE EMOTIONAL FORCE OF POETRY

We have seen how sound, language, and the shape of a poem may all work together to create the total impact of the poem. Considered individually, the rhyme scheme, imagery, figurative language, or the appearance of the poem are of little importance unless all of these interrelate to create an emotional response in the reader. The craft of the poem is not the poem.

In the poem "Listening to grownups quarreling," a modern poet writes of the way two children feel when caught in the vortex of their parents' quarrel:

LISTENING TO GROWNUPS QUARRELING,

standing in the hall against the
wall with my little brother, blown
like leaves against the wall by their
voices, my head like a pingpong ball
between the paddles of their anger:
I knew what it meant
to tremble like a leaf.

Cold with their wrath, I heard
the claws of the rain
pounce. Floods
poured through the city,
skies clapped over me,
and I was shaken, shaken
like a mouse
between their jaws.

Ruth Whitman (124)

A teacher could destroy the total impact of this poem for children by having them count the number of metaphors in it, looking at their increasing force and power. Children should have a chance to hear it, comment on it if they wish. Perhaps it could be read with a group of poems all related to feelings. With more than half the marriages in this country ending in divorce, children frequently are caught in the middle, "shaken, shaken" by the experience. All elements of this poem work together to create the feeling of being overpowered by a quarrel between those you love most and feeling helpless in the face of it.

Good poetry has the power to make the reader moan in despair, catch the breath in fear, gasp in awe, smile with delight, or sit back and wonder. For poetry heightens emotions and increases one's sensitivity to an idea or mood.

Teachers need to be able to identify the characteristics of good poetry in order to make wise selections to share with children. They need to know the various kinds of poetry and the range of

QUESTIONS FOR EVALUATING POETRY FOR CHILDREN

- How does the rhythm of the poem reinforce and create the meaning of the poem?
- If the poem rhymes, does it sound natural or contrived?
- How does the sound of the poem add to the meaning? Is alliteration used? Onomatopoeia? Repetition?
- Does the poem create sensory images of sight, touch, smell, or taste? Are these related to children's delight in their particular senses?
- What is the quality of the imagination in the poem? Does it make the child see something in a fresh new way, or does it rely on old tired clichés?
- Is the figurative language appropriate to children's lives? Are the similes and metaphors those that a child would appreciate and understand?
- What is the tone of the poem? Does it patronize childhood by looking down on it? Is it didactic and preachy? Does it see childhood in a sentimental or nostalgic way?
- Is the poem appropriate for children? Will it appeal to them, and will they like it?
- How has the poet created the emotional intensity of the poem? Does every word work to heighten the feelings conveyed?
- Does the shape of the poem, the placement of the words, contribute to the meaning of the poem?
- What is the purpose of the poem? To amuse, describe in a fresh way, comment on humanity, draw parallels in our lives? How well has the poet achieved this purpose?

content of poetry for children. Then they can provide children with poetry that will gradually develop an increasing sense of form and appreciation. The questions given above for evaluating poetry may be helpful. All these questions would not be appropriate to use for every poem. However, they can serve as a beginning way to look at poetry for children. Myra Cohn Livingston[6] always makes two requests of her students; these are their guideposts for writing poetry: "(1) Tell me something I have never heard before or (2) Tell me something I already know in a new way." This approach gets at the very essence of imaginative poetry.

Forms of Poetry for Children

Children are more interested in the "idea" of a poem than in knowing about the various forms of poetry. However, teachers will want to expose children to various forms of poetry and note their reactions. Do these children like only narrative poems? Do they think all poetry must rhyme, or will they listen to some free verse? Are they ready for the seemingly simple, yet highly complex form of haiku? Understanding of and appreciation for a wide variety of poetry grow gradually as children are exposed to different forms and types.

BALLADS

Ballads are narrative poems that have been adapted for singing or that give the effect of a song. Originally, they were not made or sung for children but were the literature of all the people. Characteristics of the ballad form are the frequent use of dialogue in telling the story, repetition, marked rhythm and rhyme, and refrains that go back to the days when ballads were sung. Popular ballads have no known authors, as they were handed down from one generation to the next; the literary ballad, however, does have a known author. Ballads usually deal with heroic deeds and include stories of murder, unrequited love, feuds, and tragedies.

[6]Myra Cohn Livingston, "What the Heart Knows Today" in Nancy Larrick, ed., *Somebody Turned On a Tap in These Kids* (New York: Delacorte Press, 1971), p. 12.

Children in the middle grades enjoy the amusing story of the stubborn man and his equally stubborn wife in "Get Up and Bar the Door" (26) As in many ballads, the ending is abrupt, and the reader never does find out what happened to the two sinister guests, other than that the good husband finally locked them all in the house together! "The Outlandish Knight" (248) and "Robin Hood and the Widow's Sons" (248) will appeal to youngsters' sense of poetic justice; while true love reigns in "The Bailiff's Daughter of Islington" (248), "Robin Hood and Allan-a-Dale" (248), and "Lochinvar" (204). All these ballads would enrich a study of the middle ages, when ballads were most popular.

Ballads from the United States include the well-known story of the dying cowboy in "The Streets of Laredo" (240). Brinton Turkle has illustrated a picture-book edition of Stephen Vincent Benét's literary ballad, *The Ballad of William Sycamore* (1790–1871). Unlike the dying cowboy, William Sycamore was a frontiersman who was killed by an unbroken colt, but he died content:

. . .

Now I lie in the heart of the fat, black soil,
Like the seed of a prairie-thistle;
It has washed my bones with honey and oil
And picked them clean as a whistle.

And my youth returns, like the rains of Spring,
And my sons, like the wild-geese flying;
And I lie and hear the meadow-lark sing
And have much content in my dying.

Go play with the town you have built of blocks,
The towns where you would have bound me!
I sleep in the earth like a tired fox.
And my buffalo have found me.

Stephen Vincent Benét (20)

Other literary ballads that are appropriate for use with children include "A Legend of the Northland" (248) by Phoebe Cary and "Beth Gêlert" (248) by William Spencer. The first ballad tells of the origin of a redheaded woodpecker from a selfish old woman; while the latter ballad is the appealing story of a faithful dog. Older children will enjoy the poignant tale of "The Ballad of the Harp-Weaver" (240) by Edna St. Vincent Millay.

NARRATIVE POEMS

The narrative poem relates a particular event or episode or tells a long tale. It may be a lyric, a sonnet, or written in free verse; its one requirement is that it *must* tell a story. Many of children's favorite poems are these so-called story poems. One classic that has been enjoyed for years is Browning's "The Pied Piper of Hamelin" (35). This poem has been richly illustrated in a single tale by Donna Diamond, presenting a striking contrast to the traditional pictures of the Pied Piper done by Kate Greenaway (36) in 1899 and still available from her original publishing house, Warne.

Another well-loved narrative poem is "A Visit from St. Nicholas" (64) by Clement Moore, known to children as "'Twas the Night Before Christmas." Moore created the prototype for the North American Santa Claus in this poem that was first published in 1823. Both Tasha Tudor (192) and Tomie de Paola (191) have created lovely old-fashioned picture-book editions of *The Night Before Christmas*. Still another traditional favorite that has been made into a single picture book illustrated by Diane Stanley is James Whitcomb Riley's humorous story, *Little Orphant Annie* (221). Other traditional favorites include Laura E. Richards' ironic tale "The Monkeys and the Crocodile" (10), Eugene Field's "The Duel" (64), and the swashbuckling "Pirate Don Durk of Dowdee" (56).

One of the favorite narrative poems of young children is the simple story of the parents who lovingly pretend to look for their child in the poem "Hiding" (9) by Dorothy Aldis. The triumphant ending of "The Little Turtle" (46) who caught a mosquito, a flea, and a minnow, "But he didn't catch me," always delights younger children. A. A. Milne's poems of a lost mouse, "Missing" (188), and the disappearing beetle, "Forgiven" (188), are also favorites with this age group.

Six-, 7-, and 8-year-olds delight in Milne's "The King's Breakfast" (188) and "King John's Christmas" (188), those petulant kings, one of whom wants a "bit of butter" for his bread and the other one, a big red India-rubber ball.

Another favorite story-poem for this age group is Karla Kuskin's ridiculous tale of "Hughbert and the Glue" (128). The long narrative story of "Custard the Dragon" by Ogden Nash has been humorously illustrated by Quentin Blake in the book *Custard & Company*. John Ciardi's story of the disastrous day "Mummy Slept Late and Daddy Fixed Breakfast" (136) continues to be a favorite among children, even though it perpetuates the stereotype of the mother as the only one capable of making waffles and the father as somewhat of a dolt in the kitchen.

Without a doubt the all-time favorite narrative poems of children today are the outrageously funny ones in Shel Silverstein's *Where the Sidewalk Ends* and *The Light in the Attic*. Some of their favorite story verses include "Sick" (235), in which Peggy Ann McKay claims to have every known symptom of dreadful diseases until she realizes it is Saturday; the sad tale of "Sarah Cynthia Sylvia Stout Who Would Not Take the Garbage Out" (235), and the man who is slowly being swallowed alive by a boa constrictor.

BOA CONSTRICTOR

Oh, I'm being eaten
By a boa constrictor,
A boa constrictor,
A boa constrictor,
I'm being eaten by a boa constrictor,
And I don't like it—one bit.
Well, what do you know?
It's nibblin' my toe.
Oh, gee,
It's up to my knee.
Oh my,
It's up to my thigh.
Oh, fiddle,
It's up to my middle.
Oh, heck,
It's up to my neck.
Oh, dread,
It's upmmmmmmmmmmfffffffffff...

Shel Silverstein (235)

Children also enjoy the story verse of Jack Prelutsky, particularly the collection of poems about the bully Harvey and the children's ultimate revenge on him in *Rolling Harvey Down the Hill*. Middle-graders delight in Prelutsky's macabre tales in *Nightmares* and *The Headless Horseman Rides*

After the death of *The Highwayman*, Charles Keeping uses negative ghostlike images in his powerful pictures. Poem by Alfred Noyes.

Tonight, both enriched with Arnold Lobel's grisly black and white illustrations.

Not all narrative poems for children are humorous. Older children, for example, respond to the pathos of "Nancy Hanks" (46). They are stirred by the galloping hoofbeats in Longfellow's *Paul Revere's Ride* (168). One of their favorite romantic tales is the dramatic *The Highwayman* by Alfred Noyes, which has been illustrated in two stunning picture-book editions, one by Charles Mikolaycak (200) and one by Charles Keeping (199). After the death of the highwayman and his black-eyed Bess, Keeping reverses his striking pictures from black on white to a ghostly white on black. This is a dramatic edition which pictures the tragedy and darkness of this tale of love, suicide, and haunting.

One of the best ways to capture children's interest in poetry is to present a variety of narrative poems. Teachers will want to build a file of story poems appropriate to the interests of children in their classes and use them to introduce poetry to children.

LYRICAL

Most of the poetry written for children is lyrical. The term is derived from the word "lyric," and means poetry that sings its way into the minds and memories of its listeners. It is usually personal or descriptive poetry, with no prescribed length or structure other than its melody.

Much of William Blake's poetry is lyrical, beginning with the opening lines of his introductory poem to *Songs of Innocence:* "Piping down the valleys wild / Piping songs of pleasant glee" (136). Stevenson's poems have a singing quality that makes them unforgettable. Everyone knows the poem "The Swing" and "The Wind" (136) and the mysterious "Windy Nights" (240). In Stevenson's poem "Where Go the Boats?" the tempo of the words reminds one of the increasing swiftness of the flow of the river toward the sea:

> Dark brown is the river,
> Golden is the sand.
> It flows along forever,
> With trees on either hand.
>
> Green leaves a-floating,
> Castles of the foam,

> Boats of mine a-boating—
> Where will all come home?
>
> On goes the river
> And out past the mill,
> Away down the valley,
> Away down the hill.
>
> Away down the river,
> A hundred miles or more,
> Other little children
> Shall bring my boats ashore.
>
> Robert Louis Stevenson (239)

Older children enjoy the lyrical beat of Masefield's "Sea-Fever" (10) or Allan Cunningham's "A Wet Sheet and a Flowing Sea" (26). The singing, soaring flight of a "Kite" (16) is described by Harry Behn, as is its sudden fall into a tree. Both boys and girls respond to the strong beat and internal rhyme of "The Lone Dog" that will have no master but himself. The first verse provides an example of its rhythm:

> THE LONE DOG
> I'm a lean dog, a keen dog, a wild dog, and
> lone;
> I'm a rough dog, a tough dog, hunting on my
> own;
> I'm a bad dog, a mad dog, teasing silly sheep;
> I love to sit and bay the moon, to keep fat souls
> from sleep.
>
> Irene Rutherford McLeod (101)

Lyrical poetry is characterized by this singingness of words that gives children an exhilarating sense of melody.

LIMERICK

A nonsense form of verse that is particularly enjoyed by children is the limerick. This is a five-line verse with the first and second line rhyming, the third and fourth agreeing, and the fifth line usually ending in a surprise or humorous statement. Freak spelling, oddities, and humorous twists characterize this form of poetry. David McCord in his book *Take Sky* suggests that "a limerick, to be lively and successful, *must* have *perfect* riming and *flawless* rhythm." He gives several suggestions of how to write a limerick using the limerick form itself.

> The limerick's lively to write:
> Five lines to it—all nice and tight.
> Two long ones, two trick
> Little short ones; then quick
> As a flash here's the last one in sight.
>
> David McCord (172)

Modern writers continue to produce limericks, as we have seen. William Jay Smith (236) uses this form regularly; Myra Cohn Livingston has written an amusing book of her own limericks titled *A Lollygag of Limericks*, illustrated by Joseph Low. Arnold Lobel wrote and illustrated a most delightful book of limericks about pigs. Appropriately titled *The Book of Pigericks*, it contains this "tongue-in-cheek" account of one very large pig:

> There was a stout pig from Oak Ridge
> Who stepped heavily onto a bridge
> When she heard a loud CREAK,
> She cried, "Gad, but it's weak!"
> So she tiptoed the length of that bridge.
>
> Arnold Lobel (165)

It is difficult to imagine Lobel's limericks without his amusing illustrations. From *The Book of Pigericks.*

His illustrations of humanized pigs are as funny as the limericks.

Children in the middle grades enjoy writing limericks, whether based on nursery rhymes, pigs, or their own names. It is certainly a far easier form for them to write than the highly abstract form of the haiku.

FREE VERSE

Free verse does not have to rhyme but depends on rhythm or cadence for its poetic form. It may use some rhyme, alliteration, and pattern. It frequently looks different on a printed page, but it sounds very much like other poetry when read aloud. Children who have the opportunity to hear this form of poetry will be freed from thinking that all poetry must rhyme. The teacher may read them some of the descriptive and arresting poems written by Hilda Conkling when she was a child. Boys and girls enjoy listening to the way this young child describes a "Mouse" (10) in his "gray velvet dress" or "Little Snail" (240), whose house doubles as an umbrella in the rain. Many of Valerie Worth's deceptively simple *Small Poems* are written in free verse. For example, her fine metaphorical description of "chairs" makes them come alive.

> Chairs
> Seem
> To
> Sit
> Down
> On
> Themselves, almost as if
> They were people,
> Some fat, some thin
> Settled comfortably
> On their own seats,
> Some even stretch out their arms
> To
> Rest.
>
> Valerie Worth (257)

While much of Eve Merriam's poetry rhymes, she has also written free verse. Her well-known poem "How to Eat a Poem" (183) is written in free verse. Langston Hughes' melodic "April Rain Song" (117) is another example of the effective use of free verse. Probably one of the best-known poems of our day is "Fog" (109) by Carl Sandburg. This metaphorical description of the fog characterized as a cat is written in free verse.

HAIKU

Haiku is an ancient Japanese verse form that can be traced back to the thirteenth century. There are only seventeen syllables in the haiku; the first and third lines contain five syllables, the second line seven. Almost every haiku may be divided into two parts; first, a simple picture-making description that usually includes some reference, direct or indirect, to the season; and second, a statement of mood or feeling. A relationship between these two parts is implied, either a similarity or a telling difference.

The greatest of haiku writers, and the one who crystallized the form, was Basho. In his lifetime Basho produced more than 800 haiku. He considered the following poem to be one of his best:

> An old silent pond . . .
> A frog jumps into the pond,
>   splash! Silence again.
>
> Basho (17)

The silence reverberates against the sudden noise of the splash, intensified by the interruption. Richard Lewis collected the haiku for *In a Spring Garden*, a book that Ezra Jack Keats illustrated with stunning pictures featuring silhouettes projected against a background of marbelized paper. Older students in middle school would enjoy attempting this form of poetry and using the same media employed by Keats. However, the meaning of haiku is not expected to be immediately apparent. The reader is invited to add his or her own

How lovely,
Through the torn paper window
The Milky Way.

—*Issa*

The nightingales sing
In the echo of the bell
Tolled at evening.

—*Ukō*

Ezra Jack Keats creates dramatic effects with marblized paper collage. This was one of the first books of haiku to break with traditional Oriental design. From *In a Spring Garden* edited by Richard Lewis.

associations and meanings to the words, thus completing the poem in the mind. Each time the poem is read, new understandings will be developed. Harry Behn has written a haiku to explain the deeper meanings of this form of poetry:

A spark in the sun,
this tiny flower has roots
deep in the cool earth.

Harry Behn (17)

Haiku is deceiving in that the form appears simple, yet, it requires much from its reader. Unless children have reached the Piagetian level of formal operations in their thinking, haiku may be too abstract a form of poetry for them to fully understand. The common practice of asking young children to write haiku suggests that teachers do not understand its complexity. In this case, short is not simple!

CONCRETE POETRY

Many poets today are writing picture poems that make you see what they are saying. The message of the poem is presented not only in the words (sometimes just letters or punctuation marks) but in the arrangement of the words. Meaning is reinforced, or even carried, by the shape of the poem. We have seen how Lillian Morrison formed her poem about "The Sidewalk Racer" into the shape of a skateboard (page 405) and how "Fueled" by Marcie Hans was written to resemble half of a tree (page 404). Robert Froman has created picture poems about pollution, traffic, loneliness, skyscrapers, fire hydrants, and a garbage truck for his book *Street Poems*. One that will please children particularly pictures a candy bar in words (see bottom of this page).

Froman has continued his innovative way of *Seeing Things* in a book by that title. An excellent source of concrete poetry is A. Barbara Pilon's book, *Concrete Is Not Always Hard*. Younger children will enjoy "Lick Smack" and "Ice Cream," while middle-graders will be amused by "Apfel" by Dohl and "Showers, Clearing Later in the Day" by Merriam, which is made entirely with exclamation points and asterisks.

Once children have been exposed to concrete poetry, they invariably want to try writing some of their own, and that is fine. However, some children become so involved in the picture-making process that they forget that the meaning of the poem is carried by both words and arrangement. If emphasis is placed on the meaning first, then the shaping of the words will grow naturally from the idea of the poem. In the words of Pilon, "Concrete is not always hard"; frequently it is simply fun!

WELL, YES
Candy bar————

Too much.

Too much.

But I'll have one more.

Robert Froman (87)

SELECTING POETRY FOR CHILDREN

Children's Poetry Preferences

Children's interest in poetry has been the subject of many research studies starting in the early 1920s. The interesting fact about all these studies is the similarity of their findings and the stability of children's poetry preferences over the years. Before conducting her own research on children's response to poetry, Ann Terry[7] summarized the findings of these earlier studies:

1. Children are the best judges of their preferences.
2. Reading texts and courses of study often do not include the children's favorite poems.
3. Children's poetry choices are influenced by (1) the poetry form, (2) certain poetic elements, and (3) the content, with humor and familiar experience being particularly popular.
4. A poem enjoyed at one grade level may be enjoyed across several grade levels.
5. Children do not enjoy poems they do not understand.
6. Thoughtful, meditative poems are disliked by children.
7. Some poems appeal to one sex more than another; girls enjoy poetry more than boys.
8. New poems are preferred over older, more traditional ones.
9. Literary merit is not necessarily an indication that a poem will be liked.

In her national survey of children's poetry preferences in fourth, fifth, and sixth grade, Terry[8] found much consistency with the results of these earlier studies. Narrative poems, such as Ciardi's "Mummy Slept Late and Daddy Fixed Breakfast" (42), and limericks, including both modern and traditional, were the favorite forms of poetry for children. Haiku was consistently disliked by all grade levels. Elements of rhyme, rhythm, and sound increased children's enjoyment of the poems, as evidenced by their preference for David McCord's "The Pickety Fence" (176) and "Lone Dog" (176). Poems that contained much figurative language or imagery were disliked. Children's favorite poems at all three grade levels contained humor or were about familiar experiences or animals. All children preferred contemporary poems containing modern content and today's language more than the older, more traditional poems.

Carol Fisher and Margaret Natarella[9] surveyed the poetry preferences of first-, second-, and third-graders, using the same schools and techniques as the Terry study. Again, they found children in these grades also preferring narrative poetry and limericks, followed by rhymed verse, free verse and lyric poetry, with haiku ranking last. Both studies found children liked poems that were funny and poems about animals and familiar experiences. The younger children enjoyed poems about strange and fantastic events, such as "The Lurpp Is on the Loose" (216) by Prelutsky and Nash's "Adventures of Isabel" (214), while the older children opted for more realistic content. Younger children appeared to like more traditional poems than the older children did. However, they insisted that poetry must rhyme, and all of the traditional poems did. Thus they could have been selecting on the basis of rhyme rather than content. Again a consistent finding of this study was that adults cannot accurately predict which poems children will like.

How then can one most effectively select poetry for children? Certainly a teacher will want to consider children's needs and interests, their previous experience with poetry, and the types of poetry that appeal to them. A sound principle to follow is to begin where the children are. Using some of the findings from the research mentioned above, teachers can share poems that have elements of rhyme, rhythm, and sound, such as "Galoshes" (46) or "The Pickety Fence" (170). Teachers can read many narrative verses and limericks and look for humorous poems and poems about familiar experiences and animals. Finally, teachers should share only those poems that they really like themselves; enthusiasm for poetry is contagious. Teachers will not want to limit their sharing only to poems that they know children will like. For taste needs to be

[7]Ann Terry, *Children's Poetry Preferences: A National Survey of the Upper Elementary Grades* (Urbana, Ill.: National Council of Teachers of English, 1974, 1984), p. 10.

[8]Ann Terry, *Children's Poetry Preferences.*

[9]Carol J. Fisher and Margaret A. Natarella, "Young Children's Preferences in Poetry: A National Survey of First, Second and Third Graders," *Research in the Teaching of English,* vol. 16 (December 1982), pp. 339–353.

developed, too; children should go beyond their delight in humorous and narrative poetry to develop an appreciation for variety in both form and content. We want children to respond to more poetry and to find more to respond to in poetry.

It may well be that the consistency in children's poetry preferences over the years simply reflects the poverty of their experience with poetry. We tend to like the familiar. If teachers only read traditional narrative poems to children, then these children will like narrative poems. Or having had little or no exposure to fine imaginative poetry, children may not have gone beyond their natural intuitive liking for jump-rope rhymes or humorous limericks. In brief, the results of the studies of children's interests in poetry may be more of an indictment of the quality of their literature program than of the quality of their preferences. We need to ascertain children's poetry preferences *after* they have experienced a rich, continuous exposure to poetry throughout the elementary school. It is hoped that as children have increased experience with a wide range of quality poetry by various poets, they will grow in appreciation and understanding of the finer poems.

Poets and Their Books

Recent years have seen an increase in the number of writers of verse for children and the number of poetry books published for the juvenile market. Poetry itself has changed, becoming less formal, more spontaneous and imitative of the child's own language patterns. The range of subject matter has expanded with the tremendous variation in children's interests. It is difficult to categorize the work of a poet on the basis of the content of his or her poems, for many poets interpret various areas of children's experience. However, an understanding of the general subject matter of the works of each poet will help the teacher select poems and make recommendations to children.

HUMOROUS VERSE

In every preference study that has been done, children prefer narrative rhyme and humorous verse. Today the popularity of the verse of Shel Silverstein and Jack Prelutsky attests to this. The use of imaginative symbols and vivid imagery and metaphor mark the difference between real poetry and verse. The versifiers provide instant gratification but leave the reader with little to ponder about. However, since children begin here in their enjoyment of poetry, it seems appropriate to start this section with writers of humorous verse.

Almost all poets have written some humorous verse, but only a few have become noted primarily for this form. In the nineteenth century the names of Edward Lear and Lewis Carroll became almost synonymous with humorous nonsense poems. Although Lear did not create the limerick, he was certainly master of the form, as we have seen (see Chapter 3). His narative verse includes the well-known "The Owl and the Pussycat" (214), "The Jumblies" (140), "The Quangle-Wangle's Hat" (56), and "The Duck and the Kangaroo" (140). His limericks, alphabet rhymes, and narrative poems have been compiled into one book, *The Complete Nonsense Book* (140). Each absurd verse is illustrated by the poet's grotesque drawings, which add greatly to Lear's humor. Myra Cohn Livingston, in her book *How Pleasant to Know Mr. Lear,* has provided a new arrangement of Lear's poems that reflect biographical details of his life. For example, in Lear's self-portrait he described himself as having an "elephantine nose." Livingston then put together his many limericks and poems that showed his preoccupation with noses and explained this in her introduction to the chapter. This new structure does give us a fresh look at Lear's work.

Several of our modern poets are following in the tradition of Lear. William Jay Smith included limericks, rhyming ABC's, and imaginary dialogue in much of his nonsense verse. The best of his poetry has been reissued in a new *Laughing Time* illustrated with amusing pictures by Fernando Krahn. His poems "Elephant," "Rhinoceros," and the "Coati-Mundi" are much fun and would add to a unit on zoo animals. The two books by the Danish-American poet N. M. Bodecker, *Hurry, Hurry, Mary Dear!* and *Let's Marry Said the Cherry,* are filled with happy nonsense and tongue-twisting word play. Bodecker's poetry and clever line drawings reflect a variety of moods from the ridiculous advice of the grandfather who told everyone to hold on to his hat when losing one's head to the joyous welcome to Spring included in "Good-by My Winter Suit" (27). His delightful play on words is seen in his series of "if" verses for

"If I Were an Elephant" (28). Children would enjoy making their own "if rhymes" after hearing this nonsense verse. Bodecker has also written a book of limericks with the title *A Person from Britain and Other Limericks*. In *Pigeon Cubes* his poetry is more satirical and adult.

The sophisticated light verse and limericks of Ogden Nash appeal to both adults and children. They delight in "The Panther," "The Centipede," and "The Eel." Young children enjoy his longer narrative poems, including "The Adventures of Isabel," who eats a bear, and the sad demise of "The Boy Who Laughed at Santa Claus." These poems appear in *The Moon Is Shining Bright as Day*. Quentin Blake illustrated a new edition of Nash's poems under the title of *Custard & Company*. It includes the long narrative verse about the cowardly dragon and some eighty-four other poems.

Quentin Blake is also the illustrator for the very British verse of humorist Michael Rosen. His narrative poems are witty, frequently featuring funny situations that occur within family relations. Children love the two brothers' verbal argument about cleaning the "fluff" out from under the bed or the race to get undressed so you don't have to be the last one and have to turn off the light. Both of these poems appear in *You Can't Catch Me*. Other books of his include *Mind Your Own Business, Wouldn't You Like to Know*, and *Quick, Let's Get Out of Here*.

John Ciardi's poetry for children also is often based on humorous family situations. His book *You Know Who* is filled with sly descriptions of different "someones" and their behaviors. *The Monster Den*, the book about his own children, has more appeal for parents than children. Many of Ciardi's poems are enjoyed by boys and girls with enough sophistication to appreciate their tongue-in-cheek humor. One fourth grade's favorite was about the disastrous custard made by "Some Cook" (39), while all children enjoy "Mummy Slept Late and Daddy Fixed Breakfast" (136). *Doodle Soup* is a delicious bowl of nonsense, cautionary tales, and other humorous poetry. Children would enjoy taking parts to read the amusing tale of "All I Did Was to Ask My Sister." Frequently, children feel like the poem "The Best Part of Going Away Is Going Away From You," while they would agree with his advice in "A Lesson in Manners" in which he tells them never to be bad before being fed. Humorous poetry characterizes his other books, which include *I Met a Man; The Man Who Sang the Sillies;* and *You Read to Me, I'll Read to You*. Sophisticated Victorian-type illustrations by Edward Gorey complement Ciardi's spoof on parent-child relations today.

X. J. Kennedy has a wonderfully weird sense of humor. His poems in *The Phantom Ice Cream Man* and *One Winter Night In August* are almost all nonsense jingles. Many like "Mother's Nerves," "Father and Mother," and "A Social Mixer" are grisly indeed and appeal to children's primitive humor. Two poems, "The Up-to-Date Giant" and "Terrible Troll's Tollbridge," in *One Winter Night* would enrich a folktale unit. And children would love to draw their version of some of Kennedy's imaginary creatures like the "The Muddheaded Messer," the bird that lives in dresser drawers and delights in messing them up. David McPhail, who illustrated both these books with wacky drawings, wisely did not illustrate this poem. In *The Forgetful Wishing Well*, Kennedy writes more serious poetry that is true to the experience of children growing up. He does include some very funny portraits of people like "Agnes Snaggletooth" and "Wilberforce Fong."

Dennis Lee, a Canadian humorist, writes rollicking nonsense that children love. His best-known poem is "Alligator Pie," found in a collection by the same name. *Garbage Delight* contains poems with strong rhythm and a kind of grisly humor. Children love "The Last Cry of the Damp Fly," the long narrative "Inspector Dogbone Gets His Man" (who turns out to be Dogbone himself), and the title poem "Garbage Delight." Lee is quoted as saying that he writes as a "35-year-old children."[10] One of the many children inside of him came up with the verse "I Eat Kids Yum Yum!" Lee's *Jelly Belly* is his delightful collection of original nursery rhymes, finger plays, and counting-out rhymes (see Chapter 4).

Much of what children consider funny is frequently sadistic and ghoulish. Jack Prelutsky's macabre poems in *Nightmares* and *The Headless Horseman Rides Tonight* and Lobel's black and

[10]Dennis Lee, "Roots and Play: Writing as a 35-year-old Children," *Canadian Children's Literature*, no. 4 (1976), pp. 25–58.

white illustrations are splendidly terrifying. One seventh-grade teacher of children in the inner city maintained that these books got her through her first year of teaching! Prelutsky is also a master at creating such zany imaginary creatures as "The Wozzit" who is hiding in the closet, "The Grobbles" who quietly wait to gobble someone up, and "The Lurpp Is on the Loose." These all appear along with *The Snopp on the Sidewalk* in a book by that name. He creates softer more lovable creatures in *The Baby Uggs Are Hatching,* including "The Sneezysnoozer," "The Dreary Dreeze," and "The Sneepies":

The Sneepies, lying in a heap,
are almost always fast asleep.
Deep inside my dresser drawer
they sleep and sleep, but do not snore.

The Sneepies, lying in a pile,
are still and silent all the while.
They stay beside my underwear . . .
I wonder why they like it there.

Jack Prelutsky (206)

Prelutsky has written some light-hearted realistic verse for younger children about special holidays and seasons. These include some useful poems in *It's Halloween* and *It's Thanksgiving* and some very amusing ones in *Rainy Rainy Saturday, It's Snowing! It's Snowing,* and *What I Did Last Summer.* All ages will enjoy Prelutsky's large collection of more than 100 new poems titled *The New Kid on the Block,* which includes humorous realistic poems such as "I'm Disgusted with My Brother" or "My Sister Is a Sissy," plus many funny characters and more zany creatures. James Stevenson's cartoonlike illustrations add to the fun of these verses, which frequently appeal to the young child's somewhat primitive sense of humor.

Shel Silverstein's *Where the Sidewalk Ends* was on the *New York Times* best-seller list for many months. It is the one poetry book that all teachers, children, and parents seem to know. Librarians complain that they can't keep the book on the shelf, no matter how many copies they have. Here you meet a boy who turns into a TV set, a king who eats only a "Peanut-Butter Sandwich," and those three characters "Ickle Me, Pickle Me, Tickle Me Too." Much of the humor of these poems is

James Stevenson's cartoon drawing for the cover of *The New Kid on the Block* reflects the child appeal of Jack Prelutsky's humorous verse.

based on the sounds of words, the preposterous characters, and amusing situations. While some verses are slightly unsavory, others surprise you with their sensitivity, such as "Invitation," "Listen to the Mustn'ts," and the title poem, "Where the Sidewalk Ends." *The Light in the Attic* is more of the same and equally popular.

Poetry is neglected in our schools today, but there is no dearth of humorous verse. Children take to it as they do to a Big Mac, fries, and a shake. And like a McDonalds meal it is enjoyable but not memorable–certainly not nutritious enough for a steady diet.

INTERPRETERS OF THE WORLD OF CHILDHOOD

Robert Louis Stevenson was the first poet to write of childhood from the child's point of view. *A Child's Garden of Verses,* published in 1885, continues in popularity today. Stevenson was himself a frail child and spent much of his early life in bed or confined indoors. His poetry reflects a solitary childhood, but a happy one. In "Land of Counterpane" and "Block City," he portrays a resourceful, inventive child who can create his own amusement. He found playmates in his shadow, in his dreams, and in his storybooks. The rhythm of Stevenson's "The Swing," "Where Go the Boats," and "Windy Nights" appeals to children today as much as to the children of a century ago. Currently, some ten illustrated editions of *A Child's Garden of Verses* are in print. They range in interpretation from Tasha Tudor's (238) quaint pastel pictures that portray Stevenson as a young child to Brian Wildsmith's (239) edition that is a brilliant kaleidoscope of color.

Perhaps the best-loved of British children's poets is A. A. Milne. Some of his poems show perceptive insight into the child's mind, such as "Halfway Down" and "Solitude." "Happiness" captures a child's joy in such delights as new waterproof boots, a raincoat, and hat. Told in the first person, "Hoppity" reveals a young child's enjoyment of the state of perpetual motion! The majority of Milne's poems are delightfully funny. The poetry from both of Milne's poetry books has now been collected into one volume titled *The World of Christopher Robin*. Illustrations by Ernest Shepard seem to belong with Milne's poetry as much as Pooh belongs with Christopher Robin; it is hard to imagine one without the other.

Another well-loved British poet for children is Eleanor Farjeon. Her knowledge and understanding of children's thoughts and behavior are reflected in her books, *Eleanor Farjeon's Poems for Children* and *The Children's Bells*. The simple poem "New Clothes and Old" (63) tells of a child's preference for old things. "Over the Garden Wall" (63) is a hauntingly beautiful poem that makes the reader feel as lonely as the child who is left out of the ball game on the other side of the wall. This poet also wrote the lovely nature poem "The Night Will Never Stay" (63) and the graphic description of "Mrs. Peck-Pigeon" (63) (page 397).

Before her death in 1965 Eleanor Farjeon had received notable recognition for her poetry and prose. She was the first recipient of the international Hans Christian Andersen Medal in 1956; and in 1959 she received the Regina Medal for her life's work. A prestigious British award "for distinguished services to children's books" that bears the name of this well-known poet and writer is given annually. No other poet who has written exclusively for children has received such recognition.

Dorothy Aldis was one of the first American poets to celebrate children's feelings and everyday experiences with simple childlike verses. With rhyme and sing-song meter, she captures the child's delight in the ordinary routines of home life, as in "After My Bath" (9), "Going to Sleep" (9) and even brushing the teeth:

SEE I CAN DO IT
See, I can do it all myself
With my own little brush!
The tooth paste foams inside my mouth.
The faucet waters rush.

In and out and underneath
And round and round and round:
First I do my upstairs teeth
And then I do my down—

The part I like the best of it
Is at the end, though, when, I spit.

Dorothy Aldis (9)

Aldis is particularly sensitive to the emotions of childhood in "Bad," "Alone," and "No One Heard Him Call." Family relationships are lovingly portrayed in "Little," "My Brother," and "Hiding." Poems from the first four books by Dorothy Aldis were collected in a single volume entitled *All Together*, which can still be found in most library collections.

Primary-grade children also enjoy Rachel Field's poems. The book simply titled *Poems* includes her first book of poetry, *The Pointed People*, and also *Taxis and Toadstools*. Many of these poems are written from the city child's point of view, including "Skyscrapers," "Taxis," "City Rain," and "Snow in the City." However, Rachel Field spent four months of every year on an island off the coast of Maine, hence the "toadstools" in one book's title. Field immortalized the experience of sleeping on an island in her poem: "If Once You Have Slept on an Island." Other favorite country poems are "Roads," with its surprise ending, and "General Store," with its "tinkly bell" and "drawers all spilly." The warning conveyed in "Something Told the Wild Geese" may have provided the signal for Field to return to the city and her "Taxis."

James Tippett wrote poems about the city and traveling in his books *I Go A-Traveling, I Spend the Summer,* and *I Live in the City.* His images are clear and childlike, whether he is describing a "cricket" or the "underground rumbling" of the subway. His poem "Sh" deals with one of the problems of a boisterous child who lives in an apartment. "Ferry-Boats" evokes the constant shuffling to and fro of the boats, while the increasing speed of engines is reflected in the tempo of "The Trains." A new collection of his best-loved poems is titled *Crickety Cricket!* Mary Chalmers' little detailed pencil sketches seem just right for these poems for the young child.

Mary Ann Hoberman writes lively rhythmical verse for young children. The poems in the collection *Yellow Butter Purple Jelly Red Jam Black Bread* range from such delightful nonsense as "The Llama Who Had No Pajama" to the swinging rhythm of "Hello and Goodbye" (see page 397). "Brother," which is a favorite with children, utilizes a theme common to homes and described in picture books: "sibling rivalry."

BROTHER

I had a little brother
And I brought him to my mother
And I said I want another
Little brother for a change.

But she said don't be a bother
So I took him to my father
And I said this little bother
Of a brother's very strange.

But he said one little brother
Is exactly like another
And every little brother
Misbehaves a bit he said.

So I took the little brother
From my mother and my father
And I put the little bother
Of a brother back to bed.

Mary Ann Hoberman (97)

Primary children also enjoy the long sustained poems in Hoberman's picture book *A House Is a*

House for Me. In this book she plays with the concept of houses, including regular houses and animals' houses, and then looks at other possibilities, such as a glove becoming a house for a hand and a pocket as a house for pennies. Once children hear these poems, they like to make up their own "house" poems. All of Hoberman's poetry can be distinguished by its fast-paced rhymes and marked rhythms.

Another joyous book is *Honey, I Love* by Eloise Greenfield, who has a great capacity for speaking in the voice of a young black child. This little book of sixteen poems includes a chant, a jump-rope rhyme (see page 398), and thoughtful observations on such experiences as dressing up ("I Look Pretty") or thinking about a neighbor who left a nickel as a "Keepsake" before she died. The Dillons' illustrations are as sensitive as these poems which celebrate the rich content of a child's world.

Karla Kuskin also sees with the eyes of a child as she creates her well-known poems. Her childlike verses from *In the Middle of the Trees* and *The Rose on My Cake* are a welcome addition to poetry for younger children. These contain such favorites as "Lewis Had a Trumpet" and "I Woke Up This Morning," which tells of a young child who does nothing right all day. Her book *Any Me I Want to Be* is written from the point of view of the subject. Instead of writing how a cat or the moon or a pair of shoes appear to her, the poet tries to get inside the object and be its voice. Children then enjoy guessing what the verse is about. In *Near the Window Tree* the poet attaches a note to each of her poems explaining what prompted her to write it. This was in response to the number of letters she receives from children asking her where she gets her ideas. Her most popular poems have been reissued in a book titled *Dogs & Dragons Trees & Dreams.* This lively collection includes such narrative poems as "The Bear with the Golden Hair" and many other poems that contain both fun and wisdom. One thoughtful one is:

THE QUESTION

People always say to me
"What do you think you'd like to be
When you grow up?"
And I say "Why,
I think I'd like to be the sky

Or be a plane or train or mouse
Or maybe a haunted house
Or something furry, rough and wild . . .
Or maybe I will stay a child."

Karla Kuskin (128)

Something Sleeping in the Hall is a collection of easy-to-read poems about all kinds of pets. Six- and 7-year-olds would like to write about the pets, big or small, that might be "sleeping in their halls" after reading this delightful book. Karla Kuskin illustrates all her own poetry books with tiny precise pen-and-ink drawings. She designed the artwork for the NCTE Poetry Award and then was the third recipient of that coveted prize.

Long before the black experience became a popular topic, Pulitzer Prize-winner Gwendolyn Brooks wrote poignant poetry about black children living in the inner city. *Bronzeville Boys and Girls* contains some thirty-four poems, each bearing the name, thoughts, and feelings of an individual child. There is "John, Who Is Poor"; "Michael," who is afraid of the storm; and "Otto," who did not get the Christmas presents he had hoped for. But there is some joy—the happiness that "Eunice" feels when her whole family is in the dining room; "Beulah's" quiet thoughts at church; and "Luther and Breck," who have a make-believe dragon fight. Unfortunately, this poet wrote only one volume of poetry for children during her lifetime.

Nikki Giovanni is well known for her adult poetry, but she has also written for children. *Spin a Soft Black Song* has been reissued with new illustrations. "Poem for Rodney" expresses both a child's point of view and an adult's. Rodney is tired of everyone asking him what he is going to do when he grows up; his reply is simply that he'd like to grow up. Rodney's answer is typical of childhood; but projected against adults' knowledge of life in the ghetto, it carries a more pathetic plea.

Arnold Adoff writes strong poems about the inner thoughts and feelings of a girl born of a mixed marriage. His words in *All the Colors of the Race* spatter across the page and make you slow down as you read them in order to emphasize the meaning of each word. His poem "The way I see any hope for later" is one that everyone should read and heed:

THE WAY I SEE ANY HOPE FOR LATER
The way I see any hope for later,
we will have to get

over this color
thing,
and stop looking

at how much brown
or tan there is
in
or on   this
woman
or that   man.
And stop looking

at who is a woman
and
who is a man.

Stop looking.
Start loving.

Arnold Adoff (2)

Adoff has also written *Make a Circle Keep Us In, Outside Inside Poems,* and *I Am the Running Girl,* which describes his daughter's dedication to the sport. *Eats* celebrates food and is filled with poems that delight youngsters. One of them even gives a recipe for "Peanut Butter Batter Bread."

Beginning in the 1920s Langston Hughes was the first to write poems of black protest and pride. It was his voice that asked: "What Happens to a Dream Deferred?" and reminded the world that: "I, too, sing America." Some of his poems are bitter, proud, and militant; others are as soft and sensitive as his lovely tribute "My People." Lee Bennett Hopkins has compiled an anthology of Hughes' poems, including the ones listed, that speak directly to young people of today. The title of this book, *Don't You Turn Back,* is from a line of Hughes' most poignant poem, "Mother to Son." One of the characteristics of childhood is its ability to dream dreams and sustain hopes. But Hughes pictures the emptiness of a world without dreams:

DREAMS
Hold fast to dreams
For if dreams die
Life is a broken-winged bird
That cannot fly.

Hold fast to dreams
For when dreams go
Life is a barren field
Frozen with snow.

Langston Hughes (117)

This collection contains such well-known poems as "The Negro Speaks of Rivers," "April Rain Song," and "I, Too, Sing America." Some of Ann Grifalconi's finest woodcuts illustrate this outstanding book.

The poems by Cynthia Rylant in her book *Waiting to Waltz* capture the essence of growing up in a small town in Appalachia. Her vivid images chronicle the minor crises that make up a childhood: the day a girl's mother runs over "Little Short Legs," the black dog down the road; the time the girl loses the spelling bee; and her dismay at being reprimanded for swearing. The most poignant poem of all describes her mixed feelings when she hears that her long-absent father has died:

FORGOTTEN

Mom came home one day
and said my father had died.
Her eyes all red.
Crying for some stranger.
Couldn't think of anything to do,
so I walked around Beaver
telling the kids
and feeling important.
Nobody else's dad had died.
But then
nobody else's dad had worn
red-striped pajamas
and nobody else's dad had made
stuffed animals talk
and nobody else's dad had gone away
nine years ago.
Nobody else's dad had been so loved
by a four-year-old.
And so forgotten by one
now
thirteen.

Cynthia Rylant (227)

Stephen Gammell's soft pencil drawings are as sensitive as these poems, each picturing a fleeting moment of childhood—until suddenly it is gone.

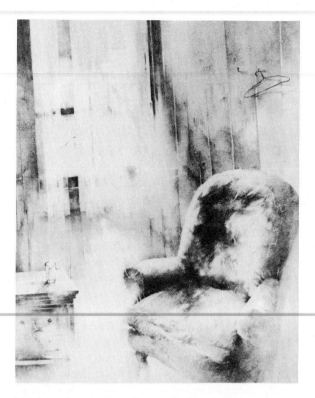

Stephen Gammel's soft pencil drawing of an empty chair captures the poignancy of Cynthia Rylant's poem "Forgotten." From *Waiting to Waltz*.

POETS OF NATURE

Children, like poets, are very attuned to the world around them. They are fascinated by the constant changes in nature and enjoy poems that communicate their delight in the first snow, for example, or their sense of wonder when they touch a pussy willow or hear a foghorn or see a deer.

Aileen Fisher is adept at observing both nature and children. She views the natural world through the eyes of the child, preserving a remarkable sense of wonder. Her poems are filled with sensory imagery, as in this verse:

PUSSY WILLOWS

Close your eyes
and do not peek
and I'll rub Spring,
across your cheek—
smooth as satin,
soft and sleek—

close your eyes
and do not peek.

                              Aileen Fisher (74)

Fisher's comparisons are simple and fresh, very much within the experience of a child. In the poem "Sky Net," she describes a spider as a "fisherman of the sky," while the constant maneuvering of bees from clover to hive is referred to as an "Airlift." Most of her nature poems are in *Cricket in a Thicket; In the Woods, in the Meadow, in the Sky;* and *Feathered Ones and Furry.* While some of these books are out of print, Aileen Fisher created 140 new nature poems for her more recent collection *Out in the Dark & Daylight.* Poems about children's activities are found in the delightful anthology *In One Door and Out the Other,* illustrated by Lillian Hoban. Her longer narrative poems are told in lilting verse and include *Listen, Rabbit; Going Barefoot; Where Does Everyone Go?; Like Nothing at All; I Like Weather;* and *In the Middle of the Night.* Beautifully illustrated by such well-know artists as Adrienne Adams, Symeon Shimin, and Leonard Weisgard, these books are usually presented to children as picture storybooks. Aileen Fisher was the second recipient of the award for Excellence in Poetry for Children given by the National Council of Teachers of English in 1978.

Lilian Moore describes the changing moods and seasons of both the city and the country in her short-lined free verse. Her poems frequently appeal to the senses as she talks about the moaning of foghorns or the "tree-talk" or "wind-swish" of the night. One that children enjoy is:

ENCOUNTER
We both stood
heart-stopping
still,

I in the doorway
the deer
near
the old apple tree,

he
muscle wary
straining
to hear

I holding breath
to say
do not fear.

In the silence
between us
my thought said
stay!

Did it snap
like a twig?
He rose on a curve
and fled.

                              Lilian Moore (194)

A former teacher, reading specialist, and editor who lived in the city, Lilian Moore now lives on a farm in the country. Her poetry reflects these experiences in her knowledge of what children enjoy and her close observations of her surroundings. Many of her poems from her earlier books have been included in a book titled *Something New Begins.* Lilian Moore is also a recipient of the NCTE Poetry Award.

Thanks to Lee Bennett Hopkins, who collected the best of Harry Behn's poems in a book titled *Crickets & Bullfrogs & Whispers of Thunder,* children can read some of Behn's lyrical poems on nature which describe "kind" trees, the "River's Song," and thunder as a grumbling dragon. "The Errand" narrates the kind of quiet peak experience we can all recall from childhood, important to our growing up, unimportant to everyone else. Behn's poem "The Lake," with its upside-down images, would be a fine accompaniment to reading the lovely picture book *Dawn* by Shulevitz.

THE LAKE
Rippling green and gold and brown
On a silver twilight upside down,
Laurels and beeches and pines awake
A ruffle of eddies along the lake.

Fluttering shadows slowly stir
Birch reflections into fir
As something rustles, a fish, or a frog,
Or a muskrat under a hollow log.

Then, nothing moves, no paw or fin,
No drifting feather's slightest din

Disturbs one planet gleaming bright
And motionless in the lake of night.

Harry Behn (16)

The poetry of Elizabeth Coatsworth reflects the moods and perceptions of an astute observer of nature. Her delicate and beautiful verse reveals a deep love of nature and animals. She frequently employs a pattern of comparison in her poems. For example, she contrasts the different kinds of snow storms of "January," those that are quiet and still with those that are blown in by a blustery wind. In "Morning and Afternoon" she describes morning as having nimble feet while the afternoon is drowsy. And in "Song of the Rabbits Outside the Tavern" she contrasts the warm cozy inside with the wild cold outside. Perhaps her best-known poem of contrast is the one that compares the beauty of the swift with that of the slow:

POEM OF PRAISE
Swift things are beautiful:
Swallows and deer,
And lightning that falls
Bright-veined and clear,
Rivers and meteors,
Wind in the wheat,
The strong-withered horse,
The runner's sure feet.

And slow things are beautiful:
The closing of day,
The pause of the wave
That curves downward to spray,
The ember that crumbles,
The opening flower,
And the ox that moves on
In the quiet of power.

Elizabeth Coatsworth (43)

Unfortunately, Coatsworth's books *Poems, Summer Green*, and *The Sparrow Bush* are out of print. However, they are still in many libraries and her work is frequently anthologized.

In contrast to Elizabeth Coatsworth, Ted Hughes, the British poet, writes of the harsher side of nature. Two of his books, *Season Songs* and *Under the North Star*, have been handsomely illustrated with stunning watercolors and drawings by

The poetry of Ted Hughes and the full color paintings of Leonard Baskin capture the essence of the cruelty and beauty of nature in the barren land *Under the North Star.*

the well-known artist Leonard Baskin. Hughes' poetry is strong, pungent, and earthy. He writes in free verse of the wild animals' cruel struggle to survive. His language in "The Snow-Shoe Hare" (118A) provides unforgettable images, such as describing the snowshoe hare as a "left-behind snowflake," "his own sudden blizzard." Children in the middle grades will be challenged by the unique image-making quality of this modern poet.

Carl Sandburg made two collections of his poetry with young people in mind, *Early Moon* and *Wind Song*. Both of these are still available in paperback. In *Wind Song*, the vivid imagery of "Haystacks," "Night," and "River Moons" will help students see through the eyes of a well-known poet. Lee Bennett Hopkins has made a handsome new edition of selected poems of Carl Sandburg titled *Rainbows Are Made*, illustrated with six of Fritz Eichenberg's wood engravings—themselves as powerful as some of Sandburg's poetry. This collection includes selections from *The People, Yes* and poems about nature, people, the seasons, the sea, and the stars. Old favorites such as "Arithmetic," "Phizzog," and "Buffalo Dusk" are here. But children may become newly acquainted with "Doors," "Pencils," and "The Young Sea" as well. This handsome book will introduce them to the thoughtful, quizzical nature of Carl Sandburg's poetry.

Many poems of Robert Frost are both simple enough for a child to understand and complex enough for graduate study. Before his death, Frost selected some of his poems to be read to, or by, young people. Interestingly, the title of this collection, *You Come Too,* was taken from a line of "The Pasture," the first poem in this book and the introductory poem of the very first book of Frost's

Fritz Eichenberg's wood engravings for *Rainbows Are Made*, a new collection of poetry by Carl Sandburg, are as powerful as some of the poems selected by Lee Bennett Hopkins.

ever to be published. Upon initial reading this poem seems no more than a literal invitation to join someone as he cleans the pasture spring. However, the poem takes on more meaning when viewed in the context of its placement; the trip to the pasture to clean the spring may well be an invitation to the enjoyment of poetry itself—"you come too!" Robert Frost seems to have had a preoccupation with clearing muddied waters, and it is significant that his last book for adults was titled *In the Clearing*. By reading *You Come Too*, children can enjoy "The Runaway," "Dust of Snow," "The Last Word of a Bluebird," and "The Pasture" on their level of understanding. Older children will begin to comprehend the deeper meanings in "Mending Wall," "The Road Not Taken," and "The Death of the Hired Man." The poetry of Robert Frost is for all ages.

VERSATILE POETS

It is almost impossible to characterize the wide variety of poems produced by certain poets. David McCord's poetry, for example, ranges in subject matter from poems about everyday experiences to nature poems to verses about verse. He plays with sound in "The Pickety Fence" and "Song of the Train"; with form, including couplets, quatrains, limericks, and triolets, in "Write Me a Verse"; and with words and their meanings in many of his poems, for example "Glowworm," "Ptarmigan," and "Goose, Moose and Spruce." He can write with a lively wit or quietly enter the serious inner world of the child. For example, in "This Is My Rock" he reflects the feelings of all children who have a special place they love.

THIS IS MY ROCK
This is my rock,
And here I run
To steal the secret of the sun;

This is my rock,
And here come I
Before the night has swept the sky;

This is my rock,
This is the place
I meet the evening face to face.

David McCord (171)

Every Time I Climb a Tree and *The Star in the Pail* by McCord were among the first poetry books to be illustrated by a well-known picture-book illustrator, Caldecott award-winning Marc Simont. The title of McCord's first book is *Far and Few, Rhymes of Never Was and Always Is.* All ten of his volumes of poetry are still in print. In 1980, he produced still another book, *Speak Up: More Rhymes of Never Was and Always Is. One at a Time* is a collection of all of his poems (except those in the 1980 book). It is appropriate that this book was published in the same year that David McCord received the first award for Excellence in Poetry for Children given by the National Council of Teachers of English.

Eve Merriam has written a trilogy of books for children about the nature of poetry, including *There Is No Rhyme for Silver, It Doesn't Always Have to Rhyme,* and *Catch a Little Rhyme.* Her poetry has a lilt and bounce that will capture the most disinterested child's attention, beginning with "How to Eat a Poem." Such poems as "Metaphor," "Cliché," "Simile," and "Onomatopoeia" are excellent for the language class. The poems in *Catch a Little Rhyme* are for children in the primary grades. City boys and girls who are accustomed to slum clearance will appreciate "Bam Bam Bam." Humor is found in "Teevee" and "Alligator on the Escalator." In her books *Finding a Poem* and *Out Loud* Merriam continues her interest in playing with language and at the same time shows her interest in social concerns and political satire. Many of these poems show a caustic wit while revealing the commercialism of our times.

Blackberry Ink, on the other hand, is a joyous collection of bouncy rhymes for younger children. A take-off on the well-known finger play is her rhyme of five little monsters making a pudding. She writes of Bella who got soaking wet because she would not use her new umbrella. Children will enjoy the sensory images of the title poem, "Blackberry Ink."

. . .

Look at my teeth,
They're raspberry red.
Look at my fingers,
They're strawberry pink.
Look at my mouth,

It's huckleberry purple,
Look at my tongue,
It's blackberry ink.

Eve Merriam (178)

Jamboree: Rhymes for All Times is a fine paperback collection of some of Eve Merriam's most popular poems. Here you will find "Mean Song," "Teevee," and "A Commercial for Spring." But here too you will find "The Stray Cat," the ugly city cat that its finder names "Beauty." Eve Merriam has also written biographical poems in *Independent Voices* and *I Am a Man: Ode to Martin Luther King, Jr.,* which appeared in picturebook format. Obviously, Eve Merriam is a versatile poet who writes on many subjects, including social protest and how poetry means. She uses rhyme, free verse, and concrete verse. She is probably one of the most anthologized of contemporary poets for children.

Another NCTE Poetry Award winner is Myra Cohn Livingston, a prolific and versatile writer of poetry for all ages of children. She handles a variety of styles and forms masterfully, including rhymes, free verse, limerick, triolet, haiku, concrete poems, and others. Her first books of poetry appealed more to the younger child and included such well-known poems as "Whispers," "The Night," and "Bump on My Knee." Many of these poems for younger children have been gathered together in a small-sized book, *A Song I Sang for You,* illustrated with Margot Tomes' appropriately naive black and white illustrations. In *Worlds I Know,* Livingston echoes the emotions of slightly older children. Here she talks about the aunts and uncles that people a child's world and "The Grandfather I Never Knew." "Secret Door" and "Secret Passageway" would intrigue children.

SECRET DOOR

The upstairs room
has a secret door.
Dad says someone
used it for
some papers many years ago,
and if I want to, I can go
and bring a treasured thing
to hide
and lock it up
all dark inside

and it can be
a place for me
to open
with
its
tiny
key.

Myra Cohn Livingston (164)

Livingston's other books, such as *O Sliver of Liver,* reflect the moods and feelings of older students in the middle grades, although the title poem surely captures the reactions of most children to the thought of liver. "Mad Song" and "Never" (a warning about telling secrets) also have high appeal for the young adolescent. Her love of dogs, nature, and ecological concerns forms constant themes in some of her most vivid poems, as in the poem titled "Only a Little Litter," when she asks the man in the moon how he likes all the litter left by the moon landings.

Increasingly, Livingston is combining her poetry with fine illustrations. Three of her books have been illustrated with striking color paintings by Leonard Everett Fisher. In the first two, *A Circle of Seasons* and *Sky Songs,* the abstract artwork almost overpowers her fine poetry; however, in *Celebrations* both the art and the poems present a moving panorama of sixteen holidays, including Martin Luther King Day, Columbus Day, Presidents' Day, and all birthdays. Not only is Myra Cohn Livingston a versatile poet, but she is also a well-known anthologist and teacher of creative writing to children.

Anthologies of Poems for Children

Today poetry anthologies do not stay in print as long as they used to because time limits are usually placed on permissions to use certain poems. This has meant the publication of fewer large anthologies and the proliferation of many specialized collections containing fewer than twenty poems. For this reason only a selected number of anthologies will be reviewed here, while others will be found on the table on page 427.

COMPREHENSIVE POETRY COLLECTIONS

Every family will want to own at least one excellent anthology of poetry for children, while teach-

---

EVALUATING POETRY ANTHOLOGIES

- What is the age-level appeal of this book?
- How many poems are included?
- What type of poems are included?
- How many poets are represented?
- What is the quality of the poetry?
- Are recent contemporary poems included, as well as old favorites?
- What is the subject matter of the poems?
- How are the poems arranged and organized?
- How adequate are the indexes in helping the reader find a poem?
- How helpful are the introduction and commentaries?
- Has the compiler achieved the stated or implied purpose in making the collection?
- Are the illustrations and format appropriate for the poems and age appeal of the collection?

---

ers will want to have several, including some for their personal use and some for the children. In selecting a general anthology of poetry, the above evaluations need to be considered.

Many parents and teachers will be attracted to the large *The Random House Book of Poetry,* with its 572 poems selected by Jack Prelutsky and profusely illustrated with Arnold Lobel's lively pictures. If children have only known Shel Silverstein's and Prelutsky's humorous verse, this is a good place to begin. Though much of the book is dominated by humorous verse (some thirty-eight poems by Prelutsky himself), fine poems by Robert Frost, Eleanor Farjeon, Emily Dickinson, Dylan Thomas, and others are interspersed with them—a little like putting a bunch of beautiful cold grapes on a plate of fudge: you hope they will be tasted even if they don't go together. Arnold Lobel's humorous full-color illustrations will also draw children to this anthology.

An equally fine collection of poems is Joanna Cole's *A New Treasury of Children's Poetry.* The subtitle "Old Favorites and New Discoveries" describes the more than 200 poems included in this comprehensive collection. Beginning with poems for the very young, Cole wisely includes riddles, jump-rope rhymes, nonsense verse, and some of the poems of Shel Silverstein, N. M. Bodecker, and David McCord. Thus the poems move from the very simple to the more complex, making the collection a wonderful one for a family to own. Brief but thoughtful introductions provide the reader with fine criteria for the selection of poetry. The following is a sample:

ANIMAL FAIR

The poems I like best about animals are the ones that describe something familiar in a new way. For instance, in his poem about a field of chirping crickets, David McCord calls them "ticket-takers" because they sound like so many conductors punching tickets on a train. In the poem "Catalogue" Rosalie Moore says, "Cats sleep fat and walk thin." If you have a cat, you know this is true, but you probably never thought to say it exactly that way.

Sometimes a poem can change the way we see an animal. I never feed white ducks in a pond without thinking they are like toys with "yellow rubber-skinned feet"—the way they are described in Valerie Worth's poem "Duck."[11]

Knock at a Star is subtitled "A Child's Introduction to Poetry." Selected by the well-known adult poet and anthologist X. J. Kennedy and his wife Dorothy, this is a memorable collection of poetry for children 8 years old and up. The poets represented range widely from such adult poets as James Stephens, Emily Dickinson, Robert Frost, and William Stafford to children's poets Aileen Fisher, David McCord, and Lillian Morrison. Many familiar poems are here, but most of them are new and fresh to children's collections. The three section headings in this book also are addressed to children; they provide an understanding of how poetry does what it does: (1) What Do Poems Do? (make you laugh, tell stories, send messages, share feelings, start you wondering); (2) What's Inside a Poem? (images, word music, beats that repeat, likenesses); (3) Special Kinds of Poems. Teachers, librarians, and parents as well as children can learn from this wise book which teaches at the same time that it develops enthusiasm for poetry.

One of the most exciting modern anthologies is

Reflections on a Gift of Watermelon Pickle and Other Modern Verses by Dunning, Lueders, and Smith. Illustrated with superb photographs surrounded by much white space, this anthology appeals to the eye as well as the ear of older students in middle school. They will take delight in "Sonic Boom" by John Updike, "Ancient History" by Arthur Guiterman, "Dreams" by Langston Hughes, and "How to Eat a Poem" by Eve Merriam. They will appreciate the honesty and realistic viewpoint of "Husbands and Wives," in which Miriam Hershenson tells of couples who ride the train from station to station without ever speaking to each other. The sharply cynical "Forecast" by Dan Jaffe suggests that when the end of the world does come, humankind will probably hear about it on the weather report on television. But the poems of despair are balanced in this fine anthology with poems of hope and beauty. Children's eyes need to be opened to the natural beauty around them. Even in the squalor of a tenement there is joy in laughter, the delight of a smile, the warmth of love, and the beauty of neon signs against a summer's black night. Robert Francis' "Summons" can be an invitation to see more clearly, to live more fully; it can be an invitation to poetry itself. It is representative of the quality of poetry found in *Reflections on a Gift of Watermelon Pickle*.

SUMMONS

Keep me from going to sleep too soon
Or if I go to sleep too soon
Come wake me up. Come any hour
Of night. Come whistling up the road.
Stomp on the porch. Bang on the door.
Make me get out of bed and come
And let you in and light a light.
Tell me the northern lights are on
And make me look. Or tell me clouds
Are doing something to the moon
They never did before, and show me.
See that I see. Talk to me till
I'm half as wide awake as you
And start to dress wondering why
I ever went to bed at all.
Tell me the walking is superb.
Not only tell me but persuade me.
You know I'm not too hard persuaded.

Robert Francis (60)

[11]Joanna Cole, *A New Treasury of Children's Poetry* (New York: Doubleday, 1984), p. 61.

COMPREHENSIVE POETRY ANTHOLOGIES

COMPILER	TITLE	AGE LEVEL	DESCRIPTION
Ann McGovern	*Arrow Book of Poetry*	8–12	Reissued by Scholastic, an indispensable paperback to use in the classroom with children. Includes more contemporary poems than traditional. Examples are such favorites as "The Cat Heard the Catbird," "Nancy Hanks," "The Pickety Fence."
Nancy Larrick	*Piping Down the Valleys Wild*	8–12	A distinctive collection of some 250 poems ranging from traditional to such modern poets as Kuskin, Milne, Merriam, Livingston, plus favorites by Frost and Sandburg.
Jack Prelutsky	*The Random House Book of Poetry*	7–12	See text.
Joanna Cole	*A New Treasury of Children's Poetry*	8–12	See text.
X. J. Kennedy, Dorothy M. Kennedy	*Knock at a Star*	9–12	See text.
Lilian Moore	*Go with the Poem*	9–12	An unusual collection of poems by an award-winning poet. Includes poems from Shel Silverstein to Robert Frost. Poetry of both city and country is represented.
Dennis Saunders	*Magic Lights and Streets of Shining Jet*	9–12	A former teacher from England collected some 40 poems which are particularly useful in class, providing sections on seasons, weather, animals, colors. Lovely full-page photographs illustrate these fine poems.
Mary Alice Downie, Barbara Robertson	*The New Wind Has Wings* *The Wind Has Wings*	8–12	Two fine Canadian collections illustrated with unusual collage pictures by the well-known illustrator Elizabeth Cleaver. Includes such exciting poems as "There's a Fire in the Forest" and "Rattlesnake."
John L. Foster	*First Book of Poetry* *Second Book of Poetry* *Third Book of Poetry* *Fourth Book of Poetry*	8–12	Each of these paperback books from England contains nearly 100 modern poems that would be enjoyed beginning at 8 years old and becoming progressively more complex for older students. The content is contemporary, including both British and American poets.
Mercer Mayer	*A Poison Tree*	9–12	An unusual anthology of some 20 poems that reflect strong emotional feelings. Each poem is beautifully illustrated with a black and white pencil sketch by Mercer Mayer.
Nancy Larrick	*Crazy to Be Alive in Such a Strange World*	10–up	An anthology for students in middle school and high school. Contains many contemporary poems from Shel Silverstein to John Updike. Sensitive photographs mirror the content and feeling of the poems.
Zena Sutherland, Myra Cohn Livingston	*Scott Foresman Anthology of Children's Literature*	all ages	Myra Cohn Livingston was responsible for selecting this outstanding collection of poetry in the first 150 pages of this 1,000-page anthology. Unfortunately, the poetry section cannot be purchased separately.
Edward Blishen	*The Oxford Book of Poetry for Children*	8–12	Recently reissued, this collection of such traditional poets as Lear, Carroll, de la Mare, Stevenson, even Shakespeare and Shelley, has been beautifully illustrated by Brian Wildsmith.

The City
David Ignatow

If flowers want to grow
right out of the concrete sidewalk cracks
I'm going to bend down to smell them.

Lee Bennett Hopkins selected some thirty poems to celebrate the change of seasons in *The Sky is Full of Song*. Dirk Zimmer created full-color linocuts for this small but distinguished anthology.

SPECIALIZED COLLECTIONS

As poetry permissions become more difficult to obtain for long lengths of time and more expensive, anthologists have turned to making small specialized collections. Most of these are organized for a particular age level or around certain subjects, such as dogs or seasons. Some are related to the ethnic origin of the poems, such as poetry of Native Americans or poems that celebrate the black experience. Others include a particular form of poetry, such as haiku or limericks. Rather than describe each of these specialized anthologies, we show the range and number of them in a chart.

SPECIALIZED COLLECTIONS OF POETRY

SUBJECT	COMPILER/POET	TITLE	AGE LEVEL	DESCRIPTION
Poems about children's daily experiences	Jill Bennett	*Tiny Tim*	5–7	A former primary teacher has selected a group of silly poems with rollicking rhymes which will appeal to the young child. Funny droll colored pictures by Helen Oxenbury add to the fun.
	Cynthia Mitchell	*Under the Cherry Tree*	5–7	Includes melodic poems by T. S. Eliot, Robert Graves, James Reeves. Children will enjoy the rich sound of the language and the glowing watercolors of Satomi Ichikawa.

SPECIALIZED COLLECTIONS OF POETRY (continued)

SUBJECT	COMPILER/POET	TITLE	AGE LEVEL	DESCRIPTION
Poems about children's daily experiences	Jill Bennett	Roger Was a Razor Fish Days Are Where We Live	5–7	Illustrated by Maureen Roffey, these books include an eclectic collection of nursery rhymes and verses by David McCord, Aileen Fisher, Myra Cohn Livingston.
	Sara and Stephen Corrin	Once Upon a Rhyme	6–8	Illustrated by Jill Bennett, this collection of about 100 poems contains many narrative verses.
	Lee Bennett Hopkins	Surprises	6–8	With unerring taste for good poetry and what children enjoy, Hopkins has selected nearly 40 poems that children can read.
		Morning, Noon and Nighttime, Too	6–8	Again Hopkins has selected over 40 excellent poems that take us through a child's day.
		By Myself	6–8	Contains 16 poems that describe children's thoughts and feelings.
	Michael Hearn	Breakfast, Books & Dreams	8–12	A day in the life of a brother and sister, including dismal school lunches, hours in the science lab, fights over TV and housework, in 20 poems. Superb brown and white etchings by Barbara Garrison.
Night poems	Nancy Larrick	When the Dark Comes Dancing	5–8	Subtitled "a bedtime poetry book," contains some 45 poems by such well-known poets as Aileen Fisher and Karla Kuskin, plus songs and familiar nursery rhymes.
	Siv Cedering Fox	Blue Horse and Other Night Poems	5–8	This poet has created vivid images of children's thoughts and dreams in some 14 poems. Powerful black and white pictures by Donald Carrick capture these dream images.
	Helen Hill, Agnes Perkins, Alethea Helbig	From Dusk to Dawn: Poems of Night	9–12	A rich collection of poetry that celebrates the night and nighttime activities.
	Nancy Larrick	Bring Me All Your Dreams	10–up	Includes a wide range of exciting poems by many contemporary poets. Dreams include daydreams, wishes, night dreams.

SUBJECT	COMPILER/POET	TITLE	AGE LEVEL	DESCRIPTION
Poetry of nature and seasons	Lee Bennett Hopkins	*The Sky Is Full of Song*	6–8	A jewel of a book: poems about the seasons described from a young child's point of view.
	Lee Bennett Hopkins	*Moments*	8–12	An excellent collection of seasonal poems, including selections from Lilian Moore, Emily Dickinson, Robert Frost.
	Lee Bennett Hopkins	*To Look at Anything*	8–12	Illustrated with photographs of gnarled stumps and branches that look like the theme of the poem, this book invites children to look carefully at the image in the poem and picture.
Holiday collections	Myra Cohn Livingston	*Christmas Poems* *Thanksgiving Poems* *Easter Poems* *Valentine Poems*	6–10	Small collections, beautifully illustrated and chosen to capture the child's delight in various seasons.
	Lee Bennett Hopkins	*Beat the Drum, Independence Day Has Come* *Good Morning to You, Valentine* *Hey-How for Halloween* *Merrily Comes Our Harvest In* *Sing Hey for Christmas Day*	6–10	Each of these illustrated books contains a fine collection of some 20 poems.
	Myra Cohn Livingston	*Callooh! Callay! Holiday Poems for Young Readers*	8–12	Some 80 poems about 15 different holidays.
	Myra Cohn Livingston	*O Frabjous Day, Poetry for Holidays and Special Occasions*	10–up	A fine collection for middle graders. Includes poems on usual holidays and some for "The New Year," "Birth," even "Assassinations."
	Myra Cohn Livingston	*Why Am I Grown So Cold? Poems of the Unknowable*	10–up	Contains some 150 ghostly poems. Some are appropriate for Halloween but many can be read throughout the year. Children would enjoy comparing the four poems about haunted houses.
	Sara and John E. Brewton	*Shrieks at Midnight: Macabre Poems, Eerie and Humorous*	8–12	An excellent collection that includes many eerie poems, plus ironic take-offs on nursery rhymes and other humorous poems.
Humorous poems	William Cole	*Oh, What Nonsense!* *Oh, How Silly!* *Oh, That's Ridiculous!*	7–12	These collections contain some of Shel Silverstein's verses and children's other favorites.

SUBJECT	COMPILER/POET	TITLE	AGE LEVEL	DESCRIPTION
	William Cole	*Poem Stew*	6–12	A hilarious feast of poems about food. Children love this collection.
	John E. Brewton, Lorraine A. Blackburn	*They Discovered a Head in the Box for the Bread*	6–12	Humorous limericks that delight all children.
	Sara and John E. Brewton	*Of Quarks, Quasars and Quirks: Quizzical Poems for the Supersonic Age*	10–up	Lighthearted poems that are both humorous and scientific.
	Myra Cohn Livingston	*What a Wonderful Bird the Frog Are*	8–up	A collection filled with verse as zany as the title poem. Includes limericks, amusing epitaphs, and the wit of such poets as Ogden Nash, David McCord, John Ciardi.
Poems about sports	Lillian Morrison	*Sprints and Distances, Sports in Poetry and Poetry in Sports*	10–up	Serious and humorous poetry about every imaginable kind of sport.
	Lillian Morrison	*The Sidewalk Racer*	8–up	Lillian Morrison has written her own poems to celebrate sports from sidewalk racing to boxing to surfing.
	Alice Fleming	*Hosannah the Home Run!*	8–up	Includes some 34 poems on a variety of sports.
Poems about animals	Lee Bennett Hopkins	*A Dog's Life* *I Am the Cat* *My Mane Catches the Wind: Poems about Horses*	6–10	Each of these collections of some 20 to 25 poems is well illustrated with appealing full-page illustrations.
	William Cole	*Good Dog Poems* *The Poetry of Horses*	8–up	More comprehensive anthologies for older children, containing about 100 poems each.
	William Cole	*The Birds and Beasts Were There*	10–up	Distinguished woodcuts complement this collection of over 300 poems.
	Adrienne Adams	*Poetry of the Earth*	8–up	These poems were selected and illustrated by an artist. The result is a handsome collection of some 33 poems about a variety of animals, butterflies, and birds.
	Nancy Larrick	*Room for Me and a Mountain Lion*	10–up	Superb poetry about open space, animals, and humans. These poems will speak to young persons of all ages.
City poems	Lee Bennett Hopkins	*Song in Stone, City Poems*	8–up	Some 20 poems capture images of pigeons, oil slicks, umbrellas, skyscrapers. Illustrated with fine black and white photographs.

431

SPECIALIZED COLLECTIONS OF POETRY (continued)

SUBJECT	COMPILER/POET	TITLE	AGE LEVEL	DESCRIPTION
	Nancy Larrick	On City Streets	10—up	The first and most exciting anthology of city poems. Selected with the help of some 100 city students.
Ethnic poetry	Arnold Adoff	My Black Me	8—up	A collection of contemporary poems that mixes black pride with power and protest. Brief biographical notes on each of the poets add interest.
		I Am the Darker Brother: An Anthology of Modern Poems by Black Americans	10—up	Contains some of the best-known poetry of Langston Hughes, Gwendolyn Brooks, and Countee Cullen, as well as some modern poets.
	Hettie Jones	The Trees Stand Shining	8—up	A handsome picture book of chants and songs of the North American Indian.
	Aline Amon	The Earth Is Sore	8—up	Poetry and prose from early speeches of Native Americans. Beautifully illustrated with natural collages of leaves, pine needles, even a spider web.
	Knud Rasmussen	Beyond the High Hills	10—up	Superb full-color photographs add to the beauty of these Eskimo poems and chants. The traditional struggle against the elements is the theme of many of the poems.
	James Houston	Songs of the Dream People	10—up	Contains chants of both Indians and Eskimos. Striking illustrations of artifacts of various groups.
Haiku	Richard Lewis	In a Spring Garden	8—up	Beautiful full-color illustrations by Ezra Jack Keats make this a particularly fine introduction to the haiku form.
	Kazue Mizumura	Flower Moon Song	8—up	A charming book of 30 original haiku and woodcuts, both created by this Japanese-born American.
	Harry Behn	Cricket Songs More Cricket Songs		Two fine collections of haiku sensitively translated by a poet.
	Ann Atwood	Haiku: The Mood of the Earth Haiku Vision Fly With the Wind, Flow with the Water		Exquisite full-color photographs reflect the images of these original haiku.

A Visit to William Blake's Inn by Nancy Willard is the first poetry book to receive the Newbery Award. In the same year the illustrators for this book, Alice and Martin Provensen, received a Caldecott Honor Award.

PICTURE-BOOK EDITIONS OF SINGLE POEMS

Traditionally, poetry books have had few illustrations in order to enable the reader to create vivid images on the screen of his or her imagination. This concept has changed, and today we have such books as the *Oxford Book of Poetry for Children* edited by Edward Blishen, which is profusely illustrated with Brian Wildsmith's brilliant pictures. It was inevitable that poetry should also follow the trend to single-poem editions already established by the many beautifully illustrated editions of single fairy tales and folk songs.

The first book of poetry to be presented with the Newbery award is *A Visit to William Blake's Inn* by Nancy Willard. In the same year that it received the Newbery, illustrators Alice and Martin Provensen received a Caldecott Honor award. Inspired by Blake's work, Nancy Willard created a book of magical poems about life at an imaginary inn run by William Blake himself. In this inn a rabbit shows you to your room and makes the beds. Two mighty dragons are the bakers, and a bear, a tiger,

and the King of Cats appear to be inhabitants. While each poem is separate, together they create a story of all the activities going on in this remarkable place. Children ages 8 and up will be intrigued by the detailed pictures of the inn and its guests. They will particularly enjoy the poems "A Rabbit Reveals My Room" and "The King of Cats Sends a Postcard to His Wife."

Susan Jeffers has illustrated two well-known poems in picture-book format. Her illustrations for Frost's *Stopping by Woods on a Snowy Evening* evoke the quiet stillness of the forest in contrast to the staid New England Village. No one can illustrate deep woods as well as Jeffers. She uses this vision again as she illustrates Longfellow's *Hiawatha*. Here she pictures the romantic Indian which is in keeping with Longfellow's poem and time. Lovely pictures of Nokomis and a growing Hiawatha hold children's interest. The artist is not always consistent in portraying the age of the Indian lad, however; he seems older, then younger, before he reaches his manhood and leaves the tribe.

In some instances these stunning picture books

PICTURE-BOOK EDITIONS OF SINGLE POEMS

POEM, POET	ILLUSTRATOR	AGE LEVEL	DESCRIPTION
Little Orphant Annie, James Whitcomb Riley	Diane Stanley	6–8	Stanley creates a proper Victorian setting for this tale of what happens to naughty children.
Casey at the Bat, Ernest Thayer	Wallace Tripp	8–up	The humorous illustrations of the despair of Mudville the day Casey strikes out add to this popular poem.
Paul Revere's Ride, Henry Wadsworth Longfellow	Ann Rockwell	8–up	Childlike illustrations of the Old North Church and New England houses look like children's block villages and capture the essence of this well-loved historical legend. A map shows the routes of Paul Revere and Dr. Prescott.
The Microscope, Maxine Kumin	Arnold Lobel	8–up	Small black and white sketches detail the Dutch setting where Anton Leeuwenhoek invented the first microscope.
The Scroobious Pip, Edward Lear	Nancy Burkert	8–up	Delicate line drawings and full-color paintings illustrate this long nonsense poem by Lear.
Hawk, I'm Your Brother, Byrd Baylor	Peter Parnall	8–up	This fine story poem tells of a young Indian boy who frees a hawk to live once again in the wild.
The Best Town in the World, Byrd Baylor	Ronald Himler	8–up	A young girl tells of the way her father remembered the wonderful town where he grew up in the Texas hills where the dogs were smarter, the chickens laid more eggs, and the people knew how to make the best chocolate cake in the world.
Hiawatha, Henry Wadsworth Longfellow	Susan Jeffers	7–up	See text.
Hiawatha's Childhood, W. H. Longfellow	Errol Le Cain	7–up	Indian designs and borders are handsome, but Hiawatha appears as stereotyped as a Walt Disney character.
The Highwayman, Alfred Noyes	Charles Keeping	10–up	Illustrations are stunning, though somewhat grim for children.
The Highwayman, Alfred Noyes	Charles Mikolaycak	10–up	Not as graphic as Keeping's illustrations, these seem more symbolic. In black and white, they have a splash of scarlet running through them changing from the joyful red ribbons of Bess, the landlord's daughter, to the red blood of the highwayman.
Stopping by Woods on a Snowy Evening, Robert Frost	Susan Jeffers	10–up	See text.
A Visit to William Blake's Inn, Nancy Willard	Alice and Martin Provensen	8–up	See text.
Birds, Beasts and the Third Thing, D. H. Lawrence	Alice and Martin Provensen	10–up	The Provensens have illustrated some of the poems by D. H. Lawrence with richly painted pictures of the poet's childhood.

will create a new interest in a poem like *Hiawatha*. In other situations it might be more appropriate to share the poem before showing the pictures to enable children to create their own images. Sometimes turning the pages to look at the illustrations interrupts the flow of the poem. This is particularly true of *Stopping by Woods on a Snowy Evening*. Teachers and librarians will need to make this decision for themselves before they share a picture-book version of a poem.

SHARING POETRY WITH CHILDREN

Developing Enjoyment of Poetry

THE MISUSE OF POETRY IN THE CLASSROOM

Very young children respond spontaneously to the sensory-motor action of "Ride a Cock Horse" or "Peas porridge hot / Peas porridge cold." They enjoy the damp adventures of poor old Dr. Foster, and they delight in the misfortune of "The Three Blind Mice." Children in the primary grades love to pantomime "Hiding" (9) by Dorothy Aldis or join in the chant of "Cheers" (184) by Eve Merriam. The young child naturally delights in the sound, the rhythm, the language of poetry.

However, at some time toward the end of the primary grades, children begin to lose interest in poetry. The poet William Jay Smith comments: "How natural and harmonious it all is at the beginning; and yet what happens along the way later to make poetry to many children the dullest and least enjoyable of literary expressions?"[12] Norvell, in his extensive study of children's reading interests, indicated that boys and girls begin to show a dislike for both juvenile and adult poems between grades three and five.[13] Terry[14] also re-

ported a decreasing interest in poetry as children progressed through the middle grades, with fourth-graders evidencing more interest in poetry than sixth-graders. These findings suggest that rather than develop enjoyment of poetry, many teachers may actually destroy children's natural liking for this form of literature.

There are several ways in which teachers have alienated children from poetry. Poor selection of poetry is one of the most common mistakes made by both teachers and textbook publishers. The Tom study[15] found that teachers in the middle grades read many more traditional poems than contemporary ones that would be more suited to the modern child's maturity, experiences, and interests. Sentimental poems or poems that are about childhood rather than for children will turn today's young people from poetry very quickly. Poems that are too difficult, too abstract for children to understand, will also be rejected.

Several studies have indicated teachers' neglect of poetry. Terry[16] found, for example, that over 75 percent of the teachers in the middle grades admitted reading poetry to their children only once a month or less. Children can hardly be expected to develop a love of poetry when they hear it less than nine times a year! It is also possible to hear too much poetry, particularly at one time. Teachers who read poetry for one hour or have every child read one poem on a Friday afternoon are contributing to children's dislike of poetry as much as those who simply neglect it.

Another way to create distaste for poetry is by requiring memorization of certain poems, usually selected by the teacher. When everyone has to learn the same poem, it is especially dull. Many children do enjoy memorizing favorite poems, provided it is done voluntarily and that they may select the poem. But choosing to commit a certain poem to memory is quite different from being required to do so.

Too detailed analysis of every poem is also detrimental to children's enjoyment of poetry. An appropriate question or comment to increase meaning is fine; but critical analysis of every word in a

[12]Virginia Haviland and William Jay Smith, *Children and Poetry* (Washington: Library of Congress, 1969), p. iv.
[13]George W. Norvell, *What Boys and Girls Like to Read* (New York: Silver Burdett Company, 1958), p. 26.
[14]Ann Terry, *Children's Poetry Preferences: A National Survey of the Upper Elementary Grades* (Urbana, Ill.: National Council of Teachers of English, 1974, 1984), p. 29.

[15]Chow Loy Tom, "Paul Revere Rides Ahead: Poems Teachers Read to Pupils in the Middle Grades," *The Library Quarterly*, vol. 43 (January 1973), pp. 27–38.
[16]Terry, p. 53.

poem, every figure of speech, and every iambic verse is lethal to appreciation. Everyone knows that if the point of a joke has to be explained, it is no longer funny. If one has to explain a poem, its beauty and resultant mood will vanish.

CREATING A CLIMATE FOR ENJOYMENT

There have always been teachers who love poetry and who share their enthusiasm for poetry with students. These are teachers who make poetry a natural part of the daily program of living and learning. They realize that poetry should not be presented under the pressure of a tight time schedule, but should be enjoyed every day. Children should be able to relax and relish the humor and beauty that the sharing of poetry affords.

Such teachers will provide an abundance of many poetry books and not rely on a single anthology which may overpower children with its sheer quantity of poems. Students will be encouraged to buy their own copies of some of the fine paperback collections such as *The Arrow Book of Poetry* by McGovern, Nancy Larrick's *Piping Down the Valleys Wild,* or *Reflections on a Gift of Watermelon Pickle* by Dunning and others. Beautiful poetry books such as Ann Atwood's *Haiku: Mood of the Earth* or *Of Quarks, Quasars and other Quirks* by Brewton and others could be featured in the science and math centers. In a primary classroom David McCord's wonderment about "The Shell" (172) could be displayed with a group of shells or his poem about a "Cocoon" (170) might be taped to the screen cage where a cocoon awaits spring hatching. Evidence of enjoyment of poetry should not be limited to one time or place.

The book center should contain many poetry books. One fifth- and sixth-grade class that really makes poetry central to their curriculum has more than 200 poetry books in the classroom. They also have a listening area where children can hear poets reading from their own works on tapes or recordings. A bulletin board displays a list of children's current favorite poems, along with paintings and copies of their own poetry work. Many teachers and children have enjoyed setting up displays of real objects and pictures of a predominant color to highlight their favorite poem from *Hailstones and Halibut Bones* by Mary O'Neill.

A brief visit to a classroom, library, or school will reveal whether poetry is "alive and well" in that place, or sadly neglected and dying. A faculty might evaluate their own school by determining where they would place themselves on the continuum presented in the chart for "Developing Enjoyment of Poetry" that follows. Teachers might also evaluate their own practices against those described as producing dislike or delight.

FINDING TIME FOR POETRY

Teachers who would develop children's delight in poetry will find time to share it with them during some time each day. They know that any time is a good time to read a poem to children, but they will especially want to capitalize on such exciting experiences as the first day of snow, a birthday party, or the arrival of a classmate's new baby brother. Perhaps there has been a fight in the playground and someone is still grumbling and complaining— that might be a good time to share poetry about feelings. The teacher could read Eve Merriam's "Mean Song" (184) or Karla Kuskin's "I Woke Up This Morning" (128) and then everyone could laugh the bad feelings away. Poetry can also be thought of as a delicious snack to nibble on during transition times between going out to recess or the last few minutes of the day. Anytime is a good time for a poetry snack!

Such teachers frequently read poetry cycles, three or four poems with the same theme. One teacher capitalized on children's interest in "special places." She shared Byrd Baylor's poetic story *Your Own Best Secret Place* with a group of third-graders. Then during the week she read such poems as "This Is My Rock" (170) by David McCord, "Tree House" (235) by Shel Silverstein, "Secret Place"(9) by Dorothy Aldis, and others. Later children wrote about their own secret places in both prose and poetry. Children also enjoy selecting a particular subject and creating their own poetry cycles from anthologies in the library or classroom.

One way to be sure to share poetry every day is to relate children's favorite prose stories to poetry. One teacher who keeps a card file of poems always slips one or two cards into the book that is to be shared that day. For example, after sharing *Whistle for Willie* by Ezra Jack Keats, "Whistling" (21)

DEVELOPING ENJOYMENT OF POETRY

AWAY FROM *DISLIKE* OF POETRY	TOWARD *DELIGHT* IN POETRY
Away from selecting only traditional poems	Toward selecting modern contemporary poems
Away from adult selection of "appropriate poems"	Toward beginning with students' interests—nonsense verse, narrative verse, jump-rope rhymes, song lyrics
Away from teacher neglect and fear of poetry	Toward teachers and children discovering and enjoying poetry together
Away from reading poetry only once a month or less	Toward daily sharing of poetry
Away from study about a poem	Toward experiencing the poem
Away from dissection and analysis	Toward questions that contribute to the meaning and enjoyment of the poem
Away from teacher presentation of poetry from a single anthology	Toward use of many poetry books, records, and cassette tapes of poets reading their own works; student-recorded tapes with appropriate backgrounds of music or sound; slides, filmstrips, and pictures
Away from poetry presented in isolation	Toward poetry related to children's experiences, classroom activities, favorite books, art, music, drama, and so on
Away from required memorization of assigned poems	Toward voluntary memorization of self-selected poems
Away from required writing of poetry	Toward student's selection of the form of poetry as the most appropriate one for his or her thoughts
Away from assigned writing of a poem	Toward keeping a poetry journal

by Jack Prelutsky, "Where Is It?" (9) by Dorothy Aldis, and "Whistling" (72) by Aileen Fisher could be read. Teachers in the middle grades could read *Dawn* and share Harry Behn's poem about the reflection of "the lake" (see page 421). The grandfather in Betsy Byars' book *The House of Wings* was very similar to "Birdfoot's Grampa" in his desire to help the wounded crane. Children might talk about how our earth would be different if everyone acted as Sammy's grandfather and Birdfoot's Grampa.

BIRDFOOT'S GRAMPA

The Old Man
must have stopped our car
two dozen times to climb out
and gather into his hands
the small toads blinded

by our lights and leaping
like live drops of rain.

The rain was falling,
a mist around his white hair,
and I kept saying,
"You can't save them all,
accept it, get in,
we've got places to go."

But, leathery hands full
of wet brown life,
knee deep in the summer
roadside grass,
he just smiled and said,
"They have places to go, too."

Joseph Bruchac (193)

Librarians and teachers will want to make their own poetry/prose connections. We hope the chart on the next four pages will get them started.

Other subjects in the curriculum can be enriched with poetry. A "science discovery walk" could be preceded or followed by Moffitt's poem "To Look at Anything" (60). A math lesson might be introduced with Carl Sandburg's "Arithmetic" (60). Many poems may enhance the social studies, including those found in Eve Merriam's *Independent Voices* and *I Am a Man: Ode to Martin Luther King, Jr.* Janet Gaylord Moore relates art and poetry in her magnificent book for older students titled *The Many Ways of Seeing*. Physical education is well served by two excellent poetry books, *Sprints and Distances* by Lillian Morrison and *Hosannah the Home Run* by Alice Fleming. Older children will enjoy the superb tension captured by Hoey's basketball poem, "Foul Shot" (60). Every taut move of the player is felt as he prepares to make the free throw that can win the game. "Base Stealer" (60) by Robert Francis is another poem that combines sports with poetry. All areas of the curriculum can be enhanced with poetry; teachers should realize that there are poems on *every* subject from dinosaurs to quasars and black holes.

POETRY/PROSE CONNECTIONS*

Primary

SUBJECT/THEME	AGES	POEMS	BOOKS
Be Yourself	6–8	"Changing" (97), Mary Ann Hoberman "Everybody Says" (9), Dorothy Aldis "The Question" (128), Karla Kuskin "Who Am I?" (114), Felice Holman "When I Am Me" (99), Felice Holman	*Alexander and the Wind-Up Mouse,* Leo Lionni *Dandelion,* Don Freeman *No More Baths,* Brock Cole *The Little Rabbit Who Wanted Red Wings,* Carolyn Bailey *Sylvester and the Magic Pebble,* William Steig
Bears	5–7	"Algy Met a Bear" (23), Anon. "The Bear with Golden Hair" (128), Karla Kuskin "Oh, Teddy Bear" (211), Jack Prelutsky "Fuzzy Wuzzy Was a Bear" (46), Anon. "Koala" (130), Karla Kuskin	*The Bear's Toothache,* David McPhail *Corduroy,* Don Freeman *Ernest and Celestine,* Gabrielle Vincent *Ira Sleeps Over,* Bernard Waber *The Three Bears,* Paul Galdone
Bedtime/Dreams	5–7	"Bedtime" (10), Eleanor Farjeon "Conversation" (172), David McCord "The Middle of the Night" (138), Karla Kuskin "Bedtime Stories" (49), Lilian Moore "The Llama Who Had No Pajama" (97), Mary Ann Hoberman	*Clyde Monster,* Robert Crowe *Bedtime for Frances,* Russell Hoban *The Napping House,* Audrey Wood *There's a Nightmare in My Closet,* Mercer Mayer *What's Under My Bed?* James Stevenson

*References for prose will be found after the chapter references on poetry.

Primary

SUBJECT/THEME	AGES	POEMS	BOOKS
Color	5–7	"A Yell for Yellow" (184), Eve Merriam "The Cheerful Blues" (186), Eve Merriam "Lullaby" (184), Eve Merriam "Winter Cardinal" (194), Lilian Moore *Hailstones and Halibut Bones* (202), Mary O'Neill	*The Great Blueness*, Arnold Lobel *The House of Four Seasons*, Roger Duvoisin *Little Blue and Little Yellow*, Leo Lionni *The Mixed-Up Chameleon*, Eric Carle
Death/Loss	7–8	"For Mugs" (151), Myra Cohn Livingston "For a Bird" (158), Myra Cohn Livingston "Skipper" (34), Gwendolyn Brooks "When My Dog Died" (46), Freya Littledale	*The Accident*, The Carricks *Mustard*, Charlotte Graeber *The Tenth Good Thing About Barney*, Judith Viorst
Family	5–7	"Little" (9), Dorothy Aldis "The Dinner Party" (9), Dorothy Aldis "My Brother" (214), Marci Ridlon "Grandma Gurney" (23), A. E. Dudley "Father" (46), Myra Cohn Livingston	*A Chair for My Mother*, Vera Williams *I Love Gram*, Ruth Sonneborn *Kevin's Grandmother*, Barbara Williams *Mr. Rabbit and the Lovely Present*, Charlotte Zolotow *Say It*, Charlotte Zolotow
Feelings	6–8	"When I Woke Up This Morning" (128), Karla Kuskin "When I Was Lost" (214), Dorothy Aldis "Wrong Start" (214), Marchette Chute "A Small Discovery" (177), James Emannuel "I'm in a Rotten Mood" (211), Jack Prelutsky	*Alexander and the Terrible, Horrible, No Good, Very Bad Day*, Judith Viorst *The Hating Book*, Charlotte Zolotow *Lost in the Museum*, Miriam Cohen *Will I Have a Friend?*, Miriam Cohen
Folktales	7–8	"Look Cinderella" (158), Myra Cohn Livingston Fairy tales: 4 poems (249), Judith Viorst "Terrible Troll's Tollbridge" (123), X. J. Kennedy "A Visit to the Gingerbread House" (123), X. J. Kennedy "In Search of Cinderella" (234), Shel Silverstein "Spaghetti" (235), Shel Silverstein	*Cinderella*, Grimm Bros., illustrated by Nonny Hogrogian *Three Billy Goats Gruff*, Marcia Brown *The Frog Prince*, Paul Galdone *Sleeping Beauty*, Warwick Hutton *Strega Nona*, Tomie de Paola
Secret Places	7–8	"Hideout" (74), Aileen Fisher "Secret Place" (9), Dorothy Aldis "Tree House" (235), Shel Silverstein "Up in the Pine" (99), Nancy Kingman Watson "Solitude" (188), A. A. Milne	*Your Own Best Secret Place*, Byrd Baylor *The Little Island*, Golden MacDonald *Come Away from the Water, Shirley*, John Burningham

Primary

SUBJECT/THEME	AGES	POEMS	BOOKS
Sibling Rivalry	5–7	"Brother" (97), Mary Ann Hoberman "I'm Disgusted With My Brother" (211), Jack Prelutsky "For Sale" (235), Shel Silverstein "Satellite, Satellite" (184), Eve Merriam "Moochie" (92), Eloise Greenfield	*Baby Sister for Frances*, Russell Hoban *If It Weren't For You*, Charlotte Zolotow *She Come Bringing Me That Little Baby Girl*, Eloise Greenfield *Peter's Chair*, Ezra Jack Keats *Titch*, Pat Hutchins
Vacations	7–8	"Driving to the Beach" (99), Joanna Cole "Until I Saw The Sea" (99), Lilian Moore "Pretending to Sleep" (99), Judith Thurman "Encounter" (194), Lilian Moore "Picnic" (9), Dorothy Aldis	*Dawn*, Uri Shulevitz *Time of Wonder*, Robert McCloskey *One Morning in Maine*, Robert McCloskey *Sleep-Out*, The Carricks

Middle Grades

SUBJECT/THEME	AGES	POEMS	BOOKS
Change	10–12	"The Errand" (16), Harry Behn "Change" (114), Charlotte Zolotow "Running Away" (130), Karla Kuskin	*After the Goatman*, Betsy Byars *The Stone-Faced Boy*, Paula Fox *From the Mixed-Up Files of Mrs. Basil E. Frankweiler*, Elaine Konigsburg *Tuck Everlasting*, Natalie Babbitt
Courage and pride	10–12	"Mother to Son" (117), Langston Hughes "Troubled Mother" (117), Langston Hughes "I Too Sing America" (117), Langston Hughes	*Sounder*, William Armstrong *Roll of Thunder Hear My Cry*, Mildred Taylor
Decisions	11–12	"The Way Things Are" (161), Myra Cohn Livingston "The Road Not Taken" (89), Robert Frost "Traveling Through the Dark" (48), William Stafford	*The Cry of the Crow*, Jean George *Sarah, Plain and Tall*, Patricia MacLachlan *Jacob Have I Loved*, Katherine Paterson *Homecoming*, Cynthia Voigt
Guilt	11–12	"Little Things" (1), James Stephens "Forgive My Guilt" (177), Robert P. Tristram Coffin "A Poem for Carol" (177), Nikki Giovanni	*The Cry of the Crow*, Jean George *One-Eyed Cat*, Paula Fox
American Indian	10–12	"Our Books" (9A), Aline Amon "The Earth Is Sore" (9A), Aline Amon "Circles" (230), Carl Sandburg	*The Sign of the Beaver*, Elizabeth Speare

*References for prose will be found after the chapter references on poetry.

POETRY/PROSE CONNECTIONS* (continued)

Middle Grades

SUBJECT/THEME	AGES	POEMS	BOOKS
The Future	11–12	"Where Will We Run To?" (121), X. J. Kennedy	*The Green Book,* Jill Paton Walsh
		"Neuteronomy" (255), Eve Merriam	*Z is for Zachariah,* Robert C. O'Brien
		"Fantasia" (180), Eve Merriam	
		"The Measure of Man" (180), Eve Merriam	
		"After a Freezing Rain" (77), Aileen Fisher	
Loss	10–12	"I Loved my friend" (46), Langston Hughes	*Bridge to Terabithia,* Katherine Paterson
		"Simple Song" (177), Marge Piercy	*The Sign of the Beaver,* Elizabeth Speare
			A Sound of Chariots, Molly Hunter
Reverence for life	12–13	"To Look at Anything" (60), Robert Francis	*A Wizard of Earthsea,* Ursula Le Guin
		"Birdfoot's Grampa" (193), Joseph Bruchac	*Dawn,* Uri Shulevitz
		"The Earth Is Sore" (9A), Aline Amon	*The House of Wings,* Betsy Byars
		"Hurt No Living Thing" (214), Christina Rossetti	*The Talking Earth,* Jean George
Holocaust/War	11–12	"I Never Saw Another Butterfly" (119)	*Friederich,* Hans Richter
		"Fear" (119)	*Anne Frank: Diary of a Young Girl*
		"My Spoon Was Lifted Up" (53), Naomi Reolansky	*Hiroshima No Pika,* Toshi Maruki
			Rose Blanche, Christophe Gallaz and Roberto Innocenti

Finding the right poem for the right moment requires preparation and planning. Many teachers make their own collection of poems either on cards or in a notebook. These can be categorized in ways that teachers find the most appropriate for their own styles of teaching. A particularly useful reference that should be in every elementary school library is the *Index to Poetry for Children and Young People: 1976–1981* compiled by Brewton, Blackburn, and Blackburn, which indexes some 110 collections of poetry, including many discussed in this chapter. The poems are listed by subject, author, first line, and title. The index is updated every five years, so earlier editions are useful for finding somewhat older poems.

Children also need time to read and share poetry. One middle-grade group reserves 15 to 20 minutes a day when everyone reads poetry—a kind of "sustained silent poetry time." Frequently children work in pairs, for once they have found a poem they particularly like it is only natural that they want to share it. Children also enjoy making their own personal anthologies of favorite poems.

Students also can be encouraged to find poems that they think complement particular books. One fifth-grader chose Felice Holman's poem "Who Am I?" to go with the Prydain series by Lloyd Alexander:

WHO AM I?

The trees ask me,
and the sky,
and the sea asks me
    Who Am I?

The grass asks me,
And the sand,
And the rocks ask me
    Who I am.

The wind tells me
At nightfall,
And the rain tells me
    Someone small

Someone small
Someone small
    But a piece
        of
          it
          all.

                    Felice Holman (114)

I chose this poem to go with the Prydain Chronicles because in these books Taran is searching for who he is and how he fits into the world.

                    Eric Lease
          Ridgemont Elementary School
               Mt. Victory, Ohio
   Peg Reed, Peggy Harrison, teachers

PRESENTING POETRY TO CHILDREN

Poetry was meant to be recited or read aloud. Not all children have the skill in reading or the background of experience to read poetry effectively, but they all can enjoy listening to poetry. Teachers will want to read or recite many poems to them at first. There is no substitute for hearing poetry shared by an enthusiastic teacher and if she or he "knows it by heart," children are delighted. If each teacher would be willing to memorize two or three favorite poems, saying them to children from time to time—again and again, the way we sing songs—children would soon know them, too. If each teacher in each grade made a gift of these two or three poems, then at the close of seven years of elementary school children would know some fifteen or twenty poems by heart. They would have caught them from enthusiastic teachers. They would then stay for life, effortlessly, the way children know jump-rope rhymes, songs, and commercials.

Poetry should be read in a natural voice with emphasis placed on the meaning of the poem rather than the rhyme. In this way the singsong effect that is characteristic of most children's reading of poetry is avoided. Generally, the appropriate pace for reading poetry is slower than for reading prose. It is usually recommended that a poem be read aloud a second time, perhaps to refresh children's memories, to clarify a point, or to savor a particular image. Most poetry, especially good poetry, is so concentrated and compact that few people can grasp its meaning in one exposure. Following the reading of a poem, discussion should be allowed to flow. In certain instances discussion is unnecessary or superfluous. Spontaneous chuckles may follow the reading of Starbird's "Eat-it-all Elaine" (214), while a thoughtful silence may be the response to Coffin's "Forgive My Guilt" (177). It is not necessary to discuss or do something with each poem read other than enjoy it.

One way to interest children in poetry is to help them to know something about the poets by sharing some of the fine sound filmstrips available. "First Choice: Poets and Poetry" (Pied Piper Productions) features five well-known poets, Karla Kuskin, Myra Cohn Livingston, David McCord, Eve Merriam, and Nikki Giovanni. These filmstrips tell something of each poet's life style and his or her views on writing; they show the poet reading some of his or her poems and invariably interest middle-graders in reading more of their poetry. "Poetry Explained" by Karla Kuskin (Weston Woods) is also a very helpful filmstrip for middle-graders. "Pick a Peck o' Poems," (Miller Brody) geared toward younger students, consists of six filmstrips dealing with animals, ecology, weather, the city, and two on the tools of poetry. For any teacher worried about presenting poetry, this may be the place to begin. Then gradually as children show their delight in poetry, a teacher will be more willing to become involved.

There are many records and tapes of poets reading their own poems (see Hunt's *A Multimedia Approach to Children's Literature*, which lists some 348 sound recordings).

Records and tapes allow children to hear live poets; they also provide an opportunity for them to hear different interpretations of poems; and they give children a chance to replay a poem as often as they wish. Recordings may supplement the teacher's presentation, but they should never substitute for it. There is no substitute for a teacher reading and enthusiastically sharing poetry with a class.

Involving Children in Poetry

Assuming that the goal of teachers and librarians is not only to introduce poetry to children but to develop a love of poetry in them, how should they do it? The first principle, as we have seen, is to immerse children in poetry from kindergarten onward. Read it to them every day. Read several poems with the same theme and contrast them. Combine poetry and prose. Make poetry a part of every content area. Provide many poetry books in the classroom, along with time to read them and share them. Teachers need to convey enthusiasm for poetry by reading it well and often. Only then will poetry become alive and grow in our schools.

However, teachers want to know more; they want to know what to do with poetry that is positive. They want to know how to involve children in poetry.

DISCUSSING POETRY

After teachers or librarians have shared a poem with children, they frequently will discuss it. They may want to link it to other poems children have read, comparing and contrasting how the poet dealt with the concept. Suppose a second-grade teacher reads the picture book *The Accident* by the Carricks to children. She or he may want to follow that book with Livingston's poems "For Mugs" (151) and "For a Bird" (158). Children could then compare how the person in the poems felt about the dog, Mugs, and the little bird. Were they as hurt by their loss as Christopher was when Bodger was struck by a truck? How much detail can an author and artist give? How much can a poet? With many such discussions children will eventually see how poetry has to capture the essence of a feeling in very few words and how important each of the words must be. Starting then with the content (children will want to tell of their experiences of losing pets—and they should have a chance to link these real-life experiences with literature), the teacher may gradually move into a discussion of the difference between prose and poetry. Discus-

sion should center on meaning and feelings first. Only after much exposure to poetry does a teacher move into the various ways a poet used to create meaning.

Children may help each other to find meaning in a poem. In the following taped discussion, the teacher was not present. He had previously taped two poems and made printed copies for each child. He told the children to discuss the poems among themselves while the tape recorder was still on. Most of the discussion centered around one poem, "The Bully Asleep." Here is a short episode from the transcript of four 11-year-old English girls.

THE BULLY ASLEEP
One afternoon, when grassy
Scents through the classroom crept,
Bill Craddock laid his head
Down on his desk, and slept.

The children came round him:
Jimmy, Roger, and Jane;
They lifted his head timidly
And let it sink again.

"Look, he's gone sound asleep, Miss,"
Said Jimmy Adair;
"He stays up all the night, you see;
His mother doesn't care."

"Stand away from him, children."
Miss Andrews stooped to see.
"Yes, he's asleep; go on
With your writing, and let him be."

"Now's a good chance!" whispered Jimmy;
And he snatched Bill's pen and hid it.
"Kick him under the desk hard;
He won't know who did it."

"Fill all his pockets with rubbish—
Paper, apple-cores, chalk."
So they plotted, while Jane
Sat wide-eyed at their talk.

Not caring, not hearing,
Bill Craddock he slept on;
Lips parted, eyes closed—
Their cruelty gone.

"Stick him with pins!" muttered Roger.
"Ink down his neck!" said Jim.
But Jane, tearful and foolish,
Wanted to comfort him.

John H. Walsh

When the following extract begins, the four girls have already been talking for several minutes. They have asked themselves whether a teacher would in real life have noticed that a boy had fallen asleep in a lesson.

1. Well the teacher's bound to notice.

2. Yes, really . . . because I mean . . . I mean if . . .

3. Or she could have gone out because someone had asked for her or something . . . she probably felt really sorry for him so she just left him . . . The teachers do . . .

4. What really sorry for him . . . so she'd just left him so they could stick pins in him.

5. Oh no, she probably . . . with the "whispered" . . . said "whispered" . . .

6. Yes.

7. Yes, but here it says . . . um . . . [rustling paper] . . . oh " 'Stand away from him children.' Miss Andrews stooped to see."

8. Mm.

9. So you'd think that she would do more, really.

10. Yes . . . you'd think she'd um . . . probably wake . . . if she would really felt sorry for . . . sorry for him she'd . . .

11. She'd wake him.

12. [cont.] . . . wake him.

13. Oh no! . . . No, she wouldn't send him home alone . . . because . . . nobody's . . .

14. His mother's bad.

15. Yes.

16. His mother would probably go out to work.

17. Yes, he'd get no sleep at home if his mum was there.

18. Might have to . . . might have to turn out and work.

19. It might be . . . his mother's fault that really he's like this.

20. Oh it will be . . . It always is.

21. Look here, it says um . . . "His eyes are . . ." Where is it? "His dark eyes cruel and somehow sad." [Referring to the second poem]

22. I think that just puts it, doesn't it?

23. Yes.

24. There's always something like that. [Pause]

25. He's unhappy. [Whispered][17]

The four girls move from discussing teachers to discussing mothers. Notice that no single child has a clear concept of the meaning of the poem, but together they build meaning. Notice too how these girls go back and forth between their knowledge of the world and the world of the poem.

An example of a more directed poetry lesson with fifth- and sixth-grade American children is given in the extract that follows. Here the teacher is leading a discussion on Sandburg's poem "Phizzog" which she has just read to the class. While she accepts all comments, it is obvious that she is trying to help children build an understanding of the imaginative quality of poetry, the freshness of expression that startles, for example.

PHIZZOG

This face you got,
This here phizzog you carry around,
You never picked it out for yourself,
        at all, at all—did you?
This here phizzog—somebody handed it
        to you—am I right?
Somebody said, "Here's yours, now go see
        what you can do with it."
Somebody slipped it to you and it was like
        a package marked:
"No goods exchanged after being taken away"—
This face you got.

Carl Sandburg (109)

[17]Douglas Barnes, *Communication to Curriculum* (London, New York: Penguin Books, 1976), pp. 25–27.

Jim: In the beginning when you started it, I didn't understand it. But I thought it was like um, he was giving away something. When he was at the end, um, it was like he was saying something about your face um, how you would, I forget. Now I think I understand. At the beginning it was strange.

Teacher: So, what do you think . . . You are saying they are talking about what? You said it.

Jim: Like a face—

Teacher: Any other comments about it?

Aaron: It kind of sounds like that it is your face and you can't get rid of it or something—there's . . .

Teacher: Go ahead—I want you to talk with one another—not to me. Okay?

Jimmy P.: Like you said, it is your face and you can't take it away or whatever. I think it really means, you said that it is your face and you can't take it away or give it away. That's about what it is but I think it really means . . .

Teacher: Jim, what did you say?

Jim P.: Like here is something God gave me.

Jimmy R.: And you can't . . . well you can't destroy it.

Teacher: How does that hit the rest of you? They're saying that it is talking about a face and God gave it to you and there is nothing you can do about that.

Jimmy P.: If you don't like it, you can—

Jimmy R.: It's just here. That's all.

Mike H.: Yeah.

Teacher: How else might we tell? If you have controversy in your groups or you don't understand, what do we do?

Boy: We go back to it.

Teacher: Want to go back to the poem and think about this again? [reads poem aloud]

Jimmy P.: Now I understand. Like Jimmy R. said, this is the way I figured. Like God gave it to you and it is like a package or something you can't exchange or anything—still phizzog is kind of . . .

Teacher: What do you think, Stacie?

Stacie: I think it is saying that you're an original and you can't return it even though you might like to exchange it—the expression . . . that you got.

Teacher: All right.

Stacie: Because you are locked in.

Robin: They give you an expression.

Teacher: Go ahead, Robin. You get an expression and you can't do anything about it. When we went back to read this poem we were looking for the meaning of the word phizzog.

Jimmy: It sounds like . . .

Jennifer R.: Your face. Your expression . . . What it does . . .

Teacher: You mean you are saying it's another word for face?

Children: Yeah.

Teacher: All right. Let's read through those first few lines. "This face you got, this here phizzog you carry around."

Many voices: Yeah. You carry your face around . . .

Teacher: It's just another word for face. What do you think about this as a poem?

Jimmy P.: It's different.

Stacie: It uses a different word. Instead of saying face it keeps repeating phizzog.

Teacher: Where do you think he got that word?

Carrie: He made it up.

Teacher: Maybe.

Mandy: It gets your attention.

Jimmy P.: When you say phizzog, you want to know what phizzog is.[18]

While the teacher did not give the children her meaning for "phizzog," she did keep asking them questions to get them to create their own meanings. Notice that she reread the poem twice and went back to a line one other time. Together teacher and children created meaning for this poem.

[18]Amy A. McClure, "Children's Responses to Poetry in a Supportive Literary Context" (unpublished dissertation, The Ohio State University, Columbus, 1984).

WRITING POETRY

Using Models from Literature

After hearing Mary O'Neill's poems about color in *Hailstones and Halibut Bones* children are frequently inspired to write their own feelings about a particular color. The first time they try this, they are apt to make a kind of grocery list of all the objects that are a particular color. By returning to the book they can begin to appreciate the craft of the poems, realizing that all lines do not begin in the same way. They see that the poems contain objects which are that color but also describe the way the color made the poet feel, smell, and taste. One sixth-grader made several revisions of her poem before she was satisfied with it.

MY RED MOOD

Red is the heat from a hot blazing fire,
a soft furry sweater awaiting a buyer.
Red is the sweet smell of roses in the spring,
Red are my cheeks that the winter winds sting.

After their teacher read aloud Mary Ann Hoberman's *A House Is a House for Me*, 5- and 6-year-olds dictated and illustrated their ideas of other things that could be houses.

Martin Luther King, Jr., Lab School, Evanston, Illinois. Esther Weiss, teacher.

Red is a feeling that rings deep inside
When I get angry and want to hide.

Red is a sunset waving good-bye.
Red is the sunrise shouting "Surprise!"

> Treeva
> Ridgemont Elementary School
> Mt. Victory, Ohio
> Peg Reed, Peggy Harrison, teachers

Looking at the way other poets have described color may extend children's thinking. Examples are Rossetti's well-known poem "What Is Pink?" (214), Lilian Moore's "Red" (194), David McCord's "Yellow" (172), and Eve Merriam's "A Yell for Yellow" (184).

After hearing Rumer Godden's translation of de Gasztold's *Prayers from the Ark* (90), a group of 8-, 9-, and 10-year-olds composed prayers for other animals:

God, I am but a wiggling worm.
Who sees beauty in me?
I am brown and squishy,
    and they feed me to the fish.
Is it because of *that;* they say I have no beauty?
They laugh and scream and run away.
I ask nothing of you
    but that you consider my humble plea.
Dress me in riches!
Feed me apples!
So that people will not say "worm holes" in disgust
    or fear that I might still be there.
I am just a worm,
    your creation to plow the earth
        So why do I bother?

> Lisa Schiltz, age 10
> Martin Luther King, Jr., Lab School
> Evanston, Ill.
> Barbara Friedberg, teacher

One group of 7-year-olds was delighted with Mary Ann Hoberman's witty, informative poems about *Bugs* (95). Their favorite was the rhythmical poem titled "Clickbeatle," with its catchy internal rhyme. Several of the children worked together to write and decorate their own version, which is pictured on this page. Sixth-graders on a three-day camping trip also enjoyed some of the poems in *Bugs*. They responded to the final line in the poem about a "Cricket" which asks how the world would seem if you became a cricket. A verse from one child's poem, "I am a Cricket," reads:

I am a cricket.
I get stepped on and crunched
In the middle of eating
My lunch.

Jacqueline Kirchner
Worthington, Ohio Public Schools
Mary Karrer, librarian

This same group of campers wrote their feelings about climbing trees after their days in the woods and listening to David McCord's poem, *Every Time I Climb a Tree*. One of their poems follows:

When I climb a tree
I feel very free.
The wind in my face
The world in its place.
Yes, I feel so free
When I'm in my tree.

Kim Krause

Using one of Hoberman's poems from *Bugs* as a model, 7-year-olds wrote and illustrated their own version.

Upper Arlington Public Schools, Ohio. Marlene Harbert, teacher.

One child's poem reflected her response to prose. Delighted by the book that her teacher was reading to the class, *Hurry Home, Candy* by Meindert DeJong, this 9-year-old chose to put her thoughts into poetic form.

THE LOST DOG
On a cold chilly night
A little dog wandering
  with a wounded leg.
A soft gentle voice
Rang out of the night
Hurry Home Candy
Candy Come Home
A platter of meat
  at the doorstep
A big house all of his own
The lonely lost dog was home!

Kelly Wood
Upper Arlington Public Schools, Ohio
Susan Lee, teacher

Another student wrote a poem based on Jean George's *The Cry of the Crow* and Robert P. Tristram Coffin's poem "Forgive My Guilt" (177). While the work was his own, he carefully acknowledged the sources of his ideas, something we could teach all children to do.

THE CRY OF THE CROW
I sat in a tree
Waiting for a bird.
That day I sighted
Three large crows.

I sighted them with my gun,
I squeezed the trigger,
One wing pulled
From a bird's body.

I still hear
The cry of that crow.
As it haunts me forever.

Matt Jennings
Ridgemont Elementary School
Mt. Victory, Ohio
Peg Reed, Peggy Harrison, teachers

Thoughts about this poem came from *Cry of the Crow* and "Forgive My Guilt" by Jean Craighead George and Robert P. Tristram Coffin.

Different forms of poetry may offer poetic structures to children and serve as models for creative poetry writing. Haiku frequently releases children from the problem of rhyme and focuses on the idea of the poem. However, this form of poetry has been overused with students too immature to understand the beauty of its concise thought and high level of abstraction. Frequently, the writer must imply a relationship between two disparate ideas, events or scenes. These events must have some relationship to nature and take place at the present moment. To make matters even more complex, all these rules must be followed within a pattern of seventeen syllables, although an occasional deviation is allowed in English haiku. Obviously, haiku is not simple to write. Only when children are ready for the formal discipline imposed by haiku should they try it. Some middle-graders are challenged by it; others are only confused. Certainly, primary-grade children who are still at the cognitive level of concrete operations should not be asked to try anything so abstract and foreign to their way of thinking. The examples below illustrate two 12-year-olds' success in writing haiku:

> The cabin is small
> in the vast whiteness. Only
> the smoke reveals it.

Carol Bartlett

> The leaves on a tree
> Rustle, impatient, restless,
> Waiting to fall off.

Patti Krog
Boulder Public Schools, Colorado
Allaire Stuart, teacher

Sustained Poetry Writing

Using models may be a way to get children started in writing poetry. It provides the opportunity to "write like a poet" and the given structures usually produce an acceptable poem. In no way does this approach help a child *think* like a poet. That may happen after much sustained writing and revisions.

In a small rural school in Ohio, two teachers, Peg Reed and Peggy Harrison, have a year-long poetry program with their combined group of fifth- and sixth-graders. Amy McClure[19] spent a year studying this poetry program and then writing an ethnographic research report on it. Thus we have a detailed picture of the program and how the children develop as writers.

They begin by reading poetry aloud several times a day. The classroom collection of over 200 poetry books is extensive. Children read poetry for some 10 to 15 minutes a day and keep poetry journals in which they write every day. They do not have to produce a poem a day—they can list possibilities, revise a poem they have been working on, or invite one of their friends to critique a poem. The rule about critiquing is that the writer reads the poem aloud and the peer listeners must respond to the meaning, not the mechanics, of the poem. Spelling, corrections, arranging the lines of the poem, etc., are done in later revisions. This daily attention to writing poetry has brought amazing changes in the children's writing. At first the children felt all poetry had to rhyme and produced the kind of distorted verses that make no sense but are driven by rhyme. At the beginning of the year, one child wrote the following poem:

> POPCORN
> It's hot, hot in the pot
> Out on the floor
> Crashed open the door
> Down the road
> Covered a toad
> Hot, hot, in the pot.

Ronnie

As the year progressed and Ronnie participated in regular critiquing and peer-sharing activities his understanding of poetry changed. He no longer thought all poetry had to rhyme. In April he wrote this poem in response to seeing a dog killed on the highway.

> CROSSING THE LINE
> The children prayed
> For the dog
> For that day
> It crossed the line

[19]McClure, "Children's Responses. . . ."

And in an instant
Lay helpless,
Seeping life.

Ronnie

When Ronnie was interviewed and asked what had made the difference, he replied:

Last year I used to write three-line poems, you know. But this year I started writing poetry with meaning. Just coming to groups and getting to talk with friends—watching other people write poetry . . . talking with the group in the morning . . . Well, we'd get some crazy ideas and some good ideas about poetry and someone might pick up on different subjects . . . I guess I just know more this year . . . I know about poetry and authors and how they write . . .[20]

The children in this class were frequently admonished to write about what they knew best. They were rural children and thus frequently wrote about their rural environment. One child described a tractor combine he had seen in this way:

COMBINE
Scissoring the weedy ground
Shaving it
And spitting it out
Taking it
For a day's harvest.

Eddie Perkins[21]

Another student wrote over 400 poems in the two years in which he was in this class. He created a book about *Bats and Owls* which his friend illustrated with lovely black and white pencil drawings. One of the poems in that book reads:

A BAT
A bat
Feeds lavishly
On moths

And beetles
Flies loops
And twirls
Catches bugs
From behind
When the sun
Rises faintly
The bat
Retires to rest

Charles Phipps, Jr.[22]

Children work carefully, revise frequently as they create their poems. After one child had gotten up before dawn and driven in to Columbus with her parents, she jotted down her first reactions to the sunrise. Over a period of three months she came back to this poem and reworked it. Angela's rough draft read as follows:

SUNRISE (rough draft)
The sun is slowly rising
Over the horizon
A bird chirps its song
While other birds join in
As the sun rises higher,
The world wakes
To sun rays on
Their windows.

Three months later her sixth and final draft read:

BREAKFAST
The sun preys
Upon the night
As it tiptoes to the horizon.
Big, yellow bite; by big, yellow bite,
The sun swallows the night.

Angela[23]
Grade 6

These children know the hard work and the delight in finding just the right word. Rather than militating against a love of poetry, this year-long poetry study has developed one. When interviewed

---

[20]McClure, p. 285.
[21]First quoted in *The WEB: Wonderfully Exciting Books,* edited by Charlotte Huck and Janet Hickman (Columbus: The Reading Center, The Ohio State University, Summer, 1983), p. 35.

[22]*The WEB: Wonderfully Exciting Books* (Summer, 1983), p. 36.
[23]McClure, p. 398–399.

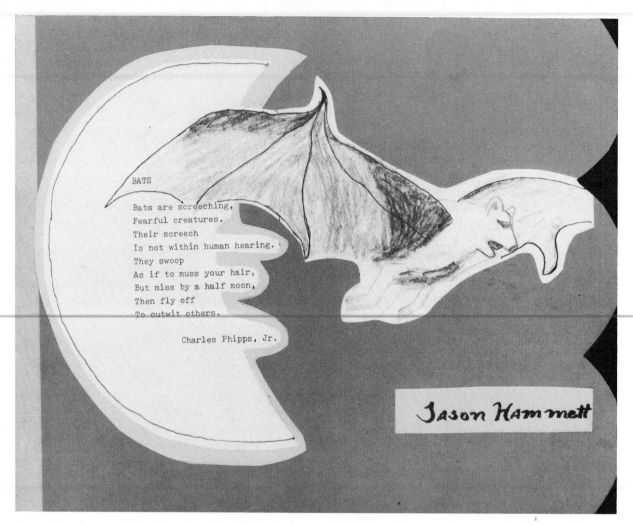

```
BATS

Bats are screeching,
Fearful creatures.
Their screech
Is not within human hearing.
They swoop
As if to muss your hair,
But miss by a half moon,
Then fly off
To outwit others.

                Charles Phipps, Jr.
```

Jason Hammett

One of the poems about bats created by Charles Phipps, Jr., and illustrated by his friend, Jason Hammet, for their book on Bats and Owls. Notice how the pages are cut like owl's feathers.

Sheryl Reed and Peggy Harrison, Teachers, Ridgemont Elementary School, Mt. Victory, Ohio.

by McClure, the children made the following statements:

I like both [books and poetry]. I like to read a book, then maybe write a poem about it and see if maybe they fit . . . but I also like to read just to read it.

Aaron

I like poetry that has deep meanings, but I like all kinds.

Jeremy

I like how it rhymes and goes around in your head. Sometimes I can't stop thinking about it.

Angela

I prefer to read books first, then save the best [poetry] for last!

Carrie[24]

These children may not become poets, but they have developed a deep love for poetry. Writing

[24]McClure, p. 305.

honest poetry that reflects their thoughts and feelings has helped to develop their appreciation for poetry.

CHORAL READING

The reading and sharing of poetry through choral speaking is another way to foster interest in poetry. Choral speaking or reading is the interpretation of poetry by several voices speaking as one. At first, young children *speak* it as they join in the refrains. Middle-grade children may prefer to *read* their poems. They are not always read in unison; in fact, this is one of the most difficult ways to present a poem. Four types of choral speaking are particularly suited for use in the elementary school. In the first, the "refrain" type, one person (teacher or child) reads the narrative and the rest of the class joins in the refrain. Another way, called antiphonal, is to divide the class into two groups. For example, in reading Rose Fyleman's "Witch, Witch" (22) one group can ask the witch the questions and the other group can give her answers. An effective approach with young children is the "line-a-child" arrangement, where different children say, or read, individual lines, with the class joining in unison at the beginning or end of the poem. "One, Two, Buckle My Shoe" is a good rhyme to introduce this type of choral reading. The dialogue of David McCord's "At the Garden Gate" lends itself to this approach for children in the middle grades. A more difficult and formal version of this method is part speaking. Groups are divided according to the sound of their voices into high, middle, and low parts. The poem is then interpreted much as a song might be sung in parts. This is usually done with mature groups and is the method utilized by verse-speaking choirs. Another difficult method is to have children say the whole poem in unison, giving just one interpretation.

Many variations to these approaches will be used by creative teachers and children. A certain sound that complements both rhythm and the meaning of the poem may be an accompaniment; for example, "clickety clack" from the sound of Tippett's "Trains." One group may repeat this phrase as another group says the words of the poem. Another poem that provides an interesting sound is "What the Gray Cat Sings" by Guiterman. Alternate groups or solo voices could say the verses with the entire class joining in the cat's weaving song—"Pr-rrum, pr-rrum, thr-ree, thr-reads, in the thr-rum, Pr-rrum!" This would be a wonderful poem to share after reading Ashley Bryan's West Indian folktale, *The Cat's Purr*.

It is great fun to read Livingston's "Street Song" (161) while eating potato chips. The bag can pass from one group to another with each verse, or one person can start it and pick up a friend to walk along to the rhythm. Children love to think of sounds to go with this poem from "crunch crunch" to "smack smack." Be sure to bring a bag of potato chips to class the day you read this poem!

STREET SONG

O, I have been walking
with a bag of potato chips,
me and potato chips
munching along,

walking alone
eating potato chips,
big old potato chips,
crunching along,

walking along
munching potato chips,
me and potato chips
lunching along.

Myra Cohn Livingston (161)

Children also enjoy planning how to read Prelutsky's "The Grobbles" (216). One person can be the innocent soul walking through the woods while individual children can each give a line describing the grobbles. Then the poem can grow with scary intensity as the person walks closer to the grobbles:

THE GROBBLES

The grobbles are gruesome	(Child 1)
The grobbles are green	(Child 2)
The grobbles are nasty	(Child 3)
The grobbles are mean	(All)
The grobbles hide deep	(Child 4)
in a hollowy tree	
just waiting to gobble	(All)
whomever they see	

I walk through the woods   (Solo)
for I'm quite unaware
that the grobbles are waiting   (All)
to gobble me there
they suddenly spring   (1st 4 voices)
from their hollowy tree
Oh goodness! the grobbles   (Solo)
are gobbling m . . .

Jack Prelutsky (216)

This interpretation of how to read "The Grobbles" is only one of many that could be developed. After you have worked with children in choral reading, they will suggest variations of different ways to interpret poems. Try these out and see which ones are the most pleasing to the ear and the most appropriate for the meaning of the poem. More serious poetry can also be read effectively. Lew Sarett's "Four Little Foxes" (255), Elizabeth Coatsworth's "Sea Gull" (255), or Merriam's "Neuteronomy" (255) all lend themselves beautifully to choral speaking.

The values of choral reading are many. Children derive enjoyment from learning to respond as a group to the rhythm and melody of the poem. They learn much about the interpretation of poetry as they help plan various ways to read the poem. Shy children forget their fears when participating with the group, and all children learn to develop cooperation as they work together with a leader to present a poem. It is necessary to remember that the process of choral reading is much more important than the final product. Teachers must work for the enjoyment of poetry, not perfection of performance. Too frequently choral reading becomes a "stunt" or a quick way to entertain a P.T.A. group. If teachers and children are pressured for a "production," interpretation of poetry will be exploited for unnatural ends.

Boys and girls should have many opportunities to share poetry in interesting and meaningful situations, if they are to develop appreciation for the deep satisfactions that poetry brings. Appreciation for poetry develops slowly. It is the result of long and loving experience with poetry over a period of years. Children who are fortunate enough to have developed a love of poetry will always be the richer for it.

SUGGESTED LEARNING EXPERIENCES

1. Begin a poetry collection for future use with children. Make your own filing system. What categories will you include? Indicate possible uses for some poems, possible connections with prose, ways to interpret poems.
2. Make a study of one poet. How would you characterize his or her work as to both style and usual content? What can you find out about his or her background? How are these experiences reflected in the poetry?
3. Make a cycle of poems about one particular subject—for example, houses, secret places, the city, loneliness. Share these with the class.
4. Bring your favorite children's poem to present to the class or to tape record. Invite class members to evaluate both your selection and presentation.
5. Select three different kinds of poems and read them to a group of children. Record their responses. What poems had the greatest appeal? Why?
6. Select one or two poems that contain figurative language. Share them with children at different developmental stages. When do children appear to understand the metaphors being used? One way to link into their understanding is to ask them to draw a picture of the images they see.
7. Find a poem to go with a passage in a book or your favorite picture book.
8. Compare two general anthologies of poetry, using criteria suggested in the text.
9. Select several poems you think would lend themselves to choral reading. Work with a group of children or classmates in planning ways to present one of these poems. If possible, tape record these interpretations.
10. Make a survey of the teachers in an elementary school to see how often they read poetry to their students, what their favorite poems are, what their favorite sources for poetry are. Make a visual presentation of your results.
11. Listen to some recordings of poetry read by authors and by interpreters. Contrast the

presentations and appropriateness of the records for classroom use. Share these with children. Which ones do they prefer?

12. Try writing some poetry yourself. You may want to use some experimental verse forms, such as concrete poetry or found poetry.

RELATED READINGS

1. Chukovsky, Kornei. *From Two to Five*, translated and edited by Miriam Morton. Berkeley: University of California Press, 1963.
   This is a classic review of the young child's delight in poetry. Written by a well-known Russian poet, it emphasizes that poetry is the natural language of little children.

2. Fisher, Carol J., and Margaret A. Natarella. "Young Children's Preferences in Poetry: A National Survey of First, Second and Third Graders," *Research in the Teaching of English*, vol. 16, no. 4 (December 1982), pp. 339–354.
   Using Terry's research as a model, this study researched the poetry preferences of *primary* children. Findings were almost identical to the Terry study done eight years earlier.

3. Hopkins, Lee Bennett. *Pass the Poetry, Please*, rev. ed. New York: Harper & Row, 1987.
   This revised edition of a well-known book presents a wealth of ideas for making poetry come alive in the classroom. It contains suggestions for sparking children's interest in writing poetry. It also includes interviews with more than twenty contemporary poets.

4. Koch, Kenneth. *Wishes, Lies, and Dreams: Teaching Children to Write Poetry*. New York: Chelsea House (distributed by Random House, 1971; also available in paperback).
   Koch describes the success he had in teaching children from grades one through six to write poetry in P.S. 161 on New York's Lower East Side. People have criticized his techniques and results. However, he did get children who had written very little of anything before to attempt to write verse.

5. Livingston, Myra Cohn. *The Child as Poet: Myth or Reality?* Boston: The Horn Book, Inc. 1984.
   Livingston disputes the widely believed statement that the child is a natural poet. She also reacts strongly to some of the techniques used in teaching children to write poetry today. Her earlier book on this subject, unfortunately out of print, *When You Are Alone/It Keeps You Capone: An Approach to Creative Writing*, gave a positive description of a poetry-writing program which produced quality writing.

6. McClure, Amy. "Children's Responses to Poetry in a Supportive Literary Context." Unpublished dissertation. Columbus: The Ohio State University, 1984.
   This ethnographic research study has captured the magic worked by two superb fifth- and sixth-grade teachers in a year-long poetry program in a rural setting.

7. Merriam, Eve. *Finding a Poem*, illustrated by Seymour Chwast. New York: Atheneum, 1970, pp. 58–67.
   In the last section of this book, a well-known poet recounts her composing process of the poem "Landscape." She includes all her revisions and her thoughts about the poem. This is excellent to use with children, for it shows that all poets struggle to make their poems say just what they want.

8. Terry, Ann. *Children's Poetry Preferences: A National Survey of Upper Elementary Grades*. Urbana, Ill.: National Council of Teachers of English, 1974, reissued 1984.
   These findings from a national survey of children's poetry preferences emphasize the importance of selecting appropriate poems if we wish to increase children's enjoyment of poetry. In the last chapter, the author makes recommendations for ways classroom teachers can create a poetry program.

9. *The WEB: Wonderfully Exciting Books*. Columbus: The Reading Center, The Ohio State University.
   Published four times a year, this periodical includes teachers' and librarians' reviews of books, along with children's responses. Each issue also contains a "web" of possible

activities to do with a single book, theme, or special genre of literature. Back issues are available, including one on *Poetry on Parade* (Fall 1979) and one in which the two teachers studied in the McClure research project were interviewed (*Journeys*, Summer, 1983).

REFERENCES

1. Adams, Adrienne, compiler and illustrator. *Poetry of Earth*. Scribner, 1972.
2. Adoff, Arnold. *All the Colors of the Race,* illustrated by John Steptoe. Lothrop, 1982.
3. _____. *Eats: Poems,* illustrated by Susan Russo. Lothrop, 1979.
4. _____, ed. *I Am the Darker Brother: An Anthology of Modern Poems by Black Americans*. Macmillan, 1970.
5. _____. *I Am the Running Girl,* illustrated by Ronald Himler. Harper, 1979.
6. _____. *Make a Circle Keep Us In,* illustrated by Ronald Himler. Delacorte, 1977.
7. _____, ed. *My Black Me*. Dutton, 1974.
8. _____. *Outside-Inside Poems,* illustrated by John Steptoe. Lothrop, 1981.
9. Aldis, Dorothy. *All Together,* illustrated by Marjorie Flack, Margaret Frieman, and Helen D. Jameson. Putnam, 1925, 1952.
9A. Amon, Aline, adapter and illustrator. *The Earth Is Sore: Native Americans on Nature*. Atheneum, 1981.
10. Arbuthnot, May Hill, ed. *Time for Poetry,* 4th ed. Scott, Foresman Lothrop, 1976.
11. Atwood, Ann. *Haiku: The Mood of the Earth*. Scribner, 1971.
12. _____. *Haiku Vision*. Scribner, 1977.
13. _____. *Fly with the Wind, Flow with the Water*. Scribner, l979.
14. Baylor, Byrd. *The Best Town in the World,* illustrated by Ronald Himler. Scribner 1983.
15. _____. *Hawk, I'm Your Brother,* illustrated by Peter Parnall. Scribner, 1976.
16. Behn, Harry. *Crickets & Bullfrogs & Whispers of Thunder: Poems & Pictures by Harry Behn,* edited by Lee Bennett Hopkins, illustrated by Harry Behn. Harcourt, 1984.
17. _____, translator. *Cricket Songs*. Harcourt, 1964.
18. _____, translator. *More Cricket Songs: Japanese Haiku*. Harcourt, 1971.
19. _____. *The Wizard in the Well*. Harcourt, 1956.
20. Benét, Stephen Vincent. *The Ballad of William Sycamore (1790–1871),* illustrated by Brinton Turkle. Little, Brown, 1972.
21. Bennett, Jill, compiler. *Day Are Where We Live,* illustrated by Maureen Roffey. Lothrop, 1982.
22. _____, compiler. *Roger Was a Razor Fish,* illustrated by Maureen Roffey. Lothrop, 1981.
23. _____, compiler. *Tiny Tim,* illustrated by Helen Oxenbury. Delacorte, 1981.
24. Bierhorst, John, ed. *In the Trail of the Wind: American Indian Poems and Ritual Orations*. Farrar, Straus, 1971.
25. Blake, William. *Songs of Innocence,* music and illustrations by Ellen Raskin. Doubleday, 1966 (1789).
26. Blishen, Edward, compiler. *Oxford Book of Poetry for Children,* illustrated by Brian Wildsmith. Watts, 1963, re-issued by P. Bedrick Books, 1984.
27. Bodecker, N. M. *Hurry, Hurry, Mary Dear! And Other Nonsense Poems*. Atheneum, 1976.
28. _____. *Let's Marry Said the Cherry, and Other Nonsense Poems*. Atheneum, 1974.
29. _____. *A Person from Britain and Other Limericks*. Atheneum, 1980.
30. _____. *Pigeon Cubes and Other Verse*. Atheneum, 1982.
31. Brewton, John E., and Lorraine A. Blackburn, eds. *They've Discovered a Head in the Box for the Bread and Other Laughable Limericks,* illustrated by Fernando Krahn. Crowell, 1978.
32. Brewton, Sara, et al., eds. *Of Quarks, Quasars and Other Quirks: Quizzical Poems for the Supersonic Age,* illustrated by Quentin Blake. Harper, 1977.

33. Brewton, Sara, and John E. Brewton, compilers. *Shrieks at Midnight: Macabre Poems, Eerie and Humorous,* illustrated by Ellen Raskin. Crowell, 1969.

34. Brooks, Gwendolyn. *Bronzeville Boys and Girls,* illustrated by Ronni Solbert. Harper, 1965.

35. Browning, Robert. *The Pied Piper of Hamelin,* illustrated and retold by Donna Diamond. Holiday, 1981.

36. _____. *The Pied Piper of Hamelin,* illustrated by Kate Greenaway. Warne, 1889.

37. Ciardi, John. *Fast and Slow,* illustrated by Becky Gaver. Houghton Mifflin, 1975.

38. _____. *I Met a Man,* illustrated by Robert Osborn. Houghton Mifflin, 1961.

39. _____. *The Man Who Sang the Sillies,* illustrated by Edward Gorey. Lippincott, 1961.

40. _____. *The Monster Den,* illustrated by Edward Gorey. Lippincott, 1966.

41. _____. *You Know Who,* illustrated by Edward Gorey. Lippincott, 1964.

42. _____. *You Read to Me, I'll Read to You,* illustrated by Edward Gorey. Lippincott, 1962.

43. Coatsworth, Elizabeth. *Poems,* illustrated by Vee Guthrie. Macmillan, 1958.

44. _____. *The Sparrow Bush,* illustrated by Stefan Martin. Norton, 1966.

45. _____. *Summer Green,* illustrated by Nora Unwin. Macmillan, 1948.

46. Cole, Joanna. *A New Treasury of Children's Poetry,* illustrated by Judith G. Brown. Doubleday, 1984.

47. Cole, William, compiler. *The Birds and Beasts Were There,* illustrated by Helen Siegl. World, 1963.

48. _____. *A Book of Animal Poems,* illustrated by Robert Andrew Parker. Viking, 1973.

49. _____, ed. *Good Dog Poems,* illustrated by Ruth Sanderson. Scribner, 1981.

50. _____, compiler. *Oh, How Silly!,* illustrated by Tomi Ungerer. Viking, 1970.

51. _____, compiler. *Oh, That's Ridiculous!,* illustrated by Tomi Ungerer. Viking, 1972.

52. _____, compiler. *Oh, What Nonsense!,* illustrated by Tomi Ungerer. Viking, 1966.

53. _____, ed. *Pick Me Up a Book of Short Short Poems.* Macmillan, 1972.

54. _____, ed. *Poem Stew,* illustrated by Karen Ann Weinhaus. Lippincott, 1981.

55. _____, ed. *The Poetry of Horses,* illustrated by Ruth Sanderson. Scribner, 1979

56. Corrin, Sara, and Stephen Corrin. *Once Upon a Rhyme: 101 Poems for Young Children,* illustrated by Jill Bennett. Faber & Faber, 1982.

57. de Regniers, Beatrice Schenk. *A Bunch of Poems and Verses,* illustrated by Mary Jane Dunton. Clarion, 1977.

58. Downie, Mary Alice, and Barbara Robertson, compilers. *The New Wind Has Wings,* illustrated by Elizabeth Cleaver. Oxford, 1984.

59. _____, *The Wind Has Wings,* illustrated by Elizabeth Cleaver. Oxford, 1978.

60. Dunning, Stephen, Edward Lueders, and Hugh Smith. *Reflections on a Gift of Watermelon Pickle and Other Modern Verses.* Scott, Foresman, 1966.

61. Esbensen, Barbara Juster. *Cold Stars and Fireflies,* illustrated by Susan Bonners. Crowell, 1984.

62. Farjeon, Eleanor. *The Children's Bells.* Walck, 1960.

63. _____. *Eleanor Farjeon's Poems for Children.* Lippincott, 1951, 1985.

64. Ferris, Helen, compiler. *Favorite Poems Old and New,* illustrated by Leonard Weisgard. Doubleday, 1957.

65. Field, Rachel. *Poems.* Macmillan, 1964.

66. _____. *The Pointed People.* Macmillan, 1924.

67. _____. *Taxis and Toadstools.* Macmillan, 1926.

68. Fisher, Aileen. *Cricket in a Thicket,* illustrated by Feodor Rojankovsky. Scribner, 1963.

69. _____. *Feathered Ones and Furry,* illustrated by Eric Carle. Crowell, 1971.

70. _____. *Going Barefoot,* illustrated by Adrienne Adams. Crowell, 1960.

71. _____. *I Like Weather,* illustrated by Janina Domanska. Crowell, 1963.

72. _____. *In One Door and Out the Other: A Book of Poems,* illustrated by Lillian Hoban. Crowell, 1969.

73. _____. *In the Middle of the Night,* illustrated by Adrienne Adams. Crowell, 1965.

74. _____. *In the Woods, in the Meadow, in the Sky,* illustrated by Margot Tomes. Scribner, 1965.

75. _____. *Like Nothing at All,* illustrated by Leonard Weisgard. Crowell, 1962.

76. _____. *Listen, Rabbit,* illustrated by Symeon Shimin. Crowell, 1964.

77. _____. *Out in the Dark and Daylight*, illustrated by Gail Owens. Harper, 1980.
78. _____. *That's Why*. Nelson, 1946.
79. _____. *Where Does Everyone Go?*, illustrated by Adrienne Adams. Crowell, 1961.
80. Fleming, Alice. *Hosannah the Home Run: Poems about Sports*. Little, Brown, 1972.
81. Foster, John L. *First Poetry Book*, illustrated by Martin White, et al. Oxford, 1982.
82. _____. *Fourth Poetry Book*. Oxford, 1983.
83. _____. *Second Poetry Book*, illustrated by Martin White and Joseph Wright. Oxford, 1982.
84. _____. *Third Poetry Book*. Oxford, 1983.
85. Fox, Siv Cedering. *The Blue Horse and Other Night Poems*, illustrated by Donald Carrick. Seabury, 1979.
86. Froman, Robert. *Seeing Things*. Crowell, 1974.
87. _____. *Street Poems*. McCall, 1971.
88. Frost, Robert. *Stopping by Woods on a Snowy Evening*, illustrated by Susan Jeffers. Dutton, 1978.
89. _____. *You Come Too*, illustrated by Thomas W. Nason. Holt, 1959.
90. Gasztold, Carmen Bernos de. *Prayers from the Ark*, translated by Rumer Godden, illustrated by Jean Primrose. Viking, 1962.
91. Gay, Zhenya. *Jingle Jangle*. Viking, 1953.
91A. Giovanni, Nikki. *Spin a Soft Black Song: Poems for Children*, illustrated by George Martins. Hill and Wang, 1971, 1985.
92. Greenfield, Eloise. *Honey, I Love: And Other Poems*, illustrated by Diane and Leo Dillon. Harper, 1978.
93. Hearn, Michael, ed. *Breakfast, Books and Dreams*, illustrated by Barbara Garrison. Warne, 1981.
94. Hill, Helen, Agnes Perkins, and Alethea Helbig, eds. *Dusk to Dawn, Poems of the Night*, illustrated by Anne Burgess. Crowell, 1981.
95. Hoberman, Mary Ann. *Bugs*, illustrated by Victoria Chess. Viking, 1976.
96. _____. *A House Is a House for Me*, illustrated by Betty Fraser. Penguin, 1982.
97. _____. *Yellow Butter Purple Jelly Red Jam Black Bread*, illustrated by Chaya Burstein. Viking, 1981.
98. Hopkins, Lee Bennett, ed. *Beat the Drum: Independence Day Has Come*, illustrated by Tomie de Paola. Harcourt, 1977.
99. _____, ed. *By Myself*, illustrated by Glo Goalson. Harper, 1980.
100. _____, ed. *Creatures*, illustrated by Stella Ormai. Harcourt, 1985.
101. _____, ed. *A Dog's Life*, illustrated by Linda Rochester Richards. Harcourt, 1983.
102. _____, ed. *Good Morning to You, Valentine*, illustrated by Tomie de Paola. Harcourt, 1976.
103. _____, ed. *Hey-How For Halloween!*, illustrated by Janet McGaffrey. Harcourt, 1974.
104. _____, ed. *I Am the Cat*, illustrated by Linda Rochester Richards. Harcourt, 1981.
105. _____, ed. *Merrily Comes Our Harvest In: Poems for Thanksgiving*, illustrated by Ben Schecter. Harcourt, 1978.
106. _____, ed. *Moments: Poems about the Seasons*, illustrated by Michael Hague. Harcourt, 1980.
107. _____, ed. *Morning, Noon and Nighttime, Too*, illustrated by Nancy Hannaus. Harcourt, 1980.
108. _____, ed. *My Mane Catches the Wind: Poems about Horses*, illustrated by Sam Savitt. Harcourt, 1979.
109. _____, ed. *Rainbows Are Made: Poems by Carl Sandburg*, illustrated by Fritz Eichenberg. Harcourt, 1984.
110. _____, ed. *Sing Hey for Christmas Day!*, illustrated by Laura Jean Allen. Harcourt, 1975.
111. _____, ed. *The Sky Is Full of Song*, illustrated by Dirk Zimmer. Harper, 1983.
112. _____, ed. *A Song in Stone: City Poems*, photographs by Anna Held Audette. Crowell, 1983.
113. _____, ed. *Surprises*, illustrated by Megan Lloyd. Harper, 1984.
114. _____, ed. *To Look at Anything*, photographs by John Earl. Harcourt, 1978.

115. Houston, James, ed., illustrator. *Songs of the Dream People: Chants and Images from the Indians and Eskimos of North America*. Atheneum, 1972.
116. Hubbell, Patricia. *Catch Me a Wind*, illustrated by Susan Trommler. Atheneum, 1968.
117. Hughes, Langston. *Don't You Turn Back*, edited by Lee Bennett Hopkins, illustrated by Ann Grifalconi. Knopf, 1969.
118. Hughes, Ted. *Season Songs*, illustrated by Leonard Baskin. Viking, 1975.
118A. _____. *Under the North Star*, illustrated by Leonard Baskin. Viking, 1981.
119. *I Never Saw Another Butterfly: Children's Drawings and Poems from Terezin Concentration Camp, 1942–1944*. Schocken Books, 1978 (1964).
120. Jones, Hettie, ed. *The Trees Stand Shining*, illustrated by Robert Andrew Parker. Dial, 1971.
121. Kennedy, X. J. *The Forgetful Wishing Well: Poems for Young People*, illustrated by Monica Incisa. Atheneum, 1985.
122. _____. *One Winter Night in August and Other Nonsense Jingles*, illustrated by David McPhail. Atheneum, 1975.
123. _____. *The Phantom Ice Cream Man*, illustrated by David McPhail. Atheneum, 1979.
124. Kennedy, X. J., and Dorothy M. Kennedy, compilers. *Knock at a Star: A Child's Introduction to Poetry*, illustrated by Karen Ann Weinhaus. Little, Brown, 1982.
125. Kumin, Maxine. *The Microscope*, illustrated by Arnold Lobel. Harper, 1984.
126. Kuskin, Karla. *Alexander Soames, His Poems*. Harper, 1962.
127. _____. *Any Me I Want to Be*. Harper, 1972.
128. _____. *Dogs & Dragons Trees & Dreams: A Collection of Poems*. Harper, 1980.
129. _____. *In the Middle of the Trees*. Harper, 1958.
130. _____. *Near the Window Tree*. Harper, 1975.
131. _____. *The Rose on My Cake*. Harper, 1964.
132. _____. *Something Sleeping in the Hall*. Harper, 1985.
133. Larrick, Nancy, ed. *Bring Me All of Your Dreams*, photographs by Larry Mulvehill. M. Evans, 1980.
134. _____, ed. *Crazy to Be Alive in Such a Strange World: Poems about People*, photographs by Alexander L. Crosby. Evans, 1977.
135. _____, ed. *On City Streets*, photographs by David Sagarin. Evans, 1968.
136. _____, ed. *Piping Down the Valleys Wild*, illustrated by Ellen Raskin. Delacorte, 1968.
137. _____, ed. *Room for Me and a Mountain Lion: Poetry of Open Space*. Evans, 1974
138. _____, compiler. *When the Dark Comes Dancing*, illustrated by John Wallner. Philomel, 1983.
139. Lawrence, D. H. *Birds, Beasts and the Third Thing*, illustrated by Alice and Martin Provensen. Viking, 1982.
140. Lear, Edward. *The Complete Nonsense Book*. Dodd, Mead, 1946.
141. _____. *A Book of Nonsense*. The Metropolitan Museum of Art, A Studio Book. Viking, 1980.
142. Lear, Edward, and Ogden Nash. *The Scroobious Pip*, illustrated by Nancy Ekholm Burkert. Harper, 1968.
143. Lee, Dennis. *Alligator Pie*, illustrated by Frank Newfeld. Macmillan of Canada, 1974.
144. _____. *Garbage Delight*, illustrated by Frank Newfeld. Houghton Mifflin, 1978.
145. _____. *Jelly Belly*, illustrated by Juan Wijngaard. Macmillan of Canada, 1983.
146. Lewis, Richard, ed. *In a Spring Garden*, illustrated by Ezra Jack Keats. Dial, 1964.
147. Livingston, Myra Cohn, ed. *Calloeh! Callay! Holiday Poems for Young Readers*, drawings by Janet Stevens. Atheneum, 1978.
148. _____. *Celebrations*, illustrated by Leonard Everett Fisher. Holiday, 1985.
149. _____. *A Circle of Seasons*, illustrated by Leonard Everett Fisher. Holiday, 1982.
150. _____, ed. *Christmas Poems*, illustrated by Trina Schart Hyman. Holiday, 1985.
151. _____. *4-Way Stop and Other Poems*, illustrated by James J. Spanfeller. Atheneum, 1976.
152. _____, compiler. *How Pleasant to Know Mr Lear!* Holiday, 1982.
153. _____. *A Lollygag of Limericks*, illustrated by Joseph Low. Atheneum, 1978.
154. _____. *The Malibu and Other Poems*, illustrated by James Spanfeller. Atheneum, 1972.

155. _____. *Monkey Puzzle and Other Poems,* illustrated by Antonio Frasconi. Atheneum, 1984.

156. _____, ed. *O Frabjous Day! Poetry for Holidays and Special Occasions.* Atheneum, 1977.

157. _____. *O Sliver of Liver,* illustrated by Iris Van Rynbach. Atheneum, 1979.

158. _____. *A Song I Sang to You: A Selection of Poems,* illustrated by Margot Tomes. Harcourt, 1984.

159. _____. *Sky Songs,* illustrated by Leonard E. Fisher. Atheneum, 1984.

160. _____, ed. *Thanksgiving Poems,* illustrated by Stephen Gammell. Holiday, 1985.

161. _____. *The Way Things Are and Other Poems,* illustrated by Jenni Oliver. Atheneum, 1974.

162. _____, ed. *What a Wonderful Bird the Frog Are.* Harcourt, 1973.

163. _____. *Whispers and Other Poems,* illustrated by Jacqueline Chwast. Harcourt, 1958.

164. _____, ed. *Why Am I Grown So Cold? Poems of the Unknowable.* Atheneum, 1984.

165. Lobel, Arnold. *The Book of Pigericks.* Harper, 1983.

166. Longfellow, Henry Wadsworth. *Hiawatha,* illustrated by Susan Jeffers. Dial, 1983.

167. _____. *Hiawatha's Childhood,* illustrated by Errol Le Cain. Farrar, Straus, 1984.

168. _____. *Paul Revere's Ride,* illustrated by Nancy Winslow Parker. Greenwillow, 1985.

169. _____. *Paul Revere's Ride,* illustrated by Paul Galdone. Crowell, 1963.

170. McCord, David. *Every Time I Climb a Tree,* illustrated by Marc Simont. Little, Brown, 1967.

171. _____. *Far and Few, Rhymes of Never Was and Always Is,* illustrated by Henry B. Kane. Little, Brown, 1952.

172. _____. *One at a Time,* illustrated by Henry B. Kane. Little, Brown, 1977.

173. _____. *Speak Up: More Rhymes of Never Was and Always Is,* illustrated by Henry B. Kane. Little, Brown, 1980.

174. _____. *The Star in the Pail,* illustrated by Marc Simont. Little, Brown, 1975.

175. _____. *Take Sky,* illustrated by Henry B. Kane. Little, Brown, 1961.

176. McGovern, Ann. *The Arrow Book of Poetry.* Scholastic Book Club, 1985.

177. Mayer, Mercer, ed., illustrator. *Poison Tree and Other Poems.* Scribner, 1977.

178. Merriam, Eve. *Blackberry Ink,* illustrated by Hans Wilheim. Morrow, 1985.

179. _____. *Catch a Little Rhyme,* illustrated by Imero Gobbato. Atheneum, 1966.

180. _____. *Finding a Poem,* illustrated by Seymour Chwast. Atheneum, 1970.

181. _____. *I Am a Man: Ode to Martin Luther King, Jr.,* illustrated by Suzanne Verrier. Doubleday, 1971.

182. _____. *Independent Voices,* illustrated by Arvis Stewart. Atheneum, 1968.

183. _____. *It Doesn't Always Have to Rhyme,* illustrated by Malcolm Spooner. Atheneum, 1964.

184. _____. *Jamboree: Rhymes for All Times,* illustrated by Walter Gaffney-Kassell. Dell, 1984.

185. _____. *Out Loud,* illustrated by Harriet Sherman. Atheneum, 1973.

186. _____. *There Is No Rhyme for Silver,* illustrated by Joseph Schindelman. Atheneum, 1962.

187. Michels, Barbara, and Bettye White. *Apples on a Stick: The Folklore of Black Children,* illustrated by Jerry Pinkney. Coward-McCann, 1983.

188. Milne, A. A. *The World of Christopher Robin,* illustrated by E. H. Shepard. Dutton, 1958.

189. Mitchell, Cynthia. *Under the Cherry Tree,* illustrated by Satomi Ichikawa. Collins, 1979.

190. Mizumura, Kazue. *Flower Moon Snow: A Book of Haiku.* Crowell, 1977.

191. Moore, Clement Clarke. *The Night Before Christmas,* illustrated by Tomie de Paola. Holiday, 1980.

192. _____. *The Night Before Christmas,* illustrated by Tasha Tudor. Rand McNally, 1975.

193. Moore, Lilian. *Go with the Poem.* McGraw-Hill, 1979.

194. _____. *Something New Begins,* illustrated by Mary J. Dunton. Atheneum, 1982.

195. Morrison, Lillian. *The Sidewalk-Racer and Other Poems of Sports and Motion.* Lothrop, 1977.

196. _____. *Sprints and Distances, Sports in Poetry and Poetry in Sport,* illustrated by Clara Ross and John Ross. Crowell, 1965.
197. Nash, Ogden. *Custard & Company,* selected and illustrated by Quentin Blake. Little, Brown, 1980.
198. _____, compiler. *The Moon Is Shining Bright as Day.* Lippincott, 1953.
199. Noyes, Alfred. *The Highwayman,* illustrated by Charles Keeping. Oxford, 1981.
200. _____. *The Highwayman,* illustrated by Charles Mikolaycak. Lothrop, 1983.
201. O'Neill, Mary. *Fingers Are Always Bringing Me News,* illustrated by Don Bolognese. Doubleday, 1969.
202. _____. *Hailstones and Halibut Bones: Adventures in Color,* illustrated by Leonard Weisgard. Doubleday, 1961.
203. _____. *Words Words Words,* illustrated by Judy Prissi-Campbell. Doubleday, 1966.
204. Petitt, Dorothy. *Poems to Remember.* Macmillan, 1967.
205. Pilon, A. Barbara. *Concerete Is Not Always Hard.* Xerox Education Publications, 1972.
206. Prelutsky, Jack. *The Baby Uggs Are Hatching,* illustrated by James Stevenson. Greenwillow, 1982.
207. _____. *The Headless Horseman Rides Tonight,* illustrated by Arnold Lobel. Greenwillow, 1980.
208. _____. *It's Halloween,* illustrated by Marylin Hafner. Greenwillow, 1977.
209. _____. *It's Snowing! It's Snowing!,* illustrated by Jeanne Titherington. Greenwillow, 1984.
210. _____. *It's Thanksgiving,* illustrated by Marylin Hafner. Greenwillow, 1982.
211. _____. *The New Kid on the Block,* illustrated by James Stevenson. Greenwillow, 1984.
212. _____. *Nightmares: Poems to Trouble Your Sleep,* illustrated by Arnold Lobel. Greenwillow, 1976.
213. _____. *Rainy Rainy Saturday,* illustrated by Marylin Hafner. Greenwillow, 1980.
214. _____, ed. *The Random House Book of Poetry for Children,* illustrated by Arnold Lobel. Random House, 1983.
215. _____. *Rolling Harvey Down the Hill,* illustrated by Victoria Chess. Greenwillow, 1980.
216. _____. *The Snopp on the Sidewalk and Other Poems,* illustrated by Byron Barton. Greenwillow, 1977.
217. _____. *What I Did Last Summer,* illustrated by Yossi Abolafia. Greenwillow, 1984.
218. Rassmussen, Knud. *Beyond the High Hills: A Book of Eskimo Poems,* photographs by Guy Mary-Rousselière. World, 1961.
219. Reed, Gwendolyn. *Out of the Ark: An Anthology of Animal Poems,* illustrated by Gabriele Marqules. Atheneum, 1968.
220. Ridlon, Marci. *That Was the Summer,* illustrated by Mia Carpenter. Follett, 1969.
221. Riley, James Whitcomb. *Little Orphant Annie,* illustrated by Diane Stanley. Putnam, 1983.
222. Rosen, Michael. *Quick, Let's Get Out of Here,* illustrated by Quentin Blake. Dutton, 1984.
223 _____. *Mind Your Own Business,* illustrated by Quentin Blake. S. G. Phillips, 1974.
224. _____. *Wouldn't You Like to Know,* illustrated by Quentin Blake. Dutton, 1980.
225. _____. *You Can't Catch Me,* illustrated by Quentin Blake. Dutton, 1983.
226. Russo, Susan. *The Moon's the North Wind's Cooky: Night Poems.* Lothrop, 1979.
227. Rylant, Cynthia. *Waiting to Waltz: A Childhood,* illustrated by Stephen Gammell. Bradbury, 1984.
228. Sandburg, Carl. *Early Moon,* illustrated by James Daugherty. Harcourt, 1930.
229. _____. *The People, Yes.* Harcourt, 1936.
230. _____. *Wind Song,* illustrated by William A. Smith. Harcourt, 1960.
231. Saunders, Dennis. *Magic Lights and Streets of Shining Jets,* photographs by Terry Williams. Greenwillow, 1977.
232. Schweitzer, Byrd Baylor. *One Small Blue Bead,* illustrated by Symeon Shimin. Macmillan, 1965.
233. Sheldon, William, Nellie Lyon, and Polly Ronault, compilers. *The Reading of Poetry.* Allyn and Bacon, 1963.

234. Silverstein, Shel. *A Light in the Attic*. Harper, 1981.
235. _____. *Where the Sidewalk Ends: Poems and Drawings*. Harper, 1974.
236. Smith, William Jay. *Laughing Time*, illustrated by Fernando Krahn. Delacorte, 1980.
237. Snyder, Zilpha. *Today Is Saturday*, illustrated by John Arms. Atheneum, 1969.
238. Stevenson, Robert Louis. *A Child's Garden of Verses*, illustrated by Tasha Tudor. Oxford, 1947 (1885).
239. _____. *A Child's Garden of Verses*, illustrated by Brian Wildsmith. Oxford, 1966 (1885).
240. Sutherland, Zena, and Myra Cohn Livingston. *The Scott, Foresman Anthology of Children's Literature*. Scott, Foresman, 1984.
241. Thayer, Ernest. *Casey at the Bat*, illustrated by Paul Frame. Prentice-Hall, 1964.
242. _____. *Casey at the Bat: A Ballad of the Republic, Sung in the Year 1888*, illustrated by Wallace Tripp. Coward, 1980.
243. Thurman, Judith. *Flashlight and Other Poems*, illustrated by Reina Rubel. Atheneum, 1976.
244. Tippett, James S. *Crickety Cricket! The Best-Loved Poems of James S. Tippett*, illustrated by Mary Chalmers. Harper, 1973.
245. _____. *I Go A-Traveling*, illustrated by Elizabeth T. Wolcott. Harper, 1929.
246. _____. *I Live in the City*. Harper, 1927.
247. _____. *I Spend the Summer*. Harper, 1930.
248. Untermeyer, Louis, ed. *The Golden Treasury of Poetry*, illustrated by Joan Walsh Anglund. Golden Press, 1959.
249. Viorst, Judith. *If I Were in Charge of the World and Other Worries*, illustrated by Lynne Cherry. Atheneum, 1982.
250. Wallace, Daisy, ed. *Ghost Poems*, illustrated by Tomie de Paola. Holiday, 1979.
251. _____, ed. *Giant Poems*, illustrated by Margot Tomes. Holiday, 1978.
252. _____, ed. *Monster Poems*, illustrated by Kay Chorao. Holiday, 1976.
253. _____, ed. *Witch Poems*, illustrated by Trina Schart Hyman. Holiday, 1976.
254. Willard, Nancy. *A Visit to William Blake's Inn*, illustrated by Alice and Martin Provensen. Harcourt, 1981.
255. Wilner, Isabel, compiler. *The Poetry Troupe: An Anthology of Poems to Read Aloud*. Scribner, 1977.
256. Worth, Valerie. *More Small Poems*, illustrated by Natalie Babbitt. Farrar, Straus, 1976.
257. _____. *Small Poems*, illustrated by Natalie Babbitt. Farrar, Straus, 1972.
258. _____. *Still More Small Poems*, illustrated by Natalie Babbitt. Farrar, Straus, 1978.

PROSE REFERENCES

Alexander, Lloyd. The Prydain Chronicles. Holt, 1964–1968.
Babbitt, Natalie. *Tuck Everlasting*. Farrar, Straus, 1975.
Bailey, Carolyn. *The Little Rabbit Who Wanted Red Wings*, illustrated by Chris Santos. Platt and Munk, 1978.
Baylor, Byrd, and Peter Parnall. *Your Own Best Secret Place*. Scribner, 1979.
Brown, Marcia. *Three Billy Goats Gruff*. Harcourt, 1957.
Brown, Palmer. *Hickory*. Harper, 1978.
Burningham, John. *Come Away From the Water, Shirley*. Harper, 1977.
Byars, Betsy. *After the Goat Man*, illustrated by Ronald Himler. Viking, 1974.
_____. *The House of Wings*, illustrated by Daniel Schwartz. Viking, 1972.
_____. *The Midnight Fox*. Avon books, 1975.
Bryan, Ashley. *The Cat's Purr*. Atheneum, 1985.
Carle, Eric. *The Mixed-Up Chameleon*. Crowell, 1984.
Carrick, Carol, and Donald Carrick. *The Accident*. Seabury, 1976.
_____. *Sleep Out*. Seabury, 1973.
Caudill, Rebecca. *A Pocketful of Cricket*, illustrated by Evaline Ness. Holt, 1976.
Cohen, Miriam. *Lost in the Museum*, illustrated by Lillian Hoban. Greenwillow, 1979.
_____. *Will I Have a Friend?*, illustrated by Lillian Hoban. Macmillan, 1967.
Cole, Brock. *No More Baths*. Doubleday, 1980.

Crowe, Robert. *Clyde Monster,* illustrated by Kay Chorao. Dutton, 1976.

DeJong, Meindert. *Hurry Home, Candy.* Harper, 1953.

de Paola, Tomie. *Strega Nona.* Prentice-Hall, 1975.

Duvoisin, Roger. *The House of Four Seasons.* Lothrop, 1956.

Fox, Paula. *One-Eyed Cat.* Bradbury, 1984.

_____. *The Stone-Faced Boy,* illustrated by Donald A. Mackay. Bradbury, 1968.

Frank, Anne. *Anne Frank: Diary of a Young Girl.* Doubleday, 1952.

Freeman, Don. *Corduroy.* Viking, 1968.

_____. *Dandelion.* Viking, 1964.

Galdone, Paul. *Frog Prince.* McGraw, 1975.

_____. *The Three Bears.* Seabury, 1972.

Gallaz, Christophe, and Roberto Innocenti. *Rose Blanche,* illustrated by Roberto Innocenti. Creative Education, 1985.

George, Jean. *The Cry of the Crow.* Harper, 1980.

_____. *Julie of the Wolves,* illustrated by John Schoenherr. Harper, 1972

_____. *The Talking Earth.* Harper, 1983

Graeber, Charlotte. *Mustard,* illustrated by Donna Diamond. Macmillan, 1982.

Greenfield, Eloise. *She Come Bringing Me That Little Baby Girl,* illustrated by John Steptoe. Lippincott, 1974.

Grimm Brothers. *Cinderella,* illustrated by Nonny Hogrogian. Greenwillow, 1981.

_____. *The Frog Prince,* illustrated by Paul Galdone. McGraw-Hill, 1975.

Hoban, Russell. *A Baby Sister for Frances,* illustrated by Lillian Hoban. Harper, 1970.

_____. *Bedtime for Frances,* illustrated by Garth Williams. Harper, 1960.

Hunter, Molly. *A Sound of Chariots.* Harper, 1972.

_____. *A Stranger Came Ashore.* Harper, 1975.

Hutchins, Pat. *Titch.* Macmillan, 1971.

Hutton, Warwick. *Sleeping Beauty.* Atheneum, 1979.

Keats, Ezra Jack. *Peter's Chair.* Harper, 1967.

Konigsburg, Elaine. *From the Mixed-Up Files of Mrs. Basil E. Frankweiler.* Atheneum, 1967.

Krauss, Ruth. *A Hole Is to Dig,* illustrated by Maurice Sendak. Harper, 1982.

Le Guin, Ursula. *A Wizard of Earthsea,* illustrated by Ruth Robbins. Parnassus, 1968.

Lionni, Leo. *Alexander and the Wind-Up Mouse.* Pantheon, 1969.

_____. *Little Blue and Little Yellow.* Astor-Honor, 1959.

Lobel, Arnold. *The Great Blueness and Other Predicaments.* Harper, 1968.

McCloskey, Robert. *One Morning in Maine.* Viking, 1952.

_____. *Time of Wonder.* Viking, 1957.

MacDonald, Golden, pseud. (Margaret Wise Brown). *The Little Island,* illustrated by Leonard Weisgard. Doubleday, 1946.

MacLachan, Patricia. *Sarah, Plain and Tall.* Harper, 1985.

McPhail, David. *The Bear's Toothache.* Little, Brown, 1972.

Maruki, Toshi. *Hiroshima No Pika.* Lothrop, 1980.

Mayer, Mercer. *There's a Nightmare in My Closet.* Dial, 1968.

Moore, Janet Gaylord. *The Many Ways of Seeing: An Introduction to the Pleasures of Art.* World, 1969.

O'Brien, Robert. *Z is for Zachariah.* Atheneum, 1975.

Paterson, Katherine. *Bridge to Terabithia,* illustrated by Donna Diamond. Crowell, 1977.

_____. *Jacob Have I Loved.* Crowell, 1980.

Richter, Hans. *Frederich.* Holt, 1970.

Shulevitz, Uri. *Dawn.* Farrar, Straus, 1974.

Sonneborn, Ruth. *I Love Gram,* illustrated by Leo Carty. Viking, 1971.

Speare, Elizabeth. *The Sign of the Beaver.* Houghton Mifflin, 1983.

Steig, William. *Sylvester and the Magic Pebble.* Windmill, 1969.

Stevenson, James. *What's Under My Bed?* Greenwillow, 1983.

Taylor, Mildred. *Roll of Thunder, Hear My Cry.* Dial, 1976.

Vincent, Gabrielle. *Ernest and Celestine.* Greenwillow, 1982.

Viorst, Judith. *Alexander and the Terrible, Horrible, No Good, Very Bad Day,* illustrated by Ray Cruz. Atheneum, 1972.

_____. *The Tenth Good Thing About Barney,* illustrated by Erik Blegvad. Atheneum, 1971.

Voigt Cynthia. *Homecoming*. Atheneum, 1983.

Waber, Bernard. *Ira Sleeps Over*. Houghton Mifflin, 1972.

Walsh, Jill Paton. *The Green Book*, illustrated by Lloyd Bloom. Farrar, Straus, 1982.

Williams, Vera B. *A Chair for My Mother*. Greenwillow, 1982.

Williams, Barbara. *Kevin's Grandmother*, illustrated by Kay Chorao. Dutton, 1975.

Wood, Audrey. *The Napping House*, illustrated by Don Wood. Harcourt, 1984.

Zolotow, Charlotte. *The Hating Book*, illustrated by Ben Shecter. Harper, 1969.

_____. *If It Weren't for You*, illustrated by Ben Shecter. Harper, 1969.

_____. *Mr. Rabbit and the Lovely Present*, illustrated by Maurice Sendak. Harper, 1962.

_____. *Say It*, illustrated by James Stevenson. Harper, 1980.

9

CONTEMPORARY
REALISTIC FICTION

small group of seventh-graders read Katherine Paterson's *The Great Gilly Hopkins* for an in-depth reading group. One of their options when they finished the book was to write about ways they were like Gilly or ways in which they were different from Gilly. One girl wrote the following:

GILLY IN ME

I think I am a lot like Gilly in some ways. One way is everything somebody says I can't do, I have to show them that I can do it or something like it. I think Gilly and I feel the same way about foster parents. If I had foster parents, I probably would feel that my mother would come and get me; but I wouldn't run away or steal money.

In school I don't act like she does, going to the principal or slipping notes in teacher's books. It seems she doesn't like to be with her friends. I like to be around with my friends. I don't like to be by myself. I think Gilly gets mad easy. I get mad easy like getting called names. I always have to call them a name back.

Amy Kauffman
Delaware Public Schools, Ohio
Christy Slavik, teacher

Obviously, Amy had identified with the character of Gilly Hopkins. By contrasting her perception of herself with Gilly, she learned more about Gilly and developed insight into her own personality.

A well-written contemporary story should do more than just mirror modern life. It should take children inside a character and help them understand the causes of behavior, while at the same time it can take them outside themselves to reflect on their own behavior. *The Great Gilly Hopkins* had opened a window of understanding for Amy and let her view herself and the world with slightly changed perception.

REALISM IN CONTEMPORARY CHILDREN'S LITERATURE

Realistic fiction may be defined as imaginative writing that accurately reflects life as it was lived in the past or could be lived today. Everything in such a story can conceivably have happened to real people living in our natural physical world, in contrast to fantasy, where impossible happenings are made to appear quite plausible, even though they are not possible. Historical fiction (see Chapter 10) portrays life as it may have been lived in the past, while contemporary realism focuses on the prob-

lems of living today. Though other genres in children's literature, such as fantasy, enjoy popularity, it is realistic fiction that consistently leads in studies of children's preferences. One librarian maintains that the most common request of middle-grade girls is for "a book about a girl like me."

The books discussed in this chapter may be categorized as contemporary realistic fiction for children. Many of these are stories about growing up today and finding a place in the family, among peers, and in modern society. All aspects of coping with the problems of the human condition may be found in contemporary literature for children. In addition, books that are humorous or reflect special interests—such as animal or sports stories and mysteries—are also classified as realistic literature and so are included in this chapter.

The content of contemporary realism for children has changed dramatically in the past twenty years. A discussion of some of these changes was included in Chapter 1, while Chapter 3 identified recent trends in publishing books for children. These changes have provoked controversy among writers, critics, librarians, teachers, and parents. For this reason attention will be given to some of the values of contemporary realism for children and some of these issues.

Values of Contemporary Fiction

Realistic fiction serves children in the process of understanding and coming to terms with themselves as they acquire "human-ness." Books that honestly portray the realities of life may help children toward a fuller understanding of human problems and human relationships and, thus, toward a fuller understanding of themselves and their own potential. In describing her purpose in writing for children, Nina Bawden states:

> If a children's writer presents his characters honestly and is truthful about their thoughts and their feelings, he is giving his readers "a means to gain a hold on fate" by showing them that they can trust their thoughts and their feelings, that they can have faith in themselves. He can also show them a bit of the world, the beginning of the path they have to tread; but the most important thing he has to offer is a little hope, and courage for the journey. [1]

This is not a function unique to contemporary realism. Other types of books can show children a slice of the world. Some fantasy may be nearer to the truth than social realism, while biography and autobiography frequently provide readers with models of human beings who offer hope and courage for the journey. The ability to maintain one's humanity in the midst of degradation becomes clear in Esther Hautzig's autobiography of her exile in Siberia, *The Endless Steppe*. The psychological importance of facing one's fears,

even going to meet them, is as much the theme of the high fantasy *A Wizard of Earthsea* by Le Guin as it is the message of the modern story of *The 18th Emergency* by Byars. However, most children appear to identify more readily with characters in books of modern realism than with those of historical fiction or fantasy. The horror of man's inhumanity to man overpowers the reader of Clark's *To Stand against the Wind*; and Arrick's *Chernowitz!* reveals the immediacy of the insidious sickness of prejudice in suburbia. Thus, modern realism may help the child to enlarge and deepen compassion and to see the world from a new perspective.

Realistic fiction may reassure young people that they are not the first in the world to have to face problems. They may read of other children whose parents have gotten a divorce in Blume's *It's Not the End of the World* or who are terrified of older siblings in Adler's *Get Lost, Little Brother*. Knowledge that you are not alone brings a kind of comfort. James Baldwin recognized the power of books to alleviate pain when he said:

> You think your pain and your heartbreak are unprecedented in the history of the world, but then you read. It was books that taught me that the things that tormented me the most were the very things that connected me with all the people who were alive, or who had ever been alive. [2]

Realistic fiction can also illuminate experiences that children have not had. It is probably far more important for the child who has loving parents, who has never known hunger, and whose only household chore consists of making a bed to read Fran Ellen's story in *The Bears' House* by Sachs than for a child of poverty to read this book. Realistic fiction, then, becomes one way of experiencing worlds we do not know.

Some books also serve as a kind of preparation for living. Far better to have read Paterson's *Bridge to Terabithia* or Voigt's *Dicey's Song* than to experience at 10 or 12 the death of your best friend or your mother. While death is a part of everyone's life, for many years this was a taboo subject in children's literature. Yet, as children face

[1]Nina Bawden, "Emotional Realism in Books for Young People," *The Horn Book Magazine* (February 1980), p. 33.

[2]James Baldwin, "Talk to Teachers," *Saturday Review* (December 21, 1963), pp. 42–44, 60.

the honest realities of life in books, they are developing a kind of courage for facing problems in their own lives. Madeleine L'Engle, whose *Meet the Austins* was among the first works of modern children's literature to treat the subject of death, maintained that "to pretend there is no darkness is another way of extinguishing light."[3]

Realistic fiction for children does provide many possible models, both good and bad, for coping with problems of the human condition. As children experience these stories, they may begin to filter out some meaning for their own lives. This allows children to organize and shape their own thinking about life as they follow, through story, the lives of others.

Issues Relating to Realistic Fiction

There is more controversy surrounding the writing of contemporary realistic fiction for children than perhaps any other kind of literature. Everyone is a critic of realism, for everyone feels he or she is an expert on what is real in today's world. But realities clash, and the issue of "what is real for one may not be real for another" is a true and lively concern. Another question relates to how real, how graphic can writers of children's books be? What is appropriate for children? Are there limits of good taste, for example? A third question centers on the negative aspects of how certain groups are presented, particularly sex-role stereotyping. Another issue relates to how realism is presented to children. Many authors become didactic when writing of the social problems of today. Their stories are overpowered by social themes of alienation, drugs, or ecology. Finally, much controversy centers on the authorship of these books. Must a story be derived from personal experience—can only blacks write about blacks, women about the girls they were, men about boys, and so on? What is the role of imagination in the writing of realistic fiction? These are some of the questions that seem uniquely related to contemporary realism in writing for children. They need to be examined.

[3]Madeleine L'Engle, in a speech before the Florida Library Association, Miami, May 1965.

WHAT IS REAL?

The question of what is "real" or "true to life" is a significant one. C. S. Lewis, the British author of the well-known Narnia stories (see Chapter 7, "Modern Fantasy"), described three types of realistic content:

> But when we say, "The sort of thing that happens," do we mean the sort of thing that usually or often happens, the sort of thing that is typical of the human lot? Or do we mean "The sort of thing that might conceivably happen or that, by a thousandth chance, may have happened once?"[4]

Middle-graders reading the Narnia series know they are fantasy and couldn't happen. You don't go into a closet and find yourself welcomed to the snow-covered land of Narnia by a faun! Things like that just don't happen, even if the faun is amazed to see you and has a book in his library titled *Is Man a Myth?* However, middle-graders may read such stories as Vera and Bill Cleaver's *Where the Lilies Bloom* or Cynthia Voigt's *Homecoming* and believe that a family of children could survive in contemporary society if led by a young but determined sister. These well-written books cast believable characters in realistic settings facing real problems. But an adult reader might question whether this is the sort of thing that "by a thousandth chance, may have happened once."

HOW REAL MAY A CHILDREN'S BOOK BE?

Controversy also centers on how much graphic detail may be included in a book for children. How much violence is too much? How explicit may an author be in describing bodily functions or sexual relations? These are questions that no one would have asked twenty years ago. But there are new freedoms today. Childhood is not the innocent time we like to think it is (and it probably never was). Although youth may not need protection, it does still need the perspective that literature can give. A well-written book makes the reader aware of the human suffering resulting from inhumane acts by others, whereas television and films are more apt to concentrate on the acts themselves.

[4]C. S. Lewis, *An Experiment in Criticism* (Cambridge, England: Cambridge University Press, 1961), p. 57.

The TV newscasts of the local Saturday night killings or the body count in the latest "peace keeping" effort seldom show the pain and anguish that each death causes. The rebuilding of human lives is too slow and tedious to portray in a half-hour newscast. Even video games are based on violence. The winner of the game is the one who can eliminate or destroy the "enemy." Reasons or motivations are never given, and the aftereffects are not a part of the game.

Between 1950 and 1984, the average time of television watching in households increased from 4 hours to over 7 hours per day.[5] One authority has estimated that the average child in the United States witnesses some 18,000 video acts of violence between the ages of 3 and 17.[6] Such mayhem and tasteless brutality blunt one's sensibility and make violence seem commonplace.

By way of contrast to the media world, a well-written story will provide perspective on the pain and suffering of humankind. In a literary story the author has time to develop the characters into fully rounded human beings. The reader knows the motives and pressures of each individual and can understand and empathize with the characters. If the tone of the author is one of compassion for the characters, if others in the story show concern or horror for a brutal act, the reader gains perspective.

A story which makes violence understandable but not condonable is Vera and Bill Cleaver's *Grover*. In one brutal scene, the children sneak over to the house of a woman who has mistreated Grover and kill her prize turkey. Yet the reader knows it is not a wanton act of revenge. Grover's mother had cancer, and she has killed herself. His father, wallowing in his own grief, shows no compassion for his son's feeling. Grover seeks the companionship of his friends Ellen Grae and Farrell, who are talked into cleaning up the yard of the town's meanest and stingiest person. She puts them to work and then finds ways to criticize them. She recognizes Grover as "the kid whose mother blew her brains out." When the children inadvertently frighten her tom turkey, she starts in again on Grover, telling him: "Suicide is a coward's way." The children leave without being paid, but the next morning at dawn they return and Grover cuts the head off the turkey. Ellen Grae tries to talk him out of it and Farrell is horrified as he avoids watching. Finally, Grover hits the bird with his hatchet and severs its head:

> His head, the eyes horribly bulging, fell to the ground and his body jerked out of the hands that held it and flew up into the air and came down again and started dancing around. But after a minute or two it gave a big convulsive shudder, which sent some more blood spraying, collapsed, and was finally dead.
>
> They left it for Betty Repkin to find.
>
> On the way back down the hill Ellen Grae didn't speak to Grover nor did Farrell.[7]

Against the background of Grover's silent suffering and the mean words of the woman, the reader sees the killing of the turkey as a kind of catharsis for Grover. Somehow he can't take any more. It is almost as if he had to fight death with death. Later he says he is sorry he killed the turkey. The explicit details are necessary in this scene, and they do serve a purpose. Slowly Grover is putting the pieces of his mother's death into a framework that he can understand. *Grover* is a story about death and how it affects the strong and the weak. It is not a sentimental story but a strong one that suggests we all have to wrestle with the grim reality of our lives in the ways that we know best.

In an article on violence in children's books, James Giblin, a children's book editor, identifies six criteria by which he evaluates violence in the manuscripts he receives. These criteria are worthy of careful consideration:

1. *Appropriateness.* Very few subjects are inappropriate in themselves; it is all in how the author treats them.
2. *Realism.* Does the author portray the necessary facts of the situation, ugly as they may be?

[5]Marie Winn, *The Plug-In Drug* (New York: Viking, 1977), p. 77; Television Bureau of Advertising (477 Madison Avenue, New York, NY 10022), January 1984 report.

[6]Frank Mankiewicz and Joel Swerdlow, *Remote Control: Television and the Manipulation of American Life* (New York: Times Books, 1978), pp. 15–72.

[7]Vera Cleaver and Bill Cleaver, *Grover,* illustrated by Frederick Marvin (Philadelphia: Lippincott, 1970), p. 95.

3. *Honesty*. Does the author portray fully and fairly both sides of a conflict, the many dimensions of a personality?
4. *Depth*. Does the author present a textured, many-leveled experience?
5. *Emotion*. Does the author write with feeling and emotion?
6. *Thoughtfulness*. Does the author evince a spirit or breadth that extends beyond the particular subject. Does he or she help the child develop a perspective?[8]

The same criteria are appropriate for evaluating explicitness in sex and bodily functions in books for children. Betty Miles raises this issue in *Maudie and Me and the Dirty Book*. When seventh-grader Kate Harris teams up with a classmate to read aloud to first-graders, one of her choices—about a puppy being born—triggers a discussion among the 6-year-olds about human birth and conception. While Kate handles the discussion with poise, a parent complaint eventually brings about a town meeting concerning what is appropriate in the elementary classroom curriculum. Miles treats the topics of conception, birth, and censorship in an open and forthright way.

Frankness in discussing sexuality is even more evident in books addressed to a young adolescent audience. John Donovan's *Remove Protective Coating a Little at a Time* concerns the physical and emotional maturing of 14-year-old Harry. Harry can't communicate with his businessman father or his mother, who is dealing with a nervous breakdown. His preoccupation with his developing sexuality leads him to consult his best friend, who asks if he ever gets "hard-ons." Later, Harry attempts to have intercourse with Marilyn, the "sure score" at summer camp: "Harry tried. He thought of every wonderful thought he had ever had about sex, but nothing happened . . . Harry sat, silent, his shorts still tangled around his ankles."[9] While Harry remains at a distance from his parents, a friendship with an eccentric old woman he meets in the park provides him with some reassurance. The vivid writing has the impact of modern poetry. Explicit references to sex are not inserted for shock value but as a necessary part of Harry's understanding of his growing up in today's world.

SEX-ROLE STEREOTYPING

Since children's books have always reflected the general social and human values of a society, it is not surprising that they are now being scrutinized closely for sexist attitudes. The raised general consciousness level of the children's book world is reflected in the increasing number of books that present positive images of girls and women.

However, teachers, librarians, authors, and editors are more aware of racial stereotyping than of sex prejudice. (Racism in books is discussed in the section "Appreciating Racial and Ethnic Diversity" later in this chapter.) All stereotyping is dehumanizing, for it treats individuals as a group without regard to individual differences, personalities, or capabilities. A book may be considered sexist if women and girls are exclusively assigned traditional female roles or if men and boys are expected to behave in certain prescribed ways, always assuming leadership roles and the exclusive rights to certain professions.

The difficulty in decrying a book as sexist is the fact that stereotypes develop from what was once considered the norm. One hundred years ago in this country most women were housewives; the agrarian society depended on them. We should not reject such a fine book as *The Witch of Blackbird Pond* (Speare) because the heroine's greatest problem appears to be whom she will marry. In 1688 Kit had little other choice. We can, however, delight in her rebellion against the strict Puritan way of life in Connecticut, in her courageous friendship with the Quaker "witch" Hannah, and in her compassion for the child Prudence. Again there is no point in denouncing fairy tales for their sexist portrayal of beautiful young girls waiting for the arrival of their princes or for evil stepmothers or nagging wives. Such stories reflect the longings and beliefs of a society long past. To change the folktales would be to destroy our traditional heritage. A book should not be criticized, then, for being historically authentic or true to its traditional genre. However, we have every right to be critical when such stereotyped thinking is perpetuated in contemporary literature. Today's books must reflect a more liberated point of view; they must

[8]James C. Giblin, "Violence: Factors Considered by a Children's Book Editor," *Elementary English*, vol. 1 (January 1972), pp. 64–67.
[9]John Donovan, *Remove Protective Coating a Little at a Time* (New York: Harper & Row, 1973), pp. 12–14.

reflect the assumption that a wide range of occupations, education, speech patterns, and futures is possible for all persons, regardless of race, sex, creed, or age.

Sex discrimination permeates our modern society to the point where it is seldom questioned. It is not surprising, then, to find examples of sex prejudice in books for children. But well-written contemporary literature must do more than mirror society; it must make its own comment about it and help the reader view society in a new perspective. In *Up a Road Slowly,* published in 1966, Irene Hunt has helped the reader to see many dimensions to the character Uncle Haskell. Despite the fact that he is an alcoholic and a pathological liar, he can be kind and helpful to his niece Julie. Because he is a sympathetic character, his advice to Julie carries more importance for her and, unfortunately, the reader. As Julie talks about her future, notice Haskell's answer:

"If I [Julie] ever have a boy, I'm going to see that he gets the blame for the things he does just as much as the girls do," I said.

"You're never going to get the chance to have a boy if you don't do something about that truculent little chin of yours." He got to his feet, hoisted the golf bag to his shoulder; and stooped to tweak my nose. "Accept the fact that this is a man's world and learn to play the game gracefully, my sweet." [10]

This is the kind of advice you might expect from the Uncle Haskells of this world, but both Julie and the author appear to accept it, for they make no rejoinder.

Despite such deprecating passages in some books, there are other children's books that do provide a positive image of women. In Burch's story, *Queenie Peavy,* Queenie throws rocks and spits tobacco, but she also shows compassion for a classmate who faints from hunger. Gradually, Queenie learns that she doesn't have to fight the world because her father is in prison. She loses some of her antagonism, but she never loses the integrity of her own person.

Many books of children's literature present the "Tomboy Turned Beautiful Young Woman"

theme. *Kick a Stone Home* by Smith does not follow this typical pattern. Fifteen-year-old Sara is a good football player and boys *want* her on their team. However, she does not date the team members, she has few friends, and is still recovering from her parents' divorce of three years ago. She is unsure of everything except her vocation, having decided to be a veterinarian. How Sara gradually comes to terms with herself and her emotions makes for a well-written story of the difficulties of early adolescence. It may be, however, that the author has worked too hard to prove that her heroine is different from other girls, thereby making Sara too unique. This may be a problem for authors writing about a controversial subject. (See Chapters 7 and 10 for other stories with strong female characters.)

In preparing a revised list of non-sexist books about girls titled *Little Miss Muffet Fights Back,* the editors indicate what they looked for:

- Girls and women who were active, interested and interesting people involved in exciting work and adventures
- Stories of girls and women with positive personality characteristics—intelligence, independence, warmth, bravery, strength, and competence
- The portrayal of positive adult female roles other than that of mother in which girl characters *were* ambitious and also took pride in their own achievements
- Authors' explicit comments on sex discrimination where required by the plot
- Books that dealt thoughtfully with the problems of friendship and of loving other people, in which romantic love is not portrayed as a girl's only satisfaction
- Writing of quality and literary merit and valid themes which combine to delight and inspire readers [11]

Boys, too, have been victimized by sex-role stereotyping in children's literature. They have been consistently reminded that boys don't cry, for example, so that it is a relief to find in stories such

[10] Irene Hunt, *Up a Road Slowly* (Chicago: Follett, 1966), p. 31.

[11] Feminists on Children's Media, *Little Miss Muffet Fights Back.* rev. ed. (Whitestone, NY 11357: Feminist Book Mart [162-11 Ninth Avenue], 1974), pp. 18–20.

as Clymer's *Luke Was There* that tough Julius cries openly when he voluntarily returns to the children's home and finds his favorite social worker is there. In Graeber's story of *Mustard*, both parents and 8-year-old Alex grieve together for the death of their beloved old pet cat. Boys have frequently been stereotyped in animal stories as having to kill an animal they have loved as their initiation into manhood. In Rawlings' *The Yearling*, Jody is ordered to shoot his pet deer because it is destroying the family's crops. At the book's end he recalls his love for his pet: "He did not believe he should ever again love anything, man or woman or his own child, as he loved the Yearling. He would be lonely all his life. But a man took it for his share and went on."[12] In Gipson's *Old Yeller*, after the boy shoots his possibly rabid dog, his father tells him to try to forget and go on being a man. Stories such as these must cause us to question the way in which some of our best literature conditions boys to be hard and strong.

However, in books that are designed to *combat* stereotypes, of whatever kind, there is a very real danger that the author will attempt to preach or teach. The book written solely to promote an ideological position—such as a non-sexist book, or a story showing the evils of prejudice, or the narrow-mindedness of suburbia—may be overpowered by its theme, didactic in its approach. The writing in such made-to-order books is usually sharply contrasted with the writing in books that have grown from the author's own experiences and feelings.

THE BACKGROUND OF THE AUTHOR

A related controversy swirls about the racial background of the author. Must an author be black to write about blacks, Chinese to write about Chinese, Native American to write about Native Americans, and so on? As Virginia Hamilton states:

> It happens that I know Black people better than any other people because I am one of them and I grew up knowing what it is we are about . . . The writer uses the most comfortable milieu in which to tell a story, which is why my characters are Black. Often being Black is significant to the story; other times, it is not.

The writer will always attempt to tell stories no one else can tell.[13]

One point of view urges that only minority authors should be the writers of so-called ethnic books. Certainly it is generally accepted that an author can write best about what he or she has experienced. Yet the hallmark of fine writing is the quality of the imagination with which that writing is involved. Imagination is not the exclusive property of any race or sex but the universal quality of all fine writers. Black authors and artists are not going to want to be limited to writing only about the black experience, nor should they be limited in this way. We need to focus on two aspects of every book: (1) What is its literary merit? and (2) Will children enjoy it?

In preparing her bibliography of *The Black Experience in Children's Books*, Augusta Baker used another criterion for selecting books, namely their contribution to the Black Experience:

> Blacks and whites have each, from their own vantage point, made a contribution to the "Black Experience" in the past and in the present and they will both contribute in the future. Work of an author or artist, black or white, has been included and recognized wherever it has demonstrated a sensitivity to the black man's striving to fulfill the American dream or attempting to maintain his identity, with dignity, in the total human community.[14]

CATEGORIZING LITERATURE

Reviewers, educators, and curriculum-makers may often categorize books according to their content. Categorizing serves textbook authors by allowing them to talk about several books as a group. It serves educators who hope to group books around a particular theme for classroom study. While one person might place Paterson's *Bridge to Terabithia* in a group of books about "making friends," it could just as easily be placed in another group: "growing up," "learning to accept death," or "well-written books." It is a disservice both to book and to reader if we apply a label and imply

[12]Marjorie Kinnan Rawlings, *The Yearling,* illustrated by Edward Shenton (New York: Scribner, 1938), p. 400.

[13]Virginia Hamilton, "Writing the Source: In Other Words," *The Horn Book Magazine,* vol. 54 (December 1978), p. 618.
[14]Augusta Baker, *The Black Experience in Children's Books* (New York Public Library, 1984), p. iii.

that this is what the book is about. Readers with their own purposes and backgrounds will see many different aspects and strengths in a piece of literature. It is helpful to remember that our experiences with art occur at many different, unique, and personal levels. While teachers may wish to lead children to talk about a particular aspect of a book, they will not want to suggest that this is the only aspect worth pursuing.

A second issue in the categorizing of literature relates to its appropriateness for a specific age level. Realistic fiction is often categorized as for upper elementary or middle grade and junior high or young adult (YA) readers. Yet, anyone who has spent time with 9- to 14-year-old readers has surely noticed the wide ranges of reading interests, abilities, and perceptions present. Betsy Byars' *The Pinballs* and Judy Blume's *Are You There, God? It's Me, Margaret* have challenged and entertained readers from fourth grade through high school. To suggest that these titles are "for 10- to 12-year-old readers" would ignore the ages of half of the readership of these popular authors.

In this chapter, books are arranged according to categories based on theme and content merely for the convenience of discussion. They could have been rearranged in many other ways. The ages of main characters are noted, where appropriate, as a clue to potential use in classrooms. In some instances we have also noted, with references to actual classroom teachers' experiences, at which grade levels certain titles seem to have greatest impact.

BECOMING ONE'S OWN PERSON

The story of every man, every woman is the story of growing up, of becoming a person, of struggling to become one's own person. The kind of person you become has its roots in the experiences of childhood—how much you were loved, how little you were loved; the people who were significant to you, the ones who were not; the places you've been, and those you did not go to; the things you wanted, and the things you did not get. Yet a person is always more than the totality of these experiences; the way a person organizes, understands, and relates to those experiences makes for individuality.

Childhood is not a waiting room for adulthood but the place where adulthood is shaped by one's family, peers, society, and, most importantly, the person one is becoming. The passage from childhood to adulthood is a significant journey for each person. It is no wonder that children's literature is filled with stories of growing up in our society today.

Living in a Family

Within the family the human personality is nurtured; here the growing child learns of love and hate, fear and courage, joy and sorrow. The first "family-life" stories tended to portray life without moments of anger and hurt, emphasizing only the happy or adventurous moments. Today the balance scale has tilted in the other direction, and it is often more difficult to find a family story with well-adjusted children and happily married parents than it is to find a story about family problems.

In earlier stories like Eleanor Estes' pre-television era books *The Moffats*, *The Middle Moffat*, and *Rufus M.*, parents tend to recede into the background and the emphasis is on the children's fun and problems. Elizabeth Enright's *The Saturdays* portrays the close-knit Melendy family in New York in the early 1940s. Their plan to pool allowances so that each child in turn may enjoy a special Saturday excursion sends one to an art museum, another to the opera, one to the circus, and one to the beauty salon. Sidney Taylor's *All-of-a-Kind Family* series recreated family life in a Lower East Side Jewish home in the 1930s. Titled "all-of-a-kind" because all are girls until a baby boy comes along, the children understand that this also means that they are Jewish and "we're all close and loving and loyal—and our family will always be that." Descriptions of Jewish feasts and holy days contribute much to readers' understanding of one family's religious faith. Children still enjoy these series, set as they are in the "olden days," and adults often point to them as evidence of the pleasures of a less fast-paced life. However, many young readers prefer stories of today's children whom they might meet in the neighborhood, the shopping center, a playground, or the classroom. These more recent books have included adults with both strengths and weaknesses and show children interacting with them. In some almost "formula stories," parents and adults are depicted as completely inept and unable to cope with or understand their children. It would seem that a balance is needed if children are to see life wholly and gain some perspective from their reading.

FAMILY RELATIONSHIPS

Episodic stories centered comfortably in a warm family setting are often the first chapter-book stories younger children approach. Johanna Hurwitz has created a *Busybody Nora* and her younger brother *Superduper Teddy*. Nora shows her growing independence as she knocks on doors of friends in her New York City apartment building to get contributions for the "Stone Soup" she and her mother are making for a group dinner. Teddy ventures forth to feed a neighbor's cat all by himself. An added bonus for readers is the children's grandfather, who retells folktales as if he personally knew the characters, such as Jack (of beanstalk fame) and Cinderella. Hurwitz also includes many other references to the literature of childhood.

Following in a similar tradition, Christine McDonnell presents six chapters in the lives of first-grader Ivy and her school friend the obstreperous Leo in *Don't Be Mad, Ivy*. Ivy's dilemmas, such as her reluctance to part with a toy bulldozer which is a birthday present to another child, or her "borrowing" of a friend's stuffed bear, are very true to 6- and 7-year-olds. Leo's story is told in *Toad Food and Measle Soup;* the title represents his misinterpretation of his mother's vegetarian venturing into cooking with tofu and miso soup. In *Lucky Charms and Birthday Wishes,* Emily starts a new school year, discovers an intriguing dollhouse, and for her birthday receives a hand-made rag doll which becomes an important link with her grandmother. Both Hurwitz and McDonnell write humorous, sensitive, and perceptive stories about everyday occurrences in the lives of 6- to 8-year-olds.

Beverly Cleary's stories about Ramona continue to be enjoyed both by children of Ramona's age and by older children who have younger siblings or who remember "how I used to be." These stories present a family coping with a working mother; a father who loses his job and, in a later book, returns to college; older and younger sister

disagreements; and all of the feelings that accompany family crises. Cleary's humorous stories concern "the problems which are small to adults but which loom so large in the lives of children, the sort of problems children can solve themselves."[15] In *Ramona the Pest*, Ramona can hardly wait for kindergarten to begin so that she can share her doll with the green hair, named "Chevrolet" after her aunt's car. The green hair is a result of the doll's encounter with soap and Dutch Cleanser. In *Ramona and Her Mother,* Ramona worries that her mother doesn't love her as much as she loves Beezus, her older sister. *Ramona and Her Father* are more frequently together now that she returns from school to find him waiting for telephone calls about jobs he has applied for. She is embarrassed about the makeshift sheep costume her overworked mother creates for her role in the Christmas Pageant. However, the advice of "The Three Wise Persons" helps her change her mind.

Ramona Quimby, Age 8 marks Ramona's arrival in third grade. There she enjoys her teacher's DEAR time (Drop Everything and Read) and stages a hilarious parody of a cat food commercial for her book report. Once again Cleary reassures us through Ramona that even happy families sometimes have bad moments together. In *Ramona Forever,* Ramona's favorite aunt is married, the family's pet cat dies, and Mrs. Quimby is expecting a new baby. After the family thinks of all kinds of appropriate male names, Roberta arrives. Still a third-grader, but a more mature *older* sister now, Ramona continues to be her irrepressible dramatic self. Ramona and her family are people worth knowing.

Lois Lowry's *Anastasia Krupnik* is the only girl in fourth grade whose name will not fit on the front of a sweatshirt. During Poetry Week at school, her teacher prefers the rhymed doggerel of her classmates to Anastasia's free verse. And to top off the list of "Things I Love / Things I Hate" which Anastasia keeps, one of the things she is sure she is going to hate is the arrival of a new baby brother. In an effort to appease her, Anastasia's parents let her choose the baby's name and she considers the worst one possible. But the death of her grandmother gives Anastasia some

[15]Beverly Cleary, "The Laughter of Children," *The Horn Book Magazine,* vol. 58 (October 1982), p. 557.

thoughts about the importance of family and of memories—and the new baby becomes Sam after her grandfather, met only through the reminiscences of the grandmother. Anastasia's ever-changing lists appear at the end of each chapter and are humorous exclamation points to the preceding events. Each succeeding novel in the Anastasia series chronicles some new quandary—a move to Boston, a stint as a maid, a growing need to talk to someone who understands, and a chance to manage the household while her mother is away. In Lowry's stories, the Krupnik parents treat Anastasia and her brother with openness, humor, and respect; they are both literate and concerned parents whose careers as artist and English teacher do not interfere with their interactions with Anastasia. Lowry has a gift for natural-sounding dialogue and situational humor, anchored by keen observations of human nature and family relationships. Anastasia's writing abilities both as journal-keeper and list-maker provide many moments of humor, insight, and inspiration to other young writers.

A very different family life is portrayed by Paula Fox in *The Stone-faced Boy.* Gus, a middle child, has learned to keep an expressionless face when his brothers and sisters tease him, thus earning himself the nickname "stone-face." During a great snowstorm, his visiting aunt gives him a geode. That night Gus is talked into rescuing a stray dog that his sister has found in a fox trap. Although Gus is terrified, he does rescue the dog and the experience changes him so that when his brother goads him to break open the geode, he refuses:

> He knew how the stone would look inside, but he didn't choose to break it open yet. When he felt like it, he would take the hammer and tap the geode in such a way that it would break perfectly . . .[16]

Behind the stone face lies a personality as intact and as perfect as the crystals of the geode in this story of a boy finding himself amidst the turmoil of family living. C. S. Adler's *Get Lost, Little Brother* also presents a boy, 11-year-old Todd, whose efforts to protect a small island he has

[16]Paula Fox, *The Stone-faced Boy,* illustrated by Donald A. Mackay (Englewood Cliffs, N.J.: Bradbury, 1968), p. 106.

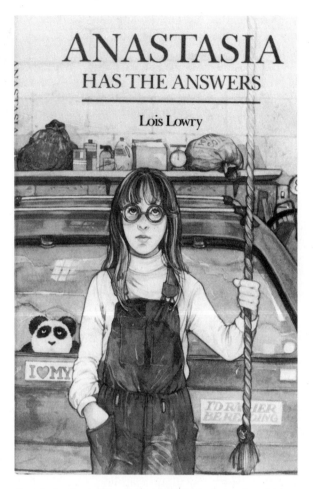

Anastasia Krupnik's determination to learn to climb a rope leads to unexpected fame in this sixth story from Lois Lowry's popular and humorous series. Jacket art by Diane DeGroat.

"claimed" eventually earn him the respect of his older brothers.

In *Tough Tiffany* by Belinda Hurmence, 11-year-old Tiff likes to think of herself as "tough," able to deal with any situation. She is the youngest of six children, and most of her problems are concerned with the everyday business of just getting along—with all her sisters in an overcrowded bedroom; with the bill collectors who fail to appreciate Mama's creative budgeting; with her Granny Turner, who is often irascible when Tiff goes to her house to help out. The most troubling situation, however, is the family's disagreement over her sister Dawn, 15, pregnant, and having a hard time deciding what to do with her life. The strength of this North Carolina family's ties is a theme the author emphasizes in Granny Turner's stories about family history and in the Turner reunion. Contemporary dialogue and black dialect expressions, plus personal idioms, help to define the characters and make lively reading.

A mother-and-daughter relationship is the center of M. E. Kerr's novel with the deliberately shocking title of *Dinky Hocker Shoots Smack.* Actually, Dinky, the very fat daughter of a social "do-gooder," does not shoot smack; but she does spend a great deal of her time eating and watching her tropical fish! Mrs. Hocker hardly notices her daughter until the night that Mrs. Hocker is to receive the Good Samaritan Award. Then the words "Dinky Hocker Shoots Smack" mysteriously appear on sidewalks, curbstones, and buildings all over Brooklyn Heights. Dinky has painted them there while the banquet was in progress. Horrified, Mrs. Hocker turns her attention from trying to cure drug addicts in the community to the needs of her own daughter. Caustic and witty, Kerr has written a sad social commentary on our times. Dinky's rebellion reflects the desperate need of all children to have their parents see them as individuals.

No book has revealed the complexities of sibling rivalry with as much depth as Paterson's *Jacob Have I Loved.* Louise is convinced that she lives in her twin sister's shadow. Caroline, her beautiful blonde delicate sister, is the talented one who leaves their island home of Rass each week to take piano lessons. Louise, or "Wheeze," the hated name Caroline has given her, believes her sister has stolen her parents' affection, her friends Call and the Captain, and her chance for an education. Her half-crazed Bible-quoting grandmother recognizes her burning resentment of Caroline and taunts her with the quote "Jacob have I loved but Esau have I hated." Louise is horrified when she looks up the passage to find that the speaker is God. So now, like the Biblical Esau, even God must see her as the despised elder twin.

Paterson has skillfully woven this Bible story of Esau, first born, who was tricked into giving up his birthright to Jacob, the younger of the twin brothers, into this modern novel of sibling rivalry. Only maturity and a family of her own can help Louise to put her hatred and resentment of her sister to rest. The novel ends on a theme of reconciliation as Louise, now a midwife in a mountain community, fights to save the life of the weaker second-born baby of a pair of twins.

In her Newbery acceptance speech for *Jacob Have I Loved,* the author, herself the middle child of five, said: ". . . among children who grow up together in a family there run depths of feeling that will permeate their souls for good and ill as long as they live."[17]

EXTENDED FAMILIES

The extended family of grandparents, uncles, aunts, or cousins often plays a significant role in a child's developing perceptions of the world. Children's literature presents other adults, and sometimes even children, acting in the place of absent or incapacitated parents.

In Eleanor Clymer's book the responsibility for *My Brother Stevie* is given to 12-year-old Annie Jenner. In fact, the last thing her mother told Annie before she left was to "Take care of your brother." Stevie is 8 years old and "full of the devil." Grandmother, who has reluctantly taken the children to live with her in a big city project apartment, can't cope with Stevie, either. He breaks into candy machines and throws rocks at trains, and Annie is frightened. Then Stevie gets a new teacher, Miss Stover, and Annie has someone who can help her with him. Stevie does behave better in school until suddenly Miss Stover is called home, and Stevie reverts to his old ways. Annie devises a desperate scheme resulting in a train ride to Miss Stover's house in the country. Stevie changes, but so, too, does his grandmother, as Annie's notes show:

> So now everything is pretty much the same as before, but not quite the same, because as I said, we did this thing [the train ride] and it made us all a little different.[18]

This is an honest, realistic story that shows the influence of each character on the others.

In *The Thunder-Pup* by Janet Hickman, the out-

[17]Katherine Paterson, "Newbery Medal Acceptance" in *Gates of Excellence* (New York: Elsevier/Nelson Books, 1981), p. 118.

[18]Eleanor Clymer, *My Brother Stevie* (New York: Holt, Rinehart and Winston, 1967), p. 75.

come of Linnie McKay's longing for a dog seems to depend on her great-aunt and her grandfather, who are as much a part of the family as her parents or her brother. Sharp-tongued Aunt Em is strongly opposed to dogs, but easy-going Granpop manages to keep secret his discovery that Linnie and a friend are hiding two stray pups in a neighbor's garage. Although Linnie believes that her tenth birthday gift will be a "legitimate" puppy, her parents have planned a different sort of surprise: they will move into a more spacious house of their own, away from Granpop and Aunt Em, who, in Linnie's eyes, "belonged with every day the way a sink belongs in a kitchen." Readers in the 8- to 11-year-old range can take satisfaction from Linnie's determination to keep one of the strays and from the courage she finds to face her fear of storms. This is a warm and humorous book that effectively portrays the tensions and special affections of three generations in one household. In an earlier book about the McKay family, *The Stones*, Granpop and Aunt Em are surrogate parents for Linnie and her brother Garrett while their mother works and their father is missing in action in World War II.

Patricia MacLachlan's *Arthur for the Very First Time* chronicles the summer of a 10-year-old boy. From the moment his parents drop Arthur at the farm of his idiosyncratic Uncle Wrisby and Aunt Elda ("shaped like an uncertain circle, made up of large shifting spaces like an easy-to-color coloring book"), he begins to change. His aunt and uncle speak French to a pet chicken, sing to a pig, and allow Arthur to check off the foods he doesn't like to eat. Always an observer, Arthur keeps copious notes in his journal: "I write about people, things I see, everything I think about," he tells his uncle. Uncle Wrisby is not impressed. Neither is his new friend Moira. Refusing to call Arthur anything but "Mouse," she accuses him of spending so much time writing in his journal that he doesn't really see what is going on around him. Arthur engineers and builds a pigpen and is justifiably proud, but Bernadette the pig will have nothing to do with the new location until a fierce storm drives her into it to give birth to her litter. When Arthur saves the first piglet from dying and protects Bernadette from the rain with Moira's help, she later excitedly tells everyone "Arthur did it . . . Arthur really *did* it." She has called him "Arthur" for the very first

time. MacLachlan's story is full of warmth, humor, and quirky characters, both human and animal. While the book has much to say about the values of *doing* as opposed to *observing*, it also suggests that what is important or real is often at first difficult to see. Her writing respects readers' intelligence. In Betsy Byars' *The House of Wings*, Sammy's parents leave him behind with his aged grandfather, a recluse in an old run-down house, while they go ahead to find a place to stay in Detroit. When Sammy refuses to believe his grandfather and tries to follow them, the old man runs after the furious boy. But in the midst of the chase he calls him to come and look at a wounded crane. Together the two of them catch the crane and care for it. Suddenly the boy desperately wants his grandfather to know him the way he knows birds:

> He wanted his grandfather to be able to pick him out of a thousand birds the way he could pick out the blackbird, the owls, the wild ducks. . . . He said, "My name's Sammy."[19]

His grandfather looks at Sammy and then, instead of calling him "Boy," calls him "Sammy," and the relationship is sealed. This is one of Betsy Byars' best books. Her two characters are well drawn: the eccentric old man, more interested in birds than in his grandson; the boy Sammy, furious at being left, uncertain of himself, and desperately wanting to love and be loved. Keith Robertson's *In Search of a Sandhill Crane* is a slower-moving story than *The House of Wings*, but it has some of the same characteristics.

A memorable girl is Eleanor Cameron's main character in *That Julia Redfern*. Julia throws herself into her activities, whether borrowing her older brother's bicycle or "skinning the rabbit" on the playground climber. "You live too hard, Julia," says her mother. One day, after Julia falls and knocks herself out, she dreams a curious dream about her father, who is away in World War I. In it, he tells her to "remember to tell Mama to go through my papers." Julia's dream results in the posthumous publication of her father's short story. Julia's imaginative gifts flower in the second book in the time sequence, *Julia and the Hand of God*,

[19]Betsy Byars, *The House of Wings*, illustrated by Daniel Schwartz (New York: Viking, 1972), p. 141.

when she is given an elegant leather-bound journal as a birthday gift by her favorite uncle. There she chronicles the loss of her friend Maisie for so simple an act as cremating a mouse in her mother's saucepan and the wonder of escaping a forest fire in the Oakland hills. *A Room Made of Windows* is the way Julia describes her new room after her family moves to another house. There, she continues to develop her perceptive capabilities as well as her writing skills. Family ties and tensions are skillfully revealed, and Cameron's superb writing allows the reader to share not only Julia's world but also her unique perception of it. Potential readers may want to be alerted to the fact that the earliest book, *A Room Made of Windows*, features Julia at 12, while the most recent ones, *That Julia Redfern* and *Julia's Magic*, take readers back to Julia's early childhood.

Both Rachel's mother and grandmother have warned Rachel not to question her great-grandmother Nana Sashie about the past. It only depresses her, they say; talk about school. But school bores Rachel and one day when Nana Sashie lets drop the fact that she and her family didn't just leave Russia, they escaped, Rachel is suddenly drawn into an exciting tale of family history. *The Night Journey* is Nana Sashie's harrowing story of the escape of 9-year-old Sashie and her family from the persecution of the Jews in czarist Russia in 1900. Kathryn Lasky has wisely framed this story in a contemporary family setting complete with Rachel's trials over a school production of *Oklahoma*. Chapters alternate; one is set in present time and the next is part of Nana Sashie's continuing story of the family's flight disguised as itinerant Purim players. As they make their way toward the border, they need to carry enough gold to pay the driver of the cart of chicken crates under which they are hidden and they need to bribe the treacherous border guards. By slipping from Rachel's present-day concerns to her hearing of Nana Sashie's story each evening, Lasky lets readers who might not normally read historical fiction be gently moved into it, as is Rachel. Trina Schart Hyman's bold black and white drawings help children visualize places, characters, and the family samovar which plays an important role in both past and present times. This is an excellent story to read aloud in conjunction with a study of family history. Lisl Weil's *Esther* tells the story

upon which the Purim play so essential to the family's escape is based (see Chapter 6).

In *Homecoming*, Cynthia Voigt introduces a most remarkable family of four children in search of a relative with whom to live. When 13-year-old Dicey realizes her mother has abandoned the family, she assumes the role of a parent and decides she and her two brothers and sister must walk south along the Connecticut shoreline to Bridgeport, where Great Aunt Cilla lives. With little money and a paper bag full of clothes, the children start their long walk, living on store-bought doughnuts, apples, and milk or by fishing. They sleep in abandoned houses, in the woods, and at a state park. They manage to supplement their meager cash supply by carrying bags for customers at a grocery store. Dicey holds her family together until they arrive at their Great Aunt Cilla's house only to discover that she has died and Cousin Eunice, a self-absorbed and fussy woman, now lives there. Dicey accepts Eunice's reluctant offer to take them in but is uneasy about it. While the younger children become involved in summer church activities, Dicey keeps house and works part-time as a helper in a grocery store. Then Dicey makes two discoveries—she has a grandmother living in Maryland that no one ever told her about; and Eunice has decided to adopt the family, all but the mercurial 6-year-old Sammy. So, determined to keep her family together, Dicey once again sets out to move the children to Maryland. After a series of adventures and a harrowing escape, the children reach their goal, only to find that their grandmother, an eccentric, independent, and angry old lady, wants nothing to do with them. Hoping to win her approval, the children pitch into the work of keeping up the huge run-down farmhouse and garden, quickly growing to love the place and the nearby ocean. But they are less sure of their grandmother. Ten-year-old James asks Dicey:

> "Do you like her?" Dicey considered this. "You know? I could. I mean, she's so odd and prickly. She fights us, or anyway I feel like I'm fighting her and she's fighting back, as if we both know what's going on but neither of us is saying anything. It's fun . . . but she's a good enemy—you know? . . . So she might make a good friend."[20]

[20]Cynthia Voigt, *Homecoming* (New York: Atheneum, 1981), p. 289.

When Gram and Dicey finally settle into a tentative relationship, Dicey sees that Gram does care about her family and that she wants them to stay.

While the previous lengthy story focuses on Dicey Tillerman and her family's survival, *Dicey's Song* is considerably shorter and centers on the growth of the four children and their developing relationship with their grandmother. Nine-year-old Maybeth tackles her reading problem with James' help while James struggles to balance his insatiable mind with a desire for friendship. Sammy's belligerence is gradually subdued; and Gram emerges as a strong-willed, stubborn, but loving and courageous woman. However, it is Dicey's story: she must learn to let her family grow in independence, accept her growth toward maturity, and acknowledge that others are important to her. Both books concern distinct, strongly realized and vulnerable characters who change gradually as a result of each encounter. *Dicey's Song,* a Newbery award-winner, is full of warmth as the Tillermans and Gram learn to be a family. It is this feeling of family which allows the children, and the reader, to accept their mother's death at the story's end.

In *A Solitary Blue,* Voigt develops the story of Jeff Green, a minor character in *Dicey's Song.* Again the story is about the gradual development of a loving relationship, this one between a boy and his uncommunicative father. After his mother Melody left home for good when he was 7, Jeff became so fearful of losing his father that he has become an expert in anticipating his needs and never disturbing him. Father and son continue their emotionless co-existence until the summer Melody invites her son to Charleston. Jeff is overwhelmed by his mother's beauty and apparent love for him. He allows himself to feel and becomes vulnerable once again. The next summer, however, his visit is a disaster. His mother spends all her time with Max, a journalist, traveling to investigate one social cause after another. Jeff, left alone, makes daily trips to an uninhabited island in a Carolina marsh. Here he feels a kind of kinship with a solitary blue heron.

Once home, Jeff sinks into a deep depression. His father recognizes what has happened, for Melody nearly destroyed him in the same way. Reaching out to his son at last, Jeff's father buys for the two of them an old hunting cabin on a point where a creek enters the Chesapeake Bay. It

The four abandoned Tillerman children look for some sign of acceptance from a grandmother they have just walked hundreds of miles to meet. Jacket art by Ted Lewin.

is here that Jeff meets Dicey Tillerman and becomes an accepted visitor in their home. *A Solitary Blue* is a remarkable novel. Its major theme is love in all of its various forms—love that can't be expressed, learning to love, manipulative love, and the depth of real love between a father and a son.

FAMILIES IN TRANSITION

With nearly one out of every two marriages now ending in divorce, it is only natural that books attempt to describe children's pain and suffering in living through their parents' separation. Peggy Mann's *My Dad Lives in a Downtown Hotel* lets the reader *feel* the pain of the situation. Joey is awkward and self-conscious in talking to his dad in the rather sterile surroundings of a hotel room. His mother has difficulty in telling Joey about the divorce, but gradually Joey begins to accept his situation. He realizes he is not alone when Pepe Gonzalez (whose father is still in Puerto Rico) tells him there are fifty-three kids in his block living in a house with no father, and so the two of them decide to form a club.

Several titles by popular authors of books for middle-grade readers also deal with divorce. Beverly Cleary won the Newbery award for *Dear Mr. Henshaw,* the story of Leigh Botts, a child of divorce. The plot is skillfully revealed through a series of letters to an author, Mr. Henshaw. Required to write a letter to his favorite author, sixth-grade Leigh writes Mr. Henshaw and asks for an immediate answer to ten questions. Mr. Henshaw responds with ten questions of his own. In the process of answering these questions (his mother says he has to) Leigh reveals how much he misses his truck-driver father and Bandit, his dog; his concern over who is stealing food from his lunch box; and his many attempts to write a prize story for the yearbook. While not as humorous as some of Beverly Cleary's other books, this one is more thoughtful and certainly presents an honest picture of a child living in a single-parent home. Leigh learns that there are some things he can't control (like his parents getting back together again), but he does figure out a way to scare away the lunch box thief and receives, not first place, but honorable mention for his story titled "A Day on Dad's Rig." Cleary's ear for portraying the way children think and speak is remarkably true.

Judy Blume's character Karen Newman thinks it is the end of the world when her father decides to go to Las Vegas to get a divorce. Suddenly she decides that if she could only get her parents together, they would change their minds. Her plan of showing them her Viking diorama isn't very successful, but when her brother Jeff runs away, they have to get together. Karen then learns that some very nice people are just impossible when they are together. She finds out that as much as she thought divorce was the awful end, *It's Not the End of the World.* This is one of Blume's best books. The characters are well realized, and she has realistically described the tension of the situation. In typical Blume fashion, real humor relieves the seriousness

of the problem. *I, Trissy* by Norma Fox Mazer is also a girl's first-person account of the problems of being caught somewhere between divorced parents. Simultaneously funny and heartbreaking, this is another popular "divorce story" for middle-graders.

Paula Danziger writes for a slightly older reader as she tells of the effects of divorce on 14-year-old Phoebe. Torn between her interior decorator mother and her painter father, each weekend she rides *The Divorce Express,* a bus which seems full of children shuttling between separated parents. Her new friend Rosie, who is in the same predicament, tells her:

> Don't be depressed . . . I've been living with it for years. You'll get used to it . . . [Y]ou know all those novels about divorce? They're mostly for the kids who are just starting it. There should be one about a kid who's lived with it for a long time. Then you'd see that we all survive it.[21]

Phoebe does survive. She becomes involved in her father's rural life, takes an active part in a cafeteria boycott at school, and begins what promises to be a good relationship with a boy. Throughout the book, Phoebe plays with anagrams, rearranging PARENTS to form ENTRAPS, for instance. By the story's end, she has learned that if she takes the letters in DIVORCES and rearranges them, she can spell DISCOVER. A sequel, *It's an Aardvark-Eat-Turtle World,* seems strained in comparison.

Betsy Byars frequently writes of children caught in complicated family situations. In *The Animal, the Vegetable, & John D Jones,* she explores the way tragedy can bring out emotions that are often concealed. Sixth-grader Clara and her older sister Deanie are delighted to be spending a vacation with their divorced father until they make the discovery that a woman friend of their father's and her son, John D, will be joining them. John D, who has "the constant companionship of the most intelligent, witty, and creative person in the world—himself," is also not pleased. He plans to spend the entire vacation as an observer, reading books, playing with his electronic games, and working on his book, which has chapters such as "Simple Ways to Get What You Want." It is not

21Paula Danziger, *The Divorce Express* (New York: Delacorte Press, 1982), p. 57.

until Clara is swept out to sea on a rubber raft that John D and Deanie reveal their feelings about themselves and their relationship with Clara. Byars has a keen ear for dialogue and is able to tell this serious story with humor and insight.

Children who must handle difficult situations are another theme of Betsy Byars' novels. Eleven-year-old *Cracker Jackson* suspects his much-loved former babysitter Alma is being abused by her husband. Since Alma has warned Cracker to "keep away or he'll hurt you," he sends his friend Goat on trumped-up errands to Alma's house to check on her. It is with Goat's help that Jackson tries to drive Alma in his mother's car to a shelter in the next town. But, in a classic response of battered wives, Alma backs out and insists on going home. The effect this has on Jackson causes his mother to intervene not quite in time to save Alma from one last violent episode, but soon enough to save her life and to relieve Jackson of the sense of responsibility which he has been carrying. In *The Night Swimmers*, three children are raising themselves while their father tries to pursue a career as a country-western singer. Retta cooks her special spaghetti for her brothers (noodles and tomato soup) and thinks of ways they can entertain themselves, such as swimming in neighbors' pools at night. It is only after the boys begin to move away from her to make friends on their own and her youngest brother nearly drowns that Retta realizes she will have to let them grow up. Like Jackson, she will also need some adult help to cope. As is typical of Byars' writing, deft touches of humor in dialogue, apt imagery or comparisons, and incidents which characters remember relieve the tension and make these stories popular with fifth- and sixth-graders.

Alternative life styles in a family have been explored in some contemporary books for children. One of the most sophisticated and amusing is Norma Klein's *Mom, the Wolf Man and Me*. Twelve-year-old Brett tells the story of her life with her never-been-married mother, who is a freelance photographer. Brett prefers their casual unscheduled life style to the restrictions that she imagines having a father and being part of a conventional family would bring. And so, though she likes Theo, the man with the wolfhound, she tries unsuccessfully to prevent a marriage. Klein describes Brett's anger, feelings of rejection following her mother's announcement, and gradual acceptance of the marriage. This is a frank and honest book that may shock, but it does portray life as it is for some contemporary families. Despite the unconventional family life, this is a warm story that shows much love and caring among its unorthodox characters.

Vera and Bill Cleaver have often looked at the harsher realities of life in their books—suicide, retardation, theft, and death. In *I Would Rather Be a Turnip*, they explore the problems created in a family when an older sister's child born out of wedlock comes to live with them in a small town. Annie is upset when she learns that 8-year-old Calvin is coming to live with them and is determined to hate him. Only as she sees the senseless prejudice of others toward the loving, amiable Calvin does Annie admit to herself how much she really likes him. Her change of heart is also influenced by a fair-minded black housekeeper who is sensitive to both children and to the situation. The authors show compassion and humor in the tone of this story.

Blowfish Live in the Sea by Paula Fox is told in the first person from 13-year-old Carrie's point of view. Her half-brother Ben, 19, is a college dropout whose main preoccupation is to scribble "blowfish live in the sea" on old envelopes, oak tables, or dusty windows. This piece of information is important to Ben because it represents his final disillusionment with his own father. Near the end of the story the reader finds out that his father had sent him a blowfish when Carrie was born, saying that it had come from the upper reaches of the Amazon; so Ben's knowledge of the real source of blowfish indicates his resentment of a father who is less than honest. Carrie, who loves Ben, agrees to go with him to meet his father for the first time. They find him in a rundown Boston boarding house. He is unreliable, drinks too much, and is a pathetic character. Ben no longer resents him and decides to stay and help him with the motel, his latest business venture. Carrie realizes that Ben has known what kind of a person his father was for a long time; this makes Ben's decision to try to help his father all the more poignant.

FOSTER CHILDREN

While placing children in foster homes is somewhat common in today's society, it is rare to find a sympathetic treatment of the many conflicting emotions the situation generates. Shirley Gordon tells a simple story of *The Boy Who Wanted a Family*. Seven-year-old Michael has been bounced around from foster home to foster home and would love to have a real family of his own. When he is taken by his social worker to Miss Graham's, he seems to have found the mother of his dreams, but first he must wait one long year for the final adoption papers to go through. The straightforward, uncomplicated plot and predictable ending make this a popular book with second- and third-graders. They can identify with Michael's dreams and apprehensions and are relieved when he finds "his own family."

The emotions engendered on all sides when the Sorenic family accepts Chad as a foster child are presented realistically in C. S. Adler's *The Cat That Was Left Behind*. Initially, Chad is convinced that he and his real mother will be reunited and that the Sorenics are one more temporary stop. While Mr. Sorenic and his son over-enthusiastically try to entice Chad into their summer vacation games, Chad prefers his private thoughts, the company of a loner cat, and an old fisherman down at the pier. Chad admires the cat's independence and would like to be equally free of his emotional encumbrances. As the cat gradually comes to trust and depend on Chad for food and affection, Chad, too, is becoming more and more attached to the Sorenic family. When the Sorenics invite Chad to join their family and try to help Chad find his cat, he realizes that he has come to care about this family and agrees to join it. While the cat can get along on its own without love and care, Chad cannot. The parallel situations of Chad and the abandoned cat are woven together in such a way as to develop insight in both the reader and the protagonist.

Leave it to Betsy Byars to write about three neglected children placed in a foster home in a way that is both poignant and humorous. In *The Pinballs,* Carlie is a tough, likable 12-year-old girl who has been repeatedly beaten up by her third stepfather. She endures her world by watching television and making caustic comments. Harvey arrives at the Masons' in a wheelchair because his alcoholic father accidentally ran over him and broke both his legs. The third child in this mismatched group is Thomas J., an 8-year-old boy

The jacket artist has symbolized Betsy Byars' concept of foster children as pinballs shot into the maze of society. Art by Ruth Sanderson.

going-on-eighty. Elderly twin spinsters had tried to raise him without notifying the authorities, so Thomas J. had never gone to school. Carlie maintains that they are all "'. . . just like pinballs. Somebody put in a dime and punched a button and out we come, ready or not, and settled in the same groove.'"[22] By the end of the story, Carlie has learned that life is determined not only by blind chance but also by initiative, for it is her creative planning that finally breaks through Harvey's depression and gives him some reason to

[22]Betsy Byars, *The Pinballs* (New York: Harper & Row, 1977), p. 29.

live. By including Thomas J. in her plans, Carlie makes him feel important, too. Carlie's change, from a defensive self-centered person to a compassionate human being, is gradual and believable, and she never loses her comical perspective on life. Middle-grade students enjoy hearing this story read aloud and meeting this fine cast of characters.

In Katherine Paterson's story, *The Great Gilly Hopkins* is not nearly the likable character that Carlie is; in fact, she is about as nasty as any 11-year-old child can be when she first arrives at her new foster home. She can't bear the huge, semiliterate Maime Trotter and her "retard" son, and so she sends a letter to her beautiful mother in California greatly exaggerating her situation. When she steals over one hundred dollars of Trotter's foster-care money and tries to buy a ticket to California, she is stopped by the police. Then she learns of the real love and trust that this woman has for her as she refuses to let the social worker move Gilly to yet another home. It is too late, however, as Gilly receives an answer to her letter in the form of a visit from her grandmother who she never knew existed. Gilly learns then that one has to accept responsibility for one's own actions. Trotter reminds her that life is tough: "Nothing to make you happy like doing good on a tough job, now, is there?" These larger-than-life characters are superbly drawn and most believable. Children delight in the swearing, self-sufficient young Gilly, but they will admire the more mature Gilly who has to learn her lessons the hard way. Slavik has shown that one of the consistent themes in Paterson's writings is that main characters always get their wishes—but not in the way they expected.[23] Gilly longed for a permanent home and family. At the end of the story her wish comes true, but it is a home with her grandmother, not with Courtney, the beautiful idealized mother she has created in her dreams. However, life with Maime Trotter, in which she had learned to accept and give love for the first time, made her ready for her real family. The reader knows that Gilly is capable of healing the hurt in Nonnie's life and that her own will be healed in the process.

[23]Christy Richards Slavik, "The Novels of Katherine Paterson: Implications for the Middle School." Unpublished doctoral dissertation, The Ohio State University, 1983.

Living with Others

Three- and 4-year-olds show momentary concern for their sandbox companions, but it is not until children go to school that the peer group becomes important. By the time children approach the middle elementary grades, what other children think is often more significant than what parents or teachers think. By the time children reach middle school or junior high school, the place in the peer group is all-important. Several authors are especially sensitive to these patterns in childhood society—finding acceptance among peers and making, or keeping, friends.

FINDING PEER ACCEPTANCE

The classic example of children's cruelty to others who are "different" is the well-known story of *The Hundred Dresses* by Eleanor Estes. Wanda Petronski, a Polish girl from a poor, motherless family, attempts unsuccessfully to win a place in the group by telling of the hundred dresses she owns. However, she wears the same faded blue dress each day and is taunted by the other girls. After she moves away, her hundred dresses are presented in an art context—one hundred fine drawings. The girls understand, too late, but it is Maddie, also poor, who worries the most as she recalls the way the teasing had started. She realizes her own cowardice:

> She had stood by silently, and that was just as bad as what Peggy had done. Worse, she was a coward. At least Peggy hadn't considered they were being mean, but she, Maddie, had thought they were doing wrong.[24]

Written over forty years ago, this story seems didactic when compared to more contemporary fiction. However, children still respond to its forceful message.

If one can believe the story of *Blubber* by Judy Blume, modern children can be much more vicious to each other than Peggy and Maddie were to Wanda. When fat, 10-year-old Linda Fischer gives her class report on "Whales," Caroline writes a note saying: "Blubber is a good name for her." In

[24]Eleanor Estes, *The Hundred Dresses*, illustrated by Louis Slobodkin (New York: Harcourt, 1944), p. 49.

no time everyone in the class reads the note and Linda is christened "Blubber." The cruelty is relentless and overdone; even the teachers appear to be totally unaware of the cruelty of the group. In fact, the teachers seem like stereotyped cardboard figures who never see a child as an individual and who use outmoded discipline techniques. At the end of the book the narrator of the story becomes the next victim of the leader's cruelty. While few of the characters have any redeeming qualities, this story does show how individuals may be manipulated by a strong leader. The book would have been strengthened if there had been even one sympathetic character who questioned such treatment. A discussion of the book could bring out the following points: Who could have stopped the cruelty to Linda? How could this be done? What could Linda have done, herself? What could the adults have done? Did anyone show any compassion?

Harriet the Spy by Louise Fitzhugh is the still popular story of a precocious child who finds difficulty in relating to her parents and her peers. The author presents the story in first-person narrative and through the device of Harriet's diary. Harriet keeps careful notes about her parents, her peers, and the eccentric people she observes on her after-school "spy route" in her New York neighborhood. Her nurse, Ole Golly, has been Harriet's sole source of security; when she leaves, Harriet is very lonely. Her sophisticated parents are too busy to give her more than superficial attention until she gets into trouble. When her classmates find Harriet's journal, they form an exclusive "Spy Catchers Club" to retaliate against Harriet. While Harriet is hurt by their treatment, she is never overcome. However she does follow Ole Golly's advice—that sometimes you have to lie a little—and prints a retraction of her statements in the school news. Basically, Harriet remains uncompromising and determined, but she has gained some understanding and wisdom. Underlying the humor of this story is a serious study of the way children respond to teachers, to their cliques, and to their cruelty to each other.

Two books by Mary Stolz may be read together, but the sequence in reading *A Dog on Barkham Street* and *The Bully of Barkham Street* seems unimportant. The same characters and events are treated in each book, but from different points of view. In the first story, *The Dog on Barkham Street,* Edward is frightened of Martin, the bully next door, who threatens him each day. When his uncle comes with his collie dog to visit the family, he helps Edward learn how to handle a bully. When he leaves, he gives Edward what he has always wanted, his own dog. In the other book, *The Bully of Barkham Street,* the reader learns that Martin Hastings had once had a dog but that his parents had given it away when Martin had failed to care for it. Now the reader knows why Martin is so resentful of Edward and his collie dog. There are moments of understanding among Martin's teacher, his sister, his mother, and his neighbors. Children can develop fresh insights into human behavior by reading both these stories of the same episodes told from two different points of view.

Martin, ex-bully and now 13 years old, struggles to lose his old reputation in *The Explorer of Barkham Street.* He no longer gets into trouble at school and has been dieting; his teacher has introduced him to the joys of reading (and daydreaming) about explorers. While old problems continue to plague Martin, he begins to understand that he can be an explorer, and the discovery will be his own real self. Although there are touching scenes and a satisfying end, there is no strong line of suspense leading to an action climax. This book may be enjoyed for its characters, vivid imagery, and for the unforced, sometimes funny, dialogue. A rich discussion could center on Martin's fears and dreams, how these changed, and why.

MAKING FRIENDS

Making friends as an important part of children's lives is often one of the themes depicted in a realistic fiction story. Several recent titles suggest the special friendship between boys and girls. Patricia Reilly Giff's "Kids of the Polk Street School" series is much-loved by second- and third-grade readers. Johanna Hurwitz warmly portrays the friendship which develops between Aldo Sossi and DeDe when he attends a new school. There he receives a nickname, *Aldo Applesauce,* but DeDe convinces him that even an offensive nickname has its value: "Everybody in the school knows you better if you have a nickname. It's sort of like being famous." Aldo agrees that this might be true since some of the sixth-grade boys now say hello to Aldo, a lowly fifth-grader. The resourceful DeDe helps Aldo evade a lunchroom prank, but it is Aldo who convinces DeDe that she doesn't have to wear a fake mustache in order to retain her connection to a divorced father. Aldo was introduced to readers in *Much Ado About Aldo*, which explains his becoming a vegetarian out of concern for the crickets in a class terrarium. In *Aldo Ice Cream*, Aldo tries to save enough money to buy his older sister an ice cream freezer for her birthday. Gentle humor characterizes these three books in which Aldo's family is portrayed as a warm, supportive one. Aldo's friendliness and his willingness to go out on a limb for people and ideas he believes in make him a character worth knowing.

Two other fifth-grade friendships are presented in Betsy Byars' *The Cybil War*; the first is a longstanding one between Simon Newton and Cybil Ackerman, and the other is a rocky one between Simon and his supposed best friend, Tony Angotti. Tony can't seem to resist putting words in Simon's mouth and lying to others about what he has said. When Tony announces that Cybil will go to the movies on an afternoon first date with him only if Simon will escort Cybil's best friend Harriet, Simon resignedly agrees. He thinks that taking Harriet to the movies, however, is like going out with a teacher or being chaperoned by the principal. Later, when Simon discovers that Cybil was tricked into going on the date by another of Tony's lies, he gathers the courage to set things right with Cybil. His triumphant bicycle ride with Cybil past Tony's house provides a satisfying conclusion to this tale of a friendship. While this story does not show the complexity of plot or serious theme of Byars' *The Pinballs* or *Summer of the Swans*, it does capture the feelings of 10- to 11-year-olds first reaching out to persons of the opposite sex. Byars' use of humorous, contemporary dialogue and her skill in characterization give depth to this popular story.

Without bringing in the elements of first love, Marjorie Weinman Sharmat also deals with rivalry and friendship between boys and girls. Sixthgraders Maggie Marmelstein and Thad Smith walk a fine line between enemy and friend because of their knowledge of each other's secrets in *Getting Something on Maggie Marmelstein*. When Maggie becomes the class newpaper's mystery columnist, Thad and his friends set out to uncover the columnist's identity in *Mysteriously Yours, Maggie Marmelstein*. While these stories may not provide much challenge to fifth-graders, they read smoothly. Recipes figuring in the plot are featured at each story's conclusion so that interested cooks may try their hands at making Mrs. Marmelstein's baked goods.

Wallis Greene has moved too many times and hates the prospect of trying to make friends in her new suburban neighborhood where all the streets are named for flowers and the houses all look alike. In Ellen Conford's novel, Wallis would do *Anything for a Friend*. When she meets Stuffy Sternwood, who is training his pet worms on the sidewalk, she likes him well enough to talk to him about finding friends. He assures her that a Halloween party seance will bring her friends and Wallis agrees to try it. Even though she discovers that Stuffy has charged admission to her party, she does make friends, including an unwanted one. When her father is transferred to California and the family is to move again, Wallis is angry and disappointed until she begins to realize that if she has made friends here, she can do it once more. Frequently, authors such as Conford, Judy Blume, Stella Pevsner, Paula Danziger, or Lila Perl have included the development of peer relationships and friendships as one of the themes in their popular novels about and for 10- to 14-year-olds.

Almost all children long for a "special friend," someone to fool around with, to call on the phone, or to "sleep over" with. *A Girl Called Al* turned out to be this kind of friend for the unnamed narrator of her story:

> Al is a little on the fat side, which is why I didn't like her right at first . . . She is the only girl in the whole entire school, practically, with pigtails . . . She has gone to a lot of different schools. She has a very high I.Q., she says, but she doesn't work to capacity. She says things like this all the time but I don't like to let on I don't always know what she is talking about.[25]

The two girls become fast friends; their third best friend is Mr. Richards, the assistant superintendent of their building. He lets them strap rags to their shoes and skate on his kitchen floor to polish it. And when the school won't let Al take shop, he helps both girls build a bookshelf. The girls find

[25]Constance Greene, *A Girl Called Al*, illustrated by Byron Barton (New York: Viking, 1969), pp. 10–11.

him after he has had a heart attack and get their mother to call the doctor. They visit him once in the hospital before he dies in his sleep one night. Their friendship with each other and Mr. Richards has been a part of their growing-up process. Less than a year passes during Constance Greene's four-book series about Al. In *Alexandra the Great*, Al eagerly prepares to join her father for a vacation, but her mother's bout with pneumonia forces Al to face a most difficult decision. The first-person telling of these stories adds to their contemporary sound and enables Greene to portray complex feelings and relationships with ease and humor.

Emily Blair was an only child until that amazing summer when she and her mother and father moved into an eighteen-room house and her four cousins came to stay with them. Not only did Emily have an instant family but she discovered Kate, a very special person who wrote poetry as she did. In *Look through My Window*, Jean Little has created the life that an only child might hope for. This is an affectionate story with real characters who come alive. Passages that are serendipitous for book lovers are Emily and Kate's rapt discussions about the books they love. In *Kate*, a sequel, the difficulties of friendship is one theme, while Kate's search for her identity through her father's Jewish background becomes another.

A strong relationship between *Ellen Grae* and her friend Grover is at the heart of Vera and Bill Cleaver's novel. Ellen has always entertained Grover and Mrs. McGruder (the woman with whom she stays since her parents are divorced) with her wild tales. For example, she tells them both about a man who was asphyxiated because he kept his car windows shut in the summer so people would think he had an air-conditioned car. It is no wonder, then, that no one will believe her when she reveals the dreadful secret of her friend Ira, a mentally retarded man who lives in an old tin shack by the river. Ellen's conscience is relieved by her confession and, at the same time, she is freed of the guilt of telling Ira's secret. Unfortunately, in the sequel, *Lady Ellen Grae*, the authors decide to tame Ellen by sending her to Seattle to visit her aunt. Although Ellen is a strong heroine who is not easily tamed, the reader has every right to ask if girls must be "tamed" in today's world.

Imaginary play is the basis for the slowly

In helping his little sister cross the swollen stream, Jess exercises the new self-confidence which was part of his friend's legacy. Illustration by Donna Diamond from *Bridge to Terabithia* by Katherine Paterson.

developing friendship between 10-year-old Jess Aarons, an artistic boy who is a misfit in his family, and Leslie Burke, a newcomer who is a misfit in school. Her parents, both writers, have moved to rural Virginia in pursuit of a simpler life style. In Katherine Paterson's Newbery award book, *Bridge to Terabithia*, these two lonely children invent a kingdom based on Leslie's image of Narnia and other fantasy worlds in literature. Their "Terabithia" is a real place, however, a private hideout in the woods reached by swinging on a rope across a dry creek bed.

On a day when spring rains have turned the creek into a torrent, Leslie goes alone to their meeting place and is drowned. As Jess works through his complex feelings of grief, he comes to see a more supportive side of his usually unsympathetic family and realizes that Leslie's gifts to him—a wider perspective and confidence in his own imaginative powers—are gifts that last, and can be shared.

> Now it occurred to him that perhaps Terabithia was like a castle where you came to be knighted. After you stayed for a while and grew strong you had to move on. . . . Now it was time for him to move out. She wasn't there, so he must go for both of them. It was up to him to pay back to the world in beauty and caring what Leslie loaned him in vision and strength.[26]

With lumber given him by Leslie's father, Jess builds a bridge to Terabithia, a safe entry for his younger sister May Belle as he leads her into the shining kingdom with the unspoken hope that her world, like his own, will grow. By asking fourth- and fifth-graders if there are any other "bridges" in this story, teachers have allowed children to discuss the many emotional or metaphorical bridges portrayed in Paterson's beautifully written story.

A strong friendship that revolves around the secret play activities of intelligent children is presented in a Zilpha Snyder story. April and Melanie invent *The Egypt Game* that eventually includes six of the neighborhood children playing in an abandoned storage yard. The game is just good fun until a child is murdered in the neighborhood and outdoor play is forbidden. Later, parents became more lax and April is attacked one night when she goes out into the yard for a book she had left. Four-year-old Marshall screams, the professor, who had been secretly watching their Egypt game for weeks, calls for help, and the murderer is apprehended. Then the children find out how important their game had been in restoring the professor's interest in living. Snyder presents distinct characters from a variety of ethnic backgrounds. Despite the grim circumstances surrounding their Egypt Game, their imaginative play has not visibly suffered—they are thinking of playing "Gypsies" next.

Growing toward Maturity

In building a concept of self, each person comes to answer such questions as: "What kind of person

[26]Katherine Paterson, *Bridge to Terabithia*, illustrated by Donna Diamond (New York: Crowell, 1977), p. 126.

am I?" "What are my roles in society to be?" "What do others think of me?" The self is built through reactions and interactions with people, places, and things. The child creates the concept of what he or she is: a worthy person; a person who can succeed; a person who is loved; who can, in turn, respect and love others, while receiving these impressions from others.

As children grow toward adulthood, they may experience brief moments of awareness of this growth process. A conversation, an experience, or a book may bring the sudden realization that a step has been taken to a new level of maturity, and there is no turning back. This step may be toward adult responsibility or acceptance of one's developing sexuality or vocational choice. This process of "becoming," of finding the unique core of self, is not easy. In literature, there are models of ordinary boys and girls who find the courage to change and grow, or to stand firm despite pressures.

DEVELOPING SEXUALITY

Recent research (see Chapter 2) indicates that boys and girls are growing up physically and psychologically faster than ever before. Girls, particularly, are reaching puberty during the elementary school years rather than during junior high school or high school, as their mothers did. The first story to discuss menstruation was *The Long Secret* by Louise Fitzhugh, first published in 1965. In this story Janie, Harriet's scientific friend, very matter-of-factly explains menstruation to Harriet and Beth Ellen. Beth Ellen's grandmother had given her false information, so Janie corrects it. The conversation is childlike and funny. None of the girls are pleased with the prospect, but take some satisfaction in the fact that when they have their periods they'll get to skip gym. By way of contrast, Margaret, in the story *Are You There God? It's Me Margaret* by Judy Blume prays for her period because she doesn't want to be the last of her secret club to start menstruating. She regularly does exercises which she hopes will increase her size 28 bust and she practices wearing a sanitary napkin! Mixed with her desire for physical maturation is a search for a meaningful relation with God. Adults find this book very funny and reminiscent of their own pre-adolescence, but it is extremely serious for 10- and 11-year-old girls who share Margaret's concern for their own physical maturation.

Judy Blume has also written a book about the physical and emotional maturing of a boy, *Then Again, Maybe I Won't*. One strand of the story concerns the sexual awakening of Tony, a 13-year-old boy who is embarrassed and concerned about erection and nocturnal emissions. The other concerns the conflicts that Tony feels about his family's sudden adoption of a new life style when they move from a cramped two-family house in Jersey City to an acre of land on Long Island. Tony is painfully aware of the effects money has on his family. At the end of the book Tony is making a better adjustment, but at the same time the reader wonders if he has sold out to suburbia, as he looks forward to the new swimming pool that his father has ordered. The title, *Then Again, Maybe I Won't*, conveys the same ambiguity as the direction of Tony's life. There is no doubt that Tony has achieved physical maturation, but will he be able to sustain his personal values in the difficult task of growing toward psychological and emotional maturity?

In C. S. Adler's *The Once in a While Hero*, Pat, a seventh-grader, is also asking questions. He is confused about his own sexuality. His two best friends are Susan and Lucy; his longer hair and pleasant demeanor make him look more like a girl; the class bully McGrew pushes him around and calls him "Pattycakes." When Pat volunteers to be a new boy's buddy and guide for a week, it seems that he will be a tormenter, too. The first thing Mud Muldowny says to Pat is "You gay or something?" However, Pat begins to feel sorry for Mud, whose parents verbally abuse him. Pat's avoidance of conflict comes to an abrupt end when, during a school party, McGrew is made to apologize for destroying part of the decorations which Susan and Lucy have made. Pat witnesses the apology, and, to save face, McGrew tries to force Susan to dance. Angered and in defense of his friend, Pat punches McGrew in the nose and thereby earns respect from Susan, his classmates, and Mud. But Pat and the reader are left to wonder if fighting makes a boy more manly. His gentle father asks Pat what is more important to his self-respect—to defeat someone or to stand up to them? Pat decides that, while he is glad to have been brave, he will be content to be himself, a once-in-a-while hero.

A more direct treatment of a boy's concern with his own sexuality is found in *I'll Get There, It*

Better Be Worth the Trip, John Donovan's sensitively told story of a 13-year-old boy's brief sexual encounter with a schoolmate. Readers see Davy Ross as a lonely boy living with his divorced mother and his much-loved dachshund, Fred. He makes friends with Altschuler and one day when they are playing with Fred in Davy's apartment, impelled by an "unusual" feeling, the two exchange a kiss. After that, they pretend to box, "like tough guys." A later incident causes Davy's mother to call his father to come and have a talk with him. Davy's sympathetic and understanding father makes him feel better, but Fred is run over in the street and the inconsolable Davy has a fight with Altschuler. Later, while the two boys agree to respect each other, Davy has lost Fred and his childhood in the encounter. His concern for the future is captured in the second part of the novel's title.

Charles Norstadt, like Davy, is searching for love and his self-identity when he meets *The Man without a Face*. In Isabelle Holland's story, Charles is trying to find a way to escape from living at home with his four-times-married mother and his nasty older sister, Gloria. So he arranges to be tutored by a local writer, known as "the man without a face," in hopes of getting into boarding school. Charles slowly grows to respect Justin McLeod, who has a badly scarred face. This respect deepens into love as he finds he can communicate with and trust Justin. Intense problems with his family drive him to Justin for physical and emotional comfort. The homosexual experience is treated with sensitivity, and the reader understands the situation in the context of the story. While Charles passes his exams and goes off to school, he later realizes how much Justin has taught him about accepting consequences for his own actions. By the end of the story, Charles is beginning to accept himself in this finely written young adult novel.

The previous titles have been criticized for presenting homosexual relationships as of no lasting significance, as exacting terrible prices, and as typically between males.[27] An exception to this kind of formula is Nancy Garden's *Annie on My Mind*, which presents a friendship between two girls, high school seniors, that grows gradually and realistically into mutual physical attraction; the

[27]Frances Hanckel and John Cunningham, "Can Young Gays Find Happiness in YA Books?" *Wilson Library Journal* (March 1976), pp. 528–534.

two girls are still together with a promise of happier times during their freshman year in college. The age of the characters in these novels, as well as the subject matter, marks them for junior high or high school age students. However, for young adults, at a time when sexuality is a constant concern, it is helpful to have young adult novels that portray gay relationships as one facet of life today.

FINDING ONE'S SELF

Most of the stories of physical maturing also suggest a kind of emotional maturing or coming to terms with one's self. The process of becoming a mature person is a life-long task that begins in the latter stages of childhood and continues for as long as a person lives. Many stories of children's literature chronicle the steps along the way to maturity.

A growing point in Maria's life is achieved when she learns that to be an artist one has to paint what is true. When her art teacher at the museum asks each of the children to paint their own houses Maria is ashamed—she can't paint the shabby tenement that is *Maria's House*. At first she decides to paint a storybook house, one she wished she lived in. But then Maria remembers what her proud mother, who works hard to pay for her art lessons, has told her—that art has to be honest. Jean Merrill has written a one-dimensional yet forthright and simple story about one child's decision.

In Betsy Byars' *After the Goat Man*, Harold's summer has been a miserable one of dieting and doing nothing except play Monopoly with his friend, Ada. And then Figgy, grandson of the old eccentric that everyone calls "The Goat Man," joins their Monopoly games. Figgy is alone in the world except for his grandfather, who turned strangely quiet when the government forced him to give up his old cabin in order to make room for a new super highway. Figgy knows his grandfather is going to take his gun to the cabin to protect it. He blurts out the story to Harold and Ada, who say they will ride their bikes to the cabin and help Figgy get his grandfather. While Figgy rides double behind Harold, Harold loses control of the bike and has an accident. He is knocked out momentarily, but Figgy breaks his leg and cries for his grandfather. Harold goes alone to get the old man, worrying all the way there that the Goat Man will shoot him. Once at the cabin he has a sudden awareness of what the place means to the old man.

A moment of awareness and empathy proves to be a beginning step toward maturity for Harold.

In *The 18th Emergency* Betsy Byars has written a very funny book with the serious theme of facing up to one's responsibility. Benjie (better known as Mouse) and his best friend Ezzie have defined seventeen emergencies based upon old adventure movies—impossible situations with miraculous escapes. But neither of them can think of an escape for the eighteenth emergency—what to do about Marv Hammerman, the biggest and, Mouse thinks, the stupidest boy in school. Mouse writes Marv Hammerman's name under Neanderthal Man on the evolution chart in the school hallway; his pleasure is short-lived, however, when he turns to find Marv glaring at him. Instead of facing the danger calmly, as Ezzie has taught him for the seventeen other emergencies, Mouse flees for his life, avoiding Hammerman for two days. Finally Mouse seeks Hammerman out and asks to get it over with. Afterwards, Mouse tells Izzie it was "a sort of honorable thing."

> "Hammerman? Honorable?"
>
> Mouse nodded. He knew that he was not going to be able to explain it to Ezzie. He wasn't even sure he understood it himself now. But at the moment when he and Marv Hammerman had met in front of the Rialto, it had been clearly and simply a matter of honor.[28]

Being willing to face problems and certain pain rather than running away represents one aspect of growing up.

Another aspect of growing up, accepting people as they are, including small pretenses and idiosyncrasies, is one of the themes of E. L. Konigsburg's *Journey to an 800 Number*. Hiding behind his prep school blazer, Maximilian Stubbs is spending the summer months with his father Woody, while his mother remarries. Max is a self-proclaimed expert on "normal" and "first class," both of which he is sure his father is not. Woody, a camel-keeper, moves through the Southwest giving rides at shopping centers or making appearances at dude ranches, state fairs, and conventions. Max's disdain for his father and his father's life is revealed in his quick quips and disparaging remarks. When Max meets a Mexican family, friends of Woody

[28]Betsy Byars, *The 18th Emergency,* illustrated by Robert Grossman (New York: Viking, 1973), p. 106.

who run a taco stand at the state fair as their vacation from melon picking, he immediately makes wrong judgments of them. He also uncomfortably realizes that even the youngest of the children knows more about life and how to do things than he does. Throughout the summer, Max meets others who care deeply about Woody and who seem able where Max is not. Only when Max discovers the facts about his real parentage is he able to show the love he has come to feel for Woody and to accept the love Woody has been showing him all along. Konigsburg's first-person narrative is sharp, humorous, and insightful. The gradual revelation to Max of the strange and wonderful possibilities in a world outside prep school suggests to him new definitions of "normal" and "first class."

Robert Burch has told the poignant story of *Queenie Peavy,* a 13-year-old nonconformist living in a small Southern town during the Depression. Queenie carries a large chip on her shoulder, defying her teachers and being deliberately mean to her classmates because they torment her about her father, who is in jail. But the reader also sees another side of Queenie, who lives for the day when her father will get his parole from jail. Once home, however, he ignores Queenie. When Queenie sees that he has broken his parole, she finally sees the man as he is: irresponsible, not put upon by others, but making his own choices—the wrong ones. Queenie, responsible for setting a trap so that Cravey Mason falls and breaks his leg, fears being sent to the reformatory. So she decides to prove she can behave properly for an entire day. Both the school principal and a wise judge recognize Queenie's good qualities and see that she is not sent to reform school. When her friend faints from hunger, Queenie goes along to the doctor's office and is very helpful. He offers Queenie a part-time job. With the help of sympathetic adults, Queenie is on her way to becoming a responsible, mature person.

Gilly Ground is also a loner, a youth torn between his desire for freedom and his longing for peace and security in Julia Cunningham's *Dorp Dead.* Kobalt's house seems a haven of peace after the noise and clamor in the orphanage where Gilly had first lived. But gradually Gilly realizes that he is a "royal prisoner" in this house, just as much as he was an inmate of the orphanage. Kobalt does provide warm clothing, good food, and fine shelter for Gilly, but no love. Gilly is taken care of, but eventually he acquires the same dull look in his eyes that he had first noticed in the eyes of Kobalt's unresponsive dog Mash. Gilly's attempt to make friends with the dog is his first reaching out. His one other connection is the mysterious hunter whom he first meets at the stone tower.

Gilly recognizes the terror of his situation when Kobalt beats the dog, saying. "Mash must learn to die." The boy finally escapes and goes down the hill, presumably to find the hunter and a new life. He makes one brief stop at Kobalt's house and scribbles a last defiant message on Kobalt's door: "Dorp Dead." Only years later does he realize that one of the words is misspelled. *Dorp Dead* is an intense and complicated allegorical novel for children. Gilly Ground represents all youth caught between a need for security and freedom; Kobalt, the ladder-maker, is the epitome of all evil that wants to control. The hunter whose gun has no bullets may represent love or the meaning of life. Cunningham explains him in this way:

> I think the Hunter is no more or less than that person or, if one is lucky, persons who pass through every life for a moment, or sometimes longer, and give it strength and meaning. Why didn't he have a name? I guess I did not give him a name because he has so many.[29]

Come to the Edge, also by Cunningham, is another story of a boy's attempt to find himself and learn to accept and return love.

Another psychologically complex novel, *One-Eyed Cat* by Paula Fox, begins when 11-year-old Ned Wallis receives from his favorite uncle an unexpected birthday present—an air rifle. But Ned's minister father banishes the gun to the attic until Ned is older. Longing to shoot just once, Ned steals forth at night and fires toward something moving near a shed. He is immediately guilt-stricken. Was it an animal? As he broods on his disobedience, he begins to lie and each lie "makes the secret bigger." He can't confide in his mother, who is wheelchair-bound by arthritis, or in the temperamental housekeeper Mrs. Scallop or in his preoccupied father. As he carries his uncomfortable secret, Ned seems most at ease at the house of

29Julia Cunningham, "Dear Characters," *The Horn Book Magazine,* vol. 43 (April 1967), p. 234.

an elderly neighbor, Mr. Scully, for whom he does household chores and odd jobs after school. There he and the old man see a sickly one-eyed cat whom they feed and observe during the winter. When Mr. Scully suddenly suffers a stroke and is taken to the hospital, Ned is afraid he has lost both his friend and the cat. Finally, on a visit to the home where Mr. Scully, now speechless, resides, Ned gathers enough courage to tell his guilty secret to his friend. This release brings a change in Ned and enables him to repair the pains of separation. Although Mr. Scully dies, the cat returns in the spring with its own family, and his mother is able to ease her pain somewhat with a new treatment. Ned's rich interior monologues contrast with his inability to talk; this motif of being unable to speak about some of life's most important moments recurs throughout the story. Paula Fox's carefully chosen images, such as "people aging the way trees do, getting gnarled and dried out" or "the gun was a splinter in his mind" lend real depth to this perceptive and well-written story. Although it is set in 1935, children are not likely to see the book as historical fiction but rather as a story of one person's moral dilemmas which spiral round him as a result of his disobedience and lying.

James Johnson has always been content to stay at home singing only for his grandmother while the rest of his family travel about in Appalachia as country singers. But when he is persuaded by his family to join them, and his mother decides that his stage name should be Jimmy Jo, even his grandmother's belief that James "has the gift" doesn't prevent his being unsettled. In *Come Sing, Jimmy Jo*, Katherine Paterson tells a believable story of James and his struggle to grow. Singing before an audience terrifies him at first, but as he comes to enjoy it, his young mother actually seems to resent his popularity with the fans and his father refuses to defend him against her. James longs for his grandma and country life and when a man claiming to be his real father turns up at the school yard several times, James retreats from everyone. But courage comes from two surprising sources. One is his friendship with and respect for Eleazer Jones, a classmate who is uncowed by the seeming power of adults; the other source is his own sudden clear understanding of the complexities and endurance of love. After he confronts his real fa-

ther and his own love and need for his stepfather, James is able to say to himself, "I done it. I growed up." Paterson writes with understanding of an 11-year-old's need for a home place and his search for independence and self-knowledge.

Manolo is a Spanish boy who has to decide whether to follow his own conscience or to conform to community expectations. *Shadow of a Bull* by Maia Wojciechowska describes the darkening shadow of Manolo's fear of failure to be like his father, a famous bullfighter. Everything and everybody remind Manolo of his destiny to face his first bull at the age of 12. On the night before his test, Manolo's mother tells him how tired his father had been after the bullfights, but she also tells him his father did what he wanted to do. What he did was for himself. Manolo prays for bravery to stand his ground, not to be saved from wounds or death. When he meets a famous critic before the bullfight, Manolo hears the words he should have heard earlier:

> "A man's life is many things. Before he becomes a man, he has many choices: to do the right thing, or to do the wrong thing; to please himself, or to please others; to be true to his own self, or untrue to it. . . . Real courage, true bravery is doing things in spite of fear, knowing fear. . . . Be what you are, and if you don't yet know what you are, wait until you do. Don't let anyone make that decision for you."[30]

Manolo proves himself by fighting the bull long enough to show his skill and bravery; then he makes his choice. He turns the fight over to his friend Juan, while he goes and sits with the doctor. His future will be healing, not killing. For Manolo it took far greater courage to say no, to be what *he* wanted to be, than to follow in his father's footsteps.

More than anything else Rudi Matt in Ullman's *Banner in the Sky* wanted to follow in his father's footsteps. His burning desire is to climb the Citadel that claimed his father's life, the mountain that no other guide has dared to climb. Although his mother and uncle have forbidden him to climb, when Rudi learns that an Englishman plans to climb the Citadel, he leaves work and goes to join

[30]Maia Wojciechowska, *Shadow of a Bull*, illustrated by Alvin Smith (New York: Atheneum, 1964), pp. 145–146.

the climber, only to find that his uncle has agreed to go with the Englishman and Saxo, a guide from another village. Rivalries and prejudice shadow the four as they set out to reach the summit. Captain Winters, the Englishman, becomes ill, and according to the code of the mountains, the guide must remain with his "Master" if he is sick or injured. Saxo cannot resist his own ambition and sets out alone to reach the top, but Rudi leaves his uncle and Winters to pursue the guide. When Saxo falls near the summit, Rudi faces a terrible decision—to go on to the top or to help Saxo. There is a way out, but it is down, not up. Although the book is not set in modern times, there are few clues to tie Rudi's story to history. On the contrary, his hopes and the hard reality of the choice he faces seem quite contemporary to today's students.

SURVIVAL STORIES

Survival stories have powerful appeal to children in middle grades. Numerous stories in all genres portray a single child or a small group of children, without adults, in situations that call for ingenuity, quick thinking, mastery of tools and skills, and strength of character. Survivors return to civilization or their former lives knowing that they have changed as a result of their experiences. In primitive societies, surviving a hazardous experience often marked the transition from childhood to adulthood. Today we have forms of this in "survival training" conducted in schools, camps, or juvenile homes. Children in middle grades avidly read survival stories and wonder "Could I do it? How? What would I do in this same situation?"

Armstrong Sperry's quintessential survival story *Call It Courage* begins and ends in the manner of a story told in the oral tradition:

> It happened many years ago, before the traders and the missionaries first came into the South Seas, while the Polynesians were still great in numbers and fierce of heart. But even today the people of Hikueru sing this story in their chants and tell it over the evening fires. It is the story of Mafatu, the Boy Who Was Afraid.[31]

Taunted for his fears, Mafatu sets out to conquer his dread of the water by sailing to some other is-

[31]Armstrong Sperry, *Call It Courage* (New York: Macmillan, 1940), p. 7.

Mafatu has conquered his fear of Moana, the sea god, and has survived many trials. He returns home triumphant. From *Call It Courage* by Armstrong Sperry.

land alone, accompanied by his pet albatross and his dog. On a distant island his character gradually develops as he proves his courage to himself by defying a tabu and stealing a much-needed spear from an idol, by fighting dangerous animals and escaping from cannibals. These heroic deeds, which represent the many faces of courage, build his self-esteem. As in so many survival stories, having proven to himself that he could carve out an existence, Mafatu is ready to return to his former life as a changed person who knows his own worth. The first paragraph of the book is repeated at the end—only the last sentence is left off.

Another exciting story of survival is Jean George's Newbery award-winning story, *Julie of the Wolves*. Miyax, the Eskimo heroine of this beautiful story, finds herself alone on the Alaskan tundra. She realizes that her salvation or her de-

Miyax mourns the wanton killing of Amaroq, leader of the wolves. Illustration by John Schoenherr from *Julie of the Wolves* by Jean Craighead George.

struction depends upon a nearby pack of wolves. Julie (Miyax is her Eskimo name) watches the wolves carefully and gradually learns to communicate with them by glance, movement, and caress until Amaroq, their leader, acknowledges her as a friend. Because of the wolves Julie survives and finds her way back to civilization. But it is that civilization that kills Amaroq, as white hunters wantonly shoot him down from a plane for the "sport" of killing. Much of the story is based on research on wolves conducted at the Arctic Research Laboratory.[32]

In contrast to Julie, Billy Wind, a Seminole Indian girl who had been to school at the Kennedy Space Center, scoffs at the legends of her ancestors. As her punishment she is sent to stay in the Everglades for one night and two days to see if she then will believe in talking animals and little people who live under the ground. She is caught in a swamp fire and survives by hiding in one of the caves used by her ancestors. With the help of a pet otter, a baby panther, and a turtle, Billy Wind lives through a hurricane and a tidal wave. After nearly twelve weeks in the wilderness, she returns home convinced the animals do talk:

> . . . for they knew everything: how to keep warm, predict the storms, live in darkness or blazing sun, how to navigate the skies, to organize societies, how to make chemicals and fireproof skins. The animals know the Earth as we do not.[33]

And the message she receives from Burden, her turtle, is the theme Jean George wishes to convey to her readers in this book, *The Talking Earth:* "It's the earth that matters. . . . It's all we've got. Dig it lovingly."[34]

My Side of the Mountain, also by Jean George, is a book about a city boy who chooses to spend a winter alone on land in the Catskills once farmed

[32]See "Newbery Award Acceptance" speech by Jean Craighead George in *The Horn Book*, vol. 49 (August 1973), pp. 337–347.

[33]Jean Craighead George, *The Talking Earth* (New York: Harper, 1983), p. 141.
[34]George, *The Talking Earth*, p. 148.

James Houston's illustrations reflect the style of the Inuit people among whom he has spent many years. From *Frozen Fire* by James Houston.

by his ancestors. Armed with knowledge from reading about how to survive on the land, he makes a home in a hollow tree, sews buckskin clothing, and lays up stores for winter. He writes in his journal, observes the birds, and keeps occupied with the chores of living. In the early spring a young news reporter discovers him, and Sam realizes he is now ready to be found. In this modern "Robinson Crusoe" story the details are so vividly related that the reader feels he is on the mountain with Sam. Once again, Jean George has drawn upon her naturalist background to provide a backdrop of authentic facts of nature.

Canadian author James Houston has based his survival story, *Frozen Fire*, on the actual survival story of a boy in the Canadian Arctic. Two boys, Matthew Morgan and his Inuit friend Kayak, set forth on a snowmobile to search for Matthew's prospector father, whose plane has been downed by a snowstorm. Careless securing of the cap of a gas can leaves them stranded seventy miles from Frobisher Bay. Kayak is able to use the skills taught him by his grandfather and helps both boys eventually to walk out on the ice, where they are seen and rescued. They discover that Matthew's father has also been saved. Houston's crisp telling and cliff-hanger chapter endings make this a fast-paced story. Having spent twelve years among the Inuit people, he is able to weave aspects of a changing Eskimo culture and folk wisdom into the text. *Black Diamonds: A Search for Arctic Treasure* continues the adventure of the two boys as they help Matthew's father in searching for gold.

Felice Holman has written a grim story of survival in New York City, *Slake's Limbo*. Slake is a 13-year-old nearsighted orphan who lives with his aunt and thinks of himself as a worthless lump. Slake has no friends; his vision makes him a poor risk for any gang, and a severe reaction to smoke and drugs makes him useless in other ways. Hunted and hounded for sport, Slake takes refuge in the subway, staying for 121 days. He makes a little money reselling papers he picks up on the trains until he gets a job sweeping up at one of the lunch counters. His home is a little hidden cave in the subway wall where he spreads newspapers to sleep. One day when the subway repair crew comes through, Slake realizes that his "home" will be destroyed. Then he becomes ill and is taken to the hospital, where he is given nourishment and proper eyeglasses. Later he slips out of the hospital and his first reaction is to return to the subway but when he hears a bird sing, he looks up and decides he could perhaps exist on the roofs of some of the buildings: "He turned and started up the stairs and out of the subway. Slake did not know exactly where he was going but the general direction was up."[35]

This story's tone stands in sharp contrast to the two children who decide to run away from home and live in comfort in the Metropolitan Museum of Art! Claudia's reasons for running away are based on what she considers injustice—she had to both set the table and empty the dishwasher on the same night while her brothers did nothing. But Claudia is also bored with the sameness of her straight-A life; she wants to do something that is different and exciting. She chooses her brother Jamie to go along with her because he has money—$24.43. Claudia is a good organizer, and the two of them take up residence in the museum, even taking baths in the museum's fountain, where Jamie finds another source of income—pennies thrown in the pool. They take their meals at the automat and the museum's cafeteria and join the tour groups for their education. It really isn't exciting until Claudia becomes involved in the mystery surrounding the statue of a little angel. The children's research finally takes them to the home of Mrs. Basil E. Frankweiler, who arranges for Claudia to return home the way she had hoped she would—different in some aspect. Now she is dif-

35Felice Holman, *Slake's Limbo* (New York: Aladdin, 1986), p. 117.

ferent because she knows the secret of the angel. In return for this knowledge the two children tell Mrs. Frankweiler the details of their survival. She carefully records it and then writes their story in *From the Mixed-Up Files of Mrs. Basil E. Frankweiler*. This story-within-a-story is a sophisticated and funny account by E. L. Konigsburg of two very modern and resourceful survivors.

There are intriguing patterns in stories of survival. Many deal with questions and themes basic to humankind. Some survival stories suggest that surviving with another person provides comforting benefits as well as difficulties. Questions readers might ask while comparing survival stories of all genres include: What qualities make one able to survive? How does surviving an ordeal change a person's outlook? After basic wants are satisfied, what other needs do survivors seem to have? Which is more difficult, physical survival or emotional survival? What role does art or beauty play in the survivor's ability to endure?

COPING WITH PROBLEMS OF THE HUMAN CONDITION

People in all times and places must cope with problems of the human condition—birth, pain, loneliness, poverty, illness, and death. Children do not escape these human problems; but literature can give them windows for looking at different aspects of life, show them how some characters have faced personal crises, and help them ask and answer questions about the meaning of life.

In discussing the psychological significance of children's literature, Jacquelyn Sanders points out:

> Areas of life that are difficult . . . if avoided will not be understood; if simply presented will only be badly handled; but a valuable service can be rendered if these areas are presented together with help in learning how to cope with them.[36]

David Elkind, also a psychologist, warns that we may be overburdening our children with the ills of society before they have an opportunity to find themselves. He says:

> This is the major stress of the literature of young children aimed at making them aware of the problems in the world about them before they have a chance to master the problems of childhood.[37]

Certainly teachers and librarians should balance the reading of "problem books" with those that emphasize joy in living.

Physical Disabilities

Good stories of physically disabled persons serve two purposes. They provide positive images with which disabled youngsters may identify, and they may help physically unimpaired children to develop a more intelligent understanding of some of the problems that disabled persons face. In stories, disabilities should "neither be exaggerated nor ignored, neither dramatized nor minimized, neither romaticized nor the cause for devaluation."[38] It is particularly important that stories of disabilities be well written, not sentimental or maudlin. They should not evoke pity for what children with disabilities cannot do, but respect for what they *can* do. As in all well-written stories, characters should be multi-dimensional persons with real feelings and frustrations. The author should be honest in portraying the condition and future possibilities for the character. Illustrations should also portray disabilities in an honest and straightforward manner.

Literary treatment of disabilities may rely on time-honored themes: a disabled person has special powers, grace, or a predetermined destiny; a disabled person serves as a catalyst in the maturation of others; a disability is a metaphor for society's ills, such as a blind person who can "see" what others do not choose to acknowledge or are too insensitive to see. Occasionally, disabilities are somewhat misleadingly portrayed as being able to be overcome with determination, faith, and grit.[39] In

[36]Jacquelyn Sanders, "Psychological Significance of Children's Literature" in *A Critical Approach to Children's Literature*, Sara Innis Fenwick, ed. (Chicago, The University of Chicago Press, 1967), p. 17.

[37]David Elkind, *The Hurried Child: Growing Up Too Fast Too Soon.* (Reading, MA: Addison-Wesley Publishing House, 1981), p. 84.

[38]Barbara H. Baskin and Karen H. Harris, *Notes from a Different Drummer: A Guide to Juvenile Fiction Portraying the Handicapped* (New York: R. R. Bowker Company, 1977), p. xv.

[39]Baskin and Harris, chapter 2.

the hands of a fine writer, themes such as these avoid becoming clichés and may present the reader with fresh insight into coping with the human condition.

Difficulties faced by a family in helping a baby who has cerebral palsy are sensitively portrayed by Marie Killilea in her book *Karen*. When the parents learn that Karen may never walk, they help an older sibling understand and accept her sister. When Karen gets braces and struggles to walk, Marie is told that it is no kindness to do things for her or Karen will not learn to do them for herself. The faith expressed by the family and Karen herself culminates in a beautiful moment at Christmas when she balances on one foot to lean toward the creche.

In another story of a child who has cerebral palsy, a family has to learn to give love, but not too much help. Jean Little's characterizations in *Mine for Keeps* are believable portraits. When Sally returns from a school for the disabled to live at home, she attends regular school and meets many problems. A dog that may be hers "for keeps" helps her gain physical skill and emotional courage. Sally grows in maturity when she forgets about her problems and helps a boy who has been ill to find happiness and confidence.

Ivan Southall has vividly portrayed some of the desires and frustrations of a boy with a mild spastic condition in *Let the Balloon Go*. John Sumner attends a regular school in Australia and, except for occasional and unpredictable spasms and stuttering, he is like any other 12-year-old boy. And yet he has no friends. The children avoid him and his over-anxious mother keeps telling him what he can't do. John longs to be free, to do what he wants. And one day, when he is home alone for the very first time, he does; he climbs a very tall tree all by himself. He once heard a man say that a balloon isn't a balloon until someone cuts the string. John has cut the string that bound him to his house and mother; at last he is truly free to grow in his own way.

In *The Alfred Summer*, Jan Slepian presents a 14-year-old boy with cerebral palsy who also chafes resentfully at the strings that he feels bind him to his over-protective mother and ignoring father. Lester describes himself self-mockingly as a walking "perpetual motion machine." When he falls, and someone asks him "Are you okay?" Lester thinks:

Now here's the thing: I want to say, sure I'm okay, or, that's all right, I'm fine. Something like that. Well, if he has an hour or two to spare I'll get it out. I might in that time be able to tell him what's on my mind. In other words . . . in other words I have no words. Or none that I can get out without looking as if I'm strangling. . . .[40]

Lester one day makes a friend of Alfred, a retarded boy whom he sees collecting tin foil from the gutters. Alfred's total acceptance of him frees Lester, and the two discover a third friend in Myron. As the three friends make a boat, each accomplishes something he thought he could not do and gains some self-respect. When the boat is finally launched, it sinks, but Myron and Lester realize that what they have built over the summer is much more important than a leaky old boat. By using Lester as a narrator in several chapters, Slepian injects humor and insight into this well-characterized, compassionate story. The sequel, *Lester's Turn*, is told entirely from Lester's point of view as he grows in independence.

In *Keeping It Secret*, Penny Pollock suggests some of the problems posed for 11-year-old Wisconsin by her having to wear a hearing aid. Though everyone in her old school knew about and accepted the fact that she wore the aid, Wisconsin is apprehensive about facing a new school and new classmates. Her parents try to reassure her, but the first day at school is marred when one of the sixth-graders teases her about her name. Her older brother adjusts easily, but for Wisconsin it takes time to overcome her distrust of the overtures of her classmates. It is her determination to play baseball, in spite of her over-protective father's wishes, that helps her overcome her self-consciousness and acknowledge that her classmates knew about her hearing loss all along. Pollock treats hearing impairment in a straightforward manner, detailing Wisconsin's sensitivity to clapping and loud noises, her problems in hearing soft sounds, and her fear that her hearing aid will fall out when she participates in sports or that a battery will suddenly fail and there will be no place to change it discretely. While Donna Diamond's pictures depict the characters in realistic detail, there is unfortunately no illustration of

[40]Jan Slepian, *The Alfred Summer* (New York: Macmillan, 1980), p. 3.

Wisconsin wearing the hearing devices that are such an important part of her story.

Veronica Robinson's *David in Silence* tells of a boy who learns to live with the disability of being profoundly deaf. Set in modern England, the story has plenty of action as the children make overtures to a new boy who can only make grunting noises. David is delighted when Michael learns sign language so he can communicate through his wall of silence. The world of deafness, with its absolute absence of sound, is made quite clear to the reader. When David's actions in playing football are misinterpreted and he doesn't read lips clearly, the other boys become angry. When they chase him, David runs away and hides. Tension mounts as he moves into a dark tunnel of a canal and is overcome by a mirage of ugly faces. The other boys eventually come to accept David and to have a new awareness of the joy of hearing, but David remains in his silent world. (See also Riskind's *Apple Is My Sign*, Chapter 10, which portrays a boy learning to live among the hearing in one of the first schools for hearing-impaired children.)

A popular story of a boy who is blind is *Follow My Leader* by James Garfield. Jimmy tries to duck an exploding firecracker, but it is too late. "The world exploded in a white flash. Deafening thunder smashed against his ears. Then the light was gone, and the sound was gone. Everything became very dark, very quiet."[41] Eleven-year-old Jimmy's world was to remain dark forever, but it is far from quiet as he learns to eat, to walk, to read, and to use the dog Leader as his constant guide and companion. At the guide school Jimmy receives a warning about the sharp corner on a mantelpiece. When he suggests they put a piece of sponge on it the director asks: "Do you expect the world to pad its corners for you, just because you're blind?" The details of learning braille and of the training received at the guide-dog school are fascinating. Overcoming his hatred of Mike, the boy who threw the firecracker, is very difficult for Jimmy. However, Jimmy visits Mike and they agree: "You can't be happy until you quit hating." Here is a good story, one that communicates the feelings of those who must learn to live without sight. (See Chapters 10 and 11 for other books about people with disabilities or impairments.)

41James B. Garfield, *Follow My Leader* (New York: Viking, 1957), p. 14.

Developmental Disabilities

The opening line of *Take Wing* by Jean Little reads: "James had wet the bed again." As usual, 7-year-old James calls on his sister Laurel to help him, rather than on his mother. For Laurel has a special way and a special love for this younger brother who is "different." Laurel has always tried to hide her fear that he isn't quite normal. Her mother won't talk about him and her father is too busy to notice how slow and unsure his son is. When Laurel's mother breaks her hip, her Aunt Jessica comes to stay at their house. Aunt Jessica recognizes that Laurel is carrying too much responsibility in having to care for James and finally an appointment is made for him to have an examination at the medical clinic. Their findings confirm Laurel's fears that her brother is retarded, but he is also educable. This is as much Laurel's story as James'. By refusing to face the facts of James' disability, the family had overburdened his older sister. The symbolic title, *Take Wing*, refers to Laurel's freedom to begin to have a childhood of her own, to make friends, and to grow.

Betsy Byars won the Newbery award for her story about an adolescent girl and her retarded brother in *Summer of the Swans*. Sara felt very much like the ugly duckling during that difficult fourteenth summer. She had wept over her big feet, her skinny legs, and her nose, even over her gross orange sneakers. But when her retarded brother got lost in the woods, her tears vanished in the terror she felt for Charlie. In her anguish Sara turned to Joe Melby—whom she had despised the day before—and together they found Charlie. It was the longest day of the summer and Sara knew that she would never be the same again. Like the awkward flight of the swans with their "great beating of wings and ruffling of feathers," Sara was going to land with a long perfect glide. Sara's love and fright for her brother's safety had helped her break through her moody adolescent shell.

One of the best stories of a retarded child is Wrightson's *A Racecourse for Andy*. Andy is presented as a likable child with friends, not as a pathetic loner. In a make-believe game, Andy thinks he has purchased a racetrack, but the community helps to preserve Andy's dignity while relieving him of his seeming responsibility of ownership. On one level, the story is amusing, but on another, his friends' real concern for Andy and their discussions about ownership raise this story to a higher plane.

It is summertime when 10-year-old Jill is *Between Friends,* following a family move. Anxious to make friends, Jill nonetheless initially avoids Dede's first overtures because Dede has Down's syndrome. But because there is no one else in the neighborhood her own age, Jill reluctantly becomes Dede's friend. Relying heavily on dialogue, Sheila Garrigue explores one child's growing understanding of what retardation means, both to Dede and to her mother. When Dede provides a sympathetic hand to Jill following the sudden death of a neighbor, Jill regards her friendship with Dede in a new light. While many of the adults as well as Jill's school friends display unbelievably cruel attitudes about Down's syndrome, Jill makes a courageous decision to accept Dede's invitation to attend her school's Christmas party. There, she sees first hand all that these "special" children have accomplished, shares Dede's pride in the flowers she is raising, and interacts successfully with several of her classmates. In addition, she discovers that her fears about being able to handle this visit were based on her own misunderstandings. Since Jill chooses to attend Dede's party rather than go to see a ballet with some of her snobby, cliquish classmates, she makes an important statement about what is important "between friends." In another book Marlene Shyer examines the complex feelings of a boy, Neil, as his mentally retarded 13-year-old sister returns home in *Welcome Home, Jellybean.* Upper elementary readers can identify with the concerns, feelings, and doubts of both Jill and Neil as they build these special relationships.

The ambivalent feelings of a rebellious 15-year-old toward her retarded 11-year-old brother are examined with compassion in Colby Rodowsky's novel, *What About Me?* It seems to Dorrie that her own life is swallowed up in the family's constant concern for Fred. Her frustration and anger boil to the surface as expressions of hatred for her brother; yet when she is left alone with him and his heart condition becomes critical, she finds herself caring for him, loving him, just as her parents would have done. In the story's poignant resolution Fred dies and, like Dorrie, the reader is left to consider what it means to grow up in a family that includes a retarded child.

Sue Ellen Bridgers in *All Together Now* portrays an important summer in 12-year-old Casey Flanagan's life. Casey, whose mother works at two jobs while her father is away in the Korean War, has come to spend the summer with her grandparents in a small southern town. There she meets Dwayne Pickens, a retarded man her father's age, who's "got the mind of a twelve-year-old. Retarded but harmless. He likes baseball and toys just like a boy would. He goes all over town on his own. Everybody knows him so he never gets into any real trouble."[42] Their friendship grows when Dwayne, who dislikes girls but mistakes Casey for a boy, includes her in his baseball playing. Soon they are sharing outings to the race track, the beach, movies, and endless baseball sessions, often with Casey's feisty Uncle Taylor. When Dwayne's brother suddenly decides to have Dwayne quietly institutionalized, Taylor is instrumental in shaming him into reconsidering. Casey contracts what may be polio and her anxious family sits with her through several terrible August days. During her long convalescence, it is Dwayne who faithfully visits, having forgiven Casey for being a girl, and keeps her spirits up. By the summer's end, Casey has grown in awareness of herself and the nature of friendship. "Having responsibility made people responsible. Having someone to love gave you a chance to be loved yourself."[43] Humorous and sometimes poignant subplots involving Casey's observations and interactions with adults make this a complex and richly characterized novel. Bridgers reveals the characters' thoughts and feelings with a shifting viewpoint, allowing readers to consider the potential of human relationships in this well-crafted story for middle-school readers.

Mental Illness

Few stories about mental illness have been written for the elementary school child. In the title of the book, *(George),* E. L. Konigsburg has let the name with parentheses stand for Ben's alter ego, a real and constant companion. Ben had managed to keep his schizophrenic symptoms to himself until he entered sixth grade. Then, because of the fear that he might to be sent away to live with his fa-

[42]Sue Ellen Bridgers, *All Together Now* (New York: Knopf, 1979), p. 7.
[43]Bridgers, p. 229.

ther and stepmother and the pressure of knowing that his lab partners are stealing equipment from chemistry class to make LSD, George begins to speak out loud. Part of this story is very witty, as is typical of Konigsburg's stories, but part is very serious. George and Ben finally become one again and the book ends on a cheerful note of recovery.

Thirteen-year-old Carrie Stokes, in Zibby Oneal's *The Language of Goldfish,* does not like what is happening to her. She wishes her family could return to the days when they lived in a cramped Chicago apartment rather than in an affluent suburb. If only things didn't change, she would still be close to her sister Moira, and they would share all that they had as children. Instead, Carrie is under pressure by her mother and sister to wear more appropriate and stylish clothes, to go to school dances, and, somehow, be someone Carrie feels she is not. When she attempts suicide from a pill overdose, her mother still avoids dealing with the real Carrie. Gradually, as Carrie mends, she is able better to understand her mother's denial. She is helped in this by a therapist, a trusted art teacher, and a new friend, the neighbor boy. Finally, she learns to accept changes in others and herself. As in Judith Guest's popular adult novel, *Ordinary People,* a young person endures and recovers from a mental illness, while those closest display various ways in which they, too, cope with mental illness.

While there are few books about mentally ill children, there are several that present a child or children dealing with a mentally ill parent. Voigt's *Homecoming* and *Dicey's Song,* for instance, portray the after-effects of a depressed mother's abandonment of her children. Bruce Brooks, in *The Moves Make Man,* shows through the eyes of a compassionate and articulate boy narrator how the mental breakdown of his friend's mother nearly brings about the breakdown of the friend as well. Jocelyn Riley's *Only My Mouth Is Smiling* follows 13-year-old Merle Carlson as she accompanies her psychotic mother and two siblings to camp in Wisconsin following her mother's argument with their grandmother. When they finally move into a small rented house in town, Merle enjoys making friends until her mother's increasingly erratic behavior becomes more difficult to conceal. Eventually, Merle realizes she and her family cannot cope alone and a social worker intervenes. While

the story ends with hope, the family will have to learn to live with their mother's illness. Merle's story is continued in *Crazy Quilt.* Sue Ellen Bridgers' *Notes for Another Life* portrays the effects of a father's incurable mental illness and a mother's inability to cope with 13-year-old Wren and her older brother. While memorable grandparents help, it is up to Wren to make important decisions about her future in this young adult novel.

Aging and Death

In the early part of this century the aging and death of loved ones were accepted as a natural part of a child's first-hand knowledge. In most instances the modern child is removed from any such knowledge of senility and death. Few grandparents stay with their families any more, living instead in retirement homes or whole "cities of leisure worlds." When older relatives become ill they are shunted off to hospitals and rest homes. Few persons die at home today, and many children have never attended a funeral. Seldom is death discussed with children. There is enough genuine mystery about death, without hiding it under this false cloak of secrecy.

Gradually, realistic fiction for children is beginning to reflect society's new concern for honesty about aging and dying. We have begun to move from a time when the subject of death was one of the taboos of children's literature to a time when it is being discussed openly and frankly.

AGING

Many recent picture books have portrayed young people learning to accept older people as they are or to recall them fondly as they were (see Chapter 5, "Picture Books About Older People.") Realistic fiction portrays older people in all their rich variety, as treasured grandparents, as activists or as passive observers, as senile or vitally involved in events around them, and as still valuable contributors to a society they have helped to build.

The Hundred Penny Box by Sharon Bell Mathis tells of the love between Great-great-Aunt Dew, an aged black woman, and Michael, a young boy. Aunt Dew is a hundred years old and she keeps a box full of pennies, one for each year of her life. Michael loves to count them out while Aunt Dew tells him the story behind each one, relating it to life and historical events. Michael's mother wants to give the old box away but Michael plans a special hiding place for it. This story is remarkable for presenting three different viewpoints on the aged: Aunt Dew who is content to sing her long song and recall the past with her pennies, Michael's mother who has to take care of her, and Michael who loves her but in his childlike way also wants to be entertained by her story-telling. The Dillons have captured these sharply contrasting feelings in their fine black and white pictures.

A few stories tell of a child's relationship with a loved older person and the problems that occur as that person becomes ill or senile. This is the theme of Rose Blue's book *Grandma Didn't Wave Back.* Ten-year-old Debbie used to hurry home from school and wave at her grandma, who would be waiting at the window of their third-floor apartment. But then one day Grandma doesn't wave back because she is feeling sick and becoming very forgetful. Some of Debbie's friends now say that her grandma is crazy, which hurts Debbie's feelings. After Grandma is found wandering the street at night, Debbie's parents find a nursing home for her. Debbie is horrified by their actions but when she goes to visit her grandma she finds that the Shore Nursing Home is very elegant, with a lake view. As Debbie leaves, Grandma waves to her from her window. This is a very idealized treatment of the subject of aging, but it might lessen the concerns of some children.

In *A Figure of Speech* by Norma Fox Mazer the problems of an older person in the home are presented more realistically. The theme that an older person is a person—not a senior citizen, a cliché, or figure of speech—is made very clear. This is a touching and poignant story of Jenny's love for her grandfather, who is tolerated by his family and then pushed aside when the older son and his wife come home to live. The book ends tragically with the death of the old man. It is certainly a fine story to promote discussion of the way in which society treats older persons.

There are also books that portray older people as active, lively, and interesting. Often children discover this, much to their surprise. In Lowry's *Anastasia Again,* Anastasia devises a scheme for involving her grouchy older neighbor with a group of lively older people at a local Senior Citizen center. In Clifford's *The Rocking Chair Rebellion,*

14-year-old Opie (short for Penelope) volunteers at the Maple Ridge Home for the Aged when a former neighbor takes up residence there. She eventually is instrumental in helping several of the residents to leave and set up their own group home in her neighborhood. Although events are somewhat improbable, both Lowry and Clifford present older people as diverse, intelligent, active, and interesting as potential friends. In Delores Beckman's *My Own Private Sky,* 11-year-old Arthur Elliott is deeply affected by Jenny Kearns, his nontraditional 60-year-old babysitter who makes squaw tea on a wood stove which she insists on keeping in her city apartment. She also takes care of her old father, the last pony circuit rider alive. From interaction with these and other characters, Arthur gains self respect and courage, which he is able to return full measure to Jenny by the story's end.

Another book which suggests that generations have much to offer each other is Walter Dean Myers' *Won't Know Till I Get There.* Fourteen-year-old Steve Perry's family, who are black, decide to take in a foster child, but the one they are assigned is a street-tough 13-year-old named Earl Goins. When Earl and Steve trespass through a railroad yard with some of Steve's friends, Steve decides to show off and spray-paint a car with the name of his imaginary gang. They are caught by the transit police and eventually sent before a judge who sentences them to "volunteer" at an inner-city home for older people. There they become involved in the "seniors' " efforts to run the home themselves rather than move to larger facilities. Narrated by Steve, the story takes on a humorous upbeat style. The gradual revelation to Steve that "the more I get to know them the more I see them as individual people" is very believable. Realistically, the seniors do not get to keep their city-owned home and disband in the end, but Steve does gain a foster brother who needs him.

DEATH AND DYING

A child's first experience with death is frequently the loss of a pet. While picture books for younger children portray this experience with younger protagonists, several longer books have depicted slightly older children dealing with the death of a pet. In *The Growing Time* by Warburg, Jamie's old collie dog King dies and Jamie is desolate.

Eventually, the family buys Jamie a puppy, but he doesn't even want to look at it. In the middle of the night, however, the new pup cries and needs someone to love it. Jamie comes downstairs to comfort and claim him.

Charlotte Graeber's *Mustard* tells the story of a beloved old cat's eventual death from a series of strokes. Eight-year-old Alex stubbornly refuses to believe that his cat is dying. His father says "I wish I could tell you Mustard will be okay, but we can only hope." After the sympathetic veterinarian puts Mustard to sleep, Alex tearfully helps his father bury the cat in the back yard. When he and his father go to the animal shelter to donate some of Mustard's things, they both agree that it is hard to consider another new cat. Alex thinks that maybe next Easter they will come back to the shelter, "But now he only had room for remembering Mustard." Emotions are portrayed honestly: both adults shed tears over their 14-year-old cat's death and Alex isn't ready yet to accept another pet. Donna Diamond's soft charcoal drawings portray family members and Mustard with warmth and truth.

A Taste of Blackberries by Doris Smith is a believable story of the sudden death of a young boy. Jamie and his friends are catching Japanese beetles for Mrs. Houser when Jamie shoves a slim willow limb down a bee hole. The bees swarm out and Jamie is stung. Allergic to bee stings, Jamie screams and gasps and falls to the ground. His best friend thinks he is just showing off until the ambulance arrives. Jamie is dead by the time they get to the hospital. His friend goes to the funeral, and the author graphically describes his reaction to seeing Jamie:

> There was Jamie. He was out straight with one hand crossed over his chest. He didn't look like he was asleep to me. Jamie slept all bunched up. Jamie looked dead.[44]

After the funeral Jamie's friend picks blackberries because the two of them had planned to do so together. He shares his berries with Jamie's mother, who is very loving to him. Because the story is told in the first person, the reader views death through

[44]Doris Buchanan Smith, *A Taste of Blackberries*, illustrated by Charles Robinson (New York: Crowell, 1973), p. 34.

The veterinarian shares a poignant moment in Alex's gradual realization of his old cat's inevitable death. Illustration by Donna Diamond from *Mustard* by Charlotte Graeber.

a child's eyes. Simple, yet direct, this story seems very real. While Paterson's *Bridge to Terabithia* is discussed under the heading of "Developing Friendships," many readers would categorize it as a book about the death of a child, since Jess must eventually reconcile himself to the loss of his friend Leslie.

Robbie Farley felt that breaking his arm on the first day of summer vacation was the most terrible thing that could happen to him. But he finds out that *There Are Two Kinds of Terrible* when his mother goes to the hospital for tests and dies of cancer. Peggy Mann details Robbie's grief, anger, and bewilderment at his mother's sudden death. What makes it even harder to bear is that Robbie feels he doesn't really know the cool stranger who is his father. The adjustment to his loneliness and his father is slow and painful for them both. This is an honest and an intensely moving story of one boy's loss of his mother. *Grover*, by the Cleavers, reports the anger and frustration felt by a young boy following his mother's suicide. Grover, too, had a difficult time relating to his father.

Another story that tells of a boy's emotional reconciliation following the death of a parent from cancer is told in Jean Little's *Mama's Going to Buy You a Mockingbird*. Eleven-year-old Jeremy and his little sister have spent an uneasy summer at their cottage with an aunt while their father has an operation in a nearby Canadian city. When his father returns, weak and pale, to the cottage, Jeremy refuses to believe what he now senses. His father and he one evening share a sighting of two owls and his father commemorates the event with the gift of a small carved owl to Jeremy. Later in the fall when his father dies, Jeremy is unable to look at the owl and hides it on his bookshelf. He thinks

> Forgetting *was* the easiest way. When he forgot Dad was dead, when he forgot Dad altogether and concentrated on other things, then life was easier. When something made him think of his father—birds flying south, a song the two of them had liked coming over the radio, the sight of Dad's name written in the front of a book—he felt so mixed-up, lonely and scared that he wished with all his heart that he had not been made to remember.[45]

His new but tentative friendship with a lanky classmate Tess and a move to a new apartment where he adopts a grandfather help cheer him. But he still faces the coming Christmas holiday with dread. It is only when he begins to think of the feelings of others that he can finally hold the small owl and realize the "more difficult" joy that remembering brings. Jean Little crafts an extraordinary story out of richly observed detail, humor, and the emotions of this loving family's reconciling themselves to their loss. A plus for readers are the many references to other novels and poems with which Jeremy and his sister are familiar.

Another fine story, *Home from Far*, also by Jean Little, portrays a girl's resentment and anger following the death of her twin brother. With the arrival of two foster children, Jenny and her mother begin to gain perspective on each other's actions and feelings.

In *Beat the Turtle Drum* by Constance Green,

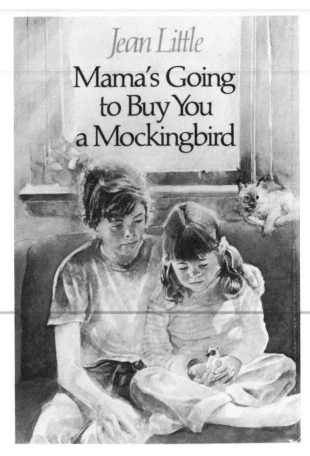

A dying father's gift of a polished stone owl helps Jeremy through his grief to newfound strengths. Jacket art by Leoung O'Young.

the reader has a chance to know 11-year-old Joss before the accidental fall from a tree that results in her death. Told from the point of view of her 13-year-old sister Kate, this is the story of the happy summer when Joss saved her money and finally rented a horse—and then the accident happened. Kate loved her "horse-happy sister" and so will the children who read about her. They will feel the tragedy of Joss' death almost as much as Kate and her parents.

A Summer to Die, by Lois Lowry, is also the story of two sisters, Molly the beautiful and popular blonde, and 13-year-old Meg who wears glasses and Molly's hand-me-down clothes. Jealous of Molly, Meg fights with her constantly until Molly becomes sick, and the doctor discovers she has leukemia. The author juxtaposes birth and

---

[45]Jean Little, *Mama's Going to Buy You a Mockingbird* (New York: Viking Kestrel, 1984), p. 151.

death when Meg is asked by a young couple to photograph the delivery of their first child at home. Meg is awed by the wonder of the birth and forced to consider death not as an end but as a new beginning. This story seems somewhat contrived in parts. The author has carefully detailed the various stages of dying but not made the reader feel for Molly or her family.

Previously discussed books deal with a child who recovers from the death of a friend, sibling, parent, or grandparent. *Hang Tough, Paul Mather* tells a memorable story of a boy who is anticipating his own death. Alfred Slote writes of Paul, a Little Leaguer who develops leukemia. The family moves from California to Michigan to be close to the university hospital where Paul will have special treatments. He is not supposed to play baseball, but the neighborhood team needs a pitcher for their big game. Paul slips out without his parents' knowledge, forges the permission slip, and pitches a great game. However, he is hit in a head-on collision and nearly passes out. His father has found out where he is and takes him to the hospital for a long stay. Once there, he has a young doctor who becomes his friend. Their discussion of death is one of the most honest in children's literature. Paul gets out of the hospital in his wheelchair, at least long enough to watch and help win another game. While Paul sounds hopeful at the end of the story, he is back in the hospital and his condition has worsened.

Two books for older readers discuss the impact of an awareness of death on life's possibilities. Pearl S. Buck's classic story *The Big Wave* offers hope, even though the villagers live under constant fear of death from the earth's volcanic eruptions or the tidal waves of the sea. When a big wave does come, it engulfs the homes and the people who live on the beach. Kino's friend Jiya loses his entire family and comes to stay with them. Kino's father tries to help him understand how to console Jiya:

> "Ah, no one knows who makes evil storms, " his father replied. "We only know that they come. When they come we must live through them as bravely as we can, and after they are gone, we must feel again how wonderful is life. Every day of life is more valuable now than it was before the storm."[46]

Jiya chooses to "live" again, returns to work, and laughs, because he does not want others to feel sad because he is sad. Eventually, he decides to return to the sea as a fisherman and builds a house down on the beach. Life goes on.

Another powerful story which asserts that coming to terms with death can be an affirmation of life and hope is Madeleine L'Engle's *A Ring of Endless Light*. Vicky Austin, whom readers met in *Meet the Austins,* begins her sixteenth summer at graveside services for a family friend who has suffered a heart attack after rescuing a spoiled teenager from an attempted suicide. While Vicky is already grieving for the impending death of her family's beloved grandfather, she tries to understand what mortality and immortality mean. She also deals with the attentions of three different young men. Zachary, the boy who attempted the suicide, is rich, impulsive, and exciting; Leo, whose father had tried to save Zachary, is plain and awkward but also reliable and candid; and Adam, a marine biologist studying the communication of dolphins, is warm, kind, and intensely eager to involve Vicky in his research after he sees her natural ability to communicate with dolphins. When the death of a child numbs Vicky, it is her experience with the dolphins that brings her back. Throughout the story shines the "ring of endless light" which her grandfather has been leading her to see. He tells Vicky, in the depths of her grief and denial:

> "You have to give the darkness permission. It cannot take over otherwise . . . Vicky, do not add to the darkness . . . This is my charge to you. You are to be a light-bearer. You are to choose the light."[47]

LIVING IN A PLURALISTIC SOCIETY

In a true democracy it is essential that we learn to respect and appreciate the diversity of all cultures within our pluralistic society. Books can never substitute for first-hand contact with other people, but they can raise the consciousness level of children and deepen their understanding of cultures that are different from theirs. Rather than falsely pretend

[46]Pearl Buck, *The Big Wave* (New York: John Day, 1947), p. 30.

[47]Madeleine L'Engle, *A Ring of Endless Light* (New York: Farrar, Straus & Giroux, 1980), p. 318.

that differences do not exist, children need to discover what is unique to each group of persons and universal to the experience of being human.

Appreciating Racial and Ethnic Diversity

The Civil Rights Movement of the 1950s led to the publication of many books about integration (see Chapter 3). These books tended to emphasize similarity of groups, rather than racial or ethnic identity. The Black Movement of the 1960s, Native American or Hispanic activism, and, more recently, the arrival of Asians from many different countries have created the need for books that authentically capture the unique experience and contributions of all minority groups.

Recognizing that books for children can be powerful socialization tools, various minorities have become more critical and demanding in how their culture should be represented in literature for children. At this time in our history it is necessary to evaluate literature about minority people according to not only its general literary value but also the image of the minority group presented by the text and illustrations.

GUIDELINES FOR EVALUATING MINORITY LITERATURE

While the emphasis should be placed on the selection of quality literature, the following guidelines[48] may be useful in evaluating minority literature:

1. *Diversity and range of representation.* In the portrayal of any minority group we need to look for a wide range of representation among the books about that particular race or ethnic group. Though many of the books of the black experience understandably have slum settings or rural backgrounds, more and more blacks are entering the middle and upper economic status. We need to have stories that reflect this reality of upward mobility. Many migratory

workers are Mexican Americans, but many Hispanics also hold positions of authority that have nothing to do with following crops. Koreans and Cambodians may work in factories, but many are doctors, teachers, or business owners, as well. Only when a collection of books about a particular group offers a wide spectrum of occupations, educational backgrounds, living conditions, and life styles will we honestly be moving away from stereotyping in books and offer positive images of minority groups.

2. *Avoidance of stereotyping.* Literature should portray the range of family groups, living conditions, occupations, and life styles of minorities. Not all Puerto Ricans live in basement apartments, nor are all black families parented by a single mother living in Harlem. All decisions in a Native American family are not made by men, nor do all Native Americans live on reservations. Sexist portrayals are to be avoided, especially those that assume that men are active, stoic, and hard-working, while women are passive and busy coping with life in the home. Illustrations should avoid stereotyping by portraying the distinctive yet varied characteristics of a group or race so that readers know they are looking at a black, a Laotian, an Hispanic, or a Native American. The portrayal of stereotypical articles should be avoided, such as the sombrero and poncho, a feathered headdress and moccasins, or "pickaninny pigtails" so often pictured in children's literature of earlier decades. A more subtle kind of stereotyping presents street, city, and store scenes picturing only whites. Further discussion of stereotyping may be found in Chapter 5, "Picture Books," and in Chapter 11, "Informational Books."

3. *Language considerations.* Derogatory terms for particular racial groups should not be used in stories about minorities unless these are essential to a conflict in the story or used in a historical setting. Even then, it should be made clear that these are unacceptable terms that cast more aspersion on the speaker than the person spoken to. Another consideration is the use of dialect or "broken English." Some recent

[48]More detailed guidelines may be found in Augusta Baker, *The Black Experience in Children's Books,* New York Public Library, 1984; "Checklist for Evaluating Chicano Material" in *Bulletin: Interracial Books for Children,* vol. 5, 1975; and Rudine Sims, *Shadow and Substance: Afro-American Experience in Contemporary Children's Fiction* (Urbana, Ill.: National Council of Teachers of English, 1982).

books about blacks have made a conscious effort to reproduce the cadence and syntax of certain black language patterns without resorting to stereotyped dialect or phonetically written spellings. Spanish words used in the context of the dialogue do not need English translations if the book truly represents Latinos. Children today need to understand that no language is any better or worse than any other and that regional speech or a dialect is a perfectly adequate mode of communication.

4. *The perspective of the book.* In evaluating a book about minority groups we need to ask if it truly represents a black experience or perspective and so on. This is a difficult guideline to define because we don't want to suggest only one kind of black experience, for example. At the same time we must consider from whose perspective the book is told. If the major theme of the story is a Latino's desire to master the English language to become "one of us," we may be certain that that story is being told from a white perspective. We need to look to see who solves the problems in stories. Do characters from the represented minority groups take the initiative in problem-solving, or is the solution provided by paternalistic whites? Does the story provide a positive image of the minority group, or a negative one? Is racial pride apparent in the story? How authentic are the details of the story to the experience of the represented minority?

These are some of the questions and guidelines that may be used in evaluating the books in this section. No one is free from his or her own particular bias or background, however. Teachers or librarians in specific school settings may want to apply other or additional criteria for the books they select. The essential point is to provide books about minorities for *all* children. Books can be a moving force in developing children's appreciation for our pluralistic society.

BLACK EXPERIENCES IN BOOKS FOR CHILDREN

In the last decades many fine books have been published which reflect the social and cultural traditions associated with growing up as a black child in America. This "culturally conscious fiction," says Rudine Sims, has certain recurring features which offer all children, but especially black children, a perspective in fiction that is uniquely Afro-American. In culturally conscious fiction there often appear references to distinctive language patterns and vocabulary; relationships between a young person and a much older one; extended or three-generational families; descriptions of skin shades and positive comparisons made, such as "dark as a pole of Ceylon ebony"; and acknowledgement of Afro-American historical, religious and cultural traditions.[49]

Today, there are many picture books, some with extended text, which portray this black experience for younger children (see Chapter 5). For instance, in four short chapters, Lucille Clifton traces the history of *The Lucky Stone* through slave times, emancipation, the early 1900s, and into Tee's hands. Three of the stories are told to Tee as she sits on the porch with her great-grandmother. The black stone, with the letter "A" scratched on it, began as a sign of the location of a young slave girl who hid in a cave to avoid detection. It becomes a talisman to Tee's great-grandmother when she is given it by the now-grown former slave. The fourth chapter, told by Tee, tells how the lucky stone comes into her possession. This story makes eloquent use of oral storytelling traditions and begs to be read aloud.

Black experiences, in both rural and city locations, are portrayed in books for middle elementary school children, as well. *Nellie Cameron* is a 9-year-old girl, one of six children in a black family living in Washington, D.C. Nellie is in third grade and can scarcely read. This makes her feel "dumb," particularly when her older brother is considered brilliant. The school gives her little help:

They kept promoting her at school, always telling her she was dumb and keeping her with the dumb kids. Nellie didn't think she was dumb. . . . She did her numbers pretty well. But reading was like a mountain she would never cross. She could see the top and it

[49]Rudine Sims, *Shadow and Substance: Afro-American Experience in Contemporary Children's Fiction* (Urbana, Ill.: National Council of Teachers of English, 1982), pp. 49–77.

was beautiful, but she had no idea how to get up there.[50]

Then Miss Lacey's reading clinic opens and Nellie has a second chance with a teacher she loves. Miss Lacey tape records her speech and gives Nellie confidence. The teacher types her stories out as her reading "book" and, gradually, Nellie learns to read. At the end of the story, when no one seems really interested that she can read or that she's going to be promoted, Nellie proves to herself that she is still important in the family by running away to a friend's house. The family's relief at discovering she is all right, even Mama's spanking, assures Nellie of who she is.

Older children can experience the good times that 12-year-old Beth Lambert has with her first "crush" on a boy in rural Arkansas. *Philip Hall Likes Me. I Reckon Maybe* by Bette Greene is an episodic novel about a spunky, energetic girl and her friend Philip. They set up "The Elizabeth Lorraine Lambert & Friend Vegetable Stand," capture chicken thieves, picket a local merchant for selling them bad merchandise, and compete in a calf-judging contest that Beth wins. Beth apologizes to Philip and says she should have let him win, which makes him angry. Later he says, "all you been doing lately is winning, and that ain't hard to live with. Hard thing is losing." Beth suggests they enter the square-dance contest so they can win or lose together. Beth Lambert has the spunk of a Queenie Peavy without Queenie's chip on her shoulder. This lively story was an Honor Book for the Newbery award. In a sequel, *Get On Out of Here, Philip Hall,* Beth's belief in herself is tested when she assumes she will win a leadership award given by her church.

Virginia Hamilton is the first black author to receive the Newbery award. One of her early books, *Zeely,* is still one of the best loved by children. Spending the summer at her uncle's farm, 11-year-old Geeder Perry meets the proud and beautiful Zeely Taber. Zeely is more than six and a half feet tall and is very thin and dark. Geeder finds a picture of a Watusi Queen and imagines that Zeely is also a queen. Only Zeely herself can bring Geeder back to reality by discovering the real

beauty of being what you are. This is a story that is full of dignity, beauty, and mystery.

Using the device of a secret diary about her "special days," Eloise Greenfield has presented an intimate picture of the peak experiences of Doretha, called *Sister* by her family. The diary begins when Doretha is age 10 and details the sudden death of her father while they are all attending a picnic. At age 11 Doretha learns the family's story of her freedom-fighting ex-slave ancestor. When she is 12 she records her tears and her mother's disappointment when her mother's friend jilts her. Throughout the book Doretha worries about her alienated sister, but gradually, Doretha emerges from the pages of her book and from her role of sister, to become a very real person in her own right.

The realities of ghetto culture are also depicted in some books about blacks. The impact of gangs on individuals is the theme of Paula Fox's *How Many Miles to Babylon.* Ten-year-old James is sent on a school errand, and instead runs off to a deserted house where he is found by a gang of boys who steal dogs. They force James to go to Coney Island where they keep him a prisoner. He finally manages to escape, sets the dogs free, and returns home to find his mother is back from the hospital.

Walter Dean Myers sets his stories in a ghetto, but he portrays a less grim, even humorous, city life while acknowledging that not everyone in the city lives in a "safe house." In *Fast Sam, Cool Clyde, and Stuff,* Stuff and his gang of friends, the Good People, join a basketball team at the youth center, inadvertently become involved with drugs, and try to help a former friend, a young addict. Sam argues that walking away from him would be "walking away from ourselves." Coming from the same background, Sam can't see "how it can't happen to one of us." This same sense of interdependence is found in Myers' *Won't Know Until I Get There.* Myers makes his stories sparkle with the keen observational powers, antics, and verbal wit of his boy narrators.

A bold and honest story about a 13-year-old boy is Alice Childress' *A Hero Ain't Nothin' But a Sandwich.* How to salvage Benjie, who is well on his way to being hooked on heroin, is the theme of this Harlem tale. The story is told from many different points of view—from those of Butler Craig,

[50]Michelle Murray, *Nellie Cameron* (New York: Seabury, 1971), p. 31.

Benjie's "stepfather"; Jimmy Lee Powell, Benjie's friend; Benjie's mother, Rose; Walter, the pusher; and Benjie himself. All of these people have important things to say about Benjie and their relationship with him. They also reveal differing viewpoints on life in Harlem. Jimmy Lee tells how hard it is to be a friend to someone on drugs:

> Friendship begins to split when one is caught in a habit and the other not. I've seen it time and time, needles divide guys, because the user rather be round another junkie.[51]

Butler saves Benjie's life one night and Benjie looks to him as to a father, someone who would believe in him. At the end of the story Butler is waiting for Benjie to come from the rehabilitation center— Benjie is late, and both Butler and the reader hope that he makes it. This is a tough, yet very tender, young adult story that may shock some readers and save others.

The Planet of Junior Brown by Virginia Hamilton is a far more complex and symbolic story than her *Zeely*. The main theme in *Planet* is our need for each other. Although the book is titled *The Planet of Junior Brown* there are really three planets in the book—all complementing each other until they physically and ideally come together at the end of the story. The first planet is a huge mass added to the plastic solar system that Mr. Poole and Buddy have set up in the school basement. Like the 300-pound Junior, the planet is larger than anything else in the solar system. By creating this planet for Junior, Buddy is trying to tell him that Junior, too, can belong. The second set of planets is the sanctuaries for homeless boys throughout the city, where leaders teach their charges, who have no home or family, to survive from day to day. All the planets and people ultimately come together in the final planet of Junior Brown, and it is here in this new planet that the reader sees what the future or new world can be— a place where everyone belongs, where people have learned to live for each other, not for themselves.

M.C. Higgins, the Great, which won both the Newbery award and the National Book Award, is the story of 13-year-old Cornelius Higgins and his

family, who live just below a strip mine in the Appalachian hills of Ohio. M.C. dreams of getting his family away from the danger of the slow-moving slag heap that threatens to engulf their home. His place of refuge, where he can survey his domain and also rise above his problems, is a 40-foot steel pole. It is from this height that he discovers two strangers entering the valley. One is a "dude" who M.C. imagines will make his mother a singing star and enable the family to move. The other is Lurhetta, a young wanderer who awakens M.C.'s initiative and his realization that both choice and action lie within his power. M.C. begins to see that running away from the mountain, or swaying above it on a pole, will never solve his problems. Finally, his father helps him build a wall to hold back the slag by giving him the tombstone of the slave who had run away to the mountain and started the family. Again Virginia Hamilton has created a symbol-filled book that speaks to both the uniqueness of the black experience and the universal concerns of all human beings (see "Historical Fiction," Chapter 10, for other stories that depict black experiences).

BOOKS ABOUT OTHER MINORITIES

There are far better quality and greater range in books about blacks than there are for other minorities. Many of the books about Latinos, for example, have forced stories that are thin in content and characterization; frequently they perpetuate stereotypes rather than dispel them. A favorite theme for stories about Puerto Ricans is that of overcoming language problems. Children are pictured as being miserable and having no friends until they learn to speak English properly. In *Candita's Choice* by Lewiton, a Puerto Rican refuses to speak at all until she can speak well enough to make the teacher proud of her. This same theme is apparent in the title of Bouchard's book, *The Boy Who Wouldn't Talk.* Carlos' family has moved from Puerto Rico to New York City and he is so confused and frustrated with his language problem that he, too, decides to give up talking—in English *and* Spanish. Finally, he meets Ricky Hermandez, a blind boy who asks for directions in order to get home. Ricky cannot read the signs or pictures that Carlos makes for him, thereby forcing Carlos to talk. The theme of Mohr's *Felita* seems to be "stick to your own kind." The family moves to a new neighbor-

[51]Alice Childress, *A Hero Ain't Nothin' But a Sandwich* (New York: Coward, 1973), p. 87.

hood and encounters such hatred from their new neighbors that they return to their former apartment in the ghetto with relief.

Other Latino stories suffer from the same shallowness as some of the slight stories of the Puerto Ricans. *Go Up the Road* by Lampman tells of the dream of Yolanda Ruiz to finish grade school. But every year the family goes north up the road to harvest the crops, and Yolanda would have to leave school early. She is doing fourth-grade work for the third time because of this and prays to pass into the fifth. Then her Uncle Luis, a logger in a small Oregon town, dies, and so they all go to help his widow and children. Much to their surprise Uncle Luis' family is far better off than the Ruizes. Yolanda has a good school experience and is tutored so she can pass into fifth grade. Her papa decides to "stabilize," to find a job and remain in Oregon. This story seems somewhat patronizing. Yolanda has none of the spunk of Janey Larkin, the heroine in the classic migrant story *Blue Willow* by Doris Gates. Janey's only friend in that story is a Mexican-American girl. A comparison of the two stories would be interesting.

One of the most widely read stories about persons of Spanish descent in this country has been the award-winning . . . *And Now Miguel* by Joseph Krumgold. Miguel is the middle brother of an Hispanic family living on a New Mexico sheep ranch. Pedro, the younger brother, seems satisfied with what he has, but Miguel thinks his 19-year-old brother, Gabriel, can do everything and has everything he wants. Miguel expresses the problem of all who feel "in between":

> Both of them, they are happy. But to be in between, not so little any more and not yet nineteen years, to be me, Miguel, and to have a great wish—that is hard.[52]

Miguel has one all-consuming desire, and that is to be able to go with the men when they take the sheep to the Sangre de Cristo Mountains. His prayers are answered, but not as Miguel wished.

While both realistic and historical fiction have often presented the Native American as the "ignoble savage," recent stories seek to redress that injustice (see Chapter 10). In the ever-dwindling number of books portraying contemporary Native Americans, a frequent theme is a child's conflict in balancing the dominant culture and the traditional Native American one.

When Thunders Spoke by Virginia Driving Hawk Sneve is representative of "identity" books. Young Norman Two Bull is the third generation of his family to live on the Dakota (Sioux) reservation. His mother wears hose and heels to entertain the ladies' society and disapproves of Norman's grandfather, Matt Two Bull, who clings to the old customs. Norman goes to Thunder Butte, a site of many traditions and finds agates which he trades to a thoroughly unlikable white trader. He also finds a relic, an old *coup* stick which he gives to his grandfather. The trader proposes a quarry as a way to benefit the Indians since Norman found the agates there, but he wants mostly to advance his own interests. However, the Butte is sacred ground and Norman's grandfather does not approve. Together Norman and his father return the *coup* stick, and the reader is left with the impression that the traditional beliefs are still revered.

In *The Potlatch Family*, Evelyn Sibley Lampman explores the changing attitudes of Plum Longor, a 14-year-old who has little interest in her Chinook heritage until her brother comes home from the war. He convinces many of their relatives and friends, who had long since left the reservation and tried to win full acceptance in white society, that it is time to capitalize on the contemporary interest in ethnic origins. Plum is horrified at first by his suggestion that they hold a weekly potlatch, or traditional feast, as a tourist attraction. His enthusiasm, however, and the community spirit fostered by their preparations change Plum's thinking. Like others in the project, she learns more about her own background and no longer thinks of it as something to hide. This story has some predictable images—Plum's drunken father, for instance, who recovers too remarkably. But there are interesting relationships also: Plum has to overcome some prejudices of her own to accept the friendship of a white girl, and the contrasting portrayal of grandmothers shows how wide the differences can be among those who wear white society's label of "Indian."

Grandfather Tayhua makes many comments about his dissatisfaction with white society in Craig Kee Strete's *When Grandfather Journeys*

[52]Joseph Krumgold, . . . *And Now Miguel*, illustrated by Jean Charlot (New York: Crowell, 1953), p. 9.

into Winter. For his grandson Little Thunder he draws the traditional signs for eagle and bear and deer and then the signs of the white man: a dollar sign, a TV antenna, a car, and an "F" for Little Thunder's grade in the white man's school. There is humor and irony in many of Tayhua's spirited statements:

> "Whole world jumping up and down and real air to breathe yet people sitting under TV cow like newborn calf that don't know it can walk." . . . "Be careful in your dealings with white people. It is said the large print giveth and the small print taketh away."[53]

There is excitement as Tayhua rides a wild stallion "to the ground" at the yearly horsebreaking and gives the prize, the horse, to Little Thunder. However, the punishing ride breaks the old man physically, and he dies soon afterward. This book has as much to say about death and dying as it does about the conflict of cultures.

While Asian-Americans, one of the fastest-growing minorities in North America, have been portrayed in picture books for younger children, there are very few stories about them for middle-graders. Several well-written accounts of life in the Japanese relocation camps during World War II have been written (see Chapter 10). *Child of the Owl* by Laurence Yep is the fine story of a Chinese-American girl who finds herself and her roots when she goes to live with Paw Paw, her grandmother, in San Francisco's Chinatown. When Barney, Casey's gambling father, winds up in the hospital after having been beaten and robbed of his one big win, he first sends Casey to live with her Uncle Phil and his family in suburbia. Casey doesn't get along with Uncle Phil's family and they are horrified by her, so she is sent to Chinatown. At first Casey doesn't like the narrow streets and alleys or the Chinese schools. But Paw Paw tells her about Jeanie, the mother Casey never knew, about her true Chinese name, and the story of the family's owl charm. Gradually she comes to like it all and to realize that this place that was home to Paw Paw, Jeanie, and Barney is her home, too.

Child of the Owl is as contemporary as the rock music that Paw Paw enjoys and as traditional as the owl charm, but Casey and Paw Paw are true originals.

Bette Bao Lord's title *In the Year of the Boar and Jackie Robinson* reflects the melding of two cultures, Chinese and American, which takes place when Bandit Wong and her mother join her father in New York City in 1947. While refrigerators and washing machines are strange mysteries to the 10-year-old, bubble gum and roller skating are welcome novelties. When school starts, Bandit (now known as Shirley Temple Wong) has a difficult time becoming accepted by her fifth-grade class-mates until she excels in hitting a ball. Then she is nicknamed Jackie Robinson and the year promises to be a good one. Marc Simont's warm and humorous drawings are perfect for this episodic family story.

Respecting Religious Backgrounds

Although the United States was founded on a belief in freedom of religion, misunderstanding and religious prejudice have persisted in our society. *Hannah Elizabeth* by Rich is the quiet story of a year in the life of a 10-year-old Indiana Mennonite. She has to learn to accept the taunts of school-mates because her father refused to fight in the war. Many quotations from the Bible and parts of sermons are included, as well as accounts of fun in family life. Hannah Elizabeth attends a movie and party with her music teacher, but realizes she is not being a good Mennonite. Faced with conflicting values, she has no difficulty in choosing.

Three stories detail the lives of girls who belong to the "plain people." Adjustment to the conflicting values of her Amish home and the school "outside" is also difficult for Esther, the central character in *Plain Girl.* Sorenson writes sensitively of a father's disappointment when his son leaves the religious community, and his fear when his daughter goes to the public school. As Esther grows up, she discovers that people who wear pink, blue, and red may be as kind and good as those who wear plain clothing. When her brother finally returns, the young people recognize they may need to change outward symbols, such as haircuts and use of machinery, but they can keep the inner values of their religion. *Shoo-Fly Girl* by Lois Lenski also portrays life in an Amish family. Shoo-Fly's encounters with the outside world bring confusion, and she prefers home.

In Eiveen Weiman's *Which Way Courage?*, Courage Kunstler feels increasingly at odds with the Amish standards that govern her family. By those, she should be preparing for marriage, but Courage dislikes cooking and sewing and is not yet attracted to any boy. She wishes to continue her schooling, but the Amish traditionally leave school at her age. It is only after Jason, her beloved younger brother, dies that Courage considers alternatives for the future. Her father had refused to seek medical help for Jason's illness, and so Courage defied him by taking Jason to the hospital where he died. Now, realizing she will not soon be ready for marriage and that she has serious doubts

about her father's calm acceptance of "God's will," she chooses to leave her family and the community. She will be "shunned" just as her father's brother was when he, too, made the same choice, and it is to his family that she will go. The simple, hard-working life of this Amish family is portrayed with warmth and sympathy. Weiman uses the Amish speech cadences, patterns, and vocabulary to help create a vivid portrait of the Kunstler family.

In *A Promise Is a Promise*, Molly Cone helps children understand the Jewish faith. Essentially, this is the story of Ruth Morgen's growing understanding of the meaning and history of her religion. Ruthy's preparation for her Bas Mitzvah is interwoven with the decisions she must make about daily relationships with people. Ruth is concerned about an eccentric, lonely neighbor whose cats bother another neighbor. Ruthy promises Mr.

The dual meaning of the title is evident as Courage Kunstler looks away from her Amish family toward the possiblity of a different way of life. Jacket art by Michael Garland.

Hainey she will care for his cats when he goes to the hospital, and when he returns briefly to close his house forever, she promises to find a home for them. Ruth's problems in finding a home for the cats become intertwined with her questions about the meaning of Judaism. The customs of the Jewish holidays and religious service are described in this sensitive story of a girl growing up.

Two novels realistically present the effects of anti-Semitism on two boys and their families. *Berries Goodman,* in Emily Neville's story, reminisces about his friendship with a Jewish boy, Sidney, and a neighboring family's prejudice against Jews. While his mother acquiesces in "agreements" made by the real-estate agency for which she works, Berries is hopeful evidence that the next generation will not carry these same senseless prejudices. Parents in Fran Arrick's *Chernowitz!* take a more active stand when a school bully begins to harass the family. Ninth-grader Bobby Cherno retaliates against the bully by making it appear that he stole a radio at school. But his victory holds no savor as Bob realizes that his action was wrong. Through Bob's parents, Arrick suggests that what may change attitudes is to make prejudicial acts visible in the community so that others' avoidance of conflict will not lead once again to history's repetition of itself.

Appreciating Regional Differences

In a time when cultural diversity and a constantly mobile population may convince children that "everyone lives as I do," there are still regions noted for their own unique features. The name of Lois Lenski is closely associated with the term "regional fiction," for she was one of the first authors to write of children who lived in particular regions of our country. Lenski would go to live in a community and observe as an anthropologist might observe, listening to the people, asking them to tell what had happened in their lives. Then she would weave the facts into an interesting plot centering around one family. Her *Strawberry Girl* describes life in the central Florida backwoods early in the twentieth century. In *Judy's Journey,* one of the first stories about migrants, conditions were so bad for Judy's sharecropper family, that they had to sell their possessions and follow the crops. Athough Judy herself does not show much charac-

ter change, she does effect change in the family's condition. This is characteristic of many of Lenski's regional stories.

The Cleavers' story *Where the Lilies Bloom* is a well-known tale of Appalachia. The tortuous death of Roy Luther from "worms in the chest" puts the full responsibility for the survival of the family on Mary Call, his 14-year-old daughter. She and Romey, her younger brother, carry Luther up the mountain in a wagon and bury him so the "county people" will not find out that they are orphaned and separate them. Then Mary Call strives to keep her "cloudy-headed" older sister, Devola, and her two younger siblings alive through the winter. Mary Call's fierce pride gives her fortitude to overcome such things as a severe winter, a caved-in roof, and the constant pretense that Roy Luther still lives. At 14, Mary Call's strength and responsibility have made her old before her time, but she pulls the family through the crisis:

> My name is Mary Call Luther, I thought, and someday I'm going to be a big shot. I've got the guts to be one. I'm not going to let this beat me. If it does, everything else will for the rest of my life.[54]

Mary Call and her family do survive, through wildcrafting on the mountains, through scheming, and pure grit. The authors have captured the beauty of the Smokies and of this memorable family who live in what an old hymn calls the land "Where the Lilies Bloom So Fair." Mary Call's story is continued in *Trial Valley,* but this sequel seems more contrived and less believable than the first book. Other authors, such as James Still, Rebecca Caudill, Cynthia Rylant, and Mildred Lee, have also set stories of characters from poor but self-respecting families in the mountains of Appalachia.

Robbie Branscum sets her novels in the rural Arkansas she knew as a child. Told in humorous, robust, and sometimes salty dialect, her stories present families eking out a living in the Arkansas hills. In *The Murder of Hound Dog Bates,* 13-year-old Sassafras Bates is sure that one of his three guardian aunts has poisoned his only friend, his pet dog. To discover which of the three it was,

---

[54]Vera Cleaver and Bill Cleaver, *Where the Lilies Bloom* (New York: Lippincott, 1969), p. 144.

Sass enlists the help of an itinerant, Mr. O'Kelly, who betrays him by falling in love with the youngest of the three aunts. However, when the real murderer finally is revealed, Sass is able to forgive. On the dog's grave marker, Sass states that Hound Dog Bates "committed suicide by his own mouth fer a-eatin' thing or things unknown t' be pizen." In earlier stories, Branscum has traced the growing up of a 13-year-old girl in *Toby, Granny and George*. Sequels *Toby Alone* and *Toby and Johnny Joe* tell of the death of her beloved grandmother, her growing independence, and her love for the gentle, once-mute boy, Johnny Joe.

Understanding Various World Cultures

There is an increasing number of fine informational books about life in other countries (see Chapter 11). However, as children are studying Australia or countries of Africa or Europe, they should be made aware of the stories that provide the feelings of people, as well as the nonfiction that provides the facts. It is impossible to describe all the books about various countries in this section, but outstanding ones will be mentioned. Again, it is good to remind children that a single book cannot convey a complete picture of a country. In order to make this point clear, children might consider what books, if any, they would like to have sent to other countries as *representative* of life in the United States.

Ann Nolan Clark's *To Stand Against the Wind* begins in America but flashes back quickly to the Vietnamese conflict. On the traditional Vietnamese Day of Ancestors, 11-year-old Em tries, despite his despair as the new head of the family, to write down his memories of the places, people, and events in the time before he came to America. While the remnants of his family, two old people and his elder sister, kneel in silence before the Altar of the Ancestors, Em thinks wistfully, "Maybe if I remember all of them now, just sit here and remember them . . . it will be like washing my memory clean. Maybe I will never need to think of them again."[55] He recalls his home village in the Mekong Delta, its rhythmical life based on planting and harvesting of rice, his sister's wartime

wedding festivities, and his father and brother departing to join the army. He remembers his two first friends, an American war correspondent named Sam, and the family water buffalo, both of whom perish when the buffalo is shot by Americans because it is a potential source of food for the advancing Viet Cong. While the story is told in several long flashbacks, it has narrative power because of this grounding in one family's life. The tragedies of war are seen in the effects it has on this family of ten people. Clark includes well-researched details of Em's daily routine, old family customs, and Vietnamese traditions. At the story's conclusion, Em has remembered all—but has recorded nothing. Finally he writes down a proverb he had learned from his father. His grandmother places it on the Altar of the Ancestors with all the other poems, part of the family history she has carried with her to the new home: "It takes a strong man to stand against the wind."

The Land I Lost: Adventures of a Boy in Vietnam by Quang Nhuong Huynh is a series of portraits remembered from the author's home village in the central highlands of Vietnam. Although it is "endless years of fighting" that make his homeland lost, his reminiscences barely mention war. Instead, his stories focus on people: farmers, hunters, bandits, his karate-expert grandmother, his older cousin who could capture pythons and train birds to sing popular tunes. Animals figure significantly in every episode—as pets, workers, or as formidable enemies. Tank, the family water buffalo, has knives strapped to his horns to help him defend the village herd from marauding tigers. Barriers are erected in the river to keep crocodiles from snatching luckless bathers. Vo-Dinh's illustrations capture the menace and fascination of many of these encounters. Each episode is sparely told, often humorous, and infused with the elusive meanings of folklore. *The Land I Lost* personalizes the Vietnamese people and may help children become acquainted with what has so often been represented as an alien land.

The Leopard by Cecil Bodker is an exciting story about a young Ethiopian boy who knew too much—he knew that it was the blacksmith who was stealing the cattle under the guise of being a leopard. When Tibeso reveals this knowledge, the smith binds and gags Tibeso and takes him to a deserted village where he will be at the mercy of

[55]Ann Nolan Clark, *To Stand Against the Wind* (New York: Viking, 1978), p. 29.

the wild animals and spirits of the night. In the end the smith is killed by a leopard, a fitting retribution. Written by a Danish author who had lived in Ethiopia, this story portrays some modern aspects of East African life overlaid with the traditional superstitions of the mountain villagers.

It would be interesting for children to compare the slow-moving, mystical story *Secret of the Andes* by Clark with the modern frightening tale *Pulga* by S. R. Van Iterson. *Secret of the Andes* appears to be realistic fiction, yet elements of legend and fantasy are included in this story of an Indian boy who is chosen to be the one who shall know of the secret gold and llama herd of the Incas. The pace of this award-winning book is as slow as his climb up the mountain trails, but the author's descriptions provide moments of real beauty. The mystery of Cusi's identity supplies the suspense of the story. *Pulga*, "flea" in Spanish, tells of a street urchin hired to accompany a trucker on dangerous runs from Bogotá to the coast. The story presents a vivid if unflattering picture of life in Colombia written by a Dutch author living in Bogotá.

Ivan Southall, an Australian, is known for his survival stories, such as *Hill's End* and *Ash Road*. *Josh* is the story of the psychological and physical survival of a 14-year-old city boy who goes to visit the country town that was settled by his great-grandfather Plowman. The people he meets there all baffle him and seem uncivilized. Josh is a dreamer and a poet, a boy who seems to do everything wrong. During the three days of his visit, encounters with the young people of Ryan Creek move from veiled hostility to open violence. Told from the point of view of Josh, this is a fascinating tale of a boy's struggle to survive in a world he doesn't understand. His Aunt Clara says Josh has been just what the small town needed—a catharsis. But for Josh it has been more than he can bear. He cuts his stay short and starts walking back to Melbourne town. This story won the English Carnegie Medal in 1971. It paints a vivid picture of contrasting values and backgrounds in Australia.

From Norway, by way of a British translation, comes Karin Lorentzen's story of *Lanky Longlegs*, a 9-year-old girl named Di who does not like the nickname given her by Martin, a new boy in school. When Di's dog has puppies (with Di eagerly watching the whole process), Martin is allowed to buy one and their friendship improves. The somber counterpoint to these everyday events is that Di's beloved 2-year-old brother Mike is slowly dying of a blood disease. After his death, Di dreams that he has disappeared into a sunbeam, but her real comfort comes from Martin, who brings a gift for the last pup in the litter, which Di will keep. This book is different in tone and in choice of detail from many U.S. treatments of a similar subject. Two particular strengths are the portrayal of Di's parents, who are able to love and grieve at the same time, and Jan Ormerod's engaging illustrations of Di, Mike, and the puppies.

Malcolm Bosse has written a story for older readers which ably portrays a boy's childhood in India and his early adolescence in a small midwestern American town. Motherless 14-year-old *Ganesh* is named for an elephant-headed Hindu god but is also known as Jeffery Moore. Bosse details in this three-part story the daily routines Jeffrey shares with his ascetic father before his death. After Jeffrey attends to the ceremonial cremation of his father, he leaves to join his aunt in America. In part two, Jeffrey lives in a ramshackle but sturdy old house built by his great-grandfather and begins to make friends with his classmates. However, the government has announced plans for a new highway, which will mean that he and his aunt will be evicted and the house destroyed. In the third section, Jeffrey, who has come to love the old house, involves his school friends in a quiet protest and a hunger strike. This practice, called "Satyagraha," is viewed with incredulity, anger, and finally respect by various members of the community. Eventually, Jeffrey, now known by his Indian name Ganesh, is allowed to keep the house and the highway is rerouted. Ganesh shares some of his Hindu practices and beliefs with his American friends, introducing them to mantras, vegetarianism, fasting, and Yoga. But they also give to him a gradual respect and tolerance which becomes active support for his cause. It is in this development of understanding and sensitivity that the book's strength lies.

Jan Mark was awarded a Carnegie Medal for *Thunder and Lightnings*, a story of friendship between two British boys. Andrew, newly moved from the city, doesn't quite know what to make of his new classmate, the unconventional Victor. Victor wears several layers of clothes and has a wonderful disorderly bedroom full of model planes suspended from the ceiling. In school, the two friends join forces to prepare a report on Lightnings, the planes Victor so loves, in spite of Victor's reluctance to "learn things" for school rather than find out simply because he is fascinated. Jan Mark provides a contrast between the two boys' attitudes as well as between Andrew's warm but chaotic household and Victor's impeccably clean and sterile one. As Victor introduces Andrew to the many kinds of aircraft which come and go from a nearby field, Andrew begins to understand Victor and his passion for planes. Humorous and subtle word play plus a contemporary British school and family setting give this story a gentle grounding in another culture. But the book is concerned with the fine-tuning of observational powers—seeing what is actually there, whether drawing fish, church priories, or airplanes—and sensing what may not be readily apparent: our need to care and be cared about.

Handles, also by Jan Mark, introduces Erica Timperley, an 11-year-old who loves motorcycles. At home, she only gets to be near them in a city parking garage, but on a country holiday she meets Elsie Wainwright, the enigmatic owner of Mercury Motorcycles, a dingy repair shop. In Erica's eyes, Elsie is the ruler of a fascinating kingdom. She finds irresistible his quirky sense of humor and his habit of substituting imaginative "handles" for the real names of people who come and go in his muddy yard. Erica longs to be part of that kingdom, with a handle of her own, a satisfaction which eludes her until her last visit. As in her previous books, Mark plumbs the depths of everyday experience and observes minute detail. Her choice of words is one of the book's chief strengths as well as its chief challenge. The combination of British slang plus regional dialect and idiom is difficult, but context and a glossary of colloquial terms will help readers appreciate Mark's sensitive story about feelings and how the use of language defines the user.

Erica longs for a nickname, a "handle" that will mark her acceptance as one of the group at the Mercury Motorcycles garage.

POPULAR TYPES OF REALISTIC FICTION

Certain subjects of realistic fiction are so popular with children that they ask for them by name. They want to read a good animal (usually dog or horse) story; a sports book (baseball or football story); a "funny" book (humorous fiction); or a good mystery. Many of these stories are not the quality of literature that we would hope children will read, at least not to the total exclusion of other books. Yet many of them serve the useful function of getting children "hooked" on books so that they then move on to reading better literature. Teachers and librarians need to identify these popular kinds of books so as to be able to recommend other titles when children are ready for them. They also need to know some of the outstanding books among these popular types in order to help children grow in their reading.

Humorous Stories

Children like to laugh. The humorous verses of a Silverstein or a Prelutsky represent children's favorite poetry (see Chapter 8). Collections of jokes and riddles circulate at all levels of the elementary school. The snappy retorts of Carlie in Byars' *The Pinballs* or the ludicrous situations presented in Daniel Pinkwater's stories are related from child to child. Humorous realistic fiction often presents characters involved in amusing or exaggerated predicaments which are then solved in clever or unique ways. Often these stories are episodic in plot structure; each chapter might stand alone as a complete story.

The "Amelia Bedelia" stories are an easy-to-read series that feature the literal-minded maid of the Rogers family. Amelia follows Mrs. Rogers' instructions to the letter. She can't understand why Mrs. Rogers wants her to dress the chicken or draw the drapes, but she cheerfully goes about making a pair of pants for the chicken and drawing a picture of the drapes. Her wonderful lemon meringue pie saves the day—and her job. Peggy Parish has written several Amelia Bedelia books, illustrated by various artists, in which the maid continues to misinterpret English expressions. These modern noodlehead stories include *Teach Us, Amelia Bedelia; Thank You, Amelia Bedelia;* and *Amelia Bedelia Helps Out* and are very funny to those who are just themselves learning to understand that simple words in special combinations have special meanings.

Young readers who ask for "longer books" have found repeated satisfaction with Carolyn Haywood's enduring and humorous series about "Little Eddie" or "Betsy." Eddie is portrayed as a typical American boy whose passion for collecting usually turns a profit for him. Betsy involves her friends and family in neighborhood and school activities. While the dialogue seems dated and the incidents often pedestrian, these stories provide a safe, predictable experience for fledgling readers.

Beverly Cleary has written a genuinely funny

series of books about a very normal boy named *Henry Huggins.* In the first book Henry's problems center on a stray dog named Ribsy and Henry's efforts to keep him. In *Henry and Beezus,* Henry's major interest is in obtaining a new bicycle. At the opening of the Colossal Market he is delighted when he wins one of the door prizes and then horrified to find out it is $50 worth of Beauty Shoppe permanent waves, facials, and false eyelashes! Cleary's intimate knowledge of boys and girls is very evident as she describes their problems, adventures, and hilarious activities. Her contribution to the literature of childhood was recognized when she received the Laura Ingalls Wilder Award in 1975.

Peter Hatcher's endless problems with his 2-year-old brother, Farley Drexel Hatcher, better known as Fudge, are humorously told in Judy Blume's book *Tales of a Fourth Grade Nothing.* One of the funniest episodes in the book concerns Peter's pet turtle, Dribble. Fudge insists that he didn't chew the turtle when Peter questions him: "'No chew, no chew, Gulp . . . gulp . . . all gone turtle. Down Fudge's tummy.'"[56] After a hurried trip to the hospital and doses of castor oil, milk of magnesia, and prune juice, the turtle is out. Since Peter is such a good sport, his parents give him a new dog which he proceeds to name Turtle to remind him of his loss. In the sequel, *Superfudge,* Peter narrates further complications in his life—new baby sister Tootsie, new school, and new friends—when his family moves to New Jersey. Peter's exasperating encounters with his brother are made public when Fudge begins kindergarten in the school where Peter is a sixth-grader. Dialogue and plot unfold in these entertaining stories in ways that resemble television situation comedies. While Fudge's outrageous antics may seem unbelievable to an adult, readers of 7 to 12 assure us that Judy Blume "tells it like it is."

How to Eat Fried Worms by Thomas Rockwell is a very funny and vividly told escapade. After an argument climaxed by a dare and a $50 bet, Billy plans to eat fifteen worms in fifteen days. They are fried, boiled, and smothered with catsup, horseradish, and other toppings. Each ingestion becomes

---

[56]Judy Blume, *Tales of a Fourth Grade Nothing,* illustrated by Roy Doty (New York: Dutton, 1972), p. 111.

more bizarre the closer Billy comes to winning his bet. The brief chapters, extensive and amusing dialogue, and the plot make this a favorite story of less able middle-grade readers.

The classic of modern humorous stories is Robert McCloskey's *Homer Price*. The six chapters of this book present extravagant yarns about life in Centerburg, as aided and abetted by Homer and his friends. Probably the favorite Homer Price story is that of the doughnuts. Homer helpfully offers to make some doughnuts in his uncle's new doughnut machine. A rich customer volunteers to make the batter and Homer is doing beautifully, until he realizes he can't stop the machine! The shop becomes full of doughnuts and then, after his uncle finally stops their manufacture, there is the problem of how to dispose of them. The missing bracelet of the woman who had helped to make the doughnuts supplies the answer. *Centerburg Tales* continues the adventures of Homer Price. Keith Robertson's *Henry Reed* stories, illustrated by McCloskey, present another entrepreneur who would have made a fine friend or competitor to Homer Price.

One of the funniest books to be published for children in many years is Barbara Robinson's *The Best Christmas Pageant Ever*. The six Herdman children are the terror of the public school, so it is not surprising that they extend their reign of terror to Sunday School and take over the Christmas pageant. The poor unsuspecting substitute teacher cannot understand why only the Herdmans volunteer for parts in the pageant, unaware that they have threatened to stuff pussy willows down the ears of any children who raise their hands. Since the Herdmans have never heard the Christmas story before, their interpretation is contemporary, humorous, and surprisingly close to the true meaning of Christmas.

The humor in one of Robert Burch's novels is in part due to his creation of a modern Mary Poppins-like caretaker who seems able to do anything. When *Ida Early Comes over the Mountain*, things begin to change for the four motherless Sutton children. Unconventional in appearance, Ida is over six feet tall, wears overalls and brogans, and has an unruly thatch of red hair. She seems to have been and done many things, can unerringly toss coats and hats onto shelves and racks, would rather read the funnies aloud than do dishes, and is un-

cowed by Aunt Earnestine's pointed remarks and disapproval of noise and levity. As Ida joins the family, laughter, joking, and joy return to the Sutton family, and Aunt Earnestine returns to the city. When the summer ends, Ida agrees to accompany the timorous twins, Dewey and Clay, to the first day of school. There, however, when older children make fun of Ida's apearance, the oldest Suttons betray Ida by refusing to get involved. The old Ida seems buried until Randall enlists her aid in a demonstration of cattle roping at a school assembly, with hoped-for and surprising results. Ida helps the Suttons celebrate the holidays and finally wins Aunt Earnestine's gratitude in a hilarious sequel, *Christmas with Ida Early*. While the pranks, some of the slapstick humor, and the Depression setting may remind readers of Robert Newton Peck's *Soup* series, Burch draws his characters with warmth and sympathy lacking in those created by Peck.

In the Bagthorpe Saga, Helen Cresswell presents a family in which anything might happen—and usually does. Poor *Ordinary Jack* thinks he has no distinguishing qualities ("strings in his bow") to compete with in this brilliantly talented British family. His father is a television writer; his mother writes "Stella Bright," an advice column; and his three siblings avidly pursue interests in sports, painting, music, and ham radios. With the secret advice and help of his favorite Uncle Parker, Jack decides to develop an ability to prophesy as a way of demonstrating his uniqueness. And it nearly convinces his amazed family.

Absolute Zero features Jack's much-maligned dog, who rises to fame as a result of the family's competition to win prizes by entering contests. Cresswell's humor derives from her ability to involve her zany characters in preposterous situations while writing with understatement and restraint. When Jack and Uncle Parker attempt to train the lethargic Zero to sit up, Jack must model the act:

"Now," whispered Jack to Uncle Parker, "you say, 'Up!' and I'll sit up and beg. If I do it and he doesn't, you say 'Good boy!' and pat my head, and give me the biscuit."

Uncle Parker nodded. He delved in the bag and came up with a chocolate digestive which he broke in half.

"Right."

He held the biscuit aloft halfway between Jack and Zero.

"Up. Sit up. Beg. Good boy—boys, rather."[57]

Other books in the series pit the Bagthorpes against obnoxious relatives, send the family into frantic self-sufficiency preparations, and chronicle in two books their ill-fated holiday in a haunted house in Wales.

There are certainly aspects of many other books that let the reader laugh. Roald Dahl's stories and Robert Newton Peck's *Trig* and *Soup* series, for instance, often portray adults in absurdly humorous situations that children find funny. Cleary's series about Ramona Quimby allows readers a good chuckle for how it "used to be when I was little." Betsy Byars' apt turns of phrase and choices of situation cause readers to smile in recognition. Humorous books need no justification in the school other than that they provide pure enjoyment for the reader. Often humorous books provide a healthy contrast in a reading diet that may be overburdened with books dealing with contemporary social problems. The enjoyment of books through laughter forms an important part of the foundation in a child's developing love of reading.

Animal Stories

Stories about animals provide children with the vicarious experience of giving love to and receiving devotion and loyalty from an animal. Frequently, these animal tales are really stories of the maturing of their major characters. For example, the well-loved story of *The Yearling* by Marjorie Kinnan Rawlings is as much the story of Jody's growth and realization of the consequences of giving love as it is the story of a boy's discovery and raising of a pet deer. Sterling North's *Rascal: A Memoir of a Better Era* presents a boy who shares happy outings with his father, worries about his older brother serving in World War I, builds a canoe in the living room, and raises a crow and a raccoon as pets. But Sterling gradually and painfully realizes that his beloved companion raccoon, Rascal, belongs and will survive only in the wild.

Children seek in animal stories characters who face risks and meet the challenge of taming or raising an animal. This challenge is accepted by Mandy in Jean Craighead George's *The Cry of the Crow*. Frequently left on her own by her three brothers, Mandy is used to roaming the marshes and piney woods around her family's Florida strawberry farm. She cannot accept her father's and brothers' killing of the crows to save maturing berry crops. So, when she happens upon a baby crow, the sole survivor of a shotgun blast to its nest, she names it Nina Terrance and secretly begins to raise it. As Nina Terrance grows, it learns to imitate some human speech sounds, while Mandy recognizes many of the calls by which the crows communicate. Soon Mandy is torn between keeping Nina Terrance as a pet and releasing her to join the other migrating crows. Weighing heavily on Mandy, too, is the threat that Nina Terrance will seek revenge if she discovers who shot her nest. Eventually, Mandy must face the consequences of her choices. The humorous anecdotes involving crows, as well as the actual material on which the story is based, come directly from George's own experiences with crows and her careful research. As is frequently the case with her novels, readers learn as much about the natural world as they do about people who engage in difficult choice-making.

The companionship between a South Australian boy and his pet pelican, Mr. Percival, is poetically told in Colin Thiele's *Storm Boy*. With a friend he soon trains the pelican to drop a fishing line out beyond the breakers so that he and his father can fish even on stormy days. It is this skill that enables Mr. Percival to save a wrecked tugboat crew by dropping a line over the boat's bow. When Mr. Percival is killed by a hunter, Storm Boy decides to accept the captain's offer to send him to boarding school in Adelaide. But Storm Boy and his friend back home do not forget: "And everything lives on in their hearts—the wind-talk and wave-talk, and the scribblings on the sand; the coorong, the salt smell of the beach . . . and the long days of their happiness together."[58] This Australian classic was

[57]Helen Cresswell, *Absolute Zero* (New York: Macmillan, 1978), p. 24.

[58]Colin Thiele, *Storm Boy*, illustrated by John Schoenherr (New York: Harper & Row, 1978), p. 62.

recently re-illustrated in distinctive pen-and-ink drawings by John Schoenherr.

Incident at Hawk's Hill by Allan Eckert is based on an extraordinary incident that took place in Canada in 1870. It is the story of 6-year-old Ben, who was adopted and protected by a female badger. A shy and lonely child, Ben wanders away from Hawk's Hill, the family farm, and is given up for lost after two days and nights of searching. But Ben is found alive weeks later by his older brother, who has to fight off the badger to get to the boy. At first Ben is as wild and silent as the badger, but they take him home only to have the badger come to their house the next day. The badger stays, and finally Ben begins to talk, to tell his family all about his experiences. This is a hauntingly beautiful story of a family's love for their shy child and his strange protector. Although few children will find this book on their own, it would make a good choice for reading aloud to fifth- or sixth-graders.

Hanno, a gorilla that escapes from the London Zoo, was a "pet" of Ping, a Chinese refugee, for only two days, but a strange bond exists between the two. *A Stranger at Green Knowe* is one of L. M. Boston's few realistic stories about the old English mansion which is the mysterious setting of many of her fantasies (see Chapter 7). The story begins in Africa with the early life and capture of the gorilla. Ping admires the gorilla in the zoo; and he learns a great deal about the animal as he talks with the keeper. The concrete walls and steel bars of Hanno's cage recall Ping's life in refugee camps. When Ping hears that the huge animal has escaped from the zoo, he plans a place for him on a hidden island in the river. Hanno finds the place and the food that Ping has left there. Ping plays with the huge beast and tries to keep the police from discovering the "refugee." The boy is foolhardy, yet this mystical understanding between the two refugees protects him. An exciting climax brings death to the gorilla and hope that Ping has found a happy refuge. *Gorilla Gorilla*, an informational book by Carol Fenner, could be shared along with this story.

Horse and dog series comprise a great number of animal stories and are favorites of intermediate children. The easiest series are C. W. Anderson's *Billy and Blaze* picture story-books for readers who are eager for more text but are not yet ready for longer chapter books. Walter Farley's popular series begins with *The Black Stallion*, the only survivor, along with Alec Ramsey, of a shipwreck. The boy secretly trains him to run in the Derby. Other titles in the series, such as *Son of Black Stallion* and *The Black Stallion's Filly*, emphasize horse training and racing, with the people characters as mere shadows.

Marguerite Henry's well-researched horse stories provide an authentic background for her accounts of horses and people. *Misty of Chincoteague* is a descendant of the Spanish horses that struggled ashore after a shipwreck near Assateague Island. When the wild horses are herded ashore each year and sold, Paul and Maureen have their hearts set on buying a horse and her colt. Although they are able to train both, the mother escapes, but Misty remains with her human friends. *Stormy, Misty's Foal*, continues the story. *King of the Wind*, a Newbery award-winner, tells of the devotion of a deaf-mute Arabian boy who stays with a horse until it dies. In *Mustang, Wild Spirit of the West*, Henry writes as if Annie Bronn Johnston is telling of her fight to protect wild horses of the western ranges. Based on a true story of mustangs being hunted by plane and truck to be sold as dog food, this story engages the reader in concern for the struggles of this endangered group.

Dogs respond to human affection and return it warmly. This bond of love is one of the themes in Taylor's *The Trouble with Tuck*. Like Marguerite Henry, Theodore Taylor based his novel on a true story. Helen lacked self-confidence until she became involved in raising Tuck, a beautiful golden Labrador given to her by her parents. Tuck once saved Helen from drowning and is devoted to her. By the time Helen reaches 13, Tuck has grown totally blind. Rejecting the advice of the veterinarian to give Tuck to the university for research or have him put to sleep, Helen finds an alternative—she obtains a Seeing-Eye dog for Tuck. Jealous and confused, Tuck refuses to accept this stranger until Helen's patient and innovative training methods teach Tuck to follow the guide dog. As the two dogs parade before Helen and her proud family, the reader rejoices in both canine and human triumphs.

In Jane Resh Thomas' *The Comeback Dog*, Daniel must decide if he is once again going to risk his love on a dog who has already rejected him. While 9-year-old Daniel is still grieving for the loss of his old dog, Captain, he discovers a starved and nearly drowned English setter in the culvert near his family's farm. He brings the dog home, calls it Lady, and nurses her back to health, assuming that she will return his love in the same way Captain did. But Lady, who has been mistreated, cringes from Daniel's touch and refuses to wag her tail for him. One day, in anger at her lack of affection, Daniel yanks Lady's chain.

> "What's the matter with you," he said. "I'm the one who fed you when you were half dead."
>
> "You can't squeeze blood out of a turnip, Daniel," said his mother quietly at the kitchen door.
>
> "What's that supposed to mean?"
>
> "You can't get love by force, if she's not willing."[59]

Daniel angrily unleashes the choke chain that holds Lady and she bounds away over the fields. She is gone, only to return a week later bristling with porcupine quills. Sympathetic parents who show their love finally help Daniel to show his. Troy Howell's frequent illustrations, believable dialogue, and short chapters make this book easily approached by independent 7- or 8-year-old readers.

Meindert DeJong's moving story *Hurry Home, Candy* tells of another dog's search for love and security. Candy had first been owned by two children and punished with a broom by their impatient mother. Finally, he would sleep: "A troubled broom-haunted sleep in which his paws twitched nervously because in his sleep he was fleeing from the fretful broom."[60] In a storm Candy is separated from the family, and fear of a broom across the ditch prevents him from crossing to them. Alone, hungry, lost, and sorrowful, he at last finds shelter with a man, a retired captain turned artist. One night, the artist interrupts some thieves, and the news story brings the original owners. But the children want only the reward, not the small dog. Candy hides again, but is drawn to the house by hunger. Once more, a broom stands between the dog and love and security. The captain discovers

the source of the dog's fear; at the same time he gains understanding of his own. The big man tosses the broom aside, and the dog edges his way to food, to love, and home. Mary Stoltz has written a similar though shorter story of a cat's journey through the lives of many humans in her fantasy, *Cat Walk*. It is the cat's desire for a name and his remembrance of his animal friend that propel him to continue his search for a happy home.

Heroic dogs who overcome obstacles are the subject of popular animal stories for children. Sheila Burnford's book of three runaway pets is an odyssey of courage and endurance, as a young Labrador retriever, an old bull terrier, and a Siamese cat make *The Incredible Journey*. Left with a friend of their owner, the animals try to reach their home more than 250 miles away. Hunger, storms, dangerous river crossings, and fights are the nearly insurmountable problems of these three animals. Their survival and care for each other make a remarkable story.

Where the Red Fern Grows by Wilson Rawls is a heartwarming but sentimental tale of the love between two hound dogs and their master. Young Billy trains his two dogs, Old Dan and Little Ann, to be the finest hunting team in the Cherokee county of the Ozarks. Twenty-five sets of hounds are entered in the big coon hunt. After five nights of hunting, catching the coons, skinning them, and turning in the hides, Billy's hounds win $300 and the first-place cup. During the hunt Old Dan and Little Ann nearly freeze to death after getting lost during an unexpected blizzard. When the family decides to move from the Ozarks to Oklahoma, Billy plans to remain behind with his beloved grandfather and the two dogs. But when both dogs die, one defending Billy against a mountain lion attack and one pining away, he regretfully joins his family's departure. Billy's decision is reaffirmed when a legendary red fern springs up at the dogs' gravesite. This story is memorable to 10-, 11-, and 12-year-olds for its warmth and the strong portrayal of devotion between humans and animals.

Occasionally, books intended for an adult audience become part of the reading of older children. Jack London's *Call of the Wild* was written for adults but is read by some middle-grade students. The men in the story are ruthless and the dog Buck returns to the wildness of nature just as the men revert to force and cruelty to survive. Jim Kjel-

[59] Jane Resh Thomas, *The Comeback Dog*, illustrated by Troy Howell (Boston: Houghton Mifflin, 1981), p. 45–47.

[60] Meindert DeJong, *Hurry Home, Candy*, illustrated by Maurice Sendak (New York: Harper, 1953), p. 39.

gaard communicates a love of wilderness through exciting dog stories like *Big Red*, a tale of an Irish setter groomed for championship showing who, along with his 17-year-old trainer, faces the bear Old Majesty. Farley Mowat's *The Dog Who Wouldn't Be* tells of his boyhood on the Saskatchewan prairie in the company of his "Prince Albert retriever" named Mutt and a score of other animal pets. In his shorter novel, *Owls in the Family*, Mowat recounts in hilarious detail his adventures in acquiring and training two pet great horned owls, the intrepid Wol and his timid companion, Weeps.

Sports Stories

Sports fiction for children reflects their energetic participation and interest in a variety of individual and team sports. Recent fiction, while continuing to include team sports such as baseball, football, soccer, and basketball, now includes books about such popular individual sports as tennis, running, gymnastics, dirt-bike racing, and swimming. Fiction, biography, and informational books about sports extend and enrich the personal experiences of the child who participates in or observes sports.

It is difficult to find well-written sports stories. Most of the characters are flat, one-dimensional figures. The dialogue tends to be stilted, and the plots predictable. Nevertheless, children continue to select these stories because they are so personally involved and interested in the activities.

While there are now many more sports stories that feature girls in sports, the female athlete has made little impact on formula sports fiction. The same clichés—making the team through hard work or overcoming fear and triumphing over pain—are prevalent in both stories for boys and stories for girls. One important change, however, is that with the advent of Title IX, girls on boys' sports teams are no longer greeted with disbelief and protest.[61]

Matt Christopher's many sports stories include titles for young readers as well as for those in middle school. Christopher's books depend on accounts of games or sports for their interest, but problem themes are usually developed as well. For example, in *Dirt Bike Racer*, a boy finds a dirt bike in the bottom of a lake and restores it to working order. But the job he takes to earn money for bike parts is with an old man whose jealous nephew begins to make trouble. In *Wild Pitch*, Eddie, who resents girls playing in the baseball league, accidentally injures Phyllis when he makes a wild pitch. As he works through his feelings of guilt, he begins to understand how important playing baseball has been to Phyllis and he helps her regain her former confidence and skill by working out with her regularly. Christopher always describes something of the thrill of the play and action of a sport—whether hockey, swimming, running, or baseball.

A more serious story that portrays characters of real depth and understanding is *Thank You, Jackie Robinson* by Barbara Cohen. While the story takes place in 1947–1948, it is written in the first person and told as a reminiscence to a contemporary child. Sam Green is the only son of a Jewish widow who runs an inn in New Jersey. He doesn't care much about sandlot ball, but he can recite the batting order and play-by-play for every Dodgers game since the time he became a fan. Sam's best friend is the inn's black cook, Davy, who takes Sam to his first Dodgers game. The two see other games together, and the hero of all the games for both of them is Jackie Robinson. In midseason Davy has a heart attack. Sam gathers his courage, buys a baseball, and goes alone to a Dodgers game, where he asks Jackie Robinson to autograph a ball for Davy. Then Davy's son-in-law, Elliott, helps Sam sneak into the hospital in a laundry cart so he can personally present the ball to Davy:

> There was no magic in the ball. He loved it, but there was no magic in it. It was not going to cure him, the way deep down in my heart I had somehow thought it would. I knew that, my whole self knew that now.[62]

This book succeeds at many levels; first as a warm and understanding consideration of friendship, second as a realistic presentation of death, and third as a backward look at Jackie Robinson and

[61]Robert E. Unsworth, "First Baseperson? Heroines in YA Sports Fiction," *School Library Journal*, vol. 27 (May 1981), pp. 26–27.

[62]Barbara Cohen, *Thank You, Jackie Robinson*, illustrated by Richard Cuffari (New York: Lothrop, 1974). p. 11.

the Brooklyn Dodgers during the height of their baseball fame.

Alfred Slote's fine book, *Hang Tough, Paul Mather,* is about the Little Leaguer who had leukemia. It was discussed among the books that dealt with death. Another excellent baseball story by Slote is titled *My Father, the Coach.* The story is a familiar one—the rookie team beats the league champions. However, the team they most want to beat is the one sponsored by the bank and coached by its vice-president, who patronizingly makes it clear each day that Willie Corkins is only a parking lot attendant and hardly a suitable coach. Out of loyalty to their coach the team proves the vice-president wrong.

R. R. Knudson presents high-schooler Suzanne Hagan's progression of interests from football in *Zanballer,* through her battle to gain acceptance on the boys' basketball team in *Zanbanger.* When a dislocated shoulder prevents her from continuing to play basketball in *Zanboomer,* she takes up distance running, using a plan mapped out by her friend Arthur Rinehart. He is repaying a debt he incurred when Zan helped the skinny Rinehart win a grade-school weight-lifting contest in *Rinehart Lifts.* Knudson sometimes relies on journal entries, first-person narrative, and fragments of thought and sentences to create likable characters with loyal friendships that transcend age and sex boundaries often typical of sports fiction.

Several writers enjoy putting characters in atypical situations and considering what might happen. Mel Cebulash's fictional speculation about the first woman to break into major league baseball is chronicled in several stories. *Ruth Marini, Dodger Ace* and *Ruth Marini of the Dodgers* both relate Ruth's difficulties in being accepted for what she can do for the team, not for who she is or what she represents. Thomas Dygard, in *Rebound Caper,* shows how jokester Gary Whipple's thinking changes when he is benched by the high school basketball coach and joins the girls' basketball team. At first, Gary enjoys the stir he creates; but protests from other teams, his girlfriend's growing impatience, and the weakening unity of both girls' and boys' teams all threaten to make Gary's caper "rebound." Finally, Gary has to try to undo what he has done. In Dygard's *Winning Kicker,* place-kicker Kathy Denver joins the football team in spite of the coach's initial reluctance. A broken ankle finally removes her from the season's closing games but not before she has won the respect of team and coach. Dygard's contemporary, dramatic, and action-packed stories also examine some of the psychological consequences of participating in athletics today.

Rosemary Wells grounds *When No One Was Looking* in 14-year-old Kathy Bardy's tennis talent. Kathy is working her way up the New England Lawn Tennis Association's tournament ladder. But she still has to struggle with family tension and jealousy, her inability to pass algebra, and a possible new boyfriend. When Kathy's powerful opponent Ruth is discovered drowned in an over-chlorinated pool at the club, Kathy must not only clear herself but she must also deal with her own suspicions of who might have murdered the girl. In explaining to her coach, she says:

> I don't care anymore . . . the fun's gone out of it . . . all I could think about, over and over in my mind, was that maybe somebody who cares about me, maybe even somebody who loves me . . . did this thing for me. . . .[63]

When all are finally cleared and Ruth's death is declared an accident, a last question to the police chief provides Kathy with the answer she really did not want to find. She realizes that her atonement may be to bear this guilty secret forever. While Wells writes engagingly about the details of tennis tournaments in this sports mystery, she also asks important questions about choices and sacrifices family, friends, coaches, and the athlete herself must make in order to play competition tennis.

Mysteries

Most children enjoy mystery stories during some period in their lives. Even very young readers demand them, and so whole series of *I Can Read* mysteries are available with such titles as *The Case of the Cat's Meow* (Bonsall) or *The Secret Three* (Myrick) about a boys' club which communicates by means of coded messages. Elizabeth Levy's

---

[63]Rosemary Wells, *When No One Was Looking* (New York: Dial, 1980), p. 177.

Something Queer at the Lemonade Stand is one in a series of her neighborhood mysteries exuberantly illustrated in cartoon style by Mordicai Gerstein. These easy-reading mysteries often welcome younger children to reading longer books.

Slightly older children usually become the mystery buffs who delight in reading one Nancy Drew book after another. These have predictable plots, cardboard characters, stilted dialogue, and cliché-ridden prose. Most librarians and teachers will not order these books, yet they continue to sell well. Obviously, they must be doing something right! Rather than discount all mysteries, teachers and librarians should look for better-written mysteries and other books that contain elements of mystery, in order to capitalize on children's interests.

Two popular mystery series give the reader a chance to match wits with clever boys. Both boys and girls enjoy the Encyclopedia Brown stories by Donald Sobol. In *Encyclopedia Brown Takes a Case,* Mr. Brown, chief of police of Idaville, brings home all the cases his men cannot solve. When he comes home for dinner he describes them to his son, Encyclopedia Brown, who usually solves them before it is time for dessert. Each Encyclopedia Brown book presents ten cases whose solutions are included in the back of the book. Seymour Simon, author of many nonfiction titles (see Chapter 11), also features short mysteries in his Einstein Anderson series. In *Einstein Anderson Lights Up the Sky,* the brainy Einstein applies his knowledge of science to show that mysterious UFOs are really spotlight reflections off low nighttime clouds and "solves" another nine problems. While each series features both consistent format and a continuing cast of characters, Einstein's incidental jokes, puns, and riddles in each chapter and the scientific observations give this series extra appeal and depth.

The McGurk Organization operates out of McGurk's basement with help from Willie, Wanda, Brains, and Joey, who tells the stories since he is the resident word expert. A hidden note in E. W. Hildick's *The Case of the Felon's Fiddle* leads the group through a series of clues to the whereabouts of a cache of uncut diamonds. In a mystery closer to home, *McGurk Gets Good and Mad* because an open house at his headquarters is sabotaged by planted mice. The many novels in the series are carefully constructed and the five children glean in-

formation, conduct research, deduce solutions, and rely on a network of friends to solve mysteries. Hildick has also written *Manhattan Is Missing*, the very amusing tale of a missing Siamese cat entrusted to an English family when they sublet the owner's New York City apartment. "Operation Catnet" is initiated by Peter Clarke, his brother Benjie, and friend Hugh in an effort to recover the prized cat. The dialogue and characterization in this story are distinctive.

In addition to sports stories and stories involving magic, Scott Corbett has written several straightforward mysteries featuring Roger Teale, a skinny 12-year-old detective. In *The Case of the Silver Skull,* Roger overhears robbery plans during a Home and Garden tour. The robbers nearly pull away with their loaded truck before Roger is able to foil their plans. In *The Case of the Gone Goose,* he is concerned with discovering who killed two prize geese.

Attics in two mystery stories hold clues to the past and keys to the future for two horse-loving girls. In Rumer Godden's *The Rocking Horse Secret,* 8-year-old Tibby is bored living in a wing of the Pomeroy mansion with her housekeeper mother. Then she discovers a rocking horse in an attic playroom. One day while playing in the forbidden room, she is dismayed to see the horse's tail fall off, revealing a piece of paper that looks like an important letter. She repairs the damage and hopes no one will notice. Later, when old Miss Pomeroy dies, terrible changes occur in the household brought about by her shrewish nieces who stand to inherit the mansion unless a will is found. In an exciting conclusion, it falls to Tibby to produce the will and keep the house from being destroyed. *The Horse in the Attic* by Eleanor Clymer is an old painting which, when restored, proves to be an important work of a long dead local artist. Twelve-year-old Caroline tracks down the painting's "bloodlines" and when she agrees that the family should sell it, the proceeds suggest that her father might be able to make a career of painting and that Caroline might continue to develop her skills in horseback riding. Both Clymer and Godden create memorable characters and provide satisfying endings sure to delight middle elementary mystery- and horse-lovers.

More complex mysteries, which involve subplots

and character development relating to larger themes, are those by Phyllis Whitney. Overcoming a physical handicap in *The Mystery of the Haunted Pool* and developing respect for a blind girl in *Secret of the Emerald Star* are subplots in two Whitney books, both of which won the Mystery Writers' "Edgar" for excellence in the juvenile category. The idea that the blind do not want pity is made very clear in *Secret of the Emerald Star,* for example:

> A real friend isn't someone who is sorry for you. I hate people who drool because I'm a poor little blind girl. Or the others who act as if I were a genius because I can walk across a room by myself. They're the ones who think about blindness all the time. And that's silly because I don't. Or anyway, I wouldn't if they didn't push it at me so much.[64]

Two ecological mysteries center around birds, but factual information does not overwhelm the story. Felice Holman's *Elizabeth and the Marsh Mystery* solves the origin of a strange call emanating from a marsh—that of a sandhill crane. *Who Really Killed Cock Robin?* by Jean George suggests the interconnectedness of humans and nature when a robin, the city's symbol, suddenly dies. After an investigation, a team determines that pesticides, parasitic flies, mercury, and other causes had all contributed to its death. Both stories feature many of the elements children enjoy in mysteries: suspense, danger, and a child involved in problem-solving.

The Museum of Natural History is the setting for a double mystery told by Georgess McHargue in the book *Funny Bananas.* Ben Pollock spends almost all of his after-school hours in the museum because his scientist parents both work there. One day he learns of some mysterious goings on—the feathers of the red jungle fowl have been destroyed, and the information desk has been ransacked, the wastebasket dumped, and some "funny bananas" found. At first Ben suspects Carmen, a girl who has been acting strangely. But when Ben convinces her that he is trying to help her, the two become allies as they look for her coatimundi, a little South American animal that she has let loose in the museum. While they are chasing him, they run right into a thief! The atmosphere of the museum and the characterizations of the children are very believable. This is an exciting mystery that involves real characters, an animal, and a thief.

The House of Dies Drear by Virginia Hamilton is a compelling story of the weird and terrifying happenings that threaten a black professor and his family, who are living in a house that was a former Underground Railway station. The brooding old house holds many secrets for Thomas Small and his family, who find they are being threatened by dangers from within and without their home. This is a finely crafted novel with enough suspense to hold every reader.

Philippa Pearce's *The Way to Sattin Shore* is the satisfying story of a girl's longing to understand the mystery surrounding the disappearance of her father the day she was born. Her mother and her grandmother both tell her that he is dead. Kate believes them until she discovers that the tombstone in the cemetery is her uncle's, not her father's, as she had thought. The clues to the mystery ebb and flow like the tide in which she learns her uncle drowned. The tension between her mother and disagreeable grandmother rises, and her older brother reveals that they had once lived somewhere else—at Sattin Shore. Kate rides her bicycle alone to the shore and discovers a grandmother she didn't know she had. Through her own determination and initiative she does find her father and brings about a reunion with her mother. While the plot provides suspense, it is the author's skill in creating believable relationships among the characters and a haunting sense of place that you admire. The eerie loneliness of the shore is as threatening as Kate's dark, unhappy home. It is up to Kate to discover what happened on that beach the day she was born that has so engulfed them all.

Ellen Raskin cut apart the words to "America the Beautiful" and dispersed them among sixteen characters to begin her "puzzle-mystery," *The Westing Game.*[65] Heirs to the estate of millionaire

---

[64]Phyllis A. Whitney, *Secret of the Emerald Star,* illustrated by Alex Stein (Philadelphia: Westminister, 1964). p. 99.

[65]See Ellen Raskin, "Newbery Medal Acceptance," *The Horn Book Magazine,* vol. 55 (August 1979), pp. 385–391.

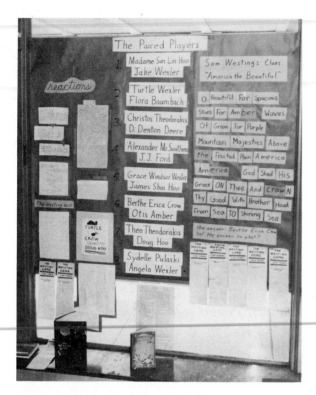

Readers keep track of Ellen Raskin's intricate mystery, *The Westing Game,* by listing character pairs, assembling cut-up clues, and making predictions.

Pat Enciso, teacher. Barrington Road Elementary, Upper Arlington, Ohio, Public Schools.

Samuel W. Westing are invited to the reading of his will: a directive to discover the identity of his murderer and a series of clues cleverly hidden within the will. Characters, all with their own physical, moral, or emotional imperfections, play in pairs. They include a judge, a Chinese restauranteur, a dressmaker, a track star, a 15-year-old palsied boy, a reluctant bride-to-be, and a 13-year-old terror, Turtle Wexler. It is Turtle who begins to link clues and discover patterns as she and readers piece together Westing's amazing game. In a tightly constructed story divided into many short sections, Raskin piles detail upon detail; rereading shows that what appears to be insignificant always proves otherwise. Warmly realized characters interrelate and grow in this Newbery award-winner.

But it is Turtle who, unbeknownst to any of the other players, quietly solves the puzzle and bicycles up to the Westing house to receive her prize in the satisfying ending.

A haunting story that has many elements of mystery is *The Witch's Daughter* by Nina Bawden. Perdita, the so-called "daughter of a witch," is a lonely orphan who is shunned by the village children because of her odd clothes, strange green eyes, shy manner, and sensitivity to nature. She has never been to school but has deep knowledge of the outdoors and expresses a special awareness of the needs of the blind girl Janey, who comes with her family to the Scottish island for a holiday. Perdita is treated kindly by the mysterious Mr. Smith, who has rented a cottage and fishes for lobsters although he does not like lobster. Tim, Janey's brother, puts the pieces of the puzzle together, but the adults will not accept his theory of the stolen jewels. A strange visitor deliberately leaves the children in a cave, but blind Janey leads them to safety. Perdita's shyness is finally overcome in a moment of sharing with Janey. This is a beautiful, almost mystical tale of danger to innocents.

Another story by Bawden, *Squib,* also has a mysterious plot. In the park Kate and Robin find an extremely shy little boy who has odd eyes and a bit of a bruise on one leg. He doesn't talk to them, but he does play with them. Kate is determined to find out more about the odd little frightened boy that they nickname Squib. Her curiosity draws her into a terrifying situation, but eventually she does save Squib. All Nina Bawden's books have well-drawn characters with believable, yet exciting plots.

The criteria for evaluating all fiction should be used in considering popular stories, with the recognition that the major appeals are fast action, straightforward plot, humor, and suspense. Children develop skills in rapid reading, building vocabulary, and noting details as they read popular fiction. Interest in reading as a pleasurable activity may begin with these books and be extended to other types of literature if children's choices are not criticized. Children should have a wide variety of these books from which to select, and teachers should share those quality books which they know have elements of the popular.

SUGGESTED LEARNING EXPERIENCES

1. Select a current theme in realistic fiction such as foster children, divorce, or immigration. Find some nonfiction that can be used with the fictional books.
2. Select books about a minority group. Find poetry, biographical material, historical fiction, and informational books that would extend the use of these books.
3. Find articles on censorship. Make a list of controversial books that are currently being censored. Compare your ideas with the evaluations used for censorship.
4. Select a topic such as loneliness, death, physical disability, or friendship. Talk to a group of children to explore with them the personal experiences they may have had in the selected area. What misconceptions are expressed? What books have they read dealing with the topic? How else have they received information about the subject?
5. Compare the treatment of a topic such as death of a pet, a child, or a grandparent in a picture book, a book for intermediate-grade children, poetry, and an informational book.
6. Select several books dealing with a particular minority group. What stereotypes do you find in the books? What are the prevalent themes in the books? Compare and evaluate books using the criteria in this chapter.
7. Compare several humorous stories. What kinds of things are funny, such as slapstick, exaggerated characters, puns or other word play, situations, or satire? Could you rank these books from less to greater sophistication according to the types of humor on which they rely?
8. Discuss with peers or a small group of children a novel such as *The Way to Sattin Shore* (Pearce), *Arthur for the Very First Time* (MacLachlan), *A Ring of Endless Light* (L'Engle), or *Jacob Have I Loved* (Paterson). How is the main character influenced by other characters in the book? When the child main character becomes an adult, which of these other characters might he or she want to thank? Why?
9. Compare the relationships of parents and children in several titles from the section "Living in a Family."
10. Compare several survival stories. After basic wants are satisfied, what else does a surviving person seem to need? What qualities does each person possess or develop in order to survive? How does (or may) surviving change a person?

RELATED READINGS

1. Baskin, Barbara H., and Karen H. Harris. *More Notes from a Different Drummer: A Guide to Juvenile Fiction Portraying the Disabled.* New York: Bowker, 1984.
   Annotations and analysis of more than 300 books published between 1976 and 1981, plus two introductory chapters that provide context, background, and excellent evaluative criteria. This supplements *Notes from a Different Drummer* (Bowker, 1977), which covered titles published from 1940 to 1975.
2. Bernstein, Joanne E. *Books to Help Children Cope with Separation and Loss,* 2nd ed. New York: Bowker, 1983.
   This wide-ranging annotated bibliography combines some 200 of the most lasting titles from the first edition with over 400 new annotations. Helpful sections include ones on mental illness, bibliotherapy, child abuse, and a useful directory of organizations.
3. *The Black Experience in Children's Books.* New York: New York Public Library, 1984.
   This annotated list is the third revision of the 1971 publication edited by Augusta Baker. The number of books has been increased to 400; it is arranged by geographical areas (the U.S., South and Central America, Africa, etc.) and includes all genres.
4. Dreyer, Sharon Spredeman. *The Bookfinder: A Guide to Children's Literature About the Needs and Problems of Youth Aged 2–15,* Volumes I and II. Circle Pines, Minn.: American Guidance Service, 1981.
   Nearly 700 titles are indexed and annotated under headings that suggest a range of typical and difficult problems in growing up which children experience: Responsibility, Parental Absence, School Achievement, Handicaps, Friendship, etc. The introduction

includes ways teachers might use the text in planning thematic studies or counselors and parents might help children develop understandings through discussion of books.

5. Lass-Woodfin, Mary Jo, ed. *Books on American Indians and Eskimos: A Selection Guide for Children and Young Adults.* Chicago: American Library Association, 1978.

An annotated bibliography of some 750 titles that identifies the understandings and information available from each story. Ratings for quality and reading level are included.

6. Newman, Joan E. *Girls Are People Too! A Bibliography of Nontraditional Roles in Children's Books.* Metuchen, N.J.: Scarecrow Press, 1982.

The major criterion for inclusion in this list of 500 titles is the female character's nontraditionalism. Works are classified as fiction or nonfiction, by age group (preschool–grade 3 and grades 4–9), and by minority (black, Native American, handicapped). An appendix chronicles notable events and personalities in the history of women.

7. Rees, David. *Painted Desert, Green Shade: Essays on Contemporary Writers of Fiction for Children and Young Adults.* Boston: The Horn Book, Inc., 1984.

Rees critiques the work of thirteen American and British writers, focusing new light on such authors as Betsy Byars, Katherine Paterson, Jan Mark, Robert Westall, Virginia Hamilton, and John Rowe Townsend.

8. Rudman, Masha K. *Children's Literature: An Issues Approach,* 2nd ed. Lexington, Mass.: D.C. Heath, 1984.

A critical examination of children's books in terms of how contemporary social problems are treated. Nine issues, among them war, sex, old age and death, minorities, divorce, and females, are examined. Evaluation criteria, numerous examples from children's books, and annotated suggested readings help illuminate educator awareness.

9. Sims, Rudine. *Shadow and Substance: Afro-American Experience in Contemporary Childen's Fiction.* Urbana, Ill.: National Council of Teachers of English, 1982.

The author surveys 150 books published between 1965 and 1979 which portray contemporary black-American experience. She categorizes images portrayed in three sections: fiction with a social conscience, "melting pot" fiction that essentially assumes a cultural homogeneity, and "culturally conscious fiction." Five black-American authors are discussed against a backdrop of other contemporary authors.

10. Stensland, Anna Lee. *Literature By and About the American Indian.* Urbana, Ill.: National Council of Teachers of English, 1979.

A critically annotated bibliography of nearly 800 titles rated according to the images of Native Americans presented and the text suitability for elementary, junior high, or senior high readers.

11. Tway, Eileen, ed. *Reading Ladders for Human Relations,* 6th ed. Washington: American Council of Education, 1981.

This is a unique and invaluable bulletin on the use of trade books in the classroom to promote better human relations. Annotated lists are provided for different age levels on five subjects: "Growing Into Self," "Relating to Wide Individual Differences," "Interacting in Groups," "Appreciating Different Cultures," and "Coping in a Changing World."

REFERENCES[66]

Adler, C. S. *The Cat That Was Left Behind.* Houghton Mifflin, 1981.
_____. *Get Lost, Little Brother.* Clarion, 1983.
_____. *The Once in a While Hero.* Coward, 1982.
Anderson, C. W. *Billy and Blaze.* Macmillan, 1936.
_____. *Blaze and Thunderbolt.* Macmillan, 1955.

[66]All books listed at the end of this chapter are recommended subject to the qualifications noted in the text. See Appendix for publishers' complete addresses. References to books of other genres are noted in parentheses.

Arrick, Fran. *Chernowitz!* Bradbury, 1981.

Bawden, Nina. *Squib.* Lippincott, 1971.

_____. *The Witch's Daughter.* Lippincott, 1966.

Beckman, Delores. *My Own Private Sky.* Dutton, 1980.

Blue, Rose. *Grandma Didn't Wave Back,* illustrated by Ted Lewin. Watts, 1972.

Blume, Judy, *Are You There, God? It's Me, Margaret.* Bradbury, 1970.

_____. *Blubber.* Bradbury, 1974.

_____. *It's Not the End of the World.* Bradbury, 1972.

_____. *Superfudge.* Dutton, 1980.

_____. *Tales of a Fourth Grade Nothing,* illustrated by Roy Doty. Dutton, 1972.

_____. *Then Again, Maybe I Won't.* Bradbury, 1971.

Bodker, Cecil. *The Leopard,* translated by Gunnar Poulsen. Atheneum, 1975.

Bonham, Frank. *Durango Street.* Dutton, 1965.

_____. *Mystery of the Fat Cat,* illustrated by Alvin Smith. Dutton, 1968.

_____. *The Nitty Gritty,* illustrated by Alvin Smith. Dutton, 1968.

Bonsall, Crosby. *The Case of the Cat's Meow.* Harper, 1965.

Bosse, Malcolm. *Ganesh.* Harper, 1981.

Boston, L. M. *A Stranger at Green Knowe,* illustrated by Peter Boston. Harcourt, 1961.

Bouchard, Lois. *The Boy Who Wouldn't Talk,* illustrated by Ann Grifalconi. Doubleday, 1969.

Branscum, Robbie. *The Murder of Hound Dog Bates.* Viking, 1982.

_____. *Toby Alone.* Avon, 1980.

_____. *Toby and Johnny Joe.* Avon, 1981.

_____. *Toby, Granny and George.* Avon, 1977.

Bridgers, Sue Ellen. *All Together Now.* Knopf, 1979.

_____. *Notes for Another Life.* Knopf, 1981.

Brooks, Bruce. *The Moves Make the Man.* Harper, 1984.

Buck, Pearl. *The Big Wave.* John Day, 1947.

Burch, Robert. *Christmas with Ida Early.* Viking, 1983.

_____. *Ida Early Comes over the Mountain.* Viking, 1980.

_____. *Queenie Peavy,* illustrated by Jerry Lazare. Viking, 1966.

Burnford, Sheila. *The Incredible Journey,* illustrated by Carl Burger. Little, Brown, 1961.

Byars, Betsy. *After the Goat Man,* illustrated by Ronald Himler. Viking, 1974.

_____. *The Animal, the Vegetable, & John D Jones,* illustrated by Ruth Sanderson. Delacorte, 1982.

_____. *Cracker Jackson.* Viking, 1985.

_____. *The Cybil War,* illustrated by Gail Owens. Viking, 1981.

_____. *The 18th Emergency,* illustrated by Robert Grossman. Viking, 1973.

_____. *The House of Wings,* illustrated by Daniel Schwartz. Viking, 1972.

_____. *The Night Swimmers.* Delacorte, 1980.

_____. *The Pinballs.* Harper, 1977.

_____. *The Summer of the Swans,* illustrated by Ted CoConis. Viking, 1970.

Cameron, Eleanor. *Julia and the Hand of God,* illustrated by Gail Owens. Dutton, 1977.

_____. *Julia's Magic,* illustrated by Gail Owens. Dutton, 1984.

_____. *A Room Made of Windows.* Little, Brown, 1971.

_____. *That Julia Redfern,* illustrated by Gail Owens. Dutton, 1982.

Cebulash, Mel. *Ruth Marini, Dodger Ace.* Lerner, 1983.

_____. *Ruth Marini of the Dodgers.* Lerner, 1983.

Childress, Alice. *A Hero Ain't Nothin' But a Sandwich.* Coward, 1973.

Christopher, Matt. *Dirt Bike Racer,* illustrated by Barry Bomzer. Little, Brown, 1979.

_____. *Wild Pitch.* Little, Brown, 1980.

Clark, Ann Nolan. *Secret of the Andes,* illustrated by Jean Charlot. Viking, 1952.

_____. *To Stand Against the Wind.* Viking, 1978.

Cleary, Beverly. *Dear Mr. Henshaw,* illustrated by Paul O. Zelinsky. Morrow, 1983.

_____. *Henry and Beezus,* illustrated by Louis Darling. Morrow, 1952.

_____. *Henry Huggins,* illustrated by Louis Darling. Morrow, 1950.

_____. *Ramona Forever,* illustrated by Alan Tiegreen. Morrow, 1984.

_____. *Ramona and Her Father,* illustrated by Alan Tiegreen. Morrow, 1977.

_____. *Ramona and Her Mother,* illustrated by Alan Tiegreen. Morrow, 1979.

_____. *Ramona Quimby, Age 8,* illustrated by Alan Tiegreen. Morrow, 1981.

_____. *Ramona the Brave*, illustrated by Alan Tiegreen. Morrow, 1975.

_____. *Ramona the Pest*, illustrated by Louis Darling. Morrow, 1968.

Cleaver, Vera, and Bill Cleaver. *Ellen Grae*, illustrated by Ellen Raskin. Lippincott, 1967.

_____. *Grover*, illustrated by Frederic Marvin. Lippincott, 1970.

_____. *I Would Rather Be a Turnip*. Lippincott, 1971.

_____. *Lady Ellen Grae*, illustrated by Ellen Raskin. Lippincott, 1968.

_____. *Trial Valley*. Lippincott, 1977.

_____. *Where the Lilies Bloom*, illustrated by James Spanfeller. Lippincott, 1969.

Clifford, Eth. *The Rocking Chair Rebellion*. Houghton Mifflin, 1978.

Clifton, Lucille. *The Lucky Stone*, illustrated by Dale Payson. Delacorte, 1979.

Clymer, Eleanor. *The Horse in the Attic*, illustrated by Ted Lewin. Bradbury, 1983.

_____. *Luke Was There*, illustrated by Diane de Groat. Holt, 1973.

_____. *My Brother Stevie*. Holt, 1967.

Cohen, Barbara. *Thank You, Jackie Robinson*, illustrated by Richard Cuffari. Lothrop, 1974.

Cone, Molly. *A Promise Is a Promise*, illustrated by John Gretzer. Houghton Mifflin, 1964.

Conford, Ellen. *Anything for a Friend*. Little, Brown, 1979.

Corbett, Scott. *The Case of the Gone Goose*, illustrated by Paul Frame. Little, Brown, 1961.

_____. *The Case of the Silver Skull*, illustrated by Paul Frame. Little, Brown, 1974.

Cresswell, Helen. *Absolute Zero*. Macmillan, 1978.

_____. *Bagthorpes Abroad*. Macmillan, 1984.

_____. *Bagthorpes Haunted*. Macmillan, 1985.

_____. *Bagthorpes Unlimited*. Macmillan, 1978.

_____. *Bagthorpes v. The World*. Macmillan, 1979.

_____. *Ordinary Jack*. Macmillan, 1977.

Cunningham, Julia. *Come to the Edge*. Pantheon, 1977.

_____. *Dorp Dead*, illustrated by James Spanfeller. Pantheon, 1965.

Danziger, Paula. *The Divorce Express*. Delacorte, 1982.

_____. *It's an Aardvark-Eat-Turtle World*. Delacorte, 1985.

DeJong, Meindert. *Hurry Home, Candy*, illustrated by Maurice Sendak. Harper, 1953.

Donovan, John. *I'll Get There, It Better Be Worth the Trip*. Harper, 1969.

_____. *Remove Protective Coating a Little at a Time*. Harper, 1973.

Dygard, Thomas J. *Rebound Caper*. Morrow, 1983.

_____. *Winning Kicker*. Morrow, 1978.

Eckert, Allan, *Incident at Hawk's Hill*, illustrated by John Schoenherr. Little, Brown, 1971.

Enright, Elizabeth. *The Saturdays*. Holt, 1941.

Estes, Eleanor. *The Hundred Dresses*, illustrated by Louis Slobodkin. Harcourt, 1944.

_____. *The Middle Moffat*, illustrated by Louis Slobodkin. Harcourt, 1942.

_____. *The Moffats*, illustrated by Louis Slobodkin. Harcourt, 1941.

_____. *Rufus M.*, illustrated by Louis Slobodkin. Harcourt, 1943.

Farley, Walter. *The Black Stallion*, illustrated by Keith Ward. Random, 1944.

_____. *The Black Stallion's Filly*, illustrated by Milton Menasco. Random, 1952.

_____. *The Blood Bay Colt*, illustrated by Milton Menasco. Random, 1950.

_____. *Son of the Black Stallion*, illustrated by Milton Menasco. Random, 1947.

Fenner, Carol. *Gorilla Gorilla*. Random, 1973. (Informational)

Fitzhugh, Louise. *Harriet the Spy*. Harper, 1964.

_____. *The Long Secret*. Harper, 1965.

Fox, Paula. *Blowfish Live in the Sea*. Bradbury, 1970.

_____. *How Many Miles to Babylon?*, illustrated by Paul Giovanopoulos. D. White, 1967.

_____. *One-Eyed Cat*. Bradbury, 1984.

_____. *The Stone-faced Boy*, illustrated by Donald A. Mackay. Bradbury, 1968.

Garden, Nancy. *Annie on My Mind*. Farrar, Straus, 1982.

Garfield, James B. *Follow My Leader*. Viking, 1957.

Garrigue, Sheila. *Between Friends*. Bradbury, 1978.

Gates, Doris. *Blue Willow*, illustrated by Paul Lantz. Viking, 1940.

George, Jean. *The Cry of the Crow*. Harper, 1980.

_____. *Julie of the Wolves*, illustrated by John Schoenherr. Harper, 1972.

_____. *My Side of the Mountain*. Dutton, 1959.

_____. *The Talking Earth*. Harper, 1983.

_____. *Who Really Killed Cock Robin?* Dutton, 1971.

Giff, Patricia Reilly. *Kids of Polk Street School Series.* 12 titles. Dell, 1985.

Gipson, Fred. *Old Yeller,* illustrated by Carl Burger. Harper, 1956.

Godden, Rumer. *The Rocking Horse Secret,* illustrated by Juliet S. Smith. Viking, 1978.

Gordon, Shirley. *The Boy Who Wanted a Family,* illustrated by Charles Robinson. Harper, 1980.

Graeber, Charlotte. *Mustard,* illustrated by Donna Diamond. Macmillan, 1982.

Greene, Bette. *Get On Out of Here, Philip Hall.* Dial, 1981.

_____. *Philip Hall Likes Me. I Reckon Maybe,* illustrated by Charles Lilly. Dial, 1974.

Greene, Constance C. *Al(exandra) the Great.* Viking, 1982.

_____. *Beat the Turtle Drum,* illustrated by Donna Diamond. Viking, 1976.

_____. *A Girl Called Al,* illustrated by Byron Barton. Viking, 1969.

Greenfield, Eloise. *Sister.* Crowell, 1974.

Hamilton, Virginia. *The House of Dies Drear,* illustrated by Eros Keith. Macmillan, 1968.

_____. *M. C. Higgins, the Great.* Macmillan, 1974.

_____. *The Planet of Junior Brown.* Macmillan, 1971.

_____. *Zeely,* illustrated by Symeon Shimin. Macmillan, 1967.

Hautzig, Esther. *The Endless Steppe.* Harper, 1968. (Historical Fiction)

Haywood, Carolyn. *"B" Is for Betsy.* Harcourt, 1968 (1939)

_____. *Betsy's Busy Summer.* Harcourt, 1956.

_____. *Eddie and His Big Deals.* Morrow, 1955.

_____. *Little Eddie.* Morrow, 1947.

_____. *Snowbound with Betsy.* Morrow, 1962.

Henry, Marguerite. *King of the Wind,* illustrated by Wesley Dennis. Rand McNally, 1948.

_____. *Misty of Chincoteague,* illustrated by Wesley Dennis. Rand McNally, 1947.

_____. *Mustang, Wild Spirit of the West,* illustrated by Robert Lougheed. Rand McNally, 1971.

_____. *Stormy, Misty's Foal,* illustrated by Wesley Dennis. Rand McNally, 1963.

Hickman, Janet. *The Stones,* illustrated by Richard Cuffari. Macmillian, 1976.

_____. *The Thunder-Pup.* Macmillan, 1981.

Hildick, E. W. *The Case of the Felon's Fiddle,* illustrated by Lisl Weil. Macmillan, 1982.

_____. *McGurk Gets Good and Mad,* illustrated by Lisl Weil. Macmillan, 1982.

_____. *Manhattan Is Missing,* illustrated by Jan Palmer. Doubleday, 1969.

Holland, Isabelle. *The Man without a Face.* Lippincott, 1972.

Holman, Felice. *Elisabeth and the Marsh Mystery,* illustrated by Erik Blegvad. Macmillan, 1966.

_____. *Slake's Limbo.* Scribner, 1974.

Houston, James. *Black Diamonds: A Search for Arctic Treasure.* Atheneum, 1982.

_____. *Frozen Fire.* Atheneum, 1977.

Hunt, Irene. *Up a Road Slowly.* Follett, 1966.

Hurmence, Belinda. *Tough Tiffany.* Doubleday, 1980.

Hurwitz, Johanna. *Aldo Applesauce,* illustrated by John Wallner. Morrow, 1979.

_____. *Aldo Ice Cream,* illustrated by John Wallner. Morrow, 1981.

_____. *Busybody Nora,* illustrated by Susan Jeschke. Morrow, 1976.

_____. *Much Ado About Aldo,* illustrated by John Wallner. Morrow, 1978.

_____. *Superduper Teddy,* illustrated by Susan Jeschke. Morrow, 1980.

Huynh, Quang Nhuong. *The Land I Lost,* illustrated by Vo-Dinh Mai. Harper, 1982.

Kerr, M. E. *Dinky Hocker Shoots Smack.* Harper, 1972.

Killilea, Marie. *Karen,* illustrated by Bob Riger. Dodd, Mead, 1954.

Kjelgaard, Jim. *Big Red,* illustrated by Bob Kuhn. Holiday, 1956.

Klein, Norma. *Confessions of an Only Child,* illustrated by Richard Cuffari. Pantheon, 1974.

_____. *Mom, the Wolf Man and Me.* Pantheon, 1972.

_____. *Naomi in the Middle,* illustrated by Leigh Grant. Dial, 1974.

Konigsburg, E. L. *From the Mixed-Up Files of Mrs. Basil E. Frankweiler.* Atheneum, 1967.

_____. *(George).* Atheneum, 1970.

_____. *Journey to an 800 Number.* Atheneum, 1982.

Knudson, R. R. *Rinehart Lifts.* Farrar, Straus, 1980.

_____. *Zanballer.* Harper, 1972.

_____. *Zanbanger.* Harper, 1977.

_____. *Zanboomer*. Harper, 1978.

Krumgold, Joseph. *. . . And Now Miguel*, illustrated by Jean Charlot. Crowell, 1953.

_____. *Onion John*, illustrated by Symeon Shimin. Crowell, 1953.

Lampman, Evelyn Sibley. *Go Up the Road*. Atheneum, 1973.

_____. *The Potlatch Family*. Atheneum, 1976.

Lasky, Kathryn. *The Night Journey*, illustrated by Trina Schart Hyman. Warne, 1981.

Le Guin, Ursula. *A Wizard of Earthsea*, illustrated by Ruth Robbins. Parnassus, 1968. (Fantasy)

L'Engle, Madeleine. *Meet the Austins*. Vanguard, 1960.

_____. *A Ring of Endless Light*. Farrar, Straus, 1980.

_____. *A Wrinkle in Time*. Farrar, Straus, 1962. (Fantasy)

Lenski, Lois. *Judy's Journey*. Lippincott, 1947.

_____. *Shoo-Fly Girl*. Lippincott, 1963.

_____. *Strawberry Girl*. Lippincott, 1945.

Levy, Elizabeth. *Something Queer at the Lemonade Stand*, illustrated by Mordicai Gerstein. Delacorte, 1982.

Little, Jean. *From Anna*, illustrated by Joan Sandin. Harper, 1972.

_____. *Home from Far*, illustrated by Jerry Lazare. Little, Brown, 1965.

_____. *Kate*. Harper, 1971.

_____. *Look Through My Window*, illustrated by Joan Sandin. Harper, 1970.

_____. *Mama's Going to Buy You a Mockingbird*. Viking, 1984.

_____. *Mine for Keeps*, illustrated by Lewis Parker. Little, Brown, 1962.

_____. *Take Wing*. Little, Brown, 1968.

London, Jack. *The Call of the Wild*, illustrated by Charles Pickard. Dutton, 1968 (1903).

Lord, Bette Bao. *In the Year of the Boar and Jackie Robinson*, illustrated by Marc Simont. Harper, 1984.

Lorentzen, Karin. *Lanky Long Legs*, translated by Joan Tate, illustrated by Jan Ormerod. Atheneum, 1983.

Lowry, Lois. *Anastasia Again!*, illustrated by Diane de Groat. Houghton Mifflin, 1981.

_____. *Anastasia, Ask Your Analyst*. Houghton Mifflin, 1984.

_____. *Anastasia at Your Service*, illustrated by Diane de Groat. Houghton Mifflin, 1982.

_____. *Anastasia Has the Answers*. Houghton Mifflin, 1986.

_____. *Anastasia Krupnik*. Houghton Mifflin, 1979.

_____. *Anastasia on Her Own*. Houghton Mifflin, 1985.

_____. *A Summer to Die*, illustrated by Jenni Oliver. Houghton Mifflin, 1977.

McCloskey, Robert. *Centerburg Tales*. Viking, 1951.

_____. *Homer Price*. Viking, 1943.

McDonnell, Christine. *Don't Be Mad, Ivy*, illustrated by Diane de Groat. Dial, 1981.

_____. *Lucky Charms and Birthday Wishes*, illustrated by Diane de Groat. Viking, 1984.

_____. *Toad Food and Measle Soup*, illustrated by Diane de Groat. Dial, 1982.

McHargue, Georgess. *Funny Bananas: The Mystery at the Museum*, illustrated by Heidi Palmer. Holt, 1975.

MacLachlan, Patricia. *Arthur for the Very First Time*, illustrated by Lloyd Bloom. Harper, 1980.

Mann, Peggy. *My Dad Lives in a Downtown Hotel*, illustrated by Richard Cuffari. Doubleday, 1973.

_____. *There Are Two Kinds of Terrible*. Doubleday, 1977.

Mark, Jan. *Handles*. Atheneum, 1985.

_____. *Thunder and Lightnings*, illustrated by Jim Russell. Harper, 1979.

Mathis, Sharon Bell. *The Hundred Penny Box*, illustrated by Leo and Diane Dillon. Viking, 1975.

Mazer, Norma Fox. *A Figure of Speech*. Delacorte, 1973.

_____. *I, Trissy*. Delacorte, 1971.

Merrill, Jean. *Maria's House*, illustrated by Frances Gruse Scott. Atheneum, 1974.

Miles, Betty. *Maudie and Me and the Dirty Book*. Knopf, 1980.

Mohr, Nicholasa. *Felita*, illustrated by Ray Cruz. Dial, 1979.

Mowat, Farley. *The Dog Who Wouldn't Be*. Little, Brown, 1957.

_____. *Owls in the Family*. Little, Brown, 1961.

Murray, Michelle. *Nellie Cameron*. Seabury, 1971.

Myers, Walter Dean. *Fast Sam, Cool Clyde, and Stuff*. Viking, 1975.

_____. *Won't Know Till I Get There*. Viking, 1982.

Myrick, Mildred. *The Secret Three*, illustrated by Arnold Lobel. Harper, 1963.

Neville, Emily C. *Berries Goodman*. Harper, 1965.

North, Sterling. *Little Rascal*, illustrated by Carl Burger. Dutton, 1965.

_____. *Rascal: A Memoir of a Better Era*, illustrated by John Schoenherr. Dutton, 1963.

Oneal, Zibby. *The Language of Goldfish*. Viking, 1980.

Parish, Peggy. *Amelia Bedelia*, illustrated by Fritz Siebel. Harper, 1963.

_____. *Amelia Bedelia Helps Out*, illustrated by Lynn Sweat. Greenwillow, 1979.

_____. *Teach Us, Amelia Bedelia*, illustrated by Lynn Sweat. Greenwillow, 1977.

_____. *Thank You, Amelia Bedelia*, illustrated by Fritz Siebel. Harper, 1964.

Paterson, Katherine. *Bridge to Terabithia*, illustrated by Donna Diamond. Crowell, 1977.

_____. *Come Sing, Jimmy Jo*. Dutton, 1985.

_____. *The Great Gilly Hopkins*. Crowell, 1978.

_____. *Jacob Have I Loved*. Harper, 1980.

Pearce, Philippa. *The Way to Sattin Shore*, illustrated by Charlotte Voake. Greenwillow, 1983.

Peck, Robert Newton. *A Day No Pigs Would Die*. Knopf, 1972.

_____. *Soup*, illustrated by Charles Gehm. Knopf, 1974.

_____. *Trig*, illustrated by Pamela Johnson. Little, Brown, 1977.

Pollock, Penny. *Keeping It Secret*, illustrated by Donna Diamond. Putnam, 1982.

Raskin, Ellen. *The Westing Game*. Dutton, 1978.

Rawlings, Marjorie Kinnan. *The Yearling*, illustrated by Edward Shenton. Scribner, 1938.

Rawls, Wilson. *Where the Red Fern Grows*. Doubleday, 1961.

Rich, Elaine Sommers. *Hannah Elizabeth*, illustrated by Paul Kennedy. Harper, 1964.

Riley, Jocelyn. *Crazy Quilt*. Morrow, 1983.

_____. *Only My Mouth Is Smiling*. Morrow, 1982.

Riskind, Mary. *Apple Is My Sign*. Houghton Mifflin, 1981. (Historical Fiction)

Robertson, Keith. *Henry Reed, Inc.*, illustrated by Robert McCloskey. Viking, 1958.

_____. *Henry Reed's Baby-Sitting Service*, illustrated by Robert McCloskey. Viking, 1966.

_____. *Henry Reed's Journey*, illustrated by Robert McCloskey. Viking, 1963.

_____. *In Search of a Sandhill Crane*, illustrated by Richard Cuffari. Viking, 1973.

Robinson, Barbara. *The Best Christmas Pageant Ever*, illustrated by Judith Gwyn Brown. Harper, 1972.

Robinson, Veronica. *David in Silence*, illustrated by Victor Ambrus. Lippincott, 1966.

Rockwell, Thomas. *How to Eat Fried Worms*. Watts, 1973.

Rodowsky, Colby F. *What About Me?* Watts, 1976.

Sachs, Marilyn. *The Bears' House*, illustrated by Louis Glanzman. Doubleday, 1971.

Sharmat, Marjorie W. *Getting Something on Maggie Marmelstein*, illustrated by Ben Shecter. Harper, 1971.

_____. *Mysteriously Yours, Maggie Marmelstein*, illustrated by Ben Shecter. Harper, 1982.

Shyer, Marlene. *Welcome Home, Jellybean*. Scribner, 1978.

Simon, Seymour. *Einstein Anderson Lights Up the Sky*, illustrated by Fred Winkowski. Viking, 1982.

Slepian, Jan. *The Alfred Summer*. Macmillan, 1980.

_____. *Lester's Turn*. Macmillan, 1981.

Slote, Alfred. *Hang Tough, Paul Mather*. Lippincott, 1973.

_____. *My Father, the Coach*. Lippincott, 1972.

Smith, Doris Buchanan. *Kick a Stone Home*. Crowell, 1974.

_____. *A Taste of Blackberries*, illustrated by Charles Robinson. Crowell, 1973.

Sneve, Virginia Driving Hawk. *When Thunders Spoke*, illustrated by Oren Lyons. Holiday, 1974.

Snyder, Zilpha K. *The Egypt Game*, illustrated by Alton Raible. Atheneum, 1967.

Sobol, Donald. *Encyclopedia Brown Takes a Case*, illustrated by Leonard Shortall. Nelson, 1973.

Sorenson, Virginia. *Plain Girl*, illustrated by Charles Geer. Harcourt, 1955.

Southall, Ivan. *Ash Road*, illustrated by Clem Seale. St. Martin, 1965.

_____. *Hill's End*, illustrated by Clem Seale. St. Martin, 1963.

_____. *Josh*. Macmillan, 1972.

_____. *Let the Balloon Go*, illustrated by Ian Ribbons. St. Martin, 1968.

Speare, Elizabeth George. *The Witch of Blackbird Pond*. Houghton Mifflin, 1958. (Historical Fiction)

Sperry, Armstrong. *Call It Courage*. Macmillan, 1968.

Stolz, Mary. *The Bully of Barkham Street*, illustrated by Leonard Shortall. Harper, 1963.

_____. *Cat Walk*, illustrated by Erik Blegvad. Harper, 1983. (Fantasy)

_____. *A Dog on Barkham Street*, illustrated by Leonard Shortall. Harper, 1960.

_____. *The Explorer of Barkham Street*, illustrated by Emily A. McCully. Harper, 1985.

Strete, Craig Kee. *When Grandfather Journeys into Winter*, illustrated by Hal Frenck. Greenwillow, 1979.

Taylor, Sidney. *All-of-a-Kind Family*, illustrated by Helen John. Follett, 1951.

_____. *All-of-a-Kind Family Uptown*, illustrated by Mary Stevens. Follett, 1958.

_____. *More All-of-a-Kind Family*, illustrated by Mary Stevens. Follett, 1954.

Taylor, Theodore. *The Trouble with Tuck*. Doubleday, 1981.

Thiele, Colin. *Storm Boy*, illustrated by John Schoenherr. Harper, 1978.

Thomas, Jane Resh. *The Comeback Dog*, illustrated by Troy Howell. Houghton Mifflin, 1981.

Ullman, James Ramsey. *Banner in the Sky*. Lippincott, 1954.

Van Iterson, S. R. *Pulga*. Morrow, 1971.

Voigt, Cynthia. *Dicey's Song*. Atheneum, 1983.

_____. *Homecoming*. Atheneum, 1981.

_____. *A Solitary Blue*. Atheneum, 1984.

Warburg, Sandol Stoddard. *The Growing Time*, illustrated by Leonard Weisgard. Harper, 1969.

Weil, Lisl. *Esther*. Atheneum, 1980. (Traditional)

Weinman, Eiveen. *Which Way Courage?* Atheneum, 1981.

Wells, Rosemary. *When No One Was Looking*. Dial, 1980.

Whitney, Phyllis A. *The Mystery of the Haunted Pool*, illustrated by H. Tom Hall. Westminster, 1960.

_____. *Secret of the Emerald Star*, illustrated by Alex Stein. Westminster, 1964.

Wojciechowska, Maia. *Shadow of a Bull*, illustrated by Alvin Smith. Atheneum, 1964.

Wrightson, Patricia. *A Racecourse for Andy*, illustrated by Margaret Horder. Harcourt, 1968.

Yep, Laurence. *Child of the Owl*. Harper, 1977.

10 HISTORICAL FICTION AND BIOGRAPHY

T he author of an historical novel visited a public library's after-school program to meet with a group of children. In her talk she described the research she had done to establish an authentic Civil War background for her book. To make the efforts seem more concrete, she had brought along many examples of source material: maps, reproductions of nineteenth-century photographs, books and pamphlets, and a three-ring binder bulging with notes. One 10-year-old girl regarded this display with a troubled expression, and when time came for questions quickly raised her hand.

"You found out a lot of things that you didn't put in the book, didn't you?" she asked. The author agreed, and the girl smiled. "Good!" she said. "If you had put all *that* stuff in, there wouldn't have been any room for the imagining!"

This child intuitively knew that historical fiction must draw on two sources, fact and imagination—the author's information about the past and his or her power to speculate about how it was to live in that time.

Biography for children also draws on both sources. Although biography is by definition a nonfiction genre, in actual practice much of the biography available for children uses the imaginative techniques of fiction. Both biography and historical fiction have narrative appeal. By personalizing the past and making it live in the mind of the reader, such books can help children understand both the public events that we usually label "history" and the private struggles that have characterized the human condition across the centuries.

HISTORICAL FICTION

Historical Fiction for Today's Child

Historical fiction today is not as automatically popular as it was a generation ago. Modern culture greatly values the here and now, and by natural inclination children look forward rather than back. School curricula that put less emphasis on the study of history may account for some loss of interest. Whatever the reason, most librarians and teachers find that, in general, contemporary realism and fantasy are in greater demand than historical fiction for independent reading.

In a reflective look at his half-century career in writing, the distinguished British author Geoffrey Trease reminds us:

Historical fiction makes special demands, and it has always been a minority taste, though the minority has often been a very strong one. . . . Indisputably, historical stories are in the commercial doldrums just now, but it seems to me that, no less indisputably, they offer literature of value in a form that can never be totally obsolete.[1]

The challenge for teachers and librarians is to bring this enduring "literature of value" to its audience.

VALUES OF HISTORICAL FICTION

Historical novels for children help a child to experience the past; to enter into the conflicts, the suffering, the joys, and the despair of those who lived before us. There is no way that children can feel the jolt of a covered wagon, the tediousness of the daily trek in the broiling sun, or the constant

[1]Geoffrey Trease, "Fifty Years On: A Writer Looks Back," *Children's Literature in Education*, vol. 14 (Autumn 1983), p. 156.

threat of danger, unless they take an imaginative journey in such books as *Trouble for Lucy* by Carla Stevens or *Beyond the Divide* by Kathryn Lasky. Well-written historical fiction offers young people the vicarious experience of participating in the life of the past.

Historical fiction encourages children to think as well as to feel. Every book set in the past invites a comparison with the present. How would the children who became "bondsmen" in Avi's *Night Journeys* be treated today? What contemporary parallels come to mind with Paul Fleischman's description of the plague mentality of Philadelphia in the throes of the yellow fever epidemic of 1793, in *Path of the Pale Horse*? Opportunities for critical thinking and judgment are built into the many novels that provide conflicting views on an issue and force characters to make hard choices. Readers of *My Brother Sam Is Dead* by the Colliers can weigh Sam's Patriot fervor against his father's Tory practicality as young Tim tries to decide which one is right. Or they can agonize with Binnie Howe over the question of "turning out" on strike with the other millworkers in Athena Lord's *A Spirit to Ride the Whirlwind*.

An historical perspective also helps children to see and judge the mistakes of the past more clearly. They can read such books as Paula Fox's *The Slave Dancer* or *Journey to Topaz* by Yoshiko Uchida and realize the cruelty that man is capable of inflicting on other men, whether by slavery, persecution, or the assignment of American-Japanese to "relocation centers." Such books will quicken children's sensibilities and bring them to a fuller understanding of human problems and human relationships. We hope they will learn not to repeat the injustices of the past. Many years ago George Santayana cautioned: "Those who cannot remember the past are condemned to repeat it."

Stories of the past will help children see that times change; nations do rise and fall; but the universal needs of humankind have remained relatively unchanged. All people need and want respect, belonging, love, freedom, security, regardless of whether they lived during the period of the Vikings or the pioneers or are alive today. It matters not how many different "Little Houses" the Ingalls family lived in as long as Pa's fiddle sang a song of love and security in each one. Children today living in tenements, trailers, or suburban homes seek the same feelings of warmth and

family solidarity that Laura Ingalls Wilder portrayed so effectively in her Little House series.

Historical fiction also enables children to see the interdependence of humankind. In the well-known words of John Donne, "no man is an island." We are all interconnected and interrelated. We need others as much as Matt needed Attean and Saknis in Elizabeth George Speare's *The Sign of the Beaver* or Annie deLeeuw needed the Dutch Oosterveld family when she and her sister had to hide in *The Upstairs Room* by Johanna Reiss. Such books also dramatize the courage and integrity of the thousands of "common folk" who willingly take a stand for what they believe. History does not record their names, but their stories are frequently the source of inspiration for books of historical fiction.

Children's perceptions of chronology are inexact and develop slowly. Even so, stories about the past can develop a feeling for the continuity of life and help children to see themselves and their present place in time as a part of a larger picture. The four interconnected tales in *Lost and Found* by Jill Paton Walsh provide this sense for younger elementary children. In each story a child loses an object that is found by another child in the same place hundreds of years later. For readers, the objects form a chain that links the Stone Age with the present.

The need for a sense of continuity is stated eloquently by the character of King Alfred in *The Namesake* by C. Walter Hodges:

. . . Every man is a part of the bridge between the past and the future, and must feel how it stretches out both ways before and behind him. Whatever helps him to feel this more strongly is good.[2]

The reading of historical fiction is one way to help children develop this sense of history and to begin to understand their place in the sweep of human destiny.

TYPES OF HISTORICAL FICTION

The term *historical fiction* can be used to designate all realistic stories that are set in the past. Even though children tend to see these in one undif-

[2]C. Walter Hodges, *The Namesake: A Story of King Alfred* (New York: Coward McCann, 1964), pp. 166–167.

ferentiated category (since all the action happened "in the olden days" before they were born), students of literature will want to keep in mind that various distinctions can be made on the basis of the author's purpose and the nature of the research and writing tasks required.

In the most obvious type of historical fiction, an author weaves a fictional story around actual events and people of the past. *Johnny Tremain* by Esther Forbes, the story of a fictional apprentice to Paul Revere, is a novel of this sort. The author had previously written a definitive adult biography of Revere and had collected painstakingly accurate details about life in Boston just before the Revolutionary War: the duties of apprentices, the activities of the Committee for Public Safety, and much, much more. Johnny Tremain's personal story, his development from an embittered boy to a courageous and idealistic young man, is inextricably connected with the political history and way of life of his place and time.

In other stories of the past, fictional lives are lived with little or no reference to recorded historical events or real persons. However, the facts of social history dictate the background for how the characters live and make their living; what they wear, eat, study, or play; and what conflicts they must resolve. Patricia MacLachlan's *Sarah, Plain and Tall* is a book of this type. The demands of life on the great mid-American prairie before the advent of mechanized farming and the practice of advertising for mail-order brides provide the frame for this moving story of a family that needs a mother. Authors who write within this generalized frame of social history have more freedom to imagine their story, since they are not bound to the chronology of specific historical events.

If we look at the author's task in another way, we can see that some deliberately reconstruct, through research, the life and times of a period long past. Others re-create, largely from memory, their own personal experiences of a time that is "history" to their child audience. The Little House books, for example, are all based on actual childhood experiences in the life of their author, Laura Ingalls Wilder, or that of her husband. Such books require searching the memory for details and then the sorting and imaginative retelling of significant events, but extensive research is seldom done.

Some books with remembered settings, like Esther Hautzig's *A Gift for Mama*, provide few clues for child readers as to the period. Although this story takes place in Poland before World War II, children are more likely to enjoy it as a realistic glimpse of a loving family than a story of long ago. Conversely, a purely contemporary story about a significant event may endure until it acquires historical significance. *Snow Treasure* by Marie McSwigan is the exciting story of Norwegian children who strapped gold bullion under their sleds and slid down the hill to the port past the watchful Nazi commandant. Written as realism in 1942, this book is read by children today as historical fiction.

Some essentially historical stories defy commonly accepted classifications. A few authors tell stories of the past within the guise of another genre to draw the hesitant reader in more quickly. Kathryn Lasky's *The Night Journey* (see Chapter 9) is one example of a contemporary novel with significant historical content. Fantasy devices are used to transport the main character (and the reader) from the present day to a carefully researched past in such books as Janet Lunn's *The Root Cellar* and *A Girl Called Boy* by Belinda Hurmence (see Chapter 7). E. L. Konigsburg's unique story of Eleanor of Aquitaine, *A Proud Taste for Scarlet and Miniver*, combines fantasy, historical fiction, and biography. Categorizing books like these is far less important than bringing them to the attention of children, for they all tell good stories and make their subjects memorable.

No type of historical story is intrinsically better than another. However, the type of story might influence a teacher's selection process when choosing books for specific classroom purposes. And, in applying the criteria for evaluating historical fiction which are described in the following section, standards of authenticity must be applied most rigorously to stories that give a prominent place to real people and real events.

CRITERIA FOR HISTORICAL FICTION

Books of historical fiction must first of all tell a story that is interesting in its own right. The second, and unique, requirement is balancing fact with fiction. Margery Fisher maintains that fact must always be subordinated to the story:

> For the more fact (the author) has to deal with, the more imagination he will need to carry it off. It is not

enough to be a scholar, essential though this is. Without imagination and enthusiasm, the most learned and well-documented story will leave the young reader cold, where it should set him on fire.[3]

Historical fiction does have to be accurate and authentic. However, the research should be thoroughly digested, making details appear as an essential part of the story, not tacked on for effect. Mollie Hunter, a well-known Scottish writer of fine historical fiction for children, maintains that an author should be so steeped in the historical period of the book that "you could walk undetected in the past. You'd wake up in the morning and know the kind of bed you'd be sleeping in, . . . even to the change you'd have in your pocket!"[4] The purpose of research, she has said, is:

> . . . to be able to think and feel in terms of a period so that the people within it are real and three-dimensional, close enough to hear the sound of their voices, to feel their body-warmth, to see the expression in their eyes.[5]

Although fictional characters and invented turns of plot are accepted in historical novels, nothing should be included that contradicts the actual record of history. If President Lincoln was busy reviewing Union troops in Virginia on a given day in 1863, an author cannot "borrow" him for a scene played in New York City, no matter how great the potential dramatic impact. It breaks the unwritten contract between author and reader, especially a naive child reader, to offer misinformation in any form.

Stories must accurately reflect the spirit and values of the times, as well as the events. Historical fiction can't be made to conform to today's more enlightened point of view concerning women or blacks or knowledge of medicine. You can't save George Washington with a shot of penicillin any more than you can have the black mother in Armstrong's *Sounder* become a black militant in the 1890s. Characters have to act in accordance with the values and beliefs of the time. The father of Brink's *Caddie Woodlawn* allowed her to be a tomboy while she was growing up in the Wisconsin backwoods, but she had to become a "proper lady" during the Victorian era; there was no other choice.

The historian Christopher Collier, who has collaborated with his brother James Lincoln Collier on several novels set during the era of the American Revolution, maintains that authors should pay careful attention to historiography, ". . . that is, the way that professional historians have approached and interpreted the central episode of the story."[6] Collier believes that authors should weigh opposing views on the causes or meaning of a conflict and decide which should be predominant in the story, but also find a way to include the other significant interpretations. One way is to have different characters espouse different points of view. However, fiction that draws the reader into the thoughts and feelings of a central character cannot be truly impartial. In the middle of a massacre scene, a bleeding settler who cries ". . . but the Indians are only fighting for what is theirs!" will sacrifice the story's credibility. Many fine books, like Anne Eliot Crompton's *The Ice Trail* and Avi's *The Fighting Ground,* do let the reader feel more than one side of an issue. But for a more objective viewpoint, teachers and librarians will want to provide a variety of books, each with its own approach to the topic.

The authenticity of language in historical fiction should be given careful attention. We have no record of how people in other times actually talked, but the spoken word in a book with an historical background should give the flavor of the period. However, too many "prithees" and "thous" will seem artificial and may discourage children's further reading. Some archaic words can be used if they are explained in the content. For example, the book *The Cabin Faced West* notes that George Washington "bated" at the Hamiltons. The author, Jean Fritz, makes it very clear by the action in the story that "bated" meant "stopped by for dinner."

Some words commonly used in earlier times are offensive by today's standards. Authors must con-

---

[3]Margery Fisher, *Intent upon Reading: A Critical Appraisal of Modern Fiction for Children* (New York: Watts, 1962), p. 225.
[4]In a lecture given in Columbus, Ohio, November 1968.
[5]Mollie Hunter, "Shoulder the Sky" in *Talent Is Not Enough* (New York: Harper & Row, 1976), pp. 43–44.

[6]Christopher Collier, "Criteria for Historical Fiction," *School Library Journal*, vol. 28 (August 1982), p. 32.

sider whether or not it would be misleading to omit such terms entirely and how necessary such language is for establishing character. In Sheila Garrigue's *The Eternal Spring of Mr. Ito,* residents of Vancouver in the panic of late 1941 contemptuously refer to their Japanese neighbors as "Japs." It would have defeated the purpose of the story to portray the residents as more understanding and compassionate than they actually were. In Ouida Sebestyen's *On Fire,* the Haneys curse and swear and use bigoted terms for blacks, including "sambos" and "jigaboos." Although we recognize this as contemptible language, it does fit the setting, an early twentieth-century mining town, and the characters who use it. When the two Haney brothers tip the balance from criminality toward human decency, their way of speaking also shows some change. Well-written historical fiction also makes use of figurative language that is appropriate for the times and characters in the story. For example, in Haugaard's superb Viking story, young Hakon comments on the plan of attack with an appropriate metaphor: "A plan should be whole and tight like a cooking pot, and ours seemed to me to resemble a fishing net."[7] An inappropriate use of language will jar the reader and make the story less believable. In John Christopher's first book of historical fiction, *Dom and Va,* Dom, a young man of prehistoric times, thinks to himself: "It was no good. The die had been cast when he took her away."[8] This reference to casting a die seems curious and out of place, given the characterization of Dom as a club-wielding savage with no knowledge of crafts or entertainment.

A book of historical fiction should do even more than relate a good story of the past authentically and imaginatively. It should illuminate the problems of today by examining those of other times. The themes of many historical books are such basic ones as the meaning of freedom, loyalty and treachery, love and hate, acceptance of new ways, closed minds versus questing ones, and, always, the age-old struggle between good and evil. Many tales of the past echo recent experience.

[7]Erik Christian Haugaard, *Hakon of Rogen's Saga,* illustrated by Leo and Diane Dillon (Boston: Houghton Mifflin, 1963), p. 96.
[8]John Christopher, *Dom and Va* (New York: Macmillan, 1973), p. 95.

GUIDES FOR EVALUATING HISTORICAL FICTION

- Does the book tell a good story?
- Is fact blended with fiction in such a way that the background is subordinate to the story?

- Is the story as accurate and authentic as possible?
- Does the author avoid any contradiction or distortion of the known events of history?
- Are background details authentic or in keeping with accurate information about the period?

- Does the story accurately reflect the values and spirit of the times, or is it written from the point of view of today's perceptions?
- Are different points of view on the issues of the time presented or acknowledged?

- Is the dialogue constructed so as to convey a feeling of the period without seeming artificial? Does it reflect character as well as setting?
- Is the language of the narrative appropriate to the times, drawing figures of speech from the setting?

- Does the theme provide insight and understanding for today's problems as well as those of the past?

The parallels between the departure of the Roman legions from England, as depicted by Rosemary Sutcliff in her book *The Lantern Bearers,* and the departure of the United States armed forces from Vietnam are striking. The "boat people" fleeing the Asian wars have kinship with the plague survivors of Ann Turner's *The Way Home* and with Felice Holman's *The Wild Children* as all struggle to preserve their humanity as well as their lives. Many of the social problems portrayed in historical novels still provoke thought today. *A Gathering of Days* by Joan Blos or *Prairie Songs* by Pam Conrad could be used in a discussion of women's roles. All these books are capable of shedding light and understanding on the problems of today.

To summarize, historical fiction must first meet the requirements of good writing, but it demands special criteria beyond that. In evaluating historical fiction the reader will want to consider whether the story meets these specialized needs.

Historical fiction can dramatize and humanize the sterile facts of history. It can give children a sense of participation in the past and an appreciation for their historical heritage. It should enable the child to see that today's way of life is a result of what people did in the past and that the present will influence the way people live in the future.

In the following sections, books are discussed chronologically, according to the periods and settings they represent. Another way to approach the historical fiction genre is to look at common topics or themes as they are presented in different settings across the centuries. For examples of titles grouped in this way, see the chart on page 555.

Stories of Prehistoric Times

Anthropologists and geologists are slowly uncovering scientific data that make it possible to imagine how life in prehistoric times might have been. Authors and their readers have been fascinated with trying to reconstruct the mind and feelings of primitive people. How did they discover that there were others living in the world? Were all the tribes at the same level of development, or did different groups mature ahead of others? What happened when two groups met? These and other questions have provided the stimulus for some remarkably fine stories.

One Small Blue Bead by Schweitzer is a poetic picture book that describes prehistoric times among a tribe that is convinced they are the only people in the world. One man thinks differently and yearns for others of his kind. His chores are willingly assumed by a boy to enable the old man to roam free in quest of knowledge. As the boy goes about his daily chores, he wonders, too:

> I wonder . . . I wonder
> If on some far hillside
> There is a boy
> who sits alone.
> And thinks the same thoughts
> As my own.
> I wonder if he wonders if
> There's a boy with thoughts like his.[9]

The boy's faithfulness is rewarded as the man returns with a boy from another tribe, who gives

[9]Byrd Baylor Schweitzer, *One Small Blue Bead,* illustrated by Symeon Shimin (New York: Macmillan, 1965), p. 18.

him one small blue bead. This is a moving story of unselfishness and man's quest for the unknown. It will be understood and appreciated by children as young as 7.

Most stories of prehistoric times, however, feature adolescent characters and are better suited for upper elementary and middle-school readers. One such is *The Memory String* by Chester Osborne, set 30,000 years ago on the Siberian peninsula. Darath yearns to be a great hunter like his father, but the tribe needs his quick mind and understanding of numbers to be put to use in the role of shaman. From his grandfather he must learn the Moon Sticks for keeping track of time, the medicines for healing, and the stories of the Memory String that keep the people's history. All this must be mastered quickly, for Darath's people intend to leave their increasingly crowded territory in search of a legendary "Other Valley" to the east, where game is plentiful. With his sister's help, Darath finds the way for their people across the land bridge that joined Asia and North America at that time. This is a good story of endurance and survival that celebrates the power of superior thinking over superior strength or numbers.

T. A. Dyer's *A Way of His Own* also deals with early people of North America, a small band of hunters and gatherers on an inland prairie. According to their way, they abandon young Shutok because he cannot keep up and because they believe his crippled back houses an evil spirit responsible for all their misfortunes. But Shutok, a well-developed character with great determination, does not die as expected. He is joined by the escaped slave girl Uita, and together the two outcasts kill the fearsome jaguar that invades their cave, struggle against bitter cold and hunger, and live to reclaim a position of worth with Shutok's people. The story is fast-paced, with lively dialogue, and could serve a younger audience than *The Memory String.*

The story of a boy who stands out because of his talent for drawing is told by Rosemary Sutcliff in *Sun Horse, Moon Horse.* Lubrin is the son of an early chieftain of the Iceni, the Horse People of the chalk downs of England. When invaders imprison his people and the leader demands that Lubrin draw a huge horse on the hillside, the boy bargains freedom for his tribe. He agrees to cut a likeness of a horse into the white chalk half a hill high if the

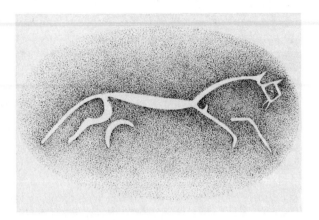

In *Sun Horse, Moon Horse* Rosemary Sutcliff speculates on the origin of a horse image carved in the chalk downs of England. Art by Shirley Felt.

Iceni are allowed to go north with enough stallions and brood mares to establish a new herd. But the image is to be a horse-god, incomplete without the quickening force of human blood. Lubrin gives his life as well as his art for his people in this powerful story of sacrifice and the demands of creativity. The author's fascination with the beautiful ancient White Horse of Uffington led her to write this tale speculating about its origin.

In *The Stronghold*, Mollie Hunter has created a character whose courage and imagination override a handicap. Coll's achievement is his plan for protection against the raiding Romans—the "brochs" or strongholds of stone that remain to intrigue present-day visitors to the North of Scotland. This is a story of conflict between tribal life and the religious domination of the Druids. It is also a story of devotion as Coll makes a daring attempt to save the girl he loves from Druid sacrifice. The power of the setting and of the language helped to make this novel a Carnegie award winner.

The Faraway Lurs by Harry Behn is a hauntingly beautiful story of the love between a young Stone Age girl, Heather, and Wolf Stone, son of the chieftain of the Sun People. One morning Heather hears the great bronze trumpets (called lurs) of the warlike Sun People, who have camped beside a lake near her village. Later, she meets Wolf Stone in the forest, as he searches for the mighty tree that her peaceful Forest People worship. The two fall in love, but there is no solution

for them other than death in this Romeo and Juliet story of the Bronze Age. The author was inspired to tell Heather's tale after a journey to Denmark to visit the birthplace of his mother. An important archeological find had been made on a nearby farm when they discovered the "wet grave" of an 18-year-old girl perfectly preserved for some 3,000 years. Behn listened to the details of her burial and then wrote his own interpretation of what might have happened. In his foreword Behn points out the relative brevity of human history and the slow progress in human relations since Heather's time.

Stories of the Old World

Children in the United States are more interested in stories of the American frontier, the Civil War, or World War II than they are in the fiction of ancient or medieval days. Increasingly, however, as we have access to books published in England and Europe, plus those written in the United States, there is a growing body of fine historical fiction of the Old World.

ANCIENT TIMES

The ancient world of Egypt with all of its political intrigue provides a rich background for Eloise McGraw's story of a slave girl, *Mara, Daughter of the Nile*. Mara, the mistreated slave of a wealthy jewel trader, is bought by a mysterious man who offers her luxury in return for her services as a spy for the queen. On a Nile riverboat Mara meets Lord Sheftu, who employs her as a spy for the king. In this exciting and sinister story of espionage and counterespionage, the transformation of Mara from a selfish, deceitful slave to a loyal and courageous young woman is made slowly and believably.

The Greek general Themistokles is the connecting link for three independent stories told in *Children of the Fox* by Jill Paton Walsh. Each story is a first-person account by a young fictional narrator who has a part in real events, such as the defeat of the Persian ships at Salamis or the general's ruse for rebuilding the walls of Athens without Spartan consent. These smoothly written stories give intriguing glimpses of three different life styles in ancient Greece. An afterword provides more of the political and military history of the time.

Daniel Bar Jamin has but one all-consuming

purpose in his life, to avenge the cruel death of his father and mother by driving the Romans out of his land of Israel. First with an outlaw band, and then with a group of boy guerrillas, Daniel nurses his hatred and waits for the hour to strike. He takes comfort in the verse from II Samuel 22:35—"He trains my hands for war, so that my arms can bend a bow of bronze." Seen as a symbol for what no man can do, *The Bronze Bow* is the title for Daniel's tormented journey from blind hatred to his acceptance and understanding of love. Only after he has nearly sacrificed his friends and driven his sister, Leah, deeper into mental darkness, does he seek the help of Simon's friend, Jesus. After he pours out his troubles and hatred, Jesus tells him:

> It is hate that is the enemy, not men. Hate does not die with killing. It only springs up a hundred-fold. The only thing stronger than hate is love.[10]

The healing strength of Jesus cures Leah and, at that moment, Daniel can forgive the Romans. He understands at last that only love can bend the bow of bronze. Each character stands out in this startling story of the conflict of good and evil.

A bear, a boy, and a holy man are strange traveling companions in Peter Dickinson's novel set in sixth-century Byzantium, *The Dancing Bear*. Silvester, a young Greek slave, is very happy at his master's large house, where he plays with Lady Adriane, the master's daughter, learns Latin and medicine, and has the sole responsibility of training Bubba, the bear, to dance. Silvester's world is destroyed on the night of Lady Adriane's betrothal feast, when a group of Huns enter the house, slaughter most of the guests, and eventually carry the girl away. Silvester takes Bubba to go in search of Adriane. They are joined by Holy John, who uses unorthodox methods in trying to convert the Huns to Christianity. The three are successful in finding and freeing the Lady Adriane. However, the real accomplishment of the quest is the freeing of Silvester from his literal and psychological bondage to slavery. Gradually, as he learns to act and think like a free man, he loses "the look of a slave." This is a heady tale, rich in humor, high adventure, imagination, and historical detail.

VIKING ADVENTURES

While ancient civilizations flourished and decayed in Egypt, Greece, and Rome, the beginnings of European history were just stirring in England, Scotland, and the Scandinavian countries. The stories of the Vikings are a part of the eerie half-light of the predawn of history, when facts were recorded only in legend and song. In *Viking Adventure*, Clyde Bulla has made the Vikings live for 8- and 9-year-olds. This is the story of young Sigurd, who joins the crew of a ship that sails to verify Leif Ericson's discovery of Wineland a century earlier. After enduring the hardships of the voyage, and witnessing the treacherous murder of his captain, Sigurd escapes from the ill-fated ship and is the only survivor of the trip to the New World. Returning home at last, he asks the old bard to instruct him in writing and reading so that he may record for others what he has seen.

Erik Haugaard has written two superb stories of the Vikings that sing with the cadences of traditional sagas—*Hakon of Rogen's Saga* and *A Slave's Tale*. In the first story Hakon is sure that his island home, Rogen, is indestructible—had it not been in his family for nine generations? But his widowed father has rashly kidnapped a chieftain's daughter for his new bride. With the spring thaws comes vengeance, and Hakon is an orphan at the mercy of his evil uncle. Treated as one of his uncle's slaves, Hakon hides in the mountains while Rark and others loyal to his father come to his aid. At last, grown wise beyond his years, Hakon achieves his birthright along with his manhood. Having tasted the bitter gall of enslavement, his first act is to free Helga, the slave girl with whom he had been reared, saying:

> That is everyone's birthright, his freedom, and the gods have only one message for us, that we must live.[11]

A Slave's Tale continues the story of Hakon and Helga. Anxious to keep his word to Rark, to return the former slave to his homeland, Hakon embarks for Brittany. Helga, determined not to be left alone, stows away on board the ship. All goes well

---

[10]Elizabeth George Speare, *The Bronze Bow* (Boston: Houghton Mifflin, 1961), p. 224.

[11]Erik Christian Haugaard, *Hakon of Rogen's Saga*, illustrated by Leo and Diane Dillon (Boston: Houghton Mifflin, 1963), p. 132.

on the trip until they reach their destination. New priests do not trust the Vikings and unknowingly aid in a tragic plot to kill Rark and the others. Only Hakon, Helga, and two others make their escape to the ship and the handful of men left to guard it. The basic theme of *A Slave's Tale* is still freedom. Haugaard explores the various dimensions of enslavement: the slavery of the mind that will not let Helga forget that she was once a slave; or the slavery of power, the desire to possess all. These books speak to all ages, as profound in the depth of their darkness as in the extent of their light.

The well-known English writer Henry Treece has produced a number of stories about the Vikings, including a trilogy on the life of one warrior, *Viking's Dawn, The Road to Miklagaard,* and *Viking's Sunset.* Like Haugaard, Treece writes with a poetic terseness that captures the epic tone of the Old Norse sagas.

TALES OF EARLY BRITAIN

No one has surpassed Rosemary Sutcliff in her ability to re-create the life and times of early Britain. More remarkable, she writes of the native peoples of Britain and of the Roman occupation forces with equal skill and sympathy. *Song for a Dark Queen* tells of Boudicca, legendary Queen of the Iceni, who led a tribal revolt against the Romans in 62 A.D. Her motives are explained in terms of her fiery character and the ways of her tribe; for since the Iceni apparently passed royal lineage from mother to daughter, Boudicca's mistreatment at the hands of Roman officials and the rape of her daughters are not just personal humiliations, but violations of the tribe. The fighting is cruel and bloody, the outcome devastating; but the narrator of the book, the Queen's Harper, balances the harshness of the tale with the lyricism of his telling.

In Sutcliff's *Frontier Wolf,* set nearly 300 years later at a Roman outpost near present-day Edinburgh, the point of view is that of Alexios, a young Roman officer who must earn the respect of the native British warriors in his new command among the troops known as Frontier Wolves. His friendship with the sons of a Clan chieftain comes to a tragic end when one of the brothers "borrows" a superior officer's horse. The conflict that follows becomes part of a larger uprising in which Alexios loses the fort but gains a reputation for courage and loyalty. This book stresses the demands of leadership and the value of respect and friendship.

The Eagle of the Ninth, The Silver Branch, and *The Lantern Bearers* form a trilogy that describes the period when Britain was ruled by Romans. In the third book the last of the Roman auxiliaries set sail in their galleys and abandon Britain to internal strife and the menace of invasion by Saxons. At the final moment, one Roman officer decides that his loyalties lie with Britain rather than the legions. Aquila returns to his family villa only to have all that he loves destroyed by the Saxons. His father is killed, his sister captured, and he is enslaved by a band of invaders. Three years later he escapes his thralldom, but it is many years before he can rid himself of the black bitterness of his sister's marriage to a Saxon. At last, Aquila finds a measure of contentment, learned partly from the kind and gentle Brother Ninnias, partly from the loving loyalty of his British wife, Ness, lastly for his part in saving his sister's son, an enemy Saxon. As Aquila looks to the future, his old friend reflects his thoughts and the theme of this fine book:

> I sometimes think that we stand at sunset. . . It may be that the night will close over us in the end, but I believe that morning will come again. Morning always grows again out of the darkness, though maybe not for the people who saw the sun go down. We are the Lantern Bearers, my friend; for us to keep something burning, to carry what light we can forward into the darkness and the wind.[12]

This is historical fiction that may cast a light into the shadows of the past and illuminate the path ahead, for there is always hope for the future in Rosemary Sutcliff's books.

MEDIEVAL TIMES AND TALES

In the Dark Ages, the chivalrous deeds of the knights were a window to the light. Young children of 7 and 8 are intrigued with stories of the days of knighthood. Some of them will be able to read Bulla's *Sword in the Tree,* which is the story

---

[12]Rosemary Sutcliff, *The Lantern Bearers,* illustrated by Charles Keeping (New York: Henry Z. Walck, 1959), pp. 250–251.

of a boy who saved his father and Weldon Castle by bravely going to King Arthur. Through treachery, Shan's uncle makes his own brother a captive and takes control of the castle. Remembering where he hid his father's sword in a tree, Shan establishes his identity as the rightful owner of Weldon Castle. This is an easy-reading book with excitement on every page. It has more than just a lively plot, however, for it presents an interesting picture of the justice of the time.

The entertainers of medieval times were minstrels, whose special way of life provides a natural frame for journey or chase stories. Thirteenth-century England is the setting for the Newbery award-winner *Adam of the Road* by Elizabeth Janet Gray. It is the story of Adam, his minstrel father Roger, and Adam's devoted dog Nick. Nick is stolen on their way to the great Fair of St. Giles. In the frantic chase that follows, Adam is separated from his father. It takes a whole long winter to find both Nick and Roger again. Adam has many adventures and some disasters, but he learns that the road is home to the minstrel and that people, generally, are kind.

A few early minstrels were women. When author Dorothy Van Woerkom learned that the court of King Edward I included two whose names were Pearl in the Egg and Matill Makejoye, she decided to write about the kind of lives they might have led. *Pearl in the Egg* is the story of a runaway orphaned serf girl who conceals herself in a minstrel troupe and there discovers her own musical talent. Her courage and compassion are shown when she risks discovery to secure help for a party of horsemen injured along the road, for one of them is Sir Geoffrey, her rightful owner. For her part in saving him she earns her freedom.

A traveling minstrel of a different sort, a charismatic musician with an uncanny ability to manipulate people, is the most compelling character in Gloria Skurzynski's *What Happened in Hamelin*. Research into the historical background of the Pied Piper legend undergirds this account of mass kidnapping in a German town in the year 1284. The story is narrated by Geist, the baker's apprentice, who is befriended by a flute-playing stranger called Gast. Gast is a plotter who convinces the boy to use tainted flour to bake treats for the town's children. Afterward Gast claims to ease their pain with his music, but instead lures them

Gloria Skurzynski's novel of the thirteenth century provides a plausible explanation for the Pied Piper legend. Jacket art by Friso Henstra.

away to be sold as serfs to a distant nobleman. This story is as fascinating as the piper's tunes in its creation of plausible motives and explanations for the legend. Parallels with modern child abuse, misuse of drugs, and large-scale fraud might be discovered by older students discussing this novel.

Marguerite de Angeli has written many books, but her finest is *The Door in the Wall*, a Newbery award-winner. Setting the book in fourteenth-century England, de Angeli has painted in words and pictures the dramatic story of Robin, crippled son of Sir John de Bureford. Robin is to become a page to Sir Peter de Lindsay. He becomes ill with a strange malady, however, and is taken to the monastery by Brother Luke. There, Robin learns many things: to whittle, to swim, to read, to write, and above all to have patience—all "doors in the wall," according to Brother Luke. For:

> Whether thou'lt walk soon I know not. This I know. We must teach thy hands to be skilled in many ways, and we must teach thy mind to go about whether thy legs will carry thee or no. For reading is another door in the wall, dost understand, my son?[13]

Robin does learn to walk, but only with the aid of the crutches that he makes with his own hands. When he is well enough to travel, Brother Luke takes him to Sir Peter's castle. Robin is fearful of the reception a page on crutches might receive, but Sir Peter assures him that there are many ways to serve. It is during a siege of the castle that Robin finds a way to aid the king. Finally, Robin, or Sir Robin as he becomes for his exploits, is reunited with his father and mother. Robin's rebellion, final acceptance, and then challenge to live a rich life *with* his handicap should provide inspiration for children today.

THE EMERGENCE OF MODERN EUROPE

Poland is the setting for Eric Kelly's Newbery award-winner *The Trumpeter of Krakow*. This is a complex tale of the quest for the shimmering Great Tarnov Crystal, coveted by a Tartar chieftain for supposed magical powers and zealously guarded by the ancestral oath of a Ukrainian family. Joseph and Elzbietka save the crystal through their knowledge of history. Ever since the Tartars had sacked the city of Krakow in 1241, the Trumpeter had ended the Heynal on a broken note to commemorate the steadfast soldier of that time who defiantly played the hourly hymn and was killed in the midst of his playing. The year is now 1461 and once again the Tartars are in the city. This time it is only a small band of them who are seeking the Tarnov Crystal, but they have captured Joseph's father. When it is the time of the second hour, Joseph is allowed to play the Heynal so no one will suspect anything is wrong. Joseph, however, signals for help by playing the hymn through to its completion, something that had not been done for 200 years. The background of fifteenth-century Eastern Europe is vividly portrayed.

In *A Boy of Old Prague*, Ish-Kishor has told the grim story of a sensitive, intelligent, but quite uneducated peasant boy, Tomas, who grows up accepting without question the harshness of the sixteenth-century feudal system in Poland. Tomas is equally accepting of all that he hears about the Jews in the Ghetto, believing them to be the foredoomed property of the Devil. Imagine his horror, then, when he is caught stealing a roast chicken from the kitchen for his ill and starving mother and is sentenced to act as a bond servant to an old Jew in the Ghetto. However, Reb Pesach and his beautiful granddaughter Rachel are kind to Tomas. Gradually, the boy allows himself to think and feel as his heart tells him. After a cruel pogrom of the Jews instigated by the young lord whose affections Rachel had rejected, Tomas searches for "his family" amidst the bodies on the streets and those left charred by the human bonfire in the marketplace. He clings to the hope that some of the Jews escaped and ends his story with a moving plea for understanding that speaks as forcefully to our times as it does to sixteenth-century Prague:

> Perhaps some day I shall find them again. . . I shall find them and I shall help them and work for them with my two strong hands, and among us we shall learn that the god of mercy is the same God, no matter where we find him.[14]

The political and personal intrigues surrounding the imprisonment of Mary, Queen of Scots are the focus of Mollie Hunter's *You Never Knew Her As I Did!* The narration is in the voice of young Will Douglas, page to the queen's custodian at the island castle of Lochleven. The action centers on attempts by Mary's supporters to rescue her and ends with a moment of triumph as she rides free before the battle that is to decide her fate. But the book is actually Will's memoir; and his postscript, which mentions her long captivity in England, is full of grief at the news of her death. Hunter's interpretation of the tragic queen leaves the reader with an appreciation for her matchless courage, unusual beauty, and ability to command the devotion of her followers.

---

[13]Marguerite de Angeli, *The Door in the Wall* (New York: Doubleday, 1949), p. 28.

[14]Sulamith Ish-Kishor, *A Boy of Old Prague*, illustrated by Ben Shahn (New York: Pantheon, 1963), p. 90.

Erik Haugaard has written two fine stories set at the time of the English Civil War. Both *A Messenger for Parliament* and its sequel, *Cromwell's Boy*, are framed as the memoirs of Oliver Cutter of Boston, who rode as a messenger and spy for the Parliamentary army and then for Oliver Cromwell himself. On one level these are satisfying personal stories of a motherless boy with a ne'er-do-well father who finds amidst his adventures the warmth and loyalty of new comrades as well as an heroic father-figure in Cromwell. On another level they are a record of the politics and conflict of the time, presenting the case for the Parliamentary rebellion, but not glossing over the suffering that it brought. Haugaard's books consistently emphasize the grief war brings to common people. This theme is eloquently stated in *Cromwell's Boy* by young Oliver's friend, a blacksmith:

> "The high and mighty never ask what they trample down. . . Sometimes I think that if they left us alone, we would be better off. But they never will. The world is the anvil, and they are the hammer, and we are in between, getting all the blows."[15]

Leon Garfield writes with similar excitement about life in England during the eighteenth century. While he captures the flavor of the times and vividly describes the grim social conditions of the poor, he does not include any known historical events. Rather, his books have a Dickensian flavor compounded of violence, suspense, and intrigue. *Smith* is the story of a 12-year-old pickpocket in the grimy, shadow-filled underworld of eighteenth-century London. *Jack Holborn* is a story of a young orphan seeking his identity. He stows away on a ship attacked by pirates, endures bloody battles and a terrible shipwreck, marches through the sodden jungles of Africa, and witnesses the horrors of a slave market and a murder trial at Old Bailey in London. There is no doubt that these are exaggerated, swashbuckling tales, yet Garfield is a masterful storyteller. The larger-than-life drama reminds one of the Gothic novels of Joan Aiken. In contrast to Aiken's books, however, Garfield provides a real eighteenth-century setting. Certainly readers would get a feel for the times: its cruelty to children, the poor, and prisoners; its lawlessness; and its daily life.

A younger audience can get a taste of Garfield's distinctive style in *Fair's Fair*, a brief Christmas-time story with a Victorian setting. This rags-to-riches tale begins:

> Jackson was thin, small and ugly, and stank like a drain. He got his living by running errands, holding horses, and doing a bit of scrubbing on the side. And when he had nothing better to do he always sat on the same doorstep at the back of Paddy's Goose, which was at the worst end of the worst street in the worst part of town.[16]

One of the few stories of early Russia for English-speaking children is E. M. Almedingen's *The Crimson Oak*. A peasant boy named Peter has a chance encounter with the exiled Princess Elizabeth, saving her from the charge of a bear, but must wait for her return to power before speaking of his deed. The political climate of Russia in 1740 is repressive; Almedingen's characters speak with fear and hatred of the Secret Chancery that enforces its own punitive rule. Peter is caught up in this nightmare of injustice when his great desire to learn to read brings him to the attention and the suspicion of the Chancery. Arrested, beaten, and imprisoned in a dungeon without trial, the boy does learn his letters from a fellow prisoner. Peter's eventual rescue is dramatic, and his second meeting with Elizabeth, now the empress, brings more reward than he had hoped, for she promises that he will go to school. Grim moments in this book are balanced by the dream-come-true ending and the presence of compassionate characters who care about Peter and his cause.

Stories of the New World

COLONIAL AMERICA

The varied settings and conflicts of colonial America have inspired an unusually large number of books about this period. *A Lion to Guard Us* by Clyde Bulla tells of three motherless London children who sail to Jamestown in hopes of finding

[15]Erik Christian Haugaard, *Cromwell's Boy* (Boston: Houghton Mifflin, 1978), pp. 206–207.

[16]Leon Garfield, *Fair's Fair*, illustrated by S. D. Schindler (New York: Doubleday, 1983), unpaged.

their father, who has gone ahead to the new colony. When the ship is wrecked in a storm near Bermuda, the children manage to save their own treasure from home, a lion's head door knocker. The voyagers survive on the bounty of the island while other ships are built to take them to Virginia. There the children do find their father, weak and ill, one of the few who survived the Starving Time of 1609–1610. Young Jemmy hangs the lion's head on a peg above the door latch, a symbol of home. The story is told in a straightforward way, centering on Amanda, the oldest child, whose earnest efforts keep the family together. The carefully limited historical detail and simple writing style make this book a real find for readers as young as 7 or 8.

Many informational books tell us what the Pilgrims did, but there are few records that tell how they felt about what they did. *The Thanksgiving Story* by Alice Dalgliesh details the life of one family on the *Mayflower*, including their hardships on the voyage and during their first winter. It tells, too, of joy in the arrival of their new baby, of spring in their new home, of planting, harvest, and giving thanks. The large stylized pictures by Helen Sewell capture the spirit of American primitive paintings. Meadowcroft's book, *The First Year*, describes the hardships of the Pilgrims in a way that makes them real people to 7- and 8-year-olds.

Eight-year-old Love Brewster provides a glimpse of many of the Pilgrims, or "Saints" as they preferred to be called, in his description of his family's life in *The House on Stink Alley* by F. N. Monjo. This book presents the Pilgrims as refugees in Leyden, Holland, just before they sailed to America. It is an unusual view of the Plymouth settlers, with Love's innocent voice giving poignant emphasis to the dangers and injustices faced by his printer father and the other dissenters. Robert Quackenbush's illustrations take their heavy style and grim content (including hangings and beheadings) from woodcuts of the time.

One of the liveliest stories about the Pilgrims is *Constance: A Story of Early Plymouth* by Patricia Clapp. Written in the form of a diary, the story of Constance Hopkins, daughter of Stephen Hopkins, begins in November of 1620 on the deck of the *Mayflower* and ends seven years later with her marriage in Plymouth to Nicholas Snow. Constance describes the grim first winter at Plymouth with its fear of the Indians, the deaths of many of the colonists, and the difficulties with the English backers of the settlement. The device of a diary allows the author to use first-person narrative, which creates an immediate identification of the reader with Constance. An excellent romance, this story reminds one of *The Witch of Blackbird Pond* by Speare, but is all the more fascinating for being the story of real people.

The Puritans soon forgot their struggle for religious freedom as they persecuted others who did not follow their beliefs or ways. Older girls will thoroughly enjoy the superb story of *The Witch of Blackbird Pond* written by Elizabeth Speare. Flamboyant, high-spirited Kit Tyler is a misfit in the Puritan household of her aunt and stern-faced uncle. For Kit is as different from her colorless cousins as the bleak barren shore of Wethersfield, Connecticut, differs from the shimmering turquoise bay of Barbados that had been her home for sixteen years. The only place in which Kit feels any peace or freedom is in the meadows near Blackbird Pond. And it is here that she meets the lonely bent figure of Quaker Hannah, regarded as a witch by the colonists. Here, too, Kit meets Nathaniel Eaton, the sea captain's son, with his mocking smile and clear blue eyes. Little Prudence, a village child, also comes to the sanctuary in the meadows. One by one, outraged townspeople put the wrong things together and the result is a terrifying witch hunt and trial. The story is fast-paced and the characters are drawn in sharp relief against a bleak New England background.

Although the subject is the same, the tone of *Tituba of Salem Village* by Petry is as forbidding as the rotten eggs found on the steps of the bleak parsonage the day that the Reverend Samuel Parris, his family and slaves, John and Tituba, arrive in Salem Village in 1692. Tituba, too, has come from sunny Barbados and then been sold as a slave to a self-seeking, pious minister. The fact that Tituba is both a slave and a black makes her particularly vulnerable to suspicion and attack from the obsessed witch-hunters in Salem. A sense of foreboding, mounting terror, and hysteria fills this story of great evil done in the name of God.

A different look at the Salem witch trials is provided by Patricia Clapp in *Witches' Children*. The first-person narrator is Mary Warren, a bond servant and one of ten girls who are "possessed."

Mary admits to herself that the ravings began as "sport," a way to vent boredom and high spirits, and grew into group hysteria. When she tries to explain, she is not believed and is herself accused. In spite of the grim subject the story moves at a fast and readable pace. A comparison of *Tituba of Salem Village* with *Witches' Children* would provoke much critical thinking by mature readers, especially in considering the two characterizations of Tituba.

During the eighteenth century, colonists pushed farther and farther into the wilderness. Many favorite stories have been set within this background. Jean Fritz has written the poignant story of lonely 10-year-old Ann Hamilton, who was the only girl in the wilderness of early western Pennsylvania. The title of this book, *The Cabin Faced West*, characterizes Ann's father's attitude toward the family's new adventure. They were not to look back to the past, but forward; and so he built the cabin facing west. Ann grows to hate the word "someday," as she hears it again and again. Someday she will have books to read; someday they will have windows in the cabin; and someday there will be a special occasion to use the linen tablecloth and the lavender flowered plates. All the "somedays" seem so very far away to Ann. At last, however, a special occasion does happen. George Washington stops at the Hamilton cabin for dinner. Ann wears ribbons in her hair and sets the table in the way she has longed to do. This final episode is based on fact and really happened to Ann Hamilton, who was the author's great-great-grandmother.

Another lonely girl has been immortalized for children of 7 and 8 by Alice Dalgliesh in her popular book, *The Courage of Sarah Noble*. This is the true and inspiring story of 8-year-old Sarah, who accompanies her father into the wilderness to cook for him while he builds a cabin for their family. Many times Sarah has to remind herself of her mother's final words to her when she left home: "Keep up your courage, Sarah Noble!" Sarah has reason to remember when she hears the wolves howl outside the campfire or when alone one day she is suddenly surrounded by Indian children. The real test of her courage is faced when her father tells her that he must leave her with Tall John, a friendly Indian, while he returns to Massachusetts for the rest of the family. Symbolic of Sarah's courage is the cloak that Sarah's mother had fastened around her just before she left home. When her family are finally reunited in their new home in the wilderness, Sarah is secure in the knowledge that she has "kept up her courage."

The situation in *The Sign of the Beaver* by Elizabeth George Speare is much like that of Sarah Noble's story, as young Matt is left to tend the new cabin in Maine territory while his father goes back to Massachusetts for the rest of the family. Matt eventually learns essential survival skills from Attean, grandson of the chief of the Beaver clan. The story explores their growing friendship, their changing attitudes, and the shifting balance between their two cultures. (See Chapter 12 for a Web of discussion and extension ideas on this book.)

Other books, like *The Matchlock Gun* by Walter D. Edmonds, show that the differences between white and Native American people could not always be bridged. This book, based on the experiences of a Dutch family living in the Hudson Valley in 1756, focuses on the terror as well as the courage of settlers who were victims of fierce Indian raids. This is much more than an exciting adventure story in which a child kills three marauders to protect his baby sister and wounded mother. The characters are very real and true to life. Readers sense the anxiety of the parents when they hear of the Indian raid and can share the fear that seems to fill the silence in the tiny cabin:

> There was only the note of the wind in the chimney and the feeling of it on the roof, like a hand pressed down out of darkness. It was easy to think of it passing through the wet woods, rocking the bare branches where only the beech trees had leaves to shake.[17]

This story, which won the Newbery award in 1941, has since been criticized for presenting the Indians as bloodthirsty savages and for having a child shoot them. Obviously, this account of events is told from the colonists' point of view. Other stories, representing an Indian point of view, will be discussed in the section on American Indians.

Two books by Avi dramatize the plight of inden-

---

[17]Walter D. Edmonds, *The Matchlock Gun*, illustrated by Paul Lantz (New York: Dodd, Mead, 1941), p. 14.

tured servants in colonial America and the problems of conscience caused by their attempted escape. In *Night Journeys*, orphaned Peter York is taken into the family of Mr. Shinn, a stern Pennsylvania Quaker who is a Justice of the Peace. Peter helps him search for two escaped bondsmen and is distressed to find that they are both children. Peter is finally able to help both runaways get safely past the searchers. In the brief but moving resolution Peter finds that his Quaker guardian has shared his compassion for the unfortunate children and will welcome him home with real affection. The sequel, *Encounter at Easton*, tells what happened to the escapees through the device of testimony at a trial. This book has suspense, adventure, and a tragic ending. Both are strong in creating a sense of the times and the terrain with its rugged beauty and ghostly fogs.

THE REVOLUTIONARY ERA

One of the best-known stories of the American Revolution for children is *Johnny Tremain* by Esther Forbes. Johnny Tremain is a silversmith's apprentice, a conceited, cocky young lad who is good at his trade and knows it. The other apprentices are resentful of his overbearing manner and determined to get even with him. Their practical joke has disastrous results, and Johnny's hand is maimed for life. Out of a job and embittered, Johnny joins his friend Rab and becomes involved in pre-Revolutionary activities. As a dispatch rider for the Committee of Public Safety he meets such men as Paul Revere, John Hancock, and Samuel Adams. Slowly, gradually, Johnny regains his self-confidence and overcomes his bitterness. Rab is killed in the first skirmish of the Revolution, and Johnny is crushed, but not completely. Somehow, this greatest of blows makes him a man of fortitude and courage, a new man of a new nation.

For Johnny Tremain, the decision to join the Patriot cause was clear. In many other books, because the Loyalist tradition and point of view are presented in a more compelling way, the characters are perceived to have a more difficult choice. In *John Treegate's Musket* by Leonard Wibberly, the title character is a solid citizen of Boston who has fought for his king at the Battle of Quebec. Not until he sees hundreds of troops marching through a peaceful countryside to seize two men does he arm himself and join his son Peter to fight the British at the Battle of Bunker Hill. In *Early Thunder* by Jean Fritz, 14-year-old Daniel adopts his father's loyalty to the king. Daniel hates the rowdy Liberty Boys who creep up on Tory porches and distribute their "Liberty Gifts" of garbage or manure, but becomes equally disillusioned by the British attitudes. Daniel's struggle to sort out his loyalties will help children see that issues in war are seldom clear-cut.

My Brother Sam Is Dead by the Colliers tells of conflicting loyalties within a family and the injustices that are always inflicted upon the innocent in time of war. Sam is the only member of his Connecticut family who is fighting for the rebel cause. Ironically, it is Sam who is falsely accused of stealing his own cattle and is executed as an example of General Putnam's discipline. No one will believe the real facts of the case, for despite Sam's excellent war record, his family are Tories. This story takes on special poignancy because it is told by the younger brother, Tim, who loves and admires Sam.

Some of the same dreams of glory that drew Sam into the Patriot army plague 13-year-old Jonathan in *The Fighting Ground* by Avi. In 1778, near Trenton, Jonathan desperately wants to be in on the "cannons and flags and drums and dress parades. . . . O Lord, he said to himself, make it something *grand!*"[18] Sent to find if the tolling bell at the tavern means bad news, Jonathan agrees to go with a few volunteers to head off a small band of approaching enemy soldiers. Caught up in a real battle and captured by Hessians who seem no worse than the Patriot corporal who enlisted his aid, Jonathan does not know which way to turn. The action takes place in little more than one day, with the text divided into many short segments labeled as to the hour and minute. This makes the book look simpler than it is, for although the print is not dense on the page, there are strong emotional demands on the reader.

On Ocracoke, off the North Carolina coast, the islanders have no intention of taking part in the war at all. Then British raiders steal the community pigs and murder the deaf-mute woman who tended them. Angered, the islanders vow to retaliate by donating their two precious barrels of salt

[18]Avi, *The Fighting Ground* (New York: Lippincott, 1984), p. 9.

In *This Time, Tempe Wick*, a spunky young girl prevents mutinous Revolutionary soldiers from taking her horse by hiding it in her bedroom! Illustration by Margot Tomes from the book by Patricia Lee Gauch.

to the American army at Valley Forge. Daring boatman Erskin Midgett is chosen to get them there by way of Pamlico Sound and Chesapeake Bay. When he decides to take his son along, the conflict becomes *George Midgett's War* in Sally Edwards' tale of a treacherous journey through poorly charted territory and a special relationship between a man and his son. The Midgetts' story serves as a reminder that some choices in wartime are made on the basis of personal loyalties rather than devotion to a cause.

The title character in Scott O'Dell's *Sarah Bishop* hates war, and with good reason. Her father, a British Loyalist, dies after being tarred and feathered by Patriot sympathizers. Her brother dies on a British prison ship, and Sarah herself is arrested on a false pretense. She escapes and flees to the Connecticut wilderness, where she struggles against the elements instead of soldiers. Her biggest battle is with herself, however, as she brings herself to face the world of towns and people once again. This story is based on the experiences of a real Sarah Bishop during the Revolutionary period.

Not all young women saw themselves as defenseless victims, however. One of the most unusual stories from this period is *I'm Deborah Sampson: A Soldier in the War of the Revolution*. Patricia Clapp's novel closely follows the real-life adventures of a young New England woman who, posing as a man, served for more than a year in the Continental army. She lived in the men's barracks, fought in several skirmishes, and was wounded—all undetected until she was hospitalized and mistaken for dead in a Philadelphia epidemic. Another little-known story of the American Revolution is that of a spunky young girl named Tempe Wick, who hid her horse in her bedroom for three days to save it from Revolutionary soldiers looting the countryside around their New Jersey camp. Finally, when a soldier demanded to search the house, the feisty Tempe threw him out in the snow. This humorous legend of the Revolutionary War is told by Patricia Lee Gauch in a brief book, *This Time, Tempe Wick?*

Few stories are available about the role of blacks during the Revolutionary era. The Collier brothers

JUMP SHIP TO FREEDOM

James Lincoln Collier · Christopher Collier

A black youth's winning of justice for himself is set against the failure of the Constitutional Convention to abolish slavery. Jacket illustration by Gordon Crabb.

have featured black characters in several books, however, including a trilogy that deals with the wartime problems of blacks in the Northern colonies and their futile hope for a guarantee of liberty under the new government. In *Jump Ship to Freedom* the memory of the late Jack Arabus, who had won his freedom in the courts as a result of his service in the Continental army, serves as inspiration for his son Dan. The boy's first problem is keeping the soldiers' notes earned by Jack to buy his family's freedom away from Captain Ivers and his greedy wife. Even if the notes can be saved, they may be worth nothing under the terms of the new Constitution just being written. Exciting action brings Dan as a messenger to the site of the Constitutional Convention. Because he is bringing important word about the slavery compromise (which will, ironically, set up a fugitive slave law),

he gets to meet George Washington, Alexander Hamilton, and other statesmen. He is also threatened by Captain Ivers, but a friendly Congressman intervenes to arrange Dan's freedom. This book has a strong theme in Dan's growing belief in himself and his abilities. The other titles in this trilogy are *War Comes to Willy Freeman* and *Who Is Carrie?*, each featuring a young black woman as the central character. In all their books, the Colliers provide detailed authors' notes to explain their background sources. For this series the notes also explain their choice of language, including the liberal use of the term "nigger" in dialogue.

Novels about Revolutionary America offer an intriguing variety of points of view. Individual books will help children feel the intense emotions of the time, but the impact of several read for comparison and contrast will be much greater. Children can also increase their frame of pertinent information about a time period in this way. Knowing more background each time, they will read each succeeding book with greater ease.

AMERICAN INDIANS

In earlier stories the American Indians are often seen as cruel, bloodthirsty savages attacking small groups of helpless settlers. The provocation for the attacks is seldom given. Thus, in Edmonds' story *The Matchlock Gun*, the reader can only guess the Indians' reasons for wounding Edward's mother and burning their cabin. In Field's *Calico Bush*, the Indians seem equally cruel as they burn the settler's house. Other stories, however, such as *The Ice Trail* by Crompton, portray Indians in more three-dimensional terms, showing their amazing generosity in some situations, their integrity, and the motivation for many of their actions. Finally, in a few books like Baker's *Killer-of-Death*, O'Dell's *Sing Down the Moon*, and Highwater's *Legend Days*, the shocking story of the white man's destruction of the Indians' way of life is told from the Indian perspective.

Many stories that present fully developed Indian characters are of white captives who observe and gradually come to appreciate the Indian way of life. Seven- and 8-year-old boys and girls thoroughly enjoy Anne Colver's *Bread and Butter Indian*. Too young to understand her parents' fear of Indians, Barbara befriends a hungry Indian, offering him the bread and butter with which she was having a tea party for her imaginary friends. One evening at dusk, Barbara is kidnapped by a strange Indian. How the "bread and butter" Indian comes to her rescue makes a satisfying, exciting climax. Williams' illustrations of the simple joys of a pioneer child are as warm and reassuring as this story of an incident that really happened. The story of this family is continued in *Bread and Butter Journey*. A story of Indian capture for more mature readers is *Calico Captive* by Elizabeth Speare. This fictionalized account of several captives taken to Montreal and sold as slaves is based on a diary kept in 1754.

In *The Ice Trail*, Anne Eliot Crompton has told the story of an Abenaki captive near Lake Champlain in the early 1700s. Called Tanial by his captors, Daniel Abbott has lived for five years with the family of Awasos, who had saved his life during the raid in which the boy's brother and sister were killed. Tanial comes to share the Indians' view of white people in general:

> They were rough giants, loud, harsh, even to each other. They gave nothing away, even to the needy ones among them. Each family lived in its own closed house, hoarding goods and food to itself.[19]

Even though the Abenakis are generous and loyal, Daniel secretly longs to feel safe among his own kind. When Awasos does not return from the hunt and another brave proudly displays the unusual "axes" he has earned in a trade, Daniel recognizes a means for escape. The blades are ice skates, and Daniel, unlike the Indians, knows how to use them. Based on the legendary account of an Indian captive from New Hampshire, this book stands out for the quality of its writing and for the characterization of Daniel/Tanial as a product of two cultures.

Conrad Richter's classic story of a young Indian captive, *The Light in the Forest*, was written for adults but has been enjoyed by older children. In this story True Son, a white boy reared by an Indian chief, is forced to return to his original home. His love and loyalty for his Indian parents and his rejection of the white man's civilization arouse heart-wrenching conflicts. Although he runs away and rejoins the Indians, he betrays the tribe and is condemned to die. His Indian father rescues him but imposes the most severe punishment of all—banishment from the tribe and the forest forever. Forced back to the white man's trail, the boy, who truly felt he was Indian, faces unbearable loneliness:

> Ahead of him ran the rutted road of the whites. It led, he knew, to where men of their own volition constrained themselves with heavy clothing like harness, where men chose to be slaves to their own or another's property and followed empty and desolate lives far from the wild beloved freedom of the Indian.[20]

The sense of inevitable tragedy that governs the end of this book is in marked contrast to the hopeful resolution of *The Ice Trail*.

One of the most popular stories about Indians is Scott O'Dell's Newbery award book, *Island of the Blue Dolphins*. Based on fact, the story concerns Karana, an Indian girl who lived alone on an island off the coast of California for some eighteen years. Following an attack by Aleuts who had come to kill otters, all of Karana's people leave their island home by boat. When Karana realizes her young brother is left on the island, she jumps overboard and returns to him. Within a few hours the boy is killed by wild dogs, and memories of the tribe are all Karana has left. Despite her despair when she realizes the boat will not return, Karana creates a life for herself. She makes a house and utensils, and fashions weapons, although in so doing she violates a taboo. Eventually she makes friends with the leader of the dog pack, and thereafter enjoys his protection and companionship. When Spanish priests "rescue" Karana, she leaves in sadness. The reader may question whether she will find as much happiness at the mission with human companionship as she had known alone on the island. The question is answered in a sequel, *Zia*, in which Karana's last days are witnessed through the eyes of her niece.

A moving story of Apache rivalry with the white man is paralleled by an inner story of conflict between two young boys in *Killer-of-Death* by Bet-

---

[19]Anne Eliot Crompton, *The Ice Trail* (New York: Methuen, 1980), p. 13.

[20]Conrad Richter, *The Light in the Forest* (New York: Knopf, 1953), p. 179.

ty Baker. The long feud between the medicine man's son and Killer-of-Death quickly disappears when they see most of their people killed like rabbits at the feast the white trader has planned so carefully. Broken and disheartened, the remnants of the tribe are moved to a reservation. The missionary asks Killer-of-Death to send his son to the white man's school. For two days the father fasts. He waits for the spirits to speak his name and to provide an answer. Finally, the sign comes in the brilliant dawn of the new day. Might there be a renewal of the people in the same way? Killer-of-Death makes his decision: he will send his son to school.

Scott O'Dell's title *Sing Down the Moon* takes on tragic significance when compared to the Southwest Indians' creation myths which tell of "singing up the mountains." O'Dell's book describes the "Long Walk," the disastrous 300-mile forced march of the Navajo from their canyon homes to Fort Sumner. Held as virtual prisoners from 1863 to 1865, more than 1,500 of the Navajos died, and many others lost the will to live. This moving story is told from the point of view of Bright Morning, who somehow maintains her hope for a better future. Tall Boy, the proud and handsome youth who is to become her husband, was once wounded by a Spaniard's bullet, but being held in the American fort causes an even greater injury to his spirit. Only through Bright Morning's urging does he make the effort to escape. The young couple return to a cave in their familiar canyon to begin a new life with the son that is born to them. This is a haunting story told in spare prose that reflects the dignity of the Navajo people.

In *Only Earth and Sky Last Forever* by Nathaniel Benchley, Dark Elk, a fictional character, moves through real events. Written for older children, this is the first-person account of a youth who wants only to live free and unshackled on the remaining Indian land and marry Lashuka. He joins Crazy Horse's troops in order to prove himself a warrior worthy of her. Jubilant with the knowledge that Long Hair and his men have been "rubbed out" at Little Big Horn, Dark Elk helps to pursue some of Major Reno's men who are hiding across the river. He discovers the damage done to one of the Indian camps, and finds that tragically, Lashuka is among the dead.

Jamake Highwater brings his own strong cultural perspective and gift for vivid language to a powerful novel of the Northern Plains Indians, *Legend Days,* the first book of the Ghost Horse Cycle. The central character, Amana, is a girl who attains adolescence and young adulthood while the buffalo herds dwindle and her people are no longer able to withstand white traders, settlers, soldiers, and government. Told to run and hide from the hideous smallpox that kills almost everyone in the winter camp, Amana survives and is given a vision that fills her with the power and the song of the fox. These sacred gifts that enable her to hunt or to go to war eventually bring her legendary status among her people. But when her elderly husband is trampled by buffalo, she is left with no family and no one to take her in, for the men consider her responsible for her husband's death. To Amana, abandoned, only the symbolic appearance of a fox suggests any hope of survival. This grim story is infused with the spiritual strength of Amana and her people. The characters' visionary experiences are not set apart from the other events of their lives. This lack of separation between the spiritual and material embodies an Indian point of view. The aged Crow Woman mourns the breakdown of this relationship between the people and their world:

"... I do not want to see my people fading away day by day. I would rather be free of this bad life. I would rather remember the land as it was when I was a girl: when each tree told me its secret and the animals gave us power and vision."[21]

Mature readers will also enjoy the highly fictionalized biography of *Ishi, Last of His Tribe* by Theodora Kroeber. Most of the Yahi Indians of California had been killed or driven from their homes by the invading gold-seekers and settlers during the early 1900s. A small band resisted their fate by living in concealment; but everywhere it seemed that Saldu (white people) had come. One by one Ishi's family dies, and, at last, he is the lone survivor of his tribe. Hungry and ill, he allows himself to be found. Haltingly, he tells his story to an anthropologist who takes him to live at the

21Jamake Highwater, *Legend Days* (New York: Harper & Row, 1984), p. 140.

University of California's museum. Here he dwells happily for five years helping to record the language and ways of the Yahi world.

THE AMERICAN FRONTIER

No other period in United States history has been more dramatized by films and television than that of the westward movement of the American pioneer. For this reason even 7-year-olds have some background for stories about the pioneers. One favorite for younger children is *Caroline and Her Kettle Named Maud* by Miriam E. Mason. Caroline is a pioneer tomboy who longs for a real gun for her birthday—like her seventeen uncles. Instead, she receives a copper kettle that proves just as effective as a gun in capturing the wolf that threatens the family cows.

Another book about a pioneer family that can be enjoyed by 8- and 9-year-olds is Susan Kirby's *Ike and Porker*. Eleven-year-old Isaac Burk wants to prove to his father that he can take his place with the other men on the yearly hog drive, and he dreams of carving "1837—Ike saw Chicago" on the log where he keeps track of special events. But when he starts off on his own with Porker, a favorite runt pig, he finds more danger on the trail than he had expected. Discovered and sent home, Ike is relieved to know that his father has a real concern for his safety.

In *The Lone Hunt,* William Steele writes vividly of a boy's yearning to take a man's part in the last buffalo hunt held in Tennessee in 1810. Ever since his father died, Yance Caywood has had to help his mother with fetching, carrying, and hoeing, while his older brother did the plowing and hunting. At last, Yance is allowed to go on the buffalo hunt, taking along his well-loved hound dog Blue. It is a long trail, and one by one the men drop out. When the snow begins, the last one turns back, but not Yance. His lone hunt through the wilderness takes courage, ingenuity, and fortitude. Yance kills his buffalo, but loses his dog to the frozen river. Pride in his accomplishment is overshadowed by his grief for his dog. Yance is grown up when he returns from the hunt. Other frontier stories by Steele include *Winter Danger, The Buffalo Knife, Flaming Arrows,* and *Trail through Danger.* His books include excitement, authentic detail, and much backwoods wisdom. Steele often wrote from a frontiersman's point of view about the conflicts between settlers and Indians, a common theme in pioneer stories.

By the mid-nineteenth century, the far western frontier was in California and Oregon. *Trouble for Lucy* by Carla Stevens uses information from first-person accounts of the Oregon Trail in 1843 to set the scene for each of its brief chapters. Appropriate for 8- and 9-year-old readers, the story focuses on Lucy's efforts to keep her fox terrier puppy from being a nuisance to the oxen and drivers. When he gets lost in a storm and Lucy follows, she and the pup are rescued by friendly Pawnees. Lucy's mother is too busy to scold her, however; she is having a baby in the family's covered wagon, which has been drawn out of the line of march and sits alone on the prairie. There is no pretending here that the pioneers' way was easy, yet the story is more concerned with the universal feelings of childhood than it is with hardship.

The story of a brother and sister who survive an Indian attack on a wagon train is told in Louise Moeri's *Save Queen of Sheba.* King David, 12 years old and named from the Bible, is injured and must struggle to keep going in the hope of finding his parents; the added burden of watching out for his little sister, Queen of Sheba, is almost too much. She is a character to be remembered for her petulance and her dangerously stubborn independence. When she manages to slip away from him, most readers of King David's age have no trouble sympathizing with his temptation to go on without her. This is a taut and suspenseful story of survival that has special intensity because the cast of characters is limited to two.

Kathryn Lasky's *Beyond the Divide* is a dramatic story for mature readers about an Amish father and daughter bound for the California Gold Rush. The plain ways of Meribah Simon, 14, are thought peculiar by some of her fellow travelers, but she makes many friends among them. The author creates a community of characters who bring very different pasts and problems to the challenging journey they share. Because they do seem like a community, it is all the more shocking that they should decide to abandon Will Simon along the trail when his wagon is disabled and he seems too weak to continue. Angry and disillusioned, Meribah elects to stay with her father. From that point the story hinges on her efforts to save him, and then herself. She is forced to shoot a mountain man who is about to attack her and fights off vultures to get food from the carcass of a deer. With help from a mapmaker who had traveled with the wagon train and from the gentle Indians of Mill Creek who feed her and take her in, Meribah does survive to choose for herself what sort of life she wants.

A less demanding story for older readers is Evelyn Sibley Lampman's *Bargain Bride,* which is set at the end of the way west, in Oregon Territory. Since married homesteaders are eligible for more land than single ones, young Ginny's guardians are able to profit from marrying her off at the age of 10 to a middle-aged farmer. But on her fifteenth birthday, when her husband comes to claim her, Ginny becomes a widow and discovers that property brings problems as well as status. The reader is shown a broad range of values in the frontier community, from independence and adventuring spirit to prejudice and pettiness. Despite some grim circumstances the tone of the book is upbeat, and there is a satisfying conclusion in which Ginny decides who will share her future.

The Texas frontier has provided a distinctive setting for many exciting stories. One of the best known is Gipson's *Old Yeller,* the story of a boy's integrity and love for his dog on an early Texas homestead. Patricia Beatty's *Wait for Me, Watch for Me, Eula Bee* takes place at the time of the Civil War, when the absence of men who had joined the Confederate army made West Texas homesteads especially vulnerable to Indian attack. Lewallen's mother, brother, and uncle are killed by Comanches, but he and his 3-year-old sister, Eula Bee, with her bouncy red curls that fascinate the warriors, are taken captive. When Lewallen manages at last to escape, he vows to return for his sister. Many months later he makes good his promise, but Eula Bee has forgotten him and has to be carried away, kicking and struggling. Long after they have reached safety, she is won to remembrance by the chance hearing of a song, the popular tune "Lorena," which Lewallen had whistled over and over during their captivity to assure her he was near.

Since civilization grows with a ragged edge, nineteenth-century frontier stories are set in widely scattered locations. Some settlers moved with the wilderness, like Pa Ingalls in what may be the best loved of all American historical fiction, the nine "Little House" books by Laura Ingalls Wilder. These stories describe the growing up of the Ingalls girls and the Wilder boys. In the first book of the series, *Little House in the Big Woods,* Laura is only 6 years old; the last three books—*Little Town on the Prairie, These Happy Golden Years,* and *The First Four Years*—tell of Laura's teaching career and her marriage. Based on the author's own life, these books portray the hardships and difficulties of pioneer life in the 1870s and 1880s and describe the fun and excitement that was also a part of daily living in those days. Throughout the stories the warmth and security of family love runs like a golden thread that binds the books to the hearts of their readers. There are floods, blizzards, grasshopper plagues, bears and Indians, droughts and the fear of starvation; but there is the wonderful Christmas when Laura receives her rag doll, the new house with real windows, trips to town, and dances. Best of all, there are the long winter evenings of firelight and the clear singing of Pa's fiddle. These mean love and security whether the home is in Wisconsin, the wild Kansas country, as described in *Little House on the Prairie,* in the Minnesota of *On the Banks of Plum Creek,* or *By the Shores of Silver Lake* in Dakota Territory. Children who read these books sense the same feelings of love and family solidarity experienced by Laura in the closing pages of *Little House in the Big Woods:*

> But Laura lay awake a little while, listening to Pa's fiddle softly playing and to the lovely sound of the wind in the Big Woods. She looked at Pa sitting on the bench by the hearth, the firelight gleaming on his brown hair and beard and glistening over the honey-brown fiddle. She looked at Ma, gently rocking and knitting.
>
> She thought to herself, "This is now."
>
> She was glad that the cosy house, and Pa and Ma and the firelight and the music, were now. They could not be forgotten, she thought, because now is now. It can never be a long time ago.[22]

The last book of the series describes *The First Four Years* following Laura's and Manley's marriage in

[22]Laura Ingalls Wilder, *The Little House in the Big Woods,* illustrated by Garth Williams (New York: Harper & Row, 1953, 1932), p. 238.

A tender Christmas scene exemplifies the warmth and simple joy of pioneer living.

1885. The manuscript for this story was found among Laura's papers after her death in 1957. Garth Williams has illustrated a uniform edition of all the books in the series. His black and white pictures capture the excitement and terror of many of the episodes in the books, but they also convey the tenderness, love, amusement, and courage that were necessary requisites to the life of the early settlers.

Another favorite book of pioneer days is *Caddie Woodlawn* by Carol Ryrie Brink. While this story takes place in the Wisconsin wilderness of the 1860s, it is primarily the story of the growing up of tomboy Caddie. She had been a frail baby, and so Caddie's father had persuaded her mother to allow her to be reared more freely than her older sister Clara, who was restricted by the rules of decorum for young ladies. Caddie was free to run about the half-wild Wisconsin frontier with her two brothers. Their escapades and adventures read like a feminine *Tom Sawyer*. Caddie is a self-willed, independent spirit who is assured a memorable place in children's literature. In a second edition of this classic pioneer story, illustrations by Trina Schart Hyman picture Caddie as a spirited young girl.

THE CIVIL WAR ERA

The Slavery Issue

Many stories of the pre-Civil War period relate to slavery and the activities of the Underground Railroad, when people faced the moral issue of breaking laws out of their compassion for humankind. F. N. Monjo titled his easy-reading book *The Drinking Gourd*, after the "code song" that the slaves sang. The song was used to point the direction for escape by following the North Star, using the Big Dipper as a guide. The words to the song are included in this short story of how a young mischievous boy helps a family on their way to freedom.

In Marguerite de Angeli's book *Thee, Hannah!*, a young Quaker girl helps a black mother and her child to safety. While Hannah is a Quaker, she does not willingly wear Quaker clothes. She particularly despises her stiff, drab bonnet that does not have flowers and a brightly colored lining like that of her friend Cecily. Yet it is her bonnet that identifies her as a Quaker and one who would be trusted to give aid to a runaway slave. Later, when the blacks are safe and tell Hannah this, Hannah's feelings toward her hated bonnet change.

In *Brady*, Jean Fritz tells the story of a very believable boy who discovers his father is an agent for the Underground Railway. His parents had not told him of their forbidden activities, for Brady just cannot keep a secret. However, Brady, always curious, discovers the secret for himself. On the very night that had been set to transfer a slave to the next station, his father suffers a broken leg during a fire in the barn. On his own, Brady carries out the plan for moving the slave. When his father hears of his son's resourcefulness, he asks for the family Bible and painstakingly writes the following inscription on the page reserved for significant events in family history: "On this day the barn burned down and Brady Minton did a man's work."[23]

A fugitive slave whom Catherine never meets brings changes to her life in *A Gathering of Days: A New England Girl's Journal, 1830–32* by Joan Blos. She and her friend Cassie agonize over a plea for help slipped into her writing book when she leaves it in the woods. They have heard about slavery and the abolition movement from their teacher, yet their activities are circumscribed by strict but loving families. Finally compassion and a sense of justice outweigh their respect for authority, and they leave food and a quilt where the fugitive will be sure to find them. Much later a packet arrives from Canada with a cryptic message and two bits of lace as a thank you; the runaway is safe and free. Meanwhile Catherine must piece a new quilt to replace the one she had given away. The story requires more of Catherine—she must learn to accept her father's new wife, bear Cassie's death, and take first steps toward a life of her own. This book, which won both the Newbery Medal and the American Book Award, uses the journal format for unusual authenticity. Catherine's vocabulary as well as the ideas and attitudes she reports are accurate reflections of the time and the rural New Hampshire setting.

Jessie Bollier is a 13-year-old white boy who is shanghaied in New Orleans and made to join the crew of a slave ship. In this grim story by Paula Fox, Jessie is forced to play his fife and "dance the slaves" so their muscles will remain strong and they will bring a higher price on the slave market. Jessie, *The Slave Dancer,* is young, innocent, and still capable of feeling shock. Everyone else on board the ship is so hardened as to be indifferent to human suffering. And this is the real message of the story, the utter degradation that eventually engulfs everyone connected with slavery—from the captain to the black Portuguese broker to the depraved Ben Stout and even to Jessie himself. For at one point Jessie is surprised to find himself hating the blacks; he is so sick of the sight, smell, and sound of their suffering that he wishes they did not exist. In one of the most compelling and symbolic scenes in the book Jessie is forced into the hold of the ship to look for his fife. Here he must touch, literally step on, the black bodies, so crowded together that there is no room to walk. Jessie's descent into that hold somehow represents the descent of the whole of humankind.

In her Newbery Medal acceptance speech, Paula Fox wrote about the theme of *The Slave Dancer:*

> Slavery engulfed whole peoples, swallowed up their lives, committed such offenses against their persons that in considering them, the heart falters, the mind recoils. . . .
>
> There are others who feel that black people can be only humiliated by being reminded that once they were brought to this country as slaves. But it is not the victim who is shamed. It is the persecutor who has refused the shame of what he has done and, as the last turn of the screw, would burden the victims with the ultimate responsibility of the crime itself.
>
> When I read the records of the past, . . . I perceived that the people who had spoken so long ago of every conceivable human loss were not only survivors, but pioneers of the human condition in inhuman circumstances.[24]

The Civil War

There are many fine stories for children about the Civil War itself. Most of these describe the war in terms of human issues and suffering, rather than political issues. One long-time favorite is William O. Steele's *The Perilous Road,* a thought-provoking story of a boy caught between the divided loyalties of the Civil War. Chris Brabson, not quite 12, lives in Tennessee and is certain that he hates the Union troops. When Yankee raiders steal his family's newly harvested crops, the Brabsons' only horse, and his new deerskin shirt, Chris is determined to have revenge. He reveals the position of a Union wagon train to a person he believes is a spy. Too late, he realizes that his brother, who is with the Union troops, could be with the group. Chris tries to find his brother to warn him and is caught in a bitter battle at dawn when the Confederates make a surprise attack. Chris realizes the full meaning of his father's words: "Like I told you before, war is the worst thing that can happen to

---

[23]Jean Fritz, *Brady,* illustrated by Lynd Ward (New York: Coward McCann, 1960), p. 219.

[24]Paula Fox, "Newbery Award Acceptance," *The Horn Book Magazine,* vol. 50 (August 1974), pp. 348, 349.

RECURRING THEMES IN HISTORICAL FICTION

THEME	TITLE/AUTHOR	SETTING
The clash of cultures	*The Faraway Lurs*, Behn	Prehistoric Denmark
	Frontier Wolf, Sutcliff	Roman Britain
	The Sign of the Beaver, Speare	Maine Territory, 1760s
	Children of the Wolf, Yolen	India, 1920s
The human cost of war	*Cromwell's Boy*, Haugaard	English Civil War
	My Brother Sam Is Dead, Collier and Collier	American Revolution
	The Slopes of War, Perez	U.S. Civil War
	The Eternal Spring of Mr. Ito, Garrigue	Canada, World War II
In quest of freedom	*The Dancing Bear*, Dickinson	Byzantium, 6th century
	Hakon of Rogen's Saga, Haugaard	Viking times
	Jump Ship to Freedom, Collier and Collier	U.S., 1780s
	North to Freedom, Holm	Europe, 1940s
Overcoming handicaps	*A Way of His Own*, Dyer	Prehistoric America
	The Stronghold, Hunter	Early Scotland (Orkney Islands)
	Door in the Wall, de Angeli	Medieval England
	Apple Is My Sign, Riskind	U.S., early 1900s

folks and the reason is it makes most everybody do things they shouldn't."[25]

Conflicting loyalties of a different sort are explored in Janet Hickman's *Zoar Blue*. In an Ohio village of German immigrants who share property communally and have strict religious principles, the question is whether allegiance to the Union can take precedence over responsibility to the community. Despite bitter family feelings, John Keffer is one of a few young men who run away to join the Union army. His story is intertwined with that of an orphaned girl, Barbara, who has been brought up by the Zoarites but who has also run away, hoping for a better life with relatives in Pennsylvania. The two young people nearly meet at Gettysburg and from there each is drawn in unexpected ways back to Zoar. This well-plotted story invites the reader to consider familiar events of the war from the perspective of its unusual but authentic background.

The high drama of the three-day battle of Gettysburg is the focus of *The Slopes of War* by N. A. Perez. Buck Summerhill returns to Gettysburg, his home town, as a soldier in the Army of the Potomac and loses his leg in the fight for Little Round Top. His sister Bekah cares for a wounded Union officer, Captain Waite, upstairs in the family's home while injured Rebels are taken into the parlor. She is delighted when her favorite cousin Custis, a Virginian, slips away from the Rebel camp during the night to visit her, but he is killed the next day on Culp's Hill. Custis' brother Mason is one of the few Confederates to survive Pickett's famous, futile charge on the last day of the battle. Bekah's 12-year-old brother Leander sees enough of this fighting and its terrible aftermath to convince him that war is not the glorious thing he had anticipated. As Captain Waite tells him, " '. . . that's what war is all about, Leander . . . an accumulation of *little* deaths that piles up into enormous grief.' "[26] (See the chart "Recurring Themes in Historical Fiction" for books about other times that carry a similar message.) This book is packed with authentic information about real officers and battle strategies, as well as several threads of fictional story line.

[25]William O. Steele, *The Perilous Road*, illustrated by Paul Galdone (New York: Harcourt Brace Jovanovich, 1958), pp. 188–189.

[26]N. A. Perez, *The Slopes of War* (Houghton Mifflin, 1984), p. 138.

In *Orphans of the Wind*, Erik Haugaard has told the story of the Civil War from various points of view expressed by an English crew when they discover that the ship they are sailing is a blockade runner. Finally, a crazed carpenter sets fire to the old brig, and the men rush for the lifeboats. Four of the young sailors who land on the Southern coast are determined to walk north until they can join the Union. They decide it will be easier to hide *in* the Southern army than to hide *from* it, so they enlist and move rapidly to the North. They are caught in the Battle of Bull Run, and one of them is killed. The other two do join the Union army, while Jim, the 12-year-old boy in the story, sails once again, but this time on an American ship. There is much strength and sensitivity in this story.

The effect of the war on a frontier family in Illinois has been told by Irene Hunt in the fine historical novel *Across Five Aprils*. Jethro Creighton is only 9 years old at the outbreak of the war that at first seemed so exciting and wonderful. But one by one Jethro's brothers, cousins, and his beloved schoolteacher enlist in the Northern army. His favorite brother, Bill, after a long struggle with his conscience, joins the South. As the war continues, Jethro learns that it is not glorious and exciting, but heart-breaking and disruptive to all kinds of relationships. Although the many letters used to carry the action of the story to different places and provide historical detail make difficult reading, this is a beautifully written, thought-provoking book.

Rifles for Watie by Harold Keith tells of the life of a Union soldier and spy engaged in fighting the Western campaign of the Civil War. Jefferson Davis Bussey, a young farm boy from Kansas, joins the Union forces, becomes a scout, and quite accidentally a member of Stand Watie's Cherokee Rebels. Jeff is probably one of the few soldiers in the West to see the Civil War from both sides. This vibrant novel is rich in detail, with fine characterizations.

In the story of 12-year-old Hannalee Reed from Roswell, Georgia, *Turn Homeward, Hannalee* by Patricia Beatty, Hannalee, her little brother Jem, and hundreds of other young millworkers are branded as traitors for making cloth and rope for the Confederacy. They are sent north to work in mills in Kentucky and Indiana or hired out as servants to northern families. Hannalee has a harsh employer and misses Jem, who has been taken to work on a farm. She runs away, disguises herself as a boy, finds her brother, and together they make their way home to burned-out Roswell. There is great pride and family feeling built into Hannalee's character. Although she learns that there are good Yankees and bad Yankees, her loyalties are firmly in the South. This book emphasizes the point that few Southerners were slaveholders, and it forces readers to consider the war's effects on the common people of the South—a good balance for the many books that present Northerners' views. Like all of Beatty's books, this one was meticulously researched and includes a long, informative author's note.

THE UNITED STATES THROUGH 1900

Stories of the Civil War and westward expansion constitute the settings for the bulk of children's historical fiction of the nineteenth century. Stories of the late nineteenth and early twentieth centuries frequently concern private lives rather than public events. They create a feeling for the period and take a look at a different kind of frontier—the long process of developing a young country.

Farming the vast mid-American prairies put special demands on families. In a beautifully written short novel by Patricia MacLachlan, motherless Anna and Caleb are delighted when Papa's advertisement for a mail-order bride brings *Sarah, Plain and Tall* to their prairie home. Sarah comes from the coast of Maine, and she brings mementos of the sea she loves, her gray cat Seal, a moon shell for Caleb, and a round sea stone for Anna. She has agreed only to a month's visit, and the children, who quickly learn to love her lively, independent ways, are afraid that they will lose her. On the day that Sarah goes to town for colored pencils to add the blue, gray, and green of the ocean to the picture she has drawn of the prairie, they realize that she will stay. She misses the sea, she tells them, but she would miss them more. The rhythm and lyrical simplicity of the writing are especially effective when read aloud.

In *Prairie Songs* by Pam Conrad, Louisa and Lester are also drawn to a newcomer, the beautiful, cultured wife of the new doctor in Howard County, Nebraska, who has come to live in the next soddy. The story is told through Louisa's eyes and reflects her wonder at the back-East world of wealth and learning that Mrs. Emmeline Berryman represents. But when the doctor's wife loses her premature baby after a long and difficult labor, Louisa is shocked by the gradual changes in her behavior. Always distraught, Mrs. Berryman is terrified out of all reason one winter day by the visit of two Indians. It is shy little Lester who later finds her where she has fled, sitting in the snow, frozen to death. Louisa's narration is vivid, and her casual acceptance of life in a soddy points up the irony of Mrs. Berryman's inability to cope. The woman Louisa had admired could not match her own mother in strength of spirit or the special kind of beauty that made Louisa feel good inside. A good picture-book accompaniment for these books about the prairie would be Ann Turner's poetic *Dakota Dugout.* Ronald Himler's drawings show both the beauty and the ruggedness of living in a sod house sandwiched between the wide prairie and the endless sky.

Patricia Beatty has written many authentic, interesting stories of both the Northwest and Southwest in the 1890s. In *Red Rock over the River,* she has chosen Fort Yuma, Arizona, in 1881 as the setting. Thirteen-year old Dorcas is the narrator of this exciting tale, but Hattie Lou Mercer, the tall half-Indian housekeeper, is the real heroine. She encourages Dorcas to visit the infamous Arizona Territorial Prison, where the two of them write letters for illiterate prisoners. She also includes Dorcas in a daring rescue of her half-brother from the prison and their escape via a gas circus balloon!

Good fun and tongue-in-cheek humor enliven the story of *Mr. Mysterious and Company* by Sid Fleischman. In this book a delightful family of traveling magicians journeys to California in the 1880s in their gaily painted wagon, making one-night stands in many frontier towns. All the children share in the magic show in a fine family story that carries the flavor of life in frontier towns of the West. The same author's equally entertaining *Humbug Mountain* features the family of an itinerant newspaperman. His son Wiley is the deadpan narrator of a wild string of adventures on the Missouri River complete with outlaws, a bogus Gold Rush, and the discovery of a petrified man. There is an underlying comment about human gullibility and greed in this funny, fast-paced story.

Not all stories of this period take place in the West, however. Although set in the early 1900s,

The birds visited me,
there was no one else,
with Matt all day in the fields.
A hawk came, snake in its claws,

A good picture book can help older children visualize the setting in related novels. Ann Turner's *Dakota Dugout* is a fine companion piece for stories set on the prairie. Illustration by Ronald Himler.

Mary Riskind's *Apple Is My Sign* is less an historical novel than a story of a 10-year-old deaf child learning to live among the hearing with his disability. Harry Berger, called "Apple" because of his family's orchards, is sent to a school for the deaf in Philadelphia. While his whole family is deaf, Harry is the first one to go away, and his early days at the school are difficult and lonely. During the fall, however, Harry discovers many doors open for him, learns a new game called football, and makes new friends. He tells his family that he thinks he'd like to be a teacher, but a family friend signs "Hearing best teacher." His mother, however, reassures Harry: " 'I-f you want teach deaf, must try. That's-all. Never know, i-f never try. In head must think can. Brave.' "[27] Riskind conveys the rapidity of signed talk by approximating its actual

[27]Mary Riskind, *Apple Is My Sign* (Boston: Houghton Mifflin, 1981), p. 119.

meanings, eliminating the little words or word endings, as signers do, and spelling out meanings for which there are no signs. Through Harry's story readers may come to realize that opportunities for the handicapped have changed over the years. Some other books that place handicapped children in historical settings are Irene Brown's *Before the Lark,* which deals with a girl's desire to conceal or heal her harelip, and Carol Carrick's *Stay Away from Simon!,* a brief story about the reactions of a girl in the early nineteenth century to a mentally handicapped neighbor.

INTO THE TWENTIETH CENTURY

Immigrants

Immigrants who came to North America in the nineteenth and early twentieth centuries had many different origins and various destinations. Still, they shared common dreams of a better life and faced similar difficulties in making a place for themselves in a new country.

The problems of the MacDonald children in Margaret Anderson's *The Journey of the Shadow Bairns* are compounded by the death of both father and mother before the family has a chance to set sail from Glasgow. Elspeth, 13, is determined not to be separated from 4-year-old Robbie. Knowing her father's plans for homesteading in western Canada, Elspeth contrives to get herself and her brother past the authorities and on board ship. She makes up the game "shadow bairns" (shadow children) to encourage Robbie to be quiet and keep out of sight of the immigration officials. Together they manage the voyage and the long train trip across Canada, but their troubles increase when they reach Saskatchewan Territory. Elspeth falls ill, her money is stolen, and Robbie disappears. It is many weeks later that she finds him, plus a permanent home for them both. This story highlights the uncertainties and misinformation that immigrants had to deal with, but its most memorable images are of Elspeth, resourceful and determined, and Robbie, clinging to his toy Pig-Bear.

Linda Lehmann has based her books *Better Than a Princess* and *Tilli's New World* on the experiences of her own German immigrant mother. The second book begins just after 7-year-old Tilli, who had been left behind in Europe, joins her parents on their little Missouri farm in the 1880s. The book's episodic plot follows Tilli's desire for

Wendy Watson's illustrations for *First Farm in the Valley: Anna's Story* reflect Anne Pellowski's emphasis on family unity and Polish heritage, as shown in this Name Day celebration.

an education and the struggles of her hardworking family. They suffer the loss of two infant sons, and there is a wrenching moment at the story's end when a third child nearly drowns in the well. Little is mentioned of the larger world in which Tilli's family lives, but through its personal dramas the book will help 9- and 10-year-olds feel what an immigrant child's life was like.

If it weren't for the references to the Polish language and Roman Catholic faith, *First Farm in the Valley: Anna's Story* might almost be mistaken for another book about Laura Ingalls and her family. Instead, this is a story by Anne Pellowski based on the 1870s childhood of her great-aunt, the daughter of a Polish immigrant in Wisconsin. The chapters are short episodes geared to the satisfactions of younger elementary children. Anna, just ready to start school, is a spunky heroine who dares to climb the roofbeam of a house to get a bag of nails or brave a hailstorm to bring home the sheep. There is a strong sense of family and of community with neighbors who keep the traditions of Poland alive in the New World. Other books by Pellowski deal with succeeding generations of this extended family.

Most of the books about immigrants focus on older children or teenagers, with considerable emphasis on social and political issues. There are many intertwining stories in *Voyage* by Adèle Geras, which examines the hopes and dreams of Jewish immigrants from Eastern Europe as they sail for America. Red-haired Mina and her "different" little brother Eli provide a focus, but the characters range from infants through two generations of adults. Mr. Kaminsky, who had survived a pogrom, dies aboard ship; Golda Schwartz is eager to join her husband so that he can see their baby for the first time; 18-year-old Rachel is falling in love. The discomforts of their voyage in steerage and the tragic pasts of many are in sharp contrast to their impossibly high expectations for life in America. The book ends without revealing the overcrowded tenements and economic hardships awaiting them in turn-of-the-century New York.

These conditions are clearly spelled out in Judie Angell's *One-Way to Ansonia*, which traces seven years in the life of a Russian Jewish immigrant family on New York's Lower East Side. At the center is Rose, who is plump, musically talented, brash, and eager for education despite the scoffing of friends and family. She has been sent out to work for pay since the age of 8 and has chosen herself a husband at 14 to avoid an arranged marriage. Still, Rose is determined to believe that there are other ways to live. It is sheer strength of spirit that takes her out of her close-knit, tradition-bound neighborhood at last, to buy a one-way ticket for an unknown Connecticut town where she hopes to make an easier life for herself, her husband, and their infant son. This story is similar in structure to *Voyage*, using short episodes with little transitional narrative. The two books have such complementary content that it would be especially productive to read them as a pair for discussion or other follow-up activities.

In Laurence Yep's books, *The Serpent's Children* and *Mountain Light,* the nineteenth-century Chinese refer to American as "the land of the Golden Mountain." Although these stories are set mainly in China, the promise of the California gold fields is part of the theme as well as the plot. *Mountain Light* includes graphic descriptions of the repugnant conditions on an immigrant ship from Hong Kong to San Francisco and the infighting among clans and factions that carried over from China to the New World. Yep's earlier book, *Dragonwings*, gives a more detailed picture of Chinese immigrants in San Francisco after 1900.

Black Americans

The history of black Americans from the late 1800s to the middle of the twentieth century is a bitter record of high hopes brought low by prejudice, hatred, and greed. Because novels that explore these situations examine issues that are still sensitive today, critics with a sociological point of view sometimes disagree about the merits of the books. Some question the authenticity or appropriateness of attitudes portrayed for today's children. Others point to the inherent drama of the stories and their intended themes of tolerance and understanding. In the books that follow, memorable characters face the uncertain future common to black Americans in the South during the first half of this century.

One of the most moving stories of this time period is the Newbery award-winner *Sounder* by William Armstrong. This is the stark tale of a black sharecropper and his family who endure cruel injustice with dignity and courage. When the father is thrown into jail for stealing a ham for his starving family, his big hunting dog, Sounder, is cruelly wounded by the sheriff. The dog never bays again until years later, when his master returns. As in the story of Odysseus, the dog is the first to recognize the man. Crippled from a dynamite blast in the prison quarry, the father has come home to die. The story would be one of deep despair except for the fact that during the boy's long searches to find where his father is imprisoned, he meets a kind schoolmaster who enlarges his world by educating him and offering some hope for the future. This is a family that has the courage and faith to endure within a setting so inhuman that they seem to be nameless in contrast to their dog. They do not fight back because they cannot fight back—not in the rural South near the end of the nineteenth century.

Come by Here by Olivia Coolidge depicts a black family living in Baltimore in the early 1900s. Minty's parents are both killed in a bizarre accident, and she is shuffled from one relative to another, none of whom really want her. Finally, she is sent unannounced to her Grandma Minty in the country town of Cambridge, where there is enough compassion to make room for her and the hope that, like her mother, she may make something of herself. This book presents a grim picture of city survival that is every bit as cruel as the rural setting is in *Sounder*.

In Ouida Sebestyen's compelling *Words by Heart*, black Ben Sills has moved his family to an all-white community in the West and taken a job as hired hand to rich Mrs. Chism. The hatred and resentment of her tenant farmer, Mr. Haney, and his son Tater grow as Ben proves himself honest and hard-working, which the Haneys are not. Ben's oldest child, Lena, also proves herself an eager, keen-minded student whose ability to recite Bible verses "by heart" wins a contest at the book's opening. Even though the family begins to settle in and make progress against their neighbor's uneasiness, the animosity of the Haneys remains. Angered when Lena's father is given a fence-mending job his own father had neglected, Tater rides out with a gun and shoots Ben as he works, but is himself nearly killed in a fall from his horse. It is Lena who finds them and loads both into the wagon—her dying father and the injured boy whom he has struggled to keep alive. This is a stunning act of mercy, in keeping with the characterization of Ben Sills as a man of faith and strength. Ben's forgiveness convinces Lena, in spite of her grief, not to accuse Tater of the killing, to ". . . let God handle it. . . . [Papa] said we couldn't give up on—that person."[28]

Sebestyen has followed the fortunes of Ben Sills' white adversaries, the Haneys, in a sequel, *On Fire*. Tater's guilt and the family's flight to a mining town in Colorado are seen through the eyes of Sammy, a younger brother who idolizes Tater. Coarse expressions of bigotry, callous attitudes, and violent situations in keeping with the setting are offset somewhat by the clear-thinking character of Yankee Belew, an older girl who takes Sammy under her wing. This is a book full of complex moral dilemmas. Even mature readers may need to sort out its implications in discussion with the teacher or other adult.

Mildred Taylor, one of the first black authors to win the Newbery award, has written with special understanding about the black experience in rural Mississippi during the 1930s. *Roll of Thunder, Hear My Cry* is the story of the Logan family, their pride in the land they have owned since Reconstruction, and their determination not to let injustice go unchallenged. The crucial action in the narrative is the conflict that 9-year-old Cassie observes in the adult world around her: night-riders who terrorize the black community; her mother's teaching job gone as a result of her efforts to organize a boycott of the store whose white owners are among those night-riders; her father's dramatic part in rescuing a black teenager, T.J., from a lynch mob. The grim nature of the events is offset by the portrayal of the family caught up in them, the warmth of their concern for one another, the strength of their pride, and their courage.

A direct sequel, *Let the Circle Be Unbroken*, follows the tragic trial of T.J. and carries Cassie's family saga into 1935. Cassie continues to be a witness to the victimization of poor sharecroppers, both black and white, the beginnings of unionization, and the first attempts at black voter registration. It is the family that sustains all through these difficult times, made more so by Stacey's running away to find work. The complex social issues and human relationships in this book make it better suited to middle school or junior high school readers. A younger audience could be introduced to the Logan family in Taylor's *Song of the Trees*, which has the format of a short illustrated book.

In the prejudiced climate of tidewater North Carolina in the 1930s, children were expected to acquire bigotry as part of their growth into adulthood. At 11 years old, however, Harrison Hawkins, who is white, and Kitty Fisher, who is black (and a boy), can still be best friends. In *Circle of Fire* by William H. Hooks, these two join forces to help a band of Irish tinkers camped on the Hawkins property escape the wrath of the Ku Klux Klan. The theme of the horrors of intolerance is doubled in force by having two sets of victims, the tinkers who are actually harassed and beaten, and the blacks, whose fate is implied in every threat of the Klan. This story has a dramatic climax that makes the setting seem real and immediate.

The World in the Twentieth Century

STORIES FROM MANY COUNTRIES

Four brief books by Alan Garner, known collectively as the Stone Quartet, celebrate continuity

---

[28]Ouida Sebestyen, *Words by Heart* (Boston: Atlantic, Little, Brown, 1979), p. 129.

and change in the lives of several generations of craftsmen in an English village. *The Stone Book*, set well before the turn of the century, is the story of Mary, who cannot read but asks her father for a book. Her father is a master stonemason, unlettered, with no ordinary book to give her. Instead, he takes her deep into a crevice of the malachite mine near their cottage to read the secrets of the rocks, as his father had once taken him. Squeezing alone through a space too small for an adult, Mary discovers a cave with mysterious and wonderful records of life: footprints in the clay floor, the figure of a huge bull painted on the wall, and the outline of a hand that just matches her own in size. Later her father carves for her a small book of stone, split so that the back shows the outline of a fossil fern. " 'It's better than a book you can open,' said Father. 'A book has only one story.' "29

The companion volumes, *Granny Reardun, The Aimer Gate,* and *Tom Fobble's Day,* all have boys as protagonists. Garner's style is rich in implication and suggestion. All four books are vivid, with human feelings and untold secrets that require the reader to make many inferences and still make do with ambiguity at the end. Coupled with the use of local idiom and family by-words, this makes the reading harder than it looks. But by avoiding the straightforward explicitness of most historical fiction, Garner is able to call up the poetic, mystical quality of those moments when we begin to apprehend our own connection to the past.

John Rowe Townsend has written stories of rugged city realism in England. In *Dan Alone*, he paints a vivid picture of slum life before World War II. Eleven-year-old Dan, a runaway, ends up in the Jungle, a squalid, dangerous district with fancy street names: Camellia, Hibiscus, or Orchid. There he learns to fend for himself, joins a disreputable family, and contributes to it by begging in the streets and singing outside saloons. He forms a friendship with another homeless child, Olive, whom he comes to care about. Eventually, his reunion with his mother, the discovery of his real father, and Olive's joining of the group provide Dan with the family he has always dreamed about. Townsend makes statements about human

nature that are both humorous and compassionate in this fast-moving story.

India is the setting for Jane Yolen's *Children of the Wolf,* which is loosely based on diary and newspaper accounts of two feral children found in the jungle in the 1920s. An author's note explains the liberties she has taken with these reports, and that the original story was thought by some to be a hoax. The book is a fascinating re-creation of time and place and offers much to be discussed with children. Fourteen-year-old Mohandas, the fictional narrator who befriends the wolf-girls Amala and Kamala in the orphanage where they are taken, is a well-developed character. Portrayed as a boy with a great fascination for words, he understands the Scottish missionary's insistence that the power of language will release Kamala from her animal state. Through Mohandas' thoughts and actions, readers may also discover an underlying theme about the imposition of one culture on another.

Edward Fenton's *The Refugee Summer* takes place in a Greek village near Athens during the summer of 1922. War between Greece and Turkey over disputed territory in Anatolia sends refugees to Athens and thus touches the lives of four American children spending the summer abroad with their families. They become friends with Nikolas, the son of their Greek housekeeper, and in the course of their play form a secret society, with code names and a secret language, for the purpose of standing against all injustice and suffering. They finally find their own project, a family of refugee children from Smyrna. Nikolas and the others feed and hide them while they get an adult friend to advertise for their relatives. When the refugees tell the other children how they were separated from their parents as they escaped the disaster at Smyrna, the listeners are awed:

> Nikolas, in the middle of the silence, suddenly understood that what he had just heard was history. What was boring was all the talk about kings and ministers and politicians. Real history was what Sotiris and Frosso and Diamondo had lived through.30

In Russia in the early 1920s, political oppression led to the unexplained disappearance of entire

29Alan Garner, *The Stone Book* (London: Fontana Lions, 1979), p. 58.

30Edward Fenton, *The Refugee Summer* (New York: Delacorte, 1982), p. 226.

families. Occasionally children were left behind and had to fend for themselves, banding together in street gangs called *bezprizorni*. This is the story told in Felice Holman's *The Wild Children*, which follows the fortunes of 12-year-old Alex to Moscow and finally to freedom in Finland, by way of St. Petersburg. Alex is fortunate in attaching himself to a group whose leader, Peter, is shrewd and strong. Thievery and trickery are their chief means of survival, but at least Peter keeps a sort of order among them with his rules: no drugs, no liquor, and no killing. In their cellar crypt in Moscow they are hungry, cold, and filthy—but also free, as Peter reminds them. When Alex remembers his former teacher's stories about places where people did not have to be slaves of the government, he urges them on to find the secret emigration network which she has mentioned. This is a hard-hitting story made bearable by its hopeful ending.

A critically acclaimed book from Sweden is Harry Kullman's novel for adolescents, *The Battle Horse*. Set in Stockholm during the 1930s, this powerful story focuses on a teenagers' game patterned after medieval jousting tournaments. Here the children of working-class families are "horses" who carry prep school "knights" on their backs for hand-to-hand combat in a makeshift area between apartment buildings. The theme is strongly stated: " 'One day we horses will travel over the Seven Seas like Gulliver and we won't carry the rich and powerful on our backs any more.' "[31] Frank language and a tragic ending help to mark this book for older readers.

THE WORLD AT WAR

Recent years have witnessed almost a deluge of stories about World War II. Oddly enough, very few books for children about World War I have been published. It may be that a generation of freedom in writing realistic stories has allowed authors to write truthfully about the horror and grimness of war. In these stories the common enemy is war itself. While most of them depict man's inhumanity to man, they also show many individual acts of humanity and extreme courage.

Escape and Resistance

Some of the most popular war stories are about families that escaped to freedom or endured long years of hiding from the Nazis. *Journey to America* by Sonia Levitin tells of a German-Jewish family who become refugees when Hitler comes to power. Papa goes ahead to the United States, but Mama and the girls must wait in Switzerland. There Mama is an alien and cannot work, and other living arrangements are made for the children. After a difficult separation, all the family is reunited in America. Simple language and the emphasis on family solidarity and mutual love make this story appealing for 8- to 10-year-olds.

Along with its intriguing title, *When Hitler Stole Pink Rabbit* by Judith Kerr also has the validity of solid detail that comes from personal experience. This is the story of another family's escape to Switzerland and their trials in trying to earn a living there, then in France, and finally in England. Again, this is a pre-war story taking place in the 1930s. It is a happier account than *Journey to America;* yet as they leave France for England, Anna wonders if they will ever really belong anywhere. And her father says: " 'Not the way people belong who have lived in one place all their lives. But we'll belong a little in lots of places and I think that may be just as good.' "[32]

Others made their escape by hiding for the duration of the war. *Anne Frank: The Diary of a Young Girl* is the classic story of hiding from the Nazis. Autobiographical, this is a candid and open account of the changes wrought upon eight people who hid for two years in a secret annex of an office building in Amsterdam and were ultimately found and imprisoned by the Nazis. Anne's diary reveals the thoughts of a sensitive adolescent growing up under extraordinary conditions. No one who lived in the annex survived the war except Anne's father. He returned to their hiding place and found Anne's diary. When it was published, it became an immediate best-seller and was translated into many languages. Its popularity continues today, an appropriate tribute to Anne Frank's amazing spirit.

[31]Harry Kullman, *The Battle Horse*, translated by George Blecher and Lone Thygesen-Blecher (Scarsdale, N.Y.: Bradbury Press, 1981), p. 183.

[32]Judith Kerr, *When Hitler Stole Pink Rabbit* (New York: Coward McCann, 1972), p. 186.

The Upstairs Room by Johanna Reiss is a moving account of the author's own experiences when she and her sister were hidden by a farm family, the Oostervelds. The girls spent most of the time in an upstairs room so that they wouldn't be seen. The greatest excitement occurs when German soldiers make the Oosterveld house their temporary headquarters. Mostly, however, this is a story of the reactions of all the characters in close confinement and secrecy—the irritability, tension, and fear. The real delight of the book is the Oosterveld family with their plain-folks values, salty language, and generosity. When the town is liberated and Annie can go outside at last, Johann's pride in what his family has done is obvious as he brags to neighboring farmers:

> "We had 'em for over two years. They're good girls. We didn't tell anybody about 'em. Don't be mad. It would've been too dangerous if we had told everybody in Usselo. I know you're special, but don't forget I was responsible for them. No, I was never afraid. Not once. Hey, Groothius, take a look at my girls."[33]

Annie's story is continued in *The Journey Back*, which shows the after-effects of war on her family and her difficulties with a perfectionist stepmother.

One of the best survival stories is *The Endless Steppe* by Esther Hautzig. This is the author's own account of growing up in a slave labor camp in Siberia. The Rudomins, a wealthy Jewish family, lived in Vilna, a city in Poland. The Russians occupy Vilna and confiscate the family business; and then one day they arrest the whole family as "capitalists and therefore enemies of the people." They are shipped in filthy, stiflingly hot cattle cars across the barren flat land that is to be their home for five endless years—Siberia. Despite the poverty and privation, Esther manages to satisfy her adolescent needs and to find hope in a hopeless situation. When they are finally allowed to go back to Poland, she finds she is sad to leave the place she had once hated:

> I said good-by to the steppe—to the wind and the snow and the heat and the monotony. And to its space that had at first filled me with so much terror and later had quieted and soothed me. I said good-by to the unique beauty of the steppe.[34]

During the time they were in Siberia, the Nazis had entered Poland and killed all their Jewish relatives and friends; in retrospect they consider themselves supremely lucky to have been deported to "The Endless Steppe." The ending of this story is less grim than that of the diary of *Anne Frank*, but both stories are a tribute to the courage of the human spirit.

Uri Orlev's story, *The Island on Bird Street*, takes the reader into an almost deserted Polish ghetto where Alex, not yet 12, has an ingenious hiding place high in the ruins of building No. 78. His mother, a Zionist, has disappeared, and his father is taken away by the Germans along with the last workers cleared from the ghetto. But Alex's instructions are to wait for his return at No. 78—for a day, a week, or even a year, if necessary. As the months pass he proves to be a clever and courageous survivor, avoiding detection even when German soldiers come to blast open a secret bunker under the cellar. Although forced to take on grim responsibilities, Alex has a childlike side; he is deeply attached to his pet mouse, Snow, and risks discovery to play with other children beyond the ghetto wall. The story ends as Alex and his father, now a part of the underground, are miraculously reunited. The author's confident tone comes from experience; he spent two years in hiding in the Warsaw ghetto as a child.

Frequently refugees were helped to flee or hide from authorities by common folk who did what they could to resist the invaders. Many stories relate the roles that children played in helping these resisters. Two stories of enduring popularity with younger readers are Claire Bishop's *Twenty and Ten*, in which French orphans manage to hide ten Jewish children during a Nazi investigation; and Marie McSwigan's *Snow Treasure*, which tells how a brave group of Norwegian children helped to smuggle gold out of the country. A fine book for older children is Alki Zei's *Petros' War*, a winner of the Mildred L. Batchelder Award for outstand-

---

[33]Johanna Reiss, *The Upstairs Room* (New York: Crowell, 1972), p. 188.

[34]Esther Hautzig, *The Endless Steppe* (New York: Crowell, 1968), p. 239.

ing books translated from a foreign language. The story, set in Athens, presents Petros as a witness to the Italian and German occupations. Two of the boy's friends are killed for their part in resistance activities, but despite the grimness of the story the author never loses the child's point of view.

Some of the most dramatic stories of young people who lived through the conflict in Europe are autobiographical. However, they employ many of the techniques of fiction, including the creation of dialogue. Ilse Koehn's *Mischling, Second Degree* describes her childhood of active participation in the Hitler Youth movement, made ironic by the secret kept even from her at the time: her father's mother was Jewish, and Ilse would have been classified as an enemy of the Third Reich had the fact been known. In Emma Macalik Butterworth's *As the Waltz Was Ending*, an autobiographical account of growing up in Vienna, 8-year-old Emmy auditions for and is accepted by the selective Vienna State Ballet School, but the fairy-tale quality of her life is shattered by the ugliness of politics and the crush of war. Her childhood pains with the *barre* exercises pale beside her adolescent struggles to survive air raids, food shortages, and, finally, kidnap and rape by Russian soldiers. Aranka Siegal's own story of her Hungarian childhood, *Upon the Head of the Goat*, is filled with dread, for the Davidowitz family is Jewish, The final scene is emotionally shattering, as Piri, her mother, brother, and two sisters are forced to board a train for a destination with a name that is unfamiliar to them—Auschwitz. Books such as these require maturity of their readers, whatever their age level.

War compounds the misery of homeless Italian children in a fine historical novel by Erik Haugaard. *The Little Fishes* are the pathetic children of Naples who have no homes, no families, no friends. Three of them wander about Italy, begging food, hoping to find a home, and get caught in the midst of war. Guido, the oldest boy, somehow stays alive and develops a mature wisdom for one so young. When he is asked why after all their suffering he cannot hate, he replies:

> "The war . . . the suffering, it must have a point and if I hate that man who only saw that we were dirty . . . then I would be like him. And all we had gone through would be as meaningless as the seasons are

to the sheep. It is understanding . . . that makes the difference between us and the animals."[35]

Children in Asia also suffered during the war years. *The House of Sixty Fathers* by Meindert DeJong is an example of a book that does not glorify war; it clearly, vividly tells of the horror of bullets coming in your direction and of the pains of hunger. DeJong's descriptions of Tien Pao's fear, loneliness, and hunger are starkly realistic but couched in terms that even 9- or 10-year-olds can well understand. The Chinese boy and his family flee before the Japanese invasion, but they are separated. Clutching his pet pig, Tien Pao struggles on, not knowing where to go. He finds a U.S. flier and helps him survive. The boy is taken to the barracks and becomes a mascot of the soldiers, his sixty fathers. Although it seems impossible, he continues to believe his parents will be found. In a rather contrived but satisfying ending he does identify his mother from a plane as she is working on the construction of an airfield.

A few Western children, mainly those of missionary parents, were trapped in Asia during World War II. In *The Bombers' Moon* Betty Vander Els tells the story of Ruth and her little brother Simeon, who must go to an emergency boarding school as the Japanese invaders come closer to their home in China. During the long separation from their parents, they endure falling bombs, a terrifying airlift over the Himalayas to India, and the stress of dealing with one new "home" after another. More than three years later, months after the war's end, Ruth and Simeon are reunited in Shanghai with their parents and a new little brother. Unlike many books about World War II, this one has characters who do not grow into adolescence during the story. Thus their natural outlook is not on the political or moral issues of war, but on its immediacy of emotions and images. The author has a gift for expressing the children's own view of their world, including their very real affection for China.

Many authors from England have written about children's experiences there at the time of the

[35]Erik Christian Haugaard, *The Little Fishes*, illustrated by Milton Johnson (Boston: Houghton Mifflin, 1967), p. 213.

bombing raids. Susan Cooper's *Dawn of Fear* and Robert Westall's *The Machine Gunners* are frequently read by young adolescents. One of the best selections for elementary readers is Nina Bawden's *Carrie's War,* about three children who are evacuees living in a Welsh mining town. Nick and Carrie, brother and sister, are sent to live with stern Mr. Evans and his sister, Auntie Lou. Another evacuee, Albert Sandwich, lives at the bottom of Druid's Grove with Mr. Evans' older sister, the invalid Dilys. Brother and sister haven't spoken since Dilys married the mine owner's son, shortly after their father's death in the mine. The story moves ahead on two levels—the family's feud and the children's involvement in it. The characters are seen from a child's eye view, with a child's perception of adults. This is a remarkable story that tells much more of the personal wars of living both as children and adults than of the war of bombs and blitzes.

An unusual story that concerns itself with the aftermath of war is *North to Freedom* by Anne Holm. A boy named David is given a chance to escape from the prison camp in eastern Europe where he has lived for most of his twelve years. He has no knowledge of his own background or of the world at large and no feeling about people except that no one can be trusted. Although David is able to read and has learned to speak seven languages from the other prisoners, much of his learning has been without the essential experience that brings meaning. He finds it difficult to relate to the world, avoids people, and makes only tentative gestures toward others. Slowly, his trust in human beings grows, and with it the desire to live and be a part of the world of sunshine, beauty, and color that is in such contrast to the drabness of the prison camp. David's change from an imprisoned creature completely shut off from normal human feelings to a responsive and responsible boy makes for a remarkable story.

Impact of the War in the Americas

While thousands of American families lost sons, fathers, and husbands in World War II, North Americans never endured the physical horror of war in our land. For this reason, perhaps, we have fewer stories about the impact of the war in the West.

The Cay by Theodore Taylor is both a war survival story and one of overcoming prejudice. After the Germans torpedo the freighter on which Phillip and his mother are traveling back home to the United States from wartime Curaçao, Phillip finds himself cast up on a barren little Caribbean Island with an old black man named Timothy. A blow on the head during the wreck has left Phillip blind and completely dependent on Timothy. Both the prejudiced Virginian and the unschooled West Indian are products and prisoners of their backgrounds. Although Phillip gradually begins to understand and trust the wisdom and selflessness of Timothy, his way of overcoming his prejudice is to make Timothy white in his mind. In return, Timothy forces him to make fish nets, to find his way around the camp, to survive without him. And following the hurricane in which Timothy bears the brunt of the storm while protecting him, Phillip has to live without him, for Timothy dies. Phillip is finally rescued and his sight restored after three operations. This story of a color-conscious white boy and a self-sacrificing black was not meant to provide a model for today's living; what it does do is present an exciting account of survival in the Caribbean in 1942. One of the few stories detailing a gradual loss of prejudice, it emphasizes human interdependence in time of crisis.

The Summer of My German Soldier by Bette Greene is the story of 12-year-old Patty Bergen, who is Jewish and the awkward, elder daughter of a small-town Arkansas department-store owner. Her mother and father fight and are cruel to Patty. Except for the real love of Ruth, the Bergens' black cook, Patty lives in a loveless situation. Perhaps this explains her compassion for a handsome, well-educated German prisoner of war named Anton who lives in a prison camp near town and comes to her father's store. Patty begins to think of him as her friend and later, when she sees him running down the railroad tracks, she offers him the safety of her special hideout room over the garage. Only after Anton has gotten away and is captured elsewhere is Patty's role in his escape uncovered. She is arrested and sent to a Reform School, clinging to the knowledge that one day she will be free to leave her family and become a "person of value," a term Anton had used.

Citizens of the United States can take no pride in

The little-known history of the internment of the Japanese in the United States during World War II is sensitively told in *Journey to Topaz* by Yoshiko Uchida. Illustration by Donald Carrick.

the treatment of Japanese-Americans at the beginning of the war against Japan. In *Journey to Topaz,* Yoshiko Uchida has given a fictionalized account of her family's evacuation and internment. Yuki's father, a businessman, is taken away from his family on the very day of Pearl Harbor. It is almost a year before he is paroled. Yuki and her mother and older brother are taken first to a temporary center, a converted racetrack where their "apartment" is a hastily partitioned stall area in one of the stables. The walls have been so sloppily whitewashed that the bodies of cockroaches still cling to the boards. The latrines have no doors, and the mealtime lines are interminable. At the "permanent" camp in Topaz, Utah, Yuki's friend Emi's grandfather is shot by a guard, who sees him looking for arrowheads and thinks he is trying to escape. The author writes the story in a restrained way, with no bitterness. The quiet courage, dignity, and loyalty with which this Japanese family endures their unjust internment makes its own statement to the reader.

Citizens of Japanese descent in Canada were subjected to similar treatment. Sheila Garrigue's *The Eternal Spring of Mr. Ito* helps the reader experience the passionate anti-Japanese feeling along the Pacific Coast even as it demonstrates the blamelessness of those who were shunned, jeered, vandalized, and interned. Sara has come from England to spend the war years with her uncle's family in Vancouver. When her cousin's fiancé is killed in the Japanese attack on Hong Kong, Sara's feelings are torn between grief for the family and sympathy for their loyal Japanese gardener, Mr. Ito. Unable to face the shame of internment, he spends the last days of his life hiding in a cliff-side cave. The ancient bonsai pine that Mr. Ito guards has been in his family for centuries and stands for all that is dignified and enduring in the Japanese way of life. It would be interesting to discuss with children other objects and actions in the story that have symbolic meaning, such as Uncle Duncan's stoning of the bonsai trees in his own garden. A powerful companion for Garrigue's book would be the short illustrated first-person account of *A Child in Prison Camp* by Japanese-Canadian artist Shizuye Takashima.

Well-written historical fiction like that reviewed in this chapter may enable children to see the continuity of life and their own places in this vast sweep of history. The power of good historical fiction can give children a feeling for a living past. History can become an extension of their own personal experiences, rather than a sterile subject assigned to be studied in school. Such books can offer children a new perspective by which they come to realize that people make and shape their destinies through the decisions and actions of each individual. The events that are happening today do become the history of tomorrow.

BIOGRAPHY

In children's literature, biography bridges the gap between historical fiction and informational books.

A life story may read like fiction; but, like nonfiction, it will center on facts and events that can be documented. In spite of the factual focus, writers of biography for children have been allowed more freedom in the use of fictional techniques than those who write for adults. As a result, children's biographies show a wide range of factual orientations, from strict authenticity to liberal fictionalization.

Authentic biography corresponds to that written for adults. A book of this type is a well-documented, carefully researched account of a person's life. Only those statements that are actually known to have been made by the subject are included in the conversation. Jean Fritz is the best-known author of authentic biography for children. Her books about famous figures of the American Revolution, including *And Then What Happened, Paul Revere?* and *Will You Sign Here, John Hancock?* are based on detailed research. No dialogue has been invented, no incidents made up to prove a point. When quotation marks are used, it indicates that, according to record, these actual words were spoken or written. Milton Meltzer's book, *Dorothea Lange: Life through the Camera,* is another example of excellent authentic biography.

Fictionalized biography is grounded in thorough research, but lets the author dramatize certain events and personalize the subject rather than present the straight reporting of authentic biography. Fictionalized biography makes use of the narrative rather than the analytical approach. Children come to know the character of the subject as it is presented through actions, deeds, and conversations. In fictionalized biography the author may invent dialogue and even include the unspoken thoughts of the subject. These conversations may be based on actual facts taken from diaries, journals, or other period sources. In Johanna Johnston's *Harriet and the Runaway Book: The Story of Harriet Beecher Stowe and Uncle Tom's Cabin,* Harriet's sister-in-law urges her on in words that closely paraphrase the written record: " 'If I could use a pen as you can, I'd write something to make people *feel* what a dreadful thing slavery is.' "[36] But the ordinary, everyday dialogue, such as Harriet's remarking on the number of pigs in Cincinnati or telling her children to be good is composed of reasonable speculation about what small talk might have been made under the circumstances.

The same distinction between authentic and fictionalized applies in theory to autobiography. *Self Portrait: Trina Schart Hyman* by Hyman is an example of authentic autobiography; it features straightforward narrative with many illustrations to document the artist's development. However, most people who write about their own lives for children do so in memoirs told in story form, with re-created conversation.

Not everyone agrees where to draw the line between fictionalized biography or memoirs and historical fiction. When Jean Fritz wrote about her childhood in China and her much-longed-for trip to the United States in *Homesick: My Own Story,* she found that her "memory came out in lumps" and finally chose not to worry about exact sequence. She telescoped events of all her childhood into a two-year span:

> . . . but they are all, except in minor details, basically true. The people are real people; the places are dear to me. But most important, the form I have used has given me the freedom to recreate the emotions that I remember so vividly. Strictly speaking, I have to call this book *fiction,* but it does not feel like fiction to me. It is my story, told as truly as I can tell it.[37]

The library cataloging information in the front of the book designates it as fiction, but many readers will think of it as the autobiography of Jean Fritz. The inclusion of a section of family photographs from their days in China strengthens the book's claim to authenticity. Fritz's humor, her depth of feeling, and her vivid portrayal of the turmoil in China during in 1920s make *Homesick* worth reading, regardless of the label that is put on it. Older readers and adults may enjoy a sequel, *China Homecoming,* that is clearly nonfiction.

Biographical fiction consists entirely of imagined conversation and reconstructed action. An exam-

---

[36]Johanna Johnston, *Harriet and the Runaway Book: The Story of Harriet Beecher Stowe and Uncle Tom's Cabin* (New York: Harper & Row, 1977), p. 53.

[37]Jean Fritz, *Homesick: My Own Story* (New York: Putnam, 1982), Foreword.

HOMESICK
My Own Story
BY JEAN FRITZ

Illustrated by Margot Tomes

Jean Fritz's story of her own childhood brings to life China in the 1920s.

ple is Robert Lawson's funny *Ben and Me,* the story of Benjamin Franklin as told by his good friend Amos, the mouse who lived in Franklin's old fur cap. The facts of Franklin's life are truly presented, but Amos takes the credit for most of his accomplishments! Lawson used the same tongue-in-cheek pattern for his readable *Mr. Revere and I,* the story of Paul Revere as told by his horse, Scheherazade.

Biography for Today's Child

Publishers of biography for children have been quick to capitalize on trends in the social studies curriculum as well as shifts in children's interests. In the mid-1970s, many biographies about leaders in the American Revolution appeared in connection with the Bicentennial. Another identifiable trend has been the increase of titles that relate to the study of blacks and, to a lesser degree, other minorities—such as Native Americans and Mexican-Americans. More stories of famous American women are being written. Publishers have recognized children's tremendous interest in sports and entertainment figures by producing biographies of Dorothy Hamill, Fernando Valenzuela, Bill Cosby, and many others.

In recent years these new biographies of popular-culture celebrities and other contemporary figures have greatly outnumbered those of historical subjects. Although the trend is toward an authentic treatment and an objective, almost journalistic style, many of the books are superficial in scholarship as well as poorly written. A great number of biographies are published as parts of series, and the result is often life stories tailored to fit certain format specifications rather than explored in all their uniqueness. Virginia Witucke's study of biographies published in a single year noted these and other trends. She concluded that children "are not being well served by biography" and that ". . . all too rarely did an author present a picture of a human being whom a reader could like and respect and want to know more about."[38]

In spite of the fact that many mediocre biographies are written for children, there are also some fine ones, both authentic and fictionalized. The task of the teacher and librarian is to begin to distinguish among them.

CRITERIA FOR JUVENILE BIOGRAPHY

The criteria for evaluating biographies for boys and girls differ somewhat from those established for juvenile fiction. They also diverge from generally accepted patterns for adult biography. Children read biography as they read fiction—for the story or *plot.* Children demand a fast-moving narrative. In biography, events and action become even more exciting because "they really happened." Thus, children like biography written as a story with continuity; they do not want just a collection of facts and dates. An encyclopedia gives

[38]Virginia Witucke, "Trends in Juvenile Biography," *Top of the News,* vol. 37 (Winter 1981), p. 163.

them facts in a well-organized fashion. Biography, to do more than this, must help them to *know* the person as a living human being.

Choice of Subject

Formerly, most biographies for children were about familiar figures of the past in the United States, particularly those whose lives offered the readiest action material, such as Daniel Boone or Abraham Lincoln. In recent years, however, there has been an increase in biographies of poets, authors, artists, musicians, and humanitarians. With these, children may begin to appreciate the challenges of the mind and spirit, as well as heroic physical accomplishments. World figures have also received more emphasis than previously; for example, two fine biographies, *Juarez, Man of Law* by Elizabeth de Treviño and *Sadat: The Man Who Changed Mid-East History* by George Sullivan suggest the widened concerns of our pluralistic society. The current trend toward biographies of contemporary figures, persons in the sports or entertainment world, and especially of young celebrities reflects the influence of the mass media.

For many years biography for children was limited to those subjects whose lives were considered worthy of emulation. This is no longer always true. There are books about such unsavory persons as Jesse James or Billy the Kid in *Western Outlaws* by Frank Surge, *Traitor: The Case of Benedict Arnold* by Jean Fritz, or *Hitler, Mad Dictator of World War II* by John Devaney. Such controversial persons as Fidel Castro, Ho Chi Minh, and Lenin have all been subjects of juvenile biographies. As long as the biographies are objective and recognize the various points of view concerning the subjects, these books can serve a useful purpose in presenting a world view to boys and girls.

Biographies of less-well-known figures or subjects whose accomplishments are highly specialized also have value for children. Marshall Taylor, a champion cyclist at the turn of the century when bicycle racing was a popular sport, was the first black person to ride in integrated races. Mary Scioscia's *Bicycle Rider* makes a story of his first victory, focusing on family values and pride of accomplishment. Magician Sigmund Neuberger, known in the 1890s as "The Great Lafayette," is all but unknown today, yet children can enjoy the account of his career and his unusual canine assistant in I. G. Edmonds' *The Magic Dog*.

A sense of discovery is added to the satisfaction of a good story where children read about intriguing but little-known lives. Children have a right to read biographies about a wide range of subjects—famous persons, great human beings who were not famous, and even anti-heroes.

Accuracy and Authenticity

Accuracy is the hallmark of good biographical writing, whether it is for adults or children. More and more writers of juvenile biography are acknowledging primary sources for their materials either in an introductory note or an appended bibliography. Conscientious authors of well-written children's biographies frequently travel to the locale of the setting in order to get a "feeling" for a place. They visit museums in order to study actual objects that were used by their subjects; they spend hours poring over original letters and documents. Much of this research may not be used in the actual biography, but its effect will be evidenced by the author's true insight into the character of the subject and by the accuracy of the historical detail.

The same kind of careful research should be reflected in the accuracy of the illustrations that convey the time, place, and setting. The costumes of the period, the interiors of the houses, the very utensils that are used must be authentic representations. Even the placement of illustrations may affect their accuracy, since children presume that text and pictures that occur together belong together. In Mervyn Kaufman's biography of *Jesse Owens*, illustrated by Johnson, the description of Owens' Olympic triumph in Germany is unfortunately accompanied by a picture of the stadium at his home university in Ohio.

But most difficult of all, perhaps, is the actual portrayal of the subject. There are many paintings and even photographs of some of our national heroes, yet some are more appropriate for use than others. In Thomas Fleming's biography of George Washington, *First in Their Hearts*, only photographs of portraits that were made by artists who were *contemporaries* of Washington were used. Fleming also indicates which of the paintings were considered good likenesses of Washington by members of the family. Interestingly, the family never liked the Stuart portrait, which serves as the well-known image on the dollar bill, since Washington was suffering from an ill-fitting set of false teeth at the time the portrait was made. The teeth fit so poorly that they had to be held in place with bands of cotton, which caused a distortion of his mouth.

Photographs provide authentic illustration for many biographical accounts of more recent presidents, such as *The Life and Words of John F. Kennedy* by James Wood, published soon after Kennedy's death. An interesting combination of modern photographs and drawings from rare books showing the same terrain is used to illustrate the authentic biography of *The Discoveries of Esteban the Black* by Elizabeth Shepherd. Maps of the routes taken by the Spanish explorers are also included.

An authentic biography must be true in every detail. A fictionalized biography must also be true to the factual record, and any invented dialogue or background detail must be plausible and true to the times. Yet the truth of what is included in a biography does not quite answer the entire question of its accuracy. Sometimes what is left out is just as important as what goes in.

Formerly, authors of biographies for children avoided writing about certain aspects in the lives of their subjects. For example, in writing a biography of Alexander Hamilton that was published in 1958, authors Anna and Russel Crouse did not say that he was an illegitimate child. They did not alter any of the facts of his life, but simply never referred to his parents as husband and wife. In a later biography, *Odd Destiny, A Life of Alexander Hamilton* by Milton Lomask, the fact of Hamilton's illegitimacy is mentioned on the very first page.

Serious critcism has been leveled at those biographies of Washington and Jefferson that did not include the fact that they owned many slaves. More recent biographies, even those for younger children, do include this information. In the note appended to the end of the biography of Jefferson titled *Grand Papa and Ellen Aroon*, Monjo points out that Jefferson's will did provide for freeing his personal slaves, but since all of his property (including slaves) was mortgaged and he was in debt, it was not possible to free the majority of them. The book also credits Jefferson with prohibiting slavery in the Northwest Territory and indicates his distress at the fact that his condemnation of slavery was struck from the original draft of the Declaration of Independence.

Certain biographers when writing for younger children may present only a portion of a person's life. In planning their picture book of *Abraham Lincoln*, the D'Aulaires deliberately omitted his assassination and closed the book with the end of the Civil War. The authors' purpose was to present the greatness of the man as he *lived,* for too frequently, they believed, children remember only the manner of Lincoln's death. There is a danger, however, that omissions may over-simplify and thereby distort the truth of a person's life. The critic Jo Carr has argued that it is better not to offer biography to young children at all than to present them with unbalanced portraits distorted by flagrant omissions.[39]

For many years it was thought that children were only interested in reading about the childhoods of great men and women and that the complexities of adult activities would hold no interest for them. For this reason many earlier biographies focused primarily on childhood pranks and legends that suggested future accomplishments, but neglected or rushed through the real achievements of later life. The current emphasis on authentic biography has reversed this trend, since it is much more difficult to find primary source material about a subject's childhood than about his or her adult life. Increasingly, the best authors respect children's right to read honest, objective biographies that tell all the truth and document their writing with source notes or a bibliography.

Style

The author's language is especially important to biography because it bears the burden of making the subject seem alive and sound real. Documented quotes should be woven smoothly into the narrative. When dialogue is invented, it should have the natural rhythms of speech, regardless of the period it represents. Stilted writing creates an impression of wooden characters, as in the following version of George Washington's proposal to Martha Custis:

> One night George went to a party
> And he danced with a young woman.

[39] Jo Carr, "What Do We Do About Bad Biographies?," *Beyond Fact: Nonfiction for Children and Young People* (Chicago: American Library Association, 1982), pp. 119–129.

Her name was Martha.
"How pretty you are!" said George.
He went to see her many times.
"Will you marry me?" he said.
"Will you be my wife?"
"Yes," said Martha, "I will be your wife."[40]

Believable dialogue characterizes the picture-book account of Haydn's composition of his famous "Farewell" symphony in David and Joe Lasker's *The Boy Who Loved Music*. Karl, a young horn player in Haydn's orchestra, is at supper with the other musicians and complains of the prolonged stay at Esterhaza castle decreed by their patron, Prince Nicolaus:

"It's not fair!" he yelled, stamping his feet. "Prince Nicolaus has no right to keep us here this long!" The laughing stopped. Everyone felt as Karl did.

"It's late October," said Xavier. "I haven't seen my family for seven months."

"Alas," Haydn sighed, "just look at this leathery old chunk of cow! Try eating these miserable apple fritters!"

Karl sat down and looked out the window . . . . "Oh," he said, "I wish I could say farewell to this place."[41]

The choice of narrator, or point of view, is also an important consideration in the style of a biography. Rather than write about the childhood of a famous person, a recent trend has been to tell his story from the point of view of a child who was close to the adult character. F. N. Monjo was particularly successful in using this approach when writing about Franklin's visit to France with his grandsons in *Poor Richard in France* and in seeing Jefferson through the eyes of his granddaughter in *Grand Papa and Ellen Aroon*. Such a point of view allows the reader to see greatness through the loving eyes of a grandchild. These are joyful, child-like biographies that present authentic facts from a perspective that will capture the imaginations of 7- to 9-year-olds.

[40]Gertrude Norman, *A Man Named Washington*, illustrated by James Caraway (New York: Putnam, 1960), unpaged.
[41]David Lasker, *The Boy Who Loved Music*, illustrated by Joe Lasker (New York: Viking Press, 1979), unpaged.

A more dispassionate, third-person point of view is generally used for authentic biography. Yet even here, the narrator's tone pervades the presentation. Whatever the form or viewpoint, the background materials should be integrated into the narrative with smoothness and proportion. The judicious use of quotes from letters or journals may support the authenticity of biography, but it should not detract from the absorbing account of the life of the subject. Children enjoy a style that is clear and vigorous. The research must be there, but it should be a natural part of the presentation.

Characterization

The characterization of the subject of a biography must be true to life, neither adulatory nor demeaning in tone. The reader should have the opportunity to know the person as a real human being with both shortcomings and virtues. In order to emphasize the worthiness of their subjects, juvenile biographers sometimes portray them as too good to be true.

Jean Fritz is one author who manages to create vivid portraits of great figures without according them pseudo-sainthood. She has presented Paul Revere as a busy and sometimes forgetful human being in her humorous yet authentic picture-book biography *And Then What Happened, Paul Revere?* He didn't always meet his deadlines, once producing a hymn book some eighteen months after he had promised it! A dreamer, he even left one page in his "Day Book" simply for doodling. The author does not debunk her character; she simply makes him come alive by admitting his foibles, as well as describing his accomplishments.

Comparing two or more biographies of the same subject is one way of understanding the importance of characterization. In Jean Fritz's *The Double Life of Pocahontas*, the Indian princess is a lively child but a tragic young woman, torn by divided loyalties and betrayed kinships in two cultures. Taken to England as the wife of John Rolfe, she realizes that her people will not accept change as easily as the English think. Thus she dreads returning to Jamestown because conflict there seems inevitable. In the simpler text of *Pocahontas* by Jan Gleiter and Kathleen Thompson, on the other hand, there is no suggestion that the Indian girl has any personal struggle with the confusing roles she is asked to play. Her feelings about going to

England as well as her willingness to stay there come only from a desire "to help people to learn to understand each other."[42] The first portrait of Pocahantas, less lofty, is certainly more believable in human terms because it is more complete.

Jean Fritz's characterization of the famed explorer in *Where Do You Think You're Going, Christopher Columbus?* emphasizes both his courage and his huge pride. The author's sense of irony and her wry humor guard against overdramatizing Columbus' greatness. Alongside the reports of his impressive discoveries are the reminders that he was consistently mistaken about them and fierce in protecting his own personal interests:

> Indeed, Colba [Cuba] *had* to be China, just as this *had* to be the Indies. Columbus had been born to find the Indies. His whole life couldn't be a mistake: God couldn't be wrong. But in case anyone disagreed with him, Christopher Columbus had his entire crew sign an oath, swearing that Colba was part of a continent. The crew was told that if any of them ever denied this, he would have his tongue cut out.[43]

Asking students to describe what kind of person Columbus seems to be at various points during the reading of this book may help them appreciate the complexities of his character.

Biography must not degenerate into mere eulogy; re-examining should not become "debunking." The background of subjects' lives, their conversations, their thoughts, and their actions should be presented as faithfully to the facts as possible. The subject should also be seen in relationship to his or her times, for no person can be "read" in isolation.

Theme

Underlying the characterization in all biography—whether it be authentic, fictionalized, or biographical fiction—is the author's interpretation of the subject. No matter how impartial an author may be, a life story cannot be written without some interpretation. The very selection of facts that a

[42]Jan Gleiter and Kathleen Thompson, *Pocahantas*, illustrated by Deborah L. Chabrian (Milwaukee: Raintree Children's Books, 1984), p. 32.
[43]Jean Fritz, *Where Do You Think You're Going, Christopher Columbus?*, illustrated by Margot Tomes (New York: Putnam, 1980), p. 54.

Margot Tomes' illustration reflects one of the many moods of the volatile Christopher Columbus in *Where Do You Think You're Going, Christopher Columbus?* by Jean Fritz.

biographer chooses may limit the dimensions of the portraiture or highlight certain features. In this context every author walks a thin line between theme and bias. Time usually lends perspective and objectivity, but contemporary biography may tend more toward bias. Teachers and librarians need to help children realize that all biographies have a point of view determined by their authors. Again, a comparison of several biographies of the same person will help children discover this fact.

Frequently in juvenile biography, the theme will be identified in the title as in *Martin Luther King: The Peaceful Warrior* by Ed Clayton or *I'm Nobody! Who Are You? The Story of Emily Dickinson* by Edna Barth. Both these titles contain double meanings and point up the theme of the books. The title of the biography of Dickinson reflects the retiring attitude of the New England poet who in later life became a recluse. It is also, however, the title of one of Dickinson's well-known poems.

The remarkable story of Annie Sullivan, Helen Keller's teacher, is told in a biography appropriately titled *The Silent Storm*. Annie's early life had left permanent scars on her spirit: "On the surface, at least, she became more sure of herself, more poised, but underneath there was still the silent storm."[44] Yet her adversities prepared her to face and understand the wild tornado that was young Helen Keller.

There is a danger in oversimplifying and forcing all facts to fit a single mold. An author must not re-create and interpret a life history in terms of one fixed picture. The most common people have several facets to their personalities; the great are likely to be multi-dimensional. The perceptive biographer concentrates on those items from a full life that helped to mold and form that personality. It is this selection and focus that create the theme of the biography.

[44]Marion Brown and Ruth Crone, *The Silent Storm*, illustrated by Fritz Kredel (Nashville, Tenn.: Abingdon, 1963), p. 189.

Types of Presentation and Coverage

Writers of adult biography are bound by definition to an attempt at re-creating the subject's life as fully as possible, with complete detail and careful documentation. Writers of children's biography, however, may use one of several approaches. The resulting types of biography need individual consideration, for each offers to children a different perspective and a different appeal.

PICTURE-BOOK BIOGRAPHIES

A biography cast in picture-book form may span the subject's lifetime or a part of it; it may be directed to a very young audience or to a somewhat older one; it may be authentic or fictionalized. Whatever the case, it remains for the pictures to carry a substantial part of the interpretation. Leonard Marcus points out:

Illustrations, then, contribute more to a picture book biography than occasional picture-equivalents of the

GUIDES FOR EVALUATING JUVENILE BIOGRAPHY

• *Choice of Subject:*
Does the subject's life offer interest and meaning for today's child?
Will knowing this historical or contemporary figure help children understand the past or the present?
Can the subject's experiences widen children's views on the possibilities for their own lives?

• *Accuracy and Authenticity:*
Do text and illustrations reflect careful research and consistency in presentation?
Does the author provide notes about original source material, a bibliography, or other evidence of documentation?
Are there discrepancies of fact in comparison with other books?
Are there significant omissions which result in a distorted picture of the subject's life?

• *Style:*
Are quotations or dialogue used in such a way that the subject is brought to life?
Does the choice of narrator's point of view for a fictionalized biography add to the story?
Is the author's style clear and readable, with background material included naturally?

• *Characterization:*
Is the subject presented as a believable multi-dimensional character, with both strengths and weaknesses?
Does the author avoid both eulogizing and debunking?

• *Theme:*
Does the author's interpretation of the subject represent a fair and balanced approach?
Does the author avoid oversimplifying or manipulating the facts to fit the chosen theme?

author's words. They traffic to some degree in unnameable objects, states and feelings. . . . Along with what it tells us about the values, temperament and concerns of a biography's central character, fine illustration also puts us in contact with an individuality—and a form of praise—that is esthetic.[45]

This sense of heightened perception comes with the illustrations by Alice and Martin Provensen for their Caldecott award-winner, *The Glorious Flight: Across the Channel with Louis Blériot, July 25, 1909*. Papa carries himself with intrepid grace in his unsuccessful attempts to fly, and the pictures that show him above the Channel use contrast and perspective to convey the elation and danger of flight. Many historical and background details appear in the illustrations without being mentioned in the text, inviting speculation, inferences, and discussion. Even the front hardcover binding of this book contains new picture material that will contribute to children's feeling for the time and place.

Joe Lasker's vivid pictures illustrate the military feats of a classic hero, *The Great Alexander the Great*. Since these were real battles which became legendary, it seems appropriate that the art depicts both intense human drama and the hovering presence of the mythical gods of Greece. This imaginative element also reflects the text, since the story makes clear that Alexander and his men were influenced by their beliefs. Another source of appeal for primary children is Lasker's attention to the mighty animals of the story, especially Alexander's faithful horse Bucephalus and the huge war elephants of India.

The charming, sometimes idealized pictures of Ingri d'Aulaire and Edgar Parin d'Aulaire serve to make their books appealing to an audience not yet able to read the text. This husband-and-wife team has written and illustrated beautiful picture-book biographies, including *George Washington; Abraham Lincoln*, for which they received the Caldecott award in 1940; *Buffalo Bill; Pocahontas; Columbus; Benjamin Franklin*; and *Leif, the Lucky*. Full-page colored lithographs printed by

The legendary Alexander the Great proves his courage at an early age by gentling the war horse Bucephalus in this painting by Joe Lasker. From *The Great Alexander the Great*.

the old stone process appear on every other page. Large black and white pictures are on alternate pages, and many small pictures are interspersed throughout these books.

In the brief, easy-vocabulary picture biographies by Aliki, the childlike illustrations create a feeling of true Colonial primitives. In *The Story of Johnny Appleseed*, this author-illustrator has captured the humor and simplicity of the legendary pioneer. Similar simplicity is communicated in *A Weed Is a Flower, The Life of George Washington Carver*. Again, Aliki has made meaningful for the youngest reader the inspiring story of a man who was born a slave but lived to become one of the greatest research scientists in the United States. Another picture biography by the same author is *The Many Lives of Benjamin Franklin*.

The mood or tone of a biography can be quickly established by its pictures. A glance at the gray tones of Lee J. Morton's illustrations for *The Freedom Ship of Robert Smalls* by Louise Meriwether lets us know that this account of a slave who com-

[45]Leonard S. Marcus, "Life Drawings: Some Notes on Children's Picture Book Biographies," *The Lion and the Unicorn*, vol. 4 (Summer 1980), p. 17.

mandeered a Confederate gunboat is a serious tale, despite its triumphant ending. A similar glance at F. N. Monjo's *Poor Richard in France* shows at once the high good humor of Brinton Turkle's illustrations, which match the lively tone of the text. Among the scenes are ones that show Franklin taking off his clothes in the ship's cabin for his daily "air bath," giving a French lady a polite kiss on the neck with rather obvious satisfaction, playing chess with Madame Brillon while she soaks in her bathtub, and dancing wildly to celebrate the news of the American victory at Saratoga.

In Jean Fritz's *What's the Big Idea, Ben Franklin?*, the droll pictures by Margot Tomes emphasize another side of Franklin's character—his ingenuity. Trina Schart Hyman's illustration of Samuel Adams thumbing his nose at the British flag helps set the tone for Fritz's biography, *Why Don't You Get a Horse, Sam Adams?* The same illustrator and author highlight their subject's vanity and penchant for flourishes in *Will You Sign Here, John Hancock?* Tomie de Paola's pictures for *Can't You Make Them Behave, King George?* emphasize Fritz's humor as she helps readers think of the unpopular English monarch in a new way.

A few picture books for older children focus on a subject's work and philosophy rather than his life. Ernest Raboff's series, "Art for Children," presents commentary and full-color reproductions of the work of great artists, along with brief biographical sketches. *Paul Klee, Marc Chagall,* and *Pablo Picasso* are among the subjects. Ann Atwood and Erica Anderson have used breathtaking color photographs to call attention to the words and work of Albert Schweitzer in *For All That Lives.*

SIMPLIFIED BIOGRAPHIES

Not all children who have an interest in biographical information are in full command of the skills of reading. Some of these children are beginning readers; some read independently but are not ready for a long or complex text; some are older children with specialized interests but low skill levels. Various kinds of simplified biographies, usually short and with many illustrations, have been published in response to the needs of these children.

For beginning readers there are a number of biographies with limited vocabularies. One of the

Gwenda Blair's simple biography will help children make the connection between *Laura Ingalls Wilder,* the adult writer, and Laura Ingalls, the pioneer child. Illustration by Thomas B. Allen.

disadvantages of this kind of writing, however, is that it does frequently sound stilted. Often the sentences are set up line by line for ease of reading, rather than in paragraph form. Unfortunately, this creates a choppy effect. This type of jerky sentence pattern is avoided in Gwenda Blair's *Laura Ingalls Wilder,* "A Beginning Biography" from Putnam. The vocabulary is more demanding than the size of the print would indicate. However, children know the details of this author's life so well from her stories and from television that the material already seems familiar, and this familiarity makes for easy reading. The smooth narrative covers the entire span of Laura's life in sixty-four pages, half of which are taken up by Thomas B. Allen's fine black and white drawings.

Few writers can produce a book that is both easy to read and admirable for its style. F. N. Monjo did it in his "I Can Read History Book," *The One Bad Thing about Father.* "Father" is

Theodore Roosevelt, and the one bad thing about him, in his son Quentin's eyes, is that he is President of the United States and thus the whole family—including irrepressible sister Alice—must live in the White House.

> Some man once asked Father why
> he didn't do something about Alice.
> Father said, "I can do one of two things.
> I can be President of the United States.
> Or I can control Alice.
> I cannot possibly do both."[46]

Although easy-to-read biographies must be simplified, they should not be oversimplified. It is important to give children a basis for understanding cause-and-effect relationships and for getting the meaning of unfamiliar terms. In *Abraham Lincoln: For the People* by Anne Colver, little explanation of the Civil War is given, and war is introduced with the very brief sentence: "When the Civil War began the President was even busier."[47] Credence is given to the now-disproved story that Lincoln composed the famous Gettysburg Address while riding on a train. When the Lincolns go to the theater the text states: "The President and Mrs. Lincoln sat in a box."[48] No picture shows the Lincolns in their box seats, so one wonders what images young readers who are not familiar with the legitimate theater will derive from this statement!

Many simple biographies, as in this last example, are not just for beginning readers but are directed toward an 8- or 9-year-old audience. Clyde Bulla has written two very popular biographies for new readers, *Squanto, Friend of the White Man* and *John Billington, Friend of Squanto*. The true story of Squanto is one that has always appealed to children, for it is filled with adventure, anxiety, and pathos. They identify readily with this Indian who was kidnapped by English explorers and spent some eight years in England. Another account which is simply told but difficult to put down is McGovern's *The Secret Soldier:*

The Story of Deborah Sampson. Dressed as a man, Deborah Sampson fought in the American Revolution, managing to escape detection for more than a year. Newly proficient readers will appreciate the detail about Deborah's childhood as well as the format which breaks the text into manageable parts. An even simpler account of Deborah's life, told in lively, direct fashion by Bryna Stevens, is *Deborah Sampson Goes to War*.

The "Crowell Biography" series, with an emphasis on contemporary figures and those from minority populations, is directed to the 7- to 10-year-old age level. Though the books are produced by a variety of authors and illustrators, the formats are uniformly brief and are enhanced by many pictures. Eloise Greenfield has written the story of *Rosa Parks*, the black woman whose refusal to move to the back of a bus in Montgomery, Alabama, triggered events that grew into the Civil Rights Movement. Other books in this fine series include *Ray Charles* by Sharon Bell Mathis, *Leonard Bernstein* by Molly Cone, *The Mayo Brothers* by Jane Goodsell, *Jim Thorpe* by Thomas Fall, *Marian Anderson* by Tobi Tobias, *Cesar Chavez* by Ruth Franchere, *Mary McLeod Bethune* by Eloise Greenfield, and *Malcolm X* by Arnold Adoff.

Some simplified biographies fall into the high interest–low reading level category, where the most popular subjects seem to be from the sports and entertainment worlds. The text in these books may be very brief and illustrations or photographs may be used very liberally. In short, the books are designed to catch and keep the eye of the reluctant or less able older reader. Astronauts have celebrity status as well as the ability to serve as models of extraordinary achievement, making them natural choices for books of this kind. The tragic loss of the space shuttle Challenger and its crew focused new attention on the qualities of men and women willing to risk their lives for space exploration and may make these biographies of particular interest. *Sally Ride, Astronaut: An American First* by June Behrens has a bright photograph on the cover and many photos throughout. There are only three unbroken pages of text in the entire book. With this heavy emphasis on pictures, it seems strange that a page which reports nothing but Sally Ride's meeting and marriage with fellow astronaut Steven Hawley includes not a photo of the husband or the

[46]F. N. Monjo, *The One Bad Thing about Father,* illustrated by Rocco Negri (New York: Harper & Row, 1970), p. 38.

[47]Anne Colver, *Abraham Lincoln: For the People,* illustrated by William Moyers (Champaign, Ill.: Garrard, 1960), p. 60.

[48]Colver, p. 72.

wedding but a snapshot of Sally, her parents, her sister and brother-in-law, and the family dog. This is a very readable book, however, one that is simple in sentence structure but doesn't avoid the multi-syllable vocabulary it takes to describe an astronaut's work. *Space Challenger: The Story of Guion Bluford* by Jim Haskins and Kathleen Benson gives an account of the first black American in space, who was once told by high school counselors that he was "not college material." This book has a somewhat longer text and more vivid writing, including quotes. It is divided into short chapters. The photographs are all in one special section, however, which makes the reading seem more dense.

The "Sports Star" series from Harcourt Brace Jovanovich is available in paperback and provides an appealing visual layout to entice young fans into hearing more about their favorites. Many sports are represented—soccer, hockey, gymnastics, and tennis, as well as basketball, baseball, and football. Several women athletes are included. Unfortunately the writing in some of these books is heavily influenced by the sportscaster tendency to "hype" a subject. In *Wayne Gretzky* by S. H. Burchard we are told that Wayne's father was "an amazing teacher," that Wayne's hockey shot was "incredibly accurate," and that the Edmonton Oilers had "a sensational season." In addition, the page 2 photo of Gretzky, credited to a newspaper source, provides a puzzling composite view; his left and right legs are wearing different uniforms! Older children do appreciate these personal close-ups of sports heroes, but it is unfortunate that such a useful concept has not been executed with more care to produce really fine books.

PARTIAL BIOGRAPHIES

One of the liberties allowed juvenile biographers is the freedom to write only part of the story of a subject's life. Authors are able to focus, if they wish, on a time of high drama and let the demands of constructing a good story help set the time frame for the book. David Kherdian deals with only a portion of the life of Veron Dumehjian, his mother, in *The Road from Home: The Story of an Armenian Girl*. What is central to the story is her family's suffering in the massacre and dispersal of Armenians by the Turks. If those events had been related as only a small part of her life experiences,

their impact and historical significance might have been dulled. Kherdian also chose to assume his mother's first-person point of view, which adds passion and immediacy to this fictionalized biography.

Some partial biographies do furnish information about the subject's entire life, but focus on a few incidents that are particularly memorable. *Mumbet, The Story of Elizabeth Freeman* by Harold Felton has two central incidents. The first and most striking tells how Bet, a slave in a well-to-do Massachusetts household in 1781, convinced a lawyer to appeal to the courts in her behalf. Her case for freedom rested on the grounds that the new state constitution guaranteed freedom and equality to all. After the court ruled in her favor, Bet worked as a paid nurse in her lawyer's household and during Shays' Rebellion helped to protect his family, his silver, and his favorite horse from marauding ruffians—with the aid of a shovel and a hatpin!

She Never Looked Back is both title and theme for Sam and Beryl Epstein's account of Margaret Mead's work in Samoa. There are brief references to her early life and a summary of her later achievements, but the substance of the book describes Mead's first field work in the South Pacific and the important contributions to our understanding of other cultures that were the result. This book is one of a series of "Science Discovery Books"; partial biography seems a natural choice to serve that purpose. Another book in the series, *Truth on Trial: The Story of Galileo Galilei* by Vicki Cobb, covers a longer period of time but focuses on those details which lead up to Galileo's confrontation with the Church for the "crime" of teaching that the planets revolve around the sun.

Other biographies are incomplete for the simple reason that a full treatment of the subject's complex life would make a book too long and unwieldy for young readers. There are several such biographies of Abraham Lincoln, for instance. Carl Sandburg wrote a partial biography for children titled *Abe Lincoln Grows Up*. It was made from the first twenty-seven chapters of the first volume of the longest and most definitive of biographies of Lincoln for adults, Sandburg's *Abraham Lincoln: The Prairie Years*. For his juvenile biography Sandburg included Lincoln's birth and boyhood until he was 19 and "grown up." In singing prose that begs to be read aloud, the author describes Lincoln's desire for knowledge:

And some of what he wanted so much, so deep down, seemed to be in books. Maybe in books he would find the answers to dark questions pushing around in the pools of his thoughts, and the drifts of his mind.[49]

Lincoln's departure for the White House marks the end of a fine book by Olivia Coolidge called *The Apprenticeship of Abraham Lincoln.* Exacting scholarship went into the preparation of this authentic biography. For all the detail that describes him, Lincoln remains something of an enigma, a man who " . . . could put on dignity like a coat, yet shirtsleeves remained his natural costume."[50] This book is written for young adults, though upper elementary school students might be interested in comparing the first chapter with other accounts of Lincoln's childhood.

Two appealing biographical works about real young people in history serve to provide a limited but interesting view of famous figures who were close to them. Harriot Washington was one of several nieces and nephews who became wards of George Washington when their parents died. *Uncle George Washington and Harriot's Guitar* by Miriam Anne Bourne is based on Washington family letters written between 1790 and 1795. It shows Harriot as an obedient, lonely pre-adolescent at Mount Vernon, caring for two little cousins and longing for an instrument and music lessons. Our perception of "Uncle Washington," who finally provides the wanted guitar, is enlarged by this first-hand look at his enormous family responsibilities. This is a book that younger middle-graders can read for themselves.

Barbara Brenner's *On the Frontier with Mr. Audubon* is technically a partial biography of apprentice painter Joseph Mason. As a young teenager he accompanied John James Audubon on an expedi-

tion down the Mississippi River to collect and make life drawings of birds. Mason actually did supply some of the backgrounds for Audubon's *Birds of America* although his name did not appear on the finished paintings. Brenner used Audubon's diary to reconstruct the activities of their trip, then re-created the story as a journal that the apprentice might have kept, focusing on Audubon's obsession with his work:

How I hate this boat life! . . . I am sick of Mr. John James Audubon, too, if the truth be known. All *he* cares about are *his* precious *birds* and *his* painting. . . . The cabin always and forever smells of dead birds. By the time the Great Artist is finished with them, they have set up such a stink in here one can scarcely stand it.[51]

Black and white reproductions of Audubon drawings and other period prints authenticate the setting.

COMPLETE BIOGRAPHIES

Complete biography spans its subject's lifetime. It may be relatively simple or difficult, authentic or fictionalized. Whatever the case may be, the reader should expect a view that has some depth, some balance, some sense of perspective. Among types of biographies, this category has traditionally been the largest, although in recent years trends have favored other kinds of presentations.

Doris Faber's *Eleanor Roosevelt, First Lady of the World,* is an example of a biography that is complete and authentic, but not too difficult for most readers in the upper elementary grades. Since it is only fifty-seven pages long, it is not a detailed biography. However, the author has chosen facts and incidents that interest a young audience. To illustrate the interfering ways of Eleanor's mother-in-law, for instance, Faber relates that she once hired a strict and insensitive nursemaid for her grandchildren; but Eleanor showed her developing independence by replacing "Old Battle-Ax" with a gentler woman. Scandals, troubles, and criticisms are not omitted, but Eleanor's deep need to do useful work, her organizational skills, and her

[49]Carl Sandburg, *Abe Lincoln Grows Up,* reprinted from *Abraham Lincoln: The Prairie Years,* illustrated by James Daugherty (New York: Harcourt, Brace, 1928), p. 135.
[50]Olivia Coolidge, *The Apprenticeship of Abraham Lincoln* (New York: Scribner, 1974), p. viii.

[51]Barbara Brenner, *On the Frontier with Mr. Audubon* (New York: Coward, 1977), p. 41.

The composition of this picture leads the eye not to Franklin and Eleanor Roosevelt, but to their wedding guest, Uncle Teddy, who stole the show. Illustration by Donna Ruff for *Eleanor Roosevelt, First Lady of the World* by Doris Faber.

compassion for others are emphasized. This is not the sort of book that will furnish students with detailed reference material for a report on the accomplishments of Eleanor Roosevelt, as a "complete" biography for adults might do. Instead, it fulfills another important function—to convey to children the spark of a human personality behind a name mentioned briefly in their social studies text.

Some of Jean Fritz's picture-book biographies could be classified as complete since they deal with the subjects' entire life spans, but she has also written longer books about Benedict Arnold in *Traitor*

and General Thomas J. Jackson in *Stonewall*. Both deal with complex characters in an even-handed way. In *Traitor*, Fritz's deft portrait of Benedict Arnold as a young man—daring, ambitious, fond of lavish living—helps to explain some of the puzzling contradictions of his later life. The detailed accounts of Arnold's military heroics may surprise students who know his name only as a synonym for treachery. *Stonewall* contrasts the general's heroic Civil War battle field behavior against his personal idiosyncrasies. The man who kept his line "standing like a stone wall" at Manassas prescribed unusual diets for himself (stale bread and lean meat, or lemons to suck) and lived by arbitrary, self-imposed rules for posture, prayer, and every other form of human conduct. Throughout the book the authentic narrative is enlivened by personal observations and quotes from Jackson's contemporaries. Sources for these quotes are listed in a bibliography of nearly forty items. Like her other biographies, *Stonewall* demonstrates the author's high standards for careful scholarship as well as vivid writing.

Among the many complete biographies for children are a few that have been awarded the Newbery Medal. One of these is the story of a little-known black pioneer of freedom. *Amos Fortune, Free Man* by Elizabeth Yates is the moving account of a common man who lived simply and greatly. Born free in Africa, he was sold as a slave in North America. In time he purchased his own freedom and that of several others. When he was 80 years old, Amos Fortune purchased twenty-five acres of land in the shadow of his beloved mountain, Monadnock—Indian for "the mountain that stands alone." Like Monadnock, Fortune stood alone, a rock of strength and security for all those he loved.

Children who have a special interest in the arts may be intrigued by another Newbery winner, *I, Juan de Pareja*. Since so little is known about the life of Velasquez and his celebrated black assistant, Elizabeth Borten de Treviño had to invent a great deal of material for her story. The fascination of Juan's life lies in his beginnings as a slave, his secret and remarkable talent for his master's business of painting, and the growth of their relationship from master and slave to equals and friends.

Frequently, biographers choose subjects who are credited with unique achievements, whatever the field. Most authors would be dubious about writing an interesting biography for children about a mathematician, but Jean Lee Latham was challenged. She studied mathematics, astronomy, oceanography, and seamanship. Then she went to Boston and Salem to talk with descendants of Nathaniel Bowditch and to do research on the geographical and maritime backgrounds of her story. The result of all this painstaking preparation was the Newbery award-winner *Carry On, Mr. Bowditch*, the amazing story of Nat Bowditch, who had little chance for schooling but mastered the secrets of navigation and wrote a textbook that was used for more than 100 years.

COLLECTIVE BIOGRAPHIES

Many children looking for biographical information want brief material about specific people or about specific endeavors. Literally hundreds of collective biographies have been published to meet this need. In scope and difficulty they run the gamut—some have one-paragraph sketches of many subjects, others have long essays on just a few. Like other books, collective biographies must be judged on more than title and appearance. *America's First Ladies 1789 to 1865* by Chaffin and Butwin promises to tell about the presidents' wives, but in reality tells more about the presidents themselves. Hettie Jones uses a bit of song lyric for her title, *Big Star Fallin' Mama: Five Women in Black Music*. The book gives information about the development of Afro-American music and in the process tells the sometimes tragic stories of five singers: Ma Rainey, Bessie Smith, Mahalia Jackson, Billie Holiday, and Aretha Franklin.

Love and Rivalry: Three Exceptional Pairs of Sisters is the enticing title Doris Faber uses for an authentic collective biography for older readers and adults. Her subjects are Catherine Beecher and Harriet Beecher Stowe, Charlotte Cushman and Susan Cushman Muspratt, and Emily Dickinson and Lavinia Dickinson. By presenting all three double portraits in one book, Faber invites the reader to compare the sisters' relationships as well as the subjects themselves. Another fascinating collection of New England women is presented in *The Mill Girls* by Bernice Selden. The three subjects, little known today, all worked as young women in the textile mills of Lowell, Massachusetts, and went on to make their mark in education, women's suffrage, and labor reform. All told, there are so many collective biographies that teachers and librarians may find it helpful to use a reference such as Silverman's *An Index to Young Readers' Collective Biographies*,[52] which includes thousands of men and women in hundreds of books.

AUTOBIOGRAPHIES AND MEMOIRS

Life stories are often recalled and written down by the subjects themselves, as autobiographies or memoirs. Some children's books based on autobiographical material have been discussed earlier in this chapter as historical fiction. Autobiography has advantages and disadvantages similar to those of informational books of eyewitness history—the warmth and immediacy of personal detail, but a necessarily limited perspective. The criterion of objectivity is reversed here; it is the very subjectivity of this sort of biography which has value. But children do need to be aware of the inherent bias, and they may be encouraged to look to other sources for balance.

Autobiographies by creators of children's books provide an easy introduction to this specialized form of writing. A "Self-Portrait Series" from Addison-Wesley gives book illustrators a chance to use their art as well as their words in telling their own stories. Children who are familiar with several of the books illustrated by Margot Zemach should be able to pick out scenes and characters from them which are incorporated in *Self-Portrait: Margot Zemach*. The tone of the text, as well as the art, provides clues to character; *Self-Portrait: Trina Schart Hyman* is sometimes breezy, sometimes intense; *Self-Portrait: Erik Blegvad* is careful and reflective.

Three popular authors focus their life stories on their writing experiences, explaining along the way the process of writing a book and adding advice for students who dream of writing for publication. *How I Came to Be a Writer* by Phyllis Reynolds Naylor reveals the same wit as her realistic novels. *Chapters: My Growth As a Writer* is Lois Duncan's account of her early successes and later development. Roald Dahl in *Boy: Tales of Childhood* recounts stories of his early family life and

[52]Judith Silverman, *An Index to Young Readers' Collective Biographies*, 3rd ed. (New York: Bowker, 1979).

incidents from his boarding school days, including one that became a scene in one of his own novels.

Biographies of all types give children a glimpse of other lives, other places, other times. The best of them combine accurate information and fine writing in a context that children enjoy—the story that really happened. Both biography and histori-cal fiction serve to put facts into a frame of human feeling. Children may come to know about histori-cal events or contemporary figures from textbooks, but literature that touches this content will bring them a different quality of knowing—more inti-mate and more memorable. All children deserve to have such books as part of their experience.

SUGGESTED LEARNING EXPERIENCES

1. Read four or five books about one particular period or place and chart the references to kinds of food, clothing, houses, transportation, language, and so on. Evaluate which books give the most authentic picture.
2. Prepare a decorated portfolio or box of materials of a particular event or period of time to help children build background for selected books of historical fiction. You may want to include copies of newspaper clippings; artifacts; an annotated bibliography; copies of appropriate paperback books; and examples of art, music, and handcrafts. Plan activity cards for children's use and extension of these materials.
3. Work with classmates or middle-grade students in role-playing dramatic confrontations in historical fiction. Some possible choices would be the witch trial of Kit Tyler in *The Witch of Blackbird Pond* by Speare or Sam Meeker's argument with his father about going to war in *My Brother Sam Is Dead* by the Colliers.
4. Collect examples of dialogue and descriptive language from several books of historical fiction. You might want to include something by Patricia Beatty, Alan Garner, or Rosemary Sutcliff in this sample. What techniques do the authors use to indicate the setting?
5. Compare the values and attitudes of Catherine in *A Gathering of Days* by Joan Blos with those of a young heroine in a contemporary novel, such as Dicey in *Dicey's Song* by Voigt. What are their hopes and expectations? How do they express themselves? How are their priorities different or alike?
6. Look at the selection of biographies in a school library. Make a checklist of how many biographies are about men. About women. What people have been the subject of many biographies? Few? One? What contemporary figures are presented in these biographies?
7. Gather several picture-book biographies or simplified biographies with many illustrations. What information appears in the pictures but not the text? How do the illustrations help create focus and characterization?
8. Select several biographies of one subject, such as Helen Keller. Make a chart to compare information, omissions, point of view of author, documentation. Read related biographies, such as *The Silent Storm* by Brown and Crone, to find out about Helen Keller through her teacher, Annie Sullivan. Make a list of books that might extend this focus—such as biographies of Louis Braille (*Touch of Light* by Neimark), informational books about seeing-eye dogs, and fictional accounts of blindness such as *Follow My Leader* by Garfield.

RELATED READINGS

1. Aiken, Joan. "Interpreting the Past," *Children's Literature in Education*, vol. 16, no. 2, Summer 1985, pp. 67–83.
   From a personal perspective the author discusses the attraction of history and the importance of bringing children to it through stories. Her definition of historical fiction, however, includes one type in which the writer reshapes history to suit his or her own ends.

2. Collier, Christopher. "Johnny and Sam: Old and New Approaches to the American Revolution," *The Horn Book Magazine,* vol. 52, April 1976, pp. 132–138.
   One of the co-authors of popular novels about the Revolution discusses three historiographic interpretations of that conflict and contends that modern historical fiction should not present historical events in simple or one-sided terms.
3. Fritz, Jean. "The Very Truth" in *Celebrating Children's Books,* ed. by Betsy Hearne and Marilyn Kaye. New York: Lothrop, Lee and Shepard, 1981, pp. 81–86.
   One of the very best writers of juvenile biography addresses the issue of censorship and discusses the necessity for telling all the truth.
4. Haugaard, Erik Christian. " 'Before I Was Born': History and the Child," *The Horn Book Magazine,* vol. 55, October 1979, pp. 514–521.
   The author writes of the relationship between history and truth and makes an eloquent case for the values of history in showing that people always have choices.
5. Hunter, Mollie. "Shoulder the Sky" in *Talent Is Not Enough.* New York: Harper & Row, 1976, pp. 31–56.
   A fine writer reveals her sense of history as human drama while discussing several issues critical to historical fiction, including the portrayal of violence and the relationship of contemporary attitudes to those of the past.
6. *The Lion and the Unicorn,* vol. 4, no. 1, Summer 1980.
   This entire issue is devoted to Biography for Young People. Of special interest are Elizabeth Segel's article about a biography of Beatrix Potter, Leonard Marcus' comments on picture-book biographies for children, and an interiew with Milton Meltzer by Geraldine DeLuca and Roni Natov.
7. Segel, Elizabeth. "Laura Ingalls Wilder's America: An Unflinching Assessment," *Children's Literature in Education,* no. 25, Summer 1977, pp. 63–70.
   Segel examines the values portrayed in the Little House series, particularly *Little House on the Prairie,* and points out that Wilder, through the character of Laura, not only presented the attitudes and beliefs of nineteenth-century America but also questioned them.
8. Trease, Geoffrey. "Fifty Years On: A Writer Looks Back," *Children's Literature in Education,* vol. 14, no. 3, Autumn 1983, pp. 149–159.
   This article reflects the author's long career, enabling him to trace changes in his own writing as well as trends in the publishing and popularity of historical fiction.

REFERENCES

HISTORICAL FICTION

Almedingen, E. M. *The Crimson Oak.* Coward McCann, 1983.
Anderson, Margaret J. *The Journey of the Shadow Bairns.* Knopf, 1980.
Angell, Judie. *One-Way to Ansonia.* Bradbury, 1985.
Armstrong, William H. *Sounder,* illustrated by James Barkley. Harper, 1969.
Avi (Wortis). *Encounter at Easton.* Pantheon, 1980.
_____. *The Fighting Ground.* Lippincott, 1984.
_____. *Night Journeys.* Pantheon, 1979.
Baker, Betty. *Killer-of-Death,* illustrated by John Kaufmann. Harper, 1963.
Bawden, Nina. *Carrie's War,* illustrated by Colleen Browning. Lippincott, 1973.
Beatty, Patricia. *Red Rock over the River.* Morrow, 1973.
_____. *Turn Homeward, Hannalee.* Morrow, 1984.
_____. *Wait for Me, Watch for Me, Eula Bee.* Morrow, 1978.
Behn, Harry. *The Faraway Lurs.* Putnam, 1982. (1963)
Benchley, Nathaniel. *Only Earth and Sky Last Forever.* Harper, 1972.
Bishop, Claire Huchet. *Twenty and Ten,* as told by Janet Jolly, illustrated by William Pène du Bois. Viking, 1964.
Blos, Joan W. *A Gathering of Days: A New England Girl's Journal, 1830–32.* Scribner, 1979.
Brink, Carol Ryrie. *Caddie Woodlawn,* illustrated by Kate Seredy. Macmillan, 1936.

_____. *Caddie Woodlawn*, illustrated by Trina Schart Hyman. Macmillan, 1973.

Brown, Irene Bennett. *Before the Lark*. Atheneum, 1982.

Bulla, Clyde Robert. *A Lion to Guard Us*, illustrated by Michele Chessare. Crowell, 1981.

_____. *The Sword in the Tree*, illustrated by Paul Galdone. Crowell, 1956.

_____. *Viking Adventure*, illustrated by Douglas Gorsline. Crowell, 1963.

Butterworth, Emma Macalik. *As the Waltz Was Ending*. Four Winds, 1982.

Carrick, Carol. *Stay Away from Simon!*, illustrated by Donald Carrick. Clarion, 1985.

Christopher, John. *Dom and Va*. Macmillan, 1973.

Clapp, Patricia. *Constance: A Story of Early Plymouth*. Lothrop, 1968.

_____. *I'm Deborah Sampson: A Soldier in the War of the Revolution*. Lothrop, 1977.

_____. *Witches' Children*. Lothrop, 1982.

Collier, James Lincoln, and Christopher Collier. *Jump Ship to Freedom*. Delacorte, 1981.

_____. *My Brother Sam Is Dead*. Four Winds, 1974.

_____. *War Comes to Willy Freeman*. Delacorte, 1983.

_____. *Who Is Carrie?* Delacorte, 1984.

Colver, Anne. *Bread and Butter Indian*, illustrated by Garth Williams. Holt, 1964.

_____. *Bread and Butter Journey*, illustrated by Garth Williams. Holt, 1970.

Conrad, Pam. *Prairie Songs*, illustrated by Darryl Zudeck. Harper, 1985.

Coolidge, Olivia. *Come by Here*, illustrated by Milton Johnson. Houghton Mifflin, 1970.

Cooper, Susan. *Dawn of Fear*, illustrated by Margery Gill. Harcourt, 1970.

Crompton, Anne Eliot. *The Ice Trail*. Methuen, 1980.

Dalgliesh, Alice. *The Courage of Sarah Noble*, illustrated by Leonard Weisgard. Scribner, 1954.

_____. *The Thanksgiving Story*, illustrated by Helen Sewell. Scribner, 1954.

de Angeli, Marguerite. *The Door in the Wall*. Doubleday, 1949.

_____. *Thee, Hannah!* Doubleday, 1949.

DeJong, Meindert. *The House of Sixty Fathers*, illustrated by Maurice Sendak. Harper, 1956.

Dickinson, Peter. *The Dancing Bear*, illustrated by John Smee. Little, Brown, 1972.

Dyer, T. A. *A Way of His Own*. Houghton Mifflin, 1981.

Edmonds, Walter D. *The Matchlock Gun*, illustrated by Paul Lantz. Dodd, Mead, 1941.

Edwards, Sally. *George Midgett's War*. Scribner, 1985.

Fenton, Edward. *The Refugee Summer*. Delacorte, 1982.

Field, Rachel. *Calico Bush*, illustrated by Allen Lewis. Macmillan, 1931.

Fleischman, Paul. *Path of the Pale Horse*. Harper, 1983.

Fleischman, Sid. *Humbug Mountain*, illustrated by Eric Von Schmidt. Atlantic, Little, Brown, 1978.

_____. *Mr. Mysterious and Company*, illustrated by Eric Von Schmidt. Little, Brown, 1962.

Forbes, Esther. *Johnny Tremain*, illustrated by Lynd Ward. Houghton Mifflin, 1946.

Fox, Paula. *The Slave Dancer*, illustrated by Eros Keith. Bradbury, 1973.

Frank, Anne. *Anne Frank: The Diary of a Young Girl*, rev. ed., translated by B. M. Mooyart, introduction by Eleanor Roosevelt. Doubleday, 1967.

Fritz, Jean. *Brady*, illustrated by Lynd Ward. Coward McCann, 1960.

_____. *The Cabin Faced West*, illustrated by Feodor Rojankovsky. Coward McCann, 1958.

_____. *Early Thunder*, illustrated by Lynd Ward. Coward McCann, 1967.

Garfield, Leon. *Fair's Fair*, illustrated by S. D. Schindler. Doubleday, 1983.

_____. *Jack Holborn*, illustrated by Anthony Maitland. Pantheon, 1965.

_____. *Smith*, illustrated by Anthony Maitland. Pantheon, 1967.

Garner, Alan. *The Aimer Gate*, illustrated by Michael Foreman. Philomel, 1979.

_____. *Granny Reardun*, illustrated by Michael Foreman. Philomel, 1978.

_____. *The Stone Book*, illustrated by Michael Foreman. Philomel, 1978.

_____. *Tom Fobble's Day*, illustrated by Michael Foreman. Philomel, 1979.

Garrigue, Sheila. *The Eternal Spring of Mr. Ito*. Bradbury Press, 1985.

Gauch, Patricia L. *This Time, Tempe Wick?*, illustrated by Margot Tomes. Putnam, 1974.

Geras, Adèle. *Voyage*. Atheneum, 1983.

Gipson, Fred. *Old Yeller*, illustrated by Carl Burger. Harper, 1956.

Gray, Elizabeth Janet. *Adam of the Road*, illustrated by Robert Lawson. Viking, 1944.

Haugaard, Erik Christian. *Cromwell's Boy*. Houghton Mifflin, 1978.

_____. *Hakon of Rogen's Saga,* illustrated by Leo Dillon and Diane Dillon. Houghton Mifflin, 1963.

_____. *The Little Fishes.* Houghton Mifflin, 1967.

_____. *A Messenger for Parliament.* Houghton Mifflin, 1976.

_____. *Orphans of the Wind,* illustrated by Milton Johnson. Houghton Mifflin, 1966.

_____. *A Slave's Tale,* illustrated by Leo Dillon and Diane Dillon. Houghton Mifflin, 1965.

Hautzig, Esther. *The Endless Steppe: Growing Up in Siberia.* Crowell, 1968.

_____. *A Gift for Mama,* illustrated by Donna Diamond. Viking, 1981.

Hickman, Janet. *Zoar Blue.* Macmillan, 1978.

Highwater, Jamake. *Legend Days.* Harper, 1984.

Hodges, C. Walter. *The Namesake: A Story of King Alfred.* Coward McCann, 1964.

Holm, Anne. *North to Freedom,* translated by L. W. Kingsland. Harcourt, 1965.

Holman, Felice. *The Wild Children.* Scribner, 1983.

Hooks, William H. *Circle of Fire.* Atheneum, 1984.

Hunt, Irene. *Across Five Aprils.* Follett, 1964.

Hunter, Mollie. *The Stronghold.* Harper, 1974.

_____. *You Never Knew Her As I Did!* Harper, 1981.

Ish-Kishor, Sulamith. *A Boy of Old Prague,* illustrated by Ben Shahn. Pantheon, 1963.

Keith, Harold. *Rifles for Watie.* Crowell, 1957.

Kelly, Eric P. *The Trumpeter of Krakow,* rev. ed., illustrated by Janina Domanska. Macmillan, 1966 (1928).

Kerr, Judith. *When Hitler Stole Pink Rabbit.* Coward McCann, 1972.

Kirby, Susan E. *Ike and Porker.* Houghton Mifflin, 1983.

Koehn, Ilse. *Mischling, Second Degree: My Childhood in Nazi Germany.* Greenwillow, 1977.

Konigsburg, E. L. *A Proud Taste for Scarlet and Miniver.* Atheneum, 1973.

Kroeber, Theodora. *Ishi, Last of His Tribe,* illustrated by Ruth Robbins. Parnassus, 1964.

Kullman, Harry. *The Battle Horse,* translated by George Blecher and Lone Thygesen-Blecher. Bradbury, 1981.

Lampman, Evelyn Sibley. *Bargain Bride.* Atheneum, 1977.

Lasky, Kathryn. *Beyond the Divide.* Macmillan, 1983.

Lehmann, Linda. *Better Than a Princess.* Lodestar/Dutton, 1978.

_____. *Tilli's New World.* Lodestar/Dutton, 1981.

Levitin, Sonia. *Journey to America,* illustrated by Charles Robinson. Atheneum, 1970.

Lord, Athena V. *A Spirit to Ride the Whirlwind.* Macmillan, 1981.

McGraw, Eloise Jarvis. *Mara, Daughter of the Nile.* Coward McCann, 1953.

MacLachlan, Patricia. *Sarah, Plain and Tall.* Harper, 1985.

McSwigan, Marie. *Snow Treasure,* illustrated by Mary Reardon. Dutton, 1942.

Mason, Miriam E. *Caroline and Her Kettle Named Maud,* illustrated by Kathleen Voute. Macmillan, 1951.

Meadowcroft, Enid. *The First Year,* illustrated by Grace Paull. Crowell, 1946.

Moeri, Louise. *Save Queen of Sheba.* Dutton, 1981.

Monjo, F. N. *The Drinking Gourd,* illustrated by Fred Brenner. Harper, 1970.

_____. *The House on Stink Alley: A Story About the Pilgrims in Holland,* illustrated by Robert Quackenbush. Holt, 1977.

O'Dell, Scott. *Island of the Blue Dolphins.* Houghton Mifflin, 1960.

_____. *Sarah Bishop.* Houghton Mifflin, 1980.

_____. *Sing Down the Moon.* Houghton Mifflin, 1970.

_____. *Zia,* illustrated by Ted Lewin. Houghton Mifflin, 1976.

Orlev, Uri. *The Island on Bird Street,* translated from the Hebrew by Hillel Halkin. Houghton Mifflin, 1984.

Osborne, Chester G. *The Memory String.* Atheneum, 1984.

Paton Walsh, Jill. *Children of the Fox,* illustrated by Robin Eaton. Farrar, Straus, 1978.

_____. *Lost and Found,* illustrated by Mary Rayner. André Deutsch, 1984.

Pellowski, Anne. *First Farm in the Valley: Anna's Story,* illustrated by Wendy Watson. Philomel, 1982.

Perez, N. A. *The Slopes of War.* Houghton Mifflin, 1984.

Petry, Ann. *Tituba of Salem Village.* Crowell, 1964.

Reiss, Johanna. *The Journey Back.* Crowell, 1976.

_____. *The Upstairs Room*. Crowell, 1972.
Richard, Adrienne. *Pistol*. Little, Brown, 1969.
Richter, Conrad. *The Light in the Forest*. Knopf, 1953.
Riskind, Mary. *Apple Is My Sign*. Houghton Mifflin, 1981.
Schweitzer, Byrd Baylor. *One Small Blue Bead*, illustrated by Symeon Shimin. Macmillan, 1965.
Sebestyen, Ouida. *On Fire*. Atlantic, 1985.
_____. *Words by Heart*. Atlantic, Little, Brown, 1979.
Siegal, Aranka. *Upon the Head of the Goat: A Childhood in Hungary, 1939–1944*. Farrar, Straus, 1981.
Skurzynski, Gloria. *What Happened in Hamelin*. Four Winds, 1979.
Speare, Elizabeth George. *The Bronze Bow*. Houghton Mifflin, 1961.
_____.*Calico Captive*, illustrated by W. T. Mars. Houghton Mifflin, 1957.
_____. *The Sign of the Beaver*. Houghton Mifflin, 1983.
_____. *The Witch of Blackbird Pond*. Houghton Mifflin, 1958.
Steele, William O. *The Buffalo Knife*, illustrated by Paul Galdone. Harcourt, 1952.
_____. *Flaming Arrows*, illustrated by Paul Galdone. Harcourt, 1957.
_____. *The Lone Hunt*, illustrated by Paul Galdone. Harcourt, 1956.
_____. *The Perilous Road*, illustrated by Paul Galdone. Harcourt, 1958.
_____. *Trail through Danger*, illustrated by Charles Beck. Harcourt, 1965.
_____. *Winter Danger*, illustrated by Paul Galdone. Harcourt, 1954.
Stevens, Carla. *Trouble for Lucy*, illustrated by Ronald Himler. Clarion, 1979.
Sutcliff, Rosemary. *Frontier Wolf*. Dutton, 1981.
_____. *The Eagle of the Ninth*, illustrated by C. W. Hodges. Walck, 1954.
_____. *Knight's Fee*, illustrated by Charles Keeping. Walck, 1960.
_____. *The Lantern Bearers*, illustrated by Charles Keeping. Walck, 1959.
_____. *The Silver Branch*, illustrated by Charles Keeping. Walck, 1959.
_____. *Song for a Dark Queen*. Crowell, 1979.
_____. *Sun Horse, Moon Horse*. Dutton, 1978.
Takashima, Shizuye. *A Child in Prison Camp*. Tundra Books, 1971.
Taylor, Mildred. *Let the Circle Be Unbroken*. Dial, 1981.
_____. *Roll of Thunder, Hear My Cry*, illustrated by Jerry Pinkney. Dial, 1976.
_____. *Song of the Trees*, illustrated by Jerry Pinkney. Dial, 1975.
Taylor, Theodore. *The Cay*. Doubleday, 1969.
Townsend, John Rowe. *Dan Alone*. Lippincott, 1983.
Treece, Henry. *The Road to Miklagaard*. S. G. Phillips, 1957.
_____. *Viking's Dawn*. S. G. Phillips, 1956.
_____. *Viking's Sunset*. Criterion, 1960.
Turner, Ann. *Dakota Dugout*, illustrated by Ronald Himler. Macmillan, 1985.
Uchida, Yoshiko. *Journey to Topaz*, illustrated by Donald Carrick. Scribner, 1971.
Van Woerkom, Dorothy. *Pearl in the Egg: A Tale of the Thirteenth Century*, illustrated by Joe Lasker. Crowell, 1980.
Vander Els, Betty. *The Bombers' Moon*. Farrar, Straus, 1985.
Westall, Robert. *The Machine Gunners*. Greenwillow, 1976.
Wibberley, Leonard. *John Treegate's Musket*. Farrar, Straus, 1959.
Wilder, Laura Ingalls. *The First Four Years*, illustrated by Garth Williams. Harper, 1971.
_____. *The "Little House" Series*, illustrated by Garth Williams. Harper, 1953.
   By the Shores of Silver Lake (1939).
   Little House in the Big Woods (1932).
   Farmer Boy (1933).
   Little House on the Prairie (1935).
   Little Town on the Prairie (1941).
   The Long Winter (1940).
   On the Banks of Plum Creek (1937).
   These Happy Golden Years (1943).
Yep, Laurence. *Dragonwings*. Harper, 1977.
_____. *Mountain Light*. Harper, 1985.
_____. *The Serpent's Children*. Harper, 1984.
Yolen, Jane. *Children of the Wolf*. Viking, 1984.
Zei, Alki. *Petros' War*, translated from the Greek by Edward Fenton. Dutton, 1972.

BIOGRAPHY

Adoff, Arnold. *Malcolm X,* illustrated by John Wilson. Crowell, 1970.

Aliki (Brandenberg). *The Many Lives of Benjamin Franklin.* Prentice-Hall, 1977.

_____. *The Story of Johnny Appleseed.* Prentice-Hall, 1963.

_____. *A Weed Is a Flower, The Life of George Washington Carver.* Prentice-Hall, 1965.

d'Aulaire, Ingri, and Edgar Parin d'Aulaire. *Abraham Lincoln,* rev. ed. Doubleday, 1957.

_____. *Benjamin Franklin.* Doubleday, 1950.

_____. *Buffalo Bill.* Doubleday, 1952.

_____. *Columbus.* Doubleday, 1955.

_____. *George Washington.* Doubleday , 1936.

_____. *Leif, the Lucky.* Doubleday, 1951.

_____. *Pocahantas.* Doubleday, 1949.

Barth, Edna. *I'm Nobody! Who Are You? The Story of Emily Dickinson,* illustrated by Richard Cuffari. Seabury, 1971.

Behrens, June. *Sally Ride, Astronaut: An American First.* Children's Press, 1984.

Blair, Gwenda. *Laura Ingalls Wilder,* illustrated by Thomas B. Allen. Putnam, 1981.

Blegvad, Erik. *Self-Portrait: Erik Blegvad.* Addison-Wesley, 1979.

Bourne, Miriam Anne. *Uncle George Washington and Harriot's Guitar,* illustrated by Elise Primavera. Coward McCann, 1983.

Brenner, Barbara. *On the Frontier with Mr. Audubon.* Coward McCann, 1977.

Brown, Marion, and Ruth Crone. *The Silent Storm,* illustrated by Fritz Kredel. Abingdon, 1963.

Bulla, Clyde Robert. *John Billington, Friend of Squanto,* illustrated by Peter Burchard. Crowell, 1956.

_____. *Squanto, Friend of the White Man,* illustrated by Peter Burchard. Crowell, 1954.

Burchard, S. H. *Wayne Gretzky* (Sports Star Series). Harcourt, 1982.

Chaffin, Lillie, and Miriam Butwin. *America's First Ladies, 1789 to 1965.* Lerner, 1969.

Clayton, Ed. *Martin Luther King: The Peaceful Warrior,* 3rd ed., illustrated by David Hodges. Prentice-Hall, 1968.

Cobb, Vicki. *Truth on Trial: The Story of Galileo Galilei,* illustrated by George Ulrich. Coward McCann, 1979.

Cone, Molly. *Leonard Bernstein,* illustrated by Robert Galster. Crowell, 1970.

Coolidge, Olivia. *The Apprenticeship of Abraham Lincoln.* Scribner, 1974.

Dahl, Roald. *Boy: Tales of Childhood.* Farrar, Straus, 1984.

De Treviño, Elizabeth Borten. *I, Juan de Pareja.* Farrar, Straus, 1965.

_____. *Juarez, Man of Law.* Farrar, Straus, 1974.

Devaney, John. *Hitler: Mad Dictator of World War II.* Putnam, 1978.

Duncan, Lois. *Chapters: My Growth As a Writer.* Little, Brown, 1982.

Fall, Thomas. *Jim Thorpe,* illustrated by John Gretzer. Crowell, 1970.

Edmonds, I. G. *The Magic Dog.* Lodestar/Dutton, 1982.

Epstein, Sam, and Beryl Epstein. *She Never Looked Back: Margaret Mead in Samoa,* illustrated by Victor Juhasz. Coward McCann, 1980.

Faber, Doris. *Eleanor Roosevelt, First Lady of the World,* illustrated by Donna Ruff. Viking Kestrel, 1985.

_____. *Love and Rivalry: Three Exceptional Pairs of Sisters.* Viking, 1983.

Felton, Harold W. *Mumbet, The Story of Elizabeth Freeman,* illustrated by Donn Albright. Dodd, Mead, 1970.

Fleming, Thomas J. *First in Their Hearts, A Biography of George Washington.* Norton, 1968.

Franchere, Ruth. *Cesar Chavez,* illustrated by Earl Thollander. Crowell, 1970.

Fritz, Jean. *And Then What Happened, Paul Revere?,* illustrated by Margot Tomes. Coward McCann, 1973.

_____. *Can't You Make Them Behave, King George?,* illustrated by Tomie de Paola. Coward McCann, 1976.

_____. *China Homecoming.* Putnam, 1985.

_____. *The Double Life of Pocahontas,* illustrated by Ed Young. Putnam, 1983.

_____. *Homesick: My Own Story,* illustrated by Margot Tomes. Putnam, 1982.

_____. *Stonewall,* illustrated by Stephen Gammell. Putnam, 1979.

_____. *Traitor: The Case of Benedict Arnold.* Putnam, 1981.

_____. *What's the Big Idea, Ben Franklin?*, illustrated by Margot Tomes. Coward McCann, 1976.

_____. *Where Do You Think You're Going, Christopher Columbus?*, illustrated by Margot Tomes. Putnam, 1980.

_____. *Why Don't You Get a Horse, Sam Adams?*, illustrated by Trina Schart Hyman. Coward McCann, 1974.

_____. *Will You Sign Here, John Hancock?*, illustrated by Trina Schart Hyman. Coward McCann, 1976.

Goodsell, Jane. *The Mayo Brothers*, illustrated by Louis S. Glanzman. Crowell, 1972.

Greenfield, Eloise. *Mary McLeod Bethune*, illustrated by Jerry Pinkney. Crowell, 1977.

_____. *Rosa Parks*, illustrated by Eric Marlow. Crowell, 1973.

Haskins, Jim, and Kathleen Benson. *Space Challenger: The Story of Guion Bluford*. Carolrhoda Books, 1984.

Hyman, Trina Schart. *Self-Portrait: Trina Schart Hyman*. Addison-Wesley, 1981.

Johnston, Johanna. *Harriet and the Runaway Book: The Story of Harriet Beecher Stowe and Uncle Tom's Cabin*, illustrated by Ronald Himler. Harper, 1977.

Jones, Hettie. *Big Star Fallin' Mama: Five Women in Black Music*. Viking, 1974.

Kaufman, Mervyn. *Jessie Owens*, illustrated by Larry Johnson. Crowell, 1973.

Kherdian, David. *The Road from Home: The Story of an Armenian Girl*. Greenwillow, 1979.

Lasker, David. *The Boy Who Loved Music*, illustrated by Joe Lasker. Viking, 1979.

Lasker, Joe. *The Great Alexander the Great*. Viking, 1983.

Latham, Jean Lee. *Carry On, Mr. Bowditch*, illustrated by John O'Hara Cosgrave II. Houghton Mifflin, 1955.

Lawson, Robert. *Ben and Me*. Little, Brown, 1951 (1939).

_____. *Mr. Revere and I*. Little, Brown, 1953.

Lomask, Milton. *Odd Destiny, A Life of Alexander Hamilton*. Farrar, Straus, 1969.

McGovern, Ann. *The Secret Soldier: The Story of Deborah Sampson*, illustrated by Ann Grifalconi. Four Winds, 1975.

Mathis, Sharon Bell. *Ray Charles*, illustrated by George Ford. Crowell, 1973.

Meltzer, Milton. *Dorothea Lange: Life through the Camera*, illustrated by Donna Diamond, photos by Dorothea Lange. Viking, 1985.

Meriwether, Louise. *The Freedom Ship of Robert Smalls*, illustrated by Lee Jack Morton. Prentice-Hall, 1971.

Monjo, F. N. *Grand Papa and Ellen Aroon, Being an Account of Some of the Happy Times Spent Together by Thomas Jefferson and His Favorite Granddaughter*, illustrated by Richard Cuffari. Holt, 1974.

_____. *The One Bad Thing about Father*, illustrated by Rocco Negri. Harper, 1970.

_____. *Poor Richard in France*, illustrated by Brinton Turkle. Holt, 1973.

Naylor, Phyllis Reynolds. *How I Came to Be a Writer*. Atheneum, 1978.

Provensen, Alice, and Martin Provensen. *The Glorious Flight: Across the Channel with Louis Blériot*. Viking, 1983.

Raboff, Ernest. *Marc Chagall*. Doubleday, 1968.

_____. *Pablo Picasso*. Doubleday, 1968.

_____. *Paul Klee*. Doubleday, 1968.

Sandburg, Carl. *Abe Lincoln Grows Up*, reprinted from *Abraham Lincoln: The Prairie Years*, illustrated by James Daugherty. Harcourt, 1928.

Scioscia, Mary. *Bicycle Rider*, illustrated by Ed Young. Harper, 1983.

Selden, Bernice. *The Mill Girls*. Atheneum, 1983.

Shepherd, Elizabeth. *The Discoveries of Esteban the Black*, maps by William Steinel. Dodd, Mead, 1970.

Stevens, Bryna. *Deborah Sampson Goes to War*, illustrated by Florence Hill. Carolrhoda Books, 1984.

Sullivan, George. *Sadat: The Man Who Changed Mid-East History*. Walker, 1981.

Surge, Frank. *Western Outlaws*. Lerner, 1969.

Tobias, Tobi. *Marian Anderson*, illustrated by Symeon Shimin. Crowell, 1972.

Wood, James Playstead. *The Life and Words of John F. Kennedy*. Scholastic, 1966.

Yates, Elizabeth. *Amos Fortune, Free Man*, illustrated by Nora S. Unwin. Dutton, 1950.

Zemach, Margot. *Self-Portrait: Margot Zemach*. Addison-Wesley, 1978.

INFORMATIONAL BOOKS

I n Jean Rogers' fictional story *The Secret Moose*, Gerald finds a huge animal with a wounded flank lying in a snowbank not far from his backyard in Fairbanks, Alaska. It is his own secret discovery which he does not want to share, but he *is* concerned and curious. He calls his mother at the library where she works and asks her to bring home an informational book that will tell "all about a moose." From the pictures Gerald realizes that his moose is a female, and he reads that she will use her ears to signal when she is happy, fearful, or angry. Gerald visits the stranded moose again and again, cutting willow branches for her to eat and keeping close watch on her ears. He observes many of the things he has read about, like her huge appetite and calm cud-chewing. What he hasn't expected is the sudden appearance of her wobbly baby, looking "like a bundle of sticks." By the time the moose and her calf move on, as Gerald has known they must, his mother has located a copy of the book that he can keep for his own. In his room Gerald finds the page that shows the map of Alaska and studies the area marked as the moose's range:

He thought about the moose and her calf browsing there, chewing the tender ends of miles and miles of willow, sleeping in the thickets with the sun warm on their backs, pulling at the grass that was getting thicker and greener every day.

Gerald smiled, turned the page, and settled down to read the book again.[1]

Informational books can play a special and very satisfying role in children's lives and in their learning. The right book at the right time can be a treasure, as the moose book was for Gerald. Every child needs a teacher or librarian who will play the role of Gerald's mother and provide that book.

[1]Jean Rogers, *The Secret Moose*, illustrated by Jim Fowler (New York: Greenwillow, 1985), p. 64

INFORMATIONAL BOOKS FOR TODAY'S CHILD

New worlds and new interests lie waiting for children between the covers of recent informational books. The secrets of mummies, micro-photography, and making maple sugar have all been revealed in attractive and inviting formats in Patricia Lauber's *Tales Mummies Tell,* Barbara Wolberg's *Zooming In: Photographic Discoveries under the Microscope,* and Kathryn Lasky's *Sugaring Time.* Informational books also offer children new perspectives on more familiar topics. *Growing Older* by George Ancona can help children appreciate their grandparents' generation; *How It Feels When Parents Divorce* by Jill Krementz presents a broad range of children's feelings in their own words. Some informational books, like the pop-up anato-

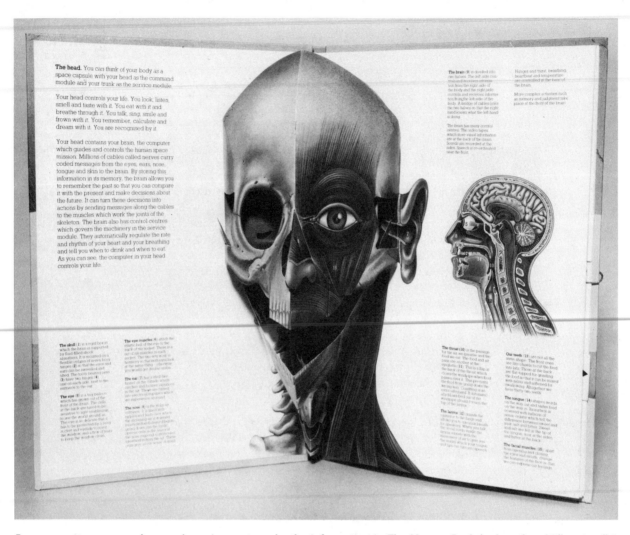

Pop-ups, cutaways, overlays, and moving parts make the information in *The Human Body* by Jonathan Miller visually exciting. Designed by David Pelham.

my of *The Human Body* by Jonathan Miller, have tremendous eye appeal and invite browsing. Others are designed to reward sustained attention, like Constance Irwin's book about the Vikings in America, *Strange Footprints on the Land*.

Certainly there are more fine informational books, with a wider variety of forms and topics, than ever before. However, such books have still not earned their fair share of critical attention and recognition. Author Betty Bacon has pointed out that nonfiction books won the Newbery Medal only six times in fifty-eight years, and those

winners were history or biography in which the chronological narrative form is very much like fiction.[2] This is quite a contrast to the situation in literature for adults, where authors like John McPhee and Tracy Kidder regularly win critical acclaim for their work, and nonfiction frequently dominates the best-seller lists.

One critic who has given close attention to informational books for children is Jo Carr. Teach-

[2]Betty Bacon, "The Art of Nonfiction," *Children's Literature in Education*, vol. 12 (Spring 1981), p. 3.

ers and librarians who want to choose the very best books available can be guided by her view that a nonfiction writer is first a teacher, then an artist, and should be concerned with feeling as well as thinking, passion as well as clarity.[3] Specific criteria can be used to help identify this level of achievement. Being familiar with these criteria and with the types of books in which information is presented will make it easier to choose the best books at the right time.

Criteria for Evaluating Informational Books

A consideration of the following points should help teachers and librarians in the evaluation of informational books. No hierarchy of values is implied in the order of discussion, although accuracy is always of primary importance. The reviewer will need to judge the various elements; there is no definite "scoring," for a book's major strengths may far outweigh a few minor weaknesses.

ACCURACY AND AUTHENTICITY

Qualifications of the Author

Informational books are written by people who are authorities in their fields; or they are written by writers who study a subject, interview specialists, and compile the data. A few, like naturalist Jean Craighead George, are both specialists and writers. It is always a good idea to check the book's jacket copy, title page, introduction, or "About the Author" page at the back for information about the author's special qualifications, often expressed in terms of professional title or affiliation. Expertise in one field does not necessarily indicate competency in another, however, so we expect a high degree of authenticity only if the author has limited the book to what appears to be his or her specialty.

If a book is written not by an expert in the field but by a "writer," facts can be checked by authorities and the authority cited. For example, the book *The Amazing Dandelion* by Millicent Selsam, with striking magnified photographs by Jerome Wexler, acknowledges that both text and pictures were checked by the president of the New York Botani-

cal Gardens. Add to this the knowledge—available in a note at the end of the book—that the author herself is not only a specialist, trained in botany, but also a writer who has produced many children's science books, and we can select this book with considerable assurance that the content is accurate. Selsam is only one of a number of authors who have earned the reputation of writing dependably good informational books. When in doubt, teachers and librarians are likely to turn first to writers who have proved their integrity with facts—Isaac Asimov, Herbert Zim, Seymour Simon, Edwin Tunis, Milton Meltzer, and Genevieve Foster, among others. But authorship, while it may be a valuable rule of thumb, is a dangerous final criterion. Each book must be evaluated on its own merits.

Accuracy of Facts

Fortunately, many of the errors of fact in children's informational books are minor ones. Gerald Johnson's book *The Presidency* mentions that the President's home is called the White House, " . . . although its official name is the Executive Mansion . . ."[4] Natalie Miller's *Story of the White House* plainly states that "White House" was made the official title by an Act of Congress in 1902, a fact easy to corroborate in various reference sources. Children who have access to a variety of books on one topic should be encouraged to notice discrepancies and pursue the correct answer, a valuable exercise in critical reading.

Errors that teachers and children may recognize are less distressing than those that pass for fact because the topic is unfamiliar or highly specialized. Then the reader must depend on a competent reviewer to identify inaccuracies. Ideally, a book with technical information should be reviewed by someone with expertise in that field. *Appraisal: Children's Science Books* is a periodical that offers paired reviews, one by a science professional, one by a teacher or librarian. *The Horn Book Magazine* singles out science books for special reviewing efforts, although other nonfiction in included. *School Library Journal* often provides helpful criti-

---

[3]Jo Carr, "Writing the Literature of Fact," in *Beyond Fact: Nonfiction for Children and Young People* (Chicago: American Library Association, 1982), pp. 3–12.

[4]Gerald W. Johnson, *The Presidency* (New York: Morrow, 1962), p. 11.

cism. *Social Education* and *Science and Children* magazines also give some attention to appropriate books. Generally speaking, science books are more likely to be challenged by experts than those about history or other topics in the humanities.

Being Up-to-Date

Some books that are free of error at the time of writing become inaccurate with the passage of time, as new discoveries are made in the sciences or as changes occur in world politics. Books that focus on the past are less likely to be rapidly outdated, although new discoveries in archaeology or new theories in history and anthropology may call for a re-evaluation of even these materials. On the other hand, books that focus on areas of vigorous research and experimentation, such as viruses and disease or space technology, are quickly outdated. Lee Priestley's 1979 book, *America's Space Shuttle,* could only anticipate events which are now history. Steven Lindblom makes the engaging admission in his 1985 book, *How to Build a Robot,* that anything written about robot technology will be out of date by the time it reaches the reader. It is worth noting, however, that the latest trade books are almost always more up-to-date than the latest textbooks or encyclopedias.

It is also difficult, but important, to provide children with current information about other countries where national governments are emerging or where future political developments are uncertain. In the 1970s the situation in Southeast Asia changed so rapidly that often only the daily news could provide completely up-to-date information. Denis J. Hauptly's *In Vietnam* traces the long history of conflict in that country and indicates that the end of the story has not yet been written, which is one way of putting the present in perspective and calling attention to change.

Books about minority cultures need to include material on contemporary experience, as well as heritage. Too many studies of American Indians, for example, have dealt only with Indian life when the country was being explored and settled. It is refreshing now to have stories like Bernard Wolf's *Tinker and the Medicine Man,* which shows a modern Navajo family interested in preserving traditional ways but willing to live in a trailer dur-

ing the school year so that the children need not be separated from their parents.

Including All the Significant Facts

Though the material presented in a book may be current and technically correct, the book cannot be totally accurate if significant facts are omitted. Twenty-five years ago science books that dealt with animal reproduction frequently glossed over the specifics of birth or mating. In McClung's *Possum,* the process is explained as: "All night long the two of them wandered through the woods together. But at dawn each went his own way again. Possum's babies were born just twelve days later."[5] Fortunately, changing social mores which struck down taboos in children's fiction also encouraged a new frankness in books of information. For instance, close-up photographs and a forthright text in *My Puppy Is Born* by Joanna Cole show the birth, delivery, and early development of a dachshund's litter.

Human reproduction and sexuality have so often been distorted by omissions that books with accurate terminology and explicit information are particularly welcome. An attractive book designed for parents to share with young children is Stein's *Making Babies,* which deals head-on with questions that adults often find difficult to answer. After suggesting an uncomplicated way to explain the mechanics of intercourse the author says: "It is sensible and honest to add that, because it feels nice, people make love together even when they are not starting a baby."[6] This book is part of the *Open Family* series, which also includes *About Handicaps* and *About Dying,* a topic often camouflaged by euphemisms. For older children, Eda LeShan offers a frank and helpful discussion of reactions to grief in *Learning to Say Good-By.*

The honest presentation of all the facts contributes to an effect of realism as well as to total accuracy. This is true in historical or cultural accounts as well as in the sciences. Alex Bealer's chronicle of the Cherokee removal in *Only the Names Remain:*

[5]Robert McClung, *Possum* (New York: Morrow, 1963), p. 41.
[6]Sara Bonnett Stein, *Making Babies,* photographs by Doris Pinney (New York: Walker, 1974), p. 38.

The Cherokees and the Trail of Tears is made to seem dramatic and immediate by the richness of detail. We learn that Andrew Jackson himself crossed out a treaty provision allowing Cherokee families to own Georgia farms, that soldiers sent to the Indian cabins forced even the sick out of their beds to march to the stockades, that government contractors supplied the journeying Cherokees with rotten meat and weevily corn. It is interesting to compare this authentic tale with Scott O'Dell's fictionalized account of the similar plight of the Navajos in *Sing Down the Moon* (see Chapter 10).

Avoiding Stereotypes

A book that omits significant facts tells only part of the truth; a book that presents stereotypes pretends, wrongly, to have told the whole truth. One subtle but very common sort of stereotyping is by omission. The illustrations in science books, for instance, often create the impression that scientists must be male Caucasians, since so few women or minorities are pictured. A new level of awareness, however, has brought about the publication of books that, without fanfare, show women in a greater variety of roles. Examples are the doctor in Rockwell's picture book, *My Doctor,* or the surveyor in Gail Gibbons' *New Road!* Some books are directed toward combating stereotypes. The series titled *What Can She Be?* by Esther and Gloria Goldreich features a woman as an architect, a newscaster, a veterinarian, and in other equally significant occupations. The cover of *Careers in a Medical Center* by Mary Davis shows a black doctor and a white child; the fact that this picture is so uncommon as to be worth mentioning indicates how far we have to go in dealing with stereotype by omission.

Perhaps the most blatant form of stereotyping occurs in books about other lands. Children can be taught to be alert to sweeping general statements such as this one found in an older book, *Looking at Italy:* "Those who live in the north are tough, and make good businessmen. Those of the south are easy going and less efficient."[7] It is difficult to portray a country or region accurately in all its diversity of terrain, people, industry, housing, and such. One solution to the problem is exemplified by Julia Singer's *We All Come From Someplace: Children of Puerto Rico,* which uses photographs to show differing life styles in a fishing village, a city, a mountain village, and a sugar-mill town. The brief text is written as the first-person narration of the children whose homes are described. Another way to deal with diversity without presenting stereotypes is to limit the scope of the book as Tom Shachtman has done in *Growing Up Masai.* Defining a cultural group rather than a nation indicates that the author will be able to maintain a clearer focus.

Using Facts to Support Generalizations

A proper generalization, to be distinguishable from stereotype or simple opinion, needs facts for support. Ron Roy begins his book *Move Over, Wheelchairs Coming Through!* in this way:

> Thousands of kids are wheelchair users. These young people are disabled, but in most cases their disabilities have not stopped them from doing the things they want to do.[8]

The entire book is organized to support this point. Seven young wheelchair users were photographed and interviewed; an essay about each one shows their mobility and determination.

Laurence Pringle says in *The Only Earth We Have* that meat-eating birds at the end of food chains have been seriously affected by biocides. Three pieces of evidence are offered: the large amounts of DDT found in the bodies of dead eagles and in eggs that did not hatch, the lowered population of eagles and ospreys in areas where DDT is heavily used, and the thriving bird population in areas relatively free of biocides. Critical readers need to be aware of generalizations and judge for themselves if adequate facts are offered for support.

[7]Rupert Martin, *Looking at Italy* (Philadelphia: Lippincott, 1966), p. 12.

[8]Ron Roy, *Move Over, Wheelchairs Coming Through!,* photos by Rosmarie Hauserr (New York: Clarion Books, 1985), p. 1.

This photo of a wheelchair user leading the neighborhood fun shows a positive image of a handicapped child. Photo by Rosmarie Hausherr from *Move Over, Wheelchairs Coming Through!* by Ron Roy.

Making the Distinction between Fact and Theory

Careful writers make careful distinctions between fact and theory; but, even so, children need guidance in learning to recognize the difference. Often the distinction depends on key words or phrases—such as "scientists believe," "so far as we know," or "perhaps." Consider the effect of the simple phrase "may have" in this description of a prehistoric reptile: "Pterodactyls lived near the shores of prehistoric seas and may have slept hanging from tree branches by their feet, like bats."[9] Some dis-

[9]David C. Knight, *"Dinosaurs" That Swam and Flew*, illustrated by Lee J. Ames (Englewood Cliffs, N. J.: Prentice-Hall, 1985), p. 39.

cussion of different kinds of possible evidence might be in order as children are led to see that one half of this statement is presented as fact, the other as theory. Although the word "theory" is not used in Julian May's *The Warm-Blooded Dinosaurs,* the title and text stress that this is a new idea, and that the answers to certain puzzling questions fit better with the new idea than with the old notion of dinosaurs as cold-blooded.

While it is important to distinguish between fact and theory in all of the sciences, and the social sciences as well, the matter receives most attention in books dealing with evolution and human origins. In some communities this remains a sensitive topic, but it would seem that children everywhere have a right to information about scientists' discoveries and theories regarding our origins. *Why Things Change: The Story of Evolution* by Jeanne Bendick has a particularly good explanation of time relationships, as well as appropriate examples which demonstrate the meaning of such terms as "evolve," "adapt," and "extinct."

Avoiding Anthropomorphism

In poetry and fiction the assignment of human feelings and behavior to animals, plants, or objects is called personification—an accepted literary device that may be used with great effect. In science, however, the same device becomes unacceptable and is known as *anthropomorphism*. In a book that purports to be an informational book, this seems to say to the child: "You really do not have the intelligence or interest to understand or accept straightforward information." Science writer Millicent Selsam addressed the problem of interpreting what animals do in one of her early books on animal behavior:

> It is hard to keep remembering that animals live in a different kind of world from our own. They see, hear, smell, and taste things differently. And they do not have human intelligence or emotions, so we must avoid interpreting their behavior in terms of our own feelings and thoughts. For example, it looks to us as though parent birds are devoted to their young in the same way that human parents are devoted to theirs. But only experimental work can show whether this interpretation is true.[10]

Knowing that young children perceive new things in terms of their own experiences and feelings, however, writers of books directed to this audience often give names to their animal characters and express behavior in a child's terms. In *Biography of a Polar Bear* by Barbara Steiner there comes a point during young Nanook's first experience with seal fishing when, like a child, he "could not sit still any longer." Very rarely are animal books at this level completely free of anthropomorphic touches. Carol Fenner's excellent book *Gorilla Gorilla* does report only the observable behavior of an animal born wild, captured, and kept in a zoo; yet an undercurrent of emotion in

the text allows the reader to suppose how such a creature feels.

Closely related to anthropomorphism is another error called *teleological explanation of phenomena*. Briefly, teleology attempts to account for natural phenomena by assigning a humanlike purpose to the plants, animals, or forces involved. Science books should not suggest that leaves turn toward the light in order to bask in the sun or that Mother Nature, capitalized and personified, is at work carving the walls of canyons. While such a description has a certain poetic effect, it also conveys a basically unscientific attitude.

CONTENT AND PERSPECTIVE

Purpose

It is futile to try to pass judgment on the content of an informational book without first determining the purpose for which the book was designed. Identifying the scope of the book lets us know what we can reasonably expect. A quick look at Anita Gustafson's *Some Feet Have Noses* shows that this is a fascinating collection of specialized facts for browsing, whereas both the title and appearance of Helen Sattler's 316-page *The Illustrated Dinosaur Dictionary* indicate a comprehensive treatment of the topic. Titles can be misleading, particularly those that promise to tell "all about" a subject but offer limited coverage instead. At best, titles both indicate the scope of the book's content and pique the reader's curiosity, as do John J. Loeper's *Going to School in 1876* and *Body Noises* by Susan Buxbaum and Rita Gelman. More about the scope and purpose of informational books can be found in the section "Types of Informational Books," beginning on page 605.

Intended Audience

Before evaluating content we have to know not just for what the book was intended, but for whom. Book jackets or book reviews often indicate an age range according to reading level or interest. It is difficult to know whether one or both of these factors are reflected in the age recommended. Generally, the readability level of a book is not as important as its content in relation to the reader's actual interest in a subject. Older students and adults may turn to children's informational books for introductory material on an unfamiliar

---

[10]Millicent Selsam, *Animals as Parents*, illustrated by John Kaufmann (New York: Morrow, 1965), p. 16.

topic. In using informational books, children will read "beyond their abilities" when reading for particular facts. Children will frequently turn to difficult books if they contain many pictures or useful diagrams. At the same time, vocabulary, sentence length, size of type, and the organization of the book are factors to be considered. When children see crowded pages, relatively small type, and few pictures, they may reject a book which contains useful information.

The choice of topic, then, is an important factor in determining whether a book will be suitable for its intended audience. Books for young children most often reflect their basic egocentric concerns and their curiosity about themselves and other living things. It is a mistake to assume that they will not be interested in other subjects, however. Although *In the Driver's Seat* by Ron and Nancy Goor is best for independent readers, many younger children find the photographs of race cars, eighteen-wheelers, and the Concorde jet very appealing. On the other hand, books that look like picture books are not always for primary audiences. *Shakespeare's Flowers* by Jessica Kerr, for example, is handsomely illustrated in delicate, glowing colors, but the content serves a mature and rather specialized audience.

Examples chosen by an author to illustrate concepts have a great deal to do with the level of cognitive development needed for comprehension of the book. In *Less Than Nothing Is Really Something,* with a picture-book format, Froman has considered the child's need to think in terms of the concrete and to manipulate objects. His explanation of negative integers asks children to recall their experience with thermometers, with steps descending below ground level, with the astronauts' countdown to blast-off. He also includes number lines to make and games to play.

Adequate Coverage

Recognizing the purpose of a book and its intended level, the reader has a basis for deciding if the author has said too much about his topic or too little. *The Bread Book: All about Bread and How to Make It* by Carolyn Meyer is an example of a book that looks at its topic from every conceivable angle. Nearly one hundred pages of legends, traditions, history, recipes, bakery techniques, and international types might become tedious if not for

the author's lively narrative style and humorous drawings.

Other topics, like the history of a nation, might require many more pages in order to allow even brief attention to all the significant material. History textbooks have earned particularly harsh criticism for faulty coverage,[11] and good trade books are needed to fill in the gaps. Gerald Johnson expressed the need for careful writing in the introduction to his book, *America Is Born:*

> Part of the story is very fine, and other parts are very bad, but they all belong to it, and if you leave out the bad parts you never understand it all.[12]

The author who fails to acknowledge more than one viewpoint or theory fails to help children learn to examine issues. Even young children should know that authorities do not always agree, though the context may be very simple. In *A Book about Pandas,* Gross reports:

> The zoo keepers in China say that female pandas are friendlier than male pandas. Other zoo keepers do not agree. They say that pandas are like people—every one is different.[13]

Various theories about the origin of Stonehenge are presented in *The Mystery of Stonehenge* by Branley. Without bias, the author discusses the studies and conclusions of scientists from several fields and sums up: "But Stonehenge remains a challenge. Its mysteries may be locked forever within the silent stones."[14]

Demonstration of Scientific Method

Since we are concerned about *how* as well as *what* children learn, it is important to note what kind of thinking a book encourages, as well as the body of fact it presents. Informational books should illustrate the process of inquiry, the excitement of

[11]See Frances FitzGerald, *America Revised* (Boston: Atlantic-Little, Brown, 1979).

[12]Gerald Johnson (in an introductory letter to Peter). *America Is Born*, illustrated by Leonard Everett Fisher (New York: Morrow, 1959), pp. viii–ix.

[13]Ruth Belov Gross, *A Book about Pandas* (New York: Dial, 1972), unpaged.

[14]Franklyn M. Branley, *The Mystery of Stonehenge,* illustrated by Victor Ambrus (New York: Crowell, 1969), p. 47.

discovery. Children in the upper elementary grades are fascinated by the dramatic account of *Thor Heyerdahl: Viking Scientist* by Wyatt Blasingame, a story which embodies the spirit of scientific investigation. *Pack, Band and Colony: The World of Social Animals* by Judith and Herbert Kohl describes the community structure of wolves, lemurs, and termites. In the process it describes the work of the naturalists who have observed them in field environments. This book gives its readers a good idea of what scientists must think about as well as what they do.

While these are fine accounts of the scientific method at work, the reader's involvement is still a vicarious one. Some books are designed to give children more direct experience with the skills of inquiry. The series, *A First Look at . . .* by Selsam and Hunt is particularly good for helping the primary-grade child develop his ability to observe and classify. In *A First Look at Leaves,* instead of pointing out that a ginkgo leaf resembles a fan, the authors direct the reader to find the leaf that looks like a fan, a mitten, a needle; clear line drawings of ginkgo, sassafras, and pine appear on the same page. Other books in this series are about fish, mammals, insects, and birds.

Experiment books for all ages should avoid the "cookbook" approach that simply tells, step-by-step, what to do. Instead, children should be guided in problem-solving through the strategies of open-ended questions, guides to observation, and suggestions for further study. All these are employed by Joan Rahn in *Seeing What Plants Do* and *More about What Plants Do,* both for middle readers. The questions to guide observation are particularly good—clear and direct, but allowing children to report their results as they see them. Expected outcomes and the reasons behind them are discussed in a separate section at the end of the book. On a simpler level, Vicki Cobb suggests experiments for observing the growth of mold in a book with a high-appeal title, *Lots of Rot.* A reference section at the end, with the heading "Which Little Rotters Did You Grow?," provides word and picture clues for identifying eight varieties of mold, mildew, and bacterial decay.

The scientific method applies to the social sciences, too, but there are fewer books in this area designed to help children learn and use the inquiry approach. Jane Strivastava's *Statistics,* for primary-grade children, is much livelier than its title indicates. It helps the reader learn to take samples, to gather data, and report it through simple charts and graphs. This is a most useful tool for children learning to explore their environment. Jean Fritz has illustrated techniques of historical research in a fictionalized account that children like very much; it is called *George Washington's Breakfast.* The story illustrates the role of perseverance and good luck in problem-solving. After young George, who is trying to find out what George Washington customarily ate for breakfast, has asked questions, exhausted library resources, and gone on a futile fact-finding trip to Mt. Vernon, he happens to find the answer in an old book about to be discarded from his own attic. Intermediate children can find out about using primary sources for studying local history in a slim volume by Kay Cooper called *Who Put the Cannon in the Courthouse Square?* The lists and charts in this book also serve as a handy reference for teachers.

Interrelationships and Implications

A list of facts is fine for an almanac, but most informational books are not almanacs. They should be expected to put facts into some sort of perspective. Basic information about geology is related to common urban sights in *City Rocks, City Blocks and the Moon* by Gallob. Intriguing black and white photographs compare an ancient fossil to a dog's footprints in wet cement; show weathered gravestones and brownstone houses as well as more conventional rock specimens; and, finally, contrast the type of rocks found on the moon with those found on the earth. In a book about ecology, *The Living Community,* Hirsch states: "A poet once said that one could not pluck a flower without troubling a star. This is another way of saying that the living and the nonliving are linked together."[15] Interrelationships of a different sort are pointed out in Foster's *Year of the Pilgrims, 1620,* a horizontal history that helps children see the cultural context of a major event. Her brief account of the Pilgrims' journey and its background is given perspective by the descriptions of Shakespeare, Galileo, and other great artists and scientists

[15]S. Carl Hirsch, *The Living Community, A Venture into Ecology,* illustrated by William Steinel (New York: Viking, 1966), p. 17.

of the day; even more significant is the inclusion of material that shows powerful contemporary kingdoms in Africa, India, China, and Japan. Other books by Foster provide similar treatment for *Year of Columbus, 1492* and *Year of Lincoln, 1861.*

The relationship of science and technology to society is a crucial one, and many recent information books have taken part of this problem as a focus. Laurence Pringle has written about health hazards in the environment in *Lives at Stake,* discussing the implications of recent technological developments for public health and safety. Because issues such as these involve politics, economics, and sensitive social factors, authors must make special efforts toward a complete, fair presentation. *The Nuclear Question* by Ann Weiss exemplifies this even-handed approach in covering the benefits and dangers of nuclear power. However, even those books which are not specifically designed to call attention to the related social problems of science and technology ought to acknowledge that such problems do exist. Where the uses of science have serious implications for society, the relationships should be made clear.

STYLE

Clarity and Directness

Books that present information through the veil of fiction generally do not succeed in either category, although some of them are widely circulated. *Peter Gets the Chickenpox,* first published in 1959, went into its eighth printing in 1970. Its didacticism recalls the informational books of the last century, however: "If new spots come, that's nothing to fear./It's customary for repeated crops to appear."[16] The awkward verse is a distraction, and children will certainly not care much about Peter as a character. Authentic stories, however—as opposed to such a contrived one—are welcomed by children. When David Mangurian went to the highlands of Peru to gather material for *Children of the Incas,* he lived with an Indian family and tape recorded long conversations with their 13-year-old son, Modesto. The boy's own words, translated and edited, make up the main text of the

photographic essay that resulted. Modesto's account of life in his village has a clarity that speaks directly to child readers and effectively presents the desired information.

The use of precise language and specific detail is another important factor in clarity. Nothing is vague in Miriam Schlein's description of a vampire bat's dinner in *Billions of Bats.* She names the animals that are likely prey ("a horse, a cow, a donkey, or even a chicken"), describes the approach and the bite ("only about a tenth of an inch long"), and goes on to explain how the bat curves its tongue into a funnel shape and sucks in blood ("for about a half hour"). The language is simple and direct, giving the reader a clear picture of the process.

Level of Difficulty

Although vocabulary does have to be within the child's range, books for primary-grade children need not be restricted to a narrow list of words. New terms can be explained in context as in one of the *I Can Read* series by Selsam. In her book *Benny's Animals and How He Put Them in Order,* the museum professor says: "Another pile will be Amphibians—animals that live in the water when they are young and on land when they are grown up. Those are your frogs and toads."[17] Context does not serve to explain everything, however; a writer aware of the background of the intended audience will take pains to make new words clear. When a writer does not make that effort, it can pose enormous difficulties for the reader. Consider the background that a child would need to visualize this description of New Zealand:

> Gorse and broom cover the weathered hills in the south but toward the west coast sounds, or Findland, alternating hills and mountains rise beyond canyons, carved by rapidly flowing rivers, until heavy forest is reached."[18]

In the unlikely event that a child knew about "gorse," "broom," "sounds," and "weathering," he or she would still be put off by the length and

[16]Marguerite Rush Lerner, *Peter Gets the Chickenpox,* illustrated by George Overlie (Minneapolis: Lerner, 1959), unpaged.

[17]Millicent Selsam, *Benny's Animals and How He Put Them in Order,* illustrated by Arnold Lobel (New York: Harper & Row, 1966), p. 47.
[18]Edna Kaula, *The Land and People of New Zealand* (Philadelphia: Lippincott, 1964), p. 15.

complexity of the sentence. Too many ideas and concepts are compressed into a brief space; this kind of density makes very difficult reading.

Words that look unpronounceable are another stumbling block for most children. A glossary is helpful, but youngsters who are intent upon a book's content may not take time to look in the back. In *City Rocks, City Blocks and the Moon*, Gallob shows one way to solve the problem in a heading that reads: "Gneiss (say 'nice')."

Reader Involvement

> Sometimes, when someone has done something very nasty to you, something mean and rotten and unfair, you might say:
> "YOU'RE A REAL SKUNK!"
> Why do you say that?
> What's so bad about skunks?[19]

There are three good ways to get reader involvement, and Schlein has used all three in these opening lines for *What's Wrong with Being a Skunk?*: writing in a conversational tone; using the second person, "you"; and asking questions. The book continues as a superb example of lively language, as well as a clear and accurate presentation of facts about skunks.

Children may be more quickly drawn into an informational book by a sense of immediacy in the writing. The use of present tense sometimes serves this purpose. *Chimney Sweeps* by James Giblin begins with a present-tense account of a modern chimney sweep at work. Parts of the book are cast in past tense to present facts about chimneys and sweeps, but the author returns to present tense and second person to describe a typical day in the life of a "climbing boy" in 1800. He invites the reader to participate:

> Then imagine that you are one of three climbing boys working for a master sweep. You are eleven years old and have been cleaning chimneys ever since you were six, when your parents sold you to the master.
> It is 4:30 in the morning when the master comes down into the cellar to wake you.[20]

Children reward the author's efforts with this book by becoming deeply involved in the unusual topic.

Vivid Language

The writer of informational books uses the same techniques as the writer of fiction to bring a book to life, although the words must be accurate as well as attractive. Imagery is used to appeal to the senses, frequently to sight, as in Kathryn Lasky's lyrical *Sugaring Time*:

> Fog swirls through the valley and up into the meadow, covering the hills and mountaintops beyond. Everything is milky white. Snow-covered earth and sky melt together. Pines appear rootless, like ghost trees, their pointy tops wrapped in mist.[21]

Metaphorical language, since it is based on comparison, can be used to contribute to clarity in nonfiction. Carol Carrick's *Octopus* helps the reader visualize that creature's underwater existence through similes: " . . . the octopus floated down over the lobster like a sinister parachute . . . ." and " . . . she crept spider-like over the bottom of the sea."[22] In his appealing and detailed book, *Chipmunks on the Doorstep*, Edwin Tunis aptly compares the little animal's seemingly insecure posture to "an egg balanced on its small end."

One of the effects of style is cadence. In scenes of action, suspense and excitement are created by the pace of the writing and the precise use of verbs. In *Bear Mouse*, Freschet makes the reader hold his breath:

> At the edge of the meadow, a bobcat slunk low.
> He crept forward, toward the mouse.
> Slowly, nearer and nearer crept the bobcat.
> Now he was close enough—
> He pounced![23]

While children will probably not be able to describe an author's style, they will certainly

---

[19]Miriam Schlein, *What's Wrong with Being a Skunk?*, illustrated by Ray Cruz (New York: Four Winds, 1974), unpaged.
[20]James Cross Giblin, *Chimney Sweeps*, illustrated by Margot Tomes (New York: Crowell, 1982), p. 17.

[21]Kathryn Lasky, *Sugaring Time*, photographs by Christopher G. Knight (New York: Macmillan, 1983), unpaged.
[22]Carol Carrick, *Octopus*, illustrated by Donald Carrick (New York: Seabury, 1978), unpaged.
[23]Berniece Freschet, *Bear Mouse*, illustrated by Donald Carrick (New York: Scribner, 1973), unpaged.

respond to it. They will know that a well-written informational book somehow does not sound the same as an encyclopedia essay, and they will enjoy the difference.

ORGANIZATION

Structure

Even though a book is vividly written, accurate, and in command of its topic, children will not find it very useful unless it also furnishes a clear arrangement of information. Every author must choose a structure or organizing principle as a basis for presenting facts. Nancy Winslow Parker uses the sequence of the alphabet to organize a collection of facts in *The United Nations from A to Z*. This is a structure that allows little attention to the relationship among facts, but it provides a good format for browsing and is easily understood by children.

Ann McGovern effectively uses the relatively loose structure of questions and answers in her book . . . *If You Lived with the Sioux Indians*. Recognizing what kinds of things children want to know, the author provides answers for: "Where would you sleep?" "Were grownups strict?" "Was there time for fun?" Also included are more conventional questions about hunting and ceremonies and war. Melvin Berger's *Computers: A Question and Answer Book*, a much longer book, adds another level of organization by grouping the questions into six chapters, such as "How Do Computers Work?" and "How Do You 'Talk' to a Computer?"

A common and sensible arrangement for many books, especially about history or biological processes, is based on chronology. Marchette Chute has presented the growth of the right to vote in this way in *The Green Tree of Democracy*, which traces the franchise in the United States from the Jamestown colony to the Voting Rights Act of 1970. A very precise chronology of the development of a chick within the egg is made wondrously clear through descriptions and unique photographs in Geraldine Flanagan's *Window into an Egg: Seeing Life Begin*.

Regardless of the topic, the general survey type of book should have a system of headings that will help the reader get an overview of the content. *Grocery Store Botany* by Joan Rahn, a brief book that investigates the botanical characteristics of common produce items, has large boldface headings for "Roots," "Stems," "Leaves," and so on. Within each category, activities are set apart under the subheading "Something to Do." The longer the book and the more complex its topic, the greater its need for manageable division. In John Roberson's comprehensive *Japan: From Shogun to Sony, 1543–1984*, the chapter titles ("A Closed World," "The Gates Forced Open") help to indicate the organization. Within chapters, extra space between paragraphs indicates changes in the direction of the discussion. Subheadings, however, are more helpful as indicators of structure, especially for less practiced readers.

Reference Aids

With the exception of certain simple and special types, factual books should offer help at both front and back for the reader who needs to locate information quickly. Since it is important for children to develop reference skills early, a table of contents and an index should not be omitted from books for primary-grade readers. *Construction Giants* by Ross Olney has a relatively simple text in spite of the difficulty of some of the words necessary in describing the machines. The table of contents clearly lists five major headings (one is a Foreword); the index is clearly set in a typeface as large as the text, with plenty of leading between the lines. The heading "credits" on the index page, however, may require some explanation. The title "Photo Credits" would have been clearer to the intended readers of this book.

An index will be truly useful only if it is complete and has necessary cross references. It is difficult to think of the possible words children might use to look up a topic or to answer a question, yet writers should consider as many possibilities as would seem reasonable. Someone who wanted to find out about "language," "talk," "sound," or "speech" of dolphins would probably look under l, t, or s. In Patricia Lauber's *The Friendly Dolphins*, the topic is finally found under "d" as "dolphin talk." In this same book the words "size," "eyes," and "baby" are omitted, although there is information on these aspects of dolphin life.

Other helpful additions to a book are glossaries, bibliographies, suggestions for further reading and informational appendixes. If children are to understand the method of inquiry, they need to learn that a writer uses many sources of information. Yolen's bibliography for *Ring Out! A Book of Bells* lists twenty-seven entries dating from 1848. Suggestions for further reading by children are most helpful if separated from the adult's more technical resources. While many recent informational books include bibliographies, annotated entries are still unfortunately the exceptions rather than the rule.

Appendixes are used to extend information in lists, charts, or tabulations of data that would seem cumbersome within the text itself. *Commodore Perry in the Land of the Shogun*, Rhoda Blumberg's award-winning account of the opening of Japanese harbors to American ships, seems all the more credible because of the documents and lists presented in the appendixes. Having read that lavish gifts were exchanged during the negotiations, children can discover in Appendix C that the emperor was offered more than thirty items, including two telegraph sets, a copper lifeboat, champagne, tea, muskets, swords, and two mail bags with padlocks.

ILLUSTRATIONS AND FORMAT

Clarification and Extension of Text

In our visually oriented culture, readers of all ages demand that a book's illustrations make it more interesting and attractive. In an informational book, the illustrations must do that, and much more. One of their basic functions is to clarify and extend the text. *Saturn: The Spectacular Planet* by Franklyn Branley would not be so spectacular without the photographs taken by Voyager 1 and Voyager 2, but it also has drawings and diagrams that help make complicated ideas about gravitation and planetary movement more understandable. Cutaway views and clear labeling are other good features of the pictures in this book. The more abstract the topic, the more important it is that pictures help children "see" explanations. Latitude, longitude, and other mapping concepts, for instance, are often hard for children to grasp, so it is especially important that they be illustrated clearly, as Harriet Barton has done for Jack Knowlton's introductory book, *Maps and Globes*. These big, bright pictures use color to focus atten-

Within a week of Commodore Perry's arrival, pictures of the Black Ships and "hairy barbarians" were hawked in the streets and sold in shops. They were also reproduced on souvenir banners, scrolls, fans, and towels. Above you can see one of the more flattering portraits of the Commodore.

Reproductions of the art of the time capture the Japanese point of view and lend extra credibility to this account of *Commodore Perry in the Land of the Shogun.* From the book by Rhoda Blumberg.

tion on the equator, contour lines, and other specific aspects of simplified maps.

Illustrations are especially important in clarifying size relationships. The beautiful paintings by Kenneth Lilly for *Large as Life: Nighttime Animals Life Size* by Joanna Cole have special impact because each figure is exactly the size of the animal it represents. Children could measure the pictures to compare the size of the tiny elf owl with the fruit bat or the giant toad. Not many topics lend themselves to life-size portrayals, of course, and that makes it important for artists to find other ways to be clear.

Photographs and drawings often show magnified parts or wholes, in which case some information should be given about actual size. A photograph of air pollution particles in *The Only Earth We Have* by Laurence Pringle is clearly identified as having been magnified several thousand times. A pictured comparison of the subject with an object familiar to children is also effective. A huge museum skeleton of Tyrannosaurus is put into perspective in a photograph that shows a boy gazing up at it in *To Find a Dinosaur* by Dorothy Shuttlesworth.

While in many books the illustrations extend the information of the text, adding detail, in others the illustrations themselves provide the bulk of the information, making the text subordinate. Shirley Glubok's series about the art of various cultures and countries, for instance, is centered on photographs which show examples of many different forms of art. *The Art of the Spanish in the United States and Puerto Rico,* like Glubok's other volumes, includes only a brief commentary; children will learn primarily by studying the pictures of paintings, furniture, textiles, tinware, homes, churches, and so on.

Suitability of Media

Illustrations in any medium can be clear and accurate, but one medium may be more suitable than another for a given purpose. Photographs are necessary for the verité essay by Bernard Wolf, *Don't Feel Sorry for Paul,* which tells the story of a congenital amputee, born with incomplete hands and feet. Drawings or paintings could not as effectively show the nuances of posture and expression that make this book an accurate, moving account of a handicapped child. *Find the Hidden Insect* by Joanna Cole and Jerome Wexler also depends on its photography to show how successful insects can be in concealing themselves in their natural environment. Since the photos are in black and white, the emphasis is on camouflage through shape and pattern. Color would have made this good book even better.

Three-dimensional illustrations are used for clarity and interest in some books of information. People of all ages are fascinated by the paper engineering in *The Human Body* by Jonathan Miller, designed by David Pelham. This goes beyond the entertainment value of a "pop-up" book; its movable parts reveal more about anatomy than flat pictures can possibly do. For instance, one double

The artist's point of view makes the reader feel like a builder on the uppermost scaffold of a cathedral. From *Cathedral* by David Macaulay.

spread of the torso allows the reader to flip back the muscular diaphragm, spread the rib cage to reveal the lungs, and open the lungs to study their connection to the heart. Other body systems are layered at different elevations from the open page to show their relative positions within the body. Alice and Martin Provensen also use three-dimensional, movable pictures for their book *Leonardo Da Vinci,* to celebrate as well as to demonstrate the inventiveness of this great artist and scholar.

Diagrams and drawings have an impact of their own and also have many uses especially appropriate to science books. It's helpful to have X-ray eyes for seeing the skeletons in living things, which the artist is able to give us for Herbert Zim's book, *Bones.* Diagrams can reduce technological processes to their essentials or show astronomical relationships that represent distances too great to be photographed. Diagrams are also fine for giving directions, and they can be charming as well as clear. This is true of Byron Barton's work for Seymour Simon's popular *The Paper Airplane Book,* where scenes are interspersed with how-to drawings to enliven the text.

Sometimes an artist's perception is vital to the purpose of a book. *Cathedral: The Story of Its Construction* is a venture in architecture, engineering, and esthetics that relies on the author's fine pen-and-ink drawings for its effect. David Macaulay pictures his creation at various stages during the building; his choice of views puts the reader into the action and gives stunning contrasts of massive proportions and minute detail. A similar format and the same standard of excellence can be found in other books by the same author, including *City, Castle, Pyramid, Underground,* and *Unbuilding.*

The astonishingly precise watercolors in Anne Ophelia Dowden's *Wild Green Things in the City: A Book of Weeds* bear part of the author's message—weeds are beautiful—in a way that lesser illustrations could not have done. The delicacy and sensitivity of these pictures may help urban children find the same qualities in their own environments. By the same token, the strong lines and contrasts of Leonard Everett Fisher's scratchboard illustrations in Milton Meltzer's *All Times, All Peoples: A World History of Slavery* underscore the violence and grim nature of the subject matter.

Captions

Children need to be able to look at an illustration and know what they are seeing, and that requires wise use of captions and labels. Some writers use the text itself, if it is brief, to explain the pictures, eliminating the need for additional captions. The words of Patricia Lauber and the photographs of Jerome Wexler are combined in this way for *Seeds: Pop . Stick . Glide,* a handsome book that explains how plant life spreads. The arrangement of the text on the page and occasional references like "As you can see . . . " or "In this photo, . . . " help readers get maximum information from the illustrations as well as from the writing. Millicent Selsam also uses text as caption in *The Amazing Dandelion,* and even though the text is briefer, some of the photographs include labels printed directly on their surfaces. A series of frames showing the various parts of an opening flower is especially clear—a bracket and label indicate the length of the *style* at the end of the *anther tube,* and progressive close-ups show the separating *stigma* at the tip

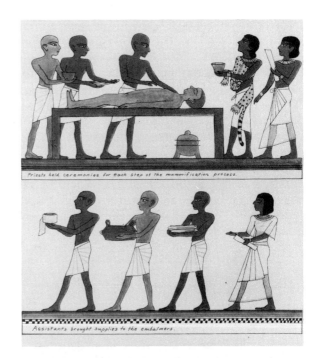

The format and the style of the illustrations are an important reflection of content in Aliki's book *Mummies Made in Egypt.*

and the grains of *pollen* along its sides. These distinct parts are plainly identified. Since children learn much by reading captions and studying illustrations, it seems fair to demand that both be clear, as they are in this book.

Format

The total look of a book is its format, involving type size, leading, margins, placement of text and pictures, and arrangement of front and back matter—these include title and copyright pages in the front and indexes, bibliographies, and other aids at the back. *A Great Bicycle Book* by Jane Sarnoff and Reynold Ruffins has something of the design of a comic magazine. A more formal presentation might have made the book less "busy," but would also have lessened its appeal. The bonus space of a book's endpapers is sometimes blank but can be used to convey the general theme of the book or to add in some way to the information. In Robert Cohen's *The Color of Man* children's faces at the front, representing different races, are contrasted with the faces of the elderly at the back. *Mummies Made in Egypt* by Aliki incorporates hieroglyphic writing on the dedication and half-title pages, and many of the illustrations are arranged like the friezes that decorated the tombs of antiquity. The content of the book is so fascinating to students that they may not appear to pay conscious attention to its format. However, they do respond to this open, inviting look and to the extra information in the captions.

Even a book that is sparingly illustrated may be notable for its overall design. Spacious margins and tastefully ornamented headings can make a long text seem less forbidding. The format of an informational book is an asset if it contributes to clarity or if it makes the book more appealing to its audience.

All the criteria for evaluating informational books which have been discussed in this chapter are of general importance. Obviously, though, some will be more crucial than others for certain types of books or for specific topics. The intended use of a book—for reference, study, read-aloud, or browsing—and the age and experience of its audience influence the relative importance of the various criteria. In using the following guides for evaluating informational books, remember that not every question will apply to every book and that books can be "good" in different ways and for different purposes.

GUIDES FOR EVALUATING INFORMATIONAL BOOKS

• Accuracy and Authenticity:
Is the author qualified to write about this topic? Has the manuscript been checked by
   authorities in the field?
Are the facts accurate according to other sources?
Is the information up-to-date?
Are all the significant facts included?
Do text and illustrations reveal diversity and avoid stereotypes?
Are generalizations supported by facts?
Is there a clear distinction between fact and theory?
Do text and illustrations omit anthropomorphism and teleological explanations?

• Content and Perspective:
For what purpose was the book designed?
Is the book within the comprehension and interest range of its intended audience?
Is the subject adequately covered? Are different viewpoints presented?
Does the book lead to an understanding of the scientific method? Does it foster the
   spirit of inquiry?
Does the book show interrelationships? Do science books indicate related social
   problems?

• Style:
Is information presented clearly and directly?
Is the text appropriate for the intended audience?
Does the style create the feeling of reader involvement?
Is the language vivid and interesting?

• Organization:
Is the information structured clearly, with appropriate subheadings?
Does the book have reference aids that are clear and easy to use, such as table of
   contents, index, bibliography, glossary, appendixes?

• Illustrations and format:
Do illustrations clarify and extend the text?
Are size relationships made clear?
Are media suitable to the purposes for which they are used?
Are illustrations explained by captions or labels where needed?
Does the total format contribute to the clarity and attractiveness of the book?

Types of Informational Books

Anyone who chooses informational books for children will soon notice several subgenres or recognizable types with common characteristics. Knowing about these types will help the teacher and librarian provide balanced and rich resources for learning as they choose particular books for particular purposes.

CONCEPT BOOKS

Concept books explore the characteristics of a class of objects or of an abstract idea. Most of the informational books intended for very young children are of this type. Typically they cover such concepts as size, color, shape, spatial relationships, self, and family. Concept books for this age are discussed at length in Chapter 4. For school-age children, concept books begin with what is already familiar and move toward the unfamiliar, some by showing new ways to consider well-known materials, others by furnishing new and different examples or perspectives. Such books are often useful as idea sources for classroom experiences and discussion.

One good book for discussion is Peter Spier's *People,* an oversize picture book that appeals to many different ages as it celebrates the possibilities for variation among the more than 6 billion human beings who live on earth. Spier's drawings include many shapes and colors of ears, eyes, and noses; costumes, shelters, and pastimes from around the world; architecture, alphabets, and foods. Although the author emphasizes the uniqueness of individual appearances and preferences, the concept of universality is implicit in the book.

The concept in Jan Adkins' *Inside: Seeing beneath the Surface* has to do with curiosity and imagination as well as with perception. His subjects for cutaway drawings stretch children's thinking about the insides of things, helping them to visualize and generalize. Cross-section views of an apple pie and a hero sandwich lead to more involved subjects like an ocean liner and a tunnel-and-duct system beneath a city street.

A beautiful but difficult book is *The View from the Oak* by Judith and Herbert Kohl. In leisurely, readable prose, the authors examine the concept of "umwelt," or the world of a living thing as experienced by that creature in terms of its own unique

sensory limits. Fascinating bits of information about such diverse animals as wood ticks and oryx antelopes may be gained here, as well as an ethological perspective. This is the first nonfiction book for children to have received the National Book Award.

A growing number of books for children deal with concepts related to self. One of these is Eda LeShan's *What Makes Me Feel This Way?* which will help children in the upper elementary grades sort out their own experiences and feelings. These books can be used to help children learn to discriminate and generalize, using the kind of thinking crucial to concept development.

INFORMATIONAL PICTURE BOOKS

More and more books of information are lavishly illustrated or published in picture-book format. Many concept books, especially those for younger children, also fit the picture-book category. A few informational books are truly representative of picture storybooks.

One of the first modern picture storybooks, *Pelle's New Suit* by Elsa Beskow, came to this country from Sweden nearly fifty years ago. That story shows a little boy getting wool from his pet lamb, then having it carded, spun, dyed, woven, and finally taken to the tailor for a new suit. Interesting parallels may be drawn between this classic and *"Charlie Needs a Cloak"* by Tomie de Paola, which also presents, as a story, basic information about making wool into cloth. Happily, this is one of the exceptions to the rule that says information is distorted by a veil of fiction. The story of Charlie's cloak is enhanced by humor, and the illustrations serve to emphasize the steps in the cloth-making process. De Paola's *The Quicksand Book* combines cartoon-style dialogue with hand-lettered charts and diagrams. Bright, funny pictures show Jungle Boy's haughty rescue of Jungle Girl, his later comeuppance, and an unlikely monkey taking tea. The sense of narrative along with attractive formats makes these books satisfying as picture storybooks as well as informational resources.

Two beautiful picture books about the medieval period present informational detail and the ambiance of the times even more effectively in their illustrations than in the text. Joe Lasker's *Merry Ever After: The Story of Two Medieval Weddings* contrasts the world of the nobility with that of the peasants by focusing on two typical couples betrothed as children and married as teenagers. Readers must consult the pictures as well as the story to get the full description of the two life styles. Aliki's *A Medieval Feast* shows the nobility of a manor house and their serfs preparing for a visit from the king and queen and their large entourage. A flurry of hunting, fishing, and harvesting is followed by scenes in the great kitchen and then the banquet presentation of such foods as a roast peacock reassembled with its feathers and a castle molded of pastry. Both of these picture books are standouts for their glowing, jewel-like colors and the use of decorative symbols and designs from the medieval period.

The more common form of informational picture book does not tell a story, but the text does depend in large part on the illustrations. *When Clay Sings* by Baylor calls attention to the Indian heritage of the Southwest United States through its rhythmic, dramatically arranged text. But the substance of the book rests with Bahti's illustrations of the motifs found on shards of ancient pottery: turtles, butterflies, monsters, hunters, abstract designs. Peter Parnall's ink and watercolor pictures of the plants and animals in a marsh enhance the lyrical, scientifically accurate text of *Between Cattails* by Terry Tempest Williams. Unusual perspectives and partial backgrounds help the reader focus on selective details like the ruby eyes of Western grebes in a courtship dance or the root systems of pond grasses. The artistry and design of books like these make them fine picture books as well as fine informational books.

Many informational picture books, despite oversize format and lavish illustration, are not directed to primary-grade children. David Macaulay's *City* and *Cathedral* are books of this type. The pictures in William Kurelek's *Lumberjack* are paintings, not so strict in representation but nevertheless accurate in portraying the operations of a lumberjack before the advent of the mechanical tree harvester. The variety of scenes, rich in color and feeling, makes this book perhaps more memorable for its art than its information. Two volumes by the Swiss artist Jörg Müller, *The Changing City* and *The Changing Countryside*, are really portfolios rather than books. In each, a series of foldout paintings show the many ways in which "pro-

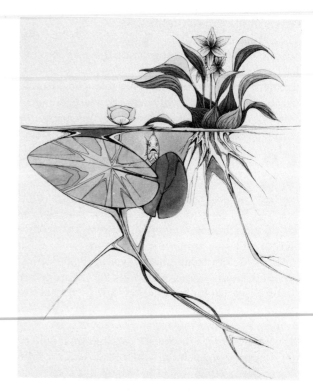

The striking design of Peter Parnall's illustration focuses attention both above and below water. From *Between Cattails* by Terry Tempest Williams.

gress" affects the environment. John Goodall's *The Story of an English Village* is a picture book with no text except for a series of decorative labels that identify the changing centuries from the fourteenth to the twentieth. All the pictures represent the same village crossroads and a particular house with alternating exterior and interior scenes plus half-page inserts to show different activities within that setting. These wordless sociology books are particularly good resources for discussion with older children who have some prior knowledge of history.

PHOTOGRAPHIC ESSAYS

Many informational picture books display photographs in a significant way, but only some of these can be called photographic essays. Although the books by Selsam about plant growth (*Cotton*, for example) depend on Wexler's photographs for clarification and support of the text on every page, they are not photographic essays. The essay relies on the camera in different ways: to particularize general information, to document emotion, to assure the reader of truth in an essentially journalistic fashion. Bernard Wolf's *Don't Feel Sorry for Paul*, the story of a boy who wears a prosthesis on his right arm, is an outstanding example of the form.

Sensitivity and vitality in George Ancona's photographs make *Handtalk: An ABC of Finger Spelling and Sign Language* by Charlip and Miller more than a specialized ABC book. Inspired by the language of the deaf, this is a unique volume about communication, made memorable by the expressive photo demonstrations of the language in action. Teachers and librarians will want to call attention to *Handtalk* when children read stories such as *David in Silence* (see Chapter 9) or biographies of Helen Keller. In *Koko's Kitten* by Francine Patterson, the photographs by Ronald Cohn serve to assure the reader of truth, for the story of this lowland gorilla who learned sign language and grieved for the death of a pet cat might be dismissed as fiction by a careless reader. These full-color photos also document the emotion of the story as they show the huge primate cuddling her tiny pet and later signing her distress. The arrival of a new kitten some months later provides a happy ending.

Numerous photographic essays present to children the way of life in other lands. Both Mangurian's *Children of the Incas* and Shachtman's *Growing Up Masai*, mentioned earlier in this chapter, are strengthened by the impact of the photographs. It is one thing to describe the struggles of traditional cultures in words, quite another to show the eloquent faces and postures that reveal individual people. Catherine and Alan Sadler's *Two Chinese Families* is another book that looks at a distant culture through a close-up view of particular members. This is an account of the family life of two children in the city of Guilin in southern China. Although some glimpses of the city and countryside are included, most of the photos feature the children and their everyday activities.

One photographic essay with great human interest appeal is *Oh, Boy! Babies!* by Alison Herzig and Jane Mali, with photos by Katrina Thomas. This book documents a special course in infant care given for fifth- and sixth-graders at an all-boys' school. The participants practiced skills like carrying, feeding, and bathing on live infants at varying stages of development. The photos show a wide range of expressions for both the boys and the babies, although the final emphasis is on how much they enjoyed one another. These pictures are also clear enough to serve a how-to-do-it function for such processes as cleaning and diapering. As a bonus for schools that might want to consider offering a similar course, the book incorporates plenty of detail about the structure and organization of this one.

IDENTIFICATION BOOKS

In its simplest form an identification book is a naming book, and this may well be the first sort of book that a very young child sees. But just as children grow in their ability to discriminate and classify, so do naming books become more detailed, precise, and complex. The range is very wide. *Tool Book* by Gail Gibbons shows simple drawings of common tools in bright colors, with appropriate labels. A phrase or two describes the common function of all those displayed on a double spread. This is information for the youngest child. Older children will find more information and precisely detailed pictures in Jan Adkins' *Toolchest*. The plane in this handsome book has all its parts labeled, and five variations of the basic tool are shown. Young children enjoy the beautiful watercolors and rhythmic text of *Houses from the Sea* by Goudey. The delicately colored illustrations by Adrienne Adams relate familiar objects, one by one, to the names of shells. At the end of the book a double-page picture of all the shells serves for quick comparison and identification. *How to Be a Nature Detective* by Selsam teaches observation skills as it helps beginning readers identify some common animal tracks.

When a child brings a stone, a leaf, or a wriggling snake to school and asks, "What is it?" the teacher or librarian has a built-in opportunity to introduce books to help that child discover the answer. Millicent Selsam and Joyce Hunt have written a series that is useful in teaching younger children how to examine a specimen and pick out the features that will be important in making an identification. Harriet Springer's line drawings show basic shapes and textures but eliminate the confusion of variable detail. *A First Look at Insects* and *A First Look at Shells* are two of the many titles in this outstanding process-oriented series. Under some circumstances it is wise to have fairly comprehensive references such as the *Golden Nature Guide* series by Zim and others. These small pocket books are crammed with information.

LIFE-CYCLE BOOKS

A fascination with animals is one of the most general and durable of children's interests, beginning very early and often continuing through adolescence into adulthood. There is an eager audience for factual books that describe how animals live, with an emphasis on the inherent story element. These books cover all or some part of the cycle of life, from the birth of one animal to the birth of its progeny or the events of one year in the animal's life or the development of one animal throughout its lifetime. While the animal subject can sometimes be given a name, it may not be given powers of speech or human emotions. Even so, an accounting of authentic behavior often produces the effect of characterization; thus children frequently read these books as "stories" rather than as references.

Life-cycle books for young children are usually picture books as well; and the best are notable for both illustration and text. Soft blues and browns color the woodcuts in *The Mother Owl* by the Hurds, which traces a year in the mother screech owl's life, measured from one nestful of eggs to the next. The same author and illustrator have produced *The Mother Whale.* Both these books emphasize the continuity of the life pattern.

Susan Bonners' *A Penguin Year* has striking illustrations of black and white with blue shadings that emphasize the cold of the Antarctic. The narrative follows a pair of Adélie penguins from their winter home on an ice floe to the mainland rookery where they mate and take turns warming their eggs in a stony nest. Efforts to protect and bring food to the new chicks consume the summer, with its dangers from skua gulls and quick snowstorms. When autumn arrives (in March), the pair leave their young, now able to fend for themselves, and return to the open sea. Although the author has assigned the descriptive names "Scarred-wing" and "Brush-tail" to the parent penguins, this is a straightforward scientific account. *Wild Mouse* by Irene Brady combines observations reported

diary-fashion with sketches showing the arrival and development of three tiny mice produced by a "he" who turned out to be a "she." This is the story of a reproductive cycle rather than a full life cycle, for the book ends when the offspring are gone from the nest and the mother appears to be "tubby" again.

Longer life-cycle stories are often stories of survival against the elements and enemies in the environment. The early books by John and Jean George, such as *Vison the Mink* and *Vulpes the Red Fox,* remain outstanding examples of this type. Holling C. Holling's beautifully illustrated *Minn of the Mississippi* and *Pagoo,* which trace the life histories of a turtle and a crawfish, are unique survival stories. Contemporary concerns about the environment and endangered species of wildlife are reflected in a number of life-cycle stories. Robert McClung, author of many books of this type, has written *Rajpur: Last of the Bengal Tigers,* which dramatizes the precarious existence of all these huge cats through several years in the life of one hypothetical animal.

Occasionally a book is structured around a life span that is not that of an animal. *Oak and Company* by Richard Mabey follows one tree through 238 years of life, tracing the huge oak's influence on plants and animals that live in, on, and around it. The beautiful illustrations by Clare Roberts are a notable feature of this book.

EXPERIMENT AND ACTIVITY BOOKS

To some children the word "science" is synonymous with "experiment," and certainly experience is basic to scientific understandings. Many basic informational books suggest a few activities to clarify concepts; in contrast, experiment books take the activities themselves as content.

For very young children, experiments and directions for simple observation may be presented in a picture-book context where the illustrations show interest and enjoyment as well as proper procedure. Seymour Simon's *Soap Bubble Magic,* illustrated by Stella Ormai, is a book of this kind. Simon's directions encourage children to watch carefully and think about what happens:

Dip the loop into the soapy water.
Slowly wave the loop through the air.
What happens?

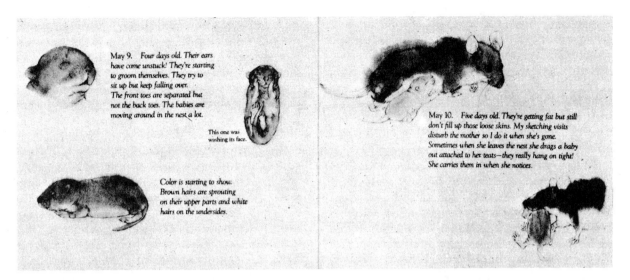

May 9. *Four days old. Their ears have come unstuck! They're starting to groom themselves. They try to sit up but keep falling over. The front toes are separated but not the back toes. The babies are moving around in the nest a lot.*

This one was washing its face.

Color is starting to show. Brown hairs are sprouting on their upper parts and white hairs on the undersides.

May 10. *Five days old. They're getting fat but still don't fill up those loose skins. My sketching visits disturb the mother so I do it when she's gone. Sometimes when she leaves the nest she drags a baby out attached to her teats—they really hang on tight! She carries them in when she notices.*

Children who read Irene Brady's *Wild Mouse* may want to keep their own dated and illustrated records of observations of the growth and development of other animals.

Quickly wave the loop through the air.
What happens now?
Does moving fast make more bubbles
than moving slowly?
Which way makes bigger bubbles?[24]

Many experiment books for older children also focus on one subject or one material. Henry Smith's *Amazing Air* suggests a wide range of experiments (on electrolysis, flight, and lung capacity, for instance), but all are designed to explore the properties of air. The directions are well illustrated, and the materials needed are clearly listed. Another outstanding book that provides experiments to help students understand one topic is Irwin Math's *Wires and Watts: Understanding and Using Electricity*.

Some of the most engaging books of science experiments are those by Vicki Cobb. An interesting approach to chemistry is found in *Science Experiments You Can Eat*, a book that is fun for children old enough to handle various cooking procedures safely. Bits of the history of technology accompany the experiments in *The Secret Life of School Supplies*, which explores the properties and processes necessary to make ink, paper, chalk, glue, crayons, erasers, and other common classroom items. *The Secret Life of Cosmetics* follows the same format with a topic that may attract students who would not usually pick up a book of chemistry experiments. *Chemically Active! Experiments You Can Do at Home* is arranged so that one experiment leads directly to the next. All these books by Cobb are designed with a commentary to link the experiments so that they can be read straight through for information as well as used to guide the actual procedures.

General experiment books, which include several experiments on varied topics, are also available. An excellent book to encourage independent activity is *Science Teasers* by Rose Wyler and Eva-Lee Baird. Experiments are grouped under such titles as "Space Age Puzzles," "Magic—or So It Seems," "Weighty Problems," and "Trick or Tease." Seymour Simon's books about "Einstein Anderson," such as *Einstein Anderson Sees Through the Invisible Man*, also fit the category of science puzzles and teasers (see Chapter 9).

Some books that suggest experiments also include experiences of other kinds, along with collections of interesting facts, anecdotes, or other material. These books which encourage children to explore a topic through a broad range of activities have gained popularity in recent years. *Good for Me! All about Food in 32 Bites* by Marilyn Burns

[24]Seymour Simon, *Soap Bubble Magic,* illustrated by Stella Ormai (New York: Lothrop, 1985), pp. 14–15.

is a compilation of facts, learning activities, experiments, and questions that may lead to further investigation. This is one of many titles from the "Brown Paper School Books" series, which consistently uses this format.

Sandra Markle's *Exploring Winter* includes simple experiments, such as putting one hand in hot water, the other in cold, then noticing which one feels colder when placed in lukewarm water. This book also has charts of good and poor heat conductors, riddles about insulation, recipes for bird food, directions for a winter scavenger hunt, weather myths, suggestions on melting snow to examine it for pollutants, and dozens of other ideas. Books like this make good browsing and are a source of possible projects for individual study or for activities that might be tried and discussed in class. Teachers as well as students appreciate the variety and creativity of the ideas. However, it is important to remember that activity books are not designed for reference. There is seldom an index, and headings may have more entertainment value than clarity. For easy access to specific information, other types of books are required.

DOCUMENTS AND JOURNALS

An important contribution to literature for children in recent years has been the publication of books based on original documents and journals. Excellent historical material is presented by E. Brooks Smith and Robert Meredith in *Pilgrim Courage,* which uses Governor Bradford's journal as its source. An adaptation for primary-grade children titled *The Coming of the Pilgrims* is somewhat less satisfactory since it is not clear which words are exactly quoted and which are paraphrased.

A few notable books provide reproduction of primary sources as a background for the study of black history. Meltzer has compiled three volumes under the title *In Their Own Words, A History of the American Negro,* divided by time periods, 1619–1865, 1865–1916, 1916–1966. The sources include letters, speeches, excerpts from books, court testimony, and the like. Lester's extraordinary *To Be a Slave,* a Newbery Honor Book in 1969, combines the verbatim testimony of former slaves with the author's own commentary:

To be a slave. To be owned by another person, as a car, house or table is owned. To live as a piece of property that could be sold—a child sold from its mother, a wife from her husband . . .

To be a slave was to be a human being under conditions in which that humanity was denied. They were not slaves. They were people. Their condition was slavery.[25]

Oral history has become increasingly important as a way to document the details of everyday life in the recent past. Alvin Schwartz's *When I Grew Up Long Ago: Older People Talk about the Days When They Were Young* is like having a conversation with several articulate great-grandparents at once. The interview material has been edited and arranged so that different people's recollections about a single topic like school or work can be presented together. George Ancona's *Growing Older* is another book in which the subjects speak for themselves about their early lives as well as their current occupations. Contemporary photographs are contrasted in most cases with childhood photos. Both these books encourage children to interview older people and create their own documents of oral history.

Russell Freedman is an author who frequently uses photographs from archival sources to document the historical information in his books. *Immigrant Kids* includes reproductions of photos of passengers on the steerage deck of an immigrant liner in 1893, street scenes from New York City's Lower East Side in 1898, school scenes, and many views of children at work. *Children of the Wild West* furnishes photographs from a time and place where cameras were scarce. Children interested in the westward movement in the United States can study the pictures as well as the text of this book for information. Photos of families with their covered wagons clearly show modes of dress and meager possessions. Log cabins, sod houses, and schoolrooms can be compared and described. The pictures of native American children in tribal dress and at government boarding schools are particularly interesting as documents.

[25]Julius Lester, *To Be a Slave,* illustrated by Tom Feelings (New York: Dial, 1968), p. 28.

The use of archival photos can lend authenticity and immediacy to historical information. From *Immigrant Kids* by Russell Freedman.

Laura Ingalls Wilder fans will be interested in a book called *West from Home: Letters of Laura Ingalls Wilder, San Francisco 1915*. The letters were written to the author's husband while she was visiting her daughter Rose and attending the 1915 Panama Pacific International Exposition. The first-hand detail provides personal insights, as well as a measure of the country during that year. There is similar documentary value in Wilder's *The First Four Years*, a journal-like account discovered as a handwritten manuscript among the author's posthumous papers. In this book, which tells of the first years of the Wilders' married life on a claim that had to be made into a farm, the reader can see the problems, attitudes, and some of the philosophies of another time. It is this information without benefit of an intermediary that is the unique contribution of documentary literature.

Unbound facsimile documents relating to special topics such as slavery or the Pilgrim fathers, collected in packet form, are available for older students. See the section on "Jackdaws" in Chapter 13 for more about these materials and their classroom adaptations.

SURVEY BOOKS

The purpose of a survey book is to give an overall view of a substantial topic and to furnish a representative sampling of facts, principles, or issues. Such a book emphasizes balance and breadth of coverage, rather than depth. *Farm Animals* by Dorothy Hinshaw Patent describes several kinds of animals found on a farm, including the birds that might be in the barnyard, animals used for meat, those that produce milk, and working animals. Although some information is given about specific breeds, a child focusing on a single animal like the horse or the cow would need to go on to other sources. Hilda Simon's topic is narrower in *Snakes: The Facts and the Folklore*, but the range of information marks this too as a survey. Various chapters cover folklore, evolution and anatomy, four broad categories of species, tips on keeping pet snakes, and the geographical range of common snakes in the United States. Detailed drawings in full color provide guides to identification and add greatly to the appeal of this comprehensive book.

A few books attempt to give children a survey of the important people, places, and events in the history of the world. Van Loon's *The Story of Mankind* was the first book to interpret world history to children in an interesting and informational fashion. This book, a pioneer in the field and the winner of the first Newbery award in 1922, is now available in a revised edition. Genevieve Foster has made notable and unique contributions to children's literature with her horizontal treatments of history in several books that present a time slice of the world as it was. In *George Washington's World*, *Abraham Lincoln's World*, *The World of Captain John Smith*, and *The World of William Penn*, this author writes of political affairs, economics, culture, and religion in relation to the span of one man's life. Foster's *Birthdays of Freedom*, now available in a single well-indexed volume, describes important people, places, and events in the development of individual liberty from the time of the earliest people to July 4,

1776. A different historical perspective is offered by Italian artist Piero Ventura in his book *Great Painters,* which chronicles much of the history of art through reference to the lives and words of more than seventy painters. Ventura's own illustrations add liveliness and humor to this fairly extensive overview. The appended information on styles, periods, and biographical data for the artists is a ready reference source.

Some survey books are quite brief, like the "Living World" series by Clive Catchpole. Unpaged and in picture-book format, *Deserts, Grasslands, Jungles,* and *Mountains* serve only to introduce the land-forms, climate, vegetation, and animal life of the respective geographical areas. Other survey books may be long and comprehensive, serving as encyclopedias of their chosen topics. These function as reference books, like *A Field Guide to Dinosaurs* by the Diagram Group or Zander Hollander's *The Baseball Book.* Survey books are available at many different levels of complexity and reading difficulty. A teacher or librarian may need to help children skim to find those that are most appropriate for their use.

SPECIALIZED BOOKS

Specialized books are designed to give specific information about a relatively limited topic. These are books that satisfy particular interests; they are more likely to be used intensively than extensively, on a one-time basis rather than as a frequent reference. For example, Caroline Arnold's *Saving the Peregrine Falcon* describes the work of California scientists attempting to preserve this species by retrieving and caring for eggs which have become too thin-shelled to survive under ordinary conditions in the wild. This will be useful information for children studying endangered species.

Many specialized books provide extensions of content areas which are frequently part of the elementary social studies curriculum. *The First Thanksgiving Feast* by Joan Anderson dispels myths about that event which are common to many classrooms. George Ancona's photographs record a re-enactment of the early celebration by staff members at Plimouth Plantation in Massachusetts, a living history museum. Costumes and period details have been carefully re-created. John Loeper's *Going to School in 1876* gives detailed information about an intriguing specific aspect of nineteenth-century history. A study of the Plains Indians with upper-grade children would be enhanced by the use of David and Charlotte Yue's *The Tipi: A Center of Native American Life.*

Many specialized books are geared to the personal interests of children. *What Has Ten Legs and Eats Corn Flakes?* by Ron Roy is about acquiring and caring for three small pets that would be reasonably easy to keep in close quarters. This book has good advice for classroom pet-keeping as well as for apartment dwellers or others with limited space. An older child with a weight problem can find straightforward, sensible information about diet and nutrition in Gilbert's *Fat Free.* Part of the value of this book for young people is that it sets up some acceptable guidelines for determining whether or not the worrier really does have too much padding. Another book that may satisfy an older child's special personal need is Jill Krementz's . . . *How It Feels When Parents Divorce.* This collection of true first-person statements by children from diverse backgrounds and circumstances reassures readers that they are not alone. The photo-portraits of the commentators add immediacy and the sense that a real conversation is taking place. Children beginning dance lessons will have a reason to look closely at the photos that compare ballet to everyday movement in *At Every Turn! It's Ballet* by Stephanie and Daniel Sorine. Whatever the child's interest, it is likely that a specialized book can be found to extend it.

CRAFT AND HOW-TO BOOKS

From chocolate-pudding fingerpaint to chess, a fascinating array of crafts and activities is featured in books that give directions for making and doing. Pride of accomplishment is emphasized in Harlow Rockwell's *I Did It,* a just-right combination of easy words and simple directions for primary-grade children. The six activities range in difficulty from making grocery-bag masks to baking bread. Another book geared to younger children is Marc Brown's *Your First Garden Book,* with directions for window-sill, backyard, and sidewalk gardens, plus bright pictures full of good humor.

Practical Puffins are sturdy paperbacks designed for use by children aged 7 to 12. This series features clearly labeled illustrations and well-written instructions for such projects as *Kites: To*

Make and Fly and *Out in the Wilds: How to Look After Yourself.*

Cookbooks for children ought to have sparkling, clear directions and adequate warnings about the safe use of tools and equipment. *The Fun of Cooking* by Jill Krementz offers clearly written directions followed by sequential photos of children preparing the recipes they have themselves recommended. Safety tips are outlined in the front of the book opposite the contents page, and reminders are added at appropriate points within the instructions for each recipe.

Some of the most intriguing recipe and craft books have special ties to other books for children. Three books by Virginia Ellison appeal to lovers of Winnie the Pooh. *The Pooh Cook Book* delights all ages, although older children can manage the recipes better. *The Pooh Party Book* does have some recipes but focuses on five celebrations with such enticing names as "A Honey-Tasting Party" and "Woozle-Wizzle Snow Party," complete with instructions for invitations, decorations, and games. *The Pooh Get-Well Book: Recipes and Activities to Help You Recover from Wheezles and Sneezles* features simple crafts, games, and recipes for "Strengthening Things to Eat and Drink." Another popular character who has suggested a cookbook is Peter Rabbit. The illustrations in Arnold Dobrin's *Peter Rabbit's Natural Foods Cookbook* are from the original Beatrix Potter books, complementing the theme of simple goodness from nutritional recipes. Two other literature-based recipe collections are Barbara Walker's *The Little House Cookbook: Frontier Foods from Laura Ingalls Wilder's Classic Stories* and *The Louisa May Alcott Cookbook,* compiled by Gretchen Anderson, which furnishes period recipes for foods mentioned in Alcott's *Little Women* and *Little Men.* Children may be surprised to learn that the author of the Alcott cookbook conceived the idea and tested the recipes when she was only 9 years old.

How-to books cover a great range of topics. Children interested in miniatures can turn common cast-off materials into simple dollhouse furniture according to the directions in *Dollhouse Magic* by P. K. Roche. As is sometimes the case with how-to books, children spend more time with the photographs and drawings than with the text and, using the pictures as guides, come up with adaptations of the suggested items. More care is required in following the instructions for crocheting, knitting, and weaving in Carolyn Meyer's *Yarn: The Things It Makes and How to Make Them.* The same would be true of prospective chess players using Jane Sarnoff's *The Chess Book* for learning the basics of this challenging game.

Many craft books seem to recommend themselves for classroom use. *Right Angles: Paperfolding Geometry* by Jo Phillips is useful for working out mathematical concepts with younger children. Elsie Ellison's *Fun with Lines and Curves* shows upper elementary school children how to draw beautiful geometric designs with lines, angles, and arcs. Directions are also given for working designs in colored yarn or thread. The relationship of art to the social studies is emphasized in *How To Make 19 Kinds of American Folk Art from Masks to TV Commercials* by Jean and Cle Kinney. Directions for pinprick pictures, wax fruit molds, Indian beading, candle-dipping, toy carving, cartoon animation, and the like are combined with photographs of early products and comments about the times that produced them.

Some craft books deal so specifically with approaches and techniques common to the activity-centered classroom that it is likely they will be used as much by teachers as by individual children. The Parents' Nursery School book *Kids Are Natural Cooks: Child-tested Recipes for Home and School Using Natural Foods* is an example. With recipes planned for variation and experimentation, young children are encouraged to work with adults in growing sprouts, grinding peanuts, making vegetable soup, and other basic experiences. Helen Sattler's *Recipes for Art and Craft Materials* will prove indispensable to teachers. Included are a variety of basic substances that children can make for their own use—such as paste, modeling and casting compounds, papier-mâché, inks, and dried-flower preservatives. In Ann Wiseman's informal but comprehensive *Making Things: The Hand Book of Creative Discovery* (two volumes), the commentary is directed to adults who work with children. Although the hand lettering is sometimes difficult to read, the drawings and ideas are clear and most notable for the emphasis on discovery and innovation. There are suggestions for fingerpainting with chocolate pudding, for cutting the basic shapes of African dashikis and Mexican rebozos, for weaving proof of the binomial theorem in red and black yarn, and for making improvised tools. In accord with the possibilities suggested, the last page bears the epigram "Never End."

USING LITERATURE ACROSS THE CURRICULUM

One of the important components of a literature program (see Chapter 12) is using literature across the curriculum. If children are to become real readers, they should meet good books not only at reading time, but also as they study history, science, the arts—all subject areas. Outstanding informational books, those that might fit author John McPhee's term "the literature of fact," are the most obvious places to begin in choosing titles to use across the curriculum.

Informational Books in the Classroom

FUNCTIONS OF INFORMATIONAL BOOKS

As in any genre, the best informational books should be appreciated for their artistry. Good writing, fine illustration, and high-quality bookmaking all have intrinsic aesthetic value. And, like fiction, informational books can provide satisfactions and delight to interested readers. Informational books are a bit different, however. They also fulfill special teaching functions that need to be considered in planning classroom materials and activities.

Serve as Curriculum Content Resources

The information in trade books is a major content resource for the curriculum. Elementary school textbooks are frequently overgeneralized or oversimplified in the attempt to keep them reasonably short and readable. A selection of informational books can provide the depth and richness of detail not possible in textbook coverage of the same topic. The latest informational books are also likely to be more up-to-date than textbooks, since the process of producing and choosing textbooks may take many months or even years. The adopted series then may not be revised, or replaced, for quite some time. However, new trade books on popular or timely topics appear every year.

Many teachers would use an up-to-date informational book like *Space Telescope* by Franklyn Branley to supplement the science textbook. Others might completely bypass the textbook and assemble many books about space and the solar system (probably including such titles as Seymour Simon's *The Long View into Space* and Patricia Lauber's *Journey to the Planets*) to provide information much richer than the text could offer.

Develop Critical Thinking

The availability of several informational books on a single topic is important for teachers to consider because it presents ready-made opportunities to encourage critical reading. When children's information all comes from one source, they are likely to accept the author's facts, attitudes, and perspectives without question. Two or more books provide a built-in comparison. Nine- or 10-year-olds studying foods, for instance, could find information about bread in Geoffrey Patterson's *All about Bread* and also in *The Bakers* by Jan Adkins. But which book will be better as a source of background? Which will be more help in a bread-baking project? Were the authors guided by different purposes? Does either one express a strong point of view? Ask children to consider Adkins' description of a supermarket shelf: "Hundreds of colorful plastic wrappers hold bread not much more nourishing and only a little tastier than medical cotton."[26] Encouraging children to ask themselves questions like these will help them make practical and critical judgments about what they are reading.

Using informational books leads to varied opportunities for teaching critical reading in context rather than with skill sheets or sterile exercises. One sixth-grade teacher who had talked with her students about the characteristics of good informational books found them complaining about the quality of some of the titles in the school library. This grew into a project in which all the students participated, comparing and scoring library books about common sixth-grade research topics. One outcome, in addition to the children's increased awareness, was a "wish list" asking the librarian to purchase additional books about castles, endangered wildlife, and other subjects.

At the pre-reading level, children can compare books read aloud by the teacher, look critically at the illustrations, and decide which ones give them

[26]Jan Adkins, *The Bakers* (New York: Scribner, 1975), p. 11.

needed information. A kindergarten teacher who shared several books about tools with her children asked them to decide which book's pictures did the best job of showing how the tools worked. To check their judgment, they took turns at the classroom workbench, under adult supervision, trying out the tools.

Most teachers or librarians who encourage the critical comparison of books find that helping children construct a chart of similarities and differences is an aid to clear thinking. The most challenging part is developing good categories. The teacher may start with basic identifying information (Title, Author, Illustrator) and draw descriptive categories from discussion with the children. Questions such as "What did you notice first about this book?" or "Were the same things important in both books?" can be used as a start. Eight-year-olds comparing *The Milk Makers* by Gail Gibbons and *Dairy Farming* by Geoffrey Patterson might notice that the Gibbons book includes diagrams of a cow's stomachs, but the other doesn't. However, the Patterson book has more information about the history of dairy cattle. A very simple type of chart would list various points covered in the books down the side of a large sheet of paper. Children would then check under the appropriate titles (written across the top) to indicate whether those points were included in each book. In more complete charts, students may supply descriptive detail about content, illustrations, or format; or they may quote brief examples of text. If chart-making is first done with the teacher, children may find it easier to do other comparisons independently or with a small group.

Suggest Areas and Methods of Study

Authors of fine informational books approach their material in interesting ways that may be easily adapted for the classroom. Although it's more usual to find good books that support a lesson, it's also possible for a good book to suggest a lesson. *Tiger Lilies and Other Beastly Plants* by Elizabeth Ring combines science and language study as it examines plants named for their similarity to certain features of animals. A one-page description faces an illustration showing the plant and the animal together for tiger lilies, elephant's ears, skunk cabbage, snake gourd, and several others. This attractive book may remind the teacher that there is much to be learned about the naming of things in

Science and language study are successfully combined in Elizabeth Ring's *Tiger Lilies,* a book on the origin of plant names. Illustration by Barbara Bash.

nature. Children could pursue a search for other plants with animal names or go on to look for animals with unusual names of their own. Ring's book could be the catalyst for a broad study of names and naming or the basis for a single session with the teacher borrowing the book's technique; that is, using pictures of animals to help clarify the names which they have lent to other things.

Middle-school teachers can discover a new twist for social studies projects in Catherine Noren's *The Way We Looked: The Magic and Meaning of Family Photographs*. This book suggests how to look at old portraits and snapshots as a source of inferences about relationships and life styles (How close do people stand? How formal are the poses?) or level of prosperity (What condition are the subject's clothes and shoes?). One intriguing bit of information about photo studio props commonly used during different decades of the late nineteenth century suggests a way for students to estimate the date of old photographs. Birds, palm trees, and bicycles, for instance, were characteristic props of the 1890s.

For young children, concept books often lead to

ideas for good classification activities. One kindergarten teacher was inspired by the categories used by Joan Rahn in *Holes*, such as "Holes That Hold Things" and "Holes That Let Some Things Go Through But Not Others." She listed each category on chart paper, then divided her class into teams to search the classroom for examples to complete the chart.

Provide Guides for Children's Reporting

Children who have searched for information on a topic need to synthesize and report their learning. Although they will need to have some experience with conventional, straightforward summaries, they can also borrow other forms of reporting from informational books. Some of the possibilities are ABCs, question-and-answer formats, guided tours, diaries, and life stories of plants, animals, or machines. Not only is this usually more fun, it often encourages more of the kind of thinking the teacher is trying to promote. For example, studying a natural environment should help children see the interdependence of living things. Interdependence is the focus that Jean George has taken in her nature story *One Day in the Alpine Tundra*. This huge concept is manageable because all the action is focused on one day's time. Birds and animals prey upon one another, a storm arises, and a falling boulder causes a chain reaction of changes on the face of the tundra. Children using this frame to write their own "One Day in the Rain Forest" or "One Day on the Beach" would need to sift through all their information and decide what things might really happen during the course of twenty-four hours and how each event would affect others. More about reports based on the structures and formats of children's books, with examples of student work, is included in Chapter 13.

CHOOSING INFORMATIONAL BOOKS FOR THE CLASSROOM

Children do not find the most exciting informational books just by chance. Some of these books need to be singled out for prominent attention in the school library, but generally the books we most want children to discover should be brought directly to the classroom and made readily available for browsing, reference, and in-depth study. This requires an investment of time by the teacher for tracking down and selecting titles. Unfortunately, textbooks and curriculum materials give few hints about children's books available in their topic areas. Librarians can direct teachers to standard reference sources and bibliographies, but it is also important for the teacher to watch for new books with particular potential for the classroom.

Two annual book lists prepared by content-area specialists in cooperation with the Children's Book Council identify the best of the new books for the sciences and for social studies. The "Outstanding Science Trade Books for Children" list is published each year in *Science and Children* magazine; "Notable Children's Trade Books in the Field of Social Studies" appears annually in *Social Education*. Another source that many teachers find helpful is *The Kobrin Letter*,[27] a newsletter published ten times a year. Each issue reviews new informational books alongside older ones on several topics—books about train travel, for instance, or wild cats or dealing with divorce.

Choosing books to serve the purposes of both teachers and children is just as important as selecting for quality. Much of the planning and selecting should be done before beginning a study, although children will raise questions and develop interests along the way that require new resources.

Defining some subtopics for a major study will make it easier to find appropriate books. One group of primary teachers who planned together for a science-focused unit study of "Water" made a list that included the following content areas:

Bodies of water
    fresh-water rivers and ponds
    salt-water seas and oceans
Water transportation
Water formations
    the water cycle
    fog/mist, rain, snow
Water creatures
    fish, birds, mammals, amphibians
Children's experiences with water
    playing in snow, watering seeds
    making soup, taking a bath

Books for information-gathering and for support of the observations and investigations planned in each area were then assembled so that children could begin their study with rich resources.

This kind of pre-planning, especially at the

[27]*The Kobrin Letter*, Beverly Kobrin, Editor, 732N Greer Road, Palo Alto, California 94303.

upper grade levels, eliminates the frustrations of children who are asked to research a topic only to find that books are not available to answer their questions. Cooperation and communication between the teacher and the librarian are essential in order to make the right books accessible at the right time.

Regardless of the topic to be studied, teachers may need to consider common purposes and functions of informational books so that their choices will represent a wide range of possibilities. The following checklist can be used as a reminder:

- Books to attract attention to the topic
- Books for browsing and exploring content
- Books with read-aloud possibilities
- Books for independent reading at varying levels of difficulty
- Basic reference books
- Books with enough information for in-depth study
- Books with a limited focus for very specific interests
- Books to guide activities and experiments
- Books that can be readily compared
- Books that introduce new perspectives or connections
- Books to accommodate new and extended interests

A selection of quality informational books representing these categories will support children's growth in reading and appreciation for good writing as well as their development of understandings within the content area.

Integrating Fact and Fiction

Using literature across the curriculum may begin with informational books, but it certainly does not have to end there. Many picture books, poems, traditional stories, novels, and biographies are natural choices for extending children's interest or knowledge base in a subject area. However, literature should never be distorted to fulfill the purposes of an informational lesson. One student participant from a university read Taro Yashima's *Crow Boy* to a class of 9- and 10-year-olds. When she finished the book she told the children that the story took place in Japan and asked them if they knew where Japan was. There was a mad dash for

the globe to see who could be the first to locate Japan. Then the participant went on to ask what Japan was, finally eliciting the answer she wanted—"an island." Next she asked what appeared to be a very unrelated question: "Why did Chibi have a rice ball wrapped in a radish leaf for his lunch instead of a hamburger?" The children were baffled. Finally, the participant gave them a brief but erroneous geography lesson in which she told them that since Japan was an island it was very wet and flat so the Japanese people could only raise rice, not beef for hamburgers! And there the matter was left—a miserable geography lesson which had somehow moved from Japan to growing rice but had lost Crow Boy and the class along the way. The student's university supervisor finally stepped in to save the day by helping the children talk about Chibi's loneliness and the artist's use of space and visual symbols.

Literature across the curriculum does not mean forcing connections, as the student in this example attempted to do. Nor does it mean reading a nature poem for literal information about a bird's habitat or using sentences from a favorite story as the basis for language drill or diagramming sentences. It does mean recognizing that some pieces of literature have a strong background of fact and provide a unique human perspective on historical, scientific, and technological subjects.

Watership Down by Richard Adams, for instance, encompasses a thorough knowledge of the biology of rabbits within an imaginative adventure story. Through its description of the society and group dynamics of the warren, it offers a commentary on human problems and organizations. *The Bomber's Moon* by Betty Vander Els tells a suspenseful story of two children separated from and finally reunited with their parents at the time of World War II. This story incorporates a great deal of background information on the war in Asia and the geography of China and India as the children are moved from place to place to avoid the fighting. Even a slim picture book like *Watch the Stars Come Out* by Riki Levinson has a base of historical information in the illustrations of Diane Goode, which show an immigrant ship, the Statue of Liberty, and street scenes on New York's Lower East Side.

Students would not use these books to gather facts in their research on rabbits, World War II, or immigrants. Even so, they are important books for

FACT AND FICTION: BOOKS TO USE TOGETHER

LEVEL	TITLE/AUTHOR	GENRE
Grades K–2	*The Goodnight Circle*, Lesser	Informational
	Ways Animals Sleep, McCauley	Informational
	The Sun's Asleep behind the Hill, Ginsburg	Picture book
	The Moon's the North Wind's Cooky, Russo	Poetry
Grades K–2	*Flash, Crash, Rumble and Roll*, Branley	Informational
	All Wet! All Wet!, Skofield	Picture book
	Where Does the Butterfly Go When It Rains?, Garelick	Picture book
	Rain, Spier	Picture book (wordless)
	Rainy Rainy Saturday, Prelutsky	Poetry
Grades 2–5	*Spider Magic*, Patent	Informational
	Someone Saw a Spider, Climo	Traditional
	Charlotte's Web, White	Fiction
Grades 3–6	*. . . If You Lived with the Sioux Indians*, McGovern	Informational
	The Tipi, Yue	Informational
	Buffalo Woman, Goble	Traditional
	The Ring in the Prairie, Bierhorst	Traditional
	The Earth Is Sore, Amon	Poetry
Grades 5–7	*The Luttrell Village: Country Life in the Middle Ages*, Sancha	Informational
	The Door in the Wall, de Angeli	Fiction
	Queen Eleanor, Brooks	Biography
	A Proud Taste for Scarlet and Miniver, Konigsburg	Biographical fiction/fantasy
	Great Grandmother Goose, Cooper	Traditional verse
Grades 5–8	*The Secret Language of Snow*, Williams and Major	Informational
	Julie of the Wolves, George	Fiction
	Wolfman: Exploring the World of Wolves, Pringle	Informational
	Under the North Star, Hughes	Poetry

children who are studying these topics to discover. Fiction gives a perspective that allows us to know facts in another way. It is especially important for children to confirm what they are learning from informational sources by meeting similar ideas in the more human frame of literature.

Pulling together fiction and nonfiction selections that work well together is an ongoing process for most teachers. A record of titles should be kept so that these books can be shelved or displayed together when appropriate. A few sample groupings are shown in the chart here.

Combining fact and fiction resources on a large scale can lead to the creation of an integrated theme unit encompassing learnings in all subjects. The focus topic may be taken from the sciences (Color, for example), from history or social studies (Colonial Life or Houses), or from language and the arts (Signs and Symbols), but it must be broad enough to allow students to develop in many skill areas as they work through a wide range of interrelated content, using trade books and other materials. Textbooks are used as reference resources, if at all. This challenging but satisfying way of teaching requires a thorough knowledge of children's literature.

Fine informational books and related books of fiction are important to the curriculum whether they serve as the major resource or as supplements to formal instructional materials. Enthusiastic teachers who have learned to recognize the best and to choose wisely for a variety of purposes will put children in touch with an exciting and satisfying way to learn.

SUGGESTED LEARNING EXPERIENCES

1. Talk to a group of children to find what special interests or hobbies they have. Make a survey of nonfiction to see what informational books might enrich these interests. Plan a display of some of these books for a classroom or library interest center.
2. Select several informational books on one topic—such as ecology, the solar system, or China. Evaluate them, using the criteria in this chapter. Plan activity cards or questions which would interest children in the books and help them use the books more effectively.
3. Working with one child or a small group of children, select a craft or activity book that seems suited to their age level. Watch carefully as children follow the directions given. What difficulties do they have? What questions do they ask? Could you make the directions clearer, safer, or more imaginative?
4. Select a country such as Ghana in West Africa. Look at social-studies texts and encyclopedias. Compare the information in these books with recent informational books. Read some of the Anansi folktales to see what additional insights can be gleaned from them about the Ashanti society.
5. Work with a group of children in writing an informational book modeled after one of the documentary accounts or a photo essay using their own snapshots. What kinds of research and choices are involved in following the form?
6. Choose one informational book with potential for interconnections in many subject areas, such as Aliki's *Mummies Made in Egypt*. Plan questions and activities; choose other literature to help children explore some of the related topics such as building the pyramids, writing with hieroglyphics, using preservatives, or the art of ancient Egypt.
7. Develop and use with children a learning activity that will encourage critical reading of informational books. Focus on identifying authors' point of view, comparing authenticity of sources, verifying facts, and the like.
8. Begin a file of fact/fiction pairs that could be used in science, social studies, the arts, or language study. Consider the different perspectives that children will draw from each.

RELATED READINGS

1. "Aspects of Children's Informational Books," John Donovan, guest ed. *Wilson Library Bulletin*, vol. 49:2 (October 1974), pp. 145–177.

   Almost the entire issue of this well-known periodical is devoted to an analysis of children's informational books. Zena Sutherland's excellent article, "Information Pleases—Sometimes," gives criteria for evaluating informational books and takes issue with some of Margery Fisher's criteria in *Matters of Fact*. Olivia Coolidge describes the process of writing authentic biography in her article, "My Struggle with Facts." In an essay, "To Each Generation Its Own Rabbits," Dennis Flanagan, editor of *Scientific American*, shows how *Watership Down* by Richard Adams embraces the two worlds of science and literature. Other articles relevant to this chapter are included in this fine special issue.
2. Carr, Jo, compiler. *Beyond Fact: Nonfiction for Children and Young People*. Chicago: American Library Association, 1982.

   This excellent collection of articles is headlined by a section called "Nonfiction Writing: Books As Instruments of Intelligence," which includes the title piece "Beyond Fact" by Milton Meltzer and a thought-provoking comparison of several books on one topic, "Out in Space" by Denise Wilms. Other sections cover science, history, biography, and controversial books. Lead articles by Carr for each section raise many discussion-worthy points. Appendixes list nonfiction winners of book awards and professional books and journals.
3. Cleaver, Betty P., Barbara Chatton, and Shirley Vittum Morrison. *Creating Connections: Books, Kits, and Games for Children*. Chicago: Garland, 1986.

   This resource guide emphasizes the integration of materials across the curriculum, including the connections to be made between fact and fiction. Six topics of study— Appalachia, bodies, cities, monsters, oceans, and sound—are outlined in detail, with an annotated list of books, kits, and games.

4. Fisher, Margery. *Matters of Fact: Aspects of Non-fiction for Children*. New York: Crowell, 1972.

   This authoritative book by an English author provides criteria for judging and selecting nonfiction books for children. The first chapter describes the various types of informational books, while the following chapters take an in-depth look at books about particular themes—such as bread, cowboys, honeybees, and atoms. Three chapters are devoted to an analysis of biographies about Bach, Helen Keller, and Abraham Lincoln. While many of the books discussed are British, publishers in the United States are given where appropriate. This work has become a standard in the field.

5. "Informational Books for Children," Geraldine DeLuca and Roni Natov, eds. *The Lion and the Unicorn*, vol. 6 (1982).

   This theme-centered issue features Patricia Lauber's thoughts on "What Makes an Appealing and Readable Science Book?" and two interviews with science writers Seymour Simon and Anne Ophelia Dowden. This last piece is one of the few to offer insight into the process of illustrating a science book. Other articles and reviews of professional books are also of interest.

6. Lamme, Linda Leonard. "Literature throughout the Curriculum" in *Learning to Love Literature: Preschool through Grade 3*, Linda Lamme, ed. Urbana, Ill.: National Council of Teachers of English, 1981, pp. 47–54.

   Lamme identifies literature to use in all curricular areas of an early childhood program and discusses criteria specific to that age level. Titles are listed for mathematics, language arts, reading, social studies, science, art, music, physical education, cooking, and other activities.

REFERENCES

INFORMATIONAL BOOKS

Adkins, Jan. *The Bakers*. Scribner, 1975.
_____. *Inside: Seeing beneath the Surface*. Walker, 1975.
_____. *Toolchest*. Walker, 1973.
Aliki (Brandenberg). *A Medieval Feast*. Crowell, 1983.
_____. *Mummies Made in Egypt*. Crowell, 1979.
Ancona, George. *Growing Older*. Dutton, 1978.
Anderson, Gretchen. *The Louisa May Alcott Cookbook,* illustrated by Karen Milone. Little, Brown, 1985.
Anderson, Joan. *The First Thanksgiving Feast,* photographs by Goerge Ancona. Clarion, 1984.
Arnold, Caroline. *Saving the Peregrine Falcon,* photographs by Richard R. Hewett. Carolrhoda, 1985.
Baylor, Byrd. *When Clay Sings,* illustrated by Tom Bahti. Scribner, 1972.
Bealer, Alex W. *Only the Names Remain: The Cherokees and the Trail of Tears,* illustrated by William Sauts Bock. Little, Brown, 1972.
Bendick, Jeanne. *Why Things Change: The Story of Evolution,* illustrated by Karen Bendick Watson. Parents', 1973.
Berger, Melvin. *Computers: A Question and Answer Book*. Crowell, 1985.
Blasingame, Wyatt. *Thor Heyerdahl: Viking Scientist*. Lodestar/Dutton, 1979.
Blumberg, Rhoda. *Commodore Perry in the Land of the Shogun*. Lothrop, 1985.
Bonners, Susan. *A Penguin Year*. Delacorte, 1981.
Brady, Irene. *Wild Mouse*. Scribner, 1976.
Branley, Franklyn. *Flash, Crash, Rumble and Roll,* illustrated by Barbara and Ed Emberley. Crowell, 1985.
_____. *The Mystery of Stonehenge,* illustrated by Victor Ambrus. Crowell, 1969.
_____. *Saturn: The Spectacular Planet,* illustrated by Leonard Kessler. Crowell, 1983.
_____. *Space Telescope,* illustrated by Giulio Maestro. Crowell, 1985.
Brown, Marc. *Your First Garden Book*. Little, Brown, 1981.
Burns, Marilyn. *Good for Me! All about Food in 32 Bites*. Little, Brown, 1978.

Buxbaum, Susan Kovacs, and Rita Golden Gelman. *Body Noises,* illustrated by Angie Lloyd. Knopf, 1983.

Carrick, Carol. *Octopus,* illustrated by Donald Carrick. Seabury, 1978.

Catchpole, Clive. *Deserts,* illustrated by Brian McIntyre. Dial, 1984.

_____. *Grasslands,* illustrated by Peter Snowball. Dial, 1984.

_____. *Jungles,* illustrated by Denise Finney. Dial, 1984.

_____. *Mountains,* illustrated by Brian McIntyre. Dial, 1984.

Charlip, Remy, and Mary Beth Miller. *Handtalk: An ABC of Finger Spelling and Sign Language,* photographs by George Ancona. Parents', 1974.

Chute, Marchette. *The Green Tree of Democracy.* Dutton, 1971.

Cobb, Vicki. *Chemically Active! Experiments You Can Do at Home,* illustrated by Theo Cobb. Lippincott, 1985.

_____. *Lots of Rot,* illustrated by Brian Schatell. Lippincott, 1981.

_____. *Science Experiments You Can Eat,* illustrated by Peter Lippman. Lippincott, 1972.

_____. *The Secret Life of Cosmetics,* illustrated by Theo Cobb. Lippincott, 1985.

_____. *The Secret Life of School Supplies,* illustrated by Bill Morrison. Lippincott, 1981.

Cohen, Robert. *The Color of Man,* photographs by Ken Heyman. Random, 1968.

Cole, Joanna. *Find the Hidden Insect,* photographs by Jerome Wexler. Morrow, 1979.

_____. *Large as Life: Nighttime Animals Life Size,* illustrated by Kenneth Lilly. Knopf, 1985.

_____. *My Puppy Is Born,* photographs by Jerome Wexler. Morrow, 1973.

Cooper, Kay. *Who Put the Cannon in the Courthouse Square?,* illustrated by Anthony Accardo. Walker, 1985.

Davis, Mary. *Careers in a Medical Center,* photographs by Milton J. Blumenfeld. Lerner, 1973.

de Paola, Tomie. *"Charlie Needs a Cloak."* Prentice-Hall, 1974.

_____. *The Quicksand Book.* Holiday House, 1977.

Diagram Group, The. *A Field Guide to Dinosaurs.* Avon, 1983.

Dobrin, Arnold. *Peter Rabbit's Natural Foods Cookbook.* Warne, 1977.

Dowden, Anne Ophelia. *Wild Green Things in the City: A Book of Weeds.* Crowell, 1972.

Ellison, Elsie. *Fun with Lines and Curves,* illustrated by Susan Stan. Lothrop, 1972.

Ellison, Virginia. *The Pooh Cook Book,* illustrated by Ernest H. Shepard. Dutton, 1969.

_____. *The Pooh Get-Well Book: Recipes and Activities to Help You Recover from Wheezles and Sneezles.* Dutton, 1973.

_____. *The Pooh Party Book.* Dutton, 1971.

Fenner, Carol. *Gorilla Gorilla,* illustrated by Symeon Shimin. Random, 1973.

Flanagan, Geraldine Lux. *Window into an Egg: Seeing Life Begin.* Young Scott, 1969.

Foster, Genevieve. *Abraham Lincoln's World.* Scribner, 1944.

_____. *Birthdays of Freedom: From Early Man to July 4, 1776.* Scribner, 1973.

_____. *George Washington's World.* Scribner, 1941.

_____. *The World of Captain John Smith 1580–1631.* Scribner, 1959.

_____. *The World of William Penn.* Scribner, 1973.

_____. *Year of Columbus, 1492.* Scribner, 1969.

_____. *Year of Lincoln, 1861.* Scribner, 1970.

_____. *Year of the Pilgrims, 1620.* Scribner, 1969.

Freedman, Russell. *Children of the Wild West.* Clarion, 1983.

_____. *Immigrant Kids.* Dutton, 1980.

Freschet, Berniece. *Bear Mouse,* illustrated by Donald Carrick. Scribner, 1973.

Fritz, Jean. *George Washington's Breakfast,* illustrated by Paul Galdone. Coward McCann, 1969.

Froman, Robert. *Less than Nothing Is Really Something,* illustrated by Don Madden. Crowell, 1973.

Gallob, Edward. *City Rocks, City Blocks and the Moon.* Scribner, 1973.

George, Jean Craighead. *One Day in the Alpine Tundra,* illustrated by Walter Gaffney-Kessell. Crowell, 1984.

George, John, and Jean George. *Vison the Mink.* Dutton, 1949.

_____. *Vulpes the Red Fox.* Dutton, 1948.

Gibbons, Gail. *The Milk Makers.* Macmillan, 1985.

_____. *New Road!* Crowell, 1983.

_____. *Tool Book.* Holiday House, 1982.

Giblin, James Cross. *Chimney Sweeps*, illustrated by Margot Tomes. Crowell, 1982.

Gilbert, Sara. *Fat Free: Common Sense for Young Weight Worriers*. Macmillan, 1975.

Glubok, Shirley. *The Art of the North American Indian*. Harper, 1964.

_____. *The Art of the Spanish in the United States and Puerto Rico*, designed by Gerard Nook, photographs by Alfred Tamarin. Macmillan, 1972.

Goldreich, Gloria, and Esther Goldreich. *What Can She Be? A Newscaster*, photographs by Robert Ipcar. Lothrop, 1973.

Goodall, John. *The Story of an English Village*. Atheneum, 1979.

Goor, Ron, and Nancy Goor. *In the Driver's Seat*. Crowell, 1982.

Goudey, Alice E. *Houses from the Sea*, illustrated by Adrienne Adams. Scribner, 1959.

Gross, Ruth Belov. *A Book about Pandas*. Dial, 1972.

Gustafson, Anita. *Some Feet Have Noses*, illustrated by April Peters Flory. Lothrop, 1983.

Hauptly, Denis J. *In Vietnam*. Atheneum, 1985.

Herzig, Alison Cragin, and Jane Lawrence Mali. *Oh, Boy! Babies!*, photographs by Katrina Thomas. Little, Brown, 1980.

Hirsch, S. Carl. *The Living Community: A Venture into Ecology*, illustrated by William Steinel. Viking, 1966.

Hollander, Zander, and Phyllis Hollander. *The Baseball Book: A Complete A to Z Encyclopedia of Baseball*. Random, 1982.

Holling, Holling C. *Minn of the Mississippi*. Houghton Mifflin, 1951.

_____. *Pagoo*. Houghton Mifflin, 1957.

Hurd, Edith Thatcher. *The Mother Owl*, illustrated by Clement Hurd. Little, Brown, 1974.

_____. *The Mother Whale*, illustrated by Clement Hurd. Little, Brown, 1973.

Irwin, Constance. *Strange Footprints on the Land: Vikings in America*. Harper, 1980.

Johnson, Gerald W. *America Is Born*, illustrated by Leonard Everett Fisher. Morrow, 1959.

Kerr, Jessica. *Shakespeare's Flowers*, illustrated by Anne Ophelia Dowden. Crowell, 1969.

Kinney, Jean, and Cle Kinney. *How to Make 19 Kinds of American Folk Art from Masks to TV Commercials*. Atheneum, 1974.

Knight, David C. *"Dinosaurs" That Swam and Flew*, illustrated by Lee J. Ames. Prentice-Hall, 1985.

Knowlton, Jack. *Maps and Globes*, illustrated by Harriet Barton. Crowell, 1985.

Kohl, Judith, and Herbert Kohl. *The View from the Oak*, illustrated by Roger Bayless. Sierra Club/Scribner, 1977.

_____. *Pack, Band, and Colony: The World of Social Animals*, illustrated by Margaret LaFarge. Farrar, Straus, 1983.

Krementz, Jill. *The Fun of Cooking*. Knopf, 1985.

_____. *How It Feels When Parents Divorce*. Knopf, 1984.

Kurelek, William. *Lumberjack*. Houghton Mifflin, 1974.

Lasker, Joe. *Merry Ever After: The Story of Two Medieval Weddings*. Viking, 1976.

Lasky, Kathryn. *Sugaring Time*, photographs by Christopher G. Knight. Macmillan, 1983.

Lauber, Patricia. *The Friendly Dolphins*, illustrated by Jean Simpson and Charles Gottlieb. Random, 1963.

_____. *Journey to the Planets*. Crown, 1982.

_____. *Seeds: Pop . Stick . Glide*, photographs by Jerome Wexler. Crown, 1981.

_____. *Tales Mummies Tell*. Crowell, 1985.

LeShan, Eda. *Learning to Say Good-By: When a Parent Dies*, illustrated by Paul Giovanopoulos. Macmillan, 1976.

_____. *What Makes Me Feel This Way?* Macmillan, 1972.

Lesser, Carolyn. *The Goodnight Circle*, illustrated by Lorinda Bryan Cauley. Harcourt, 1984.

Lester, Julius. *To Be a Slave*, illustrated by Tom Feelings. Dial, 1968.

Lindblom, Steven. *How to Build a Robot*. Crowell, 1985.

Loeper, John J. *Going to School in 1876*. Atheneum, 1984.

Mabey, Richard. *Oak and Company*, illustrated by Clare Roberts. Greenwillow, 1983.

Macaulay, David. *Castle*. Houghton Mifflin, 1977.

_____. *City: A Story of Roman Planning and Construction*. Houghton Mifflin, 1974.

_____. *Pyramid*. Houghton Mifflin, 1975.

_____. *Cathedral: The Story of Its Construction*. Houghton Mifflin, 1973.

_____. *Unbuilding*. Houghton Mifflin, 1980.

_____. *Underground*. Houghton Mifflin, 1976.

MacCauley, Jane R. *Ways Animals Sleep*. National Geographic, 1983.

McClung, Robert. *Rajpur: Last of the Bengal Tigers*, illustrated by Irene Brady. Morrow, 1982.

McGovern, Ann. *. . . If You Lived with the Sioux Indians*, illustrated by Bob Levering. Four Winds, 1974.

Mangurian, David. *Children of the Incas*. Four Winds, 1979.

Markle, Sandra. *Exploring Winter*. Atheneum, 1984.

Math, Irwin. *Wires and Watts: Understanding and Using Electricity*, illustrated by Hal Keith. Scribner, 1981.

May, Julian. *The Warm-Blooded Dinosaurs*, illustrated by Lorence F. Bjorklund. Holiday, 1978.

Meltzer, Milton. *All Times, All Peoples: A World History of Slavery*, illustrated by Leonard Everett Fisher. Harper, 1980.

_____. *In Their Own Words: A History of the American Negro 1619–1865*. Crowell, 1964.

_____. *In Their Own Words: A History of the American Negro 1865–1916*. Crowell, 1965.

_____. *In Their Own Words: A History of the American Negro 1916–1966*. Crowell, 1967.

Meyer, Carolyn. *The Bread Book: All about Bread and How to Make It*, illustrated by Trina Schart Hyman. Harcourt, 1971.

_____. *Yarn: The Things It Makes and How to Make Them*, illustrated by Jennifer Perrott. Harcourt, 1972.

Miller, Jonathan. *The Human Body*, designed by David Pelham. Viking, 1983.

Müller, Jörg. *The Changing City*. Atheneum, 1977.

_____. *The Changing Countryside*. Atheneum, 1977.

Noren, Catherine. *The Way We Looked: The Meaning and Magic of Family Photographs*. Dutton, 1983.

Olney, Ross R. *Construction Giants*. Atheneum, 1984.

Parents' Nursery School. *Kids Are Natural Cooks: Child-tested Recipes for Home and School Using Natural Foods*, illustrated by Lady McCrady. Houghton Mifflin, 1974.

Parker, Nancy Winslow. *The United Nations from A to Z*. Dodd, Mead, 1985.

Patent, Dorothy Hinshaw. *Farm Animals*, photographs by William Munoz. Holiday, 1984.

_____. *Spider Magic*. Holiday, 1982.

Patterson, Dr. Francine. *Koko's Kitten*, photographs by Ronald H. Cohn. Scholastic Hardcover, 1985.

Patterson, Geoffrey. *All about Bread*. André Deutsch, 1984.

Phillips, Jo. *Right Angles: Paper-folding Geometry*, illustrated by Giulio Maestro. Crowell, 1972.

Practical Puffins Series. *Kites* by Jack Newnham. Penguin Books, 1977.

_____. *Out in the Wilds* by McPhee Gribble Publishers, illustrated by David Lancashire. Penguin Books, 1977.

Priestley, Lee. *American's Space Shuttle*. Messner, 1979.

Pringle, Laurence. *Lives at Stake: The Science and Politics of Environmental Health*. Macmillan, 1980.

_____. *The Only Earth We Have*. Macmillan, 1969.

_____. *Wolfman: Exploring the World of Wolves*. Scribner, 1983.

Provensen, Alice, and Martin Provensen. *Leonardo DaVinci*. Viking, 1984.

Rahn, Joan Elma. *Grocery Store Botany*, illustrated by Ginny Linville Winter. Atheneum, 1974.

_____. *Holes*. Houghton Mifflin, 1984.

_____. *More about What Plants Do*, illustrated by Ginny Linville Winter. Atheneum, 1975.

_____. *Seeing What Plants Do*, illustrated by Ginny Linville Winter. Atheneum, 1972.

Ring, Elizabeth. *Tiger Lilies and Other Beastly Plants*, illustrated by Barbara Bash. Walker, 1984.

Roberson, John R. *Japan: From Shogun to Sony 1543–1984*. Atheneum, 1985.

Roche, P. K. *Dollhouse Magic: How to Make and Find Simple Dollhouse Furniture*, photographs by John Knott, drawings by Richard Cuffari. Dial, 1977.

Rockwell, Harlow. *I Did It*. Macmillan, 1974.

_____. *My Doctor*. Macmillan, 1973.

Roy, Ron. *Move Over, Wheelchairs Coming Through!*, photos by Rosmarie Hausherr. Clarion, 1985.

_____. *What Has Ten Legs and Eats Cornflakes?*, illustrated by Lynne Cherry. Clarion, 1982.

Sadler, Catherine Edwards, and Alan Sadler. *Two Chinese Families*. Atheneum, 1981.

Sancha, Sheila. *The Luttrell Village: Country Life in the Middle Ages*. Crowell, 1982.

Sandler, Martin W. *The Way We Lived: A Photographic Record of Work in a Vanished America*. Little, Brown, 1977.

Sarnoff, Jane. *The Chess Book*, illustrated by Reynold Ruffins. Scribner, 1973.

_____, and Reynold Ruffins. *A Great Bicycle Book*. Scribner, 1973.

Sattler, Helen Roney. *The Illustrated Dinosaur Dictionary*, illustrations by Pamela Carroll, Anthony Rao, and Christopher Santoro. Lothrop, 1983.

_____. *Recipes for Art and Craft Materials*. Lothrop, 1973.

Schlein, Miriam. *Billions of Bats*, illustrated by Walter Kessell. Lippincott, 1982.

_____. *What's Wrong with Being a Skunk?*, illustrated by Ray Cruz. Four Winds, 1974.

Schwartz, Alvin, collector and ed. *When I Grew Up Long Ago: Older People Talk about the Days When They Were Young*, illustrated by Harold Berson. Lippincott, 1978.

Selsam, Millicent E. *The Amazing Dandelion*, photographs by Jerome Wexler. Morrow, 1977.

_____. *Animals as Parents*, illustrated by John Kaufmann. Morrow, 1965.

_____. *Benny's Animals and How He Put Them in Order*, illustrated by Arnold Lobel. Harper, 1966.

_____. *Cotton*, photographs by Jerome Wexler. Morrow, 1982.

_____. *How Kittens Grow*, photographs by Esther Bubley. Four Winds, 1973.

_____. *How to Be a Nature Detective*, illustrated by Ezra Jack Keats. Harper, 1966.

Selsam, Millicent, and Joyce Hunt. *A First Look at Insects*, illustrated by Harriet Springer. Walker, 1974.

_____. *A First Look at Leaves*, illustrated by Harriet Springer. Walker, 1972.

_____. *A First Look at Seashells*, illustrated by Harriet Springer. Walker, 1983.

Shachtman, Tom. *Growing Up Masai*, photos by Donn Renn. Macmillan, 1981.

Shuttlesworth, Dorothy E. *To Find a Dinosaur*. Doubleday, 1973.

Simon, Hilda. *Snakes: The Facts and the Folklore*. Viking, 1973.

Simon, Seymour. *Einstein Anderson Sees through the Invisible Man*, illustrated by Fred Winkowski. Viking, 1983.

_____. *The Long View into Space*. Crown, 1979.

_____. *The Paper Airplane Book*, illustrated by Byron Barton. Viking, 1971.

_____. *Soap Bubble Magic*, illustrated by Stella Ormai. Lothrop, 1985.

Singer, Julia. *We All Come from Someplace: Children of Puerto Rico*. Atheneum, 1976.

Smith, E. Brooks, and Robert Meredith. *The Coming of the Pilgrims, Told from Governor Bradford's Firsthand Account*, illustrated by Leonard Everett Fisher. Little, Brown, 1964.

_____. *Pilgrim Courage*, illustrated by Leonard Everett Fisher. Little, Brown, 1962.

Smith, Henry. *Amazing Air*. Lothrop, 1983.

Sorine, Stephanie Riva. *At Every Turn! It's Ballet*, photographs by Daniel S. Sorine. Knopf, 1981.

Spier, Peter. *People*. Doubleday, 1980.

Stein, Sara Bonnett. *About Dying*, photographs by Dick Frank. Walker, 1974.

_____. *About Handicaps*, photographs by Dick Frank. Walker, 1974.

_____. *Kids' Kitchen Takeover*. Workman, 1975.

_____. *Making Babies*, photographs by Doris Pinney. Walker, 1974.

Steiner, Barbara A. *Biography of a Polar Bear*, illustrated by St. Tamara. Putnam, 1972.

Strivastava, Jane J. *Statistics*, illustrated by John J. Reiss. Crowell, 1973.

Tunis, Edwin. *Chipmunks on the Doorstep*. Crowell, 1971.

Van Loon, Hendrik W. *The Story of Mankind*, rev. ed. Liveright, 1972.

Ventura, Piero. *Great Painters*. Putnam, 1984.

Walker, Barbara M. *The Little House Cookbook; Frontier Foods from Laura Ingalls Wilder's Classic Stories*, illustrated by Garth Williams. Harper, 1979.

Weiss, Ann E. *The Nuclear Question*. Harcourt, 1981.

Wilder, Laura Ingalls. *The First Four Years*, illustrated by Garth Williams. Harper, 1971.

_____. *West from Home: Letters of Laura Ingalls Wilder, San Francisco 1915*, Roger MacBride, ed. Harper, 1974.

Williams, Terry Tempest. *Between Cattails*, illustrated by Peter Parnall. Scribner, 1985.

_____, and Ted Major. *The Secret Language of Snow*, illustrations by Jennifer Dewey. Sierra Club/Pantheon, 1984.

Wiseman, Ann. *Making Things: The Hand Book of Creative Discovery*. Little, Brown, 1973.

Wolberg, Barbara J. *Zooming In: Photographic Discoveries under the Microscope*, photographs by Dr. Lewis R. Wolberg. Harcourt, 1974.

Wolf, Bernard. *Don't Feel Sorry for Paul*. Lippincott, 1974.

_____. *Tinker and the Medicine Man*. Random, 1973.

Wyler, Rose, and Eva-Lee Baird. *Science Teasers*, illustrated by Jerry Robinson. Harper, 1966.

Yolen, Jane. *Ring Out! A Book of Bells*, illustrated by Richard Cuffari. Seabury, 1974.

Yue, David, and Charlotte Yue. *The Tipi: A Center of Native American Life*. Knopf, 1984.

OTHER REFERENCES

Adams, Richard. *Watership Down*. Macmillan, 1974.

Amon, Aline, adapter and illustrator. *The Earth Is Sore: Native Americans on Nature*. Atheneum, 1981.

Beskow, Elsa. *Pelle's New Suit*. Harper, 1929.

Bierhorst, John, ed. *The Ring in the Prairie*, collected by Henry Rowe Schoolcraft, illustrated by Leo and Diane Dillon. Dial, 1970.

Climo, Shirley. *Someone Saw a Spider: Spider Facts and Folktales*, illustrated by Dirk Zimmer. Crowell, 1985.

Brooks, Polly Schroyer. *Queen Eleanor: Independent Spirit of the Medieval World*. Lippincott, 1983.

Cooper, Helen. *Great Grandmother Goose*. Greenwillow, 1978.

de Angeli, Marguerite. *The Door in the Wall*. Doubleday, 1949.

Garelick, May. *Where Does the Butterfly Go When It Rains?*, illustrated by Leonard Weisgard. Scholastic, 1970.

George, Jean Craighead. *Julie of the Wolves*. Harper, 1972.

Ginsburg, Mirra. *The Sun's Asleep behind the Hill*, illustrated by Paul Zelinsky. Greenwillow, 1982.

Goble, Paul. *Buffalo Woman*. Bradbury, 1984.

Hughes, Ted. *Under the North Star*, illustrated by Leonard Baskin. Viking, 1981.

Konigsburg, E. L. *A Proud Taste for Scarlet and Miniver*. Atheneum, 1973.

Levinson, Riki. *Watch the Stars Come Out*, illustrated by Diane Goode. Dutton, 1985.

O'Dell, Scott. *Sing down the Moon*. Houghton Mifflin, 1970.

Prelutsky, Jack. *Rainy Rainy Saturday*, illustrated by Marilyn Hafner. Greenwillow, 1980.

Robinson, Veronica. *David in Silence*, illustrated by Victor Ambrus. Lippincott, 1966.

Rogers, Jean. *The Secret Moose*, illustrated by Jim Fowler. Greenwillow, 1985.

Russo, Susan. *The Moon's the North Wind's Cooky: Night Poems*. Lothrop, 1979.

Skofield, James. *All Wet! All Wet!*, illustrated by Diane Stanley. Harper, 1984.

Spier, Peter. *Rain*. Doubleday, 1982.

Vander Els, Betty. *The Bombers' Moon*. Farrar, Straus, 1985.

White, E. B. *Charlotte's Web*. Harper, 1952.

Yashima, Taro. *Crow Boy*. Viking, 1955.

3

DEVELOPING
A LITERATURE
PROGRAM

PLANNING
THE LITERATURE PROGRAM

Students in a fifth- and sixth-grade class unanimously agreed that *The Pinballs* by Betsy Byars was their favorite book. Their teacher then asked them to discuss *The Pinballs,* telling what it was that made them like it so much. Part of their discussion follows:

Lenny says, "This is the best book I've ever read. I'd like to know Harvey because I'd like to cheer him up." He decides that "He shows real courage because he has two broken legs." Barb adds, "All the kids do because they have to go to a foster home." "So does Thomas J. because the twins are going to die and he has to go to the hospital to see them," says Will.

Jack talks about Carlie, saying, "She's really funny because she's so rude." The teacher suggests that a book that is "basically serious can have funny elements." Tom says, "You know that Carlie is a tough dude."

Then Tom goes on to explain the title by saying, "Carlie thinks they're pinballs because they are always being thrown around like pinballs."

By April of that year eighteen of the class had read *The Pinballs*. They also were reading other Betsy Byars books; thirteen had read *Summer of the Swans*, eight *Goodbye, Chicken Little*.[1]

These children had read many books (from 24 to 122 over the year), yet they singled out *The Pinballs* as their favorite. While it is still difficult for them to articulate why they like the story, they have moved beyond the usual circular kind of statement, "I liked it because it was good." They are beginning to recognize the importance of character development and readily identified with Carlie and Harvey. Lenny, who was not a particularly good reader and had read few books, empathizes with Harvey to the point of wanting to comfort him. Suburban children, they have extended their horizons to imagine the courage it would require to live in a foster home away from your family and to have to visit the dying in the hospital. Tom attempts a rough statement of the meaning of the title without any prompting.

In this class, book discussions occurred every day during the last 15 minutes of an hour-long period for sustained silent reading. The children readily supported each other in their selection of books and in their evaluations in a way that we have referred to as a "community of readers." It is obvious from their discussion that they were gaining a greater sense of form and were beginning to see more in books than just story.

[1]Based on children's comments recorded by Susan Hepler in "Patterns of Response to Literature: A One-Year Study of a Fifth and Sixth Grade Classroom," unpublished doctoral dissertation, The Ohio State University, 1982.

It takes time for reading and literature to grow in a classroom. The children in this classroom had for the most part been exposed to good literature throughout their school attendance. The teacher had been working on a literature-based reading program over a period of several years. Her major goal was to develop children who could read and who loved reading. From this base she added a growing appreciation for and understanding of good literature.

PURPOSES OF THE LITERATURE PROGRAM

Each school staff will want to develop its own literature program in terms of the background and abilities of the children it serves. Teachers need to know their children and the potential of their material and have an understanding of the structure of literature; then they will be free to make the right match between child and book. This chapter can suggest guidelines and give examples, but it cannot prescribe *the* literature program that would work with all children. The four purposes of a literature program—discovering delight in books, interpreting literature, developing literary awareness, and developing appreciation—can be achieved through varied methods and materials.

Discovering Delight in Books

One of the major purposes of any literature program is to provide children with the opportunity to experience literature, to enter into and become involved in a book. The title of *Hooked on Books* by Fader and McNeil comes close to describing this goal. A literature program must get children excited about reading, turned on to books, tuned into literature.

One of the best ways to interest children in books is to surround them with many of the finest. Give them time to read and a teacher who regularly reads to them. Expose them to a wide variety of literature—prose and poetry, realism and fantasy, contemporary and historical fiction, traditional and modern. Provide time for children to talk about books, to share them with others, and to interpret them through various creative activites. Let them see that adults enjoy books too. One 6-year-

old and his teacher were reading Lobel's *Frog and Toad Are Friends* together. When they came to the part where Toad is experiencing his "sad time of day" (waiting for the mail that he never receives), the teacher burst out laughing. The 6-year-old looked up at her and said: "I didn't know grown-ups liked books!" If children are to like books they must be with adults who enjoy them.

The first step in any literature program is to discover delight in books. This should be the major purpose of the literature program in the elementary school and should not be hurried or bypassed. Delight in books only comes about through long and loving experiences with them.

Interpreting Literature

Wide reading is necessary for creating interest in books, but children need to have an opportunity to have in-depth experiences with books if they are to grow in their responses to literature. The teacher and child can talk about the personal meaning a story might have for his or her own life. The fifth- and sixth-graders described in the opening of this chapter might well have reflected on a comparison between times when Carlie brashly got her way and times when good things happened to her because she became more thoughtful of others. Just as Lenny wanted to comfort Harvey, they could discuss the different kinds of experiences they might have given Thomas J. to make up for the childhood he had missed. As children begin to see the causes for certain kinds of behavior they may develop more insight into others. When children relate what they are reading to their background of experience, they internalize the meaning of the story. Louise Rosenblatt was one of the first to remind us that the reader counts as much as the work that is being read. "The literary experience," she says, "must be phased as a *transaction* between the reader and the text."[2]

With elementary school children, it is best to begin with their personal response to the story (see Chapter 2). Only if a question appears to be appropriate for the background of the children does the teacher pursue the question of how the author or illustrator creates meaning. A question about the events that helped produce Carlie's character development would have been appropriate for the discussion of *The Pinballs*, for example.

Another way children could have been helped to identify with the characters in *The Pinballs* would have been to have dramatized certain scenes such as Carlie and Thomas J.'s visit to the hospital to see Harvey or Carlie's talk with Thomas J. at the end of the story when she is trying to prepare him for school. Another group of children might write essays on why they were like or not like particular characters in this story. All these activities would add to the interpretation of the story and deepen children's response to it.

Developing Literary Awareness

Children in the elementary school can't help but develop some literary awareness. However, knowledge about literature should be secondary to children's wide experiencing of literature. Too frequently, we have substituted the study of literary criticism for the experience of literature itself. Attention to content should precede consideration of form. However, some literary understanding increases children's enjoyment of books. Some 7- and 8-year olds are excited to discover the different variants of "Cinderella," for example. They enjoy comparing the various beginnings and endings of folktales and like to write their own. Obviously, some of this delight has been derived from knowledge of folklore. Teachers need to know something of the structure of literature in order to provide children with a frame of reference to direct their insights. Children, however, should be led to discover these literary elements gradually, and only as these elements shed light on the children's understanding of the meaning of the story or

[2]Louise M. Rosenblatt, *Literature as Exploration* (Appleton-Century, 1938, Noble and Noble, 1968), p. 35.

poem. Knowledge of the structure of a discipline frees a teacher in her or his approach to teaching. Knowing literature, she or he may tune in to where the children are and extend their thinking and understandings. The teacher does not have to rely on the questions in a literary reader; she or he is free to ask questions directly related to the needs of the children in the class.

TYPES OF LITERATURE

During the time children are in elementary school they will develop some understanding about types of literature or various genres. The primary child can usually differentiate between prose and poetry, between fiction and nonfiction, between realism and fantasy. The young child will not use those words, nor is it important to do so. He or she probably will tell you that Carle's *The Very Busy Spider* "tells a story," while *The Spider* by Margaret Lane "just tells you about spiders." This represents a beginning step in the development of a useful classification system. Later as children begin to use the library, they will learn that nonfiction includes informational books and biography. They will discover that poetry and traditional literature—including folktales, legends, and myths—have their own classifications.

Children do not need to learn all these classifications. An understanding of the various types of literature will develop as teachers and librarians introduce a variety of books to children. When children have had free access to the school library media center for six or seven years, they will have discovered the various types of books and their classifications. A framework for thinking about literature will develop gradually as children consider what kinds of stories they particularly like or what kinds of information they need for a particular purpose. Such knowledge will also be useful when children begin evaluating books. Then they discover, for example, that the characters in fairy tales are usually flat, two-dimensional characters because they represent goodness (the fairy godmother) or wickedness (the stepmother). These are seen in sharp relief to the characters in realistic fiction, who grow and change and are a mixture of good and bad. Again, this kind of understanding is developed over a period of time with much experiencing of a wide range of literature.

ELEMENTS OF LITERATURE

Knowledge of the components of literature—such as the traditional constants of plot, characterization, theme, style, setting, and point of view of the author—comes about gradually. Some children are intrigued with knowing about such literary devices as symbols, metaphors, imagery, use of flashbacks, and so on. Such knowledge can be forced, taught superficially without children really understanding the relationship between the use of the device and the author's meaning. But this kind of knowledge is more appropriate for the teacher, who can ask questions that might help children discover meaning. Focus should be primarily on the personal meaning of the content. Discussion of literary form should only be introduced where it leads to a richer understanding of a book, and then only after children have had time to respond to it personally.

THE PLACE OF CLASSICS

Some literature programs recommend a sequence of particular books for study at each age level. It is the position of these authors that there is no one book, or twenty books, or one hundred books that should be read by all children. There are many books that it would be unfortunate if children missed, but none that should be required of all. Knowledge of certain literary classics of childhood—such as *Alice's Adventures in Wonderland* or *The Wind in the Willows*—is enriching, but not absolutely essential to one's development. What is important is that we give children rich experiencing of literature at various stages of development.

Knowledge of time-tested works of prose, and poetry—such as Mother Goose rhymes, fables, myths, and Bible stories—does provide a background for understanding many literary allusions. "Don't count your chicks before they hatch," "a matter of sour grapes," "dog in the manger," "Midas touch," "the voice of Cassandra" are all examples of often-used expressions derived from literature. However, the reason they continue to be used is that their meanings have significance for today's living. Teachers who know literature will share appropriate literary classics with children because they are still *good stories,* not because they are the source of literary allusions. If children are not ready "to connect" with these stories, then such stories would have little meaning for them and would be an inappropriate literature experience.

So much depends on the teacher's understanding of children and knowledge of literature.

KNOWING AUTHORS AND ILLUSTRATORS

Study of the works of particular authors has characterized the teaching of literature at the secondary level more frequently than in the elementary school. Children enjoy knowing something about authors and illustrators as they read their books. Teachers and librarians will always want to tell children the name of the author and illustrator of a book as they introduce it. They may ask children if they know any other books that this particular person has illustrated or written. Some children delight in being able to recognize the artwork of Tomie de Paola or Leo Lionni or Pat Hutchins. They are beginning to recognize the style of an artist's work and this should be encouraged. Middle-grade children frequently discover favorite authors. They want another book by Lois Lowry, another Judy Blume, or another Daniel Pinkwater. They may be reading series books, and so they ask for another one of the Narnia series (C. S. Lewis), the Prydain series (Alexander), or the Little House books (Wilder). Some children develop special interests in sports stories, mysteries, or "Choose Your Own Ending" books. These are all ways that children categorize books. They show that children are developing a framework for literature, a way of thinking about books. Knowledge about particular books, authors, and the craft of writing will come about as children find increasing satisfaction in a range and diversity of works. Such knowledge should not be the primary focus of the literature program. It will occur as a natural result of real experiencing of books.

Developing Appreciation

The long-term goal of a literature program is the development of a lifetime pattern of preference for reading quality literature. James Britton maintained that in a quality reading/literature program "a student should read *more books* with satisfaction . . . [and] he should read books with *more satisfaction.*"[3] This emphasis on both wide reading

[3]James Britton, "The Nature of the Reader's Satisfaction" in *The Cool Web: The Pattern of Children's Reading* by Margaret Meek, Aidan Warlow, Griselda Barton (New York: Atheneum, 1978), p. 110.

and in-depth reading is characteristic of a literature program that develops fluency and appreciation.

Margaret Early[4] has suggested that there may be three developmental and sequential stages in the growth of appreciation:

1. The stage of unconscious enjoyment
2. The stage of self-conscious appreciation
3. The stage of conscious delight

The first stage is similar to the notion of discovering delight in literature, becoming engaged with it. At this level children read or the teacher reads to them for their enjoyment. They seldom touch on the way the author has created meaning. The reader in the second stage is interested in more than plot, asking why and looking below the surface of a story for deeper meanings. She enjoys exploring the story to see how the author, poet, or artist has reinforced the meaning by the text or art. The third stage describes the mature reader who finds delight in many kinds of literature from many periods of time, appreciating the best of each genre and author. Obviously, not even college students or many adults ever reach this level of conscious delight.

A literature program for the elementary school should focus on the first stage of unconscious enjoyment. If all children could be given the opportunity to find enjoyment in literature, they would be building a firm foundation for literary appreciation. As children are encouraged to interpret the meaning of the story or poem, through discussion or creative activities, some of them may be entering the second stage of self-conscious appreciation. As children respond to literature, discuss how they feel about the story and what it means to them, they may be ready to deal with the "whys" of their feelings and the ways the author or artist created those feelings. Children will need guidance from teachers and librarians as they begin to refine their understandings and become more discriminating readers.

In summary, the literature program in the elementary school will give children experiences that will contribute to these four purposes:

1. Discovering delight in books
2. Interpreting literature
3. Developing literary awareness
4. Developing appreciation

CREATING THE LEARNING ENVIRONMENT

It is possible to walk through any elementary school and tell something about the quality of education just by observing what appears to be honored in that school. If books are honored, they will be displayed throughout the classrooms and in the library. Each classroom will have a cozy reading corner or loft that provides a comfortable quiet place for reading. Good collections of books will be in each classroom as well as the library media center. Children's interpretations of books, both artistic and written, will be displayed on the bulletin boards. Attractive murals of favorite storybook characters, houses from fairy tales, or something about an author might be featured. Walk through your school and library and determine what is considered most important, basal readers or trade books; workbooks or children's own writing; commercial art on holidays, ABC cards, number cards, or children's own artistic interpretations and written work. The learning environment is readily discernible in any school or classroom.

The School Environment

Children learn what they live. Increasingly, educators are concerned that the quality of living in a school be equal to the quality of learning in that school. The physical environment of the school provides the context for that learning, but it is only one aspect of it. What teachers really believe in and want for their students will usually be taught.

COMMITMENT TO LITERATURE

Every primary-grade teacher sees himself or herself as a reading teacher who is truly committed to

[4]Margaret Early, "Stages of Growth in Literary Appreciation" in *The English Journal,* vol. 49 (March 1960), pp. 161–166.

Each classroom should have an inviting reading corner or a loft that provides a comfortable quiet place for reading.

Roy Wilson, teacher. Dhahran Hills Elementary School, Dhahran, Saudi Arabia.

teaching each child to read. In fact, in many of our primary grades over one-half of the school day is devoted to the teaching of reading. Ironically, once children reach the middle grades, teachers provide little time for children *to read,* maintaining that the curriculum is too crowded with other important subjects. Yet this is the very time when children build power in reading; when they discover the real joy of reading; in brief, when they *learn to love reading.* This is also the time when children can begin to develop taste in reading and become discriminating readers of fine literature. Teachers must commit themselves not only to teaching children to read but to helping children become readers—children who can read, will read, and will want to read. Such a commitment requires the creation of an environment that will encourage, enrich, and extend the readers' experiences with good books. Only then will children begin to develop a lifetime habit of reading.

The school will provide libraries to make fine books and quality multi-media readily accessible to children and faculty. Library media programs will be closely identified with the total instructional program. No longer will teachers rely on a single textbook to provide all the information that is needed in science or social studies. Children will use many books in all the content fields. The integration of print and non-print materials will be used to extend learning. Individualized, small-group, and large-group instruction will rely on a wide range of materials and a variety of books.

All teachers and librarians must have a strong commitment to literature. Few children discover books by themselves; in most instances, a parent, teacher, or librarian has served as the catalyst for bringing books and children together. As children grow up seeing significant adults as readers, they become readers. Find a teacher who is enthusiastic about children's books and you will find a class of

FAIRY TALE REVIEW

Gingerbread Man Escapes From Oven

Last Friday at 3:00 p.m a gingerbread man escaped from an oven. As he ran down the road, people who happened to be passing by joined in the chase. It was a long chase because everybody but the gingerbread man was getting tired.

Finally at 3:30 p.m the gingerbread man reached the river where he met a fox. The gingerbread man was last seen being taken across the river by the fox. He was wearing a button coat when last seen. If you have seen him, please notify the local authorities.

Gingerbread man when last seen

Bean Stalks Go Crazy

Two years ago, Jack cut down a bean stalk. Now the bean stalk has grown back and more stalks are sprouting.

The farmers love it because it has so many beans. The stalks have even lifted a few houses off the ground.

A wild bean stalk growing like crazy

Wolf Blows Down Pig's House

Yesterday, after the three little pigs went grocery shopping, the wolf came over and tried to blow down the pig's house. After many attempts, the wolf succeded. Minutes later, the wolf collapsed from loss of breath. When the pigs returned, they called an ambulance and "Hines Lumber and Brick Co." The pigs did not press charges; instead, they made the wolf pay for their new house. The wolf was treated and released from the hospital.

Fourth- and fifth-graders created a fairytale newspaper to sum up their study of these stories.

Martin Luther King, Jr., Laboratory School, Evanston, Illinois, Public Schools. Ellen Esrick, reading teacher.

Sports:

Tortoise Beats Hare

Last Sunday at Riverfront Stadium, the race between the tortoise and the hare began – and it was a good one too! It was suppose to be an easy race for the hare but the tortoise caught him by suprise.

The hare took a big lead early in the race. When the race was half over, the hare, thinking that he had it made, stopped to rest.

While the hare rested, the tortoise passed him up. The tortoise had already passed the finish line by the time the hare was ready to start again. It was an exciting race for sure.

Jack and Jill Break Record and Crown

Jack and Jill ran up the hill in record time. Unfortunately they fell down and broke their crown. Both are in critical condition.

Fisherman Makes Record Catch

A poor fisherman caught a five hundred pound fish yesterday breaking the world's record. The fisherman had to throw the fish back because it was magical, and catching magical fish is against the law.

Martin Luther King, Jr., Laboratory School, Evanston, Illinois, Public Schools. Ellen Esrick, reading teacher.

children who enjoy reading. Invariably, the teacher who reads, who knows books, and who shares this enthusiasm with students will inspire a love of reading.

WHOLE-SCHOOL PROGRAM

Many schools have made the development of readers as their top priority. As a total school faculty they have met and planned certain activities to promote children's interest in reading.

One school planned a whole-school unit on fairy tales. Children from kindergarten through sixth grade studied fairy tales, beginning with the traditional folktales and moving through the myths. They created a Fairy Tale Museum with such objects as "The Very Pea Which Disturbed the Princess' Sleep" and the golden ball which the Frog Prince retrieved for the spoiled princess. A Fairy Tale Newspaper included interviews with Cinderella and the Pied Piper, Classified Lost and Found Ads including an ad for a found glass slipper, a Society Column, and a Sports page describing the race of the hare and tortoise. Older children created their own mythological characters and stories. Different groups dramatized such traditional tales as "The Three Billy Goats Gruff" and "Little Red Riding Hood." This whole-school emphasis created a unity among the children and an appreciation for their traditional literary heritage.

Another school offered many different mini-courses in literature during Book Week. Children met and made puppets in one course, created a flannel story in another. Many children wrote their own stories in one course. Then, in another, they were introduced to the use of collage, marbleized papers, and ink prints made from styrofoam meat platters. Another course offered book binding so that children ended the week with their own bound and illustrated books. Different teachers volunteered to offer the various courses at different times. Some gave mini-courses on particular genres of books, like folktales or poetry. Others offered drama and choral speaking. In this particular school, children have an opportunity to do these things frequently. However, the mini-courses given near the beginning of school focused attention on bookmaking and provided children with skills they used throughout the year.

Some schools have organized book clubs for children interested in in-depth reading of particular books. Teachers, librarians, or interested parents have sponsored such clubs, which can meet after school if busing does not create a problem; otherwise book clubs meet during lunch or even during the day. Several leaders have found it helpful to establish a few guidelines from the beginning. Two that seem essential are: (1) Everyone agrees to read the chosen book. (2) Everyone agrees to write some questions about it. Some persons may have been trained as leaders for "The Junior Great Books" course sponsored by The Great Books Foundation.[5] They may be willing to meet with a group of children if their parents agree to buy the books. A school faculty will want to discuss this possibility among themselves.

In one school the parents and children created the "Book Nook," a tiny paperback bookstore literally made from a broom closet. They decorated it will Maurice Sendak posters and a charming hanging lamp and even turned the old sink into a "trading pot" where children could place a "used" paperback and exchange it for another. The whole school takes justifiable pride in this paperback bookstore. In another school the parents made a large wooden case on wheels that can be opened to create a bookstore anywhere in the building. Closed, it can be pushed flat against a wall. Parents will need help in getting such bookstores started and assuming responsibility for their operation. The librarian, a teacher who knows books, parents, and one or two children could serve as the selection committee to order new books. If teachers and parents support the store in the beginning, it will sustain itself once children know its regular hours and can find the books they want to buy and read.

PLANNING FOR AUTHOR/ILLUSTRATOR VISITS

Increasingly, schools have budgeted money to pay for an author or an illustrator to come and visit. The prospect of having a "real live author" come for a school visit is exciting and motivates students to read his or her books in anticipation of meeting the author. However, it takes good planning to use a visit to full advantage and make it a learning experience for all students.

[5]The Great Books Foundation, 40 East Huron Street, Chicago, Illinois 60611.

A converted broom closet becomes a busy paperback bookstore.

Martin Luther King, Jr., Laboratory School, Evanston, Illinois. Photographed by Fred P. Wilken.

The usual procedure for contacting an author or illustrator is to call the person in charge of promotion for his or her publisher and ask about availability, fees, travel arrangements, etc. Sometimes it is possible to arrange a visit in conjunction with another previously scheduled appearance in your area. This usually cuts down on the major travel expenses, although the author's fee must be paid.

It is essential that planning be done with teachers and children several months before the visit. There is no point in having an author or illustrator unless all the children who will be meeting him or her know the books. With authors of books for middle-graders this means obtaining many copies of their books, arranging for in-depth discussions of the books, perhaps showing films or filmstrips about the author. It might be wise to keep a running list of questions to ask the author as children are becoming acquainted with the books.

Several schools got together and invited Tomie de Paola to visit them when he was going to be at a conference in their area. His books were displayed in the Learning Center and in many of the classrooms. The children made murals of their favorite books, cooked pasta with a parent, and even wove a cloak for *"Charlie Needs a Cloak"*. First-graders made a list of their expectations of Tomie de Paola based on their knowledge of his books—what he would look like, what he would be like. Children thus became acquainted with all the books of one artist and had a chance to talk to him about his life and work. (See color section II.)

As Marilyn Parker says in describing a visit of Madeleine L'Engle in an article in *The WEB*, ". . . the actual event of an author's visit should be something like the tip of an iceberg—the most visible part of something much broader and deeper."[6] It is the preparation for the visit that provides the real learning experiences. As children focus on the work of one author or illustrator and have an opportunity to meet him or her, they have their first-time glimpse into the literary world.

The School Library Media Center

CHANGING NAMES, CHANGING FUNCTIONS

The confusing array of names for what used to be called "the library" reflects the expansion of services and materials now expected of that institution. Once a school was proud if it could boast of its own library and trained librarian. Now, however, the emphasis is on a media center for each school which contains books, film, tapes, slides, videotapes, computers, software, projectors, laminating machines, and listening and viewing centers. Such centers have variously been called The Instructional Materials Center, The Instructional Media Center, The Learning Center, The Media Center, and The Library Media Center. The term "media specialist" is often substituted for the older term "librarian." Arguments and justifications for the use of each of these terms have been delineated and debated. Each name carries certain connotations and limitations. Many, including The American Library Association, would opt for the best of both worlds by using the term Library

[6]Marilyn Parker in *The Best of the WEB, 1976–1982* (Columbus: The Reading Center, College of Education, The Ohio State University, 1982), p. 69.

A beautifully designed school library media center can become the focal point of the school.

Davenport Ridge School, Stamford, Connecticut. Photographed by Martin Tornallyay; from *School Media Quarterly*.

Media Center or just Library. Children, parents, and teachers know the meaning of the term "library." Public libraries have added videos, computers, and many other visual materials to their collections and instituted some amazing new services while still maintaining their original names of "library."

The name is not as important as the materials and services. For the purposes of this text the term "library media center" will be used to designate the place where teachers, children, and parents may expect to find a rich collection of carefully selected and arranged materials of communication, and a staff of experts who know these materials and their potential for use with children. The primary purpose of this center, regardless of its name, is to provide the best services and materials to facilitate real learning for children.

The library media center should be open all day every day to serve students in its unique way. Story hours or lessons on library skills can take place in a special area of the room and still leave the rest of the resources free for others to use. Children can learn without the immediate presence of a teacher or librarian. A trained aide can help children find relevant books, films, types, and records. Parents have served most effectively as volunteers in the school media center. Children increase in their ability to do independent study by using a variety of sources. An abundance of materials should be readily and freely available.

Increasingly, new school library media centers have become the focal point of many schools, with classrooms radiating out from them. The space should be as flexible and fluid as possible to allow for growth and change. The environment should encourage free access to materials at all time. Children flow in and out, doing projects, finding resources, making their own books, producing films. As the library media center becomes more closely identified with the total instructional program, it becomes more integrated into the total school environment.

THE SCHOOL LIBRARY MEDIA COLLECTION

Each school, regardless of enrollment, must have an adequate collection of both print and nonprint materials. The actual quantity of material in the basic collection will depend on the enrollment of the school, range of grades, variety of subjects taught, and special needs of the students. The national guidelines agreed on in *Media Programs: District and School*[7] suggest that schools with 500 or fewer students should have a minimum collection of 20,000 items, or forty per student. They recommend a base collection of some 8,000 to 12,000 volumes of books, with filmstrips, films, slides, videotapes, audiotapes, software, models and sculptures, and specimens making up the rest of the collection. Although published in 1975, these guidelines are still endorsed.

Regardless of how varied the materials, books will continue to be an essential source of information and pleasure. It is a known fact that children who have continuous access to a good school library media center staffed by qualified personnel generally read two to three times as many books as those who have only a classroom collection or are served by a central collection for an entire school

system. Children also read a greater variety of materials when they have access to their own school library media center.

Collections of quality media can be rich resources for extending and enriching the literature program, as well as other areas of the curriculum. Films, filmstrips, videotapes, slides, discs, and audiotapes may be used to introduce a poem or book, to develop meaning, to provide background, or to present literature in another form. The quantity of media available today requires entire books for their evaluation. The references at the end of this chapter are excellent resources to look for detailed description of various media.

THE LIBRARY MEDIA SPECIALIST AND THE MEDIA PROGRAM

The library media specialist[8] plays a very important role in the quality of learning and living that

---

[7]American Association of School Librarians, American Library Association, and Association of Educational Communications and Technology, *Media Programs: District and School* (Chicago: American Library Association; Washington: Association for Educational Communications and Technology, 1975), pp. 70–81.

[8]The terms "library media specialist" and "librarian" will be used interchangeably to denote the person who is responsible for directing the school library media program. It is assumed that such a director would have had training as a school librarian and a media specialist and in many instances would also have a teaching certificate.

GENERAL CRITERIA FOR EVALUATING MEDIA

General criteria appropriate for evaluating most media include such considerations as the following:

- *Proper medium:* Is this medium (slides, filmstrip, film, recording, etc.) the best and most appropriate form to present this particular content?

- *Quality of content:* Is the content of this presentation accurate, authentic, up-to-date? Does it give an overview of the particular topic or an in-depth investigation of one aspect? If a filmed version of a story, how true to the original source is this presentation?

- *Point of view:* Is the material presented in a biased manner, presenting only one side of an issue, or are various points of view included? Is the presentation complete, or is any important information left out?

- *Technical quality:* How good is the photography, the color, the sound? How clear are the captions (if used), the voice quality, the sequencing of the events? Are the unique capabilities of the particular medium used to good effect?

- *Relevance:* How relevant is this presentation to the particular unit of study? How suitable is it both in length and content for the intended age group? Does it present information not found elsewhere? What will children gain from viewing or hearing this presentation?

- *Possible use:* Would this be best used as an introduction to a subject, to stimulate interest during the study, or to provide a synthesis of knowledge? Should it be presented to the whole class, small group, or used individually?

takes place in the library media center, the school, and the community. Serving as a full-time contributing faculty member, the librarian works with children, teachers, parents, and volunteer and professional aides. Specialized training provides background knowledge of children's books and all media for instruction, library media procedures, knowledge of children's development and behavior, understanding of various teaching methods, and knowledge of school curriculum needs and organization. Increasingly, the library media specialist is called on to give leadership not only in providing the materials for instruction but in shaping the curriculum itself. The library media program should be an integral part of the total school program. Working with teachers, the media specialist needs to be responsive to the curricula and instructional needs of the school. What units of study are the teachers planning to initiate this year? Books, films, tapes on this subject should be gathered together for the teachers' and children's use. Bibliographies of print and nonprint materials based on units of work should be developed cooperatively with teachers. Read-aloud lists should be shared. The function of the library media program should be to help the school achieve its goal of a quality education for the children it serves.

The library media center should be open all day and before school and after school for children, teachers, and parents to use. While certain events must be scheduled and arranged for—such as a story time for a group of primary-grade children, the showing of a special film, or the visit of an author or artist—these can usually take place in a special listening or viewing area of the center and not interfere with its ongoing use. Individuals, groups, or even complete classes should feel free to come to the library media center whenever a need or desire arises, without making previous arrangements. In addition, the library media specialist will set aside certain periods each week to conduct special activities—such as book introductions, a group study of library media skills, or story hours for those teachers requesting them. Both teachers and the library media specialist should be involved in the initiation of learning and the extension of that learning. Ideally, interests and learning will flow from the classroom to the center and from the center to the classroom.

The Classroom Environment

AN ENTHUSIASTIC TEACHER

The most important aspect of the classroom environment is the teacher. He or she creates the climate of the classroom and arranges the learning environment. If the teacher loves books, shares them with children, provides time for children to read and a place for them to read, children will become enthusiastic readers. The teacher who reads to the children every day, talks about books and characters in books as if they were good friends, and knows poems and stories to tell is serving the class as an adult model of a person who enjoys books. One teacher regularly used to read a new children's book while her class was reading. She would keep the book in an old beat-up briefcase that she delighted in carrying. A kind of game she played with her 7- and 8-year-old students was to keep the book hidden from them. Their delight was to find out what book she was reading, so they could read the same one. Of course they always found out, which was what she had in mind in the first place. Walk into any classroom and you can tell if the teacher really respects the reading of books. You can look at the teacher's desk or ask the children what book their teacher is reading to them. You can see what provisions have been made to have books in the classroom; you can look at the quality of the books and talk to children about which ones they have read. Enthusiasm for books is contagious; if the teacher has it, so will the children.

THE CLASSROOM BOOK COLLECTION

If we want children to become readers we must surround them with books of all kinds. We know that wide reading is directly related to accessibility; the more books available and the more time for reading, the more reading children will do.

Books should be a natural part of the classroom environment. There should be no argument as to whether to have a classroom collection of books or a library media center; both are necessary. Children should have immediate access to books whenever, wherever they need them.

The books in the classroom collection will vary from those in the library media center. Many classrooms have an extensive paperback collection

(400–500 titles). Frequently, there are five or six copies of the same title, so several children can read the same book and have an in-depth discussion of it.

The classroom teacher will also want to provide for a changing collection of books. These books will be related to the ongoing social studies or science programs. The librarian may provide a rolling cart of materials that will enhance children's study of a particular interest in social studies, science, or math. If the library media center does not have particular books that the children or the teacher need, they may be obtained from local public libraries or from a book-mobile. Some state libraries will send boxes of books to teachers in communities that are not serviced by public libraries.

A few schools and some individual teachers using a literature-based reading program have been successful in obtaining the funds usually spent on basal readers and workbooks to purchase more trade books for their classroom collections. It took one school three years to make this policy switch, but they were finally successful.

CREATING A CLASSROOM READING CENTER

Most teachers try to create an inviting reading area where children may go to read. This area should be somewhat secluded and outside the general traffic pattern. It is usually marked off with shelves where trade books are attractively displayed. A rug provides quiet and comfort. Many centers have bean-bag chairs, pillows, a rocking chair, and sometimes a comfortable couch for reading. In order to mark off a reading area, one teacher of 8- and 9-year-olds clipped paperback books to clothespins and hung these by strings suspended from the ceiling. Another group of 7- and 8-year-olds made a quilt of textile crayon squares depicting their favorite stories. This then became a gay divider for their reading center. Some schools have constructed study lofts in classrooms for the reading area.

Children develop more interest in books when they share in the planning of a reading center. One group of 8-year-olds utilized an unused cloak room for their reading center. With the aid of the custodian they built and painted bookshelves. Others designed unbleached muslin curtains that were decorated with crayon drawings of their favorite characters from books. A mother provided a hooked rug and a rocking chair to complete the homey aspect of this reading center. Another school changed a storage closet that was between three rooms into a small primary-grade book center. Good lighting, carpeting, and some bookcases made this a quiet, comfortable place for children from several classrooms to meet and share books together.

Inventive teachers and children will enjoy planning for and creating their own attractive reading areas.

DISPLAY TECHNIQUES

Teachers will want to feature particular books by displaying them on top of bookselves or on the shelves with their covers facing outward. Old, dirty-covered books placed so one can read only the titles on the spines do not capture the attention of children.

Department stores feature what they want to sell by arranging interesting displays; teachers should do the same. It takes very little time to collect five or six good Halloween stories and poetry books and place them with a pumpkin on a table that has been covered with a piece of orange or black cloth. All the books by one author or illustrator could be exhibited together, along with a picture of the writer or artist. Children might decide on a "book of the week" which could have a special place of honor. One group of 8- and 9-year-olds moves their favorite books to the window sills for display. One fifth-grade classroom has books in three places, the reading area, a table of books concerned with whatever focus unit they are studying, and a special place for books they have written and bound themselves. To be effective, displays should be changed frequently.

Trade books should be an integral part of the total environment of the room. A new book on hamsters might be placed by the hamster cage, Selsam and Hunt's *A First Look at Bird Nests* near two found nests. Many books would be used in a study of Alaska, but in order to highlight a few, the teacher might display a soapstone sculpture with Glubok's *The Art of the Eskimo* and some of the exciting books by James Houston, such as *Long Claws: An Arctic Adventure*.

Whenever possible, teachers should try to involve children in the process of selecting, obtaining, and arranging books for the reading center.

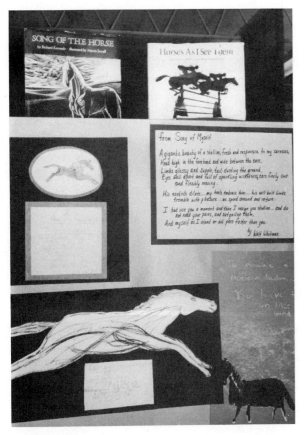

Books, poetry, and children's work make an attractive classroom display.

Marlene Harbert, teacher. Barrington Road Elementary, Upper Arlington, Ohio Public Schools.

Children may review new books and share in their selection. Excitement mounts as they unpack boxes of books, whether they come from the library or directly from the publisher. They may help with book arrangement and display. One group of three kindergarten children carefully rearranged the books on display in their room into the following categories:

- ABC Books and Mother Goose Rhymes
- Books by Leo Lionni
- Fat Books
- Little Books
- Books with Pretty Front Covers

The teacher was using the first group of books with the class. The second grouping represented their on-going study of the work of one illustrator. The last three categories were obviously theirs, but the process of rearranging the books forced them to look at each one, to discuss it and come to some tentative conclusion about its size or content. Besides their own childlike categories, they learned that books could be classified by type (genre) and author. What a simple but useful learning activity!

SHARING LITERATURE WITH CHILDREN

From the time of the earliest primitive fire circle to the Middle Ages—when minnesingers and troubadours sang their ballads—to the modern age of television, people have found delight in hearing stories and poems. Since literature serves many educational purposes in addition to entertainment and enjoyment, teachers should place a high priority on sharing literature with children. Boys and girls of all ages should have the opportunity to hear good literature every day.

Reading to Children

One of the best ways to interest children in books is to read to them frequently from the time they are able to listen. Pre-schoolers and kindergarten children should have an opportunity to listen to stories two or three times a day. Parent volunteers, high-school students, college participants—all can be encouraged to read to small groups of children throughout the day. Children should have a chance to hear their favorite stories over and over again at a listening center. The child from a book-loving family may have heard over one thousand bedtime stories before she ever comes to kindergarten; while some children may never have heard one.

One excellent teacher of kindergarten and first-grade children had this to say about the importance of sharing books with her children.

I read to my children a lot—a whole lot! I'll read anywhere from one to three stories at a time. Sometimes I'll reread a favorite story twice. And I read four to five times a day. I read to the whole group, to small groups of four of five children and to individual

Yarl Corbie

Milo Halperin

After the teacher read the description of Yarl Corbie in Hunter's *A Stranger Came Ashore,* an 11-year-old drew his interpretation of this mysterious Scottish schoolmaster who looked like a raven.

Barbara Friedberg, teacher. Martin Luther King, Jr., Laboratory School, Evanston, Illinois, Public Schools.

children. While I'm reading to the groups I'll encourage them to join in on the refrains. With individuals I may point to words, talk about what a word is. Sometimes I'll frame a word with my hands or put it on the board. I put songs, poems and refrains on chart paper so children will try to read them by themselves. And I'll read stories over and over again, just the way children hear bedtime stories. It is not unusual for me to read a book twenty times in one month![9]

[9]Interview with Kristen Kerstetter in *The Best of the WEB, 1976–1982,* Susan Hepler, ed. (Columbus: The Reading Center, College of Education, The Ohio State University, 1982), pp. 2–3.

Teachers accept the idea of reading a story at least once a day to the primary-grade child. Increasingly, the daily story hour is advocated by almost all authorities in reading. The research done by Cohen, Durkin, Clark, Thorndike and Wells reported in Chapter 4 emphasizes the importance of reading aloud to all children not only for enjoyment but also for their growth in reading skills. Reading to children improves children's reading.

Unfortunately, the practice of a daily story hour is not as common in the middle grades as in the primary grades. Yet, we know that it is just as essential. Reading comprehension is improved as students listen to and discuss events, characters, and motivation. They learn to predict what will happen in such exciting tales as Hunter's *A Stranger Came Ashore.* They increase their vocabulary as they hear fine texts such as Steig's well-known picture book *Amos & Boris* or Ursula LeGuin's remarkable fantasy *A Wizard of Earthsea.* This is the time that the teacher can introduce children to various genres of books like historical fiction, fantasy, biography, and poetry, which the children might not be reading.

Primarily, however, the read-aloud time will cause children to want to read. Once a child has heard a good book read aloud, he or she can hardly wait to savor it again. Reading aloud thus generates further interest in books. Good oral reading should develop a taste for fine literature.

SELECTING BOOKS TO READ ALOUD

Teachers and librarians will want to select books to read aloud in terms of the children's interest and background in literature and the quality of the writing. Usually, teachers will not select books that children in the group are reading avidly on their own. The story hour is the time to stretch their imaginations, to extend interests, and to develop appreciation of fine writing. If children have not had much experience in listengin to stories, begin where they are. Appreciation for literature appears to be developmental and sequential. Seven and 8-year-olds who have had little exposure to literature still need to hear many traditional fairy tales, including *Hansel and Gretel, Sleeping Beauty,* and *Rapunzel.* They delight in picture-story books like *Harry the Dirty Dog* by Zion, *Doctor De Soto* by Steig, and *Stevie* by Steptoe. Other children of the same age who have had much exposure to litera-

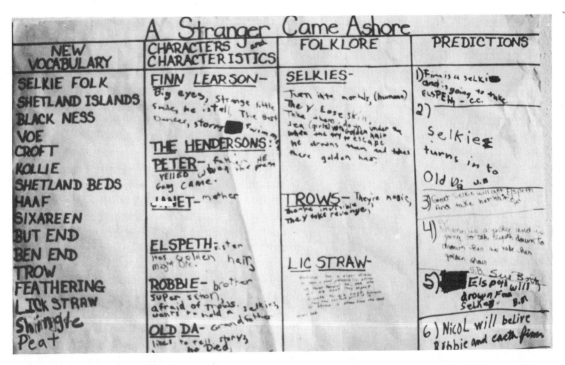

In order to help fifth graders with the Scottish vocabulary and folklore of Hunter's *A Stranger Came Ashore,* the teacher made this chart and encouraged children to add to it as she finished reading aloud each chapter.

Linda Charles, teacher. Highland Park Elementary School, South-Western City Schools, Grove City, Ohio.

ture may demand longer chapter books like *Ramona Forever* by Cleary, *James and the Giant Peach* by Dahl, or *The 18th Emergency* by Byars.

In the writers' experience, children tend to enjoy fantasies if they are read aloud. The subtle humor of Milne's *Winnie-the-Pooh* may be completely lost when the child is reading alone; when shared by an appreciative teacher-reader, the awkward but well-meaning "Pooh of Very Little Brain" and the dismal Eeyore become well-loved personages to 7- and 8-year-olds. The mysterious snow-shrouded pictures of *The Polar Express* by Van Allsburg would intrigue children of this age. They could discuss the ending of this story and ponder the question of the origin of the Christmas bell. The symbolism seen in Trina Schart Hyman's powerful pictures for Hodge's adaptation of *Saint George and the Dragon* needs to be shared and discussed with 8- and 9-year-olds.

There is a real place for sharing some of the beautiful picture books with older children as well

as younger ones. *Dawn* by Uri Shulevitz creates the same feeling visually as one of Emily Dickinson's clear, rarefied poems. It is a literary experience for all ages, but particularly for anyone who has felt "at oneness" with the world before the sunrise. Both Marcia Brown's fable *Once a Mouse* and Donald Hall's *Ox-Cart Man* are more appropriately shared with older children.

The teacher should strive for balance in what is read aloud to children. Children tend to like what they know. As they are introduced to a variety of types of books, they will broaden their base of appreciation. If 11- and 12-year-olds are all reading contemporary fiction, the teacher might read Lloyd Alexander's *Westmark,* a novel of political intrigue of a land and time that exist only in the author's mind. The fine-honed writing of Patricia MacLachlan's *Sarah, Plain and Tall,* the story of a mail-order bride and the family who longed for a new mother, could be shared with children as young as third grade and as old as sixth. Most of these books are too good for children to miss and should be read aloud to them.

Primary-grade teachers will read many books to their children, certainly a minimum of two to three a day. Middle-grade teachers may present parts of many books to their students during book talks or as teasers to interest children in reading the books. But how many books will teachers read in their entirety? An educated guess might be that starting with 8-year-olds—when teachers begin to read longer, continuous stories to boys and girls—an average of some five to six books are read aloud during the year. This means that for the next four years, when children are reaching the peak of their interest in reading, they may hear no more than twenty or so books read by their teachers! Certainly those books must be selected with care in terms of their relevance for the particular groups of students and for the quality of their writing. A suggested list of books to read aloud is included on the endpapers of this book to serve as a possible guide to selection. Notice that the age groups overlap deliberately. There is no such thing as a book for 5-year-olds or 10-year-olds. It is important to stress that. Very popular books such as those by Dr. Seuss or poems by Shel Silverstein do not appear on our Read-Aloud Lists since children will have read them on their own. Only a teacher who knows the children, their interests, and their background of experience can *truly* select appropriate books for a particular class.

We note with concern the increasing number of teachers who want to read such complex stories as *Tuck Everlasting* by Babbitt, *A Wrinkle in Time* by L'Engle, or *The Pinballs* by Byars to 6- and 7-year-olds. While children this age may become involved in the plots of these well-written stories they will certainly miss much of the deeper meaning reflected in their themes, such as the burden of immortality, the overcoming of evil with love, or the courage of children surviving family rejection and cruelty. Read at the appropriate developmental levels, these books could provide the basis for serious in-depth discussion and study. The period for reading children's literature appears to have decreased as more and more 12- and 13-year-olds begin to read best-sellers and other books written for adults. The inappropriate selection of books for reading aloud by both parents and teachers may contribute to this erosion of childhood.

There is a difference, however, between what parents may choose for family reading and what is appropriate for classroom sharing. Parents have the advantage of knowing all the books that children have enjoyed at home. In a family sharing of *Charlotte's Web,* the 5-year-old enjoys the humor of these talking barnyard animals while an 8-year-old may weep at Charlotte's death. The closeness of a family unit helps all members to find enjoyment in a read-aloud story regardless of age level. The teacher, on the other hand, has to consider children's background in literature or lack of background as he or she selects appropriate books to capture their attention.

A read-aloud program should be planned. What books are too good to miss? These should be included in an overall plan. Teachers should keep a record of the books that they have shared with the children they teach and a brief notation of the reaction of the class to each title. This would enable teachers to see what kind of balance is being achieved and what the particular favorites of the class are. Such a record would provide future teachers with information as to the likes and dislikes of the class and their background of exposure to literature. It also might prevent the situation that was discovered by a survey of one school in which every teacher in the school, with the exception of the kindergarten and the second-grade teachers, had read *Charlotte's Web* aloud to the class! *Charlotte's Web* is a great book, but not for every class. Perhaps teachers in a school need to agree on what is the most appropriate time for reading particular favorites. Teachers and librarians should be encouraged to try reading new books to children, instead of always reading the same ones. But some self-indulgence should be allowed every teacher who truly loves a particular book, for that enthusiasm can't help but rub off on children.

TECHNIQUES OF READING ALOUD

Effective oral reading of a story is an important factor in capturing children's interest. Some teachers can make almost any story sound exciting, while others plod dully through. The story-teller's voice, timing, and intonation patterns should communicate the meanings and mood of the story. Conversation should be read naturally, and volume varied with the content of the story. Humor, mystery, disgust, and other feelings can all be communicated through the tone of the reader's voice. Effective reading suggests that the teacher should be familiar with the story. Certainly his or her enthusiasm for the book will be communicated. It is good for children to see teachers moved by a story. One teacher of our acquaintance says he has never yet been able to finish *Where the Red Fern Grows* by Rawls without shedding a tear. Others find White's *Charlotte's Web* or Paterson's *Bridge to Terabithia* equally hard to finish. Literature should communicate feelings, real feelings. A well-read story can move us to tears or laughter.

The following guidelines for reading aloud may prove useful. You will want to check the list before selecting and reading a story to a whole class.

Storytelling

A 5-year-old said to his teacher: "Tell the story from your face." His preference for the story *told* by the teacher or librarian instead of the story that is read directly from the book is echoed by boys and girls everywhere. The art of storytelling is frequently neglected in the elementary school today. There are so many beautiful books to share with children, we rationalize, and our harried life allows little time for learning stories. Yet children should not be denied the opportunity to hear well-told stories. Through storytelling, the teacher helps transmit the literary heritage.

Storytelling provides for intimate contact and rapport with the children. No book separates the teacher from the audience. The story may be modified to fit group needs. A difficult word or phrase can be explained in context. For example,

GUIDELINES FOR READING ALOUD

1. Select a story appropriate to the developmental age of the children and their previous exposure to literature.
2. Determine whether you will share the book with the whole class, a small group, or an individual child.
3. Select books that will stretch children's imagination, extend their interests, and expose them to fine art and writing.
4. Read a variety of types of books to capture the interests of all.
5. Remember that favorite stories may be reread.
6. Plan to read aloud several times a day.
7. Be sure to select a story that you like so you can communicate your enthusiasm.
8. Choose a story or chapter that can be read in one session.
9. Be sure you have read the book and are familiar with the content.
10. Seat the children close to you so all can see the pictures.
11. Hold the book so children can see the pictures at their eye level.
12. Be sure your voice communicates the mood and meaning of the story and characters.
13. You may want to introduce books in various ways:
    Through a display
    By a brief discussion about the author or illustrator
    By asking children to predict what the story will be about through looking at the cover and interpreting the title
    By linking the theme, author or illustrator to other books children know
14. With longer chapter books, children may be encouraged to discuss the progress of the story or perhaps predict the outcome at the end of the chapter.
15. After finishing a book, children may want to discuss it by linking the story with their own experiences or other literature. Not all books have to be discussed to be enjoyed, however.
16. Each teacher should keep a list of the books read aloud to the whole class. This can be passed on to the next teachers.

in telling the story of *The Three Wishes* by Gal-done, "black pudding" could be quickly explained as another word for sausage before continuing the story. Stories can be personalized for very young children by substituting their names for those of the characters. Such a phrase as "and, David, if you had been there you would have seen the biggest Billy Goat Gruff. . . ." will redirect the child whose interest has wandered. The pace of the story can be adapted to the children's interests and age levels.

SELECTING STORIES TO TELL

Stories that are to be told should be selected with care. Stories worth the telling have special characteristics that include a quick beginning, action, a definite climax, natural dialogue, and a satisfying conclusion. It is best to select stories with only three or four speaking characters. Such folktales as "The Three Billy Goats Gruff," "Chicken Little," and "Cinderella" are particular favorites of younger children. The repetitive pattern of these tales makes them easy to tell. Originally passed down from generation to generation by word of mouth, these tales were polished and embellished with each retelling. *Gone Is Gone* by Gág, *The Mousewife* by Rumer Godden, and "Elsie Piddock Skips in Her Sleep" from Colwell's collection, *A Storyteller's Choice,* exemplify other favorite tales to tell.

Ashley Bryan's wonderful retelling of the pourquoi West Indian story *The Cat's Purr* begs to be told to 7-, 8-, and 9-year-olds. The sound effects of the animals, the rich use of language, and the drama of the tale of rat stealing cat's drum all make this an exciting tale to tell. The admonition "Remember now, don't rap it or beat it or tap it or poke it. Just stroke it gently. And don't let anyone else play it," sets the stage for the action and would have to be memorized to maintain the flavor of the story. However, the whole story would not have to be memorized, just the refrains. Children this age also enjoy some of the tall tales about American folk heroes such as Paul Bunyan, Pecos Bill, and John Henry. Incidents from biographies and chapters from longer books may be told as a way of interesting children in reading them.

A literary story that is known for its rich language and fine illustrations like Steig's *Amos &*

Public libraries have reached out to the preschool child. Youngsters are entranced as they listen to the librarian.

Mary Wilson Branch, Orange County Free Library, California, Oakley Stephens, librarian.

Boris is better read aloud than told. Besides, the pictures form an integral part of this literary picture book and need to be shared with children. It is best to select a story for telling that sounds like a "told tale" and can stand alone without pictures.

GUIDES FOR TELLING STORIES

From the time of the early minstrels, storytelling has been considered an art. For this reason many teachers have been afraid to attempt it. However, the classroom teacher is an artist in working with children and should have no fear in telling stories to them. Enjoyment of the tale and knowledge of children will help to convey enthusiasm and appreciation for the story. All life experiences enrich the interpretation of the story. Sensitivity to textures, line, pattern, color, and rhythm helps the storyteller to convey details and images. Skill in storytelling requires a rich vocabulary and enjoyment of words and language patterns. The teacher must be able to identify with the setting and characters of the story in order to communicate the spirit and feelings expressed in the tale.

If the teacher knows and enjoys the story, techniques will come naturally. The story, however, should be carefully prepared. The teacher needs to be thoroughly familiar with its plot, characters, and the flavor of its language; but it need not be memorized. In fact, memorization often results in a stilted, artificial presentation. There is the added danger of being completely confused when a line is forgotten. The storyteller should first visualize the setting; imagine the appearance of the characters, their age and costume; and plan an introduction that will set the mood of the story. It may be wise to learn the pattern of some introductions, such as, "Once there was, and once there wasn't. . . . " If there are repeated chants or refrains, these should be memorized. Outline the sequence of events, including major incidents, the climax, and conclusion. Master the structure of a story by reading it from beginning to end several times. Experienced storytellers allow two to three weeks to make a story their own. They learn the story as a whole, not in parts, and practice telling it to themselves, their family, in fact, anyone who will listen.

The good storyteller does not call attention to herself but to the story. She should use a pleasant, low-pitched voice with enough volume to be heard easily. Gestures, if used at all, should be natural for the storyteller and appropriate to the action of the story. The storyteller is not an actor but the channel through which the story is told. Many storytellers believe sound effects should be omitted. If the lion roars, the narrator should not attempt an imitation of a roar, but the idea can be conveyed as the word "roared" is given a deeper tone and increased volume. The r sound may be exaggerated so the lion "urroarrd." Writers and such well-known storytellers as Ruth Sawyer and Augusta Baker suggest variations in pitch, tone, and volume of voice in accordance with the mood of the story to make it more effective. Well-timed pauses may help listeners anticipate a climax. No amount of study of these techniques will substitute for actual practice. With experience comes assurance and a willingness to experiment. Tape recordings can be made to evaluate storytelling skills. A very brave storyteller may be willing to have her presentation videotaped for later group critiquing.

Marie Shedlock, a well-known storyteller, advised her students to learn no more than seven stories a year, while she herself perfected three stories each year. A repertoire of some twenty stories of different types will serve the librarian and teacher very well. By learning a few stories at first and adding to the repertoire each year, the teacher and the librarian will soon have a rich resource for literature.

FELTBOARD STORIES

Storytelling may be varied by using a flannel- or feltboard. To tell a feltboard story, the scenery or characters of a story may be made of flannel, felt, or paper. As the story is told, the figures are placed in the proper positions on the board. If the figures are made of paper, strips of flannel attached to the reverse side will cause them to adhere to the feltboard. Gluing felt to the inside of an artist's cardboard portfolio and trimming it with tape is an easy way to make a feltboard. Felt is more durable for the board than flannel. Feltboards may also be purchased commercially. Hook-and-loop boards that use velcro enable the teacher to hang larger objects on the board. Boards already constructed can be ordered, or the material can be purchased for a home-made one. Magnetic boards can also be used to tell visual stories.

Some tales are more suitable for feltboard presentation than others. The stories should be simple and have few characters. Not every incident or scene in the story needs to be included. Detailed settings are too difficult to recreate. While some rapid changes can be portrayed on a feltboard, most physical action is better dramatized. The cumulative tale, or one in which elements are added, is usually quite appropriate for a felt-story presentation. For example, in what better way could Gág's *Nothing at All* complete his metamorphosis from a round ball to the shape of a dog, to a live dog with spots, tongue, ears, and tail that wags? Similarly, children delight in watching the appearance and disappearance of the red wings on the rabbit in Bailey's *The Little Rabbit Who Wanted Red Wings*. Two versions of the Jewish folktale *Could Anything Be Worse?,* as retold by Hirsh and as *It Could Always Be Worse* by Zemach, lend themselves well to telling on a feltboard. This is the tale of the man who complains that his house is too small and so he goes to the rabbi to ask for advice. The rabbi suggests he invite the chickens into the house, then the cow, then his wife's relatives, and so on. When the man can no longer stand it, the rabbi suggests he take them out one by one. When they are at last alone, both the man and his wife appreciate all the room they now have in their house! This story can be easily shown by making a simple outline of the house, adding all the animals, and then taking them out again!

One of the advantages to the storyteller in using a feltboard is that the figures can be arranged in sequence and thus serve as cues for the story. It is essential to *tell* the feltboard story. If the teller tries to read it and manipulate the figures, he is helplessly lost in a tangle of pages and felt characters. While telling a feltboard story, remember to look at the children rather than the board.

The feltboard story is an attention-getting device. Children are intrigued to see what will appear next. As soon as the storyteller is finished, children like to retell the story again in their own words. This is an excellent language experience and should be encouraged. Children also like to make and tell their own stories.

Try to keep all the pieces of a feltboard story together in a plastic bag clearly marked with the title of the story. If possible, also put a paperback copy of the book or story in the bag to keep the memory of it fresh and to share with the children after the story has been told. If teachers or librarians just make two feltboard stories a year, they will soon build a collection of tales to share. These are fun to make and even more fun to share with an enthusiastic audience. Storytellers have their own favorites, but the ones listed below seem particularly well suited for a feltboard presentation. Each one includes some magical change which would be hard to dramatize in another way.

BOOK TALKS

Librarians and teachers frequently make use of a book talk as a way of introducing books to children. The primary purpose of a book talk is to interest children in reading the book themselves. Rather than reveal the whole story, the book talk tells just enough about the book to entice others to read it. A book talk may be about one title; it may be about several unrelated books that would have wide appeal; or it may revolve around several

SUGGESTED STORIES FOR THE FELTBOARD

Bailey, Carolyn Sherwin. *The Little Rabbit Who Wanted Red Wings*, illustrated by Dorothy Grider. Platt & Munk, 1945.

Domanska, Janina. *The Best of the Bargain*. Greenwillow, 1977.

Duvoisin, Roger. *Petunia*. Knopf, 1950.

Freeman, Don. *Dandelion*. Viking, 1964.

Gág, Wanda. *Nothing at All*. Coward McCann, 1928.

Galdone, Paul. *The Three Wishes*. McGraw-Hill, 1961.

Ginsburg, Mirra. *Mushroom in the Rain*. illustrated by José Aruego and Ariane Dewey. Macmillan, 1974.

Hirsh, Marilyn, *Could Anything Be Worse?* Holiday, 1974.

Hogrogian, Nonny. *One Fine Day*. Macmillan, 1971.

Kent, Jack. *The Fat Cat: A Danish Folktale*. Scholastic, 1972.

Krasilovsky, Phyllis. *The Man Who Didn't Wash His Dishes*, illustrated by Barbara Cooney. Doubleday, 1950.

Lionni, Leo. *Frederick*. Pantheon, 1967.

————. *Little Blue and Little Yellow*. Astor-Honor, 1959.

Nic Leodhas, Sorche, *Always Room for One More*, illustrated by Nonny Hogrogian. Holt, 1965.

Seuss, Dr., pseud. (Theodor Geisel). *The 500 Hats of Bartholomew Cubbins*. Vanguard, 1938.

Tresselt, Alvin. *The Mitten*, illustrated by Yaroslava. Lothrop, 1964.

Turkle, Brinton. *Do Not Open*. Dutton, 1981.

Waber, Bernard. *"You Look Ridiculous," Said the Rhinoceros to the Hippopotamus*. Houghton Mifflin, 1966.

Wood, Audrey. *The Napping House*, illustrated by Don Wood. Harcourt, 1984.

Zemach, Margot. *It Could Always Be Worse*. Farrar, Straus, 1976.

Zion, Gene. *Harry the Dirty Dog*, illustrated by Margaret Bloy Graham. Harper, 1956.

books which have a similar theme, such as "getting along in the family" or "courage" or "survival stories."

The book talk should begin with recounting an amusing episode or with telling about an exciting moment in the book. The narrator might want to assume the role of a character in a book, such as Julie in *Julie of the Wolves* by Jean George, and tell of her experience of being lost without food or a compass on the North Slope of Alaska. The speaker should stop before the crisis is over or the mystery solved. Details should be specific. It is better to let the story stand on its own than to characterize it as a "terribly funny" story or the "most exciting" book you've ever read. Enthusiasm for the book will convey the speaker's opinion of it. This is one reason why book talks should be given only about stories the speaker genuinely likes. Children will then come to trust this evaluation. It is best if the book is on hand as it is discussed, so that the children can check it out as soon as the book talk is finished.

A good book talk takes time to prepare, yet it is well worth the preparation if children are drawn into reading the book. Some teachers and librarians find it is helpful to tape their book talks in order to listen to and evaluate them. Children who missed the talk might be encouraged to listen to the tape. A list of the books included in the book talk can be made available to children following the talk, so they can remember the names of the titles. Remember, the effectiveness of a book talk is judged by the number of children who want to read the books after they have been introduced.

PROVIDING TIME TO READ AND DISCUSS BOOKS

One of the primary purposes of giving book talks, telling stories, and reading aloud to children is to motivate them to read. A major goal of every school should be to develop children who not only can read but who *do* read—who love reading and will become lifetime readers.

Unfortunately, schools spend so much of their time teaching the skills of literacy that they fail to develop truly literate persons who read widely and thoughtfully on many diverse subjects. The report of The Commission on Reading titled *Becoming a Nation of Readers*[10] showed how little time students spend in reading both in school and out of school. According to this report, a typical primary class has only 7 or 8 minutes per day for silent reading, while middle graders averaged only 15 minutes. In a study of fifth graders' out-of-school reading, 50 percent of the children read books for an average of 4 minutes per day or less, in contrast to the 130 minutes per day spent watching TV. "For the majority of the children, reading from books occupied 1 percent of their free time or less."[11]

To become a fluent reader, it is essential to practice reading from real books that capture the interest and imagination of children. No one could become a competent swimmer or tennis player by practicing 4 minutes a day. Schools have little influence on the out-of-school life of their students, but they do control the curriculum in school. If we want children to become readers, we must reorder our priorities and provide time for children to read books of their own choosing every day.

Sustained Silent Reading

Recognizing this need, many teachers have initiated a sustained silent reading (SSR) time. The name is somewhat formidable, suggesting more pain than pleasure. Teachers have used other names such as "Recreational Reading," "Free Reading," or even the acronym D.E.A.R. (Drop Everything and Read) used by the teacher in *Ramona Quimby, Age 8* by Cleary. Whatever the name, however, this is a time when everyone in the class (in some instances, the entire school) reads, including the teacher. SSR times have been successfully established in kindergarten through middle schools. Usually, one time period is lengthened gradually from 10 minutes a day to 20 to 30 and, in some fifth- and sixth-grade classes, 45 minutes per day. Some teachers allow children to read in pairs, recognizing the social nature of reading. A classroom collection of books supplemented by library books is essential for a successful SSR time.

[10]Richard C. Anderson, et al., *Becoming a Nation of Readers* (Washington: National Institute of Education, 1984).
[11]Anderson, p. 77.

Children need time to share their books, talk about favorites, and to become a "community of readers."

John Muir School, Madison, Wisconsin. Photo by Kathryne Lee.

One fourth and fifth grade took the last 15 minutes of the day following a 45-minute sustained silent reading time to share their impressions of their books. Everyone in the class knew what everyone else was reading, they knew each other's favorite books, and they could recommend books to each other based on their known interests. As students talked about the books they were reading, others gave such supporting comments as "Oh, that's such a neat story" or "another book by Betsy Byars that you'd enjoy reading is *Cracker Jackson*." Time for such talk is essential to developing interest in reading books and creating a literate society within the classroom.

The value of such a quiet time for children to read books of their own choosing is that it develops fluent readers. Only as students have an opportunity to practice the skills of reading by actually reading books they enjoy do they ever become readers. In overemphasizing the teaching of reading skills, schools have failed to develop children who know the joys of reading. Before television, children used to read for enjoyment at home. Since this is no longer happening, time needs to be provided for it in school if we want to become a "nation of readers."

Time for Talk about Books

Equally important as time for wide reading is time to talk about books children have found exciting. Shirley Brice Heath maintains that our schools teach literacy skills but seldom give attention to the context for developing literate behavior.[12] Only as students have an opportunity to share their response to books, discuss their favorites, and link them to other literature do they become a community of readers.

GUIDING IN-DEPTH STUDY OF BOOKS

If children are to have an opportunity for wide reading, it should be balanced by an in-depth study of books. Such a study could be based on a single book, books by one author or illustrator, a genre of books like folktales or historical fiction of one period, or a focus unit based on content or theme, such as books about monsters or survival stories.

Webbing Techniques

One way to begin planning any study of books is to make a web of all the possibilities inherent in one book or several. A web is a kind of visual brainstorm that helps to generate ideas and link them to a theme or central focus. The idea of webbing a book or group of books was first developed for the third edition of this text in 1976. *The WEB* is also the title of a journal edited by the authors, published quarterly by Ohio State University since the summer of 1976.[13] This periodical reviews books and always includes a web of books with each issue.

No two webs are alike. They should be based on the interests and capabilities of the children who

---

[12]Shirley Brice Heath, "Being Literate in America: A Sociohistorical Perspective." Keynote address for Annual Meeting of National Reading Conference, November 1984, published in *NCR Yearbook*, 1985.

[13]*The WEB* (Wonderfully Exciting Books), Charlotte Huck and Janet Hickman, eds. (Columbus: The Reading Center, The Ohio State University, 1976–).

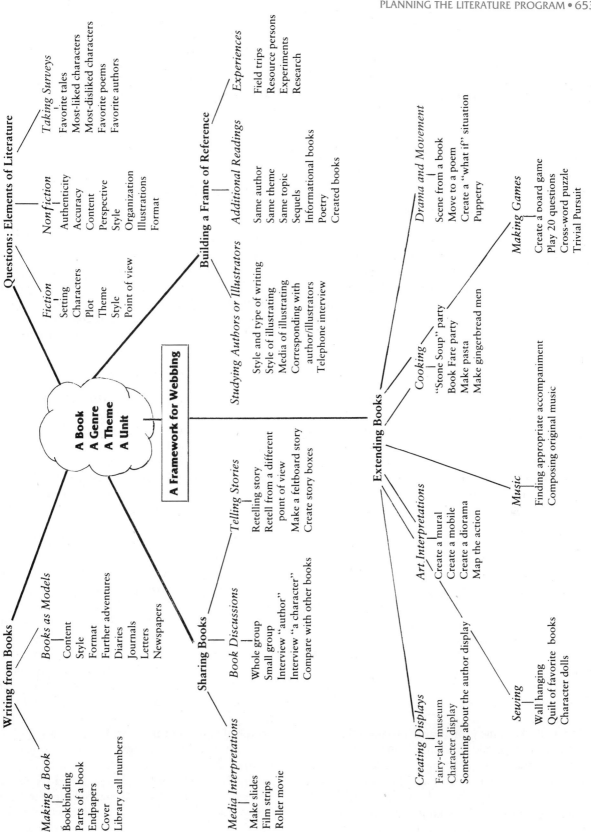

Questions: Elements of Literature

Taking Surveys
Favorite tales
Most-liked characters
Most-disliked characters
Favorite poems
Favorite authors

Nonfiction
Authenticity
Accuracy
Content
Perspective
Style
Organization
Illustrations
Format

Fiction
Setting
Characters
Plot
Theme
Style
Point of view

Building a Frame of Reference

Experiences
Field trips
Resource persons
Experiments
Research

Additional Readings
Same author
Same theme
Same topic
Sequels
Informational books
Poetry
Created books

Studying Authors or Illustrators
Style and type of writing
Style of illustrating
Media of illustrating
Corresponding with
author/illustrators
Telephone interview

A Framework for Webbing

A Book
A Genre
A Theme
A Unit

Writing from Books

Books as Models
Content
Style
Format
Further adventures
Diaries
Journals
Letters
Newspapers

Making a Book
Bookbinding
Parts of a book
Endpapers
Cover
Library call numbers

Sharing Books

Book Discussions
Whole group
Small group
Interview "author"
Interview "a character"
Compare with other books

Telling Stories
Retelling story
Retell from a different
point of view
Make a feltboard story
Create story boxes

Media Interpretations
Make slides
Film strips
Roller movie

Extending Books

Drama and Movement
Scene from a book
Move to a poem
Create a "what if" situation
Puppetry

Making Games
Create a board game
Play 20 questions
Cross-word puzzle
Trivial Pursuit

Cooking
"Stone Soup" party
Book Fare party
Make pasta
Make gingerbread men

Music
Finding appropriate accompaniment
Composing original music

Art Interpretations
Create a mural
Create a mobile
Create a diorama
Map the action

Creating Displays
Fairy-tale museum
Character display
Something about the author display

Sewing
Wall hanging
Quilt of favorite books
Character dolls

will be using the ideas. These suggested ideas should also utilize the strengths of the book or books. No web is meant to be followed exactly or totally. After all the possibilities have been considered, a teacher might circle the ones that would be new experiences for his or her students or that best fit the theme of the web.

When designing a web, it is helpful to have several adults work together to plan and refine the suggestions. A good web takes time to develop and requires a broad range of knowledge. For this reason, it is usually not advisable to have children construct webs. They frequently do not know the possibilities for related readings, the strengths of the book or books, or what is appropriate for class activities. As a result, they tend to reduce the study of a book to curriculum subject areas such as language arts, social studies, science, and art and music, whereas one of the real advantages of a well-planned web is that it helps to cut across these curriculum areas.

A teacher or librarian needs to be completely familiar with the content, the relevancy, the literary strengths of a particular book or genre before discussing it in depth with a small group or class. The very fact of having mapped the possibilities in a web enables the teacher to link the potential of the book with children's interests, past experiences, and growing abilities.

The web shown here provides a "Framework for Webbing," indicating the kinds of subheadings that might be devised when working with a single book, a genre, or a particular theme of books, such as survival stories, or a unit on such topics as houses or water. Not all these suggestions would be appropriate for each selected book or topic, nor for all ages. They can, however, serve as a guide for the persons doing the planning, who could then select on the basis of their knowledge of children and books. (See pages 660 and 665 for other webs.)

Questioning Techniques

In the well-planned literature program teachers and librarians would listen to children's responses to books and question them less. Listen to a tape of a teacher and group of children discussing a book and you will probably hear more teacher talk than child talk. Yet we know that there is real value in having children talk their way through to the meaning of a story or poem. As children become more interested in books and are allowed to explore various interpretations in supportive open discussions, there is less need for detailed question-and-answer sessions.

Some children do need guidance in thinking about a book, however. Sometimes only one question—such as "What did this book make you think about?"—is enough to help a child put the book into some kind of perspective. A teacher or librarian may help a child begin to formulate a frame of reference for books with such questions as "Can you show me another book that Leo Lionni has illustrated?" Or "Which do you like the best, the Prydain series or the Narnia series? Why?" It is possible to ask too many questions about one book and so kill the child's interest in it. On the other hand, some superficial questions may simply become routine and not extend children's thinking or sharpen their observations.

PURPOSES OF QUESTIONING

Questions will vary according to the purposes that the teacher has in mind for a particular class and book. The teacher may emphasize the content of the book, the quality of writing, or the children's comprehension of the story. For example, after planning the web for *The Sign of the Beaver* (pages 660-661), the teacher may decide that the most important point to emphasize in a discussion about this book would be the changing relationships between Matt and Attean, the Indian boy. Children might be asked to find the passages in the book that show a beginning change in Matt's understanding of Attean's dislike of the white settlers. A list of the gifts that each of the protagonists gave each other could show the outward signs of this internal change in relationships. If the teacher wanted to broaden the discussion of the coming together of two diverse cultures to today's world, she or he could ask children to apply what they have learned from this story to present cultures and the mutual distrust of the two most powerful nations of the world.

Another purpose for the discussion might emphasize the quality of writing in this Newbery Honor Book. Children could be asked to note the frequent use of signs and symbols in this story. They might look at the various ways Elizabeth Speare reflected the time period in the creation of the setting and the style of writing. Further discussion of the requirements of authentic historical fiction might be discussed. The value of a web is that it enables a teacher to decide what areas most need to be discussed—then questions can be focused on these areas to create greater understanding.

Placing a book within a literary framework means discussing other books by the same author or comparing other books with the same theme. Children need to see that books are seldom considered in isolation but are evaluated against other books that are similar in purpose.

TYPES OF QUESTIONS

Questions need to be evaluated in terms of the levels of thought that they require from the respondent. Teachers can be taught to ask questions which demand a higher level of thought than simple recall or yes/no answers. These higher cognitive level questions have been developed by various psychologists, reading experts, and educators.[14] Norris Sanders' sequential hierarchy based on Bloom's *Taxonomy of Educational Objectives* is representative of the cognitive levels of questions. Sanders defined his categories as follows:[15]

1. *Memory:* The student recalls or recognizes information.
2. *Translation:* The student changes information into a different symbolic form or language.
3. *Interpretation:* The student discovers relationships among facts, generalizations, definitions, values, and skills.
4. *Application:* The student solves a lifelike problem that requires the identification of the issue and the selection and use of appropriate generalizations and skills.
5. *Analysis:* The student solves a problem in the light of conscious knowledge of the parts and forms of thinking.

6. *Synthesis:* The student solves a problem that requires original, creative thinking.
7. *Evaluation:* The student makes a judgment of good or bad, right or wrong, according to standards he or she designates.

Though these categories can apply to all kinds of studies, examples will be given for literature questions based on the story of *Cinderella* (Perrault), illustrated by Susan Jeffers:

- *Memory:* This type of question involves a simple recall of the story, such as naming characters, recalling incidents, or describing setting.

  Question: Cinderella's godmother warned her that she must be home from the ball at what time?

- *Translation:* Requires student to recast an idea into another mode or form of communication, such as moving from the printed word to pictorial or graphic. Includes such forms as drama or making a model, diagram, or map. The student is not asked to elaborate or interpret the idea, just present it in a different form.

  Question: Dramatize the scene where Cinderella is helping her stepsisters to prepare for the ball. In what ways can you show how they mock her?

- *Interpretation:* Several kinds of thinking are represented in this category, including seeing relationships among characters, determining the reasons (or cause and effect) for certain behavior or events in a story, comparing and contrasting variants of a folktale or books with similar themes, forming generalizations concerning books of a certain type or by a certain author.

  Question: What reasons might Cinderella's stepsisters have for treating her the way they did?

- *Application:* These questions require students to make a direct application of knowledge, skills, or criteria learned in one situation to another.

  Question: What might be some examples of the Cinderella story in today's life? What kind of work

---

[14]A summary of the research on questioning is given in the ERIC report *Questioning: A Path to Critical Thinking* by Leila Christenburg and Patricia P. Kelly (Urbana, Ill.: ERIC Clearinghouse on Reading and Communication Skills and the National Council of Teachers of English, 1983).

[15]Norris M. Sanders, *Classroom Questions, What Kinds?* (New York: Harper & Row, 1966), p. 3.

might a modern Cinderella be expected to do? What would be today's equivalent of going to the ball and winning the attention of the prince?

- *Analysis:* Analysis questions emphasize elements, form, and organization of a story or poem.

Question: What are the personality traits of Cinderella which would make the prince fall in love with her? Contrast these with the personality traits of her stepsisters.

- *Synthesis:* These questions require the student to put together elements and parts of poems and literature in such a way as to create a unified, unique structure. Many of the activities suggested in Chapter 13 call for synthesis on the part of the student.

Question: If we were to make a fairy-tale museum, what objects might be used to represent the story of Cinderella?

- *Evaluation:* These questions require a judgment of the value or quality of the writing based on established criteria. The criteria are either known or developed first; then books, poems, art, films, and so on are judged on how closely they meet the criteria.

Question: Compare this version of Cinderella with *Walt Disney's Cinderella* and the one illustrated by Marcia Brown. Could you rank these from 1 through 3 (3 being the highest) on the basis of the illustrations? What are your reasons for these decisions? Can you now order them on the basis of the quality of the language? Again what are your reasons?

Questioning hierarchies have also been developed for assessing reading comprehension. These usually overlap with the cognitive hierarchies. For example, many reading texts suggest there are three levels of questions, those calling for:

1. Literal comprehension
2. Interpretative comprehension
3. Critical or evaluative comprehension

Questions may also be classified as narrow or broad, or convergent or divergent. The convergent question seeks one "best" or "right" answer, while divergent questions suggest more than one acceptable response. Convergent questions tend to focus on memory or simple recall, while divergent questions promote higher levels of thinking. However, many divergent questions may be built on the answers to a few convergent ones. For example in the questions suggested for *The Sign of the Beaver* (page 657) a listing of all the gifts might later help children to categorize them into tangible and intangible gifts, which is both an interpretation and analysis task.

The chart of questions for *The Sign of the Beaver* illustrates how the various categories for questioning overlap and also relate to literary elements. In asking a question about the symbolic meaning of the tale of *The Sign of the Beaver*, for example, the teacher would be asking children to relate the theme of the story to the title; at the same time they would have to call up other "signs" in the story and analyze them in order to interpret their meaning. Various children would have different meanings for the signs, so the question would be a divergent one. In developing questions, teachers need to be aware of all the various types, plus the literary elements necessary for developing an appreciation of the book. It takes time to develop good questions.

No one has ever determined a correct sequencing of questions for literature—if there is such a thing. Generally, it is recommended that the teacher ask questions that lead children back to the book rather than away from it, at least at first. Discussions that speculate about what might have happened or use the book as a springboard for children to discuss similar situations seem to be more appropriate for the end of the discussion rather than the beginning. For example, in the questions for *The Sign of the Beaver*, questions 5, 8, and 9 lead students away from the book, while the other questions send them back to the book. They were placed on the chart in the order of the cognitive levels of thinking required to answer the questions, but in a discussion of the book they might better be asked last.

CHILDREN'S QUESTIONS

Children derive real value from developing their own questions for a book. One teacher who regularly uses children's literature as the content of her

QUESTIONS FOR AN IN-DEPTH STUDY OF *THE SIGN OF THE BEAVER*

		SEQUENTIAL HIERARCHIES		NONSEQUENTIAL HIERARCHIES	
		Cognitive Levels of Questions	Reading Comprehension	Literary Appreciation	Type
1.	Make a chart of the exchange of gifts in this story. What gifts did Matt give to the Indians? What gifts did Attean give to Matt? What gifts did Matt make for each of his family?	Literal	Memory	Plot	Convergent
2.	Map the trip that Matt's father made from Massachusetts to Maine and back again.	Translation	Memory	Setting	Convergent
3.	Retell the scene in Chapter 6 where Matt gave the Indians his book as Attean would have told it to his friends back in the Indian village.	Translation	Interpretation	Point of View	Divergent
4.	Trace the development of friendship between Matt and Attean. What events or passages in the book show a change of ideas about their culture?	Interpretation	Interpretation	Character Development	Divergent
5.	Suppose you were lost in the woods in Maine today. What survival skills would you need to know? Would they be different from those Matt and Attean needed?	Application	Interpretation	Links to Life	Divergent
6.	Why did Elizabeth Speare title this book *The Sign of the Beaver?* What other "signs" were seen in this book? Try creating another title for this story.	Analysis	Interpretation	Theme	Divergent
7.	Write chapter headings for each of these chapters.	Synthesis	Interpretation	Plot Development	Divergent
8.	What other survival stories do you know? How are they different or similar to *The Sign of the Beaver?*	Synthesis	Interpretation	Literary Links	Divergent
9.	Which of these survival stories seem the most believable? Why? Which ones required the greatest courage?	Evaluation	Evaluation	Literary Criticism	Divergent

reading program frequently asks children to write questions when they have finished reading a book. Then she compiles all their questions, and they see if they can answer them in a discussion.

One group of third- and fourth-graders read their own paperback copies of *Abel's Island* by William Steig. They were encouraged to write questions in the margins of their books and underline favorite passages or particularly descriptive ones in order to make the book theirs through their responses. When they finished the book, they wrote questions to be used in an imaginary interview with Abel by reporters of "The Mossville News." Their questions were compiled and given to "the reporters" as suggestions for their interview. Some of their questions follow:

QUESTIONS FROM "THE REPORTERS OF *THE MOSSVILLE NEWS*" TO ABEL

1. Why did you go after Amanda's scarf in a raging storm?
2. In the beginning, how did you try to get back?
3. How did you feel after you realized you were unable to get back?
4. How long did you live on the island?
5. What did you learn on the island?
6. How will your life in Mossville be different now because of your experience on the island?

QUESTIONS FOR AMANDA AFTER ABEL'S RETURN HOME

1. What did you do while Abel was missing?
2. How will your life be different now that Abel has returned?

Third- and fourth-graders
Martin Luther King, Jr., Laboratory School
Evanston, Illinois, Public Schools
Ellen Esrick, teacher

After the children interviewed Abel, the group discussed the questions themselves. One questioning technique this teacher always uses is to develop one or two questions that cannot be answered in the book. The last question for Abel and the two devised for Amanda require children to continue the story in their imagination.

If children are given the opportunity to develop thoughtful questions and to evaluate their questioning techniques, their questions will improve. Look at the questions a group of sixth-graders

developed for Speare's *The Witch of Blackbird Pond*. This time they needed no such framing device as provided by the reporter interview.

STUDENT QUESTIONS DEVELOPED FOR
THE WITCH OF BLACKBIRD POND

1. In what ways do you think Kit *cast a spell* on the children she taught?
2. If Kit's grandfather could give her advice, what might he tell her about *teaching*?
3. The author does not tell you why William did not appear when Kit was in the shed or as a defendant at the pre-trial. What reasons can you give which might explain his apparent "uncaring" behavior?
4. What do you think Kit found most difficult about her new life?
5. Why do you think Goodwife Cruff, as well as several others in Wethersfield, *wanted* to believe that Hannah and Kit were witches and punish them?
6. What is your opinion of how the Puritans think about (1) religion, (2) the home, (3) school, (4) punishments, and (5) girls? What are some similar beliefs we hold today? What are some of today's beliefs that certain groups are trying to change?
7. What do you think Hannah Tupper's *real magic* was?
8. How do you interpret Hannah's statement to Kit when she said: "But remember, thee has never escaped at all if love is not there"? (p. 170)
9. Why do you think Kit strongly resisted her impulse to tell Mercy that John loved her? Even when she thought John might never return, why do you think Kit still kept the secret?
10. Hannah Tupper (p. 97) said to Kit: "The answer is in thy heart. . . . Thee can always hear it if thee listens for it." What do you think she meant? How did Kit follow her advice?

Sixth-graders
Martin Luther King, Jr., Laboratory School
Evanston, Illinois, Public Schools
Ellen Esrick, reading teacher

In-Depth Study of One Book: *The Sign of the Beaver* by Elizabeth Speare

There is more to the study of a book than just developing questions. The web on *The Sign of the Beaver* shows the many possibilities for study and

Four children worked together to create *The Sign of the Beaver Catalog.* Notice their symbolic drawing of the clasped hands for the back of their cover.

Marlene Harbert, teacher. Barrington Road Elementary, Upper Arlington, Ohio Public Schools.

extensions inherent in this book. One group of third- and fourth-graders made this book the focus of their curriculum work for some eight weeks. Several children built a fragile but authentic model of Matt's cabin filled with all the provisions he had obtained in anticipation of his family's return. You could lift off the roof of this model cabin and see the cradle Matt had made for the expected baby, the drying ears of corn, the new wooden bowls, the snowshoes propped against the wall. Every detail mentioned in the book was reflected in this three-dimensional translation of the story. Another group was equally successful in creating a model of the Indian village.

Stories

What does this book have to say about the importance of stories and storytelling? Does it have anything in common with *The Green Book?* (Walsh)

How might Matt tell his story when he is a grandfather?

What books does Matt's family own? Can you find any parallels between *The Sign of the Beaver* and *Robinson Crusoe?* (Defoe)

What stories did Attean's family tell?

What traditional tales might they have known? Read folktales of the Northeastern Indians: *The Talking Stone* (deWit)

Changing Relationships

Trace the development of friendship between Matt and Attean. What events or passages from the story show a change in ideas about each other's culture?

Think about Matt and Attean as teacher and student.
How did Matt become a better teacher? How would you teach someone to read?
What did Attean teach Matt? How did he conduct the lessons?

Discuss the changes in the balance between the Beaver clan's existence and the coming of white settlers.

What other changes do you see in characters' attitudes toward one another?

Survival

What survival skills did Matt develop? Which did he learn by observation?

Without the Indians, what might have happened to Matt?

Read other stories of survival
My Side of the Mountain (George)
The Talking Earth (George)
Brothers of the Heart (Blos)
The Courage of Sarah Noble (Dalgliesh)
How does the predicament of the main character in any of these books compare to Matt's?

Try out some of Matt's survival skills. What did he cook? What were common foods in colonial times?

Make johnnycake
The Heritage Sampler (Hoople)
Slumps, Grunts and Snickerdoodles (Perl)

Growing Up

How does Attean mark his preparation for manhood? What tests must he pass?

What does Matt do that shows he is a man? Which of his actions earns the respect of Attean's people?

THEMES AND MOTIFS

Signs and Symbols

What makes *The Sign of the Beaver* a good title?
How many examples of signs and symbols can you find in the book? Which are Indian signs? Signs of the white man? Animal signs?

Animals

How are animals important to this story?
Make a chart picturing the animals. Describe their role in the story's events; explain what that shows about setting, character, or theme.

Gifts and Exchanges

What gifts are given in this story by Matt? by the Indians? Think of some that are not material things.

What gifts would you have to share with a friend like Matt or Attean?

What gifts did Matt make for his family? What does that show you about how he felt?

Freedom

Who is more free, Matt or Attean?

As winter sets in, Matt's snowshoes "set him free." What other things gave him more freedom?

Setting
Map the trip that Matt's father made from Maine to Massachusetts and back.
Make a time line showing events during Matt's long wait. How many ways could you represent time passing?
Make an illustrated catalog of items that would have been familiar to Matt but are not common today. Consider tools, household items, clothing, see *Colonial Living* (Tunis)

Arrange a display of artifacts (or make your own reproductions) of colonial life or the Northeast Indians.
Build a model of Matt's cabin, or Attean's village. Compare and discuss—what differences in life style are dictated by your shelter and its surroundings?

The Sign of the Beaver
by Elizabeth Speare
A Web of Possibilities

Other Books by Speare
Calico Captive
    Compare portrayal of Native American characters with Attean and family
The Witch of Blackbird Pond
The Bronze Bow

Other Books about Clash of White and Indian Cultures
    in colonial times
        The Double Life of Pocahontas (Fritz)
        The Light in the Forest (Richter)
    in contemporary U.S.
        Johnny Stands (Paige)

Predictions
What does the cover make you think the book will be about?
Read and predict from chapter endings what might happen in following chapter.
Make up your own chapter titles.

Pace of Plot
How long are the chapters?
What kinds of things happen as the chapters end?
How do "cliff-hangers" help to keep the reader interested?

Foreshadowing
What bits of warning does the author give that there might be trouble from a bear? that something might happen to Matt's father's gun?
Can you find early clues for other events?

STYLE AND TECHNIQUE

Use of Language
Notice descriptions that are comparisons (simile and metaphor). Compile a list, suggest others of your own.
    Why would the author say that the gun was smooth as a silk dress rather than shiny as a no-wax floor?
How does the author make Attean's speech different from Matt's? What problems do you think an author has in deciding how people might have talked more than 200 years ago?
Keep a journal for Matt that tells his feelings about passing events.
Write a story about Matt's family. How might they have felt about being separated from Matt?

From *The WEB: Wonderfully Exciting Books*, Charlotte Huck and Janet Hickman, eds. Columbus: The Ohio State University, vol. 8, no. 2, Winter 1984.

Much writing took place in relationship to this book. Four children created an illustrated catalog of the items Matt used in the story. A table of contents listed four categories: Clothing, Personal Possessions, Hunting Tools, Gifts. Each page pictured an object and description of how it related to the story. For example, in the section on gifts, a picture of snowshoes had this description:

The snowshoes set Matt free.
He was happy. For the first time since
Attean and Attean's Family left.
Attean's Grandfather gave Matt the
snowshoes.

Under a picture of a cradle appeared this written description:

Before whiteness came Matt made a
cradle for his new baby brother or
sister. It was made of wood and it
rocked. The cradle even had a
headboard.

Third- and fourth-graders
Barrington Road School
Upper Arlington, Ohio
Marlene Harbert, teacher

The cover of this catalog had a picture of Matt's log cabin on the front, and the back symbolically represented the friendship of Matt and Attean by showing two hands clasping, one white for Matt, the other the darker tan of the Indian boy, Attean. The book was dedicated to the author, Elizabeth Speare, and a Prologue gave a brief summary of the story.

Children also created maps of this story and wrote descriptions of how they made their model canoes, the cabin, and Indian village. One boy reflected the thoughts of Matt after the Indians had left him all alone:

ALL ALONE AGAIN

I must have been all around the forest today searching for a sign that the Indians would come back, just something . . . a sign. But as I searched my thoughts were discouraged. I had just passed all of my memories—everything it seemed, a mark in the underbrush from the dead bear exactly where it fell. I walked to the village or what it used to be. The once busy city was now reduced to a circle of crushed brush and a number of smaller circles in the grass. Also scattered around were chips of birch bark. I sat down in the circle where Saknis' teepee was. There was a pile of black sticks in the center of the teepee, crumbling to ashes. I walked sadly away from the village remains. Then I realized I was missing the Indians even more than my own family. I wondered if my parents would come back and if they didn't what would I do? Right then I started to wish I had gone with the Indians. Sadly I walked back to the cabin.

I head my dog yelping at the door. He sure didn't know the predicament we were in. Then I thought of Robinson Crusoe. In my own way I was a Robinson Crusoe except my Friday left. I was alone, but if someone can survive alone I can. I have been taught by the Indians, masters of the forest. The air froze around me and snow began to fall. I feared for myself. I wondered how I would reach my traps for food, how I would live in this snow with my worn moccasins and short pants. But my overpowering wonder was—how would I survive?

Jamie Parson
Barrington Road School
Upper Arlington, Ohio
Marlene Harbert, teacher

It is obvious that these 8- and 9-year-olds gained much personal satisfaction and knowledge from their in-depth study of this book.

In-Depth Study of a Picture Book: *Where the Wild Things Are* by Maurice Sendak

Most primary-grade children love this particular book and ask to have it read again and again. A teacher might well increase children's enjoyment of this story by helping them to discover the layers of meaning in it and how the author-illustrator conveyed these meanings. After reading the story and sharing the pictures, the following questions might guide children's discoveries about this book:

What kind of a story is this?

Children will probably respond with such expressions as "funny," "scary," "make-believe."

Could this story really happen? Where?

Most of the action in this story took place in Max's imagination. While it is a make-believe story or fantasy, children might well say that it could have happened in Max's mind, but not in "real life."

What kind of a boy is Max? How do you know?

Children will give their varied impressions. Some will think he is naughty, others that he has a vivid imagination and a good sense of humor. One child may call attention to the expression on Max's face in the fifth picture in the book. Another may point out that Max is enjoying making up this story.

How did Max treat the Wild Things? Why do you suppose he treated them this way?

Children will remember that Max tamed the wild beasts by "the magic trick of staring into all their yellow eyes without blinking," and then led them in their "wild rumpus." Finally, he sent them off to bed without their suppers. Children will recognize that Max did to the Wild Things the very same things that had been done to him.

Was Max happy with the Wild Things?

The Wild Things all went to sleep and Max became lonely. Most of all he "wanted to be where someone loved him best of all," so he went home.

What did Max find waiting for him in his room? Who brought it? What does it mean?

Most children infer that Max's mother brought him his supper, but they do not always see that by this action, she is conveying her love and forgiveness. Actually, the warm supper symbolizes reconciliation, but children will usually tell you that it means "she isn't mad at him anymore," which is the same thing in more childlike language.

Let's look at the first picture. What do you see there? Do you see these things anywhere else in the story? What about the drawing Max made that is in the next picture? Do you see this anywhere else in the book?

Children will discover that Max is building a tent and has a toy wild thing in the first picture, and that he has drawn a picture of a wild thing in the second. Both of these pictures foreshadow coming events in the story. Children enjoy making the connection to later episodes.

What do you notice about the size of the pictures? (Go through the book quickly so children can see the pictures increasing in size.) Why do you think Maurice Sendak made them this way? What happens to the size of the pictures when Max returns to his room?

Children will notice that the pictures become larger and larger as Max's dream becomes more fantastic. They become smaller after Max returns home, but never as small as the first pictures; just as Max will never be quite the same boy after his fantasy.

What did you notice about the color of these pictures? Why do you suppose Sendak chose those colors?

Most of the colors used are greens and blues. Children may decide these convey the idea of a jungle, or a dream, or night.

At this point the teacher or librarian might want to help children summarize all the different ways that the author-illustrator has created the same meanings in pictures as in the story. Some observations might be that the illustrator can convey exaggeration and characterization in pictures. The gradual disappearance of Max's room into the forest pictures Max's journey into the world of his imagination. Size of pictures and colors are both important to the story. Pictures can be used to foreshadow events.

Following the sharing of this story children might want to dance their own "wild rumpus," paint pictures, or devise costumes. On other days the teacher might link this story to other monster stories or other books about dreams or share other stories by Sendak.

In-Depth Study of Characterization: *The Great Gilly Hopkins* by Katherine Paterson

After children have heard the first chapter of *The Great Gilly Hopkins,* the teacher or librarian could plan to discuss the many different ways the author reveals the character of Gilly.

The discussion could begin by asking the children how you get to know a person. They could imagine a new student had just entered class and then they could list all the ways you might find out about him or her. Possible responses might include:

Look at her, describe her.
Listen to what she says, how she talks.
Ask someone who previously knew her about her.
See how she reacts in school.
See what she does after school.
Find out how she treats other people.

Students might discuss the limitations of first impressions, that you need to see a person over time in many situations before you can really know him or her. Then the discussion could turn to the many ways an author uses to reveal character.

Using paperbacks of *The Great Gilly Hopkins*, ask the students to reread Chapter 1 and underline the different passages that tell something about the character of Gilly. Students could discuss the various ways the author is helping the reader get to know Gilly.

The following passages[16] are illustrative of what the students might identify:

1. Gilly calmly pinched a blob of gum off the end of her nose. There was no use trying to get the gum out of her hair. She sat back and tried to chew the bit she had managed to salvage. It stuck to her teeth in a thin layer. [Describing the character]

2. "This will be your third home in less than three years. . . . I would be the last person to say that it was all your fault. The Dixons' move to Florida, for example. Just one of those unfortunate things. And Mrs. Richmond having to go to the hospital." [Giving past history and implied innuendo]

3. Standing on the porch, before she rang the bell, Miss Ellis took out a comb. "Would you try to pull this through your hair?" Gilly shook her head. "Can't." "Oh, come on, Gilly—" "No. Can't comb my hair. I'm going for the Guinness Record for uncombed hair." [Letting the character talk; showing what others think of her]

4. "I am not nice. I am brilliant. I am famous across the entire county. Nobody wants to tangle with the great Galadriel Hopkins. I am too clever and too hard to manage. Gruesome Gilly, they call me." [Showing the character's evaluation of herself]

5. She waited until Mrs. Trotter and Miss Ellis were talking, then gave little W.E. the most fearful face in her repertory of scary looks, sort of a cross between Count Dracula and Godzilla. The little muddy head disappeared . . . She giggled despite herself. [Showing how the character treats others, particularly a fearful little boy]

6. She could stand anything, she thought—a gross guardian, a freaky kid, an ugly, dirty house—as long as she was in charge. [Showing the character's real motivation]

Gilly's larger-than-life character is revealed in this opening chapter. The reader learns of her past, how she has bested her past three sets of foster parents. We see her defiance of Miss Ellis and her cruelty to William Ernest, Mrs. Trotter's other foster child. Her interior monologue reveals her overrated opinion of herself and her disparaging observations of others. As she herself says, "I am not nice."

Students could be helped to determine the influence of such persons as W.E., Maime Trotter, Mr. Randolph, Miss Harris, and Agnes Stokes on the gradual character *development* of the Great Gilly. Slowly and believably the author dismantles her tough exterior to reveal a lovable streak in the gutsy Gilly.

After a group of sixth-graders had discussed the characterization of Gilly, they wrote about the ways in which they were like or not like Gilly. Amy's essay was titled:

GILLY IN ME

I think I am a lot like Gilly in some ways. One way is everything somebody says I can't do, I have to show them that I can do it or something like it. I think Gilly and I feel the same way about foster parents. If I had foster parents, I probably would feel that my mother would come and get me; but I wouldn't run away or steal money.

[16]Katherine Paterson, *The Great Gilly Hopkins* (New York: Crowell, 1978), pp 1–6.

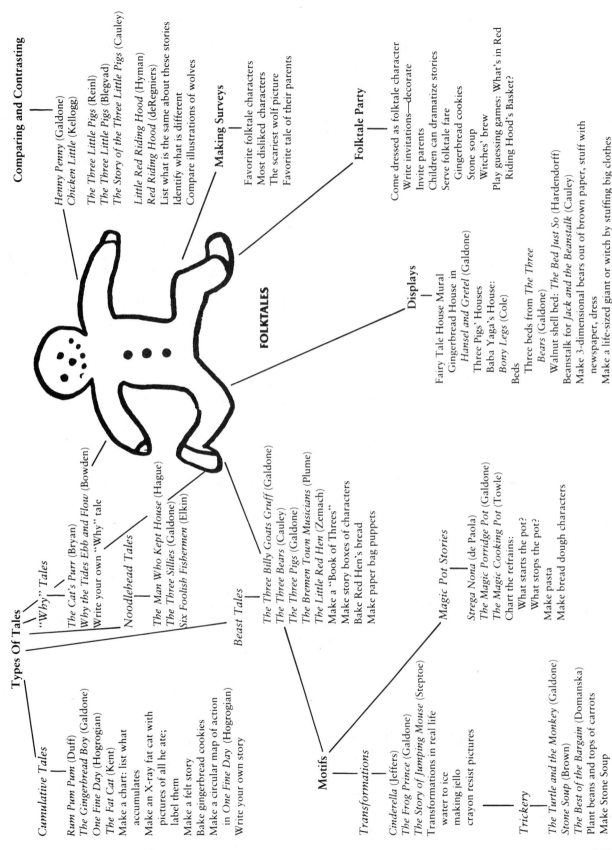

Comparing and Contrasting

Henny Penny (Galdone)
Chicken Little (Kellogg)

The Three Little Pigs (Reinl)
The Three Little Pigs (Blegvad)
The Story of the Three Little Pigs (Cauley)

Little Red Riding Hood (Hyman)
Red Riding Hood (deRegniers)
List what is the same about these stories
Identify what is different
Compare illustrations of wolves

Making Surveys

Favorite folktale characters
Most disliked characters
The scariest wolf picture
Favorite tale of their parents

Folktale Party

Come dressed as folktale character
Write invitations—decorate
Invite parents
Children can dramatize stories
Serve folktale fare
  Gingerbread cookies
  Stone soup
  Witches' brew
Play guessing games: What's in Red
  Riding Hood's Basket?

FOLKTALES

Displays

Fairy Tale House Mural
Gingerbread House in
  Hansel and Gretel (Galdone)
Three Pigs' Houses
Baba Yaga's House:
  Bony Legs (Cole)
Beds
  Three beds from *The Three
    Bears* (Galdone)
  Walnut shell bed: *The Bed Just So* (Hardendorff)
Beanstalk for *Jack and the Beanstalk* (Cauley)
Make 3-dimensional bears out of brown paper, stuff with
  newspaper, dress
Make a life-sized giant or witch by stuffing big clothes

Types Of Tales

Cumulative Tales

Rum Pum Pum (Duff)
The Gingerbread Boy (Galdone)
One Fine Day (Hogrogian)
The Fat Cat (Kent)
Make a chart: list what
  accumulates
Make an X-ray fat cat with
  pictures of all he ate;
  label them
Make a felt story
Bake gingerbread cookies
Make a circular map of action
  in *One Fine Day* (Hogrogian)
Write your own story

"Why" Tales

The Cat's Purr (Bryan)
Why the Tides Ebb and Flow (Bowden)
Write your own "Why" tale

Noodlehead Tales

The Man Who Kept House (Hague)
The Three Sillies (Galdone)
Six Foolish Fishermen (Elkin)

Beast Tales

The Three Billy Goats Gruff (Galdone)
The Three Bears (Cauley)
The Three Pigs (Galdone)
The Bremen Town Musicians (Plume)
The Little Red Hen (Zemach)
Make a "Book of Threes"
Make story boxes of characters
Bake Red Hen's bread
Make paper bag puppets

Magic Pot Stories

Strega Nona (de Paola)
The Magic Porridge Pot (Galdone)
The Magic Cooking Pot (Towle)
Chart the refrains:
  What starts the pot?
  What stops the pot?
Make pasta
Make bread dough characters

Motifs

Transformations

Cinderella (Jeffers)
The Frog Prince (Galdone)
The Story of Jumping Mouse (Steptoe)
Transformations in real life
  water to ice
  making jello
  crayon resist pictures

Trickery

The Turtle and the Monkey (Galdone)
Stone Soup (Brown)
The Best of the Bargain (Domanska)
Plant beans and tops of carrots
Make Stone Soup

In school I don't act like she does, going to the principal or slipping notes in teachers' books. It seems she doesn't like to be with her friends. I like to be around with my friends. I don't like to be by myself. I think Gilly gets mad easy. I get mad easy like getting called names; I always have to call them a name back.

Amy Kauffman
Granville Public Schools, Ohio
Christy Slavik, teacher

In-Depth Study of One Genre: Folktales

The Web on Folktales on page 665 suggests the rich possibilities inherent in the study of one genre of literature. This particular web was devised for children ages 5 and 6. A study of more complex fairy tales or myths could be done with slightly older children. Other literature genre that are appropriate for unit study might be fantasy, biography, or poetry.

This web provides for a serious look at the types of folktales and certain motifs found in tales that would appeal to young children, such as trickery, transformations, and magic pot stories. Before starting such a study, it might be wise to find out what background of experience children have had with these tales. No longer can teachers assume children will know these traditional stories—many do not.

One kindergarten–first grade group began their study of folktales with reading all the "three" stories in which three animals are the major characters. They then made their own *Book of Threes* with prints of the three bears, three pigs, and three Billy Goats Gruff. The characters were cut out of styrofoam trays and then painted and printed on brown paper. Another group made "before" and "after" pictures for their *Book of Transformations*. One page showed the ugly duckling and then the swan, another pictured a pumpkin and mice changed into Cinderella's coach and horses.

They also compared various versions of "Little Red Riding Hood" and "The Three Little Pigs," looking for the scariest wolf picture. The traditional story of *Henny Penny* was contrasted with Kellogg's very funny modern variant titled *Chicken Little* and Jan Ormerod's dramatization of *The Story of Chicken Licken*. A simple chart helped them see likenesses and differences in two versions of *The Three Little Pigs*. (See page 703.) They discussed both text and illustrations and then took a survey, placing a picture of themselves on the chart below the title of their choice. They also conducted home surveys to determine the favorite folktale of their parents. Instead of worksheets, they drew pictures of their favorite characters in folktales and their most disliked characters (see facing page).

The teacher and children developed charts on special folktale words. The one titled "The Land of Once Upon a Time" contained such words as golden eggs, mirror, poison apple, a royal pea, etc. Children had illustrated these words with their own cut-out pictures. Another chart listed "Good Guys and Bad Guys." Little Red Riding Hood, the cobbler and his wife, and the woodman were listed as "good guys," while the wolf and the troll had the distinction of being "bad guys." Around the room were quotations and refrains from folktales, such as "Not by the hair of my chinny chin chin" and "Who's been tasting my porridge?" and "Fee Fi Fo Fum, I smell the blood of an Englishman." The captions read "Who Said It?"

The children created their own story—"The Runaway Pizza"—based on the story of *The Gingerbread Boy*. Their teacher copied it in a big book which they illustrated and then read many times.

Not only did children learn about folktales in this study, but the unit gave them a real reason for reading, writing, dramatizing, taking surveys, baking, and making various art projects. The children learned that folktales had been told for many years and that even their parents and grandparents knew some of them. They discovered certain patterns in the stories like the use of three; and they learned what to expect from such characters as the wily fox or wolf, the youngest, the princess, etc. Most importantly, they found out that books were a source of pleasure and that learning to read was fun.

DIFFERENT PLANS FOR LITERATURE PROGRAMS

The authors of this text believe that there is no *one* literature program for all. We do believe in the *values* of literature for *all children*, however, and

Kindergarten children illustrate their most disliked or favorite fairytale character.

Martin Luther King, Jr., Laboratory School, Evanston, Illinois, Public Schools. Deborah Kaplan, teacher.

recognize that different teachers will have different literature programs. The following three plans are descriptive of the various ways we have seen literature incorporated into the elementary curriculum.

Each plan involves more than just the teaching of literature; it reveals the philosophy of the school system, beliefs about children's learning, and the teaching of reading and literature. Variations of each plan are seen as teachers move toward inclusion of more literature within the curriculum.

Literature as a Separate Program

Some schools see literature as something special to be taught in a separate program. These schools may buy sets of paperback books which are then assigned to each grade level and used for literature study. Some schools, particularly middle schools, may have a literature anthology which is used. There is a special time period for literature study, usually no more than once a week. Frequently students read the books or poems aloud and then they are discussed from a literary point of view. Selected books are used for the development of specific literacy understandings. Sendak's *Where the Wild Things Are* might be presented as a model of a recurring theme in literature of "a journey away from home and safe return." It may be compared with Potter's *The Tale of Peter Rabbit*, which has a similar plot structure. In-depth studies of other elements of literature, such as characterization or settings, various genres of literature, classics of children's literature, or books by one author, are other choices for unit studies.

An example of such a planned program was the so-called "Nebraska Curriculum"[17] developed with funds from the U.S. Office of Education in the

[17]*A Curriculum for English*, The Nebraska Curriculum Development Center (Lincoln: University of Nebraska, 1967).

First-graders illustrated this chart about various cumulative foktales. In the process they learned the sequence of each tale plus linking all tales of a particular type together. Later the chart helped them to retell the stories in their proper sequence.

Joetta Beaver, Teacher, Barrington Road School, Upper Arlington Public Schools, Ohio.

late 1960s. In this Elementary School Program, a spiral curriculum based on genre study such as historical fiction, fantasy, myth, and poetry was developed, with representative titles given for each grade level. Literature was considered as separate from reading. This program had several faults: (1) it assumed one literature program would be appropriate for all children in the United States regardless of differences in background, experience, or interest, (2) it emphasized literary criticism more than response and enjoyment, and (3) as a separate program it was to be taught on top of everything else required in the elementary school.

Schools have frequently included literature as a separate program for gifted children. The rationale to support this approach is that only students of high intelligence who are already good readers will have the scholarship necessary for the study of literature. Such an approach is elitist in concept and not an acceptable rationale from the authors' point of view. If literature is good for some children, it should be good for all.

Other schools have created special-interest groups for literature. These may operate as a "pull-out program" when certain children meet with a teacher or the librarian for an in-depth study of literature. Sometimes these groups meet voluntarily after school or during lunch hour. This is also the basis for the Junior Great Books Program which may meet in schools, public libraries, or community centers and is taught by specially trained leaders. In the Junior Great Books program, children meet and discuss selected literary works which are purchased through the Great Books Program. Other "special-interest" groups choose the books they will read together. Grades are usually not given for work in these literature groups.

Reports on these special literature programs are usually enthusiastic and exciting, as one would expect when the groups are made up of volunteers or talented children. The question remains: Are these the only children who deserve to know literature?

Integrating Literature with a Basal Reading Program

Basing their methods on recent research that emphasizes the significant impact of literature on helping children learn to read and become fluent readers, more and more teachers are integrating literature into their basal reading programs. Publishers, too, draw selections of prose and poetry from children's literature for the content of their texts. Increasingly, one book-length story is included in each basal text in order to give children experience in reading a whole book. Many publishers also are advocating a strong read-aloud program to accompany their basal reading programs.

The two aspects of a literature program that most teachers find time to incorporate into their basal reading programs are a read-aloud time and a sustained silent reading time. Teachers usually have a Sustained Silent Reading (SSR) period every day. Names vary from SSR to free-reading time to "Otter Time" (our time to enjoy reading). The purpose of such a period is to provide children time to read self-selected books in an atmosphere in which everyone is reading and enjoying the process, including the teacher. SSR time also provides children with an opportunity to practice their reading and develop fluency. Since they usually only read one story a day in their basal readers, they need this time to read widely.

To be successful, an SSR period requires a quantity of interesting, exciting books for children to read. Where basal readers take a large share of the funds for materials, teachers have had to find various ingenious ways to obtain books. Some of these include borrowing many books from the school library to initiate a classroom library, borrowing particular books from public libraries for certain children, involving parents or the PTA in setting up a Book Fair, the profits of which go for classroom libraries, and initiating the idea of a child giving the class a "birthday book" with a name plate in it, rather than a school birthday party. Teachers who know books have also been successful in obtaining some good ones at discount bookstores and second-hand bookstores. Another successful way to obtain books is to participate in book clubs. As children sign up for particular books, the teacher may receive bonus books for the classroom library.

Time is a constant problem in many classrooms, particularly when teachers meet with three to four reading groups a day. While the teacher works with these children, the rest of the class are assigned workbook pages and worksheets. In Anderson's report to the nation on reading practices, he maintains that 70 percent of students' reading instructional time is spent on these activities and that classroom research suggests the amount of time devoted to workbook-worksheet activities is unrelated to year-to-year gains in reading proficiency.[18] He maintains that students should do more reading and writing during this time. Some teachers have been successful in substituting some of the literature extension activities suggested in the next chapter—having children write their own stories and create their own books rather than fill in worksheets, for example.

Some teachers are trying innovative ways to provide more time for children to read real books for their reading instruction. For example, some teachers eliminate some sections or stories in the basals or have the children read them more quickly in order to complete them earlier in the year, then children begin to read sets of paperback trade books. Other teachers alternate the reading of paperbacks with the basal readers. Some teachers feel more comfortable in letting the best readers read trade books independently while still keeping the slower readers in the basals. An alternate plan, and one the authors endorse, is to give the poorest readers many easy real stories to generate enjoyment and fluency. One fifth-grade teacher let her lowest reading group read the paperback of *Stone Fox* by Gardiner. They became so enthusiastic about their reading time that every other group wanted to read paperbacks, too.

Textbooks are used in social studies, science, mathematics, health, and language arts. While some teachers try to relate their read-aloud book to their social studies or science, there is little time to share the fine informational books which would support the use of literature across the curriculum.

The use of the school library is usually directly related to the school curriculum. In textbook-oriented classrooms, there is less reliance on other resource books. Time in the library may be limited to a scheduled half hour per week for children to select and check out books. Older children frequently receive lessons on the use of the library and reference tools during their library time. This limits the time when the librarian might read stories and poems or talk with children about exciting books. In some instances librarians are expected to meet with forty to fifty classes per week, sometimes in two or more schools, give grades to children on library skills, and order materials! Other librarians have been more successful in seeing their major role as interesting children in books and promoting wide reading.

Evaluation of children's progress in a basal reading program is usually determined by the level of book they can read successfully and their performance on the publishers' tests which accompany the basals. Some teachers do try to keep a record of the titles and number of books read by each child during SSR time. Unfortunately, a few teachers still make a chart of the number of books read by each child and reward the child reading the greatest number of books. Whole schools promote independent reading with read-a-thons, book week activities, or book character days.

Teachers who want to incorporate more literature into their reading programs need to experiment with ways that are comfortable for them and still meet the expectations of the schools. If they are willing to risk new approaches, they may find their children are enjoying reading more and becoming real readers, rather than children who simply know the skills of reading.

A Literature-Based Reading Program

More and more schools are moving to a literature-based reading program in which trade books are used for all aspects of reading, the instructional program as well as the recreational program. Basal readers and workbooks are not used and funds usually appropriated for their purchase go for obtaining large classroom libraries of 400 to 500 books. Classrooms are "flooded" with books. There are books in an attractive reading corner, sets of paperback books for in-depth study, and a changing collection of books obtained from the school library and public libraries on whatever unit of study is in progress. Books are displayed along with children's work. Children's interpretations of books, book surveys, big books are seen throughout the room. Few commercial charts or pictures are seen; only quantities of children's work with captions, labels, or writing on it.

Knowing the research on the importance of

[18]Anderson, *Becoming a Nation of Readers,* p. 76.

reading aloud in developing concepts about print, a sense of story, prediction of plot, and understanding of characters, teachers read aloud to primary children two and three times a day. They frequently reread favorite stories until children almost know them by heart. Parent aides are encouraged to read aloud to small groups of children. Frequently, teachers establish a "buddy system" when older children may read with one or two younger ones.

After primary children have heard a predictable story several times, the teacher may make it into a big book and have a shared reading time with the whole class. The book is introduced and discussed in almost the same way that a parent will read a bedtime story. Children are encouraged to join in on the refrains, point to particular words, and discuss the process of reading itself—where to begin reading or how a particular word is recognized. These big books are then read over and over again by the teacher and the children.

Shared writing is done in much the same way as shared reading. Children and teachers may use the language pattern of such well-known stories as *Brown Bear, Brown Bear* by Martin to create alternative texts which they can easily read. For example, in the folktale unit described in this chapter, one group of children changed the brown bear pattern to reflect the story of *The Three Bears* with the sentences:

Papa Bear, Papa Bear,
What do you see?
I see Mama Bear
Looking at me.

Mama Bear, Mama Bear
What do you see?
I see Baby Bear
Looking at me [etc.]

Kdg./First grade
Highland Park School
Grove City, Ohio
Kristen Kerstetter, teacher

Rather than work on worksheets or workbook activities, children do a variety of things. Some may be seen reading from the big books, others may be reading individually with the teacher, while still others may be busy reading or writing stories of their own. Many of the literature extension activities described in the next chapter are done during this "worktime." Quiet talk about books flows as children create murals or map the action of a story.

An SSR or independent reading time is provided every day. Frequently, however, children read quietly in pairs. Time for discussion of books almost always follows these periods in a literature-based reading program.

The in-depth study of the books of one author, a genre of books, or one book begins as early as the kindergarten. With older children sets of such paperbacks as *Tuck Everlasting* by Babbitt, *The Sign of the Beaver* by Speare, *The Pinballs* by Byars, and many others are used for literature study with inter-students. While all children are involved in groups of in-depth reading, the groups are not formed on the basis of ability but of interest in the book.

Reading and writing across the curriculum are characteristic of this integrated program. Children do research in informational books on the particular class unit. Library skills are learned in the process of using many books and reference books for children's projects. The library is open all day long for children to use as they research particular topics. Parent assistants may help children in one part of the room to find their materials if the librarian is reading a story or sharing a filmstrip.

Teachers and children keep records of children's reading. An individual file on each child contains samples of his or her story writing, artwork, and research reports from the beginning of school. These are shared with parents during individual conference times. Book reports are not required, since children are sharing books in a variety of ways. Teachers know what children are reading because they are reading and reacting to their reading journals each week (see Chapter 13). All children know what others are reading because they discuss their books every day. Children frequently recommend books to others, as they know each other's reading interests. These children become a community of readers as they discuss and recommend particular titles. Books are an essential part of their lives.

Interest in books is seen in the entire school. Bulletin boards in the library, the halls, outside the principal's office display children's extensions of books. If an author is coming for a visit the whole school prepares for it with a study of his or her books, displaying banners and artwork and dramatizing stories, cooking, or doing puppetry.

Such support means that the faculty and ad- ministration have made a commitment to seeing literature as the way to teach children to read, to motivate them to read, and to provide a legacy of reading satisfactions for them. In such a program, they know children learn to read and learn to love reading. Their goal is to help children become life- time readers.

SUGGESTED LEARNING EXPERIENCES

1. Spend a day in an elementary school. Focus on the environment for learning, the physical environment, the intellectual climate, the emotional climate. Describe the quality of living and learning in the school. Support your descriptions with careful observations.
2. Visit an elementary school and focus on the provisions for a literature program. Does the teacher read to the children? What is read? What are the children reading? What books are available for them to read? How often are these books changed?
3. Spend a day in a school library media center. What does the librarian do? What questions do the children ask?
4. Draw a floor plan of a classroom you would hope to have as a teacher. Plan the reading areas and list what you would have in them.
5. Visit the children's rooms of several different libraries and compare what you see. What books are children reading, taking home? May they check out nonprint materials? Talk with children's librarians. What innovative practices have they initiated? What plans for the future do they have?
6. Using the Framework for Webbing, choose a book, genre, or unit to web for a particular age level. If possible work out some of the planned activities with children.
7. Plan an in-depth study using the types of questions described in the chapter.
8. Examine literature readers, sample kits of literature, and published units on literature. Note the purposes, content, plans of organization, and activities. Analyze the types of questions that have been prepared.
9. Look at several state and local curriculum guides for the elementary school and see what suggestions they give for teaching literature. Literature may be included in the guides for reading or language arts.

RELATED READINGS

1. American Association of School Librarians, American Library Association, and Association for Educational Communications and Technology. *Media Programs: District and School.* Chicago: American Library Association and Washington: Association for Educational Communications and Technology, 1975.
   This bulletin sets out the guidelines for the development of school library media programs. Published in 1975, the guidelines are still endorsed by the above three associations.
2. Anderson, Richard C., et al. *Becoming a Nation of Readers.* Washington: U.S. Department of Education, The National Institute of Education, 1984.
   This Report on The Commission of Reading has assembled some startling facts on the teaching of reading. Research on the impact of reading aloud and the reduced time of children's reading both in school and out of school suggests some major reforms in the teaching of reading. This report is available also from NCTE and IRA.
3. Barton, Bob. *Tell Me Another.* Markham, Ontario: Pembroke Publishers Limited, 1986. Distributed in U.S. by Heinemann Educational Publishers.
   A well-known Canadian storyteller provides a very useful book on storytelling and

reading aloud at home, at school, and in the community. Filled with practical suggestions, stories, and poems, this is a rich resource for the classroom teacher.

4. Bauer, Caroline Feller. *Handbook for Storytellers*. Chicago: American Library Association, 1977.

   This text provides a lively personal account of ways to tell stories. Besides the traditional approach to story-telling the author suggests many kinds of multi-media aids such as flannelboard stories, stories for the overhead projector, and the use of films.

5. Bodart, Joni. *Booktalk 2. Booktalking for All Ages and Audiences*. New York: The H. W. Wilson Company, 1985.

   The first part of this book provides a how-to-do-it manual on all aspects of giving a book talk, while the last section contains some 250 book talks contributed by librarians throughout the country.

6. Gillespie, John T. *Administering the School Library Media Center*, rev. ed. New York: R. R. Bowker, 1983.

   This is a comprehensive book which details the principles and practices of creating, organizing, and managing a school media program. It provides criteria for selecting and purchasing educational materials and audiovisual equipment.

7. Hunt, Mary Alice, compiler. *A Multimedia Approach to Children's Literature*, 3rd ed. Chicago: American Library Association, 1983.

   This is a selected list of films, filmstrips, and recordings based on children's books. For the teacher or librarian who wishes to use media to enhance literature, this book is essential.

8. Kimmel, Margaret Mary, and Elizabeth Segel. *For Reading Out Loud! A Guide to Sharing Books with Children*. New York: Delacorte Press, 1983.

   This is a practical and usable manual for reading aloud to elementary school children. Written by two professors of children's literature, the text contains a section on the values of reading aloud and in-depth reviews of some 140 potential read-aloud titles. Picture books are not included. A unique feature includes the estimated total reading time for particular books, with recommendations for appropriate "stopping places."

9. Larrick, Nancy. *A Parents' Guide to Children's Reading*, 5th ed. New York: Bantam Books, 1982.

   Now in its fifth edition, this guide has served parents well for nearly thirty years. Not only does the author suggest excellent books for children, but she suggests the best ways to share them at different age levels.

10. Malloch, Jean, and Ian Malloch. *Books Alive! A Literature-Based Integrated Program*, Teacher's Guides 4, 5, 6. Doubleday Canada Limited, 1986.

    An excellent teacher's guide for conducting a literature program focusing on selected read-aloud books and related reading for children. Each featured book is introduced with a WEB chart and suggestions for teaching. Helps teachers think through the logistics of such a program, including daily planning and evaluation.

11. Moss, Joy F. *Focus Units in Literature: A Handbook for Elementary School Teachers*. Urbana, Ill.: National Council of Teachers of English, 1984.

    This is an excellent guide for the teacher who wants to incorporate literature in his or her classroom. The text includes guides for developing questions and some thirteen literature units for grades one through six based on such subjects as Pig Tales, Friendship, and Dragons. An indispensable book for teachers.

12. Sawyer, Ruth. *The Way of the Storyteller*, rev. ed. New York: Viking, 1962.

    A great storyteller shares her experiences and pictures storytelling as an art. A classic in the field, the book includes helpful advice on selection and eleven stories often told by the author. Weston Woods Studios has produced a record album entitled *Ruth Sawyer, Storyteller*, which includes her comments on storytelling and her rendition of four stories.

13. Sive, Mary Robinson. *Selecting Instructional Media: A Guide to Audiovisual and Other Instructional Media Lists*, 3rd ed. Littleton, Colo.: Libraries Unlimited, 1983.

    A list of over 400 selected lists of AV and other instructional media for K–12 is provided in this useful book. Three kinds of lists are included: comprehensive lists, lists by subjects, and lists by media. The criteria used by each compiler are noted.

14. Trelease, Jim. *The Read-Aloud Handbook*, updated ed. New York: Penguin, 1985.

    A revised edition of a popular handbook for parents and educators. This book was on the *New York Times* best-seller list for nineteen weeks. Trelease shares his tremendous enthusiasm for reading aloud and his own special treasury of over 300 annotated titles for read-alouds: wordless books, picture books, fairy tales, novels, poetry, and anthologies.

15. Van Orden, Phyllis J. *The Collection Program in Elementary and Middle Schools.* Littleton, Colo.: Libraries Unlimited, 1982.

This text describes the ideal school library media program and provides excellent criteria for the selection of all kinds of materials.

16. *The WEB: Wonderfully Exciting Books,* edited by Charlotte Huck and Janet Hickman. Columbus: The Reading Center, The Ohio State University.

First published in 1976, this periodical is published four times a year; each issue contains a web of books related to some unit. In addition, teachers and librarians review new books and frequently include suggested activities and children's response to them.

REFERENCES

Alexander, Lloyd. *The Black Cauldron.* Holt, 1965.
_____. *The Book of Three.* Holt, 1964.
_____. *The Castle of Llyr.* Holt, 1966.
_____. *The High King.* Holt, 1968.
_____. *Taran Wanderer.* Holt, 1967.
Babbitt, Natalie. *Tuck Everlasting.* Farrar, Straus, 1975.
Bailey, Carolyn S. *The Little Rabbit Who Wanted Red Wings,* illustrated by Chris Santos. Platt, 1978.
Blegvad, Erik. *The Three Little Pigs.* Atheneum, 1980.
Blos, Joan. *Brothers of the Heart.* Scribner, 1985.
Bowden, Joan. *Why the Tides Ebb and Flow.* Houghton Mifflin, 1979.
Brown, Marcia. *Once a Mouse.* Atheneum, 1982.
_____. *Stone Soup.* Scribner, 1947.
Bryan, Ashley. *The Cat's Purr.* Atheneum, 1985.
Byars, Betsy. *Cracker Jackson.* Viking, 1985.
_____. *The 18th Emergency.* Penguin, 1981.
_____. *Goodbye, Chicken Little.* Harper, 1979.
_____. *The Pinballs.* Harper, 1977.
_____. *Summer of the Swans.* Viking, 1970.
Carle, Eric. *The Very Busy Spider.* Philomel, 1984.
Carroll, Lewis, pseud. (Charles L. Dodgson). *Alice's Adventures in Wonderland,* illustrated by John Tenniel. Macmillan, 1963 (1865 and 1872).
Cauley, Lorinda Bryan. *Jack and the Beanstalk.* Putnam, 1983.
_____. *Goldilocks and the Three Bears.* Putnam, 1981.
Cleary, Beverly. *Ramona Forever.* Morrow, 1984.
_____. *Ramona Quimby, Age 8.* Morrow, 1981.
Cole, Joanna. *Bony Legs,* illustrated by Dirk Zimmer. Scholastic, 1983.
Colwell, Eileen. *A Storyteller's Choice,* illustrated by Carol Barker. Walck, 1963.
Dalgliesh, Alice. *The Courage of Sarah Noble,* illustrated by Leonard Weisgard. Scribner, 1954.
Dahl, Roald. *James and the Giant Peach,* illustrated by Nancy Burkert. Knopf, 1961.
Defoe, Daniel. *Robinson Crusoe,* illustrated by Lynd Ward. Junior Illustrated Classics Series. Grossett, 1952. (1719)
de Paola, Tomie. *"Charlie Needs a Cloak".* Prentice-Hall, 1974.
_____. *Strega Nona.* Prentice-Hall, 1975.
deRegniers, Beatrice Schenk. *Red Riding Hood,* illustrated by Edward Gorey. Atheneum, 1977.
deWit, Dorothy. *The Talking Stone: An Anthology of Native American Tales and Legends.* Greenwillow, 1979.
Disney, Walt. *Walt Disney's Cinderella.* Golden Press, 1950.

Domanska, Janina. *The Best of the Bargain*. Greenwillow, 1977.

Duff, Maggie. *Rum Pum Pum: A Folk Tale from India,* illustrated by José Aruego and Ariane Dewey. Macmillan, 1978.

Elkin, Benjamin. *Six Foolish Fishermen,* illustrated by Katherine Evans. Children's Press, 1957.

Fritz, Jean. *The Double Life of Pocahontas,* illustrated by Ed Young. Putnam, 1983.

Gág, Wanda. *Gone Is Gone*. Putnam, 1960.

_____. *Nothing At All*. Putnam, 1941.

Galdone, Paul. *The Gingerbread Boy*. Clarion, 1975.

_____. *The Turtle and the Monkey*. Houghton Mifflin, 1982.

_____. *The Three Wishes*. McGraw-Hill, 1961.

_____. *The Three Sillies*. Houghton Mifflin, 1981.

_____. *The Three Little Pigs*. Clarion, 1970.

_____. *The Three Billy Goats Gruff*. Clarion, 1973.

_____. *The Three Bears*. Scholastic, 1973.

_____. *The Magic Porridge Pot*. Clarion, 1976.

_____. *Henny Penny*. Clarion, 1968.

Gardiner, John. *Stone Fox,* illustrated by Marcia Sewall. Harper, 1980.

George, Jean Craighead. *Julie of the Wolves*. Harper, 1972.

_____. *My Side of the Mountain*. Dutton (paperback), 1975.

_____. *The Talking Earth*. Harper, 1983.

Glubok, Shirley. *The Art of the Eskimo*. Harper, 1964.

Godden, Rumer. *The Mousewife,* illustrated by Heidi Holder. Viking, 1982.

Grahame, Kenneth. *The Wind in the Willows,* illustrated by E. H. Shepard. Scribner, 1940. (1908).

Grimm, Brothers. *The Frog Prince,* illustrated by Paul Galdone. McGraw-Hill, 1975.

_____. *Hansel and Gretel,* illustrated by Paul Galdone. McGraw-Hill, 1982.

_____. *Rapunzel,* illustrated by Felix Hoffman. Harcourt, 1961.

_____. *Sleeping Beauty,* retold and illustrated by Trina Schart Hyman. Little, Brown, 1974.

Hague, Kathleen. *The Man Who Kept House*. Illustrated by Michael Hague. Harcourt, 1981.

Hall, Donald. *Ox-Cart Man,* illustrated by Barbara Cooney. Viking, 1979.

Hardendorff, Jeanne. *The Bed Just So*. Scholastic, 1977.

Hirsh, Marilyn. *Could Anything Be Worse?* Holiday, 1974.

Hodges, Margaret. *Saint George and the Dragon,* illustrated by Trina Schart Hyman. Little, Brown, 1984.

Hogrogian, Nonny. *One Fine Day*. Macmillan, 1971.

Hoople, Cheryl. *The Heritage Sampler,* illustrated by Richard Cuffari. Dial, 1975.

Houston, James. *Long Claws: An Arctic Adventure*. Atheneum, 1981.

Hunter, Mollie. *A Stranger Came Ashore*. Harper, 1977.

Hyman, Trina Schart. *Little Red Riding Hood*. Holiday House, 1983.

Jacobs, Joseph. *The Story of the Three Little Pigs,* illustrated by Lorinda Bryan Cauley. Putnam, 1980.

Kellogg, Steven. *Chicken Little*. Morrow, 1985.

Kent, Jack. *The Fat Cat: A Danish Folktale*. Parents', 1971.

Lane, Margaret. *The Spider,* illustrated by Barbara Firth. Dial, 1983.

LeGuin, Ursula. *A Wizard of Earthsea,* illustrated by Ruth Robbins. Houghton Mifflin, 1968.

L'Engle, Madeleine. *A Wrinkle in Time*. Farrar, Straus, 1962.

Lewis, C. S. *The Horse and His Boy,* illustrated by Pauline Baynes. Macmillan, 1962.

_____. *The Last Battle,* illustrated by Pauline Baynes. Macmillan, 1964.

_____. *The Lion, the Witch and the Wardrobe,* illustrated by Pauline Baynes. Macmillan, 1950.

_____. *The Magician's Nephew,* illustrated by Pauline Baynes. Macmillan, 1964.

_____. *Prince Caspian, the Return to Narnia,* illustrated by Pauline Baynes. Macmillan, 1964.

_____. *The Silver Chair,* illustrated by Pauline Baynes. Macmillan, 1962.

_____. *The Voyage of the "Dawn Treader,"* illustrated by Pauline Baynes. Macmillan, 1962.

Lobel, Arnold. *Frog and Toad Are Friends*. Harper, 1970.

MacLachlan, Patricia. *Sarah, Plain and Tall*. Harper, 1985.

Martin, Bill, Jr. *Brown Bear, Brown Bear, What Do You See?*, illustrated by Eric Carle. Holt, 1983.

Milne, A. A. *Winnie-the-Pooh*, illustrated by Ernest H. Shepard. Dutton, 1926.

O'Neill, Mary. *Hailstones and Halibut Bones*, illustrated by Leonard Weisgard. Doubleday, 1961.

Ormerod, Jan. *The Story of Chicken Licken*. Lothrop, 1986.

Paige, Harry. *Johnny Stands*. Warne, 1982.

Paterson, Katherine. *Bridge to Terabithia*, illustrated by Donna Diamond. Crowell, 1977.

_____. *The Great Gilly Hopkins*. Crowell, 1978.

Perl, Lila. *Slumps, Grunts and Snickerdoodles: What Colonial America Ate and Why*, illustrated by Richard Cuffari. Clarion, 1975.

Perrault, Charles. *Cinderella*, retold by Amy Ehrlich, illustrated by Susan Jeffers. Dial, 1985.

Plume, Ilse. *The Bremen Town Musicians*. Doubleday, 1980.

Potter, Beatrix. *The Tale of Peter Rabbit*. Warne, 1902.

Raboff, Ernest. *Pablo Picasso*. Doubleday, 1982.

Rawls, Wilson. *Where the Red Fern Grows*. Doubleday, 1961.

Reinl, Edda. *The Three Little Pigs*. Picture Book Studio, 1983.

Richter, Conrad. *The Light in the Forest*, illustrated by Warren Chappell. Knopf, 1966.

Selsam, Millicent, and Joyce Hunt. *A First Look at Birds' Nests*, illustrated by Harriet Springer. Walker, 1984.

Sendak, Maurice. *Where the Wild Things Are*. Harper, 1963.

Shulevitz, Uri. *Dawn*. Farrar, Straus, 1974.

Speare, Elizabeth. *The Bronze Bow*. Houghton Mifflin, 1961.

_____. *Calico Captive*. Houghton Mifflin, 1957.

_____. *The Sign of the Beaver*. Houghton Mifflin, 1983.

_____. *The Witch of Blackbird Pond*. Houghton Mifflin, 1958.

Steig, William. *Abel's Island*. Farrar, Straus, 1976.

_____. *Amos & Boris*. Farrar, Straus, 1971.

_____. *Dr. DeSoto*. Farrar, Straus, 1982.

Steptoe, John. *Stevie*. Harper, 1969.

_____. *The Story of Jumping Mouse*. Lothrop, 1984.

Towle, Faith M. *The Magic Cooking Pot*. Houghton Mifflin, 1975.

Tunis, Edwin. *Colonial Living*. Crowell, 1976.

Turkle, Brinton. *Deep in the Forest*. Dutton, 1976.

_____. *Do Not Open*. Dutton, 1981.

Van Allsburg, Chris. *The Polar Express*. Houghton Mifflin, 1985.

Walsh, Jill Paton. *The Green Book*, illustrated by Lloyd Bloom. Farrar, Straus, 1981.

White, E. B. *Charlotte's Web*. Harper, 1952.

Wilder, Laura Ingalls. The *Little House* Series, illustrated by Garth Williams. Harper, 1953.
 By the Shores of Silver Lake (1939).
 Little House in the Big Woods (1932).
 Little House on the Prairie (1935).
 Little Town on the Prairie (1941).
 The Long Winter (1940).
 On the Banks of Plum Creek (1937).
 These Happy Golden Years (1943).

Williams, Margery. *The Velveteen Rabbit*, illustrated by William Nicholson. Doubleday, 1922.

_____. *The Velveteen Rabbit*, illustrated by Michael Hague. Holt, 1983.

Zemach, Margot. *It Could Always Be Worse*. Scholastic, 1979.

_____. *The Little Red Hen*. Farrar, Straus, 1983.

Zion, Gene. *Harry the Dirty Dog*, illustrated by Margaret Graham. Harper, 1956.

13

EXTENDING AND EVALUATING CHILDREN'S UNDERSTANDINGS OF LITERATURE

I hear, and I forget
I see, and I remember
I do, and I understand.

Chinese Proverb

T ime and again Piaget emphasized the active role that the child plays in his own learning and the role of activity in that learning. "Knowledge is derived from action," he maintained. "To know an object is to act upon and to transform it. . . . To know is therefore to assimilate reality into structures of transformation, and these are the structures that intelligence constructs as a direct extension of our actions."[1]

We know that it is important for children learning basic math concepts to manipulate concrete materials. In a similar way, children extend their understanding of literature when they have an opportunity to represent and manipulate the elements of literature in some concrete form. This might mean re-creating story characters and scenes in their own drawings or paintings, reconstructing plot through drama or puppetry, making a story of their own that incorporates the original author's theme or style, or even talking about a story with other readers. These activities may be fun, but they constitute a serious kind of play in which children learn how a story is put together and achieve a fuller grasp of its meaning. Properly planned and guided, such activities are a natural and childlike alternative to formal literary analysis, which is essentially an adult pursuit.

When children work with books in ways that are meaningful to them—through art or music activities, drama, talk, writing, or crafts, there is more at stake than better cognitive understandings about literature. Activities that extend literature encourage greater satisfaction with books by providing an outlet and encouragement for personal response. To interpret a book is to know it, to make it a memorable experience.

Just as children should be given a choice of books to read, so, too, should they be given a choice of various ways to interpret and extend a book. Not all children should have to write a letter to the author or give an oral book report or create a diorama. Many options should be open to the child to find a satisfying way to share a book. Children should also be allowed the option of *not* sharing their reading. Some stories or poems are too special, too personal to be shared. The child may want to savor them, to read them again and again in order to hold their thoughts close. A teacher should know the children in the class well enough to know what will help each student have memorable experiences with books. A teacher should encourage those activities that will enhance children's delight in books, make them want to read more and better books, and at the same time discourage any requirements, such as the weekly book report, that will make children actually dislike reading. The activities suggested in this chapter are planned to increase children's enjoyment and understanding of books.

[1]Jean Piaget, *Science of Education and the Psychology of the Child* (New York: Orion, 1970), pp. 28–29.

EXTENDING LITERATURE THROUGH ART AND MEDIA

Flat Pictures and Collage

Too frequently, children are given crayons and manila paper and told to make a picture of any story they like. This vague direction, coupled with a lack of interesting and varied materials, will produce nothing but dull, sterile pictures. Children must be "filled to overflowing" before they can create. They should have many materials constantly and freely available to them—including chalk, paint, colored tissue papers, scrap materials, yarn, steel wool, buttons, clay, junk for construction work, and papier-mâché.

The teacher's role is to design a rich environment for creativity by providing materials, challenging children's thinking, and honoring children's work. Teachers can help children think about their stories or poems by asking such focusing questions as:

- What would be the most appropriate material for you to use for your picture?
- What colors do you see when you think of this story?
- How will you portray the main character? How old is he or she? What does he or she wear?
- Where does the story take place? When? How could you show this in your picture?

In follow-up discussions when children show their work to the class, teachers may encourage them to talk about choices and reactions with such questions as:

- Why did you choose to illustrate this scene or characters?
- Why did you choose those particular materials?
- How did you make that part of your picture?
- Did you discover anything in making this picture?
- How does this help us see the book?

In this way children are encouraged to reflect on or appreciate their own work and that of others. In addition, the teacher gains valuable insight into children's thinking.

Often children seek to replicate pictures. A third-grader carefully re-creates a sunrise beautifully portrayed in watercolor by Shulevitz in *Dawn*. A fifth-grader struggles to reproduce the jacket illustration of Mazer's *I, Trissy* for her poster advertisement of the book. While this copying is a natural tendency of children (and a time-honored way in which artists have gained mastery), they may be encouraged to follow their own visions as well.

Some books invite children to create new visual forms. *Your Own Best Secret Place* by Baylor features Parnall's drawings of several private hideaways, and children may be eager to draw their own hideaways. A teacher may also encourage children to experiment rather than copy by suggesting interesting alternatives. One teacher provided second-graders with ink and straws which the children used to blow a monster shape which could have come from the magic bottle in Turkle's *Do Not Open*. The study of one illustrator might culminate in making pictures, characters, or a mural in the manner of that illustrator: the highly patterned surfaces of Pat Hutchins or the brightly bordered work of Vera Williams.

Murals

Murals provide children with opportunities to work and plan together. These collaborative efforts need explicit blueprints, and teachers may suggest that children make preliminary drawings or sketches before beginning. Lightly chalked areas on the final mural paper help children visualize the overall picture. An easier form of mural is one that is assembled from children's artwork cut and pasted to the background. Older children may also discuss how variation in size and shading, or overlapping, creates the illusion of depth.

Murals may be organized around events in one story, a synthesis of children's favorite characters, or a topic or theme of study. One fourth-grade class made individual collage representations of houses from favorite folktales which were later glued in place along a winding road. Baba Yaga's chicken-footed house from Russian folktales stood between the witch's house from "Hansel and Gretel" and the giant's castle from "Puss in

Seven-year-olds create a collage interpretation of *Hi, Cat!* by Ezra Jack Keats. Notice the use of rich material.

Barrington Road School, Upper Arlington Public Schools, Ohio. Marlene Herbert, teacher.

Boots." A written explanation for each house accompanied the mural.

By providing a variety of materials for collage and some organizing assistance, a teacher can help children successfully create eye-catching murals. Backgrounds may be quickly filled in with printing, using sponges dipped in paint for leaves and bushes or potato-printed tree shapes. It is important, both as a writing opportunity and for the many people who will view it, to complete the display of a mural with an explanation.

Media Exploration

A teacher can also make use of a child's desire to replicate an illustrator's way of working by encouraging children to explore various media. After seeing Lionni's *Swimmy,* a group of primary children printed with lacepaper doilies and watercolors to create similar underwater effects. Older children used dampened ricepaper, ink, and watercolor to try to capture some of the gentleness of the traditional Japanese painting techniques used by Susan Bonners in *Panda* and by Suekichi Akaba

in his illustrations for *The Crane Wife* by Yagawa. These children attempted to answer for themselves the question "How did the illustrator make the pictures?"

Techniques that easily translate to the elementary classroom include scratchboard, marbleized paper, and many varieties of printing. Leonard Everett Fisher is a master of scratchboard illustration, and older children may discover his work in books such as *The Railroads,* part of his "Nineteenth Century America" nonfiction work. Marcia Sewall's illustrations for Kennedy's poetic *Song of the Horse* show how long fluid lines and short contour lines depict the movement of horse and rider over the land. Barbara Cooney's scratchboard illustrations for *The Little Juggler* and *Chanticleer and the Fox* (Chaucer) make use of color separations to achieve color. Though schools may buy commercially prepared scratchboard, similar results may be achieved by crayoning heavily on shiny-surfaced cardboard; then cover the crayon with India ink dabbed on with a cotton ball; allow to dry throughly, then scratch designs or illustrations through the ink with pin or scissor points. Since this process is tedious, the technique is more suited for older children. A simpler "crayon resist" can be done by applying watercolor over a crayon drawing, a particularly effective way of producing nighttime effects.

Marbleized paper has frequently been used in endpapers of well-made books. Fine examples of the art may be seen in Nonny Hogrogian's endpapers and illustrations for the Grimm tales *The Glass Mountain* and *The Devil with the Three Golden Hairs.* Ezra Jack Keats often featured marbleized paper in his books that are illustrated in collage. In a filmed interview (Weston Woods), Keats demonstrated how he made this special paper for backgrounds of such books as *Dreams* and *In a Spring Garden,* edited by Richard Lewis. Children can create marbleized paper, using any paper and one of several kinds of color. Fill disposable or old baking pans with water and drop the color on the water surface. Oil-based paint (which may be thinned slightly with turpentine) or acrylic paint works well. Some types of poster paint and India ink also give good results. Place a piece of paper face down on the water and floating color, being careful not to trap air bubbles between paper and water. Gently lift the paper and hang it to dry. Colored chalk as floating color poses fewer cleanup problems for younger children. Chalk may be grated over the water with a small piece of window screen or an old sieve. Results must be sprayed with fixative when dry. Marbleized paper may be cut and used in collage or in the making of books as endpapers and covers (see Bookmaking).

Various printing techniques, from the thumbprint illustrations in *Ed Emberley's Thumbprint Book* to the woodcuts of Evaline Ness in *Sam, Bangs and Moonshine,* are often used in picture books. Cardboard cuts were used by Blair Lent in *The Wave* by Hodges and in *John Tabor's Ride.* In this printing process, the printing block or plate is built by gluing pieces of cardboard or textured material to a piece of heavy backing cardboard. Ink is worked into or rolled onto the plate and a print is taken or "pulled" off the plate.

While woodcuts and linoleum blockprints are seldom practical or safe for elementary children, similar effects may be achieved with printing plates made from plastic foam meat or fruit trays. Lines may be incised in the plate with dull pencils or ball-point pens. Excess foam may be cut away with scissors. Grease should be washed from the foam before water-based printing ink is rolled on. Hope Meryman's woodcuts for the folktale *Akimba and the Magic Cow* by Rose are black line on buff or white, but children may wish to add color by hand to their prints.

Each year fewer picture books have decorated endpapers, but occasionally teachers and children discover exceptions. The repeated figure of the resolute old Mrs. Brubeck in Sewall's endpapers from *The Story of Old Mrs. Brubeck and How She Looked for Trouble and Where She Found Him* by Segal or the rows of saucy pigs Tony Ross presents in his updated version of *The Three Little Pigs* suggest that children could decorate endpapers in geometric patterns for their own handmade books. They might also create an endpaper design in honor of a favorite book or story. A reliable plate which will not disintegrate after hard use may be made from pieces of bicycle inner tubes and rubber cement. Apply cement both to a solid backing such as a wood block and to any shapes cut from the tube and print as with any other block. While this technique takes some careful planning, the block will stand up to many printings in the classroom.

Illustrators Leo and Diane Dillon inform the reader on the copyright page in *Why Mosquitoes Buzz in People's Ears* by Aardema that they applied watercolors with an airbrush. A stencil print allows children to blend colors for a "finger airbrush" technique. A figure is cut from a piece of heavy paper, leaving the figure (positive) and the figure's shape (negative). The edges of either one are heavily chalked and the figure or shape is laid on a clean piece of paper. By holding the chalked paper stationary and gently brushing the chalk dust off onto the clean paper, an image shape or its outline is formed. Using different colors of chalk creates surprising shadows and shadings. Even primary children enjoy imitating with this technique the trailing, fading smoke Donald Crews creates with an airbrush for *Freight Train.*

Eye-catching displays may be assembled when children's efforts at working in the manner of a well-known illustrator are mounted carefully and placed alongside the book that inspired the work. Explanations written by children help clarify for parents and other classroom observers how the work was created. (See Chapter 5 for other examples of media use.)

Marcia Sewall's silhouettes for *The Story of Old Mrs. Brubeck* searching for trouble repeat the theme of this amusing tale. Children can look at endpapers and try to create some that would complement their own stories.

Dioramas and Displays

A diorama is a three-dimensional scene often including objects and figures. This technique, frequently used in museums to illustrate habitat groups or to re-create historical events, can be adapted for classroom use. Using cardboard boxes or shoeboxes placed on one side, children can recreate a memorable scene from a book. Using the description of the tiny Clock family's household which Mary Norton described in *The Borrowers*, a student "borrowed" similar materials to furnish her diorama.

A two-part division of a box allows a child to contrast two events or settings. For instance, *The Little House* by Burton could be depicted in its first pastoral setting before the city grew around it and again afterwards. What was important to the beautiful and musically talented Caroline in Paterson's *Jacob Have I Loved* could be contrasted with what was important to Louise.

A scene set in miniature and viewed through a narrow opening becomes a peep show. Numerous poems or nursery rhymes may be portrayed in this way. Children might enjoy portraying a secret place in this manner after hearing Byrd Baylor's *Your Own Best Secret Place.*

Children should be encouraged to make every part of the diorama, as commercial figurines and objects usually tend to cheapen a display or lessen the involvement of the child. By emphasizing accuracy of detail, a teacher can encourage children to return to the book frequently to check information. The actual diorama is not nearly so important as the process of making it and the result it has upon children's enthusiasm for and understanding of books.

Table scenes or displays also help children recall incidents or characters in literature. One group of 7-year-olds made papier-mâché whales, facsimile supplies that accompanied Amos, and models of the good ship *Rodent* as described in Steig's humorous fable *Amos & Boris*. These were placed in front of a painted scene of the luminous ocean sparkling in the moonlight.

Displays may also represent a synthesis of what children know about a topic. One primary group of children displayed under a list of "Books We Know About Bears" such titles as Flack's *Ask Mr. Bear*, Hayes' *Bear by Himself*, McPhail's *Fix-It*, Browne's *Bear Hunt*, and Galdone's *The Three Bears*. Intermingled in the display of books were children's stuffed toy bears and craft items "made by bears" from Cartlidge's *The Bears' Bazaar*. On the bulletin board near the display were letters that bears wrote to children and a poem children had composed following the pattern from Martin's *Brown Bear, Brown Bear, What Do You See?* Surveys had been made of favorite bear books and the number of different teddy bears in the class.

Books displayed with pictures and objects seem to invite children and adults to linger and look. By allowing children to make the collection and display, a teacher helps them make connections among books and between literature and their own lives. While locked glass cases may be appropriate for some materials, inviting displays in the classroom make knowledge tangible and accessible to children in ways that many "hands-off" displays do not.

Story Retelling Aids

Children love to retell stories to each other and aids help them recall parts of the story or focus on

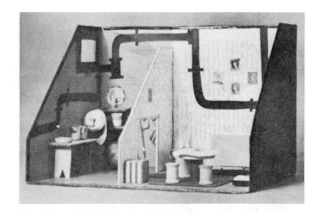

The Borrowers' kitchen and living room are illustrated in a diorama that shows the pipes, wallpaper made from a letter, postage-stamp pictures, bottlecap dishes, thimble pails, gauze hand towels, half of a manicure scissors used to cut raw potato, and a supply of pins used by Pod for climbing.

Constructed by Phyllis Morales, student, The Ohio State University.

the sequence of events. One skillful kindergarten teacher discovered the power of a **story box** to turn children into story-tellers:

October 20: I sat in front of the class and introduced the cast of characters for Galdone's *The Little Red Hen*. These were all stuffed animal toys and i used an invisible seed, some tall grasses, a tiny bag of white flour, and a loaf of bread for props. At the end of my puppet show I boxed up the cast and props and labelled the box "The Little Red Hen." I put it in the reading corner for anyone who wanted to tell that story. Throughout the morning small groups of children made time to check it all out. Some just fingered the plush toys, examined the bag of flour, and smelled the loaf of unsliced bread. But Allison organized Jamie, Jeffrey, Viviana, and Joey each to be an animal while she spoke the part of the hen. This play was for themselves, not demanding or even needing an audience, the children were unaware of observers. The box is a great idea; there seems to be great ceremony in unpacking and packing up the kit.[2]

Feltboards also provide a chance for children to practice telling stories more easily. Once they have

[2]Jinx Bohstedt, "Old Tales for Young Tellers," *Outlook*, no. 33 (Fall 1979), p. 34.

An older child has made a felt story of Hirsh's *Could Anything Be Worse?,* which she shares with a group of primary-grade children.

Worthington Hills School, Worthington, Ohio. Mary Karrer, librarian.

seen their teacher tell a story with feltboard figures (see Chapter 12), they are eager to try their hands at making them. Teachers and librarians often need to help children talk through the requirements of making a felt story. Not every detail need be shown or the pieces of the story become difficult to handle. Tips such as the piling up of characters in the order in which they will appear in the story help productions go more smoothly. Feltboard figures may be placed on the overhead projector to create a story in silhouette. Figures may also be cut from cardboard or heavy paper and moved without a hand showing if wire or straws are attached to the cardboard. Where color is needed, sheets of tinted acetate may be used for such stories as Lionni's *Little Blue and Little Yellow.*

A third story retelling aid is a child-made **map of the action** or **time line** of the events of the story. Older children frequently turn these story organizers into game boards (see Games). Seven- and 8-year-olds can map the action of *Three Ducks Went Wandering* by Roy, for instance, arranging the ducks' encounters with the bull, the foxes, the hawk, and the snake so that the wanderers end where they began, in the safety of their mother's nest. Simple stories with a journey or excursion for the action are easy to map. *Rosie's Walk* by Pat Hutchins is another good choice. (See page 691.)

A **box movie** represents a fourth way teachers help children remember stories. Children simply illustrate important scenes from the book and these pictures are arranged in sequence. Each child tells the part of the story which his picture represents as his picture passes on the "screen." A simple box movie may be constructed by attaching dowel rods or pieces of broom handles for rollers at either side of a suit box, carton, or wooden fruit box. An old window shade or a strip of shelf paper can be used for the children's illustrations of the sequence of events in the story. Each end of the strip is fastened to a roller. One child rolls the paper by turning the rod as the narrator relates the story. Edging paper with masking tape will make the "film strip" more durable.

If children have made individual pictures of certain scenes, it is a good idea to mount them on the paper and then secure the edges with masking tape. This prevents the pictures from tearing or catching on the roller. It is easier for a group of children to work on a box movie if the scenes are rolled from side to side rather than from top to bottom. In making a horizontal movie the entire roller may be pinned to a bulletin board or taped to the chalkboard and several children can work at once. To make individual "movies," drawings or pictures in a series can be made on a strip of adding-machine tape and pulled through slits cut in a heavy paper envelope. Many stories lend themselves to box-movie treatment. Longer stories or even chapter books may be rendered in this way, causing children to use the techniques of summary and synopsis.

Flip books are another simple aid to the sequencing of stories. One primary teacher glues key scenes from familiar picture books or folktales to tag board and orders the pictures on a ring. Four- and 5-year-olds flip the pictures and tell each other the story.

Story retelling aids help young children, children who have heard few stories read aloud, or children who have a less well-developed sense of how stories work to recall important aspects of a story.

The teacher may introduce or demonstrate story boxes, feltboards, maps of the action, box movies, and flip books to children. However, children who create their own story retelling aids are developing important abilities. They are learning to return to a story for information and confirmation, to extract important points, to sequence events, to visualize the story, and to become sensitive to the language of the storyteller.

Slides, Filmstrips, and Movies

Making slides provides children with a chance to visualize the key scenes in a story, select scenes that advance the plot, and consider other aspects of the story that are important, such as character, setting, and sequence of events. Since slides are only 2" × 2", they require small drawings similar to those found in cartoons. While this accounts for some of the appeal of slide-making, it also limits the activity to children above 8 who can do such fine work. Children do initial planning using a ditto sheet of slide frames so that editing can occur before actual drawing begins. After completing the slides as detailed in the handwritten directions, children may tell the story as the pictures are projected, or they may tape the story to accompany the slides. Almost any story with action is appropriate for a slide presentation. Some that seem particularly well-suited are well-known folktales like "Cinderella" and "The Little Red Hen" or some of the Anansi tales; such modern tales as *Dr. DeSoto* (Steig), *The Garden of Abdul Gasazi* (Van Allsburg), or *Harry, the Dirty Dog* (Zion); and episodes from longer stories like *James and the Giant Peach* (Dahl), some of the escapades from *Ralph S. Mouse* (Cleary) or *A Bear Called Paddington* (Bond).

Other ways to make slides involve photography. Younger children's pictures may be photographed and made into a slide show. Older children could illustrate their favorite poems by taking appropriate photos using slide film. This requires them to consider the theme, mood, and tone of the poem and demands a high level of ability to take effective pictures. For schools that have a 35mm camera for children's use, such an activity would be valuable in extending children's interest in both poetry and photography.

✳ Slide Making ✳

<u>Transparency Technique:</u>

You need • transparency film • slide frames • pencils • ditto of 2" x 2" boxes • scotch tape or an iron • permanent marking pens (fine point) • thermofax machine • scissors •

① Using the ditto of 2" x 2" boxes, plan the illustration and lettering of the slides. On the final drawing or lettering use a <u>lead</u> pencil to outline everything that needs to show, including the outer slide frame line.

② Run the ditto and a transparency through a thermofax machine. Set the machine on the setting for transparencies. This process transfers the pencil markings from the ditto to the transparency.

③ Use permanent colored marking pens to complete the illustrations. One particularly well lasting and bright brand is Staedtler lumocolor (permanent), available at Art Supply Stores.

④ Cut each illustration to a 2" x 2" size. Make sure they are not too large. Position the slide in the slide frame. Secure it with scotch tape on the three open sides, or apply heat carefully to the edges with the iron tip.

Marilyn Parker, Columbus School for Girls, Ohio.

Another way to make slides is to lift an image from a color or black and white picture on clay-coated paper. The steps involved in this process are:

MAKING SLIDES FROM MAGAZINE PICTURES

Materials

Clear contact paper (available from hardware and housewares stores)
2" × 2" color transparency frame
Magazines with slick, colored pictures (clay base)
Small pan of water; drop of liquid detergent
Iron
Spoon
Clear plastic spray

Procedures

Pull contact paper from its adhesive backing
Apply contact paper to 2" × 2" clay-base picture
Rub contact paper with spoon over entire picture, making sure there are no air bubbles
Cut out
Place in warm soapy water and in 2 or 3 minutes peel off the back and let transparency dry
Place between slide frames
Iron just the edges of the frame closed
May be sprayed with plastic spray

Since it is difficult to find such very small pictures, children can create a mood with different colors and textures without using actual pictures. Magazines that provide successful picture transfers include *National Geographic, Better Homes and Gardens, Newsweek, People, Sports Illustrated,* and others.

Children enjoy making new filmstrips from old ones which have been dipped in a small pan of bleach to remove old emulsion. The blank filmstrip is then washed under clear water, dried with a soft cloth, and left to dry overnight. Children can then draw their own pictures right on the filmstrip, using every four sprocket holes as guides for one frame. Captions may be interspersed between pictures; as with slides, planning sheets help children discuss options before they begin. Allow for a "leader" at the beginning and end of stories. Temporary colors may be made from nonpermanent felt-tip markers and, in some cases, pen and pencil. Plastic spray will make them permanent. Acrylic inks, paints, and permanent marker pens may also be used, but if spilled they cannot be removed. Filmstrips have the advantage of being compact and easy to handle. They are always in sequence. Slides, however, give more flexibility in arrangement and are more easily made. Creating in either form seems to fascinate children.

Movie-making is not an easy task, but video cameras have given more children a chance to experience this art. Choosing what scenes to portray and critiquing the performances give children a chance to look back at a story for important clues to characters' emotions and moods before they take on the roles. Yvonne Anderson's informative book *Making Your Own Animated Movies* describes her work with children aged 5 to 18 in creating films. In *Making Your Own Movies*, Harry Helfman gives hints on how to operate a simple, inexpensive movie camera and presents some basic techniques for shooting a film. A description of panning a picture is given, along with ways to vary the length of the shot. Considering the time involved in making movies, teachers may want to work with someone knowledgeable in the field.

EXTENDING LITERATURE THROUGH CRAFTS, COOKING, AND GAMES

Sewing and Making Things

There continues to be an interest in "creative stitchery" and once children have learned a few basic stitches, they are able to create scenes or characters from favorite books. Simple outlines of large round shapes, such as characters from McPhail's *Pig Pig Grows Up* or the overstuffed chair in Williams' *A Chair For My Mother,* are the easiest. Burton's *The Little House* could be depicted over four seasons. A stitched map done on burlap might represent the settings and journeys in the Wilder "Little House" books.

Children studying pioneers might become interested in quilts. Coerr's *The Josefina Story Quilt,* Johnson's *The Quilt Story* and Flournoy's *The Patchwork Quilt* all feature quilts with squares that mean something to their owners. Roth's *Patchwork Tales* features strong woodcuts of quilt squares by Ruth Phang which would give children examples of traditional patterns. Stories like these suggest that children could make small quilts with patterns and materials which are significant to them or which might be significant to a character about whom they are reading. In place of stitchery, many teachers let children create quilt blocks from commercial products such as "liquid embroidery" or iron-on crayon, which transfers to cloth. One group of 8- and 9-year-olds planned and made a quilt of blocks from favorite books, agreeing first not to duplicate any titles. A parent volunteer helped assemble the quilt. Certainly there are many possibilities of extending children's interest in books through stitchery.

Striking wall hangings may be made featuring sewn-on or glued-on figures. Iron-on interfacing may also be used to fix figures in place. Animals or characters may be padded with strips of cloth or pieces of foam rubber before they are sewn to the background. This gives them a slightly rounded, three-dimensional look. Varied materials, such as old sheets and colored or natural burlap, can be used as background for figures and objects that represent book characters, titles, books by one author, poetry, or Mother Goose rhymes. Felt, pieces of printed cotton, buttons, rickrack, lace, sequins, and found objects should be available for making the figures and scenery.

Making things by craft and construction can help children look again at single books or at similar features across books. A small group of second- and third-graders read books on dragons, such as *The Knight and the Dragon* (de Paola), *Everyone Knows What a Dragon Looks Like* (Williams), *Saint George and the Dragon* (Hodges), *How Droofus the Dragon Lost His Head* (Peet), and *King Krakus and the Dragon* (Domanska). They then constructed their own versions of these dragons. Some featured bumpy backs made of egg carton pieces; others were made of wood, spools, foam, and rope. Another class made monsters of discarded boxes, corrugated paper, mailing tubes, and other found objects which reflected their study of "monster books" like *The Judge* (Zemach), *The Mysterious Tadpole* (Kellogg), and *Where the Wild Things Are* (Sendak).

Many books feature interesting houses, such as Blegvad's *The Parrot in the Garret and Other Rhymes about Dwellings.* This collection of nursery rhymes about strange and curious houses such as Aiken Drum's moon house and Little King Boggen's Wonderful Baked Castle suggests that primary children would enjoy re-creating these houses or adding others familiar to them, as well. A similar compendium of houses is featured in *From King Boggen's Hall to Nothing-At-All* by Lent, which unfortunately is no longer in print. Older children have assembled and constructed Mrs. Frisby's cement-block house from *Mrs. Frisby and the Rats of NIMH* by O'Brien and Sam's tree house from *My Side of the Mountain* by George.

Often making things helps child readers authenticate a book character's experience. Just as 7-year-old Ramona enjoyed making the "longest pic-

Mama Bear and Baby Bear are featured with different versions of their story in this display. The bears were made of two pieces of large paper, stuffed with paper towels, stapled, and then dressed.

Reading Recovery Teachers, The Ohio State University.

ture in the world" and old-fashioned tin-can stilts in *Ramona and Her Father* by Cleary, second-graders are eager to replicate Ramona's pleasure by making their own stilts or pictures. Older children have created a memorial of paper-folded cranes to commemorate their reading of *Sadako and the Thousand Paper Cranes* by Coerr.

Dolls may be made to accompany children's dioramas or displayed singly in response to a book. Pipe cleaners, clay, clothespins or sticks, and pieces of cloth help children in doll-creating. Stuffed dolls, such as Semanthie from *The Cabin Faced West* by Fritz, may be made by sewing two shapes together and stuffing with foam rubber scraps, old nylon stockings, or quilt batting. Primary children have made stuffed paper figures from de Paola's *Helga's Dowry*. The 3-foot figures were painted and hung in the reading corner. Another group made a "parade of characters" following a study of the books of William Steig. These were mounted on a hall wall complete with identifying name flags and balloons.

Baker's clay provides a simple modeling clay for children to work with. Ten-year-olds used the following recipe to model favorite book characters for a literary Christmas tree:

BAKER'S CLAY
Mix 4 cups flour with 1 cup salt
Add approximately 1½ cups warm water
Knead thoroughly until smooth (5 minutes)
Shape into figures
Bake on foil-lined pan at 350° for one hour

Food coloring may be added to dough before baking, or the figures may be painted afterwards. However, the natural look of the baked dough is very attractive. If figures are to be hung, insert paper clips, leaving a small circle showing, before baking. Small pieces of dough may be stuck together before baking by moistening, with toothpick or with pipe cleaners. Baked dough may be prevented from cracking by being dipped in shellac or varnish. Refrigerated in a plastic bag, the dough can be stored indefinitely.

Cooking

Teachers recognize the values of cooking in the classroom—the math concepts used in doubling a recipe, the reading skills involved in following directions, the social skills of working cooperatively, not to mention children's satisfaction in making something for others to enjoy. Cooking that starts from a book can enrich children's experiences with literature.[3]

Several collections of recipes like MacGregor's *The Fairy Tale Cookbook* specifically reflect their literary origins. Baking "Haycorn Squash" or "Cottleston Pie" from *The Pooh Cook Book* by Ellison would add to children's enjoyment of the

[3]For other ideas, see Jo Osborne, "A Cook's Tour of Children's Cookbooks," *School Library Journal*, February 1986, pp. 28–29.

After first-graders retold and illustrated the story of *Stone Soup*, they made their own tasty soup in the same fashion. They also created a "recipe" to send home to their parents.

Hammond, Indiana, Public Schools. Sandra Isolampi, student teacher.

Pooh stories. Cauley's *Pease-Porridge Hot: A Mother Goose Cookbook* presents simple directions for such things as "The Big Bad Wolf's Little Pigs in a Blanket—Enough for Four Famished Wolves." Walker's *The Little House Cookbook* features authentic recipes for preparing all of the food mentioned in the Laura Ingalls Wilder books. Most recipes are preceded by a quote from the book in which the food appears, by historical notes, or by a Garth Williams illustration. Recipes for much of what Sam Gribley ate in *My Side of the Mountain* appear in *The Wild, Wild Cookbook*, both by Jean George. Boys might like to experiment with the three acorn recipes Sam tried. Experiences with cooking may be followed by having children write about "How We Made Sam's Sassafras Tea" or take surveys of each other to determine which recipe was best and why.

Some books include recipes following the text. *The Popcorn Book* by de Paola suggests two ways of making popcorn, while "How to Make Mama's Tea Cakes" follows the rural American story of *Over on the River* by Jackson. Other books merely suggest to the imaginative reader a possible cooking extension. Young children, after hearing Hoban's *Bread and Jam for Francis* or Sendak's *Chicken Soup with Rice*, have enjoyed making lunch. Following a study of witches in folktales, one group of second-graders, assisted by a parent volunteer, made gingerbread witches.

Older students have enjoyed literary "Book Fares" in which each person brings to the potluck something suggested by a book. Gurgi's "munchings and crunchings" from Alexander's Prydain series, Carlie's Famous Mayonnaise Cake from Byars' *The Pinballs,* tea made from an herb that Mary Call Luther might have gathered in the Cleavers' *Where the Lilies Bloom,* and Meg's liverwurst and cream cheese sandwiches from L'Engle's Time Trilogy were some of the offerings at one party. A teacher searched through cookbooks to find the recipe for the real Turkish Delight, Edmund's undoing in *The Lion, the Witch and the Wardrobe* by Lewis. She and the children were surprised to discover authentic Turkish Delight is not a familiar white taffy but is a gelatin-based candy, instead.

Cooking from literature gives children a chance to remember books with fondness. It also provides children with a reason to return to the book to authenticate information. Cooking also allows children to make a part of the book's experience a part of their own experience and to gain familiarity with mathematical skills such as measuring and doubling or halving a recipe. In addition, many natural opportunities for sensory writing and the writing of procedural directions are provided.

Games

Games provide another means of extending children's knowledge of books and authors. In planning games, children return to books—attending to the sequence of events, learning to evaluate these events in terms of progress or setbacks for the characters, and reinterpreting aspects of the story. In creating games, children become problem-solvers as they fit their literary knowledge into the pattern of the game or design new game patterns to fit their book choices. In the construction and playing of games, children satisfy a natural inclination to play with something of their own making. Games bring teachers and children together in the mutual enjoyment of books.

GUESSING GAMES AND WORD GAMES

Children enjoy "acting out" situations or scenes from books and guessing each other's choices of books. Young children may pantomime Mother Goose or folktale characters while others try to guess; older children may pantomime characters and scenes from stories, as well. Charades, which are more successful with middle-grade students, differ from pantomime in that they require the audience to guess words or syllables during the play rather than when the scene is finished. They also require more interchange between players and audience and a wider knowledge of language conventions than guessing games.

Often picture books suggest games children can repeat in their own play. For instance, *The Surprise Party* by Hutchins shows what happens to Rabbit's message, "I'm having a party tomorrow," as it is whispered from animal to animal. Children have delighted in playing this "telephone game" in a circle after hearing this story. *Uncle Elephant* by Lobel shows his nephew how to pass the time on a trip by counting houses, trees, or telephone poles. This game may save a long class bus trip for tired first-graders. Janet and Allan Ahlberg's *Each Peach Pear Plum* creates a picture from one folktale and hides a character from another tale within. "Cinderella on the stairs/I spy the Three Bears" shows the bears peeking in the window. Children might simply illustrate a favorite tale and hide another folktale character in their picture. Bound together, these drawings would make a class "I Spy" book.

A game that heightens children's observational and descriptive powers is played in Baylor's *Guess Who My Favorite Person Is.* Two players tell what their favorite things are but must be very explicit. Says the child, "In this game you can't just say it's blue. You have to say what *kind* of blue." Her partner specifies the blue on a lizard's belly, "the sudden kind of blue you see just for a second sometime." Children might enjoy adding their own favorites in this game which ends, in the book at least, when both characters choose the same favorite time of day, "now."

Riddles are fun for everyone. Children can base riddles on book characters with the question "Who Am I?" "I found a magic bone that saved me from the wolf. Who Am I?" (Pearl, the pig in William Steig's *The Amazing Bone*) or "I drive a very small motorcycle by saying Pb-bb-bb. Who am I?" (Ralph, the mouse in Beverly Cleary's *The Mouse and the Motorcycle*). Questions such as "Who Lived Here?" or "What Is It?" may also spur children to think of riddles. A collection of

DEVELOPING READERS

Learning to read and enjoy books begins in the home listening to stories read by a loving parent.

Primary children need to hear many stories read several times a day by an enthusiastic teacher.

Kristen Kerstetter, teacher, Highland Park Elementary School, South-Western City Schools, Grove City, Ohio.

Reading for pleasure usually decreases when students reach junior high school and high school, so older students must become "hooked on books" before they leave elementary school.

Martin Luther King, Jr., Laboratory School, Evanston, Illinois, Public Schools. Photo by James Ballard.

Children welcome the chance to read together and share their enjoyment of a book.

Barrington Road Elementary, Upper Arlington, Ohio, Public Schools.

PRIMARY CHILDREN INTERPRET AND EXTEND BOOKS

A kindergarten/first-grade teacher honors all stories and interpretations of "Little Red Riding Hood" by displaying them on this very tall mural.

Kristen Kerstetter, teacher, Highland Park Elementary School, South-Western City Schools, Grove City, Ohio.

Another group of six-year-olds uses tissue paper collage, paint, and crayons to tell the story of "Little Red Riding Hood." These charts were then used as "big books" and read many times.

Ava McGregor, teacher, Mt. Eden Normal School, Auckland, New Zealand.

First-graders read and heard many stories about bears. They then made bear puppets, created large stuffed bears out of brown paper, and had a special party for their favorite teddy bears.

Kristen Kerstetter, teacher, Highland Park Elementary School, South-Western City Schools, Grove City, Ohio.

Primary children studied all the books by Donald Crews. Different groups of children made special extensions of his books to share. Here a group of children make a mural filled with the many boats seen in *Harbor*.

Judith Allers, teacher, Avalon Elementary, Columbus, Ohio, Public Schools.

Children enjoy rereading the big book they made about the three bears. Bear shapes were cut from discarded meat trays and used to make the prints.

Rosalie Hoover, teacher, Celina, Ohio, Public Schools.

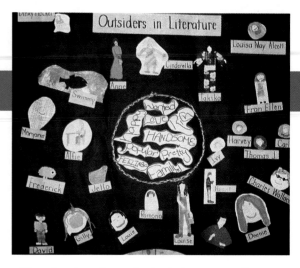

Fifth- and sixth-graders made a kind of sociogram of literature identifying the "outsiders" in various stories such as Charles Wallace, Gilly, and Carlie. Personality traits which would make you an "insider" were written in the inner circle.

Sheryl Reed and Peggy Harrison, teachers, Ridgemont Elementary School, Mt. Victory, Ohio.

Third- and fourth-graders illustrated and wrote stories about the various houses found in fairy tales, such as Baba Yaga's house, Strega Nona's, and the gingerbread house in "Hansel and Gretel."

Marlene Harbert, teacher, Barrington Road Elementary, Upper Arlington, Ohio, Public Schools.

Second- and third-graders chose their favorite books to illustrate with fabric paints. Their teacher then made a quilt of these painted squares and used it to mark off the reading area.

Highland Park Elementary School, South-Western City Schools, Grove City, Ohio. Pam Kessen, teacher.

OLDER STUDENTS EXTEND AND INTERPRET BOOKS

Literature can be used across the curriculum in all areas of study. Here we see information derived from many books in a study of chickens.

EPIC students, The Ohio State University.

Eight-, 9-, and 10-year-olds extend their knowledge of mythology by creating stories and pictures of their own mythological creatures.

Martin Luther King, Jr., Laboratory School, Evanston, Illinois. Barbara Friedberg, teacher.

Children are delighted to meet the "real live" author/illustrator Tomie de Paola, particularly when they have read his books and prepared for his visit.

Columbus School for Girls, Columbus, Ohio. Marilyn Parker, teacher/librarian.

AN AUTHOR/ ILLUSTRATOR COMES TO SCHOOL

Older students dressed a life-sized *Strega Nona* who seems to be awaiting the arrival of Tomie de Paola.

Highland Park Elementary School, South-Western City Schools, Grove City, Ohio. Photo by Barbara Peterson.

A welcome sign and a large stuffed Strega Nona and Big Anthony hang from the ceiling to greet their visitor.

Highland Park Elementary School, South-Western City Schools, Grove City, Ohio. Pam Kessen, teacher. Photo by Barbara Peterson.

Books about Strega Nona and Big Anthony were displayed with a model of Strega Nona's house.

Highland Park Elementary School, South-Western City Schools, Grove City, Ohio. Carol Blazer, teacher. Photo by Barbara Peterson.

A parent helped children make Strega Nona's famous pasta.

Highland Park Elementary School, South-Western City Schools, Grove City, Ohio. Photo by Barbara Peterson.

Children created a game and rules based on the plot of *Big Anthony and the Magic Ring*.

Highland Park Elementary School, South-Western City Schools, Grove City, Ohio.

Six- and 7-year-olds wrote fairy tales and created an unusual puppet character for each story.

Amy Nusser, teacher. Martin Luther King, Jr., Laboratory School, Evanston, Illinois, Public Schools. Photo by James Ballard.

EXTENDING BOOKS THROUGH DRAMA AND WRITING

A group of 7-year-olds dances "The Wild Rumpus" after hearing Sendak's *Where the Wild Things Are.*

West Lafayette Public Schools, Indiana. Nancy Sawrey, teacher.

After hearing the story of *The Three Little Pigs,* a first-grader made a map of the action, including placing labels on the houses and the fair.

Riverside Elementary School, Dublin Public Schools, Ohio. Deborah Moore, teacher.

literary riddles might be exchanged with another classroom or printed in the school newspaper.

Though riddles may prove less challenging for older students, Twenty Questions is a game that demands astute guessing by increasingly narrowing the field. Children quickly learn to ask selective questions like "Is it a fairy tale?" or "Does it take place in modern times?" rather than jumping to characters' names or to book titles. Questions can be answered only by "yes" or "no" responses and continue until all twenty are asked or the book title (or character) is guessed.

Literary crossword puzzles devised by children in the middle grades are another means of extending literature. Children should be instructed to ask questions concerning stories or content known to almost everyone in the class. Crossword puzzles may be enclosed in an appropriate shape, such as a book or a picture of a covered wagon for historical fiction or a space ship for science-fiction titles or characters. A teacher or librarian can make a sample crossword puzzle to show children how, but the real value is in the construction itself, which children can easily do.

BOARD GAMES AND MAPS OF THE ACTION

Children can be encouraged to construct board games or table games based on a single title or across many titles. A basic game pattern of several players moving along a channel toward a goal is familiar to most children. Players move forward by selecting a question card and answering correctly, by following directions on the board or the card, or by rolling dice or spinning a wheel. The game may be made more interesting by the addition of chance cards or choices of routes to the goal. Part of the fun of game-making is choosing the game model, designing the playing pieces, deciding on spinners, cards, or dice for movement, and constructing the playing board.

A group of 9- and 10-year-olds created a board game for Merrill's *The Pushcart War*. The players were divided into two teams: "Mighty Mammoth Truckers" and "Pushcart Peddlers." The board was divided into a road with squares marked on it. Playing with a spinner, everyone could move his or her truck or pushcart as many spaces ahead as the spin showed. If a player landed on a square marked "The Pea Shooter Campaign," he could advance five spaces if the player were a peddler; however, the truckers had to go back five spaces. Construction of the game sent children back to the book for an accurate description of both sides of this humorous battle in New York City.

Fourth-graders read Van Allsburg's *Jumanji* and made their own version of the game which, once started, must be finished. Another group of students created a game from Rockwell's *How to Eat Fried Worms*. A pot of plastic worms provided penalties for landing on certain squares and the player who reached the finish with the fewest number of worms won the game. Children will think of many books which make good games. It is helpful if game players know the book, so that clues, rewards, and penalties will be understood. However, after playing the game, children unfamiliar with the book are often motivated to read it.

Younger children may have difficulty creating an entire game from a book, but they can make maps of the action of a story. Six- and 7-year-olds might construct an overview of the forest setting from *One Fine Day* by Hogrogian. On a path trailing through the forest, they could depict the various encounters of the fox, including his meeting with the old woman and a cow; his request to the field for grass; his plea to the stream for water; his meetings with the fair maiden, the peddler, the hen, the miller; and his eventual return to the old woman who then sews his tail in place! *Rosie's Walk* by Hutchins could be depicted on a map of the barnyard. Mapping the action sends children back to the book to fix the order of events in a particular setting.

CARD GAMES

Card games allow children to classify titles or aspects of titles and to synthesize information across books. These games may be created from commercially made blank playing cards or from posterboard. The backs of the deck may be ink-stamped or potato-printed with a design if desired. This makes it easier to keep cards of one deck from becoming mixed with cards of another. Though a teacher may prepare these games, children will learn as much by creating games as they will by playing them. Card games based on pairs include "Old Maid" and "Concentration." Young children might use Mother Goose rhymes to find pairs such as Jack and Jill, Bo Peep and sheep, or Miss Muffet and a spider. Older children could summon pairs from a wider repertoire: Frog and Toad, Cupid and Psyche, Peter and Fudge, or Laura and Almanzo. There are as many versions of this game as there are readers in the classroom!

The game of "Authors" can easily be constructed using thirteen authors' names with four of their book titles in each group. The entire deck is dealt and players take turns asking each other: "Please give me any Betsy Byars." Play continues until all cards have been gathered into "books" and the player who has the greatest number of "books" wins. "Go Fish," a game familiar to most children, is also based on thirteen groups of four. Starting with five cards, players ask, "Any Byars?" before drawing a card from the pile. Of course the game may be made more challenging by creating groups of four from a genre. For instance, folktales might provide categories of fours like magical objects, giants, witches, flying things, or noodleheads. Groups of four might come from thirteen single titles. Each set of cards includes a character (Claudia), an object (the "angel" statue), a setting (the Metropolitan Museum), and the author and title (E. L. Konigsburg's *From the Mixed-Up Files of Mrs. Basil E. Frankweiler*), for instance.

Other games, such as "Lotto" or "Bingo," provide models on which games may be based. Titles, authors, characters, settings, or words from a current topic of study are placed on 3 × 3 or 5 × 5 grids. A caller reads matching identification cards while players place markers over the proper squares. A winner is declared when a player has one horizontal, vertical, or diagonal row covered with markers.

Commercially prepared games relating to children's literature are also available. However, children derive many values through the process of constructing their own games. When they plan puzzles, riddles, and games, they recall what they have read; they make new categories of what they know; and they make what they know fit the patterns of a game. In addition, children suggest to each other new reading material and the rereading of already familiar material. It is important to remember that the purpose of making and playing these games is to stimulate children's reading and thinking, not to hasten their mastery of the isolated details of literature.

EXTENDING LITERATURE THROUGH MUSIC AND MOVEMENT

Picture-Book Editions of Single Songs

Among the many values of song books in the classroom is their use as predictable and familiar reading material (see Chapter 4). In recent years, there have been numerous fine picture-book interpretations of such well-known songs for young children as *London Bridge Is Falling Down* by Peter Spier, *Roll Over!* by Merle Peek, and *Pop! Goes the Weasel and Yankee Doodle* by Robert Quackenbush. In addition, picture books for young children feature familiar counting songs such as Berniece Freschet's *The Ants Go Marching* or John Langstaff's *Over in the Meadow*. To children who are already familiar with the song, the text of these books presents easy and enjoyable reading.

Songs that follow a cumulative pattern challenge singers to remember the order in which events occur. Diane Zuromskis' *The Farmer in the Dell*, Pete Seeger's *The Foolish Frog*, Jeanette Winter's or Aliki's *Hush, Little Baby*, and Nadine Wescott's *The Old Lady Who Swallowed a Fly* are good candidates for feltboard or box movie storytelling aids. If children help to create these, they are less likely to get lost in the song.

Another strongly patterned song, Langstaff's *Oh, A-Hunting We Will Go*, includes such new child-created verses as "We'll catch a bear/And put him in underwear." Children can easily add their own new verses to this pattern after they enjoy reading what other children have done.

Many familiar folk songs have been researched and presented in authentic historic detail by such illustrators as Robert Quackenbush, Peter Spier, Tomie de Paola, and Aliki. Quackenbush's *Skip to My Lou* depicts the disasters surrounding a young woman's engagement party—flies were in the buttermilk, rats ate the sandwiches, and she lost her partner. However, she soon found another one, "and a better one, too." Directions follow for the square dance popular in 1832 which was done to this tune. Quackenbush's *Clementine* is a melodrama that takes place in a mining town. Aliki's illustrations for *Hush, Little Baby* and *Go Tell Aunt Rhody* reflect early American art in quilt-patterned endpapers and the paint-on-boards method of early limner painters. De Paola's version of Sara Josepha Hale's *Mary Had a Little Lamb* is framed by an interesting discussion of the disputed authorship of this childhood song and its first appearance in McGuffey's *Reader* in 1830. Spier presents *The Star-Spangled Banner* and *The Erie Canal* with historical background so that the songs almost become an informational book, too. These various editions help a teacher connect children with the many folk songs which are a part of the American folk tradition when they study American history.

In addition to the classroom extensions suggested, children may enjoy making their own book versions of other traditional songs like "Home on the Range," "Where Have All the Flowers Gone," or "Old Dan Tucker." Scott R. Sanders has invented details and told his own stories for twenty folk songs in *Hear the Wind Blow: American Folk Songs Retold*. Some of these long and often funny stories would inspire fifth- and sixth-graders' imaginations.

Linda Lamme has suggested several criteria for evaluating song picture books. She looks for books in which page-turning does not interrupt stanzas or verses, music is included, the lyrics are repeated on a single page at the end of the book, and accurate information is presented if the song is of historical interest.[4] Books that lack accompanying

[4]Linda Leonard Lamme, "Song Picture Books: A Maturing Genre of Children's Literature," *Language Arts*, vol. 56 (April 1979), p. 405.

musical score, such as *All the Pretty Little Horses* by Jeffers or *Fiddle-i-Fee* by Stanley may, nonetheless, be useful if children already know the music.

Matching Music and Literature

The process of identifying appropriate music to accompany prose and poetry selections helps children appreciate mood and changes of tone in book literature and music. Second-graders discussed the kind of music that could accompany the action of Sendak's *Where the Wild Things Are*. They recognized and created music with increasing tempo and volume, followed by a quiet conclusion of the story. Older children might enjoy reading one of Prelutsky's *Nightmares* poems to music of their own choosing. A teacher might let children listen to Grieg's "In the Hall of the Mountain King" or Wagner's "Valkyrie's Ride" and ask children which of Prelutsky's poems best suit these pieces.

Many themes or subjects featured in literature have counterparts in music. For instance, the quiet awakening of the day in *Dawn* by Shulevitz might be compared to the "Sunrise" movement from the *Grand Canyon Suite* by Grofé or to Cat Stevens' rendition of Eleanor Farjeon's poem "Morning Has Broken." Teachers can encourage older students to develop their sensitivity to recurring themes in art by juxtaposing literature and music. Other suggestions are given in Chapter 8, "Poetry."

Composing Music

Poetry may be set to music as children create melody and identify the rhythmical elements. One group of talented 7-year-olds wrote their own sad tale of a princess who was captured during a battle and taken from her palace. Her knight-in-arms wandered the lonely countryside in search of her, while the poor princess grieved in her prison tower for him. The children made up a theme for each of the main characters, which they repeated during the various movements of their composition. The story was first told to their classmates and then the song was played on the autoharp and glockenspiel. Older students composed a three-movement rhythmic symphony for Ged in Le Guin's *A Wizard of Earthsea*. A recorder flute repeated

Ged's theme in appropriate places in this percussive piece. When literature is the inspiration for children's composition of songs, both literature and children's appreciation for music will be enriched in the process.

EXTENDING LITERATURE THROUGH DRAMA

Forms of Drama

Books become more real to children as they identify with the characters through creative drama. Young children begin this identification with others through *dramatic play*. A 5-year-old engaged in impromptu play may become an airplane zooming to the airport built of blocks; another assumes the role of mother in the play house. Sometimes children of this age will play a very familiar story without adult direction. For example, "The Three Billy Goats Gruff" and "The Three Bears" are often favorites. Dramatic play represents this free response of children as they interpret experience.

Dramatic improvisation is very similar to dramatic play in that it is characterized by spontaneous dialogue and action. Younger children usually require some encouragement—such as puppets, props (a stethoscope to suggest a doctor), bits of costume (a long skirt for grandmother). With slightly older children, situations, time, and setting may be determined with the children's help. (See "Storytelling Devices," Chapter 12, for other suggestions.) When working with a group of 8-year-olds, Dorothy Heathcote[5] asked the students three questions: whom they wanted their play to be about, when it took place, and what their central problem was. The students decided their story was going to be about a king who lived in the "olden days." Their problem was that their king was dying; in fact, he was "dying of death" (almost always fatal!). Because Heathcote took their suggestions very seriously, these children worked out a moving scene in which six of them carried their

[5]Dorothy Heathcote, in a workshop for the In-Service Language Arts Project at The Ohio State University, Columbus, Spring 1971.

dying king to a kind of ceremonial spot (which was the teacher's desk) to determine the future of the tribe. These 8-year-olds believed in the story they had improvised; they attended to their king with proper concern. No longer third-graders, they were chieftains of long ago and their king was dying. Questions from the teacher forced them to make decisions and commitments about their situations; the rest came from their imaginations.

Creative drama is structured and cooperatively planned playmaking. It is usually developed from a simple story, folktale, or poem or from scenes from a long book. It goes beyond dramatic play or simple improvisation in that it has a form with a beginning, middle, and end. The dialogue is always created by the players, whether the content is taken from a story, poem, or chapter of a book. Occasionally, children may create an original story based on such familiar characters as those in the "Little House" series by Laura Ingalls Wilder. Perhaps they would like to imagine the kind of a birthday party that would be given for *Ramona Quimby, Age 8* by Cleary. While these are creative experiences, some structure is known about the characters or the situation. Most teachers and some children prefer the security of the story structure to complete improvisation.

Pantomime is a useful form in beginning creative drama. In preparation for acting out Leo Lionni's story *Frederick,* a group of 6-, 7-, and 8-year-olds pantomimed the role of the mice. They scurried and scuttled about the room, busily gathering their winter supplies. Later, the role of Frederick was added, and again all the rest of the children played at being mice. Only after the children had thought about their roles as mice was dialogue included. Children may also pantomime small portions of a scene in order to understand and feel a character more deeply. For example, a group of 9-year-olds pretended they were the evil witch from "Snow White." They pantomimed waking up in the morning and then standing before a mirror to ask the well-known question of who was the fairest in the land. Pantomime can be an essential step in the development of believable creative drama with children.

Moving from pantomime to the extemporaneous dialogue of creative drama is an easy transition. Scenes should be kept quite short. Many children should have an opportunity to "play" the scene, which will vary slightly each time. Staging is simple; props are negligible; and additional characters may be added as the play is developed. After playing each scene the children are guided by the teacher in evaluating the characterization and plot development. A new cast is chosen and the scene is played again.

Children play out the story as if they "believe" in the roles they assume. The teacher's major concern is with the process and values for the children involved. While occasionally a play developed creatively may be shared with another classroom, the value of creative drama lies in the *process of playing* and does not require an audience. A more formal production may grow out of creative dramatics, but then its primary purpose becomes entertainment, not expression. For such a production children plan more elaborate settings, acquire props, and wear costumes. Although the lines may become "finalized" as the scenes are rehearsed, they are neither written nor memorized.

Formal plays requiring memorization of written scripts have no place in the elementary school. When children are limited by pre-planned dialogue, there is little or no opportunity for them to think through the reactions of the characters to the situation. Creativity is further limited when elementary school children attempt to write scripts. Usually their writing skill is not equal to the task of natural dialogue. Also, the time required to compose scripts often becomes so frustratingly long that interest in the play is killed.

Even when formal productions are developed creatively, there are several cautions to be considered. The child who has developed a sincere belief in a role may, when costumed, become overly concerned with the trappings of the part. The regal queen who gracefully mounted the throne during a rehearsal may remain a chubby 9-year-old fussing with her mother's long skirt in an audience situation. Rehearsing for a perfect play on a P.T.A. program produces tense teachers and tense children. There is real danger of exploiting children when the teacher decides to "put on" the perfect play for parents and guests. It would be far better to educate parents as to the values of creative drama and let them enjoy the spontaneity of a childlike performance.

Values of Creative Drama

The many values of creative drama suggest its significance for the elementary school curriculum. The child broadens living and learning experiences by playing the roles of people in the past, in other places, and in different situations. In creating plays children obtain information and utilize their understandings from social studies and science classes. Language skills are developed through this form of creative expression. Tensions may be released and emotional and social adjustments can be fostered through creative dramatics. For example, the child who consistently seeks attention through "show-off" behavior may gain attention legitimately in creative drama. The child who identifies with characters who are alone or scorned gains new insights and understandings of human behavior and becomes more sensitive to the needs of others. Since there is no written script in creative drama, the players are forced to "think on their feet" and draw on their inner resources. Skills for democratic living are developed through cooperative planning of action and characterization. Developing the ability to accept and give criticism in the informal evaluation period, which should follow each playing, is an important concomitant of learning. The greatest value of creative drama lies in the process of doing it, the experience itself. Finally, interpretation of literature through drama brings children joy and zest in learning and living, while broadening their understandings of both literature and life.

Dramatizing Stories

The first step in dramatizing narratives is the selection of a good story to read or tell to children. Many teachers and librarians have their favorite stories for dramatizing. However, some titles will be suggested here as particularly good starters.

Very young children of 3 through 5 will become involved in dramatic play, but they usually do not have the sustained attention to act out a complete story. They may play a part of a favorite folktale (for example, "The Three Billy Goats Gruff" crossing the bridge), but they seldom will complete a whole story. And no one should expect them to do so.

Primary-grade children enjoy playing simple stories such as *The Great Big Enormous Turnip* by Tolstoy, *Caps for Sale* by Slobodkina, or *Six Foolish Fishermen* by Elkin. The teacher or librarian might read aloud *The Great Big Enormous Turnip* while six children pantomime being the old man, the old woman, the little granddaughter, the black dog, the house cat, and the mouse. Stopping at appropriate points when the old man calls to his wife for help allows the designated child to create the dialogue.

Folktales are also a rich source of dramatization. They are usually short, have plenty of action, a quick plot, and interesting characters. A favorite is *Stone Soup* by Marcia Brown. This is the story of three jovial French soldiers who trick an entire village into providing them with the ingredients for soup, which the soldiers claim to have made from three large stones. The story naturally divides into three parts—the first scene with the soldiers approaching the village; the making of the soup with the villagers' help, of course; and the last scene when the soldiers leave. Children can decide which scenes they want to play first. Usually they like to play the part where the stone soup is made. With some preliminary discussion of the characters of the soldiers and the villagers, the children may decide who will provide certain ingredients for the soup. Discourage them from actually bringing carrots or barley; instead, ask them to describe their contributions so others can almost smell and taste them. If the action lags, the teacher may enter the play and add a particularly nice morsel of beef, for example, telling how she just happened to have found one piece stored in the cellar. The playing may stop at an agreed-upon signal such as: "I never thought I'd live to see the day when you could make soup out of stones," and the soldiers' reply: "It's all in knowing how!" Following the evaluation period in which the teacher points out some of the good features of the playing (for example, "I liked the way George showed us he was an old man by the way he leaned on his cane" or "How could you tell Ann was cutting carrots?"), the teacher can ask children to tell what they noticed about individual interpretations. Additions to the playing can be discussed and the play then repeated with another group.

Other folktales that children enjoy dramatizing include *The Three Wishes* by Galdone. This is the well-known story of the couple who were granted three wishes. While dreaming and planning how they will use their wishes, the husband foolishly wastes one of his. His wife becomes so angry at him that she wishes a link of sausage will stick to the end of his nose. After much pulling and struggling, they have to use their last wish to correct the second wish, and all their wishes are used up! This can be a lively story, and children love to play it. Another very funny one is the tale titled "Who Will Wash the Pot?" in the book *The Lazies* by Ginsburg. In this story the couple argue all day over who is going to wash the pot after they have eaten the cereal. They have agreed that the first one who speaks will have to wash it. The villagers think they are ill, but it is the mayor who knows how to get them to talk!

Stories from myths, such as "Pandora's Box" or "King Midas' Touch" are fine material for 9- to 11-year-olds to dramatize. Middle-grade children also enjoy presenting parts of books to each other in the form of debates, interviews, or discussions. A group of sixth-graders debated one of the issues raised in Key's science-fiction novel, *The Forgotten Door*: "Resolved: The boy Jon should be turned over to the military intelligence." Three children on either side raised important issues of individual rights and national security in the course of the dialogue. Another group of students in roles of various characters gave advice to an empty chair representing Winnie Foster in Babbitt's *Tuck Everlasting*. They voiced advantages and disadvantages of Winnie's living forever if she chose to drink water from a magic spring. By assuming the roles of other characters in Paterson's *Come Sing, Jimmy Jo* students might tell an imaginary James what they like about him or how they think he has changed in the several months in which the book takes place. Teachers can help children focus on important and complex issues which characters face in literature by providing these opportunities to explore ideas. This exploration is often a precursor of children's developing ability to discover themes in literature or factors which influence characters to change.

Puppetry

Many children will "lose themselves" in the characterization of a puppet while hidden behind a puppet stage, although they may hesitate to express ideas and feelings in front of the class. Through puppetry, children learn to project their voices and develop facility in varying voice quality to portray different characters. For example, a rather quiet, shy child may use a booming voice as he becomes the giant in "Jack and the Beanstalk." Puppetry also facilitates the development of skills in arts and crafts. Problems of stage construction, backdrops for scenery, and the modeling of characters provide opportunities for the development of creative thinking. A well-played puppet show will extend children's appreciation and interpretation of stories and make literature a more memorable experience for them.

Beginning in the kindergarten with the construction of paper-bag or simple stick figures, puppetry can give pleasure to children throughout the elementary school. Materials and types of puppets will range from the simple to the complex, depending on age and the child.

The techniques of creative dramatics should be followed as puppet plays are created cooperatively by children and teachers. It is highly recommended that children "play out" stories before using their puppets. Written scripts are not necessary and may prove very limiting. Playing the story creatively will allow the child to identify with the characters before becoming involved with the creation and mechanical manipulation of the puppet.

SELECTING STORIES

The techniques of puppetry are most appropriate for certain stories. For example, a group of 7-year-olds presented a puppet show based on Rudyard Kipling's *The Elephant's Child*. At the appropriate moment the crocodile pulled the elephant's short stocking nose into the familiar elongated trunk. Such action would be nearly impossible for live actors to portray. Another group of 10-year-olds used marionettes to capture the hilarious action of the laughing-gas birthday party described in Travers' *Mary Poppins*. Again, this scene would be difficult to portray in any other dramatic form. Other stories that lend themselves to interpretation through puppetry are *The Fat Cat* (Kent), *The Gingerbread Boy* (Galdone), *Rosie's Walk* (Hutchins), *Frederick* and *Alexander and the Wind-Up Mouse* (both by Lionni).

CONSTRUCTING PUPPETS AND STAGES

Numerous books are available that tell children how to make puppets, marionettes, and stages. Young children enjoy making simple cardboard figures that can be stapled to sticks or to tongue depressors. Paper bags stuffed with old stockings or newspaper may be tied to represent a puppet head and body. Ears, hair, aprons, and so on may be attached to create animals or people. By placing a hand in a sock or paper bag, the child can make the puppet appear to talk by moving fingers and thumb.

A very simple puppet may be created by using a pingpong ball for a head and a plain handkerchief. The index finger can be inserted in a hole in the ball; the handkerchief is then slit and slipped over the puppeteer's hand. Two rubber bands secure the handkerchief to the thumb and second finger, thereby making the arms of the puppet. Puppets that are somewhat more complex to construct may have heads of papier-mâché, potatoes, styrofoam balls, or other materials. Cloth bodies can be cut and sewn by the children. Cardboard cylinders and small boxes can be used to create animal puppets. Yarn, fuzzy cloth, or old mittens make good cover materials for animals.

Finger puppets can easily be made with bodies of finger-sized cylinders stapled at the top. Faces may be glued to the cylinder top or painted on the cylinder itself. These simple puppets make fine storytelling aids for younger children. A stage can be made by turning a table on its side. The puppeteer sits or kneels behind the table top. Another simple stage can be created by hanging curtains so they cover the lower and upper parts of a doorway. A table, cardboard, or side of a large box can also be placed in a doorway. This type of stage is particularly good because children waiting their turns at the side of the stage are hidden from view. Older children can construct a framework for more durable puppet stages. Permanent stages that can be moved from room to room should be available in the school and can often be made by parent volunteers. Screens or hinged wings may be placed at the side of such a puppet stage. Cloth, paper, or old window shades can be painted for background material. The educational values of planning and creating a puppet show far outweigh the time and effort required to produce it.

EXTENDING LITERATURE THROUGH RESOURCES AND COLLECTIONS

Artifacts and Collections

Items or artifacts mentioned in books often seem strange to children even if explained in context. A child who read that Ma Ingalls cooked prairie dinners in a spider might be puzzled until she could see this three-legged pan in a reference such as *Colonial Living* by Tunis. Hefting a modern-day cast-iron replica would give a child a sense of the endurance of these utensils. A child who read Mollie Hunter's *The Third Eye* might be surprised to see that a corn dolly that villagers made is not braided from corn as we know it but is instead a wheat weaving. Each object, although a small part of the story, nonetheless connects reader experience with a part of the real world.

A class collection or "museum" may involve children in assembling book-related materials on a larger scale. Second-graders studying pioneers, for example, made and collected items which pioneers may have taken west with them: a wooden spoon, a corn husk doll, a flour sack, or a wagon wheel. As the teacher read aloud *Trouble for Lucy* by Stevens, children added to the display their facsimile of the wagon master's log, a bouquet of wildflowers gathered by those who walked beside the moving wagons, and a "letter" from Marcus Whitman detailing his experiences with the wagon train. Labels were made for each article as it joined the display.

Collections can by created across books, as well. While a "Book Fare" represents a collection of food from many books (see "Cooking"), a museum from realistic fiction might include Peter's turtle from Blume's *Superfudge* or Trissy's cape from Mazer's *I, Trissy*. A folktale museum made by one group of older students included a pea slept on by the princess, Hansel's chicken-bone substitute for his finger, and a feather left behind by the crane wife. Labels were made for each article and its donor. For instance, one read "This is the needle that pricked Sleeping Beauty's finger. It is donated by her great-great-grandaughter, Princess Marie Elizabeth."

The collection and display of book-related materials allow children to re-create parts of the book actively. In addition, they help children listen by allowing them to visualize more readily the scenes of the book. Collections across books give children a chance to recall books, to synthesize knowledge about characters, motifs, themes, genres, and authors. And once again they remember in the presence of others their pleasurable experiences with reading.

Maps and Time Lines

Many authors of historical fiction include geographical maps to help the reader locate the story setting. Others make sufficient reference to actual places so that children may infer a story location by careful reading of both story and map. One group of students marked on a road map of Pennsylvania the probable routes westward that two pioneer families took in the 1780s. Ann Hamilton's journey from Gettysburg to Hamilton Hill in *The Cabin Faced West* by Fritz was represented; Barbara Baum's long walk from Bedford through Fort-Franklin to Mead's Crossing was recorded from *Bread-and-Butter Journey* by Colver. Students deduced that town names change and were pleased to discover that modern-day Franklin and Meadville were once Barbara's wilderness destinations. The movement of the Wilder family in the "Little House" books of Laura Ingalls Wilder may be followed on a map. Many of the literary accounts of immigration to this country can be traced on world maps, using pins and yarn.

Maps may also help children look across genres. For example, following a study of folktales of the world, a group of second- and third-graders used an overhead projector to trace a large map of the world. On this they represented the origin of each folktale with a symbol or character from that tale. The lengthy key explained the source of the symbols. The domains of American tall-tale heroes could easily be located on a map, as could cross-cultural variants of cumulative or pourquoi tales. (See Chapter 6 for charts of "Some American Tall-Tale Heroes" and suggested groupings of variants in "Cross-Cultural Study of Folktales.") Activities such as these help children see and appreciate cultural diversity yet similarity of pattern in literature.

Older children often make detailed maps of ima-ginary "countries of the mind," as in Alexander's *Westmark,* Le Guin's *A Wizard of Earthsea,* or McKillip's *The Riddlemaster of Hed.* While fantasy provides ample opportunities for children to design their own maps imaginatively, realistic fiction may be mapped, as well. In making maps children must return to the book to consider the location of key events and the relationship of multiple settings in the book.

Time concepts are difficult for children to grasp until sometime near the end of the concrete operational stage of thinking or the beginning of formal operations (ages 11 to 12). During this period, time lines may help students organize events in a person's life as represented in a book. Time lines also allow children to represent a synthesis of events in several books. A time line from Jean Fritz's *And Then What Happened, Paul Revere?* might include the date of his birth, the date Paul took over his father's business, the summer spent in the army, his famous ride, and his death in 1818. Events in the lives of Revere's contemporaries, such as Benjamin Franklin or George Washington, might be more easily compared if they were placed on a time line of the same scale as Revere's.

Placing book events in the world's time challenges even sophisticated readers to select relevant events in both the book and human history. A stratified time line allows children to separate groups or types of events from others. While *Friedrich,* Richter's story of a Jewish boy caught in pre-World War II Germany, contains a "chronology" of dates in a reference at the back of the book, students might represent selected governmental decrees on one stratum of a time line. A second stratum might represent the number of Jews living in the Third Reich according to yearly censuses. A third stratum might list important events in Friedrich's life. In this way children could see more clearly the political events against which Friedrich's tragic life was played out.

In making time lines, children need to agree on a scale so that events may be clearly shown by year or by decade, for instance. Time lines may be made of string from which events and years are hung. If children make time lines on a long roll of paper, entries may be written on cards and placed temporarily along the line. In this way, corrections or realignments may be made easily. In addition to returning children to a book to focus on the se-quence of events, making time lines and maps gives children practice with two important tools which readers use to make meaning.

Jackdaws

The term "jackdaw" comes from the British name for a relative of the crow that picks up brightly colored objects and carries them off to its nest. Commercially prepared jackdaw collections have been developed for use in high school social studies courses. These collections, based on an historical event or period, include facsimile copies of diaries, letters, newspaper articles, advertisements, and other evidence from the time.[6]

Teachers of elementary school children have modified this concept to suit activities and discussion with younger children. These teacher-made collections assemble resource materials which they and children can handle in discussion, in display, or in actual construction and use. A jackdaw for Paterson's *The Master Puppeteer*, set in a Japanese puppet theater of the early 1600s, included photographs of a samisan player and a puppet with its operators, a first-hand account of a Japanese bath, a synopsis of a typical play, and a short glossary of key words such as *ronin, sake,* and *Daimyo*. Articles and documents that accompanied Yep's *Dragonwings* included reproductions of rare photographs of turn-of-the-century San Francisco's Chinatown, photographs of contemporary newspaper accounts of Chinese-built airplanes, a kite like the one Moon Shadow flew, and some green tea. Often sources for the factual material on which an historical fiction title is based are given in an author's note. Some jackdaws may then include copies of these actual source materials or may be created as "facsimiles" by children.

Teacher-made jackdaws may have a list of contents so that inventory is simple. Suggested uses for the parts of the jackdaw and a bibliography of related literature save time if teachers share jackdaws among themselves.

Part of the challenge and fun of making a jackdaw is locating the material. One teacher gave

---

MAKING A JACKDAW

Though each book may suggest specific items or references to assemble, this list points to general considerations and suggests some ways of representing information.

- Recipes from the book's time (a typical dinner; a menu for a celebration)
- Price lists of commonly purchased goods then and now (milk, shoes, a dozen eggs, car)
- A time line of the book's events
- A time line of the period surrounding the book's events
- A map, actual or imagined, of the setting
- A letter, diary, log, or news article which could have been written by or about a book character
- A Xerox of an actual book-related news article or document
- Artwork from the period (painting, architecture, sculpture)
- Songs, music, or dances from the book's setting (sheet music or words, tapes)
- Clothes of characters of the period (paper dolls, catalog format, collage)
- Something about the author of the book[7]
- A list of other fiction; other nonfiction references.

---

fifth-graders a chance to make jackdaws based on historical fiction. After extensive research from a variety of sources each group assembled five items from a list similar to "Making a Jackdaw."

Helping children make connections between literature and their own experiences is an important teacher role. However, teachers need to recognize when enough is enough. Said one fifth-grader after a six-week study of Wilder's *Farmer Boy*, "I hate this book." If teachers' first priority is in the fostering of children's love of reading, they will be less likely to overburden children with factual inquiry. Teachers who appreciate the child's desire to know as a prior condition of learning can appreciate Louise Rosenblatt's criterion for the usefulness of background information: "[I]t will have value only when the student feels the need of it and when it is assimilated into the student's experience of particular literary works."[8]

---

[6]Available from Social Studies School Series, 10000 Culver Blvd., Culver City, California 90230.

[7]See Appendix B, "Information about Authors and Illustrators," for sources.
[8]Louise Rosenblatt, *Literature as Exploration* (New York: Noble and Noble, 1976), p. 123.

EXTENDING LITERATURE THROUGH WRITING

Children's written work should grow out of their own rich experiences, whether these experiences are with people, places, and things, research and observation, or literature. The content of writing may come from many sources in the classroom. Nearly all of the literature extensions discussed in this chapter have accompanying writing possibilities. A display of media experiments in printing or collage, for example, needs written introduction and explanations. Cooking and games can be accompanied by directions, rules, or recipes. The patterns in marbleized paper may suggest free verse or haiku. Role-playing provides a natural rehearsal for first-person writing in such forms as diaries, logs, letters, or eye-witness accounts.

While the content for children's writing is all around us in the classroom, it is literature which gives children a sense of how the written word sounds and looks. Frank Smith suggests that the role of literature in a writing program is central:

> Reading seems to me to be the essential fundamental source of knowledge about writing, from the conventions of transcription to the subtle differences of register and discourse structures in various genres.[9]

When children have a chance to become writers themselves, they begin to notice how other authors work. While literature suggests the many forms which stories, information, or poetry may take, it is only as children experiment with the model that they begin to develop a sensitivity to the conventions of the form. This awareness in turn allows them to bring a wider frame of reference to the reading and writing that follow.

Children in elementary classrooms should have an opportunity to experience a variety of well-written fiction, poetry, and nonfiction. At the same time they can be encouraged to develop an appreciation of language and form through writing. In this way, children develop a diverse writing repertoire, a sensitivity to language, and an increasing control over the power of words.

[9]Frank Smith, *Writing and the Writer* (New York: Holt, Rinehart and Winston, 1982), p. 177.

Reading and writing are closely intertwined; as the child writes she reads what she has written. Also her writing will be influenced by the literature she has heard and read.

Dhahran Hills Elementary School, Aramco, Saudi Arabia. Roy R. Wilson, Jr., teacher.

Developing Sensitivity to Language

Children's appreciation of the writing of others increases as they listen to many fine stories, read widely themselves, and have many opportunities to create their own stories and poems. Skill in descriptive writing may be developed by helping children to become aware of the power of words in conveying sensory images. After a story has been finished, the teacher and children may reread and relish particularly enjoyable words, phrases, or paragraphs.

Children's use of sensory langue in their writing requires many first-hand experiences of touching and feeling and savoring textures, sounds, colors, shapes, rhythms, and patterns. Literature, too, can sharpen sensitivity to nature, people, and relationships. Rich sensory imagery helps children "see" the world around them in new perspectives. For example, Rebecca Caudill in *A Pocketful of Cricket* presents the last days of August as experienced by a small boy, Jay. His experiences are familiar to many children.

> He walked along the lane on the side of a hill. The dust under his feet felt soft and warm. He spread his toes and watched the dust squirt between them. . . .
>
> A hickory tree grew beside the lane. Its branches cast a dark pool of shade on the hillside. Nuts grew among its leaves.
>
> With a stick Jay knocked a nut from a low branch.
>
> He picked up the nut and smelled the tight green hull that enclosed it. The smell tingled his nose like the smell of the first frost.
>
> Jay put the nut in his pocket.[10]

One group of second-graders made a list of what Jay noticed, heard, smelled, and touched in his walks through the fields and woods. They then went out into the fall afternoon to record what they could observe with all their senses.

Children would need to have many more experiences with literature and language before they could fully appreciate the description of another August day. Natalie Babbitt recreates an oppressively still day full of foreboding as the opening scene of *Tuck Everlasting:*

> The first week of August stands at the very top of the summer, the top of the live-long year, like the highest seat of a ferris wheel when it pauses in its turning. The weeks that come before are only a climb from balmy spring, and those that follow a drop to the chill of autumn, but the first week in August is motionless, and hot. It is curiously silent, too, with blank white dawns and glaring noons, and sunsets smeared with too much color. Often at night there is lightning, but it quivers all alone. There is no thunder, no relieving rain. These are strange and breathless days, the dog days, when people are led to do things they are sure to be sorry for after.[11]

A child's interest in words begins in the cradle and proceeds into adulthood. Great-Uncle Magnus Pringle in Mahy's *Ultra-Violet Catastrophe* loves important-sounding words like, "Seismological Singularity" or "Ultraviolet Catastrophe" and his grand-niece Sally agrees. Teachers can support children's natural fascination with words, word play, and word usage in many ways. A teacher of first-graders read aloud Zolotow's *Say It!* and children discussed what the mother and little girl saw on their fall walk.

> When I asked if there were any words or phrases that they especially liked, several children mentioned *splendiferous.* We then talked about what it meant. After such responses as "wonderful" and "beautiful," Meredith suggested that it was made up of two words, *splendid* and *terrific,* and by putting them together, they were better than when they were alone. The class then discussed what they thought would be a splendiferous day. Their ideas included sunny, warm, bright, fun, time to play, and time to be free.
>
> On one or two occasions after this discussion a child commented that it was a splendiferous day.[12]

Another teacher read aloud *Amos & Boris* by William Steig. Following a discussion, the children wrote a diary such as Amos the whale or Boris the mouse might have. After the children had written their first entries, a visitor to the class discussed the rich use of language in *Amos & Boris.* He had copied his favorite expressions from the book on cards, and he shared these with the group. They included:

> He loved to hear the surf sounds . . .
> the bursting breakers
> the backwashes with rolling pebbles.
>
> In a few minutes Boris was already in the water, with waves washing at him, and he was feeling the wonderful wetness.
>
> "Amos, help me," said the mountain of a whale to the mote of a mouse.[13]

The children then wrote the second entry in their diaries. The contrast between their first writing

[10]Rebecca Caudill, *A Pocketful of Cricket,* illustrated by Evaline Ness. (New York: Holt, Rinehart and Winston, 1964), unpaged.

[11]Natalie Babbitt, *Tuck Everlasting* (New York: Farrar, Straus & Giroux, 1975), p. 3.

[12]Joetta M. Beaver, "*Say It!* Over and Over," *Language Arts,* vol. 59 (February 1982), p. 144.

[13]William Steig, *Amos & Boris* (New York: Farrar, Straus, & Giroux 1971), unpaged.

A Comparison Of TWO Versions Of
THE THREE LITTLE PIGS

Questions	Illustrators		
	DON MADDEN	PAUL GALDONE	
How were the pictures made?	Pen and Ink	Pen and Ink	Same
Why did the three pigs leave home?	They wanted to build their own houses. Everyone was happy.	Mother had no money or food. The pigs had to build their own houses. Everyone was sad.	Different
What did the pigs use to build their houses?	First Pig ~ Straw Second Pig ~ Sticks Third Pig ~ Bricks	First Pig ~ Straw Second Pig ~ Sticks Third Pig ~ Bricks	Same
What happened to the first pig?	He ran to the woods.	The wolf ate him.	Different
What happened to the second pig?	He ran to the woods.	The wolf ate him.	Different
How did the wolf try to fool the third pig?	He didn't try to fool the pig. He just came down the chimney.	1. He asked the pig to meet him at Mr. Smith's turnip field. 2. He asked the pig to go to Merry-garden with him to get apples. 3. He asked the pig to go to the fair with him.	Different
How did the story end?	The wolf fell in the pot but the pig didn't eat him.	The wolf fell in the pot and the pig ate him.	Different
What language did you find interesting?	First words: Once upon a time... Last words: That was the end of the wolf. Refrains: I'll huff and I'll puff and I'll blow your house in. Not by the hair of my chinny-chin-chin.	First words: Once upon a time... Last words: And he lived happily ever after. Refrains: I'll huff and I'll puff and I'll blow your house in. Not by the hair of my chinny-chin-chin.	Same Different Same Same
Which version did you like best? Why?	Four children liked Don Madden's version the best.	Three children liked Paul Galdone's version the best.	

Even very young children can compare two versions of the same story noting differences in illustrations, plots, and use of words. Children voted on which story they liked best and included their reasons by their pictures.

Columbus, Ohio, Public Schools. Arleen Stuck, teacher.

and their second, below, shows the influence of simply calling attention to Stieg's rich use of language.

Dear Diary,

It was Tuesday two days after I saved Amos. We are just starting to be getting acquainted.

Amos told me all about land, how I wish I could live on land.

I wish we could meet sometime again.

By Boris

Dear Diary,

Well its Tuesday and Amos built a ladder down the

great tunnel, well, at least that's what Amos calls it. It really is my spout.

One day we had a feast. We had a fat juicy lobster, some plump juicy sea cucumbers, some meaty clams and some sand-breaded fish. After that we were so full and tired we talked and talked and finally we went to sleep happy.

Well, Bye
Boris (Chris ———)

Barrington Road School
Upper Arlington, Ohio
Carolyn Fahrbach, teacher
Roy Wilson, Ohio State University supervisor

All of the students showed a richer use of language in their second entries. They used such words from the book as "sand-breaded" and "sounded," but they used them in ways meaningful to their entries. The amount of writing also increased.

The sequence of this writing is also important to note. On the first day nothing much was said to call children's attention to Steig's use of language. It was suggested that they might want to retell the story from the point of view of one of the characters and in diary form. This recasting of the story appeared to be enough of a challenge for their first attempts. The following day, however, after they had mastered the diary form, attention was given to the rich use of language, and this was directly reflected in their second entries.

While use of figurative language and dramatic expression occurs frequently in literature, certain books invite teachers and students to play with language. After hearing Hoberman's *A House Is a House for Me*, first-graders listed other possible "houses," such as: "Arms are houses for hugs," and "buns are houses for hamburgers." Wildsmith's *Birds* and *Wild Animals* have suggested to second-graders the many names by which animals may be grouped—in herds, prides, flocks, or troupes, for instance. Children made a class book of their own group names for animals, including "a scent of skunks" and "a patrol of penguins." Thayer's *Try Your Hand* illustrates the many idiomatic expressions that involve hands: an old hand, a hand of cards, a big hand, and so forth. Children studying the human body created a body-shaped poster on which were located expressions related to body parts which they had collected, such as, "broken-hearted," "a green thumb," and "a nose for news." Stories written in dialect provide another chance for teachers to call attention to figurative language. One group of children who had read James Still's Appalachian-dialect retelling of *Jack and the Wonder Beans* made a chart that called attention to Still's creative use of language.

THE BOOK SAYS	WE SAY
"Now, hit come a rough winter. Cold as doorknobs."	It was a cold awful winter.
"Airy a one"	A single one
"She sizzled like a red-hot horseshoe in the cooling tub."[14]	She was mad; madder than a hornet.

Children who, at third grade, have had experiences such as this are later much more readily sensitive to the figurative language in a novel by Betsy Byars such as *The 18th Emergency* ("Ezzie was swinging his hand in the air like an upside-down pendulum so that he could get Mr. Stein's attention"[15]) or in one by Katherine Paterson, *Bridge to Terabithia* ("hot as popping grease" and "mad as flies in a fruit jar"[16]).

An individual or class notebook of interesting passages and descriptive phrases provides another way to develop awareness of language. One group of 12-year-olds each chose a particular theme—such as hope, love, fear, courage—for a whole year and kept a section in their notebooks of appropriate passages. The selections for "fear" included these quotes:

> Still I believe I know what courage is: it is to smile when fear has locked all smiles within your breast. If you have learned to be alone without fear, then no man can call you weak. . . . Many a strong man trembles when night has made him a small island in the ocean of darkness and the hooting owl is heard.[17]

[14]James Still, *Jack and the Wonder Beans*, illustrated by Margot Tomes (New York: Putnam, 1977), unpaged.
[15]Betsy Byars, *The 18th Emergency* (New York: Viking, 1973), p. 66.
[16]Katherine Paterson, *Bridge to Terabithia*, illustrated by Donna Diamond (New York: Crowell, 1977), p. 1.
[17]Eric Haugaard, *Hakon of Rogen's Saga*, illustrated by Leo and Diane Dillon (Boston: Houghton Mifflin, 1963), pp. 37, 79.

. . . fear isn't necessarily a bad thing. It's a result of aiming high.[18]

Literature as Model

STORY FRAMES

Ideally, we hope that children will write, out of their own experiences and emotions, about the things that matter to them. Unless children have been in classrooms or homes that value this kind of writing, many will need some help in starting to write. Stories with strong organizational patterns often free children from an overwhelming set of problems—how to begin, organize, sustain, or end writing. By giving children a chance to "write your own versions," teachers may free them to write.

Particular books, stories, or poems are useful in helping children to start. In addition, children's writing may give the teacher information about what children do or do not understand. The pattern of the book *Someday* by Zolotow inspired several 7-year-olds to think of their "someday" hopes and desires. Some of the children were not mature enough to catch the irony of this story and simply drew pictures and dictated stories of what they hoped to be "someday." Others recognized that the wishes were highly improbable. One girl's telling statement has a message for all of us who are interested in bringing children and books together. She wrote simply:

Someday when I have
nothing to do, I'm
going to read a book
instead of watch T.V.

Columbus Schools, Ohio
Annie Roseboro, teacher

Very young children could use the labeling or scrapbook format of Wolf's *Her Book* or Maris' *My Book* to create their own catalog of possessions. However re-creating the half-page format of *My Book* may be beyond the skills of most 5- or 6-year-olds.

Two clearly patterned books by Judi Barrett, *I*

[18]Sylvia Louise Engdahl, *Enchantress from the Stars*, illustrated by Rodney Shackell (New York: Atheneum, 1970), p. 72.

Hate to Take a Bath and *I Hate to Go to Bed*, present in the first half the reasons for hating baths or bedtime. The second half, however, is hinged with "But if I have to . . ." and then all the advantages follow. Children have enjoyed creating other books about two-sided situations like going to summer camp, piano lessons, grandparents' house, soccer practice, or the arrival of a new baby. The pattern of *Fortunately* by Remy Charlip stimulated two 8-year-old girls to write their own "fortunate" and "unfortunate" incidents:

GOING TO SCHOOL
One day unfortunately, I woke up.
Fortunately I got dressed.
Unfortunately I was tired.
Fortunately I went downstairs to eat breakfast.
Unfortunately my Mom wasn't there.
Fortunately my breakfast was on the table.
Unfortunately my breakfast was cold.
Fortunately I wasn't hungry.
Unfortunately I was late for school.
Fortunately I could ride my bike.
Unfortunately my bike tire popped.
Fortunately I could run.
Unfortunately I skinned my knee and it held me back.
Fortunately I finally got to school.
Unfortunately it was Saturday.
Fortunately I went back to bed.
  The End

Paige Pierman and Kristy Klein
Barrington Road School
Upper Arlington, Ohio
Sherry Goubeaux, teacher

Another book that provides an excellent story is *Alexander and the Terrible, Horrible, No Good, Very Bad Day* by Judith Viorst. Children in the middle grades delight in detailing their terrible, horrible, very bad days. One child gave a new creative twist to this pattern as she wrote about "The Wonderful Magnificent Day."

Byrd Baylor's *Everybody Needs a Rock* gives the reader serious rules to consider in selecting favorite rocks. Children have added their own rules for rock selection, and others might follow the pattern, creating rules for selecting a special tree or shell. A group of 9-year-olds listened to Baylor's *Your Own Best Secret Place* and talked about the many kinds of secret places people have. After the class discussion one boy's version of "My Own Best Secret Place" described how he got to the place, what it felt like to be there, and how it looked.

My own best Secret place
To get to my secret place you have to go down the basement steps turn right go in the door on the south wall turn left go up the ladder crawl in the big hole in the wall and there is my Secret place. It feels good to be in my Secret place becaus the cool air wash's away all my troubles into the back of my head. I have a nice soft carpet that I sit on so the hard tough rocks on the floor dont irritate me. When I go in my Secret place I turn on my light and read a book with my troubles tucked in the back of my head.

Barrington Road School
Upper Arlington, Ohio
Marlene Harbert, teacher

Often a particular aspect of a book may suggest writing ideas. *Anastasia Krupnik* by Lowry keeps lists such as "Favorite Words," "Things I Love! Things I Hate!" If children, like Anastasia, kept lists on topics of their own choosing, in time one list might serve as the skeleton of a composition. Alphabet books centered on topics, such as Isadora's *City Seen from A to Z*, Azarian's *A Farmer's Alphabet*, or Musgrove's *From Ashanti to Zulu*, present organizational patterns for conveying information. Children may use this form as an alternative to stolid reports. Primary children hearing stories of wishes, such as *Do Not Open* by Turkle, *The Three Wishes* by Galdone, or *The Old Woman Who Lived in the Vinegar Bottle* by Godden, could create their own class book of wishes.

Many books invite continuations or further adventures. Children acquainted with Ramona might create another chapter in the Quimby family saga now that baby sister Roberta has joined the family. *The Mysteries of Harris Burdick* by Van Allsburg are fourteen drawings supposedly left with a publisher. Each drawing is accompanied by a tantalizing phrase: The House on Main Street, "It was a perfect lift-off" shows the house levitating; a sleeping "Archie Smith, Boy Wonder," is approached by small circles of light asking "Is he the one?" Children would have a challenging time finishing what the illustrator has started here.

The story frames and story starters suggested here allow children to enter more easily into writing. In classrooms rich in experiences, teachers can make use of writing models along with all the writing opportunities that the classroom already provides. Teachers have no need, then, to assign one topic to all children but can draw instead on what each child has become involved with. Teachers can facilitate children's writing by using what Donald Graves has termed "process conferences":

> Teachers using this method help students by initiating brief individual conferences *during* the process of writing, rather than by assigning topics in advance of writing and making extensive corrections after the writing is finished.[19]

The teacher leads students to develop authoritative voices and an awareness of what they already know. Teachers can also encourage children to talk to each other about their writing in small groups to try out their ideas. In addition, by allowing children to share and display their writing in the classroom, the teacher honors their work and provides acknowledgment that child writers are engaged in worthwhile, interesting, and entertaining endeavors.

[19]Donald Graves, *Balance the Basics: Let Them Write* (New York: Ford Foundation, 1978), p. 19.

FORMS OF LITERATURE AS FRAMES

As children become familiar with many types of literature—fables, folktales, myths, and poetry, for instance—they are able to experiment with these forms in their own writing. One child heard his teacher read Arnold Lobel's *Fables* aloud in September. Then he read it himself and over the next five weeks produced a total of seven fables. One example was:

A BULL STORY

One day a bull feeling both strong and mean came down into the valley. To his surprise, there was another bull down there looking as strong and mean as he. They challenged each other to a fight. They killed each other and neither of them carried on a happy life.
Moral: You can't win against an equally equipped opponent.[20]

Working from the moral back to the story, one group of 12-year-olds decided to create other modern versions of fables. They thought of appropriate stories for such well-known morals as "Beauty is only skin deep" and "Don't cry wolf unless you mean it."(See "Fables," Chapter 6, for stories suggesting other morals.)

Middle-graders have also enjoyed retelling familiar folktales in modern settings, as Myers does in *Sidney Rella and the Glass Sneaker*. Others have retold part of a tale from the point of view of another character, as the third little pig does in Sara Henderson Hay's poem, "The Builders."[21] One fifth-grade boy wrote his version of "The Three Little Pigs" from the wolf's point of view. His wolf arrives at the third little pig's house in a Corvette, but the pigs are ready:

Then the pigs pulled a low blow on me. I was trying to come down the chimney when the pig put hot water under me and I was burnt. I lost some fur and a

couple of teeth and had whiplash for about a month. Naturally, I'll take them to court.

Highland Park Elementary School
Grove City, Ohio
Mike Neidig, teacher

A very funny story to use as a starter for writing modern fairy tales is *Jim and the Beanstalk* by Raymond Briggs. This is a modern version of "Jack and the Beanstalk" in which the giant is a pitiful old man who used to like fried boy, but now needs false teeth, glasses, and a wig. Jim is so successful in restoring the giant's lost youth that he has to run for the beanstalk when the giant's appetite returns. Children who have noticed the ways storytellers personalize details, begin and end with traditional phrases, or include refrains are more likely to become adventuresome in their own retellings.

Other forms of traditional prose—tall tale, pourquoi story, or myth—may serve as models for children's writing. However, it is essential that many literary examples of a form be shared and discussed with children before their writing so that they may notice patterns and elements from experience with the form, rather than from "recipes."

Teachers can capitalize on children's interest in comic book forms by encouraging them to make comic sequences out of scenes from favorite stories. Conversation written in balloons allows even reluctant writers to add words to pictures. Raymond Briggs' *Father Christmas* features conversational balloons, as does Michael Margolis' *King Grisly-Beard: A Tale from the Brothers Grimm*. The Provensen's illustrations for *Aesop's Fables* and James Stevenson's stories such as *The Wish Card Ran Out!* provide useful models for this kind of writing and illustrating activity, as well. One boy made use of comic format to create a "Pooh Fun Book" that included original adventures of Pooh, a "Pooh Crossword Puzzle," Christopher Robin's Diary, Pooh's Jokes, and numbered directions for drawing Pooh plus other kinds of written discourse.

Poetry provides many opportunities for children's writing. A group of 7- and 8-year-olds studied *The Comic Adventures of Old Mother Hubbard and Her Dog*, illustrated by Tomie de Paola. They created additional verses such as "She

[20]Fredrick R. Burton, "The Reading-Writing Connection: A One-Year Teacher-as-Researcher Study of Third–Fourth Grade Writers and Their Literary Experiences," unpublished doctoral dissertation (Columbus: Ohio State University, 1985), p. 166.
[21]Sara Henderson Hay, "The Builders," in *Reflections on a Gift of Watermelon Pickle* edited by Stephen Dunning, Edward Lueders, and Hugh Smith (Glenview, Ill.: Scott, Foresman and Company, 1966), p. 40.

went to the orchard to get him a cherry. / But when she got back, he was being scary." And "She went to the hen house to get him an egg. / But when she got back, he was holding his leg." After reading *The Book of Pigericks* by Lobel, a small group of fourth-graders wrote their own "Bugericks." Suggestions for other ways to encourage children's writing with poetry may be found in Chapter 8.

Extending Forms of Writing

While it is true that most children usually start by writing stories, they should be given many opportunities to write other forms as well. Writing a character's diary or journal lets a child assume that character's point of view. Reporting a book's events in newspaper-article format allows a child to concentrate on what is happening in the story. Children can develop practical writing skills as they write directions for a literature-based game or describe how they made a diorama. All levels of writing may spring from a child's involvement with literature, and teachers need to develop a capacity to help children discover writing opportunities. Once again we suggest that children need experiences with a form before they are able to take it on in their own writing. Children who have never looked beyond the comic section of the newspaper should not be asked to write folktale characters' "Letters to Ann Landers" or entries for the "obituaries" column without prior experience with the form of today's newspapers!

LOGS, DIARIES, AND LETTERS

Once children can assume another point of view, they are able to retell a story in the first person. Forms such as a character's "thought ramblings" (interior monologues), logs, diaries, or letters allow children to enter the emotions and experiences of that character. Young children typically have more difficulty sustaining a story from another's point of view. They may meet two points of view in such books as *Mouse and Tim* by McNulty, which presents the same occurrances as told by a boy and the mouse he captures in the barn.

Older children, however, read many books written in first-person narrative forms. Much of current realistic fiction is narrated by the main character. *I, Trissy* by Mazer not only "types" her story, she writes it in a series of letters, plays, memos, and even a "last will and testament." The story line in the comic *Slaves of Spiegel* by Pinkwater is revealed in short log or diary entries written by several characters, police blotter notes, eyewitness accounts, news articles, and posters. Children are quick to notice these conventions and enjoy imitating them.

Diary-writing characters are often found in literature. Children who have heard *My Side of the Mountain* by George read aloud notice that Sam Gribley's diary and a newspaper article are part of the way the story unfolds. Children might continue Sam's diary or write a newspaper account of interviews with Sam about his experiences. Ann Hamilton in *The Cabin Faced West* by Fritz kept a diary and wrote letters to friends back east. Children might continue the correspondence or write another character's diary, such as Andy's or Ann's mother's. Irene Brady's drawings and log for the *Wild Mouse* she observed might provide a format for children's observations of other animals.

Logs or diaries can be created for characters who never kept them. David, who escaped from a concentration camp and made his way *North to Freedom* (Holm), might well have kept a record of his trip. What if Matt in Speare's *The Sign of the Beaver* had kept a diary of his lonely vigil in the log cabin in the 1700s waiting for his family to arrive? What would he have said about Attean when he first met him? How would his journal entries have changed by the story's end? Orphaned 13-year-old Elspeth in *The Journey of the Shadow Bairns* by Anderson might have confided her fears to her diary as she traveled with her 4-year-old brother from Scotland to Canada in search of relatives. Writing activities like these help children organize the story chronology while attending to character attitudes and changes. They also may encourage children to locate themselves more quickly in a story they hear read aloud by the teacher over time.

Children also can assume the voice of inanimate objects or animals in logs, letters, or diaries. Ramona's cat, Picky-Picky, suffered his own deprivations and adventures when Ramona's father lost his job in *Ramona and Her Father* by Cleary. How would Picky-Picky tell his story? One teacher of second-graders who were familiar with the Paddington series by Michael Bond sent home a stuffed Paddington Bear with a different child each weekend. Paddington's diary, as written by his child friend, became an important part of the next week's writing and was read aloud to the class.

Children might also write imaginary correspondence between several characters. This would require a good understanding of each character and the ability to be flexible enough to capture different points of view. Seven- and 8-year-olds might write a letter to *Stevie* by Steptoe from Robert. They could speculate as to whether Robert would tell Stevie that he missed him. Some could then assume the role of Stevie and answer the letter. Irene Hunt's story *Across Five Aprils* includes many letters from the Illinois farm boys involved in the Civil War, but none from Jethro, the 9-year-old boy who is left home alone. Children might compose a packet of the letters Jethro could have written to his brothers and to his beloved schoolteacher. *Dear Mr. Henshaw* by Cleary is told entirely in a one-sided correspondence between a boy and an author whom he admires. Children might try this retelling of a part of a story in several letters. What would Jimmy Jo have written to his grandmother back home while he was trying to fit in with his family of country-western singers in *Come Sing, Jimmy Jo* by Paterson?

Letters written and sent to authors and illustrators can be encouraged rather than assigned if a child or groups of children have read and are enthusiastic about books by that author. Authors appreciate the inclusion of self-addressed, stamped envelopes, and they appreciate child candor and individuality above a "canned letter" copied from the chalkboard. Requests for pictures or biographical information should be addressed to publishers, while letters to authors or illustrators should be addressed to them in care of the publisher. (See Appendix C for publishers' addresses.)

NEWSPAPERS AND NEWSCASTING

By putting themselves in the role of reporters from newspapers or television news, children can "cover" the events in a book. An interview with Abel after his year-long stay on *Abel's Island* by Steig might include his advice on how to survive. A series of news accounts of *The Pushcart War* by Merrill could present amusing battles between the mighty trucks and the puny pushcarts in New York City. News coverage of Clara's day-long ocean float in *The Animal, the Vegetable & John D Jones* by Byars could include eye-witness accounts of the rescue and an interview with Clara and her sister Deenie. Fourth-graders created a Camazotz newspaper as part of their activities while the teacher read aloud *A Wrinkle in Time* by L'Engle. Their work reflected an awareness of what life might be like on a planet where all persons were required to behave similarly.

As a way of looking across or back upon what children know in literature, teachers may help children organize a group newspaper. Sections could include news stories, editorials, announcements. a fashion or society page, sports, lost and found, Letters to the Editor, advice, obituaries, and so forth. Content could be drawn from a particular genre, such as realistic fiction or folktales. One folktale newspaper, for instance, featured an advertisement for "Big Anthony's Carry-Out Pasta: All You Can eat!," a breaking-and-entering report at the home of the Three Bears, and a review of so-

---

BOOKS THAT MODEL DIARY, LETTER, OR JOURNAL FORMATS

Blos, Joan. *A Gathering of Days: A New England Girl's Journal, 1830–1832.* Scribner, 1979. (Gr. 4 up)

Brenner, Barbara. *On the Frontier with Mr. Audubon.* Coward, 1977. (Gr. 4 up)

Cleary, Beverly. *Dear Mr. Henshaw.* Morrow, 1983. (Gr. 3–6).

DuPasquier, Philippe. *Dear Daddy . . .* Bradbury, 1985. (Gr. 1–3)

Frank, Anne. *Anne Frank: The Diary of a Young Girl.* Doubleday, 1952. (Gr. 5 up)

George, Jean Craighead. *My Side of the Mountain.* Dutton, 1959. (Gr. 4–6)

Glaser, Diana. *The Diary of Trilby Frost.* Holiday, 1976. (Gr. 7 up)

Mazer, Norma Fox. *I, Trissy.* Delacorte, 1971. (Gr. 5 up)

O'Brien, Robert C. *Z for Zachariah.* Atheneum, 1975. (Gr. 5 up)

Orgel, Doris B. *The Devil in Vienna.* Dial, 1978. (Gr. 6 up)

Sachs, Marilyn. *Dorrie's Book.* Doubleday, 1975. (Gr. 4–7)

Williams, Vera B. *Three Days on a River in a Red Canoe.* Greenwillow, 1981. (Gr. 2–4)

ciety doings at Cinderella's ball. It takes time to develop a successful newspaper, as children must sift through what they have read to recall specific events. If column headings are posted around the classroom, ideas may be noted and children can paste up their rough drafts of articles for reading by the rest of the "newspaper staff." Parents, teacher aids, or high school typing students may often be persuaded to help with typing if the newspapers are to be duplicated for each student.

DIRECTIONS, EXPLANATIONS, SURVEYS, AND REPORTS

Nearly all of the literature extensions in this chapter have accompanying writing possibilities. Children who write directions for designing and printing from plastic foam trays need to write procedures concisely for others to follow. Directions for a literary game give children an opportunity to write with clarity and precision. If others can play the game by following what the game-maker has written, then the directions have succeeded.

Explanations and descriptions help others understand what children have created or accomplished. If students' work is displayed for a wider audience, as in school corridors or the library, then children understand the necessity for informative writing to speak clearly for them in their absence. In addition, displays provide a natural encouragement for children to revise and recopy, if necessary, for this public writing. Teachers can help children write longer and more complete descriptions by asking such questions as: How did you do this? What materials did you use? What part of the book is this based on? Why did you choose it? One such discussion produced the writing shown here from two second-grade boys.

Literary surveys give children experiences with the representation of findings in graphs. One group of 11- and 12-year-olds surveyed each other on such topics as "Which Judy Blume books have you read?," "How many books did you read in March?," and "Have you read any books from these series: Trixie Belden, Nancy Drew, the Hardy Boys?" Data were presented in pie and bar graphs, averages, and percentiles in a variety of interesting displays.

A group of first-graders responded to *The Biggest House in the World* by Lionni through a variety of media and math activities. They took surveys of children's preferences for color, kind,

We made a diorama of Nantucket Harbor. We started with a cardboard box. Then we cut out some houses and then we made the whale and glued the whale on at an angle then we painted the whale black. We were going to make the under ground city but it was to hard to make. We had trouble on the whale we kept making the whale smaller. And we had trouble on the dock And sky and clouds because it was very hard. The windows on the houses were hard to. We painted the clouds 4 times.

Third-graders wrote this candid explanation for their diorama constructed after reading Blair Lent's *John Tabor's Ride*.

Dustin DeStefano and Jason Bump, Highland Park Elementary School, Grove City, Ohio. Patty Driggs, teacher.

and size of house (one, two, or three stories). Their concept of the word "house" was enlarged to include the "houses" of a snail and turtle (shells). A bulletin board displayed the results of these extensions from a single book.

Other surveys have been made of how frequently and how long each teacher reads aloud to the class or where and when children's favorite places and times are to read. Children doing survey research will learn much about conducting and organizing the results of a survey. In addition, a teacher learns more about a reading profile of the class from these surveys. Teachers may help children state questions clearly so that answers can be categorized and counted. Discussing ways of representing information, such as bar or circle graphs, keys and use of symbols, will help children create more visually interesting survey charts.

The writing of reports is a time-honored school activity that often produces stilted writing beginning with "My report is on . . ." and featuring copied phrases from encyclopedias. Teachers may help children organize informational writing into

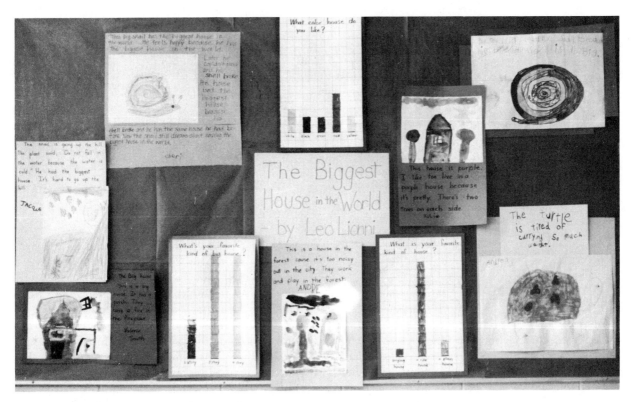

A first-grade group responded to Lionni's book by making pictures and surveys of their favorite colors, sizes, and kinds of houses.

Barrington Road School, Upper Arlington Public Schools, Laurie Mahla, EPIC Student Teacher, The Ohio State University.

more interesting forms with the help of some unusual formats found in modern nonfiction. Seymour Simon's *Animal Fact/Animal Fable* presents a statement to be judged true or false by the reader like "porcupines shoot their quills." Turning the page, the reader sees a two-paragraph answer beginning with "Fable. Porcupines cannot really shoot their quills." Diane DeGroat provides several types of illustrations for each statement and information: a humorous literal interpretation (the porcupine has a bow), a straightforward picture (the porcupine in a tree), and a close-up (of a porcupine's quill tip). Children could arrange some information on nearly any topic into an illustrated fact/fable format.

The close-ups, labeled parts of drawings, and box-and-arrow sequences found in *Snake Secrets* by Roever show how text and illustrations work together. Ann McGovern's *If You Lived with the Sioux Indians* uses questions and answers to convey information. Brady's *Wild Mouse* and Spier's

Tin Lizzie suggest two different ways of treating life cycles. Brady records daily happenings in journal and sketch format; Spier provides a narration of the "life" of an automobile.

As a deterrent to copying, one teacher helped children organize what they know about elephants. After reading fiction and nonfiction, discussing information, and taking an observational trip to the zoo, the teacher asked small groups of students to write, on 3 x 5 pieces of paper, notes of what they knew. The class then organized the notes into such piles as "Uses of Trunk"; "Asian vs. African Elephants"; "Elephant Families"; and "Famous Elephants." Following this organization, children then found it less difficult to write from what they knew rather than from what they had copied.

Another child who was much impressed with the design of Holling's *Paddle-to-the-Sea* cast her report on Lake Superior in a similar format. Information about this lake was recounted by a whitefish named Blanco.

The Wilderness Island

One night passed and Blanco could see a shape of an Island. He Knew that this was Isle Royale because Toro told him he would pass many islands in Superior but this was the largest. It covered 843 square miles of land and water area. Blanco heard a motor, then a splash, and saw a seaplane. A few minutes later he saw a yacht. Blanco noticed that there were no cars on Isle Royale, just alot of wilderness with very thick forests of hardwoods and conifers. Blanco was swimming very close to shore and saw beavers, muskrats, a coyote and a wolf. He didn't see a moose but he sure did hear one.

Johanna Frank
Barrington Road School
Upper Arlington, Ohio
Pat Enciso, teacher

The illustrations for this fourth-grader's book borrowed from Holling: borders were decorated and a map delineated Blanco's daily position; a three-part diagram of a working lock, an overhead view of an oreboat, and "About the Author" completed this wonderful alternative to a report.

Children are sensitive to the way information is presented but are often not encouraged to make use of what they know in school writing. Paul, a 7-year-old, studied the format of *The Reasons for Seasons* (Allison), which begins with "How to Use This Book":

> This is not a regular page 1 to page 128 book. The pages are to be used in any order you like. So if you want to, jump in at the middle—or somewhere near the end.[22]

Paul wrote his own "Fun Book" at home, which began:

> This is not a regular book if you want to you can skip to the middle or somewhere near the end or you can just work your way through anyway its fun.[23]

[22]Linda Allison, *The Reasons for Seasons* (Boston: Little, Brown, 1975), p. 5.
[23]Glenda Bissex, *GNYS AT WRK: A Child Learns to Read and Write* (Cambridge: Harvard University Press, 1980), pp. 156–157.

Teachers can encourage children to be sensitive to form in informational as well as in fictional writing by calling attention to some of the conventions by which infromation is conveyed.

Literature provides all kinds of book-related writing possibilities whether the books come before, during, or after children begin to write. Teachers with well-balanced writing programs will want to provide children with many opportunities to write and read across the whole spectrum of discourse.

Bookmaking

Nothing motivates children to write as much as the opportunity to create, bind, and illustrate a book of their own. Teachers need to learn how to bind books themselves before attempting to teach children. Materials for bookbinding should be made constantly available so that children can make books as the need arises. Most bookmaking materials can be readily purchased (see below), but parents may contribute leftover fabric pieces for book covers to ease classroom budgets.

Since bookbinding involves time and some expense, it should be reserved for the carefully planned, written, and illustrated book. Children should look at the way beautiful books are made, the various media used, the carefully designed endpapers or title pages, the placement of the words, and so forth, before they complete their own work. Marbleized paper or colored paper may be bound into the book as endpapers or children may create their own repeated patterns to symbolize the story. Many children enjoy planning dedications and jacket copy for their books, as well. As children create their own books, they learn much about the care and design that have gone into the books they read. Making a book of their story gives children a legitimate reason to revise, correct, and recopy.

Before binding a book, children can be encouraged to sketch a "dummy" or practice book. There, illustrations are roughed out and lines are drawn where text will be written or typed. In *Her Book* by Janet Wolf, the book's dummy serves also as endpapers, and children may wish to compare Wolf's dummy with the more detailed final illustrations as they work on their own books. Aliki's *How a Book Is Made* gives children an excellent overview of the creation and publication of a children's book.

Nothing motivates children to write as much as the opportunity to create, bind and illustrate their own books.

Ridgemont Elementary School, Mt. Victory, Ohio. Sheryl Reed and Peggy Harrison, teachers. Photo by Ann Dunetz.

✶ Book Making ✶

① Plan your story and illustrations carefully in a "dummy" or practice book. Decide what size your book should be. Then cut paper for pages that is twice the width and the same height as the size you want. Cut half as many pieces as pages you need. Remember to allow for the title pages. Cut two pieces of the same or another color or kind of paper for the end papers. Fold the paper to form pages, placing the end papers on the outside. Complete your pages so that they are just the way you want them!

② Fold the completed pages evenly and either hand or machine stitch up the center.

③ Place the open pages on the material that you will use for the cover. Cut the material to a size approximately two inches larger on all sides than the open pages. Press the fabric flat with the iron.

④ Cut two pieces of cardboard, each just slightly larger than a single book page. These will form the support for the cover.

⑤ Cut four large pieces of Dry Mounting Tissue. Make two pieces the size of the cardboard and two pieces the size of a single page. Also, cut several small strips of Dry Mounting Tissue approximately 2"×½".

⑥ Place the cover material on a flat surface face down. Position the Dry Mounting Tissue (cardboard size) on the material. Now place the cardboard pieces on top. Leave a space between the cardboard pieces to allow for the pages and for the book to open and close.

⑦ With an iron, set on low, carefully press the cardboard. This will mount the material to the cardboard.

⑧ Place the small pieces of Dry Mounting Tissue between the cardboard and the material and use the iron again to adhere the two. Begin with the corners. Then fold the top, bottom and sides until your book cover is completed!

⑨ Place the two remaining pieces of Dry Mounting Tissue on the cardboard side of the book cover. Position the sewn pages in the middle. Press the first and last pages down to form end papers. Use the iron to mount the pages to the cover.

Marilyn Parker, Columbus School for Girls, Ohio.

Materials for bookmaking include paper for pages, paper for endpapers, a threaded needle, cover material (such as cotton fabric, wallpaper, or Contac paper), and cardboard. In addition, an iron and dry-mount tissue (available from photographic supply houses) or white glue and water are needed.

EVALUATION AND RECORD-KEEPING

For years, educators have sought to evaluate children's reading by many methods that purport to be reliable and objective.[24] However, what these tests evaluate is such a narrow part of the whole process we know as "reading" that the essential character of one child reading is lost. Multiple-choice and short-answer questions following the reading of short paragraphs hardly define what a child has learned as a result of all he or she encounters in the course of reading. Information gained by these tests does little to help the classroom teacher plan programs that lead students to become more satisfied, more widely adept readers. Evaluation of children's reading should start with some knowledge of where individual children are starting; observation and evidence of the child's understandings and abilities as revealed by discussion, classroom interactions, solicited and unsolicited responses to books; and evidence of changes, or growth, in that child's knowledge, appreciation, understandings, and abilities in reading. Needless to say, this "naturalistic" method of assessment demands that a teacher constantly sharpen observational skills, develop some means of record-keeping, and be able to recognize important signs of insight and growth in the learners he or she teaches.

Determining Children's Literary Background

Begin where children are. This maxim applies to literature as well as any other area. In planning a literature program, a staff or teacher must first consider what the children's previous experiences with literature have been. Has the child been fortunate enough to have come from a home where reading is valued, where there are many books? Has a child been read to regularly? Or is school the child's first introduction to books? What have previous teachers read aloud to these children? What common experiences, such as author or illustrator studies or thematic groupings in literature, have these children had?

Teachers may want to take an informal survey or inventory of their children's backgrounds in literature. They may construct their own or use those which have already been published.[25] These inventories are not tests of children's literary knowledge but are simply informal surveys to see what kind of exposure children have had to literature. They may be given informally to younger children and duplicated or read aloud to middle-grade children. The results of these inventories would help the teacher identify strengths and gaps in children's exposure to literature. This would, in turn, be helpful in planning a literature program for them. For example, if children showed little knowledge of some of the well-known folktales, teachers could plan a folktale study, since these tales appeal to many age groups. If middle-grade students did not know Scott O'Dell's *Island of the Blue Dolphins* or had never heard of the novels of Betsy Byars, a teacher might have information on what to read aloud or introduce to the class.

Appreciation for literature seems to be developmental. If children have not had the opportunity to laugh at the antics of *Harry the Dirty Dog* by Gene Zion when they are 5 or 6, they need the experience at 7 or 8. If they have not met "Mother Goose" before they come to school, then early primary grades need to supply this cornerstone of literature. We need research on the sequential stages of appreciating literature, but we have some evidence to show that children must go through the "picture storybook stage," the "nonsense verse stage," even the "series book stage" if they are to become active, involved readers. Knowing where to start, then, is the value of finding what children's exposure to literature has been.

Record-Keeping

As a school year begins, it is important to have some record-keeping systems already in place which are simple and consume as little completion time as possible. In this way, information from the very first days of school may be compared as a child progresses, and the teacher will be better able to plan future curriculum.

[24]See David W. Moore, "A Case for Naturalistic Assessment of Reading Comprehension," *Language Arts*, vol. 60, no. 8. (November/December, 1983), pp. 957–969, for a thorough and concise description of the history of reading evaluation strategies in the United States.

[25]See Charlotte S. Huck, "An Inventory of Children's Literary Background" in the Guidebook to *Ventures*, Book 4; "An Inventory of Students' Literary Backgrounds" in the Skill Book for *Dimensions*, Grade 7 (Glenview, Ill.: Scott, Foresman, 1966).

WORK FOLDERS

A simple folder for saving dated copies or originals of children's work is often easiest. If the child does not have access to this folder, teachers might also include dated notes, anecdotes, or observations. One first-grade teacher noted that two weeks after she had read Alvin Tresselt's *It's Time Now* to the class,

> John pointed happily to Mrs. M.'s maternity shirt and said "Look, it's just like that book you read us." He recalled our discussion of the meaning of the phrase "the wind bellied out the curtains" when we read *It's Time Now*.

What better evidence could a teacher have of the lingering of literature in a child's mind?

Polaroid snapshots of children's work which is especially significant can be included to help a teacher recall a mural, sculpture, display, or other article that can't be saved. Children enjoy having access to their work and are pleased to have a place to store what might become lost or tossed away. Many children proudly take these folders home at the end of the school year. For the teacher, however, they become a means of comparing the child's previous work with her present accomplishments, a helpful tool in parent conferences, and a valuable means of sharpening a teacher's observational skills.

READING RECORDS

Asking children to make formal notes (title, author, main characters, plot, how I liked the book, etc.) often defeats novice readers and destroys their enthusiasm for what they have read. However, unless a teacher has an idea of what children choose to read and finish during SSR or at home, information and a source of important dialogue with the child is lost. One primary teacher simply walked around her silently reading class each week and noted on a class roster what each child was reading. Over a period of weeks she had amassed some interesting patterns.

A middle-grade teacher gave students 6 x 8 cards, a new one each month, where children simply wrote the title and author of each book they finished. The teacher or student could see at a glance what authors or genres the child knew, how many books he had read, etc. As the monthly cards accumulated, students were pleased to notice patterns in their own reading, used their cards to recommend titles and authors to other readers, and took pride in their accomplishments. With knowledge gleaned from the cards, the teacher was able to assemble small groups to discuss patterns in what they had read. One small group of fifth- and sixth-grade girls discussed patterns in animal stories:

> Usually someone is finding an animal or getting them at the time. They never have them to start with. Usually the animal gets hurt in a lot of stories. The main characters won't accept what their parents say and they're usually very defensive about their animal. Like someone will say "Why don't you get rid of them or kill them?" and they'll say "Not on your life."[26]

JOURNALS

Another means of keeping in touch with students as they read is to provide them with some time to react in writing. The student may simply "talk" on paper about whatever she has read; or the teacher may ask framing questions: Tell me about your reading this week; What decisions does a character have to make in the book you're reading? Tell about a funny part in a book you've read; or, Write about a book character who has shown great courage. The teacher then collects the journals and reacts positively and briefly to the child's statements: "You are reading some wonderful books this week" or "That courageous act reminds me of what the girl did in *Cry of the Crow*. That's another good one by Jean George." Since these are unpolished and ungraded writings, they often provide insight into children's thinkings. Fifth-grader Kevin, after weeks of writing two or three sentences about his reading, suddenly wrote a long entry based on his discovery of patterns in the books of Mitsumasa Anno. A partial section read:

> In the Anno books besides putting fairy tale characters in, he puts things like Beethoven playing the pi-

[26]Susan Ingrid Hepler, "Patterns in Response to Literature: A One-Year Study of a Fifth and Sixth Grade Classroom," unpublished doctoral dissertation (Columbus: Ohio State University, 1982).

ano and Shakespeare making a play. A boy climbs on a fence and there is a lady taking a bath. They also have clocks with four hands and a couple of his books have optical illusions like children throwing rings on top of a church steeple. *Anno's Italy* is the funniest of the bunch. The only one I haven't read is *Anno's Alphabet*. (They are all by Mitsumasa Anno. He has a foreign name I think.) [Writes his teacher: He is Japanese.] They are really good, really funny, and have super illustrations.

Kevin Carpenter
Barrington Road School
Upper Arlington, Ohio
Lois Monaghan, teacher

The teacher's comments shared his enthusiasm. While this seems like such a small piece of what a teacher does, it sets the teacher up as someone who is interested in what children think about their reading. And it gives a teacher a valuable chance to rejoice, advise, suggest, connect, question, and gently value the efforts children make to become readers.

INTERVIEWS

A time-consuming process, talking with children can nonetheless reveal children at their growing edges. (See Chapter 12 for more group discussion ideas.) A personal interview, if tape-recorded, gives the teacher time to reflect on what a child knows. Often these are conducted in the presence of some books the child has recently read as the mere presence of a book seems to act as a catalyst for some readers. Conversation may be simply a recounting of plot for many children. It may be a chance for the teacher to ask some specific questions: Could there be any other bridges in Katherine Paterson's *Bridge to Terabithia*? Now that you've read four books by Judy Blume, could you recognize one she wrote even if you didn't see the author and title? How would you know? Or it may be a chance for a teacher to make quiet observations about the guidance of a student. In many classrooms, students never have a chance to talk alone with the teacher except in disciplinary situations. Interviews can be exceptionally rewarding to both participants.

OTHER RECORD-KEEPING AIDS

Teachers have tape-recorded children's book discussions (see "Collecting Children's Responses,"

Chapter 2) and have used these as a way of listening more closely to what often happens very quickly in a small group.

Computer programming exists which would enable children to enter the data from, for instance, their reading records. The teacher could easily determine who has read *My Side of the Mountain* by George before she decided to read it aloud to the class. She could also determine popular authors. Children could enter pocket reactions to what they had read as a means of providing other children with reading suggestions. Computer records, too, might be used school-wide to keep track of books teachers have read aloud to the whole class. While computer records cannot replace the work folder, interview, or journal exchange, they could provide help in collecting records and reader reactions.

Evaluating Children's Literary Understandings

Evaluation of a child's understandings must be seen in light of developmental patterns, as discussed in Chapter 2. In addition, the teacher must consider a child's understandings as revealed in discussion with the group, in creating products such as murals or imaginary diaries discussed previously, and in some linear sort of way. What did the child start with? What does she know now? What accumulates long after this moment has passed?

Though the following list of understandings is by no means exhaustive, it may suggest how teachers might look at what children know following a study, for example, of the books of Ezra Jack Keats. Do they notice that:

- Many books feature a character named Peter. Other characters overlap, too.
- Stories are set in the city, in apartment buildings, in the street.
- Illustrations are often collage, using materials, newspaper, wallpaper, marbleized paper, and some paint.
- There are some ideas here. "Giving up things that you've outgrown is part of growing up" from *Peter's Chair;* "There are many things to do outside when it snows, but you can't save snowballs!" from *The Snowy Day.*

In addition, would children be able to pick out a Keats illustration from ones by Vera B. Williams

GUIDE FOR EVALUATING GROWTH OF CHILDREN

1. Does the child love one book, many books, reading in general?
2. Does the child become easily involved or easily distracted in reading a book?
3. Does the child predict, question, and confirm his way through a book?
4. Does the child prefer one genre, author, or illustrator over others? Is she aware of her preference? Can she recognize characteristics of genre, author, or illustrator?
5. Is the child a flexible reader who reads easily in several genres? Who reads often and quickly?
6. Can the child select books which satisfy him? Is he open to suggestions from other readers?
7. What kinds of understandings and awarenesses do the child's products reveal?
8. Does the child visualize, identify with, become involved with, or understand the motives of characters?
9. Does the child visualize settings?
10. What connections does the child make between a particular book and others by the same illustrator or author? Of the same genre? With the same theme? What patterns does she see?
11. What kind of thematic statements does the child make? Can he see a book title as a metaphor for a larger idea?
12. What connections does the child make between literature and life?
13. What questions does the child's reading raise for her?
14. What literary elements such as prologues, unique dedications, interesting chapter titles, language use, or narrative style does the child notice?
15. How are these reading patterns changing as the school years progress?
16. Is the child voluntarily reading more at school? At home?
17. Is the child responding to a greater range and complexity of work?

or John Burningham? Would they remember Keats' name? Understandings such as these would not be easily revealed in a multiple-choice test. But, as children discussed their choices for materials they used in making a picture "Like Ezra Jack Keats did," a teacher would see what children had noticed and remembered. When children went to the media center, a teacher might observe whether they asked the librarian for Keats' books by title, or by author. Later a teacher might hear a child say about another book, "That's just like *Peter's Chair*. She gave her little sister something she had outgrown."

Third-graders who studied folktales might be expected to recognize

- Some common tales.
- Typical characters and settings.
- Typical traits of characters.
- That there are formal beginnings, endings, refrains, and other characteristics of folktale language.

- Basic themes such as "Good is always rewarded" or "Little but honest wins over big," although they may not be able to state them succinctly.
- That popular tales such as "Cinderella" exist in many versions and variants.
- Some commonly recurring patterns, or motifs, such as magical objects, trickery, noodleheads, or wishes.

Children's own versions of folktales would reveal much about what they understood. So might their dramatic productions or their play on the playground.

Older students who had read Betsy Byars' novels, such as *The Pinballs*, *The Night Swimmers*, or *Cracker Jackson*, might be expected to be able to state, in comparing them, such patterns as humor in the midst of serious or tragic situations; children on their own without much adult or parental supervision; rural and southern settings; themes dealing with growing up; or main characters who can remember interesting incidents about their pasts.

Children's products also reveal understandings and growing edges. Did the "story map" of "The Gingerbread Boy" include all the important incidents? Could the child maintain Amos' point of view in his diary from *Amos & Boris* (Steig)? Did the child's version of *The Way to Start a Day* suggest a sensitivity to Byrd Baylor's use and arrangement of words? How did the student's two-part diorama reflect the contrasting settings of seashore and prairie in Patricia MacLachlan's *Sarah, Plain and Tall*? What teachers choose to evaluate depends on what they are hoping to have children understand after reading a book or pursuing a thematic study. It is helpful to list some goals and understandings, based on the evaluative criteria for a particular genre or the particular strengths and content of the theme, before sitting down to evaluate.

Evaluating Children's Growth

Throughout this text, we have suggested that children's learnings accrue, reorganize, and reformulate based on their own growth both as children and as readers. While observation and evaluation are daily tasks for teachers, it is the long-range goal of creating enthusiastic, versatile, and skillful readers that should be the teacher's focus. By becoming documenters of children's encounters with literature, we become better observers. Observations of change, then, provide us with clues to a child's growth. The following "Guide for Evaluating Growth of Children" provides a beginning set of questions to guide observations. The most important questions we can ask are often not the easiest to answer. What is a child building? What kind of framework is the child creating based on his experiences? How is this sense of literature changing?

GUIDE FOR EVALUATING A LITERATURE PROGRAM

AVAILABILITY OF BOOKS AND OTHER MEDIA

1. Is there a school library media center in each elementary school building? Does it meet American Library Association standards for books and other media?
2. Are there a professionally trained librarian and adequate support staff in each building?
3. Does every classroom contain several hundred paperbacks and a changing collection of hardbacks?
4. Are reference books easily accessible to each classroom?
5. May children purchase books in a school-run paperback bookstore?
6. Do teachers encourage children to order books through various school book clubs?
7. May children take books home?
8. Has the school board made some provision for keeping library media centers functioning during vacation periods?
9. Are children made aware of the programs of the public library?

TIME FOR LITERATURE

10. Do all children have time to read books of their own choosing every day?
11. Do all teachers read to the children once or twice a day?
12. Do children have time to discuss their books with an interested adult or with other children every day?
13. Are children allowed time to interpret books through art, drama, music, or writing?
14. Do children seem attentive and involved as they listen to stories? Do they ask to have favorites reread?
15. Is literature a part of all curricular areas, across the curriculum?

GUIDE FOR EVALUATING A LITERATURE PROGRAM (continued)

MOTIVATING INTEREST

16. Do teachers show their enthusiasm for books by sharing new ones with children, reading parts of their favorite ones, discussing them, and so on?
17. Do classroom and library displays call attention to particular books?
18. Are children encouraged to set up book displays in the media center, the halls, and their classrooms?
19. Does the media specialist plan special events—such as story hours, book talks, sharing films, working with book clubs?
20. Do teachers and librarians work with parents to stimulate children's reading?
21. Are special bibliographies prepared by the librarians or groups of children on topics of special interest—such as mysteries, animal stories, science fiction, fantasy, and so on?
22. Are opportunities planned for contacts with authors and illustrators to kindle interest and enthusiasm for reading?

BALANCES IN THE CURRICULUM

23. Do teachers and librarians try to introduce children to a wide variety of genres and to different authors when reading aloud?
24. Do teachers share poetry as frequently as prose?
25. Do children read both fiction and nonfiction?
26. Are children exposed to new books and contemporary poems as frequently as some of the old favorites of both prose and poetry?
27. Do children have a balance of wide reading experiences with small-group, in-depth discussion of books?

EVALUATING GROWTH OF CHILDREN

28. Are children encouraged to keep records of their own reading?
29. Do these records go into each child's cumulative file so that the next teacher knows what the child has read?
30. Do teachers give children an "Inventory of Literature" to determine their background of exposure to books?
31. Do teachers record examples of children's unsolicited responses to literature, as seen in their play, talk, art, or writing?
32. Do teachers save or record examples of children's solicited responses?
33. Are children allowed to respond to books in a variety of ways (art, drama, writing), rather than by required book reports?
34. Is depth of understanding emphasized, rather than the number of books read?
35. Are children responding to a greater range and complexity of work?
36. What percentage of the children can be described as active readers? Has this percentage increased?
37. Are some children beginning to see literature as a source of life-long pleasure?

EVALUATING THE PROFESSIONAL GROWTH
OF TEACHERS

38. Are teachers increasing their knowledge of children's literature?
39. What percentage of the staff has taken a course in children's literature in the past five years?
40. Are some staff meetings devoted to ways of improving the use of literature in the curriculum?
41. Do teachers attend professional meetings that feature programs on children's literature?
42. Are in-service programs in literature made available on a regular basis?

GUIDE FOR EVALUATING A LITERATURE PROGRAM (continued)

43. Are such professional journals as *Language Arts, The Horn Book,* and *Children's Literature in Education* available to teachers?
44. Are professional books on children's literature available in each elementary school?
45. Have the teachers and librarians had a share in planning their literature programs?
46. Do teachers feel responsible not only for teaching children to read but for helping children find joy in reading?

Evaluating the Literature Program

It is as easy to identify a school in which literature is an integral part of the curriculum as it is to recognize a home where books are loved and valued. However, since this text has not recommended any body of content that all children must learn, but rather has suggested that each school should plan its own literature program, the questions on pages 718–720 might serve as guidelines in both the planning and the evaluation stages.

The best evaluation of the impact of a literature program for today's children will be their reading habits as adults. One of the challenges of education is to teach skills, attitudes, and appreciations so that children will continue to make reading an integral part of their lives. It lies within the power of every teacher and librarian to give children a rich experience with literature. We must do more than teach children to *read*; we must help them to *become readers*, to find a lifetime of pleasure in the reading of good books. To the teacher is granted the opportunity to become the piper who leads children into the world of books. It is exciting and deeply satisfying to become such a piper, "piping down the valleys wild."

SUGGESTED LEARNING EXPERIENCES

1. Give a literature inventory to a group of children and draw some conclusions about their previous exposure to literature. Plan what you think might be a rich literature program for them.
2. Working alone or in a small group, select a book or poem and extend it through one of the suggested activities in this chapter. Bring your finished product to class and be prepared to suggest what values this activity might have for children.
3. Write something to go with the above product: a story, a poem or directions for what you did or problems faced. Mount and display your work and writing. Of what value would this follow-up in writing be for children? What other types of writing might you have done?
4. In a small group, choose a book and list scenes or opportunities for drama—interviews, debates, imaginary conversations, and so forth. Which possibilities seem to have the greatest potential for depth? Why?
5. Try an activity suggested in this chapter with children. Evaluate the children's understandings and your role in their learning. What next steps might you take?
6. Working in a small group, choose a chapter book or a picture book and suggest a variety of activities which would extend children's understanding and appreciation of the book. Be prepared to explain how each activity might extend children's thinking or enjoyment.
7. Write your own version of one of the story frames or experiment with a writing form such as a diary based on a novel you have read. What observations can you make about your own writing process? How does this inform your teaching?
8. Using the "Guide for Evaluating a Literature Program," visit an elementary school and evaluate its program. Certain members of the class could be responsible for finding the answers to certain sections of the Guide. Combine your findings in a report and make recommendations concerning the literature program of that school.

RELATED READINGS

1. Bauer, Caroline Feller. *Celebrations: Read-Aloud Holiday and Theme Book Programs.* Bronx, N.Y.: H. W. Wilson Company, 1985.

Ideas for grouping prose and poetry selections, bulletin board designs, treats, activities, and further readings are suggested for sixteen celebrations. Some of the topics are Baseball, Gone Fishin', Pigmania, Grandparents, and Nothing Day. Useful in planning thematic studies, this material is keyed to three ability levels.

2. Blatt, Gloria T., and Jean Cunningham. *It's Your Move: Expressive Movement Activities for the Language Arts Class*. New York: Teachers College, Columbia University, 1981.

   This is a helpful guide to integrating expressive movement with literature and language arts. Explicit movement lessons are provided, plus suggestions on using them in interpreting poetry and incidents from literature such as Homer Price's doughnut machine. Photographs of children doing expressive movement are included.

3. Currell, David. *Learning with Puppets*. New York: Play, Inc., 1980.

   Clear, concise directions for making all kinds of puppets—rod, glove, shadow, finger, marionette—with drawings illustrating each step. Instructions are included for presenting shows and making various kinds of stages.

4. Davies, Geoff. *Practical Primary Drama*. Portsmouth, N. H.: Heinemann, 1985.

   Written by an experienced drama teacher in the primary school, this book includes practical suggestions on how to prepare and conduct drama sessions. Various ways of starting drama are detailed, and examples from classrooms in which Davies has taught are featured in this small but useful book.

5. John, Liz, and Cecily O'Neill, eds. *Dorothy Heathcote: Collected Writings on Education and Drama*. Portsmouth, N. H.: Heinemann, 1984.

   This volume collects articles, lectures, and notes of Dorothy Heathcote, a well-known figure in the field of drama. Here she explains her pioneering approach to learning through drama and her deep commitment to the proper training of teachers. An important reference.

6. Paulin, Mary Ann. *Creative Uses of Children's Literature*. Hamden, Conn.: Library Professional Publications, 1982.

   This mammoth collection has six sections: introducing books to children, enhancing books through music, puppetry, experiencing art through picture books, and two others. Within each section books are grouped according to common themes like birthdays, various individual animals, monsters, or holidays and according to some uncommon ones: "drawings come to life," "books about the color blue," or "magic numbers." A subject index (from "Abandonment" to "Zuni Indians") and annotations for nearly 6,000 titles are included.

7. Renfro, Nancy. *Puppetry, Language, and the Special Child*. Austin, Texas: Nancy Renfro Studios, 1984.

   Featuring the works of teachers and others who have successfully implemented programs of puppetry, dance, and storytelling as a means of self-expression for children with impairments, this book includes many activities, resources, and bibliographies for those who work with special-needs children.

8. Somers, Albert B., and Janet E. Worthington. *Response Guides for Teaching Children's Books*. Urbana, Ill.: National Council of Teachers of English, 1979.

   Twenty-seven plans for integrating a book with language arts activities include summaries, initiating activities, discussion questions, and a variety of art and media, dramatic, and written extensions. Titles range from Steig's *Sylvester and the Magic Pebble* to George's *Julie of the Wolves* and additional instructional resources are noted.

9. Weiss, Harvey. *How to Make Your Own Books*. New York: Crowell, 1974.

   Both teachers and children of middle grades will want to use this book, which gives instructions for making travel journals, diaries, photo albums, scrolls, and so on. Clear directions are given for binding a variety of books.

REFERENCES[27]

Aardema, Verna. *Why Mosquitoes Buzz in People's Ears*, illustrated by Leo and Diane Dillon. Dial, 1978.

[27]All books listed at the end of this chapter are recommended, subject to the qualifications noted in the text. See Appendix C for publishers' complete addresses.

Adams, Pam. *This Old Man.* Playspaces, n. d.

Aesop. *Aesop's Fables,* illustrated by A. and M. Provensen. Golden, 1965.

Alexander, Lloyd. *The Black Cauldron.* Holt, 1965.

———. *Westmark.* Dutton, 1981.

Aliki. *Go Tell Aunt Rhody.* Macmillan, 1967.

———. *How a Book Is Made.* Crowell, 1986.

———. *Hush Little Baby.* Prentice-Hall, 1968.

Allison, Linda. *The Reasons for Seasons.* Little, Brown, 1975.

Anderson, Margaret J. *The Journey of the Shadow Bairns.* Scholastic, 1983.

Anderson, Yvonne. *Making Your Own Animated Movies.* Little, Brown, 1974.

Azarian, Mary. *A Farmer's Alphabet.* Godine, 1981.

Babbitt, Natalie. *Tuck Everlasting.* Farrar, Straus, 1975.

Bailey, Carolyn S. *The Little Rabbit Who Wanted Red Wings,* illustrated by Dorothy Grider. Platt & Munk, 1978 (1945).

Barrett, Judi. *I Hate to Go to Bed,* illustrated by Ray Cruz. Four Winds, 1977.

———. *I Hate to Take a Bath,* illustrated by Charles B. Slackman. Four Winds, 1975.

Baylor, Byrd. *Guess Who My Favorite Person Is,* illustrated by Robert Andrew Parker. Scribner, 1977.

———. *Everybody Needs a Rock,* illustrated by Peter Parnall. Scribner, 1974

———. *The Way to Start a Day,* illustrated by Peter Parnall. Scribner, 1978.

———. *Your Own Best Secret Place,* illustrated by Peter Parnell. Scribner, 1979.

Blegvad, Lenore, ed. *The Parrot in the Garret and Other Rhymes about Dwellings,* illustrated by Erik Blegvad. Atheneum, 1982.

Blume, Judy. *Superfudge.* Dutton, 1980.

Bond, Michael. *A Bear Called Paddington,* illustrated by Peggy Fortnum. Houghton Mifflin, 1960.

Bonners, Susan. *Panda.* Delacorte, 1978.

Brady, Irene. *Wild Mouse.* Scribner, 1976.

Briggs, Raymond. *Father Christmas.* Coward, 1973.

———. *Jim and the Beanstalk.* Coward, 1980.

Brown, Marcia. *Stone Soup.* Scribner, 1947.

Browne, Anthony. *Bear Hunt.* Atheneum, 1980.

Burton, Virginia Lee. *The Little House.* Houghton Mifflin, 1942.

Byars, Betsy. *The Animal, the Vegetable & John D Jones.* Delacorte, 1982.

———. *Cracker Jackson.* Viking, 1985.

———. *The 18th Emergency.* Viking, 1973.

———. *The Night Swimmers.* Delacorte, 1980.

———. *The Pinballs.* Harper, 1977.

Cartlidge, Michelle. *The Bears' Bazaar.* Lothrop, 1980.

Caudill, Rebecca. *A Pocketful of Cricket,* illustrated by Evaline Ness. Holt, 1964.

Cauley, Lorinda Bryan. *Pease Porridge Hot: A Mother Goose Cookbook.* Putnam, 1971.

Charlip, Remy. *Fortunately.* Four Winds, 1964.

Chaucer, Geoffrey. *Chanticleer and the Fox,* illustrated by Barbara Cooney. Crowell, 1982. (1958)

Cleary, Beverly. *Dear Mr. Henshaw.* Morrow, 1983.

———. *The Mouse and the Motorcycle,* illustrated by Louis Darling. Morrow, 1965.

———. *Ralph S. Mouse,* illustrated by Paul O. Zelinsky. Morrow, 1982.

———. *Ramona and Her Father,* illustrated by Alan Tiegreen. Morrow, 1977.

———. *Ramona Quimby, Age 8,* illustrated by Alan Tiegreen. Morrow, 1981.

Cleaver, Vera, and Bill Cleaver. *Where the Lilies Bloom.* Harper, 1969.

Coerr, Eleanor. *The Josefina Story Quilt,* illustrated by Bruce Degen. Harper, 1986.

———. *Sadako and the Thousand Paper Cranes,* illustrated by Ronald Himler. Putnam, 1977.

Colver, Anne. *Bread-and-Butter Journey,* illustrated by Garth Williams. Avon, 1971.

Cooney, Barbara. *The Little Juggler.* Hastings, 1961.

Crews, Donald. *Freight Train.* Greenwillow, 1978.

Dahl, Roald. *James and the Giant Peach,* illustrated by Nancy Burkert. Knopf, 1961.

de Paola, Tomie. *The Comic Adventures of Old Mother Hubbard and Her Dog.* Harcourt, 1981.

———. *Helga's Dowry.* Harcourt, 1977.

_____. *The Knight and the Dragon*. Putnam, 1980.

_____. *The Popcorn Book*. Holiday, 1978.

Domanska, Janina. *King Krakus and the Dragon*. Greenwillow, 1979.

Elkin, Benjamin. *Six Foolish Fishermen*, illustrated by Katherine Evans. Children's, 1971.

Ellison, Virginia H. *The Pooh Cookbook*. Dell, 1975.

Emberley, Ed. *Ed Emberley's Great Thumbprint Drawing Book*. Little, Brown, 1977.

Engdahl, Sylvia. *Enchantress from the Stars*. Atheneum, 1970.

Fisher, Leonard Everett. *The Railroads*. Holiday, 1979.

Flack, Marjorie. *Ask Mr.Bear*. Macmillan, 1968.

Flournoy, Valerie. *The Patchwork Quilt*, illustrated by Jerry Pinkney. Dial, 1985.

Freschet, Berniece. *The Ants Go Marching*. Scribner, 1973.

Fritz, Jean. *And Then What Happened, Paul Revere?*, illustrated by Margot Tomes. Coward, 1973.

_____. *The Cabin Faced West*, illustrated by Feodor Rojankovsky. Coward, 1958.

Gág, Wanda. *Nothing At All*. Coward, 1941.

Galdone, Paul. *The Three Bears*. Scholastic, 1973.

_____. *The Three Wishes*. McGraw-Hill, 1961.

George, Jean Craighead. *Cry of the Crow*. Harper, 1980.

_____. *My Side of the Mountain*. Dutton, 1975.

_____. *The Wild, Wild Cookbook*, illustrated by Walter Kessell. Crowell, 1982.

Ginsburg, Mirra. *The Lazies: Tales of the People of Russia*, illustrated by Marian Parry. Macmillan, 1973.

Godden, Rumer. *The Old Woman Who Lived in a Vinegar Bottle*, illustrated by Mairi Hedderwick. Viking, 1972.

Graboff, Abner. *Old MacDonald Had a Farm*. Scholastic, 1970.

Grimm Brothers. *The Devil With the Three Golden Hairs*, illustrated by Nonny Hogrogian. Knopf, 1983.

_____. *The Glass Mountain*, illustrated by Nonny Hogrogian. Knopf, 1985.

Hale, Sara Josepha. *Mary Had a Little Lamb*, illustrated by Tomie de Paola. Holiday, 1984.

Haugaard, Erik. *Hakon of Rogen's Saga*, illustrated by Leo and Diane Dillon. Houghton Mifflin, 1973.

Hayes, Geoffrey. *Bear by Himself*. Harper, 1976.

Helfman, Harry. *Making Your Own Movies*. Morrow, 1970.

Hirsh, Marilyn. *Could Anything Be Worse?* Holiday, 1974.

Hoban, Russell. *Bread and Jam for Frances*, illustrated by Lillian Hoban. Harper, 1964.

Hoberman, Mary Ann. *A House Is a House for Me*, illustrated by Betty Fraser. Penguin, 1982.

Hodges, Margaret. *Saint George and the Dragon*, illustrated by Trina Schart Hyman. Little, Brown, 1984.

_____. *The Wave*, illustrated by Blair Lent. Houghton Mifflin, 1964.

Hogrogian, Nonny. *One Fine Day*. Macmillan, 1971.

Holling, Holling C. *Paddle-to-the-Sea*. Houghton Mifflin, 1941.

Holm, Anne. *North to Freedom*. Harcourt, 1974.

Hunt, Irene. *Across Five Aprils*. Follett, 1964.

Hunter, Mollie. *The Third Eye*. Harper, 1979.

Hutchins, Pat. *Rosie's Walk*. Macmillan, 1968.

_____. *The Surprise Party*. Macmillan, 1969.

Isadora, Rachel. *City Seen from A to Z*. Greenwillow, 1983.

Jackson, Louise. *Over on the River*, illustrated by George Ancona. Lothrop, 1980.

Jeffers, Susan. *All the Pretty Little Horses*. Macmillan, 1967.

Johnson, Tony. *The Quilt Story*, illustrated by Tomie de Paola. Putnam, 1985.

Keats, Ezra Jack. *The Snowy Day*. Viking, 1962.

_____. *Dreams*. Macmillan, 1974.

_____. *Peter's Chair*. Harper, 1967.

Kellogg, Steven, *The Mysterious Tadpole*. Dial, 1977.

Kennedy, Richard. *Song of the Horse*, illustrated by Marcia Sewall. Dutton, 1981.

Key, Alexander. *The Forgotten Door*. Westminster, 1965.

Kipling, Rudyard. *The Elephant's Child*, illustrated by Lorinda B. Cauley. Harcourt, 1983.

Konigsburg, E. L. *From the Mixed-Up Files of Mrs. Basil E. Frankweiler*. Atheneum, 1967.

Langstaff, John. *Oh, A-Hunting We Will Go,* illustrated by Nancy W. Parker. Atheneum, 1974.

L'Engle, Madeleine. *A Wrinkle in Time.* Farrar, 1962.

Lent, Blair. *From King Boggen's Hall to Nothing-At-All: A Collection of Improbable Houses and Unusual Houses Found in Traditional Rhymes and Limericks.* Little, Brown, 1967.

_____. *John Tabor's Ride.* Little, Brown, 1966.

Le Guin, Ursula K. *A Wizard of Earthsea,* illustrated by Ruth Robbins. Parnassus, 1968.

Lewis, C. S. *The Lion, the Witch, and the Wardrobe,* illustrated by Pauline Baynes. Macmillan, 1968.

Lewis, Richard, ed. *In a Spring Garden,* illustrated by Ezra Jack Keats. Dial, 1976.

Lionni, Leo. *Alexander and the Wind-Up Mouse.* Pantheon, 1969.

_____. *The Biggest House in the World.* Pantheon, 1968.

_____. *Frederick.* Pantheon, 1966.

_____. *Little Blue and Little Yellow.* Astor-Honor, 1959.

_____. *Swimmy.* Pantheon, 1963.

Lobel, Arnold. *The Book of Pigericks* Harper, 1983.

_____. *Uncle Elephant.* Harper, 1981.

Lowry Lois. *Anastasia Krupnik.* Houghton Mifflin, 1981.

McGovern, Anne. *If You Lived with the Sioux Indians.* Scholastic, 1976.

MacGregor, Carol. *The Fairy Tale Cookbook,* illustrated by Debby L. Carter. Macmillan, 1982.

MacLachlan, Patricia. *Sarah, Plain and Tall.* Harper, 1985.

McKillip, Patricia. *The Riddlemaster of Hed.* Atheneum, 1976.

McNulty, Faith. *Mouse and Tim,* illustrated by Marc Simont. Harper, 1978.

McPhail, David. *Fix-It.* Dutton, 1984.

_____. *Pig Pig Grows Up.* Dutton, 1980.

Mahy, Margaret. *Ultra-Violet Catastrophe,* illustrated by Brian Froud. Parents', 1974.

Margolis, Michael. *King Grisly-Beard: A Tale From the Brothers Grimm,* illustrated by Maurice Sendak. Penguin, 1978.

Maris, Ron. *My Book.* Watts/Julia MacRae, 1983.

Martin, Bill. *Brown Bear, Brown Bear, What Do You See?* Holt, 1983.

Mazer, Norma Fox. *I, Trissy.* Delacorte, 1971.

Merrill, Jean. *The Pushcart War.* Addison-Wesley, 1964.

Musgrove, Margaret. *Ashanti to Zulu,* illustrated by Leo and Diane Dillon. Dial, 1976.

Myers, Berneice. *Sidney Rella and the Glass Sneaker.* Macmillan, 1985.

Ness, Evaline. *Sam, Bangs and Moonshine.* Holt, 1966.

Norton, Mary. *The Borrowers,* illustrated by Beth and Joe Krush. Harcourt, 1965.

O'Brien, Robert C. *Mrs. Frisby and the Rats of NIMH,* illustrated by Zena Bernstein. Atheneum, 1971.

O'Dell, Scott. *Island of the Blue Dolphins.* Houghton Mifflin, 1960.

Paterson, Katherine. *Bridge to Terabithia,* illustrated by Donna Diamond. Crowell, 1977.

_____. *Come Sing, Jimmy Jo.* Crowell, 1985.

_____. *Jacob Have I Loved.* Crowell, 1980.

_____. *The Master Puppeteer.* Crowell, 1976.

Peek, Merle. *Roll Over! A Counting Song.* Houghton Mifflin, 1981.

Peet, Bill. *How Droofus the Dragon Lost His Head.* Houghton Mifflin, 1971.

Pinkwater, Daniel M. *Slaves of Spiegel: A Magic Moscow Story.* Four Winds, 1982.

Prelutsky, Jack. *Nightmares: Poems to Trouble Your Sleep,* illustrated by Arnold Lobel. Greenwillow, 1976.

Quackenbush, Robert. *Clementine.* Harper, 1974.

_____. *Pop! Goes the Weasel and Yankee Doodle: New York in 1776 and Today with Songs and Pictures.* Harper, 1976.

_____. *Skip to My Lou.* Harper, 1975.

Richter, Hans Peter. *Friedrich.* Holt, 1970.

Rockwell, Thomas. *How to Eat Fried Worms.* Watts, 1973.

Roever, Joan M. *Snake Secrets.* Walker, 1979.

Rose, Anne. *Akimba and the Magic Cow,* illustrated by Hope Meryman. Four Winds, 1976.

Ross, Tony. *The Three Little Pigs.* Pantheon, 1983.

Roth, Susan L. *Patchwork Tales*, illustrated by Ruth Phang. Atheneum, 1984.

Roy, Ron. *Three Ducks Went Wandering*, illustrated by Paul Galdone. Houghton Mifflin, 1979.

Sanders, Scott R. *Hear the Wind Blow: American Folk Songs Retold*, illustrated by Ponder Goembel. Bradbury, 1985.

Seeger, Pete, and Charles Seeger. *The Foolish Frog*. Macmillan, 1973.

Segal, Lore. *The Story of Old Mrs. Brubeck and How She Looked for Trouble and Where She Found Him*, illustrated by Marcia Sewall. Pantheon, 1981.

Sendak, Maurice. *Chicken Soup with Rice*. Harper, 1962.

_____. *Where the Wild Things Are*. Harper, 1963.

Shulevitz, Uri. *Dawn*. Farrar, Straus, 1974.

Simon, Seymour. *Animal Fact/Animal Fable*, illustrated by Diane DeGroat. Crown, 1979.

Slobodkina, Esphyr. *Caps for Sale*. Addison-Wesley, 1947.

Speare, Elizabeth J. George. *The Sign of the Beaver*. Houghton Mifflin, 1983.

Spier, Peter. *The Erie Canal*. Doubleday, 1970.

_____. *London Bridge Is Falling Down*. Doubleday, 1967.

_____. *The Star-Spangled Banner*. Doubleday, 1973.

Stanley, Diane. *Fiddle-i-Fee*. Little, Brown, 1979.

Steig, William. *Abel's Island*. Farrar, Straus, 1976.

_____. *The Amazing Bone*. Farrar, Straus, 1976.

_____. *Amos & Boris*. Farrar, Straus, 1971.

_____. *Doctor De Soto*. Farrar, Straus, 1982.

Steptoe, John. *Stevie*. Harper, 1969.

Stevens, Carla. *Trouble for Lucy*, illustrated by Ronald Himler. Clarion, 1979.

Stevenson, James. *The Wish Card Ran Out!* Greenwillow, 1981.

Still, James. *Jack and the Wonder Beans*, illustrated by Margot Tomes. Putnam, 1977.

Thayer, Jane. *Try Your Hand*, illustrated by Joel Schick. Morrow, 1980.

Tolstoy, Alexei. *The Great Big Enormous Turnip*, illustrated by Helen Oxenbury. Watts, 1969.

Travers, P. L. *Mary Poppins*, rev. ed., illustrated by Mary Shepard. Harcourt, 1981.

Tresselt, Alvin. *It's Time Now*, illustrated by Roger Duvoisin. Lothrop, 1969.

Tunis, Edwin. *Colonial Living*. Harper, 1976.

Turkle, Brinton. *Do Not Open*. Dutton, 1981.

Van Allsburg, Chris. *The Garden of Abdul Gasazi*. Houghton Mifflin, 1979.

_____. *Jumanji*. Houghton Mifflin, 1981.

_____. *The Mysteries of Harris Burdick*. Houghton Mifflin, 1984.

Viorst, Judith. *Alexander and the Terrible, Horrible, No Good, Very Bad Day*, illustrated by Ray Cruz. Atheneum, 1972.

Wadsworth, Olive. *Over in the Meadow*, illustrated by Ezra Jack Keats. Scholastic, 1971.

Walker, Barbara. *The Little House Cookbook*, illustrated by Garth Williams. Harper, 1979.

Wescott, Nadine. *The Old Lady Who Swallowed a Fly*. Harcourt, 1980.

Wilder. Laura Ingalls. *Little House Books*, 9 volumes, illustrated by Garth Williams. Harper, 1953.

_____. *Farmer Boy*, illustrated by Garth Williams. Harper, 1953.

Wildsmith, Brian. *Birds*. Oxford, 1980.

_____. *Wild Animals*. Oxford, 1979.

Williams, Jay. *Everyone Knows What a Dragon Looks Like*, illustrated by Mercer Mayer. Four Winds, 1976.

Williams, Vera B. *A Chair for My Mother*. Greenwillow, 1982.

Winter, Jeanette. *Hush, Little Baby*. Pantheon, 1984.

Wolf, Janet. *Her Book*. Harper, 1982.

Yagawa, Sumiko. *The Crane Wife*, translated by Katherine Paterson, illustrated by Suekichi Akaba. Morrow, 1981.

Yep, Laurence. *Dragonwings*. Harper, 1977.

Zemach, Harve. *The Judge*, illustrated by Margot Zemach. Farrar, 1969.

Zemach, Margot. *It Could Always Be Worse*. Farrar, 1977.

Zion, Gene. *Harry the Dirty Dog*, illustrated by Margaret Bloy Graham. Harper, 1956.

Zolotow, Charlotte. *Someday*, illustrated by Arnold Lobel. Harper, 1965.

_____. *Say It!*, illustrated by James Stevenson. Greenwillow, 1980.

Zuromskis, Diane. *The Farmer in the Dell*. Little, Brown, 1978.

APPENDIX A **Children's Book Awards**

The **John Newbery Medal** is named in honor of John Newbery, a British publisher and bookseller of the eighteenth century. He has frequently been called the father of children's literature, since he was the first to conceive the idea of publishing books expressly for children.

The Award is presented each year to "the author of the most distinguished contribution to American literature for children." To be eligible for the award, the author must be an American citizen or a permanent resident of the United States. The selection of the winner is made by a committee of the Association for Library Service to Children of the American Library Association. There are now fifteen members on this committee. The winning author is presented with a bronze medal designed by René Paul Chambellan and donated by Frederick G. Melcher. The announcement is made in January. Later, at the summer conference of the American Library Association, a banquet is given in honor of the Award winners.

The following list of books includes the Award winners (capitalized and listed first) and the runners-up, or Honor Books, for each year. The date on the left indicates the year in which the Award was conferred. All books were necessarily published the preceding year. The name of the present publisher, if not the same as when the book was originally issued, is given in parentheses.

1922 THE STORY OF MANKIND by Hendrik Van Loon. Boni & Liveright (Liveright).
The Great Quest by Charles Boardman Hawes. Little, Brown.
Cedric the Forester by Bernard G. Marshall. Appleton.
The Old Tobacco Shop by William Bowen. Macmillan.
The Golden Fleece by Padraic Colum. Macmillan.
Windy Hill by Cornelia Meigs. Macmillan.

1923 THE VOYAGES OF DOCTOR DOLITTLE by Hugh Lofting. Stokes (Lippincott).
[No record of the runners-up.]

1924 THE DARK FRIGATE by Charles Boardman Hawes. Little, Brown.
[No record of the runners-up.]

1925 TALES FROM SILVER LANDS by Charles J. Finger. Illustrated by Paul Honoré. Doubleday.
Nicholas by Anne Carroll Moore. Putnam.
Dream Coach by Anne and Dillwyn Parrish. Macmillan.

1926 SHEN OF THE SEA by Arthur Bowie Chrisman. Illustrated by Else Hasselriis. Dutton.
The Voyagers by Padraic Colum. Macmillan.

1927 SMOKY, THE COWHORSE by Will James. Scribner.
[No record of the runners-up.]

1928 GAY NECK by Dhan Gopal Mukerji. Illustrated by Boris Artzybasheff. Dutton.
The Wonder-Smith and His Son by Ella Young. Longmans, Green (McKay).
Downright Dencey by Caroline Dale Snedeker. Doubleday.

1929 TRUMPETER OF KRAKOW by Eric P. Kelly. Illustrated by Angela Pruszynska. Macmillan.
The Pigtail of Ah Lee Ben Loo by John Bennett. Longmans, Green (McKay).

Millions of Cats by Wanda Gág. Coward-McCann.
The Boy Who Was by Grace T. Hallock. Dutton.
Clearing Weather by Cornelia Meigs. Little, Brown.
The Runaway Papoose by Grace P. Moon. Doubleday.
Tod of the Fens by Eleanor Whitney. Macmillan.

1930 HITTY, HER FIRST HUNDRED YEARS by Rachel Field. Illustrated by Dorothy P. Lathrop. Macmillan.
Pran of Albania by Elizabeth C. Miller. Doubleday.
The Jumping-Off Place by Marian Hurd McNeely. Longmans, Green (McKay).
A Daughter of the Seine by Jeanette Eaton. Harper (Harper & Row).

1931 THE CAT WHO WENT TO HEAVEN by Elizabeth Coatsworth. Illustrated by Lynd Ward. Macmillan.
Floating Island by Anne Parrish. Harper (Harper & Row).
The Dark Star of Itza by Alida Malkus. Harcourt.
Queer Person by Ralph Hubbard. Doubleday.
Mountains Are Free by Julia Davis Adams. Dutton.
Spice and the Devil's Cave by Agnes D. Hewes. Knopf.
Meggy McIntosh by Elizabeth Janet Gray. Doubleday.

1932 WATERLESS MOUNTAIN by Laura Adams Armer. Illustrated by Sidney Armer and the author. Longmans, Green (McKay).
The Fairy Circus by Dorothy Lathrop. Macmillan.
Calico Bush by Rachel Field. Macmillan.
Boy of the South Seas by Eunice Tietjens. Coward-McCann.
Out of the Flame by Eloise Lounsbery. Longmans, Green (McKay).
Jane's Island by Marjorie Hill Alee. Houghton Mifflin.
Truce of the Wolf by Mary Gould Davis. Harcourt.

1933 YOUNG FU OF THE UPPER YANGTZE by Elizabeth Foreman Lewis. Illustrated by Kurt Wiese. Winston (Holt, Rinehart and Winston).
Swift Rivers by Cornelia Meigs. Little (Little, Brown).
The Railroad to Freedom by Hildegarde Swift. Harcourt.
Children of the Soil by Nora Burglon. Doubleday.

1934 INVINCIBLE LOUISA by Cornelia Meigs. Little, Brown.
Forgotten Daughter by Caroline Dale Snedeker. Doubleday.
Swords of Steel by Elsie Singmaster. Houghton Mifflin.
ABC Bunny by Wanda Gág. Coward-McCann.
Winged Girl of Knossos by Erick Berry. Appleton.
New Land by Sarah L. Schmidt. McBride.
Apprentices of Florence by Anne Kyle. Houghton Mifflin.

1935 DOBRY by Monica Shannon. Illustrated by Atanas Katchamakoff. Viking.
The Pageant of Chinese History by Elizabeth Seeger. Longmans, Green (McKay).
Davy Crockett by Constance Rourke. Harcourt.
A Day on Skates by Hilda Van Stockum. Harper (Harper & Row).

1936 CADDIE WOODLAWN by Carol Ryrie Brink. Illustrated by Kate Seredy. Macmillan.
Honk the Moose by Phil Stong. Dodd, Mead.

The Good Master by Kate Seredy. Viking.

Young Walter Scott Elizabeth Janet Gray. Viking.

All Sail Set by Armstrong Sperry. Winston (Holt, Rinehart and Winston).

1937 ROLLER SKATES by Ruth Sawyer. Illustrated by Valenti Angelo. Viking.

Phoebe Fairchild: Her Book by Lois Lenski. Stokes (Lippincott).

Whistler's Van by Idwal Jones. Viking.

The Golden Basket by Ludwig Bemelmans. Viking.

Winterbound by Margery Bianco. Viking.

Audubon by Constance Rourke. Harcourt.

The Codfish Musket by Agnes D. Hewes. Doubleday.

1938 THE WHITE STAG by Kate Seredy. Viking.

Bright Island by Mabel L. Robinson. Random House.

Pecos Bill by James Cloyd Bowman. Whitman.

On the Banks of Plum Creek by Laura Ingalls Wilder. Harper (Harper & Row).

1939 THIMBLE SUMMER by Elizabeth Enright. Farrar & Rinehart (Holt, Rinehart and Winston).

Leader by Destiny by Jeanette Eaton. Harcourt.

Penn by Elizabeth Janet Gray. Viking.

Nino by Valenti Angelo. Viking.

"Hello, the Boat!" by Phyllis Crawford. Holt (Holt, Rinehart & Winston).

Mr. Popper's Penguins by Richard and Florence Atwater. Little, Brown.

1940 DANIEL BOONE by James H. Daugherty. Viking.

The Singing Tree by Kate Seredy. Viking.

Runner of the Mountain Tops by Mabel L. Robinson. Random House.

By the Shores of Silver Lake by Laura Ingalls Wilder. Harper (Harper & Row).

Boy with a Pack by Stephen W. Meader. Harcourt.

1941 CALL IT COURAGE by Armstrong Sperry. Macmillan.

Blue Willow by Doris Gates. Viking.

Young Mac of Fort Vancouver by Mary Jane Carr. Crowell.

The Long Winter by Laura Ingalls Wilder. Harper (Harper & Row).

Nansen by Anna Gertrude Hall. Viking.

1942 THE MATCHLOCK GUN by Walter D. Edmonds. Illustrated by Paul Lantz. Dodd, Mead.

Little Town on the Prairie by Laura Ingalls Wilder. Harper (Harper & Row).

George Washington's World by G. Foster. Scribner.

Indian Captive by Lois Lenski. Stokes (Lippincott).

Down Ryton Water by E. R. Gaggin. Viking.

1943 ADAM OF THE ROAD by Elizabeth Janet Gray. Illustrated by Robert Lawson. Viking.

The Middle Moffat by Eleanor Estes. Harcourt.

"Have You Seen Tom Thumb?" by Mabel Leigh Hunt. Stokes (Lippincott).

1944 JOHNNY TREMAIN by Esther Forbes. Illustrated by Lynd Ward. Houghton Mifflin.

These Happy Golden Years by Laura Ingalls Wilder. Harper (Harper & Row).

Fog Magic by Julia L. Sauer. Viking.

Rufus M. by Eleanor Estes. Harcourt.

Mountain Born by Elizabeth Yates. Coward-McCann.

1945 RABBIT HILL by Robert Lawson. Viking.

The Hundred Dresses by Eleanor Estes. Harcourt.

The Silver Pencil by Alice Dalgliesh. Scribner.

Abraham Lincoln's World by Genevieve Foster. Scribner.

Lone Journey by Jeanette Eaton. Harcourt.

1946 STRAWBERRY GIRL by Lois Lenski. Lippincott.

Justin Morgan Had a Horse by Marguerite Henry. Wilcox & Follett (Follett).

The Moved-Outers by Florence Crannell Means. Houghton Mifflin.

Bhimsa, the Dancing Bear by Christine Weston. Scribner.

New Found World by Katherine B. Shippen. Viking.

1947 MISS HICKORY by Carolyn Sherwin Bailey. Illustrated by Ruth Gannett. Viking.

The Wonderful Year by Nancy Barnes. Messner.

Big Tree by Mary Buff and Conrad Buff. Viking.

The Heavenly Tenants by William Maxwell. Harper (Harper & Row).

The Avion My Uncle Flew by Cyrus Fisher. Appleton.

The Hidden Treasure of Glaston by Eleanore M. Jewett. Viking.

1948 THE TWENTY-ONE BALLOONS by William Pène du Bois. Viking.

Pancakes-Paris by Claire Huchet Bishop. Viking.

Li Lun, Lad of Courage by Carolyn Treffinger. Abingdon-Cokesbury (Abingdon).

The Quaint and Curious Quest of Johnny Longfoot by Catherine Besterman. Bobbs-Merrill.

The Cow-Tail Switch by Harold Courlander and George Herzog. Holt (Holt, Rinehart and Winston).

Misty of Chincoteague by Marguerite Henry. Rand McNally.

1949 KING OF THE WIND by Marguerite Henry. Illustrated by Wesley Dennis. Rand McNally.

Seabird by Holling Clancy Holling. Houghton Mifflin.

Daughter of the Mountains by Louise Rankin. Viking.

My Father's Dragon by Ruth S. Gannett. Random House.

Story of the Negro by Arna Bontemps. Knopf.

1950 THE DOOR IN THE WALL by Marguerite de Angeli. Doubleday.

Tree of Freedom by Rebecca Caudill. Viking.

Blue Cat of Castle Town by Catherine Coblentz. Longmans, Green (McKay).

Kildee House by Rutherford Montgomery. Doubleday.

George Washington by Genevieve Foster. Scribner.

Song of the Pines by Walter Havighurst and Marion Havighurst. Winston (Holt, Rinehart and Winston).

1951 AMOS FORTUNE, FREE MAN by Elizabeth Yates. Illustrated by Nora Unwin. Aladdin (Dutton).

Better Known as Johnny Appleseed by Mabel Leigh Hunt. Lippincott.

Gandhi, Fighter without a Sword by Jeanette Eaton. Morrow.

Abraham Lincoln, Friend of the People by Clara I. Judson. Wilcox & Follett (Follett).

The Story of Appleby Capple by Anne Parrish. Harper (Harper & Row).

1952 GINGER PYE by Eleanor Estes. Harcourt.

Americans before Columbus by Elizabeth Chesley Baity. Viking.

Minn of the Mississippi by Holling Clancy Holling. Houghton Mifflin.

The Defender by Nicholas Kalashnikoff. Scribner.

The Light at Tern Rock by Julia L. Sauer. Viking.

The Apple and the Arrow by Mary Buff. Houghton Mifflin.

1953 SECRET OF THE ANDES by Ann Nolan Clark. Illustrated by Jean Charlot. Viking.

Charlotte's Web by E. B. White. Harper (Harper & Row).

Moccasin Trail by Eloise J. McGraw. Coward-McCann.

Red Sails for Capri by Ann Weil. Viking.

The Bears on Hemlock Mountain by Alice Dalgliesh. Scribner.

Birthdays of Freedom by Genevieve Foster. Scribner.

1954 AND NOW MIGUEL by Joseph Krumgold. Illustrated by Jean Charlot. Crowell.

All Alone by Clarie Huchet Bishop. Viking.

Shadrach by Meindert DeJong. Harper (Harper & Row).

Hurry Home, Candy by Meindert DeJong. Harper (Harper & Row).

Theodore Roosevelt, Fighting Patriot by Clara I. Judson. Follett.

Magic Maize by Mary Buff. Houghton Mifflin.

1955 THE WHEEL ON THE SCHOOL by Meindert DeJong. Illustrated by Maurice Sendak. Harper (Harper & Row).

The Courage of Sarah Noble by Alice Dalgliesh. Scribner.

Banner in the Sky by James Ramsey Ullman. Lippincott.

1956 CARRY ON, MR. BOWDITCH by Jean Lee Latham. Houghton Mifflin.

The Golden Name Day by Jennie D. Lindquist. Harper (Harper & Row).

The Secret River by Marjorie Kinnan Rawlings. Scribner.

Men, Microscopes and Living Things by Katherine B. Shippen. Viking.

1957 MIRACLES ON MAPLE HILL by Virginia Sorensen. Illustrated by Beth Krush and Joe Krush. Harcourt.

Old Yeller by Fred Gipson. Harper (Harper & Row).

The House of Sixty Fathers by Meindert DeJong. Harper (Harper & Row).

Mr. Justice Holmes by Clara I. Judson. Follett.

The Corn Grows Ripe by Dorothy Rhoads. Viking.

The Black Fox of Lorne by Marguerite de Angeli. Doubleday.

1958 RIFLES FOR WATIE by Harold Keith. Illustrated by Peter Burchard. Crowell.

The Horsecatcher by Mari Sandoz. Westminster.

Gone-away Lake by Elizabeth Enright. Harcourt.

The Great Wheel by Robert Lawson. Viking.

Tom Paine, Freedom's Apostle by Leo Gurko. Crowell.

1959 THE WITCH OF BLACKBIRD POND by Elizabeth George Speare. Houghton Mifflin.

The Family under the Bridge by Natalie S. Carlson. Harper (Harper & Row).

Along Came a Dog by Meindert DeJong. Harper (Harper & Row).

Chucaro by Francis Kalnay. Harcourt.

The Perilous Road by William O. Steele. Harcourt.

1960 ONION JOHN by Joseph Krumgold. Illustrated by Symeon Shimin. Crowell.

My Side of the Mountain by Jean George. Dutton.

America Is Born by Gerald Johnson. Morrow.

The Gammage Cup by Carol Kendall. Harcourt.

1961 ISLAND OF THE BLUE DOLPHINS by Scott O'Dell. Houghton Mifflin.

America Moves Forward by Gerald Johnson. Morrow.

Old Ramon by Jack Schaefer. Houghton Mifflin.

The Cricket in Times Square by George Selden. Farrar (Farrar, Straus).

1962 THE BRONZE BOW by Elizabeth George Speare. Houghton Mifflin.

Frontier Living by Edwin Tunis. World Publishing.

The Golden Goblet by Eloise J. McGraw. Coward-McCann.

Belling the Tiger by Mary Stolz. Harper & Row.

1963 A WRINKLE IN TIME by Madeleine L'Engle. Farrar (Farrar, Straus).

Thistle and Thyme by Sorche Nic Leodhas. Holt, Rinehart and Winston.

Men of Athens by Olivia Coolidge. Houghton Mifflin.

1964 IT'S LIKE THIS, CAT by Emily Neville. Illustrated by Emil Weiss. Harper & Row.

Rascal by Sterling North. Dutton.

The Loner by Ester Wier. McKay.

1965 SHADOW OF A BULL by Maia Wojciechowska. Illustrated by Alvin Smith. Atheneum.

Across Five Aprils by Irene Hunt. Follett.

1966 I, JUAN DE PAREJA by Elizabeth Borten de Treviño. Farrar, Straus.

The Black Cauldron by Lloyd Alexander. Holt, Rinehart and Winston.

The Animal Family by Randall Jarrell. Pantheon.

The Noonday Friends by Mary Stolz. Harper & Row.

1967 UP A ROAD SLOWLY by Irene Hunt. Follett.

The King's Fifth by Scott O'Dell. Houghton Mifflin.

Zlateh the Goat and Other Stories by Isaac Bashevis Singer. Harper & Row.

The Jazz Man by Mary Hays Weik. Atheneum.

1968 FROM THE MIXED-UP FILES OF MRS. BASIL E. FRANKWEILER by E. L. Konigsburg. Atheneum.

Jennifer, Hecate, Macbeth, William McKinley, and Me, Elizabeth by E. L. Konigsburg. Atheneum.

The Black Pearl by Scott O'Dell. Houghton Mifflin.

The Fearsome Inn by Isaac Bashevis Singer. Scribner.

The Egypt Game by Zilpha Keatley Snyder. Atheneum.

1969 THE HIGH KING by Lloyd Alexander. Holt, Rinehart and Winston.

To Be a Slave by Julius Lester. Dial.

When Shlemiel Went to Warsaw and Other Stories by Isaac Bashevis Singer. Farrar, Straus.

1970 SOUNDER by William H. Armstrong. Harper & Row.

Our Eddie by Sulamith Ish-Kishor. Pantheon.

The Many Ways of Seeing: An Introduction to the Pleasures of Art by Janet Gaylord Moore. World.

Journey Outside by Mary Q. Steele. Viking.

1971 SUMMER OF THE SWANS by Betsy Byars. Viking.

Kneeknock Rise by Natalie Babbitt. Farrar, Straus.

Enchantress from the Stars by Sylvia Louise Engdahl. Atheneum.

Sing Down the Moon by Scott O'Dell. Houghton Mifflin.

1972 MRS. FRISBY AND THE RATS ON NIMH by Robert C. O'Brien. Atheneum.

Incident at Hawk's Hill by Allan W. Eckert. Little, Brown.

The Planet of Junior Brown by Virginia Hamilton. Macmillan.

The Tombs of Atuan by Ursula K. LeGuin. Atheneum.

Annie and the Old One by Miska Miles. Atlantic-Little, Brown.

The Headless Cupid by Zilpha Keatley Snyder. Atheneum.

1973 JULIE OF THE WOLVES by Jean Craighead George. Harper & Row.

Frog and Toad Together by Arnold Lobel. Harper & Row.
The Upstairs Room by Johanna Reiss. Crowell.
The Witches of Worm by Zilpha Keatley Snyder. Atheneum.

1974 THE SLAVE DANCER by Paula Fox. Bradbury.
The Dark Is Rising by Susan Cooper. Atheneum.

1975 M. C. HIGGINS THE GREAT by Virginia Hamilton. Macmillan.
My Brother Sam Is Dead by James Collier and Christopher Collier. Four Winds.
Philip Hall Likes Me. I Reckon Maybe. by Bette Greene. Dial.
The Perilous Gard by Elizabeth Pope. Houghton Mifflin.
Figgs & Phantoms by Ellen Raskin. Dutton.

1976 THE GREY KING by Susan Cooper. Atheneum.
Dragonwings by Laurence Yep. Harper & Row.
The Hundred Penny Box by Sharon Mathis. Viking.

1977 ROLL OF THUNDER, HEAR MY CRY by Mildred D. Taylor. Dial.
Abel's Island by William Steig. Farrar, Straus.
A String in the Harp by Nancy Bond. Atheneum.

1978 BRIDGE TO TERABITHIA by Katherine Paterson. Crowell.
Anpao: An American Indian Odyssey by Jamake Highwater. Lippincott.
Ramona and Her Father by Beverly Cleary. Morrow.

1979 THE WESTING GAME by Ellen Raskin. Dutton.
The Great Gilly Hopkins by Katherine Paterson. Crowell.

1980 A GATHERING OF DAYS: A NEW ENGLAND GIRL'S JOURNAL, 1830–32 by Joan W. Blos. Scribner.
The Road from Home: The Story of an American Girl by David Kherdian. Greenwillow.

1981 JACOB HAVE I LOVED by Katherine Paterson. Crowell.
The Fledgling by Jane Langton. Harper & Row.
Ring of Endless Light by Madeleine L'Engle. Farrar, Straus.

1982 A VISIT TO WILLIAM BLAKE'S INN: POEMS FOR INNOCENT AND EXPERIENCED TRAVELERS by Nancy Willard. Illustrated by Alice and Martin Provensen. Harcourt Brace Jovanovich.
Ramona Quimby, Age 8 by Beverly Cleary. Morrow.
Upon the Head of the Goat: A Childhood in Hungary, 1939–1944 by Aranka Siegal. Farrar, Straus.

1983 DICEY'S SONG by Cynthis Voigt. Atheneum.
The Blue Sword by Robin McKinley. Greenwillow.
Doctor De Soto by William Steig. Farrar, Straus.
Graven Images by Paul Fleischman. Harper & Row.
Homesick: My Own Story by Jean Fritz. Putnam.
Sweet Whispers, Brother Rush by Virginia Hamilton. Philomel.

1984 DEAR MR. HENSHAW by Beverly Cleary. Morrow.
The Wish-Giver by Bill Brittain. Harper & Row.
A Solitary Blue by Cynthia Voigt. Atheneum.
The Sign of the Beaver by Elizabeth George Speare. Houghton Mifflin.
Sugaring Time by Kathryn Lasky. Photographs by Christopher Knight. Macmillan.

1985 THE HERO AND THE CROWN by Robin McKinley. Greenwillow.
The Moves Make the Man by Bruce Brooks. Harper & Row.
One-Eyed Cat by Paula Fox. Bradbury.
Like Jake and Me by Mavis Jukes. Illustrated by Lloyd Bloom. Knopf.

1986 SARAH, PLAIN AND TALL by Patricia MacLachlan. Harper & Row.
Commodore Perry in the Land of the Shogun by Rhoda Blumberg. Lothrop.
Dogsong by Gary Paulson. Bradbury.

1987 THE WHIPPING BOY by Sid Fleischman. Greenwillow.
A Fine White Dust by Cynthia Rylant. Bradbury.
On My Honor by Marion Bauer. Clarion.
Volcano by Patricia Lauber. Bradbury.

The Caldecott Medal is named in honor of Randolph Caldecott, a prominent English illustrator of children's books during the nineteenth century. This Award is presented each year to "the artist of the most distinguished American picture book for children." The following list of books includes the Award winners and Honor Books for each year. If the illustrator's name is not cited, it means the author illustrated the book.

1938 ANIMALS OF THE BIBLE, A PICTURE BOOK. Text selected from the King James Bible by Helen Dean Fish. Illustrated by Dorothy O. Lathrop. Stokes (Lippincott).
Seven Simeons by Boris Artzybasheff. Viking.
Four and Twenty Blackbirds compiled by Helen Dean Fish. Illustrated by Robert Lawson. Stokes (Lippincott).

1939 MEI LI by Thomas Handforth. Doubleday.
The Forest Pool by Laura Adams Armer. Longmans, Green (McKay).
Wee Gillis by Munro Leaf. Illustrated by Robert Lawson. Viking.
Snow White and the Seven Dwarfs translated and illustrated by Wanda Gág. Coward-McCann.
Barkis by Clare Turlay Newberry. Harper (Harper & Row).
Andy and the Lion by James Daugherty. Viking.

1940 ABRAHAM LINCOLN by Ingri d'Aulaire and Edgar Parin d'Aulaire. Doubleday.
Cock-a-Doodle-Doo by Berta Hader and Elmer Hader. Macmillan.
Madeline by Ludwig Bemelmans. Simon and Schuster.
The Ageless Story by Lauren Ford. Dodd, Mead.

1941 THEY WERE STRONG AND GOOD by Robert Lawson. Viking.
April's Kittens by Clare Turlay Newberry. Harper (Harper & Row).

1942 MAKE WAY FOR DUCKLINGS by Robert McCloskey. Viking.
An American ABC by Maud Petersham and Miska Petersham. Macmillan.
In My Mother's House by Ann Nolan Clark. Illustrated by Velino Herrera. Viking.
Paddle-to-the-Sea by Holling Clancy Holling. Houghton Mifflin.
Nothing at All by Wanda Gág. Coward-McCann.

1943 THE LITTLE HOUSE by Virginia Lee Burton. Houghton Mifflin.
Dash and Dart by Mary Buff and Conrad Buff. Viking.
Marshmallow by Clare Turlay Newberry. Harper (Harper & Row).

1944 MANY MOONS by James Thurber. Illustrated by Louis Slobodkin. Harcourt.
Small Rain. Text arranged from the Bible by Jessie Orton Jones. Illustrated by Elizabeth Orton Jones. Viking.
Pierre Pidgeon by Lee Kingman. Illustrated by Arnold Edwin Bare. Houghton Mifflin.

Good-Luck Horse by Chih-Yi Chan. Illustrated by Plato Chan. Whittlesey.
Mighty Hunter by Berta Hader and Elmer Hader. Macmillan.
A Child's Good Night Book by Margaret Wise Brown. Illustrated by Jean Charlot. W. R. Scott.

1945 PRAYER FOR A CHILD by Rachel Field. Pictures by Elizabeth Orton Jones. Macmillan.
Mother Goose. Compiled and illustrated by Tasha Tudor. Oxford.
In the Forest by Marie Hall Ets. Viking.
Yonie Wondernose by Marguerite de Angeli. Doubleday.
The Christmas Anna Angel by Ruth Sawyer. Illustrated by Kate Seredy. Viking.

1946 THE ROOSTER CROWS by Maud Petersham and Miska Petersham. Macmillan.
Little Lost Lamb by Margaret Wise Brown. Illustrated by Leonard Weisgard. Doubleday.
Sing Mother Goose. Music by Opal Wheeler. Illustrated by Marjorie Torrey. Dutton.
My Mother Is the Most Beautiful Woman in the World by Becky Reyher. Illustrated by Ruth C. Gannett. Lothrop.
You Can Write Chinese by Kurt Wiese. Viking.

1947 THE LITTLE ISLAND by Golden MacDonald. Illustrated by Leonard Weisgard. Doubleday.
Rain Drop Splash by Alvin R. Tresselt. Illustrated by Leonard Weisgard. Lothrop.
Boats on the River by Marjorie Flack. Illustrated by Jay Hyde Barnum. Viking.
Timothy Turtle by Al Graham. Illustrated by Tony Palazzo. Robert Welch (Viking).
Pedro, Angel of Olvera Street by Leo Politi. Scribner.
Sing in Praise by Opal Wheeler. Illustrated by Marjorie Torrey. Dutton.

1948 WHITE SNOW, BRIGHT SNOW by Alvin Tresselt. Illustrated by Roger Duvoisin. Lothrop.
Stone Soup. Told and illustrated by Marcia Brown. Scribner.
McElligot's Pool by Theodor S. Geisel (Dr. Seuss). Random House.
Bambino the Clown by George Schreiber. Viking.
Roger and the Fox by Lavinia R. Davis. Illustrated by Hildegard Woodward. Doubleday.
Song of Robin Hood. Anne Malcolmson, ed. Illustrated by Virginia Lee Burton. Houghton Mifflin.

1949 THE BIG SNOW by Berta Hader and Elmer Hader. Macmillan.
Blueberries for Sal by Robert McCloskey. Viking.
All around the Town by Phyllis McGinley. Illustrated by Helen Stone. Lippincott.
Juanita by Leo Politi. Scribner.
Fish in the Air by Kurt Wiese. Viking.

1950 SONG OF THE SWALLOWS by Leo Politi. Scribner.
America's Ethan Allen by Stewart Holbrook. Illustrated by Lynd Ward. Houghton Mifflin.
The Wild Birthday Cake by Lavinia R. Davis. Illustrated by Hildegard Woodward. Doubleday.
Happy Day by Ruth Krauss. Illustrated by Marc Simont. Harper (Harper & Row).
Henry-Fisherman by Marcia Brown. Scribner.
Bartholomew and the Oobleck by Theodor S. Geisel (Dr. Seuss). Random House.

1951 THE EGG TREE by Katherine Milhous. Scribner.
Dick Whittington and His Cat told and illustrated by Marcia Brown. Scribner.

The Two Reds by Will (William Lipkind). Illustrated by Nicolas (Mordvinoff). Harcourt.
If I Ran the Zoo by Theodor S. Geisel (Dr. Seuss). Random House.
T-Bone the Baby-Sitter by Clare Turlay Newberry. Harper (Harper & Row).
The Most Wonderful Doll in the World by Phyllis McGinley. Illustrated by Helen Stone. Lippincott.

1952 FINDERS KEEPERS by Will (William Lipkind). Illustrated by Nicolas (Mordvinoff). Harcourt.
Mr. T. W. Anthony Woo by Marie Hall Ets. Viking.
Skipper John's Cook by Marcia Brown. Scribner.
All Falling Down by Gene Zion. Illustrated by Margaret Bloy Graham. Harper (Harper & Row).
Bear Party by William Pène du Bois. Viking.
Feather Mountain by Elizabeth Olds. Houghton Mifflin.

1953 THE BIGGEST BEAR by Lynd Ward. Houghton Mifflin.
Puss in Boots. Told and illustrated by Marcia Brown. Scribner.
One Morning in Maine by Robert McCloskey. Viking.
Ape in a Cape by Fritz Eichenberg. Harcourt.
The Storm Book by Charlotte Zolotow. Illustrated by Margaret Bloy Graham. Harper (Harper & Row).
Five Little Monkeys by Juliet Kepes. Houghton Mifflin.

1954 MADELINE'S RESCUE by Ludwig Bemelmans. Viking.
Journey Cake, Ho! by Ruth Sawyer. Illustrated by Robert McCloskey. Viking.
When Will the World Be Mine? by Miriam Schlein. Illustrated by Jean Charlot. W. R. Scott.
The Steadfast Tin Soldier translated by M. R. James. Adapted from Hans Christian Andersen. Illustrated by Marcia Brown. Scribner.
A Very Special House by Ruth Krauss. Harper (Harper & Row).
Green Eyes by Abe Birnbaum. Capitol.

1955 CINDERELLA by Charles Perrault. Illustrated by Marcia Brown. Harper (Harper & Row).
Book of Nursery and Mother Goose Rhymes. Compiled and illustrated by Marguerite de Angeli. Doubleday.
Wheel on the Chimney by Margaret Wise Brown. Illustrated by Tibor Gergely. Lippincott.

1956 FROG WENT A-COURTIN' by John Langstaff. Illustrated by Feodor Rojankovsky. Harcourt.
Play with Me by Marie Hall Ets. Viking.
Crow Boy by Taro Yashima. Viking.

1957 A TREE IS NICE by Janice May Udry. Illustrated by Marc Simont. Harper (Harper & Row).
Mr. Penny's Race Horse by Marie Hall Ets. Viking.
1 Is One by Tasha Tudor. Oxford (Walck).
Anatole by Eve Titus. Illustrated by Paul Galdone. Whittlesey (McGraw).
Gillespie and the Guards by Benjamin Elkin. Illustrated by James Daugherty. Viking.
Lion by William Pène du Bois. Viking.

1958 TIME OF WONDER by Robert McCloskey. Viking.
Fly High, Fly Low by Don Freeman. Viking.
Anatole and the Cat by Eve Titus. Illustrated by Paul Galdone. Whittlesey (McGraw).

1959 CHANTICLEER AND THE FOX. Edited and illustrated by Barbara Cooney. Crowell.
The House That Jack Built by Antonio Frasconi. Crowell.
What Do You Say, Dear? by Sesyle Joslin. Illustrated by Maurice Sendak. W. R. Scott.
Umbrella by Taro Yashima. Viking.

1960 NINE DAYS TO CHRISTMAS by Marie Hall Ets and Aurora Labastida. Viking.
Houses from the Sea by Alice E. Goudey. Illustrated by Adrienne Adams. Scribner.
The Moon Jumpers by Janice May Udry. Illustrated by Maurice Sendak. Harper (Harper & Row).

1961 BABOUSHKA AND THE THREE KINGS by Ruth Robbins. Illustrated by Nicolas Sidjakov. Parnassus.
Inch by Inch by Leo Lionni. Obolensky.

1962 ONCE A MOUSE by Marcia Brown. Scribner.
The Fox Went Out on a Chilly Night by Peter Spier. Doubleday.
Little Bear's Visit by Else Minarik. Illustrated by Maurice Sendak. Harper (Harper & Row).
The Day We Saw the Sun Come Up by Alice Goudey. Illustrated by Adrienne Adams. Scribner.

1963 THE SNOWY DAY by Ezra Jack Keats. Viking.
The Sun Is a Golden Earring by Natalia Belting. Illustrated by Bernarda Bryson. Holt, Rinehart and Winston.
Mr. Rabbit and the Lovely Present by Charlotte Zolotow. Illustrated by Maurice Sendak. Harper & Row.

1964 WHERE THE WILD THINGS ARE by Maurice Sendak. Harper & Row.
Swimmy by Leo Lionni. Pantheon.
All in the Morning Early by Sorche Nic Leodhas. Illustrated by Evaline Ness. Holt, Rinehart and Winston.
Mother Goose and Nursery Rhymes by Philip Reed. Atheneum.

1965 MAY I BRING A FRIEND? by Beatrice Schenk de Regniers. Illustrated by Beni Montresor. Atheneum.
Rain Makes Applesauce by Julian Scheer. Illustrated by Marvin Bileck. Holiday.
The Wave by Margaret Hodges. Illustrated by Blair Lent. Houghton Mifflin.
A Pocketful of Cricket by Rebecca Caudill. Illustrated by Evaline Ness. Holt, Rinehart and Winston.

1966 ALWAYS ROOM FOR ONE MORE by Sorche Nic Leodhas. Illustrated by Nonny Hogrogian. Holt, Rinehart and Winston.
Hide and Seek Fog by Alvin Tresselt. Illustrated by Roger Duvoisin. Lothrop.
Just Me by Marie Hall Ets. Viking.
Tom Tit Tot. Joseph Jacobs, ed. Illustrated by Evaline Ness. Scribner.

1967 SAM, BANGS AND MOONSHINE by Evaline Ness. Holt, Rinehart and Winston.
One Wide River to Cross by Barbara Emberley. Illustrated by Ed Emberley. Prentice-Hall.

1968 DRUMMER HOFF by Barbara Emberley. Illustrated by Ed Emberley. Prentice-Hall.
Frederick by Leo Lionni. Pantheon.
Seashore Story by Taro Yashima. Viking.
The Emperor and the Kite by Jane Yolen. Illustrated by Ed Young. World Publishing.

1969 THE FOOL OF THE WORLD AND THE FLYING SHIP by Arthur Ransome. Illustrated by Uri Shulevitz. Farrar, Straus.
Why the Sun and the Moon Live in the Sky by Elphinstone Dayrell. Illustrated by Blair Lent. Houghton Mifflin.

1970 SYLVESTER AND THE MAGIC PEBBLE by William Steig. Windmill/Simon and Schuster.
Goggles by Ezra Jack Keats. Macmillan.
Alexander and the Wind-up Mouse by Leo Lionni. Pantheon.
Pop Corn and Ma Goodness by Edna Mitchell Preston.

Illustrated by Robert Andrew Parker. Viking.
Thy Friend, Obadiah by Brinton Turkle. Viking.
The Judge by Harve Zemach. Illustrated by Margot Zemach. Farrar, Straus.

1971 A STORY, A STORY by Gail E. Haley. Atheneum.
The Angry Moon by William Sleator. Illustrated by Blair Lent. Atlantic-Little, Brown.
Frog and Toad Are Friends by Arnold Lobel. Harper & Row.
In the Night Kitchen by Maurice Sendak. Harper & Row.

1972 ONE FINE DAY by Nonny Hogrogian. Macmillan.
If All the Seas Were One Sea by Janina Domanska. Macmillan.
Moja Means One: Swahili Counting Book by Muriel Feelings. Illustrated by Tom Feelings. Dial.
Hildilid's Night by Cheli Duran Ryan. Illustrated by Arnold Lobel. Macmillan.

1973 THE FUNNY LITTLE WOMAN by Arlene Mosel. Illustrated by Blair Lent. Dutton.
Hosie's Alphabet by Hosea Baskin, Tobias Baskin, and Lisa Baskin. Illustrated by Leonard Baskin. Viking.
When Clay Sings by Byrd Baylor. Illustrated by Tom Bahti. Scribner.
Snow-White and the Seven Dwarfs by the Brothers Grimm, translated by Randall Jarrell. Illustrated by Nancy Ekholm Burkert. Farrar, Straus.
Anansi the Spider by Gerald McDermott. Holt, Rinehart and Winston.

1974 DUFFY AND THE DEVIL by Harve Zemach. Illustrated by Margot Zemach. Farrar, Straus.
The Three Jovial Huntsmen by Susan Jeffers. Bradbury.
Cathedral by David Macaulay. Houghton Mifflin.

1975 ARROW TO THE SUN. Adapted and illustrated by Gerald McDermott. Viking.
Jambo Means Hello: Swahili Alphabet Book by Muriel Feelings. Illustrated by Tom Feelings. Dial.

1976 WHY MOSQUITOES BUZZ IN PEOPLE'S EARS by Verna Aardema. Illustrated by Leo and Diane Dillon. Dial.
The Desert Is Theirs by Byrd Baylor. Illustrated by Peter Parnell. Scribner.
Strega Nona retold and illustrated by Tomie de Paola.

1977 ASHANTI TO ZULU: AFRICAN TRADITIONS by Margaret Musgrove. Illustrated by Leo and Diane Dillon. Dial.
The Amazing Bone by William Steig. Farrar, Straus.
The Contest by Nonny Hogrogian. Greenwillow.
Fish for Supper by M. B. Goffstein. Dial.
The Golem by Beverly Brodsky McDermott. Lippincott.
Hawk, I'm Your Brother by Byrd Baylor. Illustrated by Peter Parnall. Scribner.

1978 NOAH'S ARK by Peter Spier. Doubleday.
Castle by David Macaulay. Houghton.
It Could Always Be Worse by Margot Zemach. Farrar, Straus.

1979 THE GIRL WHO LOVED WILD HORSES by Paul Goble. Bradbury.
Freight Train by Donald Crews. Greenwillow.
The Way to Start a Day by Byrd Baylor. Illustrated by Peter Parnall. Scribner's.

1980 OX-CART MAN by Donald Hall. Illustrated by Barbara Cooney. Viking.
Ben's Trumpet by Rachel Isadora. Greenwillow.
The Treasure by Uri Shulevitz. Farrar Straus.
The Garden of Abdul Gasazi by Chris Van Allsburg. Houghton Mifflin.

1981 FABLES by Arnold Lobel. Harper & Row.

The Bremen-Town Musicians by Ilse Plume. Doubleday.

The Grey Lady and the Strawberry Snatcher by Molly Bang. Four Winds.

Mice Twice by Joseph Low. Atheneum.

Truck by Donald Crews. Greenwillow.

1982 JUMANJI by Chris Van Allsburg. Houghton Mifflin.

A Visit to William Blake's Inn: Poems for Innocent and Experienced Travelers by Nancy Willard. Illustrated by Alice and Martin Provensen. Harcourt Brace Jovanovich.

Where the Buffaloes Began by Olaf Baker. Illustrated by Stephen Gammell. Warne.

On Market Street by Arnold Lobel. Illustrated by Anita Lobel. Greenwillow.

Outside Over There by Maurice Sendak. Harper & Row.

1983 SHADOW by Blaise Cendrars. Illustrated by Marcia Brown. Scribner's.

When I Was Young in the Mountains by Cynthia Rylant. Illustrated by Diane Goode. Dutton.

A Chair for My Mother by Vera B. Williams. Morrow.

1984 THE GLORIOUS FLIGHT: ACROSS THE CHANNEL WITH LOUIS BLERIOT, JULY 25, 1909 by Alice and Martin Provensen. Viking.

Ten, Nine, Eight by Molly Bang. Greenwillow.

Little Red Riding Hood by Trina Schart Hyman. Holiday.

1985 SAINT GEORGE AND THE DRAGON adapted by Margaret Hodges. Illustrated by Trina Schart Hyman. Little, Brown.

Hansel and Gretel by Rika Lesser. Illustrated by Paul O. Zelinsky. Dodd.

The Story of Jumping Mouse by John Steptoe. Lothrop.

Have You Seen My Duckling? by Nancy Tafuri. Greenwillow.

1986 POLAR EXPRESS by Chris Van Allsburg. Houghton Mifflin.

The Relatives Came by Cynthia Rylant. Illustrated by Stephen Gammell. Bradbury.

King Bidgood's in the Bathtub by Audrey Wood. Illustrated by Don Wood. Harcourt Brace Jovanovich.

1987 HEY AL by Arthur Yorinks. Illustrated by Richard Egielski. Farrar, Straus.

Alphabatics by Suse MacDonald. Bradbury.

Rumpelstiltskin by Paul O. Zelinsky. Dutton.

The Village of Round and Square Houses by Ann Grifalconi. Little Brown.

The Laura Ingalls Wilder Award is given to an author or illustrator whose books (published in the United States) have made a substantial and lasting contribution to literature for children. Established in 1954, this medal was given every five years through 1980. As of 1983, it is given every three years.

1954 Laura Ingalls Wilder
1960 Clara Ingram Judson
1965 Ruth Sawyer
1970 E. B. White
1975 Beverly Cleary
1980 Theodor S. Geisel (Dr. Seuss)
1983 Maurice Sendak
1986 Jean Fritz

The Hans Christian Andersen Prize, the first international children's book award, was established in 1956 by the International Board on Books for Young People. Given every two years, the award was expanded in 1966 to honor an illustrator as well as an author. A committee composed of members from different countries judges the selections recommended by the board or library associations in each country. The following have won the Hans Christian Andersen Prize:

1956 Eleanor Farjeon for THE LITTLE BOOKROOM. Oxford (Walck).
1958 Astrid Lindgren for RASMUS PA LUFFEN.
Rabén and Sjögren (Viking; titled RASMUS AND THE VAGABOND).
1960 Erich Kästner. Germany.
1962 Meindert DeJong. United States.
1964 René Guillot. France.
1966 Tove Jansson (author). Finland.
Alois Carigiet (illustrator). Switzerland.
1968 James Krüss (author). Germany.
Jose Maria Sanchez-Silva (author). Spain.
Jiri Trnka (illustrator). Czechoslovakia.
1970 Gianni Rodari (author). Italy.
Maurice Sendak (illustrator). United States.
1972 Scott O'Dell (author). United States.
Ib Spang Olsen (illustrator). Denmark.
1974 Maria Gripe (author). Sweden.
Farshid Mesghali (illustrator). Iran.
1976 Cecil Bodker (author). Denmark.
Tatjana Mawrina (illustrator). U.S.S.R.
1978 Paula Fox (author). United States.
Svend Otto (illustrator). Denmark.
1980 Bohumil Ríha (author). Czechoslovakia.
Suekichi Akaba (illustrator). Japan.
1982 Lygia Bojunga Nunes (author). Brazil.
Zibigniew Rychlicki (illustrator). Poland.
1984 Christine Nostlinger (author). Austria.
Mitsumasa Anno (illustrator). Japan
1986 Patricia Wrightson (author). Australia.
Robert Ingpen (illustrator). Australia.

GENERAL AWARDS

MILDRED L. BATCHELDER AWARD

Association for Library Service to Children of ALA, 50 E. Huron St., Chicago, IL 60611. For most outstanding book originally published in a foreign language in another country.

BOSTON GLOBE-HORN BOOK AWARDS

The Horn Book Magazine, Park Sq. Bldg., 31 St. James Ave., Boston, MA 02116. Currently given for Outstanding Fiction or Poetry, Outstanding Nonfiction, and Outstanding Illustration.

GOLDEN KITE AWARD

Society of Children's Book Writers (SCBW), P.O. Box 296, Mar Vista Station, Los Angeles, CA 90066. Presented annually to members whose books of fiction, nonfiction, and picture-illustration best exhibit excellence and genuinely appeal to interests and concerns of children.

INTERNATIONAL READING ASSOCIATION CHILDREN'S BOOK AWARD

International Reading Association, 800 Barksdale Rd., Newark, DE 19711. Annual award for first or second book to an author from any country who shows unusual promise in the children's book field.

NEW YORK TIMES BEST ILLUSTRATED CHILDREN'S BOOKS OF THE YEAR

The New York Times, 229 W. 43rd St., New York, NY 10036. Books selected for excellence in illustration by panel of judges.

GEORGE G. STONE CENTER FOR CHILDREN'S BOOKS RECOGNITION OF MERIT AWARD

Claremont Graduate School, Claremont, CA 91711. Given to author or illustrator of a single book or body of work with the power to please and heighten awareness of children and teachers.

UNIVERSITY OF SOUTHERN MISSISSIPPI MEDALLION

School of Library Service, Hattiesburg, MS 39406. Awarded to author or illustrator for outstanding contribution to the field of children's literature.

AWARDS BASED ON SPECIAL CONTENT

JANE ADDAMS BOOK AWARD

Jane Addams Peace Association, 777 United Nations Pl., New York, NY 10017. For a book with literary merit stressing themes of dignity, equality, peace, and social justice.

ASSOCIATION OF JEWISH LIBRARIES AWARDS

National Foundation for Jewish Culture, 122 E. 42nd St., Room 1512, New York, NY 10168. Given to one or two titles which have made the most outstanding contribution to the field of Jewish literature for children and young people. The Sydney Taylor Body of Work Award, established in 1981, is given for an author's body of work.

BAY AREA BOOK REVIEWERS ASSOCIATION AWARD

Book Section, *San Francisco Chronicle,* 901 Mission St., San Francisco, CA 94103. Honors outstanding literature originating in this section of California.

CATHOLIC BOOK AWARDS

Catholic Press Association of the United States and Canada, 119 N. Park Ave., Rockville Centre, NY 11570. Honors selected in five categories and awarded to books with sound Christian and psychological values.

CHILD STUDY CHILDREN'S BOOK COMMITTEE AT BANK STREET COLLEGE AWARD

Bank Street College of Education, 610 W. 112th St., New York, NY 10025. For distinguished book for children or young people that deals honestly and courageously with problems in the world.

CHRISTOPHER AWARDS

The Christophers, 12 E. 48th St., New York, NY 10017. Given to works of artistic excellence affirming the highest values of the human spirit.

EVA L. GORDON AWARD FOR CHILDREN'S SCIENCE LITERATURE

Helen Ross Russell, Chairman of Publications Committee, ANNS, 44 College Dr., Jersey City, NY 07305. Given by the American Nature Study Society to the body of work by an author or illustrator whose science trade books are accurate, inviting, and timely.

JEFFERSON CUP AWARD

Children's and Young Adult Roundtable of the Virginia Library Association, P.O. Box 298, Alexandria, VA 22313. Presented for a distinguished book in American history, historical fiction, or biography.

CORETTA SCOTT KING AWARDS

Social Responsibilities Round Table of the American Library Association, 50 E. Huron St., Chicago, IL 60611. Given to a black author and black illustrator for outstanding inspirational and educational contributions to literature for children.

NATIONAL COUNCIL OF TEACHERS OF ENGLISH AWARD FOR EXCELLENCE IN POETRY FOR CHILDREN

National Council of Teachers of English, 1111 Kenyon Rd., Urbana, IL 61801. Given formerly annually and presently every three years to a living American poet for total body of work for children ages 3–13.

NATIONAL JEWISH BOOK AWARDS

JWB Jewish Book Council, 15 E. 26th St., New York, NY 10010. Various awards are given for work or body of work which makes a contribution to Jewish juvenile literature.

NEW YORK ACADEMY OF SCIENCES CHILDREN'S SCIENCE BOOK AWARDS

The New York Academy of Sciences, 2 E. 63rd St., New York, NY 10021. For books of high quality in the field of science for children; three awards are given: Younger Children, Older Children, and the Montroll Award for a book that provides unusual historical data or background on a scientific subject.

SCOTT O'DELL AWARD FOR HISTORICAL FICTION

Bulletin of the Center for Children's Books, University of Chicago, 1100 E. 57th Street., Chicago, IL 60637. Selected by BCCB's Editor and Advisory Board and honors a distinguished work of historical fiction set in the New World.

PHOENIX AWARD

Alethea Helbig, 3640 Eli Rd., Ann Arbor, MI 08104. Given to author of a book published for children twenty years before which has not received a major children's book award. Sponsored by the Children's Literature Association.

PLEASE TOUCH BOOK AWARD

Please Touch Museum for Children, 210 N. 21st St., Philadelphia, PA 19103. Given to distinguished picture book that explores or clarifies a particular concept for children, 3 and up.

EDGAR ALLAN POE AWARDS

Mystery Writers of America, 1950 Fifth Ave., New York, NY 10011. For best juvenile mystery.

WASHINGTON POST/CHILDREN'S BOOK GUILD NONFICTION AWARD

Washington Post, 1150 15th St., NW, Washington, DC 20071. Given to an author or illustrator for a body of work in juvenile informational books.

WESTERN WRITERS OF AMERICA SPUR AWARD

The Western Writers of America, Inc., 508 Senter Pl., Selah, WA 98942. For best western juvenile in two categories, fiction and nonfiction.

CARTER G. WOODSON BOOK AWARD

National Council for the Social Studies, 3501 Newark St., NW, Washington, DC 20016. Presented to outstanding social science books for young readers which treat sensitively and accurately topics related to ethnic minorities.

REGIONAL AND STATE AWARDS

Awards Selected by Adults

COMMONWEALTH CLUB OF CALIFORNIA AWARDS

Commonwealth Club of California, Monadnock Arcade, 681 Market St., San Francisco, CA 94105. For finest juvenile book on any subject by a Californian.

CAROLYN W. FIELD AWARD

Youth Services Division of the Pennsylvania Library Association, 126 Locust St., Harrisburg, PA 17109. Given to a Pennsylvanian author or illustrator for distinguished children's book.

FRIENDS OF AMERICAN WRITERS AWARDS

Given to a native or resident, for at least five years, of one of the 16 midwestern states or to an author who has chosen this locale for his or her work.

FRIENDS OF CHILDREN AND LITERATURE (FOCAL) AWARD

Central Library, Los Angeles Public Library, 630 W. 5th St., Los Angeles, CA 90071. Awarded to author or illustrator who has enriched a child's appreciation for and knowledge of California.

GARDEN STATE CHILDREN'S BOOK AWARDS

New Jersey Library Association, Children's Services Section, 116 E. State St., Trenton, NY 08608. Recognize literary merit and reader popularity and are awarded to authors and illustrators.

NORTH CAROLINA LITERARY AND HISTORICAL ASSOCIATION AWARDS

North Carolina Literary and Historical Association, 109 E. Jones St., Raleigh, NC 27611. Author must have maintained residence in North Carolina for at least three years.

OHIOANA BOOK AWARDS

Ohioana Library Association, Room 1105, 65 S. Front St., Columbus, OH 43215. Awarded to an Ohio author or for the body of work of an Ohio author living in the state for at least five years.

PEN BOOK AWARDS

PEN, Los Angeles Center, 1227 Fourth St., Sanda Monica, CA 90401. Given to author from Southern California.

CARL SANDBURG LITERARY ARTS AWARDS

Friends of the Chicago Public Library, 78 E. Washington St., Chicago, IL 60602. Recipients are authors living the six-county Chicago metropolitan area.

SCHOOL LIBRARY MEDIA SPECIALISTS OF SOUTHEASTERN NEW YORK AWARD

School Library Media Specialists of Southeastern New York, P.O. Box 3401, Poughkeepsie, NY 12603. Given to author or illustrator living in a seven-county region of southeastern New York State for a body of work that is an outstanding contribution to children's and/or young adult literature.

SOCIETY OF MIDLAND AUTHORS BOOK AWARDS

Society of Midland Authors, 333 N. Michigan, Chicago, IL 60611. Awarded to a Midland author (twelve-state region) residing in, who grew up in, or has set a novel in the Midlands.

SOUTHERN CALIFORNIA COUNCIL ON LITERATURE FOR CHILDREN AND YOUNG PEOPLE AWARDS

Given to authors, illustrators, and contributors to the field of children's literature living in Southern California.

STATE HISTORICAL SOCIETY OF WISCONSIN BOOK AWARDS

State Historical Society of Wisconsin, 816 State St., Madison WI 53706. Given to a title which has made a contribution to readers' knowledge of Wisconsin.

WESTERN HERITAGE AWARDS

National Cowboy Hall of Fame and Western Heritage Center, 1700 N.E. 63rd St., Oklahoma City, OK 73111. Awarded to juvenile book that best portrays the authentic American West.

Awards Selected by Children

ARIZONA YOUNG READERS AWARD

Department of Elementary Education, College of Education, University of Arizona, Tucson, AZ 85721. Awarded every two years from a master list of titles nominated by children, finally voted on by children.

CHARLIE MAY SIMON CHILDREN'S BOOK AWARD (Arkansas)

Elementary School Council, Dept. of Education, State Education Building, 4 Capitol Mall, Little Rock, AR 72201. Arkansas schoolchildren, grades 4–6, vote from a master list of titles selected by representatives from sponsoring groups.

CALIFORNIA YOUNG READER MEDALS

California Reading Association, 3400 Irvine Ave., Suite 118, Newport Beach, CA 92660 and other sponsors. Preliminary nominations proposed by children become a master list from which a young reader medal committee determines final nominees. Children vote in four categories.

COLORADO CHILDREN'S BOOK AWARD

Colorado Council of the International Reading Association, 1100 S.E. Frontage Rd., Fort Collins, CO 80524. A list of twenty most frequently nominated books by children is the master list from which children then select one title by a living author, published within the last five years.

SUNSHINE STATE YOUNG READER'S AWARD (Florida)

Florida Association for Media in Education (FAME), and others, SSYR Committee Chairman, 630 Belmont, Temple Terrace, FL 33617.

GEORGIA CHILDREN'S BOOK AWARDS

College of Education, University of Georgia, Athens, GA 30602. Children in grades 4–7 select the Georgia Children's Book Award and those in K–3 select the Georgia Children's Picture Book Award from a list of twenty books by living authors, published within last five years.

NENE AWARD (Hawaii)

Children in grades 4–6 select a book by a living author, published within last six years.

YOUNG HOOSIER AWARD (Indiana)

Association for Indiana Media Educators, YHA Committee, 1120 E. 49th St., Marion, IN 46953. Indiana children, grades 4–8, vote for a favorite book from a list of twenty books selected by a committee. Books must be published in the five-year period preceding award. A second award is selected by grades 6–8.

IOWA CHILDREN'S CHOICE AWARD

Iowa Educational Media Association, ICCA Committee, 1500 Oakland Rd., NE, Cedar Rapids, IA 52402. Children vote for title from a list prepared by a committee from children's nominees. Two categories, grades 3–6 and grades 6–9 are awarded.

WILLIAM ALLEN WHITE CHILDREN'S BOOK AWARD (Kansas)

Emporia State University, William Allen White Library, 1200 Commercial St., Emporia, KS 66801. Schoolchildren, grades 4–8, vote for a winner from a master list of fiction, nonfiction, and poetry titles.

KENTUCKY BLUEGRASS AWARD

Northern Kentucky University, Learning Resources Center–BEP 268, NKU, Highland Heights, KY 41076. Children in grades 3–8 select a title from a booklist of titles published within a 3-year period, compiled by award committee.

MASSACHUSETTS CHILDREN'S BOOK AWARDS

Salem State College, Education Dept., Salem, MA 01970. Two awards, voted on by grades 4–6 and 7–9, are selected among both recent and older titles.

MICHIGAN YOUNG READERS' AWARDS

Michigan Council of Teachers of English, P.O. Box 892, Rochester, MI 48063. A committee of teachers selects a list from children's nominees, and children vote in two divisions, preschool–3 and grades 4–8.

MAUDE HART LOVELACE BOOK AWARD (Minnesota)

Friends of Minnesota Valley Regional Library, 100 E. Main St., Mankato, MN 56001. Winner is selected by children in grades 3–8 from a list of fifteen titles published in the previous ten years.

MARK TWAIN AWARD (Missouri)

Mark Twain Award, Box 343, Butler, MO 64730. Children in grades 4–8 vote from a master list compiled by award committee.

NEBRASKA GOLDEN SOWER AWARDS

Nebraska Library Association, Ardys Hansum, Hartman Elementary, 5530 N. 66th Street, Omaha, NE 68104. Children nominate titles for picture books, grades K–3, and fiction, grades 4–6, selected from the three-years period two years before the award is given; voting is from a master list selected by committee.

GREAT STONE FACE AWARD (New Hampshire)

New Hampshire Library Association–Children's Librarians, Barbara Young, Exeter Public Library, 47 Front St., Exeter, NH 03833. On "I Love to Read Day," usually February 14, children grades 4–6 vote on a favorite work of fiction. There is no nominees list.

LAND OF ENCHANTMENT BOOK AWARD (New Mexico)

Land of Enchantment Book Award Committee, Flo Starkey, Materials Center, Roswell Independent School District, 300 Kentucky St., Roswell, NM 88201. Students grades 4–8 select winner from list compiled by committee.

BUCKEYE CHILDREN'S BOOK AWARDS (Ohio)

State Library of Ohio, 65 S. Front St., Columbus, OH 43215. Titles selected in three divisions (K–2, 3–5, and 6–8) from children's nominations and children vote during Ohio Right to Read Week.

SEQUOYAH CHILDREN'S BOOK AWARD (Oklahoma)

Oklahoma State Department of Education, Library Resources, 2500 N. Lincoln Blvd., Oklahoma City, OK 73105. Children grades 3–6 vote from a master list of twenty titles chosen by the committee.

PACIFIC NORTHWEST YOUNG READER'S CHOICE AWARD (Alaska; Alberta Canada; British Columbia, Canada; Idaho; Montana; Oregon; Washington)

Children's and Young Adult Services Division, Pacific Northwest Library Association, c/o Children's Department, W. Vancouver Memorial Library, 1950 Marine Dr., West Vancouver, V7V 1J8, Canada. The oldest children's choice award (1940), it is selected from a master list compiled by librarians from suggestions by children.

SOUTH CAROLINA CHILDREN'S BOOK AWARD

South Carolina Association of School Librarians, P.O. Box 2442, Columbia, SC 29202. Children grades 4–8 select from a list of twenty nominees selected by adults.

THE TEXAS BLUEBONNET AWARD

Texas Bluebonnet Award Committee, School of Library Science, P.O. Box 2236, Sam Houston State University, Huntsville, TX 77341. Students in grades 3–6 who have read or heard read at least five books from a master list of titles selected by adults vote for their favorite title.

UTAH CHILDREN'S BOOK AWARD

Children's Literature Association of Utah, Dept. of Educational Studies, University of Utah, Salt Lake City, UT 84122. Children grades 3–6 vote from a master list selected from children's nominations.

DOROTHY CANFIELD FISHER CHILDREN'S BOOK AWARD (Vermont)

Vermont Department of Libraries, 138 Main St., Montpelier, VT 05602. Selected by grades 4–8 from a master list of thirty titles compiled by award committee.

WASHINGTON CHILDREN'S CHOICE PICTURE BOOK AWARD

Washington Library Media Association, P.O. Box 1413, Bothell, WA 98011. Children grades K–3 select a picture book from a list of twenty titles proposed by award committee.

WEST VIRGINIA CHILDREN'S BOOK AWARD

Main Library, O.O. Box 6069, Morgantown, WV 26506. Children grades 3–6 select from a master list of twenty fiction titles.

GOLDEN ARCHER AWARD and LITTLE ARCHER AWARD (Wisconsin)

Dept. of Library Science, University of Wisconsin-Oshkosh, Oshkosh, WI 54901. The Golden Archer Award is given to an author of recent books by children in grades 4–8. The Little Archer winner is selected by children in K–3 from picture book authors, illustrators, or a single title.

LASTING CONTRIBUTIONS OR SERVICE TO CHILDREN'S LITERATURE

CHILDREN'S BOOK COUNCIL HONORS PROGRAM

Children's Book Council, 67 Irving Place, New York, NY 10003. Honors one person for substantial and sustained contribution to books and literature at its biennial *Everychild* conference.

GROLIER FOUNDATION AWARD

American Library Association Awards Committee, 50 E. Huron St., Chicago, Ill. 60611. Given to a librarian in a community or school who has made an unusual contribution to the stimulating and guidance of reading by children and young people.

LANDAU AWARD

Salt Lake County Library System, 2197 E. 7000 S. Salt Lake City, Utah 84121. Cosponsored by the Department of Education of the University of Utah and Salt Lake County Library System. The award is given biennially to a teacher of children's literature who has most inspired students to pursue a knowledge of the field.

REGINA MEDAL

Catholic Library Association, 461 West Lancaster Ave., Haverford, Penna. 19041. For "continued distinguished contribution to children's literature."

UNIVERSITY OF SOUTHERN MISSISSIPPI CHILDREN'S COLLECTION MEDALLION

University of Southern Mississippi Book Festival, USM Library, Hattiesburg, Miss. 39401. For writer or illustrator who has made an "outstanding contribution to the field of children's literature."

OTHER ENGLISH-SPEAKING COUNTRIES

Australia

AUSTRALIAN CHILDREN'S BOOKS OF THE YEAR AWARDS

Australian Children's Book Council. Awards in three categories: Book of the Year, Picture Book of the Year, and Junior Book of the Year.

NEW SOUTH WALES PREMIER'S LITERARY AWARDS

Prizes in four categories: fiction, nonfiction, poetry, and children's books.

Canada

CANADA COUNCIL CHILDREN'S LITERATURE PRIZES

Awarded in two categories, English and French, to a Canadian author and to an illustrator.

CANADIAN LIBRARY ASSOCIATION AWARDS BOOKS OF THE YEAR FOR CHILDREN

Canadian Association of Children's Librarians, 151 Sparks St., Ottawa K1P 5E3, Canada. Awards given in two categories, French and English, for best book published by Canadian citizen.

AMELIA FRANCES HOWARD-GIBBON MEDAL

Canadian Library Association, 151 Sparks St., Ottawa K1P 5E3, Canada. For outstanding illustrations in children's book published in Canada and illustrated by native or resident of Canada.

IMPERIAL ORDER OF THE DAUGHTERS OF THE EMPIRE BOOK AWARD

Given to Canadian book by Toronto Library Board. Author or illustrator must be from Toronto area.

VICKY METCALF AWARD

Canadian Authors' Association, 131 Bloor St. W., Toronto, Ontario M5S 1R1. Given to Canadian writer for body of work.

PRIX ALVINE-BELISLE

A.S.T.E.D, 7243 rue St-Denis, Montréal, Quebec H2R 2E3, Canada. Given to author or illustrator of best Canadian book published in French in Canada.

RUTH SCHWARTZ CHILDREN'S BOOK AWARD

Canadian Booksellers' Association/Ontario Arts Council, 151 Bloor St. W., Toronto, Ontario M5S 1T6, Canada. Given to outstanding work of children's literature published in Canada by Canadian author.

Great Britain

CARNEGIE MEDAL

British Library Association, 7 Ridgmount St., London, WC1E, England. For children's book of outstanding merit.

CHILDREN'S BOOK AWARD

Federation of Children's Book Groups, 3 Marlin Close, Dawes Heath, Benfleet, Essex SS7 2TW, England. Award to best work of fiction for children to fourteen years, selected by children and adults.

KATE GREENAWAY MEDAL

British Library Association, 7 Ridgmount St., London WC1E 7AE, England. For most distinguished work in the illustration of children's books.

GUARDIAN AWARD FOR CHILDREN'S FICTION

The Guardian, 24 Weymouth St., London W1N 3FA, England. For outstanding work of fiction for children.

GARAVI GUJARAT BOOK AWARDS FOR RACIAL HARMONY

National Book League, 45 East Hill, London SW18 2QZ, England. For book promoting racial harmony.

OTHER AWARD

Children's Book Bulletin, 4 Aldebert Terrace, London SW8 1BH, England. For books of literary merit that children enjoy which are progressive in their treatment of ethnic minorities, sex roles, and social differences.

SIGNAL POETRY AWARD

Signal, The Thimble Press, Lockwood, Station road, South Woodchester, Glos. GL5 5EQ. Award for single-poet collection or anthology.

TIMES EDUCATIONAL SUPPLEMENT INFORMATION BOOK AWARDS

The Times Educational Supplement, Times Newspaper Ltd., P.O. Box 7, New Printing House Sq., Grays Inn Rd., London WC1X 8EZ, England. For distinction in nonfiction book.

WHITBREAD AWARDS

The Booksellers Association of Great Britain and Ireland, 154 Buckingham Palace Road, London SW1W 9TZ, England. For a book for children seven and up written by a British or Irish author.

FRANCIS WILLIAMS ILLUSTRATION AWARDS

National Book League, 45 East Hill, London SW18 2QZ, England. Given every 5 years to single artist.

New Zealand

RUSSELL CLARK AWARD

New Zealand Library Association, Private Bag, Wellington, NZ. For distinguished illustration by citizen or resident of New Zealand.

ESTHER GLEN AWARD

New Zealand Library Association, Private Bag, Wellington, NZ. For most distinguished contribution to children's literature by New Zealand author.

For more information about these and other awards, including complete lists of the prize winners, see *Children's Books: Awards & Prizes*, published by The Children's Book Council, 67 Irving Place, New York, NY 10003.

APPENDIX B **Book Selection Aids***

Compiled by Barbara Chatton, University of Wyoming, Laramie, WY

I. DIRECTORIES AND ADDRESS LISTS

1. *Children's Books in Print.* R. R. Bowker, P.O. Box 1807, Ann Arbor, MI 48106. Annual. $62.95.

   A comprehensive listing of children's books currently in print. Includes titles for grades K–12. Titles are arranged alphabetically by author, title, and illustrator. A list of publisher addresses is provided.

2. *Children's Media Market Place,* 2nd ed. Carol A. Emmens, ed. Neal-Schuman Publishers, 23 Cornelia St., New York, NY 10014. 1982. $29.95 paper.

   An annotated list of publishers of books and producers and distributors of nonprint materials indexed by format, subject, and special interest. Includes a directory of wholesalers, bookstores, book clubs, and children's television sources.

3. *Educational Media Yearbook.* James W. Brown and Shirley N. Brown, eds. Libraries Unlimited, P.O. Box 263, Littleton, CO 80160. Annual. 1984. $47.50.

   Includes articles, surveys, and research on various aspects of media administration, creation, and use. Has a resource list which includes over 1,000 print and nonprint items dealing with media. Lists organizations, foundations, and funding agencies for media.

   Includes articles, lists of periodicals, reference tools and producers and publishers of nonprint materials.

4. *Guide to Reference Books for School Media Centers,* 2nd ed. Christine Gehrt Wynar. Libraries Unlimited, P.O. Box 263, Littleton, CO 80160. 1981. 377 pp. $28.50.

   Includes annotations and evaluations for 2,000 useful reference tools for school media centers. Materials are arranged in order by subject. Also includes a list of sources and selection aids for print and nonprint materials.

5. *Paperback Books for Young People. An Annotated Guide to Publishers and Distributors,* 2nd ed. John T. Gillespie. American Library Association, 50 E. Huron St., Chicago, IL 60611. 1977. 232 pp. $10.00.

   Describes all the major paperback publishers in the United States and Canada. Includes distributors.

6. *Paperbound Books for Young People. Kindergarten through Grade 12,* 2nd ed. R. R. Bowker Co., Order Department, P.O. Box 1807, Ann Arbor, MI 48106. 1980. 325 pp. $9.95.

   Lists 15,000 paperback titles in print for ages preschool through grade 12, with finding and order information. Nonselective and without annotations, but is indexed by author, title, subject, and illustrator.

7. *Periodicals for School Media Programs.* Selma K. Richardson, ed. American Library Association, 50 E. Huron St., Chicago, IL 60611. 1978. 420 pp. $10.00 paper.

   Annotates a wide variety of titles suitable for school media centers including periodicals which support the curriculum, leisure reading, international, and ethnic periodicals. Includes periodicals which appeal to a range of reading interests and levels.

8. *Reference Books for Children.* Carolyn Sue Peterson and Ann D. Fenton. Scarecrow Press, P.O. Box 656, Metuchen, NJ 08840. 1981. 273 pp. $16.00.

   Contains about 900 annotated entries over a broad range of curriculum areas, collection needs, interests, and reading levels of children. Books are classified by subject. No reference to reviews of the titles, but annotations provide some guide for making selections for school collections.

9. *Selecting Materials for Children and Young Adults.* A bibliography of bibliographies and review sources, Association for Library Service to Children and Young Adult Services Division. American Library Association, 50 E. Huron St., Chicago, IL 60611. 1980. 80 pp. $7.00 paper.

   A useful selection tool, this lists tools from which to order materials in the basic curriculum areas of the collection, as well as materials in fields as various as folklore, drugs, sex education, and so on. Includes sources for both print and nonprint materials.

10. *Subject Guide to Children's Books in Print.* R. R. Bowker, P.O. Box 1807, Ann Arbor, MI 48106. Annual. $62.95.

    A companion volume to *Children's Books in Print.* Arranges all children's titles currently in print under over 6,000 subject headings. Particularly useful for finding and ordering titles on specific subjects, however titles are not annotated.

II. GENERAL SELECTION AIDS

1. *Adventuring with Books: A Booklist for Pre-K–Grade 6.* Diane Monson, ed. The National Council of Teachers of English, 1111 Kenyon Road, Urbana, IL 61601. 1985. 395 pp. $9.75.

   Annotates about 1700 children's titles published from 1981 to 1984. Annotations include summary, age levels, and prices. Contents are arranged by genre, subject, and theme. Also includes bibliography of recent works about children's literature.

2. *Babies Need Books: How Books Can Help Your Child Become a Happy and Involved Human Being.* Dorothy Butler. Atheneum. 122 East 42nd Street, New York, NY 10017. 1985. 192 pp. $5.95 paper.

* Prices subject to change

Explores the uses of books with children in the first five years. Gives characteristics of each age group along with titles of appropriate stories to share. Annotated book lists are included at the end of each chapter.

3. *Best Books for Children: Pre-school through Middle Grades,* 3rd ed. John T. Gillespie and Christine Gilbert, eds. R. R. Bowker Co., Order Department, P.O. Box 1807, Ann Arbor, MI 48106. 1985. 635 pp. $34.50.

An annotated listing of about 13,000 books which are selected to satisfy both recreational and curricular needs and interests of elementary school-age children. Books are arranged within major curriculum areas which are then sub-divided. Sections for particular kinds of fiction such as "Stories without words" or "Realistic stories" are also included. The book contains author, title, and illustrator as well as subject indexes.

4. *The Best in Children's Books: The University of Chicago Guide to Children's Literature, 1973–1978.* Zena Sutherland, ed. University of Chicago Press, Chicago, IL 60637. 1980. $25.00.

A selection of over 1,000 reviews which originally appeared in the *Bulletin of the Center for Children's Books.* An earlier edition covers 1966 to 1972. Reviews are arranged in order by author, and are indexed by title, developmental values, curriculum area, reading level, subject, and type of literature. A useful collection development tool.

5. *The Best of Children's Books 1964–1978 with 1979 Addenda.* Virginia Haviland. Library of Congress. University Press Books, 302 Fifth Avenue, New York, NY 10001.

This annotated bibliography of 1,000 titles is taken from the Library of Congress' annual guides to children's literature from the past 14 years. Books included are for ages preschool through junior high and are arranged in order by type (e.g., picture books, poetry, nature, etc.).

6. *Beyond Fact: Nonfiction for Children and Young People.* American Library Association, 50 E. Huron Street, Chicago, IL 60611. 1982. 236 pp. $12.50 paper.

Contains articles on and brief lists of high quality nonfiction for young people.

7. *Bibliography of Books for Children.* Sylvia Sunderlin, ed. The Association for Childhood Education International, 3615 Wisconsin Avenue, NW, Washington, D.C. 20016. (Revised every three years.) 1984. $10.00.

Lists the best books reviewed by *Childhood Education* over the previous two years. Books are evaluated for readability and absence of sexism and racism. Entries are annotated and grouped by age levels. Indexed and cross-referenced.

8. *Books for the Gifted Child.* Barbara Holland Baskin and Karen H. Harris. R. R. Bowker, Order Department, Box 1807, Ann Arbor, MI 48106. 1980. 263 pp. $24.95.

Critically annotates about 150 titles which would be useful in working with gifted children, ages preschool through 12. Titles are all recent. They are arranged in alphabetical order with bibliographic information and reading level included. Several chapters on the gifted are included in the book.

9. *Building a Children's Literature Collection,* 3rd ed. Harriet Quimby and Margaret Mary Kimmel. *Choice Magazine,* 100 Riverview Ctr., Middletown, CT 06457. 1986. $9.95

Recommends a core collection of children's books and reference works for academic libraries that support children's literature courses.

10. *Children and Books,* 7th ed. Zena Sutherland, et al. Scott, Foresman and Co., 1900 East Lake Avenue, Glenview, IL 60025. 1985. $26.95 text ed.

A well-known textbook of children's literature which contains bibliographies of various genres and subjects of children's literature which have been updated from previous editions.

11. *Children's Books of the Year.* Annual. Child Study Children's Book Committee. Bank Street College, 610 W. 112th Street, New York, NY 10025. 50 pp. $3.50.

A listing of about 500 titles chosen by a group of parents, librarians, and educators. Topically arranged with brief annotations. Includes ages preschool through 13. A star indicates the group felt the book was outstanding.

12. *Children's Books Too Good to Miss,* 7th ed. May Hill Arbuthnot et al. University Press Books, 302 Fifth Avenue, New York, NY 10001. 1980. 125 pp. $8.95.

Compilers, using Arbuthnot's criteria, present an annotated list of books for children from preschool to age 14. Includes both current and older titles which have worked with children.

13. *Children's Catalog,* 14th ed. H. W. Wilson Co., 950 University Avenue, Bronx, NY 10452. 1981. 1,296 pp. $54.00.

A classified (Dewey Decimal System) catalog of about 5,000 recent children's books including publishing information, grade level, and a brief summary of each title. Also includes alphabetical author, title, and subject indexes. Contains a list of publishers with addresses. Not comprehensive—lists "the best" books for children in nonfiction and fiction. New edition is issued every five years, with annual supplements in other years.

14. *Choices: A Core Collection for Young Reluctant Readers.* Carolyn Flemming and Donna Schatt, eds. John Gordon Burke, Publisher, P.O. Box 1492, Evanston, IL 60204-1492. 1984. 550 pp. $45.00.

Annotates 336 books for second- through sixth-graders reading below grade level; with plot summary, interest level, and reading level. Contains author and subject indexes.

15. *Easy Reading: Book Series and Periodicals for Less Able Readers.* Michael Graves, et al. International Reading Association, P.O. Box 8139. Newark, DE 19711. 1979. 54 pp. $4.50.

An annotated list of selected titles for middle-graders and junior high students who are not good readers.

16. *The Elementary School Library Collection,* 14th edition. Lois Winkel, ed. Bro-Dart Foundation, P.O. Box 3488, Williamsport, PA. 1984. $79.95.

A basic bibliography of materials, both print and nonprint for elementary school media center collections. Materials are interfiled and arranged by subject classification (Dewey Decimal System). All entries include bibliographic information, age level, and a brief annotation. Contains a helpful subject index as well as author and title indexes. Updated periodically with new editions.

17. *Junior High School Library Catalog,* 5th ed. H. W. Wilson Co., 950 University Avenue, Bronx, NY 10452. 1985. $80.00.

Similar to the *Children's Catalog,* but covering books for the junior high school years. Books are arranged in classified order with grade levels and short annotations. Subject, author, and title indexes are included. Issued every five years with annual paper supplements.

18. *Let's Read Together: Books for Family Enjoyment,* 4th ed. Association for Library Service to Children, American Library Association, 50 E. Huron St., Chicago, IL 60611. 1981. 124 pp. $5.00 paper.

Annotated list of books for children from preschool through age 15. Arranged in categories of interest and age level. Books are particularly suitable for reading aloud, but list is useful for helping parents to select books for their children.

19. *More Films Kids Like*. Maureen Gaffney, ed. American Library Association, 50 E. Huron St., Chicago, IL 60611. 1977. 168 pp. $12.00 paper.

Annotates 200 short films (16mm) preferred by children of elementary age during a testing period. Includes guides for classroom use, activities; and indexes films by subject. A new edition of the now-out-of-print *Films Kids Like*.

20. *A Multimedia Approach to Children's Literature*, 3rd ed. Mary Alice Hunt, ed. American Library Association, 50 E. Huron St., Chicago, IL 60611. 1983. 182 pp. $15.00 paper.

Annotated listings of over 500 books followed by annotated listings of media productions based upon the books. Many have been used with children and include their responses. Includes lists of related readings, selection aids, and publisher's addresses.

21. *Opening Doors for Preschool Children and Their Parents*, 2nd ed. Preschool Services and Parent Education Committee, Association for Library Service to Children, American Library Association, 50 E. Huron St., Chicago, IL 60611. 1981. 98 pp. $6.00 paper.

An annotated list divided into three sections: "Books and nonprint materials for parents and adults working with preschool children;" "Books for preschool children;" and "Nonprint materials for preschool children."

22. *A Parent's Guide to Children's Reading*, 5th ed. Nancy Larrick. Westminster Press, 925 Chestnut Street, Philadelphia, PA 19107. 1983. 284 pp. $12.95.

A handbook for parents suggesting appropriate titles for children's reading at each stage of their development. Contains chapters on television, language development, how reading is taught, poetry, and paperbacks.

23. *This Way to Books*. Caroline Feller Bauer. H. W. Wilson Co., 950 University Avenue, Bronx, NY 10452. 1983. 376 pp. $30.00.

A handbook of ideas for story programs, reading aloud, booktalks, poetry reading, and other activities using literature.

24. *Tied Together: Topics and Thoughts for Introducing Children's Books*. Charlotte Leonard. The Scarecrow Press, P.O. Box 656, Metuchen, NJ 08840. 1980. 261 pp. $15.00.

Puts together groups of books which can be shared in six major topic areas, each divided into sub-topics. For example, the first section, "Gifts from the Outdoors," includes lists on mushrooms, farms, trees, and so on.

25. *Your Reading: A Booklist for Junior High and Middle School Students*. The Committee on the Junior High and Middle School Booklist. National Council of Teachers of English, 1111 Kenyon Road, Urbana, IL 61801. 1983. 764 pp. $12.00.

An annotated list of books for grades 5–9, arranged in broad subject categories.

III. BOOKLISTS AND INDEXES FOR PARTICULAR SUBJECTS

a. Picture Books

1. *A to Zoo: Subject Access to Children's Picture Books*, 2nd. ed. Carolyn W. Lima. R. R. Bowker Co., P.O. Box 1807, Ann Arbor, MI 48106. 1985. 656 pp. $34.50.

Provides quite specific subject access to 4,400 picture books with cross references and full bibliographic citations. As well, the subject matter of a picture book can be discerned by looking for the entry for the book under author or title.

2. *Alphabet: A Handbook of ABC Books and Activities for the Elementary Classroom*. Scarecrow Press, P.O. Box 656, Metuchen, NJ 08840. 1984. 212 pp. $15.00.

Reviews over 200 alphabet books and provides about 80 activities to use with children from preschool to grade six.

3. *Picture Books for Children*. 2nd ed. Patricia Jean Cianciolo. American Library Association, 50 E. Huron St., Chicago, IL 60611. 1981. 254 pp. $15.00 paper.

An annotated listing of picture books divided into major subject areas such as "Me and My Family" or "The Imaginative World." Annotations include descriptions of art media, age levels, and brief synopses of plot. Material is largely new to this edition, so older editions remain useful.

4. *Picture Books for Gifted Programs*. Nancy Polette. The Scarecrow Press, P.O. Box 656, Metuchen, NJ 08840. 1981. 228 pp. $15.00.

Annotated lists of books which encourage growth of communication and thinking skills for all ages, as well as ideas for their use in classrooms and libraries.

b. Folklore and Storytelling and Reading Aloud

5. *For Reading Out Loud! A Guide to Sharing Books with Children*. Margaret Mary Kimmel and Elizabeth Segel. Dell, 245 E. 47th Street, New York, NY 10017. 1984. 240 pp. $6.95 paper.

Contains suggestions for reading aloud effectively to elementary and middle school students and an annotated list of good titles.

6. *Index to Fairy Tales, 1949–1972, Including Folklore, Legends, and Myths in Collections*. Norma Olin Ireland. 1973. 741 pp. $22.50.

Index to Fairy Tales, Myths and Legends, 2nd rev. ed. Mary H. Eastman, ed. 1926, 610 pp. $20.00.

Index to Fairy Tales, Myths and Legends. Supplement 1. Mary H. Eastman, ed. 1937. 566 pp. $20.00.

Index to Fairy Tales, Myths and Legends. Supplement 2. Mary H. Eastman, ed. 1952. 370 pp. $20.00.

Index to Fairy Tales, 1973–1977: Including Folklore, Legends and Myths in Collections. Norma O. Ireland, comp. 1979. 259 pp. $20.00.

All published by Scarecrow Press, P.O. Box 656, Metuchen, NJ 08840.

Indexes a broad number of collections of folktales and other folk literature by author, compiler, subject of tale (including characters, countries, and so on), and title of tale. Various editions cover different collections so that the total coverage is quite broad.

7. *The Read-Aloud Handbook*, rev. ed. Jim Trelease. Penguin Books, 40 W. 23rd St., New York, NY 10010. 1985. 243 pp. $6.95 paper.

Contains a rationale for reading aloud, tips for good presentations and an annotated "Treasury of Read-Alouds."

8. *Stories: A List of Stories to Tell and Read Aloud*, 7th ed. Marilyn B. Iarusso, ed. Office of Branch Libraries, New York Public Library, 45 Fifth Avenue, New York, NY 10016. 1984. $3.00.

Suggests proven stories to tell and read aloud to children. Includes poetry. Entries are briefly annotated.

9. *Story Programs: A Source Book of Materials*. Carolyn Sue Peterson and Brenny Hall. Scarecrow, P.O. Box 656, Metuchen, NJ 08840. 1980. 300 pp. $16.00 paper.

Numerous ideas and guidelines for programming for young children. Text is arranged by activity (sample programs, flannel boards, drama, puppets, etc.) Includes lists of picture books, songs with music, verse, patterns for puppets and other activities.

10. *The Story Vine: A Sourcebook of Unusual and Easy-to-Tell Stories from around the World.* Anne Pellowski. Macmillan, 866 Third Avenue, New York, NY 10022. 1984. 160 pp. $7.95 paper.

A collection of stories which can be highlighted with simple props such as string figures, picture drawings, musical instruments, or concrete objects.

11. *Storyteller's Sourcebook.* Margaret Read MacDonald, ed. Gale Research, Book Tower, Detroit, MI 48226. 1982. 750 pp. $90.00.

Provides access to folktales and folk literature in 700 collections. Tales are indexed by subject, motif, and title. Index is particularly useful in locating variants of tales.

12. *World of Storytelling.* Ann Pellowski. R. R. Bowker, Order Department, P.O. Box 1807, Ann Arbor, MI 48106. 1977. 296 pp. $19.95.

A study of storytelling throughout the world, providing history, types of storytelling, methods of opening and closing stories, use of pictures and props in storytelling, as well as a bibliography of books, periodicals, and nonprint materials related to the craft.

c. History and Biography

13. *Index to Collective Biographies for Young Readers,* 3rd edition. Judith Silverman, ed. R. R. Bowker Co., Order Department, P.O. Box 1807, Ann Arbor, MI 48106. 1979. 405 pp. $24.95.

Indexes over 7,000 biographies in 942 collections by individual names and by subject. Biographies are suitable for elementary school through junior high school.

14. Reading for Young People Series:

The Great Plains. Mildred Laughlin. 1985. 144 pp. $12.00 paper.

Kentucky, Tennessee, West Virginia. Barbara Martins. 1985. 157 pp. $12.00 paper.

The Middle Atlantic. Arabelle Pennypacker. 1980. 164 pp. $11.00 paper.

The Midwest. Dorothy Hinman and Ruth Zimmerman. 1979. 250 pp. $11.00 paper.

The Northwest. Mary Meachum. 1981. 152 pp. $11.00 paper.

The Rocky Mountains. Mildred Laughlin. 1980. 192 pp. $11.00 paper.

The Southeast. Dorothy Heald. 1980. 176 pp. $11.00 paper.

The Upper Midwest. Marion Fuller Archer. 1981. 142 pp. $11.00 paper.

All published by the American Library Association, 50 E. Huron, Chicago, IL 60611.

A series of annotated bibliographies of fiction and nonfiction for primary grades through grade ten which describe and annotate books covering the history and life of various American regions.

15. *World History in Juvenile Books: A Geographical and Chronological Guide.* Seymour Metzner, ed. The H. W. Wilson Co., 950 University Avenue, Bronx, NY 10452. 1973. 356 pp. $16.00.

Includes more than 2,700 fiction and nonfiction titles for elementary and junior high school age readers. Contains geographical and chronological listings of currently available books, with author, biographical subject, and title indexes and directory of publishers.

d. Cultural and Sexual Identity

16. *American Indian Stereotypes in the World of Children: A Reader and Bibliography.* Arlene B. Hirschfelder. Scarecrow Press, P.O. Box 656, Metuchen, NJ 08840. 1982. 312 pp. $20.00.

Contains selected articles about attitudes toward Native Americans and images of them in children's trade and text books. Includes an annotated bibliography of articles about images of Native Americans and a short list of articles, books, and current materials which convey a more positive image.

17. *A Bicultural Heritage: Themes for the Exploration of Mexican and Mexican-American Culture in Books for Children and Adolescents.* Scarecrow Press, P.O. Box 656, Metuchen, NJ 08840. 1978. 164 pp. $15.00.

Examines a selection of books about Mexicans and Mexican-Americans, critically reviewing them as to how much they adhere to false stereotypes and attitudes as well as pointing out titles which successfully portray members of these cultural groups.

18. *Bilingual Books in Spanish and English for Children.* Doris Cruger Dale. Libraries Unlimited, P.O. Box 263, Littleton, CO 80160. 1985. 163 pp. $23.50.

Annotated entries provide reviews of 254 bilingual books for preschool and elementary schoolchildren.

19. *The Black American in Books for Children: Readings in Racism.* Donnarae MacCann and Gloria Woodward, eds. the Scarecrow Press, P.O. Box 656, Metuchen, NJ 08840. 1972. 230 pp. $15.00. *Cultural Conformity in Books for Children: Further Readings in Racism.* 1977. 215 pp. $12.00.

Collections of articles in which the issue of racism in children's books is considered from a variety of points of view. Includes many citations to books of both good and poor quality which reflect positive and negative values.

20. *The Black Experience in Children's Books.* Barbara Rollock, selector. New York Public Library, Office of Branch Libraries, 8 East 40th Street, New York, NY 10016. 1984. $3.00.

An annotated list that presents titles about the Black experience in the United States as well as in other areas of the world. Criteria for selection and inclusion in the list are determined.

21. *Books on American Indians and Eskimos: A Selection Guide for Children and Young Adults.* Mary Jo Lass-Woodin, ed. American Library Association, 50 E. Huron St., Chicago, IL 60611. 360 pp. 1977. $25.00.

An annotated bibliography of over 750 titles organized to indicate aspects of Native American life. Annotations summarize and also evaluate materials as to accuracy of information and insight.

22. *Children's Books of International Interest,* 3rd ed. Barbara Elleman, ed. American Library Association, 50 E. Huron St., Chicago, IL 60611. 1985. 102 pp. $7.50 paper.

Annotates 350 titles which deal with universal themes in other cultural settings.

23. *A Comprehensive Guide to Children's Literature with a Jewish Theme.* Enid Davis. Schocken Books, 200 Madison Avenue, New York, NY 10016. 1981. 190 pp. $18.95.

Evaluates over 450 titles of fiction and nonfiction with Jewish themes for preschool through junior high. Arranged under subject categories such as fiction, history, music and dance, theology, and so on, titles are then divided either by age level, in the case of fiction, or by subheadings. Some multimedia resources are included, as well as a directory of publishers and tips on building a library collection.

24. *Girls Are People Too!: A Bibliography of Nontraditional Female Roles in Children's Books.* Joan E. Newman. Scarecrow Press, P.O. Box 656, Metuchen, NJ 08840. 1982. 195 pp. $15.00.

   A list of five hundred books with nontraditional females as characters. Most are fiction, although some nonfiction is included. Arranged by fiction, nonfiction, then by age range (preschool–grade 3, grade 4–9), then by minority groups and by handicap.

25. *Hey Miss! You Got a Book for Me? A Model Multi-Cultural Resource Collection,* 2nd ed. Joanna F. Chambers. Austin Bilingual Language Editions, P.O. Box 3864, Austin, TX 78764. 1981. 91 pp. $12.95 paper.

   A listing of 350 good multi-cultural and bilingual books and audio-visual materials. Includes mainly Spanish language with some materials in Chinese, French, Greek, and Vietnamese.

26. *A Hispanic Heritage: A Guide to Juvenile Books about Hispanic Peoples and Cultures.* Isabel Schon. Scarecrow Press, P.O. Box 656, Metuchen, NJ 08840. 1980. 178 pp. $15.00.

   An annotated subject bibliography of works about the people, history, culture, and politics in the Hispanic countries as well as works about Hispanic people in the United States. In the annotations the author indicates passages in which cultural bias and stereotyping may appear. Covers grades K–12.

27. *Indian Children's Books.* Hap Gilliland. Montana Council for Indian Education, 3311 1/2 4th Avenue North, Billings, MT 59102. 1980. 248 pp. $11.95. $7.95 paper.

   An annotated list of books about American Indians for children. Arranged by title, with indexes by tribe, region, and subject. Annotations, done largely by Native Americans or by evaluators who work with Native American children, include judgments as to whether books are historically and culturally accurate and whether they are suitable for use with Native American children. Also contains a list of publishers of books about Native Americans.

28. *Japan through Children's Literature: An Annotated Bibliography,* enlarged 2nd ed. Yasuko Makino. Greenwood, 1985. 144p. $29.95.

   Lists trade books selected from 1950 to the early 1980s and evaluates in terms of content and accuracy. Titles are grouped under headings such as Social Studies and subdivided further: History, Hiroshima, Festivals, etc. Suggested grade levels are given.

29. *Literature by and about the American Indian: An Annotated Bibliography,* 2nd ed. Anna Lee Stensland. National Council of Teachers of English, 1111 Kenyon Rd., Urbana, IL 61601. 1979. 382 pp. $9.75 paper.

   Identifies over 775 books published since 1973 including a section of books for elementary schoolchildren. Annotations describe and critique contents of books. Essays included discuss stereotypes, the themes of American Indian literature, difficulties of selecting literature which accurately depicts Native American life, and so on.

30. *Reading Ladders for Human Relations,* 6th ed. Eileen Tway, ed. National Council of Teachers of English and American Council of Education. 1785 Massachusetts Avenue NW, Washington, DC 20036. 1981. 398 pp. $10.00.

   Annotated list of titles arranged according to five basic themes: "Growing into Self;" "Relating to Wide Individual Differences;" "Interacting in Groups;" "Appreciating Different Cultures;" and "Coping in a Changing World." Covers ages preschool through high school, with books ar-

ranged in order of reading difficulty. All books are current and recommended titles.

31. *Shadow and Substance: Afro-American Experience in Contemporary Children's Fiction.* Rudine Sims. National Council of Teachers of English, 1111 Kenyon Road, Urbana, IL 61801. 1982. 112 pp. $9.00 paper.

   Annotations of 150 children's books published from 1965 to 1979 which present images of Afro-American children. Examines historical context, distortions, and social conscience as expressed in these books as well as providing some guidelines for teachers and librarians on how to make better-informed selections. Includes bibliographies and a reference list.

e. Fiction and Literature

31. *Children and Poetry: A Selective, Annotated Bibliography,* 2nd rev. ed. Virginia Haviland and William Jay Smith. Library of Congress. For sale by the Superintendent of Documents, U. S. Government Printing Office, Washington, DC 20402. 1979. 84 pp. $5.50.

   Provides discussions of the various types of poetry for children, both light and serious verse, and includes lists under several topics including "Rhymes," "Poetry of the Past," "Twentieth Century Poetry," "Anthologies," and "World Poetry."

32. *Exploring Books with Gifted Children.* Nancy Polette and Marjorie Hamlin. Libraries Unlimited, P.O. Box 263, Littleton, CO 80160. 1980. 214 pp. $18.50.

   Provides suggested units with activities and lists of books for four primary elements of literature (style, theme, character, setting). Books which stress these elements, or which can be used to motivate thinking about them, are included in the lists.

34. *Fantasy for Children: An Annotated Checklist,* 2nd ed. Ruth Nadelman Lynn. R. R. Bowker Co., Order Department, P.O. Box 1807, Ann Arbor, MI 48106. 1983. 444 pp. $29.95.

   Recommends over 1,500 fantasies for children in grades three to eight. Arranged in categories such as alternative worlds, magical toys, time travel, and so on. Books listed are all in print, with a special addenda included for out-of-print titles.

35. *Index to Poetry for Children and Young People, 1976–1981.* John E. Brewton, et al. 1983. 350 pp. $35.00.
   Index to Poetry for Children and Young People, 1970–1975. John E. Brewton, G. Meredith Blackburn, comps. 1978. $26.00.
   Index to Poetry for Children and Young People, 1964–1969. John E. Brewton, et al., ed. 1972. $20.00.
   Index to Children's Poetry. John E. Brewton and Sara W. Brewton, eds. 1942. $30.00.
   First Supplement. 1954. $18.00.
   Second Supplement, 1965. $18.00.
   All six books published by the H. W. Wilson Co., 950 University Avenue, Bronx, New York 10452.

   Each volume indexes collections of poetry by author, title, first line, and subject. Different collections are indexed in each volume. Classifies poems under a wide variety of subjects, making for easy access to poems by their topics.

36. *More Notes from a Different Drummer: A Guide to Juvenile Fiction Portraying the Disabled.* Barbara H. Baskin and Karen H. Harris. R. R. Bowker, Order Department, P.O. Box 1807, Ann Arbor, MI 48106. 1984. 495 pp. $27.50.
   Notes from a Different Drummer: A Guide to Juvenile Fiction Portraying the Handicapped. Barbara H. Baskin and

Karen H. Harris. R. R. Bowker, Order Department, P.O. Box 1807, Ann Arbor, MI 48106. 1977. 375 pp. $21.95.

Traces the history of portrayal of disabled persons in children's literature and discusses criteria for selection of contemporary titles. Includes an annotated list of about 400 titles in which disabled are portrayed, giving the type of disability, relation to the curriculum, and reading level.

f. Other Areas

37. *Accept Me as I Am: Best Books of Juvenile Nonfiction on Impairments and Disabilities.* Joan Brest Friedberg, June B. Mullins, and Adelaide Weir Sukiennik. R. R. Bowker Order Department, P.O. Box 1807, Ann Arbor, MI 48106. 1985. 363 pp. $27.50.

Contains 350 titles divided into four broad categories with author, title, and specific subject indexes.

38. *The Aging Adult in Children's Books and Nonprint Media: An Annotated Bibliography.* Catherine Townsend Horner. Scarecrow Press, P.O. Box 656, Metuchen, NJ 08840. 1982. 266 pp. $17.00.

A comprehensive list of fiction and nonprint materials about the aging adult. Lists of fiction, arranged according to age levels, include books about relationships, concerns, and activities of older people in relation to children as well as books about illness and death. Nonprint materials are largely factual in approach. No nonfiction book titles are included and the indexes are somewhat difficult to use.

39. *Best Science Books for Children: Selected and Annotated.* Kathryn Wolff, et al., eds. American Association for the Advancement of Science, 1333 H. Street NW, 8th Floor, Washington, DC 20005. 1983. 285 pp. $15.95.

An annotated list of high quality trade books in the sciences.

40. *The Bookfinder, Volume 3: When Kids Need Books: Annotations of Books Published 1979–1982.* Sharon Spredemann Dreyer. American Guidance Service, Circle Pines, MN 55014. 1985. 519 pp. $44.50. $17.95 paper.

This is the third volume of the Bookfinder series. Subject, author, and titles indexed are provided on the top half of the publication; lengthy reviews, which include subject cross-references, age levels, and specific information about the content of the book, are on the bottom half. Both fiction and nonfiction are included. The books included focus on problems children may experience, feelings, and relationships.

41. *Books to Help Children to Cope with Separation and Loss,* 2nd ed. Joanne E. Bernstein, comp. R. R. Bowker, Order Department, P.O. Box 1807, Ann Arbor, MI 48106. 1983. 439 pp. $34.95.

Includes several chapters on bibliotherapy plus annotated lists of titles in such categories as death, divorce, adoption, and foster children, and loss of mental or physical functions. 1,438 books were selected which were recommended by the *Horn Book, School Library Journal,* or *Publisher's Weekly.* Age level, interest, and reading level are included in each annotation.

42. *Careers in Fact and Fiction.* June Klein Bienstock and Ruth Bienstock Anolick. American Library Association, 50 East Huron Street, Chicago, IL 60611.

Annotates 1000 works of fiction, nonfiction, and biography which discuss careers. Oriented to a high school audience but useful for upper elementary.

43. *Celebrating with Books.* Nancy Polette and Marjorie Hamlin. Scarecrow Press, P.O. Box 656, Metuchen, NJ 1977. 184 pp. $15.00.

Suggests book titles, activities, and other means of celebrating major holidays.

44. *Celebrations: Read-Aloud Holiday and Theme Book Programs.* Caroline Feller Bauer. H. W. Wilson, 950 University Avenue, Bronx, NY 10452. 1985. 301 pp. $35.00.

Includes readings and plans for holiday activities for both well-known and Bauer's invented holiday occasions.

45. *Children's Mathematics Books: A Critical Bibliography.* Margaret Matthias and Diane Thiessen. American Library Association, 50 E. Huron St., Chicago, IL 60611. 1979. 68 pp. $6.00 paper.

Reviews almost 200 books suitable for elementary schoolchildren. Books are arranged in six major areas: Counting, Geometry, Measurement, Number Concepts, Time, and Miscellaneous. Annotations describe contents and indicate when activities are included in the text. Grade levels and ratings of quality are included for each title.

46. *Drugs: A Multimedia Sourcebook for Young Adults.* Sharon Ashenbrenner Charles and Sari Feldman. ABC-Clio/Neal-Schuman, Riviera Campus, 2040 A.P.S. Box 4397, Santa Barbara, CA 93103. 1980. 200 pp. $22.95.

Contains annotations for fiction and nonfiction as well as nonprint materials about drugs of all kinds. Guidelines for selection are carefully laid out. Also includes appendix which contains professional reading, a list of publishers, and an author, title, and subject index.

47. *Energy: A Multi-Media Guide for Children and Young Adults.* Judith H. Higgins. ABC-Clio/Neal Schuman, Riviera Campus, 2040 A.P.S. Box 4397, Santa Barbara, CA 93103. 1979. 195 pp. $22.95.

A list of both print and nonprint materials from a variety of sources including commercial, government, and trade materials for students in grades K–12. Annotations are critical, pointing out flaws in production, accuracy, or usefulness. Materials are arranged in groups by subject and then subdivided into print and nonprint formats.

48. *Fun for Kids: An Index to Children's Craft Books.* Marion F. Gallivan. Scarecrow Press, P.O. Box 656, Metuchen, NJ 08840. 1981. 340 pp. $17.00.

An index to several hundred craft books commonly purchased for library collections. Specific craft or art activities are listed with references to books in which plans and directions for the activity can be located.

49. *Health, Illness and Disability: A Guide to Books for Children and Young Adults.* Pat Azarnoff. R. R. Bowker Co., Order Department, Box 1807, Ann Arbor, MI 48106. 1983. 432 pp. $29.95.

An annotated list of over 1000 books about health issues and problems.

50. *Helping Children through Books,* rev. ed. Helen Keating Ott. Church and Synagogue Library Association, P.O. Box 1130, Bryn Mawr, PA 19010. 1979. 35 pp. $3.75.

Annotated books on contemporary problems for children in elementary and junior high school. Materials are subdivided by topic and age group under four broad categories: "Living with one-self;" "Living with others;" "Broadening one's friendships;" and "Understanding some special concerns."

51. *Index to Children's Songs.* Carolyn Sue Peterson and Ann D. Fenton. H. W. Wilson Company, 950 University Avenue, Bronx, NY 10452. 1979. 318 pp. $20.00.

Indexes over 5,000 songs in 298 children's song books, both single titles and collections. Songs are indexed by title and first line as well as by 1,000 subject headings and cross-references.

52. *Index to Handicrafts, Modelmaking and Workshop Projects.* Eleanor C. Lovell and Ruth M. Hall. 1936. 476 pp. $14.00.
Supplement, 1943. 527 pp. $14.00.
Second Supplement. 1950. 593 pp. $14.00.
Third Supplement. Harriet P. Turner and Amy Winslow. 1965, 914 pp. $18.00.
Fourth Supplement. E. Winifred Alt. 1969. 468 pp. $14.00.
Fifth Supplement. Pearl Turner. 1975. 620 pp. $20.00.
All published by F. W. Faxon Co., 15 Southwest Park, Westwood, MA 02090.
Indexes a number of craft books and a variety of children's and adult magazines for craft projects of all kinds. Arranged in order by the name of the craft with cross-references as necessary.

53. *The Museum of Science & Industry Basic List of Children's Science Books.* Bernice Richter. American Library Association. 50 E. Huron St., Chicago, IL 60611. 1985. 166 pp. $9.75 paper.
An annotated listing of 1400 science trade books for K–12 done in conjunction with the Chicago Museum of Science and Industry.

54. *Science Books for Children: Selections from Booklist, 1976–1983.* Selected by Denise Murcko Wilms. American Library Association, 50 E. Huron Street, Chicago, IL 60611. 1985. 183 pp. $15.00 paper.
A selection of reviews of science books from *Booklist* are arranged in Dewey classification order with author/title and subject indexes.

55. *Substance Abuse Materials for School Libraries: An Annotated Bibliography.* Theodora Andrews. Libraries Unlimited, P.O. Box 263, Littleton, Co. 80160. 1984. 215 pp. $22.50.
Contains 496 entries including reference works, general discussions, fiction, personal narratives, and materials on various aspects of substance abuse with appropriate age levels.

IV. INFORMATION ABOUT AUTHORS AND ILLUSTRATORS

1. *American Writers for Children before 1900.* Glenn E. Estes. Gale Research Co., Book Tower, Detroit, MI 48226. 1985. 441 pp. $88.00.
Critical biographies of 52 authors writing in the eighteenth and nineteenth centuries, including Joel Chandler Harris, Louisa May Alcott, and Hezekiah Butterworth. Full bibliographic information is given and pictures of the subjects and their works are included.

2. *Authors of Books for Young People.* Martha E. Ward and Dorothy A. Marquant, eds., 2nd ed. 1971. 579 pp. $25.00.
Supplement to the second edition. 1979. 308 pp. $18.00.
Illustrators of Books for Young People, 2nd ed. 1975. 223 pp. $15.00.
All published by Scarecrow Press, P.O. Box 656, Metuchen, NJ 08840.
Brief biographical information about authors and illustrators for children is arranged in alphabetical order by author. Includes lists of published works and references to more complete biographical information.

3. *The Illustrator's Notebook.* Lee Kingman, ed. The Horn Book, 31 St. James Avenue, Boston, MA 02116. 1978. 168 pp. $28.00.
Contains excerpts from articles by artists and illustrators which have appeared in *The Horn Book Magazine.* Articles discuss philosophy of illustration, history, its place in the arts, and the artists' experiences with various techniques of illustration.

4. *Illustrators of Children's Books 1744–1945.* Bertha E. Mahony, Louise Payson Latimer, and Beulah Formsbee, eds. 1947. 527 pp. $28.00.
Illustrators of Children's Books 1946–1956. Bertha Mahony Miller, Ruth Hill Viguers and Marcia Dalphin, eds. 1958. 229 pp. $28.00.
Illustrators of Children's Books 1957–1966. Lee Kingman, Joanna Foster and Ruth Giles Lontoft, eds. 1968. 295 pp. $28.00.
Illustrators of Children's Books 1967–1976. Lee Kingman, Grace Allen Hogarth and Harriet Quimby, eds. 1978. 290 pp. $35.00.
All published by The Horn Book, 31 St. James Ave., Boston, MA 02116.
All four volumes contain brief biographical and career sketches of artists and illustrators for children who were actively at work in this field during the period included in each volume. Articles discuss techniques, philosophy, and trends in illustration during the period. Bibliographies are included for each illustrator as well as selected bibliographies covering art and illustration of the period. Volume Four contains cumulative index.

5. *The Junior Book of Authors.* Stanley J. Kunitz and Howard Haycraft, eds. 1951. 309 pp. $18.00.
More Junior Authors. Muriel Fuller, ed. 1969. 235 pp. $16.00.
Third Book of Junior Authors and Illustrators. Doris de Montreville and Donna Hill, eds. 1972. 320 pp. $18.00.
Fourth Book of Junior Authors and Illustrators. Doris de Montreville and Elizabeth D. Crawford, eds. 1978. 370 pp. $22.00.
All published by H. W. Wilson Company, 950 University Avenue, Bronx, NY 10452.
Provides readable biographies of popular authors for young people which include, generally, a biographical statement by the author or illustrator, a photograph, a brief biography, and a list of that person's works.

6. *The Marble in the Water: Essays on Contemporary Writers of Fiction for Children and Young Adults.* David Rees. The Horn Book, 31 St. James Ave., Boston, MA 02116. 1980. 224 pp. $9.95 paper.
Includes essays on eighteen British and American authors including Beverly Cleary, Paula Fox, Judy Blume, Paul Zindel, and others.

7. *More Books by More People: Interviews with Sixty-Five Authors of Books for Children.* Lee Bennett Hopkins. Scholastic Book Service, 904 Sylvan Avenue, Englewood Cliffs, NJ 07632. 1974. 410 pp. $4.95 paper.
A sequel to the out-of-print *Books Are by People*, this volume introduces sixty-five more authors and illustrators to children. Most of the authors write for middle-grade children.

8. *Newbery Medal Books: 1922–1955.* Bertha Mahony Miller and Elinor Whitney Field, eds. 1955. 458 pp. $22.00.
Caldecott Medal Books: 1938–1957. Bertha Mahony Miller and Elinor Whitney Fields, eds. 1957. 239 pp. $22.00.
Newbery and Caldecott Medal Books: 1956–1965. Lee Kingman, ed. 1965. 300 pp. $22.00.
Newbery and Caldecott Medal Books: 1966–1975. Lee Kingman, ed. 1975. 321 pp. $22.00.
All published by The Horn Book, 31 St. James Avenue, Boston, MA 02116.

Each volume contains biographical sketches and texts of the award-winners' acceptance speeches as well as general observations of trends in the awards.

9. *Painted Desert, Green Shade: Essays on Contemporary Writers of Fiction for Children and Young Adults.* David Rees. The Horn Book, 31 St. James Avenue, Boston, MA 02116 1984. 197 pp.

Essays on thirteen British and American authors including L. M. Boston, Betsy Byars, Jane Langton, Jan Mark, Virginia Hamilton, and others.

10. *Pipers at the Gates of Dawn: The Wisdom of Children's Literature.* Jonathon Cott. Random House, 201 East 50th Street, New York, NY 10022. 1983. $19.95.

Seven essays on authors and illustrators for children focusing both on biographical information and on how these creators fit into the world of literature. Includes essays on Dr. Seuss, Maurice Sendak, William Steig, Astrid Lindgren, Achebe, P. L. Travers, and the Opies.

11. *"Profiles in Literature" Children's Authors and Illustrators on Video-cassette.* Jacqueline Shachter. Temple University, Ritter 443, Philadelphia, PA 19122. $125.00 each.

Forty-eight half-hour interviews with leading authors, illustrators, and editors of children's books. Most of the tapes are filmed in black and white, although more recent ones are in color.

12. *A Sense of Story: Essays on Contemporary Writers for Children.* John Rowe Townsend. The Horn Book, 31 St. James Avenue, Boston, MA 02116. 1973. 216 pp. $6.50.

Includes essays on nineteen English language authors for children including brief biographies, notes on their books, critical remarks, and lists of their books. Essays reflect the critical position of the author.

13. *Something about the Author.* Anne Commaire. Gale Research, Book Tower, Detroit, MI 48226. 41 volumes currently in print, added to periodically. $64.00/volume.

Clear and sizable essays on contemporary authors and illustrators. Updating allows more recent authors to be included. Contains photographs as well as reproductions from works of the illustrators. Suitable for middle grade children to use for gathering biographical information.

14. *A Sounding of Storytellers: New and Revised Essays on Contemporary Writers for Children.* John Rowe Townsend. Harper & Row, 10 E. 53rd Street, New York, NY 10022. 1979. 218 pp. $14.90.

Townsend reevaluates seven of the authors included in his earlier *A Sense of Story,* including the new ground which they have covered in more recent works. Several American authors are included in the new selections, including Vera and Bill Cleaver, Virginia Hamilton, and E. L. Konigsburg.

15. *Twentieth-Century Children's Writers,* 2nd ed. Daniel Kirkpatrick, ed. St. Martin's Press, Reference and Scholarly Division, RS-80, 175 Fifth Avenue, New York, NY 10010. 1983. 1500 pp. $65.00.

Over 700 entries give information on such writers as Maurice Sendak, Nikki Giovanni, Ted Hughes, I. B. Singer, and others. Includes critical essays and bibliography.

V. PERIODICALS

1. *Appraisal: Children's Science Books.* Children's Science Book Review Committee, 36 Cummington Street, Boston, MA 02215. Quarterly. $12.00.

Each issue contains reviews of about seventy-five children's science books. Useful for collection development in sciences and social sciences.

2. *Book Review Digest.* The H. W. Wilson Co., 950 University Avenue, Bronx, NY 10452. Ten times/year. Service basis rates quoted on request.

Evaluates about 4,000 adult and children's books per year. For those books included, provides citations from several reviews which have appeared in other review periodicals.

3. *Bookbird: Literature for Children and Young People.* Hermann Schaffstein. Verlag, D-4600 Dortlund 1, Degginstr 93, West Germany. Quarterly, $9.50.

An international periodical on literature for children containing papers, lists of prize-winning books, and lists of translated titles.

4. *The Booklist.* American Library Association, 50 E. Huron, Chicago, IL 60611. Twice/month. $40.00.

Reviews both adult and children's titles, including both print and nonprint materials. Reviews are annotated and graded by age levels and grades. Includes reviews of new selection tools. Often contains subject lists of good books in particular fields. Lists prize-winning books annually.

5. *Book World.* c/o Washington Post, 1150 15th Street, NW, Washington, DC 20071. $13.00.

A weekly supplement to the Post and several other newspapers. Reviews children's books regularly. Issues large special children's book editions in fall and spring.

6. *The Bulletin of the Center for Children's Books.* Graduate Library School, University of Chicago Press, 5801 Ellis Avenue, Chicago, IL 60637. Monthly $16.00.

Reviews current children's books with adverse as well as favorable reviews. Each entry is graded. Annotations stress curricular use, values, and literary merit.

7. *CBC Features* (formerly *The Calendar*). Children's Book Council, 67 Irving Place, New York, NY 10003. A one-time handling charge of $25.00 No annual rate.

A semi-annual newsletter about children's books, including information about special events, free and inexpensive materials from publishers, and lists of prize-winners.

8. *CM: Canadian Materials for Schools and Libraries,* Canadian Library Association, 151 Sparks St., Ottowa, Ontario KIP 583. Quarterly. $30.00.

Reviews English language materials written by Canadians or published in Canada. Evaluates books, films, filmstrips, games, and periodicals.

9. *Childhood Education.* Association for Childhood Education International. 3615 Wisconsin Avenue NW, Washington, DC 20016. Five times/year. $32.00.

Includes a column on children's books that contains annotated reviews on about twenty-five books.

10. *Children's Literature in Education.* c/o Agathon Press, 15 E. 26th, New York, NY 10010. Quarterly. $13.50.

A publication devoted to serious criticism of children's literature and commentary on the role of literature in education. Articles cover British and American literature and discuss history, children's response, use of books in classrooms, and various literary topics.

11. *Cricket Magazine.* Open Court Publishing Co., 1058 Eighth Street, LaSalle, IL 61301. Monthly. $18.50.

A literary magazine for children of elementary school age. Includes new stories and poems by well-known children's authors as well as excerpts and serializations of older pieces of literature. Includes children's reviews of books, interviews with authors, and children's writing.

12. *The Horn Book.* Horn Book, Inc. Park Square Building, 31 S. James Ave., Boston, MA 02116. Bi-monthly. $30.00.

Includes detailed reviews of children's books the editorial staff feels are the best in children's literature. Contains articles about the literature, interviews with authors, and text of important speeches in the field of literature. (Newbery and Caldecott Acceptance speeches are published in the August issue each year.) October issue gives a list of the outstanding books of the previous year.

13. *In Review: Canadian Books for Young People*. Ministry of Culture and Recreation, Libraries and Community Information Branch, Parliament Buildings, Toronto, Ontario, M7A 2R9. Bi-monthly $14.00 for three years.

Librarians review Canadian children's books. "Profile" introduces Canadian authors to children.

14. *Interracial Books for Children Bulletin*. Council on Interracial Books for Children, Inc. 1841 Broadway, New York, NY 10023. Eight times/year. $12.00.

Articles and review focus on issues of racism, sexism, handicapism, and other issues in children's literature. Attempts to establish guidelines and criteria for evaluation of children's materials.

15. *Language Arts*. National Council of Teachers of English, 1111 Kenyon Road, Urbana, IL 61801. Monthly, September through May. $30.00.

"Books for Children" section features regular reviews of new books. Several issues focus on literature and reading. Contains articles on authors, using literature in the classroom, and so on.

16. *The Lion and the Unicorn*. Department of English. Brooklyn College, Brooklyn, NY 11210. Five times/year. $4.00.

Presents articles of literary criticism of children's literature. Each issue presents a particular theme around which articles are centered.

17. *The New York Times Book Review*. University Microfilms International, 300 N. Zeeb Road, Ann Arbor, MI 48106. Weekly. $22.00.

Weekly column entitled "For Younger Readers" reviews some children's books. Two issues in fall and spring are devoted to children's books exclusively. Before Christmas, a list of outstanding books is included.

18. *Phaedrus: A Newsletter of Children's Literature*. Farleigh Dickinson University, Madison, NJ 07940. Twice/year. $5.00.

Articles emphasize research and theoretical aspects of children's literature.

19. *Publisher's Weekly*. R. R. Bowker and Co., P. O. Box 13746, Philadelphia, PA 19101. Weekly. $84.00.

Twice a year, in Spring and Fall, a "Children's Book Number" is published which includes new titles from all major publishers, as well as reviews. All issues review some children's books. Both positive and negative reviews are included. Occasionally includes feature articles on children's books and publishing for children.

20. *School Library Journal*. R. R. Bowker and Co., Box

13706, Philadelphia, PA 19101. Monthly/September through May. $51.00.

Reviews most children's books using as reviewers librarians, teachers, and critics from around the country. Includes both positive and negative reviews. Categorizes reviews by age levels. Also includes feature articles on children's literature, children's library services, technology, and nonprint materials. December issue includes a "Best Books" section.

21. *School Library Media Quarterly*. American Association of School Librarians. American Library Association, 50 E. Huron, Chicago, IL 60611. Quarterly. $20.00.

Official journal of AASL. Includes articles on book evaluation, censorship, library services, standards of service, and so on.

22. *Science Books and Films*. American Association for the Advancement of Science. 1515 Massachusetts Ave., NW, Washington, DC 20005. Quarterly, $20.00.

Reviews trade, test, and reference books for students in all grades in both pure and applied sciences. Includes nonprint materials. Indicates level of expertise required to use a piece of material. Books are reviewed by specialists in the field.

23. *Science and Children*. National Science Teachers Association, 1201 Sixteenth Street NW, Washington, DC. Eight times/year. $28.00.

Includes a monthly column which reviews books and non-print materials.

24. *Top of the News*. Association for Library Service to Children and the Young Adult Services Division of the American Library Association, 50 East Huron Street, Chicago, IL 60611. Quarterly. $20.00.

Articles on issues in children's literature, international news, text of speeches and awards, and other news about the state of children's literature are included.

25. *The WEB: Wonderfully Exciting Books*. The Ohio State University, The Reading Center, 200 Ramseyer Hall, Columbus, OH 43210. Quarterly. $10.00.

Devoted to helping teachers to incorporate children's literature into the curriculum through reviews which emphasize classroom use and through a "web of possibilities" for a major thematic area which is included in each issue. Reviews are written by practicing teachers and librarians.

26. *Wilson Library Bulletin*. The H. W. Wilson Co., 950 University Avenue, Bronx, NY 10452. Monthly, September to June. $30.00.

Includes discussions and reviews of all types of books and materials. Features a monthly column of reviews of children's books, plus articles about authors, list of awards, etc. The October issue is devoted to children's books.

APPENDIX C **PUBLISHERS' ADDRESSES***

ABINGDON PRESS; 201 Eighth Ave. S; Nashville, TN 37202.

ADAMA BOOKS; 306 W. 38 St; New York, NY 10018.

ADDISON-WESLEY; 1 Jacob Way; Reading, MA 01867.

ALPHABET PRESS; (*see* Neugebauer Press USA).

ATHENEUM PUBLISHERS; 115 Fifth Avenue; New York, NY 10003.

THE ATLANTIC MONTHLY PRESS; 8 Arlington St.; Boston, MA 02116.

AVON BOOKS; 1790 Broadway; New York, NY 10019.

BANTAM BOOKS INC.; 666 Fifth Ave.; New York, NY 10103.

PETER BEDRICK BOOKS INC.; 125 E. 23 St.; New York, NY 10010.

BELLEROPHON BOOKS; 36 Anacapa St.; Santa Barbara, CA 93101.

BRADBURY PRESS; (*see* Macmillan Publishing Co.).

BROADMAN PRESS; 127 Ninth Ave. N; Nashville, TN 37234.

DICK BRUNA BOOKS INC.; 300 Reistertown Rd.; Baltimore, MD 21208.

CAEDMON; 1995 Broadway; New York, NY 10023.

CAROLRHODA BOOKS, INC.; 241 First Ave. N; Minneapolis, MN 55401.

CHILDREN'S PRESS; 1224 W. Van Buren St.; Chicago, IL 60607.

CLARION BOOKS; 52 Vanderbilt Ave.; New York, NY 10017.

COLLINS; Collins & World (*see* The Putnam Publishing Group).

COWARD-MCCANN; (*see* The Putnam Publishing Group).

CREATIVE EDUCATIONAL, INC; 123 S. Broad St.; Mankato, MN 56001.

CROWN PUBLISHERS, INC.; 1 Park Ave., New York, NY 10016.

THOMAS Y. CROWELL JUNIOR BOOKS; (*see* Harper & Row, Publishers).

DELACORTE PRESS; 1 Dag Hammarskjold Plaza; 245 E. 47 St.; New York, NY 10017.

DELL PUBLISHING CO., INC.; (*see* Delacorte Press).

DETERMINED PRODUCTIONS; Box 2150; San Francisco, CA 94126.

ANDRE DEUTSCH; (*see* E. P. Dutton & Co., Inc.).

DIAL BOOKS FOR YOUNG READERS; (*see* E. P. Dutton, Inc.).

DODD, MEAD & CO.; 79 Madison Ave.; New York, NY 10016.

DOUBLEDAY PUBLISHING, INC.; 245 Park Ave.; New York, NY 10017.

DOVER PUBLICATIONS, INC.; 180 Varick St.; New York, NY 10014.

E. P. DUTTON & CO.; INC.; 2 Park Ave.; New York, NY 10003.

EDC PUBLISHING; 8141 E. 44 St.; Tulsa, OK 74145.

EMC CORPORATION; 300 York Ave.; St. Paul, MN 55101.

ENSLOW PUBLISHERS; Bloy St. and Ramsey Ave.; Hillside, NJ 07205.

M. EVANS & CO, INC; 216 E. 49 St., New York, NY 10017.

FABER & FABER, INC.; 50 Cross St.; Winchester, MA 01890.

FARRAR, STRAUS & GIROUX, INC.; 19 Union Sq. W.; New York, NY 10003.

THE FEMINIST PRESS; Box 311; New York, NY 10128.

FOUR WINDS PRESS; (*see* Macmillan Publishing Co.).

FUNK & WAGNALLS INC.; 52 E. 77 St.; New York, NY 10021.

DAVID R. GODINE, PUBLISHER, INC.; 306 Dartmouth St.; Boston, MA 02116.

GOLDEN PRESS; 850 Third Ave.; New York, NY 10022.

THE GREEN TIGER PRESS; 1061 India St.; San Diego, CA 92101.

GREENWILLOW BOOKS; (*see* William Morrow & Co.).

GROSSET & DUNLAP; (*see* The Putnam Publishing Group).

HARCOURT BRACE JOVANOVICH, INC.; 1250 Sixth Ave.; San Diego, CA 92101.

HARPER & ROW, PUBLISHERS; 10 E. 53 St.; New York, NY 10022.

HILL & WANG; (*see* Farrar, Straus & Giroux, Inc.).

HOLIDAY HOUSE, INC.; 18 E. 56 St.; New York, NY 10022.

HOLT, RINEHART AND WINSTON, INC.; 521 Fifth Ave.; New York, NY 10175.

HOUGHTON MIFFLIN CO.; 2 Park Ave.; Boston, MA 02107.

JEWISH PUBLICATION SOCIETY OF AMERICA; 60 E. 42 St.; New York, NY 10165.

ALFRED A. KNOPF, INC.; 201 E. 50 St.; New York, NY 10022.

LERNER PUBLICATIONS CO.; 241 First Ave. N.; Minneapolis, MN 55401.

LIPPINCOTT JUNIOR BOOKS; (*see* Harper & Row, Publishers).

LITTLE, BROWN & CO.; 34 Beacon St.; Boston, MA 02106.

LODESTAR BOOKS; (*see* E. P. Dutton & Co., Inc.).

LOTHROP, LEE & SHEPARD; (*see* William Morrow & Co., Inc.).

MACMILLAN PUBLISHING CO., INC.; 866 Third Ave.; New York, NY 10022.

JULIAN MESSNER; 1230 Avenue of the Americas; New York, NY 10020.

METHEUN INC.; 29 W. 35 St.; New York, NY 10001.

WILLIAM MORROW & CO.; 105 Madison Ave.; New York, NY 10016.

NATIONAL GEOGRAPHIC PRESS; 17 & M Sts. NW; Washington, DC 20036.

THOMAS NELSON INC.; Nelson Pl. at Elm Hill Pike; Nashville, TN 37214.

NEUGEBAUER PRESS USA; 60 Main St.; Natick, MA 01760.

THE NEW AMERICAN LIBRARY; 1633 Broadway; New York, NY 10019.

RICHARD C. OWEN PUBLISHERS, INC.; Box 819 Rockefeller Center; New York, NY 10185.

OXFORD UNIVERSITY PRESS; 200 Madison Ave.; New York, NY 10016.

PANTHEON BOOKS; (*see* Alfred A. Knopf, Inc.).

PARENTS MAGAZINE PRESS; 685 Third Ave.; New York, NY 10017.

PARKER BROTHERS PUBLISHING; 50 Dunham Rd.; Beverly, MA 01915.

PARNASSUS PRESS; (*see* Houghton Mifflin Co.).

PELICAN PUBLISHING CO., INC.; 1101 Monroe St., Box 189; Gretna, LA 70053.

PENGUIN BOOKS; (*see* Viking Penguin).

PHILOMEL BOOKS; (*see* The Putnam Publishing Group).

PICTURE BOOK STUDIO; (*see* Neugebauer Press USA).

PLATT & MUNK; (*see* The Putnam Publishing Group).

CLARKSON N. POTTER; (*see* Crown Publishers Inc.).

PRENTICE-HALL; (*see* Simon & Schuster).

PRICE/STERN/SLOAN PUBLISHERS, INC.; 410 N. La Cienega Blvd.; Los Angeles, CA 90048.

THE PUTNAM PUBLISHING GROUP; 51 Madison Ave.; New York, NY 10010.

RAND MCNALLY & CO.; Box 7600; Chicago, IL 60690.

RANDOM HOUSE, INC.; 201 E. 50 St.; New York, NY 10022.

*Note: Publishers' addresses may change. For complete and up-to-date information, see the current edition of *Literary Market Place* or of *Children's Books in Print*.

SCHOCKEN BOOKS, INC.; 62 Cooper Sq.; New York, NY 10003.

SCHOLASTIC, INC.; 730 Broadway; New York, NY 10003.

SCOTT, FORESMAN & CO.; 1900 E. Lake Ave.; Glenview, IL 60025.

CHARLES SCRIBNER'S SONS; 115 Fifth Ave.; New York, NY 10003.

THE SEABURY PRESS, INC.; (*see* Clarion Books).

SIMON & SCHUSTER, INC.; 1230 Ave. of the Americas; New York, NY 10020.

STEMMER HOUSE; 2627 Caves Rd.; Owings Mill, MD 21117.

STERLING PUBLISHING CO.; INC.; 2 Park Ave.; New York, NY 10016.

TROLL ASSOCIATES; 320 Rt. 17; Mahway, NY 07430.

TUNDRA BOOKS OF NORTHERN NEW YORK; Box 1030; Plattsburgh, NY 12901.

CHARLES E. TUTTLE CO.; INC.; 28 E. Main St.; Rutland, VT 05701.

VAN NOSTRAND REINHOLD CO., INC.; 115 Fifth Ave.; New York, NY 10003.

VANGUARD PRESS, INC.; 424 Madison Ave.; New York, NY 10017.

VIKING PENGUIN, INC.; 40 W. 23 St.; New York, NY 10010.

WALKER & CO.; 720 Fifth Ave.; New York, NY 10019.

FREDERICK WARNE & CO, INC.; 40 W. 23 St.; New York, NY 10010.

FRANKLIN WATTS, INC.; 387 Park Ave. S.; New York, NY 10016.

WESTERN PUBLISHING CO.; 850 Third Ave.; New York, NY 10022.

THE WESTMINSTER PRESS; 925 Chestnut St.; Philadelphia, PA 19107.

ALBERT WHITMAN & CO.; 5747 W. Howard St.; Niles, IL 60648.

WINDMILL BOOKS, INC.; (*see* E. P. Dutton).

ACKNOWLEDGMENTS

FOR ARTWORK FROM:

Aesop's Fables. Illustrated by A. and M. Provensen © 1965 Western Publishing Company, Inc., Reprinted by permission. *Alfie Gets in First* by Shirley Hughes. Copyright © 1981 by Shirley Hughes. Used by permission of Lothrop, Lee & Shepard Books, a division of William Morrow & Company. *Amos & Boris* by William Steig. Copyright © 1971 by William Steig. Reprinted with the permission of Farrar, Straus & Giroux. *Anastasia Has the Answers* by Lois Lowry. Jacket painting © 1985 by Diane deGroat. Reprinted by permission of Houghton Mifflin Company. *Animal Alphabet* by Bert Kitchen. Copyright © 1984 by Bert Kitchen. Reproduced by permission of the publisher, Dial Books for Young Readers. Permission granted by E.P. Dutton, Inc. *Anno's Counting Book* by Mitsumasa Anno (Thomas Y. Crowell). Copyright © 1975 by Kodansha Ltd. (Tokyo). Reprinted by permission of Harper & Row, Publishers, Inc.

Frontispiece from *The Baby's Own Aesop* by Walter Crane. Reproduced by permission of the publisher, Frederick Warne and Co., Inc. Linocut by Ashley Wolff from *The Bells of London.* Copyright © 1985 by Ashley Wolff. Used by permission of Dodd, Mead and Company, Inc. *Benny Bakes a Cake* by Eve Rice. Copyright © 1981 by Eve Rice, used by permission of Greenwillow Books, a division of William Morrow and Company. Illustration from *Ben's Trumpet* by Rachel Isadora. Copyright © 1979 by Rachel Isadora Maiorano. Used by permission of Greenwillow Books, a division of William Morrow & Company. *Between Cattails* by Terry Tempest Williams, illustrated by Peter Parnall. Illustrations copyright © 1985 by Peter Parnall. Used by permission of Charles Scribner's Sons. *Big Ones Little Ones* by Tana Hoban. Copyright © 1976 by Tana Hoban. Used by permission of Greenwillow Books, a division of William Morrow and Company. *The Book of Pigericks* by Arnold Lobel. Copyright © 1983 by Arnold Lobel. Reprinted by permission of Harper & Row, Publishers, Inc. *The Borrowers* by Mary Norton, illustrated by Beth and Joe Krush. Copyright 1952, 1953 by Mary Norton. Reproduced by permission of Harcourt Brace Jovanovich, Inc. *Bridge to Terabithia* by Katherine Paterson. Illustrated by Donna Diamond (Thomas Y. Crowell). Copyright © 1977 by Katherine Paterson. Reprinted by permission of Harper & Row, Publishers.

A Chair for My Mother by Vera B. Williams. Copyright © 1982 by Vera B. Williams. Used by permission of Greenwillow Books, a division of William Morrow and Company. *Charlotte's Web* by E.B. White. Pictures by Garth Williams. Copyright 1952 by E. B. White. Illustrations renewed 1980 by Garth Williams. Reprinted by permission of Harper & Row, Publishers, Inc. *Call It Courage* by Armstrong Sperry. Copyright 1940 by Macmillan Publishing Co., Inc. Renewed 1968 by Armstrong Sperry. Used by permission of Macmillan Publishing Co., Inc. *Cathedral* by David Macaulay. Copyright © 1973 by David Macaulay. Reprinted by permission of Houghton Mifflin Company. *Commodore Perry in the Land of the Shogun* by Rhoda Blumberg. Copyright © 1985. Used by permission of Lothrop, Lee and Shepard (A Division of William Morrow & Company). *Cornrows* by Camille Yarbrough, illustrated by Carole Byard. Copyright © 1979 by Carole Byard. Reprinted by permission of Coward, McCann & Geoghegan. *Crow Boy* by Taro Yashima. Copyright 1955 by Mitsu and Taro Yashima. Copyright renewed © 1983 by Taro Yashima. Reprinted by permission of Viking Penguin, Inc.

Dakota Dugout by Ann Turner, illustrated by Ronald Himler. Copyright © 1985. Reproduced by permission of Macmillan Publishing Company. *Dawn* by Uri Shulevitz. Copyright © 1974 by Uri Shulevitz. Used by permission of Farrar, Straus, and Giroux. *Doctor De Soto* by William Steig. Copyright © 1982 by William Steig. Used by permission of Farrar, Straus and Giroux. *The Door in the Wall* by Marguerite deAngeli. Copyright 1949 by Marguerite deAngeli. Reprinted by permission of Doubleday.

Eleanor Roosevelt, First Lady of the World, by Doris Faber, illustrated by Donna Ruff. Text copyright © Doris Faber, 1985. Illustrations Copyright © by Donna Ruff, 1985. Reprinted by permission of Viking Penguin, Inc. Illustrations by Ed Young reprinted by permission of Philomel Books from *The Emperor and the Kite* by Jane Yolen, illustration copyright © 1967 by World Publishing Company. *Ernest and Celestine* by Gabrielle Vincent. Copyright 1982 © William Morrow and Company, Inc. by permission of Greenwillow Books, a division of William Morrow & Company.

A Farmer's Alphabet by Mary Azarian. Copyright 1981 by Mary Azarian. Reprinted by permission of David R. Godine Publishers, Inc. Illustration by Wendy Watson reprinted by permission of Philomel Books from *First Farm in the Valley: Anna's Story* by Anne Pellowski, illustrations by Wendy Watson, illustrations Copyright © 1982 by Wendy Watson. *Fish is Fish* by Leo Lionni. Copyright © 1970 by Leo Lionni. Reprinted by permission of Pantheon Books, a Division of Random House, Inc. *Flying* by Donald Crews. Copyright © 1986 by Donald Crews. Used by permission of Greenwillow Books, a division of William Morrow and Company, Inc. *Frog and Toad Are Friends* by Arnold Lobel. Copyright © 1970 by Arnold Lobel. Reprinted by permission of Harper & Row, Publishers, Inc. *Frozen Fire* by James Houston. Copyright © 1977 by James Houston. Reproduced by permission of Atheneum Publishers, Inc.

Grandfather Twilight by Barbara Berger. Copyright © 1984 by Barbara Berger. Reprinted by permission of Philomel Books. *The Great Alexander the Great,* by Joe Lasker. Copyright © 1983 by Joe Lasker. Reprinted by permission of Viking Penguin, Inc. *The Green Book* by Jill Paton Walsh, illustrations by Lloyd Bloom. Pictures Copyright © 1982 by Lloyd Bloom. Reprinted with permission of Farrar, Straus, and Giroux. *The Grey King* by Susan Cooper, illustrated by Machall Heslop. Copyright © 1975 by Susan Cooper (A Margaret K. McElderry Book). Reprinted with permission of Atheneum.

Handles by Jan Mark. Copyright © 1985 by Jan Mark. Reproduced by permission of Atheneum Publishers, Inc. *Hansel and Gretel,* illustrated by Anthony Browne. Reprinted by permission of Julia MacRae Books, a division of Franklin Watts. *Hansel and Gretel* by Rika Lesser and Paul O. Zelinsky. Illustrations by Paul O. Zelinsky. Copyright © 1984 by Paul O. Zelinsky. Used by permission of Dodd, Mead & Company. *The Helen Oxenbury Nursery Story Book* by Helen Oxenbury. Copyright © 1985 by Helen Oxenbury. Reprinted by permission of Alfred A. Knopf, Inc. *Hickory* by Palmer Brown. Copyright © 1978 by Palmer Brown. Reprinted by permission of Harper & Row, Publishers, Inc. Positive and negative ink sketches by Charles Keeping for *The Highway Man* by Alfred Noyes. Illustrations Copyright © 1981 by Charles Keeping. Used by permission of Oxford University Press, England. *Homecoming* by Cynthia Voight. Jacket painting by Ted Lewin, copyright © 1981 by Ted Lewin. Reproduced with permission of Atheneum Publishers, Inc. Illustration by Margot Tomes reprinted by permission of G. P. Putnam's Sons from *Homesick, My Own Story* by Jean Fritz, drawings copyright © 1982 by Margot Tomes. *Honey, I Love and Other Love Poems* by Eloise Greenfield, illustrations by Diane and Leo Dillon. Illustrations copyright © 1978 by Diane and Leo Dillon. Reprinted by permission of Harper & Row, Publishers, Inc. *The Human Body,* text by Jonathan Miller. Designed by David Pelham, illustrations by Harry Wilcox. Copyright © 1983 by Dark Horse Productions, Limited. Reprinted by permission of Viking Penguin, Inc.

Photographs from *Immigrant Kids* by Russell Freedman. Courtesy of the National Park Service. *In a Spring Garden* edited by Richard Lewis, picture by Ezra Jack Keats. Pictures copyright ©

Quimby, Age 8 by Beverly Cleary, illustrated by Alan Tiegreen. Copyright © 1981 by Beverly Cleary. Used by permission of William Morrow & Company.

Saint George and the Dragon, retold by Margaret Hodges, illustrated by Trina Schart Hyman. Illustrations copyright © 1984 by Trina Schart Hyman. By permission of Little, Brown and Company. *Say It!* by Charlotte Zolotow. Pictures by James Stevenson, Greenwillow Books 1980, by permission of Greenwillow Books, a Division of William Morrow & Company. *Shadow* translated and illustrated by Marcia Brown from the French of Blaise Cendrars. Illustrations copyright © 1982 by Marcia Brown. Reproduced by permission of Charles Scribner's Sons. Illustration by Edward Gorey from *The Shrinking of Treehorn* by Florence Parry Heide. Illustrations copyright © 1971 by Edward Gorey. Used by permission of Holiday House. Illustration from *Sir Gawain and the Loathly Lady* retold by Selina Hastings, illustrated by Juan Wijngaard, 1985. Used by permission of Lothrop, Lee and Shepard, a division of William Morrow & Company. Linocut by Dirk Zimmer for *The Sky Is Full of Song.* Poems selected by Lee Bennett Hopkins. Illustrations Copyright © 1983 by Dirk Zimmer. Used by permission of Harper & Row, Publishers. *The Sleeping Beauty,* retold and illustrated by Warwick Hutton. Copyright © 1979 by Warwick Hutton, (A Margaret K. McElderry Book). Reproduced by permission of Atheneum Publishers, Inc. *The Snow Queen* by Hans Christian Andersen, adapted by Naomi Lewis. Illustrated by Errol LeCain. Illustrations copyright © 1979 by Errol LeCain. Reprinted with permission of Penguin Books Ltd. *The Snowy Day* by Ezra Jack Keats. Copyright © 1962 by Ezra Jack Keats. Reprinted by permission of Viking Penguin, Inc. *Song of the Horse* by Richard Kennedy, illustrated by Marcia Sewall. Illustrations Copyright © 1981 by Marcia Sewall. Reproduced by permission of the publishers, E. P. Dutton, a division of New American Library. Illustration from *Spirit Child: A Story of the Nativity,* translated by John Bierhorst, illustrated by Barbara Cooney. Copyright © 1984 by Barbara Cooney. Used by permission of William Morrow & Company. Endpaper from *The Story of Old Mrs. Brubeck* by Lore Segal, illustrated by Marcia Sewall. Copyright © 1981 by Lore Segal. Illustrations copyright © 1981 by Marcia Sewall. Reprinted by permission of Pantheon Books, a Division of Random House, Inc. *Strega Nona* by Tomie de Paola © 1975 by Tomie de Paola. Used by permission of the publisher, Prentice-Hall, Inc., Englewood Cliffs, N.J. *Sun Horse, Moon Horse* by Rosemary Sutcliff, decorations by Shirley Felts. Decorations copyright © 1977 by The Bodley Head. Reproduced by permission of the publisher, E. P. Dutton, a division of New American Library. *Sunshine* by Jan Ormerod. Copyright © 1981 by Jan Ormerod, used by permission of Lothrop, Lee & Shepard Books, a division of William Morrow & Company. *Sweet Whispers, Brother Rush* by Virginia Hamilton. Illustrations copyright © 1982 by Leo and Diane Dillon. Reproduced by permission of Leo and Diane Dillon.

The Tale of Jemima Puddle-Duck by Beatrix Potter. Reproduced by permission of the publisher, Frederick Warne & Co., Inc. *This Time, Tempe Wick?* by Patricia Lee Gauch. Illustration copyright © 1974 by Margot Tomes and used by the artist's permission. Illustration by Marcia Brown from *The Three Billy Goats Gruff* by Asbjornsen and Moe. Copyright 1957 by Marcia Brown, used by permission of Harcourt Brace Jovanovich, Inc. *Tiger Lilies and Other Beastly Plants* by Elizabeth Ring, illustrated by Barbara Bash. Walker and Company, 1984. Illustration by Tomie de Paola reprinted by permission of G. P. Putnam's Sons from *Tomie De Paola's Mother Goose,* Copyright © 1985 by Tomie de Paola.

Under the North Star, by Ted Hughes, drawings by Leonard Baskin. Text copyright © Ted Hughes, 1981. Illustrations copyright © Leonard Baskin, 1981. Reprinted by permission of Viking Penguin, Inc.

A Visit to William Blake's Inn by Nancy Willard. Text copyright © 1981, 1980 by Nancy Willard. Illustrations copyright © by Alice Provensen and Martin Provensen. Reprinted by permission of Harcourt Brace Jovanovich, Inc.

Waiting to Waltz by Cynthia Rylant, illustrations by Stephen Gammell. Illustrations copyright © 1984 by Stephen Gammell. Reprinted with permission of Bradbury Press, an affiliate of Macmillan, Inc. *We Be Warm Till Springtime Comes* by Lillie D. Chaffin, illustrated by Lloyd Bloom. Illustrations copyright © 1980 by Lloyd Bloom. Reprinted with permission of Macmillan Publishing Co., Inc. *What Happened in Hamelin* by Gloria Skurzynski. Copyright © 1979 by Gloria Skurzynski, book jacket by Friso Henstra. Used by permission of Four Winds Press, a division of Scholastic. *When I Was Young in the Mountains* by Cynthia Rylant, illustrated by Diane Goode. Illustrations copyright © 1982 by Diane Goode, Reproduced by permission of the publisher, E. P. Dutton, a division of New American Library. Illustration by Margot Tomes reprinted by permission of G. P. Putnam's Sons from *Where Do You Think You're Going, Christopher Columbus?* by Jean Fritz, illustrations copyright © 1980 by Margot Tomes. *Where the Buffaloes Begin* by Olaf Baker, drawings by Stephen Gammell. Text copyright © Frederick Warne and Company, Inc., 1981. Illustrations copyright © Stephen Gammell, 1981. Reprinted by permission of Viking Penguin, Inc. *Which Way Courage* by Eiveen Weiman. Jacket painting copyright © 1981 by Michael Garland. Reprinted with the permission of Atheneum Publishers, Inc. *Why Mosquitoes Buzz in People's Ears* by Verna Aardema, pictures by Leo and Diane Dillon. Pictures copyright © 1975 by Leo and Diane Dillon. Reproduced by permission of the publisher, Dial Books for Young Readers. Permission granted by E. P. Dutton, Inc. *Wild Mouse* by Irene Brady. Copyright © 1976 by Irene Brady. Reproduced with permission of Charles Scribner's Sons. *Winnie-the-Pooh* by A. A. Milne, illustrated by Ernest H. Shepard. Copyright 1926 by E. P. Dutton, renewed 1954 by A. A. Milne. Reproduced by permission of the publisher E. P. Dutton, a division of New American Library. *A Winter Place* by Ruth Yaffee Radin. Paintings by Mattie Lou O'Kelley. Illustrations copyright © 1982 by Mattie Lou O'Kelley. Used by permission of Little Brown and Company in association with the Atlantic Monthly Press. Illustration by Ruth Robbins from *A Wizard of Earthsea* by Ursula K. LeGuin. Map copyright © 1968 by Ruth Robbins. A Parnassus Press Book. Reprinted by permission of Houghton Mifflin Company. *The Wreck of the Zepher* by Chris Van Allsburg. Copyright © 1983 by Chris Van Allsburg. Reprinted by permission of Houghton Mifflin Company.

Illustration by Ed Young reprinted by permission of Philomel Books from *Yeh-Shen, a Cinderella Story from China* by Ai-Ling Louie, illustrations Copyright © 1982 by Ed Young. Illustration from *You'll Soon Grow into Them, Titch,* by Pat Hutchins. Copyright © 1983 by Pat Hutchins, used by permission of Greenwillow Books, a division of William Morrow & Company.

FOR PHOTOGRAPHS:

Cover and photos on pages 49, 145, 626 and two color pictures in Color Section II by James Ballard of James Ballard and Associates, Winnetka, Illinois. Part 1 photo by Kathy Woolsey. Photo on page 713 by Ann Dunetz, Kenton, Ohio. Photo on page 180 by Barbara Lovdis for International Stock Photos, New York.

FOR POETRY:

"The Ballad of William Sycamore" from *Ballads and Poems* by Stephen Vincent Benet. Copyright 1931 by Stephen Vincent Benet. Copyright © 1959 by Rosemary Carr Benet. Reprinted by permission of Henry Holt and Company. "Birdfoots Grandpa" by Joseph Bruchac from *Entering Onondaga,* Cold Mountain Press, Austin, Texas Copyright © 1975. "Boa Constrictor" from *Where the Sidewalk Ends: The Poems and Drawings of Shel Silverstein.* Copyright © 1974 by Snake Eye Music, Inc. Reprinted by permission of Harper & Row, Publishers, Inc. "The Bridge" (copyright © 1969) in the compilation *Something New Begins* by Lilian Moore. Copyright © 1982 by Lilian Moore. Reprinted by permission of Atheneum Publishers. "The Bully Asleep" from *The Roundabout by the Sea* by J. H. Walsh. Reprinted by permission of Mrs. A. M. Walsh who controls all rights. "Brother" from *Hello and Good-by* by Mary Ann Hoberman. Copyright 1959 by Mary Ann Hoberman, reprinted by permission of Russell & Volkening, Inc., as agents for the author.

"Chairs" and "Tractor" by Valerie Worth from *Small Poems*. Copyright © 1972 by Valerie Worth. Reprinted with the permission of Farrar, Straus & Giroux, Inc. "City" by Langston Hughes from *The Langston Hughes Reader*. Copyright © 1958 by Langston Hughes. Reprinted by permission of Harold Ober Associates Incorporated. "The City" by David Ignatow. Copyright © 1969 by David Ignatow. Reprinted from *David Ignatow Poems 1934–1969*, used by permission of Wesleyan University Press. This poem first appeared in *Nation*. "Country Fingers" from *Fingers Are Always Bringing Me News* by Mary O'Neill. Copyright © 1969 by Mary O'Neill. Used by permission of the author.

"Dreams" from *The Dream Keeper and Other Poems*, by Langston Hughes. Copyright 1932 by Alfred A. Knopf, Inc., and renewed 1960 by Langston Hughes. Reprinted by permission of the publisher. "Driving to the Beach" by Joanna Cole. Used by permission of the author who controls all rights.

"Encounter" from *Sam's Place: Poems from the Country* by Lilian Moore. Copyright © by Lilian Moore. Reprinted by permission of Atheneum Publishers, Inc.

"First Snow" by Marie Louise Allen from *A Pocketful of Poems*. Copyright 1939 by Harper & Row, Publishers, Inc. Reprinted by permission of Harper & Row, Publishers, Inc. "Flashlight" by Judith Thurman from *Flashlight and Other Poems*. Copyright © 1976 by Judith Thurman by permission of Atheneum Publishers, Inc. "Forgotten" by Cynthia Rylant from *Waiting to Waltz*. Copyright © 1984 by Cynthia Rylant. Reprinted with permission of Bradbury Press, an affiliate of Macmillan, Inc. "Fueled" by Marcie Hans from *Serve Me a Slice of Moon*. Copyright © 1965 by Marcie Hans. Reprinted by permission of Harcourt Brace Jovanovich, Inc.

"The Grobbles" from *The Snopp on the Sidewalk and Other Poems* by Jack Prelutsky. Copyright © 1986, 1977 by Jack Prelutsky. By permission of Greenwillow Books, A Division of William Morrow & Company.

"Hello and Good-By" from *Hello and Good-By* by Mary Ann Hoberman. Copyright 1959 by Mary Ann Hoberman, reprinted by permission of Russell & Volkening, Inc. as agents for the author. "Hushabye my Darling" by Clyde Watson reprinted from *Catch Me & Kiss Me & Say It Again*. Copyright © 1976 by Clyde Watson. Reprinted by permission of Philomel Books.

Excerpts from " 'I' Says the Poem" and "Inside a Poem" from *It Doesn't Always Have to Rhyme* by Eve Merriam. Copyright © 1964 by Eve Merriam. All rights reserved. Reprinted by permission of Marian Reiner for the author.

"The Lake" from *The Golden Hive*. Poems and pictures by Harry Behn. Copyright © 1957, 1962, 1966 by Harry Behn. All rights reserved. Reprinted by permission of Marian Reiner. "The limerick's lively to write" from *Take Sky* by David McCord. Copyright © 1961, 1962 by David McCord. Used by permission of Little, Brown and Company. "Listening to Grown Ups Quarreling." Copyright © 1968 by Ruth Whitman. Reprinted from her volume *The Marriage Wig and Other Poems* by permission of Harcourt Brace Jovanovich, Inc. Excerpt from "The Lone Dog," *Songs to Save a Soul* by Irene Rutherford McLeod. Copyright 1915 by Irene Rutherford McLeod. All rights reserved. Reprinted by permission of Viking Penguin, Inc. "Look at My Teeth" from *Blackberry Ink* by Eve Merriam. Copyright © 1985 by Eve Merriam. All rights reserved. Reprinted by permission of Marian Reiner for the author.

"Motor Cars" by Rowena Bennett from *Songs around a Toadstool Table*. Copyright © 1967 by Rowena Bennett. Used by permission of Follett Publishing Company, a division of Follett Corporation. "Mrs. Peck-Pigeon" and "Poetry" by Eleanor Farjeon from *Eleanor Farjeon's Poems for Children*. Copyright 1933, 1961 and 1938, 1966 by Eleanor Farjeon. Reprinted by permission of Harper & Row, Publishers, Inc. "My Parents Kept Me From Children Who Were Rough" by Stephen Spender. Reprinted from *Collected Poems*. Copyright 1934 and renewed 1962 by Stephen Spender. By permission of Random House, Inc.

"Night Train" reprinted from *Robert Francis Collected Poems, 1936–1976*. Amherst: University of Massachusetts Press, 1976. Copyright © 1936, 1964 by Robert Francis.

"Phizzog" by Carl Sandburg from *Good Morning, America*. Copyright 1928, 1956 by Carl Sandburg. Reprinted by permission of Harcourt Brace Jovanovitch, Inc. "The Pickety Fence" from *Every Time I Climb a Tree* by David McCord. Copyright 1952 by David McCord. By permission of Little, Brown and Company. "Poem of Praise" reprinted with permission of Macmillan Publishing Company from *Away Goes Sally* by Elizabeth Coatsworth. Copyright 1934 by Macmillan Publishing Company, renewed 1962 by Elizabeth Coatsworth Beston. "Pussy Willows" and "Skins" by Aileen Fisher. Used by permission of the author, who controls all rights.

"The Question" from *Dogs & Dragons, Trees & Dreams* by Karla Kuskin. Copyright © 1958 by Karla Kuskin. Reprinted by permission of Harper & Row, Publishers, Inc.

"Rope Rhyme" by Eloise Greenfield from *Honey I Love and Other Love Poems*. Copyright © 1978 by Eloise Greenfield. Reprinted by permission of Harper & Row, Publishers, Inc.

"The Sandhill Crane" from *The Children Sing in the Far West* by Mary Austin. Copyright 1928 by Mary Austin. Copyright renewed 1956 by Kenneth M. Chapman and Mary C. Wheelwright. Reprinted by permission of Houghton Mifflin Company. "Satellite, Satellite" an excerpt from "Mean Song" from *Jamboree Rhymes for All Times* by Eve Merriam. Copyright © 1962, 1964, 1966, 1973, 1984 by Eve Merriam. All rights reserved. Reprinted by permission of Marian Reiner for the author. "Secret Door" by Myra Cohn Livingston from *Worlds I Know and Other Poems*. Copyright © 1985 by Myra Cohn Livingston. (A Margaret K. McElderry Book). Reprinted by permission of Atheneum Publishers, Inc. "See, I Can Do It" by Dorothy Aldis from *All Together* by Dorothy Aldis. Copyright 1952 by Dorothy Aldis, copyright renewed © 1980 by Roy E. Porter. Reprinted by permission of G. P. Putnam's Sons. "Sidewalk Measles" by Barbara Hales. Used by permission of the author, who controls all rights. "The Sidewalk Racer or, On the Skateboard" from *The Sidewalk Racer and Other Poems of Sports and Motion* by Lillian Morrison. Copyright © 1977 by Lillian Morrison. By permission of Lothrop, Lee & Shepard Books, a Division of William Morrow & Company. "Sneepies" from *The Baby Uggs Are Hatching* by Jack Prelutsky. Copyright © 1982 by Jack Prelutsky. By permission of Greenwillow Books (A Division of William Morrow & Company). "A Spark in the sun" from *Cricket Songs: Japanese Haiku* translated by Harry Behn. © 1964 by Harry Behn. All rights reserved. Reprinted by permission of Marian Reiner. "Steam Shovel" from *Upper Pasture* by Charles Malam. Copyright 1930, © 1958 by Charles Malam. Reprinted by permission of Henry Holt and Company. "The Storm" by Adrien Stoutenberg, reprinted from *The Things That Are*. Copyright 1964 by Reilly and Lee Co., a division of Henry Regnery Co. "Street Song" by Myra Cohn Livingston from *The Way Things Are and Other Poems*. Copyright © 1974 by Myra Cohn Livingston. (A Margaret K. McElderry Book) Reprinted by permission of Atheneum Publishers, Inc. "Summons" reprinted from *Robert Francis Collected Poems, 1936–1976*. University of Massachusetts Press, 1976. Copyright © 1944, 1972 by Robert Francis.

Excerpt from "There Came A Day" from *Season Songs* by Ted Hughes. Copyright © 1968 by Ted Hughes. Reprinted by permission of Viking Penguin, Inc. "There was a stout pig from Oak Ridge" from *The Book of Pigericks* by Arnold Lobel. Copyright © 1983 by Arnold Lobel. Reprinted by permission of Harper & Row, Publishers, Inc. "This Is My Rock" from *Far and Few* by David McCord. Copyright 1929 by David McCord. First appeared in *Saturday Review*. By permission of Little, Brown and Company. "To Look at Anything" Copyright © 1961 by John Moffitt. Reprinted from his volume *The Living Seed* by permission of Harcourt Brace Jovanovich, Inc.

"The Way I See Any Hope for Later" from *All The Colors of the Race* by Arnold Adoff. Copyright © 1982 by Arnold Adoff. By permission of Lothrop, Lee & Shepard Books (A Division of William Morrow and Company). "Well, Yes" from *Street Poems* by Robert Froman. Copyright 1971 by Robert Froman. Used by permission of author. "Who Am I?" from *At the Top of My Voice and Other Poems* by Felice Holman. Text copyright © 1970 Felice Holman. Reprinted by the permission of Charles Scribner's Sons.

SUBJECT INDEX

AUTHOR, ILLUSTRATOR, TITLE INDEX

Numbers in bold type indicate the page where
a selection is discussed at length. The
abbreviation "il." marks pages where an
illustration is reproduced in the text.